ENCYCLOPEDIA
OF THE
FUTURE

ENCYCLOPEDIA OF THE FUTURE

Edited by

GEORGE THOMAS KURIAN

GRAHAM T. T. MOLITOR

VOLUME 1

MACMILLAN LIBRARY REFERENCE USA

SIMON & SCHUSTER MACMILLAN

NEW YORK

SIMON & SCHUSTER AND PRENTICE HALL INTERNATIONAL

LONDON   MEXICO CITY   NEW DELHI   SINGAPORE   SYDNEY   TORONTO

Copyright © 1996 by Simon & Schuster Macmillan
All rights reserved. No part of this book may be
reproduced or transmitted in any form or by any means,
electronic or mechanical, including photocopying,
recording, or by any information storage and retrieval
system, without permission in writing from the Publisher.

Simon & Schuster Macmillan
1633 Broadway, New York, NY 10019

PRINTED IN THE UNITED STATES OF AMERICA

printing number

2   3   4   5   6   7   8   9   10

LIBRARY OF CONGRESS CATALOGING-IN-PUBLICATION DATA
Encyclopedia of the future / edited by George Thomas
    Kurian, Graham T. T. Molitor.
            p.   cm.
        Includes bibliographical references and index.
        ISBN 0-02-897205-8 (set). — ISBN 0-02-897206-6 (v.1).
    — ISBN 0-02-897207-4 (v. 2)
        1. Forecasting—Encyclopedias. I. Kurian, George
    Thomas. II. Molitor, Graham T. T. (Graham Thomas Tate)
    CB158.E53 1996
    303.49'003—dc20   95-42003
                                              CIP

This paper meets the requirements of ANSI/NISO Z39.48-1992
                    (Permanence of Paper)

CONTENTS

Editorial and Production Staff

Project Editor
Scott Kurtz

Production Editor
Thomas McCarthy

Manuscript Editors
William Drennan
Lauren Long
Patrick Quigley
Carl Rieser
Joan Zseleczky

Proofreaders
Patricia Brecht
Gretchen Griffin
Gregory Teague
Beverly Moon

Production Manager
Maureen Frantino

Indexer
Katharyn Dunham

GORDON MACOMBER, *President*
PHILIP FRIEDMAN, *Publisher*
ELLY DICKASON, *Associate Publisher*

PREFACE

> "We should all be interested in the
> future because we will have to spend
> the rest of our lives there."
>
> *Charles F. Kettering*

The *Encyclopedia of the Future* is a compendium of the thoughts and forecasts of hundreds of the world's leading intellectuals—including Nobel laureates, former heads of government, and distinguished experts in many diverse disciplines. Their collective foresight provides a marvelous pool of perspectives about the most critical problems of our times. The approaching millennium provides opportune timing for such a publication.

As a reference work on impending change and the future, the *Encyclopedia of the Future* is the first of its kind, a milestone in visionary thinking. In its own way, it spans the beginning and end of time. Big Bang theorists estimate that the universe was born some 15 billion years ago. Cyril Ponnamperuma, fixing Earth's formation at 4.5 billion years ago, theorizes that primitive life emerged from Earth's primordial soup some 3.8 billion years ago. The sun's total lifetime as a star that can sustain life on Earth is about 11 billion years; approximately one-half of that destiny already has been fulfilled. Oliver Markley discusses the philosophical speculations of Olaf Stapledon covering a 22-billion-year span between First and Last Men as humans and a succession of evolutionary descendants who moved out into the universe finally die out. David Barrett's impressive chronology of the future suggests conditions resulting in the demise of humans, Earth, its galaxy, and the cosmos itself hundreds of billions of years into the future. In between this alpha and omega more than 450 articles address topics spanning the gamut of human experience, its triumphs and its troubles. Warren Wagar writes about utopia and Lane Jennings about dystopia.

Providing prediction and perspective were key goals of this undertaking. The dimensions have been articulated by a galaxy of talented writers whose creative thoughts illuminate the breadth and depth of change sweeping society.

The future is not a discrete period of time, but is part of a seamless continuum. To gain a proper understanding, one needs to set it against the backdrop of an evolutionary scale ranging from zero to infinity. The perspective that emerges is both humbling and awesome.

If Earth's history were compressed into a single year, the first eight months (about two billion years) would be completely without life. During the seventh or eighth month, only primitive life-forms would be found. During the second week in December, mammals would emerge. About fifteen minutes before the end of the last day of the year, humans finally would appear. Only during the final five seconds of the year would the written history of humanity appear.

Even more awesome is our relative position in the cosmos. It has been calculated that if a map of the known universe were 80 miles long. Earth's galaxy, the Milky Way, would take up an 8½-×-11-inch sheet. Earth's solar system would be the size of a molecule on that sheet. And Earth itself would be a speck on that molecule. Earth's galaxy is made up of 250–400 billion stars; and it is only one out of an estimated 100 billion galaxies across the universe.

On Earth, humans are among the survivors. Hard as it is to imagine, an estimated 99.9 percent of the species that ever lived on Earth were extinct by the time humans appeared. Today humans account for only one life-form among the millions of animal species on Earth, and some 1.3–2.5 billion other forms of life. Among these myriad life-forms there are 900,000 known insects (with another 1–10 million additional species yet uncataloged), 350,000 types of plants, 40–100 thousand fungi (with some 80,000 additional species yet to be classified), 22,000 different kinds of fish, and so on.

While much of this work portrays major problems and issues, we also strove to highlight triflings, recognizing how important they can be. After all, the difference between the lifeblood of plants and humans comes down to the difference of just one atom. Human hemoglobin is an admixture of 135 atoms of hydrogen, carbon, oxygen, and nitrogen clustered around a single atom of iron. Chlorophyll contains the same number of hydrogen, carbon, oxygen, and nitrogen atoms, but they are grouped around a single atom of magnesium.

Awed by huge magnitudes, the editors gained similar respect for diminutive nano-scales, for the merest of scintillas. An atom's nucleus occupies only some one-quadrillionth of its space. Scientists have peeled away at matter to identify over 100 components of subatomic structure. Nanotechnology, as Andy Hines points out, is a potential superscience in the earliest stages of its infancy. The depths and dimensions of existence are far from being fully fathomed. The mystery of life continues to unfold, and this collection of treatises helps guide readers to some of its myriad facets.

Change is a dominant theme throughout. Change, like any departure from past ways of doing things, can be disruptive—and deeply alarming. Change is born of dissatisfaction, focused by vision, and resolved by implementation. Change is pervasive. (Sometimes we fail to recognize that change is occurring until it has run its course or is receding. Once we do see it, we may not believe it. All too often, we hesitate to act on it.) Continuity, the historic norm, has been transformed. Dislocations that once took centuries or decades now occur in years or even months. While it took five months for word of Columbus's discovery of the New World to reach Spain, and Europe did not learn of Lincoln's assassination until two weeks after the event, the Wright Brothers' historic flight was cabled around the world in twelve minutes, and the world learned of—and millions actually watched—Neil Armstrong's historic first step on the moon 1.3 seconds following the momentous event. The accelerating velocity of change necessitates the need to fathom its dimensions and directions.

Aspirations cannot be fulfilled until they have been defined. Some may fret that we can never see far enough or clearly enough. But that does not mean that we should not try. Robert Kennedy once asserted, "The future is not a gift; it is an achievement." The primary mission of this Encyclopedia is to shed light upon where we might be headed or where we ought best be headed. These essays suggest where we seem to be headed and provide advance awareness to help us mend our ways or otherwise capitalize upon the moment.

Hopefully, the Encyclopedia's long-range emphasis, problem-solving approach, and multidisciplinary treatment will contribute to shaping public dialogue on important topics. The importance of vision, of goals, and hope for a better tomorrow can be traced back through the annals of history. Political leaders always have relied upon foresight. Kublah Khan, ruler of the Mongol Empire from 1260 to 1294, maintained a horde of five thousand court astrologers. The scriptures remind us: "Where there is no vision, the people perish" (Proverbs 29:18).

Contemporary politics is desperately in search of new vision, new ideologies. America's political future is analyzed here with George McGovern commenting on liberalism, William F. Buckley on conservatism, John Anderson on third political parties, Scott Erickson on political cycles, Norman Ornstein on political parties, and Richard Blades on political campaigning.

Forecasting is neither an art nor a science, although some contend that it is often a hazard. Forecasting can be characterized as an art or discipline, one hopefully on its way to becoming a science and a recognized profession. Forecasting some events or outcomes may be virtually impossible. Who could have guessed that the $6,000 invested by Queen Isabella and King Ferdinand in Columbus's voyage would lead to the discovery of the New World, or that Manhattan Island, for which Peter Minuit paid the Indians 60 guilders ($24) in 1626, would become, centuries later, one of the most valuable pieces of real estate in the world? Who would have thought that a janitor, Antony van Leeuwenhoek, could invent a compound microscope that literally changed the way the world was perceived? And, finally, who would have predicted that a sports fan from a communist country would become Pope?

On the other hand, certain trends are well defined, even if less well understood. In the United States we know with a high degree of certainty that America's population growth is slowing, and that Americans are becoming ethnically diverse, aging, marrying later, divorcing more often, spending more time in education but plagued by deteriorating outcomes. Households are becoming more diverse, smaller, busier (including dual wage-earners), are enjoying more leisure time, and are increasingly secure (thanks to the welter of welfare state supports). Economic growth is slower, driven largely by technology, burdened by debt, global-oriented, energy dependent, and environmentally concerned. The Encyclopedia covers the four Big-Es: economy, energy, education, and environment. The currents of change pose many choices.

Most entries focus on specific issues, problems, and opportunities. Toward the end of the twentieth century, the Berlin Wall fell, the Soviet Union collapsed, Yugoslavia splintered, China stirred anew, South Africa rejected apartheid, ancient religious rivalries were rekindled, and world power devolved into three dominant geopolitical spheres—the European Union, the Pacific Rim nations, and the North American colossus; some developing nations finally took off economically, while other Third World countries remained mired in poverty. Other entries attempt to make some sense out of major themes that dominated the last few decades—the death of God during the 1960s, the birth of the Information Era during the 1970s, the end of history during the 1980s, and the demise of cultures during the 1990s.

A sprinkling of articles deal with forecasting methods. They are designed to familiarize readers with some basic techniques and methodologies used in future studies.

From among the wide variety of perspectives about the future, readers can pick the kind of perspective they want and hope to see. Some futurists rely on the adage "Look before you leap," while others assert, "He who hesitates is lost." Activists maintain that "The squeaking wheel gets the grease," while others, less venturesome, maintain that "Silence is golden." Experimental types implore, "Nothing ventured, nothing gained," while the timid assert, "It's better to be safe than sorry." Absolute assurance, of course, is the prerogative of fools. Contradictions abound. Some viewpoints are optimistic, proclaiming that we live in the best of times; while others, with a more pessimistic outlook, suggest that the best of times are behind us.

Perspective is always important. Exactly how we picture things in our mind dramatically influences our conclusions. Population explosion, the inability of Earth to sustain great and growing numbers of human beings, permeates contemporary doomsaying. R. Buckminster Fuller, one of the all-time great futurists, gives us all pause: ". . . despite the hullabaloo about a world population explosion, all of humanity could be brought indoors in the buildings of greater New York City, each with as much floor room as at a cocktail party." (*Utopia or Oblivion: The Prospects for Humanity*, 1969, p. 217.) The editors have tried to make sure a variety of important views are represented, but do not necessarily endorse or subscribe to each and every article that appears.

Over the course of this project, a number of persons affiliated with or writing for it died. We want to express our great appreciation for the contributions made not only to this undertaking but to the field of future studies in general by John McHale, Cyril Ponnamperuma, Kenneth Boulding, Jan Tinbergen, John Platt, Isaac Asimov, Ralph Lenz, Robert Jungk, and Richard Critchfield.

A number of prominent futurists contributed more than one entry and also came forward with suggestions for improving work in progress: James A. Dator, David Dodson Gray, Scott Erickson, Gene Stephens, Richard Maynard, William Gahr, William Gore, Lane E. Jennings, Brian K. Toren, Richard Slaughter, Robert Ayres, Edward S. Cornish, Willis W. Harman, Hazel Henderson, Heather Hudson, Eleanora Barbieri Masini, Jean Farinelli, David Carter, Heather Hudson, Jerome C. Glenn, David Pearce Snyder, Sheldon Greenberg, Irving Leveson, James Adams, Todd Johnson, Sanford Miller, Clement Bezold, and David B. Barrett.

The dominant focus of the Encyclopedia is on the United States and English-speaking nations. Coverage of other countries and international perspectives, however, have not been neglected. The mix of articles represents an attempt to strike a balance among regions of the world, varieties of subject matter, and schools of interpretation. The selection of authors represents an innovative attempt to broaden the scope of scholarship by transcending narrow disciplinary divisions and offering the readers many examples of vibrant, cutting-edge analyses and interpretations. In some cases they go beyond that and convey something of the vitality and anticipatory excitement that the future holds.

Guided by an international advisory board that included many eminent futurists, the editors devised a conceptual scheme that tried, in Lytton Strachey's words, to exclude everything that is redundant and nothing that is significant. Given the stark limitations of space, the process of selecting topics became a rigorous exercise, consisting of both the formulation of criteria and their application to each entry. Each article was screened by the two general editors and one or more of the five working subject editors. Entries are accompanied by generally available references for the convenience of readers wishing to pursue further lines of inquiry.

The Encyclopedia uses an effective cross-referencing scheme to help the reader navigate through the maze of interrelated articles and gain an understanding of the crosscurrent of ideas and concepts that relate to the future. In addition, the index will help readers in locating topics not listed under the specific entry titles.

The Encyclopedia represents input from hundreds of persons who worked with great dedication, investing their wisdom and scholarship on the project. The members of the advisory board provided advice and encouragement whenever needed. We owe a special debt of gratitude to Phil Friedman, the publisher; Elly Dickason, the associate publisher; and Paul Bernabeo, the editor in chief. At Macmillan Library Reference, the work was shepherded by Scott Kurtz, whose skill, diligence, commitment, perseverance, fine editing skills, and intelligence provided major improvements to the work throughout.

The *Encyclopedia of the Future* offered the editors and the contributors alike an exciting challenge and insightful views into the world of tomorrow. If it does the same to the readers, we have succeeded in our task. Our hope is that readers at the end of the twenty-first century will look into it to find out what our plans and hopes were for the century that is soon to dawn.

George Thomas Kurian
Yorktown Heights, New York
October 1995

Graham Thomas Tate Molitor
Potomac, Maryland
October 1995

FOREWORD: FIVE BILLION FUTURISTS

There are, in round numbers, five billion futurists on our planet. There are so many futurists because every human carries inside her or his skull a set of assumptions about what does not yet exist.

The primitive hunter hurling a spear presupposes his prey will be at a particular spot when the spear strikes. The motorist makes thousands of assumptions about the future position of other cars. Add to that the countless everyday calculations we make about the future of our health, our children, our jobs, our favorite sports teams, our stock portfolios, bank accounts, or taxes. Together, at any given moment, they and thousands of other assumptions form our private image of the future.

Some of these presuppositions are explicit and calculated, others implicit and intuitive, often grounded in our primal emotions. Fear, for example, implies concern over something that has not yet happened. To be afraid is to anticipate. The same is true of hope. All our expectations, commands, instructions, and pleas similarly refer to states or conditions that have not yet materialized. In short, to be alive and human is to be immersed in the future.

Here, however, we will be concerned not with the five billion but with a much smaller subset—counted perhaps in the tens of thousands around the world—who today wear or bear the label "futurist."

From ages immemorial, endless efforts have been made to improve the accuracy, range, and influence of anticipatory thinking—hence the great tradition of seers, sybils, and soothsayers, prophets, prognosticators, and predictors, astromancers and geomancers, oracles and augurs, who claimed special insight into the future. Some applied objective methodologies of one kind or another; others claimed mystical revelation, or divine or subjective powers. Each civilization gave rise to its own characteristic styles and methods for grappling with what is not yet.

The spread of industrial civilization brought with it several new streams of futurist thought, including utopian and anti-utopian (dystopian) political literature, science fiction, technological forecasting, military gaming, trend extrapolation, corporate strategic analysis, and the central planning methodologies of various governments. The proponents of these and literally hundreds of other approaches and methods typically took pains to differentiate themselves from the prescientific futurists who relied on astrology, mystical revelation, entrails reading, and other varieties of crystal-ball gazing.

Starting with Rousseau and the Encyclopedists in the eighteenth century, Western intellectuals began to prefigure and critique elements of the industrial civilization just beginning to emerge. Saint-Simon, Comte, Fourier, and Prud'hon in the early nineteenth century were in turn savagely critiqued by Marx and Engels, who proclaimed the invention of "scientific socialism" and a dialectical materialism that could foreshadow the future. By the end of the nineteenth century, science fiction emerged as a separate literary genre. In the United States in 1888, Edward Bellamy's *Looking Backward* attacked the social evils of capitalist society from the vantage point of a protagonist living in the year 2000. In Europe, Jules Verne previsioned technological marvels, and far from the factories and mills of the West, K'ang Yu-wei imagined the future of a China with airplanes and telephones.

Early in the twentieth century, a school of sculptors, musicians, painters, and poets in Europe sought to capture the spirit of the emergent industrial civilization. Boccioni, Marinetti, Russolo, and Balla in Italy actually dubbed themselves "futurists." Others—poets, architects, sculptors, and theatrical designers—termed themselves "vorticists" or "constructivists." In literature three great names loomed up—H. G. Wells, Aldous Huxley, and George Orwell—each of whom powerfully shaped popular assumptions about tomorrow. Hundreds of science fiction writers followed in their wake. It was not, however, until roughly the 1960s that the current worldwide futurist movement arose, more or less simultaneously, in several countries. In France, Bertrand de Jouvenel wrote *The Art of Conjecture* and created the organization and journal still known as *Futuribles*. De Jouvenel deeply influenced the development of contemporary futurism by emphasizing the multiplicity of "possible futures."

A Dutch senator and educator, Fred Polak, wrote *The Image of the Future*, a cultural history of the future as imagined by earlier societies. Austrian journalist and political activist Robert Jungk spearheaded the broader European branch of the movement with, among other books, *Tomorrow Is Already Here*. In the United States the transplanted British economist and philosopher Kenneth Boulding published *The Meaning of the Twentieth Century*, and a group of academics, headed by sociologist Daniel Bell, created a Commission on the Year 2000.

Before long a new, highly informal futurist network began to take shape around the world. Our own experience illustrates how this network developed. In 1965 we published an article in the journal *Horizon* called "The Future as a Way of Life." The essay introduced our concept of "future shock." We described it as the personal, organizational, or social disorientation arising from the premature arrival of the future or, more precisely, from the rapid "superimposition of a new culture on an old one." Since society was going through an upheaval even deeper than the industrial revolution, we wrote, the acceleration of change would require more, not less, long-range thinking in society. We urged, among other things, the creation of an institution devoted to futurist research.

In response to that article, Arthur C. Clarke wrote, suggesting that we get in touch with a mathematician named Olaf Helmer at the Rand Corporation in California. Helmer, along with a space engineer named Ted Gordon and several other researchers, were developing a forecasting methodology called Delphi. Helmer and Gordon had also created something called the "Futures Game," an actual board game that illustrated a key futurist precept: that the occurrence of an "event" in one field raises or lowers the probabilities of events in many other fields. We obtained and played this game and many variations of it. We traveled to meet with this small group of California futurists, who felt themselves misunderstood by their colleagues at the Rand Corporation. Soon we were reading and commenting on advance drafts of their proposal to establish an independent futures think tank. Out of that initiative, in 1968, came the Institute for the Future and, later, Gordon's Futures Group. Through them we also discovered Ed Cornish, who, with his wife Sally, was thinking of starting a futures newsletter—or better yet a magazine—and an organization. This was the birth of the World Future Society and *The Futurist*.

A certain spirit of camaraderie marked this incipient futurist community. We were particularly struck by the intellectual collaboration of couples in this emerging network—Maggie and Olaf Helmer, Annie and Ted Gordon, Elise and Kenneth Boulding, Sally and Ed Cornish, and Magda and John McHale. We noted, too, the variety of their cultural and disciplinary backgrounds, ranging from mathematics and engineering to journalism and art. John McHale, for example, was by birth a Scot; his wife, Magda, a Hungarian. They were well-known avant-garde painters in Britain, cofounders of what became the international Pop Art movement, before writing important works like *The Future of the Future* and devoting themselves to futurist research on subjects ranging from basic human needs and world resources to women's rights.

In September 1966 we persuaded the New School for Social Research in New York to let us teach what may have been the first formal academic course on the future. Before long other groupings began to surface (or come to our attention) and converge—Buckminster Fuller and his many young followers, Herman Kahn and the Hudson Institute. Robert Jungk and others had already organized Mankind 2000 and in Oslo during 1967 sponsored a largely European conference on the future. Another conference was organized in Kyoto, where we came into contact with Yujiro Hiyashi, Hidetashi Kato, and Yoneji Masuda as well as with James Dator, who later became head of the World Future Studies Federation. From these initial contacts our network spread from Venezuela and India to the then-Soviet Union.

In 1970 Dator and others organized the Hawaii 2000 conference—among the first of many state and national meetings held around the world to focus on "anticipatory democracy"—a combination of futurism with the citizen participation strongly advocated in our own work. In 1970 the surprise bestsellerdom of our book *Future Shock* called broad public attention to the futurist movement. Soon the pioneers were joined by a flood of corporate strategists, teachers, environmentalists, feminists, military analysts, and religious leaders, many with fresh ideas, some no more than catalogers of the ideas of others.

By 1975, with the help of U.S. Sen. John Culver and Rep. Charlie Rose, we organized a two-day conference on "anticipatory democracy" in the United States Congress. Among those who attended that conference was a young professor who had been teaching a course based on our book *Future Shock*. His name, still unknown at the time, was Newt Gingrich, the current Speaker of the U.S. House of Representatives. Describing himself as a "conservative futurist," he has called upon Congress to judge every piece of proposed legislation according to whether it accelerates or slows the transition from a Second Wave or industrial society to a "Third Wave industrial society."

That same Conference on Anticipatory Democracy had fallout on the other side of the political spectrum as well. It led to the formation of the Congressional Clearinghouse on the Future—a group of congressional members dedicated to introducing long-range concerns into an institution noted for its myopia. In 1979 a young representative from Tennessee named Al Gore, Jr., became chair of the Clearinghouse. Later, as a senator, he cochaired the group from 1987 until 1992, foreshadowing his current interest, as Vice President of the United States, in the technologies and communications of the future. It is Gore who has placed the need for a Third Wave information infrastructure on the global agenda.

Today it is possible to identify three broad streams of thinking and writing about the future. These concern possible, probable, and preferable futures.

If we class science fiction as part of the current futures movement—and many today do not—it would largely fall into the "possible futures" category. Others who routinely explore a wide range of what-if possibilities are military contingency planners who, for example, may regard war with a current ally as highly unlikely, but nevertheless possible at some point. Those who focus on "possibles" typically believe that doing so helps decision-makers to identify more imaginative solutions to present-day problems than would otherwise be likely. In short, as impractical as a discussion of the merely possible may seem to some, "possibilists" believe their work enriches the culture and improves the decision process.

The second major stream of futurism focuses on the subset of possible futures that seem probable. Corporate and governmental clients typically call on their futurists, planners, marketers, and others to tell them the "most probable" outcome of some ongoing process. Here we find a frequent reliance on systematic methodologies, quantification, computer modeling, and a host of semi- (and, alas, sometimes pseudo-) scientific methods.

Finally, the third stream of contemporary futurist thought calls attention to "preferable" futures. In the tradition of biblical prophets who preached morality to a sinful world, works devoted to preferable futures typically begin with a forecast, paint a dire future, and propose a way to avoid it. This is a perfectly legitimate thing to do and, indeed, early warning is one of the most important of futurist tasks. Not infrequently, however, the prescription is already inherent in the diagnosis, and the work, itself, merely a propagandistic adjunct to activism.

Of course, these three categories of contemporary futurism overlap, the same report, document, or analysis often containing, at least implicitly, traces of all three. The differences are matters of emphasis and style. Regardless of their approach, however, honest futurists separate themselves from quacks by reminding their audiences that no one can "know" the future with certainty and that irrespective of how much quantification buttresses a report, analysis, or projection, futurism remains an art form—a useful art form, indeed an essential one, but an art form, nonetheless, in the sense that it necessarily rests on at least a degree of judgment, subjectivity, and values.

The historian Gertrude Himmelfarb, in her book *On Looking Into the Abyss*, points out that every work of history is, as historians have been saying since the dawn of history itself, "necessarily imperfect, tentative and partial." Why then should futurists, lacking the concrete evidence that historians can sometimes muster, be any less "imperfect, tentative and partial"?

Descriptions of possible futures, by their nature, depend more on imagination and subjectivity than on empirical fact. But even forecasts about probable futures, swaddled in numbers and computer jargon, are never wholly neutral or value-free. Values permeate the very languages we speak and the conceptual models we use, meaning that, to the degree that futurism deals with social, economic, or political matters, even "hard" forecasts have "soft" interiors. They are necessarily based on a structure of assumptions, some of which are ultimately unprovable. The choice of variables monitored or the weights assigned to them in model-making all reflect, if only indirectly, our values and hence our notions of what is preferable. And if both speculatively possible and probabilistic forecasts are less than "scientifically neutral," the same is obviously even more true for any discussion of preferable tomorrows. A preferable future is, by definition, an expression of one's values.

To say this, however, is only to say that human existence is messy and that futurists are human. And since contemporary futurism is now a global enterprise, a vast network with nodes in almost every country, it is hardly surprising that the work it produces is uneven and reflects many biases—national, ethnic, disciplinary, and even generational.

Hundreds of competing forecasting methods and models are currently in use. Many futurists focus on relatively narrow topics—the future of transportation, for example, or the future of a class of products or of a particular city or region, over a short span of time. By contrast, others attempt to anticipate change on a grand or global scale. Some analyze a few key variables—demography, technology, or economics, for example. Others synthesize data from a very wide range of fields, disciplines, and activities. Some work from computerized or printed sources alone. Others go into the field to interview change-makers and subject what they read to a "reality check." Some are theorists, while others are primarily empirical data gatherers. As in any field, there are original thinkers and there are academic mummies. There are the fools found in any human grouping, not to mention a somewhat higher than normal percentage of eccentrics or "quacks" drawn by the magical word *future*.

Despite their diversity, however, most serious futurists probably agree on a few key things: first, that no one actually can "predict" the future with certainty. Second, that "future consciousness"—an awareness of the mutability of life and the habit of conscious anticipation—is a survival trait. Next, that the planet now faces technological, environmental, and cultural changes on an unprecedented scale. Futurists have heard the skeptics who say, "All past ages also thought they were special. What's so special about now?" The answer is that never before in recorded history has the species literally had the capability of annihilating itself or of consciously altering the path of future evolution. Never has it faced global environmental challenges arising not from inexorable natural processes but from human activity itself. Which is to say that never has clarity about our possible, probable, and preferable futures been potentially more useful.

Finally, futurists share the belief that even a dim understanding of what is possible, probable, and/or preferable is better than none, because without that understanding human beings are reduced to being the objects of change, rather than its creators.

There have always been skeptics who regard any such efforts as a waste or worse. After all, the Bible warns us to "beware of false prophets." It is replete with statements like "I will raise my hand against the prophets whose visions are false, whose divinations are a lie" or against those "who dream lies and retail them." Centuries later Thomas Aquinas held that any attempt to divine the future beyond what was humanly reasonable or was revealed by God was sinful.

More recent critics, claiming scientific or philosophical support, have asserted that events are not causally connected at all, that the universe is completely governed by chance, so that the past never determines, even in part, the future. A further objection holds that the very attempt to investigate introduces a perturbation into the present. A variation of this argument holds that it is not the attempt to study the future, but the dissemination of forecasts that creates self-fulfilling or self-negating effects, thus altering the very future that is anticipated. Worse yet, any planning based on assumptions about the future is an ill-considered attempt to impose today's knowledge and values on the future.

Still others argue that, possible or not, one should not anticipate because it takes the spontaneity out of life—that, since the one prediction we can make with reasonable certainty is death, we should simply *carpe diem*.

More frivolous critics collect hilarious examples of misanticipation, real or apocryphal. There is the story about the nineteenth-century ecologist who worried that the enormous pileup of horse manure in city streets would soon drown the population—and the response from a believer in the "technological fix," who declared that the problem would be solved by the invention of "micro-horses," which would reduce the amount of oats consumed.

Critics take pleasure in reminding us of just how bad forecasts can be. They cite the committee in 1490 that advised King Ferdinand and Queen Isabella of Spain that Columbus' proposal for a westward voyage should be rejected because "so many centuries after the Creation it was unlikely that anyone could find hitherto unknown lands of any value." Or the British postmaster-general who declared in 1895 that "Gas and water were necessities for every inhabitant. . . . Telephones were not and never would be." For a more recent example of radical misanticipation, check some of the wildly exaggerated forecasts of global population growth and widespread famine made by prestigious scientific and political bodies in the mid-1960s.

Surely, prophets, predictors and futurists throughout the ages have made silly mistakes. Nevertheless, much of the criticism is misplaced or self-contradictory.

If all is chance, then the fact that some forecasts have proved even roughly on target should amaze us. Without entering into protracted debate about ancient prophesy, how does one account, for example, for Andrei Amalryk—the Soviet dissident who authored *Will the Soviet Union Survive Until 1984?* in 1969—a time when the Soviet Union was almost universally regarded as powerful and likely to endure indefinitely? Amalryk was wrong in his assumption that the breakup of the Soviet Union would be triggered by conflict with China. He was in fact a few years off on his date, but he was powerfully correct in foreseeing the ethnic and national tensions that would dismember the Soviet Empire. Was his argument right by sheer chance?

Or what about the now almost forgotten Homer Lea, who in 1909, in a remarkably prescient book entitled *The Valor of Ignorance*, warned of the great Pacific War that erupted in 1941. Lea was wrong about details and pushed his argument too far. He foresaw an actual Japanese invasion of California. But his examination of new technology, Japanese military might, and strategic requirements led him to understand the vulnerability of Hawaii and the Philippines, and other locations that later were engulfed by the Japanese in World War II. Was that, too, accidental?

Leave aside the often startling, technological, and social insights of science fiction writers from Jules Verne to Arthur Clarke and beyond. Are futurist insights the result of chance—like Shakespeare sonnets produced by the proverbial monkeys typing at random on a keyboard? Or did Homer Lea, like Amalryk, implicitly model contemporaneous forces in a way that led to powerful conclusions?

If, indeed, the future itself is a result of sheer chance, then those who get it even grossly right are all the more remarkable. On the other hand, if history is chance-less—predetermined by either God or some other prime determiner—then there was, is, and will be only one possible future, easily extrapolatable from the present.

But this "either/or" is itself deceptive. For once we step out of the Aristotelian insistence on mutually exclusive alternatives, we are free to imagine a universe in which both chance and necessity operate. It is closer to the model proposed by Ilya Prigogine, the 1977 Nobel Prize winner whose theories about nonequilibrial systems and dissipative structures not only leave room for both determinism and its opposite, but even suggest the nature of the relationship between them.

Much of the intellectual resistance to futurism derives from naive misperceptions of its functions. Over the millennia, futurists have performed multiple functions in society. They have challenged existing social institutions and practices. They have moralized—which is what the Biblical prophets did. They have inspired—as the vast utopian literature attests. They have helped planners by calling attention to potential catastrophes or to new opportunities. Like artists, they have helped broaden the public imagination, encouraging it to consider alternatives to the present. They have, more subtly perhaps, helped individuals to position themselves temporally, adding perspective to their lives. Indeed, prediction in the sense of providing "correct" forecasts may be the least important of the tasks carried out by futurists.

Yet if the history of the future is full of misanticipations, the larger and more important fact is that ordinary human beings and the race as a whole have not done a bad job of anticipating things to come—or of fulfilling their own plans and prophecies. Had that not been the case—if the hunters' spears had always missed their targets, if there were no predictability at all in our environment, or, alternatively, if ordinary people were routinely wrong in their practical assumptions—it is unlikely that the species would have survived at all. In this sense, the age-old effort to look beyond tomorrow is a survival function for human society.

Those who mock futurism, in the broad sense, are ignorant of their own reliance on it, indeed, or their own contributions to forming society's images of realities to come. They may sneer, but they cannot prevent people from struggling to make sense of tomorrow.

To stretch our collective imagination about tomorrow, to help order our images of the future, to peer forward into the mists, is one of the proudest and most essential of intellectual enterprises.

ALVIN TOFFLER
HEIDI TOFFLER

INTRODUCTION: REFLECTIONS AT THE END OF AN AGE

There is no such entity as "the future." This may be an astonishing statement in a concluding introductory essay for an *Encyclopedia of the Future.* Many writers do use the phrase "the future," as if it were a single place in near or distant time, or like a point on the horizon, to be reached by a projectile of words.

"The future" as a phrase by itself (as a philosopher would say) reifies the term, treats it as a "thing," as, somehow, a word with the power to be or to act. But there is no such independent entity. The English language requires us to use such terms as transitive—that is, to establish a following relationship. There can only be "the future *of . . .*" something: the future of the American economy, the future of the American political system, but not the "future of technology," which is too loose. In short, there has to be a boundary condition, of time and place, of a definable entity, to make sense of what we mean.

Can one talk of the "future of society"? Yes, but only if we observe a set of stipulations. A society is not an organism, a biological entity, with a homeostatic regulator (like body temperature in a human being) that seeks to maintain an equilibrium. Nor is society a "system," made up of interlocking variables, so that changes in the magnitudes of the coefficients will affect all the other variables—like an Alexander Calder mobile in motion—and thus move into a different configuration of shapes.

Society is a set of *social arrangements,* of laws and institutions, created by individuals (inherited from a previous time or re-created by agreement), to facilitate and fulfill needs, allocate social and occupational positions, educate the young, guarantee rights, and control impulses. Societies are held together by a normative series of values and authority that is accepted as legitimate by its members—unless they live under coercive and dictatorial rules and thus are not equal as members. The legitimacy of the arrangements implies a sense of justice; authority, the enforcement of such rules, implies legitimate power.

Societies are made up of different realms, each of which operates under different axial principles. The economy—the production and distribution of reciprocal goods and services—is more or less a system because of the interdependence of the economic actors. Change comes from price signals through market transaction. But the polity—the realms of law and authority—is not a system. It is an "order," created by design, a set of rules and norms to regulate the lives of individuals within the polity. In the United States, we live under a constitution, designed by the founding fathers, to establish divided powers, protect liberties, and establish rights under the rules of law. Change occurs by conflict or consensus. The culture—the realm of meanings (religious and philosophical) and of imaginative expressiveness in the arts—is even less of a system. Its meanings are transcendent. The arts are different styles, such as classical, baroque, or modern, established by artists in the exploration of form within a genre, or, as today with postmodernism, amidst the dissolution of all genres.

The point of all this is to emphasize that "societies" are not integrated and do not change by a technological wand, in undivided ways. Nor are there unified periods, radically distinct and cut off from one another by historical time, as is argued, for example, by the Marxian modes of production. If that were the case, how could one explain the persistence of the great historic religions—Buddhism, Hinduism, Confucianism, Shintoism, Judaism, Christianity, Islam—over millennia of time, when economic systems have disappeared and political systems have crumbled. Though these religions have changed in manifold ways, the great cores of belief—the Old Testament in Judaism, the savior figure of Jesus in Christianity, the concepts of karma and nirvana in Buddhism—and their great texts still compel belief today. (It is for this reason that I read with astonishment statements by Alvin Toffler such as this: "We no longer 'feel' life as men did in the past. And this is the ultimate difference, the distinction that separates the truly contemporary man from all others. . . . we have broken irretrievably with the past. We have cut ourselves off from old ways of thinking, of feeling, of adapting. We have set the stage for a completely new society, and are now racing toward it [*Future Shock*, New York: Random House, 1970, pp. 18, 19]." What, in God's name, does that mean?)

At different times and in different places, one or another of these societal realms has been dominant. Historically, most societies have been organized in empires and monarchies, so the political order has been dominant, subordinating the economy and coexisting with or seeking to vanquish religious authority. In the European Middle Ages and in theocratic Islamic societies today, the religious domain has held sway. In the modern capitalist West, the economic sphere has been primary in the shaping of society.

If societies are not unified, are there some determinate rules of social change? Again, one has to understand the different principles within each realm. Modern Western society saw, for the first time, the relative autonomy of the economic sphere separated from the state. The discovery of "the market," the production of commodities, and the rise of a new class led to the idea of the creation of wealth by private property, rather than the mercantilist state. And modern economics—which itself is only two hundred years old—had formulated the idea of productivity, the notion that, through the use of machines or new organization, one can get a more than proportional return from equal or less effort; and this became codified in the rules of economic change. Thus, if a new invention or innovation is cheaper, or better, or more efficient, then, subject to cost and a better return on investment, it will be used. There is a clear principle of substitution, and change is linear. A second feature of modern economics is that the market—in trade and production—knows no boundaries and oversteps political lines. Thus, in the search for profit, the range of economic activities moves from the regional to the national, to the international, and finally to the fully global (which differs from the international), and becomes a "single" market, for capital and commodities.

Political change—leaving aside the wars between states—has been of two kinds. The most common has been revolution: the overthrow of older privileged classes, freedom from imperial or colonial rule, or, when empires have crumbled, the creation of new states. After World War I, there was the end of the Hohenzollern, Hapsburg, and Romanov empires; after World War II, the end of Western imperialism and the creation of almost one hundred new states; and, in the last decade, the breakup of the communist empire of the Soviet Union and of Yugoslavia. It is a striking historical fact—given the histories of the Roman Empire and subsequent events up to the end of the British and Western European empires—that today, for the first time, there are no major political empires in the world. Whether China will become a new empire in the twenty-first century remains to be seen.

Where one finds stable, democratic societies—and again it is striking how few these are: the United States, the United Kingdom, and the small countries in northwest Europe—political change arises from the inclusion of previously excluded groups (such as women and blacks) into the political order; the checking of corporate economic power, as with the New Deal; the expansion of rights, such as privacy and free sexual choice; the expansion of regulatory power; and, as we have seen increasingly, the reaction to bureaucracy and the centralization of powers in government. One central theme—which was enunciated by Aristotle in his *Politics*—has been the role of inequality in creating political conflict in societies. And the first lines of Tocqueville's *Democracy in America* emphasize the novelty of the search for equality in American life. In the United States, for the past 160 years, we have been sorting out the different kinds of equality, such as the equality of all persons before the law, of civil equality in public accommodations, of voting rights, and equality of opportunity and equality of result.

Changes in culture have many different patterns. In the arts, there is no principle of substitution. Pierre Boulez does not replace J. S. Bach, but widens the esthetic repertoire of mankind. We read *The Iliad* to understand the codes of honor and shame, and the first expression of tragedy in the realization, as in the fates of Patroclus and Hector, of death before its expected time, and even the very idea of death for humans, as against the immortality of the gods. And we read *Antigone* to understand the defiance of Creon by this young woman, in order to provide a decent burial for her brothers, since decent burial, as we had already learned in *The Iliad*, is the mark of respect and of civilized behavior. It was a quest repeated two thousand years later by that extraordinary woman, Nadezhda Mandelstam, in searching for the body of her husband, the great Russian poet Osip Mandelstam, who had disappeared in the purges, killed by Stalin for the mocking poem he had written about the dictator. Art crosses time and appeals to a common human understanding. Can it be outmoded or rendered obsolete?

In the realm of "meanings," particularly religion, modernity has brought many challenges to established faiths. Most of the Enlightenment thinkers, from Voltaire to Marx, thought that religion would disappear in the twentieth century, for to them religion was superstition, fetishism, and irrational beliefs that would give way to the authority of science and rationalism. Much of this was summed up in the term *secularization*, particularly in the sociology of Max Weber. But the word *secularization*, I believe, is wrong, because it conflates two different processes: changes in *institutions* and changes in *beliefs*. It is quite evident that religion has lost much of its institutional authority, in the sense of providing a commanding set of prohibitions and permissions in many areas of life, particularly private morals. But what we have also witnessed is the multiplication of faiths, the renewal of religions, of new cults and belief systems, as a recurrent feature of life. Beliefs and faith are responses to the existential and nonrational situations—in the facts of death and tragedy and suffering—in the search for meanings beyond the mundane.

These are all multifarious and complicated sets of distinctions, and other social theorists may have different ways of ordering and distinguishing the different facets of social structure and culture. But what cannot be questioned is that any disciplined effort to understand the future configurations of different societies, or of different realms in societies, has to be rooted in history and culture, and the relevant distinctions about the phenomena that are being analyzed. Bombastic phrases, careening about like a Tom-and-Jerry cartoon in overdrive, will not do.

The engine that has driven our world in the past two hundred years has been technology—for what the new technology has given us is the possibility of the mastery and transformation of nature, and only slowly, later, the comprehension as well of the destruction of nature.

The change is marked, by conventional agreement, by the term *industrial revolution*. Yet it is striking to know how belated was the recognition of that change. The phrase, in fact, was first created by Arnold Toynbee, Sr. (the uncle of the famed historian), when in a set of lectures at Oxford, in 1886, he remarked that if we look back a hundred years, we can realize that we have been living through an "industrial revolution." But the unfortunate fact of the single phrase was that it masked two different "revolutions" that had taken place at the time: one in technology, which was the application of controlled energy to machines; the other a "social revolution" in the transformation of work and of the places where people came to live. The failure to distinguish between these two processes has often obscured the different kinds of change in society.

One of the first thinkers to pick up the thread of technology was the writer and renowned historian Henry Adams. For forty-five years, Adams pondered the past, and, as he wrote in his classic *Education* (in the third person), "after ten years of pursuit, he found himself lying in the Gallery of Machines at the Great Exposition in 1900, his historical neck broken by the sudden eruption of forces entirely new."

It was in the great hall of dynamos that this revelation took place. In the energy churning from the dynamo, Adams felt he had a metric to understand the modern world. (In the famous chapter on "The Virgin and the Dynamo," he contrasted the faith of the twelfth century, as exemplified by the cathedrals of Chartres and Mont Saint-Michel, with the power of science in the twentieth century, as exemplified by the dynamo.) In the nineteenth century, Adams wrote, society measured its progress by the output of coal. He suggested that the ratio of increase in the volume of coal power might serve as the "dynamometer of history." Between 1840 and 1900, he pointed out, coal output had doubled every ten years in the form of utilized power, each ton of coal yielding three or four times as much power in 1900 as it had in 1840. The gauge on the dynamometer of history had started out with arithmetical ratios; but new forces emerging around 1900—Adams had in mind the cracking of the world of appearances by X-rays and radium—were creating new "supersensual" forces. What all this showed, he said, was the foundation for a new social physics, for a dynamic law of history, the fundamental secret of social change—the law of acceleration.

Adams, like many writers in the nineteenth century, had been intrigued by the triadic scheme of history proposed by August Comte (who had coined the term *sociology*) in his *Cours de Positive Philosophie* (1842) involving a theological, a metaphysical, and a positive (or scientific) set of stages of the human mind. Seeking to extend this, Adams had discovered the work of Willard Gibbs, professor of mathematical physics at Yale, who in 1878 had promulgated a "law of phases" which described the transformations of matter (such as water from solid [ice] to liquid [water] to gas [steam]). Adams proposed to apply the "rule of phase to history," by taking Gibbs's mathematical formula of least squares and applying that to Western time.

If one took the year 1600 as a starting point (the work of Galileo was the benchmark), and ended in 1900, this would be the *mechanical* phase, as typified by the views of Isaac Newton and John Dalton. "Supposing the Mechanical Phase to have lasted 300 years from 1600 to 1900, the next or Electric Phase would have a life equal to $\sqrt{300}$, or about seventeen years and a half when—that is, in 1917—it would pass into another Ethereal Phase [i.e., mathematics] which, for half a century, science has been promising, and which would last only $\sqrt{17.5}$ or about four years and bring Thought to the limit of possibilities in the year 1921." Yet, since starting points are difficult to establish, even if one began a hundred years before, "the difference to the last term of the series would be negligible. In that case, the Ethereal Phase would last till about 2025."

Ingenious as this was, Adams's essay only proved that a "social physics" could not be applied to history. Yet the idea of acceleration and exponential growth intrigued scholars, and the most serious effort was made by the Yale historian of science Derek Price, who, in *Science Since Babylon* (1961) and other works, sought to chart the growth of scientific knowledge. Price took the scientific journal and the learned paper as two major indicators of knowledge, and he drew "a law of exponential increase," since the number of new journals and papers had grown exponentially rather than linearly.

Price's work was challenged by other scholars who pointed out that if he had used different starting points, growth rates would have been lower. But the major intellectual problem was the obvious proposition that no increases could continue *ad infinitum.* There had to be some ceiling or boundary conditions. This led to efforts to plot Verhulst or S-shaped sigmoid curves, where the exponential growth of an item (such as population) begins geometrically, until it reaches a "point of inflection," when the rate now reverses itself and tapers off as it reaches the ceiling limit.

The key problem with the use of S-curve analysis is that it works only within some "closed system" based on some fixed resources or physical laws, so that the "ceiling conditions" force the leveling off of the curve. Even efforts to use "piggyback" S-curves for "envelope curve" analysis founder when attempting to find the exact relations between these separate curves. In short, efforts to use such measures for purposes of prediction are very limited.

What is worse is the popular phrase "the pace of change," or, more thumpingly, "the acceleration of the pace of change." The crucial problem is that the terms lack a metric. What is being measured by the words *pace* or *acceleration?* One may run a mile in four minutes: that is a measure. Or with the calculus one can measure how quickly an automobile reaches sixty miles an hour from standstill. But what is being measured simply by the word *change*—change of what?

Even if one talks of technological change, what is being measured? Technological progress may be the better utilization of older organizations of work. It can be the replacement of a man by a machine. It can be a logical analysis in operations research or a mathematical formula such as linear programming. Clearly all these are incommensurate. Even if we were able to take all these heterogeneous modes and recombine them as homogeneous entities, such as "capital" and "labor" in an economist's production function, the subsequent measures of productivity are rough over-all measures and do not account for the exogenous role of technological innovations. (For a detailed analysis of the problems of measurement and understanding of the idea of the pace of change, see my long chapter "The Dimensions of Knowledge and Technology," pp. 167–212 in my book *The Coming of Post-Industrial Society* [New York: Basic Books, 1973], or the paperback edition with a new introduction [New York: Basic Books, 1976]. The analysis of the work of Derek Price and the examination of S-curves are on pp. 177–187.)

If one generalizes, rashly, to talk of the "pace of societal change," then these have to include political changes, such as the inclusion of minorities into the society; the sociological changes in manners and morals; the cultural changes in the breakup of ordered narrative in fiction or the introduction of abstraction in painting. Clearly there is no simple conceptual way to group all these together and find a common mensuration.

The "pace of change" remains, however, as the leading metaphor to impress people about the radical changes in their lives. But much of this is based on a simple-minded and misleading conception of history, of a once unchanging, traditional society fixed in its ways, as against a modern, fast-paced, changing society. But what periods of history and what peoples have ever lived in that presumably unchanging pattern? What peoples have escaped wars, plagues, famines, exhaustion of soils, migrations, conquests by marauding forces, enslavement, colonial conquest—the sweep of Alexander's armies across Egypt through Persia to India; or the extension of Rome from the Mediterranean to Britain; the Huns and the Mongols and the Turks swooping out of central Asia to Europe; the armies of Napoleon expanding to Egypt and to Moscow; and the imperialism of the European powers who, before World War II, ruled 80 percent of the land mass of the world and 80 percent of the world's peoples?

And if one assesses the changes in Western society since the "industrial revolution," consider this: A person born in 1800 and living to 1860 would have seen the introduction of deep coal-mining (because of steam pumps that allowed mines to be sunk hundreds of feet deep, and hundreds of thousands of men to become coal-miners); of factories with looms close by in the spacing of machines, to conserve the energy of steam, so that hundreds of workers were bunched together in such factories; or railroads, which for the first time allowed individuals to move faster than any animal, and extended the range of travel; of steamships that could bring millions of immigrants across the ocean within a sailing period of a few weeks each.

A person born in 1860 and living to 1920 would have seen electricity, which changes the character of night and day; which allows elevators to go up to fifty or more stories, in new skyscrapers; of oil and petro-chemicals which for the first time create materials not found in nature, such as plastics, and which use oil for diesel motors; or the telephone, which allows people to talk to each other readily from a distance (and increases the productivity of doctors, since an individual in a rural area does not have to hitch up a horse and wagon to come to town to summon a doctor, bring him to the farm, and then drive him back, when a telephone call can now make that summons).

Or take an individual born in 1920 and living to 1980, who would have seen automobiles and trucks, propeller planes and jet planes, television and satellite communication, atomic bombs and nuclear energy, laser-guided weapons and intercontinental ballistic missiles.

Were the "future shocks" experienced by individuals living through those six decades any less an upheaval than what may be happening in this generation?

Technology and knowledge have become crucial for the modern world, but we need to be clear what this means. Many people use the term *technology* in relation to machines. But in the past twenty-five years, there has been a crucial change in the character of technology—from a *mechanical* to an *intellectual* technology. Although mechanical technology and machines remain, of course, the newer technologies (i.e., computers and telecommunications, as well as semiautomated production systems) are "driven" by software, programming, computer languages, etc., that are dependent on work in linguistics and mathematics.

The second change is the role of theoretical knowledge, and the codification of theoretical knowledge in the development of innovation. If one looks at the major industries we still have—steel, electricity, telephone, automobile, aviation—they are all nineteenth-century industries (though steel began in the eighteenth century with Darby and the coking process, and aviation in the early twentieth century with the Wright brothers) and their products were created by "talented tinkerers" who worked independently of any comprehensive knowledge of the laws of science. Bessemer, who created the open-hearth furnace for steelmaking, knew little of the work of Sorby on metallurgical properties (Bessemer did his work hoping to win a prize offered by Louis Napoleon for a new cannon). Thomas Edison, one of the great geniuses as an inventor, having invented, among other things, the electric-light filament, the phonograph, and the motion picture, was indifferent to the work of Maxwell and Faraday on electromagnetism. And Marconi, who invented the wireless, knew little of the work of Hertz on radio waves.

All this changes in the twentieth century, in the transformation of physics following the work of Max Planck and quantum theory. In optics, for example, almost all work leads back to a paper by Albert Einstein, in 1904, on the photoelectric effect (for which he won his only Nobel Prize in 1919). Einstein showed that light was not only a wave, but also a pulse or quanta. Everything from the beams that control elevator doors, to the light meters in cameras, and, in particular, the laser (an acronym for Light Amplification Stimulated by the Emission of Radiation), invented by Charles Townes at Columbia in 1939, derives from theoretical knowledge. All the developments of computers, in particular semiconductors, leading to the transistor and the microprocessor, go back to the early work in solid-state physics and the electron-orbit models of Niels Bohr and Felix Bloch. The revolutionary changes in materials technology, in the "transmutation" of materials, derive from quantum mechanics.

Without an awareness of this change, there is no understanding of the sources of innovation and of the importance of basic science in the modern world. All this makes incomprehensible a statement by Alvin Toffler: "We are creating and using up ideas and images at a faster and faster pace. Knowledge like people, places, things and organizational forms is becoming disposable." (*Future Shock*, p. 145.)

There is a further, sociological misunderstanding of the role of technology. This goes back to the phrase "culture lag," created by the sociologist William Fielding Ogburn and used unthinkingly ever since. Ogburn argued that technology had become a leading force for change, but that social institutions and culture had failed to adapt to this, and therefore there was a "culture lag." Ogburn was a "technological determinist," a product of an era in which it was assumed that technology was beneficial and represented progress. But there is the question: Why should we accept or adopt all technological change? Technology (at best) is *instrumental* and not an end in itself. Culture is the realm of values. And for any society it has to be our values that determine whether we accept or reject a technology. The fact that it may now be possible to have an "electronic democracy" does not make it desirable. In fact, the founding fathers of the American constitution would have been horrified at that possibility. This would be a kind of "democracy of the emotions" such as Aristotle had feared. That is why the founders constructed a political order of divided powers, of checks and balances, and of a representative, rather than direct, democracy. One may, or may not, want a more participatory democracy, but it is a decision that must be derived from political theory, not push-button technology.

One of the difficulties with "futurism" as a field, as we can see in its twenty-five-year development, is that it lends itself too easily to "hype"—large claims of innovations that will change society in the twist of a gadget or the doomsday arrival of the apocalypse. Both excite the public. Yet all this discredits the enterprise.

Thirty or so years ago, the technology and popular-science magazines were buzzing about a "revolutionary" new development that would give each person the power that had hitherto been available only in large machines. This was "fractional horsepower," or small motors of one-half or one-fourth horsepower. Revolutionary? With fractional horsepower we now have electric toothbrushes and electric carving knives, as well as power saws and power tools. A convenience for some. And how quickly this has been absorbed into everyday life with nary a thought in anyone's head that it is a development that has transformed their lives.

In 1964, there was great apprehension about automation and the loss of jobs by technological displacement. An "Ad Hoc Committee on the Triple Revolution," headed by the futurist Robert Theobald and the economist Robert Heilbroner, declared that productivity was rising so rapidly that in the near future there would be a cornucopia of goods, so that the link between work and income should be severed and goods distributed freely. President Lyndon B. Johnson set up a National Commission on Technology, Automation, and Economic Progress to assess the issue. After a year of inquiry and fifteen detailed research inquiries, the Commission concluded:

> Our study of the evidence has impressed us with the inadequacy of the basis for any sweeping pronouncements about the speed of scientific and technological progress. . . . Our broad conclusion is that the pace of technological change has increased in recent decades and may increase in the future, but a sharp break in the continuity of technological progress has not occurred, nor is it likely to occur in the next decade.

In fact, much of the increase in productivity at the time occurred in agriculture, which then leveled off, while productivity in the last fifteen years in the United States has been low, about 2 percent a year, or under the historic averages of 3 percent a year. The turn in productivity, particularly in services, has given rise to renewed fears of automation, and these are equally exaggerated.

Often major expectations, much ballyhooed in their time, fail to live up to the promises. In 1948, Denis Gabor invented the hologram, the photographing of three-dimensional images, which many thought would "revolutionize" our modes of imaging, even including the changing at times of the apparent facades of buildings by holographic imaging. After forty years, holograms remain a curiosity or decorative object.

Fifteen years ago, the Japanese announced the "fifth-generation of computers," which would lead to voice recognition and direct language communication with computers. After ten years of work, the project, wildly heralded at the time, was abandoned.

Often innovations are announced as being "far ahead of their time" for many reasons. Facsimile, which is commonplace today, was available more than twenty-five years ago. Indeed, many newspapers assumed that the daily delivery of their paper would be by facsimile through television sets, because of the high cost of transportation and distribution by truck. In Japan, the *Asahi* newspaper, the largest in the world, experimented with a facsimile-delivery system to Hokkaido, in the far north, because of the lack of a tunnel connecting the two large islands of the Japanese archipelago. One can still see in Tokyo the *Asahi* newspaper facsimile as a curio, but the idea was never realized—in large measure because of the slowness and cost of facsimile then. This plan was overtaken by the different innovation of establishing printing plants in different parts of the country and, through satellite, beaming the pages of the paper to those plants for printing there. In this way, the *Wall Street Journal* has a national edition appearing at the same time around the country, as well as Asian and European editions with many of the standard pages.

Even when innovations are made, there are large barriers to their use. Most telecommunication companies in America ten years ago announced the introduction of ISDN—Integrated Services Digital Networks—which would allow for the interchange of voice, text, and image on a common channel. But each company had its own system, and it took ten years to reach a common standard for the compatibility and interconnectedness of the different systems.

Twenty years ago, Jay Forrester and others were announcing the paperless economy and the onset of electronic banking to the home. Twenty years later, major banks are again proposing the onset of electronic banking. And in fanciful fashion, the seer Marshall McLuhan predicted in the 1960s that by the year 2000 the wheel and the highway would become obsolete, giving way to the hovercraft, which would levitate on air—an instance, perhaps, of the medium creating his own medium.

The simple point of all this is not only that technological innovations are uncertain, but that the crucial onset of changes comes with *diffusion*, which is subject to the hazards of cost, old habits, legal barriers, and the like, all of which stretch enormously the time frame of social change.

The credibility of future studies depends on the validity and adequacy of its modes of analysis and the nature of its conceptual schemes. The startling beginning of modern forecasting came with the *Essay on the Principles of Population*, published anonymously by Thomas R. Malthus in 1798, and greatly expanded and altered, in his name, in 1803. Malthus was originally a church curate, and he wrote his essay as a theological-political tract against the "liberationist" views of William Godwin, the political writer and novelist, who was the father of Mary Wollstonecraft Godwin, who herself later married Percy Bysshe Shelley, who in turn endorsed his father-in-law's views. In his *Enquiry Concerning Political Justice* (1793), Godwin said that happiness would incur if one abolished marriage and the family, which constricted human passions. To answer him, Malthus declared that if all restraints on passion were removed, humanity would suffer, for population increases would soon outrun the resources to feed the burgeoning population. Malthus pointed to the New World as providing the optimum conditions of food production and said that while yields would increase arithmetically, populations would increase geometrically, and thus hunger and famine would follow. Charles Darwin said that on reading Malthus on population, he concluded that natural selection was the inevitable result of the rapid increase of all organic beings, for such rapid increase necessarily leads to the struggle for existence.

The population of the world during the time of Malthus was under one billion persons; today it is perhaps five billion. But the long shadow of Malthus reaches over two centuries. Lester Brown, the head of the Worldwatch Institute, and a leading decrier of unrestrained growth, wrote:

> As we make the transition from the third to the final quarter of this century, the world food economy appears to be undergoing a fundamental transformation. Two developments stand out. One, the comfortable reserve of surplus stocks and excess production capacity which the world has enjoyed over the past generation may now be a passing incident in history. Two, the world is becoming overwhelmingly dependent on North America for its food supplies.

This was an article, "The World Food Prospect," in *Science,* December 12, 1975. In 1995, Brown now argues that China's growing demand for grain imports could trigger price shocks, in turn causing starvation for hundreds of millions around the world (*The Economist,* June 10, 1995). In 1968, Gunnar Myrdal, later a Nobel laureate, declared that India would have trouble feeding more than 500 million people. Today, there are close to one billion Indians, and less starvation than twenty-five years ago.

We should not be Pollyannas and assume that all will always be right in the world. But we should be clear as to the reasons for change. In 1975 there was a handful of countries supplying grain to the world—Canada, the United States, Argentina, and Australia. Within twenty years, most parts of the world had become self-sufficient as to stocks of food (though not necessarily in good nutrition), and in Europe, the Common Market has faced repeated crises over the price supports for its agricultural policies and the need to cut back on food production. India, following "the green revolution," is relatively self-sufficient, though distribution remains a problem. Except for a few areas of the world, such as Bangladesh, and the occasional droughts in parts of Africa, food itself is not a worldwide problem.

In fact, the problems are more often *political,* not agricultural or technological. Burma was always a rice-exporting country, feeding large parts of Southeast Asia. But when it was taken over by a xenophobic military dictatorship, rice production collapsed, and Burma (now known as Myanmar) became a rice importer—though its rice-paddy lands remain. Ethiopia has often suffered from droughts, but a small-shopkeeper network provided buffer stocks of food for less extreme periods of famine. However, the Marxist dictatorship of Mengistu smashed the small-shopkeeper system, and Ethiopia starved. In Africa, the Sudan and Somalia fed themselves until ethnic, secessionist, and landlord conflicts devastated those countries. The situation in the former Soviet Union is markedly instructive. The wheat-growing areas of Russia—forming a triangle from Moscow to Rostov to Lake Baikal—are roughly similar to the North American wheat belt from Saskatchewan through North Dakota, though the weather is often more uncertain in Russia. Yet the productivity of North American agriculture has been four to five times that of Russia because the bureaucratic structures of state and collective farms provided few incentives, and these farms often could not obtain machinery from other government firms, so finally Russia had to enter into the world market twenty years ago to obtain sufficient grain. Geography, no; politics, yes.

In assessing modes of analysis, two further, often egregious and misleading modes should be mentioned. One is trend analysis, or "mega-trends." Trend analysis is relatively straightforward. One takes a time-line set of indicators and simply extrapolates these. The assumption is that what was true in the past will continue in the future. Yet this mode in no way identifies "system breaks" or assesses their consequences. Take one fateful trend in American economic—and social—history. From 1900 to 1942 or so, agricultural productivity in the United States averaged about 1 to 2 percent a year. In the 1940s and for more than two decades thereafter, productivity averaged 6 to 8 percent a year. What had happened was the introduction of chemical fertilizers, which increased yields enormously. As a result, from 1950 to 1970 more than twenty million persons left the farms, creating one of the largest internal migrations in American history. A large proportion of them were sharecroppers, mostly black, who were pushed off the farms as unnecessary. Sharecropping, which involved some of the most miserable social problems in the United States before World War II, was largely eliminated. Huge numbers of blacks trekked out of the South, crowding into Watts in Los Angeles, into Bronzeville in Chicago, into Harlem and Detroit. Unemployment figures soared, not because large numbers were suddenly unemployed, but because previously they had been on a farm, and as part of the household economy they were not counted. What was also true is that the runoff of chemical fertilizers from the farms polluted many of the rivers and lakes of America. In an important way, a "system break" such as the trend-line in agriculture became a "strategic site" to trace out social consequences, but such analyses are rarely done, since "futurists" are usually more eager simply to extrapolate trend-lines.

A second example is the "closed system" model. This includes the computer models initiated by Jay Forrester of M.I.T., expanded by his student Dennis Meadows, and given huge publicity in the "Limits of Growth Studies" popularized by the Club of Rome in the 1970s. Such models took a resource that presumably had finite limits—the growth in population and the growth in demand—and by plotting the interaction of these variables showed a ceiling level where the world would exhaust its resources. The Club of Rome achieved worldwide publicity because the release of its claims coincided with the "oil shock" of 1973 and the long lines at the gas stations. The oil shock, however, was not a resource problem. It was a political club wielded by a cartel, the OPEC nations, which used its then-monopoly position to sharply raise the price of oil.

Actually, the first resource that the Meadows–Club of Rome studies said would be exhausted was copper. Based on identifiable resources and growing demand, the Club of Rome predicted a ceiling on copper. The price of copper did, indeed, begin to rise. A number of oil companies, such as Arco and Sohio (later bought by British Petroleum), bought the Anaconda and Kennicott copper companies as hedges for their oil business, yet each lost several billion dollars. And for twenty years, copper has virtually been a glut on the market, and the commodity price has been constantly low. What happened? For one, the studies never built "price" into their models. With the rising prices, it became profitable to reopen old mines. In the Massai range above Lake Superior, copper, once unprofitable since it yielded only a few pounds in a ton, was extracted. Panama and Zaire began working old mines. Israel reopened mines that had been dormant since King Solomon's time. When new supply came on the market and prices tumbled, a number of these countries sought support from the United Nations, on the ground that they had invested capital to "save" the developed world.

There was still, however, the long-run question of "final" exhaustion. But here a new "surprise" entered into the equation—one that increasingly recurs in the areas of supply—namely, *technological substitution*. In this case, it was the invention of fiber optics that increasingly outmoded the old copper cables in every telecommunication system in the world, and provided cheaper, broader-banded channels for communication.

In fact, with the spread of the "materials revolution," the world need not run out of almost any natural resource—at a cost. Old natural-resource sites are becoming outmoded. More than that, in looking at metals, one does not ask specifically for steel, or zinc, or copper, but for the *properties* wanted—ductility, tensility, conductivity—and these can be supplied in different combinations and composites. In World War II, there was a rubber cartel, a copper cartel, a zinc cartel organized by countries where these natural resources were located. Today, with the exception of oil, no such cartel is possible. And oil—whose cartel is breaking up for political reasons—was possible because oil was so cheap, as against alternatives such as thermal, or shale, or solar, and possibly as against nuclear energy.

Given these cautions, what can one say about identifying social changes? It is necessary, first, to distinguish between *prediction* and *forecasting*, arbitrary as this distinction may be. Prediction is the specification of "point" events—single items or events that may occur in "the future." Yet this is inherently difficult because of the multiple intersection of different variables (as with weather prediction), even if one could plot these in "real time." The other is the limitation of information, particularly in closed arenas. This is what makes political prediction, especially about key decisions, difficult from "the outside." I call this Brzezinski's Law, in honor of my sometime colleague at Columbia who was also a member of the Commission on the Year 2000.

Zbigniew Brzezinski (before going to the White House as national security adviser to President Jimmy Carter) was once being baited on television by a hostile commentator. He asked: Professor Brzezinski, you are a Kremlinologist? Yes, was the reply, if you like that ugly word. You tell the White House what is going on in the Soviet Union? Yes, when they listen. And the interviewer then sprang his trap: Professor Brzezinski, why did you fail to predict the ouster of Nikita Khrushchev? And Brzezinski, who is quick on his feet, replied: Tell me, if Khrushchev could not predict his own ouster, how could you expect me to do so?

The answer is that such timing, when possible, is the product of "intelligence," of knowing the play of political forces and combinations within the arena of a closed circle. Could one have predicted the collapse and breakup of the Soviet Union? One could and did. There were two factors. One was economic, the increasing failure of centralized planning. The Gosplan could not make the literally millions of price decisions necessary for the allocation of resources for production (military and civilian) from a small central office, even with the (theoretical) use of computers to collect and register all the necessary price information (which the Soviet economist Leonid Kantarovich had proposed in his system of dynamic programming). Thus greater and greater inefficiencies and misuse of resources mounted.

The second was moral and political, the evident loss of legitimacy, the end of ideology, and the belief in the future which had first given hope to the adherents of the new faith system. Much of this was evident in Eastern Europe in the Hungarian, Polish, and Czech revolutions, all led by Communists and all crushed by Soviet military forces.

In short, *the process* was clear, though the exact "tipping point" could not, perhaps, have been "predicted." Equally, one cannot predict what is often the decisive role of leadership in historical situations. When the French Army in Algeria, in 1952, threatened to send paratroopers to Paris to seize the government, the continuation of Guy Mollet's weak government might not have prevented such an act. Yet the recall to power of General Charles de Gaulle with his decisive authority saved the day. One need not subscribe to a "great man" theory of history to acknowledge that the record is full of turning points, by the acts of individuals that were decisive for the fate of nations.

One can forecast when one has an *algorithm*, a decision rule that allows one, with some confidence, to identify future outcomes. Briefly, the following three are worthy of mention:

1. *Institutional stability*. In 1964, when the Commission on the Year 2000 was initiated at the American Academy of Arts and Sciences, I went to John Gardner, then the head of the Carnegie Corporation, to ask for support. The idea is an intriguing one, he said, but give me a "for instance" of serious forecasting. I recalled a remark of Bertrand de Jouvenel (in whose Futuribles project I had been a consultant for the Ford Foundation) and said: This is 1964, and there will be an election for president of the United States. There will be one in 1968, 1972, 1976 . . . 2000. He looked at me and said: That's a damned obvious prediction. And I replied: Yes, but there are now about 120 nations in the world. Of how many nations can one make such claims with confidence?

The degree of institutional stability in the United States and a handful of other democratic nations in the world—where changes of parties in office can take place peacefully through regulated competition, with no resort to force by a loser, and decisions by a Supreme Court to decide contentious issues of interest and morals—is extraordinarily rare in the world. And these conditions of stability, under the rule of law, are a condition for a tolerable life and security.

It is the failure to establish "institutional succession" that often gives rise to crises in regimes when the old leaders die and a struggle for power ensues. This was the case in Yugoslavia after the death of Tito. It was the situation in China after the death of Mao, and it may recur with the death of Deng. In Africa, where the first generation of leaders (e.g., Nkrumah in Ghana) began to weaken, military rule took over. The problem of succession may threaten the stability of countries such as South Africa, Indonesia, and Singapore, with the passing of Mandela, Suharto, and LeeKwan Yew.

2. *Structural changes.* These are changes in the demographic profiles of a society—a bunching of baby-boomers or an increase in longevity, creating a large aging population—all of which create different requirements in an educational system, health expenditures, and the like. And there are sectoral changes, such as the decline of agriculture or manufacturing, regional changes in the sites of work, and transportation patterns.

It is the awareness of such changes that makes a society flexible and responsive—when there is a political will to make such changes. The transformation of Japan from 1950 to 1990 is a relevant case in point. Japan began its recovery concentrating on textiles and cheap manufactured products based on a low-wage labor force. When Japan became undercut by Hong Kong and other countries, it moved to heavy industry—steel, shipbuilding, and automobiles—then to optics and instruments, and then, because of the oil shock and the rising costs of energy, Japan moved to electronics, computers, and knowledge-based products. There is nothing "automatic" about such progressions, but if a society wishes to make such changes, then a number of "functional requirements" come in their wake. Apart from tribal warfare, for example, Africa today is poorly placed in the world economy for lack of an adequate educational system.

3. *Structural frameworks.* This is an effort to provide a unified and comprehensive social structure based on the *logic* of a set of social principles. I offer, as a case in point, a "picture" of a postindustrial society (see Table 1 on the next page).

This is *not* a forecast of what will come. It is, rather, as I have stated, "an *as if,* a fiction, a logical construction of what *could be* against which a future social reality can be compared in order to see what intervened to change society in the direction it did take."

There are some methodological stipulations that a disciplined social science inquiry has to observe:

One has to state a *concept,* its *dimensions,* and the *indicators* (statistical, if possible) of those dimensions. Take the concept of the *postindustrial society.* These are its five dimensions:

1. Economic sector: the change from a goods-producing to a service economy.
2. Occupational distribution: the pre-eminence of the professional and technical class.
3. Axial principle: the centrality of theoretical knowledge as the source of innovation and of policy formulation for the society.
4. Future orientation: the control of technology and technological assessment.
5. Decision-making: the creation of a new "intellectual technology."

The indicators—or the range of effects—would be the changing of numbers of persons in goods production and services, the changes in the numbers of the professional and technical classes, and so on.

There also should be an effort to stipulate an axial principle—in this case, the codification of theoretical knowledge. The change in

TABLE 1. From Industrial to Postindustrial Society: General Schema of Social Change

	Preindustrial	*Industrial*	*Postindustrial*	
Regions:	Asia Africa Latin America	Western Europe Soviet Union Japan	United States	
Economic sector:	*Primary* Extractive: 　Agriculture 　Mining 　Fishing 　Timber	*Secondary* Goods producing: 　Manufacturing 　Processing	*Tertiary* Transportation Utilities *Quinary* Health Education Research Government Recreation	*Quaternary* Trade Finance Insurance Real estate
Occupational slope:	Farmer Miner Fisherman Unskilled worker	Semiskilled worker Engineer	Professional and technical scientists	
Technology:	Raw materials	Energy	Information	
Design:	Game against nature	Game against fabricated nature	Game between persons	
Methodology:	Common sense experience	Empiricism Experimentation	Abstract theory: models, simulation, decision theory, systems analysis	
Time perspective:	Orientation to the past ad hoc responses	Ad hoc adaptiveness Projections	Future orientation Forecasting	
Axial principle:	Traditionalism: Land/resource limitation	Economic growth: State or private control of investment decisions	Centrality of and codification of theoretical knowledge	

From *The Coming of Post-Industrial Society* by Daniel Bell (New York: Basic Books, 1973, p. 117).

the character of knowledge is the fulcrum of the change from an industrial to a postindustrial society.

There are two cautions to be noted. The word *society*, again, is somewhat misleading, for I am *not* proposing a *complete* change in the society—considering the disjunctions of realms vis-à-vis the polity and the culture. But one is trapped sometimes by the ubiquitous use of the word, as in *capitalist society* or *bourgeois society*. And this obscures the salient points sketched here, which are the changes in the *techno-economic structure*. These changes do not "determine" other realms of a society, but they do pose management problems, particularly for the political order that has to respond to these changes.

The second point, needless to say, is that this is not the only way one can conceptualize major structural changes in a society. Clearly there could be many others, such as one that makes market transactions, or different emphases of technology, an alternative sketch. Whatever approach is used, it needs to have a disciplined and methodologically self-conscious intellectual structure, if it is to be taken seriously.

Finally, here are three reflections on what an intellectual enterprise dealing with public policy needs to observe:

1. The frequent emphasis of futurism is to look ahead in spectacular and sweeping terms, and to neglect the more difficult, prosaic tasks of seeking to chart the *consequences* of the decisions taken now. I repeat what I wrote on the opening page of *Toward the Year 2000*, almost thirty years ago, because the argument is still relevant:

> Time, said St. Augustine, is a three-fold present: the present as we experience it, the past as a present memory, and the future as a present expectation. By that criterion, the world of the year 2000 has already arrived, for in the decisions we make now, in the way we design our environment and thus sketch the lines of constraints, the future is committed. Just as the gridiron pattern of city streets in the nineteenth century shaped the linear growth of cities in the twentieth, so the new networks of radial highways, the location of new towns, the reordering of graduate-school curricula, the decision to create or not to create a computer utility as a single system, and the like will frame the tectonics of the twenty-first century. The future is not an overarching leap into the distance; it begins in the present.

2. At the heart of any society is *trust*, the trust of a citizenry in the fairness of the courts, the truth spoken by its leaders, and a belief in the country of which they are part,

Economics, for example, is based on the idea of "stable preferences" in the actions of individuals, so that what may have been true three or four months back will be true three or six months hence. In the econometric models of forecasting, this is called the use of "lagged variables." Yet, as we saw in the rising inflation of the 1970s and '80s, people no longer believed that government policy would bear down steadily on the interest rate, but would relax every four years to obtain votes. So individuals kept on going into debt, believing that the new borrowing would wipe out the debts of the old. It took a more than 20 percent interest rate finally to break the back of inflation. In short, when the "political discount rate," so to speak, is higher than the economic discount rate, policy is in trouble.

And when a government lies to its people (as Nixon did in Watergate and Reagan did in the Iran-Contra affair), it is little wonder that distrust and paranoia spread among a population.

3. Finally, what is crucial to any society is its value system. The virtue of the market is that it coordinates human interdependence in some optimal fashion, in accordance with the expressed preferences of buyers and sellers—within a given distribution of income. Dollars are not like one man, one vote: those who have more can buy more, and can exert a greater influence in shaping the patterns of production and services.

But what ultimately provides direction for the economy is not the signals of the price system, but the value system of the culture in which the economy is embedded. One of the surprises of the past thirty years (though it was anticipated in the Commission on the Year 2000) has been the environmental movement. When swarms of insects were reducing crops, growers rushed quickly to chemical agents such as DDT. Yet as Rachel Carson pointed out in her poignant *Silent Spring* (1962), its effect was also to kill off birds that ingested the chemicals—just as, in later years, large oil spills wiped out sections of marine life. And the value of the environment began to challenge economic efficiency.

The value system of modern Western society has emphasized material growth and the increase of wealth above all other considerations. Yet these have also brought along many social costs. No society can ignore the problem of balance, of leaving the basic decisions either entirely to the market or to bureaucratic rule. These are some of the most difficult problems of political theory. They are value and communal judgments. And technology provides no answers, no matter on what wave it rides.

DANIEL BELL

Alphabetical List of Articles

A

Abortion
Arthur B. Shostack

Acid Rain
Jurgen A. Schmandt

Adult Learning
Allen Tough

Advertising
Fred Danzig

Africa
Vivian Lowery Derryck
Robert J. Berg

Agents of Change
Robert Theobald

Aging of the Population
Nestor E. Terleckyj

Agricultural Technology
Ashok K. Dhingra
David S. Weir

Air Transport
Tom Conger

Alcohol
Graham T. T. Molitor

Animal Rights
Michael W. Fox

Antarctica
Christopher Joyner

Apocalyptic Future
Lane E. Jennings

Appropriate Technology
George McRobie

Architectural Design
John P. Eberhard

Arms Race
James Adams

Art Dealers
Steven Vincent

Artificial Intelligence
Paul J. Werbos

Artificial Life
Steven Levy

Arts
Richard Kostelanetz

Asia
Yogesh Atal

Asimov, Isaac
W. Warren Wagar

Astronomy
Donald W. Goldsmith

Australia and New Zealand
Richard A. Slaughter

B

Batteries
Jerry Kline

Behavior: Social Constraints
Charles M. Johnston

Bell, Daniel
W. Warren Wagar

Biodiversity
Walter V. Reid
Kenton R. Miller

Bioethics
Clifton Anderson

Broadcasting
Edward O. Fritts

Alphabetical List of Articles

Alphabetical List of Articles

Alphabetical List of Articles

Alphabetical List of Articles

Alphabetical List of Articles

Alphabetical List of Articles

Alphabetical List of Articles

Directory of Contributors

A

Tom Abeles
Sagacity, Inc.
EXTINCTION OF SPECIES

Virginia Deane Abernethy
Vanderbilt University Medical School
FAMILY PLANNING

Clark C. Abt
Center for the Study of Small States
INTERNATIONAL TENSIONS

James Adams
Washington Bureau Chief, *Sunday Times of London*
ARMS RACE
ESPIONAGE AND COUNTERINTELLIGENCE

Arthur J. Alexander
Japan Economic Institute, Washington, D.C.
JAPAN

Roy C. Amara
Strategic Decisions Group
WORLD: PROLOGUE AND EPILOGUE

Clifton E. Anderson
University of Idaho
BIOETHICS

John B. Anderson
Former Representative from Illinois to the U.S. Congress
THIRD POLITICAL PARTIES

Martin Anderson
Stanford University
CAPITALISM

Peter Anderson
University of New Orleans
SEXUAL REPRODUCTION

Walter Truett Anderson
Meridian International Institute
GENETIC TECHNOLOGIES
GLOBAL CULTURE

Yogesh Atal
UNESCO, Paris and Bangkok
ASIA

Richard Avancino
San Francisco SPCA
PETS

Robert U. Ayres
The European Institute of Business Administration, Fontainebleau, France
INTELLECTUAL PROPERTY
RESEARCH AND DEVELOPMENT
TECHNOLOGICAL INNOVATION

B

William Sims Bainbridge
National Science Foundation
RELIGION: INSTITUTIONS AND PRACTICES

Frank Barnaby
Former Director, Stockholm Peace Research Institute
MILITARY TECHNOLOGIES

David B. Barrett
Global Evangelization Movement; Regent University
CHRISTIANITY
APPENDIX: CHRONOLOGY OF FUTURISM AND THE FUTURE
GLOBAL STATISTICS

Ellie Bator
Forum Foundation
CHURCH-STATE AFFAIRS

Gary L. Bauer
Family Research Council
FAMILIES AND HOUSEHOLDS

M. Garrett Bauman
Monroe Community College
LIBERAL ARTS

Harold S. Becker
West Yarmouth, Massachusetts
VALUES FORMATION

Directory of Contributors

Jack N. Behrman
University of North Carolina, Chapel Hill
GLOBAL BUSINESS: DOMINANT ORGANIZATIONAL FORMS

Cecil H. Bell
Forum Foundation
CHURCH-STATE AFFAIRS

Daniel Bell
American Academy of Arts and Sciences
COMMISSION ON THE YEAR 2000
INTRODUCTION: REFLECTIONS AT THE END OF AN AGE

Wendell Bell
Yale University
VALUES

Robert J. Berg
African-American Institute
AFRICA

Fred Best
Pacific Management and Resource Associates
WORKING CONDITIONS

Igor Bestuzhev-Lada
Institute for Social Research, Moscow
COMMUNISM

Clement Bezold
Institute for Alternative Futures
MEDICAL CARE PROVIDERS
PHARMACEUTICALS

Peter C. Bishop
University of Houston, Clear Lake
CHANGE

Tsvi Bisk
St.E.P. Institute, Kfar Saba, Israel
JUDAISM
MIDDLE EAST

Richard H. Blades
Political Consultant
POLITICAL CAMPAIGNING

Joseph B. Board
Union College, Schenectady, New York
SWEDEN

Elisabeth Mann Borgese
Dalhousie University, Halifax, Nova Scotia Canada
OCEANS

David B. Bostian
Herzog, Heine, Geduld
INVESTMENTS

Leon Bouvier
Tulane University
DEMOGRAPHY

Ben Bova
West Hartford, Connecticut
SPACE FLIGHT

James R. Bright
Fort Myers, Florida
SOCIAL CHANGE: UNITED STATES

Arnold Brown
Weiner, Edrich, Brown, Inc.
BUSINESS STRUCTURE: FORMS, IMPACTS

Harold O. J. Brown
Trinity Evangelical Divinity School, Rockford, Illinois
RELIGION, SPIRITUALITY, MORALITY

Robert S. Browne
Washington, D.C.
RACE, CASTE, AND ETHNIC DIVERSITY

William F. Buckley, Jr.
National Review
CONSERVATISM, POLITICAL

George Bugliarello
Polytechnic University, Brooklyn, New York
ENGINEERING

Charles Buki
American Institute of Architects
HOUSING, AFFORDABLE

Catherine G. Burke
University of Southern California
URBAN TRANSIT

William M. Burnett
Gas Research Institute
PIPELINES

C

Joseph A. Califano
Center on Addiction and Substance Abuse, Columbia University; former Secretary of Health, Education, and Welfare
HEALTH CARE COSTS

John H. Campbell
Federal Bureau of Investigation
CRIME, VIOLENT

Albert H. Cantril
Consultant in Opinion and Survey Research
SURVEYS

Richard K. Caputo
Barry University
UNEMPLOYMENT INSURANCE, WORKERS' COMPENSATION,
JOB SECURITY

David L. Carter
Michigan State University
CRIME, ORGANIZED
CRIME, VIOLENT

Vincent Casaregola
St. Louis University
MINORITIES

Michael Cassutt
Studio City, California
SPACE COLONIZATION

William B. Cate
Forum Foundation
CHURCH-STATE AFFAIRS

Bernard Cazes
Commisariat Général du Plan, Paris
FRANCE

Peggy Chaudhry
Villanova University
GRAY MARKET GOODS

Phyllis Chesler
Brooklyn, New York
WOMEN'S MOVEMENT

Bryce J. Christensen
Rockford Institute
PRESCHOOL EDUCATION

Joseph Chuman
Ethical Culture Society of New Jersey
NONRELIGIOUS BELIEFS

Mary E. Clark
Denison University
MIND: NEW MODES OF THINKING

Joseph F. Coates
Coates and Jarratt, Inc.
SCIENTIFIC BREAKTHROUGHS
WORKFORCE DIVERSITY

Vary T. Coates
U.S. Congress, Office of Technology Assessment
INFORMATION TECHNOLOGY

Bernard L. Cohen
University of Pittsburgh
NUCLEAR POWER

Robert H. Cohen
U.S. Postal Rate Commission
POSTAL SERVICES

Sam Cole
State University of New York, Buffalo
CULTURE AND SOCIETY

D. Stuart Conger
Canadian Guidance and Counseling Foundation
SOCIAL INVENTIONS

Tom Conger
Coates and Jarratt, Inc.
AIR TRANSPORT

McKinley Conway
Conway Data, Inc.
MACROENGINEERING

Michael Cook
Rockefeller University
GENETIC ENGINEERING

Blake M. Cornish
Mayer, Brown, and Platt
LAW OF THE LAND

Edward S. Cornish
President, World Future Society
FUTURISTS

George Anthony Cornish
BNA Communications
TELECOMMUNICATIONS

Frank D. Cox
Santa Barbara City College
MARRIAGE

Richard P. Critchfield
Deceased
LIFESTYLES, REGIONAL

Robert A. Cropf
St. Louis University
MINORITIES

David Crowe
National Association of Homebuilders
HOME OWNERSHIP

D

A. J. Dahl
E. I. duPont de Nemours and Company
MATERIALS: RESEARCH AND DEVELOPMENT

Directory of Contributors

Louis J. D'Amore
L. J. D'Amore and Associates
HOSPITALITY INDUSTRY: LODGINGS AND ACCOMMODATIONS

David Dalby
Observatoire Linguistique, Cressenville, France
LANGUAGES

Gordon T. Danby
Brookhaven National Laboratory
MAGLEV

Fred Danzig
Advertising Age
ADVERTISING

David R. Darr
U.S. Forest Service, Department of Agriculture
FORESTRY

James A. Dator
University of Hawaii, Manoa
LAWMAKING, JUDICIAL
WOMEN IN FUTURES STUDIES

Christopher J. Dede
George Mason University
EDUCATIONAL TECHNOLOGIES

Etel E. De Loach
Aesculapian Institute of Healing Arts
HEALTH CARE: ALTERNATIVE THERAPIES

Vivian Lowery Derryck
African-American Institute
AFRICA

Margaret de Vries
Bethesda, Maryland
MONETARY SYSTEM

Ashok K. Dhingra
E. I. duPont de Nemours and Company
AGRICULTURAL TECHNOLOGY
MATERIALS: RESEARCH AND DEVELOPMENT

Howard F. Didsbury, Jr.
Kean College
FUTURES EDUCATION

Fred DiMaria
The Quantic Group, Ltd.
CHEMICALS, FINE

Yehezkel Dror
The Hebrew University of Jerusalem
GOVERNANCE

Tom Dufficy
National Association of Photographic Manufacturers
PHOTOGRAPHY

William L. Duncan
McDonnell Douglas, Helicopter Division
FACTORIES AND MANUFACTURING

E

John P. Eberhard
Carnegie Mellon University
ARCHITECTURAL DESIGN

Roderick G. Eggert
Colorado School of Mines
MINERALS

Leon Eisenberg
Harvard University
FAMILY PATTERNS

Duane S. Elgin
Choosing Our Future, Inc.
LIFESTYLES, ALTERNATIVE

William D. Ellington
Forum Foundation
CHURCH-STATE AFFAIRS

Selwyn Enzer
University of Southern California
INTERNATIONAL TRADE: SUSTAINING GROWTH

Scott W. Erickson
Upjohn Company
FREE TRADE
POLITICAL CYCLES

Amitai Etzioni
George Washington University
COMMUNITARIANISM

Raymond P. Ewing
Issues Management Consulting Group
BUSINESS GOVERNANCE

Thomas G. Exter
TGE Demographics
MIGRATION, INTERNATIONAL

F

Jean L. Farinelli
Creamer Dickson Basford
COMPUTER HARDWARE
COMPUTERS: SAFETY

Frank Feather
GEODEVCO, Aurora, Ontario
WORKFORCE REDISTRIBUTION

Paul M. Feine
Richmond, Virginia
ELECTRIC POWER

Kenneth E. Feltman
Employers Council on Flexible Compensation
HUMAN RESOURCES DEVELOPMENT

Victor C. Ferkiss
Georgetown University
TECHNOLOGICAL DETERMINISM

Jonathan D. Fife
ERIC Clearinghouse on Higher Education
HIGHER EDUCATION

Christopher Flavin
World Watch Society
ENERGY

Joseph Flower
The Change Project
HEALTH CARE

James R. Follain
Syracuse University
HOUSING, COST AND AVAILABILITY OF

Jay W. Forrester
Massachusetts Institute of Technology
ECONOMIC CYCLES: MODELS AND SIMULATIONS

J. D. Foster
Tax Foundation
TAXES

Jib Fowles
University of Houston, Clear Lake
TELEVISION

Charles Fox
Charles Fox Associates, Inc.
COSMETICS AND TOILETRIES

Michael W. Fox
Humane Society of the United States
ANIMAL RIGHTS

J. Davidson Frame
George Washington University
TECHNOLOGY DIFFUSION

Van Arsdale France
Disney Universities
THEME PARKS AND ORGANIZED ATTRACTIONS

Robert T. Francoeur
Fairleigh Dickinson University
SEXUAL CODES

Joshua Freedman
University of California, Los Angeles
MENTAL HEALTH

Martin Friedman
New Product News
NEW CONSUMER PRODUCTS

Edward O. Fritts
National Association of Broadcasters
BROADCASTING

G

Medard Gabel
World Game Institute, Inc.
ENERGY, RENEWABLE SOURCES OF

William E. Gahr
Food and Agriculture Issues
FOOD AND AGRICULTURE

Ellen Galinsky
Families and Work Institute
CHILD CARE

Anthony E. Gallo
U.S. Department of Agriculture
FOOD DISTRIBUTION

Gary Gappert
University of Akron
CITIES

J. L. A. Garcia
Georgetown University
MORALS

Sherwin Gardner
Regulatory Policy Consulting Services
FOOD AND DRUG SAFETY

John J. Gargan
Kent State University
CLASS AND UNDERCLASS

Gary L. Geipel
Hudson Institute
GERMANY

Abraham Moses Genen
Office of the Attorney General, New York State
COMMUNICATIONS: MEDIA LAW

Directory of Contributors

Benjamin Ginsberg
Johns Hopkins University
VOTING

Dru C. Gladney
University of Hawaii
CHINA: ETHNIC REAWAKENING

Nathan Glazer
Harvard University
PLURALISM

Jerome C. Glenn
American Council for the United Nations University
DEVELOPMENT: WESTERN PERSPECTIVE
POST-INFORMATION AGE

Frank M. Go
University of Calgary
TOURISM

Michel Godet
Conservatoire National des Arts et Métiers, Paris
TECHNOLOGY AND SOCIETY

Alan Goldhammer
Industrial Biotechnology Association
GENETICS: AGRICULTURAL APPLICATIONS

Donald W. Goldsmith
Berkeley, California
ASTRONOMY

Tom Goodale
George Mason University
LEISURE TIME

Deborah Gordon
Union of Concerned Scientists
TRANSPORTATION

Theodore J. Gordon
The Futures Group
TECHNOLOGY AND SCIENCE

William J. Gore
University of Washington, Seattle
DEMOCRACY
SOCIAL DEMOCRACY

Roderic Gorney
University of California, Los Angeles
MENTAL HEALTH

David Dodson Gray
Bolton Institute for a Sustainable Future
DERIVATIVES
DISASTERS, PLANNING FOR
ENVIRONMENTAL BEHAVIOR

FUTURE: NEAR, MID-, AND LONG-TERM
NATURAL RESOURCES, USE OF
SURPRISES

Elizabeth Dodson Gray
Bolton Institute for a Sustainable Future
WOMEN AND RELIGION

Annette Green
The Fragrance Foundation
FRAGRANCE

Sheldon F. Greenberg
Johns Hopkins University
COUNTERFEITING
DRUGS, ILLICIT

Jan M. Grell
University of Akron
CHILD ABUSE

Peter C. Grenquist
Association of American University Presses, Inc.
PRINTED WORD

Linda Groff
California State University, Dominguez Hills
SOCIAL AND POLITICAL EVOLUTION

Ann Hofstra Grogg
Winchester, Virginia
MUSEUMS

Bertram Gross
Saint Mary's College of California
HUMAN RIGHTS

Steven Gurley
Population Reference Bureau
POPULATION GROWTH: WORLDWIDE

Greg Gutfeld
Prevention Magazine
EXERCISE AND FITNESS

H

William E. Halal
George Washington University
EVOLUTION, SOCIAL
INSTITUTIONS, CONFIDENCE IN
ORGANIZATIONAL COMPLEXITY

Charles Hallisey
Harvard University
BUDDHISM

Trevor Hancock
Kleinburg, Ontario
PUBLIC HEALTH

Willis W. Harman
Institute of Noetic Sciences
HOLISTIC BELIEFS
PARASENSORY PHENOMENA

Carl Haub
Population Reference Bureau
POPULATION GROWTH: WORLDWIDE

Nelson Hay
American Gas Association
NATURAL GAS

James L. Hecht
University of Delaware
RUSSIA

Hugh Heclo
George Mason University
PUBLIC ASSISTANCE PROGRAMS: SOCIAL SECURITY

Robert K. Heldman
U.S. West Communications
DIGITAL COMMUNICATIONS

Hazel Henderson
Center for Sustainable Development and Alternative
Futures
ENVIRONMENTAL INDICATORS
INFORMAL ECONOMY

Lenneal J. Henderson
University of Baltimore
RACIAL AND ETHNIC CONFLICT

Rosanna Hertz
Wellesley College
FAMILY PROBLEMS

James C. Hickman
University of Wisconsin, Madison
INSURANCE

Christopher T. Hill
George Mason University
SCIENCE ISSUES

Andy Hines
Coates and Jarratt, Inc.
MEDIA OF EXCHANGE
NANOTECHNOLOGY

Charles D. Hobbs
Public Policy and Management Consultant
SOCIAL WELFARE PHILOSOPHIES

John M. Holcomb
University of Denver
CIVIL PROTEST

R. A. Houghton
The Woods Hole Research Center
CLIMATE AND METEOROLOGY

Nils E. Hovik
Lehigh County Community College
WEALTH

Barbara Marx Hubbard
Foundation for Conscious Evolution
CONSCIOUS EVOLUTION

Lauren Huddleston
The Consortium
ENTREPRENEURSHIP

Heather E. Hudson
University of San Francisco
SATELLITE COMMUNICATIONS
SPACE SATELLITES

Gary Hufbauer
Institute for International Economics
INTERNATIONAL TRADE: REGIONAL TRADE AGREEMENTS

Kenneth W. Hunter
University of Maryland
INSTITUTIONS AND ORGANIZATIONS

Peter Barton Hutt
Covington and Burling
FOOD LAWS

Henry R. Huttenbach
City College, City University of New York
NATIONALISM

Gary Hymel
Hill and Knowlton
LEGISLATIVE AND PARLIAMENTARY SYSTEMS

I

Sohail Inayatullah
Queensland University of Technology, Australia
DEVELOPMENT, ALTERNATIVE

J

Jennifer Jarratt
Coates and Jarratt, Inc.
WORK

Directory of Contributors

Lane E. Jennings
World Future Society
APOCALYPTIC FUTURE
DYSTOPIAS

Susan Jette
Forum Foundation
CHURCH-STATE AFFAIRS

Stanley Johanson
University of Texas School of Law
ESTATE AND FINANCIAL PLANNING

Carl T. Johnson
Compressed Gas Association
INDUSTRIAL GASES

Nicholas Johnson
University of Iowa
ELECTRONIC CONVERGENCE

Todd M. Johnson
International Journal of Frontier Missions
RELIGIONS, DECLINE OR RISE OF
RELIGIONS, STATISTICAL PROJECTIONS OF

Charles M. Johnston
Institute for Creative Development
BEHAVIOR: SOCIAL CONSTRAINTS

Julia Hughes Jones
Former Auditor, State of Arkansas
WOMEN IN POLITICS

Earl C. Joseph
Anticipatory Sciences, Inc.
HEALTH CARE: TECHNOLOGICAL DEVELOPMENTS

James A. Joseph
Council on Federations
PHILANTHROPY

Nandini Joshi
Foundation for Constructive Development, Ahmedabad,
    India
INDIA

Christopher Joyner
George Washington University
ANTARCTICA

K

Robert Kalisch
American Gas Association
NATURAL GAS

John J. Karch
World Slovak Congress
EUROPE, CENTRAL AND EASTERN

David Keating
National Taxpayers Union
PUBLIC FINANCE

John P. Keenan
University of Wisconsin
SOCIAL SCIENCES

John R. Kelly
University of Illinois, Champaign
SPORTS AND GAMES, COMPETITIVE

Rita Mae Kelly
Policy Studies Organization
SEXUAL HARASSMENT

Josephine Kelsey
Kelsey Associates
INDUSTRIAL DESIGN

Miriam Friedman Kelty
National Institute on Aging, National Institutes of
    Health
ELDERLY, LIVING ARRANGEMENTS

Roger L. Kemp
Center for Strategic Planning
CITIES, NORTH AMERICAN

John W. Kendrick
George Washington University
PRODUCTIVITY

John L. Kennedy
Oil & Gas Journal
PETROLEUM

John Kettle
Futuresearch Publishing, Inc.
CANADA

Fred D. Kierstead
University of Houston, Clear Lake
TECHNOLOGICAL CHANGE

Hee Sun Kim
U.S. Postal Rate Commission
POSTAL SERVICES

Russell Kinderman
Center for Leadership Development, Commission on
    Peace Officer Standards and Training
CRIME, NONVIOLENT

Jerry Kline
John Naisbitt's Trend Letter
BATTERIES
GREEN REVOLUTION

Richard Kostelanetz
New York, New York
ARTS

Pamela G. Kruzic
U.S. Nuclear Regulatory Commission
FORECASTING METHODS

Mark H. Kryder
Carnegie-Mellon University
DATA STORAGE

George Thomas Kurian
President, International Encyclopedia Society
CLARKE, ARTHUR CHARLES
CORNISH, EDWARD
FORRESTER, JAY
FULLER, RICHARD BUCKMINSTER
MEDIA LAB
MEXICO
NAISBITT, JOHN
ORWELL, GEORGE
PENTECOSTALISM
POPULARIZED FUTURES
TOFFLER, ALVIN AND HEIDI

Sarah Claudine Kurian
Baldwin Place, New York
WOMEN'S RIGHTS

L

Gene R. La Rocque
Center for Defense Information; Rear Admiral, U.S.
Navy (Retired)
WEAPONS OF MASS DESTRUCTION

Heather Lamm
Congressional Institute for the Future
ENTITLEMENT PROGRAMS

Richard D. Lamm
University of Denver; former Governor of Colorado
CREDIT, DEBT, AND BORROWING
HEALTH CARE FINANCING

Robert W. Lamson
George Washington University
DEMOCRATIC PROCESS

F. Wilfrid Lancaster
University of Illinois, Urbana
LIBRARIES: ELECTRONIC FORMATS

Gary P. Lathan
University of Toronto
PARTICIPATIVE MANAGEMENT

Richard L. Lawson
National Coal Association
COAL

Stan Lee
Marvel Comics
COMIC BOOKS

Stuart M. Leiderman
University of New Hampshire
ENVIRONMENTAL REFUGEES
HAZARDOUS WASTES

Richard J. Leighton
Keller and Heckman
LAWYERS AND LEGAL PROFESSION

Ralph C. Lenz
Waynesville, Ohio
COMMUNICATIONS

Richard Lesher
U.S. Chamber of Commerce
WORK ETHIC

Irving Leveson
Leveson Consulting
ECONOMICS
FINANCIAL INSTITUTIONS

Steven Levy
Otis, Massachusetts
ARTIFICIAL LIFE

Michael Lind
Harpers Magazine
UNITED STATES

David F. Linowes
University of Illinois, Urbana
COMMUNICATIONS: PRIVACY ISSUES

Harold A. Linstone
Portland State University
TREND INDICATORS

Edwin A. Locke
University of Maryland
PARTICIPATIVE MANAGEMENT

Amory B. Lovins
Rocky Mountain Institute
ENERGY CONSERVATION

Marcia D. Lowe
Durham, North Carolina
PERSONAL TRANSPORT

Directory of Contributors

C. Lena Lupica
Early Signals
  SEXUAL REPRODUCTION: ARTIFICIAL MEANS

M

Timothy Craig Mack
AAI Research
  CHILDREN, LIVING ARRANGEMENTS
  DIVORCE

Christine A. R. MacNulty
Applied Futures, Inc.
  UNITED KINGDOM
  WORK, QUALITY OF

John B. Mahaffie
Coates and Jarratt, Inc.
  NATIVE AMERICANS

Spyros Makridakis
INSEAD, Fontainebleau, France
  STRATEGIC PLANNING

Jonathan M. Mann
Harvard University
  EPIDEMICS

Lynn Margulis
University of Massachusetts, Amherst
  LIFE SCIENCES

Michael Marien
Future Survey
  APPENDIX: COMMISSIONS AND WORK GROUPS ON THE
    FUTURE
  FUTURE STUDIES
  MULTIFOLD TREND

Oliver W. Markley
University of Houston, Clear Lake
  GLOBAL CONSCIOUSNESS

Elizabeth W. Markson
Boston University
  LONGEVITY

Richard Martin
Metropolitan Museum of Art
  CLOTHING

Joan Martin-Brown
United Nations Environment Programme
  ENVIRONMENTAL INSTITUTIONS

Joseph P. Martino
University of Dayton
  TECHNOLOGY FORECASTING AND ASSESSMENT

Martin E. Marty
University of Chicago
  FUNDAMENTALISM

Magoroh Maruyuma
Aoyama Gakuin University, Tokyo
  LIFESTYLES, ETHNIC

Michael Mascioni
New York, New York
  INTERACTIVE ENTERTAINMENT

Eleanora Barbieri Masini
World Future Studies Federation, Rome
  ITALY
  WOMEN AND WORK

Robert E. Maston
Futuremics, Inc.
  HOUSEHOLD COMPOSITION

Richard G. Maynard
Maynard Associates
  ON-LINE SERVICES
  SCIENCE CITIES

John McClaughry
Institute for Liberty and Community
  EXECUTIVE BRANCH

Robert M. McCord
Congressional Institute for the Future
  ENTITLEMENT PROGRAMS

Terry L. McCoy
University of Florida, Center for Latin American Studies
  LATIN AMERICA

George McGovern
Middle East Policy Council; former U.S. Senator from
    South Dakota
  LIBERALISM, POLITICAL

John McHale
Deceased
  MASS CULTURE AND ARTS

Magda McHale
State University of New York, Buffalo
  MASS CULTURE AND ARTS

Peggy McIntosh
Wellesley College
  WOMEN'S STUDIES

Kate McKeown
America China World Opportunities, Inc.
  VISIONARY THINKING

Melanie McMullen
LAN Magazine
   NETWORKING

Joseph D. McNamara
Stanford University
   LETHAL WEAPONS

Kristen McNutt
Consumer Choices, Inc.
   FOOD CONSUMPTION

George McRobie
Intermediate Technology Developmental Group, London
   APPROPRIATE TECHNOLOGY

Dennis L. Meadows
University of New Hampshire
   GLOBAL ENVIRONMENTAL PROBLEMS

Donella Meadows
Dartmouth College
   SUSTAINABILITY

Constantine Michalopoulos
The World Bank
   FOREIGN AID/ASSISTANCE

Michael Michaelis
Partners in Enterprise, Inc.
   INTEGRATED PERFORMANCE SYSTEMS

Lester W. Milbrath
State University of New York, Buffalo
   ENVIRONMENTAL POLICY CHANGES

J. A. Miller
E. I. duPont de Nemours and Company
   MATERIALS: RESEARCH AND DEVELOPMENT

Kenton R. Miller
World Resources Institute
   BIODIVERSITY

Sanford A. Miller
University of Texas, San Antonio
   FOOD ADDITIVES
   FOOD TECHNOLOGIES

Gordon Misner
University of Illinois, Urbana
   CRIMINAL JUSTICE

Lawrence E. Modisett
Portsmouth, Rhode Island
   RUSSIA

Graham T. T. Molitor
Public Policy Forecasting, Inc.
   ALCOHOL

   CHANGE, OPTIMISTIC AND PESSIMISTIC PERSPECTIVES
   CHANGE, PACE OF
   CHANGE, SCIENTIFIC AND TECHNOLOGICAL
   CONTINUITY AND DISCONTINUITY
   CRIME RATES
   ELEMENTARY AND SECONDARY EDUCATION
   ETHNIC AND CULTURAL SEPARATISM
   INFORMATION OVERLOAD
   LAWS, EVOLUTION OF
   PACESETTER GOVERNMENTS
   POLITICAL PARTY REALIGNMENT
   PUBLIC POLICY CHANGE
   RECORD SETTING
   SEXUAL LAWS
   SOCIAL CONTROLS
   TOBACCO
   VALUES CHANGE

James Monaco
UNET 2 Corporation
   MOTION PICTURES

James L. Morrison
University of North Carolina, Chapel Hill
   SCANNING

Stanley Moses
Hunter College, City University of New York
   UNEMPLOYMENT

N

Stuart S. Nagel
University of Illinois, Urbana
   JUDICIAL REFORM

John Naisbitt
Megatrends, Ltd.
   GLOBAL PARADOX

Charles B. Nam
Florida State University
   INTERNAL MIGRATION, UNITED STATES

Joseph J. Napolitano
Bryn Mawr, Pennsylvania
   NURSING

Vasudha Narayanan
University of Florida
   HINDUISM

Richard P. Nathan
State University of New York, Albany
   GOVERNMENT ORGANIZATION

P. Ranganath Nayak
Arthur D. Little Company
   MARKETING BREAKTHROUGHS

Directory of Contributors

Ruben F. W. Nelson
Square One Management Ltd.
INFORMATION SOCIETY

Kevin Nesbitt
University of California, Davis
MOTOR VEHICLES, ALTERNATIVELY POWERED

Jack M. Nilles
Jala International Inc.
COMPUTERS: OVERVIEW

Judith Norsigian
Boston Women's Health Book Collective
WOMEN'S HEALTH MOVEMENT

O

Ellen L. O'Sullivan
Southern Connecticut State University
SPORTS AND ACTIVITIES, SPECTATOR

James O'Toole
University of Southern California
MACROECONOMICS

Frank Ogden
21st Century Media Communications
HIGH TECHNOLOGY

Robert L. Olson
Institute for Alternative Futures
OZONE LAYER DEPLETION

Norman J. Ornstein
American Enterprise Institute for Public Policy
    Research
POLITICAL PARTIES

Oliver S. Owen
University of Wisconsin
GLOBAL WARMING

Le Roy Owens
Owens and Associates Consultants
ILLITERACY

P

Seymour Papert
Massachusetts Institute of Technology
COMPUTERS: SOFTWARE

Lynn Patenaude
Environment Canada, Ottawa, Ontario
SOLID WASTE

Janice E. Pearlman
New York University
MEGACITIES

Edward S. Pearsall
U.S. Postal Rate Commission
POSTAL SERVICES

Jonathan Peck
Institute for Alternative Futures
HEALTH CARE: MORAL ISSUES

W. David Penniman
North Potomac, Maryland
LIBRARIES

Jean Pennington
Center for Food Safety and Applied Nutrition
NUTRITION

Arno Penzias
AT&T Bell Laboratories
COMPUTER LINKAGE

Bonnie Penzias
Wellesley Information Systems
COMPUTER LINKAGE

John L. Petersen
The Arlington Institute
NATIONAL SECURITY

Philippe Pichat
European Institute of Business Administration,
    Fontainebleau, France
TECHNOLOGICAL INNOVATION

David Pimentel
Cornell University
SOIL CONDITIONS

Dennis Pirages
University of Maryland
RESOURCES

John Platt
Deceased
FORECASTING, DETERMINISTIC

James W. Plumb
The Greenhill Partnership
PUBLIC RELATIONS

Frederik Pohl
Palatine, Illinois
SCIENCE FICTION

Cyril Ponnamperuma
Deceased
EVOLUTION, BIOLOGICAL
EVOLUTION: LIFE-FORMS IN THE UNIVERSE

Sandra L. Postel
Worldwatch Institute
FRESHWATER

James R. Powell
Brookhaven National Laboratory
MAGLEV

Ruthann Prange
AT&T
PRIVATE ASSISTANCE PROGRAMS

Charlene C. Price
U.S. Department of Agriculture
FOOD SERVICES

Robin Thorne Ptacek
National Gallery of Art
VISUAL ARTS

Q

Dan Quayle
Hudson Institute; former U.S. Senator; former Vice
President of the United States
FAMILY VALUES

R

David L. Rados
Vanderbilt University
MARKETING

Wayne D. Rasmussen
Agricultural History Society
FARM POLICY

Nora Raum
Arlington, Virginia
NEWSPAPERS

Victoria Razak
State University of New York, Buffalo
CULTURE AND SOCIETY

Walter V. Reid
World Resources Institute
BIODIVERSITY

Ira L. Reiss
University of Minnesota
SEXUAL BEHAVIOR

William L. Renfro
Policy Analysis Company, Inc.
FORECASTING, MISTAKES IN

Malvin E. Ring
Rochester, New York
DENTISTRY

Deanna Campbell Robinson
University of Oregon
MUSIC

John P. Robinson
University of Maryland
FREE TIME

Thomas W. Robinson
U.S. State Department (Retired); American Enterprise
Institute
CHINA

John D. Rockfellow
Copenhagen Institute for Future Studies, Denmark
WILDCARDS

Harrell R. Rodgers
University of Houston
POVERTY, FEMINIZATION OF

Joseph C. Rost
University of San Diego
LEADERSHIP

Milton Rothman
Trenton State College
PHYSICS

Fabrice Roubelat
Conservatoire National des Arts et Métiers, Paris
TECHNOLOGY AND SOCIETY

Joseph R. Roy
Creamer Dickson Basford
COMPUTER HARDWARE
COMPUTERS: SAFETY

Mark A. Runco
California State University
CREATIVITY

Cheryl Russell
The Boomer Report
POPULATION GROWTH: UNITED STATES

S

Dorion Sagan
Sciencewriters, Inc.
LIFE SCIENCES

Directory of Contributors

Wendy Sanford
Boston Women's Health Book Collective
WOMEN'S HEALTH MOVEMENT

Ziauddin Sardar
London, England
ISLAM

Philip G. Satre
Promus Companies Inc.
GAMBLING

Herbert I. Schiller
University of California, La Jolla
MEDIA CONSOLIDATION

Jurgen A. Schmandt
Houston Advanced Research Center
ACID RAIN

Gregory Schmid
Institute for the Future
MANAGEMENT

Ernest Schneider
Croton-on-Hudson, New York
EUROPE, WESTERN

Frank C. Schuller
Massachusetts Institute of Technology
MOTOR VEHICLES

Peter Schwartz
Global Business Network
SCENARIOS

Richard K. Scotch
University of Texas, Dallas
DISABLED PERSONS' RIGHTS

Eric Seaborg
Free Union, Virginia
OUTDOOR RECREATION AND LEISURE PURSUITS

Glenn T. Seaborg
University of California, Berkeley
TRANSURANIUM ELEMENTS

Roger Selbert
FutureScan
CAPITAL FORMATION
SAVINGS

William J. Serow
Florida State University
INTERNAL MIGRATION, UNITED STATES

Thomas A. Shannon
Worcester Polytechnic Institute
ETHICS

Michael Sherraden
Washington University
PUBLIC ASSISTANCE PROGRAMS

Arthur B. Shostack
Drexel University
ABORTION
UNIONISM

Kristin S. Shrader-Frechette
University of South Florida
ENVIRONMENTAL ETHICS

George H. Siehl
Library of Congress
PARKS AND WILDERNESS

Paul H. Silverman
University of California, Irvine
GENETICS

W. H. Clive Simmonds
Futurescan International Inc., Ottawa
CHEMISTRY

Max Singer
The Potomac Organization
INTERNATIONAL DIPLOMACY

Nigel Sizer
World Resources Institute
DEFORESTATION

Richard A. Slaughter
University of Melbourne
AUSTRALIA AND NEW ZEALAND
FUTURES CONCEPTS

Robert H. Smith
The Futures Group
BUSINESS STRUCTURE: INDUSTRIAL POLICY

Tom W. Smith
National Opinion Research Center
SOCIAL INDICATORS

Paul Smoker
Antioch College
PEACEKEEPING

David Pearce Snyder
The Snyder Family Enterprise
HOUSING, DEMOGRAPHIC AND LIFESTYLE IMPACTS ON
PUBLIC OPINION POLLS

Richard J. Spady
Forum Foundation
CHURCH-STATE AFFAIRS

Daniel Sperling
University of California, Davis
MOTOR VEHICLES, ALTERNATIVELY POWERED

H. Brooke Stauffer
Association of Home Appliance Manufacturers
HOUSEHOLD APPLIANCES

Gene Stephens
University of South Carolina
LAW ENFORCEMENT
PRISONS

Terence Stewart
Stewart and Stewart
INTERNATIONAL GOVERNANCE AND REGIONAL AUTHORITIES

Maurice Strong
Ontario Hydro
ENVIRONMENT

T

Nestor E. Terleckyj
National Planning Association
AGING OF THE POPULATION

Leah Thayer
The Global Network; John Naisbitt's Trend Letter
ELECTRONIC PUBLISHING
GREEN REVOLUTION

Robert Theobald
New Orleans, Louisiana
AGENTS OF CHANGE

David C. Thomasma
Loyola University
DEATH AND DYING

Jan Tinbergen
Deceased
SOCIALISM

Irene Tinker
University of California, Berkeley
WOMEN AND WORLD DEVELOPMENT

Graham A. Tobin
University of Minnesota
NATURAL DISASTERS

Alvin Toffler
Los Angeles, California
FOREWORD: FIVE BILLION FUTURISTS

Heidi Toffler
Los Angeles, California
FOREWORD: FIVE BILLION FUTURISTS

Joseph P. Tomain
University of Cincinnati
NUCLEAR POWER: CON

Brian K. Toren
International Robots
ROBOTICS
TELEPHONES

Allen Tough
University of Toronto
ADULT LEARNING

Marcello Truzzi
Grass Lake, Michigan
PSEUDO-FUTURISTS

J. Y. Tsao
Sandia National Laboratories
SEMICONDUCTORS

James S. Turner
Swankin & Turner
CONSUMER PROTECTION/REGULATION

Richard E. Tustian
Lincoln Institute of Land Policy
LAND USE PLANNING

V

Charles Van Doren
Falls Village, Connecticut
LITERATURE

Ted Van Dyk
Van Dyk Associates, Inc.
EXECUTIVE BRANCH: THE PRESIDENCY

John H. Vanston
Technology Futures, Inc.
SUPERCONDUCTORS

Laurence K. Vanston
Technology Futures, Inc.
COMMUNICATIONS
SUPERCONDUCTORS

Steven Vincent
Art and Auction
ART DEALERS

Directory of Contributors

W

W. Warren Wagar
State University of New York, Binghamton
ASIMOV, ISAAC
BELL, DANIEL
FUTURISM
JOHN THE DIVINE
JOUVENEL, BERTRAND DE
KAHN, HERMAN
MORE, SAINT THOMAS
NOSTRADAMUS
OGBURN, WILLIAM FIELDING
SCHUMPETER, JOSEPH A.
SOROKIN, PITIRIM A.
SPENGLER, OSWALD
UTOPIAS
WELLS, H. G.

Robert Wagley
Wright State University
VALUES, NONWESTERN

Cynthia G. Wagner
The Futurist
PERFORMING ARTS: DANCE AND THEATER

Michael G. Walsh
Villanova University
GRAY MARKET GOODS

Richard H. Ward
University of Illinois, Chicago
TERRORISM

Michael Y. Warder
Rockford Institute
NONGOVERNMENTAL ORGANIZATIONS

Melissa G. Warren
American Psychologist
PSYCHOLOGY

David J. Webber
University of Missouri
GENETICS: COMMERCIALIZATION

Lee J. Weddig
National Fisheries Institute
FISHERIES

Murray L. Weidenbaum
Washington University
MARKETPLACE ECONOMICS

David S. Weir
E. I. duPont de Nemours and Company
AGRICULTURAL TECHNOLOGY

Paul J. Werbos
National Science Foundation
ARTIFICIAL INTELLIGENCE

Frank White
Framingham, Massachusetts
COMMUNICATIONS TECHNOLOGY
EXTRATERRESTRIAL LIFE-FORMS
SPACE TRAVEL

Keith D. Wilde
Office of the Superintendent of Financial Institutions
POLITICAL ECONOMY

Timothy Willard
National Food Processors Association
RECORDING INDUSTRY

Charles W. Williams
Charles W. Williams, Inc.
INTERNATIONAL TRADE: REGULATION

Wesley H. Williams
Charles W. Williams, Inc.
COMPUTERS: PRIVACY LAWS
INTERNATIONAL TRADE: REGULATION

A. Bruce Wilson
The Planning Forum
PLANNING

George W. Wilson
University of Indiana
DEFICITS, GOVERNMENTAL

Ian H. Wilson
SRI International
LIFESTYLES, VALUE-ORIENTED

Rosalyn A. Wilson
ENO Transportation Foundation, Inc.
RAILWAYS

Roger P. Winter
U.S. Committee for Refugees
REFUGEES

William Van Dusen Wishard
Worldtrends Research
CHANGE, CULTURAL
CHANGE, EPOCHAL
ETHNIC AND CULTURAL SEPARATISM
GLOBAL TURNING POINTS
INFORMATION OVERLOAD
MODERNISM AND POSTMODERNISM
RELIGION: CHANGING BELIEFS
VALUES CHANGE

Sylvan H. Wittwer
Michigan State University
FOOD AND FIBER PRODUCTION

Laurin A. Wollan, Jr.
Florida State University
CRIMINAL PUNISHMENT

X

Spyros S. Xenakis
U.S. Postal Rate Commission
POSTAL SERVICES

Y

Joel Yager
Neuropsychiatric Institute
PSYCHIATRY

A

Abortion

Historians in the early twenty-first century, looking back at the last quarter of the twentieth century in America, will recognize the abortion issue as one of the period's most divisive, revealing, and costly domestic controversies. They may also be able to see something barely glimpsed in the mid-1990s at the beginning of the end of the abortion wars.

The 1973 U.S. Supreme Court decision in *Roe* v. *Wade* discovered a right to privacy in the Constitution that, in effect, protected a woman's right to request the clinical termination of an unwanted pregnancy. Nearly twenty years later a Supreme Court of a different cast decided that each state could decide its own legal framework, provided that some limited access to abortion remained. Court watchers, noting that President Bill Clinton takes a "permissive" stand at sharp variance with his predecessor (George Bush), believe his Supreme Court appointments may tilt decisions in a "pro-choice" way, favoring readier access to abortion. While the privacy right itself may succumb to challenges, abortion per se is likely to remain court-protected, though increasingly infrequent—this is the major change of the late 1990s.

The antiabortion movement, thoroughly convinced that life begins at conception, and its opponents inhabit irreconcilable moral universes. More use can be expected by the antiabortion movement of research interpretations that view a fetus as a human being, with all attendant rights. As well, the movement is likely to highlight advances in neonatal technology that might enable post–twelve-week fetuses to survive in a hospital incubator. This would alleviate the need for about 12 percent of abortions in the United States, provided that a pregnant woman freely consented to the medical procedures. Overall, however, they probably will have to settle in the 1990s for no more than state-by-state inconveniences, such as parental notification and twenty-four-hour waiting periods. The nation will not permit the recriminalization of abortion.

Throughout the 1990s the culture of advanced industrial nations is likely to place a higher-than-ever value on the well-being of infants. Abortion will be viewed with sympathy when it involves the last resort of a woman unable to provide adequately for a newborn, even though support will probably be forthcoming from both public and private sources to make this choice unnecessary. This is a rare opportunity for collaboration between antiabortion and pro-choice forces that extremists on both sides are likely to thwart.

The Clinton administration is committed to ending the White House-imposed ban on federal funding for abortions requested by women too poor to afford them. To dampen opposition this administration may direct more funds than ever into research directed at improved contraception, including a "pill" for male use.

Pregnant women were prosecuted in the early 1990s to interrupt and control their use of alcohol and drugs, which harm the fetus. Some were threatened with a court-ordered abortion unless they abstained. Medical insights from prenatal research lent support here, as did the exasperation of the public with childbirths to AIDS carriers, chronic child-abusers, crack addicts, and the like. The Clinton administration, however, is likely to shift emphasis from punishment toward rehabilitation. The Supreme Court, in turn, is likely to ban forced abstention as an unconstitutional violation of an adult woman's personal rights, engendering a more deeply divided public reaction.

Although fewer than 14 percent of 1,400,000 abortions in 1991 were performed on teenagers and only 1 percent on girls under fifteen, the 1990s saw a rapid spread of state laws requiring a teen to tell her parents before obtaining an abortion. Approved in polls by three out of four Americans, these laws, especially when confined to notification rather than consent, were contingent on the ability of a lower court judge to waive the requirement in special cases. A premier example of compromise in the abortion issue, such laws are likely to remain on the books long after their applicability has dwindled or is nil.

Efforts by antiabortion forces to enforce a White House-ordered "gag rule," a ban on the mention of abortion by healthcare professionals in federally funded facilities, were ended early in the Clinton administration. Never popular with the public, opposed by civil libertarians, many physicians, and most ethicists, the "gag rule" will find few mourners aside from its original advocates.

There are no abortion clinics or participating hospitals in over 80 percent of America's counties, largely due to the efforts of abortion opponents and increasing insurance rates. Consequently a small number of illegal abortions are likely to occur throughout the 1990s in the United States. There will be countries, such as Ireland or parts of the Middle East, where contraceptives and all abortions are banned. Although medical advances are likely to reduce the death and/or sterilization toll, illegal abortions will remain a response of desperation.

The waning of the abortion issue can be traced, at least in part, to decidedly pro-choice policies initiated in 1993 by the Clinton administration. Equally significant is the substantial growth expected in the use of Norplant, the first new contraceptive technology introduced in the United States in over thirty years. A skin implant, Norplant offers up to five years of birth-control protection. Similarly, RU-486, the French abortion pill, once it gets FDA approval, should play a large role in re-

ducing requests for abortion. Finally, the continued threat of AIDS will promote school-based sex education and contraceptive use. These pro-choice policies and improved access could in a decade halve the ratio of abortions to births recorded in 1990 (344:1,000). Should the tide of politics turn conservative again, a flare-up in the abortion issue would probably follow, as new hindrances to birth control invariably have more and more anguished women seeking abortions, the right-to-lifers notwithstanding.

Historians in the twenty-first century who study abortion in post–1973 America will undoubtedly puzzle over the absence of the male from the abortion scene. They will note that the 1973 *Roe* decision required an expectant mother to decide the fate of the fetus. Exactly why the male was treated as irrelevant, was taught nothing about how to provide loving support for his sex partner, and was given no contraceptive advice to help him avoid participating in serial abortions will puzzle twenty-first-century adults. They are likely themselves to see much wisdom in fully involving both women and men in resolving a dilemma posed by their joint behavior. Male involvement in helping pursue pro-choice public policies, and a "techne fix" (Norplant and RU-486), will substantially reduce the need to resort to abortions. Bringing men in from the cold also makes a contribution to tempering the infamous and costly battle of the sexes.

The liberalization of abortion rights is part of the long-term trend of people taking responsibility for themselves and their well-being, and of the growing social and economic equality of women with men.

See also FAMILY PATTERNS; FAMILY PLANNING; FAMILY VALUES; SEXUAL CODES; SEXUAL REPRODUCTION.

BIBLIOGRAPHY

BONAVOGLIA, ANGELA. *The Choices We Made: Twenty-Five Women and Men Speak Out about Abortion.* New York: Random House, 1991.

CONDUIT, CELESTE M. *Decoding Abortion Rhetoric: Communicating Social Change.* Chicago: University of Illinois Press, 1990.

COZIC, CHARLES P., and STACEY L. TRIPP, eds. *Abortion: Opposing Viewpoints.* San Diego, CA: Greenhaven Press, 1991.

FAUX, MARIAN. *Crusaders: Voices from the Abortion Front.* New York: Birch Lane Press, 1990.

ROSENBLATT, ROGER. *Life Itself: Abortion in the American Mind.* New York: Random House, 1992.

SHOSTAK, ARTHUR B. "Abortion: Ten Cautious Forecasts." *The Futurist* (July–August 1991): 20–24.

SHOSTAK, ARTHUR B., and MCLOUTH, GARY (with Lynn Seng). *Men and Abortion: Lessons, Losses, and Love.* New York: Praeger, 1984.

TRIBE, LAWRENCE H. *Abortion: The Clash of Absolutes.* New York: W. W. Norton, 1990.

Arthur B. Shostak

Abuse, Child.

See CHILD ABUSE.

Acid Rain

Acidification of rainfall, and the potential for related damage to forests, inland water bodies, and buildings, originates and mostly occurs in highly industrialized regions. It is caused by air pollution from both stationary and mobile sources. So far, effects are most severe in Europe and the eastern parts of North America, and increasingly in southern China. With increasing industrialization, there is the concomitant potential for problems to emerge in other regions with sensitive soils and surface waters, such as those in northern and eastern parts of Latin America, western equatorial Africa, large parts of the Indian subcontinent, and Southeast Asia. Areas with naturally acidic soils, in prevailing downwind locations from urban and industrial centers, are most at risk.

The acidity of rainfall is measured in pH units, indicating the concentration of hydrogen (H) ions. Rainfall is almost always more acid than pure water with variations from region to region. However, it is generally agreed that a pH less than 5.6 is abnormally acid. Basically, pH 7 is neutral and a reduction of one pH unit represents a tenfold increase in the concentration of H ions.

A variety of pollutants contribute to acidification: sulfur dioxide (SO_2) from coal-fired power plants, nitrogen oxides (NO_x) from power plants and automobiles, and volatile organic compounds (VOC) from automobiles and natural sources. In the presence of radiation produced by sunlight, chemical reactions produce sulfuric and nitric acid.

Acid deposition occurs in both wet (acid rain) and dry forms. Acid rain makes up about half of the problem. Dry deposition, either as particulate matter or as undissolved gases, is harder to measure and tends to be deposited closer to the emission source. Because it is deposited directly onto the leaves of plants, dry deposition may be particularly important for heavily vegetated (particularly forested) areas. In addition, there also may be toxicity problems resulting from chemical interactions with soil constituents. For example, the increased solubility of metals at lowered pH levels could create the potential for contamination of drinking water and edible fish.

Evidence of accelerated forest decline during the last thirty years has accumulated in Europe and the United States. The most publicized instance of decline attributed directly or indirectly to man-made pollution occurs in the Harz, Black Forest, and Bavarian Forest in Germany. The rapid rate of decline led to public concern about the seriousness of the situation. In the late-1970s silver fir first began to show signs of damage. This was followed by Norway spruce and, in 1982, by hardwoods such as beech and oak. Damage was greatest on west-facing slopes, having the greatest effect on older trees at higher elevations. As many as 50 percent of the trees could be considered in danger. In the case of fir trees, more than 80 percent are affected. However, things may not be as bad as they

TABLE 1. The Chemical Transformation of Air Pollutants

Pollutant	Contributing Factors	End Product
NO_x	OH (in air)	HNO_3 (nitric acid)
NO_x + VOC		O_3 (ozone)
VOC	HO_2 (in air)	H_2O_2 (hydrogen peroxide)
SO_2	H_2O_2 and O_3	H_2SO_4 (sulfuric acid)
	OH + O_2 (in air)	
	Oxidants (wet surfaces)	

Source: The National Acid Precipitation Assessment Program. *Interim Assessment, The Causes and Effects of Acidic Deposition, Volume I Executive Summary.* Washington, D.C.: U.S. Government Printing Office, 1987, pp. 1–3.

seem. In recent years, forest surveys have been refined, resulting in more conservative damage estimates. It has also been established that poor forest management is a contributing factor.

Two major sources of damage were established in Germany: industrial pollution and car exhaust fumes. Car exhaust fumes often damage areas that are not close to industrial sites. Instead, they are concentrated along superhighways. In the United States, forest damage has been more limited. It is concentrated in parts of the Appalachian Mountains and New Hampshire, with smaller affected areas in California.

A large National Acid Precipitation Assessment Program was established by the U.S. Congress in 1980. It took ten years to complete and cost over $500 million. The final report confirms that acid rain harms some lakes and streams, mainly in the northeastern United States. Damage could spread to the southeastern United States.

Damage to forests is complex, because various natural and contributing factors combine to harm trees. It remains difficult to sort out causes and effects. However, it can be said with confidence that acid rain and ozone do contribute to stress on forests. Acid precipitation robs some forest soils of vital nutrients and interferes with the ability of trees to absorb those that are left. This will lead to widespread stunting of some species of trees at high altitudes over the long term. Except for red spruce, there is no convincing evidence that acid precipitation harms trees through direct chemical contact. In the short term, ozone from car exhausts is much more harmful, and has been identified as the cause of damage to southern pine forests and in the San Bernardino Mountains in California. Damage occurs mostly at high altitudes where trees are often bathed in acid mist, clouds, and fogs.

Stunting of growth of trees will result from altered chemistry of mountain forest soil. This damage has two underlying causes: (1) depletion of soil of calcium and magnesium, which are necessary for formation of chlorophyll and wood, and (2) breakdown of soil and release of aluminum. Aluminum, in turn, inhibits the ability of trees to absorb remaining calcium and magnesium. Over a period of up to fifty years this not only may disrupt the physiology of the tree, but in some cases can kill root systems outright.

The true costs of air pollution in general, and acid rain in particular, are hard to determine. In addition to damage to forests, acid rain is known to reduce crop yields and acidify lakes. If the pH of lake water drops below 5, significant death of fish will result, affecting both recreational and commercial fishing. Sulfur dioxide is also a powerful lung irritant and may be the third leading cause of lung disease in the United States. Structural damage to buildings and monuments is well documented, with damage estimates ranging from $15 million to $60 million (Schmandt et al., 1989, p. 112).

Acid rain can be transported across international boundaries, and one country can be bearing the consequences of another's emissions. Scandinavia loudly protested the uncontrolled emissions originating in the United Kingdom and other European countries that were devastating its lakes and forests. Canada became the victim of acid precipitation that originated in the United States. In 1984 Canada, West Germany, and eight other European countries signed a declaration to reduce SO_2 emissions by at least 30 percent from 1980 levels within ten years. At that time the United Kingdom and the United States were unwilling to make such a commitment, although the United Kingdom subsequently agreed to the reductions. This left the United States as the only major Western industrialized nation to maintain that there was still insufficient evidence to justify further action, which contributed to deteriorating U.S.-Canadian relations (Regens and Rycroft, 1988, pp. 150–152).

Debate about the need for additional emission controls continued well into the 1980s in the United States. The 1970 Clean Air Act ruled that high levels of air pollution, particularly in urban areas, were unacceptable and needed to be controlled. At the time, sulfur dioxide was known to be a lung irritant and other pollutants, including particulate matter, caused reduced visibility. By concentrating on ambient air quality, the act encouraged the use of tall stacks to dispose of pollution so that local air quality standards could be met. This technique resulted in the dispersion of air pollutants, which travel over long distances and undergo various chemical transformations, including the production of acidic compounds. Thus, reducing local air pollution contributed to long distance acidification.

By 1980 emissions of SO_2 and NO_x in the United States amounted to 25–27 and 21–23 million tons, respectively (Office of Technology Assessment, 1984, p. 149). Stationary sources, particularly electric utilities, were responsible for 80 percent of SO_2 emissions, while mobile sources accounted for almost half of NO_x emissions. Although SO_2 emissions were declining, with the burning of cleaner fuels and emission controls on power plants built after 1978, emissions of NO_x were on the increase (Schmandt et al., 1989, pp. 109–110).

After almost a decade of controversy with Canada, the 1970 Clean Air Act was amended in 1990 to require a 10 million ton reduction in SO_2 emissions and a 2 million ton reduction in NO_x emissions, compared with 1980 levels. Electric utility power plants are the primary focus for SO_2 emission reduction. By January 1, 2000, total emissions of SO_2 by electric utilities will be limited to 8.9 million tons. Old plants will be required to install emission control devices; others will be assigned emission allowances based on actual 1985 emissions. New plants will be required to obtain existing allowances through a system of trading credits administered by the U.S. Environmental Protection Agency.

Whether these emission reduction strategies will be effective in reducing the effects of acid rain to acceptable levels is uncertain. In recent years the debate has moved away from the specific issue of acid rain to the more general issue of transboundary air pollution, and international efforts to limit greenhouse gas emissions and global warming. Coal produces the most carbon dioxide per unit of energy. If coal is replaced by other, cleaner burning fuels in an attempt to limit global warming, this will have the added benefit of reducing SO_2 emissions.

See also ENVIRONMENT; ENVIRONMENTAL BEHAVIOR; ENVIRONMENTAL ETHICS; ENVIRONMENTAL INDICATORS; ENVIRONMENTAL POLICY CHANGES; FRESHWATER; GLOBAL ENVIRONMENTAL PROBLEMS; GLOBAL WARMING; NATURAL DISASTERS; OCEANS; OZONE LAYER DEPLETION; SUSTAINABILITY.

BIBLIOGRAPHY

MacKenzie, J. J., and El-Ashry, M. T. *Ill Winds: Airborne Pollution's Toll on Trees and Crops.* Washington, DC: World Resources Institute, 1988.

Office of Technology Assessment. *Acid Rain and Transported Air Pollutants: Implications for Public Policy.* U.S. Congress, OTA-O-204, Washington, DC: Government Printing Office, 1984.

Regens, James L., and Rycroft, Robert W. *The Acid Rain Controversy.* Pittsburgh: University of Pittsburgh Press, 1988.

Schmandt, Jurgen A.; Clarkson, Judith; and Roderick, Hilliard. *Acid Rain and Friendly Neighbors: The Policy Dispute between Canada and the United States.* Durham, NC: Duke University Press, 1989.

White, J. C. *Acid Rain: The Relationship Between Sources and Receptors.* New York: Elsevier, 1988.

Jurgen A. Schmandt

Additives, Food.

See FOOD ADDITIVES.

Adult Learning

Most knowledge and skills are learned because adults expect to use them in some practical way. As jobs generally become more complex, they require more learning. As people travel more, try to improve their relationships, take on more do-it-yourself projects, and begin new recreational activities, their learning needs to escalate.

The primary purpose of many adult education institutions is to foster such practical learning. Adults are more willing to pay for practical learning than to pay for satisfying their curiosity, puzzlement, and general learning interests. Practical, useful learning is marketed increasingly by institutions under pressure to be financially self-sufficient or profitable. Liberal arts education and education about world issues, popular well past mid-century, have been deemphasized by many institutions. Some adult educators advocate a renewed sense of social mission, with major or even radical social change as the central purpose, but most of the field shows little sign of heeding this call. Within peace and environmental education for adults, however, and within many grassroots movements, a strong commitment to fundamental social change still is central.

Demand and Populations

Demand for knowledge and skills is very high. Based on statistics for eleven countries, in any given year, 90 percent of adults, for example, engage in at least one major learning effort. They conduct an average of five such projects annually, and spend an average of one hundred hours at each one.

Demand for institutional programs to facilitate this learning is also high. These programs serve at least four target populations: (1) people who need basic skills in reading, communicating, speaking English as a second language, arithmetic, and applying for a job; (2) employed people who need to upgrade their job skills or prepare for new responsibilities as technology and the work world change rapidly; (3) professionals and experts who need to keep up with new knowledge and techniques in their fields; (4) older adults, who are becoming more numerous and more eager to learn. A wide variety of educational enterprises will provide education or training for each of these target groups, sometimes with the cooperation of governments and employers. Adult education is a vast and expanding enterprise, already much larger than elementary or secondary education.

France already requires that businesses employing over 100 workers devote 1.2–3.0 percent of wage costs to training programs. Spending on labor training programs as a percentage of GNP (c. 1991) amounted to 1.79 percent in Sweden, 1.05 percent in Germany, 0.52 percent in Canada, and 0.25 percent in the United States.

Educational Technologies

Computers have assisted instruction for more than twenty years. Using computers to link students and instructors is increasingly common in distance education. No matter how far apart they are, computers can send messages to each other instantly; the receiving computer then stores a message until the user requests it at a convenient time. Messages can be sent to one particular person in the class, or to the whole group.

Adult learners are already using teleconferencing, electronic mail, computer bulletin boards, radio and television broadcasts, video cassettes, audio cassettes, laser videodiscs, and CD-ROM reference publications. Access to data and to educational programs, as well as communication among learners, will presumably become faster and easier as technology and media develop further. Voice recognition may even eliminate the need for a keyboard. In addition, artificial intelligence may enable computers to function as sophisticated mentors to the learner, making the instruction much more individualized.

New Roles

Several new roles are likely to develop within adult learning and education during the next few decades. Counseling services may help adults choose their learning goals and broad strategy, and improve their individual competence in guiding their own learning. Because worklife now may involve three to five different jobs, each successive career is likely to require specialized training. Information services may provide data about the wide array of available opportunities and resources. Libraries and self-directed learning centers may foster the teaching, learning, and assessment tasks faced during the 70 percent of adult

learning that is self-planned. Institutional adult education may provide more help to teachers and workshop leaders who work in the informal sector. Life-planning centers may help men and women cope with a rapidly changing world beset with major problems, and decide how to make their optimum contribution toward a reasonably positive future for humankind.

See also HIGHER EDUCATION; HUMAN RESOURCES DEVELOPMENT; ILLITERACY; LIBERAL ARTS.

BIBLIOGRAPHY

BROCKETT, RALPH, ed. *Continuing Education in the Year 2000.* New Directions in Continuing Education, no. 36. San Francisco: Jossey-Bass, 1987.
GANLEY, GLADYS. *The Exploding Political Power of Personal Media.* Norwood, NJ: Ablex, 1992.
LEWIS, LINDA H. "New Educational Technologies for the Future." In Sharan Merriam and Phyllis Cunningham, eds., *Handbook of Adult and Continuing Education,* pp. 613–627. San Francisco: Jossey-Bass, 1989.
ROSSMAN, PARKER. *The Emerging Worldwide Electronic University.* Westport, CT: Greenwood Press, 1992.
TOUGH, ALLEN. "Potential Futures: Implications for Adult Educators." *Lifelong Learning* 11/1 (1987): 10–12.
——. *Crucial Question About the Future.* Lanham, MD: University Press of America, 1991.

Allen Tough

Advertising

As the twenty-first century approaches, advertising is undergoing a fundamental realignment in order to accommodate new technologies that "demassify" the media. Advertising agencies realized in the 1990s that they could not grow if they remained focused chiefly on creating campaigns for the mass network television and national magazine audiences. This is because mass media have turned to the new technology to focus more precisely on smaller niche audiences.

Advertisers, imbued for the last few decades with the "global village" ideal, now are moving toward more localized communications. Specific databases open new ways to personalize the ads sent to customers and prospects. The forces behind all this change are altered family relationships and lifestyles, new markets, changing workforce habits and schedules, and a steady flow of new products bursting from high-tech labs. Now available are fiber optics, digitalization, more compact and powerful computers, dazzling software, microwaves, and new broadcast bands to transmit information, entertainment, and advertising messages. Demassification forces television networks to work harder to deliver today's—and tomorrow's—biggest audiences to advertisers. While prime-time TV audiences have declined significantly from their pre-cable 1950–1980 glory years, network TV's viewership numbers remain formidable.

Many ad agencies, by focusing on network TV and mass audience "reach," misjudged the arrival of targeted new media options. One arena in which ad agencies faltered is that of integrated marketing, a database-driven discipline that has advertisers searching for all-encompassing promotional programs inspired by the media. Such programs in theory enable advertisers to choose from among every available promotional venue and media option, whether technologically driven or not. With truly integrated marketing programs, traditional media—print and broadcast—must compete against every other option for a share of the budget.

This is another development forcing agencies to regroup. In creating new tables of organization that bring together people with the technical skills needed to accommodate integrated marketing programs, agencies are in effect setting up "SWAT" teams (multifaceted units). New compensation packages are being designed to reward key members of these media-neutral, flexible units.

Future copywriters and artists will have skills beyond creating TV and radio commercials and writing newspaper and magazine ads. To deal with targeting, their talents will be applied to designing special events; games; data-based coupon, contest, and direct response programs; TV home-shopping programs; "infomercials"; interactive video; virtual-reality formats; "800"- and "900"-like television services; sweepstakes; and premiums.

While advertisers work through this trial-and-error period, the new media elements will show a higher rate of revenue growth than that of traditional broadcast and print media. New media will record revenue gains—much of it local in nature—significantly higher than the 3 to 4 percent associated with older media companies and agencies. Revenue growth will mean tapping into emerging new marketing categories such as computer software and hardware, consumer electronics, entertainment, personal and home security devices, home improvement, new personal-care products, energy-saving devices, grooming and apparel lines, and financial service offerings.

As they move more deeply into developing databases for targeted marketing programs that reach individual customers or prospects, advertisers will grow more interested in experimenting with cable-network channels that cater to special audiences and with "place-based" media that deliver computer-driven programs to offices, schools, colleges, department stores, shopping malls, and other public areas.

Videocassette recorders, rental movies, and videogames contribute to mass media's breakup by making it possible for people to fashion personal viewing schedules. Advertisers can reach them simply by changing the route the sales message takes: telemarketing, catalogues, sponsored information services, commercials on rental tapes, movie theater commercials, sponsored videotapes, and magazines that produce special editions for certain readers and advertisers.

Ink-jet printing technology leads to personalized editorial sections and ads in magazines, plus split runs based on reader occupation, interests, income, and zip codes. Magazine publishers show increasing interest in creating demographically designed titles and departments to attract readers with common interests—in turn attracting more advertisers. Event marketing—the sponsoring of Olympic teams, sports events, citywide music and arts festivals, special museum exhibitions, and so forth by advertisers—also represents a new challenge for ad agencies.

The hunger of advertisers for new programming that will attract new cable and microwave system subscribers will lead to growing uses of infomercials—the sponsored "entertainment" packages that are usually half-hour TV sales messages. Home shopping programs will gain in popularity as they are merged into popular entertainment formats. Such programs also will encourage more manufacturers to develop exclusive product lines for home shoppers.

As privately sponsored "information highways" become a reality, they will attract information suppliers as well as advertisers. Using telephone technology, TV, the full broadcast spectrum, and computers, these "highways" will raise new concerns over such issues as privacy, the limits of advertising in an environment of free speech, the extent to which they exclude people, and the dynamics of participatory democracy in a high-tech era.

Advertisers, capitalizing upon every new gadget and format that enables them to build closer customer relationships, will generate more intrusive advertising and promotional activity. These developments will provide more ammunition for consumer-interest groups, government officials, educators, students, social scientists—the constituency that strives to combat commercialism's inroads into everyday life. The advertising industry will never become immune from attack. While a self-regulatory system monitors the ad claims in national campaigns, this intramural program cannot deter government intervention in marketing. Regulators may agree with the theory that advertising is a form of speech that deserves First Amendment protection, but there are deep differences concerning the degree of protection it deserves. Government will be drawn into the debate as long as there are disagreements over "kidvid," or children-oriented commercials, ads and sales programs, premiums, sales promotion efforts, tobacco advertising, fitness and health claims, advertising by lawyers, doctors, and other professionals, package labeling, advertising content in terms of gender, minority representation, taste, and decency.

The new advertising media add new dimensions to the "free speech" debate. Spawned not as journalistic enterprises grounded in Fourth Estate principles and traditions, the new media often are pure sales-oriented vehicles; they may or may not contain material bordering on borrowed news interest. The program content of such media will largely determine the degree of new friction they cause between advertising and the public.

The question of tobacco companies and their right to advertise a legal product will become less pervasive. Cigarette marketers, their promotional options steadily being narrowed, will continue to focus on ways of addressing smaller niche audiences, and their ads may become more "reminders" than motivational. But as more Americans turn away from cigarettes and tobacco, tax revenues will diminish and government leaders will try to levy new "sin taxes" on other targets: beer, entertainment, distilled liquors, and, yes, even sweets. The advertising community will go on battling against such taxes, even as it argues against proposals to further reduce the tax deductibility levels of advertising costs.

See also BROADCASTING; COMMUNICATIONS: PRIVACY ISSUES; MEDIA LAB; TELECOMMUNICATIONS; TELEVISION.

BIBLIOGRAPHY

BRAND, STEWART. *The Media Lab.* New York: Viking, 1987.
CAPPO, JOSEPH. *FutureScope.* Chicago: Longman Financial Services Publishing, 1990.
MAYER, MARTIN. *Whatever Happened to Madison Avenue?* Boston: Little, Brown, 1991.
SNIDER, JIM, and ZIPORYN, TERRA. *Future Shop.* New York: St. Martin's Press, 1992.

Fred Danzig

Africa

Unlike any other area of the world, the most significant challenge for most of the fifty-three countries in sub-Saharan Africa over the next decades will be survival: survival of peoples, the environment, and states. While a number of peoples will do well, many more will not, barring a dramatic change in current trends.

The dramatic, optimistic period of independence in the 1960s, high growth in the 1970s, debt-led crisis of the 1980s, and continuing stringent adjustment in the 1990s have masked the underlying deterioration of the fundamental underpinnings of African development. The balance among the size of the population, the ability of the environment to sustain its strength, and the ability of African farmers to grow enough food for the population has begun to erode seriously. Improvements in health and education have led to sizable net increases in population at a pace far more rapid than the increase in food production.

Farmers have responded to the increase in demand for food by farming more extensively by cultivating a great deal more land and by drastically reducing the amount of time given for the land to rejuvenate its strength (fallow periods). The new land brought into cultivation is far more fragile than the old land because of its very thin layer of topsoil; it wears out fast. For the rising poor, urban populations, life could be grim indeed. Nations in particular danger of environmental crisis include the largest country on the continent, Sudan.

Consequently, experts believe that by 2025 Africa's food supply could be only 55 percent of what is required. That point may not be reached as starvation could take hold well before then. During this time period every other part of the world will be self-sufficient in food supplies. An exception will be China, which will be short of food, but which will have the purchasing power to take food from the world market—likely at the expense of Africa.

The disruptions in Africa from the ecological and food crises could be immense. An increasing cycle of drought and starvation could well take hold, transforming huge populations into wandering masses ·in search of food. International relief mechanisms may be stretched to the limits.

Part of the reason survival will be such a strong issue is that the African state has been and will continue to be weak. In the early years of the twenty-first century, African states will fall into two categories, those states that benefited from the democratization movements of the 1990s, devolving market-oriented economies and trade relations with neighboring states; and those states that were unable to change because of entrenched dictators, statist, command-driven economies, disaffected populations, and internal ethnic conflicts. The latter category of failed states will remain discrete national entities because no other nation either in Africa or the West will have the inclination to intervene. It is conceivable, however, that the urge to associate along ethnic lines could split apart a few nations. Religious fault lines may deepen as well, continuing to place great stress on countries like Sudan and its neighbors.

In failed states' quests for survival, corrupt government bureaucracies, entrenched militaries and lawless gangs of young men will mitigate against peaceful evolution of democratic governments. As these states grow more fragile, civil societies will assume larger roles.

On the other hand, a significant number of African nations will become more robust, secure, economically viable states. Led by Southern Africa (especially South Africa, Botswana, Zimbabwe, and Namibia), the successes of the 1990s—including Ghana, Benin, Uganda, and Seychelles—will be joined by other democratizing states such as Malawi, Eritrea, and possibly Côte d'Ivoire (Ivory Coast). These successes will be at the vanguard of the move to involve ordinary citizens in national governance.

Those states with oil-based economies will have the potential for enormous influence within the region. Within the next thirty years the price of oil will increase significantly, unless a viable substitute is discovered. This will increase the prospects of Nigeria, Cameroon, Angola, Gabon, and other states in which explorations will yield favorable results. But there are no guarantees that oil revenues will be spent wisely.

Africa's greatest strength will continue to be its people. Further health improvements can be expected under the dynamic leadership of UNICEF and the World Health Organization.

Africans and donors will act upon the fact that an educated population is essential for development and integration into the information century. The education of girls will be a condition of international assistance, and great leaps in female literacy will occur. Higher education will continue to be extremely costly, but democratic governments will realize that long-term survival depends on the trained labor those universities will produce.

The accelerated empowerment of women will be achieved through more widespread educational opportunities and the power of the ballot. They will continue to be the food growers in Africa, but they will be better-educated farmers, resulting in higher yields per hectare. Women will provide a new perspective on national politics as they focus on an end to corruption, better social-services delivery, and conflict resolution. They will play an increasingly important role in the growth of nongovernmental organizations.

In technology and the physical sciences, international trade and investment, and diplomacy, Africa will be the least significant part of the world, moving further behind over the next two generations. There will be huge pressure to increase investment in agricultural research, but this research will largely be performed by international and foreign institutions, not by African institutions.

Increasing marginalization will make Africa more vulnerable to outside powers. The greatest outside power will be the Bretton Woods institutions, particularly the World Bank and the International Monetary Fund, which will have relatively even more power vis-à-vis Africa than they had in the 1990s, particularly as the industrialized countries' enthusiasm for foreign aid will continue to decline.

The World Bank will want to help develop Africa's infrastructure, but national economic crises in the failed states will absorb a large percentage of funds available to Africa and minimize long-term investment possibilities for the continent as a whole. Nevertheless, for those countries on the faster track of development, there will be a boom in the development of roads, electrification, and social infrastructure, particularly schools and hospitals, funded by both multilateral and private-sector lending.

Partly in response to its economic isolation, the momentum for regional cooperation will increase in the years ahead as Africans strengthen their regional and national institutions. At the local level, civil societies and nongovernmental organizations also will flourish. This burgeoning will occur naturally in Africa's democracies, but also in its failed states as citizens will take on more and more traditional functions of the state simply to survive.

An overall gloomy assessment should not hide many encouraging developments of the early twenty-first century: self-help groups will grow in economic and political importance; local-level entrepreneurship will flourish; and ties with the African diaspora in the United States and Latin America will grow much stronger. The global communications and information revolution will strongly affect South African and other urban centers, thereby linking cities and developed subregions to the world community. Nevertheless, the majority of the continent will be bystanders and listeners in the technological/communications revolution. Absent strong economic and technological links to the wider world, Africans will turn to literature and the arts (drawing upon strong cultural traditions merging poetry, song, dance, and the life of the individual and society) as important vehicles for global linkages.

See also DEVELOPMENT, ALTERNATIVE.

BIBLIOGRAPHY

ADEDEJI, ADEBAYO, and SHAW, TIMOTHY. *Economic Crisis in Africa: African Perspectives on Development Problems and Potentials.* Boulder, CO: Lynne Rienner, 1985.

BERG, ROBERT J., and WHITTAKER, JENNIFER S. *Strategies for African Development.* Los Angeles: University of California Press, 1986.

BROWN, LESTER R., and WOLF, EDWARD C. *Reversing Africa's Decline.* Washington, DC: Worldwatch, 1985.

CHERU, FANTU. *Silent Revolution in Africa: Debt, Development and Democracy.* London: Zed Books, 1989.

ONIMODE, BADE. *A Future for Africa: Beyond the Politics of Adjustment.* London: Earthscan, 1992.

ONWUKA, RALPH I., and OLAJIDE, ALUKO. *The Future of Africa and the International Economic Order.* New York: St. Martin's Press, 1986.

SHAW, TIMOTHY M., and OLAJIDE, ALUKO. *Africa Projected: From Recession to Renaissance by the Year 2000?* New York: St. Martin's Press, 1985.

WHITTAKER, JENNIFER S. *How Can Africa Survive?* New York: HarperCollins, 1988.

Vivian Lowery Derryck
Robert J. Berg

Agents of Change

Twenty years or so ago, futurists would probably have largely agreed when asked about the process of change and how change agents operated. They would have identified a number of people who changed the dynamics of world history. They would have cited experts, scholars, theorists, artists, policy makers and planners, opinion leaders and shapers, popularizers, and the activities of interest groups. They would have broken down these groups into additional categories. For example, they might have classified theorists in terms of visionaries, philosophers, theologians, and utopians, or considered experts in terms of geniuses, leading authorities, researchers, and innovators.

Alternatively, they might have looked at the big names in history. Genghis Khan and Adolf Hitler were change agents. So were Charles Darwin, John Maynard Keynes, William Wilberforce, Harriet Beecher Stowe, Mohandas Gandhi, Martin Luther King, Saint Francis, and Queen Elizabeth I. Change agents are not intrinsically good or bad but belong to this category, because they alter dynamics, not because we either like or despise them.

But who really changes dynamics? Some authorities believe that a few key people drive history, that major figures throughout history have guided the course and direction of events. Others believe that there were particular moments in history when the future was in the balance and that a small event at those critical junctures in time could have altered the world in which we now live.

Still others see the whole process of change as random. Minor incidents clash and combine unpredictably to cause great events. A parallel is drawn with the weather. The latest thinking on this subject is that it never will be possible practically, or even theoretically, to precisely predict the weather more than a few days ahead. This belief is being popularized with an idea derived from a science fiction story—that the flapping of a butterfly's wings on one continent can eventually alter the weather on another.

A new consensus is currently developing about the issue of how change comes about. This approach argues that change today is driven by major forces that are irreversible (or at least highly deterministic), short of massive catastrophe. The technology of production and destruction, ecological constraints, increasing population, and movement toward individual freedom are pushing us in new directions. If this view is correct, we shall either adapt, moving from adolescence to adulthood, or we shall perish.

If this new understanding is valid, then today's change agents need to discern the flows of history and work with them. The effective change agent, or leader, "finds the parade" and gets in front of it. Change agents, therefore, help people clarify their real options. They also distinguish between what can and cannot be changed.

The core task of change agents, particularly in today's conditions of rapid change, is to provide people with words, images, and approaches that help grasp the directions needed if they and their children are to survive. This shift in the image of change agents is tied to a major shift in the sciences that started at the beginning of the twentieth century. Scientists such as Werner Heisenburg, Niels Bohr, and Albert Einstein showed Newtonian cause-and-effect thinking as applicable to a small range of cases rather than to all scientific phenomena.

This lesson has been fully understood in the physical sciences only in recent decades. *Chaos* by James Gleick explained this physical science theory as a profoundly new way of understanding the world. We are only just beginning to apply this way of thinking to the social sciences.

There are very practical implications that follow from this new way of looking at the world. First, the idea of strategic planning is losing ground. Nobody knows for certain how to predict events even one year ahead, and there is every reason to believe that the rapids of change will become even more unmanageable. Change agents must be more flexible than ever before.

As the emphasis shifts to a tension between top-down and bottom-up systems, more people see themselves as change agents. They aim to set up systems where opportunities are grasped as they become available and problems are resolved before they become crises. Indeed, many change agents no longer try to bring about change directly but instead work to set up systems in which others can be effective as change agents.

Perceived thus, the job of change agents is to reduce the need for their type of activity in the long run. Of course, they never will be fully successful. However, a commitment to this approach will certainly change lifestyles. Instead of seeing their activities as confined to the elite, they will aim to involve broader segments of the general population. They will be guided by the statement that "at the end of every intellectual journey lies common sense." They will explain what needs to be done in language that can be understood by anybody who cares to make the effort.

Two primary groups of change agents exist today. One group of ideologues tries to change the world so that it conforms to their sense of what is right. We are increasingly discovering that such advocacy is no longer effective. A second group aims to help people cooperate, hoping to ensure very long-term ecological balance accompanied by a higher worldwide quality of life. They also recognize a religious or broadly spiritual commitment as central to their task. The latest vision sees all citizens as players at discovering a viable future. We all have our own roles to play,

See also CHANGE; CIVIL PROTEST; MIND: NEW MODES OF THINKING; PACESETTER GOVERNMENTS; PUBLIC OPINION POLLS; RECORD SETTING; SOCIAL CHANGE: UNITED STATES.

BIBLIOGRAPHY

BATEMAN, GREGORY. *Steps Toward an Ecology of Mind.* New York: Ballantine, 1975.

GREENLEAF, ROBERT K. *Servant Leadership.* New York: Paulist Press, 1977.

MURRAY, CHARLES. *In Pursuit of Happiness.* New York: Simon & Schuster, 1988.

THEOBALD, ROBERT. *Turning the Century.* Indianapolis: Knowledge Systems, 1993.

Robert Theobald

Aging of the Population

The aging of the population in the developed industrial countries of North America, Europe, and Japan is a major global trend with implications for future economic, social, and geopolitical developments. Over the next generation, growth of the working age population will slow down significantly in all the advanced industrialized countries relative to growth in other countries.

Here, the prospective demographic developments in the United States are examined over the period from 1995 to 2025. These developments and their economic, social, and public finance implications can be assessed with some degree of confidence, though uncertainties are necessarily present. Beyond this time period, the uncertainties are much greater. By the year 2030, the last of the baby boomers will reach age 65; barring unforeseen developments, population trends will then stabilize. This analysis is based on demographic projections that embody the current "middle series" Census Bureau assumptions of birth and survival rates for specific age-race-sex population groups, but assume a higher rate of immigration that would grow in proportion to U.S. population.

The roots of future demographic changes lie deep in the past. The expected changes in the age structure of the population will reflect events as far back as World War I and immigration restrictions of the early 1920s, and especially the effects of the subsequent decline in birthrates during the Depression of the 1930s and World War II, of the "baby boom" of 1946 to 1965, and of the sharp drop in the birthrates during the 1965 to 1972 period. Birthrates and mortality rates are projected to continue to decline in the future.

Dynamics of U.S. Population Aging

The massive "graying of America," which will begin after 2007, will be the result of large num-

Aging of the Population

TABLE 1.   U.S. Population by Major Age Group and Their Growth Rates, 1995–2025

	Total	*0–19*	*20–64*	*65+*
Total Population (Thousands)				
1995	263,491	75,741	153,815	33,935
2007	295,133	82,425	174,312	38,396
2025	345,459	92,339	189,558	63,562
Annual Growth Rate (Percent per Year)				
1995–2005	0.9	0.7	0.7	2.1
1995–2007	0.9	0.7	1.0	1.0
2007–2025	0.9	0.6	0.5	2.8

Source: NPA Data Services, Inc.

bers of baby boomers growing old while the growth of younger population groups will be much slower owing to the decline of birthrates after 1965. Table 1 summarizes the projected size and growth rates of the young (under 20), the prime working age (20–64), and the elderly (65 and older) population groups. Over the entire period from 1995 to 2025, the growth rates of the young and of the prime working age populations, both averaging 0.7 percent a year, will be much lower than the 2.1 percent annual growth rate projected for the elderly population. The elderly population will almost double, while population under 65 will grow only by 30 percent. This does not mean that the old will outnumber the young. Population under 20 will still be considerably larger than population 65 and older. However, the ratio of old to young will rise from 40 percent in 1995 to 69 percent by 2025.

Growth rates of different population groups will vary significantly over shorter periods. Until 2007, the older population will grow at the same rate as the prime working-age population, because the number of persons reaching 65 during that period will come from the small age cohorts born during the Depression and World War II. After 2007, the growth rate of the elderly population will escalate to 2.8 percent a year, while growth of the young and prime working age populations will slow down considerably.

Over the entire period, 1995–2025, the growth rates of the "younger elderly" group (age 65–74) and the "older elderly" group (age 75 and older) will be the same; but within the latter group, the oldest population will grow more rapidly (see Table 2). However, until 2007, the "younger elderly" population (65–74) will grow only at 0.1 percent a year. Thereafter, its growth will accelerate sharply to 3.5 percent a year from 2007 to 2025. Population of age 75 and over will grow uniformly at 2.1 percent annually. The growth rate of population 100 and older will be very rapid, but the number of centenarians will still be small, totaling approximately 0.1 percent of U.S. population in 2025.

TABLE 2.   Age Detail of the U.S. Elderly Population, 1995–2025

	65–74	*75+*	*75–84*	*85–99*	*100+*
Population (Thousands)					
1995	18,908	15,027	11,262	3,712	53
2007	19,108	19,288	13,219	5,919	150
2025	35,599	27,963	19,844	7,682	437
Annual Growth Rates (Percent per Year)					
1995–2025	2.1	2.1	1.9	2.5	7.3
1995–2007	0.1	2.1	1.3	4.0	9.1
2007–2025	3.5	2.1	2.3	1.5	6.1

Source: NPA Data Services, Inc.

Some Possible Problems and Solutions

With increased longevity and larger numbers of elderly, there will be some changes in the lifestyle of many Americans. There will be more families and individuals with both parents and children who require personal attention. The increased numbers of the very old will probably increase the need for personal care to be provided for by relatives, or paid for through the public sector, or from the elderly's own resources. A greater proportion of wealth may be consumed by the elderly rather than being bequeathed to the next generation. This implies an increased need for personal savings by the working population.

By themselves, the demographic changes do not appear to imply big changes in the overall support ratio. The ratio of total population to population of prime working age—that is, ages 20–64, will decline from 1.71 in 1995 to 1.69 in 2007. It will then rise to 1.82 in 2025. The projected total support ratio is within the range of the past experience of 1.92 in 1970 and 1.75 in 1980. However, support requirements are shifting progressively from support of children—largely within families—to support of the elderly, largely through government and private money transfer systems. Increased consumption by the elderly will reduce the disposable income and consumption of workers.

The size of the economic burden of support placed on the working population is neither fixed nor determined only by demography. It will also depend on the rate of future economic growth and, in particular, on growth in national productivity and hence in the real earnings of workers. An increase in economic growth will expand the means available in the economy for support of the elderly. For this reason, it will be particularly important to have in effect policies that raise productivity growth. To maintain economic growth during the coming demographic transition, it will be necessary to make changes in tax, expenditure, and regulatory policies before 2007.

Apart from growth policies, two specific approaches have been initiated to limit the cost of support of the elderly population—containing the growth of health care costs and increasing the retirement age. Growth in the real cost of health care (i.e., its growth relative to growth in the general price level) has already been dampened by limits imposed both by government programs and by the private health insurance industry involving payment schedules for specific services and reviews of the choice of services.

Increasing the retirement age is more complicated. It requires changes in incentives, not only for elderly workers to increase the supply of their labor, but also changes in incentives for employers to raise their demand for older workers. Considerable proportions of workers over 40—and especially those workers over 55—who have lost jobs due to plant closings, corporate mergers, and so forth, have not been able to find new jobs and have involuntarily left the labor force. Increases in the age of eligibility for social security retirement benefits, from 65 to 67, have already been legislated and further increases may be added in the future. However, an effective increase in the retirement age will require increasing the labor force participation and employment rates of workers in the younger groups, especially those of age 55 to 64. Partly because of reduced demand by employers for older workers, participation rates of groups age 55 to 65 has been declining. Therefore, in order to assure higher employment rates for workers over 65, it will be necessary to increase employment opportunities for potential workers under 65, because employment continuity is probably the most effective means for raising the age of retirement.

See also DEATH AND DYING; DEMOGRAPHY; ELDERLY, LIVING ARRANGEMENTS; HEALTH CARE; POPULATION GROWTH: UNITED STATES.

BIBLIOGRAPHY

AUERBACH, JAMES A., and WELSH, JOYCE C., eds. *Aging and Competition: Rebuilding the U.S. Workforce.* Washington, DC: National Planning Association, 1994.

DAY, JENNIFER CHEESEMAN. *Population Progressions of the United States, by Age, Sex, Race and Hispanic Origin, 1993–2050.* Current Population Reports, No. 1109. Washington, DC: U.S. Bureau of the Census, 1993.

MANNHEIMER, RONALD J., ed. *Older Americans Almanac: A Reference Work on Seniors in the United States.* Asheville, NC: North Carolina Center for Creative Retirement, University of North Carolina; Detroit: Gale Research, 1994.

TAEUBER, CYNTHIA M. *Sixty-five Plus in America.* Current Population Reports. Washington, DC: U.S. Department of Commerce, Economics and Statistics Administration, Bureau of the Census, 1992.

TERLECKYJ, NESTOR E., and COLEMAN, CHARLES D. *U.S. Population Trends, 1995–2025.* National Economic Projections Series, Vol. 94-N-2. Washington, DC: NPA Data Services, 1995.

U.S. Senate Special Committee on Aging. *Aging America: Trends and Projections.* Washington, DC: U.S. Government Printing Office, 1991.

Nestor E. Terleckyj

Agricultural Technology

We are moving into an era where knowledge, not labor, raw materials, or capital, is the key resource. This knowledge is giving us the scientific understanding to meet the growing demands of society for a higher quality of life. At the same time, we seek a development process that is sustainable, globally competitive, and market-driven.

The opportunities afforded by competencies such as molecular biology, combinatorial chemistry, and smart materials mean that we will have new ways to fulfill the basic needs of food, fiber, and shelter. Yet, the development and commercialization of knowledge-based technologies are becoming increasingly complex as societies and markets try to balance their material needs with other priorities. The sustainability of production systems, the protection of the environment, and the preservation of natural resources are priorities that cannot be forgotten as new technologies are developed.

The balance of the scales is challenged even further by the explosion of science and technology, the escalating cost of achieving and maintaining technical leadership, and the difficulty of protecting technical leadership through intellectual property rights. The value of technological innovation must be captured to ensure continual reinvestment in our future.

How can we achieve balance? It is clear that independent, self-sufficient efforts are unlikely to keep pace with the needs of society and the leading edge of innovation. Change is clearly necessary—our processes must be reinvented so that technology is discovered and developed internationally. Former attorney general Ramsey Clark, the respected American political and social thinker, once described change in this way: "Turbulence is life force. It is opportunity. Let's love turbulence and use it for change."

The underlying turbulence or stress that is currently driving change is fundamentally related to globalization and the transition from an asset to a knowledge-based economy. Within the last five years, we have seen vast political and economic change throughout the world as countries embraced democracy and the free market system. GATT, NAFTA, and the EEC reflect a spirit of global competitiveness and cooperation unlike any we have seen in history.

People on our planet can now share knowledge with one another in an instant. Still and video images can be transmitted cost-effectively. More than forty million people are now linked through Internet, receiving information from more than 100,000 publishing sources. Many of us would not know how to function without electronic mail, faxes, and video conferencing. As business guru Peter Drucker has observed: "There will be no poor countries or industries, only ignorant ones." In other words, knowledge will be the currency of the future.

In summary, we see a world business environment that is undergoing a major transition as local economies regionalize and individual businesses globalize. Technology, capital, and information flow freely across international borders, equalizing some of the previous disparities between countries. Every business is faced with increased competition and increased customer expectation in terms of higher quality, lower prices, a demand for products tailored to individual needs, and a local source of supply. In addition, societal expectations have increased, especially regarding environmental issues and sustainable development.

Knowledge-based technologies, if used wisely and judiciously, can help restore balance (Figure 1). But to be fully effective in the current business environment, these technologies must be researched and developed by a new paradigm.

What does this new paradigm look like? Successful business and technical processes will change from vertical and country-specific to horizontal and international. By reinventing our processes, the fundamental unit of work will be international teams and affiliations tied to a global

A New Paradigm

⇩

Technology

Explosion Of Science
Technical Leadership
Intellectual Property
Sustainability
Environment
Natural Resources

FIGURE 1.   Restoring balance.

A New Paradigm
Horizontal and International Alliances
Matched Competencies
Compatible Goals

FIGURE 2. A new paradigm.

effort. Alliances will develop that match competencies and compatible goals between partners (Figure 2).

This process is illustrated by changes occurring in agriculture and the technologies being developed in response to these changes. With this level of change, independent, self-sufficient efforts are unlikely to keep pace either with the needs of society or with the leading edge of innovation.

In agriculture, change today manifests itself primarily in four areas: population growth, societal demands, the environment, and the marriage of traditional agriculture with the high-tech world of advanced chemistry, and molecular biology and information technology.

As we move into the next century, the Earth's population is forecast to double, reaching about eleven billion by the year 2050. It is important to remember that 97 percent of the world's food supply is grown on 3 percent of the Earth's surface, a relationship that is unlikely to change to any significant degree. This means that over the next fifty years or so, we will need to produce more food than in all of history. As this production task unfolds, society will require that it be accomplished while protecting the global environment and preserving natural resources such as land and water.

Over the years, agriculture satisfied these ever-increasing societal needs at an incredible rate of improved efficiency through new crops, better production, better storage, better processing, and better distribution. Agricultural chemicals have been a very significant factor in meeting society's needs—revolutionizing farming practices by reducing labor requirements, increasing crop yields, lowering food costs, and improving food quality. However, as sustainability of the environment becomes a high priority, society is expecting a continuous improvement in the environmental compatibility of these products.

What we have then is a dilemma that has brought us to an important crossroads. On one hand, there is a global ground swell of public concern about the impact of production methods in agriculture. On the other hand, there is increasing concern over the ability of the world's agriculture system to meet future food and fiber demands. The dynamics of global trade will influence the resolution of this dilemma.

What is agriculture's response? Through technology, the potential exists to develop agricultural systems that protect and enhance the global environment. Increasing the intensity of agriculture on highly productive land will reduce the environmen-

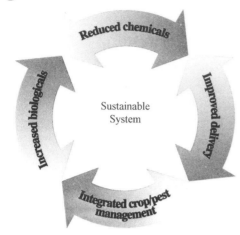

FIGURE 3. Sustainable system.

tal pressure on our forests and wetlands and allow the withdrawal of marginal lands from production. A flexible, sustainable system is being developed that includes reduced chemical input, increased biological input, improved delivery systems, and integrated crop and pest management (see Figure 3).

Although chemicals will remain the principal input, their performance characteristics are changing dramatically. They are being designed to be increasingly effective on target organisms and increasingly safe to the environment and nontarget species. They will possess high biological efficacy to minimize the amount of material introduced into the environment. They will have high specificity to target organisms, but at the same time, softness toward beneficial organisms. There will be low potential to affect surface and ground water and a degree of persistence that can be tailored to match the designed length of pest control, the cropping systems, the soil, and other environmental and food safety considerations. There will be little or no residue on treated crops and low toxicity to man, fish, and other wildlife (see Figure 4).

Quite a challenge, but much progress has already been made. Over the past fifty years, herbicide use rates have been steadily reduced. With the introduction of sulfonyureas, these rates dropped dramatically. Today, a few grams per hectare of a sulfonyurea are as effective as kilograms per hectare of the more conventional herbicides currently in use. This represents a reduction of several hundredfold in the amount of chemicals that are introduced into the environment to achieve the same level of weed control. This knowledge and performance will be prerequisites for product commercialization by the year 2000.

Another important change occurring in agriculture is the marriage of traditional agriculture with advanced chemistry, molecular biology, and information technologies. New synthetic organic techniques combined with molecular biology are increasing the availability of diverse chemistries. Molecular biology also provides an unprecedented level of understanding of key biological processes in plants, fungi, and insects.

We can now produce crops that are resistant to environmentally sound herbicides or have improved disease and insect resistance. Improved microbes for controlling insects, disease, and weeds are also being explored. Although chemicals will remain the major crop-protection technology, improved crops, biological and integrated pest management will become part of a flexible sustainable system.

Diagnostic tests are being developed for early detection of plant disease and work is continuing to better understand multigene traits such as stress, yield, nutritional content, and processing characteristics. More fruits and vegetables will be developed with improved taste, texture, shelf life, and appearance. Edible oils will be tailored with specific nutritional properties such as levels of saturated, unsaturated, and polyunsaturated fatty acids. New uses for plants in areas such as pharmaceuticals, materials, and fuels will spur tremendous opportunities for global production.

The third critical factor concerning the change in agriculture is information technology. Using microcomputers, satellites, soil and crop geographical databases, positioning technologies, decision-support systems, and automatic control of machine functions, farmers can respond to variations in soils such as water content, compaction, and fertility. They can predict leaching

The Ideal Chemical
High biological efficacy
High specificity to target organisms
Low potential to affect water
Tailored persistence
Little or no residue
Low toxicity

FIGURE 4.

and runoff potentials of nutrients and chemicals, as well as identify and measure the density of target weeds, pests, and diseases. Then using sensors, they can measure crop yields, use variable seed rates, and precisely apply fertilizer and chemicals. In other words, farming by the foot. Systems that apply this kind of precision to farming will give us the productivity and sustainability we require in the future.

In summary, there is yet another revolution occurring in farming—a blending of traditional agricultural practices with technology. We are witnessing a marriage where innovations in mechanization, seeds, fertilizer, and crop-protection chemicals are united with advanced chemistry and molecular biology. Information technology provides the interactive link that holds together the system, the facility to share questions and answers.

See also BIODIVERSITY; CLIMATE AND METEOROLOGY; DEFORESTATION; FISHERIES; FOOD AND AGRICULTURE; FOOD AND FIBER PRODUCTION; FOOD TECHNOLOGIES; FORESTRY; GENETICS: AGRICULTURAL APPLICATIONS; NUTRITION; SOIL CONDITIONS; TOBACCO.

BIBLIOGRAPHY

Burrus, Dan, and Thomsen, Patti. *Advances in Agriculture: A User Friendly Guide to the Latest Technology.* Milwaukee; WI: International Mangement, 1994.

Miller, Richard K., and Waller, Terri C. *Robotic, Vision, and AI Applications in Agriculture.* Lilburn, GA: Future Tech Surveys, 1989.

WEIR, DAVID S. "Sharing the Vision: The Shape of Things to Come." Keynote lecture, International Symposium on the Frontiers in Chemistry and Chemial Technology, Indian Institute of Chemical Technology, Hyderabad, India, March 1995.

Ashok K. Dhingra
David S. Weir

Air Transport

The direction of development for air transport technology is clear. Speed, safety, noise reduction, energy efficiency, and reliability continue to improve. Materials science contributes to smarter, lighter, and more durable aircraft frames and skins. Information technology will improve aircraft design, pilot performance, air traffic control, navigation, and the interchange among various transportation systems. More specialized aircraft, such as tiltrotors and tiltwings, will be introduced if they become cost-effective.

The schedule of specific advances is less certain than the direction of change. Visions of air transport include birdlike flight and hypersonic entry into orbit. Such visions, technologically possible within the next thirty years, must give way to the practicalities of money, needs, and priorities. Planning, designing, and producing a new commercial aircraft can cost $4 billion.

Much of aviation for the first decade of the twenty-first century is already in place. Commercial aircraft have a lifespan of thirty to thirty-five years. In 2000, the Boeing 737 and 767 and the Airbus 310 and 320s will be in their midlife. Subsonic aircraft technology is mature, and most advances will be incremental. The greatest strides will be made in systems integration and information technology. Expert systems will coordinate digital sensors, controls, and onboard and external data, and will increasingly take over control of the flight.

Revolutionary advances are expected for supersonic transport. Worldwide demand for supersonic aircraft may reach 350 aircraft between 2000 and 2010. Efficiency and noise reduction are expected to improve. A hypersonic plane that flies at Mach 5 (five times the speed of sound) could be developed and commercialized by the 2020s. Hypersonic planes would exit and reenter the atmosphere on trans- and intercontinental flights. Flight times between Europe and the United States would be two hours. The number of passengers per plane could double to 600 or more.

Military procurement and research and development drives air transport technologies and systems because performance is more important than costs. Air transport systems must be effective in battle. Aircraft are designed for acceleration and maneuverability and recently for stealth. Visions of military air power include a hypersonic intercepter, dog-fighting helicopter, and greater use of unmanned, remotely controlled aircraft. Roughly one-third of the U.S. defense budget is devoted to aviation.

Civilian use of military technologies happens only after they become cost-effective. For example, short/vertical takeoff-and-landing (S/VTOL) technology used by the military is too expensive for most civilian use. The divergence of military missions and civilian applications have reduced military-to-civilian technology transfer.

The end of the Cold War has led to military downsizing. The U.S. Air Force will soon have 2,200 fewer aircraft than in the mid-1980s.

Civilian aviation includes passenger travel, air cargo, and general aviation (private and business flying). Between 1980 and 2000, the number of takeoffs and landings in the United States by major and regional air carriers is expected to almost double to 30 million per year. Over the same time, the hours flown by major carriers may increase from 6.5 million to 13.4 million. Air travel accounted for one-fifth of all intercity passenger miles, twice the 1970 rate.

U.S. air travel will grow from 1.4 million passengers per day in 1990 to 4 million or 5 million by 2040. Revenue passenger miles for U.S. major carriers is forecast to increase from 259 billion miles in 1980 to 762 by 2000. People are increasingly financially able to see more of the country and the world. The number of trips abroad by U.S. citizens could reach 27 million by 2025, up from 15 million in 1990. Overseas travelers may take a pill or wear a skin patch to neutralize jet lag. Better understanding of chronobiology will allow circadian rhythms to be adjusted by influencing the brain's reaction to light.

World air-passenger miles could quadruple between 1990 and 2025. The strongest growth will likely be in the U.S.-Pacific Basin and Europe-Far East routes. Business globalization and the robust economies of many Asian countries will likely increase the demand for longer, faster commercial travel. Asian air travel is expected to reach up to 22 percent of the global air fleet and 42 percent of air travel by 2010. Transoceanic flights are expected to double between 2000 and 2025.

Competition is increasingly strong and international. Alliances will link airlines around the world. In the United States the large airlines will be supplemented by a growing network of regional airlines.

Air cargo and general aviation will continually grow. Air cargo growth will exceed passenger growth and could reach 5 percent of all commercial aircraft movements by 2010, up from 3 percent in 1990. Modularized container and cargo systems may help move goods from ship to plane to train to warehouse.

By the early twenty-first century, a next-generation supersonic business aircraft could be developed to carry ten business travelers at Mach 2. Personal flight in the next century could be offered by VTOL, but individually owned aircraft replacing a great number of automobiles is virtually impossible.

Aviation forecasting is vulnerable to unforeseen changes in social priorities and economics. New environmental issues could surface. Concern about aircraft noise, for example, was for the most part unforeseen. Telecommunications could reduce travel demand as video-conferencing and other electronic communications increase. Rapidly escalating fuel prices could change technology priorities. Air transport growth could overwhelm the airport and air traffic control infrastructure. Lack of adequate airport runway capacity could be the greatest constraint on growth.

Only three new airports have opened in the U.S. in the past twenty-five years: Dallas-Fort Worth, Southwest Florida Regional, and Denver International. It is unlikely that any other large new airports will be operational before 2000. Thirty-nine U.S. airports could have more than 20,000 hours of flight delays a year in air carrier operations, up from twenty-one airports in 1987. The larger airports could see delays of 50,000 to 100,000 hours annually. The National Airspace System Plan being implemented by the Federal Aviation Administration to reduce delays caused by the air traffic control system will begin to yield benefits only after the year 2000.

An obstacle to airport development or expansion is land. Expansion often is protested by citizen groups concerned about noise. About 20,000 acres of land are required for modern airports including runways, facilities, parking, and sound-buffer zones. Floating airports could be a solution to noise and land scarcity problems for coastal cities.

Information technologies will improve safety and air traffic control. Traffic management works on limited data and is constrained by the ability of air traffic controllers to manage complexity. With the introduction of more computing power and expert systems, a global, comprehensive, integrated airspace system may evolve. The next-generation air traffic control system will include real-time global positioning to a few meters and advanced weather technology. Traffic-management-center computers could use satellite and cellular technology to communicate with computers on board airplanes, as well as with other transportation modes, to improve routing efficiency.

Reducing the potential for human error will improve safety. Better presentation of data on the plane's condition will improve pilot performance. Collision avoidance technologies will improve and become more widespread. Aircraft may be dynamic structures that respond to environmental stresses. Better weather forecasting will come from using supercomputer-based modeling, smart databases, real-time data, and graphic displays. Weather forecasts could be provided in minutes rather than hours.

The adoption of new aviation technology is slow because of exacting safety standards and fear of litigation. Safety-related technology reflect the accident patterns of the preceding few years. Yet air travel remains one the safest modes of transportation available.

Hijackings and other terrorist incidents will always be a threat to aviation. The number and violence of terrorist groups continues to increase. Security systems will need to keep pace with the increasing technological sophistication of terrorists. Biological and chemical weapons are difficult to detect. Terrorists may then turn to other targets that are less protected than airplanes.

See also CHANGE, PACE OF; MACROENGINEERING; MAGLEV; RAILWAYS; SPACE FLIGHT; SPACE TRAVEL; TERRORISM; TRANSPORTATION.

BIBLIOGRAPHY

"Mach 3 Passengers? No Simple Formula." *New York Times*, January 14, 1990.

"The Sky Is Falling." *Christian Science Monitor*, November 20, 1989.

SOCHER, EUGENE. *The Politics of International Aviation*. Iowa City, IA: University of Iowa Press, 1991.

WATERS, SOMERSET R. *Travel Industry World Yearbook: The Big Picture*. Vol. 35. New York: Child & Waters, 1991.

Tom Conger

Alcohol

Alcoholic beverages have been a part of traditional cuisine and a pleasurable social amenity throughout recorded history. Alcoholic beverages, like many newly introduced consumables, were often prescribed for medical purposes. Sumerian clay tablets dating to 2100 B.C. corroborate such use, as do records of Egyptian physicians during the following millennia, revealing that about 15 percent of "prescriptions" called for alcohol.

Alcohol, once largely the province and privilege of religious orders, also played a role in divination. Priests substituted holy water with alcohol, sometimes insisting it was essential to reaching transcendent states that increased their ability to foretell the fortunes of rulers and prospects for societies.

Consumption

Alcohol used in moderation not only provides recreational diversion, but may be beneficial to health. However, alcohol abuse always has plagued society. Alcohol consumption constitutes the nation's most widespread drug problem. Despite the typical warnings of nausea and dizziness suffered by first-time users, individuals not only learn to tolerate such poisons, but can develop cravings and physical dependence tantamount to addiction.

Heavy drinking became unfashionable during the 1980s, when preventive attitudes surged. Tougher criminal laws, stiffer enforcement of them, and raising the legal drinking age to twenty-one played major roles in this change. The drinking age was raised to a minimum of twenty-one in all states by 1988. Alcohol consumption, as a result, has declined and remained relatively stable over the past fifteen years.

The rate of consumption was highest in 1810 and 1830, when U.S. per capita use amounted to 7.1 gallons of pure alcohol. By 1985, consumption had dropped to 2.58 gallons of absolute alcohol and is likely to decline by only a small amount over the next several decades.

Americans may think that what they drink is healthy, but a look at per capita consumption raises doubts (see Table 1). Consumption of all fluids in 1994 amounted to 186.2–221.4 gallons per capita. Soft drinks, 49.6 gallons of them, far and away constituted the leading beverage. Surprisingly, beer ranks second, at some 22.5–32 gallons per capita. Next comes coffee at 26–28 gallons; and finally, fluid milk, at 19.1–25.0 gallons. Soft drinks, together with bottled water (including flavored

TABLE 1.   Fluids Consumed Per Capita in the United States in 1994

Type of Liquid	No. Gallons Consumed
Soft Drinks	49.6
Alcoholic Beverages	25.4–36.7
Beer	22.5–32.0
Wine	1.6–2.7
Distilled Spirits	1.3–2.0
Coffee	26.0–28.0
Fluid Milk	19.1–25.0
Bottled Water	11.2
Tea	7.0
Juices	7.0
Powdered Beverages	6.9
Water Content from Solid Foods	34.0–50.0
Total	186.2–221.4

Source: Public Policy Forecasting, 1995; based on USDA, PPFI, and Beverage World data. (Some adjustments exclude or include minors.)

varieties), will continue to increase and lead the pack. Coffee, including all its gourmet and upscale varieties, also will experience strong growth. Beer may experience moderate growth. Fast-paced lifestyles and healthier diets will also encourage considerably higher consumption of fruit and vegetable juices.

Consumer Spending

Consumption of alcoholic beverages overall is expected to remain relatively flat, and probably decline somewhat, over the next ten to twenty years; however, expenditures are expected to continue increasing as consumers switch to more costly premium, specialty, imported, flavored, and exotic varieties.

Consumer spending for alcohol reveals a trend favoring moderate products. Consumption of distilled spirits, as a percent of alcoholic beverage sales, fell from 51 percent in 1967 to 31 percent in 1992. Beer's proportion increased from 43 percent to 58 percent. And wine outlays doubled from 6 percent to 12 percent over the same period.

Food stores overtook liquor stores and became the biggest distribution channel in 1986. USDA statistics reveal food stores sold $17.6 billion and liquor stores $17.4 billion during that year. Grocers' marketshare is certain to continue growing. Wine, for example, enjoys a profit margin of 20–30 percent compared to about 3 percent or so for overall supermarket margins. Beer, wine, and liquor constituted the fourth largest spending category in grocery store sales during 1993—$39 billion of the $423 billion sold through all grocery stores. Soft drinks ranked seventh highest at $21 billion.

Packaged goods accounted for most of 1994 outlays—$49.8 billion—with another $39.4 billion in drinking establishments. Because eating away from home is expected to continue growing, spending for drinks is likely to overtake sales of packaged goods. Eating and drinking places became the largest dollar-volume channel for alcoholic beverages in 1977, when drinks garnered $11.98 billion, liquor stores took in $11.69 billion, and food stores accounted for only $8.04 billion in sales. By 1993 the gulf had further widened: $29.7 billion for eating and drinking places (plus another $4.7 billion in hotels and motels), $21.1 billion in food stores, and $18.6 billion in liquor stores.

Controlling Consumption

During ancient times, as today, excessive drinking came under government regulation. The Code of Hammurabi established by the king of Babylonia by 1770 B.C. responded to excessive intoxication and unruliness among abusing subjects. Not so long ago, almost one-half of all police activity in the United States involved alcohol, one way or another.

Militating against unreasonable consumption of alcoholic beverages are a bevy of powerful forces. Health consequences—early deaths from alcohol-related diseases, accidents, homicides, suicides, alcoholism, birth defects, and a host of other adverse health consequences—pose the strongest imperative for reform. Property damage and added taxpayer burdens also figure prominently. Keener interest in preventive health measures, including sound nutrition, reduction of caloric intake, and the increasing incidence of obesity add to potential widespread interest in curbing and controlling—but not eliminating—alcohol consumption.

Alcohol burdens the economy by as much as $100 billion attributable to health care costs and lost productivity. There is good reason to impose additional controls and expand educational efforts that seek to modify behavior.

Government Jurisdiction—Revenues or Health Prevention

Taxation has been used to discourage consumption of alcoholic beverages for many years. By the mid-1300s, Germany imposed taxes for this purpose. "Sin taxes," designating revenue raised from alcohol, tobacco, and gambling, gain enormous momentum. Policymakers will strive toward tax levels to offset costs taxpayers otherwise would have to bear. Such taxes are likely to grow enormously. Sweden slaps high prices on alcohol sold in its state-monopoly liquor stores, and boosts prices by the drink to levels that discourage purchase—about twenty-two dollars for a double martini in Swedish restaurants.

For centuries alcoholic beverages were controlled by revenue collectors, because spirits provided a main source of government funds. Today, alcohol revenues constitute a minuscule part of total revenues, and widespread alcohol abuse justifies reassigning jurisdiction to health ministries. Sweden, the bellwether country for undertaking new government policies (*see* PACESETTER GOVERNMENTS), transferred jurisdiction to its National Board of Health and Welfare within the Ministry of Health and Social Affairs, a step certain to be emulated.

Drunk Driving

Drunken driver arrests numbered 1.52 million in 1993, down approximately 300,000 from 1990. During 1993, nearly one-fourth of all such arrests (86,570) were for persons under twenty-one. The bad news is that overall, some 42 percent of the 40,655 traffic deaths in the United States during 1994 were alcohol-related. The good news is that alcohol-related deaths dropped from 25,165 (57 percent of traffic deaths) in 1982 to 16,884 (42 percent of traffic fatalities) in 1994, which was about 600 fewer than during 1993. Total costs resulting from alcohol-related motor vehicle accidents in 1993 amounted to an estimated $26.7 billion. Sterner controls are in the offing.

Tougher Penalties

Between 1970 and 1990 literally thousands of new laws were established to deter drunk driving. Recommendations call for reducing culpable blood alcohol concentration (BAC) levels from 0.1 percent to .08 percent, and setting them even lower for repeat offenders and younger drivers. At least five states already had set BAC levels at 0.08 percent by 1993. The trend is toward ever lower tolerance levels.

El Salvador, as of 1979, dealt sternly and finally with drunk drivers whose indiscretion takes another life—death by a firing squad. This response is unlikely to be followed elsewhere.

Some 30–35 percent of all DWD (driving while drunk) drivers are repeat offenders, according to a recent Department of Transportation twelve-state report. Statistics reveal that recidivists are four times more likely than average drivers to be involved in fatal accidents. Getting them off the street is important to the public safety. Four-time offenders in some states are considered felons and subject to a minimum of two years imprisonment. Plea bargaining also is restricted for such offenses in some jurisdictions. Some states test drunk drivers for alcoholism, and require treatment for persons afflicted as well as for three-time offenders. Stiffer penalties are imposed on DWD drivers with children in the vehicle at the time of arrest.

Withdrawal of driver licenses, including immediate seizing at arrest (which is allowed in thirty-eight states as of 1995), also have been imposed; length of suspension may be pegged to the number of offenses (thirty to ninety days for first offenders, and one year for recidivists). Convicted DWD drivers who continue driving will receive much tougher penalties when caught. Some states confiscate and/or destroy license plates of multiple offenders on the spot if the violations occurred over the past three to ten years. Vehicle impoundment and confiscation has been imposed by other jurisdictions. Courts have held that taking vehicles, plates, or drivers' licenses forecloses any subsequent criminal conviction on grounds of the constitutional bar against double jeopardy (being tried twice for the same crime). Sooner or later, the Supreme Court is likely to validate such "dual" penalties, finding them to be part and parcel of a single transaction.

One state immobilizes vehicles of multiple offenders with Denver boots. An extreme recommendation involves keeping repeat offenders under intermittent surveillance. Some jurisdictions set up unannounced roadblocks, particularly in nightclub areas, to help keep drunk drivers off the road. Other states require ignition interlocks designed to prevent inebriated drivers from starting up their vehicles (twenty-nine states as of 1995). Another controversial approach involves public humiliation of offenders, such as distinctively designed or colored license plates, license plates beginning with the letter "Z," or bumper stickers warning that the vehicle is operated by a convicted DWD operator or a person driving with a restricted license.

Open containers of alcoholic beverages in vehicles are prohibited in twenty-seven states (as of 1993). At least one state exempts open containers of beer from the prohibition.

Alcohol-Related Deaths

Alcohol, as noted, is a factor in nearly half of all motor vehicle fatalities. Boating deaths attributable to alcohol abuse run about 60 percent. Alcohol also was implicated a contributing factor in approximately 10 percent of all nonvehicular deaths and 5 percent of property damage accidents. Alcohol is a factor in at least 150,000 additional deaths due to homicides, suicides, and accidents of all kinds—some 50 percent of all falls, 50 percent of fire deaths, and 50–68 percent of drownings. Alcohol figures prominently in high percentages of criminal activity in general. The impact of alcohol abuse upon battered spouses, the incidence of divorce, child abuse, and other asocial behavior also are considerations. Over the ten-year period of 1982 to 1992, alcohol-related deaths declined 27 percent.

Alcohol

Alcoholism and Related Diseases

Alcoholism afflicts anywhere from 10–11 to 14–15 million Americans over eighteen years of age. An additional 1.3 million suffer alcohol dependencies. Altogether about 8 percent of adults in the U.S. have serious problems with alcohol. Alcohol abuse or dependence is suffered by about 40 percent of all U.S. family households, according to the National Institute for Alcohol Abuse and Alcoholism. Men are more than three times as likely to be afflicted compared to women.

Federal reports link alcohol abuse to cancer of the mouth, larynx, esophagus, liver, and colon; heart disease; nervous system damage; gastrointestinal tract diseases; depression and suicide; and dangerous drug interactions.

Cirrhosis and Liver Disease

During the "dry" period of 1920 to 1933 imposed by Prohibition, mortality rates for cirrhosis and liver disease plummeted. In 1905 the rate was 14.0 per 100,000 persons, but by 1933 the rate had declined to approximately 7.0 per 100,000. Following repeal of national Prohibition, alcohol use once again began to climb, and the incidence of cirrhosis—an indicator of alcohol abuse—also began an upward climb, with current rates running at about double the level prevailing during the prohibition era (reaching 15.5 per 100,000 persons in 1970, and then declining to 11.7 by 1983).

Fetal Alcohol Syndrome

Perhaps the saddest and most dreadful consequence of alcohol abuse involves fetal injury. Fetal alcohol syndrome has ranked as the third most common cause of birth defects in the United States in recent years. Among the top three birth defects, it is the only one that is preventable. Harms posed by alcoholic beverages during conception are well known, but the severity is underestimated. Chronic heavy drinking during pregnancy can cause microcephaly, prenatal/postnatal growth deficiency, developmental delay and mental retardation, abnormalities of the extremities, and a host of other teratogenic anomalies.

Biblical scriptures warned the mother of Samson, ". . . thou shalt conceive and bear a son. Now therefore beware, I pray thee, and drink not wine nor strong drink. . . ." (Judges 13). Laws of ancient Carthage and Sparta prohibited use of alcohol by newly married couples. Warnings date way back in history, but human behavior stubbornly tends to go on in its carefree and careless manner.

Promotion

Advertising alcoholic beverages traditionally has been controlled by government. A number of precursor countries have banned all advertising of alcohol (for example, Norway). Few jurisdictions are likely to impose total advertising bans, but sharp reductions along the lines of successes established in bellwether countries like Sweden almost certainly will be followed.

Labeling Disclosures

Health-hazard warnings, akin to those required for tobacco products, also are required for alcoholic beverages. Ostensibly to avoid a "strength war" (touting alcoholic strength to attract users), the Supreme Court ruled in 1995 that decisions prohibiting beer labeling disclosing alcoholic content violated freedom of speech rights. This was not a difficult decision, since the Bureau of Alcohol, Tobacco, and Firearms (BATF) rules already required such declarations for wine and spirits. During the 1980s leading retailers in Denmark voluntarily undertook to label the caloric content of alcoholic beverages, a lead that other calorie-counting and health-conscious nations will follow.

Availability

A number of jurisdictions restrict sales of hard liquors to government-run stores, which are purposely limited as to number and hours of operation. Happy hours in bars have been voluntarily eliminated or restricted by statute. Dispensers of alcohol—including commercial operators as well as social hosts—have been held responsible for serving guests too much alcohol and, accordingly, are held jointly responsible for any injuries. Over the long run, availability and access to alcohol will increase, not decrease.

Excusing Behavior

Some social and medical authorities view alcohol abusers as hapless victims and blame alcohol abuse on heredity, bad genes, psychological failing (contending that chronic offenders are mentally ill), physical factors (negating volitional criminal acts by attributing them to symptomology), antisocial personality disorder (ASPD), attention deficit disorder with hyperactivity (ADD-H), addiction, chemical causes, weak tolerance levels, handicapped disablement, and so on. Efforts to explain away and otherwise excuse alcohol abuse aids and abets permissiveness to extremes. In the future, individuals increasingly will be called upon to look to themselves and take responsibility for their own actions.

See also DRUGS, ILLICIT; FOOD AND DRUG SAFETY; GAMBLING; TOBACCO.

BIBLIOGRAPHY

CAHALAN, DON. *Understanding America's Drinking Problem: How to Combat the Hazards of Alcohol.* San Francisco, CA: Jossey-Bass, 1987.

GOLDEN, SANDY. *Driving the Drunk Off the Road.* Washington, DC: Acropolis Books, 1983.

GUSFIELD, JOSEPH R. *The Culture of Public Problems: Drinking-Driving and the Symbolic Order.* Chicago, IL: University of Chicago Press, 1981.

KLINGEMANN, HARALD; TAKALA, JUKKA-PEKKA; and HUNT, GEOFFREY, eds. *Cure, Care, or Control: Alcoholism Treatment in Sixteen Countries.* New York: New York University Press, 1992.

LENDER, MARK EDWARD, and MARTIN, JAMES KIRBY. *Drinking in America: A History.* Rev. ed. New York: The Free Press, 1987.

Transportation Research Board. *Zero Alcohol and Other Options: Limits for Truck and Bus Drivers.* Washington, DC: National Research Council, 1987.

Graham T. T. Molitor

American Indians.

See NATIVE AMERICANS.

Amusement Parks.

See THEME PARKS AND ORGANIZED ATTRACTIONS.

Animal Rights

The animal rights movement and its central philosophy developed rapidly in the wake of the human rights movement during the 1970s and '80s. It directly challenged conventional, institutionalized, and even religiously sanctioned attitudes toward animals, attitudes that have been responsible for centuries of animal suffering, in the name of cus-

tom, pleasure, entertainment, profit, necessity, scientific knowledge, and purported medical progress. The movement raised questions over the ethics and moral costs to society of using animals for testing military weapons and cosmetics; of exploiting them for food and fiber; of killing them for fur and for trophies; of keeping them as pets or in zoos; or using them for students to experiment upon. The movement's radical Animal Liberation Front engaged in frequent acts of civil disobedience, first in the United Kingdom in the 1970s and later spreading to the United States. Various schools of animal rights philosophy evolved in the 1980s. A plethora of books, monographs, symposia, and college courses, indicative of the growing academic and scholarly involvement in the animal rights debate, heralded the birth of a new sensibility toward nonhuman animal life.

It should be recognized that various animals are very different from each other or from the human species. Animal rights are not the same as human rights. All nonhuman animals do, however, have the right to equal and fair consideration.

During the last decade of the twentieth century, the animal rights movement is maturing into a more unified front. Some common ground has been established with other movements, notably those of the environmental, alternative agriculture (organic, sustainable), holistic medicine, and social justice/human rights movements.

The pharmaceutical-medical-industrial complex will continue to face increasing public censure as the health of an economically and ecologically dysfunctional industrial society continues to deteriorate. Opposition toward vivisection (operating on live animals for experimental purposes) continues to intensify as the ethics, scientific validity, and medical relevance of animal experimentation and product testing are being questioned by an increasingly informed public, including physicians, veterinarians, and other professionals not beholden to establishment values.

The petrochemical-based food industry (agribusiness) complex also is facing increasing opposition from the public and from health, environmental, and agricultural experts. The justifications for using pesticides and for the proliferation of cruel factory-like methods of livestock and poultry production cannot be justified.

In response to the burgeoning animal rights movement, counter-organizations and propaganda are being developed by furriers, hunters, trappers, agribusiness, and the biomedical industrial establishment. Such trends are likely to continue.

The interconnection between animal, environmental, and human rights is leading to a convergence of once separate and often opposing movements. This convergence is best exemplified by the theory and practice of alternative, humane sustainable agriculture, which embraces concern for domestic and wild animals, for the land, for all who work the land, and for the consuming public as well.

The Humane Sustainable Agriculture movement was born in the late 1980s, as society began to face a new set of ethical, environmental, and economic questions that a new technology had spawned: genetic engineering biotechnology. The benefits of this technology to society will be dubious, and the costs and risks predictably considerable, if it is not linked with preventive, holistic medicine and health maintenance (including family planning)—and with humane sustainable agriculture. It is more likely to intensify rather than alleviate the medical and agricultural nemesis, if the core principle of animal rights philosophy—namely, respect and reverence for all life, including the land—is not incorporated into every component and direction that this new technology takes.

The early 1990s saw a U.S. biotech company develop genetically engineered pigs with human immune systems to serve as organ donors for people in need. It also saw the U.S. government refuse to sign onto an important U.N. treaty to protect biodiversity—wild creatures, plants, and their natural habitats—arguably because the U.S. biotechnology industry saw this treaty as a threat to corporate sovereignty.

In applying biotechnology to propagate endangered species, zoos claimed to be protecting species' right to life. But the animals' right to live in natural conditions, and for zoos to be more actively involved in protecting wildlife in their natural places of origin, helped unite the animal rights and environmental conservation movements. The need to kill wildlife or use biotechnology to regulate wildlife populations in sanctuaries was another issue that forced animal rights fundamentalists to think ecologically.

In a very profound sense, the animal rights movement and philosophy contributed to a shift in human perception from a chauvinistic, human-centered one to one that embraced the truly compassionate spirit of respect and reverence for *all* life. This latter world view, like the notion of animal rights, is antithetical to the technocratic, profit driven motives of corporate industrialism. If the essential unity and interdependence of all life continues to be denied into the next millennium, the destruction of the natural world will be assured.

Increasing opposition to animal rights parallels an increasing disregard for the sanctity of life by those who do not understand the egalitarian philosophy of animal rights, that is, those who continue to adhere to the chauvinistic view that animals were created for humanity's use. If this view prevails, we will be left with a wholly synthetic, bioindustrialized world, with a few scattered wildlife parks and zoological gardens, but no truly natural habitat. Eden, like Paradise, can never be regained, but the restoration and preservation of the remnants of the natural world is still feasible. Acknowledgment that nonhuman animals have rights can help society make the right choice in this direction, if not for its own survival, then for the living memory of our evolutionary history and in recognition of our biological and spiritual kinship with all life in the universe.

See also BIODIVERSITY; BIOETHICS; ENVIRONMENTAL BEHAVIOR; ENVIRONMENTAL ETHICS; EVOLUTION, BIOLOGICAL; EVOLUTION: LIFE-FORMS IN THE UNIVERSE; GENETIC ENGINEERING; HOLISTIC BELIEFS; HUMAN RIGHTS; LIFE SCIENCES; PETS; SUSTAINABILITY.

BIBLIOGRAPHY

Fox, Michael W. *Animals Have Rights, Too.* New York: Continuum, 1991.

Pringle, Lawrence. *Animal Rights Controversy.* San Diego, CA: Harcourt, Brace, Jovanovich, 1989.

Strand, Rod, and Strand, Patti. *The Hijacking of the Humane Movement.* Wilsonville, OR: Doral Publishing, 1992.

Michael W. Fox

Antarctica

Antarctica is a continent of extremes. It is the coldest, highest, driest, windiest, remotest, most desolate place on earth. There are no states in Antarctica, although seven countries—Argentina, Australia, Chile, France, New Zealand, Norway, and the United Kingdom—do claim portions of the continent as their national territory. These claims, however, are not legally recognized by any other governments. The United States and the former Soviet Union (now Russia), which maintain the largest national presence in Antarctica, do not make claims to the continent, but reserve the right to do so.

The governing mechanism for activities south of 60° south latitude is the Antarctic Treaty of 1959. This agreement today counts forty-two countries as parties, and provides for demilitarization, denuclearization, and only peaceful uses of the region. Freedom of scientific research and cooperation is stipulated, as is open, unannounced on-site inspection of bases and the obligation among parties to settle disputes peacefully.

Among treaty members, twenty-six governments have qualified as "consultative parties" by conducting substantial scientific activity in Antarctica. This special status empowers them to formulate "recommendations" as administrative policies for the treaty membership. The consultative parties have also negotiated special agreements to regulate the use of Antarctic resources, including flora and fauna (1964), seals (1972), marine living resources (1980), minerals (1988), and environmental protection (1991).

No indigenous human inhabitants reside in Antarctica, and the number of humans varies seasonally. The population, comprising wholly scientists and logistical support staff living in research stations, ranges from around 4,200 in the austral summer to only 1,100 during the winter. In 1992, twenty-three countries supported forty-three year-round stations and more than forty additional summer-only stations in Antarctica.

Living in Antarctica poses tremendous challenges. Resident scientists must cope with the severe frigid climate. Temperatures can drop below −100° F and winds often exceed 100 mph. There are also oppressive psychological pressures brought on by extended periods of isolation, six months of darkness a year, and extreme physical hardships.

Economic considerations of Antarctica are resource based. The continent itself is barren, and dominated by the enormous ice sheet that covers 98 percent of the continent. Terrestrial life consists of only a few species of lichens, mosses, and mites. The circumpolar seas, however, are superabundant in living resources. Seals, whales, birds (including penguins), fin fish, and squid are found in Antarctic waters. Key to the Antarctic marine ecosystem is krill, a shrimplike crustacean that serves as the main food source for many higher species.

Scientific research is the key for diplomatic cooperation in Antarctica. The Antarctic Treaty actually evolved from the cooperative experience of the 1957–1958 International Geophysical Year, during which the continent was a main focus of scientific attention. The twelve states participating in the IGY became the original members of the 1959 treaty.

Antarctica, the fifth largest continent, has a diameter of about 4,500 kilometers (2,800 miles) and an area of 14 million square kilometers (5.4 million square miles), about the size of the United States and Mexico combined. All but 2 percent of the continent is covered by an enormous ice sheet that extends out into the circumpolar Southern Ocean. If the Antarctic ice sheet were to melt, the amount of water released would cause the sea level to rise more than 60 meters (200 feet).

The natural resource base of Antarctica is mixed. The greatest economic potential rests in exploitation of living resources, especially by harvesting krill in circumpolar waters. Estimates of krill vary from standing stocks of 125 million metric tons to as much as 6 billion metric tons. Krill could furnish rich new sources of protein to meet the world's burgeoning demands for food. Other biological bounty available for harvest in the southern seas include fin fish and squid.

Mineral and hydrocarbon potential in the Antarctic is at present speculative. Some low-quality coal deposits are known in east Antarctica and in the Transantarctic Mountains, and scattered traces of copper, lead, molybdenum, manganese, uranium, and chromium have been found in the Antarctic Peninsula region. No petroleum or natural gas has been located beneath the mile-thick ice mantle on the continent or on the offshore Antarctic continental shelf. Even so, geologists feel that Antarctic rock structures and geophysical sediments likely contain petroleum-bearing formations.

The dominant mineral resource in Antarctica is its enormous ice sheet, the largest and oldest ice mass on the planet. This glacial sheet covers nearly all of the continent with an average thickness exceeding 2,000 meters (6,000 feet), and rises into a massive dome over the interior having a depth of 4,500 meters (14,700 feet). It is Antarctica's ice mantle that pushes up the average elevation of the continent to be the highest on earth. Antarctica's ice cap contains 75 percent of the earth's water and 90 percent of its ice.

Antarctica was formerly a region reserved for explorers, whalers, and sealers. Today, environmentalists, lawyers, scientists, and even tourists are turning their attention there. The promulgation in 1991 by the Antarctic Treaty countries of a special environmental protection agreement should facilitate preservation of the pristine nature of the southernmost continent for future generations.

BIBLIOGRAPHY

AUBURN, F. M. *Antarctic Law and Politics.* Bloomington: Indiana University Press, 1982.

BREWSTER, BARNEY. *Antarctica: Wilderness at Risk.* Wellington: Friends of the Earth, 1982.

HARRISON, A., ed. *The Experience of Antarctica: Application to Space.* New York: Springer-Verlag, 1993.

HERR, R. A.; HALL, H. R.; and HAWARD, M. G., eds. *Antarctica's Future: Continuity or Change?* Hobart: Australian Institute of International Affairs, 1990.

JORGENSEN-DAHL, ARNFINN, and OSTRENG, WILLY, eds. *The Antarctic Treaty System in World Politics.* Oslo: Macmillan/Fridtjof Nansen Institute, 1991.

JOYNER, CHRISTOPHER C. *Antarctica and the Law of the Sea.* Dordrecht: Martinus Nijhoff, 1992.

SPLETTSTOESSER, J., and DRESCHHOFF, G., eds. *Mineral Resources Potential of Antarctica, Antarctic Research Series*, Vol. 51. Washington, DC: American Geophysical Union, 1990.

SUTER, KEITH. *Antarctica: Private Property or Public Heritage?* London: Zed Books, 1991.

Christopher Joyner

Anthropology.

See SOCIAL SCIENCES.

Apocalyptic Future

Apocalypse comes from a Greek word that simply meant "unveiling." But through its association with the New Testament *Book of Revelation* (*Apokalypsis*), it has come to mean a prophecy, fiction, or vision of some final (and usually violent) end.

Speculation about endings is as basic to human nature as the search for ultimate origins. One entire branch of philosophic/religious/mythical studies called *eschatology* deals with "last things."

Ancient depictions of "the End"—the final future—generally involve a cataclysm in which Earth and humans suffer. Ultimately the outcome is considered a blessing, since it marks the final defeat of evil and the triumph of good. Even such bleak visions as the Norse *Ragnarök* (Twilight of the Gods) or the Hindu *Kali Yuga* look beyond the end of this world to a new beginning.

Visions of impending doom emerge in times of social stress. The best-known apocalyptic passages in the Old Testament (e.g., *Isaiah*, chapters 24–26, and the *Book of Daniel*) were written after Israel had already lost its political independence. A number of noncanonical apocalyptic Jewish writings date from the chaotic periods of revolt against Roman rule in Palestine (A.D. 66–70 and 132–135). Similarly, most Christian apocalyptics, including the New Testament *Book of Revelation*, date from the late first and second centuries A.D., when the Christian community was widely persecuted.

One particularly influential passage from the *Book of Revelation* (Chapter 20) contains the prediction of a perfected earthly kingdom in which the elect will reign beside the returned Messiah, before the Final Judgment. A thousand-year bridge between normal human history and the divine eternity to follow the "end of the world" is sometimes called the *chiliasm* or *millennium* after the Greek and Latin root words for one thousand. Through the centuries, the desire to realize a chiliastic or millennarian world order has spawned many secular interpretations and parallels: from utopian communities (*see* UTOPIAS) to Adolf Hitler's "thousand-year Reich."

In common usage, an apocalypse is the sudden end of a process or an era. The end in question need not be universal. Decisive battles and natural catastrophes with far-reaching impacts (such as the mass extinctions that closed certain geologic periods) can be termed apocalypses.

At least four "levels" of apocalypse seem relevant to futures research: (1) the end of the universe; (2) the end of Earth; (3) the end of a society or civilization; and (4) individual death.

The end of the universe—whether by implosion ("the Big Crunch") or exhaustion (entropy)—may appear remote in time and beyond the present power of human influence. Even so, fiction writers (e.g., Olaf Stapledon's *Star Maker* [1937]) and physicists offer intriguing material for speculation.

At the other extreme, futurists seem no more willing than others to confront the personal apocalypse: death. While life extension prospects (and their social consequences for population growth and resource scarcity) are sometimes explored, few futurists discuss how to prepare for a future that includes death.

It is the two remaining levels of apocalypse—cultural and planetary endings—that are most often addressed. Visionary warnings of impending doom attract attention, entertain, and on occasion galvanize leaders into action.

St. Augustine and other theologians believed the conversion of the Roman Empire to Christianity marked the start of the thousand-year kingdom of Christ on Earth that would end with the Last Judgment. Later, reformers like Martin Luther were convinced they were living in the era of wars and calamities described in the *Book of Revelation.* Christian sects as varied as the Jehovah's Witnesses and the Branch Davidians continue to expect the imminent coming of a Messiah and the end of the world by divine intervention. Philosophers from Kant and Hegel to Karl Marx came to regard human betterment as the ultimate goal of history, with or without divine guidance. The idea of a cataclysmic End Time was gradually replaced by expectations of inevitable improvement toward perfection—the idea of progress. But in the twentieth century, wars, social injustice, economic chaos, and unsettling scientific discoveries undermined faith in human goodness and universal order, leading many to doubt whether history has any goal at all.

Today, apocalyptic visions abound once more in fiction and popular writing. Specific mechanisms of destruction include: global war; nuclear holocaust plague; collision with a comet or asteroid and a plethora of eco-catastrophes (OZONE LAYER DEPLETION, rapid GLOBAL WARMING, mass extinctions of many species, and so forth), generally resulting from human indifference, negligence, or greed.

Secular apocalypses (including works of fiction) often seek to help prevent, mitigate, or ease cataclysmic changes. By contrast, religious apocalyptics tend to believe that the nature and scope of the coming disaster is wholly beyond human control, and urge calm acceptance, or even joy at this final fulfillment of the divine plan. Both secular and religious apocalyptics share a tone of urgency: The future they depict is close at hand—if not already beginning.

The many apocalyptic visions in modern art and literature, and the continuing popular interest in Biblical prophecy, reveal widespread dissatisfaction with present conditions and fears for the future. By helping to focus such fears, apocalyptic writings may promote prudent forethought and stimulate futures research.

See also DYSTOPIAS; EXTINCTION OF SPECIES; HUMAN RIGHTS; NOSTRADAMUS; SCIENCE FICTION; WEAPONS OF MASS DESTRUCTION; and, in the Appendix, CHRONOLOGY OF FUTURISM AND THE FUTURE.

BIBLIOGRAPHY

AUDEN, W. H., and TAYLOR, PAUL B., trans. *The Elder Edda: A Selection.* New York: Random House, 1977.

BARNSTONE, WILLIS, ed. *The Other Bible: Jewish Pseudepigrapha, Christian Apocrypha, Gnostic Scriptures, Kabbalah, Dead Sea Scrolls.* San Francisco: Harper, 1984.

BOYER, PAUL. *When Time Shall Be No More: Prophecy Belief in Modern American Culture.* Cambridge, MA.: Harvard University Press, 1992.

DAVIES, PAUL. *The Last Three Minutes: Conjectures about the Ultimate Fate of the Universe.* New York: Basic Books, 1994.

HAWKING, STEPHEN W. *A Brief History of Time: From the Big Bang to Black Holes.* New York: Bantam, 1988.

Lane E. Jennings

Appliances, Household.

See HOUSEHOLD APPLIANCES.

Appropriate Technology

The critical role of technology in economic development, and especially the importance of technology choice, was first brought into focus by the economist E. F. Schumacher, author of *Small Is Beautiful,* in the 1960s. He argued that the conventional technologies of the rich countries—large-scale, capital- and energy-intensive, and labor-saving—were singularly inappropriate for the poor countries of the world. To meet their needs, technologies must be discovered or devised that are relatively small, so as to fit into small, rural markets; they must also be simple, so that they can be operated and maintained by rural men and women; and they must be inexpensive so that they can create workplaces in very large numbers, using local raw materials. Large-scale technologies, he argued, bypass the rural poor and distort the cultures, not only the economics, of poor countries. Technology is not culturally neutral.

This was not a popular argument in the 1960s, when it was widely believed that modern technology and cheap oil guaranteed limitless economic growth for rich and poor countries alike. But by the 1980s, aid and development policies based on these notions had undeniably failed. Escalating rural poverty—more than 1.3 billion men and women could be below the poverty line by early next century—insupportable indebtedness and massive and growing unemployment in developing countries called for a radical change in approach. The central objective now must be to raise the incomes of the rural poor by equipping them with tools and machines that they can own, use, and maintain for themselves.

Appropriate Technology

A wide range of appropriate technologies is now available, along with experience of supporting services such as credit and marketing, thanks to non-profit bodies such as the Intermediate Technology Group, started by Schumacher in the 1960s and now employing some 200 engineers and other professionals, with offices in Africa, Asia, and Latin America; Appropriate Technology International in the United States; and more than 20 similar groups in Europe, Canada, and developing countries. United Nations agencies such as UNICEF, UNIFEM, UNIDO, and the ILO also are supporting work on appropriate technologies.

Small, efficient, low-cost technologies now exist for agriculture and food processing, water supply, building materials, renewable energy, health, transport, and small industries of many kinds. They enable a new workplace to be created for as little as a few hundred dollars, compared with the ten or twenty thousand dollars it takes to equip one new workplace in large-scale industry (see Carr [1985] and Smillie [1991]).

Although now widely available, such technologies have not spread rapidly in developing countries because government policies and regulations generally favor big enterprises over small, the rich over the poor, the city over the village. A large firm may borrow, for example, at only 2 or 3 percent interest, whereas the small family firm may have to pay 20 percent or much more. The biggest international lender, the World Bank, still persists with large-scale projects even when small technologies would be cheaper and more efficient and would employ more people. When such biases in favor of capital-intensive industries are removed—and they are increasingly under fire—appropriate technologies will spread rapidly through the market, allowing the poor to work themselves out of their poverty.

By the 1980s it was also becoming evident that conventional capital- and energy-intensive industries had a questionable long-term future, not only in the poor countries of the southern hemisphere but also in the rich industrialized countries of the northern hemisphere. The large-scale, oil-based industry and agriculture of the north are mostly unsustainable because they are on a collision course with the environment, which is being devastated by pollution; with people, because of growing unemployment and pervasive human health hazards; and with the world's resource base, owing to heedless overconsumption. The north's need for appropriate technologies is even more pressing than that of the south: the very existence of life on Earth may now depend upon the north's ability to replace present technologies with sustainable forms of industry and agriculture.

It is no longer enough simply to ask about any new activity, "Does it pay those who undertake it?" Answers must be obtained to three other questions as well:

- What does it do to the environment?
- What does it do to the resource base, renewable and nonrenewable?
- What are its social and political implications?

In all industrial countries, the actions needed to get a more sustainable economy and a more appropriate technological base would include:

- A determined program of energy conservation, and the hastened development of renewable forms of energy, all of which derive from the sun: direct solar power, biomass, wind, water, and geothermal energy. As energy expert Amory Lovins once remarked, solar energy won't run out, explode, or cause cancer. The nuclear lobby argues that nuclear power is also appropriate, but in fact, it may be the least appropriate technology ever created. It is very expensive, highly centralized, and authoritarian, and it poses serious danger to human life. Because nuclear wastes remain lethally radioactive for up to hundreds of thousands of years, the problem of waste "disposal" may be insoluble. A thoroughgoing policy of energy conservation on both sides of the Atlantic could result in renewables satisfying up to 60 percent of the total energy needs of most industrial countries within the first two decades of the twenty-first century. The progressive introduction of long-lasting products that can be repaired, renewed, and recycled would reduce materials and energy use, and provide work for many people in dispersed small enterprises.
- Transport policies promoting public transport, especially rail, could cut pollution and accidents. Policies favoring local economic development and small enterprises could minimize long-distance hauls of people and goods, and also bring economic activity under the control of local communities.
- Agricultural policies aimed at substituting organic husbandry for the prevalent petrochemical farming, which is bad for people and the environment.

Thus, both in the northern hemisphere and the south, sustainable life-support systems demand appropriate technologies means of producing goods and services that are human in scale and respect human needs for useful and satisfying work; that minimize damage to the environment; and that make prudent use of renewable and nonrenewable resources. This is the best way toward an economics of permanence.

See also DEVELOPMENT, ALTERNATIVE; ENERGY; ENVIRONMENT; GLOBAL ENVIRONMENTAL PROBLEMS; RESOURCES; SUSTAINABILITY.

BIBLIOGRAPHY

BROWN, LESTER, et al. *State of the World* (annual reports of the Worldwatch Institute). New York: W. W. Norton, 1990–1994.

CARR, MARILYN. *The AT Reader.* London: IT Publications, 1985. (Note: IT Publications books can be obtained from Women Ink, 777 UN Plaza, New York, NY 10017.)

JAZAIRY, IDRISS; ALAMGIR, MOHIUDDIN; and PANUCCIO, THERESA. *The State of the World Rural Poverty.* London: IT Publications, 1992.

MILES, DEREK, ed. *A Future That Works.* London: IT Publications, 1983.

SCHUMACHER, E. F. *Small Is Beautiful.* London: Sphere, 1973.

SMILLIE, IAN. *Mastering the Machine.* London: IT Publications, 1991.

STEWART, FRANCES; THOMAS, HENK; and DE WILDE, TON, eds. *The Other Policy: The Influence of Policy on Technology Choice and Small Enterprise Development.* London: IT Publications, 1990.

George McRobie

Architectural Design

As the world draws closer to becoming one global market, the practice of architecture will become international. In the future, collaboration between architectural firms in different countries will be common in building better communities and ecologically sound habitation.

New kinds of buildings and more advanced urban networks for the cities of the world will challenge the imagination and technological skills of architects everywhere. Intelligent office buildings that are responsive to workers' needs for personal control of the temperature, light, and fresh air movement in their work spaces and that provide technically advanced communications systems and computer terminals for all types of work will be the norm. Many buildings will provide spaces for living, shopping, recreation, and working within the same structure. In these buildings personal trans-

portation will consist of an elevator instead of an automobile. Clusters of these buildings will form complexes covering areas as large as several city blocks. In such complexes internal gardens and parks, playgrounds, and schools will be accessible to the people who live and work within them without reliance on public or private transportation. Public transportation will connect areas of cities such as airports and urban centers, towns and villages, and countries with rapid means of conveyance connected at transportation nodes.

Architects will design large areas of future cities as well as individual buildings. In addition, new design challenges will stem from increased concern around the world with the preservation of the environment, with the ecologically sound use of materials and methods of building with historic preservation, and with meeting the special needs of those with disabilities.

The buildings and urban complexes will apply urban planning and land use principles based on intelligent long-term use of our habitats. Urban designers will take maximum advantage of climate variations and changes in the topography of an area, especially in hilly regions and waterfronts.

One of the most significant changes will be in the design tools available to future architects. Advanced computers and ubiquitous information networks using fiber optics and satellite systems will make it possible to link all of the decision makers for a building project. The remainder of this article describes how an architect would work with such advanced technology in designing a university building in the year 2010.

The project would begin with the university planning office searching the architectural database created by scanning architectural magazines for the past twenty years and putting the information into one large graphics database for examples of university buildings with requirements similar to the planned project. When the search produces four or five comparable buildings, the planning office would invite the architects of these buildings to submit credentials over the conference phone now available in most offices.

After one firm has been selected, the university team would travel to the architectural firm's office for a design session. This session will be held in the computer simulation arena within the architect's office, containing a large computer display area, ten feet by fourteen feet in size, in full color. The board-certified master designer from the architect's office will lead the intricate operation of the arena over the next four hours, assisted by a team of specialists, each of whom has gathered critical information needed for the master design.

As the design operation begins, a large topographical plan of the entire building site will be displayed on the arena screen, with climate data, zoning regulations, local building trade practices, and many other variables superimposed in smaller windows around the large display. As design decisions are developed, each of these windows will display an assessment of the design against the particular variable considered in that window. For example, one window will continuously display the energy use characteristics of the proposed building design and show how this use fits energy standards. The master designer can fine-tune changes in the design to bring the energy use in line with standard requirements.

As the master designer begins to plan the building spaces and make materials and equipment selections, additional windows will display three-dimensional views of the interiors and exterior of the building. To one side of the arena a holographic image of the building will show it in three dimensions.

Once the master architect and the university client have agreed on the preliminary design, specialists will ready estimates of building costs based on programmed schematics for local labor, materials, and equipment. This cost estimate will include not only the cost for constructing the building, but the cost of maintaining and updating the building's materials and systems over the next thirty years.

At the end of a session lasting some four hours, the university client will be able to sign a contract to have the building designed and constructed and to keep it up-to-date for thirty years. The building firm in which the master architect is a senior partner will be prepared to sign this contract and guarantee the performance of the new building over that time span. Thus the architectural, construction, and operating team will be assuming the full responsibility on behalf of the university for providing and maintaining high-performance educational spaces over a long period of time.

Master architects with the skills and knowledge to work on such design problems will require intensive education in a university followed by many years of experience in each of the specialty areas utilized during the arena operations.

Routine in the new architecture will be involvement in the design by the would-be users and occupants, as well as by others affected by the project. New materials as well as information tools will be crucial to designs, as will the long-term so-cial commitment to recycling of both structures and materials.

See also CITIES; RESIDENTIAL ARCHITECTURE; SCIENCE CITIES; VISUAL ARTS.

BIBLIOGRAPHY

DAVIS, DOUGLAS. *Modern Redux: Critical Alternatives for Architecture in the Next Decade.* New York: Grey Art Gallery and Study Center of New York University, 1986.

PAPADAKIS, ANDREAS. *Modern Pluralism: Just Exactly What Is Going On?* New York: St. Martin's Press, 1992.

VENTURI, ROBERT. *Complexity and Contradiction in Modern Architecture.* New York: Museum of Modern Art, 1977.

WOOD, LEBBEUS. *The New City.* New York: Simon & Schuster/Touchstone, 1992.

WRIGHT, FRANK LLOYD. *The Future of Architecture.* Reprint. New York: New American Library/Dutton, 1970.

John P. Eberhard

Arms Race

The lip service that most governments paid to curbing weapons proliferation during the 1980s ended with the Gulf War. The invasion of Kuwait by Iraq in 1990 helped focus the attention of Western intelligence agencies on the problem. After the war, President George Bush promised that a "new world order" would emerge, but in fact a new arms race began in the Middle East, led by Saudi Arabia and Iran, and another arms race began in China as well.

The Western combatants meanwhile replenished the stocks that were expended in the war. When procurement decisions were made, those weapons that had performed well in the Gulf War—lasers, microcomputers, stand-off systems, Stealth technology—were ordered. The production of these new weapons brought large numbers of the most modern weapons to the market to be sold to developing countries while manufacturers also sought rich customers who could afford the new systems, thus reducing unit cost and increasing profits. The replacement of old weapons by new in the arsenals of the West and the drive by arms manufacturers to hold down unit costs by finding more customers—this is the dynamic that propels the arms race.

Within that cycle, an additional impetus drove the proliferation of conventional arms after the Gulf War. Defense contractors who supplied the allied forces during the Gulf War believed that they had a new opportunity to market weapons tested and proved in battle.

The West is not the only seller in the postwar arms bazaar. As the Eastern-bloc countries reorganize their military forces and seek new sources of foreign exchange, they will try to produce more weapons for export and also will sell weapons from existing inventories.

According to the British Defense Intelligence Agency, Russian defense exports in 1992 totaled only $2.5 billion compared with an average of $20 billion a year in the mid-1980s. The output of bombers declined from 700 in 1988 to 20 in 1992. Tank production fell from 3,500 in 1988 to 675 in 1992, and the delivery of artillery pieces fell from 2,000 in 1988 to 450 in 1992. Similar reductions in helicopters, fighter jets, and armored personnel carriers, all of which had once been mainstays of the Soviet Union's export business, also occurred.

In 1992, the United States continued to dominate the international arms market and increased its share from 49 percent in 1991 to 57 percent. The value of U.S. exports fell from $14 billion to $13.6 billion, a small reduction compared with other major arms suppliers. The overall value of arms sales to Third World countries fell by 20%.

This rapid downturn in the international defense business meant the laying off of thousands of defense workers and the restructuring of entire industries to adapt to a rapidly changing market. To fight those changes, each manufacturer and arms exporting nation tried to maintain a slice of a diminished market by reducing prices and doing barter deals. After 1990 Britain sold Chieftain tanks for $5,000. Leander frigates, which cost $30 million when new in the 1960s, were sold for $120,000, or $7 million below expectations.

The rapidly evolving conventional weapons market paralleled changes in the development of mass-destruction weapons. As of the mid-1990s, twelve developing countries—Burma, China, Egypt, Ethiopia, Iran, Iraq, Libya, Libya, North Korea, Syria, Taiwan, and Vietnam—were believed to have chemical-weapons programs. Nineteen other countries—Afghanistan, Angola, Argentina, Chad, Chile, Cuba, El Salvador, Guatemala, India, Indonesia, Laos, Mozambique, Nicaragua, Pakistan, Peru, the Philippines, South Africa, South Korea, and Thailand—were trying to obtain chemical weapons and may have succeeded. The developing countries in general had to acquire chemical-weapons capability on their own, usually illegally but frequently with the complicity of Western companies and governments that turned a blind eye because of export earnings.

As far as nuclear capabilities are concerned, the problem was less serious in that a number of countries had been persuaded to abandon their nuclear programs, and smaller countries were less likely to start the process since chemical and biological weapons offer cheaper alternatives. The Nuclear Non-Proliferation Treaty (NPT), which was signed in 1968 and came into force in 1970, was designed to keep the number of states with nuclear weapons stable at five—the United States, the Soviet Union, Britain, France, and China. The treaty calls for those who have nuclear weapons not to ship the equipment or transfer the technology necessary for other countries to develop nuclear weapons. To encourage support for the agreement, those countries that signed the NPT have been helped to develop peaceful nuclear programs.

By 1994, one hundred and forty-three countries had ratified the NPT, but some of the most important had not done so. Only recently did France, China, and South Africa indicate that they plan to abide by terms of the NPT. South Africa abandoned its nuclear program and destroyed stockpiled nuclear weapons. But Israel, India, Pakistan, Brazil, and Argentina have refused to do so. Just who has or has not signed, however, seems to have made little difference in the spread of nuclear weapons. An early signatory of the NPT, Iraq pursued an aggressive twenty-year program to obtain nuclear weapons, with much Western help, notably from Germany. India developed a nuclear capability in the early 1970s and actually tested a nuclear device. Pakistan, after more than fifteen years of trying to develop nuclear weapons has either succeeded or is on the brink of doing so. According to unconfirmed reports, Pakistan has agreed to share nuclear technology with Libya, North Korea, Taiwan, and Brazil. Among these countries, North Korea is believed to be close to achieving a nuclear capability.

In the face of nuclear proliferation, Western nations have been unwilling to address the failure of the NPT. At the fourth five-year review conference of the NPT in Geneva during August and September of 1990 some progress was made. Suppliers of nuclear materials, such as Germany and Japan, agreed to sell only to states observing internationally determined safeguards. New measures were agreed to improve the inspection capacity of the International Atomic Energy Agency. Iraq, as a signatory to the NPT, had its nuclear plant regularly inspected by the IAEA. Not inspected, however, were the centrifuge plant for enriching uranium and the factories spread around the country in which materials to be used in the manufacture of nuclear weapons were being designed and made.

If countries have been able to ignore the institutions meant to govern the spread of chemical and nuclear weapons, they have often lacked the equipment to deliver the weapons to targets. This has brought about a whole new aspect of the arms race over the past ten years as developing nations attempted to acquire ballistic missiles. By the end of this decade at least fifteen developing countries will be able to build and deploy ballistic missiles, and eight of those fifteen either have or soon will have a nuclear capability. Scud missiles are currently in service in Syria, Egypt, Iran, Libya, and Yemen, while Iraq still has a significant number of launchers and missiles.

In April 1987, the United States, Canada, France, Britain, Italy, Japan, and (then) West Germany agreed to the Missile Technology Control Regime (MTCR), intended to curb exports of missiles able to deliver nuclear weapons and of equipment that might be used to develop such missiles. (Since 1987, Spain, Australia, Belgium, Luxembourg, and the Netherlands have agreed to participate.) The participants agreed not to export rocket systems, unmanned air-vehicle systems, or their components. A number of Western intelligence agencies agreed to share information on any countries that appeared to be trying to acquire ballistic-missile technology. Even countries not participating in the MTCR have provided useful intelligence, but such actions are on a voluntary basis and rely on the good will of the volunteers.

See also INTERNATIONAL TENSIONS; MILITARY TECHNOLOGIES; TERRORISM; WEAPONS OF MASS DESTRUCTION.

BIBLIOGRAPHY

ADAMS, F. GERARD, ed. T*he Macroeconomic Dimensions of Arms Control.* Boulder, CO: Westview, 1992.
DANDO, MALCOLM, and ROGERS, PAUL. *What If . . . ?* London and New York: Brassey's/Macmillan, 1991.
HOLDREN, JOHN, and ROTBLAT, JOSEPH, eds. *Strategic Defense and the Future of the Arms Race.* New York: St. Martin's Press, 1987.
WANDER, W. JAMES, et al., eds. *Science and Security: The Future of Arms Control.* Washington, DC: American Association for the Advancement of Science, 1992.

James Adams

Art Dealers

Buying and selling art is a complicated business affected by so many variables—market conditions, the rise and fall of artists' reputations, the presence of fakes and forgeries, aesthetic tastes, and the health of the national and international economies—that accurately forecasting its future is nearly impossible. Moreover, changes in the field occurring over the next decade are likely to be small, incremental shifts that will really become important only much later in the twenty-first century.

The clearest trend among art dealers today is a movement toward ever larger, and ever smaller, organization. In the coming century, large, corporate-run art dealers with international connections will grow larger, diversifying into several fields of fine and decorative arts. Conversely, smaller, privately run dealers should also proliferate, filling in niches and needs that international art dealerships cannot. The reason for this transformation is money. Many mid-sized art galleries—especially those exhibiting contemporary art—are struggling to meet the rising costs of mounting art exhibits and maintaining expensive gallery spaces open to the public five days a week. As real estate and other business costs rise, galleries with large economies of scale, or private dealers, who often operate right out of their own dwellings and thus do not have to maintain gallery spaces, will form the backbone of the art world.

Art dealers will also seek to avoid the high cost of doing business through art fairs, trade shows where dealers rent booths and display their wares. The idea is not always to make immediate sales, but to build up the contacts and intimate relationships so important in making future transactions. Art fairs should prove increasingly popular in the future, especially if the general public becomes accustomed to attending them. Related to art fairs are exhibitions such as the one held in 1994 at the Gramercy Park Hotel in New York, where dealers pooled resources, rented several floors of rooms, and invited visitors to "drop in" to look at, or purchase, art on display in each room. Here again, the idea is to avoid the costs of maintaining an expensive art gallery.

Internationally, the picture is much more unclear. As the art market generally follows the flow of money around the world, experts agree that the rising economies of Pacific Rim countries will be crucial to art dealing in the 21st century. In the 1980s Japanese buyers spent huge amounts of money on Impressionist paintings, skewing overall prices for these works and affecting virtually every area of the art market. Should Asian buyers once again enter the market in force, their tastes could again transform the trade. For now, however, the tendency among collectors from such countries as

Korea, Taiwan, and Singapore is to purchase works from their own cultures. But this could change at any moment, if, like the Japanese, they reach out to the artworks of the West.

In Europe, the struggling nations of Eastern Europe have generally been a brake to economic prosperity—particularly in Germany—that curtails the ability of collectors and institutions in those nations to purchase art. The same holds true with South America and Mexico, whose ability to affect the trade has been considerably diminished because of their recent, drastic economic woes.

This leaves the United States. For the near future, it seems, the United States will continue to be the main engine behind the art market's rise and fall. This means, of course, that United States tastes, artists, collectors, and institutions will dominate the trade. Within the nation, however, the market's main emphasis should continue its current shift away from the cultural centers and collectors on the East Coast to newer collectors and museums in Southern California—especially Hollywood—and, perhaps, in such well-to-do Sun Belt cities as Santa Fe.

The greatest change in the art world may occur in the area of antiquities. As indigenous cultures in the Third World, as well as Native American tribes throughout the United States, actively resist the trade in their cultural property, the buying and selling of antiquities is slowly but inexorably becoming less acceptable among younger collectors. Increasingly, this trade is being criticized for fueling a black market in smuggled goods that often leaves fragile historic and archeological sites—from Cambodia to Mali to the Southwest United States—devastated by looters seeking to sell antiquities primarily to Western dealers and collectors. Even today, reputable anthropologists and archeologists, along with government officials in the United Nations and the U.S. State Department, are calling for a total moratorium on antiquities dealing—calls that will grow as sensitivities to the world's indigenous cultures increase.

See also ARTS; COUNTERFEITING; GRAY MARKET GOODS; VISUAL ARTS.

BIBLIOGRAPHY

NAISBITT, JOHN, and ABURDENE, PATRICIA. *Megatrends 2000: Ten New Directions for the 1990s.* New York: William Morrow, 1990.

PANKRATZ, DAVID B., and MORRIS, VALERIE B., eds. *The Future of the Arts: Public Policy and Arts Research.* New York: Praeger, 1990.

Steven Vincent

Artificial Intelligence

In the last ten years, the field of artificial intelligence (AI) has begun to experience a major paradigm shift. New, sixth-generation computer hardware has begun to permit a brainlike style of computing that was not feasible earlier. This could produce truly brainlike intelligent systems within the next fifty years (or sooner).

Like most new technologies, the developments in AI offer clear benefits, serious hazards, and some consequences that are difficult to evaluate. On the positive side, we will see more efficient controllers, crucial perhaps to the feasibility of gasoline-free cars, airplanes able to reach orbit, and a major reduction in chemical waste. On the negative side, the frightening scenarios depicted in movies like *Terminator 2* or *Colossus: The Forbin Project* are far more realistic than many people appreciate. On the confusing side, intelligent computer personalities can be inserted into the "information utility" or "superhighway" of the future; these systems could help students learn at their own pace, in their own way, but—depending on how they are implemented—they could also interfere with personal freedom and individual initiative. AI technologies also will contribute to the rapid growth of communications and computing, in directions that we already expect ever increasing bandwidth, improved graphics and speech recognition, virtual reality, and so on.

In the past, people have argued that humans should learn to understand themselves better before developing such potent technologies. But a deeper, more scientific understanding of intelligence is itself a crucial prerequisite to understanding ourselves better—at the personal level, the social level, and even at the spiritual level. This understanding or awareness will be the most important benefit of AI technology in the long term. Thinking about the future is an essential component of higher-order intelligence. Therefore, new technologies to predict the future are an important component of this field.

Basic Paradigms

AI is a huge field. Researchers in one part of the field generally do not know where the frontiers are in other parts. AI is divided into three major communities:

- First there is the classical or hard-core AI community, based on classical formal logic. Hard-core AI emphasizes symbolic reasoning by computer. It includes expert systems. Classical AI uses left-brain thinking. It builds computer programs that manipulate sentences of propositions. As in Aristotelian logic, all sentences must be true or false—there are no shades of gray. Classical AI is part of computer science, which mainly relies on digital logic.

- Second there is the soft computing community, which uses artificial neural networks (ANNs), fuzzy logic, and genetic algorithms. It even includes embryonic efforts to use chaos or quantum effects in computing. Soft computing has been described as right-brain thinking by computers. Soft computing is a coalition of several different emerging paradigms, thrown together for sociological reasons. These paradigms emphasize continuous variables—the degree of truth, as in fuzzy logic; the strength of a connection, as in ANNs; or the level of performance, as in ANNs or genetic algorithms. Soft computing is mainly practiced by engineers who rely on continuous variables or analog logic.

- Third are the specific-application communities—involving such areas as speech recognition, image processing, and robotics—which mix and match tools from the other communities, from statisticians, and from elsewhere.

Figure 1 illustrates some of the history behind these paradigms.

In the 1960s, when AI was new, it focused on *one* basic question: how could we reproduce "intelligence"—as we see it in the human mind—in computer systems? This leads to the question: What *is* intelligence? There were three different strategies for answering these questions.

One group said, "I can't define 'intelligence,' but I can recognize it when I see it. There are certain difficult problems—like playing a good game of chess or proving hard theorems in logic—that are known to require intelligence. By building systems to solve these specific problems, we will actually learn about intelligence in the general sense." Many early efforts—like Samuels's checker-playing program—did yield important insights. There were three specific applications—speech, image-processing, and robotics—with large commercial markets that did not care about "intelligence" as such; these areas basically split off from classical AI and brought in new techniques from statistics and elsewhere to produce practical results.

A second group argued that intelligence does not lie in specific algorithms to solve specific problems. Rather, it lies in the ability to learn or discover an algorithm, when confronted with a new problem. Algorithms are like clam shells; the life is not in the shell, but in the clam that grows the shell. To understand intelligence, we must develop systems that *learn* to solve "any" new problem—General Problem Solving Systems (GPSS). But how do engineers build a system to "solve all problems"? In practice, the GPSS people mainly focused on two specific problems with general implications: (1) the problem of symbolic reasoning—how to prove the truth or falsity of a proposition, when given a database of initial axioms or assumptions; (2) the problem of "reinforcement learning"—how to maximize some predefined measure of performance, or pleasure, or utility, or profit, over future time, in an unknown environment. Many psychologists believe that the brain is mainly a reinforcement learning machine, which needs large numbers of brain cells to *learn* to do symbolic reasoning.

A third group—the perceptron school—argued that intelligence in the brain results from connecting large numbers of neurons and adapting them over time. They borrowed a simple model of the neuron from the neuroscientists McCulloch and Pitts, and developed ways to train these neurons to recognize simple patterns. Marvin Minsky proved that the perceptron designs of the 1960s were not powerful enough for true intelligence. Nevertheless, progress quietly continued.

In 1968, one researcher combined two existing AI systems to build a flashy display for the Montreal World's Fair: (1) a language-understanding system, to take questions about baseball typed in by human beings; (2) a reasoning system, to use information in the form of axioms about baseball, stored in a database to answer the questions. This was the first expert system. The main applications of classical AI today are expert systems—systems

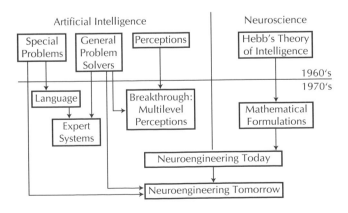

FIGURE 1.   A partial history of artificial intelligence.

in which the human expert provides the database of facts or assumptions, and the computer answers questions. Important research has focused on machine learning, based on symbolic reasoning, but practical applications are limited.

In 1974, Paul J. Werbos found a solution to Minsky's problems, by combining reinforcement learning and ANN approaches. This solution was based on a generalization of Wiener's concept of "feedback" or of Freud's concept of "psychic energy." After several applications and later papers, the idea took root and was widely popularized in 1986. The ANN field grew rapidly after that. ANNs are now best known as systems that recognize patterns in data; however, they can also perform prediction, control, reinforcement learning, data clustering, and data compression.

Fourth-generation computers are like the PC—one central processor or several processors for one computer. *Fifth*-generation computers use many processor chips strung together to achieve "massively parallel processing" (MPP). *Sixth*-generation computers use many very simple processors on a single chip (or in optics) to achieve 1,000 to 1,000,000 more throughput than fifth-generation computers, but they can only run programs designed to run on such machines (the human brain is a sixth-generation machine, which proves that sixth-generation machines can have very general capabilities). The ANN field has developed designs that begin to make good on that promise. New chips have come out that make the high throughput a reality. Brainlike throughput (or many times more) could be developed in ten years.

Application Areas

ANN-based systems already provide humanlike ability to recognize handwritten digits better than earlier methods. Designs for processing sequences of digits and letters will probably be working in ten to twenty years. In speech recognition, ANNs outperform older methods on small-scale tests, but considerable work—(perhaps twenty years of research)—will be needed to integrate this into full-fledged speech recognition.

The most important applications involve control or planning. Classical control theory—the descendant of Norbert Wiener's "cybernetics"—includes some very broad concepts in theory. In practice, the *working* designs of large-scale practical value are all based on the idea of the thermostat—a simple system, forced to stay near a fixed set point; near such a set point, all variations can be under-

stood by the use of linear techniques, used to analyze small perturbations. They are especially useful where *high efficiency* is crucial—reducing weight requirements to permit Earth-orbit capability in an airplane, reducing pollution, and so on.

Symbolic reasoning tasks are far more difficult. For example, there is great interest now in developing "intelligent agents." An intelligent agent might be a smiling face that appears on a child's computer screen at school and offers to help the child. For now, classical AI makes it possible to build usable agents even without a true brainlike learning capability. But *hybrids* of AI and ANNs can permit "adaptive interfaces," which *learn* about children over time, so as to improve performance and individualize instruction. Prototypes are being planned for about six years in the future. Some children are excited about the idea of the "happy computer"—a reinforcement learning system the sole objective of which is to make the child "happy" (i.e., to smile or to push a "happy" button on the keyboard). Unfortunately, it is easy to imagine abuses of this technology by the intelligent computer.

Practical applications of fuzzy logic mainly involve control. In fuzzy control, an expert provides a list of simple IF-THEN rules like: "If motor is hot, then turn down fuel valve." Fuzzy logic has proved superior to classical AI in interpreting such rules, which do not require elaborate reasoning to interpret.

The information utility of the future will combine many of these technologies and others. Nippon Telephone and Telegraph (NTT), the world's largest corporation, has prepared a twenty-year plan for the global information utility. In that plan, ANNs and two optical technologies are listed as the two new basic technologies required to implement the rest. Even in the short-term, improved nonlinear control will be a major issue in building such networks. Some analysts have even proposed turning the telephone network itself into a huge neural network, a kind of giant collective happy computer.

See also COMPUTERS: OVERVIEW; DIGITAL COMMUNICATIONS; INFORMATION SOCIETY; INFORMATION TECHNOLOGY; INTERACTIVE ENTERTAINMENT.

BIBLIOGRAPHY

The views expressed herein are those of the author, not of the National Science Foundation.

DEBOECK, GUIDO. *Trading on the Edge: Neural, Genetic and Fuzzy Systems for Chaotic Financial Markets.* New York: Wiley, 1994.

PRIBRAM, KARL, ed. *Origins: the Brain and Self-Organization.* Erlbaum, 1994.

———. *The Roots of Backpropagation: From Ordered Derivatives to Neural Networks and Political Forecasting.* Wiley, 1994.

WERBOS, PAUL J. "Neural Networks, Consciousness, Ethics and the Soul." In *WCNN94 Proceedings,* Hillsdale, NJ: Erlbaum, 1994.

Paul J. Werbos

Artificial Life

Can human beings create life? To some the thought is sacreligious; to others, scientifically preposterous. Life as we know it is the result of billions of years of evolution. Its beginnings on Earth are still mysterious, but undeniably impressive: Somehow, protoorganisms managed to metabolize and reproduce, maintaining a delicate molecular balance that distinguished life from anything else. We still argue about the precise definition of life, but know that of all things, life is the least trivial.

However, in the mid-1980s a new science emerged that dared, however tentatively, to presume that a second origin was possible—the creation of an artificial life. Two developments have emboldened scientists to claim that the time is right to begin creating life. First, our knowledge of biology, particularly since the discovery of DNA and its importance, has seemingly turned an important corner. Never before have we understood life so well. Second, we now have the ideal tool for creating life—the computer. Since we now know that information-processing is a critical aspect of life, it makes sense that high-powered computers can model its processes, and perhaps duplicate those processes. At a certain point, those processes may themselves qualify as "alive." Or so goes the unabashedly optimistic logic of artificial life, described by Christopher P. Langton as "the study of man-made systems that exhibit behaviors characteristic of natural living systems."

It was Langton who coined the name (often abbreviated to a-life), but the acknowledged father of artifical life is mathematician John von Neumann. Among his stellar accomplishments was his late-1940s blueprint for a "self-reproducing automaton," a creature literally made of information. It "lived" on an imaginary checkerboard, an infinite grid in mathematical space. Each square, or cell, of the grid was in one of a number of given states; a set of rules dependent on the state of its neighbors determined what state the cell would take in the

next step, or generation. After a number of generations, a "daughter" identical to the complex initial pattern would appear, with the ability to reproduce again. The process was remarkably like biological production. In the early 1960s, mathematician John Horton Conway made a much simpler "cellular automaton," calling it "Life." Though Conway's automaton is known mainly for its cult following in computer labs around the world, serious mathematical work was performed with Life. But its most striking aspect was its ability to generate unlimited complexity—even the sort of dazzling complexity associated with biology—from a few simple rules.

In the late-1970s, Christopher Langton, then a student at the University of Arizona, programmed the "Langton Loop," the simplest self-reproducing automaton to date. He did it on an Apple II. Langton became the field's chief proselytizer, and in 1987 he organized the first Artificial Life Conference. Approximately 150 biologists, computer scientists, physicists, and philosophers came to Los Alamos and instantly established the basis of a new multi-disciplinary pursuit. They shared a belief that lifelike behavior in silicon would adhere to the cellular automata methodology of using simple rules to generate complex behavior. One of the a-lifers had a slogan that could apply to artificial life studies in general: "fast, cheap, and out of control."

The most impressive work in artificial life deals in computer-based evolutionary experiments. Usually they involve some variation of the genetic algorithm, a scheme devised by University of Michigan computer scientist John Holland to approximate the mechanics of evolution in a computer program.

As a result, some of the most fascinating work in evolution is now being performed on computers. Particularly notable is Tierra, a computational environment created by Thomas Ray, a University of Delaware ecologist. A single computer-program "organism" in this digital equivalent of primordial soup can reproduce; its offspring mutate, evolve, and turn into a number of identifiable species, co-evolving with each other. Evolutionary battles are waged between hosts and parasites.

Certainly the most visually arresting experiments are those conducted by Karl Sims of Thinking Machines. Using a variation of the genetic algoritithm, Sims "evolves" striking pictures—the artist is not Sims, nor his program, but the mechanics of evolution. Sims has also used similar techniques to "train" computer-based artificial creatures to perform certain tasks, like hitting a virtual ball.

Successive generations discover more efficient ways to perform these tasks. Seeing this is like viewing a time-lapse photographic panorama of how movement evolves.

Not all artificial life is conducted inside the computer. Rodney Brooks of the Massachusetts Institute of Technology is one of several roboticists adopting an approach based on the "bottom-up" artificial life approach. Brook's six-legged robots not only look like insects, they behave like them, operating with simple rules that mimic the mechanisms of instinct. Though much less complicated than robots, which operate on the top-down approach associated with artifical intelligence, the faux creatures from Brooks's lab seem more cunning in coping with natural environments.

None of these experiments rival real life. However, the field is young and its practitioners are confident that they or their followers will cook up some indisputably living creatures. If they are successful, the implications will go far beyond science, raising such questions as: Should we regard artificial life with the same respect granted natural life? Can we control our living creations? Ominously, the closest a-life analogue to physical organisms so far are probably computer viruses. Should we even try to? As Doyne Farmer and Alletta d'A. Belin, argue, it is best not to wait until we are on the doorstep of these achievements before considering these questions. "We must take steps now to shape the emergence of artificial organisms," they write. "They have the potential to be either the ugliest terrestrial disaster, or the most beautiful creation of humanity."

See also ARTIFICIAL INTELLIGENCE; BIOETHICS; EVOLUTION, BIOLOGICAL; EVOLUTION: LIFE-FORMS IN THE UNIVERSE; EXTRATERRESTRIAL LIFE-FORMS; GENETICS; GENETIC ENGINEERING; GENETICS: COMMERCIALIZATION; NANOTECHNOLOGY; SEXUAL REPRODUCTION: ARTIFICIAL MEANS; ROBOTICS.

BIBLIOGRAPHY

FARMER, DOYNE, and BERLIN, ALLETTA d'A. "Artificial Life: The Coming Evolution." In Christopher Langton, et al., ed. *Artificial Life II: Proceedings of the Workshop on Artificial Life Held February 1990 in Santa Fe, New Mexico.* Redwood City, CA: Addison-Wesley, 1992.

KELLY, KEVIN. *Out of Control.* Reading, Mass.: Addison Wesley, 1994.

LANGTON, CHRISTOPHER. "Artificial Life." In Christopher, Langton, ed. *Artificial Life: The Proceedings of an Interdisciplinary Workshop on the Synthesis and Simulation of Living Systems.* Redwood City, CA: Addison-Wesley, 1989.

LEVY, STEVEN. *Artificial Life: The Quest for a New Creation.* New York: Pantheon, 1992.

Steven Levy

Arts

Fourteen years ago this author predicted that much of the future of art would come from two different kinds of developments—first, changes within the society of art and, second, new technological developments. An example of the first is the hypercommercialization of the established art industry. Those few artists who can sell, whether in the retail market of painting or the wholesale markets of book publishing and film, have been able to command far higher prices for themselves while earning far more than ever before for their sponsors. Given both absentee conglomerate ownership and continuing increases in production costs, this hypercommercialization is likely to escalate as well.

Will less profitable art survive, and if so, how? A dozen years ago the growth of small literary presses and alternative art galleries was a positive trend. Conventional wisdom now is that, either in spite of or because of government grants, they have largely missed the opportunity to sponsor the best new work. In art, as in corporate life, not everything survives, and that which dies is not necessarily the worst.

One paradox remains: while the number of those seriously making art in every field has increased substantially through every decade in the postwar period, the number of people becoming cultural celebrities remains remarkably few. Art has always been far more competitive than law, business, or even restaurant proprietorships; with ever more practitioners, it is now yet more competitive. If an ever smaller percentage succeeds, how will such pervasive failure affect the future making of art?

What lends perspective to this present inquiry is recognition of those technological developments that were not expected. Few could have predicted a decade ago that small, silver plastic "donuts" would have replaced larger, more substantial-looking, long-playing records. Fewer would have predicted virtual reality with its capacity to simulate three-dimensional sensory experience. Nor could we have predicted the proliferation of word-processing machines and programs.

This author failed to predict dimensions of the digital revolution in art. Few imagined the developments collectively called desktop publishing, where individuals working largely alone could produce camera-ready paper with the visual and typographic quality of "professionally printed" literature. In 1981 it was possible to compose in an electronic music studio where separate tracks of sound were laid onto multitrack tape, editing and "mixing down" a stereo version composed from many sources. By the late 1980s, most composers were sitting behind cathode ray tubes. The painstaking editing that previously took a week could be replicated on a computer screen, with portions of sounds moved around to taste within a single day.

Equally elusive were the current capabilities of CD-ROM, which can store the art of a whole museum on a single disc, or hypertext literature, whose multipath structures are best read on a computer screen, rather than on printed pages. Composers can pop into a computer a disc that plays an "imaginary orchestra" through amplified speakers. One result of most technological development is the undermining of traditional authorities. Thanks to desktop publishing, an author need not fear the printer's censorship; thanks to electronics, composers can avoid wasting time flattering orchestral conductors and other performing musicians.

Writing at the beginning of the 1980s, one could imagine better paints than the new acrylics, new sculptural materials with "the solidity of steel and the light weight of balsa wood," anthropomorphic machines that could "execute spectacular choreography better than live dancers," electronic instruments that could "imitate the richly varied sounds of a symphony orchestra," a typewriter that could "type out words as they are spoken," a television system that could "reproduce images that are present only in one's head," or computerized retrieval that could give "a writer immediate access to systemized information."

Of these speculations, only the last has been widely realized. A few have access to a computer that can type out spoken words or has the computer moxie to simulate the instruments of a symphony orchestra. The other speculations remain on our collective wish list. Technologies still have a way to go in the arts, which is another way of saying that innovative arts have a future with technologies.

One general esthetic direction is the creation of encompassing worlds. Whereas a church surrounds its visitors with largely static images, more recent environments have been filled with kinetic sources that, like a church, create an immersive sensory experience. These sources can be based upon sound, upon kinetic sculptures, upon moving pictures, or upon effective combinations of such media. Consider Frank Popper's description of an elaborate installation by Wen-ying Tsai, *Desert Spring* (1991):

> A cybernetic sculptural system that focused on the homeostatic relation of art to its environment, . . . it represented a new generation of environmental sculptures based on the concepts of stability and disturbance. The work was endowed with virtual intelligence which enabled it to maintain its internal stablity by coordinating real-time spontaneous and interactive responses that automatically compensate for changes in the environment. When spectactors enter the threshold of this darkened space, this presence is sensed by the sculpture's infra-red and audio antennae; thus, by their movement and sound, the spectators stimulate and destabilize the sculpture from normal relaxed undulation to excited rapid palpitation. It is only when the spectator leaves that the sculpture returns to its usual tranquil undulating state, as if awaiting the next round of confrontation."

Combining new technologies into an innovative integration of different media presages a future for art.

One promise of that new science called robotics is the creation of an immersive physical space in which everything literally can respond to the spectator's presence; so that every move made, from touching to simply shifting weight, triggers a perceptible change in the surroundings. The presence of such a continually responsive artistic environment—the sounds, images, and palpable objects—would become more interesting if the network of computerized responses could be frequently changed; so that the same move producing a certain response now would produce a different one later. Consider in this context the claim of virtual reality to recreate artificially the environmental experience through computer-assisted sensory stimulation.

Emerging technologies will discover content unique to each. The first function of cable television was providing cleaner images of network programs. Only later did cable transmission provide kinds of programming, beginning with locally produced shows, that would never go out on networks. With this principle in mind, consider the artist Manfred Mohr's suggestion that the most appropriate content for computer-generated visual art is not resemblances to familiar images but rules for creating art that are represented on paper through a computer-driven plotter. (One can wager that few people, if any, yet know what the ultimate content of Virtual Reality or CD-ROM might be.)

There will be progress within long-dormant technologies, such as television, beginning with an improved image closer in quality to film on larger screens and probably including dimensionality. Watch as well for developments in under-supported technologies, such as holography, which can represent images at different times in illusory space. One reason why holography has not developed is that holograms are so difficult to make. Video arrived around the same time as holography—in the middle 1960s; now there are millions of video users, nearly all of them amateur, but only a few dozen holographers, nearly all of them professional.

It is striking that new technologies which seem initially destined only for an elite few, such as the videotape camera, are successfully mass-merchandized throughout the world. One result is increasing the sheer amount of artistic experience and esthetic information available to more people around the world. The possibilities available to art a dozen years from now will be as different as those today are from a dozen years ago. Surprises are more frequent in art, because it is unencumbered by worldly needs. It does not just progress but literally jumps over fewer resistances. Even by the time this book appears, it will become apparent that this essay will have missed something important. Whatever that something is, it will probably be a joy to behold.

See also ART DEALERS; INTERACTIVE ENTERTAINMENT; LITERATURE; MUSIC; PERFORMING ARTS; PRINTED WORD.

BIBLIOGRAPHY

FRIEDHOFF, RICHARD MARK, and BENZON, WILLIAM. *Visualization: The Second Computer Revolution.* New York: Abrams, 1989.

KOSTELANETZ, RICHARD. "The Artistic Explosion (1980)." In *On Innovative Art(ist)s.* Jefferson, NC: McFarland, 1992.

———. *A Dictionary of the Avant-Gardes.* Flemington, NJ: A Capella, 1993.

MOHR, MANFRED, "System Esthetics." In Richard Kostelanetz, ed. *Esthetics Contemporary.* 2nd ed. Buffalo, NY: Prometheus, 1989.

POPPER, FRANK. *Art of the Electronic Age.* New York: Abrams, 1993.

Richard Kostelanetz

Arts, Visual.

See VISUAL ARTS.

Asia

Asia is geographically and demographically the largest continent on Earth. It is characterized by topographic and climatic extremes, differing levels of economic development, diverse systems of governance, and a variety of religions, cultures, and languages. Until the end of World War II, many Asian countries were part of Western colonial empires. Their decolonization was followed by economic development variously based on capitalist or socialist models. During the past fifty years, Asia has witnessed major wars in the Korean Peninsula and in Indochina, the creation of Bangladesh, the fall of an authoritarian regime in the Philippines, and the shift toward democracy and a free-market economy in China.

Asia accounts for 56 percent of the world's population. By the year 2025, its population could equal the present population of the entire world (some 4.6 billion), a 70 percent increase. Of this population, 48 percent (about 2 billion) will inhabit South Asia, 37 percent East Asia, and 15 percent Southeast Asia. Increased longevity and reduced infant mortality are continually changing the shape of the age pyramid. Declining mortality rates have increased the size of the elderly population (65+), which will account for 15 to 25 percent of the overall population by 2025.

Asia is rapidly urbanizing. By the year 2000, around 35 percent of the people will reside in urban areas; the number of Asian cities with one million or greater population will be 101, including 38 in China and 24 in India. Urban growth will continue to diminish agricultural land, creating more slums and squatter settlements and overwhelming city infrastructures. Urbanization seems to be an irreversible process.

Asia is in the throes of social change. Modernization has touched all spheres of social life. People are mobile—geographically, socially, and psychologically. Local communities are becoming culturally mixed. Exposure to the media has created new areas of awareness and reintroduced people to their own cultural roots. The number of nuclear families is rising with expanding groups of women in their prime reproductive ages. As a result, extended families are breaking into smaller units, through spatial separation; however, such splitting has not affected filial ties. Kinship considerations continue to take priority, even in modern business. The availability of in-laws to look after children facilitates the entry of women into the workforce. Thus families remain lineally linked.

Overconcern with economic development has caused the neglect of the social sphere. The exploding population due to changing fertility and mortality rates is contantly altering demographic patterns. The uneven distribution of the benefits of development is marginalizing populations such as women, tribal and ethnic minorities, and disabled and illiterate people. Unemployment is on the rise among the educated. Large populations live below the poverty line. Social infrastructure, including the provision of basic needs—potable water, essential sanitation, housing and transport, food, and primary education—is still very inadequate. Social discontent occasionally results in violent civil unrest, which often invokes a repressive response from the state. Such a scenario contributes to political instability and hinders economic development. Social policy will have to address these issues.

The region's economic composition is highly diverse. Roughly, it can be categorized into developed economies (Japan); newly industrialized economies (NIEs) such as the Republic of Korea, Taiwan, and Hong Kong; soon-to-be NIEs (Thailand, Malaysia, and Indonesia), developing, least developed, and landlocked economies. GNP per capita ranges from U.S. $27,305 (Japan) to U.S. $100 (Mongolia). Some countries currently exhibit a negative GDP growth. It is, however, widely acknowledged that the world's growth center is shifting to Asia. The Southeast and South Asian subregions have natural and human resources and millions of potential consumers that are attracting world attention as future markets. China, Laos, and Vietnam are moving toward capitalist economies, and new economic powers are emerging in Southeast Asia. The process of industrial restructuring is continuing in all countries. Such progress notwithstanding, there are problems of poverty and unequal distribution of income that affect the region's standard of living.

Asia is rapidly losing its forest cover—5 million hectares were lost in 1991 alone. Continued deforestation has adversely affected biodiversity: over 600 animal species and 5,000 plant species are on the verge of extinction. Soil erosion, waterlogging, and salinization are causing land degradation, and 860 million hectares are affected by desertification. Over 170 million hectares of wetland have been lost. However, strategies of sustainable development now being devised may help protect the environment from advancing industrialization and prevent the pollution of previously healthy rural areas.

With comparatively limited reserves of oil and gas, Asia depends on its coal reserves. Energy requirements are being met by fuelwood, bagasse (plant residue), and oil—the latter's importation is rising as a result. An increase in fuelwood consumption can accelerate the deforestation process, and the curtailment of its production to save the forests may cause a shortage of fuelwood.

The health situation in Asia has significantly improved in areas such as life expectancy, as reflected in the following statistics: Life expectancy is now 76 years for developed countries, 73 for NIEs, 62 for East and Southeast Asian countries, and 58 for South Asian countries. The average daily calorie intake has increased by 18 percent in the last two decades, and more and more children are being immunized against killer diseases. AIDS has become a new health threat. While in 1992 there were less than 5,000 reported AIDS cases, it is projected that by 2000 Asia will have 20 million HIV-infected cases—half of the world figure—and 90 percent of these will be in developing countries.

Education has made impressive advances. Literacy now stands at 70 percent, which still leaves 666 million people, mostly female, who are illiterate. An additional 40 million children do not attend school. Furthermore, advances in science and technology are creating new illiteracies such as "incomputeracy," a lack of basic knowledge of how to use computers. The educational systems throughout Asia need revamping—a process already begun in ex-socialist countries.

Summary

About 4.6 billion people will inhabit Asia by the year 2010, and the age pyramid will show bulges at the apex and base. Although literacy rates will go up, there still will be around 600 million adults, including 25 million adults of school-going age, who will need special programs. The increasing size of the school population will necessitate renovations and additions to existing structures; the changing science and technology profile will require the remodeling of curricula and teaching methodologies. Programs will be needed for new constituencies of illiterates. Growing urbanization will accentuate problems associated with migration, housing, family breakdown, crime, disease, and an increasing pressure on the infrastructure. Demand for higher education will rise. Increasing industrialization will pose problems for the environment. International trade will grow. Cultural identities will continue to remain strong, fostering tradition in the midst of modernity. The population growth rate may stabilize at 1 percent and near-total literacy may be attained by 2010. Sustainable development strategies may halt environmental deterioration. The opening of markets may create further interdependencies between countries and promote internal democratization. Also, remaining socialist regimes may collapse, and supranational groupings like the European Community (EC) may emerge.

Still, the alleviation of poverty may remain a difficult goal. Narrow parochial and ethnic loyalties may continue to surface. If so, Asia will maintain its cultural pluralism in a changing milieu.

See also CHINA; DEVELOPMENT, ALTERNATIVE; INDIA; JAPAN.

BIBLIOGRAPHY

ATAL, YOGESH. "Anticipating the Future: Asia-Pacific Region." *Futures Research Quarterly* (Winter 1988): 15–27.

MASINI, ELEONORA BARBIERI, and ATAL, YOGESH, eds. *The Futures of Asian Cultures: Perspectives on Asia's Futures*, Vol. 3. Bangkok: UNESCO, 1993.

United Nations Economic and Social Commission for Asia and the Pacific. *State of the Environment in Asia and the Pacific.* Bangkok: UN-ESCAP, 1990.

_____. *Towards a Social Development Strategy for the ESCAP Region.* Bangkok: UN-ESCAP, 1992.

Yogesh Atal

Asimov, Isaac (1920–1992)

This Russian-born American science fiction writer and popularizer of science was brought to the United States by his parents in 1923. Asimov published his first science fiction story in 1939. He earned a doctorate in chemistry at Columbia University in 1948 and taught at Boston University for several years before becoming a full-time writer. By the time of his death in 1992, he had published well over 400 books, most of them nonfiction. His most influential works of fiction are two series of stories and novels, one recounting the history of a far-future galactic empire in which scientific prediction of the future ("psychohistory") plays a central part, and the other exploring the interaction of human beings and robots. *Foundation* (1951), the first galactic empire novel, and *I, Robot* (1950), a collection of early robot stories, firmly established his reputation. Devoting himself chiefly to science writing and other nonfictional work from 1958 to 1980, Asimov later published a series of novels integrating his visions of galactic empire and ro-

botics, beginning with *Foundation's Edge* (1982). Several of his nonfictional titles deal with speculation about the future, such as *A Choice of Catastrophes* (1979) and (with Frederick Pohl) *Our Angry Earth* (1991). He also edited a volume of essays, *Living in the Future* (1985).

See also FUTURISTS; SCIENCE FICTION.

BIBLIOGRAPHY

ASIMOV, ISAAC. *In Joy Still Felt.* Garden City, NY: Doubleday, 1980.

_____. *In Memory Yet Green.* Garden City, NY: Doubleday, 1979.

GUNN, JAMES E. *Isaac Asimov: The Foundations of Science Fiction.* New York: Oxford University Press, 1982.

PATROUCH, JOSEPH F. *The Science Fiction of Isaac Asimov.* Garden City, NY: Doubleday, 1974.

TOUPONCE, WILLIAM F. *Isaac Asimov.* Boston: Twayne, 1991.

W. Warren Wagar

Astronomy

The fact that we observe all galaxy clusters to be receding from Earth's own Milky Way galaxy indicates an expanding universe. It also implies that the universe had an origin in time, the "Big Bang" when all matter crowded together at near-infinite density. Determination of the time of the Big Bang, currently set at about 15 billion years ago, depends on accurate measurements of the distances and recession velocities of galaxy clusters hundreds of millions, or even billions, of light years away. The next two decades should allow more accurate dating of the Big Bang to within 500 million years of its occurrence.

Formation and Development of Stars and Planets

The high temperatures within the early universe made it diffuse and unstructured. Significant clumping of matter could begin only after the radiation filling the universe ceased to interact with matter, at a time approximately 300,000 years after the Big Bang. Within the following million years, the clumps of matter that would become galaxies and galaxy clusters must have appeared. Within those clouds, subunits became individual stars. In the Milky Way, a typical giant spiral galaxy, star formation began some 12 billion years ago; and our sun and planets formed 4.6 billion years ago. The initial stages of star formation are poorly understood, although it is clear that once a clump forms that has significantly greater than average density, self-gravitation will squeeze the clump, raising its central temperature and, if the clump is large enough, initiating nuclear fusion at its center. The formation of a planetary system apparently often accompanies the formation of stars. Astronomers have found disks of material surrounding many young stars, thought to be either planets in formation or matter left over from the formation era. They have also discovered planets orbiting pulsars, the remnants of exploded stars; these planets have apparently formed from the debris of the explosion. Observations from space should reveal extra-solar planets around ordinary stars during the first two decades of the next century.

Manmade Evolution of Planets

Although most of a planet's mass lies buried below its surface, it is the surface that interacts with the universe and is most easily altered. Feedback loops present in the atmosphere, oceans, and surface of Earth demonstrate that a small initial effect can produce large consequences in a short time. For example, the addition of carbon dioxide to the atmosphere increases the greenhouse effect. In turn, this warms the planet by trapping infrared radiation from the surface and lower atmosphere. Even a small amount of carbon dioxide produces a noticeable effect. On Venus, a dense atmosphere rich in carbon dioxide keeps the planet's surface 450°C warmer than Earth. The suitable addition of small amounts of such gases into another planet's atmosphere would be relatively easy to accomplish, and could have far-ranging consequences.

Terraforming

Mars is the planet most susceptible to human-induced change. Its thin carbon dioxide atmosphere, if increased with the carbon dioxide now frozen into the Martian polar caps, could trap more heat and allow liquid water to exist (now an impossibility because of the low surface pressure). Such a project, if judged reasonable rather than environmentally unsound, could begin during the second half of the twenty-first century and might yield a planet capable of supporting human colonies.

Black Holes

A black hole is an object with such strong gravitational forces that nothing, not even light, can escape from within a critical distance from its center. Black holes can be detected by their gravitational effects on matter surrounding them that gradually spirals inward, as well as by the effects of gravity on light rays that pass close by them. Several likely black hole candidates have been identified in the Milky Way. Over the next decade several dozen more should be revealed with improved ground- and space-based observations. The Hubble Space Telescope has apparently detected a black hole of two billion solar masses in the core of the galaxy M87.

Pulsars

Pulsars, sources of regularly pulsed radio emission, arise from rapidly rotating neutron stars, the collapsed cores of stars that have exploded as supernovas. The number of known pulsars should reach several thousand by the year 2010, with many pulsars found to have planets in orbit around them.

Asteroids and Meteoroids

Debris left from the formation of the solar system 4.6 billion years ago continues to orbit the sun. Earth often intersects the orbits of small objects, called meteoroids, which produce "shooting stars" or meteors as friction consumes them high in the atmosphere. Larger objects called asteroids typically orbit between Mars and Jupiter, but some have Earth-crossing orbits. A 10-km asteroid's impact apparently caused the extinction of many species, including the dinosauria, 65 million years ago. Such impacts probably occur at 50- to 100-million-year intervals, so we may expect such an impact with 10 percent probability during the next several million years.

Space-Borne Astronomical Instruments

The heart of future astronomical observations lies in space, where the Earth's atmosphere neither blurs nor absorbs radiation from celestial objects. Since only visible light and radio waves penetrate to the Earth's surface, observation of the universe in the infrared, ultraviolet, X-ray, and gamma-ray portion of the spectrum requires that instruments be sent into orbit above the atmosphere. The Hubble Space Telescope (HST), launched in 1990, has provided important new observations in both visible light and ultraviolet radiation, especially since being fitted with a corrective optical system in

1993. Other satellites now observe the cosmos in types of radiation inaccessible to HST. The most significant new satellite should be the Advanced X-Ray Astrophysics Facility (AXAF), which may be launched by the end of this century. Ground-based telescopes, such as the giant Keck telescope in Hawaii, will remain of crucial importance in following up any discoveries made from space-borne observatories, since only they can provide large amounts of observing time for a particular project.

See also NATURAL DISASTERS; SPACE COLONIZATION; SPACE SATELLITES; SPACE TRAVEL.

BIBLIOGRAPHY

BARSTUSIAK, MARCIA. *Through a Universe Darkly.* New York: HarperCollins, 1993.

BEATTY, J. KELLY, and CHAIKIN, ANDREW, eds. *The New Solar System*, 3rd ed. Cambridge, MA: Sky Publishing, 1990.

FIELD, GEORGE, and CHAISSON, ERIC. *The Invisible Universe.* Boston: Birkhäuser Books, 1985.

GOLDSMITH, DONALD W. *The Astronomers.* New York: St. Martin's Press, 1991.

Donald W. Goldsmith

Atheism, Agnosticism.

See NONRELIGIOUS BELIEFS.

Atomic Power.

See NUCLEAR POWER; NUCLEAR POWER: CON.

Australia and New Zealand

Australia and New Zealand are two largely western societies superimposed on older traditional cultures. In global terms, they are small, isolated, and vulnerable. They have relatively limited manufacturing sectors and have specialized in the export of primary products such as beef, wool, butter, wood products, and minerals. This structural imbalance is reflected in the aphorism "tonnage out, lifestyle in." This trend is well established with, for example, the export of wood chips to Japan and the import of TV sets and VCRs. However, both countries are attempting to diversify into tourism and information products (including software and educational services). Both are likely to grow in importance.

Both countries have attained a slow rate of population growth, sensitively affected by immigration. They have aging populations with smaller groups of young people. They are both affected by persistently high unemployment, especially among the young. These trends are not expected to change in the near future.

Being geographically isolated, both countries possess unique flora and fauna. But these have suffered enormously under the impact of colonization over the last two hundred years and remain under threat from development pressures. The extinction rates of local species are expected to accelerate in the coming decades as their environment deteriorates because of salination, deforestation, urbanization, soil erosion, and pollution of lakes and rivers. Conflicts between conservation of natural resources (especially forests) and their commercial exploitation are expected to be increasingly sharp. This reflects a further growing conflict between commercial motives and a developing conservation or stewardship ethic. The latter has won some important battles, especially in Tasmania (saving the Franklin River from a hydroelectric scheme), but "resource security" legislation with an anticonservation bias has recently been enacted elsewhere in Australia.

Economic rationalism has dominated governance in both countries over the last decade, resulting in severe cutbacks of government services and reduced job security. However, its adequacy as ideology is being increasingly questioned (and may well decline). So, too, are the role and nature of economic growth. The primacy and meaning of both are likely to change drastically as the two economies come up against increasingly obvious environmental and social limits.

The key to future energy supplies in Australia and New Zealand is diversification. In the past, both countries have relied upon coal and oil, with growing investment in gas, hydroelectricity, and in the case of New Zealand, geothermal energy. In the future there will be increasing investment in energy conservation, wind power, and solar energy (both for water heating and electricity). The Australian interior, with its vast and reliable inflow of solar radiation, is an outstanding environment for the development of the latter. Many small communities there are pioneering the use of high-tech solar systems for refrigeration, power, lighting, and communications. This comparative advantage provides the potential to create an innovative edge in the years to come.

Australia and New Zealand both have conventional, high-quality education systems that still tend to be past-driven rather than future-responsive. The need to move from the former to the latter will increase as the social and economic stakes continue to grow. Both nations have a genuine interest in social justice and are taking steps to right historical injustices to the Aborigine and Maori peoples. This process will continue. In both cases, native cultures pose a challenge and a stimulus to the white majorities, who nevertheless will continue to benefit from the cultural diversification process. In New Zealand, Maori culture will continue to be a powerful social and economic force. In Australia, the impact of the Aborigines is less marked, but strong in the arts and literature.

Transport and communications will continue to be important due to geographic isolation. Efforts will continue to be made to upgrade both, particularly via satellite and other new communications technologies such as fiber optics, teleconferencing, and electronic mail. Geopolitically, the two nations will remain dependent upon the United States, particularly since the ties with Europe, and particularly with the United Kingdom, have grown more tenuous. Indeed, present indications are that Australia could become a republic around the end of the century. The ANZUS treaty (for mutual defense between the United States, Australia, and New Zealand) remains in force, despite New Zealand's stand against ships bearing nuclear weapons. On the other hand, both will continue to pursue active diplomacy and economic interests in Asia, the Pacific Basin, and Antarctica. In time, the latter may become an international conservation area, with distinct economic benefits to both countries. Science and technology are being pursued aggressively in areas such as biotechnology, food processing, and astronomy. But numerous failures to commercialize discoveries and to market them successfully imply continued dependence on high-technology work done elsewhere. (For example, the airplane flight recorder, or "black box," is an Australian invention, but it is now manufactured overseas.)

Though isolated, Australia and New Zealand are strong in culture and the arts. They possess orchestras, ballet and opera companies, and local art of the highest international standard. This is expected to continue, with the added presence of native cultures providing variety and a lively stimulus to creativity.

Future alternatives for Australia and New Zealand fall into two broad categories. (There were once three. But the scenario of a worldwide holocaust caused by conflict between the old Soviet Union and the United States can now be discounted.) First, they continue to play the old industrial game of competing in the global marketplace with better placed nations and continuing to decline economically, with growing overseas debts. In this scenario, many of the fears of social polarization, breakdown, violence, and so forth occur on a new and destructive scale (as in Los Angeles), with massive environmental deterioration. A business-as-usual outlook (which remains the commonplace assumption in many influential circles) leads in the same direction, since it contains no proven principles which can be expected to resolve the intractable problems of late-industrial life.

An alternative path involves a genuine commitment to sustainable development. In this scenario, growth is reconceptualized, environmental integrity becomes a primary social goal, and social institutions restructure away from high-consumption, rapid-throughput systems, toward more qualitative, long-term ends. Institutions of foresight become central to the functioning of each society. At present they are marginal. Australia's Commission for the Future has yet to win wide support, despite recent modest achievements such as its glossy journal *21C*. The New Zealand Commission for the Future was abolished in the late 1980s, leaving only the much smaller N. Z. Futures Trust.

In the early 1990s it seems clear that conditions will get harder for these two nations before they get easier. This is because the changes in attitude, the social and economic innovations, the processes of legislation, governance, and education, which would herald a real change of direction, show few signs of taking place. Progressive structural changes are, on the whole, still placed on the political agenda by social movements and other relatively marginal groups, and only later conceded to by reluctant governments. In other words, the ability of these two countries to assess the significance of changing global conditions, to carry out serious, high-quality futures research, and to adapt and shift toward a revised modus operandi seems limited. Hence, at present, both remain in a paradoxical situation in which social learning is achieved more effectively through disasters, depressions, violence, trauma, and environmental destruction than through applied foresight.

Times will therefore continue to get tougher for Australia and New Zealand in the foreseeable future. However, if and when a true "paradigm change" occurs—i.e., if a new or renewed world-view involving stewardship, qualitative growth, human development, and foresight can become established—then both countries will be well placed to pursue a more sustainable future. They have the skills, the intelligence, and a wide range of natural resources to participate in the creation of truly postindustrial cultures in the twenty-first century.

BIBLIOGRAPHY

BIRCH, CHARLES. *Confronting the Future: Australia and the World—the Next 100 Years*. Melbourne: Penguin Books, 1976; new ed., 1993.

DUNCAN, JAMES. *Options for New Zealand's Future*. Wellington: Victoria University Press, 1984.

"The Future of New Zealand," special issue. *Future Times* (N.Z.) (Autumn 1990).

SLAUGHTER, RICHARD A., ed. "Futures for Australia and the Pacific," special issue. *Futures* (U.K.) 22/3 (April 1990).

Richard A. Slaughter

B

Batteries

Engineers are waging a worldwide race to improve battery technology used in electric-powered vehicles and consumer products. Advances since the early 1990s offer promise that battery-powered autos will be common before 2000, utility-scale uses of photovoltaic cells could be a reality by 2015, and improved fuel cells will reach the marketplace by 2025. Two movements drive the research: growing environmental concerns and an expanding array of miniaturized electronic devices, from cellular phones and laptop computers to "smart" credit cards. Until the 1990s, only nickel-cadmium batteries (nicads) were rechargeable, presenting an environmental problem because cadmium, a toxic heavy metal, can leach into groundwater when batteries are dumped in landfills. Most disposable batteries are alkaline; new models introduced in 1993 can be recharged 25 times, compared with up to 1,000 recharges for nicads.

Searching to make rechargeables more efficient and environmentally friendly, engineers are testing combinations of plastic-like polymers, carbon materials, and metal alloys. Japanese scientists recently developed two kinds of rechargeable batteries, the nickel metal-hydride and lithium ion, said to be more efficient than nicads. A third design, lithium-polymer batteries, may offer a greater energy output than the Japanese models. In the next decade, lithium polymer, nickel metal-hydride, and lithium ions could replace nickel cadmium in reusable-battery design. Improvements in nickel-zinc batteries, boosting their lifetime from less than 200 recharge cycles to 500 cycles, might make those models viable contenders in the marketplace.

Electric Vehicles

The battery industry's greatest challenge for the 1990s is to develop an efficient, economical battery for electric cars. Stringent clean-air regulations in California require incremental improvements in auto emissions. By 1998, 2 percent of new cars and light trucks that major manufacturers sell in California must emit zero exhaust emissions. The figure rises to 5 percent in 2001 and 10 percent in 2003. Several states have adopted California's air-pollution rules. Given existing technology, only battery-powered vehicles can achieve those standards, but high price tags and limited driving range (typically 80 to 200 miles between eight-hour charges) are major barriers.

Automakers, battery manufacturers, and entrepreneurial engineers around the world hope to develop low-cost batteries with high-energy density and fast recharging capability. Japanese automakers aim to put 200,000 electric vehicles on the road by 2000. Germany's Mercedes-Benz and Volkswagen have formed a joint venture to test sixty different electric prototypes with advanced batteries. Electric Fuel Ltd., based in Jerusalem, Israel, has developed a zinc-air battery that powers a small van 200 miles on a single charge, twice the range of most other batteries. Researchers at Clark University, in Worcester, Mass., are working on a battery with six times as much power per unit of weight as current lead-acid batteries used in experimental electric vehicles. Plans call for the battery to operate at room temperature and to use low-cost materials, sulfur and aluminum. The United States Advanced Battery Consortium, a cooperative program of the nation's Big Three automakers, partly funded by the U.S. Department of Energy, electric utilities, and battery manufacturers, leads U.S. efforts.

Among various designs under consideration, engineers are looking at hybrid vehicle systems that combine features of electric and gasoline power. A hybrid vehicle uses an internal combustion engine to recharge a battery-powered electric drive system. In 1993, General Motors and Ford signed agreements with the Department of Energy to develop a hybrid vehicle within this decade.

Other university and national laboratories, including California's Lawrence Livermore National Laboratory and Tennessee's Oak Ridge National Laboratory have tested the use of flywheel-linked batteries in vehicles. The flywheel principle is based on kinetic energy, the energy of a moving object: When a force sets the heavy rim of a flywheel spinning, the wheel keeps rotating, making it a reservoir of energy. American Flywheel Systems (AFS), a Bellevue, Wash., company believes its patented device will power an electric car 350 miles on one charge and will recharge in 20 minutes. AFS and its technical partner, Honeywell, plan to build prototype batteries by 1995. Whatever their technology, electric vehicles will appear in auto showrooms in the mid to late 1990s and by 2000 could be a familiar sight on U.S. roads.

Fuel Cells

Many engineers believe the real hope for electric cars and other energy users lies in fuel cells. In the early 1990s scientists launched more than a dozen major experiments involving the use of fuel cells in vehicles.

Conventional batteries store energy and take hours to recharge; fuel cells produce energy and recharge in minutes. Like batteries, fuel cells create electricity through a chemical reaction, but they can generate electric current only as long as a stream of fuel and oxygen runs into the cells. Fuel cells do not create nitrogen oxide or sulfuric oxide, major contributors to urban smog. Their biggest drawback is cost: For fuel cells to be price compet-

itive in autos, the cost of a fuel-cell kilowatt must be slashed from almost $10,000 to $50 ($35 per unit of horsepower). Once manufacturers massproduce fuel cells, the cost should drop dramatically. Some forecasters predict that fuel cells will be a major source of electricity by 2000, with worldwide sales of $6 billion annually.

The public is most aware of fuel cells because of their use by astronauts. An alkaline potassium hydroxide fuel cell generates electricity in space shuttles. However, many scientists believe that phosphoric acid and solid-polymer fuel cells are more versatile. California's South Coast Air Quality Management District uses phosphoric acid fuel cells to generate current. Solid polymer fuel cells are starting to enter mainstream use; their first commercial applications may be in vehicles, in home cogeneration systems, and as substitutes for portable batteries.

Photovoltaic Cells

A battery-related technology, photovoltaic solar-electric cells, will come into wide use in the next decade. The price of these cells has fallen sharply since the 1960s, from $500 a watt to about $4. By the year 2000, they will power many portable electronic products, from cellular phones to "smart" credit cards with display screens. Photovoltaics' source of energy can be the sun or any low-level light. Environmental support is strong, since the cells are virtually pollution free. Because of initially high manufacturing costs, photovoltaic technology has looked mostly to rural customers for large-scale use. For "off-grid" users—homes not served by electric utilities—photovoltaic technology is economically competitive with conventional fuels. Thousands of remote towns around the world, particularly in Mexico, India, and Zimbabwe, rely on solar electrification systems. By 2000, photovoltaic energy could be highly competitive.

See also ENERGY, RENEWABLE SOURCES OF; HAZARDOUS WASTES; MOTOR VEHICLES; MOTOR VEHICLES, ALTERNATIVELY POWERED.

BIBLIOGRAPHY

KRAUSE, REINHARDT. "High Energy Batteries." *Popular Science* (February 1993).
McWHIRTER, WILLIAM. "Off and Humming." *Time* (April 26, 1993).
NEFF, ROBERT, and COY, PETER. "The High Voltage Rivalry in Batteries." *Business Week* (February 15, 1993).
SPAID, ELIZABETH LEVITAN. "Energy-Conscious Home Owners Begin to See the Light." *Christian Science Monitor*, October 12, 1993.

WALD, MATTHEW L. "Going Beyond Batteries to Power Electric Cars." *New York Times,* March 3, 1993.
———. "Imagining the Electric-Car Future." *New York Times,* April 28, 1993.

Jerry Kline

Behavior: Social Constraints

We are at a pivotal juncture in our thinking about how societies guarantee appropriate social behavior. From many directions we are confronted with phenomena that appear to reflect the breakdown of social order—the loss of clear moral codes, growing violence, and deteriorating faith in traditional leadership in almost every sphere, from politics to parenting. Moreover, the customary response to loss of order—increasing the force of traditional controls—turns out to be at best ineffective and often makes matters worse.

Grasping the significance of this apparent impasse is among the most important issues of our time. Making our way in the times ahead will require new, dynamic, and mature ways of understanding and dealing with social order.

Historically, culture imposed social constraint by three means: the state—through laws, royal decrees, and official government acts; the church through moral codes; and the community—through traditions, social mores, and norms. Throughout this century, the influence and potency of the first and second of these means have been diminishing markedly, and the effectiveness of the third has been severely challenged.

Few people today would describe themselves as having strong bonds in the community or would admit being strongly influenced by community traditions. While the church continues to be a significant force in many people's lives, it exercises considerably less control over the average person. The seven deadly sins—pride, greed, lust, envy, sloth, anger, and gluttony—have now for many been transformed into virtues. We live increasingly in an age of the individual. Individualism carried to extremes inevitably transgresses the rights of others living within the society. Striking a balance between the individual and society in general is not easy. If there is a prevailing moral code in this materialistic country, it is caveat emptor: let the buyer beware.

Of the three traditional means of social constraint, we are left to rely primarily on what is the most institutionalized, and thus best organized, to deal with a social structure defined primarily by the rights of individuals—government and the strong arm of the law. But here we encounter problems as well. A society defined by competition and legalistic rules tends to become more and more litigious and increasingly dependent on police and prisons to keep order. The outcome is governments, courts, police, and prison systems overburdened with issues or people they were not designed to handle. The resulting morass has caused these institutions to be viewed with diminishing respect, thereby impairing their ability to get the job done.

Do these trends reflect a fundamental erosion of our social fabric? This may be, but the evidence suggests that the disorder we witness is more that of transition than of disintegration. If we ignore or run away from the challenges that this disorder represents, destruction is a possible outcome.

The disorder itself may reflect important new possibilities for defining and achieving social coherence. To grasp what is being asked, we might start by looking at several areas where the loss of traditional behavioral codes affects us in particularly poignant ways.

Love is one such area. Not too long ago, we had highly reliable rules of appropriate behavior for love. Society provided us with clear gender roles and codes for how we should behave if we were just friends, dating, engaged, or married. Gender roles are increasingly being challenged and with them established assumptions about the forms that love should appropriately assume.

Many people, appropriately concerned about the breakdown of families, would argue that this is an erosion of social order. But one can argue as well that these new uncertainties reflect first tentative steps toward a new maturity in love, and a new depth and maturity in how we conceive family bonds. Surrendering gender roles moves us beyond the reality of man and woman as two predetermined puzzle parts that come together to find their "better halves" and toward the task of loving as unique, whole people. Succeeding at such a task is not easy; it requires giving up many familiar assumptions. But it offers the possibility of love that more completely embraces all we are capable of being.

We can discover a similar dynamic in almost all situations that confront us with new cultural uncertainties. The primary determinant of a healthy future on the international scene will be the degree to which we can move beyond needing the clear rules of a world defined by allies on one side and enemies on the other. One could call this a "messier" world—it certainly gets confusing and complicated if we hold to tactics of the past. But, in fact, the challenge is simply to see other of the world's people more fully for who they are. This is not easy. We must think and respond much more creatively and maturely, see and act from a bigger picture.

Most of the critical emerging social challenges require at least two kinds of social evolution. First, the critical challenges ahead require a willingness to step forward without externally defined, concretely articulated moral, legal, or scientific codes to guide us. This reflects how dynamic and creative—and interesting—reality has become. As Nietzsche said, for the truth of the future, "there is no immaculate perception."

Second, these challenges require that we find a new appreciation for our relatedness—at all levels, from family, to neighborhood, to workplace, to region, and planet. Few of the important challenges ahead are amenable to purely legalistic or institutional solutions. Our laws will be effective only to the degree that they are grounded in a new and deepened sense of human community.

In the past, culture has been like a parent, providing us with well-defined bonds of affiliation and clear codes of right and wrong to guide our actions. The critical questions ahead require a new kind of human maturity. They require that we bring a new consciousness and initiative to our bonds of affiliation, and they ask that we accept new responsibility at all levels in life's decisions—not just in the uncertainties of our personal lives, but as well in the life of our culture. This does not mean playing God, but it does mean accepting that many of the questions ahead have godlike importance and godlike consequences—and appreciating that these awesome decisions are in our hands.

See also DIVORCE; ETHICS; EVOLUTION, SOCIAL; FAMILY PATTERNS; FAMILY VALUES; MARRIAGE; MORALS; SEXUAL BEHAVIOR; SEXUAL CODES; SEXUAL LAWS; SOCIAL CHANGE: UNITED STATES; SOCIAL CONTROLS; VALUES; VALUES CHANGE; VALUES FORMATION; WOMEN'S MOVEMENT.

BIBLIOGRAPHY

BELLAH, ROBERT. *The Good Society.* New York: Random House, 1992.
ETZIONI, AMITAI. *The Spirit of Community: Rights, Responsibilities, and the Communitarian Agenda.* New York: Crown, 1993.
JOHNSTON, CHARLES M. *Necessary Wisdom: Meeting the Challenge of a New Cultural Maturity.* Berkeley, CA: Celestial Arts, 1991.
KOPP, SHELDON. *An End to Innocence.* New York: Bantam, 1978.
LAPPÉ, FRANCES MOORE. *Rediscovering America's Values.* New York: Ballantine, 1989.

Charles M. Johnston

Bell, Daniel (1919–   )

The American sociologist and futurist Daniel Bell is the son of Polish Jewish immigrants. Bell has taught sociology at several major universities, including Chicago, Columbia, and Harvard, and had an early career in journalism and policy analysis. His first major work, *The End of Ideology* (1960), was an examination of the fading of Marxism in American intellectual life and the rise of a new postideological generation for whom the radical passions of the 1930s were no longer relevant. Chairing the Commission on the Year 2000, he edited its celebrated report, *Toward the Year 2000: Work in Progress* (1968). In *The Coming of Post-Industrial Society: A Venture in Social Forecasting* (1973), he anticipated a near-future America in which the great majority of workers find employment in the professions and services. The principal source of wealth, he argues, will be information, grounded in the empirical sciences. Bell has revisited and fine-tuned his prognosis of a "post-industrial" society in his 1987 *Daedalus* article "The World and the United States in 2013." Another book, *The Cultural Contradictions of Capitalism* (1976), follows his study of the disintegration of ideology with a plea for the renewal of religious faith.

See also COMMISSION ON THE YEAR 2000; FUTURISTS.

BIBLIOGRAPHY

BRICK, HOWARD. *Daniel Bell and the Decline of Intellectual Radicalism.* Madison, WI: University of Wisconsin Press, 1986.
COATES, JOSEPH F., and JARRETT, JENNIFER. *What Futurists Believe.* Mt. Airy, MD: Lomond, 1989, chapter 7.
LIEBOWITZ, NATHAN. *Daniel Bell and the Agony of Modern Liberalism.* Westport, CT: Greenwood Press, 1985.

W. Warren Wagar

Bicycling.

See PERSONAL TRANSPORT.

Biodiversity

Biodiversity is the variety and variability of life—the sum of genes, species, and ecosystems existing in a region. It is extraordinary how little we know about the diversity of life on Earth. Only a decade ago, the best estimate was that about 3 million species coexist on our planet. Since then, an almost unimaginable array of living things has been uncovered. Tropical forests are now thought to be home to millions of undescribed species, and the deep sea floor may host hundreds of thousands, if not millions, more. Even soil samples from around the world are revealing a previously unsuspected variety of life. Estimates of the number of species on Earth now range from 10 million to 100 million, with a mere 1.4 million described and catalogued so far.

Scientists estimate that the Earth's biotic wealth stood at an all-time high when the first human beings appeared. Now it is fast declining, as a result of human activities. Around the world, habitats are being rapidly destroyed. Species are now dying out as fast as at any time since the mass extinction at the end of the Cretaceous period some 65 million years ago.

Tropical forests are home to more than half of the Earth's species, and tropical deforestation is the crucible of today's extinction crisis. About 17 million hectares of tropical forests are cleared annually. Recent estimates of this threat to biodiversity, assuming that deforestation continues at current rates, conclude that at least 5 to 10 percent of tropical forest species will either die out over the next thirty years or be reduced to such small populations that extinction will become a foregone conclusion.

Tropical species are by no means the only ones at risk. Worldwide, the temperate-zone rain forest has shrunk as much as the tropical forest. Other habitats such as wetlands and mangroves, U.S. tall grass prairies, and Central America's dry forests also have been reduced to mere remnants. Some 633 species are listed as being in danger of extinction in the United States alone, and more than 3,000 other species have been proposed for addition to this list. In the past several hundred years, at least 80 species—and possibly as many as 290—have become extinct in the continental United States and Hawaii. Worldwide, more than 700 extinctions of vertebrates, invertebrates, and vascular plants have been recorded since 1600.

Why do these losses matter? The ethical case for preserving biodiversity argues that every form of life is unique and warrants humanity's respect and that people now living have a moral responsibility to future generations to pass on the Earth's store of biotic richness undiminished from that which their forebears inherited. Many of the world's religions teach respect for life's diversity and exhort believers to conserve it. In India, certain societies established spirit sanctuaries—natural areas protected from human disturbance. In the Philippines, farmers still maintain traditional rice varieties for ceremonial occasions. In the United States, ethical, aesthetic, and scientific concerns—not economic considerations—spurred passage of the Endangered Species Act in 1973.

Biodiversity also is important because it serves as a source of economic benefits and as a reservoir of genetic variety. Humanity derives all its food and many of its medicines and industrial products from both wild and domesticated species. Economic benefits from wild species alone make up an estimated 4.5 percent of the U.S. gross domestic product. Indeed, wild species are dietary mainstays in much of the world. Fisheries, largely composed of wild species, contributed about 100 million tons of food worldwide in 1989. Biotic resources also serve human needs for recreation. Worldwide, nature tourism—a boom that has barely begun—already generates as much as $12 billion in revenues each year.

Formerly, nearly all medicines came from plants and animals, and even today they remain vital. Traditional medicine is the basis of primary health care for about 80 percent of people in developing countries, more than 3 billion people in all. More than 5,100 species are used in Chinese medicine alone, and people in northwestern Amazonia have tapped some 2,000 species for medicinal purposes.

As for modern pharmaceuticals, one fourth of all prescription drugs dispensed in the United States contain active ingredients extracted from plants. Over 3,000 antibiotics—including penicillin and tetracycline—are derived from microorganisms. Cyclosporin, developed from a soil fungus, revolutionized heart and kidney transplant surgery by suppressing the body's immune reaction. Aspirin (acetylsalicylic acid) and many other drugs that now are synthesized in factories were first discovered in nature. Compounds extracted from plants, microbes, and animals were involved in developing all of the twenty bestselling medicines in the United States, drugs whose combined sales approached $6 billion in 1988.

The stock of genetic variations within each species is another vital element of biodiversity—

and new technologies are multiplying its value. Genetic engineering made it possible to use genes from wild relatives of domesticated plants and animals to fuel such agricultural advances as modern high-yield crops and livestock. In the United States, plant breeders' use of diverse genes accounted for at least half of the doubling in yields of rice, barley, soybeans, wheat, cotton, and sugarcane between 1930 and 1980—and for tripling tomato yields and quadrupling corn, sorghum, and potato yields. Genetic diversity is needed to maintain crop yields in the face of rapidly evolving pests and diseases. Furthermore, it may prove crucial to maintaining species themselves if the worst global warming forecasts are borne out.

Today, biotechnology is opening another frontier in the exploration of biodiversity. Genetic engineering transforms the world's biota into raw material for the biotech industry. Other new technologies have sparked a resurgence in pharmaceutical companies' screening of wild species as sources of new drugs. Designing drugs from scratch has proved difficult and costly, and cures for diseases such as cancer and AIDS have eluded scientists. Nature provides a veritable storehouse of chemicals with potential medicinal uses. Of the 3,500 new chemical structures discovered worldwide in 1985, some 2,619 were isolated from plants.

It is crucial to preserve the natural wealth upon which so much of human enterprise is built. Even from an economic standpoint alone, there are benefits to maintaining biodiversity. Biodiversity provides an indispensible undergirding for future advances in agriculture, medicine, and industry that far outweigh the short-term monetary benefits obtained from cutting a forest or filling a wetland. We expose ourselves to incalculable risks by threatening the extinction of species whose role in ecosystems are not yet understood, and also future generations are robbed of the benefits that otherwise might be reaped from Earth's biotic storehouse.

For all these reasons, it is auspicious that 156 nations signed the biodiversity treaty at the 1992 Earth Summit in Rio de Janeiro. If nations now begin working together to preserve species, genes, and ecosystems around the world, this decade could mark a turning point in humanity's long history of interaction with Earth's other inhabitants.

See also DEFORESTATION; ENVIRONMENTAL BEHAVIOR; ENVIRONMENTAL ETHICS; EVOLUTION, BIOLOGICAL; EXTINCTION OF SPECIES; FORESTRY; GENETICS: AGRICULTURAL APPLICATIONS; GLOBAL WARMING; GREEN REVOLUTION; LIFE SCIENCES.

BIBLIOGRAPHY

NOSS, REED F. and COOPERRIDER, ALLEN. *Saving Nature's Legacy: Protecting and Restoring Biodiversity.* Washington, DC: Island Press, 1994.

REID, WALTER V., et al. *Biodiversity Prospecting: Using Genetic Resources for Sustainable Development.* Washington, DC: World Resources Institute, 1993.

SZARO, ROBERT, and JOHNSTON, DAVID W., eds. *Biodiversity in Managed Landscapes.* Oxford, UK: Oxford University Press, 1995.

WILSON, EDWARD O. *The Diversity of Life.* New York: W. W. Norton, 1993.

World Resources Institute, World Conservation Union (IUCN), United Nations Environment Program. *Global Biodiversity Strategy.* Washington, DC: WRI, IUCN, UNEP, 1992.

Walter V. Reid
Kenton R. Miller

Bioethics

Although the world abounds with diverse life-forms, people's awareness of the bonds linking humans and other species has been slow to develop. The concept of ecological systems did not gain widespread acceptance until the final decades of the twentieth century. By 1970 the public was aware of environmental deterioration. Danger signs were evident—more and more endangered species disappearing, chemical pollutants poisoning the planet, and new technologies posing ominous risks to living organisms. At last, large numbers of people realized that pioneer ecologist George Perkins Marsh (1801–1882) had been correct when he warned that human efforts directed at "improving" nature's ecosystems possibly might lead instead to the systems' degradation.

Out of this anxiety came *bioethics*—attempts to define modes of responsible human behavior capable of preserving the fragile ecosystems humans share with other species.

Bioethics and the New Genetics

With the advent of molecular genetics in the 1970s, bioethicists were challenged with questions concerning the environmental impact of the new plant and animal genetics. For example: In view of science's emerging capability to transform existing life-forms and also create new ones, is it possible to determine in advance which genetic engineering experiments will lead to beneficial results and which might bring on an environmental catastrophe? How can science justify introducing into the environment novel organisms that might trigger irreversible ecological changes?

Social and economic concerns were voiced as well. Among the questions asked were: Why impose onerous restrictions on biological engineering in agriculture when it can substantially increase the world's food supply? What will be the social costs of high-tech farming systems replacing the family farm and privatized biological research taking the place of public, nonprofit research? And will the Third World be able to progress if farmers there are unable to pay patent holders for the right to raise genetically improved crops and livestock?

Ethical issues of biotechnology are still being debated. Of crucial importance are (1) the maintenance of genetic diversity and (2) science's overall competence: i.e., its ability to foresee and surmount a multitude of problems that will come about as human intervention in the realm of nature becomes more extensive and pervasive. In a world that appears to be undergoing biological transformation, concerned persons are insisting that the agenda of the new genetics should include appraisal of environmental risks and planning to avoid social dislocations.

Patents of Living Organisms

Genetically engineered microorganisms may be patented, the U.S. Supreme Court ruled in the *Diamond* v. *Chakrababarty* case in 1980. This was a landmark decision, opening the way for patent protection to be extended to genetically altered plants, animals, and various types of living matter, including human and nonhuman cells.

Once the patentability of new organisms had been established, biotechnology firms intensified their development of potentially profitable materials, seeking to maximize returns on each product. This means that seed of a new plant variety—herbicide-resistant corn, for example, or drought-tolerant millet—will be marketed to large numbers of farmers. When one plant variety is grown extensively, the appearance of a new strain of virus or fungus may result in crop failure over huge acreages. Plant diseases are less likely to reach epidemic proportions when farmers grow numerous crop varieties representing a wide range of genetic backgrounds. One of biotechnology's more serious defects may be its tendency to restrict genetic diversity in some situations.

Patenting of animals has been allowed since 1987, when the U.S. Patent Office decided biologi-

cal inventions merit the same protection as mechanical inventions. In 1988, a patent was issued for the "Harvard Mouse," a genetically altered animal used in cancer research. So-called transgenic animals are useful as disease models and as sources of biologically important drugs and pharmaceuticals. In the years ahead, new biological creations may take the places of traditional farm animals. Animal welfare may become a troublesome issue, since animals are likely to be considered merely units of production on factory farms of the future.

Release of Altered Organisms

In genetic engineering's early years, American researchers were not permitted to release genetically altered organisms into the environment. Possible damage to public health and the environment, it was felt, outweighed the researchers' need for field testing. In 1978, the National Institutes of Health relaxed the rules and permitted field tests under closely regulated conditions. Two tests were conducted of a bacterium that prevents frost damage in field crops. A scheduled third test drew protests from environmentalists, and a court order issued in 1984 halted the test. Subsequently, tests of the "ice-minus" bacterium have been resumed, with no harmful results observed.

Due to intense international competition in the biotechnology industry, restrictions limiting field tests of genetically altered organisms in America and Germany have been opposed by biotech firms in the two countries. Field testing is now taking place in both nations, and restrictions may be eased further in the future. No one can say for certain that field testing will never cause serious health or environmental problems, but the biotech industry's record to date has been excellent.

Biotechnology and the Environment

Commercial-scale introduction of genetically modified organisms could result in environmental nightmares. Super-weeds might come into existence if special genes in herbicide-resistant crops were transmitted to wild species. Unexpectedly, bacteria that are benign and helpful could mutate and endanger the health of animals and humans. Although genetic engineering offers many worthwhile benefits, the possible dangers should not be overlooked. Careful monitoring of the environment will be needed in order to identify problems before they become uncorrectable.

In a positive, clear-eyed approach to biological engineering, possible environmental dangers would be taken into account as policy-makers decided which research and development areas of the new genetics should be given top priority. It would seem desirable to modify plants so that their new characteristics would enrich the environment. Instead of inviting erosion by planting annual crops, we might develop deep-rooted perennial grain crops that could protect the soil from water and wind. If we had crops that grew well on brackish soil, we could reclaim vast areas of wasteland.

Conversely, it does not seem reasonable to "improve" crops in ways that might jeopardize the environment. Genetically altered crops that are highly productive only if sustained by doses of commercial fertilizer, herbicides, and other chemicals may be poorly engineered for a system of agriculture that aspires to be sustainable and responsive to the needs of the environment. How biotechnology shapes the future will be determined by the people who set the early goals for biotechnology's development.

See also ANIMAL RIGHTS; ARTIFICIAL LIFE; ENVIRONMENTAL BEHAVIOR; ENVIRONMENTAL ETHICS; ETHICS; GENETIC ENGINEERING; GENETICS; SEXUAL REPRODUCTION: ARTIFICIAL MEANS.

BIBLIOGRAPHY

CALDWELL, LYNTON KEITH. *Biocracy: Public Policy and the Life Sciences.* Boulder, CO, and London: Westview Press, 1987.

GENDEL, STEVEN M.; KLINE, A. DAVID; WARREN, D. MICHAEL; and YATES, FAYE, eds. *Agricultural Bioethics: Implications of Agricultural Biotechnology.* Ames, IA: Iowa State University Press, 1990.

LESSER, WILLIAM H., ed. *Animal Patents: The Legal, Economic and Social Issues.* New York: Stockton Press, 1989.

REGAN, TOM. *All That Dwell Therein: Animal Rights and Environmental Ethics.* Berkeley, CA: University of California Press, 1982.

RODD, ROSEMARY. *Biology, Ethics, and Animals.* New York: Oxford University Press, 1990.

Clifton E. Anderson

Books.

See LITERATURE; PRINTED WORD.

Breakthroughs, Scientific.

See SCIENTIFIC BREAKTHROUGHS.

Broadcasting

Radio and television broadcasting ushered in the age of electronic information and entertainment beginning in the 1920s. Generations of Americans have grown up with the convenience and familiarity of broadcasting in the twentieth century. Virtually everyone watches television or listens to radio sometime during the week, a pattern that is likely to continue far into the future.

Americans are served by over 1,000 television stations and more than 11,000 radio stations, the highest per capita rate of any major country in the world. There are more households with radio (5.6 sets on average) and television receivers (98 percent penetration with 69 percent having more than one set) than with telephones or running water. The average U.S. household receives 13.3 television stations over the air. This increases to a total 39.4 channels receivable when cable is included. On average, people (two years and older) watch over thirty-five hours of television each week. More than two dozen radio stations are available to the average American, and in bigger markets (or with rooftop antennas) this rises to over eighty radio stations receivable off the air. The average person (twelve years and older) listens to over twenty-three hours of radio programming each week.

The first Golden Age of Broadcasting began in mid-century when Americans overwhelmingly adopted radio and television listening and viewing into their lifestyles. The U.S. model of commercially supported, free over-the-air broadcasting is immensely popular and has a sound economic basis. Toward the end of the twentieth century, this model began to be widely imitated around the world with much success. Unlike the United States, much of the rest of the world is dependent upon government sponsored and operated broadcasting, which provides fewer choices and insufficient amounts of popular programming. In many cases, advertising is limited or not allowed, which limits economic growth in many sectors.

From Analog to Digital

In the next Golden Age, we will do more with our radios and television sets than just watch and listen. The radio and television systems we rely on are evolving from analog to computer-based digital electronics that is dramatically changing what broadcasting can do. We will interact, transact, exchange data, personalize, customize, and integrate our media environments. The seeds of the next

Golden Age are already being planted. The far-reaching impacts of computer-based digital signal processing and compression techniques are changing assumptions about what is possible in all electronic media. The once comfortable technological policy, and economic barriers keeping industries apart are breaking down and forcing society to change as a result.

Multimedia Convergence

Under the banner of "multimedia convergence" a number of previously distinct industries are banding together in various strategic alliances, partnerships, joint ventures, mergers, and acquisitions. The rush to convergence has blurred the lines between the traditional broadcast, cable, telephone, and consumer electronics industries as each segment considers ways to not only joint venture but also to compete with each other in their traditional product-service marketplaces.

For example, telephone companies are exploring relationships with cable television and programming companies to examine ways to offer audio and video entertainment services. Cable television companies, for their part, are considering what it would take to offer competitive telephony services over their facilities. Broadcasters are exploring new opportunities with digital transmission facilities, including multimedia, interactive, and data broadcasting. Video game and CD-ROM companies are trying new means of distributing their services via broadcast, telephone, and cable systems.

The key elements of the convergence marketplace are *content, distribution,* and *processing.* From the consumers' perspective, any system or combination of systems that improves *control, choice,* and *convenience* is likely to be something they will adopt more readily. For convergence to work in the marketplace, consumers must have confidence that the different systems being offered to them by cable, telephone, broadcast, consumer electronics, and other companies can be hooked up and work together. This connectivity of systems requires standards to guarantee fully compatible interoperability. Technical standards facilitating such integration will have to be set, either by industry or by the government.

What Lies in the Future

TELEVISION

New technology-enabled advances in television permit wider and higher resolution pictures with CD-quality sound, interactivity, multiple services in the same channel, and computer data services. These technologies also provide a platform for television broadcasters to enter the age of digital data systems. All television sets (13 inches or larger) manufactured for sale in the United States since 1993 have the ability to decode closed captioning. Typically, these sets also have the ability to decode and display other kinds of information such as basic programming information (title, length, type of program), and programming guides to better serve viewers.

Interactive broadcast television companies are bringing an entirely new range of services to viewers. Using both wired (telephone or cable) and wireless (spectrum allocations) approaches, new services will allow home viewers to enjoy electronic shopping, information retrieval, interactive games, and computer-based learning. Because of more efficient utilization of the available broadcast spectrum, all these services will be offered *in addition to* the conventional television program service to which viewers have become so accustomed.

RADIO

While television often grabs the headlines and consumer attention, broadcast radio services are also undergoing rapid change due to technological advances. From basic improvements to the receivers of both AM and FM broadcast services, to data broadcast and interactive services, radio is rapidly forging its own way into the new multimedia convergence landscape.

For example, by adding a printer interface to a radio, if a listener hears something advertised that is interesting, he or she could simply push a button on the receiver to print out a coupon. Navigational information can be broadcast in part of the radio signal to augment the global positioning satellite (GPS) service many travelers use for orientation. Radio broadcasters are now planning to move from delivering an analog signal to a newer digitally formatted signal with compact disc (CD) quality to listeners. Other radio advances will combine text and graphics with audio for a multimedia-based set of services for listeners. As with television advances, these radio advanced services will be in addition to traditional services.

The Next Golden Age

Radio and television broadcasting introduced generations of Americans to electronic media systems with greater success and popularity than any other system to date. As we enter the second century of electronic and computer-based media systems, broadcasters expect to once again be at the forefront of innovation. Broadcasters will be able to flexibly offer multiple and interactive services. This may well be the next Golden Age of Broadcasting.

See also ADVERTISING; COMMUNICATIONS; COMMUNICATIONS: MEDIA LAW; COMMUNICATIONS: PRIVACY ISSUES; COMMUNICATIONS TECHNOLOGY; DIGITAL COMMUNICATIONS; ELECTRONIC CONVERGENCE; ELECTRONIC PUBLISHING; INFORMATION OVERLOAD; INFORMATION SOCIETY; MEDIA CONSOLIDATION; SATELLITE COMMUNICATIONS; TELEPHONES; TELEVISION.

BIBLIOGRAPHY

DeSonne, Marcia, ed. *Advanced Broadcast/Media Technologies*. Washington, DC: National Association of Broadcasters, 1992.

_____. *Convergence: The Transition to the Electronic Superhighway*. Washington, DC: National Association of Broadcasters, 1994.

Ditingo, Vincent. *The Remaking of Radio*. Boston: Focal Press, 1995.

Doyle, Marc. *The Future of Television*. Lincolnwood, IL: N & C Business Books, 1992.

Giller, George. *Life After Television*. New York: W. W. Norton, 1994.

Jankowski, Gene F., and Fuchs, David C. *Television Today and Tomorrow*. New York: Oxford University Press, 1995.

Edward O. Fritts

Buddhism

Buddhism began in northern India approximately 2,500 years ago with the teaching career of the Buddha ("the Awakened One"). It was displaced from India in the next few centuries but rapidly spread throughout Southeast Asia and the Far East, where it remains an important cultural and religious presence, and in the last century, it has taken root in Europe and North America, where it is practiced by immigrant and refugee communities as well as by men and women who have adopted it as a new religion. Over the centuries and in different places, many Buddhists have turned their thoughts to the future, and their ideas provide radically new perspectives.

This is especially the case when we consider our expectations about the openness of the future. The modern West routinely qualifies all predictions about the human future out of a respect for human freedom and from an awareness of the inevitability of historical change; the future is regarded as essentially open, and no prediction about the human future—as opposed to the natural world—can be made with absolute confidence. Voices from the Buddhist traditions remind us that such an orientation to the future is itself culturally determined. Traditionally, many Buddhists thought that some predictions—perhaps we might better call them prognoses—could be made without qualification.

Humans in the future will suffer, for example, just as they have in the past and as they do today. They will suffer because they will be subject to sickness, old age, and death and because they will try to live in ways that are incompatible with the nature of reality. In the modern West, questions of human finitude are often left to the natural sciences; we look to physicians and biologists to define death and its significance for us. In contrast, Buddhism from its beginnings has consistently presented itself as a medicine to cure just this kind of fundamental suffering. From the same traditional Buddhist perspective, we can also say that some individuals will be cured from suffering in the future. They will experience what the Buddha experienced in the process of his own "awakening." The course of treatment that will culminate in such experiences has already begun and continues in the present. In the traditional view of Buddhists, experiences of salvific enlightenment are only attained after lifetimes of effort, and because there are future Buddhas (Sanskrit: *Bodhisattva*) now, there will be Buddhas in the future.

We might also expect, however, that it will be even harder for men and women in the future to begin this arduous therapeutic process, because they will live in circumstances which will be less conducive to Buddhist practice. This kind of change, in the traditional view, is inevitable, and some Buddhist texts depict the Buddha himself as predicting the decline of his religion. There are various versions of his prediction in the various Buddhist traditions, but they all agree that the conditions necessary for the practice of the Buddhism will gradually deteriorate, until all outward signs of the religion disappear. The Buddha also predicted that in the more distant future another great Buddha, Maitreya, would come to teach again the eternal Truth to which humans now have access through Buddhism.

These traditional Buddhist ideas about the future illuminate a discussion about the future of the Buddhist religion. It is concerned with the more mundane aspects of Buddhist thought and practice, the vicissitudes of historical institutions, and the development of systems of thought. But in the light of the traditional view, such matters are irrelevant to what should most interest human beings. The traditional Buddhist view reminds us that an interest in Buddhism as a historical phenomenon should not prevent us from recognizing that Buddhists have valued Buddhist thought and practice for the access it gives to a transhistorical eternal Truth.

This is not to say that Buddhists themselves have not been aware of the historicity of the Buddhist religion. Indeed they have been acutely aware of historical change and especially change for the worse. In the future, we can expect them to continue to care for the Buddhist religion and to attempt to restore the damage done to it by human carelessness and malevolence. Buddhist history has been punctuated by revivals and reforms, and similar efforts will occur in the future, although it should be noted that traditional ideas about the future may provide the most compelling motivations for such reforms.

The technologies of modern communication and transportation have made Buddhists more aware of the cultural and religious diversity of the Buddhist world, and this will introduce a new component to future revivals and reforms. Attention will be given to rediscovering and preserving the essentials of Buddhist thought and practice as opposed to what has been introduced in the course of the long process of adaptation of Buddhism to local contexts. Reforms in the future may make the Buddhist world more homogeneous than it is now.

Such reforms will inevitably raise new questions about Buddhist identity, and especially, local Buddhist identities. In the nineteenth and twentieth centuries, Buddhist imagery and mores have often played an important role in the forging of new nationalist identities; to be Burmese, for example, is now often taken as meaning that one is a Buddhist. A strong, politically significant connection between local identities and Buddhism will continue as long as nationalism continues to be a potent force in the modern world. This will sometimes bring Buddhism into conflict with other modern values, such as a concern for minority rights and the structures of democracy, even as it also contradicts the more universalist aspirations generated by many Buddhist reforms.

Buddhist thought and practice will also be correlated and compared with other areas of modern life, especially those theoretically addressed by the natural sciences. In the twentieth century, there has been considerable adjustment of the Buddhist heritage to bring it more in line with a modern scientific worldview; like those in other religious communities, Buddhists have subjected their religious heritage to a process of demythologizing and rationalization. We should expect similar processes to continue wherein Buddhists review their religious tradition in the light of changing scientific orientations. A more critical attitude to the inadequacies of modern science and economics, on moral and religious grounds, has already begun and can be expected to gain momentum.

Dramatic changes in the structures of religious authority have occurred throughout the Buddhist world in the twentieth century, and these will bear fruit in the near future. There is greater emphasis on the authority of individual conscience rather than on the authority of hierarchical office. This means that we can expect a diminished role in Buddhist communities for monks and other professionally religious persons. As is the case with many other religious communities, Buddhist society is increasingly becoming secularized; this is already apparent in North America. Related to this sociological change, there is now widespread approval of a generalized probative attitude to all areas of human knowledge. A kind of "hyperrationality," in which everything is plausible until proven otherwise by trial and error, creates a context in which many practices (for example, magic and astrology) that would have seemed irrational by early twentieth-century standards are given credence and encouraged among educated people; one can expect patterns of "new-age religion" to emerge throughout the Buddhist world.

See also CHRISTIANITY; HINDUISM; ISLAM; JUDAISM; MIND: NEW MODES OF THINKING.

BIBLIOGRAPHY

GOMBRICH, RICHARD, and OBEYESEKERE, GANANATH. *Buddhism Transformed: Religious Change in Sri Lanka.* Princeton, NJ: Princeton University Press, 1988.
DUMOULIN, HEINRICH, and MARALDO, JOHN, eds. *Buddhism in the Modern World.* New York: Collier Books, Macmillan, 1976.

Charles Hallisey

Business Governance

Business governance relates to who shall govern a corporation—the owner/shareholders, management (directors and senior executives), or other stakeholders—and for what purpose?

In proprietorships and closely held corporations, the owners answer these questions as they wish, so long as they comply with existing law. However, in large publicly held corporations, these questions are complicated by corporate law strictures that separate stock ownership from business management. This arrangement permits a runaway management technocracy in many large publicly held corporations to control director nominations to their boards. Rubber-stamp control enables them to follow their own goals and to escape accountability to individual shareowners, whose holdings are too small to impact on board elections. This situation helped spark the merger and takeover frenzy of the 1980s, when outside investors decided they could manage the corporate assets to better the reward to stockholders.

Since the 1930s, a debate has raged between those who argue that management holds corporate powers in trust for shareholders only and others who hold that these powers are held in trust for society. In more recent times, the terms have changed, but not the concepts: Management holds corporate powers in trust to "maximize shareholder value" (Rappaport, 1986, pp. 1ff.); or, the powers are held in trust to balance or "to optimize the interests of its stakeholders," for example, customers, employees, shareholders, the public. (Ewing, 1987, p. 32).

The question of business governance is further complicated in the industrialized world during the last half of the twentieth century by the concentration of ownership of large corporations in a small number of institutions. The proportion of stock ownership in the United States held by institutional investors grew from 20 percent in 1970 to over 50 percent in the early 1990s. (These institutions, dominated by pension funds, hold about an equal amount of the debt of the largest American corporations.) This concentration of ownership will increase as pension funds grow and individual share ownership decreases. Britain has seen a similar trend.

In Germany, 60 percent of the share capital of large companies is controlled by the three major banks. These holdings are either direct or managed holdings of their customers that the banks vote upon.

In Japan, ownership of large companies is concentrated in the members of a small number of industrial groups, the *keiretsu*. In *keiretsu*, 20 percent to 30 percent of the share capital of member companies is owned by other members, the group's bank and trading company. Estimates of the country-wide concentration of stock ownership of the largest corporations in a small number of *keiretsu* and financial institutions range from 50 percent (Drucker, 1992, p. 236), to 66 percent (Kester, 1991, pp. 57–58).

Japanese and German banks and financial institutions are not only shareholders in their companies but also direct business partners with them. Thus, they are long-term investors in the corporations that they help govern directly through board memberships or indirectly through group affiliations. In these two countries, governance in the long-term interests of owners and society through a loose affiliation with government and labor is not at present a problem. Whether these tight relationships can survive in the world marketplace of the twenty-first century remains to be seen.

Institutional investors in the United States historically have played a passive role in corporate governance, selling their stock when they could no longer vote their proxies in favor of management. However, a more active role in the matter of corporate governance is being assumed.

Large state and municipal pension funds are becoming active in influencing board member selection, corporate policies, executive compensation, and accountability. Some critics who support corporate governance reform oppose efforts to mandate changes by government. They believe the "marketplace"—the investors—should bring about the changes through existing channels. Others are critical of large pension-fund managers taking a more active role in controlling corporate management. These fund managers can make their decisions without conferring with the individuals who own the stocks held by the funds. Institutional investors respond that they have the resources to consult with the best minds in the country and to find the best business managers in the country, if needed.

Thus, in the 1990s a major shift occurred in business governance as the pendulum began to swing away from the concept that corporate managers hold their powers in trust for the balanced benefit of stakeholders to the concept that the powers are held in trust only to maximize profits. Institutional investors, as they marshall their power to make boards and corporate executives more accountable to shareholders, will benefit individual as well as institutional shareholders. Major pension funds already have forced several corporations to take the power of nominating future directors away from corporate CEOs and place it in the hands of outside (nonemployee) directors.

Although not in place yet, the following changes are possibly—in some cases likely—to be adopted over time as the large pension funds and other institutional investors assert their voting power:

Professional Directors

As institutional investors seek to improve investment performance, they will recruit full-time professional directors, professionals who will be independent of the management but accountable to shareholders. A full-time director might serve on five or more major corporate boards, review strategic plans, debate policies, and monitor management to assure compliance. Full-time directors will be recruited from major accounting firms, business school faculties, successful management consulting firms, mid-career marketing and financial executive ranks, and so forth.

Stakeholder Directors

Many corporations already have outside directors representing minorities, women, and employees. Calls for "public directors" representing local communities, the public in general, and other interests are underway. Calls to elect directors representing the corporate customers surface periodically.

Separation of Chairmanship from CEO Position

A move is underway to reserve the board chairmanship to a full-time outside director and to relegate the senior corporate officer to the position of president and chief executive officer. The chairman's duties would relate to board leadership and strategic management. Allegiance would be to the board and corporate shareholders. The president would report to the entire board, not just to the chairman, and would be responsible for the day-to-day management of the corporation. Under this approach, the board, not the CEO, would prepare all annual reports and control all communications to shareholders. Also, outside directors would nominate and pick new CEOs, with counsel from the retiring CEO.

Restriction of Inside Directors

To strengthen shareholder governance, inside directors would be limited to the president (CEO), the chief operating officer (COO), and the chief financial officer (CFO). Another approach restricts

inside directorship to the CEO only, since all other officer expertise is on call at the will of the board.

Management theorist Peter F. Drucker believes that boards and corporate executives hold their powers in trust to "maximize the wealth-producing capacity of the enterprise" (Drucker, 1992, p. 32). He argues that this objective integrates short- and long-term results, business performance and the satisfactions of the stakeholder constituencies. It is possible that current trends in business governance will develop a new social contract between corporations and society as businesses strive to achieve Drucker's objective.

See also BUSINESS STRUCTURE: FORMS, IMPACTS; BUSINESS STRUCTURE: INDUSTRIAL POLICY; DEMOCRATIC PROCESS; GOVERNANCE; MANAGEMENT; SOCIAL DEMOCRACY.

BIBLIOGRAPHY

BERLE, ADOLF A., and MEANS, GARDINER C. *The Modern Corporation and Private Property*, rev. ed. New York: Harcourt, Brace & World, 1968.
CAYWOOD, CLARKE L., and EWING, RAYMOND P. *The Handbook of Communications in Corporate Restructuring and Takeovers*. Englewood Cliffs, NJ: Prentice Hall, 1992.
DRUCKER, PETER F. *Managing for the Future: The 1990s and Beyond*. New York: Truman Talley Books/Dutton, 1992.
EWING, RAYMOND P. *Managing the New Bottom Line: Issues Management for Senior Executives*. Homewood, IL: Dow Jones-Irwin, 1987.
KESTER, W. CARL. *Japanese Takeovers: The Global Contest for Corporate Control*. Boston: Harvard Business School Press, 1991.
RAPPAPORT, ALFRED. *Creating Shareholder Value: The New Standard for Business Performance*. New York: Free Press, 1986.

Raymond P. Ewing

Business Structure: Forms, Impacts

In a democratic society, all institutions exist at the sufferance of the public. As long as they enjoy the consent of the public, they will continue to exist. If that consent were to be withdrawn, no institution could survive. This is the social contract. It is a contract that one party, the public, can decide by itself to continue or discontinue.

It is clear, more so now than ever before, that the institution of business enjoys a high watermark of public consent. Following the virtual collapse of Marxist economics at the end of the 1980s, market-based economics reign supreme. Even in countries with little or no tradition of private enterprise, business is increasingly seen as the means to general prosperity and public well-being.

It would appear, therefore, that what some are calling "the coming golden age" for business may well come about. But keeping in mind the revocable nature of the social contract, consent has to be earned every day. In the context of rising public expectations, a heightened sense of entitlement, and growing competition, this would be a dangerous time for business to become complacent.

There are two broad categories of business structure—one is the legal entity, and the other is the operational form. Examples of the former are: the corporation, partnership, sole proprietorship, and so on. The second category is based on how the business organizes itself to perform its functions—what we call the organization chart. This includes the various departments that are set up (e.g., marketing, human resources, and the like) and their positions in the hierarchy.

Both categories are undergoing intense examination as business tries to discover how best to move into the future. The corporate form flowered in the nineteenth century, when businesses grew large and the need for capital exceeded the ability of owning individuals or families to provide. The corporate form, with its limits on individual liability, enabled the twentieth-century shift from owner-run businesses to management-run businesses.

However, that shift, from owners to managers, resulted in what many observers feel is a flaw, particularly in American business: an overwhelming emphasis on short-term profitability rather than long-term viability. In 1992, a private study group, the Council on Competitiveness, chaired by Professor Michael Porter of the Harvard Business School, said that changes intended to encourage a longer-term focus were urgently required if U.S. business was to remain competitive.

In addition, the limits on individual liability are seen as cushioning managers against accountability. As the public increasingly wants to hold leaders of all institutions accountable, this legal protection may not be in the best interests of society. Recent court decisions in the United States that allocate individual responsibility to corporate officers seem to indicate that a fundamental change is occurring in some legal aspects of incorporation.

Unincorporated businesses are those in which the company is, in effect, an extension of the individual owner or owners. Consequently, for most such forms of business there are no limits on liability. The increase in litigiousness means that this individual vulnerability is much greater than it used to be. Law firms, accounting firms, and other personal-service partnerships have become victims of what *The Wall Street Journal* has called "the perils of partnership" (Berton and Lublin, 1992). As a result of lawsuits and often huge liability judgments, many personal-service partnerships are shifting to the corporate form—a change that seems likely to continue as long as the liability and malpractice suit trend prevails. As one leader in the accounting field said, "The partnership may go the way of the dodo." However, critics of the shift say that individual liability is necessary because it enhances client confidence in the integrity of professional service.

The sole proprietorship, the legal form for most small businesses, seems likely to be the one form of business booming in coming years. The restructuring that occurred in large businesses in recent years resulted in the elimination of many managerial positions. Many of the people whose jobs were eliminated went into business for themselves, most often as sole proprietors. In response to this development, governments in many countries are increasingly encouraging the formation of such small businesses.

It is in the second category of business structure, functional structure, that the most profound changes are occurring. These changes will create business organizations vastly different from those we have known in the past.

The restructuring mentioned earlier may prove to be as revolutionary in its results as was the onset of mass production. It represents a shift from structure to function—that is, concern about providing a product or service profitably and effectively supersedes concern about the structure out of which that product or service comes. The past emphasis on structure meant that *efficiency* was the paramount objective. The present and future emphasis on process shifts the focus to *effectiveness*. The difference, as someone once said, is that efficiency means doing things right, while effectiveness means doing the right things.

Two major trends will continue to contribute to and accelerate this development. One is the extraordinary impact of communications and information technologies. American business spent almost $1 trillion on these technologies during the 1980s. In the years ahead, that immense investment will pay off in greatly increased productivity. That increase will come largely from doing more things better, with fewer people—particularly with fewer highly paid people.

One way this will be manifested is in what has been called the "framework organization" (Brown and Weller, 1984). Large companies will operate with a permanent cadre whose skill is in knowing what each particular venture will require and how to meet those requirements. They will know how to get the job done rather than how to do it. They will add people or ally with other organizations to get a particular job done, and they will disengage when that job is done.

The second driving force is competition. In the new world economic order, *competition* is the key word, and competitiveness is the key to national economic well-being. Intensified competition means that businesses have to be both more efficient and more effective to get and keep customers. One way to do that, obviously, is by keeping labor costs and overhead down.

These trends also contribute to another development that will be a characteristic of business in the future: the nomadic organization. Businesses whose primary assets are intellectual—that is, the minds of their people and the information they have—are not tied down to a place. They can easily (and profitably) move to be closer to their markets and/or cheaper labor or to respond to government pressures or incentives.

What seems increasingly likely is that the new business organization will be flexible rather than rigid, able to respond quickly to change, and pragmatic to the utmost.

See also BUSINESS GOVERNANCE; BUSINESS STRUCTURE: INDUSTRIAL POLICY; CAPITALISM; GLOBAL BUSINESS: DOMINANT ORGANIZATIONAL FORMS; MANAGEMENT.

BIBLIOGRAPHY

BERTON, LEE, and LUBLIN, JOAN S. "Partnership Structure Is Called in Question as Liability Risk Rises." *The Wall Street Journal*, June 10, 1992, pp. A1+.

BROWN, ARNOLD, and WELLER, EDITH. *Supermanaging.* New York: McGraw-Hill, 1984.

DAVIS, BOB. "U.S. Capitalism Needs Overhaul to Stay Abreast of Competitors, Report Warns." *The Wall Street Journal*, June 29, 1992, p. A2.

Arnold Brown

Business Structure: Industrial Policy

There are a variety of definitions for "industrial policy," but in its broadest form it can be defined as targeted government programs that redirect resources to maximize national productivity and/or the ability to compete internationally. In its more focused application, industrial policy usually entails a strategy of helping specific industries while at the same time phasing out low-priority industrial segments. More importantly, however, industrial policy supposedly requires *agreement* among government, industry, unions (if applicable), and financial institutions. In addition, in some manifestations, industrial policy consenses will be augmented by including representatives of national media in order to help ensure that the policy is "sold" to a country's citizenry.

While the term *industrial policy* has taken on a negative connotation in the United States during the 1980s, the practice of using government policy to strategically benefit particular industries has always been practiced. Every aspect of government action—taxation, defense spending, the management of currencies and exchange rates, the definition and enforcement of property rights, tariffs, depletion allowances, and so forth—helps or hinders, benefits or harms, one industry or another. Since the time of Ricardo, economic theory has argued that there is no neutral tax, that all forms of taxation distort market behavior in one way or another. The same may be argued for government policy.

What purports to be new in today's debate over industrial policy is the idea of *targeted* government programs. Advocates argue that there is a significant difference between past types of government policy and a formal industrial policy in that the industrial and competitive impacts in the past have generally been haphazard or even indirect consequences, and not a targeted goal. A formal industrial policy, it is argued, should select growth industries and develop programs to support them through direct government incentives.

This type of industrial policy, in one form or another, is practiced in Germany and Japan and in a number of newly industrializing countries. In Japan, the Ministry of International Trade and Industry (MITI) is the coordinating ministry for industrial policy. MITI selects high-tech industries based on various economic principles. Here, industrial policy is a strategy devised and agreed upon with a goal of facilitating growth or the phasing out of specific industrial segments. Often all that is needed is the publication of the official list of "sunrise" and "sunset" industries to start all sectors of the economy readjusting their priorities and objectives. While Japan tends to have a highly coordinated industry policy focus, other countries have opted to confine their policy to very specific enabling activities such as the U.S. space program.

Market dynamics are altering the world at such a rapid rate that the commanding economic industries of only a decade or two ago have now eroded, or have been totally transformed into almost unrecognizable organizations. In market after market, industrial deconstruction is going on at unprecedented speed. Entirely new industrial forces appear seemingly from nowhere. These changing markets are truly global in scope. Telling an export from an import is virtually meaningless, while the service industries are overwhelming manufactured goods in importance and volume. At the same time, corporations are finding it ever more difficult to calculate the impact and consequences of their own actions and are either operating on ever-shorter planning horizons, or are developing plans that appear robust over a multitude of alternative future scenarios. Their strategic focus has shifted from anticipating future risks and opportunities to developing the ability to take appropriate action whatever it might be, whenever it may be needed.

In today's dynamic competitive environment, the advocates of industrial policy favor actions that will support future growth industries; where these cannot be identified, they favor policies that will foster the emergence and expansion of creative innovation required to produce unspecified future growth industries. Thus, policy focus is shifting to support for the infrastructure of innovation, be it telecommunications, networks, university research programs, or accelerated resolution of industry standards.

The question, then, that needs to be answered is twofold: (1) should countries adopt industrial policies and (2) do industrial policies really work? The answer to the first question is relatively simple: All countries already have industrial policies in one form or another. The differences in how countries apply these policies, however, is not just cosmetic. On the one hand you have policies which "push" certain industries to achieve, for example, by picking winners and losers, as is the case in Japan. On the other hand, you have policies that "pull" new industries into the limelight. Most often this is brought about by government funding or new or improved technologies. Even in cases where governments are not actively funding new technologies, a type of industrial policy may emerge purely within the private sector (such as the Microelectronics and Computer Technology Corporation) where the government's role is the easing of regulations, rather than funding.

The answer to the second question—whether these policies really work—is more complex. For an industrial policy to work, the location, timing, and subject must all coincide. For example, contrast an industrial policy in Japan with one in the United States. In Japan, in recent years, industrial policy seemed to work because they interfaced well with the country's particular culture. MITI decides, based on a rational economic-based life cycle approach, which industries will be "sacrificed" for the good of the overall economy. Japan's approach reflects strong homogeneous social values whereby individual interests are sacrificed for the good of the nation. Conversely, in the United States, where powerful lobbyists represent the interests of specific groups or industries and individualism and entrepreneurial spirit are dominant characteristics, for a national, cohesive industrial policy even to be adopted let alone implemented, is highly problematic.

The issue of timing is also of critical importance. Industrial policies in Japan and Germany emerged after World War II when the rebuilding of entire nations was required. The economic necessity of rebuilding, coupled with a cultural imperative, allowed for targeting industrial sectors for government support and involvement. And, while this policy has worked well in the past, it remains to be seen if it will serve as well in the future. Careful assessment is complicated by the fact that the global marketplace, along with technology and diffusion rates, are changing so rapidly. In the future it may not seem wise to select a handful of industries based on a set of criteria forged from today's issues and hope that these are the industries that will continue to grow long term.

Finally, and most importantly, we have perhaps been asking the wrong question all along. If the definition of an industrial policy is "targeted government programs designed to redirect resources in a way that maximizes national productivity and/or the ability to compete internationally," then the question should not be which industries should be promoted or which technologies should we invest in. Rather, the key question is what are the *fundamental* characteristics which will allow us to maximize national productivity over the long run. When the question is asked this way, there is only one inescapable answer: a highly educated and healthy workforce. It is the investment in these two areas that will distinguish countries with a successful long-term industrial policy.

See also BUSINESS STRUCTURE: FORMS, IMPACTS; GLOBAL BUSINESS: DOMINANT ORGANIZA-

TIONAL FORMS; INTEGRATED PERFORMANCE SYSTEMS; INTERNATIONAL TRADE: REGULATION; INTERNATIONAL TRADE: SUSTAINING GROWTH; MARKETPLACE ECONOMICS; STRATEGIC PLANNING; WORKFORCE REDISTRIBUTION.

BIBLIOGRAPHY

PHILLIPS, K. P. "U.S. Industrial Policy: Inevitable and Ineffective." *Harvard Business Review* (July–August 1992): 104–112.

PORTER, M. E. *The Competitive Advantage of Nations.* London: Macmillan Press, 1990.

REICH, R. B. *The Work of Nations: Preparing Ourselves for the 21st Century Capitalism.* New York: Alfred Knopf, 1991.

THUROW, L. C. "Who Owns the Twenty-first Century?" *Sloan Management Review* (Spring 1992): 5–17.

Robert H. Smith

C

Campaigning, Political.

See POLITICAL CAMPAIGNING.

Canada

In addition to global developments affecting all countries, the outcomes of the following six situations will shape the future of Canada:

1. Conflict between French-speaking Quebec and the rest of Canada may lead the province to break away from the rest of the country and establish itself as a sovereign nation. At present Canada is 63 percent English-speaking and 25 percent French-speaking, the remainder having been raised to speak another language, most popularly Italian, Chinese, or German. If Quebec remains in Canada, French is expected to continue to lose ground. At least in the major cities, the number of people raised to speak neither French nor English is now as high as a third and rising. As in Belgium or Ireland, the main differences between the two primary linguistic groups are in language, culture, and politics rather than economics. Opinions differ on how well Quebec would do as an independent country. Its population and gross domestic product are similar to those of Sweden and Switzerland.

2. The North American Free Trade Initiative (NAFTA), which could lead to open economic borders between all the countries of the Americas, is likely to shift low-skill jobs out of Canada but should increase its exports. If, on the lines of the European model, it leads to political union, it will meet more resistance.

3. Conflict between recent and established immigrants is expected to continue. Almost all Canadians are immigrants or their descendants, but when immigration speeds up (as it did at the start of the 1990s) or when predominant immigrant origins shift quickly (as they did in the 1980s, from European to Asian, Indian, and Caribbean), intolerance rises.

4. Conflict between the aboriginal inhabitants, Indians and Inuits (Eskimos), and the rest of the population is likely to be resolved by giving native peoples a large degree of self-government and major land grants or the cash equivalent. There are about 800,000 people of aboriginal origin, or about 3 percent of the population.

5. The decentralization of government and the growth of regional autonomy and culture continue. There is some debate about how many common laws and practices are needed for Canada to remain a single nation.

6. Canada is learning to export services instead of goods. After centuries of making a living from the land, Canada's future depends on making a living by exporting services throughout the world. Only 20 percent of Canadian exports are services, as compared with 40 percent in the case of the United States and France, for example. Tourism,

banking, insurance, freight, computer software, movies, and TV are export sectors with growth potential.

Population and Demographics

Only four countries had major baby booms after World War II—Canada, the United States, Australia, and New Zealand—and Canada's was the largest in proportion to its population. In 1966, when the boom more or less ended, people born since 1946 were 42 percent of the population; in 1991, they were still 34 percent, and this group is likely to remain the largest slice of the population until at least 2015.

But like most industrialized countries, Canada is now experiencing fewer marriages, more divorce, smaller families. From 1970 to 1990, about 70 percent of the rise in population came from natural increase, the excess of births over deaths, and 30 percent came from immigration. From 1990 to 2010, immigration will bulk larger in population growth. With the birth rate declining and the aging postwar baby boomers' mortality rates rising, about 30 percent of population growth will come from natural increase and 70 percent from immigration.

Canada's population was younger than all but one of the other Group of Seven economic leaders in 1990 (the United States was the youngest, followed in order by Canada, France, Great Britain, Germany, Italy, and Japan), but over the next ten to thirty years will age faster than any of them. This is expected to create a major financial crunch for pension plans and medical care for the elderly.

Urbanization

Though Canada covers 3,800,000 square miles, 50 percent of the population lives in nine metropolises with an area of only 16,000 square miles, leaving the remaining 99.6 percent to the other half of the population. The population share of these nine metropolises is expected to increase to 70 percent by the year 2015.

Social Conditions

By American though not by European standards, Canada has a socialistic welfare net that includes government health insurance and generous unemployment insurance. In 1991 total government revenue (federal, provincial, and municipal) took a larger percentage of GNP than in Japan, the United States, or Great Britain, but a smaller percentage than in France, Germany, or Italy. The welfare state is widely popular and is likely to remain so for many years.

Economics

Canada and the United States are the first postindustrial economies in the world. In Canada, 67 percent of output and 72 percent of jobs in 1991 were in the production of services, from restaurant meals and religious services to air freight and engineering. By one calculation, a third of the national economy was delivered in the form of information—bank balances, teaching, phone calls, government statistics, etc. By 2025, according to one forecast, service production will rise to 73 percent of total output—39 percent in the form of information, 34 percent in other services—and service employment will account for 84 percent of all jobs.

Among the Group of Seven countries, the purchasing power of per-capita gross domestic product in Canada was second only to that in the United States for many years, but this is unlikely to remain true much longer. By the twenty-first century or sooner, Japan and Germany are expected to become, in personal terms, the world's richest countries.

Labor and Workforce

Once the fastest growing in the industrialized world, Canada's workforce is not expected to grow rapidly in the foreseeable future—perhaps from 13.8 million in 1991 to 16.3 million in 2010. However, as production shifts from goods to services and work therefore requires more brain than brawn, women workers will increase more quickly than men. A plausible forecast shows that by 2010, with nearly two-thirds of both men and women of working age (fifteen and over) in the labor force, women will for the first time outnumber men. Part-time workers were 16 percent of the total in 1991; by 2010 they will probably have at least 20 percent of the jobs.

Energy

Canada's energy needs are met mainly by oil and gas (69 percent); coal, hydroelectricity, and nuclear power fill the gaps. The country stands out among non-OPEC nations in having substantial reserves of both oil and gas: ten years of oil at current rates of use and twenty-six years of natural gas, which

TABLE 1. Growth Projections for Canada

Year	Population (Millions)	Median Age	Dependency Ratio*	*(In Constant 1990 US Dollars)* GDP (Billions)	Per capita GDP	Per capita Income
1990	26.5	33.3	47.8	482.5	18,100	15,900
2000	28.5	37.3	46.2	580.0	20,000	18,000
2010	30.2	40.1	46.7	750.0	25,000	22,000
2025	32.2	44.2	59.5	920.0	29,000	26,000

* Number of people aged 0–14 and 65 plus for every 100 aged 15–64.

enables it to export gas in significant quantities to the United States. Exploration will continue to expand these reserves for some years.

Education

In the mid-1980s, 44 percent of Canadians aged 20–24 were enrolled in higher education programs, compared with 57 percent in the United States and no more than 30 percent in Japan or any of the other Group of Seven countries. The proportion of young people enrolled in universities and community colleges was around 50 percent in 1991 and continues to increase, and one forecast suggests it will reach 70 percent by 2015. This quickly converts into educated workers. In 1991, over 50 percent of the workforce had some postsecondary education (more than 40 percent were university or college graduates), and this too should rise to 70 percent in 2015.

See also DEVELOPMENT: WESTERN PERSPECTIVE; FRANCE; LANGUAGE; UNITED KINGDOM; UNITED STATES.

BIBLIOGRAPHY

BARNEY, GERALD O. *Global 2000: Implications for Canada.* Toronto: Pergamon Press, 1981.

KETTLE, JOHN. *The Big Generation.* Toronto: McClelland & Stewart, 1980.

————. *Population Projections for Canada, 1986-2026.* Oshawa, Ontario: Futuresearch Publishing, 1989.

KEYFITZ, NATHAN, and FLIEGER, WILHELM. *World Population Growth and Aging: Demographic Trends in the Late Twentieth Century.* Chicago: University of Chicago Press, 1990.

Report of the Royal Commission on the Economic Union and Development Prospects for Canada. Toronto: University of Toronto Press, 1986.

"Review of Demography and Its Implications for Economic and Social Policy." In *Charting Canada's Future.* Ottawa: Supply and Services Canada, 1990.

VOYER, ROGER D., and MURPHY, MARK G. *Global 2000: Canada: A View of Canadian Economic Development Prospects, Resources, and the Environment.* Toronto: Pergamon Press, 1984.

John Kettle

Capital Formation

The days when banks were the only significant sources of investment capital are long gone. In the future, sources of investment capital are and will be diverse, various, nontraditional, innovative, dynamic, and international.

Industries around the world are constantly and continually restructuring, driven by the need to increase productivity and profitability, and thereby remain competitive. This requires massive capital needs: investment is necessary to fund the invention, discovery, innovation, and creation of new products, processes, designs, and materials (as well as the enhancement of known ones) that will drive future economic growth and wealth creation.

However, banks will still be the main sources of capital funding in the future. They are still the best and biggest reservoirs of capital and determiners of where investment capital is best utilized. In fact, banks are now flush with capital, after suffering a dearth of funds in the early 1990s. According to the Federal Deposit Insurance Corporation (FDIC), U.S. bank lending to industrial and commercial firms is more than $650 billion outstanding. This amount has grown substantially since the early 1990s and can continue to increase significantly without threatening the industry's strong capital/equity ratio.

The drawback is that banks are under enormous pressure from investors to earn a healthy return on their equity. Some observers fear that they will repeat past mistakes in a rush to deploy capital: frenzied lending into boom markets that later go bust (sovereign lending to developing countries in the 1970s, for example, or oil-producing and commercial properties in the 1980s). But with the financial deregulation that has allowed banks to branch into other businesses, interest from loans currently represents a smaller and declining proportion of bank profits. In addition, banks are now cognizant of the need to reduce their exposure to single customers, industries, and regions.

Firms in need of capital have many other options besides banks. Increasingly, large companies are completely bypassing commercial banks and directly tapping into the capital markets, finding individual, corporate, and fund investors who want to make their own investment decisions. There is also a host of new, innovative financial instruments for capital formation. The most famous of these are high-yield securities (also known as "junk bonds" to denote the high risk associated with large potential gain).

Junk bonds were created in the 1970s, when high inflation and low stock prices together made it extremely difficult to raise funds. (The more favorable tax treatment of debt over equity was also a major contributing factor.) Junk bonds filled an urgent need for financing that the regular capital market was not supplying through normal channels. In this respect they were just one in a long line of such financial innovations (even the first issues of industrial common and preferred shares of stock were considered radical and nearly worthless at the time). Contrary to popular perception, total returns on junk bonds, including all defaults, have been about the same as for higher-grade bonds. In fact, by capitalizing "less than creditworthy" companies, junk bonds made possible an explosion of innovation that propelled entire new technologies and industries (including cable television, cellular telephones, personal computers, software, and scores of others).

Indeed, the entire range of financial innovations introduced during the 1980s, including leveraged buyouts, junk bonds, mergers and acquisitions, etc., have acquired an undeserved bad reputation. Results are now in, and we can see that they were beneficial: lowering costs of capital formation, improving efficiency, and creating wealth. Was all this built on a mountain of debt? The answer is no. Total corporate debt service, at about 16 percent, is approximately the same level that prevailed in the mid-1970s. These and other innovations, which will all be growing sources of financing in the future, include second-tier lenders, sale-leasebacks, partial public offerings, credit-sensitive notes, securitization, and capital recovery.

Another permanent revolution that has come to capital formation is internationalization. As recently as 1984, financial markets remained essentially domestic. Since then, new telecommunications and information technologies—coupled with advances in financial theory, radical innovation in financial products, and a universal process of market deregulation—have transformed financial markets dramatically.

Market capitalization of the world's major stock exchanges grew from $1.7 trillion in 1978 to $10.6 trillion in 1993. Cross-border trading in corporate equities has grown from about $120 billion in 1979 to $1.3 trillion in 1992. The share of U.S. initial public offerings (IPOs) abroad increased from 1.4 percent in 1985 to 19.3 percent in 1992. The market in derivatives—which barely existed before 1980—grew to nearly $9 trillion by 1992, much of that in interest and currency swaps.

Thus, one in every five transactions in equity markets in the mid-1990s involves cross-border trading. Such investors are estimated to own 10 percent of world equities, a proportion that will rise to 15-20 percent by the end of the decade. Financial transactions with foreigners have grown by a factor of 10 or more for all major industrial economies since the early-1980s. But these developments pale in comparison to the explosion that has characterized foreign exchange markets in recent years. Current estimates cite a daily volume of more than $1.2 trillion, the equivalent of 5 percent of the world's total production of goods and services.

Venture capital has also become an important source of capital formation. After riding an up-and-down roller coaster during the 1980s, venture capital firms are again flush with funds, amassing billions of dollars yearly for investment in newer, smaller, innovative businesses with high growth potential. (Some of the most popular areas in the mid-1990s are biotechnology, computer software, media and communications, and medical devices.)

Today and in the future entrepreneurs will seek loans from private venture-capital partnerships; public venture capital funds; corporate venture capital funds; investment banks; SBICs and SSBICs (privately capitalized venture capital firms regulated by the U.S. Small Business Administration); state development agencies; clients, customers, and vendors, business incubators (private or public/private facilities that provide business development services to start-ups); and "angels," or individuals who invest in new ventures (every year about 250,000 angels pump $10 billion to $15 billion into 30,000 to 40,000 early-stage ventures).

Capital markets will expand and evolve to provide the great capital needs of future decades. New and innovative financial products and mechanisms will be devised. Financing vehicles of the future will be varied and complex, because the demand for capital in the future will be enormous and varied. Capital formation is the basis for investment, which is the basis for productivity, which is the basis for future economic growth, prosperity, and well-being.

See also CAPITALISM; DERIVATIVES; ECONOMIC CYCLES: MODELS AND SIMULATIONS; ECONOMICS; ENTREPRENEURSHIP; ESTATE AND FINANCIAL PLANNING; FINANCIAL INSTITUTIONS; INVESTMENTS; MARKETPLACE ECONOMICS; MONETARY SYSTEM; SAVINGS; WEALTH.

BIBLIOGRAPHY

"Coast-to-Coast Angels." *Inc.* (September 1993).
FISHER, ANNE B. "Raising Capital for a New Venture." *Fortune* (June 13, 1994).
FRANKEL, JEFFREY, ed. *The Internationalization of Equity Markets.* Chicago: University of Chicago Press, 1994.
"A Glut of Venture Capital?" *Fortune* (October 31, 1994).
"Seed Corn Is Back in Fashion." *Forbes* (February 27, 1995).
"Time for the Chop?" *The Economist* (February 25, 1995).
WOOLLEY, SUZANNE. "The Floodgates Inch Open." *Business Week* (1993 Enterprise Issue): 96–98.

Roger Selbert

Capitalism

At the end of the twentieth century, capitalism has evolved into a social system based primarily on individual rights, especially private property rights. Other societies, such as the former Soviet Union, China, and Castro's Cuba, share with capitalist countries the means of production, the industrial plants, the technologies of communications and transportation, and the other physical aspects of the modern industrial state. But what distinguishes a capitalist nation from a socialist, communist, or fascist nation is the extent to which property is privately owned and privately controlled.

There is, of course, a broad continuum from the more capitalistic countries—for example, the United States—to the more collectivist ones—for example, China. At the ends of the continuum the distinction is clear. Few have ever called the United States a communist or socialist society. No one has ever called the former Soviet Union, Castro's Cuba, or China a capitalist society. But in the middle of the continuum the distinctions can blur. Some European countries, while predominantly capitalistic, have major parts of their society under government control and ownership. On the other hand, a socialist country, such as India, can have significant private property rights.

The essence of economic capitalism is private property and private contracts, protected by the rule of law, including a strong criminal justice system. In a capitalist society, the economic role of government is minimized, taxes are kept reasonably low, state regulations are minor, and men and women operate freely in the marketplace. Other key elements of capitalism are a viable stock market, private ownership of the means of production and of the print and electronic media, and voluntary labor unions.

Capitalism is not new. Elements of it were present in ancient civilizations. But it was not until 1776, when Adam Smith in his seminal book *The Wealth of Nations* spelled out in comprehensive detail the theoretical underpinnings of capitalism, that it began to expand in influence. Adam Smith was one of the first to understand and identify what to many is an enduring mystery—how a complex society can and does operate successfully without constant control and regulation by government.

This "spontaneous order" of capitalism is its most powerful strength and its greatest potential weakness. Its strength derives from the natural inclination of men and women to produce and trade voluntarily and the fact that this natural activity often results in a prosperous society. Its weakness is that the complexity underlying this natural economic order is not generally understood, and the natural instinct of people is to attempt to control what they do not understand.

For the last 200 years or so, capitalism has had many competitors, particularly socialism and communism. These political-economic systems promised individual freedom, economic prosperity, a fair distribution of wealth, and personal security. After the Russian Revolution of 1917 competition among these systems largely settled into a two-sided struggle, epitomized on one side by the communist system of the Soviet Union and on the other by the capitalist system of the United States and Western Europe. That struggle metastasized into the Cold War in the late 1940s.

The dramatic internal collapse of the communist government of the Soviet Union in the late 1980s led swiftly to the freeing of Eastern Europe, as country after country discarded the communist model for the capitalist one. What fueled these changes was the clear, convincing evidence in virtually every communist nation that collectivism did not work very well.

In economic terms the contrast between collectivist and capitalist societies is sharp. In standard of living, distribution of income, and the environment, capitalist states are usually far superior to noncapitalist ones.

By no means is capitalism perfect. Whether in the United States, Japan, Britain, or the new Russia, a dynamic free economy sometimes may expand too rapidly, leading to recessions and even depressions. A free economy is oriented toward serving the needs and desires of individual citizens. Where people are free to succeed, they are also free to fail—and they sometimes do.

But the twentieth century has demonstrated, by way of what was perhaps the greatest social experiment in history, that while capitalism may not be the perfect political-economic system, so far it is the most efficacious one.

As the twentieth century closes, we are entering a new era where almost every country in the world has adopted some variant of the capitalist idea. As professor Peter L. Berger noted in his 1986 book *The Capitalist Revolution*, "Capitalism has become a global phenomenon . . . [it] has been one of the most dynamic forces in human history, transforming one society after another, and today it has become established as an international system determining the economic fate of most of mankind and, at least indirectly, its social, political and cultural fate, as well."

The changes in our political and economic thinking have been so profound that it is unlikely that we will see any significant reversals of these changes for decades. In the political and economic world, ideas, for better or worse, shape and drive people's actions. Those ideas are now set in the philosophical mold of capitalism. As these ideas unfold in terms of specific policy actions for different countries, the twenty-first century will most likely host a flowering of many variants of capitalism as nations add private property and the rule of law to their own traditions, customs, and environments.

This new developing capitalism is a powerful idea, but like all ideas, it is not necessarily permanent. Capitalism is an idea that will need constant renewal if its momentum is to continue beyond the early years of the twenty-first century.

See also COMMUNISM; DEMOCRACY; ENTREPRENEURSHIP; INFORMAL ECONOMY; MARKETPLACE ECONOMIES; POLITICAL ECONOMY; SOCIAL DEMOCRACY; SOCIALISM.

BIBLIOGRAPHY

BERGER, PETER L. *The Capitalist Revolution: Fifty Propositions about Prosperity, Equality, and Liberty.* New York: Basic Books, 1988.
FRIEDMAN, MILTON. *Capitalism and Freedom.* Chicago: University of Chicago Press, 1963.
FRIEDMAN, MILTON, and FRIEDMAN, ROSE. *Free to Choose.* New York: Harcourt Brace Jovanovich, 1980.
HAYEK, FRIEDRICH A. *Capitalism and the Historians.* Chicago: University of Chicago Press, 1963.
_____. *Road to Serfdom.* Chicago: University of Chicago Press, 1944, 1956.
SMITH, ADAM. *Wealth of Nations,* Modern Library edition. New York: Random House, 1993.
VON MISES, LUDWIG. *Human Action: A Treatise on Economics,* 3rd ed. Chicago: Contemporary Books, 1966.

Martin Anderson

CD-ROM.

See COMPUTERS: SOFTWARE; INTERACTIVE ENTERTAINMENT.

Central America.

See LATIN AMERICA.

Central Europe.

See EUROPE, CENTRAL AND EASTERN.

Change

Change was one of the two primary questions considered in the early days of social science. The first question addressed was how society achieved order (social stasis); the second was how that order changed over time (social dynamics). The subject of social change is the number, type, structure, culture, or behavior of people in groups.

Modern society places greater emphasis on change as an intrinsic characteristic. Ancient societies valued traditions and were generally suspicious of change. They viewed change as inconsequential or ephemeral in a world of permanent social arrangements. In contrast, no social or cultural fact is safe from the onslaught of change in modern society. News media chronicle the passage of change daily. Modern society has an ambivalent view of change. On the one hand there is the hope that change will bring a better world, but there is also a longing for the "good old days." Ancient societies had their good old days, or golden ages, but they were shrouded in legend and myth while our perspectives are largely based on the past one or two decades.

One difference between ancient and modern society is the speed of change. Alvin TOFFLER caught this difference in his book *Future Shock*, observing that everyone in the twentieth century experiences fundamental change in their lifetimes that redefines the basic premises of the world as it is known. With life expectancies double what they were a century ago and major changes happening more frequently, fundamental change often occurs within a generation. People born and socialized into one world-order also live and work in a completely different one before they die.

Forms of Change

Change comes in many forms. The simplest type of change is the discrete or discontinuous change that transforms everything. The Judaeo-Christian view of change includes two such times when God intervened in human history. Modern versions of discontinuous change involve the New Age beliefs that describe ongoing transformation.

Other forms of change are continuous. Most ancient societies believed decay was the fundamental form of change. They had observed the law of entropy at work positing that disorder in the universe always increases.

Other societies (such as the Hindus of India) see change as long cycles of endless recurrence. Cyclic theories form the basis of grand theories of history, such as those of Arnold Toynbee and Oswald SPENGLER. More modern cyclic concepts such as long-wave theories of Nicholai Kondratieff, Joseph SCHUMPETER, and others posit a natural period of fifty to sixty years in economic development. Each cycle is marked by characteristic types of innovation, capital investment, military conflicts and other social changes. Cyclic theories find recurring patterns in historical data and are used to forecast future change.

Beginning with the Enlightenment, change came to be seen as endless progress toward better states. Francis Bacon was the first champion of science as the key to progress. The writers of the French Enlightenment expanded Bacon's progressive theory of change. Marquis de Condorcet wrote *L'An 2200*, the first utopia set in the future. Herbert Spencer applied evolutionary theory as the mechanism of progressive change.

The modern version of the progressive theories is Alvin Toffler's concept of the information society. Toffler and others pointed out that the technological basis of society has shifted twice in human history—once with the introduction of agriculture and second with the use of machines and fossil fuels. Each change brought a significant increase in the material standard of living and a host of social changes. The third shift based on computers and electronic communication is creating a society in which information replaces material things as the primary economic asset.

Assumptions of Change

Each of these forms of change is produced by an internal or external mechanism or agent. The discrete theories often rely on outside intervention as the primary mechanism of change. Religious theorists believe that supernatural forces create the salvation events that are most significant. Other discrete theories of change see technological breakthroughs, psychological transformations or emergent paradigms as the primary force of change. Each of these interventions disrupts the continuous flow of human events.

Newer systems theories have focused on internal mechanisms of discrete change, commonly known as self-organizing systems. Ilya Prigogine pointed out how basic chemical systems can achieve a balance or rhythm under certain external conditions. René Thom, a French mathematician, popularized the concept of catastrophe, the sudden change of system behavior under extreme conditions. Sometimes catastrophes are bad, like the death of the system, but they can also be good in moving the system to higher levels. These ideas are now being tested using computer programs.

The decay theories rely on the force of entropy as their mechanism of change. Derived from the field of thermodynamics, entropy is the process by which ordered states decay to disordered states through a random process. Shuffling cards will probably never re-create the order of the cards as they came out of the box, coins are never as shiny, clothes are never as new, cars never run better than when they are newly made. Entropic theories of social change do not explain the ability of humans to create islands of order in the midst of increasing disorder. So society, a highly improbable arrangement of people and things, is organized amid increasing disorder to the physical environment, beginning with the burning up of the sun but also including the destruction of fossil energy sources, ecosystems and other species. Optimists view the future with unlimited potential for increasing order and sophistication of technology. Pessimists warn of potential limits and point to the possibility that the increasing entropy of the physical environment may someday overwhelm even the most technologically capable civilization. Entropic theories foretell the ultimate collapse of society.

The cyclic theories rely on feedback systems to create their cycles of change. Negative feedback governs a system, keeping its variables within limits. Certain systems dampen all change and eventually reach equilibrium. Other systems oscillate between two states, just as cyclic theories predict. The exact variables depend on the system under investigation. Some theories explain the peaks and troughs of capitalist change as the exploitation and then saturation of major markets. Theories of organizational development explain how some previously very successful companies became locked into old ways of doing business and are reluctant to try out or accept new approaches. Societies which are hardened by adversity and strive for excellence become less capable as affluence makes their lives easier. Each of these forms the basis for a system which repeatedly cycles through various states.

Modern progressive theories have relied on a number of mechanisms for continuous improvement. The first mechanism was rational planning. The Enlightenment theorists had an unbounded belief in the ability of human reason to understand and solve problems. That belief was later shattered by Marx's dialectical view of history and Freud's theories of the subconscious. Rational planning does create much social change, but our belief in its unbounded capability has definitely faded.

Another mechanism of change that appeared during the early industrial period was the dialectical theory of change. First enunciated by Hegel, the process was picked up by Karl Marx to describe the succession of primary social arrangements in human history. Ancient empires were marked by master-slave relations, the feudal periods by lord-serf relations and the industrial period by owner-

worker relations. Each relation, although an improvement over its predecessor, also created conditions that led to its destruction. Owners must put workers together in factories to maximize industrial productivity but in doing so they create the conditions for worker organizations and eventually revolutions. Marx's theories of industrial development are in disrepute today, not unrelated to the fall of communist societies, but his mechanism of dialectical change is still a viable theory to account for some social changes.

Biology supplied the guiding principles of other social theories of the nineteenth century. Two such theories emerged. Although both were termed evolutionary, the first set of theories is really developmental. Developmental change proceeds according to a prearranged plan or schedule. For example, humans grow from embryo to infant to adolescent to adult in a genetically programmed sequence. The simplest developmental theory of social change came from Auguste Comte, who posited three stages of human social evolution: the theological (where animistic and supernatural explanations were dominant), the metaphysical (where philosophical arguments reigned), and the positive (where science provided all explanations). The most successful developmental theory was from Herbert Spencer. He believed that societies evolved much like organisms did and that the most advanced societies were more fit for their environments than less advanced societies. Spencer's theories were used to justify all manner of oppression from colonialism to genetic explanations of social class. The developmental theories in general saw a staircase of increasing progress with modern industrial societies at the pinnacle.

Twentieth-century evolutionary theories returned to the purer form of evolution as originally proposed by Darwin. They pointed out that "fitness" was not an absolute standard, as Spencer and others believed, but rather was relative to the environment. Each species (or society) is fit for the environment it finds itself in. Thus the Kalahari bushmen are fit for African savannas just as Japan is fit for the global economy. This new interpretation took the value and directionality out of earlier developmental theories. Societies did evolve, but in no particular direction and for no particular reason. Evolutionists could not discount the tendency toward increasing complexity in modern society, but they insisted that such complexity was not necessarily good. It may just be an episode in the continuous meandering of human civilization. The question of whether human civilization (or any social change) is directed toward some final end state or whether it is a random walk for no particular reason marks the difference between these two fundamentally different interpretations of evolutionary development.

Combinations of assumptions about change are also possible and underlie some of the more modern theories of social change. One of those theories is called interrupted or punctuated equilibrium. This is a modification of traditional evolutionary theory. Darwin's theory of evolution was gradual or incremental. Each generation contributed to the change through minute, indistinguishable mutations. When geologists and biologists finally were able to examine the fossil record, however, they did not see smooth increments between successive generations. Rather they saw many generations that were identical interrupted by sharp points of change. Changed environmental conditions cause species to become extinct, opening the way for the dominance of another. This type of change may occur in social and economic organizations as well as in biological systems.

An emerging field adds another set of assumptions to the theories of social change. Called complexity theory, it is an alternative paradigm of systems behavior. Current systems theory has its roots in cybernetics and feedback as described above. The fundamental unit is the variable (pressure, temperature, population size, and so forth), a quantity that takes on a range of values. A changing variable induces changes in other variables in a domino-like fashion. Ultimately that effect returns to the originating variable, either inducing it to move further in the same direction (positive or reinforcing feedback) or to move in the direction of its initial value (negative or balancing feedback). Systems change through the effects of positive feedback yet remain stable through the effects of negative feedback.

Rather than being a system of variables, complexity theory conceives the system as a set of actors who behave according to simple rules established in their environment. Actors are independent, but come from cooperative or antagonistic relationships that give rise to mass behavior. The properties studied under traditional systems theory are emergent properties of the actions of these independent entities. In some systems, the conditions change, leading to a change in the behavior of the actors and the emergent properties they spawn. In other systems, the actors themselves learn or evolve to maximize their rewards in the environment. In most real systems, both processes occur simultaneously in a process termed *co-evolution*—the actors and their environment evolving together. Under this theory, change is the result of the mutual, continual adaptation of sets of actors with each other and their environment.

Systems of such actors (termed *cellular automata*) have been created in computer memories that act as laboratories for studying the process of social change. These actors "live" through millions of generations in a short time, evolving to sometimes advanced and complex systems of behavior. These systems demonstrate most of the forms of change described above. They can reach steady states, which may suddenly be transformed into a new system. They progress to higher forms of social organization, decay to lower forms, or endlessly cycle through alternative forms. They evolve but ultimately die.

Current Assumptions

Each of the assumptions of social change is used to form the basis of a major school of thought about the future.

Optimistic views of the future assume that the progress experienced in the industrial age will continue. Optimistic futurists include Herman KAHN, Alvin Toffler, John NAISBITT, and Julian Simon. They point to hundreds of years of continual economic growth and social development. They see no reason that human ingenuity will not continue to push the envelope of technological innovation further to solve Earth's environmental problems, provide food, shelter and employment for the billions of new people on the planet and even begin the serious colonization of outer space. They point to the as-yet unexploited potential of information technology and the biological technologies to increase economic growth and social development to unprecedented levels.

The pessimists nevertheless contend that success is in no way guaranteed. Pessimistic futurists include Lester Brown, Donella Meadows, Paul Ehrlich, and Dennis Meadows. They point out that progress is always bought with higher levels of entropy somewhere. Pessimists call for a form of society that creates no entropy on the planet itself—a sustainable society that uses land, energy and materials only in proportions that can be easily replaced. Barring that, they forecast an almost inevitable decline in standard of living as one or more critical resources diminish.

Cyclic theorists see a continual interplay between the positive and negative forces with neither permanently in place. The good times result from the successful implementation of new, powerful technologies like agriculture, fossil energy, and now telecommunications. Bad times are the transition periods between these eras when the old technology is fully exploited and the new one is not yet in place. Long-wave theorists explain our current economic difficulties as the effect of such a periodic shift. Leaving the energy-rich coal and petroleum economies of the past without having the complete information technologies of the future in place has created transition strains for businesses, workers and consumers alike. Likewise, the shift from agricultural to industrial societies elsewhere in the developing world has created even more massive dislocation, all of which however is temporary. A new information society, including all the countries of the world, will provide a return to prosperity. That prosperity, like all previous ones, is also temporary, however, eventually giving way to the transition preceding a new society, this time probably based on biological technologies.

The transformationalists harbor yet a fourth set of assumptions. They include Willis Harman, Robert Theobald, Marilyn Ferguson, Hazel Henderson, and Amitai Etzioni. They claim we are on the verge of one or more permanent, fundamental shifts in societal organization. These shifts will be the big news of the future. Some look to sustainable technologies of economic development, some to environmental collapse, some to psychological awakening, some to the reemergence of community. Whatever the source, they see another discrete jump to a completely different form of society.

Each of these theories forecasts a much different world of the future. Humans living in groups (families, small groups, organizations and societies) will be affected by such change. Some parts of the social landscape will remain the same because everything cannot change. Some continuity must exist. But those things that do are each foretold, depending on the assumptions one makes about the fundamental shape and mechanisms of change that we are experiencing.

See also AGENTS OF CHANGE; CHANGE, CULTURAL; CHANGE, OPTIMISTIC AND PESSIMISTIC PERSPECTIVES; CHANGE, PACE OF; CHANGE, SCIENTIFIC AND TECHNOLOGICAL; CONTINUITY AND DISCONTINUITY; EVOLUTION, SOCIAL; GLOBAL PARADOX; GLOBAL TURNING POINTS; INFORMATION SOCIETY; LAWS, EVOLUTION OF; PUBLIC POLICY CHANGE; SOCIAL CHANGE: UNITED STATES; TECHNOLOGICAL CHANGE; VALUES CHANGE.

BIBLIOGRAPHY

FERGUSON, MARILYN. *The Aquarian Conspiracy.* Los Angeles: Jeremy P. Tarcher, 1987.

GOLDSTEIN, JOSHUA. *Long Cycles: Prosperity and War in the Modern Age.* New Haven, CT: Yale University Press, 1988.

HARMAN, WILLIS. *Global Mind Change.* Indianapolis: Knowledge Systems, 1988.

HENDERSON, HAZEL. *Paradigms in Progress: Life Beyond Economics.* Indianapolis: Knowledge Systems, 1991.

MEADOWS, DONELLA H., MEADOWS, DENNIS L., and RANDERS, JORGEN. *Beyond the Limits: Confronting Global Collapse, Envisioning a Sustainable Future.* Post Mills, VT: Chelsea Green Publishing, 1992.

PETERSEN, JOHN L. *The Road to 2015: Profiles of the Future.* Corte Madera, CA: Waite Group Press, 1995.

THUROW, LESTER. *Head to Head: The Coming Economic Battle Among Japan, Europe and America.* New York: Morrow, 1992.

TOFFLER, ALVIN. *The Third Wave.* New York: Morrow, 1980.

Peter C. Bishop

Change, Cultural

Culture has assumed an exceptionally vital role in shaping the future. According to the cultural historian Christopher Dawson, culture is "an organized way of life which is based on common traditions and conditioned by a common environment."

The classical tradition defines culture as the search for life's highest expressions of truth and beauty. Beauty was said to be an aesthetic analogue for perfection and goodness, while ugliness was an analogue for derangement or evil. Historically, part of the function of culture has been to help the human soul discriminate between good and evil, between what is beautiful and what is ugly. Matthew Arnold described culture as "the study of perfection."

Some of the creative geniuses of culture have clearly supported such a belief. Dante expressed his purpose in writing *The Divine Comedy* as, "Make strong my tongue/That in its words may burn/One spark of all Thy Glory's light/For future generations to discern." J. S. Bach said his purpose in life was "to write well-ordered music to the glory of God."

Even eighteenth- or nineteenth-century America, while perhaps not manifesting a culture on the level of Dante and Bach, displayed a culture expressing the higher aspects of existence, as in the works of Hawthorne, Whitman, Emerson, Church,

Cole, and Innes. Europeans wrote volumes extolling Melville's *Moby Dick* as the American equivalent of Goethe's *Faust*. Nineteenth-century American culture was a culture of process and becoming; it portrayed the hope and promise of the possible.

And today we encounter the likes of *Pulp Fiction*, Serrano, and Mapplethorpe, or Madonna, Ice-T, and Michael Jackson. We see art such as abstract expressionism, which, in the words of Harold Rosenberg, seeks "liberation from value—political, aesthetic, world."

In essence, twentieth-century culture has been accepted as a capricious expression of any human instinct, no matter how base or psychotic, and regardless of its content or effect. It is a culture that acknowledges no hierarchy of values, no social or spiritual tradition; a culture that lives for the moment in a chaos of sensation. Such a culture no longer provides relevant answers to those everlasting questions of meaning and significance that confront all peoples throughout all ages.

Two thoughts may provide a clue to what is happening. First, let us reflect on Dawson's contention that culture is "based on common traditions and conditioned by a common environment."

Common traditions have been in the process of being shredded for the better part of this century. How we spend Sunday is a good example. Most civilizations throughout history have set aside a special time for renewal of the inner spiritual energies of life. In Western Christendom, that time was Sunday. Yet today, for most Americans, while Sunday may give relief from job pressures, it is just another day at the shopping mall, with scant spiritual refurbishment. Tradition has been sundered.

On the Fourth of July, a century ago, people would go to the town park and listen to a distinguished speaker orate for two or three hours on the significance of the Declaration of Independence and the Constitution. Today, the Fourth of July is good for a trip to the beach, and the vast majority of college graduates never read the two most important documents in America's history.

And as global television, computers, the Internet, faxes, cellular phones, and virtual reality increasingly link the world together as part of one intertwining electronic nervous system, tradition will continue to decrease its hold on individual emotions and loyalties, thus further affecting culture.

A second point to consider is the source of culture. Culture, whether sublime or profane, springs from the deepest recesses of the unconscious mind. It is a reflection of what is happening at the intuitive level of the human psyche. It is no use

blaming Hollywood for the wasteland of American television and movies. The fact is that what Hollywood produces somehow resonates at some deep level in the American subconscious. If it did not, people would not respond to or pay for it.

Whatever one thought of Bob Dylan singing "How does it feel/to be on your own/with no direction home/like a complete unknown/like a rolling stone?" in 1962, the fact is that Dylan's song reflected the pain, loneliness, and emptiness of a world without metaphysical anchors, a world increasingly inhabited by psychologically alienated Americans. Dylan was only the latest in a long line of twentieth-century artists and writers whose artistic efforts depicted disenchantment and disillusion with the American ideal in particular and with life in general.

If one were to try to pinpoint the starting point in America of such psychological alienation, it might actually have been Herman Melville and *Moby Dick*. *Moby Dick* is generally conceded to be the greatest product of the American literary mind. But when examined from a psychological viewpoint, *Moby Dick* takes on a different hue. Simply by starting the book with "Call me Ishmael," Melville presents us with the biblical figure of the rejected outcast, the alienated man. The opening paragraph of *Moby Dick* strikes the same note as almost all the classic examples of alienation and descent into the underworld, whether Homer's *The Odyssey*, Dante's *Divine Comedy*, or T. S. Eliot's "The Waste Land."

What we have been experiencing in the twentieth century is the breakup of the inner projections of images of spiritual and psychological wholeness. For some 1,800 years, Christianity served as the core spiritual and cultural expression of the inner subjective integrity of the Western world. But with the rise of scientific rationalism in the seventeenth century, and with the increasing emphasis on external, objective reality as opposed to an inner, intuitive reality, the Christian myth lost much of its power as the archetypal image of psychic totality.

With the erosion of the underlying archetype of Western psychological and spiritual integrity, other aspects of the unconscious mind have been activated. These other projections from the unconscious have fashioned most of twentieth-century American culture. Two of those projections are the Apocalypse, as exemplified by any number of horrific depictions of destruction, such as *Natural Born Killers*, and the *Second Coming*, as suggested by the motion picture *E.T.*

Understanding this process is critical to assessing what is happening to our culture. These issues go much deeper than "liberal" or "conservative." The issue is a transformation that is taking place at the deepest level of the unconscious mind, a shift that has been in process for well over two centuries, and expresses itself in a dramatically different style of culture. With the advent of modern means of communication and travel, this shift has gathered substantial momentum in the past nine decades.

If the universal themes of *The Odyssey* or *The Divine Comedy* or Milton's *Paradise Lost* or Eliot's poetry tell us anything, it is that a trip through the spiritual and psychological underworld of life is followed by rebirth and renewal. Thus it is that in the twenty-first century we may see the flowering of a new culture, something beyond anything expressed in America's past—poetry beyond MacLeish, literature beyond Fitzgerald, art beyond Pollack, music beyond anything produced in America in the past two centuries. For as rebirth and renewal come, they will bring with them new forms of culture that express the richest and deepest meanings of a new era of the human odyssey.

See also ARTS; CHANGE; CHANGE, EPOCHAL; CHANGE, SCIENTIFIC AND TECHNOLOGICAL; LITERATURE; MUSIC; VISUAL ARTS.

BIBLIOGRAPHY

BARZUN, JACQUES. *The Culture We Deserve*. Middletown, CT: Wesleyan University Press, 1989.

GASSET, JOSÉ, ORTEGA Y. *The Dehumanization of Art*. Princeton, NJ: Princeton University Press, 1968.

KROEBER, A. L. *Configurations of Culture Growth*. Berkeley, CA: University of California Press, 1969.

MALRAUX, ANDRÉ. *The Voices of Silence*. Princeton, NJ: Princeton University Press, 1978.

NISBET, ROBERT. *The Present Age*. New York: Harper & Row, 1988.

PANICHAS, GEORGE A. *The Reverent Discipline*. Knoxville, TN: University of Tennessee Press, 1974.

William Van Dusen Wishard

Change, Epochal

Americans are experiencing an epochal shift in society. Many of us do not even know it, although intuitively we may be aware of it. We feel a pervasive sense that life is out of control and no one is in charge. When the tectonic plates of life shift, everyone feels insecure, whether it's expressed or not. The old meanings about life no longer have the same authority. We are experiencing confusion about everything—about the economy, about education, values, sexual roles, the function of a family, about the source of authority, the role of the state, about the wellsprings of freedom, the existence of God; indeed, about the very meaning of life.

We Americans are in the midst of redefining who we are and what an "American" really is. The consequences of this redefinition go right to the core of life, affecting education, culture, and individual identity. The old perspectives—group identity, structured authority, progress as "more and more," happiness as the constant accumulation of gadgets, freedom as absence of restraint, progress in terms of technology rather than human aspirations—no longer explain life. They no longer work. So we must first find a new perspective, a new way of viewing everything—ourselves, our work, our institutions, our country.

It appears that we have come to the end of roughly a four-hundred-year period where science acted as the primary interpreter of what life is all about. This is causing a disjunction in life.

The technoeconomic realm is driven by the principle of rationality and efficiency. The political realm is theoretically driven by the principle of equality. The cultural realm is driven by unrestrained self-expression. All this leaves us groping for authority and legitimacy in the body politic, and for some transcendental belief in society at large.

For the past three hundred years, the main emphasis of Western development has been on technology and its requirements—power, motion, speed, quantification, precision, uniformity, regularity, control, standardization, and regimentation. This has been accelerated in the twentieth century by the outpouring of new technologies. What we have not realized is that technology does not simply augment existing modes of life. New technologies change the way people perceive reality. They alter our symbolic life. They create new definitions of old terms.

We assume that more technology will solve almost any problem. Clearly, technology is taking us into new realms that enhance and magnify human capabilities. While technology solves old problems, it always creates new ones, and the new ones are usually more complex than the problems solved. Technology, in and of itself, is not an expression of human purpose. It does not create any life-affirming values. It is an extension of means, not a definition of ends.

Today's human needs are overwhelmingly psychological and spiritual, not material or technological, which is why our historic interpretation of progress is largely irrelevant to our present condition. Only a framework of human purpose that gives direction to the use of technology will decide the question in favor of the human race. We must integrate the use of technology with some common affirmation of the underlying meanings that sustain human life and happiness.

The demise of many of the primary intellectual and political themes of the last two centuries has taken place partially because we have effectively reached the end of the Cartesian perspective. The Cartesian approach did more than break down scientific investigation into its discrete parts. It also separated the whole panorama of existence into segments that, by adherence to immutable laws, so it was believed, could be predicted and controlled. The aspects of reality that could not be reduced to mathematical certainty or be seen as the result of the blind operation of material forces were treated as mere subjective impressions of the human mind. Insofar as man himself was viewed as a by-product of a vast mechanical order, he was denied the link to any possible spiritual significance.

We have come to the end of this reductionist theme as a valid perspective of life. Now we are reintegrating the disparate divisions of life into a larger synthesis. We suddenly see that all things are interconnected—a view held in the West from Heraclitus in sixth-century B.C. Greece up to the time of Descartes. It becomes clear that we can only understand one phenomenon if we look at it in relationship to the totality of which it is a part, and that a complete understanding of reality must include subjective phenomena. This view is well understood in the scientific world, but its application to the social and political realms is only now coming into focus.

Thus we are seeing a shift in our understanding of nature—from solely quantitative relations that are explained by mathematical treatment, to a nature whose essence may be in some realm of reality beyond matter, some expression of reality that flows through the underlying connectivity of all life and events.

Modes of communication have historically determined the structure of cultures, of education, and even of thought and knowledge. So as our modes of communication shift, basic changes will inevitably take place in these other areas as well. The printed word emphasizes logic, sequence, exposition, detachment, and history. For example, television puts its emphasis on imagery, presentness, immediacy, and intimacy. Thus countless studies show that, as the influence of print wanes, the content of politics, religion, education, and anything else that comprises public business must change and be recast in terms that are suitable to television—which is to say that all subject matter must be recast in terms of entertainment and show business.

In education we must ask whether kids are being torn between two differing modes of knowledge transmission—print and electronic knowledge transmission. The 1950s produced the first TV generation, causing our children to be raised in a different context, with wider horizons at earlier ages than any prior generation. This change especially influences children and how they relate to time. For example, historically this has been represented by a circle, whether a sundial or a clock. Now we have the digitized watch, which gives a sense of moment, but not of the larger context in which the moment exists.

Children have always defined themselves by drawing contrasts with animals. Now, brought up with computers and computerized toys, some kids define themselves in relation to the computer. Adolescents are struggling to find their identity, not in relationship to their families or the world around them, but in relation to video games and computers.

The epochal changes raise questions about the basis of our political structure. What is the core of liberty, and how is it sustained? In a society where the primary value source (television) is collective, how does a child develop his or her individual sense of being, yet relate that being to some larger responsibility for the community? In an age of mobility and global television impressions, what can be found to help us realize a sense of roots and our unique position in both time and place? What does a student need to know when there is so much that can beknown? How does one gain self-understanding, self-control, and self-direction? What gives life its highest significance, and what saves it from meaninglessness?

Part of the cultural change is a change taking place within you and me. It is a psychological and spiritual change taking place deep within the psyche. It is in the realm of myth and symbol. Our whole understanding of who we are and what the human venture is all about will take a quantum leap forward. There is need for a sense of meaning that enables each of us to know who we are, why we are here, what we are rooted in, and what we are living for. "Know thyself" is more than just a happy aphorism. It is the precondition for the fulfilled personality. Such knowledge is at the very core of any human community—be it a family, a corporation, or a nation.

One of the great tasks of the twenty-first century will be to reconcile the extroverted tendency of the West with the introverted propensity of the East. Basically, we must find a new balance, a dynamic equilibrium between our inner and our outer life. Six thousand years of civilized life have taught us that human health and happiness depend on a certain outward expression of inner psychological wholeness, of a healthy balance between the ego and the larger self. Without such wholeness, however that may be expressed in different cultures, the personality and society disintegrate. Culture must assume again its earlier function—feeding the inner life, and encouraging psychological coherence, which is the foundation of any lasting social order.

To find such meaning and purpose, we must now give priority to the integrative elements in life—sense, wholeness, intuition, trust, communications, openness, and generosity of spirit. We must reinterpret the "why" of those ethical norms that the experience of civilized life has taught us are essential for psychological and social health and happiness.

We need to understand and develop the subjective side of life, the intuitive. We live in two worlds, the worlds of data and meaning. These two worlds must be linked together by the unity of the objective and the subjective.

Finally, we must learn to make the interconnections between people, between events, and between different categories of life, for interdependence is emerging as a dominant principle of the future.

See also AGENTS OF CHANGE; CHANGE; CHANGE, CULTURAL; CHANGE, PACE OF; CONTINUITY AND DISCONTINUITY; GLOBAL CONSCIOUSNESS; MIND: NEW MODES OF THINKING; MODERNISM AND POSTMODERNISM; POST–INFORMATION AGE; RELIGION, CHANGING BELIEFS; SOCIAL CHANGE; SOCIAL AND POLITICAL EVOLUTION; VALUES CHANGE.

BIBLIOGRAPHY

CAPRA, FRITJOF *The Turning Point.* New York: Simon & Schuster, 1982.
JUNG, C. G. *Civilization in Transition.* Vol. 10 of the *Collected Works.* Princeton, NJ: Princeton University Press, 1964.
SOROKIN, PITIRIM A. *The Crisis of Our Age.* New York: E. P. Dutton, 1941.
SPENGLER, OSWALD. *The Decline of the West.* New York: Alfred A. Knopf, 1932.
TARNAS, RICHARD. *The Passion of the Western Mind.* New York: Random House, 1991.
TOYNBEE, ARNOLD J. *A Study of History.* London: Oxford University Press, 1946.

William Van Dusen Wishard

Change: Optimistic and Pessimistic Perspectives

Human perspectives are tempered by optimism and pessimism. The optimistic outlook welcomes the opportunity to invent the future. It rejects the more pessimistic view of man as a captive of fate.

The Pessimistic Viewpoint

Peddlers of gloom and doom always have been around. Predictions of doomsday persist throughout history. The doomsayers, pessimists, and negativists include influential thinkers such as Jacques Ellul, Lewis Mumford, and Herbert Marcuse. Rousseau, Thoreau, and contemporaries like Paul Ehrlich, Jeremy Rifkin, Ralph Nader, and Barry Commoner hold forth in much the same manner. Doomsayers often play on fears of the uncertain and unknown to stir up angry and emotional responses. They champion their causes and crusades—back-to-nature movements, cultural dropping out, counterculture faddism, anti-establishment activism, and so forth. Premature in many of their conclusions, they often fail to estimate properly the capacity of the human will to alter circumstances and redirect actual outcomes.

Negative attitudes, including alienation, cynicism, disillusionment, helplessness, resignation, despair, passivity, and apathy are among the attitudes that usually creep into policy debates. Pessimism has a dark and foreboding cant to it.

Complaint and criticism seem to dominate our times. Despite the constant carping, the fact is that people live longer, work less, are healthier, have more leisure and recreation as well as better housing, clothes, and food. The list could go on. Virtually everywhere one looks, living conditions and the lot of human beings everywhere are better than they were. In fact, the average person today eats better and enjoys amenities far superior to those restricted to royalty not so long ago. Humans are relentless in their pursuit of something better.

Values, constantly evolving and ascending to new and higher planes, also are at the bottom of any such understanding. They define ideas that unleash the aspirations that eventually become the goals toward which society, as a whole, inevitably strives.

For all its shortcomings, criticism also has a positive side. Criticism tends to bare imperfections and shortcomings. By shedding light they set the stage for optimists to respond.

The Optimistic Viewpoint

The optimistic outlook is a positive one. Optimists are not disillusioned with runaway technologies, excessive economic growth, population explosions, entropy, or any of the other dreary disasters anticipated by doomsayers throughout history. What pessimists see as problems, optimists see as challenges to be overcome by conscious, deliberate, and well-planned effort.

Optimists regard alarms raised by doomsayers, pessimists, and negativists as wake-up calls. They find this discontent useful in alerting society to potential situations or shortcomings requiring attention and resolution.

Optimism is consistent with the rational tradition of Western intellectual history and the scientific method associated with ordering affairs in advanced industrialized nations. This upbeat view considers people in control of their destiny, instead of being its hapless captive. They perceive society as open to intelligent directions and management. Optimists share an abiding belief in the perfectibility of mankind. They view the future neither as inflexible and predetermined nor as unordered and chaotic.

The very size and complexity of activities, coupled with accelerating rates of change, prompt the need for more conscious direction. Impacts from far-reaching decisions have become so broad and pervasive that deliberate effort is required to contain negative effects and accentuate positive benefits.

Through a conscious, comprehensive, and careful scientific understanding of sociopolitical issue genesis and development, wiser alternatives can be selected. Anticipation of unfolding situations affords an opportunity to take steps to minimize, if not avoid, the sometimes protracted, overlapping, and always costly defense of the indefensible. Such an approach enables change—the key concept—to be accommodated with minimal disruption.

Action based on poor understanding of the forces that drive innumerable and unstructured events is likely to be ineffective. Merely muddling through—benevolent neglect, as some have described it—has become too erratic, too costly, and even too dangerous a course. Careful explication of our problems and reasoned analysis are needed now more than ever before. Management of massive modern, subtle, complex, invisible, and qualitative technologies require much more time and conscious attention. Planning, furthermore, is a necessary tool for getting things done. By anticipating problems, we are able to assess them, assign social priorities, and marshal resources to meet them. Planning provides the opportunity for ushering the desirable future into the present.

Policy makers are beginning to assume a new role as architects of destiny and are no longer willing to remain merely its passive and hapless captives. Many are expressing an interest with respect to a willed, rather than a fated future. No longer are they likely to remain victims of autonomous, directionless change. No longer willing to stand outside the process of change, they are asserting instead a desire to participate in it.

The question is not whether we can change the world, but what kind of a world we want. Fundamental change has come about only in recent times. It is not so much a change in capacity or in events as it is a change in outlook and attitude. There is a growing realization that we can manage change, not merely be managed by it.

See also AGENTS OF CHANGE; APOCALYPTIC FUTURE; CHANGE; CHANGE, CULTURAL; CHANGE, EPOCHAL; CONTINUITY AND DISCONTINUITY; DYSTOPIAS; LIFESTYLES, VALUE-ORIENTED; PUBLIC POLICY CHANGE; RELIGION, CHANGING BELIEFS; SOCIAL CHANGE: UNITED STATES; SOCIAL AND POLITICAL EVOLUTION; TECHNOLOGY AND SCIENCE; UTOPIAS.

BIBLIOGRAPHY

ARCHER, JULES. *The Extremists: Gadflies of American Society.* New York: Hawthorn Books, 1969.

CERF, CHRISTOPHER, and NAVASKY, VICTOR. *The Experts Speak: The Definitive Compendium of Authoritative Misinformation.* New York: Pantheon Books, 1984.

CETRON, MARVIN, and O'TOOLE, THOMAS. *Encounters with the Future: A Forecast of Life into the 21st Century.* New York: McGraw-Hill, 1982.

McCARRY, CHARLES. *Citizen Nader.* London: Jonathan Cape, 1972.

NAISBITT, JOHN. *Megatrends: Ten New Directions Transforming Our Lives.* New York: Warner Books, 1982.

THOMIS, MALCOLM I. *The Luddites: Machine-Breaking in Regency England.* New York: Schocken Books, 1970.

TOFFLER, ALVIN. *PowerShift: Knowledge, Wealth, and Violence at the Edge of the 21st Century.* New York: Bantam Books, 1990.

Graham T. T. Molitor

Change, Pace of

The pace of change varies by subject. Astronomically, the creation of the universe probably involves quadrillions of years. The age of the universe, it is generally thought, may be as much as 8–12 billion years, or possibly even as much as 19–20 billion years. Evolution of our sun's planetary system may have involved 4–5 billion years, and scientists predict that our planet will no longer support life as our sun dies out billions of years from now. Evolution of life-forms on Earth dates back at least 3–4 billion years.

The speed of change has increased dramatically over the years. Major change stemming from the discovery, development, and large-scale introduction of new scientific and social technologies has been steadily compressed into ever shorter periods of time. Leads and lags in application of new technologies that used to take thousands of years are accomplished in just a few years.

- 5,000 years elapsed from the time it was noted that the seed of a plant would grow and farming became widespread throughout Europe. (Grain cultivation dates back to 8500 B.C.)
- 3,500 years ago the extraction of iron from ore was discovered, but 1,000 years elapsed before this knowledge spread across the Western world.
- 1,600 years ago the first steam engine toy (aeolipile) was invented by Hero of Alexandria (c. 1000 A.D.), but not until nearly 800 years later, with the invention of Watt's steam engine (1788), did widespread use get underway.
- 112 years lapsed between the discovery of photography in 1727 and its general application by 1839 (although the principle of photography had been noted by Roger Bacon as early as 1267).
- 56 years were required to commercially capitalize on the telephone (1820–1876).
- 35 years were needed to successfully launch radio (1867–1902).
- 6 years were needed to develop the atom bomb (1939–1945).
- 3 years of work were required to introduce the integrated circuit (1958–1961).
- 2 years to launch solar batteries (mid-1960s).

Diffusion from development to commercial mass marketing in specific business sectors reveal three similar rapid-fire patterns. Take diagnostic imaging devices, for example: From the discovery of X-rays by Roentgen in 1895 (a discovery often credited with launching the Second Scientific Revolution), eighteen years lapsed before the first successful commercial application of the principle; five years for computer-aided tomography to be developed; and less than three years for magnetic resonance imaging. No matter where one looks, the pace has picked up.

Even something as apparently basic as the musical pitch of the note A is not immune to change. In fact, the pitch of A has been changed more than twenty times! Currently specified at 440 cycles per second (c.p.s.), historically, the frequency has ranged from 360 to 457 c.p.s. (360 c.p.s. in 1611; 422.5 in 1740; 421.6 in 1780; 431 in 1822; 435 in 1858; 457 in 1880; 440 in 1939). We contend with the relentless pace not only in science-based invention, but also in arbitrary standards established for the convenience of and by the whim of persons involved.

Increased Speed of Human Travel

The speed of human travel on foot remained at 3 miles per hour (m.p.h.) for thousands of years. Horse-drawn carriages and sailing ships averaged about 10 m.p.h. for about one hundred years. Automobiles accelerated the rate of travel to 50–100 m.p.h., and a rocket-powered three-wheel vehicle achieved a record speed of 739.666 m.p.h. (the fastest nonairborne speed to date). Steam-powered locomotives averaged 65 m.p.h. at the height of the age of steam, and steamboats averaged about 36 m.p.h. (The fastest modern rail train, the French TGV, has achieved a record speed of 320.2 m.p.h.).

Propeller aircraft ushered in a new pace of activity throughout the world—speeding travel up to speeds of 300–500 m.p.h.; with a world speed record of 575 m.p.h. (Mach 0.82—Mach speeds derive from Ernst Mach, an Austrian physicist who calculated the speed of sound at 766.98 m.p.h. at sea level and 15 degrees Centigrade; or about 659 m.p.h. at high altitudes). In earlier times, exceeding the speed of sound was thought to be impossible because the physical barrier, it was thought, could not be exceeded. Jet airliners boosted travel speed to more than 500 m.p.h., with the supersonic Concorde cruising at up to 1,450 m.p.h. (Mach 2.2), and Lockheed's SR-71A or "Blackbird," achieving a world record speed of 2,192.2 m.p.h. (Mach 3). Manned spaceships involve a further new frontier with speeds in excess of 20,000 m.p.h.

At first blush, and by everyday standards, it would seem that such record-shattering travel in excess of the speed of sound is far beyond most everybody's personal experience. Or is it?

Just to prove that all things are relative, consider the following. Asked if they have ever traveled at Mach 1, everyone—except travelers who can afford Concorde ticket prices and pilots of high-performance jet aircraft—will answer "no." The astounding fact is that each and every one of us is now traveling and always has traveled at speeds vastly in excess of Mach 1 because:

- Earth rotates on its axis at the equator at a speed of more than 1,000 m.p.h. and about 645 m.p.h. at the latitude of Washington, D.C.
- Earth revolves in orbit around our sun at 66,700 m.p.h.
- Earth's galaxy, the Milky Way, orbits around the center of its own galactic group once every 230 million years, traveling at a speed in excess of 492,000 m.p.h.
- Galaxies in a section of the universe measuring at least one billion light years across, which includes the Milky Way and its two satellite Magellanic Clouds, among others, are moving in the same direction at a speed of 1.56 million m.p.h.

And so it is on across the universe, with the most distant galaxies speeding away from us at nearly the speed of light, or 186,283 miles per second (in a vacuum). Although the debate is far from settled, some astronomers—rightly or wrongly—speculate that the "absolute" speed of light may be exceeded under the unique conditions of black holes by as much as sixfold! What's the cosmic rush? Where are we headed? The point made here is that perspective is largely relative.

Most everyone experiences a rapid pace of change every day, often in subjects or areas so mundane that they get scarcely a thought. The rapidity of our lives, for example, can be seen in things as familiar as supermarket shopping. Introduction of new food and household products during 1994 totaled 20,076 (15,006 foods and 5,070 nonfoods). The profusion that confronts grocery shoppers is truly formidable. Active universal-product-coded (UPC) products in grocery channels number 644,782 distinctive items! And an astounding 2,500,000 UPC-coded products are available in the distribution system. The sheer breadth of choice is awesome.

Human ingenuity is boundless, and this pace of change—new product introductions—can be expected to continue increasing. All of this is a far cry from the good old days when all phones were black, bathtubs white, checks green, and Henry Ford sold cars in any color—so long as it was black. Yesterday mustard came in one variety and one-size jar—not the hundreds of blends, variations, forms and colors, sizes and shapes of packages available today. Using the selfsame products, day in and day out, is fine for many. But for the more adventuresome—and that includes almost everybody—there is a cascade of choices and more opportunities for new experiences.

Today, most Americans are in a hurry to get things done and be on their harried way. Lifestyles cater to instant gratification, me-now, self-indulgence, living for the moment, narcissism, and self-centeredness. Instant everything is ingrained in the American experience. Americans insist upon push-button convenience, yet are too busy to be bothered with taking the time to learn how to sequentially program a video recorder.

Our ancestors waited two to three days for stagecoaches that often took weeks or months to reach final destinations. Modern Americans are frustrated if they miss one spin of a revolving door. The pony express has been displaced by airmail, which in turn is being supplanted by overnight mail, electronic mail, and instantaneous facsimile transmissions. We rely on instantaneous copies from trouble-free and push-button laser printers. Cooking from scratch, kitchen drudgery, and time-consuming household chores have been eased and simplified. The fifteen minutes required to prepare oatmeal in 1922 had been reduced to five minutes by 1939, and to a mere ten seconds during the 1980s in heat-and-serve containers (with no fuss-and-muss cleanup afterward). Motor oil changes that required a long ordeal at local service stations now take less than five minutes. One-hour dry cleaning has been available for years. One-hour photograph processing and prescription eyeglasses are more recent quick fixes.

We have even reduced the time to say or write the words describing things. We have developed a whole new language of short acronyms to speed things up—TV, VCR, CD, PC, MTV, HDTV, FAX, BMW, PCMCIA, and so on. Acronyms, however, do have excesses and limits. Long and windy titles abound in bureaucracies, especially in government and the military, where ADCOMSUBORDCOMPHIBSPAC stands for Administrative Command: Subordinate Command Amphibious Forces, Pacific Fleet. That one gives some pause for concern. There are others like it.

Politicians have degraded the style and content of political dialogue into a patter of vapid and simpleminded phrases, one-liners, sound bites, parodies, and symbols. Voter lack of attention or interest in what is being said (and by whom) and short attention spans explain this trend. While few voters could give a candidate's position on major foreign or domestic policy questions, they are apt to remember themes that captured recent elections: "Read my lips. No new taxes." Or "Where's the beef?" Or demeaning a candidate by referring to him as "Slick Willie." It's a sad day when political one-liners dominate the simplistic patter of presidential election campaigns, and the voters do not seem to want to take the time to see that the country is headed in the right direction.

See also AGENTS OF CHANGE; CHANGE; CHANGE, EPOCHAL; CHANGE, OPTIMISTIC AND PESSIMISTIC PERSPECTIVES; CHANGE, SCIENTIFIC AND TECHNOLOGICAL; CONTINUITY AND DISCONTINUITY; LAWS, EVOLUTION OF; PUBLIC POLICY CHANGE; RELIGION: CHANGING BELIEFS; SOCIAL CHANGE: UNITED STATES; SOCIAL AND POLITICAL EVOLUTION; TECHNOLOGICAL CHANGE; TECHNOLOGY DIFFUSION; TREND INDICATORS; VALUES CHANGE.

BIBLIOGRAPHY

GRUN, BERNARD. *The Timetables of History*. New York: Simon & Schuster, 1975.

KANE, JOSEPH NATHAN. *Famous First Facts: A Record of First Happenings, Discoveries and Inventions in the United States*. 3rd ed. Bronx, NY: H. W. Wilson, 1964.

TRAGER, JAMES. *The People's Chronology: A Year-by-Year Record of Human Events from Prehistory to the Present*. Revised ed. New York: Henry Holt, 1992.

Graham T. T. Molitor

Change, Scientific and Technological

Human knowledge has advanced to the point that almost anything that can be conceived can be achieved—at least within the ambit of natural laws as we understand them. In other words, technology is no longer a limiting factor. This new development ushers in a new era.

Science and technology should no longer be allowed to lead us wherever they might take us. Blind trust in technology will no longer suffice. New techniques are needed to anticipate and assess direct and indirect social, economic, and political consequences of technology. Unintended repercussions sometimes catastrophic in their sweep, need to be avoided or contained.

Haphazard technological development with smaller-scale consequences went largely unnoticed in developing countries prior to the Industrial Rev-

olution. As massive new technologies burgeoned, the need for deliberate direction and control emerged. Recognition became more widespread that some technologies could wreak horrendous destruction. Haphazard, unplanned, accidental, and negative impacts of technological and social policy no longer could be tolerated. Constraining second-order consequences and blunting potential adverse impacts before they did much damage became the focal point of these efforts. In short, society now strives toward deliberate direction of technology. Technology is no longer to be just harvested—it will have to be pruned, too.

The mere fact that a particular technology can be developed is not necessarily sufficient justification to proceed because risks of the new technological undertaking may be too great, costs, monetary as well as social, may be too high, ecological imbalances or improper conservation inherent in certain undertakings may prove disastrous, irresponsible development of finite resource may be unwise in the long run, the moral and ethical dilemmas involved with such development may be potentially catastrophic. Like so many other aspects of modern civilization, technology may be a force for good or for evil. It all depends on how the new capability is applied. Just five titanic technologies have transformed the world as we know it—the bomb, contraceptives, the computer, the rocketship, and genetic engineering.

The Nuclear Bomb

Nightmares of Hiroshima and Nagasaki, amplified by tens of thousands of remaining nuclear weapons, mean that the world still lives just moments on this side of oblivion. But at the same time the introduction of limitless and inexpensive energy from controlled nuclear fusion of hydrogen is a boon.

The Pill

The pill and a range of cheap, simple to use, and effective, birth-control methods have introduced realistic prospects for population stabilization. On the other hand, their adverse side effects cause major grief.

The Computer

Electronic data processing in all its myriad forms, and especially computers, are mainsprings of the ongoing information era. They provide a core resource akin to what steel and electric motors were to the Industrial Revolution. (Symbolic of this change is the $675 worth of steel in 1994 cars, compared with $782 of electronics.)

The Rocketship

Intercontinental ballistic missiles provide a "balance of terror." Space travel, on the other hand, is the ticket to tapping the wonders of the cosmos.

Genetic Engineering

Mapping the human genome portends human control over life itself with bright promise for eradicating disease and dysfunctions. The darker prospect is that of creating a Master Race. William Van Dusen Wishard asserts, "Biotechnology is raising ethical questions that no religious leader could have conceived. He goes on to call for technologies that enhance and assert the primacy of human qualities.

Innovation is the driving force in the economic history of advanced industrialized societies. Joseph SCHUMPETER noted that bursts of scientific invention occurred in previous historic periods of technological growth and progress, and contended that innovation itself was essentially responsible for the growth that often is attributed to other factors. Boom and bust cycles generated by new technologies destroying and replacing the old—"creative destruction," he termed it—appear to have occurred in a fifty-five-year cycle in recent history. Previous peaks of technology occurred in 1770, 1825, 1880, and 1935. That should place the current peak between 1980 and 2000. If true, this observation signals an explosive period of business growth over the next decade or so.

Where new breakthroughs are expected to occur, at least their general frontiers can be delineated. Only six key frontiers remain to be fully conquered:

The very hot and the very cold. The very hot includes plasma fusion, the fire of the stars, which is expected to be harnessed for commercial energy by 2020. The very cold involves supercool and absolute zero phenomena—cryogenics—which brightens prospects for superconductivity essential for supercomputers and energy conservation.

The very large and the very small. The very large entails fathoming far reaches of the galaxy and universe, searching out the origin of the beginning. The very small involves new capacities to measure parts per quadrillion and to plumb the inner elemental components of subatomic matter with a mind's-eye toward constructing perfect and new elements or their allotropes, then building matter onward from there. Biotechnologies and genetic engineering at the molecular level, mapping the human genome, and unravelling the mysteries of DNA also hold exciting promise. (If humans evolved from the Big Bang and possibly originated on Earth as organisms spawned electro-biochemically from the primordial soup millions of years ago, ponder the amazing feat of a mere chemical reaction actually conceiving its own origin!)

The very dense and the very diffuse. Changed states of matter and phenomena under enormous pressure or other variable physical parameters portend untold possibilities, as does unraveling the mystery of Black Holes, whose properties confound the basic natural laws we have constructed to explain reality. The very diffuse involves reaction of matter in super vacuum, including production of new materials in the near-perfect vacuum of outer space, or fully understanding the mysteries of the human psyche.

Throughout history, the expansion of scientific knowledge has always heralded social and cultural change. So, as scientific knowledge increases exponentially, we also can expect exponential social and cultural upheaval. Future economic growth will largely be dependent on staying in the forefront of new technologies.

What it all comes down to is this: the excesses that threaten society and environment increasingly need to be curbed. Up to this point, technology has been the determinant of social conditions. We are entering into a new era when just the opposite is likely to happen. Until now, man has been up against nature; from now on, he is likely to be up against his own nature as well.

Technology and its often awesome consequences assure that modern society will require more planning. We cannot wait for crises to bring issues into focus and expect to have all the time needed to respond at the last minute. Responses in such situations may be hasty and ill considered. In short, the future increasingly will be determined by forces that humans can control. Consciously forecasting such long-range impacts will require new responsibilities and keener sophistication on the part of public and private sector leaders.

See also CHANGE; POLITICAL CYCLES; SCIENCE ISSUES; SCIENTIFIC BREAKTHROUGHS; SOCIAL CHANGE: UNITED STATES; TECHNOLOGICAL CHANGE; TECHNOLOGICAL INNOVATION; TECHNOLOGY AND SCIENCE; TECHNOLOGY AND SOCIETY.

BIBLIOGRAPHY

FOSTER, RICHARD. *Innovation*. New York: Summit Books, 1986.

McHale, John. *The Future of the Future.* New York: George Brazille, 1969.

Nayak, P. Ranganath, and Ketteringham, John M. *Breakthroughs: How the Vision and Drive of Innovators in Sixteen Companies Created Commercial Breakthroughs That Swept the World.* New York: Rawson Associates, 1986.

Rogers, Everett M., and Shoemaker, F. Floyd. *Communication of Inventions: A Cross-Cultural Approach.* 2nd ed. New York: Free Press, 1971.

Vago, Steven. *Social Change.* New York: Holt, Rinehart, and Winston, 1980.

Graham T. T. Molitor

Chemicals, Fine

Fine chemicals are high-purity, high-value substances sold on specification with recognized effects in health care (22 percent), agriculture (4 percent), imaging applications (7 percent), electronics (15 percent), nutrition (5 percent), cosmetics (4 percent), and industrial applications (35 percent). Fine chemicals were $60 billion of a total $1 trillion worldwide chemical market in 1992. The fine chemical market is expected to reach $85 billion in 2000, with North America consuming one-third of that total. Fine chemicals are produced by organic and inorganic synthesis, fermentation, and extraction. Frequently, fine chemical manufacturers produce less than 10,000 kg per year of an entity, hold sole or semiexclusive rights to manufacture the substances, and supply a comparatively small number of customers, with only minimal support required after sales.

Triggers of Change

End-product usage of fine chemicals will increase rapidly, especially in electronics, agriculture, and health care. Increase in the demand for end-use products will be driven by greater automation, the need for more food in developing countries, and improved worldwide health care.

Consumers will demand environmentally safe products with less broad-scale and more tightly targeted effects. Increasingly stringent government regulations are expected in all fields. Claims for efficient environmentally sound products with fewer adverse effects will be the subject of new, more effectively enforced laws.

Technology will be developed to create new methods of manufacture that are more cost-effective, require less capital, and generate fewer undesirable by-products. These environmentally sound processes will involve biotechnology, chirality/stereospecificity (left- or right-handed molecular configurations that enhance the efficiency of end use), catalysis, and other techniques applied to both the production and refinement of end products.

Technologies will be favored that yield higher purity at lower cost and keener targeted efficacy. Closed-loop extractions, highly automated systems, and in-process, analytical self-adjusting controls will be important. Manufacturing and measurement technique improvements will change production of some specialty chemicals from an imprecise art to a more exact science.

Outcomes

There will be an increase in the cost of product and process research but more cooperation between government, university, and industrial laboratories. A wide variety of products for diverse uses will come from greater investments in tightly focused research. Potential intermediate manufacturers are expected to do less speculative development work than in the past.

The escalating cost of technical development and commercialization will cause increasing concentration in the industry through alliances and acquisitions. The market will also shift geographically to satisfy higher demand in Asia and Eastern Europe.

Sound manufacturing practices will be synchronized worldwide for both end products and intermediates. Larger manufacturers who can handle the required practices will survive and thrive. Highly potent products with keener specificity will require protection against cross-contamination, purity at point and time of use, and vendor certification. More burden will be placed on the producer regarding packaging, handling, and storage. Higher governmental and financial penalties for noncompliance, including legal liabilities and tort claims, are expected.

The use of sophisticated production controls will require increased operator skills. This will be accelerated by the availability of practical information technology. Some specialty chemicals will make the transition from performance requirements to a specifications basis.

Implications

There will be 10 to 20 percent fewer fine-chemical companies than the 10,000 currently existing firms. An increase in alliances between companies is also expected. The market will grow at 6 percent annually through 2005, but there will be high-growth niches with growth rates of 10 to 20 percent.

High expenditures for regulatory requirements will put downward pressure on research and plant expansions. To compensate for costly regulatory compliance, more operations are likely to move offshore, and there will be a tendency to outsource research and manufacturing. Cost-benefit and regulatory pressures will result in fewer new products. Those introduced will be more highly differentiated.

Agriculture, electronics, and medicinals will lead worldwide market growth. Offshore demand will increase at a greater rate in developing countries. Some specialty chemicals will make the transition to become fine chemicals, further increasing the overall size of the fine chemicals market. New investment will be needed to commercialize products made by innovative cost-benefit effective processes. This will also require additional worker training and new skills. In summary, the fine chemical market will remain important and profitable, and it will grow substantially faster than the GNP over the next decade.

See also CHEMISTRY; COSMETICS AND TOILETRIES; FOOD ADDITIVES; NUTRITION; PHARMACEUTICALS; PHOTOGRAPHY.

BIBLIOGRAPHY

Kline Guide to the Chemical Industry. Fairfield, NJ: C. H. Kline, 1990.

Stanford Research Institute. *International Specialty Chemicals.* Menlo Park, CA: Stanford Research Institute, 1993.

Fred DiMaria

Chemistry

Chemistry is the branch of natural science that investigates the composition of matter and how its atoms and molecules behave. The most remarkable "composition of matter" is the human being. Thousands of chemical reactions link themselves together within each of the 75 trillion minute cells in the human body: to support life, to digest food, to distribute energy, to produce growth, and to renew the body.

The future of chemistry, and therefore of the human race and the world, lies in better understanding of the behavior of atoms and molecules in different chemical structures: through controlled experiment and application of knowledge to chemical activity inside, on, and above the surface of our planet.

Anticipating the Future of Chemistry

There are three ways of anticipating the future of chemistry: extension of its basic theory, which leads to new experiments and new knowledge; research into problems that need solutions; and integration of theory, needs, and practice to solve problems.

Three leading trends are emerging: the intermingling of chemistry and physics in the behavior of the smallest units of electrons and nuclei; through examination of the most complex molecules such as DNA; and through understanding the behavior of complex interdependent systems—the environment. These all highlight molecular recognition: how do reacting atoms or molecules "know" which way to react? The simplest model is that of lock-and-key, but modified by the relative size, functionality, and energetics of the atoms involved.

The Experimental Route

The pioneering of a new chemical physics technique, supersonic jet laser beam spectroscopy, enabled new clusters of atoms to be detected, isolated, and described. Using carbon as the feed, a new form appeared, containing 60 carbon atoms arranged symmetrically in hexagons and pentagons to form a molecule resembling a soccer ball. Others have been discovered since. This new class of molecules is called *fullerenes,* or "buckyballs," after Buckminster FULLER and his geodesic domes. C60 occurs naturally in candle flames; C70 exists; fullerenes containing nitrogen and boron have been made; and fullerenes with water-soluble "tails" have shown activity against the AIDS virus. A new field of chemistry is opening up; much more will follow.

Superconductors that possess very low resistance to the flow of electricity afford another example of unexpected payoff from experimentation. Until recently, superconductors only functioned at temperatures close to absolute zero (–273° C). IBM, working in their Zurich, Switzerland, laboratories in 1986, announced the discovery of ceramic compositions that raised superconductors up to –118° C, and then to –23° C. Soon thereafter French researchers announced similar findings. Though difficult to fabricate, such materials can help reduce electronic transmission losses and electronic chip costs.

The rapid development of transistors was based on the ability to etch and build up ever more of them on a single wafer of silicon. It is now also possible to construct patterns by selective removal of atoms from a thin film surface. These new fields of chemistry arose from freshly discovered chemical structures in which specific atoms put in specific places achieve desired results.

The Theoretical Route

The number one killer of men and women is cancer. There is only one way to stop it—early detection. But present detection methods depend on the cancer becoming visible or palpable. Two potentially important new detection approaches are being explored. First, by comparing the infrared spectra of tissue samples with standards, the presence or absence of cancer can be verified much sooner. Second, the samples can be examined under a range of high pressures in a "diamond anvil," which enables changes in the chemical bonds within the cells to be identified. These techniques do two important things: they provide a simple, more accurate cancer test that can be automated for general use; and, by using the pressure tests, the transition from normal to cancerous tissue can be tracked at the molecular level. These could be major gains in what has until recently been a very difficult research field.

The Greatest Chemical Enigma

In the biochemical field the greatest enigma has been the composition of genomes, the key component of the cells of higher living organisms. The first results of the Human Genome Project have just been released as a partial computer listing of this composition, which researchers can access and exploit. This will undoubtedly accelerate research in this and related fields.

The Environment

The environment poses problems on an enormous scale. The present economic system reports only the results of business transactions but not their consequences, such as the accumulation of poisons and wastes in the environment which threaten future generations. Much of the public is aware, but skeptical, of these environmental dangers and of the need to deal with them: ozone loss; carbon dioxide warming of the Earth; toxic material buildup in the soil, in some atmospheres, in animals, fish, humans, or parts of the Earth.

Paul Hawken contrasts this threatening situation with the three ways that nature has coped over millions of years. Nature recycles waste as food for other species; nature runs on solar energy; nature thrives on diversity and perishes in the imbalance of an unnatural uniformity. Current economic policies are unfortunately directed toward the development of an economically based worldwide uniformity. Chemists will help to challenge this trend toward uniformity by demonstrating that diversity is the soundest future strategy to attain a sustainable Earth. Chemists will also need to make the chemical chains, cycles, and linkages in the environment easier to understand and thus help to reduce present dangers and future crises.

The Industrial Chemical Approach

The chemical industry forms another vital part of the chemical picture. After a successful shift into petrochemicals in the 1960s–1980s, the industry faces major geographical moves, to exploit cheaper natural gas in the Middle East and to meet rising demands in the Asia Pacific zone. But a global vision continues to elude international chemical companies. The obvious fact that Earth runs on the use of chemical energy has to be fully understood. Keener awareness and appreciation that all chemical energy is interlinked, whether it is in the form of ozone, carbon dioxide, gasoline, chloralkali, fertilizers, polyester, plastics, metals, colors, drugs, food, water, or pollution has to be achieved. Either those in the chemical industry today will come to grasp that these are all "one" and begin to act accordingly or, the forecast goes, the industry will be taken over by others who do!

The Pollution Case

The International Institute for Applied Systems Analysis study of the river Rhine in Europe revealed the sources, spread, and deposition of cadmium, lead, zinc, phosphorus, nitrogen, lindane, and polychlorinated biphenyls throughout the Rhine basin and into the North Sea. It showed how closely chemistry links people, agriculture, forestry, electricity, coal, water, industry and air, and what happens when we ignore this. The globe is "chemical," but we still try to treat pollution as something different.

Chemistry and Society

The underrating of the human and social aspects of society in the single-minded pursuit of economic gain is producing serious consequences. These reveal themselves in suspicion, violence, rape, murder, random killing, and ultimate degradation through ethnic and racial "cleansing." Behavior itself has a chemical basis. The primary field is that of neurotransmitters, the chemicals in the brain cells which translate "thought" into action. This field is beginning to be clarified as the separate and combined effects of serotonin, noradrenaline, dopamine, and other neurotransmitters become better understood. Better understanding of how these operate is one way of helping to reveal the causes of violence and of finding ways to dampen and eliminate them.

The Sustainability of Planet Earth

The greatest problem of all is the expansion of the human race at a rate faster than its base of natural resources, food, and energy. Much can be done and is being done to improve this situation—for example, in using solar and wind energy. But the conditions for a resilient, sustainable planet will have to be faced if succeeding generations of all living things are to coexist indefinitely into the far future. This is not just an exercise in numeration. It will involve fundamental changes in human, social, business, and political behavior that shift the focus from exploitative to sustainable ways of living. All of these changes will require the development of accurate chemical knowledge. The twenty-first century will be a busy time for chemists, chemical engineers, and chemistry!

Conclusion

Just as chemistry operates at all levels of human and natural behavior, so chemists and chemical engineers of every stripe will contribute to the transition from the discrete ways of the past toward the increasingly integrated ways and cooperation needed to enable the world to continue far into the future.

See also CHEMICALS, FINE; GENETICS; GLOBAL WARMING; NUCLEAR POWER; NUCLEAR POWER: CON; OZONE LAYER DEPLETION; PHYSICS; SCIENCE ISSUES; SUPERCONDUCTORS; TRANSURANIUM ELEMENTS.

BIBLIOGRAPHY

BEARDSLEY, TIM. "A War Not Won." *Scientific American* 270, no. 1 (January 1994): 130–138.

"The Cell: Its Secret Life." *The Economist* 329 (December 25, 1993–January 7, 1994): 109–113.

"Commercial Uses of Fullerenes." *C&EN* (November 22, 1993): 8–18.

HAWKEN, PAUL. *The Ecology of Commerce: A Declaration of Sustainability.* New York: Harper/Collins, 1993.

RESTAK, RICHARD. "Brain by Design: An Era of Molecular Engineering." *The Sciences* (September–October 1993): 27–33.

———. *Designer Brain.* New York: Bantam Books, 1994.

"Trends in Superconductivity." *Scientific American* 269, no. 12 (December 1993): 118–126.

W. H. Clive Simmonds

Child Abuse

The term *child abuse* is defined in various ways depending upon cultural setting. Basically, it involves physical or emotional maltreatment; institutional, educational, or medical neglect; and sexual harassment. At the 1991 World Summit on Children, heads of seventy-one nations committed themselves to improving the well-being of children by the year 2000. One future challenge confronting policy makers and professionals everywhere is the need to broaden public awareness and understanding of child abuse in order to stimulate prevention and treatment of the problem (Daro and McCurdy, 1992, p. 3).

Scope of the Policy Problem

All varieties of serious child abuse, including chronic paddling, spanking, beating, using children for sexual gratification, or depriving them of medical treatment and other basic necessities of life, cannot be tolerated in civilized societies. Protection of children from harm is an ethical imperative.

The U.S. Child Abuse Prevention and Treatment Act of 1974 attempted to establish uniform standards nationwide for the identification and management of child abuse cases. However, it was left to the states to determine investigative procedures and to define maltreatment. Consequently, only limited information on the scope of the child abuse problem was developed. In 1992, the National Committee for the Prevention of Child Abuse (NCPCA) collected data from all fifty states and the District of Columbia, enumerating institutional facilities and reports for the years from 1985 to 1992. NCPCA findings revealed that reported child neglect and abuse increased 50 percent over this seven-year period.

Kinds of Child Abuse and Neglect

Child abuse in the laws of all fifty states is defined broadly to cover harmful behavior impacting on a child's physical, emotional, social, and educational development and well-being. If more effective prevention and treatment services are to be provided, types of maltreatment need to be more carefully and comprehensively examined. In the United States during 1992, 1,261 children—about four children each day—died of neglect or abuse. Types of maltreatment reported in a recent year included physical abuse, 27 percent; sexual abuse, 17 percent; neglect, 45 percent; emotional maltreatment, 7 percent; and others, 8 percent. (The total percentages exceed 100 percent, because they were based on state averages.)

PHYSICAL ABUSE

Physical abuse is most generally defined as the nonaccidental injury of a child. American children today face greater risks because of rapid changes in society, altered family structure, warped values, and inadequate resources needed for nurturing. Corporal punishment is a questionable practice that in extreme forms is forbidden. Striking a child was still permitted in schools in 78 percent of the states as of 1988. Corporal punishment was still legal in some forms in most places in thirty-nine states, but it was outlawed in eleven others (as well as in other individual school districts). Three million times a year, teachers resort to corporal punishment; however, it may not be effective in preserving discipline because it treats symptoms and not underlying causes.

The United States lags behind much of the developed and developing world in prohibiting corporal punishment. Nations already prohibiting corporal punishment include the Netherlands, China, France, Spain, Austria, Denmark, Germany, the United Kingdom, and Russia.

Corporal punishment contradicts national policy dedicated to the elimination of child abuse. Eliminating corporal punishment by federally mandating appropriate disciplinary alternatives that require state and school-district compliance is one possible solution.

NECESSITY DEPRIVATION

Necessity deprivation includes denial of medical treatment because of religious convictions or because of economic inability, and also extends to include the failure to provide nourishment, clothing, shelter, or other essentials (Ingram, 1988, p. 41). In the United States, the care, custody, and nurturing of children are primarily the responsibility of parents. The doctrine of *parens patria*—the sovereign power of the state to protect people under disability, including children—limits parental autonomy to raise children as they desire. State authorities intervene when parents or other guardians fail to supply necessary medical care or to provide for a child's well-being.

The paramount criterion for state intervention is the best interest of the child. Constitutional protection of religious freedom prohibits states from interfering with religious decisions regarding medical care; nevertheless, numerous child neglect statutes impose criminal liability and provide for the removal of parental custody in life-threatening situations.

SEXUAL MALTREATMENT

The term *sexual abuse* denotes any sexually stimulating act that is inappropriate for a child's age level of development or role within the family (Brant and Tisza, 1977, p. 80). Sexual abuse occurs at all socioeconomic levels, though it is more prevalent among the poor. U.S. Department of Health and Human Services statistics reveal that 80 percent of the children sexually abused are girls. Three types of sexual behavior are identified as (1) noncontact behavior such as "sexy talk" and exposure of intimate body parts to the eyes of the victim by the perpetrator; (2) sexual contact that includes the touching of intimate body parts; (3) sexual exploitation, that is, child prostitution or the use of children in the creation of pornography.

Public awareness of child sexual abuse is increasing because of media attention, community education, and school programs. This increase probably does not reflect so much an increase in incidence as an increase in willingness to report such incidences. A recent NCPCA study sampling sixteen developed countries and fourteen developing countries indicated that 75 percent of the developed countries and 50 percent of the developing countries cited child sexual abuse as the type of maltreatment most time-consuming to professionals.

General population studies in various countries show the problem is widespread:

TABLE 1. Episodes of Sexual Abuse During Childhood

Country	Females	Males
United States	20.0%	7%
Canada	33.3%	——
Netherlands	33.3%	——
Finland	18.0%	——
Sweden	10.0%	3.3%

Source: *World Perspectives on Child Abuse*, 1992; Ronstrom, 1989, p. 125.

Evidence of incest can be found in early civilizations. Since the late 1970s, the reluctance to speak out on the subject has been lifted and the issues slowly have been uncovered, all of which has been featured in the media. Confused values, increased mobility, and society's emphasis on sexuality and performance are contributing factors to the high incidence of incest. Incest, or familial abuse, is now recognized as a national problem that deserves further investigation to devise effective legislation and strategic intervention.

Summary

Reports on child abuse continue to increase steadily, primed by growing economic stress, substance abuse, and an increased public awareness that fosters more frequent reporting of maltreatment. States continue to experience large caseload increases with little or no funding to deal with them. Despite this, states are making headway through innovative programs. Developments include home visiting services; mechanisms addressing the connection between substance abuse and child abuse; and state children's trust funds for prevention. The solution depends on implementing services, providing assistance to individual families, and improving overall living environments. Progress can be made through multifaceted approaches, including:

- A uniform system of common language, definitions, information, and technology worldwide.
- Laws that mandate the link between victim identification and family assistance.
- Increased federal appropriations to prevent and treat child neglect.
- More and better quality recidivism studies to learn more about treatment and punishment alternatives.
- Increased education of the judiciary.
- Comprehension that child abuse cannot be treated as an isolated social problem.
- Improvement of overall living environments.
- The elimination of corporal punishment.

See also ABORTION; CHILD CARE; CHILDREN, RIGHTS OF; CRIME RATES; FAMILY PROBLEMS; FAMILY VALUES.

BIBLIOGRAPHY

BRANT, R., and TISZA, V. "The Sexual Misused Child." *American Journal of Orthopsychiatry* (January 1977): 80–90.

DARO, D., and MCCURDY, K. *Current Trends in Child Abuse Reporting and Fatalities: The Results of the 1991 Annual Fifty-State Survey.* Chicago: National Committee for Prevention of Child Abuse, 1992.

INGRAM, JOHN DWIGHT. "State Interference with Religiously Motivated Decisions on Medical Treatment." *Dickinson Law Review* (Fall 1988): 41–66.

National Center on Child Abuse Prevention Research, National Committee on the Prevention of Child Abuse. *World Perspectives on Child Abuse: An International Resource Book.* Chicago: National Committee for the Prevention of Child Abuse, 1992.

RONSTROM, ANITHA. "Sweden's Children's Ombudsman: A Spokesperson for Children." *Child Welfare* 68 (March–April 1989): 123–128.

TZENG, OLIVER C. S., and JACOBSON, JAMIA JASPER, eds. *Sourcebook for Child Abuse and Neglect.* Springfield, IL: Charles C. Thomas Publishing, 1988.

Jan M. Grell

Child Care

A dramatic increase in mothers' participation in the labor force is currently in progress. In 1965, 25.3 percent of the mothers with children under six years old were in the labor force; in 1990, that figure reached 58 percent. Even more dramatic has been the rise in labor force participation for the mothers of infants and toddlers. In 1965, 21 percent were in the labor force; by 1990 that number had gone up to 54 percent. Likewise, 73 percent of mothers of children five to twelve years old were in the labor force in 1990. These increases have obviously created a greater demand for child care services, which is likely to accelerate further in the future.

Child Care Supply

Not surprisingly, the supply of child care has correspondingly increased. In 1990, there were 80,000 centers in the United States, serving between 4 and 5 million children. Between 1976 and 1990, the number of centers tripled and the number of children in centers quadrupled. Likewise, the number of family child care homes (care for children in the home of the provider) has increased, although the exact increase is difficult to discern because between 82 and 90 percent of family child care homes are not licensed or registered. It is estimated that there are 118,000 regulated homes serving 700,000 children. In addition, there are approximately 685,000 to 1.2 million family child care homes that are not licensed or registered, serving 3.4 million children (Kisker, Hofferth, Phillips, and Farquhar,

1991; Willer, Hofferth, Kisker, Divine-Hawkins, Farquhar, and Glanz, 1991).

There are indications, however, of developing gaps between supply and demand. On average, centers are filled to 88 percent capacity; between two-thirds and three-fourths of centers report having no vacancies. This problem is particularly acute for infants and toddlers (Kisker, Hofferth, Phillips, and Farquhar, 1991). For parents, the issue also seems to be a problem of locating quality care. In a nationally representative study of the U.S. workforce, 58 percent of parents looking for child care report finding no choices. The situation seems likely to exacerbate further in the years ahead.

Usage of Various Child Care Arrangements

Since 1970, the arrangements that families use to care for their children has shifted. Among families with employed mothers and preschool children, there has been a decrease in care by relatives. In 1965, 62 percent of these children under five were cared for by relatives. In 1990, that number dropped to 47 percent. Interestingly, this decrease does not represent less parental care. In 1965, 29 percent of preschool children with employed mothers were cared for by their own parents, while in 1990, that figure was 28 percent. Parents typically care for their own children while employed by working split shifts or taking their children to work. The shift in relative care, therefore, represents a sharp drop in the use of care by relatives other than parents—grandparents, aunts, and uncles. In 1965, 33 percent of the preschool children with employed mothers were cared for by their grandparents, aunts, and uncles, as compared with 19 percent in 1990.

Another notable trend is the increased use of formal child care arrangements, especially among families with children three years and older. In 1990, 14 percent of infants were in center care, 23 percent of toddlers (one- to two-year-olds) were. For children three to four years old, 43 percent were cared for in centers.

Among school-age children with employed mothers, 33 percent are cared for by their parents, 23 percent by other relatives, 3 percent by sitters, 7 percent by family child care providers, 14 percent by centers, 4 percent in self-care, and 15 percent in after-school lessons. This trend is likely to continue.

The Price of Child Care

While the demand and the supply of child care is increasing, the fees that parents pay are remaining virtually flat. Fifty-six percent of families with employed mothers and preschool children pay for child care. In 1975, parents paid $1.40 per hour for center care while in 1990, parents paid $1.67, representing an increase of $0.27 over fifteen years. For parents who used family child care, including licensed, registered, and unlicensed, the fees went from $1.29 an hour in 1975 to $1.35 in 1990, an increase of $0.06 per hour in the same fifteen years.

On average, the yearly 1990 price for all forms of care for preschool children with employed mothers was $3,150. This represents 10 percent of their family income. Low-income families, however, pay a much greater share of their family income for child care than higher-income families. Families earning less than $15,000 per year pay 23 percent while families earning $50,000 or more pay 6 percent.

Child Care Quality

There is a growing interest in the quality of child care because it has become apparent that for many children, child care is "education before school" (Galinsky and Friedman, 1993). The first national education goal states that "By the year 2000, all children will enter school ready to learn." If this country is serious about meeting this goal, then the quality of child care settings must be good. Three multisite observational studies of both center care and family child care conducted between 1988 and 1994 reveal a more dismal picture of the quality of child care. These studies indicate that 12–14 percent of the children are in child care arrangements that promote their growth and learning while 12–21 percent are in child care arrangements that are unsafe and harmful to their development. For infants and toddlers, the proportion in unsafe settings is even higher: 35–40 percent (Whitebook, Howes, and Phillips, 1990; Cost, Quality, and Child Outcomes Study Team, 1995).

These studies also uncovered the characteristics associated with higher-quality education and care. They found that children in center-based arrangements fare better emotionally, socially, and cognitively when they are in arrangements that have:

- a sufficient number of adults for each child—that is, high staff-to-child ratios
- smaller group sizes
- higher levels of staff education and specialized training
- low staff turnover and administrative stability
- higher levels of staff compensation.

Studies of center-based arrangements reveal that these characteristics of quality are interrelated. Furthermore, these studies find that quality in child care centers is affected by state regulations: children who live in states with high regulatory standards have higher-quality early care and education than children who live in states with low standards (Cost, Quality, and Child Outcomes Study Team, 1995; Whitebook et al., 1990). Not surprisingly, given the uneven quality of care, there are large variations in standards across the United States.

In family child care, children fare better emotionally and cognitively when their providers:

- are committed to taking care of children and are doing so from a sense that this work is important and it is what they want to be doing.
- seek out opportunities to learn about children's development and child care, have higher levels of education, and participate in family child care training.
- think ahead about what the children are going to do and plan experiences for them.
- seek out the company of others who are providing care and are more involved with other providers.
- are regulated.
- have slightly larger groups (three to six children) and slightly higher numbers of adults per child.
- charge higher rates, and follow standard business and safety practices.

As with center-based arrangements, studies find that these characteristics of quality go together. Providers who have one of these characteristics are likely to have others. In other words, providers who are *intentional* in their approach provide more sensitive and responsive education and care.

There are indications that the quality of care and early education is declining. Although the educational level of staff has improved, ratios and group sizes seem to be growing worse. Furthermore, a number of programs do not meet their own state standards for group size and staff-to-child ratios, especially in programs for infants and toddlers. Moreover, staff turnover is high (Kisker, Hofferth, Phillips, and Farquhar, 1991; Whitebook, Howes, and Phillips, 1990; Whitebook, Phillips and Howes, 1993).

Recent studies offer some hopeful news about quality. A study of family child care training revealed that the children were more likely to be securely attached to their providers following training, and that the quality of the caregiving en-

vironments had improved. In another study where the state had legislated higher staff-to-child ratios and higher educational requirements for staff, the changes in children's development is impressive: they are more securely attached, exhibit better cognitive and social development, are more proficient with language, and have fewer behavior problems (Howes, Smith, and Galinsky, 1994).

See also CHILD ABUSE; CHILDREN, LIVING ARRANGEMENTS; FAMILIES AND HOUSEHOLDS.

BIBLIOGRAPHY

Cost, Quality, and Child Outcomes Study Team. *Cost, Quality, and Child Outcomes in Child Care Centers*. Denver: Economics Department, University of Colorado at Denver, 1995.

GALINSKY, E., and FRIEDMAN, D. E. *Education Before School: Investing in Quality Child Care*. Commissioned by the Committee for Economic Development. New York: Scholastic, 1993.

HOWES, C.; SMITH, E.; and GALINSKY, E. *The Florida Child Care Improvement Study: Interim Report*. New York: Families and Work Institute, 1994.

KISKER, E. E.; HOFFERTH, S. L.; PHILLIPS, D. A.; and FARQUHAR, E. *A Profile of Child Care Settings, Early Education, and Care in 1990*. Vol. 1. Princeton, NJ: Mathematica Policy Research, 1991.

WHITEBOOK, M.; HOWES, C.; and PHILLIPS, D. A. *Who Cares? Child Care Teachers and the Quality of Care in America*. Final report of the Child Care Staffing Study. Oakland, CA: Child Care Employee Project, 1990.

WILLER, B., HOFFERTH, S. L.; KISKER, E. E.; DIVINE-HAWKINS, P.; FARQUHAR, E.; and GLANZ, F. B. *The Demand and Supply of Child Care in 1990*. Washington, DC: National Association for the Education of Young Children; U.S. Department of Health and Human Services, Administration on Children, Youth, and Families; U.S. Department of Education, Office of the Undersecretary, 1991.

Ellen Galinsky

Children, Living Arrangements

The living arrangements of the world's children reflect patterns of social change affecting all of us. Patterns displayed by Western nations may or may not be indicative of the world as a whole. Beyond this, available data stress children in families or alternative care. Almost no reliable data exist on the controversial status of abducted children, runaways, or children with homosexual or transracial parents. These childhood situations attract media attention disproportionate to their frequency. Many of the statistics staking out the parameters of these problems are waved about to influence policy or public opinion, and involve wishful thinking, or even outright fabrications.

The most significant of these change patterns are those relating to marriage. Substantial decreases in first marriage rates and increases in the likelihood of divorce have directly affected the nature of families with children. Other factors include falling mortality rates among married individuals and the connected decline in single-parent households plus the growth in the number of families headed by never-married mothers. Finally, the decline of U.S. female fertility rates from 3.7 children on average in 1955 to 2.0 children in 1992 may be considered an indicator of the declining importance of parenthood in modern life. What is clear, at least in Western countries, is that dramatic changes of a much broader nature are under way. Common to social trend foresight, the most reliable guess is that patterns that became evident in the 1980s will continue through to the end of the century. Concise descriptions of some important Western patterns follow.

In the United States fewer people are marrying, they are marrying later, those marrying are having fewer children, and more marriages are ending in divorce. All of these factors affect the living arrangements of children. The United States has the highest divorce rates in the world. It also suffers the most children living in poverty in any Western nation—20 percent (a 21 percent increase since 1970). In justification or explanation of these alarming statistics, it is worth cautioning that the numbers may be erroneous; comparisons may be overdrawn due to the simple fact that U.S. numbers may be more painstakingly accurate than data collected in other countries.

Children under the age of eighteen are considerably more likely to be living with only one parent today than two decades ago. In 1993, more than one in four children in the United States under eighteen lived with only one parent (27 percent), up from one in eight in 1970. The overwhelming majority of these children—87 percent—lived with their mother. An increasing percentage lived with their father—13 percent, up from 9 percent in 1970. A decade ago, a child in a one-parent family was almost twice as likely to be living with a divorced parent than a never-married parent. However, by 1993 the chances were almost even in the U.S.

In Great Britain, the change has not been as dramatic. In 1971, single mothers were only 16 percent of single-parent families, while the formerly married comprised 51 percent. By 1991, the single-mother category in Great Britain had doubled to 1 in 3. The formerly-married was steady at 52 percent of the total (the drop was in widowed parents, from 21 to 6 percent). In other industrialized countries, the single-mother category is around 20 percent and growing. Only Germany and Italy show averages under 10 percent (and some decline over the past decade).

One important phenomenon is the increase in children living within blended families with combinations of stepparents, step-siblings, and half-siblings. Altogether, this category accounted for 15 percent of all children in the U.S. in 1991.

Arrangements outside of any family connection accounted for 1 percent or less in the United States, and foster or adoptive parents for less than 2 percent. The 1993 U.S. total in foster care alone was only 440,110 out of 67.5 million children under the age of eighteen (0.65 percent). Although these numbers are proportionally small, they do represent a significant policy problem. The trend is what highlights the problem. The number of U.S. children in substitute care almost doubled in the past decade (up from 282,000 in 1982). The number of such children entering into new families through adoption dropped over the same period—from 24,000 annually in 1982 to only 17,000 in 1990. Finally, the ages of children in substitute or foster care have continued to drop, with a 12 percent increase in the number of children under five years of age occurring between 1982 and 1990.

There are clear foster-care differences between racial and ethnic groups. In the U.S., the percentages of white children in foster care dropped from 53 percent of the total in 1982 to 39 percent in 1990, while the percentages of African-American children rose from 34 percent in 1982 to 40 percent in 1990. The highest proportional increase was among Hispanic children—rising from 6 percent in 1982 to 12 percent in 1990—which is likely a reflection of evolving U.S. immigration patterns.

In 1993, one-parent families accounted for 21 percent of white children's situations, 32 percent of Hispanic children, and 57 percent of African-American children under eighteen years of age. In the case of children living with grandparents, the percentages were 4 percent of whites, 6 percent of Hispanics, and 12 percent of all African-American children.

What is becoming clear is that large numbers of children will experience a variety of family types over the course of their lives. However, research in the United Kingdom and the level of disagreement elsewhere indicates no single or straightforward relationship between family disruption, single parenthood, and outcomes for children, either positive or negative. There is no inevitable path down which any one child will travel.

In the United States, an estimated 330,000 children were homeless in 1993. Assumptions concerning associated declines in adequate education, nutrition, and health care are just that—educated assumptions. Certainly much of the homelessness associated with wars and famine throughout the world has negative consequences. According to the UN High Commission on Refugees, the tides of refugees across borders have grown tenfold from the mid-1970s—to a total of 23 million in 1993. As well, internally "displaced persons" within country borders totaled 26 million in 1993.

The challenge is to reach a clearer understanding of the effects these trends impose on the children affected. A serious debate has been raging among social scientists concerning the effects. What is the correct definition of a family? Is it bound by sexual ties, blood relation, shared space, shared resources, or all of the above? Is the "family" in decline or is it constructively evolving to meet new social conditions?

Some observers believe the modern family structure now fails to fulfill its traditional roles involving child socialization, economic cooperation, provision of affection and companionship, and the teaching of sexual mores. However, others believe that the trends described above represent movement toward flexibility and away from historically sexist and exploitive structures and situations. It is clear that ideology plays some part in how trends are characterized and how people react to them in a value-laden area such as family patterns.

Changes in Western family structure and the expanding work roles of women have increased the influence of substitute caregivers in modern children's lives. While some luminaries such as Margaret Mead have cogently argued that structured variety in caregiving patterns may in fact be a positive thing, by teaching coping skills and flexibility, it also is clear that the limitations of an inadequate institutional setting can restrain development and self-reliance.

The more interesting question is how much trends in children's living arrangements reflect changes in the underlying relationships between generations, especially as they relate to attitudes and communications. While these factors influence the tone and quality of social structures in the future, they also influence attitudes toward intergenerational commitments such as employee-employer–funded social security programs.

Debates surrounding these issues are compelling and broad-based because children's policy is such a tempting target for foresight-aided policy intervention. Observers point to past intervention failures and to a general shrinking of resources for such ill-defined programs as those aimed at providing for "our children's future." Still others note declining sympathy for children's issues generally in an era of self-absorption and social unrest. In defense of such programs and policies, proponents argue that if we could only understand the changes that families and children are undergoing and fathom their causes, perhaps "ideal" outcomes could be realized through changes in the family policies of nations. This may be part of the thinking behind the 1989 UN Convention of the Rights of the Child, which includes language on the continuity of child-family connections. Children's living arrangements and the causes giving rise to changing conditions are critical issues that demand our attention. The experiences of children indelibly shape their values and attitudes. In the clearest possible sense, "children are the future."

See also CHILD ABUSE; CHILD CARE; DIVORCE; ELDERLY, LIVING ARRANGEMENTS; FAMILY PATTERNS; FAMILY PROBLEMS; FAMILY VALUES; HOUSEHOLD COMPOSITION; MARRIAGE.

BIBLIOGRAPHY

ADAMSON, PETER, ed. *The Progress of Nations: 1994.* New York: UNICEF, 1994.

BEHRMAN, RICHARD, ed. *The Future of Children: Children and Divorce.* Los Altos, CA: Center of the Future of Children, 1994.

BURGHES, LOUIE. *Lone Parenthood and Family Disruption: The Outcomes for Children.* London: Family Policy Studies Centre, 1994.

CONODY, ANN. "Family Index," *Family Policy Bulletin,* May 1994. London: Family Policy Studies Centre, p. 16.

FURUKAWA, STACEY. *The Diverse Living Arrangements of Children: Summer 1991.* Washington, DC: U.S. Bureau of the Census, 1994.

HART, ROGER, *The Changing City of Childhood: Implications for Play and Learning.* New York: City College Workshop Center, 1986.

HEWLETT, SYLVIA. *Child Neglect in Rich Nations.* New York: United Nations Children's Fund, 1993.

KIRSCHTEN, DICK, "No Refuge," *National Journal* 26/37 (September 10, 1994): 2068.

POPENOE, DAVID, "American Family Decline, 1960–1990: A Review and Appraisal." *Journal of Marriage and the Family* (August 1993): 527.

SALUTER, ARLENE, *Marital Status and Living Arrangements: March 1993.* Washington, DC: Bureau of Census, 1994.

TATARA, TOSHIO, *Characteristics of Children in Substitute and Adoptive Care* Washington, DC: American Public Welfare Association, 1993.

Timothy Craig Mack

China

As is true of every nation, China's future is highly indeterminate, including a large number of relevant variables, most of which cannot be quantified. Trend projections are of some use: population statistics, arable land amounts, probable economic growth rates, and the like are mostly set for the next decade. Qualitative directions—type of government, ideological orientation, cultural life, and so on—can be assessed with some accuracy for the two-to-three-year future. Moreover, some measures that depend on a mixture of quantitative data and qualitative estimation can also be viewed with a degree of certainty in the period between three and ten years. These include degree of urbanization, social conditions, environmental questions, the energy and natural resource base, and education and health matters.

But the middle of the 1990s already was witnessing fundamental changes that make impossible any reasonably certain forecast of even basic aspects of life and policy in China. The most important was the end of rule, after nearly a half century, of the founding generation of communist rulers. Almost no one shared their ideological outlook yet no one equalled their personal authority. Consequently, China's political and ideological base could change enormously and rapidly in the coming years, with highly uncertain outcomes. Of nearly equal importance were the effects on society and polity of the vast economic changes since 1979.

Huge, annual economic growth rates, the engine of change for the entire post-Maoist period, could not continue. The major issue was whether a "soft landing," in terms of reduced but sustainable growth, acceptable inflation, and reconnecting the infrastructural base with the high-technology/foreign trade/international interdependence superstructure, was still possible. The alternative would be drastic, medium-term economic decline, with the concomitant dangers of mass starvation, ecological disaster, general civil disorder, and possibly even political breakdown.

At the end of the Deng Xiaoping-led decade and a half of economically driven reforms, the polity appeared stable. But that was deceptive. The near-term transition was from totalitarianism to corporate authoritarianism, therefore, with a concomitant distribution of power from center to region and locality and competition for leadership not only among those in the troika of ruling institutions (party, army, and government) but also political newcomers as private entrepeneurs, an urban middle class, and industrial workers. (The peasantry, comprising about 70 percent of the population of 1.2 billion, still lacked serious political representation.) Moreover, the party was no longer a pyramid with all power concentrated at the top, but an umbrella, spreading ever wider and thinner to contain within its bounds the swirl of politics among many organizations and factions that could eventually form the basis of a multiparty, proto-democratic polity. That was years away, however. Meanwhile, China's political options ranged from ragged party-centered authoritarianism to straight military rule (like Poland in the 1980s) to a gradual political coming apart at the seams between central and regional authorities to cautious democratization to full political disintegration.

China's economy was at once its shining light and its danger. Rates of growth for the 1978–1994 period approached 10 percent, despite a strong downturn in the late 1980s and early 1990s. With huge capital inflows (by the mid-1990s, nearly $50 billion per year), high (up to 40 percent) rates of domestic savings, gradual and successful market-directed economic reforms in agriculture, services, and industry, and an opening to the global economy that saw China become within a decade one of the globe's largest trading states ($235 billion of two-way trade in 1994), the economy grew from less than $350 billion to more than $1.5 trillion per annum (on the basis of purchasing-power parity calculations), with a per capita national income of about $1,100 to $1,200.

Coastal and southern areas grew richer much faster than northern and inland provinces, leaving geographic distribution of income highly skewed. But even the latter areas—especially the agriculturally productive countryside—more than doubled their per capita income. The Chinese people, for the first time in their history, had more than enough to eat. Total grain production continued to grow at about 4 percent per annum, to 450 million tons in 1994, and per capita production increased to about 2,700 calories per day (i.e., beyond the approximately 2,200 necessary to keep people alive and productive). Labor mobility was gradually restored, a private internal capital market was gradually created, technological modernization zoomed (although it did not fully make up for the stagnation of the 1958–1976 Maoist past), a legal basis to economic life was laid, and a massive ($500 billion over the next decade) infrastructure construction program was initiated. Most Chinese cities were in the midst of transformation, with high-rise buildings and construction cranes dominating every horizon, and traditional one-story structures rapidly disappearing beneath their shadows or being bulldozed out of existence. The Chinese consumer (now it was possible to speak of such a person) hankered to possess a television, a VCR, a motorcycle, and a washer-dryer, no longer interested in such "lower-order" items as watches, bicycles, and sewing machines.

Other areas closely connected to the economy also prospered greatly. China imported (whether by purchase or purloining) massive amounts of technology, and together with huge domestic efforts, became a technological leader in many areas. With another decade or two (presuming no major setbacks), China would be at the cutting edge in practically every area, from aircraft to computers to medicine to satellites. Chinese scientists, freed generally from ideological constraints and able to communicate with their brethren (especially those of the global Chinese diaspora) in foreign lands, quickly moved to the forefront. Numbers plus official encouragement plus wealth implied a China scientifically rivaling the United States for global primacy within a similar period. China was rapidly progressing through the communications revolution, unifying the nation as never before and bringing China in contact with places and institutions throughout the globe. The transportation system, long anachronistic, much too dependent on the railroad, with a much underdeveloped road net (to say nothing of the absence of the modern superhighway), and an air transport system fully unsuited to rapid economic growth, also began to modernize rapidly. While all these areas would take additional decades of intensive work, it became possible for the first time (at least under ideal circumstances) to move large numbers of people and goods over long distances within reasonable time.

Societal measures were equally encouraging. Average life span by 1994 reached 69 years. Reproduction rates declined swiftly to 2.07. The "life tree" of the Chinese population began to look more like that of the standard developed country, with a constricting base, relatively equal numbers of working age adults, and a growing population of the elderly. Educational attainments were increas-

ingly high: some 100 million Chinese (75 percent of the relevant age group) finished primary school, 30 million (30 percent) finished secondary school, and one million (about 2 percent) attended college. All these figures were significantly higher, year by year and group by group, than the years before the Deng-era reforms began in late 1978 and, of course, represented a sea change from the Cultural Revolution, when schools as a whole were closed for up to a decade. Literacy, at about 85 percent, was at developed-country levels. Literature and the arts, while hardly freed from party control, nonetheless experienced a flowering. Taiwan and Hong Kong served as domesticizing funnels for all kinds of foreign influences. Television, including access to international broadcasting, was available in every village throughout the land. Housing stock grew enormously, and the number of square meters per person in urban areas grew to near 7 (in 1991, up from near 4 in 1978), and above 18 (up from 8 in 1978) in rural areas. That still evidenced very crowded conditions, but was a major improvement from the Maoist quarter century.

Social mobility, in terms of class, wealth, and education, turned from socialist-commanded equality of poverty toward the high degree of differentiation characteristic of most developed societies. There was a resurgence of interest in religion in China, both in terms of undifferentiated asking of religious questions and of formal religions, especially Christianity and Islam. The movement toward a market economy caused many to think, at least, about the emergence (or reemergence, depending on appraisal of Chinese history) of a civil society in China. In sum, in comparison with the recent past, the quality of life had improved to the point where most people could pursue a variety of private interests relatively unhindered by party control or ideological interference, could concentrate on becoming wealthy if they so chose, and could look forward to a reasonably lengthy life enjoying some of the standard rewards.

But these gains came at very high cost and masked the potential for disaster. The list of ills was very long. Most important was the combination of near-universal corruption and high (in 1994, about 25 percent) inflation. That combination had brought down many a Chinese regime and, if not definitively checked, would by itself spell the end of communist rule and could bring on the chaos that all Chinese feared. But the remainder of the list was also long and equally serious: loosening controls on population growth, the product of declining party authority and inequities in the birth control policy (population totals were already several years ahead even of high-end projections); a massive internal migration problem (the "floating population," estimated at between 50 and 100 million people, moving into the cities without permanent employment); reemergence of economically based class divisions; lack of macro tools of indirect economic control coupled with increasing inability (or unwillingness) to use raw coercion; regional and local centers of economic and political power increasingly autonomous from central control; the center's declining ability to squeeze resources from lower levels; the difficult-to-overcome problem of dissolving the state-run industrial sector and overcoming the attendant "iron rice bowl" syndrome; massive infrastructure bottlenecks, especially in the rail net; power shortages (the country would have to install a new power plant every two weeks just to keep up with demand); rising crime; rural rebellions and urban worker strikes; governmental inability to fulfill grain purchase contracts; lack of a banking system and regulations suitable to a marketizing system; rampant speculation in real estate and stocks; a major capital flight problem (still hidden in 1994 but estimated at up to $40 billion); general decline in education levels and teacher numbers in the primary schools; probable unwillingness of the military to fire upon the people if they demonstrated again in massive numbers; enormous environmental and ecological problems that, if not addressed, would lead to absolute and long-term decline in food production and rise in disease incidence; and a spreading narcotics problem. This list could be lengthened practically at will. When added to the coming political transition and the impossibility of maintaining almost double-digit growth rates, these many troubles could spell disaster for China. To that—hardly a footnote—should be added the very uncertain international situation and the prospect of a much harder military and economic attitude toward the country by its neighbors and other important countries and regions, as China accelerated the process of projecting its power at ever-farther distances from its borders and into situations and disputes with which it previously had had no interest or in-volvement.

China's medium-long-term future (three to fifteen years) hinges domestically on three alternatives: continuation of economic reforms amid slow political evolution (so-called reformist authoritarian regime); conservative restoration and halting or reversal of economic reforms (a conservative repressive regime); and political decay, loss of economic control, and societal churning (a decaying regime). Internationally, three alternatives also appear: straight-line projection of the ad hoc, laissez-faire post–Cold War international situation; international systemic pulverization characteristic of massive security and economic instability; and international systemic integration on the basis of a great power-led solution to security challenges, reasonably high, all-around economic growth, and a general global movement toward democracy. China's future, a combination of these domestic and international alternatives, seems to consist of nine alternatives.

- A reformist-authoritarian Chinese regime combined with a straight-line projection of the mid-1990s international situation. This would provide China with at least a reasonable chance to develop fully economically and politically, as well as to become a global power.
- A reformist-authoritarian Chinese regime combined with international systemic pulverization would allow China for a while to modernize economically, but hold back democratization, expand its Asian purview to the point of dominating the region, but eventually spell disaster for the country as external markets would dry up, capital and technological flows would cease, and the regime would be gradually overcome by burgeoning domestic ills.
- A reformist-authoritarian China and international systemic integration providing the best chance for successful economic, social, and political modernization at least cost. A secure international atmosphere and a cooperative China would assure the continuation of reforms in all three spheres, high rates of growth, attack against the country's manifold problems, as well as a country threatening no one (except perhaps Taiwan), and acceptable to its neighbors and more distant powers.
- A conservative repressive regime associated with a straight-line projection of the mid-1990s international environment would find the world slowly but steadily becoming more unfriendly and constrictive. Feeling threatened from abroad and increasingly less able to grow economically from internal resources alone, China would enter a vicious circle: more GNP would go into the military and correspondingly less would be left for economic and social betterment. The regime would be isolated abroad and the party progressively isolated from the populace, and China would lose what chance it might have had to

modernize in the full sense of the word and become an accepted, equal partner in global affairs.

- A conservative repressive regime, if emergent along with a pulverized international system, would become an imperialist threat to all of Asia, taking Taiwan at will and making Southeast Asia into an exclusive sphere of influence. Such expansion, while probably successful for a while, would eventually spell the end of the communist regime, for the major powers would finally recover sufficiently to restore the status quo ante and perhaps even conduct highly destructive military operations against China—i.e., wage war. Confronting the need to marshal all resources for a fight for survival and faced with the inevitable internal political and economic decay, the regime would fall, and the country could descend into chaos.

- A conservative repressive regime facing international systemic integration would find life much harder much sooner. An imperialist China would be countered quickly with superior resources. The regime would thus be forced back upon itself after suffering several near-term defeats and squandering enormous resources girding for war. The party would thus confront an angry Chinese populace with nothing to show for their sacrifices. Decay and downfall would soon follow, and China would have to choose between rapid transition to democracy (with all the pitfalls associated with that movement) or, again, chaos, disunion, and possible dismemberment.

- A decaying regime linked with a straight-line extrapolation of the mid-1990s international situation would not be instantly disastrous for the regime, if only because the downward slope would be modulated by useful international economic and political influence. At least such a regime would have a chance to modify its policies in the direction pointed out by China's more successful neighbors. Indeed, it might seize the opportunity to turn around failed economic and political policies and move back to the reformist-authoritarian path, if not onto the road of full marketization and democratization, which is China's only long-term salvation.

- If a decaying regime is matched with international systemic pulverization, however, the danger quotient could rise dramatically. The question is which would decline more rapidly. In China's case, decay could proceed without much worry about international interference. Decay would not necessarily spell collapse; it could eventually lead to transformation through replacement of party rule by some more liberal form of polity, even though that be some version of authoritarianism and not necessarily democracy. But if the rate of downward drift at home were less than that internationally, China might be tempted to project its power abroad faster and farther, through Soviet-like "defensive imperialism." The outcome then would be, in all probability, systemic downfall, collision with the United States, and internal disaster. But comparative rates of decline being inherently difficult to evaluate, miscalculations on all sides would be easy to make and the danger of disaster would be high.

- The final combination would witness the coexistence of a decaying regime with international systemic integration. China would fall into crisis, and perhaps chaos, on its own. But the nation would at least address its internal problems without fear of untoward external involvement, thus providing some support for further marketization and movement toward democracy. Eventually, China—with strong international assistance—would recover sufficiently, become interdependent internationally, and return to the path of full, if postponed, modernization.

Among the nine basic possibilities, some are clearly "better" than others, in the sense of being beneficial for China and its neighbors. The reformist-authoritarian domestic alternative poses the least danger for the country, even when the international environment varies. The conservative repressive regime would be worst for China, over all three international alternatives. A decaying internal Chinese regime would fall somewhere in between. Two conclusions seem apparent. First, China's future is largely in its own hands. That was not the case before the Deng-led reform era began. The probability is that it will succeed in becoming fully modern, although the road will remain tortuous. Second, the outside world will continue to be an important influence over China, for better or worse. In that regard, if other peoples wish the Chinese well, they will take care to arrange their own affairs in such a manner as to maximize the resources available to deal with China, whether necessarily resistant to Chinese interference in their own activities or having at ready the massive level of assistance that might be required to save that country from itself.

An interesting regularity over the past half century shows up—with a massive upheaval occurring about once a decade. The revolution of 1949, the

Great Leap, the Cultural Revolution, the initiation of thoroughgoing modernization under Deng, and the Tiananmen Incident all were separated from each other by roughly ten years. The huge upsurge of economic development and the consequent sociopolitical changes of the 1990s actually began shortly after the Tiananmen Incident in 1989. That upsurge will falter after a time, and it is then that China will encounter its next great crisis. If the past pattern is any indication, that crisis could begin in the final year or two of the current millennium.

See also ASIA; CHINA: ETHNIC REAWAKENING; COMMUNISM.

BIBLIOGRAPHY

CHU, GODWIN C. *The Great Wall in Ruins: Communications and Cultural Change in China*. Albany, NY: State University of New York Press, 1993.
NAGEL, STUART S., and MILLS, MIRIAM K. *Public Policy in China*. Westport, CT: Greenwood Press, 1993.
OVERHOLT, WILLIAM H. *The Rise of China: How Economic Reform Is Creating a New Superpower*. New York: W. W. Norton, 1993.

Thomas W. Robinson

China: Ethnic Reawakening

China's future is generally thought to be as monolithic as its past, unaffected by world trends toward smaller, more ethnically defined nation-states. Officially, however, China is currently made up of 56 nationalities: one majority nationality, the Han, and 55 minority groups. The peoples identified as Han comprise 91 percent of the population from Beijing in the north to Canton in the south and include the Hakka, Fujianese, Cantonese, and other groups. These Han are thought to be united by a common history, culture, and written language; differences in language, dress, diet, and customs are regarded as minor and superficial. The rest of the population is divided into 55 official "minority" nationalities that are mostly concentrated along the borders, such as the Mongolians and Uygurs in the north and the Zhuang, Yi, and Bai in southern China near southeast Asia. Other groups, such as the Hui and Manchus, are scattered throughout the nation, and there are minorities in every province, region, and county. But even this recognition of diversity understates the divisions within the Chinese population, especially the wide variety of culturally and ethnically diverse groups within the majority Han population. These groups have recently begun to rediscover and reassert their different cultures, languages, and history. Yet, as the Chinese worry and debate over their own identity, policymakers in other nations still take the monolithic Han identity for granted.

The notion of a Han person (*Han ren*) dates back centuries and refers to descendants of the Han dynasty that flourished at about the same time as the Roman Empire. But the concept of Han nationality (*Han minzu*) is an entirely modern phenomenon that arose with the shift from the Chinese empire to the modern nation-state. For the Nationalists, the Han were seen as a unified group distinct from the "internal foreigners" within their borders—the Manchus, Tibetans, Mongols, and Hui—as well as the "external foreigners" on their frontiers, namely the Western and Japanese imperialists. The Communists later expanded the number of "peoples" from five to 56, but kept the idea of a unified Han group. The recognition of minorities, however, also helped the Communists' long-term goal of forging a united Chinese nation by solidifying the recognition of the Han as a unified "majority." The Communists incorporated the idea of Han unity into a Marxist ideology of progress with the Han in the forefront of development and civilization, the vanguard of the people's revolution. The more "backward" or "primitive" the minorities were, the more "advanced" and "civilized" the so-called Han seemed and the greater the need for a unified national identity.

Cultural diversity within the Han has not been admitted because of a deep (and well-founded) fear of the country breaking up into feuding, warlord-run kingdoms as happened in the 1910s and 1920s. China has historically been divided along north/south lines, into "Five Kingdoms" as often as it has been united. A strong, centralizing Chinese government (whether of foreign or internal origin) has often tried to impose ritualistic, linguistic, and political uniformity throughout its borders. The modern state has tried to unite its various peoples with transportation and communication networks and an extensive civil service. In recent years these efforts have continued through the controlled infusion of capitalistic investment and market manipulation. Yet even in the modern era, these integrative mechanisms have not produced cultural uniformity.

Although presented as a unified culture—an idea also accepted by many Western researchers—Han peoples differ in many ways, most obviously in their languages. The supposedly homogenous Han speak eight mutually unintelligible languages (Mandarin, Wu, Yue, Xiang, Hakka, Gan, Southern

Min, and Northern Min). Even these subgroups show marked linguistic and cultural diversity; in the Yue-language family, for example, Cantonese speakers are barely intelligible to Taishan speakers, and the Southern Min dialects of Quanzhou, Changzhou, and Xiamen are equally difficult to communicate across. Chinese linguist Y. R. Chao has shown that the mutual unintelligibility of, say, Cantonese and Mandarin is as great as that of Dutch and English, or French and Italian. Mandarin was imposed as the national language early in the twentieth century and has become the lingua franca, but like Swahili in Africa, it must often be learned in school and is rarely used in everyday life in many areas.

China's policy toward minorities involves official recognition, limited autonomy, and unofficial efforts at control. The official minorities hold an importance for China's long-term development that is disproportionate to their population. Although totaling only 8.04 percent of the population, they are concentrated in resource-rich areas spanning nearly 60 percent of the country's landmass, and exceed 90 percent of the population in countries and villages along many border areas of Xinjiang, Tibet, Inner Mongolia, and Yunnan. In recognition of the minorities' official status as well as their strategic importance, various levels of nominally autonomous administration were created—five regions, 31 prefectures, 96 counties (or, in Inner Mongolia and Manchuria, banners), and countless villages. Such "autonomous" areas do not have true political control although they may have increased local control over the administration of resources, taxes, birth planning, education, legal jurisdiction, and religious expression.

While the Han population grew 10 percent between 1982 and 1990, the minority population grew 35 percent overall—from 67 million to 91 million. The Manchus, a group long thought to have been assimilated into the Han majority, added three autonomous districts and increased their population by 128 percent from 4.3 to 9.8 million, while the population of the Gelao people in Guizhou shot up an incredible 714 percent in just eight years. Clearly these rates reflect more than a high birthrate; they also indicate "reclassification" as people redefine their nationality from Han to minority or from one minority to another. One scholar predicts that if the minority populations' growth rate continues, they will total 100 million in the year 2000 and 864 million in 2080.

Different groups within the so-called Han majority have also begun to rediscover, reinvent, and re-assert their ethnic differences. With the dramatic economic explosion in South China, southerners and others have begun to assert cultural and political differences. Rising self-awareness among the Cantonese is paralleled by the reassertion of identity among the Hakka, the southern Fujianese Min, the Swatow, and a host of other generally ignored peoples empowered in the mid-1990s by economic success and embittered by age-old restraints from the north. Interestingly, most of these southern groups traditionally regarded themselves not as Han but as Tang people, descendants of the great Tang dynasty (618–907 A.D.) and its southern bases. The 1990s may see the resurgence of Tang nationalism in southern China in opposition to northern Han nationalism.

China's economic vitality potential can fuel ethnic and linguistic division, rather than further integrating the country as most would suppose. As southern and coastal areas get richer, much of central, northern, and northwestern China is unlikely to keep up, increasing competition and contributing to age-old resentments across ethnic, linguistic, and cultural lines. Southern ethnic economic ties link wealthy Cantonese, Shanghainese, and Fujianese (also the majority people in Taiwan) more closely to their relatives abroad than to their political overlords in Beijing. Already provincial governments in Canton and elsewhere not only resist paying taxes to Beijing but also restrict the transshipment of goods coming from outside across provincial—often the same as cultural—lines.

Dislocations from rapid economic growth may also fuel ethnic divisions. Huge migrations of "floating populations," estimated to total more than 100 million nationally, are moving across China seeking employment in wealthier areas, often engendering stigmatized identities and stereotypical fears of the "outsiders" (*wai di ren*) within China. Crime, housing shortages, and lowered wages are attributed most to these people from Anhui, Hunan, or Gansu who are taking jobs from locals, complaints similar to those in West Germany about the influx of Easterners after reunification.

While ethnic separatism will never be a serious threat to a strong China, a China weakened by internal strife, inflation, uneven economic growth, or the struggle for succession after Deng's death could become further divided along cultural and linguistic lines. It was a southerner, Dr. Sun Yatsen, born and educated abroad, who led the revolution that ended China's last dynasty; and when that empire fell, competing warlords—often supported by foreign powers—fought for local turf occupied by culturally distinct peoples. And, the Taiping Rebellion that nearly brought down the Qing dynasty also had its origins in the southern border region of Guangxi among so-called marginal Yao and Hakka peoples. These events are remembered as the generally well hidden and overlooked "Others" within Chinese society begin to reassert their own identities in addition to the official nationalities. Recent moves to allow and even encourage the expression of cultural diversity, while preserving political unity, indicate a growing awareness of the need to accommodate cultural diversity. This will be important to watch as China incorporates Hong Kong, a city that operates on cultural and social assumptions very different from those of Beijing.

See also ASIA; CHINA; COMMUNISM; ETHNIC AND CULTURAL SEPARATISM.

BIBLIOGRAPHY

BANISTER, JUDITH. *China's Changing Population.* Stanford, CA: Stanford University Press, 1987.
BLAKE, C. FRED. *Ethnic Groups and Social Change in a Chinese Market Town.* Honolulu: University of Hawaii Press, 1981.
DESSAINT, ALAIN Y. *Minorities of Southwest China: Introduction to the Yi (Lolo) and Related Peoples.* New Haven: Human Relations Area Files Press, 1980.
GILL, LUANDA. *Portraits of China.* Honolulu: University of Hawaii Press, 1990.
HEBERER, THOMAS. *China and its National Minorities: Autonomy or Assimilation.* White Plains, NY: M. E. Sharpe, 1989.
SCHWARZ, HENRY G. *The Minorities of Northern China.* Bellingham, WA: Western Washington University, 1984.

Dru C. Gladney

Christianity

During the twentieth century, from 1900 to 1980, Christianity gradually lost ground to secularism, materialism, agnosticism, and atheism. Nevertheless, in 1994 it consisted of 1,905 million Christians professing to follow Jesus Christ as Son of God, Crucified Savior, and Risen Lord. These were found in 23,000 denominations in the world's 270 countries and territories, with 4.5 million full-time workers, 99,000 major institutions, and 500,000 minor institutions. Among the latter were 800 research centers that collectively had produced the mass of data on which the following trends and scenarios are based.

Immediate Prospects (During the 1990s)

This decade has witnessed a dramatic change in the fortunes for all branches of Christianity. After gradual decline from 1900 to 1970, the years 1980 to 1994 saw a radical reversal in three major geographical areas hostile to Christianity. From 1987 to 1990 the final collapse of all Eastern Europe's communist regimes took place. From 1988 to 1991 a similar collapse of the U.S.S.R. saw 30 million atheists profess allegiance to Christ and Christianity. As one illustration, in these three years the movie *Jesus* (two hours and five minutes), based on the Gospel of Luke, was seen by 85 percent of all Russians. And although mainland China remained rigidly communist, its Christian churches grew from 2 million members in 1970 to 79 million by 1984.

The decade of the 1990s has been marked by growing good relations and mutual respect between Christianity and the other great world religions, such as Islam, Hinduism, Buddhism, and Judaism. All participated in the 1993 World Parliament of Religions in Chicago, which produced strong affirmations on global ethics as well as hundreds of collaborative projects.

Short-Term Trends (to A.D. 2025)

From 1994 to 2025, Christians are likely to increase 52 percent to 3,061 million (36 percent of the world population). Some 2,280 million are expected to be practicing Christians, including 1,140 Pentecostals/Charismatics. Nearly 80 percent of them will be nonwhites in Third World countries, and 80 percent of all Christians will be urbanites. By 2025 the continent with the largest number of Christians is likely to be Africa, with 760 million. Other predictions for 2025: 9.0 million full-time workers; 2.5 billion general-purpose computers owned by Christians or churches. Projected annual income and expenditures in 2025 are as follows: personal income of all Christians, $26 trillion; church's income, $300 billion; ecclesiastical crime, $18 billion; foreign missions, $60 billion.

An indicator of the future vitality of Christianity can be seen in these projections concerning Christian literature by A.D. 2025. New commercially sold Christian book titles per year will rise from 23,400 in 1994 to 70,000 in 2025, while the number of Christian periodicals will rise from 28,000 to 100,000. Demand for Christian scriptures is likewise expected to mushroom by 2025, with projected annual sales or distribution of 180 million Bibles,

250 million New Testaments, and 4 billion Gospels in 5,000 major languages. They will be produced in many formats, including print, audio, disc, comics, Braille, sign-language, and interactive.

Christianity's expertise in modern communication techniques developed extensively from the 1950s on and will be further evident in future global broadcasting. Current projections indicate an increase from 2,860 Christian radio/TV stations, with 1,672 million monthly listeners/viewers across the world in 1994, to 10,000 stations, with 3,800 million regular listeners/viewers in 2025.

Long-Term Futures (After A.D. 2025)

Most Christian churches will continue to be heavily involved in the whole range of human and societal problems and issues. All denominations will increasingly mold their lifestyles and programs to the Bible's challenging high standards. Examination of the large number of detailed projections and miniscenarios (see CHRONOLOGY OF FUTURISM AND THE FUTURE in the appendix of this encyclopedia) indicates a reduction in conflict between science and religion.

The most likely scenario will be the rise in the number of Christians in A.D. 2200 to 4,398 millions, or 37.9 percent of the global population.

Although firmly anchored in the world, organized religions will continue to demonstrate their otherworldly aspect. In 1994, 78 percent of the world's populations—members of virtually all of the world's religions—expected the imminent return of the Christ, or (Islam) of the Mahdi, or (Buddhism) of Maitreya, or (Judaism) of the Messiah, and so on. Christians have always been futurists, expecting the Second Coming. For example, in the United States in 1993, 72 percent of people surveyed nationwide replied yes to the question "Do you believe Jesus Christ will return to earth one day?" In 1993, books in print in English included 2,000 serious titles dealing with Christian eschatology. Up to the 1900s, 80 percent of all serious or professional futurists were committed Christians, with many luminaries such as Isaac Newton (who compiled biblical commentaries on the Books of Daniel and Revelation) and mathematician John Napier (who invented logarithms to speed up his calculations on the number of the Beast in Revelation). By 1994 that percentage had dropped to 50 percent, but by 2025 it is likely to rise again somewhat to 60 percent.

See also BUDDHISM; GLOBAL CONSCIOUSNESS; HINDUISM; ISLAM; JUDAISM; NONRELIGIOUS BE- LIEFS; RELIGION, SPIRITUALITY, MORALITY; RELI- GION: CHANGING BELIEFS; RELIGION: INSTITU- TIONS AND PRACTICES; RELIGIONS, DECLINE OR RISE OF; RELIGIONS, STATISTICAL PROJECTIONS OF.

BIBLIOGRAPHY

BARRETT, DAVID. B. "Evolution of the Futurology of Christianity and Religion, 1893–1980." In *World Christian Encyclopedia: A Survey of Churches and Religions in the Modern World, A.D. 1900–2000*. New York: Oxford University Press, 1982, pp. 854–856.
_____. *Cosmos, Chaos, and Gospel: A Chronology of World Evangelization from Creation to New Creation*. Birmingham, AL: New Hope, 1987.
_____. "Annual Statistical Table on Global Mission, A.D. 1900–2025." *International Bulletin of Missionary Research*, 19/1 (January 1995): 24–25.
KÜNG, HANS. *Theology for the Third Millennium: An Ecumenical View*. New York: Doubleday, 1988.
_____. *Christianity: Essence, History, and Future*. New York: Continuum, 1995.
PHILLIPS, JAMES M., and COOTE, ROBERT T., eds. *Toward the 21st Century in Christian Mission*. Grand Rapids, MI: Eerdmans, 1993.
WUTHNOW, ROBERT. *Christianity in the 21st Century: Reflections on the Challenges Ahead*. New York: Oxford University Press, 1993.

David B. Barrett

Church-State Affairs

Emerging patterns of church and state affairs worldwide are primarily affected by the power relationships between nations and the organized churches of Christianity and Judaism in the Western religions, and Islam and others in the Eastern religions. The Western sphere of influence historically has been more sharply focused. However, the future in all regions is likely to see a rising tide of ethnicity intimately tied to religion as an organizing influence shaping state policy and identity.

Moral principles form the basis for the church. Administrative principles based on guiding moral precepts form the basis for government. The reconciliation of these two sets of principles forms a fundamental interaction influencing the governance of society. The heart of the tension lies in the diversity of church influences upon the state. Tensions increase when religious groups attempt to use the state as a conduit of power to shape human conduct. Tensions decrease when the churches maintain an ethical leadership and do not try to manage the political process.

Liberalism and fundamentalism are two trends affecting church-state relations. They constitute opposing forces. The historic tendency of churches in liberalism's sphere is to influence the state indirectly, while churches in the fundamentalist's sphere attempt to influence the state directly through actions or pronouncements.

Liberalism is a worldwide social trend that grew out of Enlightenment thought of the sixteenth, seventeenth, and eighteenth centuries following a century of religious wars in Europe. Liberalism is characterized by tolerance for opposing ideas. It is adaptive to change. It favors freedom from both traditional moral restraints and the authority of the church. Its rationalism evolved into more revolutionary, idealistic, entrepreneurial individualism within capitalistic societies benefiting from the "unseen hand" of divine Providence or the free market. Shifting toward individualism during the nonconformist movement of the 1960s, liberalism became an attitudinal trend driven by secularization, modernization, democratization, and pluralism. The recent collapse of communism, however, sparked a renewed emphasis in democracy as a precondition to the successful functioning of a society. In this social context the role of the individual as citizen of the state is to (1) contribute an opinion, (2) respond to the opinions of others, and (3) help solve problems leading to a better future.

Fundamentalism is a worldwide trend characterized by suspicion toward change. It entails a cautious reaction to rapid change in a world grown smaller through technologies. Fundamentalism uses traditional scripture to justify reversion to the past. From Right-Doctrine Protestantism to Islamic Fundamentalism, this set of attitudes emphasizes idealized traditional values and more homogeneous relationships. Some fundamentalist groups have sought to use the state as a conduit of power in the belief that it is God's will. It is likely that these groups will continue to align and develop strategies that attempt to counterbalance "a secularized society gone awry."

Theocracy is the direct influence of the church upon the state, as seen most clearly in Islamic countries where the "Word of God" reigns as law. Islam's alternative view of institutional structures and goals provides a driving force for scenarios of episodic religious-based revolutions. Rising tides of ethnicity also affect this form of Fundamentalism, which considers religion its sole, authentic source of identity. Both Liberalism and Fundamentalism affect the future of church-state relations. Churches in the liberal sphere tend to influence the state indirectly. In Fundamentalism, the influence is more direct. In a democratic society such as the United States, the crucible of power lies in the people. The First Amendment to the Constitution, which guaranteed religious freedom through the separation of church and state, created a high and impregnable wall between church and state for the first time in history. This demarcation subsequently caught on as a worldwide trend.

Fundamentalism's scenario pushes for uniform laws in the U.S. This mindset often challenges generally accepted notions of privacy and freedom of choice. The general public's weakening allegiances to both political and religious institutions since the 1960s give a stronger political edge to more strident fundamentalist agendas. Passions flare among liberals and fundamentalists at such flash points as school prayer, abortion, and cults. Religion has a profound influence on these issues and is significantly aided by high-visibility fundamentalist television ministries and mass communications.

Liberalism's influence in U.S. church-state relations is more subtle today. Concurrently church-church relations forge new processes that adapt to growing pluralism among world religions. Interfaith and interchurch councils are weaving networks in new, creative structures. These religious

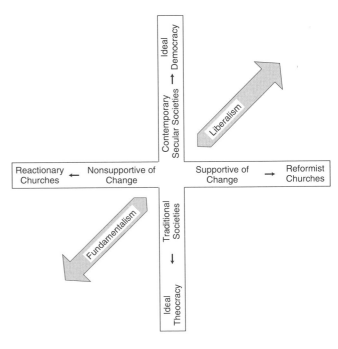

FIGURE 1. The future of church-state affairs: an axis of trends.

councils reject hierarchy, dogma, and exclusivity in favor of the inherent diversity of genuine grass-roots relationships and community building. Religion is forging new ways of resolving social issues like human rights and responsibilities, poverty, and a sustainable civilization. In this the church is teaching the state—a democracy within a democracy reshaping America. Past fractures of allegiance toward the church will mend as these processes wend their way and mature.

As the wounds of history begin to heal, relations between church and state may become intimately tied to making more apparent the Zeitgeist "the spirit of the time." We then can better anticipate the winds of change that will have shifted so unpredictably. The moral and ethical teachings of the church will then be reflected through the individual who simultaneously is a citizen of the state. The world may then become the beneficiary of true communication as the institutions of church and state are both guided by their greatest resource—human thought—which is itself guided by scripture, tradition, experience, and reason in a process of building a civilization that works for everyone.

See also CHRISTIANITY; FUNDAMENTALISM; RELIGION: CHANGING BELIEFS; RELIGION: INSTITUTIONS AND PRACTICES; RELIGION, SPIRITUALITY, MORALITY; RELIGIONS, DECLINE OR RISE OF; RELIGIONS, STATISTICAL PROJECTIONS OF.

BIBLIOGRAPHY

ALLEY, ROBERT S. *The Supreme Court on Church and State.* New York: Oxford University Press, 1988.
CORD, ROBERT L. *Separation of Church and State: Historical Fact and Current Fiction.* Grand Rapids, MI: Baker Books House, 1988.
MCCARTHY, MARTHA M. *A Delicate Balance: Church, State, and the Schools.* Bloomington, IN: Phi Delta Kappa Educational Foundation, 1983.
TIERNEY, BRIAN. *The Crisis of Church and State.* Toronto: University of Toronto Press, 1988.

Richard J. Spady
Ellie Bator
Cecil H. Bell
William B. Cate
William D. Ellington
Susan Jette

Cigarettes, Cigars.

See TOBACCO.

Cities

The future of cities is shaped by their history, location, command of technology, quality of human resources, and social institutions. Because they are built environments, cities endure for centuries, but their populations are more fluid and can dramatically change within a few decades. Cities of the future can be rich with innovation and full of individual and institutional vitality.

Alternative Urban Futures

Futurists think about the future in terms of alternatives, usually called scenarios. Arthur Shostak, the noted sociologist, once proposed seven scenarios for Philadelphia. "Conflict city" refers to the intense competition for scarce and shrinking resources awash in an atmosphere of fear and distrust, often expressed along racial and ethnic lines. Private employment decreases or moves elsewhere and the tax base is insufficient to support the public services. Detroit and Newark often are cited as conflict cities.

"Wired city" refers to the emerging Information Age where the Information Superhighway has eliminated much face-to-face communication. In the late nineteenth century, electricity and railroads helped to centralize industrial cities. In the twenty-first century computers and the new communications systems may decentralize cities. *Washington Post* journalist Joel Garreau describes this outcome as an "edge city" scenario. Edge cities already can be seen in shopping malls, electronic office complexes, and new varieties of condo-housing in the outskirts of most traditional cities. Edge cities are impersonal and lack a sense of community.

The "neighborhood city" scenario entails a return to a more human scale. The emphasis here is on self-reliance, walking-distance scale, voluntary cooperation, and decentralized leadership. Community schools become a neighborhood meeting place for several generations. Areas of Seattle, Portland, Ore., and Denver resemble this pattern.

The "conservation city" or the eco-village scenario can reflect a technological optimism and a sense of environmental frugality. Urban sprawl accompanied by loss of farmland and recreational spaces are concerns. Eco-villages feature rooftop gardens, verdant balconies, and apartment waterfalls. Conflict between increased urban densities and the preservation of urban green spaces is resolved through urban planning and managed growth policies. Urban settlements depend heavily upon access to energy and other natural resources. Boulder, Colo., and Berkeley, Calif., are examples.

Different in scale are "international cities" reflecting an emerging world systems. Cities now exist serving a global economy and society—a veritable global village where communities are linked together in a world of instantaneous intimacy. Some cities serve as headquarters or key research centers for transnational corporations. Some American industrial cities manifest a global heritage through their immigrant populations. In the twenty-first century the global connectiveness of cities will be an important element of their future. Toronto and Hong Kong represent this emerging international city scenario.

The "regional city" scenario recognizes that core areas and hinterlands also are part of a regional biosystem. Although politics and class differences have contributed to fragmenting urban communities over the last hundred years, political reformers hope to rationalize governance on a regional scale. In the 1990s environmental issues associated with air and water quality, solid waste disposal, and intermodal transportation planning compel local jurisdictions to develop new regional alliances. The regional city scenario involves a more efficient use of its space and ecology. It features cities moving from a concentric-zone model to a multiple-centers model. Cities are becoming multipolar, with a small inner center, and several edge city centers representing new clusters of urban sprawl. This scenario exists in most regions. Creating a regional forum, to devise a common vision, and to coordinating infrastructure and transportation needs are major challenges.

"Leisure city" variations include retirement communities clustered around city centers in Sunbelt states, and theme park centers (Disney World and Orlando, Fla.; Williamsburg, Va.; Aspen and Vail, Colo.). As the baby boom population ages, the future of many cities will be determined by their ability to meet retiree needs.

These scenarios represent possible futures. They are not mutually exclusive. They can and already do coexist in some places. These scenarios suggest both technological possibilities and environmental constraints.

The Urban Future

Futures research can be applied to city management, public administration, and urban planning in different ways. City governments responsible for substantial public expenditures can be subjected to rigorous cost-benefit analysis, which forces the political process to rank order capital development projects based upon assessment of economic benefits.

Cities also need to do some environmental scanning concerning the entire range of emerging issues. Emerging social, economic, political, technological, and other trends need to be regularly assessed to determine their consequences for urban life in general and for city issues in particular. Cities must also adapt a more systematic approach to information collection and interdisciplinary analysis.

Effective leadership of a city or a community requires a strong commitment to foresight. Alternative programs—including at least three different discussed scenarios—should be identified and elaborated: 1. a dynamic extension of the status quo; 2. a "better times" projection replete with growth, prosperity, and success; and 3. a "decline and shrinkage" projection where bad things happen in tough times. Current conditions and trends—for the economy, employment, public revenues, and taxes—should be projected by traditional forecasting methods. Good forecasting begins with an accurate assessment of current conditions.

Cities must also develop participatory processes to devise a strategic vision and a consensus from significant leaders, decision makers, and stakeholders in the public and private sectors. Strategic vision should include both hopes and fears. Strategic consensus to back action plans should establish priorities representing the most important concerns for immediate and long-term futures. A city needs to consider at least four major approaches to its future:

The first is a strategic perspective full of dramatic new proposals. It needs to think boldly and aggressively about its potential for the next fifty years.

Second, it needs to have a pragmatic and humane concern for immediate quality-of-life issues. People need safety and efficiency right now, not some time in the future. Quality management carries important implications for the future of a city and its reputation.

A third perspective is the investment in up-to-date technology. Efficient management requires a commitment to technocratic and innovative approaches in everything from recycling to public libraries.

Finally, there must also be utopian proposals and ideas generated by the geniuses of the community. A city must encourage its artists and poets to think beyond the mundane realities of today, go beyond the recurrent budget and election cycle, and conjure up large dreams for the human condition.

When a new global system of cities will come into being, these cities will have larger populations and provide a better quality of life through more efficient and innovative management.

See also CITIES, NORTH AMERICAN; LAND USE PLANNING; MEGACITIES; TRANSPORTATION; URBAN TRANSIT.

BIBLIOGRAPHY

BROTCHIE, JOHN. *The Future of Urban Form: The Impact of New Technology*. Tulsa, OK: GP Publications, 1991.

FATHY, TARIK A. *Telecity: Information Technology and Its Impact on Urban Form*. Westport, CT: Praeger/Greenwood, 1991.

GRAPPERT, GARY, and KNIGHT, RICHARD V., eds. *Cities in the Twenty-first Century*. Ann Arbor, MI: Books on Demand, 1992.

HALL, PETER. *Cities of Tomorrow*. Cambridge, MA: Blackwell, 1990.

Gary Gappert

Cities, North American

The year 2000, the dawn of the twenty-first century, is less than a decade away. Gone are the more stable days for local governments, when revenues were plentiful and public officials could merely adjust tax rates to balance budgets. The outside environment did not pose many significant challenges, opportunities, or threats. Public programs merely increased in response to citizens' demands for more services.

Traditional local government decision making, previously based on information obtained by projecting past trends into the future and preoccupied with the present, merely reacted to societal change. Nowadays, events and conditions are changing so rapidly that these practices are quickly becoming ineffective and obsolete.

Changes needed include greater government responsiveness, increased ethnic and racial representation, and more comprehensive taxing and spending controls. By proactively adapting to the future, elected and appointed public officials will be able to create a smooth transition to a new reality during the coming decade.

To illustrate the extent of these changing conditions, they are presented in five broad categories.

The categories include (1) political trends, (2) major demographic shifts, (3) evolving urban patterns, (4) modern technologies, and (5) contemporary economic factors influencing our local governments.

Political Trends

- More state and federal laws will usurp the home-rule powers of elected officials and serve to limit their discretion in many areas.
- Special interest groups will typically pursue their own narrow goals and will form coalitions around major community issues.
- Limited revenues mean that many political issues will have no clear-cut response.
- Citizens will demand more services, but will not want increased taxation, making it more difficult for public officials to set program priorities and balance their annual budgets.
- Responsibility will continue to shift from the federal and state governments to cities, leaving cities to solve their own problems. Many cities with a low tax-base may have to resort to service reductions.
- More minority group representatives, including women and immigrants, will get involved in the political process, placing greater demands for their representation in the workplace.
- A growing number of senior citizens will become more politically active, because they have more available time.
- Quality-of-life issues, such as those focusing on individual well-being and the state of the environment, will emerge as key areas of public concern.
- The NIMBY ("Not in My Back Yard") movement will continue to grow at neighborhood and community levels. Undesirable public services, such as jails and waste-disposal facilities, will be difficult to locate or relocate.
- Public attention will shift from national to local community issues, such as crime prevention, drug abuse, affordable housing, and shelters for the homeless.
- More coalitions and partnerships involving business, government, education, and the nonprofit sector will emerge to address local social and economic problems.
- The public will demand more "ethics-in-government" mandates to monitor the integrity of their public officials and to ensure that they do not personally gain from their government office.

Major Demographic Shifts

- Senior citizens will demand more specialized public services, such as recreational and other social programs.
- Senior citizens, many of whom are on a fixed income, will seek property tax reductions, forcing others to pay for these programs.
- The number of female heads of households is growing steadily. There will be greater demands for affordable child care and more flexible working hours in the future as this trend continues.
- An increasing number of smaller households will require more high-density residential developments, such as condominiums, townhouses, and apartments, placing greater demands on existing public services.
- There will be a greater number of women in the workforce, and they will become more politically active in the workplace. As a result, such issues as comparable pay and sexual harassment will become increasingly important.
- As the number of minority and immigrant groups increases, new demands for more specialized public services will be created. This will in turn require more bilingual public employees.
- There will be more minority and ethnic groups participating in the political process, creating growing demands for district elections and greater minority and ethnic representation in the political arena.
- Existing public officials will feel the increasing political influence of these special interest groups (for example, seniors, women, immigrants).
- Any new federal grants will be limited to those programs that help achieve national goals (such as affordable housing, lower unemployment, and shelters for the homeless).

Evolving Urban Patterns

- Urban sprawl will increase, primarily along major vehicle transportation corridors and public mass-transit routes.
- Cities will witness greater "in-fill" development in already urbanized areas. Land areas that once were marginal will be purchased and upgraded for new development.
- Older land uses, such as outdated industrial plants and commercial centers, will be upgraded and/or retrofitted with new amenities to make them more marketable and appealing to consumers.

- In central city areas, continuing high land values will lead to increased gentrification, further exacerbating the need for more affordable housing for low- to moderate-income citizens.
- Immigrant and refugee groups will relocate primarily to the city centers of large metropolitan areas.
- New "ethnic centers" will evolve in metropolitan areas. These "new" immigrants will stress the maintenance of the cultural traditions, values, and customs of their respective homelands.
- Higher energy costs and greater traffic congestion will create more political pressure for public mass-transit systems. Emphasis will be placed on multimodal systems that offer greater transportation options to the public.
- Public services will increasingly be tailored to better represent these growing minority and ethnic population centers.
- The population explosion in the suburban areas will lead to greater pressures for additional public infrastructure, with limited funds to finance these much-needed improvements.
- As the urban population shifts to suburban areas of cities, housing starts will not keep pace with this population movement, creating housing shortages in these areas.
- The shifting population, from urban to suburban areas, will create an erosion of the corporate tax base in these locations, forcing service reductions and/or tax increases.

Modern Technologies

- There will be an increased use of microcomputers in the workplace, brought about by more sophisticated systems, lower costs, and more user-friendly software.
- Policies will emerge to ensure the compatibility of computer hardware and software, which will require uniformity among applications, facilitate training, and minimize system downtime.
- Expensive standalone computer systems will disappear, due to enhanced and inexpensive networking techniques and the use of more sophisticated microcomputers.
- Information management will become necessary as computers make more information networks and databases available. The emphasis will switch from receiving "more" information to receiving "quality" information.
- Management by computer systems will become a common technique to monitor and limit energy consumption in public buildings and grounds.

- More public meetings will be aired on local public-access cable television stations. These stations will also be used to educate citizens on available services and key issues facing their community.
- Greater energy costs will continue to shape our lifestyles and technologies (for example, smaller cars, less spacious offices, new energy-saving devices, and more sophisticated building techniques).
- Advanced telecommunication systems, such as those with conference-calling and facsimile-transmission capabilities, will reduce the number of business meetings and related personnel and travel costs.
- Increased public pressure for mass transit, and greater construction costs, will lead to shorter routes in more densely populated high-traffic areas. Light-rail systems will replace the expensive underground subways of the past.
- More labor-saving devices of all types will be used, out of necessity, in order to hold down personnel costs (the largest component of any government's budget).

Economic Factors

- Ever-increasing energy costs will require the greater use of energy-conservation techniques (see above).
- Citizens will increasingly demand higher standards and accountability for air and water quality, especially in densely populated urban areas.
- Public officials will stress economic development as a vehicle to raise revenues without increasing taxes. Highly urbanized cities will have to resort to redevelopment for their financial survival.
- Since nearly every community provides the "hard" services (police, fire, and public works), there will be an increasing demand for the so-called "soft" services (recreation, museums, libraries, and cultural programs).
- Federal subsidies for mass transit in urban areas will decrease, forcing fare increases to operate these systems and to make them cost-covering.
- The public's aversion to new taxes, and higher user fees and charges, will severely limit the growth of government services.
- Taxpayers increasingly will acknowledge that it is the legitimate role of government to provide "safety net" services to citizens (that is, essential services to the truly needy).

- Limited new revenues will be earmarked for those public services and programs with the highest payoff—from both a political and productivity standpoint.
- The availability of federally funded grant programs will be limited, and greater competition will exist among cities for these funds. They will be earmarked for those cities with large low-income populations and related social and housing problems.
- The public will continue to advocate the "controlled growth" of government by opposing increased taxation and the growth of user fees and charges. They will also demand greater accountability and productivity for existing services.
- Due to more double-income families, employers will offer "cafeteria style" fringe-benefit options. Employees will also be asked to bear an increasing share of these benefit costs.
- Severe national budget deficits will continue to limit federal involvement in social programs, forcing state and local governments to pay for these services.
- Privatization trends will continue, making the private sector a provider of public services. Greater public accountability will be demanded of these "private" providers.

Change Is Essential

New models of governance are essential in times of fewer grant programs, complex and interrelated issues, fragmented and piecemeal local policies, rising citizen expectations regarding public services, skepticism of government in general, and the public's aversion to increased taxation.

Planning for change, a common practice in the private sector over the past few decades, needs to be extended to the public sector to enable government officials to adapt successfully to changing conditions. New political models must encompass multiple community issues, be nonhierarchical in nature, and help achieve a public consensus on the major issues and problems facing a municipality.

The Future

It is imperative that public officials provide comprehensive and consensus-based solutions to complex public policies. At the same time they also need to provide a collective vision for their community and its municipal organization. A shared understanding of the issues, problems, and goals facing a community not only provides a unified vision of the future, but it also helps to mobilize all available resources to effectively manage change.

It is only through the process of politically adapting our local governments to the electorate's expectations that public confidence in local government institutions can be restored.

See also CITIES; CIVIL PROTEST; INSTITUTIONS, CONFIDENCE IN; LAND USE PLANNING; MEGACITIES; TRANSPORTATION; URBAN TRANSIT.

BIBLIOGRAPHY

KEMP, ROGER L. *America's Cities: Strategic Planning for the Future.* Danville, IL: Interstate Press, 1988.
_____. *Economic Development in Local Government: A Handbook for Public Officials and Citizens.* Jefferson, NC: McFarland, 1995.
_____. *Privatization: The Provision of Public Services by the Private Sector.* Jefferson, NC: McFarland, 1991.
_____. *Strategic Planning for Local Governments: A Handbook for Officials and Citizens.* Jefferson, NC: McFarland, 1993.

Roger L. Kemp

Civil Liberties.

See COMMUNICATIONS: PRIVACY ISSUES; COMPUTERS: PRIVACY ISSUES; HUMAN RIGHTS.

Civil Protest

Among the varieties of civil protest are (1) violence; (2) nonviolent direct action, as practiced by the civil rights and peace movements; and (3) conventional collective action, including public demonstrations, boycotts, lobbying, and litigation. Such repertories span the spectrum of collective action from single-issue protests to rebellion seeking governmental overthrow.

Periods of Conflict

Conflict is pervasive. Worldwide, 5,400 political demonstrations occurring between 1948 and 1967 were documented by one study. Another identified 2,200 episodes of conflict in eighty-seven of the world's largest nations from 1961 through 1970. During the 1960s, over 500 race riots took place in the United States.

Excluding the Revolutionary War in the United States, there have been three periods of conflict: 1. the Civil War and Reconstruction Era (1850s–1876); 2. industrial and labor conflict coinciding with the era of immigration, industrial growth, and urbanization (1880s–1920s); and 3. contemporary social movements and political reaction (mid–1950s and 1960s).

Fields of Literature

Collective action and protest are the focus of three different literary fields of study: social movements, political interest groups, and violence. Three disciplines—sociology, political science, and history—are principal contributors.

Variations in Conflict

Political institutions and economic development levels affect conflict. Peaceful reformist demands are more frequent in democratic and wealthier societies. Violent revolutionary demands are more common in autocratic or elitist states, and in less developed nations (Gurr, 1989).

Grievances in developed democracies are channeled into legitimate avenues of political expression. Among the 6 million Americans who participated in the 1960s' civil protests, 80 percent did so in peaceful and legal demonstrations.

Violence used as a tool of protest carries a high degree of risk. Violence polarizes political forces, discredits its sponsors, alienates the public, invites repression, and reduces leverage by removing the uncertainty of escalation to violence others strive to avoid.

Explanations for Conflict

Breakdown theories of the 1960s concluded that urbanization and social disorganization led to urban riots. The McCone Commission (formed after the 1965 Watts riots) propounded a "riffraff" theory, contending that the rioters were a tiny faction of hoodlums, not supported by most blacks. The Kerner Commission (formed after the 1967 riots) concluded that the riots were spontaneous and unorganized voices of protest in the ghetto, reflecting the breakdown theory.

Three theories currently explain civil protest:

1. *Relative deprivation theory* maintains that protest ensues when social conditions give rise to grievances and to expectations that political systems cannot meet. Such conflict has not occurred along class lines but along ethnic, religious, and national cleavages in the United States. Civil rights and peace movement participants cut

across class lines of income and occupation. This approach also fails to explain the student and peace movements of the 1960s, which were products of affluence.

2. *Resource mobilization theory* has been the dominant explanation of collective action since 1980. Its essential assumptions are listed here:
   a. Deprivation or grievances do not automatically translate into social movement activity.
   b. Movements form on the basis of rational calculations of costs and benefits.
   c. Mobilization of resources may occur from within an aggrieved group or from external resources.
   d. The costs of participating in a movement can be raised or lowered by state support or repression.
   e. Movement outcomes are problematic; success does not automatically follow from movement activity.
   f. People do not join movements just for marginal utility but to gain solidarity or to advance a cause.
   g. Movements are of no certain size.
   h. A movement is a mediated, informal set of relationships among organizations, coalitions of organizations, and their members.
   "Movement entrepreneurs" mobilize resources and participants from social networks and capitalize upon mobilizing structures, such as lecture tours, prayer meetings, and e-mail networks. Critics contend that much protest occurs spontaneously, without the benefit of organizations, and point out that formal organizations tend to inhibit more militant protest. Relative deprivation theory may be a better explanation of American protest, and resource mobilization theory may apply more to Europe.

3. *Political opportunity* theory provides the newest explanation (Tarrow, 1994). While deprivation and organizational capacity might partially explain *why* and *how* protest occurs, political opportunity theory best explains *when* protest might occur. Four elements prompt political opportunity structures: (a) increasing access to power opens up (e.g., through electoral opportunities); (b) shifts in ruling alignments occur (e.g., when conservative Southerners left the Democratic party during the civil rights era); (c) influential allies become available (e.g., when urban liberals supported farmworker organizing and boycotts in the late 1960s); and (d) ruling elites are divided among themselves (such as during the Vietnam War era).

Arguably, if the Democratic party realigns into a more centrist party, its disaffected constituents and their allies could bolt the party and launch a wave of reformist protest. That has been a recurring pattern in American politics, just as conservative activism emerges when the Republican party moves toward the center.

Cycles of Protest

When one movement achieves gains through protest, other groups often emulate—the feminist and ecology movements followed in the wake of the 1960s' civil rights and antiwar movements.

Initiatives by one movement may generate counter-movements. Gay rights activism has mobilized conservative religious groups, and right-to-life and pro-choice groups on the abortion issue proliferate.

Impacts of Protest

Political response to social protest and allied movements entails repression and/or reform, or cooptation. Activism of any form has a long-term effect on the political socialization of its participants, and they often move on to other social movements and organizations to continue their activism. Success rates are highest among occupational groups, followed by reform groups. Socialist groups, right wing, and nativist groups have most often collapsed far short of success. Some movements, such as the women's movement, have had a long-term impact on social, political, cultural, and economic institutions.

Rebellion

Richard Rubenstein, an authority on conflict resolution, suggests four preconditions for rebellion: 1. slowing of immigration, giving identity groups the opportunity to integrate existing immigrants; 2. decline in local rates of economic growth; 3. failure of local political leaders to improve a group's status; and 4. intensified outside pressure on the aggrieved factions; e.g., through a war on crime. Open rebellion is unlikely in the United States.

Global Outlook

Sidney Tarrow also suggests the possibility that the United States has evolved into a "movement society." Single-issue groups are regularly at the forefront of civil protests. In an age of global communications and a wide array of sophisticated political tactics, genuinely transnational movements have emerged on such issues as the environment. Beyond this, global ideological and religious movements have made all nations prospective targets of terrorist activities. Recent low levels of movement violence may be giving way to more violence. Murders by fundamentalist pro-life followers may be indication of this shift. Finally, not only governments have been the targets of activism and protest. Individual companies and entire industries have been the focus of a wide range of citizen activism; this will increase with the spread of free markets.

See also CLASS AND UNDERCLASS; ETHNIC AND CULTURAL SEPARATISM; HUMAN RIGHTS; INSTITUTIONS, CONFIDENCE IN; INTERNATIONAL TENSIONS; RACE, CASTE, AND ETHNIC DIVERSITY.

BIBLIOGRAPHY

GAMSON, WILLIAM. *The Strategy of Social Protest,* 2nd ed. Belmont, CA: Wadsworth, 1990.

GURR, TED ROBERT, ed. *Violence in America: Protest, Rebellion, Reform,* Vol. 2. Newbury Park, CA: SAGE, 1989.

MORRIS, ALDON D., and MUELLER, CAROL MCCLUNG, eds. *Frontiers in Social Movement Theory.* New Haven, CT: Yale University Press, 1992.

TARROW, SIDNEY. *Power in Movement: Social Movements, Collective Action and Politics.* New York: Cambridge University Press, 1994.

ZALD, MAYER N., and MCCARTHY, JOHN D., eds. *Social Movements in an Organizational Society.* New Brunswick, NJ: Transaction Books, 1987.

John M. Holcomb

Clarke, Arthur Charles (1917–)

Born in Minehead, U.K., science fiction writer and prophet of space flight Arthur C. Clarke has been domiciled since 1956 in Sri Lanka, serving there as chancellor of the University of Moratuwa. Clarke's article "Extra-Terrestrial Relays" (1945) is believed to have been the inspiration for communications satellites (*see* SPACE SATELLITES). Clarke joined the fledgling British Interplanetary Society at age seventeen, becoming its chairman while completing his studies at King's College in London during the late 1940s. *The Exploration of Space* (1951) was the first of many books that made him a prophet of the new space age. His forays into SCIENCE FICTION earned him an international audience on the same scale as Isaac ASIMOV, Ray Bradbury, and Robert A. Heinlein. Clarke's novels include *Childhood's End* (1953), *The City and the Stars* (1956), *A Fall of Moondust* (1961), *Rendezvous with Rama* (1973), and *The Songs of Distant Earth* (1986). With Stanley Kubrick, he wrote the movie script for *2001: A Space Odyssey* (based in part on an earlier Clarke short story, "The Sentinel"). Clarke's visions of the future sometimes involve a rational "hard science" approach (e.g., *A Fall of Moondust*) and sometimes verge on a kind of New Age mysticism (e.g., *The City and the Stars*). His futurist works include *Profiles of the Future: An Inquiry into the Limits of the Possible* (1962), *The Worlds of Tomorrow* (1972), and *Life in the 21st Century* (1986). In 1980 he hosted *The Mysterious World of Arthur C. Clarke,* a television program.

See also COMMUNICATIONS TECHNOLOGY; GLOBAL CONSCIOUSNESS; SATELLITE COMMUNICATIONS.

BIBLIOGRAPHY

OLANDER, JOSEPH D., and GREENBERG, MARTIN H., eds. *Arthur C. Clarke.* Writers of the Twenty-first Century Series. New York: Taplinger, 1976.

George Thomas Kurian

Class and Underclass

Events of the final years of the twentieth century accent the continued relevance of social class to an understanding of human affairs. The collapse of the Soviet Union marked the end of a long quest for a classless utopia. Much political rhetoric in the United States is about social class. Presidents and would-be presidents pledge support for policies beneficial to a "forgotten middle class." Liberals attack conservatives for advocating tax laws favoring a monied upper class. Both vow an end to programs that foster a problem-laden underclass.

The underclass has received special attention in recent years. This is a population caught in a web of problems and destructive behaviors, such as high rates of illegitimate births, female-headed households, substance abuse, and withdrawal from the labor market. The underclass population is heavily dependent on public-sector spending to survive and imposes burdens upon public spending for special-education programs, the judicial system, and prisons.

Attention to the normal and abnormal classes is not surprising; the idea of class is fundamental to any description of societal structure. It is also central to the concept of social stratification, the placement of individuals and groups in higher- and lower-status categories. Class hierarchies reflect values and characteristics that a society considers important.

Class has been long studied. Karl Marx and his followers held that historic developments were conditioned by the economic system and its property relationships. A class order, ultimately consisting of only two elements—capitalists and workers—they prophesied, would result from the dynamics of exploitation inherent in prevailing modes of production. They maintained that, until the order is overthrown, there will be biases and inequities throughout the system.

Max Weber, and those who built upon his theoretical insights, found the world to be more complex. Social stratification involved an economic-based class component, but also status and power components. In modern, developed societies, social class status is apportioned in terms of an individual's contributions to the division of labor. The apportioned status allocates economic, social, and power positions in such a way as to assure the effective and efficient conduct of societal affairs.

Five broad classes are typically cited by researchers. The five classes and examples of sources of wealth and income include: *upper class*—inherited family wealth, investment income, corporate control; *upper middle class*—leading professions, major business ownership, executive/management positions in private and public bureaucracies; *lower middle class*—lesser professions, sales, skilled crafts; *working class*—industrial production, construction, clerical, personal service; *lower class*—unemployment or irregular employment in low-skill jobs. Daniel Rossides estimated the size of the respective classes in the mid-1990s as a percent of total U.S. population at 1–3 percent, 10–15 percent, 30–35 percent, 40–45 percent, and 20–25 percent. This distribution roughly resembles a diamond with its thicker portion below the middle.

Elements of social stratification are correlated; those ranking high in one tend to rank high in the other two. Education and hard work, for example, are prerequisites to economic success as a professional, entrepreneur, or corporate executive. The affluence of economic success allows for a lifestyle and good works that lead to high status in the local community and beyond. Prestige occupations, wealth, and high status tend to facilitate political participation. The upper and upper-middle classes are the "natural" recruitment pool for political office, and the more prestigious the office, the higher the implicit entry-level class requirement. Obviously, a reverse pattern could be traced; those ranking low in one of the social stratification elements tend to also rank low in the other two.

In the American context, evidence of a class identity and consciousness is weak. Lack of a feudal tradition inhibited the emergence of a well-defined class structure. Commentators have long pointed to the absence of a viable socialist tradition or successful working-class political party. And American culture emphasizes individualism. The lone man or woman overcoming extraordinary obstacles through hard work on the way to success continues to be a familiar theme in American literature and mythology. Where success and failure are individually based, class consciousness will not flourish.

For the future society, any upsurge in class consciousness is unlikely. Rank will be determined, as in the past, by the combined effects of achieved class and the ascribed characteristics of ethnicity, religion, race, and gender. The interaction of class and ascribed characteristics often produces a homogeneous cultural environment so that the primary agents of socialization—family, school, peers, and religion—convey a consistent message with future consequences. As Charles Murray (1984) indicates, "Young people—not just poor young people, but all young people—try to make sense of the world around them. They behave in ways that reflect what they observe." In the homogeneous environment, children, young adults, and elders receive and give cues on matters as basic as orientation to the future, work, proper behavior, admirable qualities in parents, spouses, and citizens.

The most significant developments affecting future class conditions will be economic. Transformations in a global economy have already eroded the competitive advantage of American workers. The stability of the lower-middle and working classes after World War II owed much to jobs in manufacturing. Over the course of a work life, the ambitious moved from low-skill to high-skill factory jobs. Strong unions gained good wages and extensive benefits, including medical and retirement benefits.

Future employment growth in the postindustrial economy will be bifurcated, most pronounced at the extremes on an employment-income continuum. At one end will be rewarding positions in innovative fields based on new technologies, creative development strategies, and exotic sciences. Entry-level requirements will demand extensive education, theoretical sophistication, and communication skills.

At the other end will be jobs in services and routine production. Few skills will be called for. New workers need only demonstrate promptness, an ability to deal with the public in service roles, and a capacity to cope with boredom in repetitive tasks. Most of the jobs will be part-time, at low wages, with few benefits.

If the class structure of the past resembled a diamond, that of the future will resemble an hourglass with the top part considerably smaller than the bottom. As members of the lower-middle and working classes fall into the bottom half of the hourglass, economic insecurity coupled with racial attitudes will likely further suppress working-class solidarity. For the past quarter century, racial attitudes of the white working class have been shaped by negative experiences and perceptions of breakdowns in traditional values and prominority and antiwhite working-class biases of major institutions. This has resulted in conflict over public policy for education, welfare, and affirmative action. These controversies have contributed a profound instability in American politics, evidenced in the elections of 1992 and 1994.

Developments working against the lower-middle and working classes will strengthen class consciousness in the upper and upper-middle classes. Wealth has become increasingly concentrated; by 1989 the wealthiest 1 percent of households controlled 10.9 percent of total income and 37.1 percent of total net worth.

Suburbanization has segregated populations by housing values, income, and social class. Those in affluent jurisdictions are aware of the importance of strategic thinking about life and careers. Community resources are committed to quality education, and family resources are invested in children from preschool through the best graduate and professional schools. Peers, work associates, and marriage partners come from like upper- and upper-middle-class, if not ethnic or religious, backgrounds. In the twenty-first century, the gulf between the upper and lower classes in income, lifestyle, and culture will be wider than in the past.

Of greatest concern for future elites should be the growth of the underclass. Though there is no agreement on basic causes or feasible policy solutions, underclass conditions in many central city neighborhoods are like those of a war zone: life is brutish, the young kill each other, and the old are preyed upon by their progeny. If the conditions remain unabated, the potential long-term costs are incalculable. Like their counterparts in earlier regimes, those in the upper and upper-middle classes need to be advocates for those beneath them if the order upon which their elite status rests is to be maintained.

See also DISABLED PERSONS' RIGHTS; ENVIRONMENTAL REFUGEES; ETHNIC AND CULTURAL SEPARATISM; FAMILIES AND HOUSEHOLDS; GLOBAL INEQUITIES; HOUSEHOLD COMPOSITION; HUMAN RIGHTS; MIGRATION, INTERNATIONAL; MINORITIES; POVERTY, FEMINIZATION OF; PUBLIC ASSISTANCE PROGRAMS; RACE, CASTE, AND ETHNIC DIVERSITY; RACIAL AND ETHNIC CONFLICT; REFUGEES; SOCIAL WELFARE PHILOSOPHIES; UNEMPLOYMENT; WEALTH; WORKFORCE DIVERSITY.

BIBLIOGRAPHY

DIONNE, E. J. *Why Americans Hate Politics.* New York: Simon and Schuster, 1991.

EHRENREICH, BARBARA. *Fear of Falling: The Inner Life of the Middle Class.* New York: Harper Perennial, 1990.

MURRAY, CHARLES. *Losing Ground: American Social Policy, 1950–1980.* New York: Basic Books, 1984.

REICH, ROBERT. *The Work of Nations.* New York: Vintage Books, 1992.

SOWELL, THOMAS. *Ethnic America.* New York: Basic Books, 1981.

STROBEL, FREDERICK. *Upward Dreams, Downward Mobility.* Lanham, MD: Rowman and Littlefield, 1993.

VANNEMAN, REEVE, and CANNON, LYNN WEBER. *The American Perception of Class.* Philadelphia: Temple University Press, 1987.

WILSON, WILLIAM JULIUS. *The Truly Disadvantaged: The Inner City, the Underclass, and Public Policy.* Chicago: University of Chicago Press, 1987.

John J. Gargan

Climate and Meteorology

By the year 2100, the current scientific consensus anticipates that the mean global surface air temperature will be 3° C (5.4° F) warmer (range 2–5° C [3.6–9° F] warmer) than it is today. Unless deliberate steps are taken to reduce emissions of greenhouse gases, the warming will continue well beyond 2100. If 3° C doesn't sound like much of a warming, one should recall that the mean global temperature at the time of maximum glaciation 18,000 years ago was only 5° C cooler than today. More important than the absolute rise in temperature may be the *rate* of the warming projected over the next century and beyond. The rate seems likely to be 20 to 100 times more rapid than the rate associated with the retreat of glaciers between 12,000 and 8,000 years ago. These and other long-range climatological forecasts are based on computer modeling whose reliability is steadily improving.

The warming is projected on the basis of two scientifically established facts. The first is the existence of the greenhouse effect—the heat-trapping capacity of gases in the atmosphere. The effect is natural; it is responsible for the Earth's being 33°C (59.4° F) warmer at present than it would be in the absence of the greenhouse effect. Without this natural effect, life would not exist on the planet. The second recognized fact is the increasing atmospheric concentrations of the gases responsible for the greenhouse effect. Increasing concentrations of carbon dioxide, methane, nitrous oxide, and chlorofluorocarbons (CFCs) are largely the result of industrial activity, with a smaller contribution (about 20 percent) from conversion of forests to agricultural lands. The greenhouse gas responsible for the greatest warming is water vapor. Water vapor is not directly affected by human activity, but a warming itself will increase the concentration of water vapor in the atmosphere. Thus, a human-induced warming can be expected to amplify itself through natural processes.

Under future scenarios in which current growth rates of greenhouse gas emissions are assumed to continue, the mean global temperature is predicted to increase by about 0.3°C (0.54° F) per decade over the next century. The range of uncertainty includes 0.2 to 0.5°C (0.36 to 0.9° F) per decade. The average warming will be about 1°C (1.8° F) by 2025 and 3°C (5.4° F) by 2100. Under the same scenarios, sea level is predicted to rise about 6 cm (2.34 in) per decade (range 3 to 10 cm [1.17 to 3.1 in] per decade) over the next century. The rise will amount to about 65 cm (25.35 in) by 2100.

Under different scenarios with increasing levels of controls on emissions of greenhouse gases, the predicted increase in global mean temperature is 0.1 to 0.2° C (.18 to .36° F) per decade, and the predicted rise in sea level is also reduced.

These global averages will not be observed in individual regions. Mid-latitude regions are expected to warm more than tropical latitudes. Different models of climate give a range of results. Furthermore, predictions of regional changes in precipitation and soil moisture, probably more important than temperature for most of the tropics, are even less-consistently predicted by the models. Thus, the specific changes in climate for a particular region are very uncertain.

Predictions to the year 2100 are thus not very disturbing or compelling except for low-lying coastal communities. But the fact that scientists cannot yet make specific predictions should not be confused with the possibility that the changes will be large. The possible effects include massive disturbance of climate, with associated disruption of agricultural production and political systems. The specific effects may be uncertain, but the effects upon regions already close to the edge of survival are not difficult to imagine. The world's population is expected to double in the next thirty to forty years. Is there enough arable land to provide twice the food now produced? The answer could be yes if new lands brought into agriculture were managed sustainably, but the increasing area of degraded lands in the tropics shows this not to be the case. Will new strains of crops help double production? Will the effects of the warming together with increased levels of atmospheric carbon dioxide actually increase agricultural production? Perhaps, but for how long? Add to the growing world population a changing climate with year-to-year variation in rainfall, frosts, droughts, storms, and other unpredictable events, and the picture is not reassuring.

Although not quantitative, the following aspects of climatic change are cause for concern:

- The warming is likely to be *rapid* unless major steps are taken now to reduce emissions of greenhouse gasses. The rate of the warming is expected to be more rapid than ever experienced in human history. Rapid change is difficult to foresee and prepare for, and difficult to adjust to.
- The warming will be *continuous*. Any policy of dealing with climatic change that is based on adaptation or coping will find itself several steps behind the existing climate. Rapid and continuous change together mean that adjustments to change will face continuously changing conditions. There will be no new climate to adjust to; adjustments must be to change itself.
- The changes will be irreversible within a single human generation, and probably within several generations. If the change turns out to be unacceptable, there will be no way to undo its harmful effects for decades. If all releases of greenhouse gases were stopped tomorrow, for example, the earth would continue to warm approximately 0.5°C (0.9° F) or more. The longer greenhouse gases are emitted to the atmosphere, the larger will be this commitment to a further warming. The commitment is to an additional warming that *follows* what has already

been realized. Warming continues because of the long atmospheric lifetime of most of the greenhouse gases, and because of the slow heat-absorbing capacity of the oceans. Policies proposed to reduce climatic change will affect future *emissions* of greenhouse gases. Nothing but time will be able to reduce *concentrations* of the gases that have already been released to the atmosphere.

- Finally, the change is almost *open-ended.* Carbon dioxide concentrations will not stop at a doubling, as experiments with global climate models tend to imply, unless deliberate policies are enacted to reduce further emissions. There is enough fossil fuel in recoverable reserves to raise the atmospheric concentrations of carbon dioxide by a factor of five to ten above preindustrial levels. There is enough carbon in the trees and soils of Earth to double or triple atmospheric concentrations.

These statements, although qualitative, suggest that climatic change will be difficult for most nations of the world.

See also ACID RAIN; DEFORESTATION; GLOBAL WARMING; OCEANS; OZONE LAYER DEPLETION.

BIBLIOGRAPHY

HOUGHTON, R. A. "The Role of the World's Forests in Global Warming." In: K. Ramakrishna and G. M. Woodwell, eds. *World Forests for the Future. Their Use and Conservation.* New Haven, CT: Yale University Press, 1993.
HOUGHTON, J. T.; JENKINS, G. J., and EPHRAUMS, J. J., eds. *Climate Change: The IPCC Scientific Assessment.* Cambridge, U.K.: Cambridge University Press, 1990.
SCHNEIDER, S. H. "The Greenhouse Effect: Science and Policy." *Science* 243 (1989): 771–781.
WOODWELL, G. M., and MACKENZIE, F. T., eds. *Biotic Feedbacks in the Global Climatic System: Will the Warming Feed the Warming?* New York: Oxford University Press, 1995.

R. A. Houghton

Clothing

In 1946, James Laver in *A Letter to a Girl on the Future of Clothes* wrote, "I must perforce try to deduce the shape of your clothes by what I think is likely to be the state of the world . . ." Laver argued that clothing reflected the political conditions so sensitively that clothing transformations were in tandem with political fact and discourse. While technology and other aesthetic disciplines play a

role, fashion is chiefly determined by social conditions. Standards of beauty and fashion have changed over time—from the life-affirming volume of voluptuous Rubenesque beauty in times of plague and physical peril in Europe as if to assert corpulence as the presence of the body, to modern sleek gym-toned bodies in the 1980s as a reflection of physical and aesthetic control as well as hard, lean self-control. Appearance serves as both self-image and social discourse: fashion's future is indivisibly linked to the technological and social forces patterning the future. Clothing, like society, promises to be more conformist and less expressive. In some respects, everyone comes into intimate, self-defining contact with the future first in apparel, and self-image constitutes the first social shape.

Clothing is a fixed human need arising from utility and a convention of modesty; fashion is a modern phenomenon of change. In the West, fashion arrived along with democracy at the close of the eighteenth century, when dissemination of fashion plates and massive textile production allowed the bourgeoisie to simulate court clothing. Fashion became dominant a century later as department stores, ready-to-wear clothing, and women's periodicals spread out from such fashion centers as Paris, London, and New York, and commerce inevitably replaced the court as fashion's arbiter and index. The commerce in clothing answers, however, to many other issues as well. Changing perceptions of modesty are morally induced and enforced. The first bikinis of the 1940s seemed, in their time, shocking in exposure: today, the same garments would appear demure. American beaches allowed men to go topless only gradually in the 1930s. Sexuality is conventionally associated with dress: fashion finds focus in shifting erogenous zones, probably not first determined by fashion, but by social propriety and preference. Western dress has become more or less universal, both assimilating aspects of African, Middle Eastern, and Asian apparel, and in offering solutions to clothing utility along with convenience in mass production.

Appearance may also include cosmetics and fragrance as elements of fashion. Cosmetics temporarily alter physical appearance, especially of the face. Once relentless in the pursuit of standardized beauty, cosmetics are increasingly under criticism for artificiality and deleterious personal-health and environmental effects. Moreover, some cosmetic effects are more permanently achieved through plastic surgery rather than applications of cosmetic materials. Sight and touch are essential to effective apparel, but so is scent. Fragrance has primarily been associated with the body, though by the 1990s, fragrance was also transmitted through controlled environments.

While clothing began with natural materials and thence to natural fibers, the twentieth century has seen the domination of synthetic textiles extending the potentially limited resources in natural materials. In this century, the preference has invariably (with a notable exception of some Japanese designers of the 1980s) been for natural fibers in high-end markets and synthetics for cheaper prices and markets. Furs, for example, were effectively simulated in man-made materials, but the first synthetic fur coats were thought inferior to the true furs until sentiment about animals finally reversed the aversion to the synthetic. In the 1990s, ethical value was attached to garments that were ecologically sensitive. Arguably, some synthetics were prematurely launched (polyester, for example) and failed in consumer tests of comfort. In the future, increasingly percentages of apparel materials will be man-made and will meet a standard of comfort, both resembling and feeling like natural fibers. Textile technology is producing garments that feel like silk, knitted cotton, or other natural materials and offer superior shaping, durability, and comfort. Any textile production also reaches the consumer with expectations for limited care: standard washing-machine or drycleaning care must be sufficient for textile maintenance. Hand-ironing is already recognized as too labor-intensive in pants that require no ironing and other wrinkle-resistant textiles. Alternatively, we will develop an aesthetic rationale for wrinkled clothes, because it is clear that we are not returning to a society of ironing.

Dress codes once prevailed socially and for business. For the man, the business suit was *de rigueur* almost through the twentieth century. Swelled leisure, indistinct separations of home and office, communications technology, and casual preferences are leading to the extinction of traditional business dress for both men and women. The market for tailored (suits and jackets) clothing for men is decreasing by roughly 10 percent a year in the United States, reflecting more casual lifestyles. Without specific dress codes, superfluous and uncomfortable clothing will be discarded. Hats, gloves, and accessories exist even today almost solely for utility, not for aesthetics of dress alone. Separate wardrobes of business attire and sports clothing will no longer be sustained. While special-event clothing will be retained for celebrations, there will not be the kind of clothing changes by occasion and time of day once practiced. One outfit for the entire day will suffice. Cross-training footwear and sports apparel is increasingly in evidence and gives the sign of clothing adaptable for different purposes: clothing is increasingly multi-purpose, with active sports a notable exception. Social, business, and sports occasions may be pursued in the same shoes, whereas a few decades ago footwear was distinctive to discrete activities.

Wearing apparel as a consumer-driven industry also follows demographics. An enlarged population of the aging and an enlarged population of the enlarged means fashion sizing and styling for the elderly and large sizes. Of course, older people used to wear black or otherwise discrete clothing from the population majority; by the 1970s, fashion for the elderly was no different in style from the most comfortable clothing for the general population. Clothing requires more and more convenience, e.g., Velcro fastening replacing the age-old button and the fifty-year-old zipper. The 1980s street-savvy oversized recreational clothing also recognizes the ampler, older audience as prime buyers of clothing. Conformity also means easier purchasing: sizes S, M, L, and XL allow for mail-order and computerized shopping.

Clothing technologies are seldom generated in laboratories or clinical circumstance. In the same way in which style is the elegant wearer's comportment, so clothing technology is generally tested by use. Everyday clothing is often derived from aviation, fire-fighting and other practical uniforms, and military gear rendered first in utility and thereafter for an extended, already proven, use. In addition, there is always the patina of glamour whether the trenchcoat that survived war or the astronaut outfit that sets spirits soaring.

Clothing followed in the Garden of Eden immediately upon gender differentiation and has always been a signifier of gender. To be sure, men learn from women and women from men (the former less than the latter, due to prejudice) in all fields, including fashion. The bifurcated trousers so successful for men have now been accommodated to much women's apparel. But the woman's jacket still buttons opposite to the man's. Symbolically, clothing will always express gender difference. Practically, there will be more and more uniformity, but not the arcadian unisex anticipated in the 1960s. Clothing's symbolic gender differentiation will be maintained as long as sexuality inheres to the body (and mind).

Traditionally, fashion had been thought to be determined first by the *haute couture*. Then, fashion was determined by the young. In the future, fashion will be increasingly set by the middle-aged middle class as determined by the market. Not only do the demographics indicate this change, but the erosion of home-sewing capability and the increasing mass production of fashion represent a decline in self-expression and non-conformist options. Conformity to templates of size, style, and fashion are required and—given that fashion seeks to persuade the consumer—desired.

Clothing has always been a way of altering and ameliorating appearance, humankind's most abiding mode of self-imaging. Other than the first decorations of scarification and anatomical distortion, all adorning beauty of the body was vested in clothing. By the late twentieth century, cosmetic surgery offered a significant option to alter the body, even without the stigmatic, apparent elements of body deformity in other cultures and first culture. Now, we can hope for the medical idealism that shifts the burden back to the body and away from clothing's glamorization and/or distortion. Significantly, body sculpting and alteration is likely to become the body ideal and clothing will be assumed for more practical reasons and purposes. Both self-esteem and sexual allure may seem to be enhanced in this new way. That apparel might be supplanted as the first technique of physical expression and social presentation by body refinement is not unexpected. Anthropologically, decoration began with body adornment. But clothing is not, even with plastic surgery, without its utility of temperature control, modesty, social identification, and other purposes that have been sustained from fig leaf to animal skin to kimono to denim to Lycra. If the ideal configuration of the human body is otherwise achieved in the mirror's reflection, clothing still has its important place of allowing interaction and of styling the human discourse. In *Penguin Island*, Anatole France imagined a world without clothing that was then made ludicrous by the imposition of clothes. Rather, we will need clothes, even aside from decoration and apart from variable modesty, to serve practical needs.

See also COSMETICS AND TOILETRIES; FRAGRANCES.

BIBLIOGRAPHY

Davis, Fred. *Fashion, Culture, and Identity*. Chicago: University of Chicago Press, 1992.
Hoffman, Kurt, and Rush, Howard. *Micro-Electronics and Clothing: The Impact of Technological Change on a Global Industry*. New York: Praeger, 1988.

Richard Martin

Coal

Coal is the paramount source of electric power in the United States and the primary domestic energy in both production and reserves. Comprising nine-tenths of available fuel reserves, its recoverable energy content is approximately four times the energy content of the oil reserves of Saudi Arabia. The United States is a foremost producer, user, and exporter, and the leading developer of advanced power-generation technology. Coal also supplies 44 percent of the world's electricity. United States and global reliance on coal will grow as this century closes and the next century begins.

World Energy Use—Long- and Shorter-Term Forecasts

One projection for 2050 sees overall demand rising by a factor of 4.5, with coal supplying 45 percent of all energy, its use exceeding that of oil by 2.5 times. Forecasts, each founded on different economic assumptions, vary widely. The range of most sees overall energy use as doubling or tripling through 2030. Governing actual demand will be a projected population growth of three billion in the developing na-

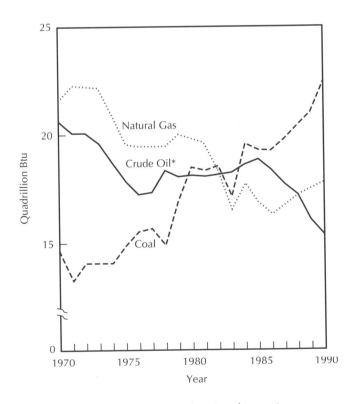

FIGURE 1. U.S. energy production by major source, 1970–1990.

tions, their economic development, economic cycles, technological advances, and the availability of a given energy. Greatest demand growth will occur in developing nations, many of which are energy-poor.

Mid-range, shorter-term forecasts see faster growth in coal than overall demand: 22 percent through 1996; 28 percent through 2000; and 45 percent through 2010. High-range projections see an end-term increase of 70 percent.

Developments of the last two decades drive the trends of the next two and set the stage for the next century. From the 1970s through the early 1990s, a series of shocks and surprises caused worldwide reappraisal and revision of plans and practices. First the Arab embargo and the Islamic revolution in Iran caused oil-related dislocations of the global economy; then the accident at Chernobyl intensified efforts to raise questions about nuclear power's safety; and, finally, the Persian Gulf War underscored the instabilities of the dominant oil-producing region. Energy security became a stronger influence—supply questions of availability, stability, and diversity assumed a vital significance. Demand for coal has grown faster in the last quarter of this century than for any other type of energy.

Forces driving coal demand include: (1) world reserves and the need for secure energy; (2) rapidly rising requirements for electric power; (3) advanced power-generation technology that resolves environmental concerns; and (4) the performance of the U.S. coal industry at home and in the world market.

RESERVES AND PRODUCTION—ENERGY SECURITY

World reserves are quite extensive. By all estimates, the amount of presently recoverable coal exceeds one trillion tons, and total reserves may approach 15 trillion tons. Recoverable reserves include all coal judged mineable with current technology at current prices; and advances in either technology or market prices can raise estimates. The worldwide recovery rate is about 50 percent. The U.S. rate is 75 percent, a result of recent modernization.

America's recoverable coal may exceed 290 billion tons, the energy equivalent of the proved world oil reserve. Oil reserves and production concentrate around the Persian Gulf. Fifty nations produce coal, the most widely distributed resource. Other major holders are the Commonwealth of Independent States (the former Soviet Union), 270 billion tons; and the People's Republic of China, 109 billion tons. Lesser holders include Australia, Canada, Germany, India, Poland, South Africa, and the United Kingdom.

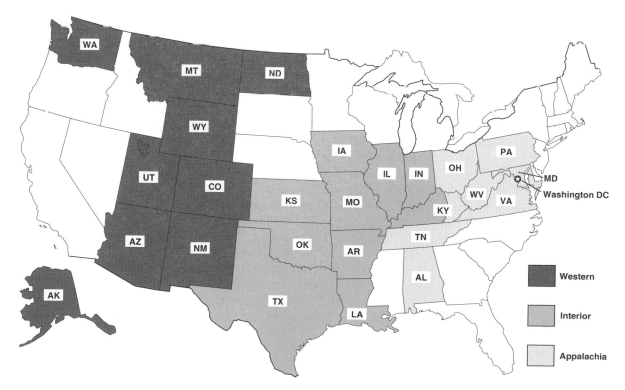

FIGURE 2.   U.S. coal-producing regions. (Source: Energy Information Administration, Office of Coal, Nuclear, Electric and Alternate Fuels.)

Richest also in energy content, U.S. deposits are in the Appalachian Basin (from Pennsylvania to Alabama); the interior (Illinois to Texas); and the West (North Dakota to Arizona). Thirty-eight states hold reserves. Foremost are Montana, Illinois, Wyoming, West Virginia, Kentucky, Pennsylvania, Ohio, Colorado, Texas, and Indiana.

World coal production increased to 5 billion tons—by 63 percent overall and 71 percent in the United States—from 1970 through 1990. Coal displaced oil and natural gas in and by power generation. The largest producers are the United States and China, both with about one billion tons, and the Commonwealth of Independent States (CIS) with 694 billion tons. Others include Australia, Canada, Germany, India, Poland, Turkey, the Czech Republic, and Slovakia.

American coal production rose from 603 million tons to one billion, including coal for export. About 60 percent of this is mined east of the Mississippi River, and more than 60 percent is from surface mines. Twenty-seven states produce coal. The top ten coal producers are Wyoming, West Virginia, Kentucky, Pennsylvania, Illinois, Texas, Virginia, Montana, Indiana, and Ohio.

At recent production levels the world has at least a 230-year supply of coal, 44 years of oil, and 56 years of natural gas. Demand will rise as other reserves diminish and prices increase. Low and stable long-term costs are significant considerations in electric power.

ELECTRIC-POWER DEMAND—WORLD AND UNITED STATES

Electric power accounts for most new energy demand, globally and in the United States. Electricity is the most efficient, economic, versatile, and cleanest end-use energy. Additions to the world generating capacity should exceed 1.4-million megawatts through 2010. One hundred developing nations account for 45 percent; the CIS and Eastern Europe, 17 percent; other industrialized nations, 19 percent; and the United States, almost 20 percent.

More power generation leads to projected world use of at least 6.2 billion tons by 1995; 6.6 billion by 2000; and 7.4 billion in 2010. Most demand will be in energy-poor developing nations and reserve-holding nations—in particular, China; the CIS, India, and the United States.

In the United States, electricity filled 24 percent of all energy demand in 1970; by 1990 it was 36 percent; and by 2010 it should be 41 percent. Coal generated more power in 1990 than all energy sources combined in 1970. Utility use increased 142 percent, from 320 million tons to 774 million. Forecasters see power production rising 30 percent to 60 percent.

The United States will require up to 233,000 megawatts of new capacity for baseload, or around-the-clock, use by 2010; the need will be in addition to gains in conservation and end-use efficiency. Forecasts say that coal will fuel at least half due to long-term fuel costs. Present capacity of all kinds is about 700,000 megawatts.

U.S. coal-burn projections are: 1.0 billion tons by 2000, 1.3 billion by 2010, and 1.6 billion by 2030. However, these estimates are based on the assumption that government policy will revive nuclear power; failing this, electric generation may call for 2 billion tons in the closing year.

Relative share of domestic power in 1990 was: 55.6 percent, coal; 20.5 percent, nuclear generation; 9.9 percent, hydroelectric; 8.7 percent, natural gas; and 4 percent, oil. Coal share will range from 50 percent to 59 percent through 2010, although a weak or failed nuclear revival could put it at 75 percent by 2030.

ADVANCED POWER-GENERATING TECHNOLOGIES

The United States leads in research, development, and demonstration. Recent government policy emphasized the Clean Coal Technology (CCT) and Coal Research programs. Goals of these programs include higher thermal efficiencies, lower capital costs, and emissions at one-tenth of current standards. First-generation technologies, in demonstration, should enter commercial use after 1995; and a second generation, in research, after 2010.

First-generation demonstrations are in the CCT program, a $5 billion joint venture with participant industries paying 60 percent. Most promising to repower old plants and for new capacity are pressurized-fluidized-bed combustion (PFBC) and integrated-gasification-combined-cycle generation (IGCC); both use the energy of combustion twice. In PFBC, steam from a boiler drives one generating turbine, and pressurized exhaust gases another; combustion is on a bed of limestone to absorb pollutants. In IGCC, gas produced from coal is burned in a generating turbine, and the hot exhaust raises steam to turn a second. The former eliminates at least 90 percent of sulfur emissions and the latter 99 percent. The first IGGC demonstration, in California, used most ranks of high- and low-sulfur coal, and bettered standards of the world's strictest emissions permit. Conventional thermal efficiency averages 33 percent; PFBC achieves 40 percent, and IGCC 42 percent.

Second-generation efficiencies range from 42 to 60 percent; applications include advanced state-of-the-art conventional generation, advanced PFBC and IGCC, fuel cells, and magnetohydrodynamics.

The efficiencies of conventional coal generation improved by factor of eight in the twentieth century; without this gain the United States might have eight times the present power costs and eight times the pollutant emissions of current concern: sulfur and carbon dioxide. With the new technologies, the cumulative gains rise to a full order of magnitude; they raise power output at still lower costs and fuel input; they reduce carbon dioxide output by up to 20 percent per unit of power in the first generation and 40 percent in the second. They deliver the ability to increase power production while answering concerns about environmental and climatic changes.

Other research goals include the production of liquid fuel, chemicals, and other products at costs equivalent to feedstock oil at $30 a barrel.

The U.S. Industry—Domestic and World Markets

The U.S. industry is the world's most modern and productive. Increased demand led to capital investment, and productivity rose 126 percent in the twelve years ending in 1990. Investment transformed the mines and the market. Forces driving modernization, and others put in motion by it, will influence demand, domestic and foreign, into the twenty-first century.

In the mines: underground, investment improved continuous miner production, and deployed 90 to 100 longwall mining systems that each can deliver more than 2,000 tons a shift; and it opened rich, new fields and new surface mines while allowing the introduction of larger equipment. Investment and productivity gains are expected to continue. Meanwhile, coal mining fatalities declined from 266 in 1970 to 66 in 1990, safety was emphasized, and coal now ranks below twenty industries in injury-incidence rate; underground mines operate at average dust levels below those scientifically determined to preclude new cases of black lung; and reclamation quickly returns all surface mines to original contour and productive use; examples of how former surface-mine sites have been put to productive use include tree farms, pasturage, cropland, and wildlife refuges.

In the domestic market, competition lowered coal prices in constant (1982) dollars in every year of the 1980s; average price was one-half that of oil, two-thirds of natural gas, even when those prices fell; and variable power-plant costs were lower than for oil, gas, or nuclear generation. Coal became the power-fuel of economic choice. As a growing economy demanded more electricity, coal units were put in service earlier and kept longer. In Ohio a contested nuclear plant was converted to coal in mid-construction. In 1993 the largest fifty planned additions to capacity were coal-fired. Meanwhile, as twenty-year use more than doubled, sulfur emissions declined; the causes of these improvements included precombustion preparation, blending, and flue-gas desulfurization.

In world production, the coal industry outdistanced others. Each American miner produces 7,800 tons of coal a year. The best available figures offer these comparisons: miners in Poland produced 432 tons; in Germany, 729 tons; in the United Kingdom, 1,400 tons; and in Australia, 5,400 tons.

The United States led in remaking the world market. Once dominated by steelmakers' needs for metallurgical coal, it now is predominantly an energy market competing with other fuels. America's ready response to sudden demand in the 1980s fostered this change; its productivity underwrites permanence and price competitiveness, answers to the security questions of availability and stability. Geographic and geopolitical distribution ensure diversity of supply. Unlike oil exporters, the principal traders are committed to free markets and competition, and reserves are not concentrated.

World trade could more than double to 900 million tons by 2020, primarily due to power in developing nations. A strong, but shorter-term, influence will be the end of production subsidies in Europe. Leading exporters are Australia, the United States, South Africa, and Canada. Others include Colombia, Venezuela, Indonesia, Poland, the CIS, and China.

Annual U.S. exports are expected to increase to 136 million tons by 2000; to 199 million by 2005; to 250–282 million by 2010; and to possibly as much as 300 million by 2020. The United States is expected to again be the number one exporter early in the period. The only net export in energy, annual coal shipments in excess of 100 million tons now add $4.5 billion to the plus side of the trade balance. Other exports will be tied to growth: precombustion preparation, and new generating technologies. Capacity additions outside the United States will be a $3 trillion market for equipment and services through 2010.

Almost nine-tenths of production goes to power generation and export. Other important domestic

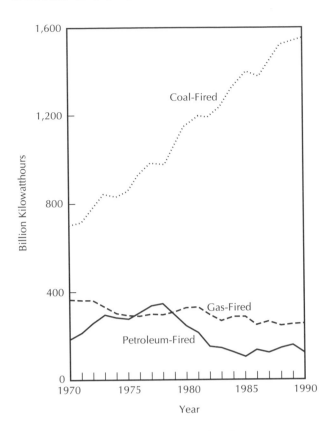

Billion Kilowatthours

Coal-Fired

Gas-Fired

Petroleum-Fired

Year

FIGURE 3. Electric utility fossil-fired steam generation by fuel type, 1970–1990. (Source: Energy Information Administration, *Annual Energy Review,* 1991.)

use includes: conversion to coke for basic steelmaking; as a source of heat or steam in the manufacture of cement, chemicals, and paper and paperboard; and for the same purposes in general industrial activity. In addition, the Dakota Gasification Company economically produces pipelinequality synthetic natural gas from North Dakota lignite, a low-rank coal; and the Tennessee Eastman Company gasifies coal to produce raw material for Kodak film and other products.

The Future

All forecasts begin with assumptions that may meet, fail, or exceed expectations as unforseeable developments of passing years prove them right or wrong. U.S. coal production passed one billion tons five years ahead of predictions made only in the mid-1980s, the result of power demand and industry performance.

Increased—or decreased—performance also may change other projections—year by year, decade by decade. Continued poverty in the developing world points to unabated population growth and global political unrest; but economic development could bring stability and lower birthrates toward the replacement-only levels of industrialized nations. Success in developing a competitive electric automobile would raise power demand above all forecasts, and also eliminate most anthropogenic carbon dioxide. Energy and advanced technology are critical in dealing with concerns, real or postulated.

The power in coal is a versatile factor in the important equations of the future. No longer the "King Coal" of 1900, nor the obsolescent resource of 1950, coal will nevertheless be a mainstay of the United States and the world in balancing and solving the problems of the twenty-first century; indeed, they may be insoluble without it.

See also ELECTRIC POWER; ENERGY; ENERGY, RENEWABLE SOURCES OF; ENERGY CONSERVATION; MINERALS; NATURAL GAS; NATURAL RESOURCES; NUCLEAR POWER; NUCLEAR POWER: CON; PETROLEUM; PIPELINES; SOIL CONDITIONS; TRANSURANIUM ELEMENTS.

BIBLIOGRAPHY

Annual Energy Outlook 1991. Washington, DC: Energy Information Administration, U.S. Department of Energy, 1991.
Annual Energy Outlook 1993. Washington, DC: Energy Information Administration, U.S. Department of Energy, 1993.
Annual Energy Review 1991. Washington, DC: Energy Information Administration, U.S. Department of Energy, 1991.
BP Statistical Review of World Energy. London: British Petroleum Company, 1990.
Coal Data: A Reference. Washington, DC: U.S. Department of Energy, 1992.
"Coal Quietly Regains a Dominant Chunk of Generating Market." *Wall Street Journal,* August 20, 1992, p. 1.
International Energy Outlook 1990. Washington, DC: Energy Information Administration, U.S. Department of Energy, 1990.

Richard L. Lawson

Comic Books

Story telling by means of illustrations has come a long way since cartoons were crudely scratched on the walls of caves by prehistoric man. It was in the 1930s that comic strips were first collected from newspapers and printed in magazine form. That was when they gained the name "comic books." More than one-quarter billion American comic books are sold annually, with the number growing all the time.

One trend that shows no sign of abating is the amazing increase in the age of readers. Where such magazines were once read primarily by children under the age of ten, ever since the 1960s the median age has been growing until it is now in the middle teens, with young adults now equaling the number of children who qualify as regular readers. As the subject matter of many comic books grows more and more sophisticated, and as the comics industry's so-called "graphic novels" are printed in ever more expensive, coffee-table editions, the time will come when comic books are no longer thought of as merely entertainment for children. Indeed, in France, Italy, and Japan, the comic book format has for many years been considered literature for adults.

The growing acceptance of comic books is something of a self-fulfilling prophecy. As their sales increase, the publishers are able to pay higher rates to their artists and writers. As these rates increase, more and better talents are drawn to the field. As the quality of the stories and artwork increases, ever more discerning readers join the legion of fans.

A spectacular new development has been a growing recognition of the value of comic book artwork. Prestigious organizations such as Sotheby's have held auctions of comic book covers and illustrated pages in which the bidding has reached into the high thousands for both illustrations and collectible comics from the last few decades. In the future, comic books will be bought, sold, and traded by investors and collectors much in the same manner as postage stamps, lithographs, and baseball trading cards are.

The coming decade will bring us more and more comic books being sold in the large, prestigious book chains. Concurrently, there will be newspaper columns that critique the latest comic book releases in the same way that columnists review motion pictures, books, and television shows. Inevitably it will follow that an Academy of Comic Book Arts will be established, along the lines of the motion picture and television academies, to give awards to the most creative and imaginative work produced by the writers, artists, inkers, letterers, and colorists, as well as the editors and art directors within the comic book industry.

Comic books will soon be taking their place on the cultural totem pole alongside of popular novels, motion pictures, and television.

What was once considered merely a product for young, naive children is increasingly becoming one of the standard literary and art forms of our time, an art form that will help to usher us into the twenty-first century.

See also FREE TIME; INTELLECTUAL PROPERTY; LEISURE TIME; LITERATURE; NEWSPAPERS; PRINTED WORD; SCIENCE FICTION.

BIBLIOGRAPHY

DANIELS, LES. *MARVEL: Five Fabulous Decades of the World's Greatest Comics.* New York: Harry N. Abrams, 1993.

HORN, MAURICE, ed. *The World Encyclopedia of Cartoons.* 6 vols. New York: Chelsea House, 1982.

JACOBS, WILL, and JONES, GERALD. *The Comicbook Heroes.* New York: Crown, 1986.

Stan Lee

Commission on the Year 2000

The Commission on the Year 2000 was the first serious effort in the United States to identify future problems confronting the society in the next thirty years. Initiated in 1965, it was chaired by Daniel BELL and comprised thirty-eight individuals from universities, government, and research organizations who occupied leading positions in these institutions.

Among the members (and their present or later positions) were William O. Baker, the head of Bell Labs; Harvey Brooks, Harvard, who headed the National Science Foundation committee that proposed the Office of Technology Assessment; Zbigniew Brzezinski, national security adviser to President Carter; Hedley Donovan, editor-in-chief, Time, Inc.; Erik Erikson, psychoanalyst; Robert Fano, director of the Laboratory of Computer Science, M.I.T.; Stanley Hoffmann, Harvard; Samuel P. Huntington, Harvard; Fred G. Iklé, Under-Secretary of Defense in the Reagan administration; Herman KAHN, a theorist on nuclear war; Wassily Leontief, Nobel laureate in economics; Ernst Mayr, biologist, Harvard; Matthew Meselson, biologist, Harvard; Daniel P. Moynihan, senator from New York; Emanuel R. Piore, chief scientist, IBM; Roger Revelle, oceanographer; David Riesman, Harvard; Eugene Rostow, dean, Yale Law School and Under-Secretary of State in the Carter administration; Krister Stendhal, dean of the Divinity School, Harvard; Robert C. Wood, Secretary of Housing and Urban Development, Johnson administration.

The commission's members felt that American society was ill-prepared to deal with social issues, because there was no mechanism to anticipate them.

The commission did not believe in "sky-writing" about "the future." As Daniel Bell wrote in the first working paper: "The future is not an overarching leap in the distance; it begins in the present . . . for in the decisions we make now, in the way we design our environment and thus sketch the lines of constraints, the future is committed."

The first efforts of the commission—working papers, transcripts of several meetings, and thirty-seven essays by members—were published in full in mimeographed form, and three thousand sets of these volumes went to individuals in universities, government, and business. A selection from these volumes was published in the September 1967 issue of *Daedalus*, the journal of the American Academy of Arts and Sciences, under the title of "Toward the Year 2000: Work in Progress," and more than 100,000 copies were sold. A hard-cover edition was published by Houghton Mifflin; and a paperback edition, later, by the Beacon Press. In addition, materials from volumes II and IIa of the working papers were revised and published independently by its authors, Herman KAHN and Anthony J. Wiener, under the title *The Year 2000*.

In laying out its agenda (I paraphrase and quote here from pp. 3–7 of the "Toward the Year 2000" report), the commission stated that the basic framework of day-to-day life has been shaped by the ways the automobile, the airplane, the telephone, and television have brought people together and increased the networks and interactions among them. The major technological changes would be in the development of computers and biomedical engineering. "We will probably see a national information-computer-utility system with tens of thousands of terminals in homes and offices . . . providing library and information services, retailing, ordering, and billing services, and the like." Biomedical work with organic transplant, genetic modification, and control of disease would produce an aging population.

In respect to structural changes the commission noted that "the centralization of the American political system has marked an extraordinary transformation of American life." A postindustrial system is reducing the role of employment in manufacturing. The older bureaucratic patterns of hierarchy may force institutions to reorganize. Individuals will face the need for renewed education. The family as a source of primordial attachment may become less important. The culture will become more hedonistic, expressive, and distrustful of authority. Further, as a result of the greater public focus on visible issues, social and political conflict may become more marked.

Thirty-one papers exploring these issues were printed in the volume. Eight further working groups were set up—one on the structure of government, chaired by Harvey Perloff; another on values and rights, chaired by Fred G. Iklé; intellectual institutions, by Stephen Graubard; the life cycle, by Kai Erikson; the international system, by Stanley Hoffmann; the social impact of the computer, by Robert Fano; science and society, by Franklin Long and Robert S. Morison; business institutions, by Martin Shubik. In all more than two hundred individuals participated in the work of these groups. A major project, *The Future of the U.S. Government*, edited by Harvey Perloff (with papers by Rexford Tugwell, John Brademas and Henry Reuss, as well as Richard P. Nathan, George C. Lodge, and others) was published in 1971. In pointing to the patchwork system of governmental units and the need for decentralization, the volume stated: "The major problem in the years ahead will be to define the effective size and scope of the appropriate social units for coping with the different levels of problems: what should be decided and performed on the neighborhood, city, metropolitan and federal levels."

In reviewing the work of the commission, thirty years later, what is most striking is the "freshness" of its observations, if only because of the persistence of the issues it identified, amidst all the flurry of words about the shock of change.

BIBLIOGRAPHY

BELL, DANIEL, ed. "Toward the Year 2000: Work in Progress." *Daedalus* 96/3 (Summer 1967).

KAHN, HERMAN, and WIENER, ANTHONY J. *The Year 2000*. New York: Macmillan, 1967.

PERLOFF, HARVEY, ed. *The Future of the U.S. Government*. New York: George Braziller, 1971.

Daniel Bell

Communications

Communications will mold the structure and essence of twenty-first-century communities, wherever they exist and whatever purposes they fulfill. Indeed, the common root of these words ties them to the concept of sharing—the exchange of ideas, information, money, goods, entertainment, and most everything else of which society is comprised. In this sense, we have always lived in an information society, but now the sharing will leave no one untouched and will interconnect everybody and everything to a much greater degree.

Major advances in communication—e.g., the appearance of oral language in tribal communities, pictographic languages such as hieroglyphics in Egypt or cuneiform in Mesopotamia, and the alphabet in Europe and Asia—have brought about dramatic changes in societies since the first spoken word. Paper preserved and spread ideas and images throughout the global community, and the printing press greatly expanded the sharing of knowledge.

Small uses were found for electrons in communications over the last century with the invention of the telegraph and telephone. Photons, hundreds of times more powerful in communication, will support the next societal revolution.

The technology of and for optical communications will connect the twenty-first-century citizen to the ideas, knowledge, and happenings of an immensely varied set of communities. The twentieth-century mind cannot yet conceive how it will cope with—or even survive the infoglut or overload inherent in so much sharing.

The term *information society* arose because information technology advances have often heralded or even brought about major societal changes. In such a society, the exchange of information is not only a decisive factor, but is overwhelmingly dominant in all facets and activities of the community.

Information exchange will consume more of our time and resources, and information systems will control an increasingly larger part of physical activities such as transportation, manufacturing, and distribution.

What now exist as numbers and words for "throughput" in the communication systems will be converted into more useful forms. First will come transformation into useful data. Next will come algorithms to process the data into information. Expert systems will translate information into intelligence. Neural systems embedded in the communications network may ultimately even impart a degree of learning to users.

Perhaps the earliest example of such systems will involve language. Of all the features defining community, a shared language is the most important. Computers capable of real-time translation will accelerate the move toward a worldwide community. Imagine a conversation by phone with anyone, anywhere, with both speakers speaking and hearing in their native languages.

Will the present generation be the last to use the printed word? In the long battle of attrition between hard copy and electronic media, the armies of print and film continue to lose both people and territory. This conflict, begun in 1837 with the telegraph, may have reached the end of the beginning in 1937 with television, and we are almost certainly near the beginning of the end today. Many battles yet remain, but the retreat by Gutenberg's legions should end this 200-year war by 2037 or thereabout. In each domain where paper and type have held advantages over electronics, continued improvements in the newer technology have eventually eliminated those advantages. The still-developing electronic network will be a faster, more accurate, more efficient, and more satisfying creator and servant of communities than ink and paper could ever be.

Newspapers may continue to be major purveyors of "news" during the near-term future. As of now, they are the principal source of expository news for both local and larger communities in contrast to the "sound bytes," "talking heads," and occasionally graphic images of television. The future presents a dilemma. Will the market for real news decline as a result of cultural change, or will the visual media find a way to deliver news with substantial content? Given the ongoing multimedia experiments and increasing capabilities of video communications, the latter seems most likely to end the newspaper dominions.

Advertising is not only a form of communication in its own right, but it also often subsidizes other communications. What mechanism would support newspapers and magazines in the absence of advertising? Home shopping will not only compete for advertising revenues, but will also reduce the economic base that purchases ads. The encroachment by electronic media upon print media will continue to be reflected in the shift of advertising revenues, a problem that will no longer be masked by overall growth in the economy.

Libraries will become less and less the storers and providers of books. As dispensers of information, they will survive if they incorporate newer methods for storage and distribution of information. However, the threat to local institutions again comes from the exponentially expanding ability of electronic media to accomplish these functions.

Continued sniping at the U.S. Postal Service will hasten its inevitable decline. E-mail and facsimiles are completing the elimination of first-class mail begun by the telephone and electronic funds transfer. In every other postal sphere concerned with the transport of communication, such as magazines, catalogues, and advertising, the transformation of these physical forms into electronically equivalent services will reduce postal carriage.

The past decade of revolutionary change in the U.S. telephone system is only a prelude to the changes of the next twenty years. Dissolution of the AT&T monolith, thought to presage the end of the world's best telephone operation, instead unleashed a torrent of advance that would have been unlikely under the old monopoly. By the year 2013 or thereabouts, every element of today's telephone system will have been completely replaced by newer technologies. Optical fiber and cellular radio will have virtually supplanted the last vestiges of the copper network. All analog elements will have long since been replaced by digital systems. Digital radio networks, including low-orbit earth satellites, will enable personal communication connections any time, anywhere, with anyone.

Two-way interactive video communications will be the new transport vehicle for many of the forms of sharing and exchange which now require the movement of people. For shopping, your fingers and eyes will do the walking and driving.

Advances in financial transaction methods will be among the most important features of the Information Society. These advances will include the ability for anyone to transfer funds anywhere, at any time. The effectiveness of media for the exchange of money will be a major influence in stabilizing world society.

Satellites, as both generators and transporters of information, will continue these functions, unseen and unappreciated. Although connections between earth and low-altitude satellites are limited to radio frequencies, laser beams between the satellites could provide worldwide broadband trunking circuits. The twenty-first century will commence with massive competition and cooperation among fiber optics, cellular radio, and satellites in meeting communication and transportation needs.

Just as Gutenberg kicked off a world revolution with movable type, and Giotto's geometry led to new concepts in visual presentation, so too photography and electronic imaging affected every aspect of society. In the future, how will the competition between film and electronics play out? Video cameras have driven out motion picture filming from all except the highest-definition recording. The realm of still photography is similarly vulnerable. A similar situation faces all recording. Can delivery from central sources, on demand, be provided at lower cost than music or video record purchase or rental?

Most, if not all, of the advances in communication technology have advanced freedom and democracy. Developments such as facsimiles, copy machines, electronic mail, home videos, and cellular phones facilitate the rapid uncontrolled distribution of information essential to informed deliberation.

Whatever the future holds for communication, it will hold for all the world communities. Even when we can do no more than define the direction that communications developments are taking, we can be sure that society will ultimately benefit, as it always has.

See also ADVERTISING; BROADCASTING; COMMUNICATIONS: MEDIA LAW; COMMUNICATIONS: PRIVACY ISSUES; COMMUNICATION TECHNOLOGY; DIGITAL COMMUNICATIONS; ELECTRONIC CONVERGENCE; NEWSPAPERS; ON-LINE SERVICES; POSTAL SERVICES; PRINTED WORD; TELECOMMUNICATIONS; TELEPHONES; TELEVISION.

BIBLIOGRAPHY

DAVIS, STAN, and DAVIDSON, BILL. *2020 Vision.* New York: Simon & Schuster, 1991.

GRANT, A. *Communication Update,* 3rd ed. Stoneham, MA: Focal Press, 1994.

LENZ, RALPH C. "Crossroads En Route to the Information Highway." *New Telecom Quarterly* (October–December 1993).

VANSTON, LAWRENCE K. "Technological Substitution in Telecom Equipment." *New Telecom Quarterly* (January–March 1994).

Ralph C. Lenz
Lawrence K. Vanston

Communications: Digital.

See DIGITAL COMMUNICATIONS.

Communications: Media Law

Social and technological advances are usually followed by legislative responses aimed at restraints that moderate social change. Legislators, torn between the public interest and special interests, usually favor the special interests. Attempts to modify the Communications Act of 1937 and coordinate it with the requirements of emerging technologies have made little progress. Distribution of limited-frequency and channel spaces overwhelmed by the increased use of interactive multimedia communications should force an overhaul of communications law by the turn of the century.

Information-based technologies, advancing at an accelerating rate, are providing more knowledge to more people than ever before in history. Mass information technologies, over the short term, tend to be concentrated in fewer hands. This trend is likely to be slowly reversed over the next decade. Antitrust laws, administered by the Federal Trade Commission, the Federal Communications Commission, and the U.S. Department of Justice, may have to be strengthened.

New services such as the Internet accelerate a trend toward ever-more information—for better or worse. Access to such services increases the availability and diversity of fact and opinion and decreases dependence on any one provider. Attempts to control and suppress the dissemination of the diverse materials will increasingly be attempted. New laws may decentralize controls over all forms of communications.

Censorship

The fear of change has always been a primary cause of censorship. Throughout history, ruling elites have used their moral attitudes and legal authority to control many information sources.

The U.S. Supreme Court has protected and expanded free expression over the past two centuries. As rights of expression expand, increased responsibility over expression must expand commensurately. The regulatory authority of the Federal Communications Commission is increasingly inadequate to resolve the abuses of socially irresponsible communication.

Books and Publications

Increasingly we may read reports of attempts by small, vocal minorities to censor what is read or taught. At times, some legislators may be foolish enough to act, but ultimately attempts to prevent the distribution, publication, and transmission of "controversial" written materials are doomed to failure.

Works of Art

No moral restraint on the arts has ever succeeded in controlling creative expression. Definitions of what art is evolve. Social, moral, and intellectual attempts to inhibit the expansion of human consciousness by imposing artificial values will continue. Top-down attempts at censorship will continue to conflict with expanding constitutional guarantees of socially responsible expression.

Teachers

Almost always, attempts to increase knowledge or information arouse cultural opposition. Increased intellectual independence inherently involves decreased reliance on and obedience of arbitrary authority. The manipulation of educational systems to advance narrowly based political agendas are underway now. Efforts by conservative religious groups to privatize schools also entail curricula control that may involve a hidden agenda to undermine the educational processes through censorship and budgetary control.

While there is an increased movement toward uniform educational standards, on-line services such as the Internet promote diversity. Public policies that encourage the proliferation of such technology-based services are being developed. As communication technologies become easier to use, broad-based public participation in education will eventually spawn a diverse, nonhierarchical, fully participatory, and truly democratic system.

Libel and Slander

Intellectual enlightenment is threatened by egalitarian tendencies to devolve to the lowest common denominator. Media pandering to the emotions, fantasies, gossip, and misinformation debase and demean a society already wallowing in superficialities. Improved ethical standards, voluntarily assumed by the media and sometimes enforced by government agencies, will help assure a more responsible media.

The U.S. Supreme Court ruled that commercial speech is not protected by the First Amendment of the Constitution if it involves the dissemination of false and misleading advertising. An increased need to broaden that rule is emerging. Viable legal standards to prevent the dissemination of libel, slander, misinformation, and fiction disguised as fact will be devised without impairing freedom of speech.

Court rulings limit the ability of public figures to obtain full legal recourse and damages for slander and libel. Mass media tend to emphasize hearsay and innuendo while shielded by defense of the public's need to know.

In an electronically interconnected society, the right of privacy will be protected. The right of the media or any agent of government to invade the privacy of any individual and disseminate personal information in the absence of a clear and present danger to the public is excessive. Allegations by public authorities affecting public policy should require corroboration. The absence of malice is less and less of a defense.

Simultaneously, the right of free expression must be protected. Attempts to suppress commentary through the courts may be mitigated by requiring the moving party to pay the defendant's court costs, legal fees, and ancillary expenses in the absence of a finding on the part of the plaintiff.

Media Complaints

Media complaints usually emanate from pressure groups pursuing self-promotion and preservation. As media outlets increase and audiences fragment, an increasing number of such groups will attempt to impose controls on the media. Over the long term, these same increases in information sources and diverse opinion should produce an enlightenment causing such problems to self-correct.

Claims of media bias will increase. Increased diversity of opinion prompts increased disagreement. There will never be complete agreement on any issue, nor should there be. Problems occur when attempts are undertaken to suppress valid, informed opinions.

Attempts to increase media holdings will increase over the short term. However, such consolidation could seriously threaten access to information and entertainment. Although attempts to control the content of what is available in such circumstances are more likely to be motivated by profit rather than ideology, the net effect could be the same as with ideological censorship: a restriction of the diversity of viewpoints accessible to the public.

Antitrust authority over media consolidations is vested in the Federal Trade Commission, the Federal Communications Commission, and the Department of Justice. Reduced competition is occurring between promoters of various transmission technologies. Market forces that might have increased diversity and reduced costs through competition have not been set into motion. Statutory limitations based on total market share and percentage of broadcast band access may have to be enacted to protect the public interest.

Consumer Fraud

Exposure to temptation in America's consumer-oriented society, which increased during the previous decade, will continue to increase. The consumer's ability to order something on impulse by telephone increases unabated. New temptation through multimedia and computer-based shopping escalates this trend. Informed decisions based upon brief and usually incomplete representations by telemarketing spokespersons is limited; comparison shopping is all but nonexistent. Full, clear, and conspicuous disclosure of the quality, price, terms of sale, and other relevant criteria to compare goods and services will have to be provided.

Protection also may be established for consumers by requiring a mandatory three-day cooling-off period following receipt of contracts for all purchases (excluding perishable items). Advertising misrepresentations concurrently dealt with by state and local authorities will be strengthened to protect private rights of action by consumers. Federal preemption is no longer viable.

Civil actions are increasingly inadequate. State and local injunctive relief and restitution orders, which have no force or effect beyond jurisdictional lines, are increasingly ignored in a highly mobile society. The capacity of mobile merchants to evade the snare of state and local laws will be countered by increasing civil and criminal jurisdiction and penalties involving fraud in interstate commerce. The act of fraud will be redefined to include any misrepresentation of goods or services, or the failure to provide goods or services under the merchant's direct control. Mere proof of the act of fraud itself, not proof of *intent* to defraud, will be sufficient to enhance criminal prosecutions and protect consumers under this new definition.

Computers

Telephone lines and modems that allow anyone to communicate with anyone else via computer also allow them to interfere with other computers. The extent of unauthorized, unwarranted, and improper incursions into business and government databases increased during the past decade. There is little doubt that such incursions will continue to increase.

Unauthorized access to a database without owner authorization violates existing federal law. Prosecutions and convictions under this law have been few and far between. Perpetrators, often students thoughtlessly acting out immature rebellions, are usually treated leniently. As technologies improve, however, the number of "white-collar criminals" may increase.

Law enforcement tends to focus on crimes of violence, all but ignoring economic crimes. Wire fraud involving improper electronic fund transfers, banking frauds, and massive telemarketing schemes get less attention. What the public and Congress have not yet meaningfully addressed is that economic crimes impose costs substantially larger than crimes involving violence.

As the methods of access to bank accounts through computers and other electronic means increase, losses increase. Most economic crimes continue to be treated as civil rather than criminal violations and may not be included in crime statistics; as a consequence, they are not dealt with in a manner that discourages their spread. Laws defining and imposing penalties for communications fraud are in the offing and will be under the concurrent jurisdiction of state and federal agencies.

Different parts of the world currently have different communication standards and interfaces involving television, computers, and virtually all other commercial factors. The development of high-definition television (HDTV) provides an example of the pushing and pulling in attempting to develop a worldwide state-of-the-art standard. Worldwide intergovernmental cooperation in conjunction with the private sector is essential to achieve uniform interfaces and standards. How soon such standards arc adopted will depend on the willingness of the various elements within the private sector to share technologies and share the costs of research and development.

See also ADVERTISING; COMMUNICATIONS; COMMUNICATIONS: PRIVACY ISSUES; COMPUTER LAWS; CONSUMER PROTECTION/REGULATION; INTELLECTUAL PROPERTY; MARKETING; TELECOMMUNICATIONS.

BIBLIOGRAPHY

BAGDIKIAN, BEN H. *The Media Monopoly*, 4th ed. Boston: Beacon Press, 1992.
BURRIS, DANIEL, with ROGER GITTENES. *Technotrends: How to Use Technology to Go Beyond Your Competition.* New York: Harper Collins, 1993.
COMBS, JAMES E., and NIMMO, DAN D. *The New Propaganda: The Dictatorship of Palaver in Contemporary Politics.* New York: Longman, 1993.
DUBLIN, MAX. *Futurehype: The Tyranny of Prophecy.* New York: Dutton, 1989.
GLASTONBURY, BRYAN, and LAMENDOLA, WALTER. *The Integrity of Intelligence: A Bill of Rights for the Information Age.* New York: St. Martin's, 1992.
YANKELOVICH, DANIEL. *Coming to Public Judgment: Making Democracy Work in a Complex World.* Syracuse, NY: Syracuse University Press, 1991.
ZALLER, JOHN R. *The Nature and Origins of Mass Opinion.* New York: Cambridge University Press, 1992.

Abraham Moses Genen

Communications: Privacy Issues

Modern society is in the midst of a technological upheaval comparable to the advent of the steam engine and electricity. By the end of the next decade, almost every U.S. business, government agency, library, school, and home will be plugged into a high-speed, interactive communications network. In this new "infostructure," a single, fiber-optic terminal will transmit words, images, music, medical information, and industrial charts. With everyone connected electronically, there will be greatly reduced need for such familiar services as mail delivery or newspapers as we know them today. People will receive personalized magazines and newspapers customized to fit their own interests. Students will communicate with teachers from home terminals and design their own individualized home-based learning programs. With telemedicine, people will get medical advice from electronic medical databanks rather than doctors.

Signal compression techniques will enable cable television companies to devote a channel for an individual customer's use, allowing personalized programming. In the next century, people from all over the world will have computer access to the 500 miles of shelved books in the Library of Congress. We will be able to order a copy of any Library of Congress holding, any painting that hangs in the Louvre, or any movie from the comfort of our living room. Electronic robots will do our research for us by scanning the contents of distant libraries without human intervention. Virtual reality systems open up opportunities for interaction with computer-modeled environments, allowing a variety of activities to be experienced without ever leaving home. Communications advances will lead to increased use of electronic money, and currency may be abandoned entirely.

These wonders of technology will bring with them increased concern for personal privacy. Unless current trends change, computers will be used to track customers' shopping, banking, and leisure habits to an even greater extent than today. Cable companies, advertisers, direct marketers, and investigative firms will seek such data, much as they do today. This information will be stored and readily available, thereby representing an ever-increasing threat to personal privacy.

Tiny, hand-held devices will allow instant communications with anyone else in the world. People will never be out of touch, and calls will be placed to individuals instead of to places as they are today. The tendency toward constant communication will lead to a communications network that will be able to locate every individual's whereabouts.

British Telecommunications PLC is spending more than $1 billion over the next several years to develop a multimedia voice, data, and video digital-transmission network called Cyclone that will encompass many of these features. After initial outlays, the cost of establishing personal communications networks will be much lower than the cost of traditional wire-based connections. Therefore, these services will be affordable for average consumers.

Meanwhile, new methods of communicating are replacing more traditional forms. Although 60–90 percent of all nonspoken communications are now paper-based, this is rapidly changing. There are already an estimated 32,000 electronic bulletin boards in North America and 45,000 worldwide. The most notable of these, the Internet, links millions of users around the world.

Taken one step further, it will soon become as easy to transmit data through the air as it is today through wires. The new wireless telephone technology will allow salespeople to carry laptop computers connected directly to their home base by radio. Airlines already enable passengers to link up with their office computers, sending and receiving e-mail messages and faxes while in the air. Future office workers will not be typing at keyboards; they will be talking to computers that will have the ability to recognize human speech.

With more of the nation's business conducted over wireless networks, computer encoding is expected to grow rapidly by having devices such as clipper chips installed to protect privacy. Clipper chips are microcircuits that scramble telecommunications by using an algorithm.

Privacy also will continue to be a fundamental workplace issue. Managers will increasingly use new surveillance technology to monitor worker behavior. While management will attempt to enhance their control over the workplace, workers will devise new methods to protect their rights.

The revolution in technology development is being stimulated by the use of fiber-optic cables—a transmitting medium with enormous capacity. Fiber-optic cable is made up of hair-thin strands of glass so pure that it is theoretically possible to "see through" about 60 miles of fiber. It is the most powerful carrier of information ever invented and currently can transmit up to a billion bits of information per second. In a few years, a bundle of fiber-optic cable just half an inch thick will carry up to 32 million conversations.

Fiber-optic advances will be accompanied by continuing advances in computer technology. Future computers may be controlled directly by human thoughts. Fujitsu, Japan's largest computer company, is developing a computer controlled by a person's thoughts and body motions. At the Nippon Telegraph and Telephone Corporation, researchers have been able to communicate brain waves to control joystick movement, and a similar project is underway at Graz University in Austria.

Researchers at the New York State Department of Health have already produced a system that allows control of a computer screen cursor by mental action alone, and University of Illinois psychologists are working on a project that allows people to type characters by spelling out words in their minds.

AT&T's new hand-held computers and notepads, such as Apple's Newton, take commands written with an electronic pen and function both as computer and communications device. By the turn of the century, we shall be able to give computers commands using voice and hand gestures, as the interface between people and machines becomes more user-friendly. People already dial telephone numbers by speaking the names of the persons they wish to call. Shoppers will browse through the contents of an entire shopping mall without ever leaving their chairs.

New developments in communications and information technology no longer take place in a linear fashion, separated by decades, with enough time in between for their implications to be sorted out. A wide range of converging technologies force us to make immediate choices, leaving considerably less time for decision-making.

In the information age, data does not move from one private space to another, but travels along networks. These networks create a connectedness that reduces individual isolation and zones of privacy.

When communication was by hieroglyphics written on stone, knowledge was extremely limited. As it progressed to communicating with pencil and paper, knowledge and its diffusion were significantly increased. Printing dramatically quickened the pace. Now, we have a quantum leap into electronic communication. How a person communicates essentially molds how one thinks, the pace at which one thinks, what one thinks, and the amount and complexity of knowledge one is able to develop. The new communication technologies will profoundly change the way we live our lives.

See also COMMUNICATIONS; COMMUNICATIONS: MEDIA LAW; COMPUTERS: PRIVACY ISSUES; INTEL-

LECTUAL PROPERTY; INFORMATION SOCIETY; MEDIA CONSOLIDATION; TELECOMMUNICATIONS.

BIBLIOGRAPHY

FLAHERTY, DAVID H. *Protecting Privacy in Surveillance Societies.* Chapel Hill, NC: University of North Carolina Press, 1989.

LINOWES, DAVID F. *Personal Privacy in an Information Society.* Report of the Privacy Protection Commission. Washington, DC: U.S. Government Printing Office, 1977.

————. *Privacy in America: Is Your Private Life in the Public Eye?* Champaign, IL: University of Illinois Press, 1989.

PECK, ROBERT S., ed. *To Govern a Changing Society: Constitutionalism and the Challenge of New Technology.* Washington and London: Smithsonian Institution Press, 1990.

David F. Linowes

Communications Technology

Communications has been essential to the evolution of human society since civilization began. As communications technologies change, so does the structure of society. However, the past century has seen extraordinary advances in the technology of communications, and none more critical than a change in the speed of transmission and the scope of coverage.

Before the advent of electrical and electronic communications, the speed of communications and transportation were equivalent. Prior to the nineteenth century, information was moved at the same rate as goods and services, which limited the potential structural options for society. If a government wanted to send out a decree, that information traveled by messenger. If a person wanted to write a friend, or a merchant wanted to conclude a trade arrangement, the same limitations prevailed for those activities as well.

Thus, the ability of human beings to collaborate and work together depended upon their ability to come together in the same place at the same time. Technological advances beginning in the mid-nineteenth century, and continuing ever since, have transformed this relationship, so that it has become possible for people to do increasingly more without being in the same physical space.

Telegraphy led the way as the first of these innovations. This technology, invented by Samuel Morse in the 1850s, allowed people to send messages by code (Morse Code) over transmission wires strung across the United States. It provided an instantaneity of communication that was revolutionary at the time but allowed for very little information to be passed from one person to another, and there was little or no interactivity in the communication. It was a *low volume/low interactivity* technology.

Since the invention of the telegraph, the trend in communications has been toward *high volume/ high interactivity*. The telephone followed the telegraph and offered a higher level of interactivity, but initially only between two people at a time. Television, in its initial broadcast format, offered high-volume but very low interactivity.

A New Era

The advent of communications satellites has ushered in a new era of opportunity in the communications field. It was first noted in the late 1940s by British scientist and author Arthur C. CLARKE that a satellite placed in geosynchronous orbit (22,500 miles from the surface) over the Earth would be essentially stationary in relationship to the planet. Such a technology could therefore be used to relay signals from one point on Earth to another.

It was in the 1960s that the first communications satellite was in fact placed in orbit. This meant that all kinds of communications, whether low volume/low interactivity or high volume/high interactivity, could be transmitted instantaneously from one person to another, almost as if time and space were irrelevant.

The revolution caused by communications satellites and global wiring of telephones and computers has created the "global village" prophesied by media philosopher Marshall McLuhan, who also wrote and lectured extensively in the 1960s. While the planet itself has not changed in size, the communications process has changed significantly, so that we interact with one another like villagers in an earlier time. The latest developments in communications technology include a convergence of all kinds of media into one so-called "electronic superhighway."

The electronic superhighway, or National Information Infrastructure (NII), is envisioned as a fiber-optic interconnection of homes, schools, and businesses, initially nationwide in the United States and eventually worldwide, capable of carrying voice, images, data, and other forms of information. After a century of communications developing separately, many will converge into one integrated system. Computers and television sets are likely to merge as well, creating the smart television at home and in the office.

Other developments are beginning to transform not only human perceptions of space and time, but of reality itself. Interconnected communications systems, such as the Internet and the World Wide Web, are called "cyberspace" by their users and represent a new frontier for human exploration and settlement. *Virtual reality* is an extension of the cyberspace concept.

Virtual reality uses communications technology to create a digital universe that humans can "enter," pseudo-physically as well as mentally. The virtual reality concept opens up the possibility of virtual communities that are disconnected in physical time and space.

Other developments in the combined technologies of computing and communications promise the use of computer "agents," or pieces of software that would roam the worldwide communications networks in search of relevant information for human users. Intelligent agents can, and probably will, begin to replace certain human functions, such as repetitive writing activities.

The specific long-term future of communications technology essentially is beyond prediction, because of the speed with which changes are taking place. For example, automatic language translators, long a goal of computer developers, now seem to be within reach. We may also witness marriages between the technologies of computers, communications, and biotechnology to produce enhanced human beings who will be able to have information communicated directly to the brain without going through the computer, television, or other media.

In general, we can see an entirely new kind of system being created on Earth, consisting of a natural system (the Earth itself), a human system (humanity), and a technosystem (the worldwide network of computer and communications technologies). This "planetary overview system" is radically unique in the history of the planet and of humanity itself.

Issues and Concerns

The evolution of communications technology brings with it many challenges. For example, will people who are attracted to the virtual reality environment become addicted to it, preferring that state to so-called "normal reality?" The individual's rights to privacy are already being called into question, as increasingly detailed personal information is put on-line in computer networks. The kinds of crime that occur in normal reality have begun to occur in cyberspace as well, and law-enforcement agencies are just beginning to understand how to cope with criminal activity in the electronic world.

Other central questions include these: As information becomes more of a commodity, broadly available around the world, how will producers of information be compensated and how will copyright be protected? What is the role of universities and other learning institutions in circumstances where much of the planet's knowledge and many of its leading thinkers are available electronically? With human population growing and with more people spending more time communicating in more ways, are we really *communicating* better—or are we apt to drown in an ever-growing load of information?

As humans have evolved over the millennia, we have been forced to confront similarly challenging dilemmas, and so far the responses to these issues has supported our evolution as a species. It is an open question, however, whether our response to the explosion in information/communication technology will have the same effect.

See also COMMUNICATIONS; DIGITAL COMMUNICATIONS; ELECTRONIC CONVERGENCE; ELECTRONIC PUBLISHING; INFORMATION OVERLOAD; INFORMATION SOCIETY; INFORMATION TECHNOLOGIES; ON-LINE SERVICES; SATELLITE COMMUNICATIONS; TELECOMMUNICATIONS; TELEPHONES; TELEVISION.

BIBLIOGRAPHY

McLuhan, Marshall. *Understanding Media: The Extensions of Man.* New York: McGraw-Hill, 1964.
White, Frank. *The Overview Effect: Space Exploration and Human Evolution.* Boston: Houghton Mifflin, 1987.

Frank White

Communism

Communism has been defined as a society or social system in which there is no private property, no differentiation among social classes, and no money, with all goods being distributed according to need. It has also been identified as the doctrine for creating such a society. The following historical summary will look at the roots of communism and attempt to show why it is a failed doctrine that appears at this point in time to have no future.

The earliest roots of communist doctrine can be found in various utopian writings by Plato, Thomas More, Tommasso Campanella, Abbé de Mably, and others. However, it was not until the second half of the nineteenth century that what we know today as communism was first formulated, chiefly by the German political philosophers Karl Marx and Friedrich Engels. After the 1917 revolution in Russia, the Marxism of Marx and Engels became the Marxism-Leninism of Vladimir Lenin. According to this doctrine, "socialism"—a term which has been used to describe an enormous variety of disparate socio + political systems—was considered to be the first stage of communism, a necessary transition between capitalism and communism.

As it was practiced and promulgated, Marxism-Leninism took on a quasi-religious character with its own canon of "holy books"—the works of Marx, Engels, Lenin, and others. Despite its dogmatic character, Marxism claimed to be the result of a scientific analysis of society and branded traditional religions as the opiate of the people. "Scientific" communism has its own philosophy of nature (dialectical materialism), philosophy of history (historical materialism), and a collection of demagogic postulates on "labor as the first vital need," "no difference between town and village," "mental and manual labor," "no state government, self-government only," and so on. But many of these postulates are empty phrases, attractive to credulous people at times, but with little or no claim to scientific validity. Slogans aside, the real essence of communist doctrine consists of the three following postulates: (1) the destratification of society to eliminate social classes; (2) the demarketization of the economy (replacing private ownership of property and a free market with state ownership of property and central planning of production and consumption); and (3) the demonetarization of finances (i.e., "soft currency," or nonconvertible bank notes that can be printed in any needed quantities irrespective of available goods, instead of the "hard currency" of a market economy). These three principles were supposed to be achieved through a "socialist revolution" and a "dictatorship of the proletariat," which in practice was tantamount to the dictatorship of a Communist party controlled by an individual dictator like Lenin or Stalin or Mao Ze Dong.

The first attempt to realize this doctrine was made by radical extremists among the social democrats of Europe at the end of World War I, in 1917 and 1918. In some countries (Germany, Hungary, and Finland), there were attempts to foment a communist revolution that failed. Only in Russia did communists actually manage to seize power. In spite of the communist victory in the 1918–1922 civil war that followed the overthrow of the czar, it soon became apparent that implementation of true communism was not viable. Renamed the Union of Soviet Socialist Republics, or U.S.S.R., Russia was thrown into a state of dictatorship, ruled by a group of zealots who undermined industry and trade, and who destroyed and robbed the peasantry, causing the total collapse of the economy. Soon thereafter most of the peasantry, constituting 85 percent of the population, rebelled against the ideologues in the Kremlin; there were workers' strikes in Moscow, Petrograd, and elsewhere, and there was mutiny in the military.

Lenin responded by declaring the New Economic Policy (1921–1929), which restored private property and entrepreneurship, hard currency, and some degree of a market economy. Nevertheless, the new ruling class, or *nomenklatura*, remained in power, and in 1929 a new dictator, Joseph Stalin, undertook a second wave of reforms. As a result, for more than sixty years, until August 1991, there existed in the U.S.S.R. a totalitarian regime with mass repressions, hard labor, compulsory Marxist-Leninist ideology, and quasi-military social relations—like those in any army barracks where any officer could bully his subordinates. During this era, 60 million people were shot or perished in prisons or in exile—nearly one out of every three Soviet citizens. Those who evaded forced labor or doubted Marxist tenets shared the same fate: imprisonment.

There was evidence from the beginning of the inability of Marxism to compete with market-based economies. But sweeping events tended to mask some of these failures. During the 1930s, when the country was preparing for the war against Germany and Japan, as well as during the war itself and the painful period of reconstruction afterward, noneconomic forces worked to preserve and prolong the status quo. However, in the mid-1950s it finally became clear to the ruling clique that economic and eventually political catastrophe was inevitable unless drastic measures were undertaken. As a result there were successive waves of attempts to revitalize socialism and make it competitive with the free-market West: the reforms of 1956–1964, 1966–1971, 1979, 1983, and 1985–1991. All of these attempts failed.

Simultaneously efforts were made to find a way out of permanent crisis by military means. After Russia's victory in World War II, won with the help of Great Britain and the United States, pro-communist totalitarian regimes were established in many countries of the world, comprising nearly one-third of the globe's population. In addition, certain alternative varieties of nineteenth-century socialism and communism began to proliferate in the form of various kinds of anarchism, guild-socialism, and Christian, Islamic, Buddhist, and African socialism. Non-Marxist totalitarianism, loosely or not at all dependent on the U.S.S.R., triumphed in Libya, Iraq, Syria, Myanmar, Iran, Ethiopia, Angola, Mozambique, and some other countries of the Third World. Numerous attempts were undertaken to expand the sphere of the "world socialist system" and satellite totalitarian regimes: the blockade of West Berlin, military adventures in Greece, Iran, Korea, Angola, an attempt to seize control of Bosphorus and the Dardanelles, the deployment of Soviet nuclear weapons in Cuba in order to blackmail the United States, and so on.In the long run, none of these attempts were successful.

By the early 1970s it became clear to the Soviet ruling clique that the arms race with NATO, which was four times more powerful economically and incomparably more powerful technologically, had been irreversibly lost. The Soviet leadership tried to counter this trend through negotiations (especially dangerous to the U.S.S.R. was the American Strategic Defense Initiative in space, which the U.S.S.R. had no means to counteract). However, the inertia of the long-lasting duel between the two superpowers continued to propel Soviet leaders toward further military adventurism, culminating with the invasion of Afghanistan, which involved the U.S.S.R. in a long, frustrating, demoralizing, and exhausting war, similar to the American experience in Vietnam.

It is important to emphasize that one of the main impulses for the last attempt to find a way out of the crisis, Gorbachev's *perestroika* (1985–1991), was an open admission of defeat in the Cold War and a last-ditch effort to save the "world socialist system" by bringing the arms race to a halt.

As is well known, totalitarianism can only flourish in an atmosphere of fear and mass repression. When fear and repression are lessened, totalitarianism inevitably collapses. The successive rebellions in Eastern Europe—East Germany in 1953, Hungary in 1956, Czechoslovakia in 1968, Poland in the late 1970s—point to the gathering momentum of the anticommunist movement in that region from year to year. There was also a steadily increasing flow of refugees to Western countries. In the second half of the 1980s, their numbers were so

significant that the Soviet government was confronted with a dilemma: either to step up the occupation of Eastern Europe to 1945 levels (and face the prospect of a world war they could not hope to win) or to capitulate. The struggle within the inner circles of leadership intensified, and the latter course was chosen. As a result, the Soviet socialist empire collapsed in 1989 followed by the disintegration of the U.S.S.R. itself in 1991 and by the virtually total rejection of the idea of communism by public opinion worldwide.

It is important to emphasize that communism is not merely an abstract idea but has constituted a global tragedy that brought grief to millions of victims throughout the world. By 1992 the world socialist empire had almost totally collapsed. Only a few separate countries retained Marxism as their official ideology—China, North Korea, Cuba, Vietnam—and they no longer constitute a united front, some of them being inimical to each other. Very close to these countries in the political, social, economic, and ideological sense are such totalitarian countries as Libya, Iran, Iraq, Syria, some of the former Soviet republics of Central Asia, and others. But these are mainly a remnant, and it is only a question of time before they return from social pathology to social norm.

Communist parties, which until recently existed in more than 120 countries, have been discredited almost everywhere that communists are not still in power, and many of them have dissolved, no longer able to turn to Moscow for subsidy of their activities. Even so, communist ideas are still rather popular among certain social and intellectual groups in the former U.S.S.R. and other countries of the world. The diehards include some members of the older generation who are used to living under totalitarianism and find it difficult to alter their mind-sets, as well as some younger people who resent the national humiliation caused by the downfall of the socialist empire. There has also been some reaction against the new varieties of corruption that have been manifest in the transition from totalitarianism to democracy. Even among those who reject communism there are those who hold the opinion that communists are not state criminals on a par with Hitler's Nazis. It will take perhaps two generations for people to adjust to the new democratic order and become real citizens of a real democracy. It will not be easy and many uncertainties remain.

See also CHINA; INTERNATIONAL TENSIONS; POLITICAL ECONOMY; RUSSIA; SOCIAL DEMOCRACY; SOCIALISM.

BIBLIOGRAPHY

BRZEZINSKI, ZBIGNIEW. *The Grand Failure: The Birth and Death of Communism in the 20th Century.* New York: Macmillan, 1990.

EDERSTADT, NICK. *The Poverty of Communism.* New Brunswick, NJ: Transaction Books, 1989.

PRYER, PETER. *The New Communism.* New York: State Mutual, 1988.

WESTOBY, ADAM. *Evolution of Communism.* New York: Free Press, 1989.

Igor Bestuzhev-Lada

Communitarianism

The communitarian movement seeks to shore up the moral, social, and political foundations of society. It builds on the elementary social science observation that people are born without any moral or social values. If they are to become civil, they must acquire values. Later, they may rebel against these values or seek to modify them, but they first must have some.

Historically, the family was the societal entity entrusted with laying the foundation for moral education. Schools were the second line of defense. Community bonds—whether clustered around religious institutions, schools, town meetings, or other establishments—served to reinforce values previously acquired. These social institutions have been the seedbeds of virtue, in which values are planted and cultivated.

In contemporary society, to a significant extent, these seedbeds have been allowed to wither. We should not be surprised, then, that the young ignore our entreaties to "just say no" to the numerous temptations society puts in their way, or when children kill children without showing remorse.

We need to restore the seedbeds of virtue if society is to regain civility. Such restoration does not entail a simple return to the traditional past, a past that had its own defects—a society that did discriminate against women and minorities and that was at least a bit authoritarian. Specifically, we need first of all to expect that both mothers and fathers be more dedicated to their children and that as a community we again value children. We must enable parents to be parents by allowing more flex time, work at home, and paid leave when children are born (as is the case throughout Europe), and by reducing the marriage penalty in the tax code.

Schools must put character education at the top of their agenda and not allow academic pressures to crowd out their civilizing agenda. Everything that happens in schools generates experiences and sends messages to the students. Are the corridors, parking areas, and cafeterias disorderly danger zones or places where people learn to respect one another? Is sport used to teach that winning is the only thing or that playing by the rules is essential? Are grades handed out on the basis of hard work— or some other social criteria? Schools need to engage in self-evaluation and line up the experiences they generate so that they will reinforce rather than undermine the educational message that they are supposed to carry.

Communities happen to a large extent in public spaces. When our parks, sidewalks, squares, and other public spaces are threatened by crime, communities are thwarted. Community policing, neighborhood crime watches, drug checkpoints, and domestic disarmament are among the new devices that may help communities recapture those spaces. Above all, we need to increase the certitude that those who commit a crime will be punished, and it may not be enough to merely increase the size of their penalty. Needless to say, if families and schools will do a better job in transmitting values, the communities' public safety burden will grow lighter.

Finally, civility requires that the vigilant protection of rights not be turned into extremism in which new rights are manufactured at will. There are reasonable limits to behavior, and the unlimited "right" to rent a car or for women to use the men's room may exceed the limits of civility. There are limitations to individual rights, and if each right is treated as an absolute, the rights of other persons inevitably are diminished.

The Constitution opens by directing the federal government to insure the general welfare, the common good. The courts have long balanced individual rights with social responsibilities. They authorized drug testing for those who have the lives of others directly in their hands, sobriety checkpoints, and screening gates at airports. A civil society requires careful nurturing of both rights and responsibilities—not the dominance of one at the expense of the other.

Communitarian ideas have long been with us. They are found in writings of the ancient Greek philosophers and the Old and New Testaments. The contemporary communitarian movement in the United States was established in 1990. Its first formal expression was the only communitarian quarterly in the world, *The Responsive Community.* In 1991 a communitarian platform was issued and was endorsed by 100 leading Americans.

In 1993 a membership organization, The Communitarian Network was established and headquartered in Washington, D.C. A book explicating its philosophy was issued: *The Spirit of Community, Rights, Responsibilities, and the Communitarian Agenda* in 1993.

See also CHANGE, CULTURAL; ETHICS; MODERNISM AND POSTMODERNISM; MORALS; POLITICAL CYCLES; POLITICAL PARTIES; POLITICAL PARTY REALIGNMENT; VALUES; VALUES CHANGE; VALUES FORMATION.

BIBLIOGRAPHY

ETZIONI, AMITAI. *The Spirit of Community: Rights and Responsibilities and the Communitarian Agenda.* New York: Crown Publishing, 1993.

HUGHES, ROBERT. *Culture or Complaint: The Fraying of America.* New York: Oxford University Press, 1993.

MAGNET, MYRON. *The Dream and the Nightmare: The Sixties' Legacy to the Underclass.* New York: William Morrow, 1993.

Amitai Etzioni

Competitive Sports and Games.

See SPORTS AND GAMES, COMPETITIVE.

Computer Games.

See INTERACTIVE ENTERTAINMENT.

Computer Hardware

Gordon Moore, cofounder of chipmaker Intel Corporation, predicted in the early 1970s that the speed of the microprocessor chip would double every eighteen months. His prediction, known as "Moore's Law," has been correct so far. Many forecasters expect Moore's Law to remain valid or nearly so well into the twenty-first century. Ironically, though, Moore himself raised doubts in 1993. If the law does hold, the computer chip—which has dramatically changed our daily lives—will continue to shape society for several decades to come.

To the consumer, the increasing speed of the computer chip is most obvious in the form of gadgets, small appliances, and personal computers. Inexpensive watches now contain functions that would have been inconceivable at any price in the mechanical-watch era. Single-lens reflex cameras,

once the bulky and expensive tools of skilled photographers, now weigh a few ounces, cost about $100, and are nearly foolproof.

Electronic games far more complex than those once played on multimillion-dollar mainframes now fit in a pocket. Also pocket-sized and affordable are navigation devices that motorists, hikers, and sailors can use to locate any point on Earth within 300 feet. These devices receive data from the global positioning system, a satellite network installed for military navigation.

During the 1960s, telephone companies rationed mobile phones and typically reserved them for physicians. The electronics occupied a big box in the trunk of a sedan. Now hand-held mobile phones are so popular that telephone companies are scrambling to keep up with the demand for additional telephone numbers, exchanges, and area codes.

In the kitchen, even children can program multiple-step cooking instructions into a microwave oven. In the home or workplace, the power of yesterday's supercomputer resides in a $2,000 desktop computer. These are the obvious and everyday points at which individuals are aware of the effect of Moore's Law. Equally significant are the behind-the-scenes effects and startling implications for the future.

Behind the scenes, speedier computer chips have enabled a worldwide revolution in manufacturing efficiency. The same technology that puts microchips into cameras and desktop computers has made the supercomputer, the mainframe, and the minicomputer so affordable and so reliable that few manufacturers still rely on a manager's pad and pencil for calculations or plans of any type. As a result, the prices of many manufactured products—from motor vehicles to ballpoint pens—have remained affordable or even fallen. It is probable that the deflationary impact of computerized manufacturing will continue far into the twenty-first century. Increasing affordability of computers enhances prospects for the rapid economic development of less developed countries.

The cost of telecommunication services will continue to fall, as they have throughout the twentieth century. The computer chip is a key reason: It provides the rapid switching that can pack more signals into existing circuits—not only in the highly promising fiber-optic and satellite circuits but also in the copper wire that the telephone companies have been installing since the late nineteenth century.

The convergence of computing, telecommunications, and entertainment is occurring. Because we can safely assume that chips will become even faster and that the bandwidth (signal-carrying capacity) of communication circuits will continue to increase rapidly, software will become the industry of the future. In a convergent world, we think of software not in the traditional narrow definition of programs for business computers, but in a broader definition that includes communications, motion pictures, musical recordings, sequencers and other music programs, games, virtual reality systems, desktop video, and electronic storage of the contents of entire public libraries.

Defined in this way, software already is the most significant export of the United States. Giant corporations—including Microsoft, Viacom, and the regional Bell operating companies—may battle for position in a highly visible way, but the future may be even brighter for a worldwide cottage industry in software. Because software is not necessarily a capital-intensive business, it holds great promise for entrepreneurs and workers in smaller and developing countries. It is already happening: Software developers are writing and exporting products from countries such as Guatemala, and the continuing robustness of the worldwide telecommunication infrastructure overcomes the transportation problems that hinder other forms of manufacturing in many countries, such as those in central Africa. It is plausible that, within the next few decades, anyone could use a converged device (whatever it may be called) to download and store almost any motion picture ever made, to correspond with friends anywhere in the world, or to look up information in a distant library—and get a passable translation done in seconds, if necessary. What we now call personal digital assistants could become mighty computers, storage devices, and telecommunications tools. For example, a person could store his or her financial records, correspondence, family photos, favorite music, and entire medical history in such a portable device.

Perhaps the most interesting societal effect of Moore's Law is its impact on large private and public organizations. So far, the computer chip has tended to empower individuals in their private lives and in the workplace, and to flatten organizations. In the private sector, for example, networks of cheaper computers enabled the massive restructuring of U.S. corporations during the 1980s and '90s. As corporations began to use desktop computers and data communication to share work-related information more widely, they needed fewer layers of middle managers, whose main job was the manual processing and distribution of information. The old organizational model was a hierarchy, in which communication was primarily vertical: managers handed down the orders and assignments, and workers handed up the feedback and results. The new organization is becoming flatter with fewer layers of management, and is using more horizontal communication. Teamwork is replacing the hierarchical, command-and-control model of the past. Bosses are learning to act more like coaches.

This horizontal trend is unlikely to reverse soon. In fact, it's highly probable that companies will outsource even more of their work to vendors—including home-based workers. Inexpensive computers and reliable satellite communication have made the home office—located in an urban area or a country town—an economical powerhouse that would have been unthinkable as recently as the early 1980s. The same horizontal trend is at work in the public sector. Computer power on the citizen's desktop—and the telecommunication services to link to other desktops worldwide—may change a citizen's relationship to government. For example, approximately twenty million people now use the Internet, an informal worldwide network made up of private and public networks. The Internet operates mostly outside the control of any government. Many observers interpret the U.S. government's interest in network-building as a defensive measure, designed to get free-market networks under government control before they become larger. Governments see worldwide private-sector networks as a threat to their power to govern.

But the network is only half of the threat to government power; the other half is electronic encryption. Personal computers have become so powerful that they can create encryption codes that even supercomputers cannot crack. As more and more citizens use encrypted electronic messages, they could hide financial transactions from the tax collector. Governments would find it difficult or impossible to collect some income taxes. Some people speculate that the end of the income tax could lead to the end of the welfare system, and that could drive some former recipients to crime and and even lead to civil war. The Federal Bureau of Investigation and the National Security Agency want computer and telecommunication companies to use encryption methods that would give a key to the U.S. government. So far, the companies have not welcomed the idea; individuals, meanwhile, already are using encryption software available on the market. However the private-public conflict may be resolved, it is clear that the computer chip will be an engine for the empowerment of individuals—from budding software entrepreneurs to billions of consumers who simply want more goods and services at less cost.

See also COMMUNICATIONS; COMPUTERS: OVERVIEW; COMPUTERS: SOFTWARE; INTERACTIVE ENTERTAINMENT; TELECOMMUNICATIONS.

BIBLIOGRAPHY

"Auctioning the Airways." *Forbes: ASAP* (April 11, 1994).
DAVIDSON, JAMES DALE, and REES-MOGG, LORD WILLIAM. *The Great Reckoning*. New York, Simon & Schuster, 1993.
"Hollywired." *The Wall Street Journal*, March 21, 1994.
"No More Moore's Law: Moore." *Electronic Engineering Times*, May 17, 1993.

Jean L. Farinelli
Joseph R. Roy

Computer Linkage

From a user perspective, we can expect Local Area Networks (LANs) to disappear. Instead of an environment that offers geographically limited access to a well-defined group of machines, users will interact with a particular "server"—irrespective of where they happen to be. And this server, in turn, will present the user with a location-independent image of the rest of the world.

Thanks to the Asynchronous Transfer Mode (ATM) transmission and switching standard (which should become the medium of choice by the mid-1990s), so-called *local* and *wide*-area networks will hand off traffic to one another with minimal notice of boundaries. At the same time, ubiquitous use of the uniform-size, limited-header, ATM cell format will support voice and video calls over virtual circuits, as well as traditional datagram traffic—thereby blurring the distinction between LANs and PBXs as well.

Finally, a steadily growing shift toward wireless access will create demand for a uniform environment—available worldwide—from users who wish to carry their "terminals" in their pockets wherever they travel. In this scenario, the server located at a user's home base in Massachusetts would, for example, arrange to have paper copies of its client's messages delivered by a laser printer in a Paris airport. When this becomes commonplace, "local" will mean "anywhere on the planet."

Electronic Mail

While most future e-mail users will continue to *receive* a large portion of their messages as typed text, much of that material will originate from other modalities. In particular, the likely emergence of low-cost, large-vocabulary speech recognition in the late 1990s will allow users to dictate messages and see the resulting text appear in real time on the screens in front of them. Furthermore, since pen-based tablets, natural-sounding text-to-speech, scanners, and recognizers will become commonplace in that same time frame, the distinction between electronic mail and other forms of communication will surely blur as time goes on. A scanned-in image sent as part of an e-mail message would turn the combination into an annotated fax, for example, but how would one characterize it with a video insert added? Tomorrow's multimedia will make such distinctions obsolete.

Since tomorrow's personal workstations must travel with their owners worldwide, they will feature built-in modems and encryption circuitry, assuring reliable connectivity from out-of-the-way places not yet served by broadband networks. Each machine's owner will obtain robust access safeguards via a combination of voice and visual recognition, together with unobtrusive conversational interrogation based on the user's profile. Conversely, that same profile will restrict access in the other direction, via customized screening of incoming messages. Indeed, the conventional (paper mail) postal service's inability to provide sensitive automatic screening may well prove a decisive handicap in the struggle to maintain economic viability vis-à-vis electronic alternatives.

National and International Networks

Given the multiplicity of networking options and user needs, it seems likely that an interoperating group of specialized networks will prevail in the coming decades. While government-supported networks will address some needs, just as Internet does today, private-sector network providers will compete with one another in providing guaranteed levels of performance, facilities management, rapid rearrangement, and other features, to an increasingly demanding body of worldwide users.

Technology of Computer Networks

Looking forward, we can expect a continued mix of optical fibers for most land-line applications, and radio for individual mobility, together with a mixture of other technologies—such as metallic cables, and through-the-air optics—for special applications. If optoelectronic device yields and packaging technologies improve markedly, costs should drop to a level that will make hundreds of megabits per second available at the desktop, along with one-hundred-times-greater bandwidths in links between network servers. Moreover, the use of so-called *soliton* pulses in lightwave systems will permit even higher speeds, by circumventing lightguide nonlinearities that would otherwise limit transmission capacity.

Digital Data

While data networks will continue to support datagram service, a connection-oriented ATM network (based on virtual circuit technology) will actually provide the underlying connectivity— thereby providing better security and consistent performance. At the same time, many applications can be expected to make direct use of the virtual circuit's separation of data and control information in its messaging format.

Data Compression

While the size of some data files in the coming decades may seem huge by today's standards, we can expect even larger traffic volume from high-resolution images in a true multimedia environment. As a result, the need to cram data as tightly as possible into undersized pipes will lose much of its urgency. In its place, the main focus of compression technology will shift toward the realistic rendition of complex three-dimensional environments, especially as virtual reality and telepresence become commonplace networking features.

See also COMMUNICATIONS TECHNOLOGY; COMPUTERS: OVERVIEW; NETWORKING; DATA STORAGE; DIGITAL COMMUNICATIONS; ELECTRONIC PUBLISHING; INTERACTIVE ENTERTAINMENT; ON-LINE SERVICES; SATELLITE COMMUNICATIONS; SUPERCONDUCTORS; TELECOMMUNICATIONS; TELEPHONES; TELEVISION.

BIBLIOGRAPHY

GILSTER, PAUL. *The Internet Navigator.* New York: John Wiley, 1993.

JUSSAWALLA, MEHEROO, ed. *Global Telecommunications Policies: The Challenge of Change.* Westport, CT: Greenwood Press, 1993.

RHEINGOLD, HOWARD. *The Virtual Community: Homesteading on the Electronic Frontier.* Reading, MA: Addison-Wesley, 1993.

RUSHKOFF, DOUGLAS. *Cyberia: Life in the Trenches of Hyperspace.* San Francisco: HarperCollins, 1994.

Arno Penzias
Bonnie Penzias

Computers: Overview

Computers have made fundamental and accelerating changes in human society since the first programmable calculators were introduced in the nineteenth century. Computers enabled the emergence of the information sector as the dominant component of the U.S. economy in the mid-1950s. In 1994, about three of every five people employed in developed countries were information workers, people whose livelihoods depended on the creation, manipulation, transformation, or dissemination of information, or operation of information machines—computers. Although not all information workers regularly used computers in 1994, by the year 2000 most will. And, at least 60 percent of economic activity will be computer-dependent.

The root of all this transformation since the 1950s is solid-state physics, particularly semiconductor technology. First transistors, then integrated circuits, the first microprocessors, memory chips, lasers, magnetic and optical storage media, and display devices—all joined a diversifying array of components and systems that proved to be irresistible to people who wanted tools to accomplish their information work. A fundamental rule of thumb in this technological explosion is Moore's law, which states: the number of components on a state-of-the-art microchip doubles every other year. What Moore's law doesn't state, but what appears to be true in practice, is that the cost of the latest chip doesn't change much. In terms of cost per unit of information processing power Figure 1 tells the story. So far, each time that there seemed to be a technological limit to the number of components per chip, there has been a breakthrough that extended Moore's law for an additional few years. However, around 2010 we may find that continuation of the bottom curve of Figure 1 may not be possible.

A similar rule holds for related technologies such as magnetic and optical storage devices. Hard discs, once considered capacious if they held ten megabytes of information, are now capable of multibillion-byte capacity—in a module 3.5 inches wide. High-density magnetic tape storage is competing with removable magneto-optical discs that begin to rival hard discs in speed and exceed them in capacity.

The central effect of these trends is that information processing power that was once reserved for very large organizations is now available on desktops, in briefcases and pockets, automobiles, washing machines, microwave ovens, and telephones.

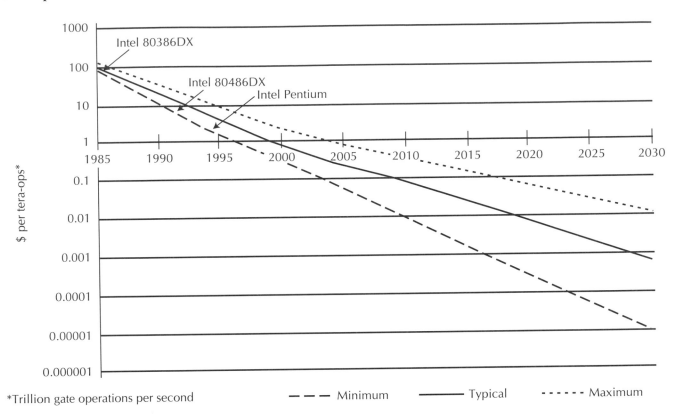

FIGURE 1.   Past and projected performance ranges for the Intel series of microchips; a similar pattern was also exhibited by the Motorola 68000 series of microchips and will likely also be exhibited by successive generations of RISC-based or other processors in the years ahead, with an evenual slowing of the pace of change.

Computers have spawned subindustries that were not even imagined at the beginning of the twentieth century.

The hierarchy of computers generally runs in decreasing order of size or processing power:

- Supercomputers
- Mainframes
- Minicomputers
- Engineering workstations
- Personal computers (PCs) and other microcomputers
- Personal digital assistants (PDAs)
- Organizers and calculators
- Embedded computers and smart devices.

In 1975, personal computers and PDAs didn't exist, the mainframe was considered to be the king of computers, and the dominant manufacturer was IBM. Supercomputers, such as the Cray series, were used primarily by the military or research organizations that required huge amounts of calculation, such as for detailed modeling of the weather. Even then, the growing power of minicomputers, led by machines produced by Digital Equipment Corporation and Data General, were eroding the market for mainframes. Workstations—microminicomputers—by Sun Microsystems and Hewlett-Packard, for example, became the powerful tools of engineers and scientists engaged in complex design projects.

By 1994, personal computers were taking market share away from workstations, minicomputers, and mainframes. The term *downsizing* applied not only to the trend of large corporations to slough off excess staff, but to the movement from mainframes to minis to workstations to PCs, and from central to local control of the organization's information activities.

Even at the supercomputer level, the effects of Moore's law are being felt. Once composed of a single, very-high-speed central processor surrounded by closely spaced memory banks (to minimize cable lengths; every foot of wire introduces a nanosecond of delay), new supercomputers are being built of large arrays of interconnected microprocessors operating in parallel. The same transformation is applying to mainframes. On the other hand, minicomputers and workstations may disappear as a class by 2000, either merging upward with mainframes or downward with high-end PCs. Whatever the nomenclature, general purpose computers will be associated with almost every office desk and laboratory bench by 2000. Personal computers are becoming more personal with the appearance of personal digital assistants (PDAs). At an introductory level in 1994, they are likely to become the equivalent, in variety and breadth of distribution, of pocket calculators by 2000, containing personal, financial, and health data, telecommunications interconnects, and a variety of information utilities for daily use.

At another level entirely, microprocessors are being incorporated into a huge variety of devices, making them "smart." Automobiles have a significant and growing number of computer-based functions, including ignition, fuel, air-conditioning, brakes, and instrument control. Many common household devices already incorporate microprocessors and "fuzzy logic" soft/firmware, enabling them to sense and react to a variety of operating conditions. Rudimentary appliance controllers have been on the market for several years, but as communications standards—and the size of the market—develop, "smart" buildings will also become increasingly common. These homes and offices will incorporate intercommunicating environmental and security devices that will run under their own programs, possibly with a central computer controller, and will also be accessible remotely via the telephone system. The new generation of digital high-definition television (HDTV) requires computer memory arrays and processing in the set to provide theater-quality viewing and sound.

The equivalent of Moore's law also is in operation for telecommunications technology. While computers, particularly personal computers, have been largely "stand-alone" machines much of the time, they are increasingly becoming interconnected via telecommunications. This fact—the jointly increasing power per dollar spent of both computers and telecommunications—has far-reaching implications.

Telecommunications using copper wires are being replaced by higher-capacity, speedier optical fibers. Huge mechanical switches for telephone interconnection have been replaced by much smaller computers. At the level of a single organization, computers interconnected by local area networks (LANs) are a large part of the trend toward elimination of mainframes. They also permit more effective operation of work groups through such means as electronic mail and joint editing of documents, spreadsheets, graphics, and other forms of analysis and documentation. Wide area networks (WANs) extend this reach to continental or global scales. Wireless data communications, first through analog, then digital cellular telephones, and next through cellular satellite transmission, extend the interconnective computer reach both to mobile offices and to rural or remote areas without wired communications access.

Computer networking in the early 1990s closely resembled the early days of the telephone industry: each network had its own set of standards and protocols, often incompatible with other networks. But as interest in networking grew, so did systems and standards for communication between computers. The technique of packet switching gave rise to a new revolution in global communication, as typified by several commercial computer networks and the Internet—an informal organization of individual computer networks that included more than two million host computers covering the globe by 1993. As this form of networking expands and evolves, it will be possible for a computer to communicate with another computer anywhere in the world. Key steps in this expansion will be the development of globally observed directory and interface protocols, and encryption techniques indecipherable by interlopers for message protection. These latter steps are necessary for effective commercial acceptance of networking.

At the first level of impact, computers alone and telecommunications-connected computers are used primarily to increase the efficiency of existing operations. After a period varying from a few months to years, new applications and configurations arise that use the improved technologies. One of the most significant of these is telework: the substitution of information technology for work-related travel—transporting the work instead of the worker. Because of these technological changes, teleworking will be a viable option for at least one-half the workforce of developed countries by 2000.

Teleworking and its major component telecommuting have a number of positive consequences for employers, employees, and the communities in which the employees live. For employers, the primary benefits include increases in worker effectiveness and teamwork, and decreases in operating costs, office space, and turnover rates. For employees, the benefits include reduced stress from commuting, increases in—and greater control over—discretionary time, access to education via interactive distance learning programs, and better family life in properly managed telework situations, without negative effects on their careers. For urban communities, reduced traffic congestion and air pollution as well as reduced crime rates are the payoff. For rural communities, these technologies bring economic revitalization and development as both work and new educational opportunities become independent of the location of the worker or student. All of these consequences have been demonstrated in the past two decades, and the growth of telecommuting applications is accelerating.

The fundamental attribute of teleworking is independence of location. Because of information technology, many work functions can be performed anywhere. This gives rise to new structure and forms of organizations. Within an organization, for example, teams can be formed that include members who may be scattered around the globe.

Traditionally, such teamwork always required a large amount of face-to-face interaction. Simple telephone communications were considered poor substitutes. Now, digital videoconferencing and other multimedia communications are becoming economically practical for general use and approximate face-to-face interaction. Network and evanescent organizations are developing globally, coalescing for particular projects, then reforming in new combinations as new opportunities arise. The objectives of these organizations can be business, government, public interest, education, or some combination.

Increased computer use causes some forms of structural unemployment. That is, some jobs disappear or are distinctly downgraded because computers take over some or all of the job's functions. For example, the traditional job functions of a secretary, once primarily involving telephone answering and text processing services, are being supplanted by computer-enabled voice mail or answering machines and PC-based text processing software operated by the originator of the message—not the secretary. One outcome of this process is for the job of secretary to disappear. Another is for the job to be upgraded or enriched: secre-

taries become administrative assistants, handle spreadsheets and database searches, act as personnel coordinators, or otherwise diversify. Although some jobs clearly become extinct because of computers, new jobs arise. For example, the professions of computer programmer, database search expert, CAD/CAM engineer, or computer graphics artist didn't exist in 1950. The central question is: Will the new jobs be more numerous and better—in terms of economic rewards and personal satisfaction—than the vanished ones? The evidence so far is that they will.

Whatever the details, everyone's life will be moderated by computers in the years to come.

See also ARTIFICIAL INTELLIGENCE; COMMUNICATIONS; COMPUTER HARDWARE; COMPUTERS: SOFTWARE; DATA STORAGE; DIGITAL COMMUNICATIONS; ELECTRONIC PUBLISHING; INFORMATION SOCIETY; INFORMATION TECHNOLOGY; TELECOMMUNICATIONS.

BIBLIOGRAPHY

DREXLER, K. ERIC. Nanosystems: Molecular Machinery, Manufacturing, and Computation. New York: John Wiley and Sons, 1992.

The Internet Unleashed. Indianapolis, IN: Sams Publishing, 1994.

NILLES, JACK M. *Making Telecommuting Happen: A Guide for Telemanagers and Telecommuters.* New York: Van Nostrand Reinhold, 1994.

NILLES, JACK M., et al. *A Technology Assessment of Personal Computers,* 3 Vols. Los Angeles: University of Southern California, Center for Futures Research, 1980.

PORAT, MARC U. *The Information Economy: Definition and Measurement.* Washington: U.S. Department of Commerce, Office of Telecommunications, 1977.

TOFFLER, ALVIN. *The Third Wave.* New York: William Morrow, 1980.

Jack M. Nilles

Computers: Privacy Laws

Today we live in the earliest stages of a new era in which information itself is considered by many the most valuable commodity of all. This view is rooted in the technological power of the computer, and its growing role in every aspect of modern life. Less noticed, but no less significant in contributing to the growing impact of the computer, is the ongoing revolution in the communications networks of today.

Evolution of the Era

An understanding of the problems that stem from such technology begins with an understanding of the evolution of this new era, the speed with which it has emerged, and the uses that are only now beginning to be understood.

In 1950, there was no such thing as the computer business. But, one year later, the first real-time computer called the Whirlwind became operational at MIT. Two years later, IBM shipped its first stored-program computer, the 701.

The rapid deployment of the computer over the thirty years from 1960 to 1990 was unimaginable. In 1960, 1,790 mainframe computers were being shipped domestically at a value approaching $600 million. Fifteen years later in 1975, the value of all computers and related peripheral equipment shipped into the U.S. market had risen to roughly $7.5 billion. But the nature and magnitude of computing power being shipped had changed dramatically. Mainframe shipments had grown to 6,790 units, but so-called minicomputers and microcomputers were also being shipped at the annual rate of 26,990 and 10,500, respectively. By 1990, the value of shipments approached $56.2 billion and included more than 7 million micros, 232,000 minis, and 12,250 mainframes. Thus, from 1975 to 1990, the economic value of computer shipments climbed by a factor of 7.4, while the raw number of units shipped jumped by a factor of more than 165! That trend has continued to the present so that by 1993, the U.S. computer industry was shipping more than 9 million computers a year, or roughly one computer for every 30 people. By the year 2000 forecasters estimate that one billion computers and smart-card computers will be in use in the United States.

To service this new industry, America's educational institutions began training men and women at an equally impressive rate. The first Ph.D. in the field of computer science was granted by the University of Pennsylvania in 1965. By 1989, 3 percent of all bachelor's degrees and more than 1 percent of all doctorates awarded annually in American universities were in the field of computer science.

For all of the impressive growth figures in the computer industry though, no single technical invention has been considered more important to the quality of life than the telephone. For years, the guiding U.S. policy for telecommunications was universal service. (In much of the developing world, that still is a goal.) To achieve that end, U.S. policy controlled telephone companies almost completely and used long distance rates to subsidize local phone service. The policy was so effective that in the 40 years between 1930 and 1970 phone service grew from a service for a very few privileged households into a standard convenience that was installed in 87 percent of all homes. Today, in the United States and most developed nations, that goal has been essentially realized. For example, telephone service now reaches more than 93 percent of all occupied houses in the United States.

A latecomer to the communications revolution, cable television now boasts penetration rates in excess of 60 percent of all households in the United States. (In 1970, only 6.7 percent of households had cable TV.)

By almost any measure, the "wiring of the modern world" has proceeded at an awesome pace.

Converging Industries

The telecommunications infrastructure is now truly global in reach. More than 280,000 miles of fiber-optic cable with virtually infinite bandwidth span the globe. This capability is augmented by wireless technologies from satellites, microwaves, and in the forseeable future, lasers. The result of this is that today there is truly no place on Earth where the telecommunications network is not available in some form.

The technological basis of communications and computers is merging. Computers were designed on a binary basis and therefore utilized digital transmission from the beginning. The public switched telephone network (PSTN) was designed as an analog transmission system to carry voice. Technically and economically, there were sound reasons for this disparate development. But, recent advances in digitalization and more powerful microprocessors have led to superior quality in digital transmission. Historically, computers had to transmit information through the PSTN by converting from digital to analog and then reconverting back to digital form at the receiving end. Clearly, the process of conversion was inefficient. With both systems using digital technology, the need for this inefficiency vanishes. Moreover, the technical base of the two industries is converging so that the sharp distinction that historically existed between telecommunications and computers as an industry is not sustainable.

The Chip Culture

Add to these facts another facet. Linked by miles of cable or wireless transmission to every conceivable type of equipment and each other, computers monitor, control, and record millions of routine events and actions every day.

Computers, in the form of microchips, have been widely integrated into almost everything that we buy or use from automobiles to refrigerators. They control the engines in the cars we drive, enhance our vision from space, monitor and direct factories, enable physicians to perform microsurgery, allow us to program VCRs, control the utilities in a house or commercial building, and more.

The Capacity for Good Versus the Potential for Evil

The technological capacity we now possess to acquire, store, retrieve, and process information opens the door to major improvements in the quality of life, but misused, it also confronts society with completely new challenges. The fact is that the current ethical, policy, and legal structure that oversees this data-intensive age is, in some key aspects, critically deficient. In order to understand this reality, policy makers, ethicists, managers, citizens, and lawmakers must now struggle with understanding the nature of the deficiencies and what to do to redress them.

Nowhere are these deficiencies more pressing than in the right to personal privacy. By all indications, most people consider personal privacy to be a fundamental right. Even the courts have recognized a right to privacy. Privacy is essential to a reasonable quality of life. Yet the precise definition of what the right to privacy covers is far from clear. The advent of the information society is posing questions about that right that have never been considered before. How we draw the line between the free use and exchange of information on the one hand, and the right to privacy on the other, will fundamentally shape our lives in the future.

Living with the Information Age

An examination of daily life reveals the collection of an ominously long and growing list of details and information about the life of the average individual: records of bill payment, medical histories, books purchased at the local store or checked out at the local library, programs watched on cable television and/or the videos rented for home viewing, courses taken in various schools attended and the grades received, employment evaluations, personal productivity statistics, items purchased at the grocery store (including products for personal use), any records related to law enforcement, tax records, driver's licenses, applications for credit, credit history, insurance policies, travel records, and so on. All of these data and more are stored somewhere in the electronic information superstructure of the modern world.

The presence of such an overwhelming amount of information and the increasingly ubiquitous nature of the telecommunications system raise three distinct threats to personal privacy.

The first is the illicit interception of personal messages and conversations by unintended parties. "Wiretapping" of course was always technically possible, but the sophistication required to do it and the legal procedures established to prevent its abuse were generally sufficient to protect privacy. As recent history has shown, however, wireless telephones open a whole new set of possibilities to would-be eavesdroppers. Likewise, E-mail systems and phone-mail systems are subject to penetration and "eavesdropping" by unintended parties.

The second, and more difficult, threat is the use or misuse of the information that can now be readily assembled about groups of people or individuals. Information has always been available, but historically the time and effort required to gather large amounts of it have provided a natural defense. Now, however, it can be assembled in relatively short periods of time. Moreover, because the incremental cost is minimal, more detailed information is routinely kept and available in hundreds of disconnected databases. That poses society with some new problems when it comes to privacy.

Consider the following examples: State governments have always maintained complete records of drivers' licenses and car tags matched to the people who own them. Such records were necessary to administer the licensing of vehicles. Historically, such records have been considered public information and hence available for public inspection on government premises. But, since it is public information, why not make it available in an easier-to-use form? At least one state now provides a complete listing of motor vehicle license plates and their owners on magnetic media for a nominal service fee. Now, a list that would have required thousands of man-hours to assemble can be acquired in virtually no time at minimal cost. An automobile dealer might acquire and use such a list to send direct mailings to all the Pontiac owners in his or her service area. Does this constitute an invasion of privacy?

On another front, one of the most popular phenomena of our time has been the rapid growth of stores that rent movies to customers. The computerized check-out systems used by most video stores provide complete and detailed rental histories for every customer. Because such information is available, political candidates, for instance, have found themselves pressed to release the history of their VCR movie rentals to the public. Is such information, privately held, a legitimate target of public political inquiry or not?

If an insurance company were to decide to use a list of subscribers to a gay magazine as a prescreening device for insurance applicants who might have AIDS, would that constitute an invasion of privacy, or illegitimate treatment of some type?

Many institutions, from hospitals to churches, keep computer records. With how much security should they be required to maintain these records? In an electronic age, unethical employees, service technicians, or others could copy and pass on detailed personal records without ever being detected. Security countermeasures exist, but as with all security systems, the costs in terms of user-friendliness and expense have to be weighed by the information provider or holder. The information holder may not always value security as much as the people on whom information is held.

The third and most potentially troubling use of information technology is to monitor the actions of others. At the extreme end, many states are experimenting with programs that place minor criminals under house arrest and monitor their whereabouts by electronic means. This is a cheaper, and in many ways better, alternative to prison. But on another more controversial front, an estimated 26 million Americans now have their work monitored by computers, and the number is climbing. These systems can be designed to keep track of productivity (keystrokes per minute or number of phone calls handled per hour) and even advise when it is time to take a break. But they also offer employers the opportunity to monitor phone conversations, track how much time employees spend in the bathroom, or enable supervisors to periodically monitor the work of subordinates while remaining undetected themselves.

Troubling Questions

Several questions arise as one considers these matters. Should the definition of "public information" change or should access somehow be limited? How safe are the security systems used now and how safe do they need to be? Should different systems be required by law to conform to certain levels of

security? Are records contained in business files, like those of the video rental store, public or private? What happens when employees or others with access to data not generally available to the public make it available to other people or the press? Should businesses have the right to sell their own customer lists and information about those customers to other parties who may want them? If so, are there any limits on how the information can be sold? Who guarantees the accuracy of information in all these sources? Who is liable for intentional or accidental harm resulting to individuals damaged by erroneous information? For example, if a hospital incorrectly identifies a person as having contracted HIV or if an erroneous credit record causes someone to be denied credit, housing, or even employment, who has legal liability? What constitutes fair or unfair use of information? How does society police the illicit sale of information? What kind of enforcement can and should governments provide for whatever body of laws emerge in this area? Does employer monitoring of work produce undue stress, and if so, are employers liable for some type of stress-related damage caused to an employee?

The list of troubling considerations is almost without limit. Some of the issues are not new, but the potential magnitude of the problem has fundamentally changed the calculus that will be applied in the legal and political system.

An Evolving Future

One of the certainties in modern life is the fact that governments at all levels will have to grapple with these issues. Tough, pragmatic standards that ensure fairness, economic affordability, enforceability, and the continued free flow of information will have to be developed. Law enforcement procedures, standards of accountability, and professional ethics all will have to evolve in the near future as public and private parties struggle with the still unwritten rules.

The bodies that will write these rules have yet to clearly assert themselves. Political bodies will certainly play a major role, but unless private industry professionals move to the foreground of the debate fairly quickly, the courts will probably assume the dominant role.

Unfortunately, that will take time. Indeed, the nature of legal systems is to proceed slowly until considered reason and case history support a well-established body of precedents. In the meantime, there are almost certain to be cases of grievous personal harm. How we deal with those cases as a society will do much to define the legitimate and illegitimate uses of information and guarantee the safeguarding of "personal" information.

See also COMMUNICATIONS: PRIVACY ISSUES; COMPUTERS: OVERVIEW.

BIBLIOGRAPHY

BLOOMBECKER, JAY, ed. *Computer Crime, Computer Security, Computer Ethics.* Santa Cruz, CA: National Center for Computer Crime, 1986.

HOFFMAN, LANCE J. *Security and Privacy in Computer Systems.* Ann Arbor, MI: Books-on-Demand, 1993.

Security and Privacy, Research In. Symposium. Los Alamitos, CA: IEEE Computer Society, 1991.

Wes Williams

Computers: Safety

The basic technology of the video display terminal (VDT), or computer monitor, was developed for television reception early in the twentieth century. Inside the VDT is a cathode-ray tube (CRT) similar to the picture tube in a television receiver. In a CRT, the cathode (an electrode in the end of the tube closer to the back of the television set or VDT) emits a beam of electrons aimed at the center of the screen. Electromagnetic deflection coils or electrostatic plates surround the neck of the tube and control the direction of the beam. At the point where it strikes the screen, the beam triggers illumination in the chemicals that coat the inside surface of the screen. The beam sweeps across the screen line by line to create an image. The image is updated a number of times per second. This "refresh rate" varies in different computer monitors, but sixty times per second is typical. The lower the refresh rate, the more the screen appears to flicker and the more fatiguing, many researchers say, the work becomes.

Researchers have estimated that more than fifty million people in the United States use VDTs every day in their work.

Historically, as more workers began to use VDTs, some workers began to complain of eye strain, headaches, and other ailments. Gradually, from the 1960s through the early 1990s, the number and variety of complaints kept rising. So did the variety of the medical diagnoses and the number of private-sector and public-sector studies of various VDT hazards. Researchers are concerned primarily about the electromagnetic fields (EMFs) generated within the VDT. During the 1970s, two landmark VDT-hazard incidents occurred in Sweden and the United States. In 1975, Swedish scientists reported that VDT operators were complaining of blurred vision and inability to focus their eyes. In 1976, two young copy editors at the *New York Times* developed opacities in both eyes—a precursor of cataracts, which rarely occur in young people. There have been many studies since, some of them in conflict. The list of ailments attributed to VDTs has grown, especially injuries to the unborn. Unions in many countries have pushed for regulatory safeguards. The regulatory leaders have been Sweden, Germany, France, the United Kingdom, and Japan. In addition, many state and local jurisdictions in the United States established regulations.

However, a clear scientific consensus still has not emerged. Some manufacturers continue to deny that VDT hazards exist; others have redesigned their products to meet the strict Swedish standards. Proper CRT design and effective shielding of electromagnetic field radiation are the key precautions. For their part, many employers are concerned for the safety of their VDT users. Some have adopted remedies, such as installing glare screens, repositioning equipment to minimize exposure, encouraging frequent breaks, and advising pregnant women on the possible dangers to unborn children. Researchers who agree that CRTs impose hazards are also concerned about larger television screens, which will become increasingly popular and affordable, and about the future widespread adoption of high-definition television (HDTV). In the United States, preschoolers watch television more than twenty hours per week on average; millions of adults watch between thirty and forty hours per week.

While this controversy may continue, it is possible that alternative technologies gradually will replace CRTs. The technologies include liquid crystal, gas plasma, and semiconductor-based displays. Unlike CRTs, these technologies do not involve significant EMF emanations. However, the widespread adoption of these technologies may be slow. They are more expensive or they lack the clarity and fast response of the better-established CRT technology. If the history of most technologies is any guide, the wider adoption of CRT alternatives may well lead to design improvements and lower costs, which in turn could accelerate their adoption. Another approach would be to reduce VDT use by increasing the use of other input technologies, such as optical character recognition scanning and voice recognition. Both technologies are burgeoning and show great promise for the future, and both offer efficiency gains aside from any relief they may offer from VDT hazards.

See also COMPUTERS: OVERVIEW; COMPUTERS: PRIVACY LAWS; TECHNOLOGICAL HAZARDS.

BIBLIOGRAPHY

"The Big Question: Is the PC Environment a Safe Place to Work?" *PC Magazine* (December 12, 1989).
"Terminal Damage." *The Jerusalem Post*, November 16, 1989.
"VDT Safety Debate Is Still Plugged In." *The Business Journal-Sacramento*, October 22, 1990.

Jean L. Farinelli
Joseph R. Roy

Computers: Software

The connotations of the word *software* range from the mundane to the metaphysical. The most commonly employed usage refers quite pragmatically to a commodity bought in retail stores to enable computers to perform particular functions, such as figuring taxes or amusing children. At the opposite end of this scale, philosophers (e.g., Daniel Dennett, Hillary Putnam, John Searle) have fiercely debated whether the relationship between mind and brain is equivalent to the relationship between software and hardware in computers.

Debates about mind as software are not without real-world significance. They have a bearing on what kind of machine, if any at all, can emulate human intelligence. In the reverse direction, such debates have influenced how psychologists think about the human mind. They are also related to a more general intellectual perspective with widespread implications for public policy and economic development: the concept of software reflects a previously unthinkable separation between the physical properties of a machine and the function that it performs. In its most abstract sense this insight can be credited to Alan Turing, who had already formulated in the 1930s the concept of a universal computing machine (known in his honor as a "Turing Machine") that could (in a certain formal sense) act like any other computing machine; in modern jargon functional differences between physically identical machines would lie in the software. The practical sweep of this idea has been enormously extended as the development of digital technologies brings more and more functionality under the rubric of "computing machine."

A simple example that will illustrate the general point is a profound shift in views (see Nicholas Negroponte, *Being Digital*) about "standards" for communication industries. Today most television sets used in the United States would not work in France, because the way signals are turned into pictures is determined by the hardware. Soon the insides of a television set will be a "universal computing machine" whose software will enable it to accept signals in whatever digital form they come. This shift will transcend not only boundaries between nations but also between such media as television, telephones, print, and personal computers.

The liberation of television from such standards as picture shape and resolution is part of a deeper evolution of the stuff of which artifacts are made. Pictures painted by stone-age artists on the walls of caves or by Picasso on canvas are all composed of atoms. What can be done with them is limited by the properties of matter. When I place a picture on my computer screen, I may see it through the mediation of a material screen, but the entity I bring (or "down-load" from a site on the Internet) is made of a different kind of stuff. It is not a physical entity but a software entity. It is not composed of atoms but of bits; and because bits are not restrained by physical laws, software entities can be transformed, transmitted, and reproduced in so nearly arbitrary ways that nobody yet has more than a glimmer of any limiting laws that may exist.

Software is seen in the largest historical perspective by recalling how early stages in human industry, indeed in civilization itself, are conventionally marked by turning points in the stuff of artifacts: the Stone Age, the Bronze Age, and the Iron Ages opened new vistas for our ancestors on the variety and complexity of life. For many millennia industry was about transforming and transporting matter. It is only in the past century that a new stuff became prominent: we moved into a period in which large fortunes were made, and world politics shaped, by dealing in energy. It appears to be a safe prediction that in the twenty-first century the third stuff in the sequence—matter, energy, software—will become dominant as measured by the numbers of people engaged and most especially as measured by the importance in shaping society.

The shift to software objects and to software tools for working with them is ubiquitous and far-reaching in its consequences. Shifting from quill pens to fountain pens to ball-point pens changed the ease but not the nature of making financial records and projections. Shifting from figures made of ink to figures made of software radically changes what can be done and who can do it. Financial deals of unprecedented complexity can be developed with a rapidity that was unprecedented even for all but the simplest transactions in the past. Moreover, such a plan can be developed by an executive with minimal arithmetical and book-keeping skills.

One of the most strikingly novel features of the pattern of appropriation is the presence of children in the population of users. Here too it is instructive to contrast the nature of previous shifts in toys—(e.g., from wooden trucks and cloth dolls to plastic forms of each—with the shift from material toys to software toys. On the economic level the importance of children as consumers of software is seen in the fact that multibillion-dollar companies in this area (e.g., Nintendo) have grown as dramatically as their counterparts (e.g., Microsoft) in business software. But the greater potential importance of the presence of software in the lives of children comes through its impact on the learning environment.

A full appreciation of the trends in software requires one to discount a phenomenon that happens to be well illustrated in the development of software for children. The uses to which software is put follow a pattern that is shared by the process of social appropriation of any new technology. The first application almost always consists of using it to achieve improvement in something that had been done before—for example, making movies by acting in front of the camera just as if it were in a theater. It took many years for anything resembling what we now call "cinema" to emerge, with all the paraphernalia of Hollywood, of stardom, of techniques such as closeups and editing that make it very different from stage acting.

An analog to photographing the stage is making software to teach children the number skills that are made unnecessary by the presence of computers. Most computer games can be seen in the same spirit, as children engaging in new action games that differ from the old simply in speed and glitter. The seeds of something more essentially different are present when children begin to take control of the computer to roam the globe on the Internet. But in the context of thinking about the development of software, the most poignant example of a new direction must be recognizing the need to create software to provide children with activities that are as natural as making drawings, making sandcastles, and making up stories. This beginning trend (see Papert, *The Children's Machine*) is significant not only because making software is new but

also because it offers children the possibility for the first time of creatively appropriating a cutting-edge technology and of sharing with the business, scientific, and engineering worlds the opportunity to carry out projects of unprecedented complexity.

See also COMPUTER HARDWARE; COMPUTERS: OVERVIEW; COMPUTERS: PRIVACY LAWS; ELECTRONIC CONVERGENCE; INTERACTIVE ENTERTAINMENT; MEDIA LAB; ON-LINE SERVICES; TELECOMMUNICATIONS.

BIBLIOGRAPHY

NEGROPONTE, NICHOLAS. *Being Digital.* New York: Bowker, 1995.
PAPERT, SEYMOUR. *The Children's Machine: Bringing the Computer Revolution to Our Schools.* New York: Basic Books, 1993.

Seymour Papert

Conflict, Ethnic and Racial.

See ETHNIC AND CULTURAL SEPARATISM.

Conscious Evolution

Conscious evolution is a new world view that has emerged in the latter half of the twentieth century. Through the development of scientific, technological, and social capabilities we have gained the power to affect our own evolution and that of life on Earth, for better or for worse. *Conscious* evolution is the effort to learn how to be responsible for guiding evolution on a planetary scale and eventually a solar system scale.

> As Dr. Jonas Salk wrote in his *Anatomy of Reality*, human beings now play an active and critical role not only in the process of their own evolution but in the survival and evolution of all living beings. Awareness of this places upon human beings a responsibility for their participation in and contribution to the process of evolution. If humankind would accept and acknowledge this responsibility and become creatively engaged in the process of metabiological evolution consciously as well as unconsciously, a new reality would emerge, and a new age could be born.

The roots of conscious evolution go back to the dawn of human awareness that this current stage of life is not ultimate, that something new is being born out of the human struggle. It has been nourished by visionaries and scientists of the human race who sensed the possibility of a quantum jump in capacity and consciousness and foresaw the possibility of the regeneration or transformation of the human race. But only now, in our lifetime, do we have the actual power to destroy or transform our world. Only now has the responsibility for conscious evolution become a pragmatic necessity for our survival and fulfillment. It is a new field, brought into focus by three radically new conditions called the "Three C's"—the new cosmology, crises, and capacities.

The New Cosmology

Conscious evolution arises from cosmogenesis, the discovery that the universe had a beginning, has been evolving for billions of years, and is evolving through us now. This awareness gives us a new identity, capability, and responsibility to be conscious coevolvers, participants in the process of creation. From the perspective of the new cosmology our future is envisioned as a continuum in the process of continuous transformation—open-ended, immeasurable, radically new, and filled with hope. This future is seen, however, as a contingency, not an inevitability. It depends on what we do. Conscious evolution makes us potentialists, not optimists. We seek to understand what is potential, good and desirable in the whole system, and how to manifest it in our lives.

The New Crises

The complex set of environmental/economic and social crises presents an unprecedented threat to our species. Never before in human history have we been required to change our behavior or suffer the destruction of our life support system within a very short time frame. This generation is called upon to manage a planetary ecology, to provide sustenance for humans throughout the world without further damage to the environment, to control population growth, to handle our own wastes, to shift from nonrenewable to renewable resources, to liberate human potential everywhere. Conscious evolution is the context for the development of these new capabilities.

The New Capacities

Advanced technologies such as microbiology, nuclear power, cybernetics, astronautics, nanotechnology, barely a generation old, give us vast new powers over the material world. We are already intervening in evolution directly. We can create new life-forms and new worlds. If we combine the *science of matter* with the *science of mind* (our potential for spiritual evolution), we see the possibility of a quantum leap from one phase of evolution to the next. Yet we are collectively without a positive vision of our future commensurate with our new powers. To envision such a future is a major emphasis for conscious evolution. In the effort to participate in the process of transformation, conscious evolution synthesizes three ways of knowing.

Conscious evolution is experienced *spiritually* as the subjective apprehension of a designing universal intelligence, a pan*en*theism, transcendent yet immanent, which is manifesting at all levels of being from the atomic to the galactic. It is experienced as our individual desire to align with the process of creation and to express that intention, or "implicate order," in our own lives as participants in the evolution of the larger community.

It is manifested *socially* in our growing efforts to design new social systems—in health, environmental protection, governance, education, business—to enhance creativity, cooperation, and sustainability.

It is discovered *experimentally* through science and technology as we learn how nature works by exploring the invisible technologies of creation, such as the gene, the atom, and the brain, so that we can coevolve with nature.

Conscious evolution can serve as a meta-discipline, a new framework to offer coherence, direction and purpose to various aspects of human endeavor. Education becomes the process of learning cosmic, personal, social, and vocational evolution, so each of us can give our creative gift to the evolution of our world. It offers to religion a new ground of the whole in which each faith can contribute its unique gift to the evolution of humanity. It provides for science a "telos" that offers the understanding and the technologies to meet an evolutionary agenda aimed at bringing about a universal future for humanity, one that is sustainable, open, and full of a wide range of choices. It gives futurism a new context and values to envision, plan, and guide us toward the next stage of our evolution.

See also EVOLUTION, SOCIAL; GLOBAL CONSCIOUSNESS; HIGH TECHNOLOGY; MIND: NEW MODES OF THINKING; NANOTECHNOLOGY.

BIBLIOGRAPHY

GROSSO, MICHAEL. *The Millennium Myth.* Wheaton, IL: Quest Books, 1995.
HUBBARD, BARBARA MARX. *The Evolutionary Journey.* Miami, FL: Evolutionary Press, 1982.

MURPHY, MICHAEL. *The Future of the Body: Explorations into the Further Evolution of Human Nature.* Los Angeles, CA: Tarcher, 1992.

ROSZAK, THEODORE. *The Voice of the Earth.* New York: Simon and Schuster, 1992.

RUSSELL, PETER. *The Global Brain Awakens: Our Next Evolutionary Leap.* Global Brain, 1995.

SALK, JONAS. *The Anatomy of Reality.* New York: Columbia University Press, 1983.

SAVAGE, MARSHALL T. *The Millennial Project: Colonizing the Galaxy in Eight Easy Steps.* Little, Brown, 1992.

STOCK, GREGORY. *Metaman: The Merging of Human and Machines into a Global Superorganism.* New York: Simon and Schuster, 1993.

Barbara Marx Hubbard

Conservatism, Political

A discussion of the future of conservatism requires attending to the elusive concept of conservatism per se. The difficulty in defining conservatism derives primarily from its frequent use as a defense of the status quo or the status quo ante. Thus, conservatism in the Kremlin embraced those who wished to return to Stalinist practices. Conservatism has also been associated with the nineteenth-century social and economic standpattism of the British. On the other hand, in some parts of the world (e.g., Latin America), the word has had no ideological overtones. And as the status quo shifts in the years ahead, the connotations of the word may well undergo corresponding transformations.

Nevertheless, it was in the United States during the New Deal years (1933–1945) that political conservatism crystallized with a new meaning that overtook competing meanings. Conservatives rallied in reaction against the centralizing tendencies of what in America came to be known as "liberalism." Up until World War I, liberalism was generally used to designate the doctrine that expanded individual liberty; and liberty was generally understood to describe protections from the oppressors of the individual. Thus, we find Woodrow Wilson pronouncing that "the history of liberty is a history of resistance . . . of the limitation of governmental power, not the increase of it."

New Deal liberals tended to approach problems on a grand scale as fit subjects for government reform. Thus, in comprehensive ways, "liberal" government undertook to mobilize the state to combat virtually all social problems—unemployment, agricultural distress, a shortage of electricity, illiteracy, malnutrition, among others.

Conservatives sought to abide by what is widely known as the rule of "subsidiarity." This principle asserts that a social problem that can be handled by the private sector should not be taken over by the public sector; and that a problem that can be handled by a lesser unit of the public sector must not be given to a more central unit. Thus, e.g., the care of children of working mothers should be a private responsibility, to be handled where possible by churches or other private associations; only if this is not possible should the responsibility be taken by the state—and last of all, by the federal government.

Since the vision of conservatism is not eschatological—i.e., it does not conceive of redemptive ends implicit in its conventions—the conservative approach to the future has tended toward the cautionary rather than the utopian. True to the concept of utopia as imagined by Samuel Butler in *Erewhon,* for conservatives an earthly utopia *is* nowhere. It does not exist at present, did not exist in an idyllic, idealized past, and will not exist in the future, especially not as a consequence of humanity being uplifted by the benign (or malevolent) authority of big government to a new plateau of enforced egalitarian tranquility.

Most conservatives are men and women who have a religious faith, and they reserve their vision of ultimates for extraterrestrial phenomena. It is for this reason that conservatism has been marked mostly by negative importunities against human inclinations, as is the case with the Ten Commandments and the Constitution, both of which emphasize that which ought *not* to be done.

The conservative believes that the threat of the omnipotent state is endemic and historically insistent, and that as a state acquires power, so the individual loses it. For that reason, it is presumptively against state action, but always allowing for the rebuttability of presumption, which is a logical rule. Conservatism believes also that in free circumstances, the social sector will mobilize to satisfy felt economic needs. During the twentieth century, conservatism addressed its Achilles' heel, unemployment, with special emphasis, developing knowledge and insights that dispelled any probability of unemployment on the scale in which it was suffered during the 1930s. Conservatism was especially alert during the years of the Cold War to urge that the protection of national sovereignty, and within it of individual liberty, justified enormous corporate sacrifices, and also justified a nuclear deterrent. It is likely to remain alert to whatever needs for similar sacrifice that may arise in times to come.

Conservatism is firmly rooted in a concept of human equality that is narrowly defined. This doctrine acknowledges the binding kinship of all men and women, and for this reason the law must not distinguish in its treatment of any human being. But within the bounds of equal protection under the law, conservatism remains obliged to respect vast differences in individual abilities, and to resist any arbitrary regulatory quagmires, such as affirmative action, that give special consideration to special minorities, or confiscatory taxation that seeks to level for the sake of levelling.

Unlike Marxism and socialism, conservatism does not attempt to solve problems it cannot solve. It presupposes limitations in human nature readily understandable to Christians who believe in original sin, otherwise deduceable by non-Christian conservatives who study the history of humanity. They know that the propensity to self-indulgence must be denied. And correspondingly, the state must be denied such powers as are necessary for authoritative action, while denying it such powers as encourage authoritarian action. Believing, then, that most problems derive from a deficiency in human nature, conservatism comes to terms, or seeks to do so, with the limitations of politics: problems are seldom "solved"; they can only be ameliorated. Someone somewhere expressed this principle by noting, "You cannot eliminate Skid Row."

Conservatives recognize that the fundamental issues are likely to remain the same, though specific contexts will certainly alter in barely imaginable ways, in response to new technologies, shifts in the dynamics of international relations in the post–Cold War era, the exacerbation or amelioration of existing social problems, or the appearance of new ones. Conservatives face the future, ever aware of the dangers of the swollen state, deriving as they do from the weaknesses of the citizens in a state, whose calling is always to struggle lest they become the subjects of the state.

See also COMMUNITARIANISM; LIBERALISM, POLITICAL; POLITICAL CYCLES; POLITICAL PARTIES; POLITICAL PARTY REALIGNMENT; THIRD POLITICAL PARTIES.

BIBLIOGRAPHY

BUCKLEY, WILLIAM F., JR., and KESLER, CHARLES R., eds. *Modern American Conservative Thought.* New York: HarperCollins, 1988.

FERGUSON, THOMAS, and ROGERS, JOEL. *The Decline of the Democrats and the Future of American Politics.* New York: Hill and Wang, 1986.

KIRK, RUSSELL. *Prospects for Conservatives,* rev. ed. Washington, DC: Regnery-Gateway, 1989.

William F. Buckley, Jr.

Consumer Protection/Regulation

"Consumption," wrote Adam Smith in *The Wealth of Nations,* "is the sole end and purpose of all production; and the interest of the producer ought to be attended to, only in so far as it may be necessary for promoting that of the consumer."

This statement, the economic corollary of Thomas Jefferson's nearly simultaneous 1776 political assertion that all governments derive "their just powers from the consent of the governed," underpins the operation of the American economy. Smith and Jefferson forged what Max Lerner called the new doctrine of "economic liberalism and freedom from governmental interference"—the driving force of the most powerful economy in history.

In the 1790s, when most Americans lived on farms or ran small businesses, Jefferson recommended a set of weights and measures standards, kicking off American consumer protection.

Economic dependence destroys political freedom according to Jefferson. Liberty rested on economically independent small businesses and farms. Weights and measures rules protect the weaker from the more powerful buyers and sellers.

Between 1800 and the end of the Civil War in 1865, America developed an industrial corporate sector, which was beset by boom and bust economic cycles, robber baron excesses, and political corruption. In 1887 Congress passed the Interstate Commerce Act, with consumer protection rhetoric, launching the thirty-year Progressive Era.

Government protection of railroad consumers—farmers, miners, businesses owners—from exploitative rates seemed an antidote to corporate abuse, but the bill passed only when railroaders saw that it helped *them.*

Legislative success with railroads led Progressives to try other regulation. These efforts led to the creation of the Federal Reserve, Food and Drug Administration, Federal Trade Commission, meat inspection, and antitrust laws, among others. Between 1887 and 1916, Congress passed fifty-six consumer laws. Still, corporations accumulated more economic power while Americans remained agrarian (60 percent lived on farms in 1900).

World War I diverted America from its regulatory binge. But in the twenty-two years following

World War I, including Franklin Delano Roosevelt's New Deal, the nation again turned to consumer protection laws, passing seventy-three new ones or 3.3 a year, as compared to 1.9 yearly by the Progressives.

New Dealer Gardner Means called Franklin Roosevelt's consumer programs "the peculiar American answer to the economic forces driving the rest of the world to choose between Communism and Fascism." Then World War II briefly led the nation away from its regulatory impulse.

After World War II (1951 to 1980) regulatory legislation got back on track with 227 new consumer laws passed—a 7.6 per year average. In the meantime, Sweden's consumer protection government (1930s to '80s) developed the world's highest standard of living.

In 1962, in a Jeffersonian vein, President John F. Kennedy announced a Consumer Bill of Rights to Congress. He also ordered expanded use of the federal weights and measures program to assure, in particular, the integrity of packaged goods, and to protect consumer rights nationwide. This Kennedy message highlighted modern consumerism. Fewer than 6 percent of postwar Americans worked on farms. Most of the rest worked for wages, many in large corporations or government. Americans expressed their economic stake primarily as consumers.

Alvin Toffler writes that "The Second Wave [industrialism], drove a giant invisible wedge into our economy, our psyches, and even our sexual selves . . . [splitting apart] production and consumption . . . that had always, until then, been one."

Industrial workers and managers struggled, obscuring the deeper conflict between producer (worker and manager) demands for higher wages, profits, and benefits and the counter demands of consumers (the same people) for lower prices.

Industrialism advanced individuals economically by raising income. Postwar consumerism built individual economic power by improving outgo. It tried modestly to narrow the price/quality and production/consumption gaps created by industrialism.

This history establishes the framework for an even more vigorous consumer protection future. Cyclical projection and precursor jurisdiction methodology developed by Graham Molitor forecast 350 to 450 new consumer laws for debate and passage between 1989 and 2018.

Early 1990s' food label, organic farming, and cable TV rules suggest the soundness of this projection and a future consumerism looking much like its past. Consumer redress, choice, safety, and information create the competition that disciplines markets. During the next twenty-five years, 350 to 450 new consumer laws and rules would regulate the Internet, finance (S&L's), trade, safety, quality and price information, privacy, and speech.

However, the current context—a global economy; the information revolution; an aging, low-birthrate population—underlines Toffler's observation that increasingly knowledge, not force or wealth, defines power and magnifies the power of consumers.

Focus on government's role, an important secondary topic, may obscure a deeper power shift from organizations toward persons that increases individual empowerment. However, certification, registration, and local regulation all increase rules while ostensibly lessening overt government control. Devolution to something other than strong federal laws, to more subtle administrative rules and decentralized decision making, shift the focus and onus of new consumer protection.

Consumers are to economics what voters are to politics. Using powerful new information tools, consumers increasingly influence markets. Consumer protection rules play a key role managing this power from knowledge. Consumer regulation faces a robust future.

See also COMMUNICATIONS: PRIVACY ISSUES; COUNTERFEITING; FOOD ADDITIVES; FOOD AND DRUG SAFETY; FOOD LAWS; GRAY MARKET GOODS; PHARMACEUTICALS.

BIBLIOGRAPHY

KOLKO, GABRIEL. *Railroads and Regulation, 1877–1916.* Westport, CT: Greenwood Press, 1970.

MOLITOR, GRAHAM T. T., and PLUMB, JAMES. "Reading the Cycles of Consumerism." *Mobius* (Fall 1989).

SMITH, ADAM. *The Wealth of Nations.* New York: Random House/Modern Library, 1937, p. 625.

"TechnoMania: The Future Isn't What You Think." *Newsweek* (February 27, 1995): 43.

TOFFLER, ALVIN. *Power Shift: Knowledge, Wealth, and Violence at the Edge of the 21st Century.* New York: Bantam Books, 1990.

———. *The Third Wave.* New York: Bantam Books, 1984.

TURNER, JAMES S. *The Chemical Feast.* New York: Grossman Publishers, 1970.

James S. Turner

Contagious Diseases.

See EPIDEMICS; PUBLIC HEALTH.

Continuing Education.

See ADULT LEARNING.

Continuity and Discontinuity

Continuity, slow evolution, and strong inertial drift are the general guiding principles of virtually all sociopolitical change. Human nature itself exhibits a natural reluctance to embrace change. These limiting influences minimize upheaval, ameliorate dislocation of established large-scale investments, limit dislocation, and minimize individual disorientation. Rapid and drastic shifts in established institutions, procedures, and other trappings of an established society disrupt social equilibrium. To temper disruptive influences a variety of conscious and unconscious social counterforces are interposed.

The rapidity, depth, breadth, and complexity of change are constantly transforming society. Change is incremental and evolutionary, and lodged upon us case-by-case and crisis-by-crisis. Pieces of the puzzle describing societies never seem to quite fit because the picture is constantly changing. When we attempt to assess the salient features of society, so much is happening in so many areas that we lose perspective and have difficulty fathoming the meaning of our times. The old moorings and familiar landmarks no longer provide the same sense of conventional reference.

Continuity

To an extent greater than most would surmise, the future already is shaped by past events. Historical momentum so strongly grips the present that many forecasters look to the past to gain a sense of the future. Confucius concurred in this approach, putting it this way: "Coming events cast their shadows before them." Auguste Comte also underscored the importance of the past by proclaiming, "No conception can be understood except through history." Leibnitz stated, "The past is pregnant with the future," and Winston Churchill asserted, "The further backward you can look, the further forward you can see."

Many other prominent thinkers have acknowledged the role the past chain of events, ideas, and leaders plays in determining the future. Isaac Newton said, "if I have seen further (than others), it is by standing on the shoulders of giants." Victor Hugo underscored the importance of ideas by as-serting, "No army can stop an idea whose time has come." Progress is the triumphant convergence of many factors.

The past chain of events, though it exerts a powerful influence in shaping future developments, is not a fatalistic force. Human willpower, properly directed, can alter the course of almost anything. As William James put it, "Man alone, of all the creatures of Earth, can change his own pattern. Man is the architect of his destiny." The future is not undiscernible or unknowable. It is an evolutionary state toward which we are ever tending.

Man-made systems, logically, are subject to greater human control than most natural systems. What humans have created, they essentially are capable of tearing asunder and refashioning according to need. Not that all man-made systems are easily manipulated. Things were easier in simpler times but are more difficult in today's complex environment.

Natural occurrences, subject to nature's whim and caprice, tend to be less predictable than man-made phenomena. Continuing advancements in knowledge, however, strip away uncertainty and enhance understanding, which advances the predictability of many natural phenomena. Satellite surveillance and massive computer surveys greatly enhance predicting weather and agricultural crop yields. Tectonic plate theories as well as sophisticated computer analysis and simulation make earthquake prediction reasonably certain.

Change is a constant and ceaseless phenomenon of societies. Society is dynamic, not static. The social systems in which we live are constantly changing, always churning, consistently in a state of flux.

Semantic gradations describe rates of change. Evolution usually connotes slow-paced change. *Revolution* is among the terms used to describe a pace of change at cataclysmic or rapid rates. Revolutionary change may characterize a single phenomenon or a considerable range of coterminous changes that radically transform. In the overall scheme of things, change occurs at an increasing tempo, covers an ever broader and more comprehensive range.

Our inspirational moments are driven by a desire to refine, extend, elaborate, and better what has gone before. The search for something better, new, or novel is constant. New high-water marks become points of departure to be surmounted. New vantage points sharpen the vision of additional peaks to be conquered. There are few limits to what the human race can achieve given imagination, understanding, and commitment to realize our goals.

Continuity and Discontinuity

The ceaseless search for perfection, improvement, doing something better gives rise to constant unrest. Events being at rest or at status quo give rise to a new unrest, and an ensuing quest for experimentation and novelty follows. New experimentation becomes the harbinger of another wave of change. This helical process usually is forward moving, ever expanding, and upward tending. As something new is mastered and widely accepted, it becomes routinized, standardized, institutionalized, normalized, and gets taken for granted. Rising expectations drive us toward higher levels. Everyone yearns for a new and better tomorrow. Eventually new heights become a mere floor, not a ceiling.

Human inquisitiveness never seems to be quite satisfied. Constantly restless, it searches for the next step forward. So ultimates often are merely temporary way stations.

Humans constantly strive for perfection. This constant upgrading assumes imperfection. Human activity almost always is fraught with faults and foibles, shortcomings and defects. Humans are destined to strive perpetually toward, but never actually to reach perfection. No matter how long and how hard the attempts to close gaps, the job never is fully or finally concluded. Even if a balanced state could be achieved, it never could be maintained. Perpetual pursuit of goals always just beyond reach indicates that the nature of change is destined to be eternal. Perfection is an ideal state or condition, an abstraction not attainable on Earth. It remains eternally elusive. The ceaseless search may be viewed as one of the greatest cosmic mysteries, or as the driving force toward human greatness.

Discontinuity

Discontinuity denotes breaks with the past involving gaps, interruptions, or even cessation. Careful examination of sociopolitical change processes, however, reveals another perspective that dispels notions of discontinuity. What are popularly perceived as discontinuities often are misleadingly based on insufficient data or incomplete analysis. Changes in human affairs involve extraordinarily long time frames. Meticulous analysis reveals patterns of constant incremental development leading to changes that dispel any notion of discontinuity.

Rarely, if ever, are there sharp and total breaks or discontinuities with the past. There are many early warnings that signal impending change. Change rarely is thrust on established systems by a single grand stroke. Instead, there are many ministeps by which the new is incorporated into the existing system. Very little that is built up over time is discarded by single bold strokes or by one fell swoop. Past traditions and established institutions are given up reluctantly. Sharp breaks with past events seldom occur. Perspective depends on how carefully one looks at the forces of change.

Few persons can afford the time or have the resources to assess societal drift fully. Demands of everyday living are so overwhelming that usually most of us see only a dizzying blur of events, not the overall pattern. This shortcoming may explain the tendency to embrace discontinuity uncritically.

What may be truly remarkable about these times is the pace and breadth of change. When so many things change so fast, there is little time to get acclimatized. Prior historical periods, changing at a slower pace and far simpler in complexity, had the benefit of thousands or hundreds of years to accommodate transformation. Contemporary society responds in periods measured by mere decades. Thus, there is ample reason for many to feel insecure, uncertain of where things are headed. Dealing with continuity is much easier than dealing with change, especially deep and pervasive change.

The future speaks to us with hundreds of signals. Society or human affairs need not drift haplessly and blindly toward tomorrow. We are not mere victims of a thousand random events. Change originates in dissatisfaction, is focused by vision, implemented by practical first steps, then confirmed and fine-tuned by implementation. The key to tracking the future is deeply and firmly embedded in the past. Continuity is a reliable guide.

The essential understanding in coping with change is to realize that there is no fixed destination—only a continuing series of way stations. Societies are dynamic, constantly changing, never the same at any two points in time. Human beings face a perpetual process of changing to and readapting to new circumstances. History entails a progressive adjustment to change, a continuous abandonment of the status quo.

See also CHANGE; CHANGE, EPOCHAL; CHANGE, OPTIMISTIC AND PESSIMISTIC PERSPECTIVES; CHANGE, PACE OF; GLOBAL TURNING POINTS.

BIBLIOGRAPHY

AUBERT, WILHELM, ed. *Sociology of Law.* Baltimore: Penguin Books, 1969.
DRUCKER, PETER F. *The Age of Discontinuity: Guidelines to Our Changing Society.* New York: Harper & Row, 1968.

HOROWITZ HAROLD W., and KARST, KENNETH L. *Law, Lawyers, and Social Change: Cases and Materials on the Abolition of Slavery, Racial Segregation, and Inequality of Educational Opportunity.* Indianapolis, IN: Bobbs-Merrill, 1969.

KAHN, HERMAN A., and BRIGGS, B. BRUCE. *Things to Come: Thinking About the '70s and '80s.* New York: Macmillan, 1972.

KAIRYS, DAVID, ed. *The Politics of Law: A Progressive Critique.* New York: Pantheon Books, 1990.

SCHUR, EDWIN M. *Law and Society: A Sociological View.* New York: Random House, 1968.'

Graham T. T. Molitor

Cornish, Edward S. (1927–)

Born in New York City, Edward Cornish is president of the World Future Society and editor of *The Futurist* (since 1966). After attending the University of Paris and Harvard University, he entered journalism as a copyboy for the *Washington Star*. In 1951 he joined the United Press Association (later known as UPI) and served in the agency's bureaus in Richmond, Va.; Raleigh, N.C.; London; Paris; and Rome. In 1957 he joined the National Geographic Society as a staff writer. There his interest turned to the new technologies and their potential impact on human life, an interest that led him to publish (irregularly) a six-page newsletter entitled *The Futurist*. Positive response to the newsletter prompted the formation of the World Future Society (WFS) on October 18, 1966, with Cornish as director; in 1967 *The Futurist* was expanded to journal size, with a more regular publication schedule. As the only president the WFS has ever had, Cornish has presided over its growth from 3,000 members in 1969 to 30,000 in 1994. Cornish brings a rare objectivity to the field and presents a balanced view of short-term futures. Cornish's many books include *The Study of the Future* (1986), *Communications Tomorrow: The Coming of the Information Society* (1982), *Careers Tomorrow: The Outlook for Work in a Changing World* (1983), *The Great Transformation: Alternative Futures for Global Society* (1983), *Global Solutions: Innovative Approaches for World Problems* (1984), *The Computerized Society: Living and Working in an Electronic Age* (1985), and *The 1990s and Beyond* (1990).

See Cornish's essay FUTURISTS in this encyclopedia.

George Thomas Kurian

Cosmetics and Toiletries

Cosmetics and toiletries in the twenty-first century, reflecting scientific strides forward, will function by reacting chemically and physiologically with skin and hair. Products will be available to increase or decrease the amount of sebum secreted from the sebaceous glands, for persons with dry or oily skin respectively. With aging the microcirculation in the skin atrophies and the skin cells are undernourished, resulting in a sallow complexion. Products will be available that will enhance the microcirculation when applied topically, resulting in a healthier skin with a rosy complexion.

The stratum corneum—the outermost dead layer of skin cells that acts as a barrier to body-moisture loss and penetration of extraneous poisons into the body—is continually being shed and new stratum corneum forms as living cells from the basal layer move upward through the epidermis. This cell "turnover time" is normally about three weeks. With aging, the cell turnover time increases and the skin becomes drier and loses its healthy glow. Products will be available that will control the skin turnover time at any safe rate desired.

Wrinkles form on aging because the collagen and elastin in the dermis become cross-linked—due to the action of free radicals—and lose their ability to act as a cushion and provide turgor to the skin. New materials will be available that when applied topically will penetrate and activate the fibroblast cells in the dermis to produce fresh new collagen and elastin. Thus it will be possible to retard wrinkle formation early on.

Dry skin is caused by overcleaning the skin with soaps and detergent products. These cleansers remove from the skin the naturally occurring humectants and barrier lipids that are required to maintain the proper amount of moisture in the stratum corneum. Today's skin moisturizers all contain water-soluble humectants and several types of oleaginous materials to enhance the skin's moisture level. In the next century products for alleviating dry skin will contain hydrogels that are capable of holding hundreds of times their weight in water and yet not be water soluble. Such materials will lay down a film on the skin that is not easily removed and will continually bathe the skin in a film of water. Dietary polyunsaturated fatty acids are required for the skin to manufacture ceramides and glycosphingolipids having the correct chemical structure and spatial configuration to provide a good moisture-loss barrier. Barrier lipids, such as ceramides and glycosphingolipids, are currently available, but the cost is exorbitant. These materials will be manufactured by genetic engineering and will become more affordable so that skin-moisturizing products will contain effective concentrations to maintain appropriate moisture levels in the stratum corneum.

Cleansing products for the hair and skin will be based on mild biodegradable surfactants that will be completely nonirritating to the skin and not defat the skin or impair the barrier layer—thus alleviating the major cause for dry skin condition. The consumer also will come to understand that an abundance of lather is not necessary to obtain good cleaning. Shampoos will be available that will clean and condition the hair without drying out the scalp. Specialty shampoos will also be available that will wave, set, or color the hair as desired.

Hair waving and hair removal will no longer depend on the use of smelly mercaptans. These functions will be accomplished by using appropriate enzymic systems that will break and remake disulfide linkages in the hair as desired or will further split the keratin protein into simple water-soluble polypeptides and amino acids.

Exposure to ultraviolet light (UV) in several discrete bandwidths is known to be the major cause for premature skin aging; excessive exposure can lead to skin cancer. Today's sunscreens, while effective screens for UVB rays (290–320 nanometers), are not very effective in screening out UVA (320–400 nm) and are completely ineffective for UVC (rays below 290 nm). While at one time UVA rays were thought of as the "tanning rays" and as not harming the skin, recent studies have shown that UVA rays penetrate more deeply than those in the UVB and that daily exposure to these can also cause premature skin wrinkles. UVC rays are normally screened out by the ozone layer in the stratosphere, but increasing damage to this protective layer will allow ever-increasing amounts of UVC to penetrate to Earth and lead to an increased incidence of skin cancer. The products of the next century will contain highly effective screens to filter out harmful UV rays in the 200 to 400 nm range of the spectrum. In addition, effective antioxidants will be present to allay the formation of free radicals—the major cause of skin aging.

Many Caucasians prefer to have a tanned look and yet do not want to expose themselves to UV sunlight without wearing a high sunscreen protective factor (SPF) preparation. This can be accomplished by using sunless self-tanning creams and lotions containing dihydroxyacetone, which reacts with several amino acids in the skin to develop a jaundiced yellow color. Products of the twenty-first century will be vastly improved and will impart a longer lasting rich bronze color to the skin, utilizing compounds that will develop substantive pigments resembling melanin—the naturally occurring pigmenting agent.

The market for nail lacquers is huge, although most nail lacquers do not wear well. The next century will bring to the consumer nail lacquers that will last for several weeks without cracking or peeling, and nail lacquer removers will be available that will not harm or weaken the nails. Today's nail strengtheners are based primarily on the use of formaldehyde, which is a potent skin-sensitizing agent and possible carcinogen. Nail strengtheners will be available based on agents that will cross-link the keratin protein of the nail without irritation or sensitization reactions.

Use of fluorides in water supplies and in dentifrices in this century resulted in a major reduction in the formation of cavities. In the next century there will be a vast improvement in the type of agents used to reduce or eliminate plaque formation, which if uncontrolled results in gingivitis and eventually periodontal disease and tooth loss. Thus, the mouthwash of the future will not only provide sustained-release control for pleasant breath but be formulated to help eliminate gingivitis and periodontal disease.

See also DENTISTRY; FRAGRANCES; OZONE LAYER DEPLETION.

BIBLIOGRAPHY

ESTRIN, NORMAN, and JUNGERMANN, ERIC, eds. *The Cosmetics Industry: Scientific and Regulatory Foundations.* New York: Marcel Dekker, 1984.

ROMM, R. *The Changing Face of Beauty.* St. Louis, MO: Mosby Year Book, 1990.

UMBACH, WILFRIED. *Cosmetics and Toiletries.* Englewood Cliffs, NJ: Prentice-Hall, 1991.

Charles Fox

Counterfeiting

Counterfeiting has become one of the world's fastest-growing methods for committing fraud. It has grown at a record pace over the past decade and will continue to flourish well into the next century.

In addition to greed, there are two primary forces that will drive growth in counterfeiting. First, people in emerging and developing nations rely on U.S. currency for security more than at any other time in history. Second, modern technology—particularly accessible low-cost items such as personal computers, imaging software, scanners, color copiers, and laser printers—make counterfeiting relatively easy. The days of the stereotypical engraver laboring in a basement to etch a perfect set of plates on behalf of an organized crime kingpin is gone. As Doug McClellan of the *Albuquerque Journal* stated, "counterfeiting has gone mainstream." Counterfeiting has become and will continue to grow as a cottage industry.

The range of products being counterfeited extends from T-shirts to auto parts and from sophisticated computer systems to telephone calling cards. In the future, growth in product copying will occur most rapidly in Asia and Eastern Europe, with the large volume of counterfeited products being exported throughout the world with relatively low risk.

Phone cards, computer software, credit cards, prescription forms, checks, securities and a myriad of other documents, as well as technology, will be targeted by counterfeiters in the United States and Western Europe. Worldwide, currency will remain the counterfeiter's staple.

Over a two-year period, the U.S. banking industry alone reported a 43 percent increase in fraud, with over 1 million reported cases and total losses in excess of $800 million. The U.S. Secret Service estimates that computer-aided forgery of bank notes may exceed $2 billion by the turn of the century. The National Research Council (National Academy of Sciences) identified counterfeiting using desktop technology as the biggest future threat to U.S. currency.

Methods of counterfeiting are being developed and refined much faster than preventive and enforcement measures can be put into place. Counterfeiting will increase rapidly in Eastern European countries, China, and other nations in which people save U.S. currency, rather than that of their own nation, as a means protecting their future. Counterfeiting U.S. dollars is a huge growth industry in emerging and developing nations, particularly those that have yet to embrace checks, credit cards, and computerized transactions as common tools of trade. In the two years from 1992 to 1993, the amount of counterfeit U.S. currency seized overseas rose from $30 million to $120 million.

Counterfeiting is and will continue to be an international problem. Mafia-like crime organizations have led counterfeiting in Eastern Europe, freely crossing national borders. But because so much of the counterfeit market is in U.S. dollars, the burden and cost for prevention and enforcement primarily falls on the U.S. government.

Methods of counterfeit prevention will continue to go high-tech. Experiments are underway to use an individual's DNA as a means for authenticating his or her identification.

Based on small computer chips, smart cards (prepaid cards containing stored values to be used at retailers) will be used with greater frequency. With smart cards, retailers receive money from the system providers, who receive money in advance from their customers. Secured data representing the value is exchanged rather than currency.

Public key cryptology and digital signatures will replace today's credit and automated teller cards as well as other means for conducting transactions. A financial institution or corporation maintains a public encryption key, while the private key is known only to the owner. What the private key encrypts, the public key decrypts and vice versa.

The United States and other nations will continue to experiment with new ways to protect their currency. New dollar designs, water marks, special inks, holographic images, polyester fibers that mar images when copied, and special fibers embedded in strategic locations on bills are some of the methods that will used more frequently.

In the United States, the Bureau of Engraving will design and issue new currency for the first time in over sixty years, with an aim toward reducing counterfeiting. The National Academy of Sciences established the Committee on Next-Generation Currency Design that will share its findings with the Bureau of Engraving. The U.S. Treasury Department has begun using security threads, visible by bright light but difficult to reproduce, and microprinting, a process for printing words so small that they cannot be duplicated easily and appear as a straight line to the naked eye. The U.S. State Department is applying the same principles to passports, and the Immigration and Naturalization Service is seeking new ways to secure cards and forms related to an individual's immigration status. In Australia, currency has been redesigned and is being printed on polymer (plastic) stock designed to make copying difficult. Other countries are making comparable changes in their currency.

Unless the computer industry undertakes more comprehensive self-regulation, there will be greater regulatory controls placed on the distribution of computer chips, in part to stem their use in product counterfeiting.

See also CONSUMER PROTECTION/REGULATION; GRAY MARKET GOODS.

BIBLIOGRAPHY

BLOOM, MURRAY T. *Money of Their Own.* Clinton, OH: BNR Press, 1983.

ROCHETTE, E. C. *Making Money.* Frederick, CO: Renaissance House, 1986.

ROWELL, ROLAND. *Counterfeiting and Forgery.* Stoneham, MA: Butterworth, 1986.

Sheldon F. Greenberg

Courts.

See CRIMINAL JUSTICE; JUDICIAL REFORM; LAWMAKING, JUDICIAL; LAWYERS AND LEGAL PROFESSION.

Creativity

Creativity should be a top priority in preparations for the future because it is critical for forecasts and possible futures and for the construction of preferable futures. Forecasts must recognize a range of possibilities, some of which are entirely hypothetical. To be considered, they must be defined. Creative thought can produce, manipulate, and evaluate hypothetical outcomes. Since the 1950s, influenced by seminal work by J. P. Guilford at the University of Southern California, creative thinking has been viewed as a divergence of thought that allows original insight and the exploration of the hypothetical.

If all relevant information is available, prediction is a matter of calculation. All trends can be used as indicators of what is to come. But the future will be significantly influenced by events about which we have virtually no clues. There are many possible futures, some of which may be largely unrelated to present trends. They are, however, anticipatable with informed and creative forecasts.

Creativity involves more than the ability to produce alternatives. It is often expressed as a kind of adaptive thinking. It is not synonymous with divergent thinking, and not just something that leads to originality. It also involves good judgment and an appreciation of useful and fresh possibilities. This adaptive facet is what makes creativity critical for studies of the future. What could be more important for the future than adaptability? As Jerome Bruner, the Harvard psychologist, suggested, we cannot predict the details of the future, so we must prepare ourselves—and our children—for the unforeseeable. Creativity is an adaptive skill that will allow individuals or organizations to cope with such unforeseeable futures.

One current research program defines creative thought as the ability to integrate and synthesize. Creative thought often uses seemingly discrepant information, such as when a physicist recognizes that light has features of both a wave and a particle. Albert Rothenberg described creative integrations as "janusian," after Janus, the Roman god who kept a simultaneous watch in two opposite directions. Others have noted the ability of creative thought to synthesize the opposites. The point is that this manifestation of creativity may be important for predicting and coping with the future, especially in the midst of the current information explosion. How can we make sense of it all? How can trends be identified? If we think of the diversification of the human population as generating a multitude of perspectives, the question becomes one of integrating diverse opinions, needs, and values. Here again, creativity can help us.

Much of the above implies educational need. The students of the last decade of the twentieth century, and those of the first years of the twenty-first, will need to be more creative than ever before. Fortunately, most educators and parents see the value of creativity. It is not always easy to appreciate or encourage the specific traits that allow creativity, such as nonconformity and independence. It may help educators to know that creativity is a reflection of psychological health. Creativity allows adaptability. Healthy individuals, organizations, and societies will undoubtedly adapt.

One of the most pertinent lines of educational research was initiated by E. Paul Torrance of the University of Georgia. His program, *Future Problem Solving*, focuses on realistic problems, with original and flexible thinking modeled and encouraged. The realistic nature of the tasks distinguishes his work, since many other creativity programs use artificial assignments. This feature also suggests that future problem solving may produce generalizable effects that are useful in the natural environment.

Most educational efforts, including Torrance's, consider creativity to be a special kind of problem solving. Here again we must be careful, for creativity is broader than problem solving; it is also problem finding and problem definition, and certainly is not always reactive. Proactive creativity can be distinguished from passive reactive problem solving. The former is particularly relevant for the construction and selection of preferable futures. Reactive creativity may be useful when dealing with problems as they arise or after the fact. Proactive creativity, on the other hand, can be used to avoid problems, or to adjust and accommodate to them.

Proactive creativity might also operate in the moral domain. Here the need to construct preferable futures is especially clear. Perhaps for this reason, this is an area of recent creativity research.

Howard Gruber and Doris Wallace edited a collection of papers on this topic, with a number of contributors noting how creativity can be used to adapt, to solve problems, and to determine directions for effort. Creativity in the moral domain might involve some problem solving, but also involves what Gruber called decisions about what ought to be done to shape the future. The alternatives may be many, if we are creative.

See also MIND: NEW MODES OF THINKING; SURPRISES; VISIONARY THINKING; WILDCARDS.

BIBLIOGRAPHY

GRUBER, H. E., and WALLACE, D., eds. "Creativity in the Moral Domain" special issue. *Creativity Research Journal* 6 (1993): 1–200.
BRUNER, J. "The Growth of Mind." *American Psychologist* 20 (1965): 1007–1017.
RUNCO, M. A., ed. *Problem finding, problem solving, and creativity.* Norwood, NJ: Ablex Publishing, 1994.
SHAW, M. P., and RUNCO, M. A., eds. *Creativity and Affect.* Norwood, NJ: Ablex Publishing, 1994.

Mark A. Runco

Credit, Debt, and Borrowing

Worldwide there has been an explosion of debt. Governments in the developed world have dramatically increased their debt (see Figure 1), though none as dramatically as the United States (Figure 2). Federal debt in 1993 stood in excess of $4.8 trillion. In the United States, the cost of servicing this debt has exploded (Figure 3), and now represents one of the largest items in the federal budget ($292 billion in 1992 and projected to reach $407 billion by 1998). Corporate debt in 1992 stood at $2.9 trillion, which represents an increasing burden to corporate earnings. American households increased their debt (home mortgages and consumer debt) almost threefold during the 1980s—from $1.3 trillion in 1980 to $3.4 trillion in 1990 and $4.2 trillion in 1993. The average U.S. household owed $35,000 by 1991, and paid interest of $3,500 per year (approximately 18 percent of its disposable income). Many Americans are going into debt to maintain their standard of living. A myriad of credit devices encourage and facilitate the accumulation of debt: credit unions, credit cards, smart cards, super-smart cards, and now debit-loaded cards.

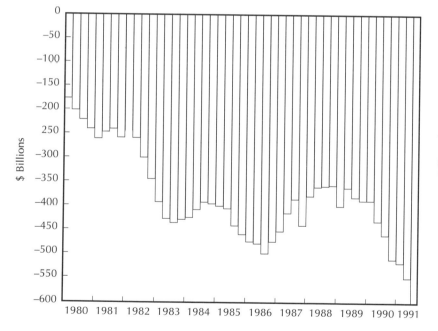

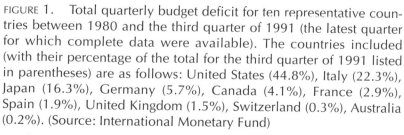

FIGURE 1. Total quarterly budget deficit for ten representative countries between 1980 and the third quarter of 1991 (the latest quarter for which complete data were available). The countries included (with their percentage of the total for the third quarter of 1991 listed in parentheses) are as follows: United States (44.8%), Italy (22.3%), Japan (16.3%), Germany (5.7%), Canada (4.1%), France (2.9%), Spain (1.9%), United Kingdom (1.5%), Switzerland (0.3%), Australia (0.2%). (Source: International Monetary Fund)

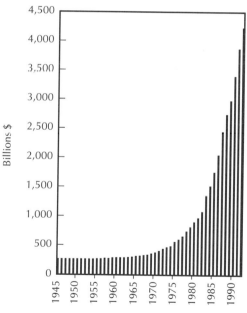

FIGURE 2. Annual gross federal debt in the United States, 1945–1992 (in billions of dollars).

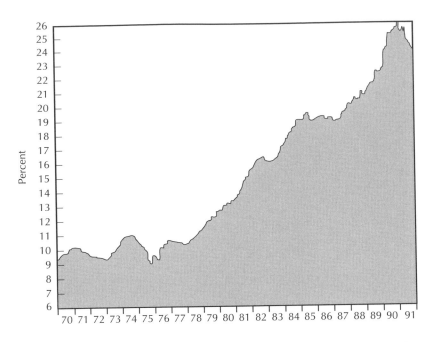

FIGURE 3. Federal government interest expense plus outlays for the Resolution Trust Corporation as a percentage of total government budget expenditures. (Source: U.S. Treasury monthly statements.)

Total debt in the U.S. is rising faster than the GNP. U.S. government debt is rising faster than the U.S. GNP, corporate debt has increased faster than earnings, and consumer debt during the 1980s grew 50 percent faster than consumer income. Total U.S. debt by 1992 stood at approximately $16 trillion.

Furthermore, that figure, however gargantuan, does not include unfunded liabilities—i.e., military and federal civil service pensions and unfunded so-

cial security, and the unfunded cost of dealing with the disposal of nuclear wastes. These considerable obligations lock into future spending and represent a "stealth budget" that does not appear in usual government estimates of the debt. However, it does represent an obligation to be paid off by future tax-payers.

Additionally there are large contingent liabilities that the government may or may not be called upon

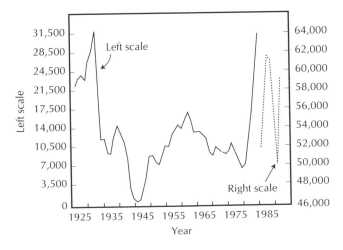

FIGURE 4. Business failures in the United States, 1925–1992. Left scale: 1925–1982; right scale: 1985–1992. (Source: Dun & Bradstreet.)

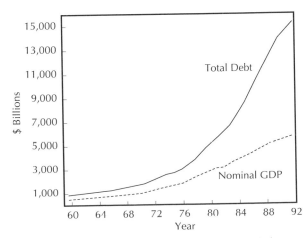

FIGURE 5. Divergence of U.S. debt and ability to serve that debt, 1960–1993. (Source: Department of Commerce, Federal Reserve Flow of Funds.)

to cover. These contingent obligations include federal deposit insurance, the Federal Pension Benefit Guarantee Fund, crop insurance, flood insurance, and the list goes on and on. Since this category is a contingent liability, it is impossible to estimate a total figure of governmental debt—but some estimates put government debt alone at $16 trillion in 1993, with total governmental and private debt considerably higher.

Business failures are on the upswing (see Figure 4). Commercial bank failures also have grown. Federal bailout of failed banks could add up to as much as $200–400 billion. Luckily, low interest rates have kept disasters to a minimum.

The question that must be asked is how long debt can go on compounding faster than income. Credit cycles inevitably end when the society runs out of credit-worthy borrowers and when creditors recognize from the t size of the total debt guarantees that much of it must be defaulted. Some believe we are in the terminal phase of a long credit expansion that has far outstripped our ability to service, let alone repay, the debt (see Figure 5). Mortgage foreclosures approached record highs as we entered the 1990s (see Figure 6).

Debt fueled the economy since the end of World War II, a trend which was greatly exacerbated in the 1980s. One author calls it the "democratization of lending and the socialization of risk" where credit is increasingly extended to less credit-worthy people and more and more debt is guaranteed by the federal government. This system allows the maximization of credit, but runs the risk of im-

ploding. Government has already guaranteed far more debt than it could practically pay off without causing an economic disaster.

The question for the future is whether the federal government, by its use of monetary and fiscal tools, can keep the accumulated debt from deflating the economy—or if the U.S. will experience an asset liquidation and deflation. Excess is usually followed by contraction.

See also DEFICITS, GOVERNMENTAL; DERIVATIVES; ECONOMIC CYCLES; PUBLIC FINANCE; SAVINGS; TAXES; WEALTH.

BIBLIOGRAPHY

DAVIDSON, JAMES DALE, and REES-MOGG, LORD WILLIAM. *The Great Reckoning*. New York: Summit Books, 1991.
FRIEDMAN, BENJAMIN M. *Day of Reckoning*. New York: Random House, 1988.
GRANT, JAMES. *Money of the Mind*. New York: Farrar Straus Giroux, 1992.

Richard D. Lamm

Crime, Nonviolent

Nonviolent crime, victimless crime, has been defined as "an illegal act in which no one is harmed, or if harm occurs it is negated due to the informed consent of the participants." This definition is predicated on the assumptions that those who provide consent are adults and that harm is caused to the person's body or psyche, property, society, or to personal freedom. Gambling, illegal drug use, pornography, and prostitution are generally classified as victimless crimes.

Types of Victimless Crime

GAMBLING

There has been a spectacular expansion of legal gaming. Industry revenues from lotteries, bingo, casino games, and horse race betting almost tripled in the 1980s to some $300 billion annually. It is forecast that spending on gambling will double by the year 2000. The FBI estimates that far more is still wagered illegally than legally.

The experience of Atlantic City and Las Vegas indicates that development of casinos in urban areas causes a change in community character, including an increase in crime and other undesirable activities such as loansharking, pickpocketing, and prostitution. It appears that there is no such thing as "painless prosperity." The cost to society is increased

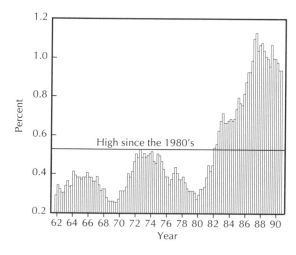

FIGURE 6. U.S. mortgage foreclosure rate, 1960–1991. (Source: Mortgage Bankers Association of America.)

violent and nonviolent crime, a threat of organized crime's participation, and potential corruption of government officials.

PROSTITUTION AND PORNOGRAPHY

Emphasis on the rights of the individual and the liberation of sexual behavior beginning in the 1960s will continue to conflict with certain community attitudes about undesirable sexual conduct. The criminal justice system will continue to struggle with the enforcement of restrictive sexual conduct statutes. Sexual acts that involve violence, incest, and acts against children will be the targets of enforcement action.

"Victimless" sexual conduct, such as prostitution and soft pornography, are considered to present less of a threat to the society. Tenderloin crimes of street prostitution, "skin flick" theaters, and adult book stores will receive little attention in "controlled" districts for two reasons: too few police resources and victimless crime by consenting adults. Senator Daniel Moynihan recently noted this as a degradation of social mores and pointed to society's "redefining deviance so as to exempt much conduct previously stigmatized."

Technological advancements in the distribution of pornography will present many problems for law enforcement. The emerging information technology will reorganize people's recreation as drastically as it has their work environment. Sexually explicit fiction and digitized photographs of naked people are common on the nation's rapidly growing computer networks, as are forums for discussing sexual fantasies.

Because of the international nature of the Internet, creators of sexually explicit material can quickly set up operations overseas or transfer their material to foreign computer networks. Enforcement officers will have to gain additional expertise in collecting evidence that can be presented in court and countering arguments about individual freedom.

Some "cybersex" advocates view virtual reality computer technology as an opportunity. One author says that ". . . ultimately consumers will have virtual reality home-entertainment centers, consisting of three-dimensional stereoscopic displays and control mechanisms, coupled with CD-ROM and some 'sexy' robust software."

Public Disobedience

Public disobedience is related to the amount of social tension in the society. The United States has been undergoing a period of declining trust in government and its ability to provide a quality of life seen by prior generations. Many young people believe that their future standard of living will be lower than that of their parents. Add the increasing legal and illegal immigration (bringing with it differing social, moral, and political views) to the widening economic chasm between rich and poor—and the social crucible will be ripe for increased public disorder. There will be increased potential for ethnic conflicts and domination by single-issue politics.

Society has been experiencing a growing disparity between the haves and the have-nots—in education, economic status, skills, and access to the political arena. As the underclass continues to struggle with the shortage of skills and education necessary to compete in the information job market, homelessness will increase. Those communities with growing shares of lower and welfare class populations and deteriorating economies will face severe budget shortages and have less ability to reverse these conditions.

The number of people in the nation without housing and jobs will result in increased visible panhandling, squatting in abandoned buildings, vagrancy in the form of wandering from place to place in search of subsistence-level existence, and increased levels of disorderly conduct, as the business community tries to have police impose some form of control.

Homelessness is a growing problem in society, and its impact will become more profound in the future as a significant law enforcement issue. Homeless children and families may become a particular concern. Many runaway youths will continue to engage in prostitution—trading sex for survival.

The recognition that a tremendous amount of money is being spent on the enforcement of drugs may force additional legalization of narcotic possession and use. States are no longer able to continue to fill jails with drug law violators while reducing sentences for violent criminals due to lack of jail space. Many leading figures call for legalization to remove the profit from the drug trade and slash drug-related crime, arguing that government efforts to eradicate drug use through punishment have only aggravated the problem. Some advocate the legalization of heroin, marijuana, and cocaine. Legalization advocates propose high taxes on legalized drugs so that the drug consumers will pay for the networks of regulation, education programs, administration, and rehabilitation efforts for those who want to escape their dependence.

Opponents say that the legalization of drugs would only create more drug users and turn casual users into addicts. Two questions will have to be addressed. First is the problem of how the new legal drugs would be controlled and distributed, and at what level of government such a system would operate. Second, as the scientific search continues for more understanding of how the brain works, some criminals will learn to alter the chemistry of moods and sexual desire.

During the 1990s, the advance of elementary genetic engineering may make it possible for the commercial production of Beta-endorphins, replacing morphine and cocaine as a local anesthetic. By the turn of the century, understanding of the body's own mood-monitoring system may progress to the point where it will be possible to reset the "chemostat" regulating the body's own production of mood-altering hormones. Scientific advances in chemical methods of altering individual mood have been adopted by the illegal drug manufacturers. The drugs may be produced so easily and changed so rapidly that society may not be able to regulate their production and use.

Crimes Against Property

Computer-related crime is one of the most challenging problems facing law enforcement today and in the future. Most people are aware of hackers: those who surreptitiously enter computer systems to destroy or steal data, intentionally and maliciously. However, of more concern are the insiders who have the confidence of management and then betray that confidence with fraud, embezzlement, larceny, and sometimes even sabotage.

The growing popularity of computers has provided the latest opportunity resource for criminal misuse. This is largely because computers are being frequently employed to provide direct access to cash or merchandise. The proliferation of smaller, more powerful computers combined with the changing nature of American business will contribute greatly to an increasing rate of computer crime. The computer literacy of the nation is rising rapidly as "user-friendly" computer hardware and software make them easier to use. The result is more savvy computer users, with access to more computers and their data, offering innumerable possibilities for data manipulation, vandalism, and theft.

The ability of local jurisdictions to comprehend, identify, investigate, and prosecute high-tech, electronic crimes—involving illegal access and transfers of monies, information altering, or sabotage—will be sorely tested.

Computer crimes fall into four main categories: internal computer disruptions such as the planting of viruses or logic bombs; telecommunicating crimes like "phone phreaking" (hacking or misusing the telephone system); computer manipulation crimes such as embezzlement or frauds; activities in support of criminal enterprises, like money laundering or selling of criminal information to criminal syndicates; and hardware/software piracy.

High-technology crimes will have a significant impact on police budgets because of the complexity of the cases. Estimates range from four months to a year for thorough investigations. Computer crimes may extend into several jurisdictions and even into other states or countries. Law enforcement strategies must include better on-site investigative ability; better ability to store properly the computer hardware and software seized in investigations; understanding between law enforcement and corporate businesses of each others' capabilities and clarification of each others' roles regarding computer-related crime; establishment of regional task forces to investigate computer crime; and ability to have contractual services for computer-related crimes in need of such expertise.

Tax Evasion

In the United States, the underground economy is estimated at between 10 and 28 percent of the gross national product. Internal Revenue Service (IRS) researchers suggest that almost all hidden labor is paid in currency and that the balance of underground activity is perhaps 50 percent cash. As the economy remains stagnant and a larger portion of the underclass struggle with reduced resources, there will be more barter for services. The exchange of services for other services siphons tax revenue from governmental entities. Law enforcement may be called upon to enforce tax collection on barter-type activity.

See also ALCOHOL; BEHAVIOR: SOCIAL CONSTRAINTS; CHILD ABUSE; CIVIL PROTEST; COUNTERFEITING; CRIME RATES; DRUGS, ILLICIT; ESPIONAGE AND COUNTERINTELLIGENCE; GAMBLING; SEXUAL CODES; SEXUAL LAWS; SOCIAL CONTROLS; TAXES.

BIBLIOGRAPHY

ALBANESE, JAY S., and PURSLEY, ROBERT D. *Crime in America: Some Existing and Emerging Issues.* Englewood Cliff, NJ: Regents/Prentice Hall, 1993.

"New Puzzle: High-Tech Pedophilia." *Los Angeles Times,* March 5, 1993.

"Pot, Heroin Unlock New Areas for Neuroscience." *Science* (December 18, 1992).

ROBERTS, SAM. *Who We Are: A Portrait of America Based on the Latest U.S. Census.* New York: Random House/Times Books, 1993.

"Tomorrow's Thieves." *Futurist* (September-October 1988).

"Trends in Crime, Punishment, Race, and Drugs: The Connections Emerge." *Future Scan* (May 17, 1993).

Russell Kinderman

Crime, Organized

Organized crime is structured, goal-directed criminal activity organized as a profit-making enterprise. The relationships and hierarchy in any organized-crime group are based largely on personalities, power, influence, success, and loyalty. Although organized-crime groups often operate somewhat like businesses, their structure is usually more unconventional. Organized crime is *profit-motivated,* attempting to earn money through unlawful means. Violence is not its goal—it is a tool used to obtain and maintain compliance in order for the organization to flourish. While the focus of this essay is on North America, organized crime exists worldwide.

The most common vision of organized crime is the "traditional" Cosa Nostra, or the Mafia, with roots in Italian and Sicilian "families." The reference to families is twofold: the first is a family of persons related by blood or marriage. The second refers to a strong kinship of trust and respect among a group of people with common (in this case, criminal) goals, values, and beliefs.

La Cosa Nostra is noteworthy because of its prominence and rapid expansion during Prohibition, when sales of liquor provided vast profits for expansion of the organization into gambling and prostitution while permitting it to maintain its interests in theft, black marketing, and loan sharking. Lucrative profits from illegitimate activities also permitted investments in legitimate businesses, blurring the distinction between lawful and unlawful activities.

The Mafia did not start during Prohibition; it simply grew during that time. It has not been eliminated—or even seriously thwarted—as a result of the convictions of high-level members in recent years. Like most large organizations, Cosa Nostra is readily able to replace its leaders with new ones from within its ranks. Recent assessments of the Mafia find that it is becoming more sophisticated in its operating practices and uses of technology. The organization grows increasingly complex as new layers of corporate entities are added, further integration with legitimate businesses proceeds, and alliances are formed with other organized-crime groups. These trends will not only continue, but are likely to grow over the next decade as social, political, and economic conditions change.

Despite the traditional view of organized crime as synonymous with La Cosa Nostra, there are other organized-crime groups, some of which have been growing rapidly recently. Among these, some but not all are ethnically based.

Latin America and the Caribbean

The organized-crime groups best known in this region are the Colombian Medellín and Cali cartels, which concentrate on the vastly profitable cocaine trafficking and money laundering. The profits from drug trafficking have been invested in legitimate businesses, stocks, and U.S. real estate. Power in these cartels is concentrated, and it is delegated to a much lesser degree than in La Cosa Nostra. Nevertheless, the Colombian groups are extensive, with regional drug distribution networks throughout North America, and possibly expanding into Western Europe via agreements with La Cosa Nostra. Beyond the Colombian cartels, there also are smaller Peruvian and Bolivian cartels involved in cocaine trafficking.

Also well known are the Jamaican "posses" which have been surprisingly evident throughout the United States, often involving Jamaican residents. These posses are involved in drug trafficking and often deal with "competitors" through violent acts including maiming and disfigurement. While the presence of Jamaican posses has diminished somewhat, they remain active in the drug trade, predominantly in large cities.

Eastern Europe and Central Asia

Ethnically based organized-crime groups in Eastern Europe and Central Asia are perhaps among the fastest growing, resulting from the breakup of the Soviet Union, the movement of Eastern European countries toward market-based economies, reduced government controls and surveillance, and changes in Western Europe associated with the European Community. European Community developments facilitating criminal activity include the virtual elimination of border controls, new laws that make international business transactions easier, and relaxed transnational monetary regulations. Organized crime may be taking more rapid advantage of these factors than legal businesses. Impact of such expansion already has touched North America and will likely increase significantly.

European organized crime has focused largely on consumer goods. Shipments of products are stolen and sold on the black market. If there is a demand for a product, it is a potential target. In one case, organized crime groups were found to have stolen radioactive material with the intent to sell it to the highest bidder. These groups also have been involved in counterfeiting various consumer goods (jeans, tennis shoes, watches, videotapes, and other consumer items), and even in the theft of counterfeit items produced by other organized-crime groups. Given the changing world economic market to one of free enterprise and consumerism, it is likely this activity will continue to expand.

Central Asian organized-crime groups, largely in the southeastern republics of the former Soviet Union, also are involved in black marketing. They tend, however, to be more actively involved in drug trafficking, terrorism, and political insurgency. Preliminary indicators suggest that the economic successes of organized crime activity may be more rewarding than any political accomplishments. Growth and expansion in these criminal enterprises can be expected.

Pacific Rim

The presence of organized-crime groups from the Pacific Rim clearly exists in North America. Hong Kong Chinese, ethnic Chinese, Taiwanese, and Thai elements exist in the United States and Canada. To a large extent their role provides "supply and support" for other organized-crime groups in Asia and the Pacific. More prevalent and better established in North America are Japanese, Vietnamese, and Korean crime groups. Their involvement in drug trafficking (mostly in heroin) has grown substantially, but they are also involved in loan sharking, black marketing, and, to a lesser degree, "protection" rackets.

Most notorious of the Pacific Rim organized-crime groups are the Japanese Triads—highly organized crime cartels characterized by loyalty, rigid structure, and aggressive ruthlessness. The focal leadership of the Triads remains in Japan; however, their presence is pervasive throughout North America. Although extremely difficult to penetrate, the Triads seem not only to have investments in legitimate businesses, both in North America and Japan, but also government ties in Japan. The sociocultural characteristics with which Japanese industry has been so successful are magnified in the Triads. As a result, they may emerge as a "world crime cartel" in the not too distant future.

Gangs

Traditionally viewed simply as groups of local, frequently violent juvenile delinquents interested in protecting their "turf," gangs are in transition. Gangs increasingly are involved in drug trafficking, theft, extortion, and other crimes at the local, regional, and national levels. It is difficult to make any meaningful generalizations about gangs as a form of organized crime, simply because they vary so much. Gangs tend to be neither very sophisticated nor well organized (e.g., the "Crips" and "Bloods" of Los Angeles). They are formed largely along racial or ethnic lines and tend to cooperate predominantly with similar ethnic groups. Alliances are generally short-term and informal. Despite these factors, a growing number of these gangs are taking on characteristics of organized crime. If these trends continue, gangs are likely to become a more dominant force, particularly at the local level.

Summary

Diverse organized-crime groups will continue to flourish for two reasons: they are profitable and are difficult to prosecute successfully. Given the diversity of the groups, increased competition for their respective "markets" is likely. While violence will always be a part of organized crime, it does not appear that the future competition will be as bloody as that between the Cosa Nostra groups in the 1920s. Rather, competition is more likely to involve aggressive marketing tactics. Organized-crime leaders of today are more sophisticated and future-oriented than their predecessors were. They recognize that violence will attract law enforcement and public attention, both of which are "bad for business." Over the years, organized-crime groups have shown creativity and resourcefulness. Intellectual property, information crimes, and high technology all appear to be areas that organized crime will pursue with vigor.

See also CRIME, NONVIOLENT; CRIME, VIOLENT; CRIME RATES; DRUGS, ILLICIT; TERRORISM.

BIBLIOGRAPHY

ABADINSKY, HOWARD. *Organized Crime*, 2nd ed. Chicago, Ill.: Nelson-Hall Publishers, 1988.

BOOTH, MARTIN. *The Triads.* London: Grafton Books, 1990.

FOX, STEPHEN. *Blood and Power: Organized Crime in Twentieth Century America.* New York: Penguin Books, 1989.

President's Commission on Organized Crime. *The Impact: Organized Crime Today.* Washington, DC: U.S. Government Printing Office, 1986.

David L. Carter

Crime, Violent

Violence is a complex social problem occurring under a wide variety of circumstances and conditions produced by the interaction of many factors. Levels of violence have increased worldwide, becoming so pervasive in America, that the U.S. Center for Disease Control now characterizes violence as a public health problem. Indeed, the leading cause of death among young black men is homicide.

Crime

Violent crime results from such varied forms of behavior and circumstances that it cannot be solved by any blanket remedy. Each type of violence must be combated through a response tailored to the special nature of the act (such as domestic violence, rape, drive-by shootings, robberies, and so forth). Violent behavior is heterogeneous, and heterogeneous approaches are needed to deal with it.

The number of assaults, homicides, robberies, and criminal sexual assaults continues to rise disproportionately to population increases. In cities such as Detroit and St. Louis, the number of violent crimes continues to rise, even though the population is decreasing.

A violent crime that emerged in the early 1990s is "car jacking." This is a robbery wherein a driver is confronted by a menacing or armed thief who steals the car. In a number of incidents victims have been assaulted or even killed. The crime attracted such notoriety that a federal law was passed prohibiting it.

Weapons

The frequency and intensity of violence is related to the availability of weapons, although weapons availability alone is not "the cause" of violence. The availability of firearms and the increased capacity of firepower, particularly in semiautomatic weapons, contributes to the seriousness of violent acts. While not as pervasive, there also has been an increase in the use of nonlethal weapons, such as knives, tear gas, and stun guns. Underscoring the awareness of growing violence, criminals have protected themselves with body armor similar to that worn by police officers.

Drug Trade

There can be no doubt that violence is escalated by drug trafficking. Violence and drugs interact in several ways, notably in the cities. National Institute of Justice Drug Use Forecasting (DUF) findings show that a high proportion of persons commit crimes while under the influence of drugs. Twenty of twenty-four cities testing arrestees for the presence of drugs found that over 50 percent of them tested positive for at least one drug. In Manhattan, DUF data showed that 79 percent of those arrested tested positive for some drug. Research further shows that a number of criminals use drugs in order to "build up their courage" to commit a crime. Criminals under the influence of drugs are likely to respond violently if confronted by a citizen or police officer.

Competing drug trafficking organizations, when attempting to dominate drug markets and to gain control of a geographic area, also resort to violence. Drive-by shootings used by competing groups to discourage competition are particularly noteworthy. While drive-by shootings are also used for other motives, they are most common in drug dealing. The Jamaican "posses" earned a notorious reputation by shooting indiscriminately at a group of people in order to be certain that their target was killed.

Human Interaction

To understand violent behavior, it is necessary to understand how people interact. Trends in violence over the past decade indicate growing tolerance for and reliance on violent behavior and aggression rather than negotiation to resolve conflict. In other words, when people engage in conflict, there is a greater tendency to resolve it through aggressive behavior rather than through negotiation. In increasing numbers, this aggression might be described as "mindless or motiveless violence." People have been killed over trivial arguments related to cooking food, possession of clothing, and spilled beer. Similarly, ramming cars, dropping objects on vehicles from expressway overpasses, and motorists shooting at each other became so commonplace that the California Highway Patrol began keeping statistics on "freeway violence."

Media portrayals of violence may contribute to aggressive behavior. Consistent exposure to violent acts in media portrayals "teach" violence as a response to conflict and people essentially "learn" aggression through sustained exposure to these actions.

Schools

Violence and aggression in the nation's schools has reached unprecedented levels. Contrary to popular belief, these problems are not limited to inner-city schools, but also encompass rural and suburban areas. Nor is the problem just in the high schools—middle and elementary schools also have experienced increases in violent behavior.

Violent acts can be characterized as "student-on-student" and "student-on-teacher" aggression. Both types have increased. The presence of guns and knives has risen significantly. One estimate from the Center for Handgun Violence is that on any given day 100,000 students go to school with a gun. The number of schools that employed security guards, established their own police force, or installed metal detectors to screen persons entering the school are further indicators of this escalating problem.

Surprisingly, drugs and violence in schools do not seem to be strongly correlated. In fact, violence and aggression appear to be more pervasive in schools than are drug and alcohol abuse. This is particularly evident when examined across all grade levels. Still, drugs and alcohol do contribute to a general atmosphere of disorder which, in turn, creates an environment conducive to violence. Other contributing factors include an increased number of children who have experienced fetal alcohol syndrome (which entails consequential behavioral problems); increasing numbers of students with attention deficit disorder; significant court and/or administrative restrictions on school disciplinary policies; reduced parental involvement in both the educational process and discipline; and changing values and lifestyles among youth. These are long-term, endemic problems which require aggressive and sustained intervention. Consequently, levels of violence, aggression, and disorder in the schools will likely continue to increase into the foreseeable future.

Terrorism

Until the carefully planned and coordinated attack on the World Trade Center in February 1994, there had been relatively few international terrorist attacks in North America, due to our comparative geographic isolation, effective intelligence operations, prevention initiatives, and limited numbers of sympathizers to the ideologies of Middle Eastern or other terrorist groups. These groups had found that terrorist targets in the United States were simply too difficult and expensive to attack. Heightened security measures in the aftermath of the World Trade Center tragedy may reinstate that opinion, but the feeling that the United States is somehow immune to terrorism has been at the very least greatly reduced, if not eliminated.

The Irish Republican Army (IRA) generally has had no desire to stage terrorism in the United States because it receives contributions and support from some members of the Irish-American community that the IRA does not want to offend. Abroad, terrorism remains an on-going problem. U.S. targets—embassies, military bases, and U.S. citizens—remain more vulnerable, but attacks are still relatively rare. Given the changes in world politics, only carefully orchestrated attacks against U.S. targets are likely to come about.

Domestic terrorism is different but still relatively rare. This encompasses violent behavior by groups in the United States who oppose American laws, policies, and sociopolitical trends. In the 1960s, extreme political leftist groups—e.g., the Weathermen and Students for a Democratic Society (SDS)—were responsible for various terrorist acts. While these groups are largely gone, they have been replaced by political ideologues, predominantly of the extreme right. Groups such as the Aryan Nations, the Order, the Covenant, Sword, and Arm of the Lord, and neo-Nazis seek a white, Protestant America with limited governmental controls. They particularly support violent acts against minorities, Jews, homosexuals, and people who support these groups. Right-wing groups are well-armed ideologues who possess the potential for increased terrorist violence, at least in geographic pockets.

Riots

Mounting evidence suggests that riots may again emerge in the United States. While the 1960s riots were focused on institutional change related to the civil rights movement and the Vietnam War, the impetus for riots in the future will be different. Deteriorating economic conditions, growing chasms between white America and people of color, decaying urban America, and the growing political power of the affluent at the expense of the shrinking middle class and the poor will ignite future riots. Moreover, according to FBI agent and futurist William Tafoya, the riots of the future will surpass those of the 1960s in duration, intensity, and violence. In the past four years there have been civil disorders in Miami, Shreveport, New York, Virginia Beach, and Los Angeles. The signs of stress are emerging on our campuses and in our cities. The future holds a strong potential for violent unrest unless actions are taken to temper the social, economic, and political strains currently emerging.

Summary

Violence is a learned phenomenon which becomes part of the behavioral pathology of a culture. It has been molded by a series of complex, interactive patterns over a generation which cannot be changed in the short term. As a result, it is unlikely that levels of violence will decrease over the next few years. Violent acts will probably increase, albeit at a slower rate, in the coming years until institutional change reshapes the behavioral patterns of the next generation.

See also CHILD ABUSE; CRIME, NONVIOLENT; CRIME, ORGANIZED; CRIME RATES; DRUGS, ILLICIT; LAW ENFORCEMENT; LETHAL WEAPONS; TERRORISM.

BIBLIOGRAPHY

BASTIAN, LISA, and TAYLOR, BRUCE. *School Crime.* Washington, DC: Bureau of Justice Statistics, 1991.

Caught in the Crossfire: A Report on Gun Violence in the Nation's Schools. Washington, DC: Center to Prevent Handgun Violence, 1991.

CROMWELL, PAUL, et al. *Breaking and Entering: An Ethnographic Analysis of Burglary.* Newbury Park, CA: Sage Publishing Company, 1991.

National Institute of Justice. *Drug Use Forecasting—Second Quarter 1992.* Washington, DC: U.S. Department of Justice, 1992.

ROHR, JANELLE. *Violence in America: Opposing Viewpoints.* San Diego, CA: Greenhaven Press, 1990.

TAFOYA, WILLIAM L. "Rioting in the Streets: Déjà Vu?" *CJ the Americas* 2:6 (1990):1, 19–23.

David L. Carter
John H. Campbell

Crime Rates

Soaring crime erodes America's social fabric. Rampant crime is associated with declining morals, breakdown of traditional values, liberalized codes that define criminal conduct more permissively, individual rights delinked from social responsibilities, pursuit of self-expression without self-control, tolerant attitudes toward criminal behavior, weak law enforcement and crime detection methods, overemphasis on criminal rights to the virtual exclusion of victim rights, and softening of penalties that detract from deterrence of criminal behavior. Further aggravating this pervasive social malaise are public indifference and tolerance for the turmoil, havoc, despair, and even death.

Rules that govern "acceptable" social behavior have been eroded. Forms of misbehavior once forbidden by criminal codes are now excused. These radical reversals in basic principles of criminal law, which reflect what society will and will not tolerate, occurred in just a few decades. The spiral downward has been swift and pervasive. The following cursory review reveals how ethics and morals that once anchored social order have been reversed.

Mugging has become so commonplace, and chances of tracking down culprits so slim, that no follow-up is likely and most of these crimes go unreported. This is a bonanza for strongarm hoodlums who shy away from burglary because mugging provides quick cash with no fencing of stolen goods, and no sting operations to get trapped by.

Unruly civil disturbances previously constituted a breach of the public peace and were repressed. All too often perpetrators are allowed to wreak destruction, take property, and otherwise threaten or endanger others. Demagogic politicians frequently encourage civil disobedience—in overly zealous pursuit of civil rights that occasionally escalate into full-scale riot and rebellion.

On a communitywide scale, looting Los Angeles-style carries personal property crimes to new heights. Offenders may be let free to run their course. Full force of repression, the kind of police response that used to be fielded to protect citizens and to cut short and deter further uprisings of a violent nature, now is downplayed, and rioters on a spree are given license to "do their thing." A hands-off attitude encourages mob frenzy. When things get out of hand and authorities no longer are able to provide protection, government lets the public absorb the brunt of the unruly mob. Rights of the mob are allowed to prevail over individual rights.

Because police shy from using whatever may be required to protect life and limb or private property, some victims in these powder kegs organize armed vigilantes. For their efforts, they sometimes wind up themselves being prosecuted for illegal conduct.

Union hooliganism far too often resorts to vandalism, sabotage, beatings, bullying, and belligerent threats. Strikebreakers often fear for their personal safety. Unions, initially intended to redress power disparities between workers and management, sometimes are intentionally used to force capitulation, even if it means forcing a business into bankruptcy or out of business. Such an abuse of power seems to be "too hot a potato" for politicians to address.

Environmental extremists seem to be given wide latitude, even when they pursue harmful tactics. Monkey-wrenching—spiking trees or sabotaging equipment, for example—sometimes causes lumberjack or sawmill worker deaths. Extremist acts in defense of admirable objectives never should be tolerated.

Parking tickets, a bane and a bother to drivers (but a boon to nearby merchants), are allowed to pile up. Scofflaws may get hailed into court when the number of tickets mount. In Tokyo, where parking tickets can draw fines of $2,000 each, a different incentive applies.

Communities into which parolees are released are forbidden from notifying neighborhoods of potential threats, even from dangerous repeat offenders. Unleashing risky repeat offenders upon an unwary community respects criminals' rights over those of the community upon whom they prey. Criminals used to go to jail—and stay there. Now, early release from prison, weekend passes, and other humanitarian-inspired methods seek to reintegrate ex-convicts into society. All too often these well-intentioned efforts go awry. In a recent presidential election, the Willie Horton incident (involving a felon parolee who committed another grievous crime following early release from prison) became a major campaign issue. At least nine states have taken steps to abolish early release from prison terms.

Vagrants and loiterers—who used to be characterized as bums, hobos, drifters, and so on—once were tossed into jail or run out of town. Now they are housed, clothed, fed, and cared for by government. Street people are permitted to construct shantytowns or hovels on public grounds in a manner that effectively runs the general public out. A long-suffering public is expected to endure these depredations. Panhandlers and beggars, once confined to skid rows, the Bowery, or similar areas, have spread communitywide. Panhandling locations even are approved by government, the only restriction being to mooch in nonthreatening ways.

Shoplifting and pilferage have reached epidemic proportions. Thieves, especially juveniles, all too often are let off scot-free or with a mere slap on the wrist. Making up losses from pilferage adds about 10 percent to retail prices. In addition, store security systems and guards, electronic or explosive-dye security tags, hidden surveillance cameras, parking lot patrols, and so on add incrementally to costs.

Usury once was the domain of loan sharks and unscrupulous predators. Pawnshops that used to extort interest on pledged goods effectively amounting to 20 percent to 25 percent or higher were largely driven out of business. At least for the present time, it has become permissible for credit card firms, banks, and other credit givers to charge exorbitant rates hovering close to 20 percent, a rate previously held to be usurious.

Debtor prisons have given way to revolving-door bankruptcy. Profligacy is rewarded by wiping the slate clean and letting perpetrators take another round at bilking honest businesses and citizens.

Automatic guns, assault rifles, machine pistols, guns with unprecedented firepower, clips that carry hundreds of rounds, and ever larger bores—all once strictly prohibited—can be openly or clandestinely purchased virtually anywhere. Kids tote deadly weapons to school. Schools respond with metal detectors, surveillance, frisking, and locker searches. Civil rights advocates wince. Worse, the number of young Americans killed by guns was up twofold, rising from 1,059 in 1970 to 2,162 in 1990. Kids accidentally shooting kids sometimes results in parents being charged with reckless endangerment. To deter such mishaps, laws require trigger guards and other locks or tamper-resistant features.

Drive-by shootings have become rites of passage for some youth gang members. "Mushrooms" or accidental victims caught in crossfire, many of them babies and children, have become all too frequent. Gun control efforts falter. More than 20,000 gun laws already on the law books in 1988 apparently have done little to stem the tide of gun violence that wracks society. Twice the number of Americans were killed by firearms at home as were killed in Vietnam (84,633 versus 46,752). In a pitiful show of political courage, politicians have zeroed in on geyserlike squirt guns and proposed legislation banning their sale. So-called super-soakers are little more than bothersome and certainly not lethal. Legislators also seek to minimize realistic mock guns and children's toy guns in committing real crimes. Because "toys" involve no deadly force potential, perpetrators can get off on reduced charges not involving real guns. Turning the tables on victims, some criminals have been able to sue police or citizens who respond to the confrontation with toy guns by shooting perpetrators. To distinguish such toys and replicas, red-tipped muzzles or other identifying marks have been proposed.

Drug abuse contributes to escalating crime. Addicts who pursue a life of crime to support drug habits have spawned the worst crime wave in U.S. history. Crime profits in 1994 worldwide amounted to an estimated $1 trillion, half of it in drugs. Illegal drugs generated an estimated $500 billion worldwide in 1954. America's most valuable crop is marijuana, with a value exceeding $32 billion in the mid-1990s. The value of the nation's most important food crops—corn at $14 billion, and soybeans at $11 billion—pale by comparison.

Some states imposed tax stamps on illegal drugs to help facilitate prosecution and seizure of untaxed drugs. Stamp collectors responded by scooping them up. Against this sordid backdrop of illicit drugs, the Presidential Commission on Marijuana and Drug Abuse Decriminalization, under President Carter, advocated decriminalization in 1977. The Netherlands tried lax enforcement, open drug areas, and clean-needle exchange between 1978 and 1995; results are unclear. A few jurisdictions tolerate or actually legalize drugs—Christiana, Denmark; North Rhine-Westphalia, Germany; and Amsterdam among them. U.S. litigation permits marijuana for medicinal purposes. As of January 1991, several dozen persons have been authorized to rely upon such therapy.

Alcohol abuse is abetted by government-run stores in some jurisdictions. At least one jurisdiction offers private government brands for exclusive sale in government-owned and -run shops (Montgomery County, Maryland). Sales of alcoholic beverages were formerly restricted to a few licensed outlets with rigidly controlled hours of operation intended to limit sales. Now alcoholic beverages are increasingly available from almost any retailer. The pain and suffering linked to alcohol abuse impose costly burdens. One of every thirteen American adults is an alcoholic. Fetal alcohol syndrome ranks as the third most common cause of birth defects, afflicting 4,000 to 12,000 victims annually.

Sobriety checkpoints attempt to stem alcohol-related motorcar mayhem. Yet, one-third of the states outlaw these checkpoints as an infringement on free movement and an invasion of privacy. Some jurisdictions make providers of excess alcohol liable for ensuing acts of their drunken guests. Taking such incidental liability one step farther, persons who fail to stop obviously inebriated individuals who come across their path (such as gas station attendants who might have an opportunity to intervene) have been held liable for ensuing damages caused by persons they failed to detain. Sweden pursues an economic route (among others) to discourage alcohol consumption. To dissuade public drinking, Swedish restaurants charge about $22 for a double martini.

Sobriety measurement devices at bars sometimes encourage "good ole boys" to vie with bar buddies to see who can consume enough alcohol to blow the meters off the scale. Unobtrusive breath analyzers built into police flashlights are assailed as an invasion of privacy or illegal search. Ignition interlocks making it difficult for inebriates to start cars may be required for drivers repeatedly convicted for driving under the influence.

Gambling, once forbidden by government, has become a government monopoly. Numbers and lotteries have been taken over by the government. Adding insult to injury, governments wantonly encourage gambling through mass advertising campaigns. All other manner of gaming, from casinos and riverboats to slots, roulette, cards, and off-track betting, is being authorized on an unprecedented scale. Legal gambling mushroomed into a $300 billion enterprise in 1992, plus another estimated $40 billion in illegal gaming. In European Union nations, gambling ranked as the twelfth-largest industry in 1989.

Government corruption, bribes, and kickbacks also have reached all-time highs. The morality of elected officials from presidents to mayors is being questioned. But despite their personal shortcomings, voters elect them.

Health insurance fraud burgeons. A few years ago an estimated $60 billion, or 10 percent of health-care costs, were siphoned off in this manner. An estimated 20 percent of all automobile insurance payments are diverted to bogus claims. Citizen attitudes toward "deep pocket" providers have waned.

White-collar crime accounts for as much as ten times the amount stolen in street crime. Yet only one of ten perpetrators receives a sentence.

Embezzlement and fraud took four times more money stealthily out of banks than robbers took out the front door during the early 1990s. And the stakes are enormous. Charles Keating's failed Lincoln Savings & Loan may have cost taxpayers up to $2 billion.

Champerty and barratry—ambulance-chasing—encourage litigation. Fomenting spurious litigation—including mass media inducements—encourages feigned injuries and frivolous lawsuits.

Enforcement of truancy laws, previously strictly enforced, has become lax. Today, when major enforcement is undertaken, it's a news event. Spanking, once used to drive home moral lessons, has been outlawed in some jurisdictions. In the name of child abuse, parents and guardians are forbidden to use physical reprimands.

Juvenile crime is largely hidden from public view. Mollycoddling may be a misguided effort intended to protect youth from notoriety that could adversely affect the rest of their lives. Because kids cannot be prosecuted as adults, callous drug dealers use them as "mules" to shield drug pushers from being charged with physical possession of illegal drugs. Only occasionally are hardened, repeat offenders, or those charged with especially horrendous crimes, tried as adults.

Law enforcement officers used to respond to violence with armed force. Now trained riot troops are armed with rubber bullets, water cannons, electronic prods, disabling "sticky-goo," and tear gas. Even regular tear gas has been judged too dangerous, and pepper compounds have been substituted. Police uniforms used to be sufficient to deter harm being directed their way. Now police wear protective vests, helmets, shields, and so on. Everyday policing involves a retreat from excessive or deadly force. "Speak first and hold fire" has become the rule, increasing chances of police officers being shot. The number of police officers shot dead in the line of duty doubled between 1961 and 1989, increasing from 73 to 146 deaths.

"Cop killer" bullets—ammunition with Teflon coatings or hollow points—are permitted. At least one jurisdiction, frustrated at an inability to directly ban guns, attempted to limit gun use by outlawing the sale of ammunition. Like so many other well-intentioned efforts, this approach has been overturned.

Historically the death penalty has had a checkered use. Between 1968 and 1976, nobody sentenced for a capital crime in the United States was executed. Since then, many states have reinstated the death penalty. In 1992, thirty-one persons were executed.

Retreat from hot pursuit is another limitation on law enforcement. High-speed chases that might expose innocent civilians to danger must be terminated. Thugs, as a result, sometimes resort to chase evasion in the sanctuary of crowded neighborhoods. Another hobbling influence involves search and seizure. Evidence gleaned is subject to severely restricting strictures.

Sophisticated crime detection methods—including DNA type matching—undergo severe impediments. Meticulous procedures and burdensome costs discourage effective use. Fingerprint use and blood sample matching have undergone similar introductory ordeals.

Myriad restraints impede policing. A "subway vigilante" (Bernhard Goetz), after being mugged several times with impunity, took things into his own hands and shot the next group of hoodlums that attempted to rob him. He was tried and convicted on a variety of charges for his "misdeed." In like manner, in the midst of the Los Angeles riots, Korean shopkeepers, upon recognizing the absence of effective police protection, organized their own armed vigilante groups.

Regular citizens have become prisoners in their own homes. They retreat into walled communities, or erect antitheft barricades and alarms to protect themselves. Organized crime and gangs rule certain neighborhoods or areas. Freedom of association protects such groups. Criminal rights prevail over the broader community interest. An overly tolerant attitude prevails in society today. Indiscriminate acceptance of any and every idea, of every act of individual expression, is, quite simply, wrong. Permissiveness—doing your own thing with impunity and total disregard for the rights of others—cannot be allowed to infringe obtrusively on and compromise or ruin the rights of others. Self-expression is no excuse for lack of self-control. The operative principle of moral codes is restraint. The fact is that toleration has its limits. Liberty is not license. Codes of acceptable behavior that have been reversed a full 180 degrees to accommodate individual rights may be swinging back to broader social obligations.

Criminals these days seem to have more going for them than their victims do. In the interest of preserving individual freedom and minimizing the potential heavy-handedness of a repressive police state, attitudes toward those accused of criminal conduct have been softened. Thus criminal codes have given way to the rights of accused (perpetrators). Bending over too far in pursuit of protecting individual freedom impairs civil liberties communitywide and threatens the lives of everybody else.

This review highlights where these changes have taken us. Criminal codes must increasingly be scrutinized as to focus. Social or community interests will have to be reasserted to make streets safe once again. Political leaders in the years ahead will be compelled to take stock and to rethink whether current trends and directions in criminal law are appropriate to the times.

See also BEHAVIOR: SOCIAL CONSTRAINTS; CHILD ABUSE; CIVIL PROTEST; COUNTERFEITING; CRIME, NONVIOLENT; CRIME, ORGANIZED; CRIME, VIOLENT; CRIMINAL JUSTICE; CRIMINAL PUNISHMENT; DRUGS, ILLICIT; LAW ENFORCEMENT; LETHAL WEAPONS; PRISONS; SEXUAL CODES; SEXUAL LAWS; SOCIAL CONTROLS; TERRORISM.

BIBLIOGRAPHY

BOUZA, ANTHONY V. *The Police Mystique: An Insider's Look at Cops, Crime, and the Criminal Justice System.* New York: Plenum Press, 1990.

CURRIE, ELLIOTT. *Confronting Crime: An American Challenge.* New York: Pantheon Books, 1985.

DIIOLIO, JOHN J., JR. *No Escape: The Future of American Corrections.* New York: Basic Books, 1991.

GORDON, DIANA R. *The Justice Juggernaut: Fighting Street Crime, Controlling Citizens.* New Brunswick, NJ: Rutgers University Press, 1990.

LURIGIO, ARTHUR J., et al., eds. *Victims of Crime: Problems, Policies, and Programs.* Newbury Park, CA: Sage Publications, 1990.

U.S. BUREAU OF THE CENSUS. *Statistical Abstract of the United States, 1994.* Washington, DC: U.S. Government Printing Office, 1994.

Graham T. T. Molitor

Criminal Justice

Technology and politics, two separate but interrelated forces, are likely to be the primary forces driving future developments in the criminal justice field. In the short run, rationality, democratic values, and compassion are likely to give way to fear, rejection of the principle of proportionality, and repression.

Fear, rationally based or not, has reinforced a social conditioning that is receptive to a variety of approaches to the crime problem. In poll after poll, "crime" has consistently ranked as the most serious or one of the most serious social problems confronting the nation. Unemployment, job security, homelessness, AIDS, and international security issues seldom evoke the same intensity of citizen concern.

Therefore, it has been the rare public official, elected or appointed, who would risk public wrath by speaking in a moderating voice or questioning public "mandates" to manage crime and delinquency concerns. Political officials responded accordingly often by simplistically trying to outdo others in being tough on crime.

Bush and Clinton crime bills created the most massive expansion of the federal role over crime control in U.S. history. This included the "invention" of more than fifty new federal capital offenses. Traditional exponents of states rights were silent on this expansion of the federal role, as were those representatives and senators traditionally opposed to the death penalty.

Conceding the many limitations of various measurement tools, there is a gap between subjective-based fear and the objective reality of crime. Nearly all the data reveals that the amount of crime actually decreased or plateaued during the 1990s. Politicians fixated on the erroneous impression of escalating crime perpetuate this myth, ignoring reality.

Explanation for this misplaced emphasis can be attributed to the increased reporting by television of spectacular and violent crimes. Body bags and SWAT teams have replaced balanced reporting of local news. Youthful violence also adds a new and terrifying element. Just as television coverage of mass starvation spurred reluctant political leaders into action in Somalia, Ruwanda, and Haiti, so, too, television images of death and violence spurred them into action in attempts to control crime.

There is no reason to believe that the social impact of television will decrease in the near future. Indeed, just the opposite can be expected with improvements in image resolution and the combination of television and computers into a new generation of user-friendly multimedia control centers, which will be common in perhaps one-third of U.S. homes and almost certainly in nearly every school. The political response to new imagery control is likely to be driven by images created by the powerful new media and enhanced by a keener texture of information.

There are related communication spin-offs in the presentation of evidence to juries and other fact finders. Simulations of crime scenes and the construction of computer-based alternative scenarios of crime reenactments have assisted juries in their decision-making role. The development of Automated Fingerprint Identification Systems (AFIS) have increased the number of identifications of suspects in murder cases, some of them inactive for many years.

Technology, of course, encompasses more than computer-based communications. DNA-testing has revolutionized the process of eliminating or including potential suspects in a variety of types of cases. In the mid-1990s, the investigation and prosecution of O. J. Simpson focused the attention of the public and the legal profession on both the value and the limitations of DNA as an investigatory and probative tool.

The deluge of communications vehicles and equipment relaying the Simpson trial proceedings to the public raised public consciousness of the value of forensic evidence. Implicitly and explicitly, this information raised questions about the scientific objectivity as well as the competence of laboratory personnel. It also highlighted discrepancies between the forensic resources available to the state (prosecution) and the defendant. This was the trial of a wealthy defendant rather than an indigent defendant. Whereas the prosecutor has access to a costly array of forensic services and the gratis testimony of experts, the defense may be limited to services costing less than $500 for an entire case! In the Simpson case, however, it was suggested that the resources of one rich defendant might actually exceed those available to the entire County of Los Angeles!

The most expensive and longest prosecution in U.S. history—the McMartin school child-abuse case (also in Los Angeles County) caused a rethinking of prosecutorial decision making. How many prosecutions can the state afford, even in aggravated cases? In its early stages, the expense of the O. J. Simpson prosecution was estimated to be in excess of $20 million.

In the early 1990s, there were a series of prosecutions of police officers and laboratory personnel—in widely dispersed parts of the nation—for tampering with, altering, or fabricating evidence in criminal trials. Although not widely publicized outside the immediate environs of the cases, the public at large has begun to understand that government investigators may not always be the objective pursuers of fact envisioned by professional standards. The public may be ready to accept the notion that some police/investigatory personnel can just as easily become "advocates," selecting and construing the evidence in a manner pursuant to their own bias of the case.

Finally, the impact of economic considerations on the criminal-justice process is largely unknown. Fiscal realities in the mid-1980s resulted in some rethinking of governmental organization and delivery of a range of criminal-justice services. This has caused some diminution in the nation's nearly 29,000 police agencies as contracts, merging or pooling of operations, consolidations of staff services, privatizations, and so on took hold.

In the 1970s fiscal as well as operational realities led a number of jurisdictions to adopt management information systems to assist in assigning priorities to both criminal investigation and prosecution. Finite resources could no longer be automatically devoted to every deserving case.

In one sense, policing/order maintenance efforts have seen a greater degree of privatization than other aspects of the criminal-justice process. The number of private-security personnel assigned duties in both residential and commercial areas was in the mid-1990s estimated to be greater than the total number of public police, which totaled approximately 600,000 nationwide.

Privatization has been tried in all other aspects of criminal justice, including prosecution and the courts in various diversion and conflict-resolution programs. Private entrepreneurs have also entered some portions of the correctional field, both in administering institutions and various probation and parole endeavors. Due-process considerations will figure prominently in whether these efforts are allowed to stand by various courts.

See also ALCOHOL; CHILD ABUSE; CRIME RATES; CRIME, NONVIOLENT; CRIME, ORGANIZED, CRIMINAL PUNISHMENT; DRUGS, ILLICIT; LAW ENFORCEMENT; LAWS, EVOLUTION OF; PRISONS; SEXUAL CODES; SEXUAL LAWS; TOBACCO.

BIBLIOGRAPHY

The Criminal Justice System and the Future. Claremont, CA: Claremont Graduate School/National Conference of Christians and Jews, June 1983.
"The Global Crime Wave." *Futurist* (July-August 1994).
STEPHENS, GENE. *The Future of Criminal Justice.* Cincinnatti: Anderson Publishing, 1992.
"Trends in Crime and Criminal Justice." *Future Scan* (February 27, 1989).

Gordon Misner

Criminal Punishment

Jails and prisons will remain the principal correctional institutions in the twenty-first century, but they will be more attractive architecturally than the traditional fortresses of the nineteenth and twentieth centuries, though still with slit or barred windows and tangles of concertina wire. More, perhaps eventually most, of the newer facilities will be privately owned and operated as the privatization phenomenon accelerates, but under close and strict governmental supervision. Inside, there will be activities very much like those of today, many of them rehabilitative, but they will be voluntary rather than mandatory. The spirit of such facilities will be more punitive, because of changing philosophical principles; the style, however, will be more humane, because of changing administrative practices.

A smaller portion of the general population will be housed in such facilities than now, but a larger portion of the population will be subject to lesser constraints and to supervision, some in newly developed circumstances. In other words (but expressed in today's numbers), fewer than 1,000,000 will be incarcerated but more than 3,000,000 will be under supervision or some other constraint. This may be the most salient characteristic of corrections in the early twenty-first century. Relatively fewer inmates will occupy celled space of the sort one finds in today's maximum and medium security prisons, though more of those, who would otherwise have been there, will instead be in somewhat lower security (even camplike) facilities. Many more will be placed in what amounts to traditional probation or parole but under more intensive supervision. What will be different for some portion of those under constraint will be facilities with electronically secured perimeters (cross the line and you die) confining inmates to grounds on which they will live in barracks, dormitories, cottages, even tents, and move about relatively freely. What will not be new for many of the supervised, except in terms of magnitude, will be the numbers placed in electronically monitored "house arrest." These two technologically based developments will greatly reduce the portion of the convict population that would otherwise be under loose or no supervision. They will experience the "net-widening" effect of the expanded capacity of additional facilities.

More convicts will be in some degree of correctional constraint under judicial or executive jurisdiction because of a growing acceptance of the idea of alternative or intermediate sanctions for many convicted criminals. This will owe partly to the availability of fail-safe electronic monitoring devices and partly to a desire to see more prisoners treated humanely. Much of this will take the form of "community service orders," often in combination with limited periods of constraint (e.g., evenings, weekends). These shifts reflect a philosophy of engaging more persons earlier in their criminal "careers" with lower levels of sanctions and measures that do not call for costly institutionalization. These shifts will also represent a blurring of the formal-informal, public-private, and central-local distinctions that have characterized governmental arrangements generally. There will be many experiments with contractual arrangements among correctional agencies and those institutions with some contribution to make to the correctional functions, such as schools, welfare organizations, and private corporations. The arm of the law, so to speak, will be longer, though the weight of its hand will be lighter for many.

Correctional philosophy as well as technological development and cost-cutting experiments will account for this. Two principles of punishment will have come to be more acceptable: (1) retribution requires the pain of liberty lost; and (2) incapacitation is cost-effective. A third may be acknowledged as well: (3) the lessons of constraint, of liberty lost, are learned by those who become aware of it by personal experience or by word of it "on the street." This means that some inmates will be behind bars or under constraint because they deserve to be, whatever the cost may be—and the public will increasingly insist on this. Others will be confined because it will be accepted that a few people, who can be identified with increasing accuracy, commit a disproportionate amount of crime, which costs victims and communities more than their incapacitation. These principles will reflect the values of the middle-aging portion of the general population, which will increase in number and no longer feel quite so outnumbered, surrounded, and daunted by the younger generation as their counterparts did in the late 1960s and '70s.

This is consistent with the movement to legislatively restrict the sentencing decision—more recently, to relax it somewhat. The trend toward increasing judicial discretion was reversed after the 1970s, when legislatures imposed mandatory sentences and/or guided discretion in sentencing (as in sentencing guidelines). The sentencing decision probably will continue to be constrained for more serious offenses, but as the level of seriousness declines, legislatures will tend to back off, in effect, to allow judges more discretion in fashioning correctional measures tailored to each individual offender.

There is a prospect, however, for movement toward even more restricted decision making. The capacity of computers to store vast amounts and kinds of information and to retrieve it instantly will make it attractive—in spite of resistance to invasions of privacy—to "assist" decisions with dossiers that provide the basis for projected penalties with much greater refinement. This, in principle, is what sentencing guidelines do with the convict's record; the practice would be merely(!) an extension of the sophistication.

The number of persons who will be subjected to correctional constraints, institutional and otherwise, is all but impossible to forecast beyond the three to five years that is the outside limit of traditional forecasting in the corrections field. In a simple world, one would project the general population for each year, noting the changing demographics as baby booms and busts mature and the prison-prone years follow the crime-prone years (15–24) by some seven or eight years. But prison population also depends on crime rates, which depend, in turn, on a complex set of factors criminologists have yet to figure out fully. However, even if demographic and crime rate projections were dependable, it would be difficult to project what has been called "the scale of imprisonment." Complicating factors include public opinion, economic conditions, and policy decisions. An example is the "war" on drugs (with mandatory penalties) that has swelled prisons with drug offenders and the more recent "truce" that has reduced prison admissions.

Changes less subtle, though also less far-reaching, can be anticipated. Technological capabilities, as ever before, will be all but irresistible. The ability to inflict pain without lasting physical effects will make corporal punishment an attractive alternative to the "pains of imprisonment" behind bars—for the convict as well as for the authorities. Capital punishment, which will continue to be important symbolically though not instrumentally, will have nearly disappeared in the United States, as in other industrialized nations. But its decline will not be so much a matter of outright abolishment, even though a constitutional peg may have been found from which to hang a decision to abolish it. Instead, it will be the continuing political ambivalence of the people, who both want and do not want the death penalty. Citizens want capital punishment on the books as a deterrent or retribution. But when it comes down to the reality of executions, they do not favor it in practice.

Rehabilitation, which fell from favor for reasons both philosophical and fiscal in the 1970s and '80s, will not make a comeback by the early decades of the twenty-first century. Should there be some major discoveries by then of why criminal conduct occurs at all, and what can be done to change the disposition to murder, rape, and rob, rehabilitative efforts would advance. But this seems unlikely in general, though some programs, such as drug treatment regimens, may prove effective.

Major discoveries with correctional implications can be anticipated in one area of crime-causation: in the biological, chemical, electrical workings of the brain. These will make it possible, hence irresistibly attractive, to treat a small number of offenders whose behavior is known to have been produced by brain malfunction. The efficacy of surgical and especially of pharmacological intervention in such cases will often overwhelm what might be called the "ethicacy" of such measures, by which we would otherwise have resisted them in the interest of the "patient's" psychological autonomy and physical integrity.

Thus, decades into the twenty-first century, the look of corrections will be very much like it is becoming as we approach the end of this century. Prisons and jails will continue to be very important, but alternatives will reduce relatively the number in such institutions. The alternatives will be attractive enough (to the authorities, not the offenders) to greatly increase the number sentenced to them rather than left in loosely supervised probation or unattended altogether. There will possibly be some high-tech corporal punishment and probably even less capital punishment than now, of any "tech" whatsoever. Rehabilitation, by and large, will be limited, at least in any therapeutic sense, and will be largely voluntary to the extent that it is practiced. In short, for corrections there will be more of the same for the most part, but with some interesting differences—much as its future has always been.

See also CRIME RATES; CRIMINAL JUSTICE; LAW ENFORCEMENT; PRISONS.

BIBLIOGRAPHY

DILULIO, JOHN J., JR. *No Escape: The Future of American Corrections.* New York: Basic Books, 1991.

DURHAM, ALEXIS M., III. *Crisis and Reform: Current Issues in American Punishment.* Boston: Little, Brown, 1994.

GARLAND, DAVID. *Punishment and Modern Society.* Oxford: Oxford University Press, 1990.

MORRIS, NORVAL, and TONRY, MICHAEL. *Between Prison and Probation: Intermediate Punishments in a Rational Sentencing System.* New York: Oxford University Press, 1990.

ZIMRING, FRANKLIN E., and HAWKINS, GORDON. *The Scale of Imprisonment.* Chicago: University of Chicago Press, 1991.

Laurin A. Wollan, Jr.

Culture and Society

As we prepare for the next millennium, issues of culture and society—ethnic conflict, extinction of indigenous peoples, language, and material culture, and the emergence of diverse new subcultures—have taken a special prominence. As one response to the growing importance of these issues, the United Nations declared the decade 1988–1997 to be the World Decade for Cultural Development and established a World Commission for Culture and Development. *Culture* is a nebulous concept with many definitions, but in the context of culture and society, it may be defined as the way people behave as communities, sharing a set of ideas, values, and beliefs about the world and practicing customs and social behaviors that help bind them as distinct groups within societies. It is these specific formations of culture that determine how different communities respond, change, and strategize about the future.

There are many forces—technological, economic, ecological, political, and demographic—that transform culture and society in diverse and contradictory ways, and in turn are transformed by them. Our increasingly globalized world market system is homogenizing production and marketing technologies, global lifestyles, and commodities. Other changes in the global economy, such as the formation of new regional blocs (Europe, North America, and Asia), for example, are realigning global relations so that national identities are becoming subordinate to global regional identities. To offset cultural and economic marginalization or loss of identity, ethnic and minority groups reinvigorate historic cultural symbols, language, religious and social rituals, and social organization. Within nation-states, demographic shifts are forcing changes to the current distribution of social, economic, and political power so that, in some areas, minorities are poised to become majorities, while in others, some marginalized peoples are barely surviving at all. Yet, as we enter the era of cyberspace, radically new worlds are being invented, hastening the pace of change for all communities as they encounter new worlds beyond their boundaries.

How are we to anticipate the future of global cultures? To answer this question, futurists may look first at the *dominant trends*, asking whether we are heading for a world we really want our children to live in. Are the *policies and responses* of governments and communities sufficient to assuage or transform these conflicts? If not, are there examples of societies and cultures that offer *the possibility of more desirable futures* that take advantage of the diversity of cultures to enrich human futures? On all such questions, the future is not clear. There is considerable dispute over the implications of the trends and countertrends, and hence over the appropriate policies. In the face of such uncertainty and ambiguity futurists often construct scenarios that portray consistent and persuasive images of alternative possible futures.

Scenarios typically are built around axial variables, such as economic or demographic growth. In our case, to develop scenarios relevant to the possible futures of culture and society, we take cultural diversity as the key variable. This variable can have both positive and negative connotations, but it is, we believe, one of the most important considerations in the shaping of the future. In what follows we begin to speculate about variations in the degree of *cultural segmentation* in societies and sketch scenarios of *cultural polarization, cultural assimilation,* and *cultural pluralism.* In these scenarios, each level of cultural polarization or harmony is linked to a corresponding political, social and technological organization. For us these scenarios represent respectively the result of present trends, present policies, and a new world that fosters, celebrates, and benefits from the diversity of human culture.

A Scenario of Cultural Polarization

Present trends are leading to a future of cultural polarization. This may seem ironic, but historically we see that the global trend toward the homogenization of production and consumption also invokes a cultural reaction. The current trends are leading to considerable income disparities within and between countries, so that some groups are increasingly marginalized. In this situation aspirations for global commodities dictated by a dominant culture cannot be fulfilled, fermenting and exacerbating conflicts between populations. Even if these material aspirations could be met, such uniformity does not provide the basis for a distinctive identity that all individuals and communities need, an identity that is lost as traditional cultures are increasingly demeaned, considered atavistic, or viewed merely as tourist attractions. Such trends will bring an inevitable increase in the kind of conflicts we see in Azerbaijan, Africa, India, Bosnia, and so on, including the inner cities of America, Brazil, and many other nations.

This kind of scenario portends an increasing polarization of attitudes, continued disregard for minority needs, and repression and ghettoization based on ethnic, religious, and national stereotypes. This has implications for other areas. For example, extended to the ecological domain, with increasing consumerism alongside increasing poverty, this future places increasing burden on both local and global environments. Extended to the demographic domain, we would expect to see continuing divergences in infant mortality, family size and life expectancy across income, gender, and ethnic groups. Extended to the political domain, we believe these trends will lead to a continuing instability in national and international economic and political structures.

A Scenario of Cultural Assimilation

Our second scenario is based on a policy that attempts to reduce potential cultural conflicts through a far more benevolent, assimilationist approach to nonmainstream cultural traditions. The primary aim is that people might live together in relative harmony. The main difference from the first scenario is that far greater emphasis would be placed on sharing the fruits of economic advance. An effort would be made to resolve ethnic and cultural conflicts by adapting education, institutions, and technologies, setting a trend toward a universal definition of skills and levels of attainment across cultures. Thus, in this future, we see that lifestyles would become more uniform. Cultural differences would be low-key and expressed through activities, such as festive days and parades. Again, there would be implications for other domains. For example, marriage across all groups would blur ethnic and racial distinctions, and differences in family size, fertility, and morbidity, would decline. Nevertheless, we would expect a convergence of lifestyles with a plethora of look-alike world cities and shopping malls. Thus, even though this scenario is more equitable and more benign toward culture, the adoption of globalized material values and technologies would regularly test the carrying capacity of the planet in specific and unpredictable ways and would not resolve the problem of a loss of individual or group identity.

A Scenario of Cultural Pluralism

What is lacking from the last scenario is that it does not view cultural diversity as a source of intellectual and social capital that can contribute to economic and social development in a substantive manner. Therefore, with our third scenario we invoke policies that foster cultural diversity, rather than cultural homogenization. These, we consider, are likely to offer a greater range of economic, social, and environmental strategic development choices for the future. The future imagined here would be one of a cultural pluralism that would be multicultural and inclusive in that development strategies would make space for, and make use of, different cultural traditions. It would involve many aspects of the second scenario while exhibiting far greater mutual respect for cultural style and traditions based on creative interchanges of ideas and perspectives. Education here would become more varied, centered on local cultural structures and local social and economic needs, but maintaining respect for the cultures of other populations and regions. Again, there are implications for other domains. For example, production systems, social organizations, and communities would be smaller and more varied, with economic exchanges based on cultural differentiation. There would be wider variations in family size and lifestyles than in the last scenario, converging with greater health and life expectancy. Because of divergence in lifestyles, technologies, and smaller decentralized organizational structures, there would be reduced environmental impacts and increased ecological stability.

Obviously, in such a short space, it is not possible to do justice to the arguments—either for or against—that underpin the above scenarios. But from a more detailed elaboration and comparison of all three scenarios, we believe a strong case can be made for the last scenario. This argues for a future based on rebuilding and strengthening the links between knowledge, technology, and the natural environment, which have deteriorated during the process of industrialization and contributed to the marginalization of traditional cultures. There is a need to combine the awareness of traditional societies of the natural environment with the innovativeness of modern societies while diminishing one-sided dependence relationships. This implies neither a return to traditional lifestyles nor a lack of change in existing societies. Rather, it recognizes that both traditional and industrial lifestyles must adapt within a development strategy that over the long term is designed to achieve a more varied and equitable path for global development.

See also CHANGE, EPOCHAL; CHANGE, OPTIMISTIC AND PESSIMISTIC PERSPECTIVES; CHANGE, PACE OF; CONTINUITY AND DISCONTINUITY; GLOBAL CULTURE; MODERNISM AND POSTMODERNISM; PLURALISM; RACIAL CONFLICT; SCENARIOS; SEXUAL CODES; SEXUAL LAWS.

BIBLIOGRAPHY

COLE, SAM. "Cultural Diversity and Sustainable Futures." In Sam Cole and Karo Yamaguchi, eds. *Paradigms for Human Development.* Special issue. *Futures* 22/9 (December 1990).

MASINI, ELEONORA BARBIERI, ed. *Futures of Culture Project: The Prospects for Africa and Latin America.* Vols. 1 and 11. Paris: UNESCO, 1991, 1992.

RAZAK, VICTORIA M., and COLE, SAM, eds. *Anthropological Perspectives on the Future of Culture and Society.* Special issue. *Futures* 27/4 (May 1995).

WALLMAN, SANDRA, ed. *Contemporary Futures: Perspectives from Social Anthropology.* London: Routledge, 1992.

Victoria Razak
Sam Cole

Data Storage

Data storage is the fastest-growing segment of the computer hardware industry. Already it is estimated to approach $100 billion a year in sales. It is estimated that as of the mid-1990s, however, less than 5 percent of information is stored electronically. As of the mid-1990s the cost of electronically storing information is comparable to the cost of storing information on paper. However, the cost of electronic storage is decreasing rapidly, and it is expected that before the turn of the century, the cost will be significantly less than on paper. As the cost of electronic storage becomes less than that of paper, one can expect the growth of the electronic data storage industry to accelerate even further.

Since 1960, electronic data storage has predominantly been by magnetic recording, either on disks or tapes, and it is likely that this will remain the main data storage technology until at least the year 2015. Since 1957 the areal storage density on magnetic disk has increased by about 500,000 times, so that it is possible to store about 50,000 pages of text on one square inch of magnetic recording medium. In spite of this amazing increase in storage density, the physical limits to storage density on magnetic media are still orders of magnitude higher than we can achieve today. In a laboratory demonstration, workers from AT&T Bell Laboratories and Carnegie Mellon University demonstrated a storage density sufficient to store more than 2 million pages of text on a square inch of a magnetic thin film (Betzig et al., 1992).

A schematic diagram of a magnetic recording head and medium is shown in Figure 1. To record information in the medium, electric current is passed through the windings on the recording head, causing it to be magnetized. Due to the gap in the recording head, the magnetic field produced by the current emanates from the head and penetrates the medium. The medium, which is a magnetic coating on either a flexible tape or floppy disk or a rigid aluminum alloy (rigid disk), is magnetized either to the right or left, depending on the direction of current in the windings around the head. The coincidence of a transition in magnetization direction with a clock pulse can be used to represent a "1," while the absence of a transition represents a "0" in a binary encoding of information. To read the stored information, the medium is moved past the head. Magnetic flux produced by the transition in the magnetization direction in the medium is picked up by the head and transformed into a voltage pulse across the windings around the head.

To achieve higher storage densities, it is necessary to make the gap in the recording head narrower, to make the medium thinner, to move the head closer to the medium, to raise the coercive force (field required to reverse the magnetization of the medium), and to increase the magnetization of the recording head. Technology in the mid-1990s is far from the fundamental limits in any of these areas. The fundamental limit to recording

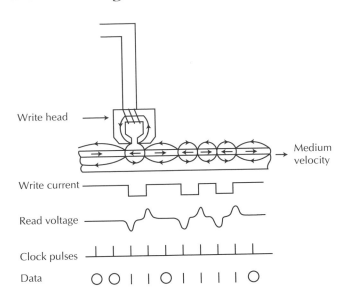

FIGURE 1. Magnetic recording system.

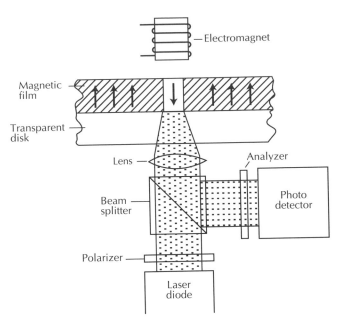

FIGURE 2. A magneto-optic recording system.

density is believed to be determined by the smallest magnetized region that will remain stable against thermal demagnetization. This limit is estimated to be about 10^{12} bits/in^2 or about 50 million pages per square inch.

It is expected that by the turn of the century the storage density on a magnetic disk will reach 5 billion bits per square inch (about 250,000 pages per square inch) (Grachowski and Thompson, 1994). Such a storage density would make possible 750-megabyte disk drives that use 1-inch disks and are put into packages scarcely larger than a microprocessor. These miniaturized drives would no longer be thought of as computer peripherals, but would be components plugged onto a board just like semiconductors chips. It is likely that several such small drives will be put onto a printed circuit board. This will make possible not only larger total storage capacities but also faster access to data, higher data rates, and improved reliability. Work with arrays of disks has shown that it is possible to organize the data in the array so that with a small amount (perhaps 20 percent) of extra storage capacity, it is possible to have one drive in the array fail and still lose no data.

Another data storage technology that is earning a growing share of the data storage market is optical recording. Optical recording uses a variety of different types of media and can be of the write-once, read-many-times variety, or the erasable variety. As of the mid-1990s, erasable optical recording uses magneto-optical storage media and is the fastest-growing segment of the optical recording market.

A schematic diagram of an apparatus for magneto-optical recording is shown in Figure 2. A laser diode provides a beam of light to write and read information in the medium. The medium is a magnetic thin film that can be magnetized either up or down, relative to the film plane. To write information into the medium, a magnetic field is applied to the medium in either the upward or the downward direction by an electromagnet, and the laser diode is pulsed. Although the medium requires a very large field at room temperature to cause it to change magnetization direction, at the high temperatures to which the focused laser beam heats it, the magnetization is easily switched. Thus, in the small region heated by the laser beam, the magnetization direction can be controlled by the applied magnetic field. In the medium, upward-pointing magnetization represents a "1" and downward-pointing magnetization represents a "0" in a binary encoding of information. To read out the information, the laser beam is used, but at reduced power, so there is insufficient heating to cause a change in magnetization direction. The laser beam is plane-polarized by a polarizer, and when it reflects from the magnetic medium, the plane of polarization is rotated either clockwise or counterclockwise, depending on whether the magnetization is directed upward or downward. This change in polarization is converted to a change in light intensity by passing the reflected beam though a second polarizer (the analyzer) and then is detected by a photodetector. Since the magnetization may be switched repeatedly by applying the magnetic field in alternating directions and pulsing the diode laser, the medium is erasable and rewritable.

The areal storage density on magneto-optical disks is, as of the mid-1990s, about the same as on a magnetic hard disk. As for the hard disks, it can be expected that the density will greatly increase to about the year 2015. Through use of shorter-wavelength lasers, improved optics, more sophisticated coding, and signal processing electronics, it is projected that at least a 32X improvement in storage density is possible.

Magneto-optical disk drives have lower data storage rates and longer access times than magnetic disk drives; however, a magneto-optical disk may be removed from the drive, much like a flexible magnetic disk can. In comparison to a flexible disk, however, a magneto-optical disk offers about 100 times more storage capacity. Thus future computer systems using large databases and images will likely use magneto-optical disk drives in place of flexible disk drives. As of the mid-1990s, the price of a magneto-optical drive is too high (about $700) for magneto-optical drives to replace flexible disk drives in low-cost systems, but magneto-optical drives are comparable in complexity to magnetic hard disk drives. Hence, as the volume of sales increases and the economics of large-volume manufacturing are realized, magneto-optical drive prices should decline to less than $500, at which point they will become much more widely used.

Other technologies, not discussed here, such as holographic storage, ferroelectric storage, and flash memory, may find application in certain market segments, but are not considered likely to displace magnetic recording as the main data storage technology until about the year 2005. The market size and investment in magnetic recording technology, its prospects for future progress, and the fact that it is actually accelerating its rate of progress, all suggest it will remain the dominant storage technology for the foreseeable future.

See also ARTIFICIAL INTELLIGENCE; CHANGE, PACE OF; COMMUNICATIONS TECHNOLOGY; COMPUTER HARDWARE; COMPUTERS: OVERVIEW; DIGITAL COMMUNICATIONS; ELECTRONIC CONVERGENCE; INFORMATION OVERLOAD; INFORMATION TECHNOLOGY; MEDIA LAB; SUPERCONDUCTIVITY; TECHNOLOGY DIFFUSION.

BIBLIOGRAPHY

BETZIG, R. E.; TRAUTMAN, J. K.; WOLFE, R.; GYORGY, E. M.; FINN, P. L.; KRYDER, M. H.; and CHANG, C. H. "Near-Field Magneto-Optics and High-Density Data Storage." *Applied Physics Letters* 61 (1992):142–144.

GRACHOWSKI, E. and THOMPSON, D. "Outlook for Maintaining Areal Density Growth Rule in Magnetic Recording." *IEEE Transactions on Magnetics* 30 (1994):3797–3800.

Mark H. Kryder

Death and Dying

Attitudes Toward Death

Attitudes toward death change in different eras and among different cultures. These attitudes, in turn, affect moral judgments about how to die with dignity and to what extent others may help us. Traditionally, physicians have considered their professional role to preserve life. This ethic led them to resist efforts to permit persons to withdraw life support in order to die. More important, preserving life and the cultural rule against killing are central values in the debate about euthanasia.

Changes in attitudes are largely caused by new technologies. Technology today has created many more opportunities for choices about how to die. The physician's duty to preserve life is not as clear-cut. Further, the patients' rights movement succeeded in placing many of these choices in the hands of patients, their families, or their surrogates. Thus, how we die is no longer a medical judgment. As it was in ancient times, it has again become personal, familial, and social.

Mortality

A major change in our time is how people die. In the past, death came to most persons rather suddenly, either from an incurable disease or accident. Because of the many possible medical interventions in the mid-1990s, about 80 percent of most people in technologically advanced countries die long, lingering deaths. This fact increases the stages of dying during which persons may make choices about their care and try to enlist their doctors and others in those decisions.

If trends continue, in the future there will be greater and greater longevity, with emphasis on improved quality of life during that period. When one's quality of life diminishes to an intolerable level, greater demand for a "decent way out" will occur. We already can detect that demand in the current debate about euthanasia.

Death and Dying

Euthanasia

Euthanasia is the controversial practice of painlessly ending the lives of people who have incurable, terminal diseases or painful, distressing, irreversible handicaps. The term comes from the Greek words for "good" and "death." There are different kinds of euthanasia.

The first is called *active* or *direct* euthanasia. This occurs when terminally ill persons ask their doctor, or in some cases, friends or relatives, to put them to death to avoid further pain and suffering. In this action, the cause of death is the direct and intentional action of the one helping the patient to die. Mercy killing takes place under similar circumstances, except that the patient is incapable of asking for a good death, for example, a severely defective newborn, or a severely demented, elderly person. Active euthanasia is by consent; mercy killing is euthanasia without consent.

Active euthanasia is illegal throughout the world, although it is tolerated in the Netherlands under strict guidelines. If physicians follow those guidelines, they are not prosecuted after the case is reported to and reviewed by the authorities. Mercy killing is always illegal. Yet when physicians, nurses, or family members are prosecuted for mercy killing, the jury often refuses to indict or convict them because of the human tragedy involved. Euthanasia and mercy killing are often compared to the atrocities of the Nazis. Some Nazi programs were mercy killing, but most were outright killing without consent. No one can support such programs.

A third form of euthanasia is called *passive* or *indirect*. This is because the intention is not to take the life of the person directly, but to withdraw an intervention that is delaying the dying process. Withholding and withdrawing treatments are not controversial when they are done through advance directives or the current wishes of the patient. The United States Supreme Court ruled in 1990 that competent persons have a right to refuse treatment at any time, even if the treatment might prolong their lives.

Withdrawal of care becomes ethically controversial when it is discussed without clear evidence of the patient's wishes. In such cases, physicians and families rely on previously expressed values or on a value history of the patient. This is combined with a poor prognosis, a calculus of risks and benefits, and of medical futility. Thus surrogates help decide when to withdraw or withhold treatment and allow the person to die.

Another method of obtaining a painless death is by self-induced euthanasia, or suicide. To avoid the possibility of pain and suffering during a suicide attempt, or the possibility of its failure, physicians have sometimes helped patients by providing the drugs or other means necessary to take their own lives. This is called physician-assisted suicide. In some cultures taking one's own life is considered a noble act. Some people think that suicide can be a decent "way out" of life today to avoid a lingering death. Except in Oregon, which has legalized physician-assisted suicide, it is illegal elsewhere. Yet a majority of the population supports the concept. A minority argues that doctors should never kill, because their training and public profession is to preserve life. However, Dr. Jack Kevorkian, a Michigan pathologist, has helped selected people suffering terminal illness to commit suicide in an effort to focus public attention on what doctors do privately and to help legalize assisted suicide in every state.

Death with Dignity

Some people think that everyone ought to have an unqualified right to die. Others limit this right to the withholding and withdrawing of care. Still others consider all forms of euthanasia to be unethical. The moral questions involved in all these actions is whether they violate the rule against killing and whether there is any valid distinction between killing and allowing someone to die. Once the understanding exists that death is a good for the patient, does the means by which this is brought about make any moral difference?

Yet persons in each group might agree that fundamental dignity is lost in contemporary modes of dying, in which people are tethered to machines. Death with dignity is hard to define because "dignity," like its companion concept, "quality of life," means different things to different people. For one person, it may mean stoically accepting one's pain and suffering; for another it may mean fighting the indignities of the disease at every step and not giving up; for another it may mean accepting one's mortality and determining ahead of time which treatments will be acceptable; for still another it may mean maintaining control throughout the dying process, even to the point of setting the time that one will die through direct euthanasia or assisted suicide. Most everyone agrees, therefore, that physicians should help people die with dignity, but the moral consequences of that assistance must be discussed with each patient.

Advance Directives

The principal way of ensuring death with dignity is through advance directives. Advance directives is a catchall term that encompasses all forms of establishing one's preferences about medical care in advance. These are not limited to the dying process, because in the United States and in other countries individuals have a right to determine their own medical care and can refuse it even if it means that they will die without it. Any discussion of preferences with one's family, friends, or doctor is a form of advance directive and should be honored.

When disputes arise or to avoid disputes altogether, one can execute a durable power of attorney for health care. This document spells out one's wishes in a legal format and designates a surrogate decision maker who will make decisions when an individual becomes incompetent. It is limited to medical decisions only, and is in force only while the patient cannot competently express his or her wishes. Some states, like Illinois, have established a set of surrogates in the law in case an incompetent patient is incapable of designating a surrogate.

A living will is a form of advance directive that covers the dying situation exclusively. It is a legal document written in advance, by which the patient determines which treatments he or she will accept or reject during the final stages of the dying process. It applies only if a person is irreversibly, terminally ill and in the final stages of dying.

In the United States, hospitals, home health institutions, and nursing homes are all legally required (in order to receive federal funds) through the Patient Self-Determination Act to notify patients prior to admission of their right to execute advance directives. Many patients decide not to do so because they either believe their family can make decisions for them or they do not want to tie the hands of their doctors. When they become incompetent, it is not always clear to the family or doctor what their wishes might be. This is a cause for confusion and anxiety at the bedside.

Hospice

An alternative to difficult hospital stays during the dying process is to choose hospice care. A hospice is a community of volunteers and professionals who help a dying patient, the family, and friends to accept death in a peaceful and dignified way. This is done by support other than most medical interventions. Comfort care, pain control, discussions of fears, assistance with unfinished business, preparation of one's will, saying good-bye, and many other compassionate actions are provided at home or in specially designated institutions.

Hospice care in the mid-1990s receives federal funding and is increasingly provided by home health-care companies, thus losing some of its former voluntary status. It is increasingly popular because it is both less expensive than hospital care and it allows loved ones to be cared for in a home environment with ready access to family and friends during the last six months of life.

Autopsies and Burial

The special circumstances of death in almost every culture call for rituals for the living. Autopsies of the dead person are done to advance the scientific understanding of disease or, in sudden deaths, to determine the cause of death or the possibility of a criminal act. Some religions oppose autopsies and embalming because these practices are thought to violate the sacredness of the body and affront the Creator.

Most often burial rites include stories about the deceased, a reminder of the journey of life (and the afterlife in some cases), and comfort or prayers for the living. The rituals are designed to show the community's support of those who must grieve. The power of grief itself demonstrates the importance of surrounding the dying with the best possible procedures of respect, support, and comfort for all.

See also AGING OF THE POPULATION; BIOETHICS; DEMOGRAPHY; GENETIC TECHNOLOGIES; HEALTH CARE: TECHNOLOGICAL DEVELOPMENTS; HEALTH CARE: MORAL ISSUES; LONGEVITY.

BIBLIOGRAPHY

BAIRD, R. M., and ROSENBAUM, S. E., eds. *Euthanasia: The Moral Issues.* Buffalo, NY: Prometheus Press, 1989.

DE VEBER, L. L.; HENRY, F.; NADEAU, R.; CASSIDY, E., GENTLES, I.; and BIERLING, G. *Public Policy, Private Voices: The Euthanasia Debate.* Toronto: Human Life Research Institute, 1992.

GAYLIN W.; KASS L.; PELLEGRINO, E. D.; and SIEGLER, M. "Doctors Must Not Kill." *Journal of the American Medical Association* 259 (April 8, 1988): 2139–2140.

GOMEZ, C. F. *Regulating Death: Euthanasia and the Case of the Netherlands.* New York: The Free Press, 1991.

GULA R. "Moral Principles Shaping Public Policy on Euthanasia." *Second Opinion* 14 (July 1990): 73–83.

HACKLER, C.; MOSELEY, R.; and YAWTER, D. E., eds. *Advance Directives in Medicine.* New York: Praeger, 1989.

HAMEL, R. ed. *Active Euthanasia, Religion, and the Public Debate.* Chicago, IL: Park Ridge Center, 1991.

HUMPHREY, D., and WICKETT, A., eds. *The Right to Die: Understanding Euthanasia.* London: The Bodley Head, 1986.

KILNER, J. *Life on the Line: Ethics, Aging, Ending Patients' Lives and Allocating Vital Resources.* Grand Rapids, MI: W. B. Eerdmans, 1992.

KOHL, M., ed. *Beneficent Euthanasia.* Buffalo, NY: Prometheus Books, 1975.

LYNN, J., ed. *By No Extraordinary Means: The Choice to Forgo Life Sustaining Food and Water.* Bloomington, IN: Indiana University Press, 1989.

MEISEL, A. *The Right to Die.* New York: John Wiley, 1989.

RACHELS, J. *The End of Life: Euthanasia and Morality.* New York: Oxford University Press, 1986.

RAMSEY, P. *Ethics at the Edges of Life.* New Haven, Conn.: Yale University Press, 1978.

THOMASMA, D., AND GRABER, G. C. *Euthanasia: Towards an Ethical Social Policy.* New York: Continuum Books, 1990.

David C. Thomasma

Debt.

See CREDIT, DEBT, AND BORROWING.

Deficits, Governmental

The federal government budget and net export deficits, the so-called twin deficits, have loomed large over U.S. economic and political policies for several decades. Their significance has long been overrated.

The first is simply the excess of federal government outlays for goods and services, subsidies, welfare, and interest over revenues, mainly from taxes, social security contributions, fines, and fees during a fiscal or calendar year. A deficit means that the government is adding more to the nation's income and expenditure than it removes, which provides a net stimulus to total spending or gross domestic product (GDP). Growth of the deficit enhances the stimulus, while a decrease contracts it. These effects create the possibility of countercyclical fiscal policies to offset increases in unemployment or inflation. A deficit is an instrument of policy, and it is either useful or detrimental, depending upon the expected state of the economy.

Despite the utility of the instrumental aspects of deficits, governments tend to seek a balanced budget as a goal rather than as a means, at least during periods of full employment and stable prices. The absolute size of deficits decreased from about $50 billion during the last three years of World War II to smallish sums averaging three to four billion dollars during the 1950s and '60s, including five years of surpluses of similar size. In the late 1970s they rose above previous highs, burgeoned to over $200 billion in the mid-1980s, and surged to $300 billion in fiscal year 1992. The 1993 deficit was $255 billion.

More meaningfully, the size of the deficit relative to the gross domestic product has ranged from a 30 percent high in World War II to a small surplus of almost 5 percent in 1948. Since 1969, when deficits came to stay, their proportions have fluctuated mostly between 3 and 6 percent. In the first three years of the 1990s, they averaged 4.5 percent, with an estimated 4 percent for fiscal 1993. They are not large by historical standards, nor are they growing relatively.

Often deficits are overstated in an important sense. In the United States, all federal outlays are treated as "current," with no distinction between those that would be constituted "capital" in business and those that would be amortized over some future period. Many other governments distinguish between current and capital expenditures and calculate deficits or surpluses accordingly. Because of its unusual accounting practice, the entire U.S. deficit is construed as *dissaving* and is subtracted from private national saving.

Besides their relatively small size, likely overstatement, and utility in offsetting recessions, deficits do not cause inflation, cannot lead to national bankruptcy, and do not shift burdens to future generations, as is so often alleged. They do add to the national debt, but since this is owned overwhelmingly by U.S. residents, firms, and government entities, the interest and principal payments represent mainly an internal transfer from U.S. taxpayers to U.S. bondholders. Excessive concerns about the deficit arise largely from false analogies with business losses, a feeling that the recent deficits are "out of control" and are somehow immoral, profligate, and evidence of failure. Nonetheless, deficits have obviously become inconvenient. There will be therefore persistent attempts to reduce and keep them as close to zero or balance as possible.

Future of the Budget Deficit

Future trends in the deficit depend upon the growth rates of receipts and outlays. On the receipts side, there is a strong correlation between the growth of nominal GDP (defined as the sum of real GDP) and inflation growth rates.

Real GDP growth averaged about 2.5 percent per year between 1973 and 1993, two decades aptly characterized as the "silent depression" or "high level creeping stagnation." But there is impressive evidence that the long decline in U.S. productivity is over and that both manufacturing and service sectors are once more highly competitive in world markets. Therefore, future real growth should easily average about 3.5–4 percent per year over the next two decades, which is less than the average for the 1950s and '60s.

Inflation will doubtless be better contained in the next two decades below levels prevailing between 1970 and 1990, when they hovered at over 6 percent per year. Thus far in the 1990s annual inflation is in the 3–4 percent range per year and falling. A reasonable long-run scenario envisages U.S. annual inflation rates of 3.5–4.5 percent per year.

Thus nominal GDP growth, to which federal revenues are closely tied, should center around 8 percent. Federal revenues may average even more than 8 percent growth with the higher tax rates established during 1993, especially if the composition of expenditures inclines toward more investment-type outlays for infrastructure and human capital, as now envisaged.

It will be more difficult to constrain the growth of federal spending much below 8 percent per year. Over three-quarters of expenditures are contractual, military, or in the form of entitlements. Further military cutbacks are less likely. Urgent initiatives in education, health, crime, environment, and so on require costly federal support.

However, the past decade has seen nominal federal outlays held to an average of less than 6 percent per year. Though painful to many programs, this rate seems sustainable for another decade or so. Thus if federal receipts and outlays grow at 8 percent and 6 percent respectively, the deficit would shrink from $255 billion in fiscal 1993 to zero in ten years. If the spread between the growth rates rises to 3 percent, a balanced budget can be achieved before the year 2001. The ratio of the deficit to GDP will fall to 2 percent or less within three to five years if the spread is 3 percent or 2 percent respectively. Beyond that time it is likely that the federal deficit can be maintained close to balance on average.

The Foreign Trade Deficit

U.S. exports of goods and services exceeded imports every year between 1946 and 1982. Net ex-

ports have been negative ever since, reaching record levels of well over $100 billion from 1984 through 1988. During this period the United States was alleged to have shifted from the world's biggest creditor to the biggest debtor, although such statements are exaggerations. Since 1988 the absolute and relative size of the net export deficit has dropped to less dramatic levels.

The share of exports plus imports to GDP more than doubled over the past two decades as more industries sought overseas markets. Future exports depend upon rates of economic growth and import accessibility among U.S. trade partners. The United States, especially if it grows as rapidly as forecast, remains a powerful magnet for imports. This implies the need for strong export growth to offset and balance trade accounts. The prospects of this occurring are favorable. The adoption of NAFTA (North American Free Trade Agreement) and GATT (General Agreement of Tariffs and Trade) and the expansion of freer trade opens up foreign markets.

The future of both deficits ultimately depends upon the growth of the U.S. economy, itself increasingly integrated with global development and growth.

There are powerful reasons for expecting the twin deficits to move toward balance. First, they are interrelated and partially interdependent. Second, there is strong public pressure for their reduction in ways that contribute to sustainable long-run growth rather than protectionism, subsidies, or increased regulation. Third, market and democratic forces unleashed since the fall of communism will add additional and compelling pressures toward balance.

The challenges to economic growth will no longer be as circumscribed as in the past. The problems of wisely "investing" a growing economic surplus and reducing rising inequality are not determined by any inherent scarcity of natural resources nor by any neo-Malthusian drive to excess procreation. They are political. The enemy is "us," as the cartoon character Pogo put it. Certainly the real enemy never was either of the twin deficits now launched upon a path toward balance.

See also CREDIT, DEBT, AND BORROWING; ECONOMIC CYCLES; PUBLIC FINANCE; TAXES; SAVINGS; WEALTH.

BIBLIOGRAPHY

EISNER, ROBERT. *How Real Is the Federal Deficit?* New York: The Free Press, 1986.
HEILBRONER, ROBERT, and BERNSTEIN, PETER. *The Debt and the Deficit.* New York: W. W. Norton, 1989.

KOTLIKOFF, LAURENCE J. "Deficit Delusion." *The Public Interest* (Summer 1986): 53–65.

WILSON, GEORGE W. "Deficits: Another Look." *Business Horizons* 31 (1988): 2–13.

George W. Wilson

Deforestation

Deforestation and degradation of the world's forests show little sign of abating.

Tropical forest loss is likely to continue into the next century at an annual rate of 15–20 million hectares, equivalent to an area about the size of the state of Georgia in the United States. Trees in the temperate zone are dying a slower death, afflicted by air pollution, which already has led to a 20–25 percent defoliation in Europe. Deforestation contributes to global warming, species extinction, loss of livelihoods and of human shelter. There are also many indirect costs. When forests are cleared, soil is no longer held by tree roots and washes away. Streams and rivers become more shallow and flood more easily. Reservoirs behind dams fill up with soil, decreasing their water-holding capacity. Forest dwellers migrate to cities. Prices increase for forest resources such as tropical timber.

Over the coming half century the last great forest countries of the world will suffer a vicious assault as timber prices rise and aggressive commercial enterprises seek to maintain timber flows. These remaining major forests are found in Brazil, Suriname, Guyana, South America, Laos, Cambodia, mainland Southeast Asia, the Russian Far East, and Zaire.

Agricultural land use will continue to expand and feed a human population that is not only growing but also seeking ever more protein and fat-rich foodstuffs. Recent studies suggest that global demand for food may triple by the year 2050. Ominously, production growth rates have declined. Forest lands, therefore, will continue to be a very tempting target for conversion to agricultural purposes.

Logging and agriculture will continue to be the major proximate causes of deforestation. The "root causes" or "drivers" of forest loss will be government policies and institutional arrangements that encourage forest clearance. These signals include enormous subsidies for agriculture. There is no comparable assistance to entrepreneurs interested in "sustainable" forest management, even though careful forest management can produce a continuous stream of timber, fruits, fiber, and medicines and also provide "environmental services."

International efforts to slow forest loss show no sign of substantial success in the near future. Some local and national efforts, however, do look promising. New logging technologies, currently seen only on the drawing board, could soon be employed in tropical forests. These might include use of lighter than air balloons to pluck trees from forests without roads and tractors that impose severe impacts and open the forests to subsequent colonization.

As indigenous peoples and other forest-land dwellers acquire greater control of the forests they inhabit, they may help to lead the way to more careful use of the resource. They will team up with businesses to capitalize upon their unparalleled knowledge of forests, and to market new foods and medicines. Genes from some forest plants might, in turn, help to increase agricultural production yields and reduce pressure for further encroachment on forest lands.

Governments will become more concerned about forest loss and implement reforms to reduce the pressure to convert forests to other land uses. Perhaps the most interesting policy options will be those that increase a forest's economic value. This is done, for example, by increasing the taxes on timber extraction so as to make wood more valuable. This stimulates conservation and promotes more careful extraction. A more far-reaching option would be to charge a fee to utility companies that rely upon forests to control the flow of water into hydroelectric dams so as to cover the "environmental service" provided by the forest. The fees, in turn, might be used to develop alternatives for small farmers who are living in the region and who might otherwise be motivated to convert the forest to agricultural uses.

Governments may also agree to a global limit on forest loss and embody those objectives in a Global Forests Convention. Such an agreement already is being debated. Developing countries that view logging forests and converting them to agriculture as good ways to finance their own national development are reluctant to agree. Such an agreement might become more attractive as developed counties, pressured by their citizens, offer funds to support forest reduction elsewhere. Thus, a multibillion dollar "Global Forests Fund" might come into being.

Much will be lost unless governments, industry, and citizens join forces to seek agreement on how to save forest resources. As many as half a billion people worldwide are directly dependent on forests for food, income, and shelter. Furthermore, tropical forests are the richest natural source of biological diversity. Disappearing at current rates, as many as 10–15 percent of the world's species may be doomed to extinction over the next twenty years. This represents an annual loss of from 8,000 to 28,000 species (the wide range reflecting uncertainty over total species numbers). While we cannot predict what *will* be done, it will become clearer to a growing number of decision makers that something *must* be done.

See also BIOETHICS; BIODIVERSITY; ENVIRONMENT; ENVIRONMENTAL BEHAVIOR; ENVIRONMENTAL ETHICS; ENVIRONMENTAL INDICATORS; ENVIRONMENTAL POLICY CHANGES; FORESTRY; GLOBAL WARMING; NATURAL DISASTERS; NATURAL RESOURCES; RESOURCES; SOIL CONDITIONS.

BIBLIOGRAPHY

ANDERSON, ANTHONY B., ed. *Alternatives to Deforestation: Steps Toward Sustainable Use of the Amazon Rain Forest.* New York: Columbia University Press, 1992.
GILLIS, MALCOLM, and REPETTO, ROBERT. *Deforestation and Government Policy.* San Francisco: ICS Press, 1988.
PITT, D. C., ed. *Deforestation: Social Dynamics in Watersheds and Mountain Ecosystems.* New York: Routledge, 1988.
World Bank. *The Forest Sector.* Washington, DC: World Bank, 1991.

Nigel Sizer

Delphi Method.

See FORECASTING METHODS.

Democracy

Democracy was devised by the Greeks over 2,000 years ago, in Athens, but the democratic regimes of the ancient world disappeared with the demise of the Roman empire. Democracy was embraced in Western societies only after the disappearance of feudalism, and its reappearance was brought about by the enfranchisement of the masses. Equally important was the willingness of Europe's emergent merchant classes to embrace public aspirations toward self-government. They came to see this as a means of establishing a civic order that would evoke broadly based public support for the kind of institutional infrastructure—such as effective transportation, nationwide monetary systems (including banks), and general education—that would sustain the market economies through which they expected to prosper.

It is often said that the reappearance of democratic government in Europe anticipated the onset of the Industrial Revolution and with it the establishment of the modern nation-state. Out of the turmoil of these times, democracy emerged, sometimes haltingly, as the dominant form of government in Western societies—not because of an intrinsic moral value or its coupling with capitalistic economies, but because it proved to be a useful vehicle for promoting egalitarian forms of societal development where "rising waters lift every ship."

Joseph SCHUMPETER, among others, would argue that the inconsistencies inherent in our conceptions of democracy are so intractable that it cannot be translated into a stable framework for an enduring system of government. While democracy's supporters claim it is superior to other forms of government because it encourages socially responsible political activity, political scientists focus on its utility as a means of bringing elected members of legislative bodies to defuse social conflict by fashioning compromises and building public consensus on basic political values from which government ultimately derives its legitimacy. Although the decision-making processes of authoritarian systems are more orderly and more fully rational in comparison with the often jumbled, sometimes haphazard, processes of a democratic assembly, the openness and permeability of representative bodies appear to be more conducive to promoting adaptive forms of social change. In a world where the quest for progress has driven rates of social change to previously unknown heights, democracy has been embraced as the preferred means of dealing with this challenge.

Nowhere is this potential more easily seen than in the American Revolution, which, de Tocqueville said, gave rebirth to democracy as a way of adapting operations of government to serve the "needs of a diverse people." Interestingly, Americans tend to view the historic thrust of this process as an effort to translate the blueprint contained in their Constitution into a fully elaborated, stable system of government.

Paradoxically, the outcome of two centuries of seeking to perfect the promise of the document produced by the Constitutional Convention of 1787 suggests that de Tocqueville may have been overly optimistic. Nor is there any doubt about the need to strengthen the governments of the rest of the Western democracies. The *pivotal issue* that preoccupies all of those concerned with the viability of this fragile institution is which among the hodge-podge of changes that have been put forward are most likely over time *to compensate for the inherent instability of participatory government.*

Basic Characteristics

Because institutional change should strengthen the mechanisms through which self-government is carried on, it would be helpful to consider first the basic elements of a democratic government. Figure 1 below summarizes these components, which come to focus around universal suffrage. As this diagram indicates, there are (1) a number of charac-

becomes critically important. The first and ultimate prerequisite of a viable democracy is that its political processes generate continuing, enduring public support for self-government. Ideally this is accomplished not by pandering to public tastes, but by promoting wide-ranging public dialogue through which majority support is generated for a relevant agenda of pertinent issues dealing with real rather than apparent needs. This in turn requires setting aside ("putting on the shelf") enough equally appealing issues to avoid overwhelming the system's limited decision-making capacity. More specifically, it is the potential (not always realized) for promulgating agendas that balance the *need for change* with the equally im-

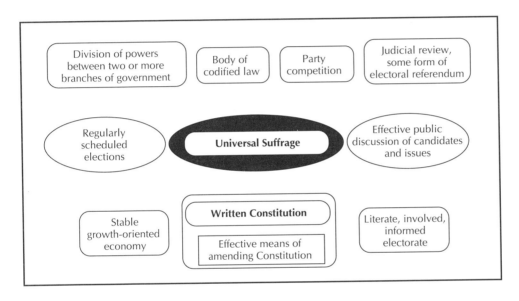

FIGURE 1. Elements of universal suffrage.

teristic structural components of democratic government that (2) have been fused into a more or less functioning whole in Western democracies, and which (3) taken together are meant to assure that the basic needs of a preponderance of the members of a society are adequately provided for (4) in a manner that is fair and just as possible.

But the hallmarks of democratic government are the manifold *political processes* that move forward within this framework; figure 2, on the next page, summarizes these.

If democracy is to serve as the means through which the competing interests that energize participatory government find ways to fuse around a familiar mix of public programs, linked together so as to sustain a rewarding way of life, the character of the politics through which this takes place

perative *need for institutional continuity* that has led mass publics in the Western democracies to support participatory government.

Democracy's Pivotal Dilemma

During those uncomfortable moments in history when controversy cannot be resolved by seeking compromises between those interests holding with existing arrangements and those demanding change, decision-makers may be driven to consider another, more rudimentary dilemma—one that runs like an earthquake faultline through the framework of democratic government. On the one hand, there are the essential needs of individuals seeking to sustain a civilized and secure way of life for themselves, including the need for food, hous-

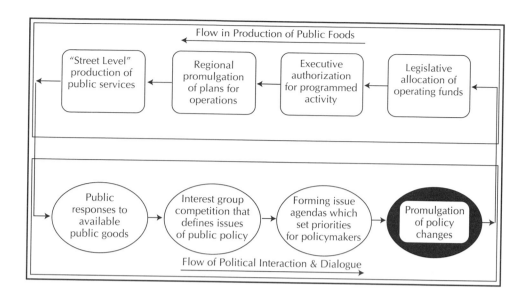

FIGURE 2. The decision making cycle: core process in democratic government.

ing, and employment. On the other, there are equally essential collective needs which, though different in character from those of individuals, are just as essential, including public safety, education, and economic growth. As societal development moves forward, *the numbers of both of these types of needs increase*, sometimes at an exponential rate. This leaves government facing not just the burden of more ponderous agendas, but the sometimes foreboding prospect of making choices about sensitive issues that exceed the public's readiness for change even though existing policies are seen as untenable.

At this point, familiar elements such as widespread participation in elections, an electorate that is motivated to become sufficiently well informed to cast meaningful votes, and a capacity for compromise become the means through which trade-offs that are binding on everyone are expected to be formed. But the transcendent challenge to participatory government is more subtle and at the same time more demanding.

- On what basis can the atomistic needs of individuals be equated with the collective needs that define the general welfare of all of the members of society?
- If elected officials and their constituents are to "keep faith" with one another, how shall the use of raw political power—which too often displaces

trust-based relationships—be constrained so as to allow those who are ruled to make truly propitious choices about who shall serve as their rulers?

Questions such as these have been of concern to both political philosophers and practitioners of politics from antiquity to the present. Even after several centuries, attempts to fashion a coherent response have failed to produce a generally accepted rationale for self-government. Instead, two contending, and in some respects incompatible, conceptions have emerged, introducing ambiguity into the very foundations of democracy.

Liberal Versus Social Democracy Perspectives

In the spirit of the dictum that "what you see depends upon where you stand," it is useful to note that these contending perspectives toward participatory government are anchored in the disjuncture between individual and collective needs. Broadly, liberals hold that public agenda should be gauged, and public programs judged, by the degree to which they meet the basic needs of the greatest number of citizens while social democrats want government programs to foster social justice and serve the long-term collective interests of society.

In Table 1, several of the more specific contradictions setting off the liberal and social democratic

TABLE 1.   Types of democracy.

	Liberal	*Social democratic*
Key Imperative	Achieve the greatest good for the greatest number, sometimes at the expense of the general welfare	Promote the general welfare of the members of society as a whole, sometimes at the expense of individuals
Central Focus	Individuals—especially their felt needs and their preferences	Collectives—especially arrangements that enhance quality of the civic order
Core Values	Liberty and opportunity	Equality and justice
Clashing Conceptions	Commonly shared ends, so pivotal to social democrats, are seen as highly symbolic and ephemeral, hence not a reliable means of identifying ways of promoting well-being	Self-interest of individuals, and especially their vaunted "preferences," seen as insubstantial, transient, and anchored in circumstances rather than enduring social values
Critical Assumption Regarding Human Nature	Each individual has the right and the capacity to delineate and pursue their own best interests	The civic order as a buffer against the "unkind blows of fate" in which everyone has an equal and common stake

conceptions of democracy are paired as a way of emphasizing the fractured nature of our understanding of self-government.

As massive social change sweeps nations toward a future where the only certainty is that familiar ways of carrying out the ordinary tasks of life can be disrupted or even displaced, social adaptivity becomes the key to the viability of government. As uncertainty builds and change carries us toward a new world order, the central challenge facing public leaders will be sorting through issues and sifting

through alternative ways of maintaining a meaningful balance between the past and the future.

Given the nature of the changes that democratic leaders will confront, it is inevitable that some of the public policy issues will raise questions about the adequacy of the form and functioning of their governments. While democracy is the accepted basis for government in the West, the responses of societies where liberal democracy is ascendant (as is the case in the United States) can be expected to differ from those where social democracy is the

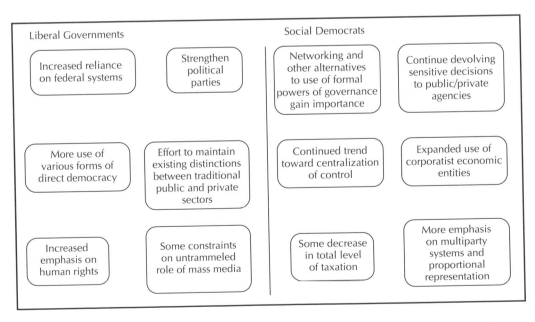

FIGURE 3.   Characteristics of liberal governments (e.g., United States, Canada, and Australia) and social democracies (e.g., Sweden, Norway, and Denmark.

basis for the organization of government (as is the case in several Scandinavian countries).

More specifically, given the fractured nature of our conceptions of democracy, it is to be expected that governments will adapt to the shifting international situation by reviewing their historical attachment to the liberal versus the social democratic versions of self-government. Figure 3 summarizes some of the lines of response they may adopt, taking into account their divergent perspectives:

In the largest sense, democracy has yet to be perfected; perhaps de Tocqueville should be faulted for insisting that this was possible. Yet the experiment with which he was so taken has demonstrated the enduring place of democracy in Western civilization, even if it has fallen short of a single, coherent framework for democratic government. History may show that Schumpeter was correct in pointing out democracy's flawed conception but erred in suggesting that this was a fatal flaw. In one sense the coexistence of two distinguishable forms of democracy in Western society, where each moves toward or away from the other as circumstances and convictions dictate, may be a living testimony to the consummate resilience of self-government.

See also CAPITALISM; DEMOCRATIC PROCESS; POLITICAL CYCLES; SOCIAL DEMOCRACY; SOCIAL AND POLITICAL EVOLUTION; VOTING.

BIBLIOGRAPHY

DAHL, ROBERT A. *Dilemmas of Pluralistic Democracy*. New Haven: Yale University Press, 1982.

HAMILTON, ALEXANDER, et al. *The Federalist Papers*. Baltimore: Johns Hopkins University Press, 1981.

PLAMENATZ, JOHN. *Democracy and Illusion*. London: Longmans, 1973.

RIKER, WILLIAM. *Liberalism Against Populism*. San Francisco: W. H. Freeman & Co., 1982.

SCHUMPETER, JOSEPH. *Capitalism, Socialism, and Democracy*. New York: Harper and Brothers, 1942.

TOCQUEVILLE, ALEXIS DE, ed. Phillips Bradley, *Democracy in America*. New York: Alfred Knopf, 1945.

William J. Gore

Democratic Process

Nations can be overwhelmed by external threats and internal vulnerabilities. If not adequately addressed, problems of security, cohesion, order, and leadership can destroy or transform any political system.

Despite trends to embrace democracy and market-oriented economies at the end of the Cold War, democratic and market-oriented outcomes are not inevitable. Other periods in history have displayed trends toward democratic governance, only to be succeeded by dictatorships and totalitarianism. Belief in the ideas of and trust in the institutions of democracy can decline if democratic political systems fail to provide an adequate level of security, order, and well-being.

One can imagine alternate scenarios for democracy in the United States and abroad, each with a different probability, impact, desirability, and feasibility. Each scenario is based on trends in, and interactions among, the various parts of the political and economic system; on trends and impacts of technology; upon internal and external threats; and upon the varying success of policies to address them:

An optimistic scenario for democracy in the United States could involve the successful resolution of domestic problems and the continued perfection of self-government and freedom under law domestically, combined with the expansion and strengthening of democracy internationally, thereby reducing the probability of war and the oppression of people by their own governments. Failures of representative democracy, rising expectations, and higher levels of education and income could lead to a greater emphasis on direct democracy under which citizens voting for specific policies would be conducted by a referendum, a process that is increasingly enabled by technology.

Possible pessimistic scenarios involve trends that could damage the old and new democracies. The end of the Cold War and a declining external threat may be followed by increased disunity within the United States. At the same time, intensification and spread of preexisting overseas conflicts based on nationality, kinship, locality, race, ethnicity, and religion might be exacerbated by the extreme application of self-determination and on the continuation of antidemocratic ideological trends.

Observers have noted a range of inadequately addressed problems that could lead, through a vicious circle of interacting causes and effects, to the erosion of democracy. Substantive problems include crime, drugs, and an urban underclass; environment-population stresses; the strains between freedom and order; rifts between the ideal of political equality and the glaring reality of extreme social inequality; and creating and maintaining unity out of diversity in the absence of a clear external threat to good response.

Defects in the process and conditions for democracy can be found in its constitution and laws, institutions, political culture, and the character of its citizens. Specific issues include declines in the effectiveness of political institutions, as well as in their legitimacy, authority, and trust; weakening of social groups intermediate between the individual and government (family, neighborhood, and voluntary associations); the depredation of citizenship, self-government, and political participation; and shortcomings of an inadequately expressed will of the citizenry, low voter turnout, weak political parties, strong lobbies, and powerful media.

Political gridlock, or the incapacity to act expeditiously and effectively may occur because of the weakness of political parties or the fact that different parties control Congress and the executive branch. Presidential democracies, in contrast to a parliamentary democracy, run an increased risk of gridlock that can provoke a constitutional crisis. The expense of elections and the skewed system for financing them create unequal access to the political process, undermine the loyalty or integrity of officeholders, and bestow undue influence upon large contributors.

The political culture (shared beliefs, attitudes, and values) may be too weak to enable the nation to strengthen the democratic process or address its substantive problems effectively. The character and political virtue of citizens and leaders may be inadequate, thereby eroding the conditions for and competency of democracy. Inadequate transmission to new citizens (native as well as foreign born) of the political beliefs, attitudes, values, skills, and character traits may jeopardize sustaining a healthy democracy. Ill-designed for the problems they purport to address, policies may be fragmented, short-range, and lacking in adequate understanding, consensus, continuity, and coordination.

A strategy for democracy could include the following elements, each of which may exist today to some degree, but in a weak and loosely integrated state:

1. Internationally, increase the spread of democracies and cooperation among them in order to strengthen democratic processes and more effectively address shared concerns.
2. Domestically, stimulate national dialogue concerning the viability and effectiveness of democracy (through periodic congressional hearings, for example) to increase understanding and agreement needed to develop strategies for strengthening democracy.
3. Report periodically on problems, indicators, and trends in democratic political systems, including options for change and improvement.
4. Synthesize and disseminate what is known about democracy (the state of the art), what additional knowledge is needed (an agenda of necessary research and experimentation), and what resources are required for implementation.
5. Analyze, evaluate, and communicate lessons learned from various attempts to improve the policy process, including efforts to enhance the institutions, social process, intellectual tools, and technologies for improved self-government, citizen education, dialogue, and deliberation.
6. Map and display policy debates (their history, status, arguments, and change agents) to improve public understanding, policy dialogue, and, it is hoped, policy outcome.
7. Create museums to inform the public about the history of self-government, freedom, and democracy, as well as about the options, arguments, and trade-offs involved in a range of public policy issues, but without becoming advocates and propagandists for any one option.
8. Support and strengthen the network of individuals and organizations working to improve democracy.

Developing strategies for survival and success of democracy is an unmet need. Within the range of possible futures, many pessimistic possibilities could be realized in the absence of adequate strategies to prevent their occurrence. The future health and survival of democratic political systems depend, in part, not only on how well substantive problems are addressed, but also on actions undertaken to protect and promote democracy itself. It is, therefore, important that we design and implement strategies at home and abroad to increase democracy's margin of safety, effectiveness, and success.

See also CONSERVATISM, POLITICAL; DEMOCRACY; LIBERALISM, POLITICAL; POLITICAL CAMPAIGNING; POLITICAL CYCLES; POLITICAL PARTIES; POLITICAL PARTY REALIGNMENT; PUBLIC OPINION POLLS; SOCIAL DEMOCRACY; SOCIAL AND POLITICAL EVOLUTION; THIRD POLITICAL PARTIES; VOTING.

BIBLIOGRAPHY

BEEDHAM, BRIAN. "What Next for Democracy?" In "The Future: An Anniversary Supplement." *The Economist* 328/7228 (September 11, 1993): 5–8.
BRODER, DAVID S. "Gridlock Begins at Home: How We Build Political Failure into the System." *Washington Post*, January 23, 1994, pp. C1–2.

KARATNYCKY, ADRIAN. "Freedom in Retreat." *Freedom Review* 25 (1994): 4–9.

LAMSON, ROBERT W. "Improving Democratic Participation." *National Civic Review* 82 (1993): 186–189.

PORTER, BRUCE D. "Can American Democracy Survive?" *Commentary* 96 (1993): 37–40.

Robert W. Lamson

Demography

Demography is about people—how many people, what kind of people, where do they live? Demography is a necessary complement to the social sciences as they attempt to better understand our economy and society.

Demography emphasizes the study of (1) the size, composition, and distribution of the population in a given area; (2) changes in population size, composition, and distribution; (3) the components of these changes; (4) the factors that affect these components; and (5) the consequences of changes in population size, composition, and distribution or in the components themselves.

Demography deals with numbers. It requires some knowledge of basic mathematics. However, demography is not dull. It is also amazingly simple. All population size and compositional change can come only from shifts in the three demographic variables: fertility, migration, and mortality.

People decide whether or not to have children and how many to have. People move once, twice, often or not at all. Sometimes people cross an international border in the process. We all die once. Yet to a considerable extent the age at which we die is dependent on social as well as biological factors. All of us, past, present, and future, are population actors and our acts determine what our society looks like—today as well as tomorrow. That in a word is what demography is all about.

If demographic behavior shifts, an area may gain or lose people. That behavior determines what kind of people live in that area—young or old, rich or poor, black or white, and so on. This is what makes demography exciting. We, as population actors, are shaping the kind of society we live in, now and in the future.

Demographic Behavior

Fertility is the major demographic act. It is a two-generational phenomenon. Potential parents, who themselves are the products of the acts of their parents, decide whether to have children and how many.

Shifts in fertility have occurred often in American history. During the 1950s and early 1960s, American women were averaging between three and four children. This was the "baby boom" era. Beginning in 1972, women averaged less than two children. Then in 1989, fertility began to rise once again and is now approaching 2.1 births per woman. Thus American women have altered their fertility behavior dramatically in a relatively brief period.

How is fertility measured? On the macro level, crude birth rates indicate how many births occur per 1,000 people in a specific year and place. In the United States, for example, the crude birth in 1992 was 16.2. There were 16.2 births per 1,000 people.

The total fertility rate (TFR), a micro measure, is more informative. The TFR takes the age-specific rates of a given year and assumes that women will follow that rate through their reproductive period. In the United States, the TFR is 2.04. If women acted according to the age-specific rates of 1992, they would have on average, just over two live births.

Even a slight change in the TFR can yield vast differences a few decades later. A Census Bureau projection illustrates this point. Assuming that mortality and migration don't change, a variation of 0.4 births per woman would result in a difference of 20 million people by 2020!

As a population act, mortality contributes to a decline in the number of people. While it is not voluntary as fertility is, many people do something that may lengthen, or shorten, their lives. Some change their health habits. Many have given up smoking, reduced their alcohol intake, exercise more frequently, and pay more attention to what they eat. The result is increased longevity. The opposite is often true. Some of us turn to violence whether on the streets or between nations. That contributes to reductions in life expectancy. Other factors contribute to variations in longevity. On the whole, women live longer than men, married people live longer than single people, and whites live longer than blacks.

The crude death rate indicates the number of deaths per 1,000 population. Here the term *crude* is particularly advisable. Everything else being equal, a population with many old people will have a higher crude death rate than one with many young people.

Life expectancy, usually at birth, is a more reliable measure of longevity. It resembles the total fertility rate in that it relies on the age-specific death rates of one year and assumes that individuals live their lives according to those rates. In the United States, life expectancy is about seventy-five years. A child born in 1992 can expect to live that many years, on average, according to the age-specific death rates of 1992.

We sometimes neglect mortality when discussing population change. It is an important variable. Again, citing from Census Bureau projections, a difference of six years in life expectancy results in a difference of eight million people within thirty years.

As a population act, migration adds one person to the place of destination and subtracts one from the place of origin. As people throughout the world move more and more, migration as a demographic variable is becoming almost as important as fertility.

The size of the United States is not determined solely by the population acts of Americans. Many people from other countries move here, either legally or illegally. Increasingly, people are coming from Latin America and Asia rather than from Europe as was the case earlier in this century. This population act affects those individuals and all Americans as well.

Holding fertility and mortality constant, a difference of 300,000 per year in immigration results in a difference of 13 million in the nation's population in 2020.

Measuring migration is not as clear-cut as fertility and mortality. Whereas births and deaths are registered in vital statistics, such is not the case with migration. Americans are free to move anywhere in the nation. Legal immigration records are maintained by the Immigration and Naturalization Service (INS) but no records are kept of people leaving the country. Finally, it is next to impossible to determine how many enter the country illegally and how many remain.

Despite these statistical difficulties, estimates are made of the extent of migration and immigration. Americans are movers. On average, Americans move thirteen times in their lives. Certain places are selected more than others. Cities are abandoned while suburbs grow; southern and western states grow as northern and eastern states decline. Even these patterns are subject to radical and quick changes as personal tastes and economic conditions vary.

In recent years, immigration has risen considerably, and today perhaps over 1 million enter the country with the intention of remaining. Together these moves—domestic and international—contribute to population growth in many parts of the country.

In sum, the size of the nation's or any region's population is determined by this complex web of population acts performed by millions of individuals. Their decisions regarding fertility and migration and their ability to postpone death all contribute to the fact that in 1990 the Census Bureau enumerated 249 million Americans.

Age Composition

Knowing about population size is important, but equally important is knowing about age composition. This characteristic is related to each of the demographic variables. Changes in the demographic variables affect a nation's age composition and, in turn, changes in age composition affect the demographic variables.

Demographically, nations can be "young" or "old." A nation is old if it has a large proportion of elderly persons in its population; it is young if it contains a large share of youths. Population pyramids are a convenient way of presenting the age-distribution profile. The shape of a pyramid yields clues concerning past levels of demographic behavior as well as information concerning current composition and possible future trends.

A close examination of the 1990 United States population pyramid shows how the baby boom period of high fertility is affecting the nation's composition. The baby boomers are now between twenty-five and forty. The baby bust period followed the boom era. Finally, there is what demographers call the baby boom echo in the ages below ten. These are the babies of the baby boom mothers. Although their fertility has remained low, their sheer numbers resulted in an increase in the *number* of births—a phenomenon called "population momentum." Even if the fertility rate is low, when there are many women of reproductive age, from the earlier generation, the number of births will increase.

It is commonly believed that reductions in mortality cause the aging of a society. Such reductions increase the average age at death and increase the number of old people. Is it reasonable to conclude that reductions in mortality cause the population to "age"? The answer is no. Indeed, reduced mortality has increased the number of young persons more than it has increased the number of older persons because typical improvements in health and medicine reduce mortality more among the young than among the old. Thus, reductions in mortality often produce a younger population. Low fertility is the principal ingredient of aging. With fewer children being born, the proportion of older persons increases.

Migration also influences age composition. Immigrants are usually disproportionately young adults, and this contributes to a younger age distribution. Internal migration plays an important role in determining the age composition of certain regions. St. Petersburg, Fla., for example, has an old population because of massive in-migration of older Americans. The demographic variables all contribute to changes in age composition. In turn age composition affects fertility and mortality.

One of the factors explaining the baby boom was the greater-than-normal proportion of women in the childbearing years as a result of high fertility in the 1920s. Fertility has climbed recently in part because of the baby boomers reaching their reproductive years. If there are many women in that stage of life, an increase in births can be expected.

Differences in age composition help explain unexpected differences in death rates. We have the strange anomaly of an advanced country like Sweden having a crude death rate of 11 while a less developed country like Mexico has a rate of 6 per 1,000. Mexico has a young population while Sweden has a much older population. Only 20 percent of Sweden's population is under fifteen and 15 percent is over sixty-five. By contrast, 46 percent of Mexico's population is fourteen or younger and only 4 percent is sixty-five or older.

There is a constant interplay between the demographic variables and the age distribution of a population. Shifts in one affect the other, and this goes on indefinitely.

Causes of Shifts in the Demographic Variables

We have discussed some of the causes of mortality shifts. Since we all die eventually, little can be done except to postpone this inevitability for as long as possible. But fertility and migration are both voluntary. We do not have to conceive children; we do not have to move.

Many factors help explain why fertility is high or low. First and foremost is marital status. While pregnancy outside of marriage is increasingly common, most births still occur within marriage. In the United States, age at marriage has risen in recent decades. On average, women marry at 23.9, men at 26.1, quite a difference from just thirty years ago, when the respective ages were 20.3 and

22.8. Women are having their children later in life and this contributes to smaller families.

Divorce rates have also climbed in recent decades and this too contributes to small families. In 1990, the divorce rate was 4.7 per 1,000 compared to only 2.2 in 1960. There are 142 divorced persons per 1,000 married persons with spouse present. In 1960, there were 35.

Together the postponement of marriage and the rapid increase in divorce contribute to the decline in fertility. Other factors are also present. Generally, the higher the education of the woman, the lower the fertility; being employed and, especially, being employed in white-collar jobs results in lower fertility. Usually, the rich have fewer children than the poor.

Moving is a voluntary decision. People usually move to better their lot in life. This often means getting a job or getting a better job. Older people are apt to move for retirement reasons. There has long been a stream of elderly migrants out of the north into the south and southwest.

International migrants also move for economic reasons. The situation in the mother country may be so bad that crossing the border may be the only solution. Sometimes, the lure of the United States suffices to entice a foreigner to immigrate. Here again, the generalization holds—people move to better their lot in life.

The Future

What does the current demographic behavior and the age-sex composition of the nation portend for the future? We will continue to grow; we will age; and we will become more ethnically diverse.

With fertility at just over 2 births per woman and with immigration at the highest levels in history, the population of the United States could reach 400 million by the middle of the next century. As the baby boomers move into retirement soon after the turn of the century, the share of the population who are elderly could rise from 11 percent today to almost 20 percent.

With immigration so high and with immigrants coming overwhelmingly from Latin America and Asia, the proportion of the society who are immigrants or their children will grow. By 2060 there may be no ethnic majority in the United States. Together low fertility among residents and high immigration will result in an ever more heterogeneous nation.

As we enter the twenty-first century, we need to be aware of the shifts already in progress because of our past and present demographic behavior. In this way we as a nation can better prepare ourselves to face the challenges that are bound to follow from such a massive restructuring of the population—all the results of countless individual population acts.

See also AGING OF THE POPULATION; CHILDREN, LIVING ARRANGEMENTS; CRIME RATES; DIVORCE; ECONOMICS; ELDERLY, LIVING ARRANGEMENTS; EVOLUTION, SOCIAL; HOUSEHOLD COMPOSITION; HOUSING, DEMOGRAPHIC AND LIFESTYLE IMPACTS OF; INTERNAL MIGRATION, UNITED STATES; LONGEVITY; MIGRATION, INTERNATIONAL; POPULATION GROWTH: UNITED STATES; POPULATION GROWTH: WORLDWIDE; SOCIAL AND POLITICAL EVOLUTION; SOCIAL CHANGE: UNITED STATES; WORKFORCE REDISTRIBUTION.

BIBLIOGRAPHY

ABERNATHY, VIRGINIA D., ed. *Population Policies: The Choices That Shape Our Future.* New York: Insight Books, 1993.

BOUVIER, LEON F. and GRANT, LINDSEY. *How Many Americans? Population, Immigration, and the Environment.* San Francisco, CA: Sierra Club Books, 1994.

HAUB, CARL and YANAGISHITA, MACHIKO. *1995 World Population Data Sheet.* Washington, DC: Population Reference Bureau, 1995.

RUSSELL, CHERYL. *The Master Trend: How the Baby Boom Generation Is Remaking America.* New York: Plenum Press, 1993.

LEON BOUVIER

Dentistry

Dentistry became a profession in 1728 when a French surgeon, Pierre Fauchard, published a monumental work that encompassed all of the dental knowledge up to that time. Theretofore, dental treatment had been provided by a variety of practitioners, from barber-surgeons to roving charlatans and mountebanks. Treatment consisted mainly of extraction; cavities were filled with a variety of worthless substances, including mouse dung, cobwebs, and tree rosins.

From the 1700s onward, dentistry moved on apace. In 1839, the first dental school in the world was founded in Baltimore. Subsequently hundreds of schools were established worldwide. Today, dental schools are affiliated with universities and require a minimum of four years of study. The eleven recognized specialties require advanced, postdoctoral study of from two to three years.

From the latter part of the nineteenth century, dentistry made very great advances. Greene Vardiman Black put its practice on a sound scientific basis. W. D. Miller promulgated the theory of the bacterio-parasitic origin of dental caries, which laid the groundwork for all further studies in the prevention of dental decay. Remarkable advances in instrumentation and materials took place, starting in the latter part of the century. The discovery of anesthesia in 1844 by the Connecticut dentist Horace Wells permitted dreaded dental procedures to be performed without pain. The introduction of vulcanized rubber, in 1851, made dentures available to the masses at a low cost. Wholesale extraction of teeth followed, and their replacement with prosthetic appliances became the most common treatment offered by dentists.

The invention of precision casting in 1907, however, stimulated a leap forward in restorative dentistry, using gold inlays, bridges, and crowns. Improvements in root-canal therapy saved countless teeth. The introduction of porcelain into restorative dentistry gave impetus to the drive for greater esthetics.

Major Advances in the Twentieth Century

The first half of this century saw the improvement of techniques and the introduction of new and better materials. Acrylic resins supplanted rubber in dentures; composite resins provided a filling material both long-lasting and tooth colored; chromium-cobalt-molybdenum alloys replaced gold in partial dentures; even amalgam was improved upon. A major breakthrough was the veneering of porcelain onto metal crowns. The most significant instrument advance was the air-driven turbine drill, introduced in 1957, with speeds of over 350,000 rpm. With vibrationless cutting, exceptionally fine tasks could be performed with a minimum of discomfort.

One of the greatest public health measures of all time, begun in the early 1950s, was the fluoridation of public water supplies. By adding sodium fluoride, in the amount of one part per million, to public water supplies, children's decay rate in those cities was cut 60 percent. The benefit of fluoride was extended by painting it onto the teeth and by adding it to toothpaste and mouthwash.

Important Recent Advances Point to the Future

Important new diagnostic techniques just coming onto the market allow earlier detection of abnormalities. An electronic cavity detector measures the density of tooth surfaces, pinpointing those that show incipient decay, since even minutely demineralized areas allow greater passage of electric current. New panoramic X-ray machines take sharper and more diagnostic radiographs with a shorter exposure, subjecting the patient to far less radiation.

Because of the reduction in tooth decay to less than half of what it had been several decades earlier, emphasis shifted to improvement of the health of the tissues investing the teeth—the bone and gums. Research identified plaque—the sticky film secreted by bacteria—as the cause of periodontal disease, and the germ *Streptococcus mutans* as the causative organism of caries. Great advances in periodontic techniques have been made in the last several decades, including an improved method of grafting bone into areas where it had been lost.

An exciting new development is the implant. Pioneered about thirty-five years ago, the technique consists of inserting into the jawbone screws, or other variously shaped devices, to which either single teeth, or multiple-tooth bridges, can be affixed. New design of the implants, and new materials, encourage osseo-integration, where bone becomes tightly bound to the implant.

Other new developments are based on the use of the computer, coupled with fiber optic imaging. A penlike camera is run around the patient's mouth, and the data "seen" by the probe is transferred to the computer, which can then do a variety of things: It can print out a chart of the mouth; it can display the current oral status on the monitor screen; and it can allow the dentist to manipulate the picture on the screen so that the patient can see exactly what the present condition is and what it will be following dental treatment. Another innovation is the use of this probe to scan a tooth that has been prepared by the dentist for a crown. This information is fed to a machine that mills a perfectly fitting crown out of a block of ceramic in about thirty minutes, allowing restorations to be completed in one sitting.

What of the Future?

Several areas of research offer the most promise for the future. Although caries has declined, it still must be treated. New filling materials will have fluoride in them, which will be continuously released. Since the causative agent of caries is known, this will lead to the development of a vaccine. Increased public education about diet and oral hygiene will dramatically alter the caries rate. The laser, already used in periodontal surgery, will be used for caries removal and tooth reduction. This, coupled with decay-dissolving liquids applied by the dentist, will do away with the need for drilling.

In the field of periodontics, new products for removal of plaque by the patient at home, will bring about a great reduction of periodontal disease. It is also likely that antiplaque agents will be incorporated into foodstuffs and chewing gum, and vaccines will also be introduced to combat the bacteria that secrete plaque. Regarding treatment, a new technique that is only now being developed will be greatly expanded. This consists of draping a tiny synthetic mesh over the root of a bone-denuded tooth; the mesh encourages growth of new bone without allowing soft-tissue encroachment into the surgical area.

The current emphasis on esthetics will lead to advances in bonding techniques. Fractured or malformed teeth will be improved by painting a tooth colored material directly on the tooth, without the need for grinding or drilling. Today, these bonding agents must be cured under a special light; bonding agents of the future will be self-hardening. Root-canal treatment will become less laborious; new methods of cleansing the canal of debris and filling it with a liquid sealer, which will harden in the canal, will mean that the number of visits for the procedure will be greatly reduced.

Orthodontic treatment, which has seen great strides, will see even more. Wires and bands, which at present are more esthetically acceptable than they had been for decades, will be improved by using almost invisible plastic bands that will be "spot-welded" onto the tooth with a laser. Miniaturization, which has brought such remarkable changes in the field of electronics, will be adapted to orthodontic treatment. Microminiature motors, powered by tiny batteries, will be placed in the mouth and will serve to apply tiny forces to move teeth more predictably and with less discomfort.

In the field of anesthesia, new techniques bode well for the future. Electric current as a pain suppressant, which has tantalized dentists for years, seems about to become a reality. Low-voltage but high-frequency current will be applied in such a way that the body's natural pain blockers, endorphins, will be released in greater numbers. Local anesthesia, which has been, for almost a century, the dentist's principal pain fighter, will be greatly improved. Intraligamentary anesthesia will become standard. With this method, a needle, almost as fine as a hair, is inserted into the exact area to be deadened, obviating the uncomfortable long-lasting numbness over a large area.

Dentistry a hundred years from now will be as unlike today's as that of the 1890s is to what is practiced now.

See also MEDICAL CARE PROVIDERS.

BIBLIOGRAPHY

CONLEY, JACK F. "Dentistry in the 21st Century." *Journal of the California Dental Association*. 22/1 (January 1994).

DEMIRJIAN, ARTO. "Teaching Dentistry in the 21st Century." *The Compendium of Continuing Education in Dentistry*. 15/1 (January 1994).

RING, MALVIN E. *Dentistry: An Illustrated History*. New York: Harry N. Abrams, 1985.

Malvin E. Ring

Derivatives

A derivative is a financial instrument for buying or selling today some future financial risk. Derivatives are an important social invention for quantifying and transferring future risks by means of financial markets. Derivatives can help individuals and companies shift future risks so as to suit their various degrees of risk-aversion.

It is vitally important with derivatives to understand that they make the world financially much safer for some—and much riskier for others who have different goals. However the underlying risk that exists in the real world is not affected at all by derivatives (any more than it is diminished by having an insurance policy).

Derivatives do not eliminate financial risk, they simply transfer it to someone who thinks they can better afford to pay, should the worst happen. In the marketplace for financial derivatives, there is always someone ready to assume such risks, in return for the chance of their making what they hope will be a very handsome financial return.

What Derivatives Are

The term *derivative* comes from the fact that, unlike most financial instruments (such as bank deposits, certificates of deposit, bonds, or stocks), derivatives have no value of their own. Whatever value they have is instead "derived" from something else. A derivative's value is linked to the underlying securities (stocks, bonds, currencies, or commodities) or securities index, and rises or falls with fluctuations in the price of the linked assets.

Derivatives are created whenever the future *price* of something is dealt with separately from the future financial *risk* involved. The underlying value is separated—the technical term is *unzipped*—from its associated risk. Suppose you are a wheat farmer about to plant a farm in wheat. Or you could equally well be acting for a large corporation that expects to receive a specified amount of future income in a foreign currency. In both cases you are taking (or *assuming*) a financial risk that what you will be paid will be the profit you anticipate, because by harvest (or payment) time that profit could be wiped out by fluctuations in the market price of wheat, or by changes in the value of the other country's currency.

How Sellers Protect Future Profits

How can you make yourself less dependent on price fluctuations (risk) in financial markets where prices of wheat, currencies, stocks, and bonds rise or fall every day?

To separate some (or all) of this financial risk from the actual work you do, you can pay someone else to assume for you some or all of that risk. You do that through what is called a financial *intermediary*. An intermediary stands between sellers and buyers in a market, "making a market" for them so that for every transaction buyers and sellers do not have to seek out each other. Using an intermediary is a quick and efficient way to get a competitive price, whether for a farmer's wheat, or for a corporation's sale, or the purchase of a foreign currency. Such an intermediary can also buy (and perhaps later resell to someone else) your risk exposure, guaranteeing you today a fixed future price for your wheat or currency.

How Buyers Stabilize Future Costs

Buyers, as well as sellers, take market-price risks. Often buyers, too, need stable, predictable prices and a known result. For example, a large baking company wants a predetermined cost of flour so it can set definite prices for its products. Or a corporation, making a commitment now to pay a large sum in a foreign currency at a future date, wants to establish today the cost for that future transaction. These buyers (like sellers) are motivated to "sell" this market-risk component of their business through an intermediary to others with different goals.

To do this, the value of a derivative is "unzipped" from whatever is being sold or bought, meaning that its value is *purely a risk-based value*. The cost of the derivative—to the farmer or to the flour company or to the company getting paid in foreign currency—is the market price of the risk exposure from which they want to shield themselves.

Derivatives are akin to insurance, except that insurance is based upon the risk being shared among a pool of similarly at-risk clients. With a derivative, risk is not pooled and not shared, but instead is pure risk—unpooled, unshared. Furthermore, derivatives expire. They are good for only a predetermined period of thirty, sixty, or ninety days, at the end of which, if you have not made a profit, you have lost everything you invested.

Trading in Pure Risk

Why would anyone ever want to assume such risks? The answer is that different investors have different objectives. Some individuals or institutions are risk averse and seek ways to shield their businesses from the risks of price changes. Others, for sufficient financial incentive, are readier to take such risks.

Those who purchase derivatives do so because they believe they have better information about overall economic conditions, the better to protect themselves. Or they may be more able to afford taking such a risk with some portion of their holdings, provided the *potential* financial return is great enough.

Still other investors or intermediaries believe that they can take such risks because they are diversified among many different kinds of risks, each of which uses only a fraction of their invested assets. They expect to lose a great deal on some of their derivatives, but they count on more than making up those losses on the rest of their derivatives. Like insurance companies, their risks are diversified, and they expect extremely generous profits in return for the package of high-risk exposures they assume.

Such investors are also attracted to the greater risks and potential returns (or losses) of the derivatives markets by a regulatory peculiarity of those markets. Purchases in derivatives markets can be more highly "leveraged" than stock-market purchases allow in the mid-1990s. Current regulations allow a 10 percent margin on derivatives but require an 80 percent margin on stock purchases. This means that $1 million invested in a derivatives market secures the purchase of a derivative worth $10 million, whereas an alternative purchase of stock requires immediate payment of 80 percent of

the total price, securing stock worth only $1.25 million. So the "action" is bigger in derivatives markets, making possible bigger profits (or losses).

Who can be a financial intermediary? In the beginning it was very wealthy individuals and large insurance companies. Both had "deep pockets"—vast financial reserves. And, in return for taking large risks with a portion of their money, they expected quick large profits (and occasional large losses, more than offset by the profits). More recently pension funds, mutual funds, large commercial banks, very large corporations, and even some college-endowment management companies have begun investing some of their money in these markets to increase returns.

The Future of Derivatives

Do derivatives have a useful social function? In the mid-1990s, Federal Reserve Chairman Alan Greenspan, testifying before U.S. congressional banking committees concerned about risks to financial institutions, repeatedly defended financial derivatives as very important and useful financial instruments.

But in late February 1995, Barings Bank, Britain's oldest and one of its most prestigious investment banks, collapsed after one of its traders bought and sold derivatives that lost more than $1,000 million in one week, wiping out the bank's total capital and forcing it into bankruptcy. What happened was that a trader in the bank's Singapore office "took a long position" on Japanese stock-index futures contracts, betting that the price of Japanese stocks would increase, and the bank would then profit from the price increase. But prices fell on the Japanese stock market and kept falling—and Barings kept buying, betting on each downward move that the "bottom of the market" had occurred. The risk of the downturn had been sold to Barings. Over one weekend, it went bankrupt.

Earlier in 1995, the municipalities, school districts, police and fire departments, and pension funds of Orange County, California, were bankrupted when the county treasurer, while investing in the risky side of the derivatives market, suffered heavy losses. Major international corporations such as Procter and Gamble have also suffered severe losses in these risk markets.

Like insurance companies, those who sell derivatives reduce someone else's exposure to future financial risks. But they can themselves sustain great losses very quickly, as well as make extremely large, quick profits. The "bottom line" is that derivatives do not eliminate future financial risk, they just redistribute it.

See also CAPITAL FORMATION; CREDIT, DEBT, AND BORROWING; ESTATE AND FINANCIAL PLANNING; FINANCIAL INSTITUTIONS; INVESTMENTS; SAVINGS; WEALTH.

BIBLIOGRAPHY

HULL, JOHN C. *Introduction to the Futures and Options Markets.* 2nd ed. Englewood Cliffs, NJ: Prentice Hall, 1995.

KOLB, ROBERT. *Understanding Options.* New York: John Wiley, 1995.

LYONS, ALLAN S. *Winning in the Options Market.* Chicago: Probus, 1994.

WEBBER, ALAN. *Dictionary of Futures and Options; 1500 International Terms Defined and Explained.* Chicago: Probus, 1994.

David Dodson Gray

Determinism.

See FORECASTING, DETERMINISTIC.

Development, Alternative

The goal of development in the Second and Third Worlds since World War II has been to create independent social institutions and to establish strong nonfeudal economies. Through massive aid and loans, it was hoped that all nations could rapidly industrialize as the West had done. Ignored, however, were the impacts of colonialism (the extraction of wealth and the creation of a collective inferiority complex), and the cultural and spiritual contradictions embedded in the Western industrial model. Development alternatives were nation-state–oriented, narrowly defined by the discipline of economics and focused on bureaucrats, capitalists, and technocrats as agents of change. Economic development merely created a new elite and further impoverished the poor.

Recent efforts to rethink development have attempted to deconstruct the power relations embedded in the idea of development itself, particularly to free development from its Social Darwinian views of past and future. Emerging models focus on the contribution of factors that have been the traditional basic materials of development: rural labor, women and children, as well as the environment.

Shifting from national, technocratic, and bureaucratic orientation—with the multinational corporation as the exemplar—alternative development approaches now focus on local peoples' organizations and international nongovernmental organizations as agents of transformation.

In contrast to the capitalist notion of development, which emphasizes freedom for capital, individual mobility, and labor mobility within nations, local models of development stress identity and survival. They focus on policies that do not degrade the environment or increase inequality among classes. These models are often nonlinear in their assumptions—that is, they are not based on the belief that there is an end stage of modernity to reach; rather they believe that all polities, individuals, and economies follow a cyclical rise and fall, expansion and contraction. Within this framework, development is not based on the extraneous values of those presently wealthy, but rather on the notion that all regions can shape their own model of the ideal society.

Local models, however, have not been able to solve the problem of globalization, or to meet the desire for Westernization among local communities. Local models, while giving communities a sense of history and pride, have failed at providing plentiful consumer goods.

The previous alternative to capitalist development, the communist model—which focused not on the idea of individual freedom leading to growth but state power ideally leading to justice—has been discarded. Communist systems at best met only survival needs, fell short of advancing well-being, and faltered in advancing economic growth.

In contrast, the new Japanese-Confucian model has attempted to perfect the traditional development paradigm without pitting the state against business and labor against management. Based on education and long-term planning cycles, the state and the corporation provide collective unity as well as hierarchical discipline. Economic growth takes precedence over identity and social freedom. However, as economic well-being has increased, the problem of individual identity has reemerged, as have spiritual needs previously relegated to history by the glitter of modernity.

Successful future development models must meet many needs: freedom, mobility, identity (above and beyond nation and ethnicity), survival, and well-being. These models must be able to provide for economic growth (supported by savings, a hard-work ethic, and an efficient distribution system), development without exploitation of people or the environment, and distributive justice. Emerging models must be eclectic, including ideas from capitalist, collective, welfare, and diverse cultural traditions. They must also include gender fairness and environmental sustainability. Decisions must include women's categories of knowledge and their important contribution to the informal home and formal exchange economy. Finally, empirical indicators of new models must include the contribution of these factors: women, community, and the environment, in such a manner as to show the imbalances caused by each model.

An emerging global alternative development model is the Progressive Utilization Theory of the Indian philosopher Prabhat Ranjan Sarkar. This model has the necessary dimensions for both strong economic growth (through the development of material, intellectual, and spiritual potentials) and for distributive justice (through economic democracy). Cooperatives make up its prime economic organization. Identity is based on spiritual, not national, character. The spiritual state is manifested by conditions of *prama*, or balance. There must be balance among and between many realms: the material and spiritual, the physical (economic balance between regions), intellectual (an eclectic or multiple view of reality), and the spiritual (in the form of individual trans-formation).

This model would encourage free trade, but under conditions of equality between nations. Until these criteria are met, regions should withhold and not export their raw materials.

Manufacturing, ideally, should be established away from populated cities in decentralized areas. Ideally, economic activity should be based on bioregions. With increased communication and trade, regions could evolve into confederations, until a true world economy emerges. The overarching goal is a world in which development is not based on the exploitation of the many for the few, nor measured in linear or materialistic terms. The past few centuries have been characterized by great imbalance. Alternative development models aim not only to restore the ancient cyclical balance but to create systems based on a dynamic view of order and disorder, of chaos and complexity.

See also AFRICA; ASIA; DEVELOPMENT: WESTERN PERSPECTIVE; INDIA.

BIBLIOGRAPHY

CARLEY, MICHAEL and IAN CHRISTIE. *Managing Sustainable Development*. London: Earthscan, 1992.

DALY, HERMAN E., and COBB, JOHN E. JR. *For the Common Good: Redirecting the Economy Towards the Community, the Environment and a Sustainable Future*. Boston: Beacon Press, 1990.

DE LA COURT, THIJS. *Beyond Brundtland: Development in the Nineties*. London, Zed Books, 1990.

HARRISON, PAUL. *The Third Revolution: Environment, Population and a Sustainable World*. New York: Tauris, 1992.

PEARCE, DAVID; BARBIER, EDWARD; and MARKANDAYA, ANIL. *Sustainable Development: Economics and Environment in the Third World*. London: Earthscan: 1991.

REDCLIFT, MICHAEL. *Sustainable Development: Exploring the Contradictions*. New York: Methuen, 1987.

SCHNEIDER, BERTRAND. *The Barefoot Revolution: A Report to the Club of Rome*. London: Intermediate Technology Publications, 1989.

World Commission on Environment and Development. *Our Common Future*. New York: Oxford University Press, 1987.

Sohail Inayatullah

Development: Western Perspective

Nine out of every ten persons under the age of fifteen are Third World citizens. The vast majority of Earth's resources also are in the developing world. How these regions and people develop will shape the twenty-first century.

The purpose of development is enlightened growth within a social setting of peace and plenty. Western development philosophy assumes that transferring the "things of development," such as schools, hospitals, machines, computers, and highways, to poorer regions inevitably leads to development. This approach has brought about some improvements. According to the United Nations Development Program's *Human Development Report* (1993), there has been some significant progress. Safe water access rose from 10 percent of population to 60 percent over the last two decades. Life expectancy increased 33 percent during the last three decades. Economic growth averaged 7 percent during the 1980s in South and East Asia, which has 66 percent of the Third World's population. Fifty countries meet their daily caloric requirements, up from 25 percent of that total in 1965. High school enrollment grew from 25 percent to 40 percent in two decades, and world military spending has begun to decline.

This "Western form of development" led to mammoth private and public debts as these countries struggled to pay for teachers, doctors, machine repairs, and road maintenance. Richer countries tax business for public revenue, but there was little business in the developing world to tax. Without a major effort to strengthen and expand the smaller economic activities and the foresight to manage the technological change, the policy of duplicating the "things of development" was doomed to failure.

Massive migration and famine in Africa; environmental time bombs inherent in rapid industrialization in China; ethnic wars in sixty countries; jobless economic growth; continued financial debt; one billion illiterate people; political instability; and the population growth rates across the Third World—all these factors will increasingly affect the richer countries. By involving themselves in efforts to solve or ameliorate these conditions through enlightened self-interest, the affluent countries will benefit themselves and the international support system.

It took the developed world one hundred years to double its per capita income, but just thirty years for some developing nations. Korea's GDP per capita was the same as Ghana's at independence. Ghana is poorer today, while Korea is a rich, dynamic country; Korea embraced technology, free market incentives, and long-term planning—and Ghana did not. About 700 American corporations have invested $4 billion in Singapore, because it has a free economy, a hard-work ethic, and enthusiastic people. Still, economic growth without increased employment should be expected to continue as the technology of automation is transferred to the less developed regions. Hence, the current unemployment rates of over 20 percent will increase until new kinds of economic activity are created.

Futurists such as R. Buckminster FULLER, Herman KAHN, and Arthur C. CLARKE have suggested that poorer regions of the world will be able to catch up with the West by "leap-frogging" past the industrial era, jumping from the agricultural to the information age. Table 1 highlights these key stages in the Western view on development.

People are "underdeveloped" both because of wrong consciousness and technology, whether in Haiti or America. Where people tend to be fatalistic, development will not happen until the grip of fatalism and dependency is broken. As long as people define the solution to their problems as outside their control, they are dependent and will remain underdeveloped. Too often poorer nations see the solutions to their problems as beyond their ability. More developed groups define a problem in such a way that it is within their ability to solve it or at least to take the first step on the road to solution.

The poorer regions of the world inherit technology and concepts from the more developed and richer regions. Those that decided to define their future and to invent their long-range strategy—for example, Japan, Mauritius, and Korea—have done well. Such long-range thinking is becoming more acceptable in development. One of the first examples of this shift in development philosophy is the UNDP's African Futures program to assist every country in Africa to develop its long-term strategy.

Meanwhile during the 1980s, the Western approach to development began shifting from bilateral aid for large-scale public-sector projects to create the "things of development" toward smaller-scale private-sector development. With this focus on private-sector growth and the new interest in long-term strategic thinking, unique market niches that are international as well as local can be anticipated. The Third World could take the initiative to form partnerships with the most advanced technological conceptual initiators to invent their future together.

See also CHANGE, EPOCHAL; DEVELOPMENT, ALTERNATIVE; ENVIRONMENTAL REFUGEES; INFORMATION SOCIETY; RELIGION: CHANGING BELIEFS; WORKFORCE DISTRIBUTION.

TABLE 1. A Simplified View of Western Development

Age (Major Activity)	Product	Wealth	Power	Location
Agricultural	Food	Land	Religion	Farm
Industrial	Machinery	Capital	State	Factory
Information	Service/Info	Access	Corporation	Office
Conscious Technology	Linkage	Being	Individual	Motion

BIBLIOGRAPHY

BOWERS, C. A. *Education, Cultural Myths, and the Ecological Crisis: Toward Deep Changes.* Albany, NY: State University of New York Press, 1993.

GLENN, JEROME C. "Economic Development in the Third World." In *Future Mind: Merging the Mystical and the Technological in the 21st Century.* Washington, DC: Acropolis Books, 1989.

Global Outlook 2000: An Economic, Social, and Environmental Perspective. New York: UN Publications, 1993.

Human Development Report: United Nations Development Program, 1990–1993. New York: UN Publications, 1993.

KENNEDY, PAUL. *Preparing for the Twenty-first Century.* New York: Random House, 1993.

PIRAGES, C. DENNIS, and SYLVESTER, CHRISTINE. *Transformation in the Global Political Economy.* New York: St. Martin's Press, 1990.

Jerome C. Glenn

Diet.

See NUTRITION.

Digital Communications

Throughout the 1930s, '40s, and '50s, communications blossomed in both the wireless and wireline worlds of radio and telephone, and later television. The predominant technologies were based upon various analog modulation/demodulation techniques as voice, data, and video signals were superimposed on high-frequency carriers and multiplexed together to be transported from here to there to everywhere. As high-wattage radio antennas were established on high-rise towers to broadcast radio frequencies long distances, the telephone took the wireline route, as telephone poles were established down country lanes, while urban cable vaults blossomed as they terminated hundreds of thousands of copper pairs, bringing analog voice conversations to large central switching offices. (In time, past the middle of the century, after Sputnik, satellites were universally deployed commercially to distribute wireless television signals to remote locations.)

Unfortunately with regard to wireline, there was considerable expense in dedicating each conversation to a single wire pair and considerable maintenance time required to hook up and hand-wire each new request for service within the cable distribution plant and main distribution frames of the central office. Here, stored program controlled (SPC) switching and service systems helped speed up the customer service changes enabling numbering changes, number translations, and new routing table updates, as well as the enhanced capability, to provide new features more easily in a timely manner. But there was still a serious need to reduce the cost of the distribution plant, improve the quality of service, and reduce the proliferation of new central switching offices requiring new blocks of the dwindling resources of seven-digit local codes.

To address these needs, especially for long distance carrier transport, AT&T introduced digital communications in the early 1970s, based upon pulse code modulation techniques developed in the 1930s by an earlier pioneer, ITT Laboratories. Here, AT&T's T1 carrier systems, operating at 1.544 million bits per second (Mb/s), were able to transport 24 voice conversations over a pair of copper wires, where each voice conversation was sampled 8,000 times per second with each sample level coded in blocks of 8 ones and zeros (bits). Hence, 8 times 8,000 or 64,000 digital bits were sent each second to represent a single-voice conversation. Thus, 24 times 64,000 bits were sent together with specialized synchronization (bits) information to formulate the T1 1.544 Mb/s transport system. Later, capabilities were expanded to T2 (6.31 Mb/s) and eventually T3 (45 Mb/s) capabilities.

It was soon noted in the mid–1970s by GTE engineers that their central offices in remote rural towns could "home in" on a single large office located usually at the county seat. Hence, they extended the digital long distance transport to the local community, as remote switching units were deployed in remote locations to "home" on centrally based units, thereby establishing digital clusters of 15 or so small towns and villages with the county seat. Thus were born integrated digital networks (IDN).

Though there were administrative economies of scale and number group savings in deploying digital to the voice world in this manner, much, much more could be achieved by integrating digital voice with the world of data. This was the purpose and charge of integrated services digital networks (ISDN). Their initial task was to enable the customer to send and receive voice or data from their location over the copper pair, and to provide the capability to take immediate advantage of shared digital transport and switching facilities. In this, the user was provided a 2B+D interface, with the B channel having the capability of sending/receiving 64,000 bits per second and the D channel enabling

16,000 bits per second of signalling and control information. Thus, the user is able to send a digital voice in one B channel, as well as simultaneous digital data in the other B channel, or have two separate voice conversations in the two B channels or digital data in both B channels at a total rate of 128,000 bits per second, while having 16,000 bits of out-of-band signalling and control information in the D channel. This D channel is also able to send data in a packet form (with information packaged in a variable or fixed number of 8 bit bytes, having a header and a tail to differentiate the beginning and end of the message; here, the D channel's transport rate for packet data was 9,600 bits per second).

Hence, this 2B+D interface was called the basic rate interface (BRI), enabling voice or data to be mixed together, or allowing two voice conversations or two data conversations to be transported. These narrowband capabilities were then augmented by a higher-speed (wideband) ISDN primary rate interface (PRI), enabling 23 B channels of 64 Kb/s and one D channel having 64 Kb/s of signalling and control information, equating to the T1 transport rate of 1.544 Mb/s.

In time, broadband capabilities will be available enabling the user network interface (UNI) to deliver 155 million bits per second (Mb/s) and 622 Mb/s to the customer over fiber-optic local loops. These optical carrier rates are multiples of OC-1 (51.8 Mb/s). It should be noted that American and European systems will be in step at the internationally agreed standard of OC-3 or 155 Mb/s, with Americans evolving from the T1 rate of 1.544 Mb/s and Europeans from the E1 rate of 2.048 Mb/s.

Here, information will be digitally transported, using the synchronous optical network (SONET) transport capabilities, enabling voice, data, text, image, and video to be dynamically modulated and multiplexed over gigabit facilities. This then will be switched utilizing asynchronous transfer mode (ATM) fast packet-switching technologies, as well as synchronous transfer mode (STM) circuit-switching capabilities. These techniques will later be complemented and extended by photonic multiple-frequency (colors) optical-electrical switching transport systems, handling terabits of information.

Using these capabilities, as fiber is delivered first to the office (FTTO), then to the residential curb (FTTC), and later to the home (FTTH), customers will be able to see four or so high-definition video channels and communicate to the world at the 155 Mb/s rate, thereby paving the way for high-definition videophone, high-speed computer-

to-computer data traffic, and the ability to dial up high-quality musical and sporting events, etc. In this manner, narrowband and broadband ISDN digital communications will establish the communications infrastructure for a new society—the information society in the twenty-first century.

See also BROADCASTING; COMMUNICATIONS; COMPUTER LINKAGES; COMPUTERS: OVERVIEW; DATA STORAGE; ELECTRONIC CONVERGENCE; INFORMATION TECHNOLOGIES; LIBRARIES: ELECTRONIC FORMATS; MEDIA LAB; NETWORKING; ON-LINE SERVICES; POSTAL SERVICES; SATELLITE COMMUNICATIONS; SPACE SATELLITES; TELECOMMUNICATIONS; TELEPHONES; TELEVISION.

BIBLIOGRAPHY

BRADLEY, STEPHEN B, HAUSMAN, JERRY A., NOLAN, RICHARD L., eds. *Globalization, Technology, and Competition: The Fusion of Computers and Telecommunications in the 1990s.* Boston: Harvard Business School Press, 1993.

CONNORS, MICHAEL. *The Race to the Intelligent State: Towards the Global Information Economy of 2005.* Oxford, U.K. and Cambridge, MA: Blackwell Business, 1993.

HARASIM, LINDA M. *Global Networks: Computers and International Communication.* Cambridge, MA: MIT Press, 1993.

JUSSAWALLA, MEHEROO, ed. *Global Telecommunications Policies: The Challenge of Change.* Westport, CT: Greenwood Press, 1993.

NORDENSTRENG, KAARLE, and SCHILLER, HERBERT I., eds. *Beyond National Sovereignty: International Communication in the 1990s.* Norwood, NJ: Ablex Publishing Corp., 1993.

PARKER, EDWIN B.; HUDSON, HEATHER; et al., eds. *Electronic Byways: State Policies for Rural Development Through Telecommunications.* Boulder, CO: Westview Press, 1992.

Robert K. Heldman

Disabled Persons' Rights

Problems of stigma and discrimination have long been associated with physical and mental impairments. Because of negative attitudes and their manifestation in architectural design and societal norms, individuals with disabilities who have been able to work and otherwise participate in public life have often been denied the opportunity to do so. For example, in a 1986 survey of working age persons with disabilities, 47 percent of the respondents stated that employers' negative attitudes about their work potential resulted in them working part-time or not at all, and 25 percent of those working reported experiencing discrimination.

The first significant laws prohibiting discrimination in access to public accommodations were the white cane and guide dog laws enacted by a few states in the 1930s and in most jurisdictions by the early 1960s. These laws prohibited restrictions on blind people using canes or guide dogs in public buildings and on streets. However, individuals with disabilities other than blindness, and blind people who did not use canes or guide dogs were not affected.

Rulings that provided equal access to public education regardless of disabling condition established by several federal court decisions during the early 1970s were broader in scope (*Pennsylvania Association for Retarded Citizens* v. *Commonwealth of Pennsylvania* and *Mills* v. *Board of Education*). Subsequently, public policies acknowledged that unfair stereotypes and discrimination were as great a problem for many people with disabilities as were their impairments.

The first two major federal laws protecting the rights of people with disabilities were passed in the early 1970s. The Rehabilitation Act of 1973 prohibited discrimination on the basis of disability by recipients of federal assistance (such as state and local governments, schools and colleges, hospitals, and public transit systems), and by federal contractors. This statute required that federally supported services be accessible and that they practice nondiscrimination in providing service and in employment practices.

The Education for All Handicapped Children Act of 1974 required equal access to public education and related services for all children regardless of their handicaps. This program led to the inclusion in regular school programs of many disabled children who had previously been segregated into special education classes or refused services altogether.

Antidiscrimination laws and rulings were the result of demands for legal protection by people with disabilities and their advocates. At least three major groups were involved. The first included concerned family members and other nondisabled advocates for people with disabilities often unable to advocate for themselves, such as children and people with severe cognitive or emotional impairments.

The second group championing disabled rights included organizations of people with disabilities who were active in lobbying on their own behalf for equal access to public life. This group of advocates, sometimes known as the disability rights movement, included groups organized around specific impairments such as blindness, deafness, or paraplegia, and coalitions including a wide range of disabling conditions. Such organizations were particularly concerned about the enactment and enforcement of prohibitions of discrimination in public accommodation, public transportation, employment, housing, and communication systems.

The third major group of advocates established the independent living movement. This movement included local self-help and advocacy groups that set up independent living centers. The centers were organized in communities around the country during the 1960s following the founding of the first such enterprise in Berkeley, California. Independent living centers seek to assist people who might otherwise be forced to live in institutional settings and are typically led by individuals who themselves have disabilities. The independent living movement has been active in promoting self-sufficiency by shifting service provision from institutional to community settings, promoting accessible housing, transportation, and employment, and giving people with disabilities more control over services they receive and those who provide them.

After the legislative gains of the 1970s, the legal status of people with disabilities as a protected minority group was tested in the courts and debated as part of the attack on government regulation during the 1980s. Overall, the case for guaranteeing people with disabilities access to public life came to be accepted across the political spectrum. Several issues were hotly contested, the most visible of which in the 1980s was the demand by disability rights groups that urban mass transit systems be made accessible through mandating wheelchair access to bus, rail, and subway systems. While the cost of transition to fully accessible systems was high and the demand uncertain, disability advocates viewed accessibility as a measure of legal equality. Critics of full accessibility argued for the alternative of separate "paratransit" systems utilizing vans and taxis, although the service provided by many such systems was often unreliable and subject to limitations on the time and purpose of travel. The debate over accessible mainstream transit versus segregated paratransit was largely resolved by the 1990s in favor of accessibility.

The landmark statute guaranteeing the rights of people with disabilities is the Americans with Disabilities Act of 1990 (ADA), which prohibits discrimination on the basis of disability in employment, public accommodation, public transportation, and telecommunications. It parallels the prohibition on racial discrimination of the Civil Rights Act of 1964. Some of the major provisions of this law include the requirement that private employers with more than fifteen workers practice nondiscrimination in hiring and make facilities and services accessible to qualified disabled employees, that all new vehicles purchased or leased by public transit agencies be accessible, that public and private providers of public accommodations practice non-discrimination and remove architectural barriers, and that telecommunications relay services for speech and hearing impaired individuals be established under the supervision of the Federal Communications Commission.

With the enactment of ADA, persons with disabilities have gained the legal right to participate in the mainstream of American society on the basis of their abilities. Rights in themselves are no guarantee of social change. Issues of participation, social integration, and independent living will continue to pose challenges for disabled individuals.

See also HEALTH CARE: MORAL ISSUES; PUBLIC ASSISTANCE PROGRAMS: SOCIAL SECURITY; SOCIAL WELFARE PHILOSOPHIES; UNEMPLOYMENT INSURANCE, WORKERS' COMPENSATION, JOB SECURITY.

BIBLIOGRAPHY

DEJONG, G., and LIFCHEZ, R. "Physical Disability and Public Policy." *Scientific American* 248 (1983): 40–49.

PERCY, STEPHEN L. *Disability, Civil Rights, and Public Policy: The Politics of Implementation.* Tuscaloosa, AL: University of Alabama Press, 1989.

SCOTCH, RICHARD K. *From Good Will to Civil Rights: Transforming Federal Disability Policy.* Philadelphia: Temple University Press, 1984.

WEST, JANE, ed. *The Americans With Disabilities Act: From Policy to Practice.* New York: Milbank Memorial Fund, 1991.

Richard K. Scotch

Disasters, Planning for

Following the devastating earthquake in Kobe, Japan, on January 24, 1995, which registered a 7.2 magnitude on the Richter scale, the city council of New York City decided that all new construction in the city will be required to have greater resistance to earthquakes. New York City does not have the tectonic activity of a truly major fault (as do California and Japan) because it is in the middle of a geologic plate. But New York City is built on geologic faults, so earthquakes do occur—about once a century. Hence the possibility cannot be ruled out of a New York City quake with an intensity measuring 5.0 on the logarithmic Richter scale (i.e., more than 100 times weaker than the Kobe quake). Its likelihood can be said to approach "zero," and yet the potential economic damage from such an occurrence was estimated at $25 billion.

To guard in this way against a peril we hope will never occur is accepted as a part of the cost of promoting public safety. Doing so is expensive, however, and it becomes a policy dilemma when such calamities are infrequent and their frequency is thought to approach zero. Fundamental questions involving risk/benefit assessment are at stake here.

The Zero-Infinity Dilemma

Rare occurrences like the Kobe earthquake force us to alter our planning for the future. It may appear that there is close to zero chance that a given hypothetical event might occur; nevertheless, when such an event does occur, the disruption it causes may be so great, conceptually, that it may seem to approach infinity—hence the concept of the "zero-infinity dilemma."

How Much Protection—and How Much Risk?

How much should society spend to protect itself now against such potentially disastrous but probably unlikely future events? In thinking about this it is helpful to examine other examples of the zero-infinity dilemma.

During World War II, scientists of the U.S. Manhattan Project thought it entirely possible—but unlikely—that exploding an atomic bomb might ignite the Earth's atmosphere and burn up all its oxygen, ending life. There are extremely important questions about whether any nation or group ever should presume to take such a risk for everyone else and for all time. But they took that risk, and their worst fears did not happen. And this fact reminds us vividly that the unlikely catastrophic event does *not* always happen.

Again, in the 1970s when natural gas began to be liquefied for transport and sale worldwide, special tankers were built to bring the liquefied natural gas (LNG) to transfer points on distant shores. One such transfer station was to be built in Everett, a working-class community adjacent to the busy Boston harbor and downtown Boston. There was speculation in some circles at the Massachusetts Institute of Technology in nearby Cambridge about what might happen if one of the LNG tankers ever were involved in a collision with another ship in Boston harbor. It was known that when a small amount of LNG was dropped into water, it exploded; also that LNG, when released from being pressurized, turned to vapor and became a dense and very combustible fog (if it did not immediately explode) which would quickly fill the harbor and downtown Boston, smothering all in its path; and finally the vapor, like all natural gas, could easily be ignited by a single spark in a great conflagration. It is characteristic of the zero-infinity dilemma that no laboratory tests, scale model tests, or even pilot plant tests can show us in advance what the full-scale event will entail. Just as no one knew in advance the consequences of the Exxon Valdez oil tanker accident off Alaska, which involved releasing a large amount of oil into the waters and fisheries of Fitzwilliam Sound, so too the consequences of a sudden large LNG release into water has still unknown consequences. The LNG terminal in busy Boston harbor has been in safe operation for the past twenty years without an LNG tanker collision.

Bad Things Do Happen

Big technology often involves big unknowns. Standard behavior of such technologies is familiar and safe, but occasionally a malfunction or accident sets in motion unprecedented and unfamiliar behaviors. Recent examples are the nuclear meltdown at the Chernobyl power plant in the Soviet Union (April 26, 1986); the Exxon Valdez oil spill (March 24, 1989); and the failure of the northeastern U.S. power-generating and distribution network on November 9, 1965. In the last instance, in 2.7 seconds more than 30 million people over 80,000 square miles were cast into darkness, and 800,000 people were trapped in New York City's subways.

It is fortunate that such events are rare. But they can and do occur. One of our most challenging responsibilities for the future is identifying such zero-infinity possibilities and then deciding how to protect society from potentially enormous disruptions and hazards, if they should ever occur.

When Those Put at Risk Are Not Those Getting Benefits

Further complicating our assessments in such matters is the frequent separation between *those who will benefit* from putting everyone at such great (but probably unlikely) risk, and all *those who will be hurt* should that worst eventuality happen. At Chernobyl, the power generated was used within the Soviet Union. But after the nuclear meltdown, the radiation that spilled into the atmosphere was transported by wind currents to points throughout Eastern and Central Europe and as far west as France and north throughout Scandinavia.

Again, the benefits are often for *those living now*, and the potential catastrophic costs or damage (if the event occurs) will be borne by *those who will live in the future*. So the intergenerational questions of the zero-infinity dilemma focus on how risks and benefits should be distributed among different generations. Earlier generations often decide these questions before subsequent generations are even born. In doing so they face difficult policy dilemmas. Do we go for the benefit now? And how concerned are we about potential downside risks that could impose great consequences on future generations? The question remains the same: How well do we guard ourselves and others against low-likelihood but very big disasters?

See also NATURAL DISASTERS; SURPRISES; WILD-CARDS.

BIBLIOGRAPHY

BERTELL, ROSALIE. *No Immediate Danger: Prognosis for a Radioactive Earth.* Summertown, TN: Book Publishing Co., 1985.
COMMONER, BARRY. *The Closing Circle: Nature, Man and Technology.* New York: Alfred Knopf, 1971.
WINNER, LANGDON. *Autonomous Technology: Technics-out-of-Control as a Theme in Political Thought.* Cambridge, MA.: MIT Press, 1977.

David Dodson Gray

Divorce

When looking at trends relating to divorce, it is immediately clear that married couples around the world now divorce and remarry in numbers that would have been beyond comprehension thirty years ago. Over the past two decades, more women raised children without marriage and many couples married later than previously. In the future, it is safe to assume that a large segment of the adult population will flow into and out of several marital categories during their lives, and the proportion of children in a traditional nuclear family will continue to decline as family patterns grow more complex.

It is very likely that marriage at later ages, no marriage, and no remarriage will continue to increase.

Divorce is not expected to exceed 60 percent and in fact is likely to decline. At least one forecast holds out 40 percent divorce rates and 65 percent remarriage rates as world maximums for the year 2000, and cohabitation among younger couples and the elderly will continue to serve as a factor in keeping official divorce rates down.

Although projecting future trends directly from past events is a complex endeavor in a time of change (especially when social trends are involved), in the case of divorce trends around the world, a look at the past may be helpful. Some dramatic changes have already occurred, and we seem to be entering a period of relative stability. Over the past several decades, we have seen major alterations, especially in the United States, of marriage patterns, childbearing, women's employment, parenting, and attitudes toward marriage. Both pro-family and anti-family forces have been at work affecting rates of divorce worldwide. These include later first marriages, delayed childbearing, and increased education and work experience among women.

Between the late 1960s and 1980, the divorce rate in the United States, for example, doubled—to the point where one out of two marriages could be expected to end in divorce. This rate of change reflects an accelerating curve, from a seven percent divorce rate in 1860 to twenty-five percent in 1945. The rate plateaued for about fifteen years, then climbed again, then plateaued again. The interesting question is whether 1995 will mark the start of another steep climb.

There continues to be an inverse relationship between age and the likelihood of divorce, and an inverse relationship between divorce and the attainment of formal educational degrees, no matter what the level of overall education. As well, premarital conception or birth of children seems to be directly related to divorce rates.

A complicating factor in forecasting social change is the interactive nature of these dynamics. For example, higher divorce rates create a larger pool of eligibles for remarriage. In 1991, more than four out of ten American marriages were second marriages or above, but the rate of remarriage after divorce has declined over the past fifteen years—while the overall divorce rate remained constant. Like many social phenomena, divorce and its counterpart, marriage, are individual decisions, resulting from individual factors, such as age, education, pregnancy, etc. Whether or not societies function as systems with discernible internal dynamics continues to be a matter of debate. It

is just as arguable that the regularities of collective behavior represent responses to common stimuli.

The differences in marriage and divorce laws among countries present challenges for international comparability of data, as does the accuracy of polling surveys. Divorced people often represent themselves as single, married, or widowed, for a variety of personal reasons. While increases in divorce rate have occurred in both developed countries other than the U.S. and undeveloped countries, the relative rates are always lower, as American divorce rates are the highest in the world (and U.S. data on divorce are the most detailed). Divorce rates in the United States are twice those in Europe, except for the countries of the former Soviet Union, which nearly match those of their former enemy. However, the marriage rates of Western and Northern Europe are about half that of the United States, producing many fewer couples to divorce. In Asia, rates range from one-fourth to one-tenth those of the United States, and are also holding steady. Data from South America show levels and patterns similar to those of Asia.

There is little information on divorce in the African countries, with only 12 percent of the nearly sixty countries in Africa providing data to the United Nations. In African countries, divorce is not a universal right for men, much less for women, and there was not the substantial increase in divorce rates during the 1970s that occurred elsewhere. In Muslim countries, women have no right of divorce whatsoever. These data highlight the differences among countries—i.e., how cultural norms strongly influence social trends like marriage and divorce. What is clear across all countries, however, is that the impacts of divorce are strikingly different between men and women, especially women with children.

In addition, it is not very accurate to speak of divorce rates or any other social trends as if a given society was wholly homogeneous, exhibiting change uniformly throughout. One area of distinctions within countries or societies in the past has been among racial or ethnic groups. This is most clearly shown in the United States, where the most detailed data exist. In all cases, changes in divorce rates have been strongly tied to rates of marriage. In 1975, there was only a 7 percent variance between the rates of black versus white women who had ever married. By 1990, only 75 percent of black women in their late thirties had ever married, compared with 91 percent of white women in the same age group—Hispanic rates were similar to those of whites. It is useful to contrast this with racial or ethnic group attitudes toward marriage. Life-long marriage continues to be the ideal among those polled on the subject, in all but about 12 percent of the population. The one exception to this was black men, where the rate of those who rejected marriage as a lifetime goal increased to 23 percent. Again, white and Hispanic rates were very similar in this area.

As important as the raw numerical data are the implications of these trends in terms of the human condition. One impact of divorce is the one-parent family, which also shows variation among racial or ethnic groups. Blacks, for example, now have the highest single-parent rates of any racial group in the U.S., with 55 percent of all American black children living with only one parent in 1990 (versus 27 percent of Hispanic and 19 percent of white families). The impact also varied by gender. Six percent of these one-parent black children lived with a father rather than a mother, as opposed to 10 percent of Hispanic one-parent families and 15 percent of whites. Estimates are that nearly half of those children alive today will spend time in a one-parent family. In Europe and elsewhere in the world, the growth of single-parent families has been much less than in the United States, with most births occurring to couples (whether married or unmarried) followed by lower rates of divorce or separation. The developed regions have the highest number of single-parent households, with Latin America and the Caribbean next, Africa third, and Asia lowest, with under 10 percent overall.

Another area of substantial change is in the growth of cohabitation, especially among older adults. This was especially true in the developed regions, Latin America, and the Caribbean. These unions remain poorly defined and largely under-reflected in public data, as they are without official beginning or end. Some estimate that as much as half of the population will experience a period of cohabitation by their mid-thirties over the next decade. When measured by such factors as births to unmarried couples, the rates are clearly rising. For example, the percentage of married births in France declined from 60 percent of the total in 1970 to 40 percent by 1980. Across regions, Africa, the Caribbean, and Europe all showed rates of over 40 percent unmarried births, in 1985, while Japan had only 1 percent of its births outside marriage. In the United States, less than 15 percent of American adults polled recently disapprove of cohabitation under any circumstances. With a growing acceptance of alternatives, the data on divorce may

have less policy impact, as living arrangements and parenting decisions come to depend less on marital status.

See also CHANGE; CHILD CARE; CHILDREN, LIVING ARRANGEMENTS; FAMILIES AND HOUSEHOLDS; FAMILY PATTERNS; FAMILY PROBLEMS; FAMILY VALUES; HOUSEHOLD COMPOSITION; MARRIAGE; SOCIAL CHANGE: UNITED STATES; VALUES; VALUES CHANGE; VALUES FORMATION; WOMEN AND WORK; WOMEN'S MOVEMENT.

BIBLIOGRAPHY

BUMPERS, LARRY L., "What's Happening to the Family? Interactions Between Demographic and Institutional Change." *Demography* 27 (1990): 483–498.

NORTON, ARTHUR J., and MILLER, LOUISA F. *Marriage Divorce and Remarriage in the 1990s.* Washington, DC: Bureau of the Census, 1992.

SEAGER, JONI, and OLSON, ANN. *Women in the World.* London, U.K.: Pluto Press, 1986.

SOUTH, SCOTT. "Racial Ethnic Differences in the Desire to Marry." *Journal of Marriage and the Family* 55 (1993): 357–370.

The World's Women, 1970–1990: Trends and Statistics, New York: United Nations, 1992.

Women's Indicators and Statistical Spreadsheet Database. New York, United Nations, 1992.

Timothy Craig Mack

Drugs, Illicit

As the twenty-first century begins, the detrimental effects of illicit drugs will touch every segment of society. There is no class, race, ethnic or age group, or geographic region immune from the human suffering, crime, violence, and devastation of illicit drugs. The impact of illicit drugs is immeasurable, with some estimates putting the cost at over $67 billion per year. Over the past decade, federal funds spent on law enforcement interdiction efforts increased 27 percent; state and local funds spent on drug control 1,000 percent; funds allocated to drug treatment 1,700 percent; and funds spent on drug treatment 400 percent.

The United States has seen a decline in the number of illicit drug users since 1979, when it peaked at 24 million, with a slight resurgence in the mid-1990s but uncertainty as to its continuation. Debate will also continue about the so-called "war on drugs" and whether a combat-like approach, with emphasis on enforcement, is more effective than a health and prevention approach.

The change toward more conservative politics in the United States will shift emphasis in dealing with illicit drugs to enforcement and incarceration from rehabilitation, harm reduction, and other alternatives to traditional approaches.

Among the most dramatic trends that will continue into the next century is the aging of current users. In the fifteen years from 1979 to 1993, rates of current illicit drug use declined among people twelve to thirty-four years of age. By contrast, use increased among people aged thirty-five and older (10 percent in 1979 to 28 percent in 1993), due in part to heavy drug use by this population in the 1960s and '70s. The decline among younger people is attributed to education, prevention, and fear of the drug-related sexually transmitted disease HIV.

While international cooperation has increased along with federal resources allocated to drug enforcement, primary responsibility for enforcement of street-level illicit drug use continues to rest with local police departments. Drug sweeps and crackdowns to reduce open-air drug markets in neighborhoods, problem-solving programs as a component of community policing, and prevention programs such as D.A.R.E. will continue to be implemented by city and county police agencies, supported by federal agencies and/or grants. The lack of resources, combined with a fragmented criminal justice system, places future odds in favor of drug merchants, according to some authorities.

The Anti–Drug Abuse Act of 1986 provided $230 million for enhanced drug enforcement by state and local law enforcement agencies. No study or other measure of effectiveness has authenticated that this infusion of funds had any significant effect on the illicit drug trade at the street (retail), wholesale, dealer, manufacturer, or kingpin level. One of the primary areas of need in coming years will be to assess the cost-effectiveness of antidrug enforcement efforts.

Some successes in reducing illicit drugs—such as international cooperation, more efficient use of interagency task forces, multilateral action against money laundering, and more stringent control of essential and precursor chemicals needed to manufacture illicit drugs—will continue into the twenty-first century. The failures will also continue.

Illicit drugs, including crops needed to produce them (coca, opium), will continue to be a financial boon to drug lords and corrupt officials in the developing nations. Hundreds of tons of cocaine and heroin will be transported into the United States, Europe, and Central Asia. Consumption of illicit drugs will increase in Latin America. Drug trafficking will expand dramatically in Eastern Europe, particularly in former Soviet states. Infusion of large amounts of money, primarily from the United States, will be the mainstay for the limited interdiction and reduction activities that occur in these countries.

Cocaine and its highly addictive derivative, crack, will remain a major high-use, high-demand product in the United States and Europe. Cocaine will remain a staple of illicit drug users, but recent decline in use among young people should continue.

Crack is a relatively new drug, first appearing on the market in the late 1980s. It is and will remain one of the fastest growing drugs in the United States. Crack is cheap. It gives a "high" that only lasts five to twenty minutes, meaning that addicts require frequent hits and will commit crimes necessary as needed to get the money they need to make a purchase. Crack usually produces a powerful chemical dependency within two weeks. A byproduct of the crack trade requiring attention well into the future is the birth of so-called "crack babies," a new population born with a dependency and other ill effects. Crack babies will require significant medical, educational, and other human service resources.

Approximately 1.3 million people—0.6 percent of the United States population—are cocaine users. Of this group, about 500,000 are considered frequent cocaine users, which means they have used it at least weekly for a period of one or more years. While the number of users remains stable, overall use of cocaine has declined steadily since 1985. This trend will continue.

Cocaine will continue to affect people of all races, ethnic groups, and socioeconomic classes. Fifty-nine percent of cocaine users are white, 23 percent are black, and 16 percent are Hispanic. A higher percentage of high school–educated people (1.3 percent) use cocaine than those with some college (0.7 percent) or a college degree (0.8 percent). These trends will continue.

To stem the volume of cocaine and other illicit drugs, increased emphasis will be placed on reducing cultivation. By 1990, every state in the United States participated in the cannabis-eradication program sponsored by the Drug Enforcement Agency, eliminating 29,000 cannabis plots and 7.3 million cultivated plants.

With most of the world's supply of coca limited to three countries (Peru, Colombia, and Bolivia), crop suppression is and will remain a potentially viable method for eradication. However, its success will continue to be hampered by political influence and corruption fostered by the drug cartels, and changing political and enforcement priorities. Due to ineffective enforcement by the government and a growing crop, Peru will remain the world's primary producer of coca well into the twenty-first century.

In past decades, most of the heroin used in the United States came from Southeast and Southwest Asia (Myanmar, Laos, Afghanistan) and Mexico. But the supply market is beginning to shift. Southeast and Southwest Asia produce white refined heroin while Mexico produces "black tar." Both of these sources will continue.

In the years ahead, an increasing volume of heroin will come from Colombia. Opium cultivation will increase in countries such as Pakistan (the fifth largest producer in the world) and Afghanistan (the second largest producer) due to limited eradication and prosecution efforts and banking regulations that allow money laundering to occur without restraint. Three-fourths of the world's opium supply is produced in an area known as the Golden Triangle (Thailand, Myanmar, Laos). Due to corruption in the government and military and direct ties between the military and growers, Myanmar will continue to grow opiates at increased rates with few, if any, constraints.

The number of heroin users in the United States is conservatively estimated at almost 2.5 million people, a fluctuating but continually growing number. Growth in the number of heroin users should continue at a steady rate well into the future, with increased reliance on smokable varieties rather than those taken through injection. Regardless of the variety, heroin will receive increased attention as its use and the subsequent number of heroin-related deaths grows.

The most common illicit drug is marijuana, used by three-fourths (77 percent) of all drug users. However, its use is in decline. Researchers debate whether the decline will continue. In 1993, 4.3 percent of the American population (approximately 9 million people) was using marijuana or hashish. This is a steady drop in use from 1985 when 9.3 percent of the population (approximately 17.8 million people) used marijuana or hashish. Despite the debate, stabilization or a small decline in the use of marijuana is expected to continue in the years ahead, with the exception of the school-age population, as new medical findings point to it being more dangerous.

There was a decline in the nonmedical use of psychotherapeutic drugs from 1985 to 1991. By 1992, the decline ceased and nonmedical use of sedatives, stimulants, and analgesics stabilized. Since then, there has been a slow increase in the illicit use of these drugs. The nonmedical use of tranquilizers has continued to decline. These trends are expected to change along with the demographics of the population.

As the population of the United States ages and the baby boomers experience some of the ailments associated with aging, illicit use and abuse of prescription medication will grow. Self-medication using legally obtained prescriptions will become more prevalent as will sharing and reselling of legally obtained medications. The market for illegally obtained prescription medications will also expand. Counterfeiting prescriptions will become a growing problem for both law enforcement and health organizations.

According to the National Household Survey on Drug Abuse, there have been no noteworthy changes in the use of hallucinogens (LSD, amphetamine variants, mescaline and peyote, and phencyclidine [PCP]) or inhalants (glue, paint, petroleum products) in recent years. As new hallucinogens and derivatives of known hallucinogens are found, there may be a wave of increased use. While the extent of use has changed little, the potency and dangers of the hallucinogens being used have increased. Health officials have estimated the potency of some forms of LSD to be ten times greater than the drug used in the late 1960s. Law enforcement has been mildly effective in supporting legislation to control ingredients used to manufacture some chemically based hallucinogens and will continue to pursue this avenue for prevention.

The correlation between illicit drugs (trafficking and use) and violence will continue into the next century. Studies of street use of illicit drugs by criminals now serving time in prison for both violent and nonviolent offenses support this. Among the approximately 400,000 men and women in local jails in the United States, 23 percent are incarcerated for drug-related offenses, representing an increase of 9 percent over a six year period.

Over half of the people incarcerated in local jails in the United States admitted to committing the offense for which they were incarcerated while under the influence of drugs, alcohol, or both. One in four convicted inmates admitted to using major drugs—heroin, cocaine, crack, LSD, or PCP—in the period prior to committing their crime.

Approximately 29 percent of jail inmates committed their crime while under the sole influence of alcohol, 15 percent under the influence of drugs and, 12 percent under the influence of both alcohol and drugs. There is no indication that the number of criminals who use drugs or the number of crimes committed by people while under the influence of drugs will decline.

Violence will continue to stem from disputes among rival street-level distributors, conflicts between buyers and sellers, domestic arguments in which one or both parties are influenced by drugs or alcohol, and confrontations between police and those involved in the drug trade. Third party injuries—including deaths to bystanders and other innocent people—will continue as low-level "franchise" dealers who deal their merchandise in neighborhoods rely on violence to resolve disputes.

As street gangs and pseudo gangs (youth modeling gang behavior) continue to emerge, there will be more franchising of the illicit drug trade. It will take its form in highly structured street markets and informal get-rich-quick schemes. Young people will assume a greater role in dealing drugs in neighborhoods, paying a percent of their profits to the person who gave them the franchise to deal. In turn, they may franchise part of their small operation to others.

This street-level franchising of the drug trade will perpetuate both wanton and planned violence. Street-level dealers will be well armed and willing to kill or maim anyone over a small amount of money or to protect his or her franchise. They will plague law enforcement agencies and their communities. In response, law enforcement agencies will expand the concept of drug market analysis to anticipate where and how the drug trade and its franchisees move, support tighter gun laws, and pursue mandatory sentences without parole for drug dealers who use weapons.

Estimates place annual spending on enforcement of the drug laws at $2–4.4 billion. The number of full-time law enforcement officers assigned to drug enforcement is small and will remain so. There are two primary reasons that more police resources will not be not assigned to address illicit drugs: declining local and federal government funds and the movement toward community policing.

As of 1990, over 3,200 law enforcement agencies in the United States operated special drug units, including 29 state police organizations. Approximately 6,000 local police officers, 3,500 sheriff's deputies, and 2,000 state police officers are assigned to drug units.

Local police will continue to focus the majority of drug enforcement efforts on street-level activities. Covert police operations designed to infiltrate cartels and large-scale drug operations drain resources, consume a great deal of time, and therefore will remain few in number.

Limited law enforcement resources combined with increased citizen fear about illicit drugs will cause an increased number of communities to turn to private or contractual security forces to provide basic protective services.

Asset forfeiture laws allow the government to seize cash, vehicles, houses, and other goods gained as a result of trading in illicit drugs. State and local laws dictate how seized assets may be used.

There has been significant debate about whether funds resulting from seized assets should be reallocated to police service or returned to the government's general fund to serve a multitude of uses. In recent years, the trend has been to allocate all or a larger portion of seized assets to law enforcement agencies, and this will continue.

A concern for the future is that the potential to seize assets may dictate how and where law enforcement agencies channel drug investigations and resources. This is of particular concern in jurisdictions in which police departments are in need of equipment and other items not available through their operating budget. Strict controls over allocation of investigative resources will be required to prevent emphasis on seizing assets as a primary thrust in conducting investigations into illicit drugs.

Drug losses in the workplace are measured in billions of dollars annually. On-the-job injuries, losses due to excessive sick leave (16 times higher than average for someone who is drug or alcohol dependent), violence, and other byproducts of drug use in the work place will continue. However, drug testing prior to and as part of employment has begun to have a positive effect. Employers will continue to screen out at-risk employees. Ultimately, drug testing of all candidates and random, select, or total testing of work forces will become commonplace.

There is a resurgence in the call for legalization and decriminalization of drugs and this will continue. The last significant movement toward legalization occurred in the late 1960s and early '70s. Current proponents discuss legalization as part of "harm reduction," the concept of supporting addicts so that they can function within the society; legalization of some drugs is required. Proponents of this approach cite less reliance on illegal drugs, more effective monitoring of addicts, reduced profits for illegal drug dealers, and less strain on the criminal justice system as benefits. The legalization and harm reduction movement will continue to gain respectability.

While theories have been put forward there has been little research to show that legalization and decriminalization of hard drugs will reduce deaths, injuries, and other crimes related to drug abuse. In Amsterdam, the Netherlands, legalization of marijuana has reduced some crimes and stabilized the number of hard drug users. According to polls, the majority of the public and elected officials in the United States do not favor legalization of drugs.

People often confuse calls for increased treatment, reduced incarceration, and rehabilitation with legalization. As traditional methods of enforcement and treatment fail to provide solutions to the problems caused by illicit drugs, additional funds will be channeled to research on legalization.

See also ALCOHOL; CRIME, NONVIOLENT; TOBACCO.

BIBLIOGRAPHY

CHAIKEN, MARCIA R. *Street Level Drug Enforcement: Examining the Issues.* Washington, DC: National Institute of Justice, U.S. Department of Justice, 1988.

International Narcotics Control Strategy Report. Washington, DC: Bureau of International Narcotics Measures, U.S. Department of State, 1993.

Drugs, Crime, and the Justice System. Washington, DC: Bureau of Justice Statistics, U.S. Department of Justice, 1992.

Sheldon F. Greenberg

Dying.

See DEATH AND DYING.

Dystopias

The concept of *dystopia* was apparently first used by English philosopher John Stuart Mill in the mid-nineteenth century. The word is formed by using the Greek root *dys-*, "with the notion of hard, bad, unlucky, etc.," to replace the first syllable in *utopia*. A synonym (also coined by Mill) is *cacotopia*. Since cacophony or dissonance are the opposites of euphony (good sound), so dystopia and cacotopia are the opposites of utopia (really *eu*-topia) meaning "good place."

Strictly defined, a dystopia is "a place or condition in which everything is as bad as possible."

Thus a dystopian vision of the future emphasizes the serious problems that may result from deliberate policies, indecision and indifference, or simply bad luck in humanity's attempts to manage its affairs.

In fiction, dystopian visions have most often taken the form of antiutopias—satirical or prophetic warnings against the proposed "improvement" of society by some political faction, class interest, technology, or other artifact. Perhaps the best known and most relentlessly bleak examples of political dystopias in fiction are Eugene Zamiatin's novel *We* (1924), and George Orwell's *Nineteen Eighty-Four* (1949).

But in the late twentieth century, dystopian visions in fiction have grown more complex, embracing such diverse ingredients as: nuclear war (Nevil Shute's *On the Beach*, 1957); overpopulation (John Brunner's *Stand on Zanzibar*, 1968); pollution (Philip Wylie's *The End of the Dream*, 1972), or cultural breakdown and subversion (Anthony Burgess's *A Clockwork Orange*, 1962).

Dystopian visions have dominated movies set in the future from the early silent classic *Metropolis* (1926) to contemporary adventure films like *Road Warrior* (1981), *Blade Runner* (1982), *The Terminator* (1984), or *Total Recall* (1990). Whether the hero triumphs or barely squeaks by, most future films leave viewers feeling that tomorrow's world is likely to be crowded, regimented, crumbling, and extremely violent. Even such relatively upbeat films as *2001: A Space Odyssey* (1968), or the fairy-tale-like *Star Wars* trilogy (1977–1983) dwell on the trials and dangers of a perilous existence.

On television, too, attempts to depict future society have generally emphasized dystopian visions. About the only "*eu*-topian" futures presented in the mass media have come from the television series *Star Trek* (1966-1969) and *Star Trek: The Next Generation* (1987-1994). But even here the belief in progress does not imply that perfection will ever be achieved.

The prevalence of dystopian future visions in fiction is not surprising. Conflict is the heart of fiction, and conflict in a perfect society is hard to find. Utopia may be a wonderful place to live in, but it often is dull to hear about or view secondhand.

Dystopian visions outside fiction presumably do not arise from any desire to entertain. True, bad news often sells better than good. But to be successful, a prophet needs to offer some hope. From the Old Testament Book of Jonah to the Club of Rome Report, *The Limits to Growth* (1972) and its 1992 sequel, *Beyond the Limits,* the point of issuing a serious warning has been to inspire timely counteraction and thereby to prevent, if possible, a dystopian vision from becoming reality. However pessimistic their predictions, most scientists and scholars who warn of impending disaster are really acting from antidystopian motives. If they did not believe there was some chance to avert disaster or shape a better future, they would not warn us.

In contrast to the numerous attempts made to establish utopian communities, there has probably never been a self-acknowledged dystopia in practice. Even most prison systems claim improvement as their goal. Just how bad must a society be to qualify as a dystopia? Also, who is to judge what is good and bad?

Aldous Huxley's novel *Brave New World* (1932) is often called a technological dystopia, but the society it describes holds more attractions for readers today (particularly young ones) than its author intended. The question arises: can dystopia and utopia exist simultaneously, depending on one's point of view?

The ancient city-state of Athens under Pericles may have seemed a near utopia to its wealthy and well-educated citizens, but the powerless and ignorant slaves whose labor made Athenian society possible experienced life very differently in that same time and place.

The value of fictional dystopias and of pessimistic warnings by scientists and scholars is to counteract the optimistic bias in human nature—the tendency to deny unwelcome truths that psychologists Margaret Matlin and David Stang identify in their book *The Pollyanna Principle* (1978). Whatever goals we set ourselves, careful planning and hard work are often needed to turn dreams into reality. Unless we face our fears, we risk becoming prematurely complacent and may fail to follow through on difficult or complex projects.

But the dystopian vision is also limiting and contains a special danger: it can poison our outlook on the present, or even prompt us to give up trying to do better. Anyone who sets out to create a believable utopia must be prepared to answer skeptics with reasoned arguments and facts. Yet we can build powerful dystopian visions in our own minds by piling up isolated pieces of bad news without ever questioning their source or relative importance in a global context.

Natural disasters, accidents, crime, war, disease, social injustice—all these and many other insults assault us daily through alarming headlines and "sound bites." Taken together, to some they convey a picture of a world where nothing works—in short, dystopia now. If we accept this image uncritically, it can make all future planning and risk-taking seem pointless.

Perhaps the secret to being a futurist lies in taking a critical view of both dystopian and utopian visions—balancing the need to prepare for the worst with a desire to achieve the best.

See also APOCALYPTIC FUTURES; CHANGE, OPTIMISTIC AND PESSIMISTIC PERSPECTIVES; POPULARIZED FUTURES; SCIENCE FICTION; UTOPIAS.

BIBLIOGRAPHY

AMIS, KINGSLEY. *New Maps of Hell: A Survey of Science Fiction.* New York: Harcourt, Brace, 1960.

CLARKE, I. F. *The Tale of the Future,* 3rd ed. London: The Library Association, 1979.

———. *Voices Prophesying War: Future Wars 1763–3749.* 2nd ed. New York: Oxford University Press, 1992. (See esp. pp. 149–153, and Chapter 6, "From the Flame Deluge to the Bad Time," pp. 165–217.)

STABLEFORD, BRIAN M. "Dystopias." In John Clute and Peter Nicholls, eds. *The Encyclopedia of Science Fiction.* 2nd ed. New York: St. Martin's Press, 1993, pp. 360–362.

Lane E. Jennings

E

Eastern Europe.

See EUROPE, CENTRAL AND EASTERN.

Eastern Religions.

See BUDDHISM; HINDUISM.

Economic Cycles: Models and Simulations

Unfavorable forces have been exerting growing pressures on the U.S. economy for decades. Government and private sector policies since 1960 have caused severe economic imbalances that may take years to correct. These imbalances include excess manufacturing capacity, rising corporate and personal debt, large trade imbalances, and chronic budget deficits.

Is such an array of forces merely a streak of bad luck or are they only multiple coincidences? Or are they connected below the surface to powerful forces of change? The best explanation may be found in a mode of behavior called the economic long-wave, popularly known as the Kondratieff Cycle, after the Russian economist, Nikolai Kondratieff.

The economic long-wave is controversial, both as to its cause and even as to its existence. Those who believe in its existence see it as a great rise and fall of economic activity, with peaks and val-leys some forty-five to sixty years apart. It is considered to be the cause of the great depressions of the 1830s, 1890s, and 1930s. The nature of the economic long-wave remains unclear in the absence of a theory on how it is generated. Instead, depressions have been attributed to accidents or mismanagement. For example, the Great Depression of the 1930s has been blamed on the mistaken policies of the Federal Reserve. Most economic theory is based on equilibrium, or steady-state, conditions that leave little room for long-term fluctuations between booms and depressions. However, at least one comprehensive and coherent theory is able to explain the economic long-wave. It is the Systems Dynamics National Model developed at the Sloan School of Management at MIT. The National Model is a computer-simulation model based on the policies followed in banks, industries, markets, and governments. The model is self-contained and operates without external inputs controlling its behavior. It generates short-term business cycles with peaks some three to ten years apart and economic long-waves with a major rise and fall in economic activity having peaks some fifty years apart.

A computer-simulation model is a theory of the behavior it creates. The structure of the model and the decision-making policies within it cause the resulting behavior. The model can be used to understand how production, investment, savings, construction, and credit can interact to produce, over many decades, great waves of excessive economic expansion and contraction.

Economic Cycles: Models and Simulations

The National Model provides a unique perspective from which to interpret the economy and understand real-world economic behavior. It sheds new light on the meaning of many puzzling and controversial things. For example, real interest rates (bank interest minus inflation) drop to low or negative values before a long-wave peak, as they did in the 1970s, and then quickly rise to high values after the peak, as they did in the early 1930s. Such interest behavior seems little affected by government policies but is deeply embedded in private sector borrowing and investment. Prices and wages rise to a maximum shortly after the peak of long-wave activity and fall during deflation after the peak, as they did sixty years ago. In the early part of a long-wave expansion money is borrowed to build factories; after the peak, depreciation cash flows and new borrowing are used for speculation in land, for corporate acquisitions, and for bidding up prices in the equities markets beyond the underlying business realities. Just before a long-wave peaks, waves of speculation move through the economy, with the run-up in agricultural land prices coming early, speculative peaks and collapses moving through other physical assets, and ending in the peak and fall of urban land prices and the Wall Street stock market.

The central long-wave driving force is overinvestment in physical capital. Construction of physical facilities increases employment and personal income, which, in turn, support more purchasing and the apparent need for still more production facilities. As the economy moves toward a peak and the need for more physical investment diminishes, government makes credit more freely available and introduces investment tax credits to sustain the boom, leading to still more excess physical investment. When prices begin to rise steeply during the late stages of an expansion, the inflation in price of physical assets encourages additional construction as a hedge against prices rising still higher. The demand for more physical capital requires expansion of the capital-producing sectors of the economy for which they also need more capital plant. This "self-ordering" process adds still more to pressures for expansion. The net result is to encourage continuation of construction well beyond actual need.

The long-wave affects the magnitude of business cycles. During long-wave expansion, a shortage of both physical plant and labor limits the overbuilding of inventories of goods and restrains excesses at top business cycles. Also, during the long-wave expansion there is an excess of consumer demand, which keeps the economy from sinking into a recession. However, conditions change after the expansion phase of the long-wave. During a long-wave peak and downturn, the short-term business cycle grows in both its up and down swings. On the up side, excess physical capacity and labor allow overexpansion of business-cycle recoveries, while on the down side, demand is no longer strong enough to avert deeper recessions.

The economic long-wave is a worldwide phenomenon. Trade and money flows lock the world economies together into about the same timing of long-wave rise and fall. There is excess production internationally. Every country is trying to solve its domestic economic weakness by exporting more than it imports, which is not possible. The total must balance.

Long-wave peaks and downturns are times of great international danger. World War I occurred at the peak of a long-wave and World War II in its valley. As internal economic and social conditions worsen, governments tend to divert the attention of their people by engaging in military adventures. A small fraction of the resources devoted to the military would help us to understand and counter the debilitating effects of business cycles. Powerful computer simulation models are available that can help governments and corporations manage complex economic and social problems.

See also CHANGE; ECONOMICS; FORECASTING METHODS; MACROECONOMICS; TREND INDICATORS.

BIBLIOGRAPHY

DEWEY, EDWARD R., and DAKIN, EDWIN F. *Cycles: The Science of Prediction.* New York: Henry Holt, 1949.

FORRESTER, JAY W. *Collected Papers of Jay Forrester.* Cambridge, MA: Wright-Allen Press, 1975.

_____. *Urban Dynamics.* Cambridge, MA: The MIT Press, 1960.

_____. *World Dynamics.* Cambridge, MA: Wright-Allen Press, 1971.

FRUMKIN, NORMAN. *Guide to Economic Indicators.* Armonk, NY: M. E. Sharpe, 1990.

GOLDSTEIN, JOSHUA S. *Long Cycles: Prosperity and War in the Modern Age.* New Haven, CT: Yale University Press, 1988.

MOORE, GEOFFREY H. *Leading Indicators for the 1990s.* Homewood, IL: Dow Jones-Irwin, 1990.

ROSS, MYRON H. *A Gale of Creative Destruction: The Coming Economic Boom, 1992–2020.* New York: Praeger; Westport, CT: Greenwood Press, 1989.

ROSTOW, W. W. *The Stages of Economic Growth.* Cambridge, MA: MIT Press, 1965.

SCHLESINGER, ARTHUR M., JR. *The Cycles of American History.* Boston: Houghton Mifflin, 1986.

SHUMAN, JAMES B., and ROSENAU, DAVID. *The Kondratieff Wave: The Future of America Until 1984 and Beyond.* New York: World Publishing/Times Mirror, 1972.

Jay W. Forrester

Economics

The early decades of the twenty-first century and the years leading up to it are likely to exhibit a new economic pattern. While retaining important features of the past, they will add new elements to produce historical uniqueness: long-term economic recovery and global growth, along with globalization, market orientation, more widespread economic development, altered industrial structures, and new cyclic manifestations.

Despite serious difficulties, in many ways this is an age of achievement. The promise awakened with the breakdown of the Berlin Wall will haltingly, gradually, but largely be fulfilled. European integration will continue to evolve and to encompass a growing number of countries and arrangements. The United States will further revitalize its economy and dramatically improve its international trade position. The world trading and finance systems will modernize with passage of the GATT agreements, expansion of IMF and World Bank activities, the North American Free Trade Agreement, and the evolution of other specialized and regional institutions.

Economic Development

Economic development will continue to spread to less developed countries, with growth increasingly rapid in large countries. The Latin American economies will undergo a broad resurgence after their long period of stagnation. The true emergence of a "Pacific century" will dawn with the rapid growth of China (see Figure 1) and the appearance of many new Asian tigers.

The United States will come out of its period of stagnation. Japan painfully will work off its speculative bubble. Europe will be forced to come to grips with rising global competition. Russia will primarily rely on markets despite traditions and nationalism that can slow or reverse progress.

Consumers and businesses, enlightened by vast information resources, will continue to grow in sophistication. Even as some advanced nations expand the role of government, reliance on markets will increase, especially in countries that depended on them least.

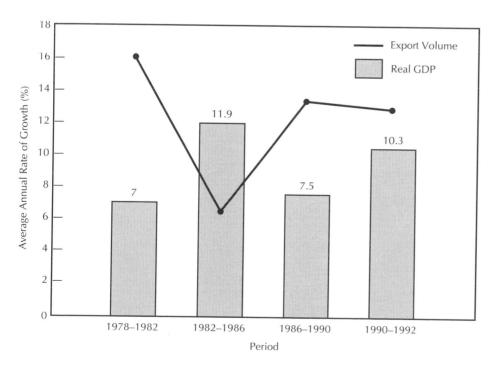

FIGURE 1.   China's gross domestic product (GDP). Source: International Monetary Fund. *World Economic Outlook,* May 1993, p. 53.

TABLE 1.   Projected World Rates of Growth of Real Gross Domestic Product

	1975–1984	1985–1994	1995–2014	Subperiod Projections	
				1995–2004	2005–2014
World	3.3%	2.9%	3.6%	3.7%	3.6%
Industrial Countries	2.5	2.5	2.8	2.9	2.7
United States	2.5	2.5	2.8	2.9	2.8
Canada	3.2	2.5	3.0	3.1	2.9
Japan	4.0	3.3	2.8	2.8	2.8
European Community	2.0	2.3	2.5	2.7	2.4
Developing Countries*	4.5	5.1	5.6	5.8	5.5
Asia†	6.3	7.4	7.0	7.2	6.7
Western Hemisphere	3.2	2.7	4.2	4.3	4.1
Countries in Transition‡	3.9	–3.3	6.0	7.0	5.5

  * Includes developing countries of Europe, the Middle East and Africa.

  ** Includes China.

  *** Former Soviet Union and Eastern Europe.

Source: Leveson Consulting projections; historical data from Council of Economic Advisors based on OECD.

Helping to propel advances (Table 1) will be the spread of economic development around the world and the resurgence of formerly communist nations. Long-term cyclic forces (i.e., upswings in cycles that last fifty to sixty years), particularly in technology, will play a major role in the global economic upswing. The Third World will be a rapidly growing source of demand for goods and capital.

Difficulties will come from heightened nationalism in many countries and regions. Local wars and revolutions, some of great international concern, will punctuate the economic landscape. More countries will break apart. Inflation may be rekindled, and protectionism will increase. Environmental actions, both beneficial and excessive, will dampen growth. Overall, however, progress will continue at a significantly more rapid pace than in the two decades following the 1973 oil shock. The United States will find that it is no longer alone at the top, but must share economic and political power with a growing number of countries and regions.

Long Economic Cycles Suggest Upswing

Herman KAHN (1979), the noted futurist, identified four major periods of the twentieth century in terms of global economic performance. The years of 1886–1913, which he called the First Good Era, were a time of rapid growth and social upheaval. The period of 1914–1947, the Bad Era, encompassed the Great Depression and two world wars. From 1948 to 1973, the world experienced a Second Good Era, a quarter century of growth more

rapid than in the 1886–1913 period. The Second Good Era was the first time that sustained economic growth reached beyond a set of no more than twenty countries. World economic development was on its way. Progress, however, came to an abrupt end with the oil shock and worldwide recession of 1973–1975, ushering in a new Era of Malaise, characterized by extensive economic readjustment on a global scale that Kahn felt was likely to extend until the year 2000. Kahn's analysis is consistent with the view that U.S. and world economic cycles tend to last for decades; however, it does not depend on any particular mechanism or insist that such cycles are necessarily automatically self-repeating.

Nicolai Kondratieff (1935) found cycles in prices and other phenomena, amplified by wars, and lasting an average of about fifty-four years. There have been many other long-cycle interpretations dealing with production (Kuznets, 1965), population and associated investment (Easterlin, 1968), capital investment, technology (Schumpeter, 1939; Freeman et al., 1982), natural resources, war, and debt (Eichengreen and Lindert, 1989).

Long-economic-cycle interpretations differ widely, but they put the latest cycle trough somewhere in the Era of Malaise, with an upswing gradually to follow.

Complexities and Challenges of Change

Europe in the early 1990s was mired in a persistent recession. Many countries, most notably Germany, experienced serious declines in competitiveness from many years of rapid wage increases, despite improvements in export sector productivity. Japan, too, faced high costs without the chance for immigration or better utilization of its female labor force to dampen wage gains, but some economic opening had begun.

The shift to capitalism in formerly communist countries came in response to: (1) decades of communism, socialism, bureaucracy, and central planning failing to cope with rapid change, (2) stultifying effects of centralized control on the human spirit, and (3) an information revolution that promoted interaction and global opportunities and advances that could be attained. Following GNP declines of as much as 50 percent, the nations of the former Soviet Union and Eastern Europe are positioned to grow by 6 percent per year or faster for at least a decade, provided they are more open to basic tenets of capitalism, including property rights and the rule of law.

The United States struggles with huge government budget deficits that are dangerous over the long run. Efforts to deal effectively with reducing them would lslow the economy for years. High debt levels continue among companies and households, and the overhang of real estate and financial problems will moderate only gradually. Ideas for dramatically raising investment and savings rates largely go unheeded.

The massive problem of rising health care costs, while particularly virulent in the United States, increasingly will be a worldwide problem as technology and expectations spread. The health care cost issue threatens to disrupt government and personal finances for generations. Containing medical costs threatens to slow national economic growth, impede innovation, and constrict job creation.

Job growth in the U.S. will be far slower than that of the period 1962–1989, when fifty million jobs were created amid a rapid influx of women and youth into the labor force. Cost-consciousness of business, advances in automation, global production shifts, increased employee benefits, and government regulation in health and other areas weaken job growth for the foreseeable future.

Wage rates in the middle of the income distribution were promoted by regulation and unionization in the 1950s and 1960s, and then eroded by large labor supplies and heightened international competition. The new emphasis on government policies toward equalizing the distribution of income can impose disincentives that work against income and job growth.

The New Social Cycle

Since 1988 the United States has shown increasing signs of going through an upswing in a social cycle described by Arthur Schlesinger, Jr. (1986, chapter 2) and others who discern thirty-year swings between liberalism and conservatism.

The new social cycle interacts with the long economic cycle. It is tempered by economic and budget limitations which deny the economic basis for costly programs. Stymied on the one front, reformers turn to issues such as insurance reform, health, abortion, employer mandates, political correctness, and the populism expressed in the 1994 congressional and local elections. There are some indications that this social cycle is becoming global in scope.

History Repeats Itself

The economic situation in the United States bears striking resemblance to conditions a hundred years ago. The depression of the 1870s was followed by two decades in which increases in output depended on rapid growth in the factors of production accompanied by little national productivity growth. There was a long period of deflation. Technology was rapidly creating new production processes and opening up markets, and exports grew rapidly. By the 1890s there was an acceleration of productivity growth. The first *Belle Epoque* also was a time of severe business cycles and great social change.

With time a new progress, the *Age of Achievement*, can emerge strongly in the 1990s and early years of the twenty-first century. During this era, developed countries will benefit significantly from progress in the developing world.

Monetary Policy Will Again Dominate Business Cycles

Inflationary pressures with strong world growth and increased vulnerability to debt and energy price shocks threaten economic stability. Business cycles are once again becoming dominated by periodic efforts to check the rise in inflation, with swings between monetary tightening and subsequent easing.

We normally would expect business cycles to be shorter and less sharp during a period of rapid economic growth and as we get farther into the upswing of a long economic cycle. However, high debt makes economies more sensitive to interest rates. Thus, the shape of what has been thought of as a four-year business cycle, while affected, may not change that much.

Economics

Corporate Restructuring

Shifts in interest rates, financial innovation, exchange rates, and the policy prompted widespread corporate restructuring. More fundamental stimuli to restructuring have been intensified international competition, slow growth and disinflation, rapid technological change, and the end of the Cold War. Major changes in the business mix have come along with mergers and acquisitions, strategic alliances, divestitures, and downsizing, both for firms and entire economic sectors.

Companies have gone back to basics, concentrating on businesses they best understand, and divesting peripheral subsidiaries and affiliates. Many start-up firms responded to new business conditions and technologies. Consequently, major consolidations occurred as firms moved from local and regional to national and international status, and as surviving winners in new industries emerged.

The Growth of Services, the Information Revolution, and the Superindustrial Society

The growth of services reflects shifting demands as societies develop. Growth of the service industries' share of output and employment has been dramatic (Fuchs, 1968). The United States has become a superindustrial society in which services are increasingly automated and efficient. The superindustrial society is an extension of the industrial revolution to the formerly lagging service sector combined with the integration of the information revolution into the entire economic and social fabric (Leveson, 1991). The superindustrial society paradigm describes a growing number of advanced nations.

Revitalization has been even more intense in manufacturing (e.g., Klier, 1993). Large improvements in productivity and growth contradict ideas about deindustrialization and decline. The expansion of service industries, the growth and role of information-based activities, and the presence of an informal economy are making it increasingly difficult to measure economic growth. Some have suggested that growth in the United States may be greater than officially reported.

Founding the Future

Prospect for two decades of higher growth in the United States and the world opens up exciting opportunities. Additional resources can be used to build future growth. However, even greater challenges lie beyond the next two decades. Their resolution also depends on the actions taken today.

Changes in the age distribution in the United States have been a spur to economic growth, but they can be expected to work in reverse when the baby boom generation retires (Social Security and Medicare Boards of Trustees, 1993). Retirement costs will impose huge, long-lasting, and negative effects on the economy after 2015, even if individuals, companies, and governments save enough. However, we do not save nearly enough. There is a high risk of a severe and extremely long-lasting depression when demographic realities clash with retirement and health care costs. Nations will be tested not only in terms of how well they do in the new global and technological environment, but also in terms of how well they prepare for the next generation. Discussions about deficits and responsibilities of generations are only a first step.

See also CAPITAL FORMATION; CHANGE, SCIENTIFIC AND TECHNOLOGICAL; ECONOMIC CYCLES: MODELS AND SIMULATIONS; INTERNATIONAL TRADE: SUSTAINING GROWTH; INVESTMENTS; MACROECONOMICS; POLITICAL CYCLES; TECHNOLOGICAL DETERMINISM; WORKFORCE REDISTRIBUTION.

BIBLIOGRAPHY

DRUCKER, PETER. *Managing for the Future: The 1990s and Beyond.* New York: Penguin Books, 1992.

EICHENGREEN, BARRY, and LINDERT, PETER H., eds. *The International Debt Crisis in Historical Perspective.* Cambridge, MA.: MIT Press, 1989.

FREEMAN, CHRISTOPHER; CLARK, JOHN; and SOETE, LUC. *Unemployment and Technical* Innovation.Westport, CT: Greenwood Press, 1982.

FUCHS, VICTOR R. *The Service Economy.* New York: National Bureau of Economic Research, 1968.

KAHN, HERMAN. *World Economic Development.* Boulder, CO: Westview Press, 1979.

KLIER, THOMAS H. "Lean Manufacturing: Understanding a New Manufacturing System." *Chicago Federal Letter* 67 (March 1993): 1–3.

KONDRATIEFF, NICOLAI D. "The Long Waves in Economic Life." *Review of Economics and Statistics* (November 1935): 105–115.

KUZNETS, SIMON. *Modern Economic Growth: Rate, Structure, and Spread.* New Haven: Yale University Press, 1965.

LEVESON, IRVING. *American Challenges: Business and Government in the World of* the 1990s. New York: Praeger Publishers, 1991.

PORTER, MICHAEL E. *The Competitive Advantage of Nations.* New York: The Free Press, 1990.

REICH, ROBERT. *Tales of a New America.* New York: Times Books, 1987.

SCHLESINGER, ARTHUR, JR. *The Cycles of History.* Boston: Houghton Mifflin, 1986.

SCHUMPETER, JOSEPH A. *Business Cycles.* New York: McGraw-Hill, 1939.

Social Security and Medicare Boards of Trustees. *Status of the Social* Security and Medicare Programs. Washington, DC: Boards of Trustees, 1993.

World Bank. *World Development Report.* Washington, DC, annual.

Irving Leveson

Economy, Informal.

See INFORMAL ECONOMY.

Educational Technologies

Of all society's institutions, schooling is among the least affected by advances in technology since the Industrial Revolution. If transported forward in time from 1850 to the present, a farmer or a banker, a factory worker or a business proprietor would find many technology-driven changes in his or her work role. In contrast, an instructor from more than a century ago would see little different in today's teaching methods. During the next several decades, however, advances in information technology could transform education as thoroughly as they have altered civilization's other human services.

Several trends in the evolution of information technology are driving its emerging impact on teaching, learning, and instructional management. Increases in the power of computers coupled with decreases in their size and cost are creating a world of "intelligent objects" with embedded microprocessors. Just as motors shrank in size and effectively "disappeared" during the Industrial Revolution, so computers are vanishing into our everyday context, supplementing physical reality with a virtual overlay of data.

Simultaneously, broad-band, wide-area telecommunications webs are interconnecting knowledge sources to create a universal information infrastructure that bridges people across time and distance. This twenty-first-century equivalent of the industrial economy's highways and railroads is emerging as a nervous system for global civilization. What do these technological trends mean for today's schools and universities?

For thousands of years, education has centered around two types of knowledge sources: the teacher lecturing and the library acting as an information extender, informing learners of experiences and ideas beyond those available firsthand. For the first time in history, information technologies have the potential to transform classrooms into reality amplifiers, in which students can synthesize knowledge from a mixture of real and simulated experiences. In such a setting, the role of the instructor shifts to that of guide and facilitator, helping students to find patterns of knowledge in a deluge of information, teaching learners how to avoid drowning in a surfeit of data.

Such an environment for learning is not a new concept in education. Learning by doing, individualized tutoring, mastering authentic skills in contexts similar to real-world settings, collaborative learning, interdisciplinary instruction, and tailoring teaching to multiple learning styles are pedagogical strategies that long predate educational devices. Sophisticated information technologies add richness, motivation, and magic to these kinds of learning experiences, as well as making them sustainable by providing extensive managerial scaffolding for teachers and administrators.

For example, today's educational television is in the process of transforming to multimedia that combine video, audio, text, images, and animations to represent knowledge in multiple ways. Over the next two decades, multimedia will in turn evolve into virtual reality, using computer actuated clothing to help immerse the learner's senses in elaborate simulated environments. Because virtual reality devices have numerous applications in business and entertainment, the demand for equipment generated by these large markets will drive prices down to a level affordable by schools and students.

As an illustration of what this might mean for education, imagine a biology student entering an immersive virtual laboratory environment that includes simulated molecules. The learner can pick up two molecules and attempt to fit them together, exploring docking sites. In addition to the interactive three-dimensional images in the head-mounted display, the gesture gloves on his hands press back to provide feedback to his sense of touch. Alternatively, the student can expand a molecule to the size of a large building and visually fly around inside it, examining the internal structure.

Another intriguing educational possibility is to create physical shapes and forms for intangible things, such as frameworks of information. The instructor could literally give a student a "piece of her mind," enabling the learner to examine patterns of interrelationships among ideas in a manner analogous to tracing bonds within a molecule. Data visualization techniques that enable mapping information from symbolic representations to geometric entities are empowering this type of simulated environment. Simultaneously, a new, nonlinear medium called "hypertext" is making the construction of rich knowledge webs much easier.

The intelligent objects mentioned earlier may appear in classrooms as smart manipulatives, providing individualized coaching for learners. As one illustration, imagine a child stacking blocks in order of size from biggest to smallest to form a tower. When he picks up a block whose size is out of sequence, it could say, "Not me," while the correct block lights up and says, "My turn."

More sophisticated "knowbots" (machine-based intelligent agents) can enhance education by making learners' information processing activities more efficient. For example, a knowbot can scan arriving electronic information for topics of particular interest to the student, selecting and filing material for future reading. Smart badges broadcasting the wearer's identity can link to smart bulletin boards that, when approached, alter their content to match that person's interests. Smart materials can unobtrusively notify a teacher when a learner seems to be unproductively floundering and appears to need help. Knowbots can even populate virtual environments with simulated personalities, allowing students to learn interpersonal skills through structured interactions with machine-based participants that model real-world situations involving teamwork.

What could block this vision from occurring? Some of the limits that may prevent this technology-intensive paradigm of teaching/learning from becoming society's dominant model for schooling are technical and economic. However, these constraints are steadily receding with price/performance improvements in information technology. The more profound barriers are psychological and political, reflecting people's unwillingness to change from familiar, if less effective, educational approaches.

Instruction based on collaborative, interdisciplinary learning about real world tasks necessitates major shifts in current schooling practices. Successful transformation to this model of teaching will require not only the widespread dissemination of sophisticated educational technologies, but also interdependent innovations in evaluation criteria and methods, class scheduling, staff development, authority structures, personnel incentives, student/teacher ratios, and the roles of parents and communities.

Technology can empower many of these shifts and can provide the managerial knowhow to make the new approach sustainable. However, the collective will to accomplish such an unprecedented change must come from a broad-based commitment to redesign education to match the requirements of the postindustrial, knowledge-based workplace. Whether this affirmation to transform will materialize over the next several decades is uncertain, but there is reason to be cautiously optimistic. If it does not, information technology will remain an ornament for the conventional classroom rather than a driving force for educational reform.

See also ARTIFICIAL INTELLIGENCE; INTERACTIVE ENTERTAINMENT; LIBRARIES; LIBRARIES: ELECTRONIC FORMATS.

BIBLIOGRAPHY

DEDE, CHRISTOPHER J. "The Future of Multimedia: Bridging to Virtual Worlds." *Educational Technology* 31 (May 1992): 54–60.

———. "Education in the Twenty-first Century." *Annals of the American Academy for Political and Social Science* 522 (July 1992): 104–115.

DEDE, CHRISTOPHER J., and PALUMBO, DAVID. "Implications of Hypermedia for Cognition and Communication." *Impact Assessment Bulletin* 9 (Summer 1991): 15–28.

WEISER, MARK. "The Computer for the Twenty-first Century." *Scientific American* 265/3 (September 1991): 94–105.

Christopher J. Dede

Elderly, Living Arrangements

It will be increasingly common for people to live into their eighties or even to become centenarians. As people plan for a longer senior period in their lives, new living arrangements will become essential.

Elderly people, a heterogeneous group, vary in needs, attitudes, and expectations about aging. Census surveys reveal that most older people prefer to retain the living arrangements established in young adulthood or middle age—owned or rented homes, often near children and relatives. Eighty percent of older persons have living children, and two-thirds live within a half hour of a child. Many will move from individual housing to alternatives that permit them to maintain their independence for as long as possible and that, when and if needed, offer graded levels of assisted living.

Demographics

The United States, long thought of as a youthful country, now has a larger proportion of middle-aged and older persons than ever in its history. Since 1980, older Americans increased by 22 percent compared with an increase of 8 percent in the under-sixty-five population. When the postwar baby-boom generation reaches age sixty-five between 2010 and 2030, the older population will experience its most rapid increase. The U.S. Census Bureau projects that by 2030, there will be sixty-six million persons older than sixty-five, or two-and-one-half times their number in 1980. Persons over sixty-five will constitute 13 percent of the population in the year 2000, and 22 percent by 2030.

The most senior segment of the older population is showing the largest change in absolute numbers. The over-eighty-five group was twenty-four times greater in 1990 than in 1900, and is projected to grow even more.

Although the data presented here are for the United States, virtually all other parts of the world are experiencing increases in the numbers of persons who live longer. In the more developed nations, the proportion of older persons is increasing faster than the birth rate.

Because men on average die at a younger age than women, older men in 1990 were about twice as likely to be married as older women (77 percent versus 42 percent), and half of older women were widows. In the same year, 5 percent of older persons had never married, and 5 percent were divorced. A pattern of survivors finding new partners to live with (if not always to marry) is likely.

Living Arrangements

Among persons over sixty-five, about 5 percent live in nursing homes. Nursing home residents include only 1 percent of sixty-five- to seventy-four-year-olds but 25 percent of persons over eighty-five. Of those in 1990. who are not institutionalized, the majority live in a family setting. Thirty-one percent live alone, and the vast preponderance of these are women.

Sandwich Generation Households

The fact that people are living longer and living in their own residences or with their adult children has spun a new phrase—"the sandwich genera-tion"—to describe the living situation of adults who are caring for both their children and their parents simultaneously. In some families the oldest generation cares for the youngest, but in others both the children and oldest adults use day-care services.

Elder Care

Because most older persons live by themselves or with family and prefer to remain in such living arrangements, it will be socially and economically desirable when assistance is needed to provide it through day care offered either within or outside of the home. Whereas in the past two decades, child care has been viewed as a pressing social-economic need, there will be a demand in the future for elder care to an extent similar to the past demand for child day care. Regular elder day care and respite care will especially be needed by multi-career households. Its very availability is likely to foster intergenerational arrangements, especially if it is offered at the same site as child care by the same provider. Even now, workplace-based elder care is becoming available and is likely to be preferable to more conventional church-based or community-based care for the same reasons that workplace-based child care is chosen, i.e., convenience, increased time with family, option of visiting with custodial person during the workday if necessary, and minimized transportation stress. It could be economically viable as an employment benefit or as a shared cost among employees.

Health-care suites—modular living units designed to fit inside an existing garage—have been proposed by Stephen Menke. They respect the preferences of the older person to remain with his or her family, allow access for the older person and caregiver, maintain privacy for older persons and the caregiver family, allow maintenance of social interactions, and are more economical than nursing-home placement.

Retirement Communities

During the past quarter century, retirement communities restricted to persons over age fifty or fifty-five, have sprung up throughout the Sun Belt and to a lesser extent in other regions. These communities provide security surveillance, houses or apartments designed for older persons, social centers, continuing-education programs, recreational facilities, and opportunities to become involved in governance.

Communities populated by persons who were in their fifties when they arrived could become depressed when large numbers of them become ill and die in their eighties. The future-oriented view aims at reserving amenities that appeal to older people and designing intergenerational and socioeconomic mixing to minimize overly homogeneous social clustering.

Communities designed for residential purposes often have restrictive zoning that precludes inclusion of elder-oriented commercial and social-support activities and services. It is imperative to have mixed zoning and tax and other economic advantages for businesses and services that locate in such communities so as to encourage commercial zones as well as age and socioeconomic integration.

Campus-Style Communities

Communities with individual and low-rise living units around green space and with some facilities for common use are patterned after school campuses and resort communities. Experience with campus-style communities is that access becomes increasingly difficult as people progress from being young-old to the oldest-old. Management and caregivers contend that campus-style communities are more costly and inefficient to service than compact high-rise or garden apartment designs that feature transport over smaller distances to get to central community social, dining, health, or commercial establishments.

Restricted Mobility Units

Many people remain mentally alert throughout their lives. Others maintain physical functioning in later years yet suffer from impaired cognitive functioning brought about by Alzheimer's disease and other dementias. Such people often are restless and may become irritable when confined. For these individuals, residential arrangements must provide for a more active lifestyle than is possible in traditional nursing-home settings. Technological devices that monitor an individual's whereabouts by telemetry can provide subjective freedom for such individuals and minimize endangerment from wandering off or failing to remember to eat or to check in with caregivers. Closed-circuit-television monitoring provides a more intrusive alternative.

Group Units

Group homes are being used increasingly to provide more homelike rather than institutional environments that still manage to meet the needs of those who require some surveillance or assistance. Group living allows members to do what they are able or prefer to do with the entire group and to benefit from what others are able to do for themselves and the others. For example, in a group situation, one member might manage household finances, another might do laundry, while another might cook or tend to each member's medications, appointments, or health routines.

Personal experience with group living in college and during one's single years may help make such arrangements more acceptable to older persons in the future. If so, they could go a long way toward providing economically feasible living arrangements, supplemented with home health care or other services as needed. They could also provide the social stimulation and companionship so often lacking among isolated elderly persons and, in the process, reduce some of the depression that accompanies a feeling of abandonment.

Progressive Care

Progressive or continuing-care communities represent an extension of retirement communities that acknowledge needs for increasingly intensive levels of assistance as persons become less independent. Continuing-care communities are able to provide the familiarity and continuity of social environment and caregiver services that enhance the quality of care and quality of life. Despite the extension of life that we have been observing, all people eventually die. Therefore, a full range of levels of caregiving services will become the norm in residential communities that are intentionally designed to serve older people. Hospices provide another option for persons who elect to die at home or in a homelike setting surrounded by family and friends.

Design Accommodation

The Americans for Disability Act of 1992 and a generation of socially conscious persons who are committed to access for persons with disabilities will result in increasing availability of living units designed to be "friendly" to the physically challenged. Design standards may change so that accessible housing will become the norm rather than the exception. Those without special needs will accommodate to altered dimensions in order to foster physical mobility for persons with special needs. Examples include wider door openings, adjustable cabinet heights and work-surface, and altered location of switches and knobs or handles that can be manipulated by people with problems in motor coordination or who are wheelchair-bound.

The simple reality that nursing-home care costs four to five times as much as home-based care, coupled with strong preferences for home-based care, will stimulate planners and designers as well as market forces to increase choices of types of living arrangements available to the diverse populations of older people.

See also AGING OF THE POPULATION; DISABLED PERSONS' RIGHTS; FAMILIES AND HOUSEHOLDS; HOUSEHOLD COMPOSITION; HOUSING: DEMOGRAPHIC AND LIFESTYLE IMPACTS; LONGEVITY; PUBLIC ASSISTANCE PROGRAMS: SOCIAL SECURITY.

BIBLIOGRAPHY

FOWLES, DONALD G., ed. *A Profile of Older Americans: 1991.* Washington, DC: U.S. Department of Health and Human Services/American Association of Retired Persons and the Administration on Aging, 1992.

TAEUBER, CYNTHIA M., ed. *Sixty-Five Plus in America.* Washington, DC: U.S. Government Printing Office, 1992.

U.S. Senate Special Committee on Aging, the American Association of Retired Persons, the Federal Council on the Aging, and the U.S. Administration on Aging. *Aging American: Trends and Projections, 1991.* DHHS Publication No. (FCoA) 91-28001. Washington, DC: U.S. Department of Health and Human Services, 1991.

Miriam Friedman Kelty

Electric Power

During the 1980s, U.S. electric utilities began changing from the vertically integrated monopolies that characterized the industry during the century since Thomas Edison established the first central generating station in New York City to a new era of competition with other energy suppliers. Companies that controlled the electric power market from generation through distribution to end users were forced to fight to retain existing customers and to win new markets.

Two federal laws passed by the Congress in 1978 were instrumental in moving electric utilities from protected markets and virtually guaranteed returns to the new world of free competition and increased efficiency, while continuing some regulation.

The Public Utility Regulatory Policies Act (PURPA) and the Powerplant and Industrial Fuel Use Act (FUA) provided the ground rules for entry of new players into the previously closed group of utilities, and set the stage for dramatic changes in electric generation sources.

PURPA encouraged the development of an entirely new class of electric power facilities: independent power projects (IPPs) and cogenerators, which utilize otherwise wasted heat or energy from industrial processes to generate power. These plants, usually smaller and able to be built more quickly than large centralized power plants, are often owned by nonutility companies. They mostly used natural gas rather than the coal and nuclear energy that still account for a majority of utility-owned power generation.

FUA provisions that discouraged use of natural gas for electric power generation were eliminated by amendment, and environmental priorities simultaneously increased demands for the use of natural gas, the cleanest fossil fuel. As a result, gas has become the fuel of choice for most new small and mid-sized generating units built, by utilities and independent firms.

For the larger generating units needed to service areas with extraordinary power needs, however, coal remains the most economical generating fuel.

Annual increases in electricity demand, which reached the 7 percent level in the early 1970s, declined to near zero in the aftermath of the 1973 Arab oil embargo. By the mid 1990s, yearly increases in power demand rebounded to the 5 percent range, and the surplus generating capacity prevalent for nearly two decades largely disappeared. Demand for electricity in traditional and new applications is likely to grow throughout the remainder of the 1990s and into the twenty-first century.

As needs for new generating capacity grow, utilities are turning toward two types of capacity enhancement that offer shorter lead times for construction and lower capital costs: purchases of power from nonutility generators, and construction of smaller generating units. The latter are usually natural gas-fired combustion turbines or combined-cycle units pairing a combustion turbine with a steam generator powered by the turbine's waste heat.

Utilities have also developed numerous "demand side management" techniques to encourage more efficient use of power. Time-of-day and seasonal pricing are designed to discourage power use at peak demand periods and to encourage customers to switch electricity use to times when overall demand is lower. This has the advantage of leveling demand peaks and valleys, making use of existing generating units more efficient, and reducing the total generating capacity needed.

Other programs pursued by some utilities offer subsidies to large users who install more energy-efficient equipment or reduce peak consumption. At the residential level, many utilities now offer rebates and other inducements for installation of peak-load controls on water heaters and other energy-intensive appliances. Other demand management programs include direct payments and offers of reduced rates to large electricity users for load-balancing actions. These incentives vary widely from state to state, as utility pricing policies are controlled by separate regulatory commissions in each state.

Construction of new power plants is now a last resort for many utilities. The high cost of new plants, the uncertainty of regulatory approval for recovery of constructions costs, the resistance of citizens to the location of new facilities in their vicinity (which has become known as the "Not In My Back Yard," or NIMBY problem), and increasingly stringent environmental regulations make demand controls and increased efficiency preferable to capacity enhancement.

Responding to environmental concerns, electric utilities moved toward burning cleaner fuels, such as natural gas, and sought acceptable ways to use conventional fuels, such as coal and oil. Coal gasification, fluidized bed combustion of coal, methods to clean coal before combustion, and "co-firing" of natural gas with coal have permitted utilities to continue using coal while observing pollutant emission limits imposed by the Clean Air Act.

Some potential environmental problems remain unresolved for electric utilities. Several methods are under development for disposal of spent fuel from nuclear reactors, but no single satisfactory method has been proven. Until the federal government decides how and where to store or dispose of radioactive waste products, nuclear utilities will continue to store spent fuel at reactor sites in protective containers.

Controversy continues over whether electromagnetic fields (EMFs) found close to electric transmission lines are harmful to the public. Scientific and academic studies have indicated that the effects of EMFs are minimal, but some environmentalists have suggested that any EMF impact is unacceptable. This question is unlikely to be resolved before the late 1990s.

Congress considered in 1993 imposing new taxes on all energy consumption, based on the British thermal unit (Btu) content of fuels and equivalent measurements for nuclear energy. The Btu-based tax, which would have significantly increased electric power costs, was voted down in favor of a levy on transportation fuels only. However, it may well resurface later in the decade for reconsideration. The United States has traditionally imposed lower taxes on energy than most other countries, and efforts to exploit this revenue source are likely to continue.

If global warming continues to be a significant environmental concern, moves toward taxation of utilities on the basis of carbon emissions, already debated during 1993 energy tax revisions, are likely to recur.

Several emerging trends will influence the electric utility industry during the latter part of the 1990s and the early years of the twenty-first century. One benchmark indicator is the extent to which a growing number of mergers can reduce inefficiencies in the national electric power supply system while avoiding antitrust objections.

Another looming question is whether the proliferation of IPPs and cogenerators during the late 1980s and early 1990s ultimately will be proven economical sources of generating capacity as reliable as utility-owned facilities. Major bond-rating agencies have questioned whether nonutility generators offer financial stability comparable to generating facilities constructed and operated by utilities. Bonds of some major utilities have been "downrated" as a result of increasing dependence on independent generators. In isolated instances, nonutility generators have been forced into bankruptcy. In such cases, utility customers of the failed generator usually have taken over the independent firm's operations, often at bargain prices compared to new construction by the utility.

Another challenge for electric utilities involves fostering the development of new "electrotechnologies" and other new uses for electric power. These innovative new uses may be offset by declines in power demand made possible by conservation efforts and the increased efficiency of electric appliances and equipment.

The single most promising area for expanded electrification is the transportation sector. State regulations pioneered in California mandating "zero-emission" vehicles impose requirements that only electric motors can meet. Already electric utilities have undertaken pilot programs to electrify commercial and industrial fleet vehicles in areas subject to intense air pollution, such as airports and densely populated urban areas. The same air quality concerns will enhance the attractiveness of electrified urban mass transit systems, including subways, light rail, and electric buses.

Business activity in the twenty-first century will inevitably depend ever more heavily on electronic data storage and retrieval, new forms of high-speed communications, and efficient manufacturing processes, all of which are dependent either largely or exclusively on electric power.

Utilities will meet these needs with a mix of traditional generating technologies and a variety of new methods now in the development and testing stages. Among those are fuel cells, which convert fuels directly into electricity without using a generating turbine; solar energy, which converts sunlight directly into electric current; wind power, which harnesses natural air currents; and geothermal energy, tapping underground heat to drive conventional turbines. None has yet proven economically viable on a commercial basis in large-scale applications, but all have proven technically feasible, and further technological advances and economies of scale are likely to make some widely available in the next century.

See also COAL; ENERGY; ENERGY, RENEWABLE SOURCES OF; NATURAL GAS; NUCLEAR POWER; NUCLEAR POWER: CON; PETROLEUM.

BIBLIOGRAPHY

CHASE, MILTON. *Electric Power: An Industry at the Crossroads.* Westport, CT: Greenwood/Praeger, 1988.

Electric Power Today: Problems and Potential. New York: American Society of Civil Engineers, 1979.

HILL, PHILLIP G. *Power Generation: Resources, Hazards, Technology, and Costs.* Cambridge, MA: MIT Press, 1977.

Paul M. Feine

Electronic Convergence

Convergence describes a number of phenomena relating to electronic technologies. It is used in the dictionary sense of "to come together," or "to unite in common interest or focus." There will be a continuing convergence of electronic components, manufactured products, the uses to which they are put, the form in which media are stored and transmitted, and the firms that manufacture the products or offer the services.

For most of the nineteenth and twentieth centuries, there were clear distinctions between vacuum tubes, wire, resistors, capacitors, relays, and switches. As tubes are replaced by transistors, and

transistors by microprocessor chips, there will be a continuing convergence of these components into single printed circuit boards and chips, and even organically grown devices.

In the early twentieth century there was a clear distinction between telegraph messages and telephonic voice messages, between print and radio, silent motion pictures and phonograph recordings. With the transformation of all media from distinct analog form into interchangeable digital bits and bytes, all messages, information, and entertainment converge into the same basic components that can be stored and transmitted, with perfect accuracy, through any medium.

By the time that television and computers came to be more widely available, in the mid-twentieth century, they were seen as two totally distinct technologies, manufactured by different firms, and serving different functions for the user. The same would be said for the telephone and cable television—the former providing voice communication between two persons, and the latter providing one-way delivery of entertainment program.

In the twenty-first century, television and computers will converge. The telephone, computer, and cable television networks will converge.

As computer screen technology improves, computer memory size and speed continue to increase, and networks have more broadband capacity, multimedia computers will become more common. They will be able to utilize both the evolving CD-ROM technology (and its successors) and wired and wireless network connections to receive the massive amounts of information necessary to create the images that were earlier called television—as well as graphics, audio only, and text files.

At the same time, increasing computational capacity will be built into television sets. Already used as a screen for the computers called video games, interactive television will involve computer-like control devices for selecting programming, making purchases, engaging in home banking, or sending other kinds of messages to and from what was earlier called a television screen.

Indeed, once telephones have screens, computers have telephones networked by the cable television companies, television sets are hooked up to the phone company, and computer networks are delivering music and video programming, these converged technologies will be virtually indistinguishable in function.

Transmission technologies will also be converging. The coaxial cable, or optic fiber, used by cable television companies—once it is designed as two-way, with some switching capability—will be able to provide voice telephone and data services. The optic fiber of the telephone company, and even its earlier twisted pair of copper wires (with compression technology), will be able to provide a video dial-tone service to carry entertainment television programming to screens normally connected to a computer, telephone, or television set—or provide a video image of the person on the other end of what was formerly a voice communication. Communications satellite technology will, as well, deliver to ever-smaller dishes the digital bits that will sort themselves out on the receiving end into voice conversations, entertainment television, faxes, printed newspapers, and data files.

Convergence will also be quite obvious and dramatic in mobile or personal wireless communications. As computers decrease in size (from mainframes, to mini, to micro, to desktop, to lugable, to laptop, to notebook, to palmtop, to wristwatch-size), they will became truly portable communications devices not only for voice, data, and faxes, but audio and video material as well. What is now thought of as a pager, notifying the owner of a received voice-phone call at another location, will add screens of sufficient size to receive text messages (not just buzz or provide a phone number or brief voice message). What began as mobile radios and mobile telephones, and subsequently evolved into voice cellular phones (actually radios) with more channels and range, will acquire screens and incorporate the ability to send and receive video and audio as well as voice, computer messages, and faxes. Personal data assistants will combine all of these functions into a single device. But all will have converged into alternatives with common features that (with low orbit and conventional, communications satellites) include global reach to personalized and global numbers (addresses).

In the broadest sense, there will also be a convergence of function between entertainment and education, or education and training. The functions of employees will converge with those of customers and suppliers (such as the bank teller's function being performed by the ATM [automated teller] machine user).

At the same time that there will be a convergence of technology, form, function, and utility, there will also be a convergence of the firms involved in providing these goods and services. Paging services will provide cellular and personal-data-assistant networks. Cellular phone companies will provide data and fax services. Computer software companies will incorporate the capacity for computers to send messages to pagers; and entertainment television, music, computer and video games, and telephone firms will enter each other's businesses.

Convergence of firms will occur in two other ways as well. There will be a growing merger movement that will produce fewer and fewer multimedia global conglomerates with ever-increasing market power and control. Such firms will combine ownership of the creative talent and intellectual property, the media manufacturing (books, newspapers, movies, videotape, computer games, and software), and distribution (over-the-air broadcasting, cable television, telephone, videotape rental) systems. In addition to this merger movement (in the sense of 100 percent ownership of subsidiaries providing vertical and horizontal integration), there will also be a growing tendency of such firms to acquire minority stakeholder investments in a wide variety of firms engaged in these converging businesses. Such investments will be both a hedge in an uncertain and rapidly changing economic environment and also an additional driving force toward corporate convergence.

Notwithstanding the movement to convergence, the mid-twentieth-century predictions of a single home computer, providing all computational functions, did not come about. With the rapidly decreasing cost and size of microprocessors they—like the electric motor technology before them—will continue to be designed, not for a single home device, but for very specific functions and implanted in a wide array of home products, from microwave ovens, furnace thermostats, videotape recorders, refrigerators, and washing machines to automobiles and other personal products used outside the home. Thus, the early twenty-first century will see, simultaneously, both the trend to convergence and the growing specialization and diversity in the use of computer and other electronic technologies.

See also BROADCASTING; COMMUNICATIONS; COMMUNICATIONS TECHNOLOGY; COMPUTER LINKAGE; DIGITAL COMMUNICATIONS; ELECTRONIC PUBLISHING; INFORMATION SOCIETY; INTERACTIVE ENTERTAINMENT; MEDIA LAB; NEWSPAPERS; NETWORKING; ON-LINE SERVICES; PHOTOGRAPHY; SATELLITE COMMUNICATIONS; TELECOMMUNICATIONS; TELEPHONES; TELEVISION.

BIBLIOGRAPHY

BAGDIKIAN, BEN H. *The Media Monopoly.* Boston, MA: Beacon Press, 1992.

HARASIM, LINDA M. *Global Networks: Computers and International Communication.* Cambridge, MA: MIT Press, 1993.

Nicholas Johnson

Electronic Publishing

So dramatically has the computer revolutionized publishing that words such as *magazine, newspaper,* and *book* are edging toward obsolescence. Tomorrow's publishers, with a few exceptions, will be purveyors of information. Unconstrained by any single delivery mode, a broad variety of text, music, and video will be merged into databases, accessible whenever and wherever the user chooses—an always open, universal-access "information library."

Production tools such as pasteboards, glue, and scissors have all but disappeared, replaced by software that fosters unprecedented experimentation, precision, and speed. The plunging prices of computers and their rapid proliferation have democratized publishing, giving millions of individuals and small businesses the means to create professional-quality newsletters, brochures, and advertisements.

In the years ahead, electronic publishing's focus will shift from the production of printed materials to the wireless and paperless dissemination of information. Using computers of all sizes and capacity—on the desktop or dashboard, in the pocket or backpack, even worn like a watch or a ring—people everywhere will have instant access to a vast array of information. What they do with that data—download, print, annotate, respond to, or transmit to colleagues in a dozen other countries—will be up to them. All information will be portable, pliable, and interactive.

The Multimedia News

In the early 1980s, the print media began experimenting with electronic distribution, prompted by surging competition, shrinking advertising revenues, and rising newsprint costs. Videotex, fax, and the floppy disk, for the most part, initially failed to attract subscribers. More user-friendly—and viable—were commercial on-line services and CD-ROM (compact disc, read-only memory). By the late 1990s, PC (personal computer) makers will equip most new personal computer models with built-in CD-ROM drives. By the dawn of the twenty-first century, all major newspaper and magazine publishers will offer interactive editions, integrating text, sound, still video, and animation. Added value will be the linchpin to electronic systems' financial success. Far more than digital displays of the printed page, the emerging media will provide an immediacy, vividness, and emotional impact unattainable in print.

Consumers tomorrow will be able to scan summaries or delve deeper into a topic, calling up a historical overview, video footage, text of a speech, charts and graphs, or related stories. By tapping a few keys, touching an icon, or speaking a command, users will respond to classified ads, buy stocks, book reservations, correspond with editors, or join electronic discussion groups. Prospective buyers can shop for advertised items, hear snippets of compact discs, or view homes.

The media will become increasingly customized—a coping response to the threat of information overload. A "personal index" will ferret out preferred topics. Formats will be as familiar (modeled on the *New York Times,* for instance) or as unique as the user wishes. For those too busy to read the news, the digitized voice of their choice will read it to them. Users will arrange news feeds for specified times of the day, such as financial data after the stock market closes.

Research and Education

Digital technologies bestow order on conducting research. The twentieth century will be the last in which students, taxpayers, engineers, reporters, or anyone else must plow through reams of paper, pore over tiny print, or even drive miles to the library—only to find that a reference is unavailable, outdated, stored away, or incomplete.

Enormous stores of information will exist in the form of portable multimedia libraries. In 1993, a CD-ROM could store 680 megabytes of data—the equivalent of 20 four-drawer file cabinets—on a single half-ounce disk. With the click of a button, users could watch an old newsreel, navigate any street in America, hear symphonic music, research a business, decipher a tax code, locate a Supreme Court decision, find an antidote, or "tour" the human anatomy.

In the years ahead, these options and many more will be available through centrally located electronic databases. Users will be able to print or download all or part of a text, image, recording, or video onto their own system. Downloading copyrighted material will require permission, licensing, or royalty payment.

Interactive multimedia will become a leading educational tool. Sound, animation, cross-referencing, and user-controlled pacing provide an engaging "flight simulator" approach to learning. Digital lessons in everything from ancient history to molecular physics will complement, and eventually replace, unwieldy, one-dimensional textbooks.

Publishers of do-it-yourself books and manufacturers of toy-model kits will supplant paper instructions with multimedia "toolkits."

Arts and Leisure

Emerging technologies will add new dimensions to the pursuit of pleasure. Books will become multimedia experiences enhanced with sideline "excursions"—supplementary music, narrative, video, related readings, or historical annotations. Readers will be able to modify text, edit photo spreads, and download passages. They will also alter contents and outcomes—solving mysteries alongside fictional detectives, for instance.

Armchair travelers will embark on electronic tours to hundreds of destinations. Publishers and travel agencies will team up to form on-line reservation and itinerary-planning services.

Marketing and Advertising

Electronic publishing will give marketers unprecedented reach, precision, and creativity—at lower expense than high-overhead stores or costly mailings. The growth of CD-ROM and completion of the data superhighway will prompt thousands of retailers to list their merchandise in "electronic catalogs." Compact, comprehensive, and easy to update, these will gain early favor among suppliers of high-volume products such as auto and appliance parts.

Multimedia marketing will tailor sales pitches to special-interest groups and even individuals. Consumers will be able to browse among products that interest them. They'll "try on" items in clothing catalogs by programming their computers with data such as height and weight. Software, music, book, and video catalogs will be encrypted so users can "sample" slivers of each item; to buy, they'll inexpensively download the items onto their systems.

Eventually, through virtual reality, shoppers will be able to simulate a product's taste, smell, or feel—such as a car's ride on a bumpy road, on a hot day.

Challenges

As new options proliferate, the major technological obstacle will be the development and implementation of industry-wide standards that let all formats and devices communicate with one another. Industry-government coalitions are working toward this goal.

The greatest challenge, of course, is consumer acceptance. Paper—user-friendly, portable, and generally serviceable—remains for most people the best way to deliver ideas and store information. Most likely, paper will never disappear, but will become just another media option, used for applications most suited to it. Its popularity will erode over time, however, as computers become more pervasive and portable, electronic data services become faster and easier to use, and the flood of paper creates a need for compressed storage.

See also COMMUNICATIONS: MEDIA LAW; COMPUTER LAWS; COMPUTER LINKAGE; COMPUTERS: OVERVIEW; COMPUTERS: SOFTWARE; INFORMATION TECHNOLOGY; INTELLECTUAL PROPERTY; INTERACTIVE ENTERTAINMENT; LIBRARIES; LIBRARIES: ELECTRONIC FORMATS; LITERATURE; MEDIA LAB; NEWSPAPERS; PRINTED WORD.

BIBLIOGRAPHY

"CD-ROM 101." *Forbes FYI*, Fall 1993.
"The Digital Press." *Forbes* (September 27, 1993).
"For Magazines, a Multimedia Wonderland." *The New York Times*, October 11, 1993.
GOODRUM, CHARLES A., and DALRYMPLE, HELEN. "The Computer and the Book." In *Books in Our Future*, ed. John Y. Cole. Washington, DC: Library of Congress, 1987.
"Publishers Deliver Reams of Data on CDs." *The Wall Street Journal*, February 22, 1993.
"The Tools of a New Art Form." *The New York Times*, September 19, 1993.

Leah Thayer

Elementary and Secondary Education

Public K–12 education costs too much and delivers too little. Educational achievement is down but spending is up. Over the past several decades education outlays have doubled or tripled—even while the number of students has shrunk—yet academic performance has declined. Spending increasing amounts of money ostensibly to improve education, only to have it grow worse, is a shortcoming that will pervade the politics of the late 1990s and beyond.

Education is one of the few endeavors where the solution for poor performance is to throw more money at it. There is no other major institution where consistent shortcoming—failure—is a perpetual excuse to increase funding. Rewarding failure sends the wrong message.

Education never has been so important. Complexity, an integral part of scientific progress that hallmarks the information era enterprise, demands more and better schooling. Knowledge, information, and education are the central resources of these times.

Less than optimal intellectual development squanders human resources and relegates the nation to second-rate accomplishment. Education provides the passport to personal advancement, increased earning ability, and is determinative of domestic well-being and international competitiveness. America may be losing the global economic race as much in the classroom as in factories and offices.

Total expenditures for public elementary and secondary schools have increased by leaps and bounds: $71.2 billion in 1960; to $144.2 billion in 1970; to $241.9 billion in 1993. Bluntly put, are we getting 3.4 times more?

A fairer evaluation expresses K–12 public education expenditures in constant 1990–1991 dollars: $201.3 billion in 1970, to $334.6 billion in 1991. On this basis, are we getting 1.7 times more?

Putting these changes in perspective, spending per pupil increased from $1,500 in 1955 to $4,500 in 1986. Are taxpayers getting 3.0 times as much for their money? Compared to other nations, spending during the early 1980s for public and private primary and secondary schools per pupil amounted to $3,843 in the United States; $2,470 in Germany; $2,438 in the United Kingdom; and $1,978 in Japan.

The baby boom echo and the influx of immigrants are expected to increase public K–12 school enrollment from 45 million in 1995 to 49.3 million by 2003. Adding further to overall education costs is the fact that kindergarten and preschooling begin at ever younger ages. By 1992, 55.7 percent of three- to five-year-old Americans attended preparatory schools (6.4 million of 11.5 million in that age group). Currently a privately financed choice, the trend in precursor countries in Scandinavia and Europe has been to provide it universally (free—or mostly so). In addition, growing numbers of American students are staying in school longer, pursuing postgraduate degrees. Starting school earlier and staying longer prolongs matriculation and increases public education costs.

General fund appropriations among the states for fiscal year 1994 averaged 41.9 percent for education (29.9 percent for grades K–12, 12 percent for higher education). When spending for a program category dominates all other government obligations, attention inevitably will be drawn to it. States provided 46.8 percent, local governments 46.3 percent, and the federal government 6.9 percent of all revenues for public K–12 school costs in 1993. Taxpayers, hard pressed by escalating costs of government, will demand a better accounting.

Illiteracy

The extent of illiteracy provides one measurement of the educational system. Literacy in the U.S. ranks a dismal forty-ninth among the 158 UN-member states! A 1993 Department of Education report estimated that 23 percent (40–44 million) Americans were illiterate (25 percent of them immigrants), and another 25.8 percent (50 million) were considered functionally illiterate. Augmented by increasing immigration, functional illiteracy in the United States is expected to grow from 60 million in 1990 to 90 million by 2000.

High School Dropouts

Another way to judge K–12 compulsory education is the number of pupils completing the curriculum. High school completion during the early 1990s was 82 percent for whites, 70 percent for African Americans, and 53 percent for Hispanics. In Japan, the number of dropouts, 12 percent, is less than half the U.S. rate of 25 percent. This poor showing is a goad to continuing improvement.

SAT Score Decline

SAT scores have dropped substantially and are not rebounding well from their low point. Verbal scores plunged from a postwar high of 479 in 1956 to 422 in 1991, and rose to 423 in 1994. Scores for mathematics dropped from a postwar high of 502 in 1963 to a low point of 466 in 1980, and then slowly rose to 479 in 1994. Until these performance levels improve, angered parents will keep the pressure on for education reform.

Intelligence Quotients

IQ scores among Asian and European youth also exceed those of U.S. counterparts. Japanese students score ten to fifteen points higher than do Americans. Asian immigrant students in the United States also outperform all other peers. In the 1988 International Assessment of Educational Programs testing science skills, American students scored last among nations that were tested. The U.S. student mean score of 474 was about one hundred points lower than the 568 score among Korean students. Part of this increase is attributed to strong will, determination, and dedication to a serious work ethic.

Other factors contributing to flagging education performance and intellectual accomplishment include more broken homes, more teenage mothers, more neglected or abused children, more abject poverty, and a deterioration of nurturing family environments. Some argue that a generation of Dr. Benjamin Spock-inspired permissiveness has contributed to the decline.

It also can be argued that overly zealous pursuit of egalitarianism contributed to educational decline. Providing the same thing for all comers— even though they are radically different and have vastly different needs—may not be wise. Mainlining dysfunctional students is counterproductive when it intrudes upon the rights of the many. A few violent, constantly noisy, interminably demanding underachievers who excessively intrude upon and impede regular class functioning shortchange the many.

Remedial Training

Remedial training provides another indication of schooling shortfall. Disgraceful numbers of entering college freshmen are required to take remedial ("bonehead") courses to bring them up to acceptable college standards. By the late 1980s, college remedial training was offered by 80 percent of all higher education institutions, and the percentage of entering freshmen taking remedial courses in 1984 was 25 percent in math, 21 percent in writing, and 16 percent in reading.

The workplace provides one final indicator of preparatory education shortcomings. Employers, finding workers ill-prepared to assume even rudimentary tasks, have increased on-the-job training. Spending levels, according to some estimates, rival public education costs. During 1990–1991, $221.6 billion went for public elementary/secondary education. A few years earlier (1989), it was estimated that business spent the equivalent of $328 billion for formal and on-the-job training.

Social Costs of Under-Education

One 1988 report estimated that an uneducated populace cost America at least $224 billion in crime, prison costs, welfare payments, incompetent job performance, and lost tax revenues. Today that economic cost might easily be doubled.

Classroom Time

Attendance in the classroom varies greatly from nation to nation. To begin with, the length of the school day of seven to eight hours in Japan compares to only six hours per day in the United States. The number of school days in attendance also differs drastically (1991): 243 days in Japan; 210 days in Germany; 192 days in the United Kingdom; and only 180 days in the United States. Summer vacations in the United States amount to twelve weeks, compared to seven weeks in Germany, and six weeks in Japan and the United Kingdom. Overall, the number of *years* of compulsory schooling completed provide an important perspective on educational achievement (1989): eleven years in the United States, ten years in Germany, and nine years in Japan. Despite the smaller number of classroom days that U.S. students receive, spending on American students was almost double that in Japan in 1985: $3,310 versus $1,805.

Teacher/Pupil Ratio

The educational establishment insisted over the years that the key to enhancing public education was a smaller teacher-pupil ratio. So the ratio was reduced. In 1960 the ratio stood at 25.8 to 1; it stood at 17.2 in 1991 and is projected to drop to 16.9 by 2004.

Questioning the teacher/pupil contention is the fact that Japan gets superior results with a much bigger classroom size. In Japan the number of students per teacher has been increasing, not decreasing. Despite the fact that Japanese classrooms are three to four times larger than in the United States, student achievement in Japan betters the United States. In 1987 there were forty-nine Japanese students for each teacher; by 1989 the ratio had been upped to sixty to one.

Core Curriculum

Shunning "basics" also contributes to lackluster educational performance. Students in other advanced postindustrial nations spend as much as twice the number of hours on basic core subjects compared to U.S. students. The situation is worsened, bit by bit, as single-issue zealots goad governments to impose ever-growing numbers of well-intentioned but nonessential courses on K–12 curricula, thereby displacing more fundamental courses. The highly regarded 1983 report *A Nation At Risk* urged a core curriculum for high schools consisting of four years of English; three years each of social studies, science, and math; two years of a foreign language, and one-half year of computer science. In 1982, only 2 percent of students satisfied this curriculum, but only 17 percent in 1990. The trend, hopefully, will continue.

Education Reform

For all the money that goes into it, American public K–12 education needs drastic reform. Something must be wrong somewhere. Instead of just running students "through the mill," much more attention must be focused on results.

Until the late 1980s, debate surrounding educational quality focused on inputs—spending levels, teacher/pupil ratios, teacher salaries, educational attainment of teachers, and so forth. Now the focus is on outcome, end results. Flagging SAT scores, comparatively lower IQ scores, and mounting illiteracy have been important catalysts. Suggestions that teachers assume an increasing responsibility for student outcomes—such as merit pay incentives—draw vitriolic response from educator unions.

Educational Bureaucracy

The proportion of nonteaching bureaucrats rose from about one-third of all full-time hires in 1960 to one-half in 1991. Public education, grades K–12, allocated full-time staff as follows:

Year	Classroom Teachers	Nonteaching Staff
1960	64.8%	35.2%
1992	55.2	44.8

A few years back one writer pointed out the disparity of overhead staff between public and private schools in New York City, where Catholic schools were administered by thirty-five bureaucrats and public schools by 20,000 nonclassroom bureaucrats. The writer pointed out that New York City education bureaucrats were more numerous than education administrators for the entire nation of France! The conclusion would seem to call for fewer frills and featherbedding, and more basics and teachers in the classroom.

High and increasing levels of education spending coupled with lesser levels of educational achievement, deplorable illiteracy/functional illiteracy rates, and lackluster SAT test scores will drive education reforms. Over the long term, the emphasis

will be less upon inputs/quantitative indicators and more upon outcomes/qualitative results. All told, education spending increasingly will have to prove itself. Results will count. Excellence in education is imperative to national survival.

See also ADULT LEARNING; EDUCATIONAL TECHNOLOGIES; HIGHER EDUCATION; LIBERAL ARTS.

BIBLIOGRAPHY

FORBES, MALCOLM S., JR. "Quality Time." *Forbes* (September 12, 1994).

KELLY, DENNIS. "Core Curriculum Toughening Up U.S. Students." *USA Today*, June 21, 1994.

PETERSON, JOHN E. "Why Schools Are Tumbling Down: The Fiscal Story." *Governing* (April 1994).

SAMUELSON, ROBERT J. "Merchants of Mediocrity: The College Board Nationalizes Grade Inflation." *Newsweek* (August 1, 1994).

SHANKER, A. "Where We Stand on the Rush to Inclusion." *Vital Speeches of the Day* (March 1, 1994).

Graham T. T. Molitor

End of the World.
See APOCALYPTIC FUTURE.

Energy

The modern energy economy was created virtually out of whole cloth in the short period between 1890 and 1910, transforming many American and European cities. On the streets, horses were replaced by automobiles, while candles and gaslights were supplanted by electric lights. Such transitions are usually driven by an array of social and economic forces, coupled with the availability of technologies that can be applied in new ways.

If these are the conditions needed for rapid change, then the final decade of the twentieth century and the first decade of the next may be as revolutionary as those of one hundred years ago. Indeed, rapid change of many kinds is already taking place, though to see it, one has to delve beneath the broad energy statistics that preoccupy most analytical efforts.

As we consider the future of the energy economy, we may learn more by studying the electronic revolution of the late twentieth century than by applying the geopolitical and geophysical framework of conventional energy analysis. Rapidly evolving technologies, many of them incorporating the latest electronics as a way of raising efficiencies and lowering costs, are now on the verge of commercializations. A variety of stronger, lighter, more versatile synthetic materials will also be applied to everything from wind turbine blades to car frames.

Such technologies are leading to a new generation of relatively small energy-conversion devices that can be mass-produced in factories—a stark contrast to the huge oil refineries and power plants that dominate the energy economy of the late twentieth century. The economies of mass manufacturing will quickly bring down the cost of the new technologies, and ongoing innovations will be rapidly incorporated in new products, in much the way that today's consumer electronics industry operates.

Efficient use of energy is the cornerstone of a more sustainable energy system. Several studies show that it should be possible to double the current level of global energy productivity—the amount of energy needed to produce a dollar of gross world product—over the next four to five decades. From light bulbs to refrigerators, many new energy-using technologies are at least 75 percent more efficient than the current standard. Even in the power industry, which has sought to improve the efficiency of its equipment for a century, the power plants that opened in the early 1990s are 50 percent more efficient than a decade earlier.

Natural gas is the second key to a sustainable world energy system. Gas is far more abundant than oil and much less polluting as well. Natural gas also lends itself to efficient applications, including potentially widespread cogeneration of electricity and heat in factories and buildings. Natural gas resources appear adequate to permit a tripling in global production by 2025. Although such estimates are somewhat speculative, our relatively conservative figures suggest that world gas consumption would peak by about 2030, fall sharply after 2050, and be largely phased out by the end of the twenty-first century.

The third step to a sustainable future is the development of carbon-free ambient energy sources such as wind and solar power. Technologies for harnessing these energy sources are advancing rapidly, and together they can provide three times as much primary energy in 2025 as nuclear power now does.

Some 20,000 wind turbines are already spread across the mountain passes of California and the northern plains of Europe, and the market is expanding at a rate of 20 percent annually. The most extensive wind development in the mid-1990s is occurring in Germany and India. The new generation wind turbines are made of high-tech synthetic materials and incorporate the latest in variable electric drives and electronic controls. As a result, wind power costs have declined by a factor of four since the early 1980s, reaching as low as four to five cents per kilowatt hour for some commercial projects in the United States—which is less than the cost of many coal-fired projects.

The cost of photovoltaic solar cells has fallen even faster—from $20 per watt in 1980 (in 1994 dollars) to $4 per watt in 1994. This has made solar electricity economical in many areas where conventional electric lines are not present. By the end of 1994, some 250,000 Third World households were using solar power. India alone accounted for 12 percent of the world market in solar cells. Even bigger projects are coming. In early 1995, Enron Corporation announced plans for several hundred megawatts of grid-connected solar power plants in India, Pakistan, and China—deals which, by themselves, could easily triple the world production of solar cells.

Solar and wind energy are far more abundant than any of the fossil energy resources in use today, and declining costs are expected to make them fully competitive in the near future. Three states alone—the Dakotas and Texas—have enough wind to provide all U.S. electricity, while a tiny fraction of the southwestern deserts could supply all the country's transportation fuel needs via solar-derived hydrogen. By 2025, renewables could displace oil as the world's second-largest energy source, providing more than half the world's primary energy, with the share rising as high as 90 percent by 2100.

The 1990s are marked by another unanticipated technological development: viable alternatives to the gasoline-powered internal-combustion engine. Lightweight hybrid-electric vehicles made of synthetic materials and run on devices such as gas turbines, fuel cells, and flywheels are about to emerge from engineering labs around the world. With fuel economies that are three to four times the current average and emissions of air pollutants that may be a mere 5 percent of currently permitted levels, these revolutionary new cars, trucks, and buses appear likely to enter the commercial market by the end of this decade, ushering in an era when automobiles can be refueled at home from the local electric or gas system.

Although an energy system this different may be hard to envision, there are no foreseen technical or economic barriers to such a transition. The projected annual growth in new renewable-energy technologies—as high as 20 to 30 percent—is actually slower than the growth rates of nuclear power in the 1960s and '70s, or of personal computers in the 1980s. By 2025, the renewable-energy industry could have annual revenues as high as $200 billion (in 1993 dollars)—twice the 1993 revenues of Exxon, the world's largest oil company.

As natural gas supplies level off or are voluntarily kept in the ground to reduce carbon emissions, a substitute will be needed in the decades ahead. The fuel most likely to fill this niche is hydrogen, the simplest of the chemical fuels—in essence a hydrocarbon without the carbon. Hydrogen is the lightest of the elements as well as the most abundant. When combined with oxygen to produce heat or electricity, the main emission product is water. Although hydrogen has a reputation as a dangerous fuel, this is largely a myth. If properly handled, hydrogen will probably be safer than the major fuels in use today.

Electricity can be used to split water molecules through electrolysis, a century-old technology already used commercially. Although it is relatively expensive today, costs would come down as the technology is scaled up. As far as water is concerned, the requirements are relatively modest. In fact, all current U.S. energy needs could be derived from just 1 percent of today's U.S. water supply. Even in most arid regions, water requirements will not be a major constraint on hydrogen production. The water needed by a photovoltaic power plant producing hydrogen is equivalent to just 2.7 centimeters of rain annually over an area the size of the plant. And in the long run, hydrogen may be derived from seawater.

As large wind farms and solar ranches appear in sunny and windy reaches of the world, they can generate electricity that is fed into the grid when power demand is high and be used to produce hydrogen when it is not. Additional hydrogen could be produced in individual homes and commercial buildings using rooftop solar cells. Hydrogen can either be stored in a basement tank or piped into a local hydrogen-distribution system.

Hydrogen could gradually fill the niches occupied by oil and natural gas today—including home and water heating, cooking, industrial heat, and transportation. Hydrogen-powered cars have already been developed by several companies, with the main future challenges being an improved storage tank and an inexpensive fuel cell engine. In addition, a new technology called a fuel cell—first used widely in the U.S. space program—can convert hydrogen to electricity via an electrochemical process, at an efficiency as high as 60–80 percent. Fuel cells could be used to provide electricity in buildings and also to power hybrid-electric cars. Several companies are already developing commercial fuel cells.

Eventually much of the world's hydrogen is likely to be carried to where it is needed through pipelines similar to those now used to carry natural gas. This is more efficient than the oil or electricity distribution systems in place today. In the early stages of the transition to hydrogen, the new energy gas can be added to natural gas pipelines in concentrations up to 15 percent—a clean-burning mixture known as hythane. Hydrogen could also be produced from natural gas, either in central facilities or gas stations. Later, engineers believe that it will not be too difficult to modify today's natural gas pipelines so that they will be able to transport hydrogen.

Over time, solar- and wind-derived hydrogen could become the foundation of a new global energy economy. All major population centers are within reach of sunny and wind-rich areas. The Great Plains of North America, for instance, could supply much of Canada and the United States with both electricity or hydrogen fuel. The pipelines that now link the gas fields of Texas and Oklahoma with the Midwest and Northeast could carry hydrogen to these industrial regions. Although renewable energy sources are more abundant in some areas than others, they are far less concentrated than oil, with two-thirds of proven world petroleum reserves being in the Persian Gulf.

For Europe, solar power plants could be built in southern Spain or North Africa. From the latter, hydrogen could be transported into Europe along existing gas pipeline routes. To the east, Kazakhstan and other semiarid Asian republics could supply energy to Russia and central Europe. For India, the sun-drenched Thar Desert is within easy range of the rest of the country. For the more than 1 billion people of China, hydrogen could be produced in the country's vast central and northwestern regions and shipped to the population centers on the coast.

How quickly might the transition unfold? When oil prices first soared in the 1970s, energy markets responded slowly at first, but then quickened. Government responses were initially misguided, but gradually the more foolish projects were abandoned, and better policies emerged. The strongest pressure to move away from fossil fuels is environmental—particularly the greenhouse effect of warming that is occurring as a result of fossil-fuel combustion. In order to stabilize concentrations of carbon dioxide in the atmosphere, we will have to move away from fossil fuels and toward the array of available, new energy technologies. The world has been laying the policy and technical groundwork for such a system for two decades; with sufficient political pressure, it could accelerate the process dramatically.

History suggests that major energy transitions—from wood to coal or coal to oil—take time to gather momentum. But once economic and political resistance is overcome and the new technologies prove themselves, things can unfold rapidly. If the past is any guide, unexpected events, new scientific developments, and technologies not yet on the drawing board could push the pace of change even faster.

This is how today's energy systems emerged at the end of the nineteenth century, and it may be the way a sustainable energy economy begins to emerge at the end of the twentieth century. If so, the coming energy revolution will have profound effects on the way all of us work and live, as well as on the health of the global environment on which we depend.

See also COAL; ELECTRIC POWER; ENERGY CONSERVATION; ENERGY, RENEWABLE SOURCES OF; NATURAL GAS; NUCLEAR POWER; NUCLEAR POWER: CON; PETROLEUM.

BIBLIOGRAPHY

FLAVIN, CHRISTOPHER, and LENSSEN, NICHOLAS. *Power Surge: Guide to the Energy Revolution.* New York: Norton, 1994.

HOFFMANN, PETER. *The Forever Fuel: The Story of Hydrogen.* Boulder, CO: Westview Press, 1981.

OGDEN, JOAN M., and WILLIAMS, ROBERT H. *Solar Hydrogen: Moving Beyond Fossil Fuels.* Washington, DC: World Resources Institute, 1989.

World Energy Council. *Energy for Tomorrow's World.* New York: St. Martin's Press, 1993.

Christopher Flavin

Energy, Renewable Sources of

"Renewable" energy sources are those sources that are not running out or limited by their total quantity, as with the remaining reserves of petroleum, coal, or natural gas. Renewable sources of energy are limited rather by the rate at which they are available or can be exploited. For example, the total amount of sunlight that shines on any given surface is limited, but it does not deplete or is not reduced in any meaningful sense through its use or "consumption." The sun is expected to keep shining for another nine to ten billion years—eight orders of magnitude longer than petroleum's expected life span.

Among the renewable energy sources are all forms of solar power, plus power derived from the wind, rivers, heat from the Earth (geothermal), waves, tides, and biomass that is either burned or turned into fuels such as ethanol. Hydrogen, the most common element in the universe, can also be used as a renewable fuel. In addition, one of the largest sources of energy today, conservation or increasing the efficiency of our current uses of energy, does not involve tapping any one source of energy but rather utilizes new technological advances. In many places in the industrial world, but especially the United States, this is the least costly and the largest energy source.

Renewable energy sources play an important role in meeting the world's energy demands, although they are not in as widespread commercial use throughout the world as the nonrenewable (depleting) energy sources. In the early 1990s, renewable energy sources supplied 8.5 percent of the world's total *commercial* energy needs. The total contribution of renewable energy to meeting the world's energy needs is much larger but much renewable energy is not bought and sold in the global marketplace. For example, most firewood that is consumed in the developing world is gathered and used by families, and it never enters the market. In today's market, the renewable energy sources are often perceived as more expensive than the main commercial energy sources. Part of the reason for this is that renewable energy sources have traditionally not been subsidized by government research, tax breaks, insurance, and other means to the extent of the nonrenewable energy sources.

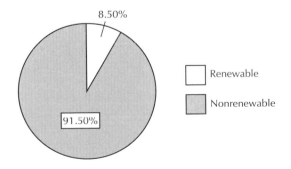

FIGURE 1.   World energy production.

That renewable energy is not commercially bought and sold as much or as often as the more "traditional" energy sources of coal, oil, and natural gas does not mean that these energy sources do not play a large role in the global economy or in the everyday lives of billions of people on this planet. Actually, solar energy supplies over 99 percent of all the energy used in the world—it just doesn't get counted in our economic accounting system. When we turn on our furnaces in the winter, we think we are heating our homes with oil or natural gas. In fact, we would be heating our homes from a −240° centigrade temperature if solar energy were not heating our planet to begin with.

Because the primary energy sources that society relies on are depleting, the price for these energy sources will increase. Eventually, with a growing world economy, the depleting energy sources will become so expensive that the conversion to renewable energy sources will become a natural process. As economic competitors seek the least-cost way of producing quality products in a global economy, the lower-cost renewable energy sources of today will become the mainstream energy sources of tomorrow. Some analysts point out that this conversion to renewable energy could happen even sooner as technological progress in this area is advancing much faster than in the nonrenewable area.

For example, electricity produced from wind energy is already competitive in many parts of the world with coal, oil, natural gas, and nuclear powered electrical plants. Solar power is also in use throughout the world as the least-cost option for producing heat and hot water. In remote regions away from the electric grid, solar-powered photovoltaic cells are also the least-cost option for producing electricity.

Hydro, or river, power has been in use for millennia, providing transportation and the power to mill grain, cut lumber, and more recently to produce electricity. The most developed of the renewable energy sources, hydroelectric power provides 18.6 percent of the world's total electric power cleanly and efficiently. Hydro power does not produce carbon to add to the Earth's warming nor does it produce any other air pollutants. However, hydro power does cause changes in ecological cycles and loss of land. The total global hydro power potential from large hydro sites is about equal to the world's current consumption of energy in all forms. Small-scale hydro power is a proven technology and can add significantly to meeting the world's need for clean energy without damaging the surrounding ecosystems.

Biomass is solar energy that has been captured and stored by nature through photosynthesis. It currently provides a significant portion of the world's energy supply: 5.7 percent of the world's total commercial energy use, primarily in the developing world. Biomass is used for energy in the form of wood, dung, crop residues, and crops that are turned into fuel alcohol, ethanol, or methane.

Geothermal energy is the heat from inside the Earth trapped at shallow depths as dry steam, wet steam, brine, hot dry rock, pressurized liquid, or magma. It has been in use since the early 1900s producing electricity. Geothermal energy currently supplies less than 1 percent of the world's electricity needs. Tapping just the molten rock in the Earth's upper ten kilometers could provide a virtually unlimited energy source capable of powering the entire world. Like other renewable energy sources, the technology that would make this an affordable option has not been fully developed.

One of the most promising renewable energy sources is hydrogen. Made from water, it could supply clean, abundant fuel for automobiles, trains, airplanes, industry, heating, and even electricity in the form of hydrogen-powered fuel cells. When "consumed," or used, hydrogen produces water (H_2O) and heat. As such, it is the cleanest of all fuels and could play a significant role in lessening the impact of global warming. It is also an ideal medium for storing other renewable energy sources such as solar and wind power; first, the solar or wind energy is converted into electricity, and then through electrolysis hydrogen is produced from water. Hydrogen has a few other advantages: Many existing energy converters can readily switch to using hydrogen fuel, and it has the greatest energy per unit mass of any chemical fuel (two and a half times the energy per unit weight of gasoline). Its major disadvantages are

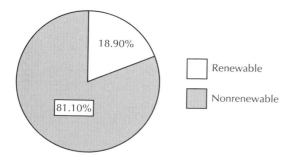

18.90%

81.10%

Renewable

Nonrenewable

FIGURE 2.   World electricity production.

that it is still too expensive to produce to compete effectively with conventional fuels, and it is so light that it is not concentrated enough to store easily.

See also ELECTRIC POWER; ENERGY; ENERGY CONSERVATION; MOTOR VEHICLES, ALTERNATIVELY POWERED; NUCLEAR POWER.

BIBLIOGRAPHY

Energy Statistical Yearbook. New York: United Nations, 1991.

JOHANNSON, THOMAS D., et al. *Renewable Energy: Sources for Fuel and Electricity.* Washington, DC: Island Press, 1993.

Medard Gabel

Energy Conservation

People do not want energy for its own sake. Rather they want the "end-uses," the services, that energy provides: hot showers and cold beer, visibility and mobility, baked bread and smelted alumina. *End-use efficiency* is defined as how much service is delivered per unit of delivered energy used. Raising that efficiency is the most important, easiest, fastest, cleanest, cheapest, and most profitable way to provide more and better energy services. With the possible exception of new doubled-efficiency electric generators, it is also by far the greatest opportunity to wring more work out of each unit of primary energy such as coal, natural gas, or crude oil.

End-use efficiency does more with less, providing unchanged or improved services with less energy and more brains. (One-third of Americans think *energy conservation* means doing less, worse, or without—privation, discomfort, and curtailment—so we avoid that ambiguous term.) During 1979 to 1986, Americans' energy savings delivered seven times as much new energy as all net increases in energy supply, just over half of which were renewable. By 1994, the United States was saving about $160 billion per year compared with the energy it would have had to buy if it were still as inefficient as in 1973. Billions of tiny choices by tens of millions of individuals—insulation, caulk guns, duct tape, plugged steam leaks, and slightly more efficient cars—were providing a new national energy "source" two-fifths bigger than the domestic oil industry.

Almost all of these savings came not from making power plants and refineries more efficient, or from reducing distribution losses in pipelines, tankers, and power lines, but from more efficient end-use. Perhaps the most spectacular example was in cars and light trucks. From 1973 to 1986, government standards were largely or wholly responsible for doubling new cars' average efficiency to twenty-nine miles per gallon (mpg). Largely in consequence, oil imports fell from 46 percent of U.S. consumption in 1977 to 28 percent five years later. By 1985, oil imports from the Persian Gulf were only one-tenth of their 1979 peak.

End-use efficiency requires consistent effort if its benefits are not to be swallowed up by growing population and affluence. Thus after 1985, oil imports rebounded as car efficiency stagnated: more than half of the mpg improvements went into making cars accelerate faster. Such choices have consequences. President Reagan's 1986 rollback of light-vehicle efficiency standards promptly doubled Gulf imports and wasted more oil than the Bush administration and the 1995 Congress hoped to find under the Arctic National Wildlife Refuge. In 1990 to 1991, many young Americans went to the Persian Gulf in 0.56-mpg tanks and seventeen-feet-per-gallon aircraft carriers, because we had not all been driving thirty-two-mpg cars. That would have been enough, had we done nothing else to eliminate the need for oil imports from the Persian Gulf. If Americans had continued to save oil as rapidly after 1985 as they did for the previous nine years, no oil from the Gulf would have been needed from then on. Not doing so increased oil-import bills and balance-of-trade deficits by $23 billion in 1993 alone. It costs roughly $50 billion every year for the peacetime readiness costs of forces earmarked for intervention in the Gulf.

How much better could we do? In the mid-1980s, about a dozen automakers demonstrated internal-combustion-engine family cars achieving 67 to 138 mpg via better aerodynamics and lighter metals such as aluminum and magnesium. At least two of these concept cars reportedly would have cost no more to make; several offered equivalent or better comfort and safety. None entered mass production. In 1993, however, a vastly larger potential emerged, properly combining the best available technologies could yield: safe, spacious, affordable, high-performance family cars that could drive coast to coast on one tank of any convenient fuel. Full worldwide use of such cars, and of analogous heavier vehicles, will ultimately save as much oil as OPEC (the Organization of Petroleum Exporting Countries) now extracts.

Such "hypercars" artfully combine two main elements. First, they replace heavy steel with extremely light but strong polymer composites, such as the carbon fiber familiar in sporting goods, to make the car lighter and cut friction with sleeker shapes and better tires. Such "ultralight" cars are twice as efficient, as General Motors demonstrated in 1991. Second, hypercars add "hybrid-electric drive": the wheels are driven by special electric motors, but the electricity, instead of coming from heavy batteries recharged from the utility grid, is made onboard from fuel as needed. Since fuel has about a hundred times as much energy per pound as batteries, this saves weight and cost. A small battery or other storage device temporarily stores braking energy, recovered when the wheel motors convert unwanted motion back into useful electricity for reuse in hill climbing and acceleration.

Adding hybrid-electric drive to an ultralight car can boost its efficiency by about 400 to 1,000 percent. The car becomes radically simpler and cheaper to build, more than compensating for its costlier materials. Its product cycle time, tooling cost, parts count, assembly labor, and space requirement are roughly one-tenth of today's cars. Starting in 1994, these potentially decisive competitive advantages led many current and potential automakers to launch major development efforts. During 1994–1995, several prototypes three to five times as efficient as production cars emerged. By the late 1990s, hypercars may well trigger the biggest shift in industrial structure since the microchip.

Light vehicles use about 37 percent of America's oil (roughly half imported at a cost of about $50 billion a year). The rest goes to heavy road vehicles, aircraft, ships, industrial heat, and feedstocks, as well as space and water heating in buildings. But even in 1988, straightforward technological improvements could have saved most of that oil very cheaply. Even before hypercars were invented, fully using mid-1980s' technologies could have saved four-fifths of U.S. oil use at an average cost of a few dollars per barrel—cheaper than drilling for more. (Today the savings would be even bigger and cheaper.) Widespread use of "superwindows"—which have heat-reflecting thin films and insulating heavy gas fillings that insulate as well as up to twelve sheets of glass—could save twice as much oil and gas as Americans obtain from Alaska.

Better yet is the recent discovery that *big energy savings can be cheaper than small ones*. For example, superwindows don't just save energy. They also provide numerous other benefits, such as efficient motors, and dimmable electronic ballasts to control fluorescent lamps; but these devices are often more than paid for by just one or two of their benefits, making their energy savings better than free.

In the early 1990s, this surprise showed up in big and small buildings, hot and cold climates, motor and lighting systems, hot-water and computer systems, and even car design. It is starting to revolutionize the way we think about the economics of end-use efficiency.

For example, a house built in Davis, California, in 1993 needed only one-fifth the energy allowed by the strictest U.S. energy code for all its major uses. Yet because it provided superior comfort with no furnace or air-conditioner, even at 113° F (45° C), it would cost, if widely imitated, about $1,800 *less* than average to build and $1,600 less than average to maintain. Rocky Mountain Institute's superinsulated, superwindowed headquarters showed this a decade earlier in a cold climate (down to –47° F, or –44° C), eliminating the furnace while *reducing* total construction cost.

Careful timing can also make big savings cheaper than small ones. More than 100,000 big all-glass office buildings need reglazing because the window seals fail after about twenty years. In one such building near Chicago, replacing the dark-bronze glass with superwindows could allow less unwanted heat but six times as much daylight (bounceable deep inside), insulate four times as well, yet cost nearly the same. The lighting and office equipment could also be made to work the same or better, look better, and use 80 percent less energy. These combined actions would reduce cooling requirements by nearly fourfold. It would then cost $200,000 less to replace the cooling system with a far smaller one nearly four times as efficient than to renovate the old one. The money saved would pay for the better lights and windows. The building's total energy use would fall by about 75 percent, repaying its investment in less than a year.

Cost-effective, state-of-the-art designs can save about 75 percent of the energy in most existing buildings. In new buildings, the savings are often even larger, and the construction cost typically goes *down*. Savings are often about 50 percent in big motor systems, rising to as much as 90 percent if the driven equipment (such as fans and ducts or pumps and pipes) can also be improved. Such savings often pay for themselves in a few years as a retrofit, and cost less than average in new construction. Office air-conditioning savings can run as high as 97 percent. Around 75 percent of all U.S. electricity can be saved at a cost several times lower than that of just *operating* a typical coal-fired power plant. Because it is cheaper to save the coal than to burn it, the resulting global warming and acid rain are abated not at a cost, but at a profit—and, being profitable, this can be done in the marketplace.

In practice, however, this huge technical potential is being achieved far too slowly because of pervasive market failures. Most states reward utilities for selling more energy, not saving it. Architects and engineers are paid for what they spend, not what they save; all two dozen parties in the real-estate process are systematically rewarded for inefficiency and penalized for efficiency. Most designers use obsolete rules of thumb, not real whole-system optimization. People buying energy efficiency typically want their money back ten times as fast as energy companies recover their investment in increased supply—equivalent to a tenfold price bias against end-use efficiency. Subsidies and asymmetrical tax rules increase that bias. Incentives are split between landlords and tenants, builders and buyers, equipment manufacturers and users. Most people have poor information about what the best buys are, where to get them, and how to shop for them. Overcoming such persistent obstacles will be a key to achieving a prosperous economy, a just society, and a secure, sustainable world.

See also ENERGY; ENERGY, RENEWABLE SOURCES OF; NATURAL GAS.

BIBLIOGRAPHY

FICKETT, ARNOLD P.; GELLINGS, CLARK W.; and LOVINS, AMORY B. "Efficient Use of Electricity." *Scientific American* (September 1990): 65–74.

HEEDE, H. RICHARD, et al. *Homemade Money: How to Save Energy and Dollars in Your Home.* Snowmass, CO: Rocky Mountain Institute; Amherst, NH: Brick House, 1995.

LOVINS, AMORY B. "The Negawatt Revolution." *Across the Board* (September 1990): 18–23.

LOVINS, AMORY B., and HUNTER, L. "Least-Cost Climatic Stabilization." *Annual Review of Energy and the Environment* 16 (1991): 433–531.

———. "Reinventing the Wheels." *Atlantic Monthly* (January 1995): 75–86.

LOVINS, AMORY B., and BROWNING, WILLIAM D. "Negawatts for Buildings." *Urban Land* (July 1992): 26–29.

Amory B. Lovins

Engineering

Engineering is involved in the extension of our biological capabilities through the design, production, and operation of artifacts, from bridges to airplanes to artificial organs. As engineering continues to carry out its historic function in the future, a number of trends will be increasingly important:

New Physical Frontiers

There will be continued expansion of the human reach into new physical frontiers—space and the oceans—way beyond what we have been able to achieve thus far. The next century will see, through engineering and intelligent management, a greater ability to utilize the oceans as sources of food and other important materials; the design of long-term human habitats in space; possibly the establishment of industries on the planets and asteroids; more ambitious explorations of the galaxy through unmanned probes; the enhanced use of space for telecommunications through satellites; and greater utilization of all the electromagnetic spectrum frequencies.

Concern with Society

Engineering has addressed societal problems throughout its history, but the complexity of the problems of the cities, poverty, health care, transportation, and employment, as well as the ambiguous attitude of society toward technology, will require new engineering skills and a clearer sense of how technology can realize its beneficial potential while minimizing negative social side effects. Crucial concerns will include the role of engineering in (1) achieving on a global scale a civilized sustainable living standard, while preserving ecology and environment; (2) addressing the structural unemployment created by increasing technological efficiencies in all sectors of employment; and (3) establishing a reasonable balance between traditional aspects of sovereignty, economics, and politics, and the profound changes created in these domains by telecommunications and information technology. The appropriateness of specific engineering projects—whether, what, how, and when to build—will be increasingly scrutinized. Also, engineers will seek a larger role in the governance of society.

Concern with Environment

Engineering increasingly will be called upon to prevent or remedy the environmental problems—such as waste, noise, air and water pollution—created by industrialization and continuing population increases. A particularly enduring set of issues is how to treat toxic waste, especially from nuclear materials.

Convergence of Engineering and Science

This is already beginning to occur. Scientists are creating tools and artifacts—in genetic engineering or in new synthetic molecules, for example—while engineers endeavor to use their techniques to understand physical and biological systems. The convergence will extend to the behavioral and social sciences, such as psychology, or to economics.

Interdisciplinary Integration

This general trend will show itself in new kinds of engineering designs, from sensors combining biological and electronic elements or concepts to a closer integration of structures and electronics in ship or aircraft design. The picture, in jest, of an airplane as a microchip with peripherals makes the point. The integration of design and flexible manufacturing will make it practical to mass-produce, individually, different parts and systems. A fundamental challenge will be how to integrate vast decentralized entities, be they computer networks, factories, or suburbs.

Blending of Biology and Engineering

Clearly manifest at the end of this century is the application of engineering to the solution of biomedical problems, from instrumentation to physiological simulations, to artificial organs and better mechanisms for the delivery of medication. The reverse direction—transfer of knowledge gleaned from biology to the design of engineering systems—will become increasingly common because of the imaginative solutions that have emerged through biological evolution, including ways to sense, to create and shape materials, to integrate systems, and to transform energy in environmentally benign ways. A big area of future engineering development is biotechnology and its transformation from a laboratory operation to widely used and large-scale industrial applications.

Intelligent Capabilities in Ever Wider Classes of Artifacts

The ability to provide flexible responses to inputs, maintain the memory of past events, and perform logical decisions will be increasingly embodied in new computing devices, in new materials, and in many other engineering systems. It will lead to myriad applications, including intelligent telecommunications networks and sophisticated and flexible robots capable of responding to a variety of human needs, e.g., as house-helpers.

Enhanced Value-Added Through Multifunctionality

Many engineered artifacts will have more than one capability, such as self-diagnosis of malfunctions and self-repair, or inherent decision making. This broad new frontier will be one of the most significant generators of new kinds of engineering design and industrial opportunities.

Relentless Pursuit of Cost Reduction

Material, manufacturing, operating, and disposal costs—a constant concern of engineers—will be reduced through simplicity of design, "just in time" techniques, modularity, new ways of enhancing maintainability and reparability, and recycling the products of design, and through a ubiquitous drive toward total quality.

Greater and Smaller Dimensions, Speed, and Power

These traditional engineering goals will lead to hypersonic commercial planes, faster land and sea vehicles, more powerful nonnuclear explosives, planes for a thousand or more passengers, transcontinental highways (e.g., in Asia) and other macroengineering projects, ever-longer bridge spans or tunnels, and faster construction and excavation methods. The traditional goals are leading to molecular composites with properties varying at the molecular scale and assembled molecule by molecule, and to molecular engines composed of a few molecules. Such developments are the extension of the submicron focus at the core of today's semiconductor industry. Defense will continue to be a major engineering arena, with an increasing shift toward smart weapons, electronic warfare, more effective navigation systems, and stronger protection for tanks. From all of this, technologies capable of both military and civilian use will emerge.

New Areas for Engineering Endeavors

Engineers will be increasingly involved in the area of services ranging from financial services (in operations and in the mathematical modeling of financial variables) to the area of security (from the design of overall security systems to that of better systems for identification and encryption of confidential data). The management of natural and human-made catastrophes and of the associated risks will be of mounting engineering concern. The complexity of today's technology and the expansion of dense human habitats increase people's exposure to potential disasters. Other new domains are exemplified by engineering and law, including issues of intellectual property and of forensic engineering. Sports engineering, an increasingly indispensable tool for competitiveness accomplished with wind tunnel tests of shapes, skiing configurations, and trajectories, will also flourish.

Globalization and Reorganization of the Engineering Process

Advances in telecommunications and information processing will transform engineering into a global process with teams working concurrently on the same design or project across the globe. This will force a rethinking of the engineering profession, from the issue of standards to the preparation of managers of global real-time engineering teams. There will be ubiquitous expert systems, much closer ties of design to production, and interpenetration of the design teams of suppliers and main project contractors.

Rethinking Engineering Education and the Role of Engineering Schools

There will be an ever greater trend toward interdisciplinarity, increasing efforts to reverse the decline of interest of American students in engineering, and efforts to remedy the underrepresentation of minorities. The number of women engineering students will equal that of men, changing the attitude of society toward engineering—and vice versa. Engineering schools will continue to seek a balance between expanding demands on the curriculum and the need to produce engineers in a reasonable number of years. They also will struggle with the conflicting needs to assert the differences between the engineering and the scientific process, while at the same time bringing engineers in closer contact with a broader range of scientific subjects. Engineering schools will develop closer ties with industry and the community and will be seen increasingly as a resource for economic and social development.

See also AIR TRANSPORT; APPROPRIATE TECHNOLOGY; FACTORIES AND MANUFACTURING; MACROENGINEERING; PIPELINES; RAILWAYS.

BIBLIOGRAPHY

BUGLIARELLO, GEORGE. "Technology and the Environment." In D. B. BOTKIN, M. F. CASWELL,, J. E. ESTES, and A. A. ORIO, eds. *Changing the Global Environment.* New York: Academic Press, 1989.

DREXLER, ERIC K. *Engineers of Creation: The Coming Era of Nanotechnology.* New York: Doubleday/Anchor Books, 1987.

NEGROPONTE, NICHOLAS. *Being Digital.* New York: Bowker, 1995.

SLADOVICH, HEDI E. *Engineering As a Social Enterprise.* Washington, DC: National Academy Press, 1991.

George Bugliarello

Entitlement Programs

In the words of Dietrich Bonhoeffer, "The ultimate test of a moral society is the kind of world it leaves to its children." Every generation of Americans has struggled to realize progress. And to date, every generation has succeeded in making America, if not the world, a better place. Yet America's current generation of leaders may be failing to meet Bonhoeffer's mandate. Many now question the future of the American dream—and the steady productivity increases on which that dream depends. Most policy analysts agree that some necessary investments in the future are today being crowded out by unnecessary and excessive government spending and borrowing.

Over the last thirty years, the federal government has racked up enormous deficits. Currently, the national debt is approximately $4.8 trillion dollars, or $18,460 for every man, woman, and child in the United States. In order to pay for annual deficits, the government borrows from the nation's pool of savings, leaving less money for private investment. Lower private investment in new equipment, technology, and worker training—that is, less investment in the future—means American industries are not as competitive as they used to be. As America's competitive edge slips away, the nation earns less money. As a result, wages go down, standards of living stagnate, and jobs become worse and harder to find, especially for young people just entering the work force.

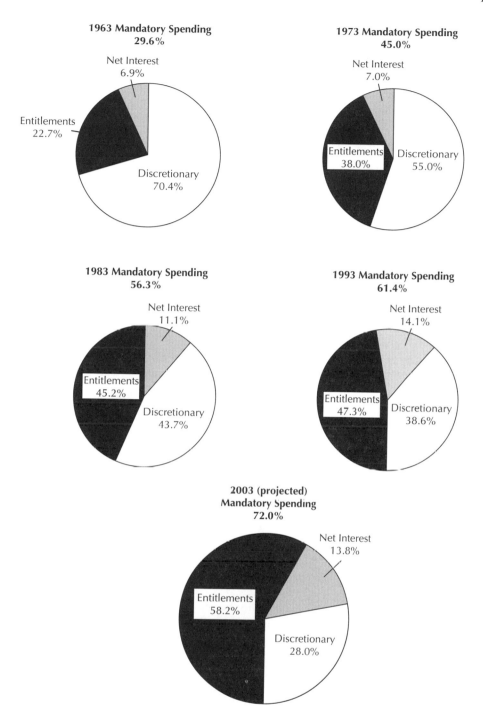

FIGURE 1.   Growth of mandatory spending in the federal budget.

The Problem

The responsibility for America's national debt rests on the shoulders of all Americans. As citizens, Americans have demanded the best of both worlds: lots of funding for many public programs, without the pain caused by higher taxes. Ironically, the lion's share of federal spending has not gone to discretionary programs—education, infrastructure, crime prevention, the environment, or even national defense. Rather, the majority of federal funds today go to interest on the national debt and to "entitlement" programs.

Entitlements are the federal government's promises to deliver benefits to anyone who meets certain eligibility criteria. Popular entitlement programs include Medicare, Medicaid, veterans benefits, Social Security, farm subsidies, and a host of other programs. Unlike "discretionary" programs (education, transportation, and so on) entitlements are funded automatically and without annual Congressional review. Entitlements have served as important sources of support for many Americans. Yet the facts regarding entitlement spending are sobering. If present spending trends continue, the United States government will simply not have enough money to deliver on its current promises very far into the next century.

- Entitlement spending and interest on the national debt together consume more than 60 percent of federal outlays today, double the percentage of just twenty-five years ago, and they are projected to exceed 70 percent of total federal outlays by 2003.
- More than three-quarters of all entitlement spending goes to just four programs: Social Security, Medicare, Medicaid, and federal pensions.
- The Public Trustees of Medicare have concluded that the Medicare Health Insurance program will run out of money by 2002 in the absence of new funding.
- By 2013, according to the Public Trustees of Social Security, Social Security will be in the red, with benefit payments exceeding the tax revenues dedicated to the program. By 2029, unless appropriate changes are made in the interim, Social Security is projected to be bankrupt.
- By 2030, projected spending for Medicare, Medicaid, Social Security, and federal employee retirement programs alone will consume all tax revenues collected by the federal government.

Many people understandably blame the national debt and deficit on "waste, fraud, and abuse" in discretionary programs. While waste, fraud, and abuse are serious problems, they are not the source of our long-term financial problems. Even if the federal government eliminates all discretionary spending—closes down Congress, the White House, and the Pentagon, stops spending on education, job training, and NASA—it would barely have enough money by 2012 to meet mandatory entitlement payments and interest on the national debt.

What this means is that just as the students of the 1990s reach the height of their careers, political leaders of the future will have to raise taxes dramatically, or there will be no money available for any discretionary program. Fifty years ago America was able to fight a world war, build an in-terstate highway system, and provide a just level of benefits. But if the United States continues down its current fiscal path, today's twenty-something generation will inherit dysfunctional entitlement programs, a deteriorating American economy, and the potential for skyrocketing taxes.

Many entitlement programs are growing at only a moderate rate. It is America's federal retirement and health costs that have exploded in recent years. Social Security was established in 1935 as a pay-as-you-go system in which each generation of workers pays, through payroll taxes during their working years, for the retirement benefits of the generation before it. Medicare has a similar design, except that a large portion of Medicare comes from general revenues. The systems were enormous successes because each generation of workers had enough children to fund its own retirement. That held true until the baby boom ended in the 1960s.

When Congress enacted Social Security there were over ten workers to support each retiree. However, in 2008 the baby boom generation will begin to retire, and in a single decade the ratio of working Americans to retired Americans will be cut by 40 percent (from a ratio of 5:1 to 3:1). In addition, thanks to the fantastic medical advances of the last 20 years, Americans are living longer, healthier lives, and as a result are collecting far more lifetime Social Security and Medicare benefits. Although most retirees believe they are simply getting back what they put into the system, the facts contradict that belief. Within a decade, a typical middle-income couple retiring in the early 1980s had already received back, with interest, the total value of their lifetime Social Security and Medicare taxes *and* the total value of their lifetime federal income taxes.

Under these demographic forces, America's federal retirement programs will be severely strained. Unless America acts soon to account for its changing demographics, the nation will face a choice between dramatic tax hikes or draconian benefit cuts.

Treading on Sacred Ground

Most national politicians treat Social Security and Medicare as the most politically unassailable federal programs. Indeed, the programs have done a tremendous amount of good and deserve respect. In 1935, the elderly, as a group, were America's poorest people. Today, they are among the nation's wealthiest. But the success of Social Security and Medicare must not mask the problems future generations face if the programs go untouched. The federal government spends nearly ten times more on every person over sixty-five than it spends on those under age eighteen. Moreover, the overall poverty rate among Americans under age six is nearly three times the rate of poverty among Americans over sixty-five.

Furthermore, Social Security and Medicare are now on a collision course with bankruptcy. The facts are backed by experts from the Congressional Budget Office, the Federal Reserve, and the Social Security Administration. Politicians are not doing these programs any favors by ignoring the experts and avoiding the programs' shortfalls. Those who promise to leave Social Security and Medicare "off the table" from government cuts are denying the overwhelming forces of arithmetic and demographics. Further, they are saddling America's future with dysfunctional programs. The longer America waits to change course, the more drastic the reforms will have to be. Postponing reform is a moral and economic assault on future generations.

The Solutions

Reducing the deficit and getting a handle on entitlement programs will not be easy. The nation's leaders cannot do it just by attacking "waste, fraud, and abuse." Nor will a slight tax increase solve the problem. Raising taxes on some groups might be justified, but if the federal government relied only on tax increases to solve long-term entitlement problems, every federal tax would have to double in order to meet spending obligations. To address America's addiction to entitlement spending and changing American demographics, American citizens will have to make some difficult choices about raising the retirement age, scaling back benefits for wealthier segments of society, and even eliminating programs that do not work. The good news is that if the nation acts quickly, it can take moderate, incremental steps to plan for a promising future.

However, if the nation fails to act quickly, the youth of the 1990s will inherit a world of crumbling entitlement programs, a burgeoning national debt, decreased national savings, and an increasing number of retirees who have unrealistic expectations. As a generation, today's young Americans cannot face that tremendous fiscal burden and still lead this nation into greatness.

See also CLASS AND UNDERCLASS; DEFICITS, GOVERNMENTAL; HEALTH CARE COSTS; HEALTH CARE FINANCING; HEALTH CARE: MORAL ISSUES; HEALTH CARE: TECHNOLOGICAL DEVELOPMENTS; HUMAN RIGHTS; PUBLIC ASSISTANCE PROGRAMS; PUBLIC ASSISTANCE PROGRAMS: ADULT CARE CENTERS; PUBLIC ASSISTANCE PROGRAMS: SOCIAL SECURITY.

BIBLIOGRAPHY

The Bipartisan Commission on Entitlement and Tax Reform. *Final Report to the President.* Washington, DC: U.S. Government Printing Office, January 1995.

_____. *Interim Report to the President.* Washington, DC: U.S. Government Printing Office, August 1994.

KOTLIKOFF, LAURENCE J. *Generational Accounting.* New York: Free Press, 1992.

LONGMAN, PHILLIP. *Born to Pay.* Boston: Houghton Mifflin, 1987.

PENNY, TIMOTHY J. *Common Cents.* Boston: Little, Brown, 1995.

PETERSON, PETER G. *Facing Up: How to Rescue the Economy from Crushing Debt and Restore the American Dream.* New York: Simon & Schuster, 1993.

Robert M. McCord
Heather Lamm

Entrepreneurship

Entrepreneurship is about individuals taking risks in business to develop and deliver innovative products and services. In doing so, entrepreneurs change people's lives and even large societies.

In the future, the entrepreneurial role will expand. The complexity of a global economy, shifting financial resources, the demand for more devices, the emergence of competitive Third World economies, and the continuing disintegration of Cold War-based policies entail new problems that will demand the kind of creative solutions that entrepreneurs can provide. However, the future entrepreneur will look different from today's typical practitioner, because the relationship between emerging enterprises and established corporate organizations will change and women and minorities will play greater roles.

Philosophically, entrepreneurs are the cowboys of the commercial world. They are driven more by a passionate desire for autonomy and belief in their product and less by profits or shareholder interests. In classic cases, they take higher than average financial risks to deliver new, innovative products and services to new, never-before-tested consumer groups. Size is a key component. Generally, entrepreneurs run small, fast, flexible organizations. In recent years, restructuring has forced some people into becoming entrepreneurs.

Entrepreneurial power in the marketplace has been documented. Between 1972 and 1982, over three million new entrepreneurial businesses were formed throughout the world, including countries with controlled economies. During that same period, a study by the U.S. Commerce Department shows that small businesses responded more quickly to market opportunities, creating more than their proportionate share of new jobs. By the year 2000, 85 percent of the U.S. labor force will work in firms employing fewer than 200 people.

In terms of innovation, a National Science Foundation study reports small firms perform better. They produced approximately four times as many innovations per research-and-development dollar as medium-sized firms and twenty-four times as many as large firms.

Today, the method, manner, and content of production is changing dramatically. Globalization is expanding the marketplace. Financial investment is shifting from developed to emerging countries. Disposable income is in the hands of more diverse and demanding consumers who seek immediate gratification. In this environment, success depends on how fast companies respond to the varied needs of new customers.

Entrepreneurs, unlike large corporations, are better equipped to move quickly to meet these demands. Big enterprises, even those with entrepreneurial founding fathers, usually are not structured for flexibility and speed. Traditional manufacturing companies are hierarchically organized for control. Even those that have flattened their organizations by eliminating management levels and introducing quality circles and teams are still encumbered and impeded by the problems of size.

While many entrepreneurs' main clients are corporations, in general these two groups operate separately in different, parallel commercial worlds. There is little cross-activity between them. Over time, successful entrepreneurial activities evolve into larger, more organized organizations that eventually "mature" and become part of the established commercial world.

In the future, this relationship will be different. The gulf between small and large corporate entities will expand. Megacorporations without national boundaries will organize to serve the demands of a global-driven marketplace for basic goods and services. Medium-sized companies without the capital to compete will merge or be forced out. However, small companies will flourish focusing on niche sectors and local needs and becoming, in the process, the hothouses for tomorrow's entrepreneurial activities.

Large companies will actively seek out these smaller businesses to form partnerships, buy intellectual properties, or simply acquire them. International entrepreneurial product brokers will represent small companies. Research and development will become less prominent in the corporate structure. The corporation will float grants, seed money, or resources to entrepreneurial groups outside its structure (or sometimes within its own ranks) to entrepreneurs who are supported by the host company and allowed to "sink or swim."

The large involvement of women and minorities in this arena is another significant development. Because of the free-form nature of the entrepreneurial process, more women and minorities are finding rewarding opportunities as they become a predominant part of this world. Today, women are starting businesses at over twice the rate of men and could own over 50 percent of U.S. small businesses by 2000.

Entrepreneurs are recognized as a dynamic factor in the marketplace—breaking norms, creating and delivering new products, and changing societies. Because of their flexibility and innovative approaches, their role will expand as opportunities to solve future problems grow in an increasingly complex global economy.

See also BUSINESS STRUCTURE: INDUSTRIAL POLICY; CAPITAL FORMATION; CREATIVITY; INVESTMENTS; RESEARCH AND DEVELOPMENT; SCIENCE CITIES; SCIENTIFIC BREAKTHROUGHS; TECHNOLOGICAL CHANGE; TECHNOLOGICAL INNOVATION.

BIBLIOGRAPHY

BROWN, JONATHAN, and ROSE, MARY B., eds. *Entrepreneurship, Networks, and Modern Business.* Manchester: Manchester University Press, 1993.

DRUCKER, PETER T. *Managing for the Future: The 1990s and Beyond.* New York: Penguin Books, 1992.

KURATKO, DONALD F., and HODGETTS, RICHARD M. *Entrepreneurship: A Contemporary Approach.* 2nd ed. Fort Worth, TX: Dryden Press, 1992.

Lauren Huddleston

Environment

Millions of people around the world gasped with wonder in 1969 as a man set foot on the dusty gray surface of the Moon. Later, they thrilled to see a televised view of their own planet from outer space—round and gleaming, awesomely finite and deceptively simple from 240,000 miles away. It was an exhilarating and sobering picture of Spaceship Earth, a depiction in which national boundaries could not be discerned. Nor could distinctions be made between the gleaming office towers and manicured lawns of the modern industrialized parts of the globe and the teeming cities, depleted forests, and degraded farmlands of the developing regions. And while that glistening orb—our Earth and our home—appeared serene, it also looked disturbingly small and fragile.

These dramatic new glimpses of Earth heightened a nascent awareness that all humankind was in the same boat—that whatever threatened a part of the planet menaced the world's inhabitants as a single community.

If Earth were photographed from the Moon today, it would look much the same. One could not see the disappearance of more than forty species of animal life or the net increase of the Earth's human population from nearly four billion to almost six billion. But it is those two trends—and the political, economic, social, and environmental stresses and tensions associated with them—that have made our world ever more fragile and vulnerable as humankind approaches the twenty-first century.

The advance of industrial civilization and the burgeoning of population in the developing countries have produced imbalances that now threaten the future of us all. The most ominous are the concentration of economic growth in the industrialized countries and population increases in the developing nations. Nearly three-quarters of the population increase of the quarter-century since 1969 occurred in the developing countries. During the same period, the gross global product rose to $20 trillion, more than 70 percent of it in the industrialized countries.

The benefits of these dramatic changes accrued largely to the minority of the world's people who live in the highly industrialized countries. The majority of the population, living in the less developed areas, received few, if any, of the benefits; yet they share disproportionately in the costs and risks. These people remain at an early stage of economic development, and many live in a state of dire and debilitating poverty in which the day-to-day imperatives of survival drive them to exploitative practices that destroy the resource base on which their future depends.

Three years after the remarkable space achievement of 1969, the international community focused more closely on Earth and its problems. The United Nations Conference on the Human Environment held in Stockholm during 1972 was the first attempt to bring a global perspective to—and obtain worldwide agreement on—the fact that humankind was on a course that could lead to ruin. A major achievement of that conference was the endorsement by 113 nations of a declaration that all humans bear "a solemn responsibility to protect and improve the environment for present and future generations."

This custodial notion was elaborated by the United Nations World Commission on Environment and Development (UNCED), headed by Norwegian Prime Minister Gro Harlem Brundtland. Its report in 1987, *Our Common Future*, calls for a full integration of the environmental dimension into all areas of political, economic, social, and industrial policy, and decision making. The result of this radical process eventually would come to be called "sustainable development." But the degradation of the Earth continued, despite the earnest declarations of the Stockholm Conference, the Brundtland Commission's reassurance that environmental responsibility and economic growth were not incompatible, and a growing public awareness of the complex and interrelated environmental issues.

Against this background the United Nations General Assembly convened a global conference on environment and development during 1992 in Brazil. Following two and one-half years of intensive preparations, the conference brought together in Rio de Janeiro leaders of virtually all the nations of the world, including more heads of state and government than had ever before come together. The 1992 UN Conference on Environment and Development was the world's first true "Earth Summit." World leaders were joined at the conference and at the accompanying "People's Summit" by unprecedented numbers of people representing a broad spectrum of nongovernmental organizations and citizen groups, and by more than twice the number of media representatives than had ever before covered a world conference. People throughout the world were attuned to the conference and its importance.

This "people-pressure" helped to move governments to agree on a declaration of principles, the Declaration of Rio, and on Agenda 21, a comprehensive program of action to give effect to these principles. Despite some compromises to achieve consensus, Agenda 21 constituted the most comprehensive and far-reaching program of action of its kind ever agreed to by the nations of the world. And the fact that this agreement was reached at the highest political level lent its pronouncements a unique authority. It presented detailed policy and action recommendations on a broad range of issues central to prospects for survival and well-being. And it did this within an integrated framework that enables our response to these issues to be guided by an understanding of the systemic linkages and interactions among them.

What all of these issues of environment and development have in common is that they must be managed on an integrated, cooperative basis, if the risks to which they give rise are to be averted or contained within tolerable limits. This will require a vast strengthening and reorientation of institutional mechanisms and capacities at every level, and an incorporation of the objectives of Agenda 21 into international agreements and arrangements involving trade, investment, and finance.

This will require the development of an effective and enforceable international legal system which will further extend into the international arena the rule of law, which is the solid basis for the effective and equitable functioning of nations. Success will require the integration of ecological disciplines into our educational system, and the additional development of the understanding and skills required to manage these issues. The values on which implementation of Agenda 21 will depend require integration into cultural and social systems. To be effective, each sector of society—business and industry, trade unions, scientists, farmers, educators, religious leaders, communicators, indigenous people, women, children, and youth—must become fully committed to and engaged in the implementation of Agenda 21.

All of the environmental deterioration we have witnessed to date has resulted from levels of population and human activity which, while unprecedentedly high, are still a great deal less than they will be in the period ahead. One of the traditional outlets for the pressures generated by population growth, conflict and economic difficulties has been migration. But today, as pressures for migration escalate, the national borders of the world are closing. Scarcely had the tearing down of the Berlin Wall in 1989 been celebrated than new barriers were being erected in Europe against the entry of the poor, the homeless, and the dispossessed from the eastern and southern parts of Europe.

A new world order must include full and fair participation by the majority of the people of the world who currently inhabit the developing countries. They must have equitable opportunities to share the benefits of technological civilization, just as they share the risks. And surely the highest priority should be accorded to eradication of the poverty that condemns so many people to suffering and hunger and is an affront to the moral basis of civilization.

As we moved through the last decade of the twentieth century, there were few signs that governments were giving priority to implementing the agreements reached in Rio. To some degree this was understandable. The changes called for at Rio were fundamental in nature and will not come quickly or easily. In addition, political leaders were preoccupied with a vast array of more immediate and compelling pressures, both domestic and international. All these factors, however, are much less important to the future of their societies than the issues addressed at Rio.

There have been some positive developments. The United Nations Commission on Sustainable Development was established as the forum for continuing consultation and cooperation and for following up and implementing the agreements reached in 1992 at UNCED. The United States in 1993 reasserted and reestablished its leadership in respect of the issues addressed at Rio by signing the Biological Diversity Convention and by setting up a new Presidential Commission on Sustainable Development. A number of countries, including China, are developing their own national "Agenda 21" in response to the global agenda. Japan, which has made great environmental strides domestically, is poised also to take on an international leadership role.

The most exciting and promising developments, however, are occurring outside of government. Since the Rio conference, there has been a virtual explosion of activities on the part of grass-roots organizations, citizen groups, and key sectors of society—including business, scientists, architects, engineers, and educators and religious leaders. Representatives of these groups returned from Rio determined to translate basic environmental themes into their own responses to Agenda 21. The Business Council for Sustainable Development comprise some sixty chief executive officers of leading transnational corporations. In its 1992 report, "Changing Course," this influential group made an important contribution to the Earth Summit, and it has been subsequently reconstituted with a commitment to bringing about the changed course it called for at Rio.

The proliferation of private initiatives and grass-roots activity has promise of infusing new energies into the political process and ensuring that the issues of Rio will be moved back into prominence in the political agenda. The pressures for follow-up and implementation of the results of the Earth Summit will increase as the necessity becomes ever more evident.

Necessity always has driven change. Throughout history, nations have demonstrated their willingness to devote the resources, establish the alliances, and make the sacrifices required to confront risks to their security. Today, as never before, the people and nations of the world are joined in facing the greatest threat ever to their common security—the threat to the capacity of our planet to sustain life as we know it. Only by forging a new global alliance, embracing North, South, East, West, rich and poor, can this challenge be met effectively. The agreements reached at the Earth Summit—the Declaration of Rio and Agenda 21—provide the foundations for the construction of this new alliance. Our common future depends on it.

See Jan Tinbergen on SOCIALISM for further discussion of the disparity between developed and developing countries. *See also* ACID RAIN; DEVELOPMENT, ALTERNATIVE; DEVELOPMENT: WESTERN PERSPECTIVE; ENVIRONMENTAL BEHAVIOR; ENVIRONMENTAL ETHICS; ENVIRONMENTAL INDICATORS; ENVIRONMENTAL POLICY CHANGES; GLOBAL ENVIRONMENTAL PROBLEMS; GLOBAL WARMING; HAZARDOUS WASTES.

BIBLIOGRAPHY

BRUNDTLAND, GRO HARLEM. *Our Common Future: Report of the World Commission on Environment and Development.* New York: Oxford University Press, 1987.

Commission on Global Governance. *Our Global Neighbourhood: The Report of the Commission on Global Governance.* New York: Oxford University Press, 1995.

MYERS, NORMAN. *Ultimate Security: The Environmental Basis of Political Stability.* New York: Norton, 1993.

SCHMIDHEINY, STEPHAN. *Changing Course: A Global Business Perspective on Development and the Environment.* Cambridge, MA: MIT Press, 1992.

SHABECOFF, PHILIP. *A Fierce Green Fire: The American Environmental Movement.* New York: Hill and Wang, 1993.

WARD, BARBARA, and DUBOS, RENE J. *Only One Earth: The Care and Maintenance of a Small Planet.* New York: W. W. Norton, 1972.

Maurice Strong

Environmental Behavior

Environmental ethics (and the behavior it engenders) involves a major shift in the frame of reference within which traditional ethics is contemplated. Ethics in Western thought has been an aspect of philosophy and theology, and it has shared their focus upon the individual and the human, describing desirable human goals, ideals, moral character, and behavior. Various theologians or philosophers have differed about important details, but always nature (or "God's Creation") was the stage or backdrop. So the focus of moral attention remained upon humans (or upon humans and God).

This traditional view has been challenged by the scientific perception that individuals (and the entire human species) participate fully in the physical and biological processes that create, sustain, and change life. We are totally within those processes, not somehow apart from or above or beneath them.

Ecology entails the systematic integration of biology, chemistry, and physics to account for the creation and stability of living communities (ecosystems) made up of many species interacting with one another and their environment. Environmental ethics no longer sees humans as separate from the rest of life around us and no longer in mastery over it all.

The biblical environmental ethic was one of "dominion." Responsible "stewardship" has been proposed as an improved biblical ethic. But stewardship still assumes that humans know enough about complex natural systems to be able to be "good stewards." Elizabeth Dodson Gray has proposed as an alternative an environmental ethic of "attunement," based upon "ecological reconnaissance," with humans aiming to attune and fit in with ecosystems, particularly those deemed unique or fragile.

We humans are making major changes to the present and future environments of the globe and its regions. A major example is certainly the rapid increase in the total human population from 2 billion (1930) to 5.3 billion (1995). Humans of a particular localized ecosystem can degrade and decrease its life-sustaining potential (or "carrying capacity"). We have done this to major worldwide systems (such as oceans, fisheries, soils, and the ozone layer in the upper atmosphere).

A major controversy within environmental ethics has been between a global and a regional focus: "spaceship ethics" is different from "lifeboat ethics." Spaceship ethics sees all on the planet as in the same boat (a single spaceship), and the needed response is conserving and sharing. Lifeboat ethics sees many boats on the sea of life (many regions, continents, ecosystems). Garrett Hardin (1976) criticizes Kenneth Boulding (1966) and R. Buckminster Fuller (1969) for not taking sufficient account of human mismanagement of shared resources. The conserving and sharing assumed by spaceship ethics, says Hardin, often works out badly in practice when a common resource (such as air, water, fisheries) is unstructured and so left to a first-come-first-served process in which human greed and desire for profit can often dominate the more noble sentiments of planetary sharing.

Hardin's lifeboat ethics is based upon a biologist's understanding of carrying capacity. Hardin proposes that spaceship Earth is akin to a naval ship. Such ships are built to be divided in emergencies into watertight compartments (regions or ecosystems) so as not to endanger the entire ship (or planet) when there is severe damage to one or more compartments.

In lifeboat ethics, each boat has the opportunity and responsibility for its own survival. It must stay within its own national or regional carrying capacity. Exporting surplus populations, Hardin says, should not in the future be a permitted solution for nations (lifeboats) that allow their populations to continue to grow. Such out-migration mattered less in the recent past when human numbers were far fewer. But as all boats approach (or pass) their various carrying capacities, each boat must take responsibility for its own people and its own viability. Not to do that would make all equally irresponsible and similarly miserable.

The assumed "care horizon" for human actions and accountability in traditional ethics was measured in one or perhaps two human lifetimes. Environmental ethicists are now reckoning with present-day responsibilities for safe long-term storage of highly toxic nuclear wastes (plutonium, for example, has a radioactive half-life of nearly 25,000 years, or three to four times longer than all of previous human civilization). So ethics now asks, what are the rights of those who are currently voiceless because they are not yet born? And again, should other species, who also have no voice in human affairs, have any say about human actions affecting the shared environment and so affecting them?

The scope of environmental ethics is so radically enlarged because both the scale and the duration of our human impacts are now so much bigger. Human actions are still important to environmental ethics. But humans are no longer assumed to be the only point of ethical concern. Human life is now seen as completely rooted in and depending upon viable ecosystems and a viable planet, so environmental ethics moves moral thinking about human actions into this wider context. Then, in that wider context, it asks the traditional sorts of ethical questions about proper human goals, ideals, moral character, and responsible behavior.

See also ENVIRONMENT; ENVIRONMENTAL ETHICS; ENVIRONMENTAL POLICY CHANGES; GREEN REVOLUTION; NATURAL RESOURCES, USE OF.

BIBLIOGRAPHY

BOULDING, KENNETH E. *Human Values on the Spaceship Earth.* New York: Council Press, 1966.
FULLER, R. BUCKMINSTER. *Operating Manual for Spaceship Earth.* Mattituck, NY: Amereon, 1969.
GRAY, ELIZABETH DODSON. "Come Inside the Circle of Creation: The Ethic of Atunement." In FREDERICK FERRÉ and PETER HARTEL, eds. *Ethics and Environmental Policy: Theory Meets Practice.* Athens, GA: University of Georgia Press, 1994.
LUCAS, GEORGE R., and OGLETREE, THOMAS W. *Lifeboat Ethics.* New York: Harper & Row, 1976.

David Dodson Gray

Environmental Ethics

In response to widespread human destruction of the environment, thinkers such as Baird Callicott, Aldo Leopold, Holmes Rolston (1988), and Paul Taylor (1986) have called for a new environmental ethic: one that is *biocentric.* They point out that all beings on the Earth are interdependent and that because of this interdependence, individualistic, *anthropocentric* (human-centered) ethics are not appropriate.

Traditional ethics or moral philosophy, especially in the West, have been anthropocentric. They teach that nonhuman beings have only instrumental value, as means to human ends, such as food. Only humans, according to anthropocentric ethics, have inherent value, or value in themselves, apart from their worth to humanity.

Proponents of biocentric ethics, on the other hand, argue for a holistic approach that recognizes the inherent value of the entire planet. They criticize the human chauvinism, speciesism, and arrogance that many humans exhibit toward nature.

Responding to the biocentric arguments, philosophers such as William Frankena and Kristin Shrader-Frechette (1991a, 1991b) claim that a genuine environmental ethic can be anthropocentric. They contend that even anthropocentric ethics condemn the greed, arrogance, and insensitivity that cause environmental destruction. Moreover, they maintain that although all environmental degradation must stop, it is not possible to give all beings on the planet equal "rights" because not all beings are equal. Tom Regan argues that if we follow biocentric ethics and claim that human rights are equal to those of all other beings, then we would become victims of "environmental fascism" (Regan, 1983, p. 262). That is, we would make all human rights to life, liberty, and dignity subject to the welfare of the environment. For example, taken to an extreme, we could kill humans to save snail darters.

Apart from whether they are anthropocentric or biocentric, most environmental ethics focus on the question of whether duties to the environment—or to other human beings—take primacy. Arguing for "lifeboat ethics," Garrett Hardin says that the planet may be thought of as a sea on which there are lifeboats. The poor of the world are falling out of their crowded lifeboats and trying to swim to the uncrowded, rich lifeboats of the developed nations. Hardin contends that genuine environmental ethics require that persons on the rich boats not help those on the poor lifeboats, because doing so would cause the rich boats to capsize as they exceeded the carrying capacity of their crafts.

Buckminster Fuller, Kenneth Boulding, and others, however, reject lifeboat ethics as unjust and argue for "spaceship ethics." They propose thinking of Earth as a finite, closed spacecraft on which we must conserve and share resources equitably if the entire craft is to survive. For proponents of spaceship ethics, planetary sisterhood and brotherhood are necessary to environmental ethics.

In addition to different general theories—anthropocentric versus biocentric, spaceship versus lifeboat—governing norms for human behavior, proponents of environmental ethics also address a number of more specific issues. Among them is the question of whether animals and/or natural objects have rights, whether there are duties to members of future generations, and whether use of technologies such as commercial nuclear power and long-lived chemical pesticides are unethical. Relentless pursuit of a balanced perspective will continue on into the future.

See also ENVIRONMENT; ENVIRONMENTAL BEHAVIOR; ENVIRONMENTAL POLICY CHANGES; GREEN REVOLUTION; NATURAL RESOURCES.

BIBLIOGRAPHY

ATTFIELD, ROBIN. *The Ethics of Environmental Concern*. New York: Columbia University Press, 1983.

HARGROVE, EUGENE. *Foundations of Environmental Ethics*. Englewood Cliffs, NJ: Prentice-Hall, 1989.

REGAN, TOM. *The Case for Animal Rights*. Berkeley, CA: University of California Press, 1983.

ROLSTON, HOLMES. *Environmental Ethics*. Philadelphia, PA: Temple University Press, 1988.

SCHERER, DONALD, and ATTIG, THOMAS, eds. *Ethics and the Environment*. Englewood Cliffs, NJ: Prentice-Hall, 1983.

SHRADER-FRECHETTE, KRISTIN. *Environmental Ethics*. Pacific Grove, CA: Boxwood Press, 1991.

———. "Ethics and the Environmental." *World Health Forum* 12 (1991b): 311–321.

TAYLOR, PAUL. *Respect for Nature*. Princeton, NJ: Princeton University Press, 1986.

Kristin S. Shrader-Frechette

Environmental Indicators

Accounts placing monetary evaluations or otherwise measuring and quantifying the value of natural resources and environmental factors shed new light on the costs of ecological depredations. Prior to this, little effort had been made to value clean air and water, other than estimating damage to buildings caused by particulates and other contaminants or health costs of these to living beings. Economists refer to such costs as "externalities" (i.e., costs of production externalized from company balance sheets, not added into prices but passed on to taxpayers and future generations). Cost calculations vary because quantifying environmental amenities, let alone the value of human life, is speculative.

The United Nations

The United Nations has promoted social indicators at least since 1954, and its latest, most comprehensive work is the UN Development Program's *Human Development Report* of 1990–1992, which introduces the new Human Development Index, a measure that specifically includes environmental indicators. Economists who deal with environmental, natural resource, or ecological matters, as well as statisticians from other disciplines, tend to resist translating pollution and resource-depletion data into monetary coefficients. Some question whether any index combining comprehensive aspects of "quality of life"—such as the UN's Human Development Index or the World Bank's Index of Sustainable Economic Welfare—can be any more meaningful than GNP. The economic approach focuses on single indices using money equivalents and weighting priorities in economic terms, for example, as between urban clean air, public health, preserving rain forests, preventing global warming, or ozone depletion on the one hand and per capita income increases on the other hand. Of course, some kind of environmental capital consumption deflator would be better than the GNP/GDP-based current accounting, which ignores environmental resources altogether.

Some scientists believe that environmental pollution and resource depletion are best left specific and "unbundled"—expressed as parts per million of pollutants in the air or water and hectares of land lost to desertification and deforestation, for example—rather than buried in some new single-index version of GNP. A broader, unbundled quality-of-life indicator that parallels but does not replace GNP is termed the Country Futures Indicators (CFI), as shown in Table 1 (see also Henderson, 1991).

OECD Environmental Indicators

Long involved in developing quantitative and qualitative measures of human conditions, the Organization for Economic Cooperation and Development also publishes its own environmental indicators. OECD has also prepared several working papers featuring environmental measurements in specific countries such as Norway (1992).

The OECD promulgated in the early 1970s the so-called polluter pays principle, which helped legitimize and implement the collection of pollution cost data. This led to the introduction of pollution levies on polluters. Eighty-five different so-called green taxes in effect during 1992 fall into four categories: (1) emissions of pollutants such as carbon dioxide, nitrogen oxides, or toxic waste; (2) the depletion of natural resources, for example, mining; (3) generation of waste, for example, over-packaging; and (4) planned obsolescence, for ex-

TABLE 1. Country Futures Indicators*

Beyond money-denominated, per-capita averaged growth of GNP

Reformulated GNP to Correct Errors and Provide More Information	*Complementary Indicators of Progress Toward Society's Goals*
• *Purchasing power parity (PPP).* Corrects for currency fluctuations. • *Income distribution.* Is the poverty gap widening or narrowing? • *Community-based accounting.* Complements current enterprise-basis. • *Informal, household-sector production.* Measures all hours worked (paid and unpaid). • *Deduct social and environmental costs.* A "net" accounting avoids double counting. • *Account for depletion of nonrenewable resources.* Analogous to a capital-consumption deflator. • *Energy input/GDP ratio.* Measures energy efficiency, recycling. • *Military/civilian budget ratio.* Measures effectiveness of governments. • *Capital asset account for built infrastructure and public resources.* Many economists agreed this is needed; some include environment as a resource.	• *Population.* Birthrates, crowding, age distribution. • *Education.* Literacy levels, school dropout and repetition rates. • *Health.* Infant mortality, low birth weight and weight/height/age correlations. • *Nutrition.* Calories per day, protein/carbohydrates ratio, etc. • *Basic services.* Access to clean water, etc. • *Shelter.* Housing availability/quality, homelessness, etc. • *Public safety.* Crime. • *Child development.* World Health Organization, UNESCO, etc. • *Political participation and democratic process.* Amnesty International data, money-influence in elections, electoral participation rates, etc. • *Status of minority and ethnic populations and women.* Human rights data. • *Air and water quality and environmental pollutions levels.* Air pollution in urban areas. • *Environmental resource depletion.* Hectares of land, forests lost annually. • *Biodiversity and species loss.* Canada's environmental indicators. • *Culture, recreational resources.* Jacksonville, Fla., etc.

*From *Paradigms in Progress: Life Beyond Economics* by Hazel Henderson (1991). Table copyright © 1989 Hazel Henderson, used with permission.

ample, throw-away lighters, one-time cameras, and so on. Green taxes could become so large a revenue source that eventually they may replace income taxes.

National Experience

Exemplary of future environmental accounting is *A Report on Canada's Progress toward a National Set of Environmental Indicators* (1991). Forty-three specific indicators in eighteen issue areas, including air and water quality, solid wastes, and contamination in species of bird and fish are represented.

New Zealand reformulated national accounts by adding to GNP/GDP accounts a capital-asset account that represents the value of infrastructure (public buildings, railroads, highways, dams, ports, bridges, etc.). Most nations do not carry such assets on the balance sheet (as do corporations) in order to arrive at a country's "net" worth. This omission led to poor maintenance, short-term thinking, and under-investment in public sector goods and services. Possibly, this concept will be broadened to include environmental assets, such as forests. The Netherlands is overhauling its GNP/GDP accounts, along with over twenty other countries, including Germany, France, Denmark, Canada, Venezuela, India, and Indonesia. Japan deducts social and environmental costs of urban congestion in calculating its GNP/GDP.

Natural Resource Accounting

Progress in natural resource accounting has accelerated since 1990, mainly in valuing forest resources. Institutions now studying and producing natural resource accounting models include the following:

- UN-ECOSOC (New York)
- United Nations Environment Program (New York and Nairobi, Kenya)
- The World Bank (Washington, D.C.)
- World Resources Institute (Washington, D.C.)
- Organization for Economic Cooperation and Development (Paris and Washington, D.C.)
- World Wildlife Fund International (Gland, Switzerland)
- European Association for Bioeconomic Studies (Milan, Italy)
- International Society for Ecological Economics (Solomons, Maryland)
- Worldwatch Institute (Washington, D.C.)
- Environment Canada (Ottawa)

- ECOTROPIC (Rio de Janeiro)
- Wuppertal Institute for Climate, Environment, and Energy (Germany)
- New Economics Foundation (London)
- International Academy of Environment (Conches, Switzerland)

Life Cycle Accounting

Another tool in the growing array of environmental indicators is life cycle accounting. This method fully accounts for natural resources and their conservation spread over the useful life of products and services. This approach accurately balances the often high initial costs of resource-conserving technologies with the net savings they produce over their period of use. For example, a house built to rely on solar energy may be less expensive than a conventional house when savings in energy bills are costed out over the life of the structure, even though the initial cost of such a house would be high.

Unit-Waste Pricing

Unit-waste pricing, also known as full-cost pricing, refers to prices of products that fully account for and include social and environmental costs. Calculating longer-term costs or costs displaced to other regions (transborder pollution or depredation of the global commons, for example) is exceedingly difficult.

Green Indices

Green indices appeared during the 1990s. *The Green Index, 1991–1992* is a state-by-state guide to environmental health in the United States, published by the Institute for Southern Studies in Durham, N.C., and the Island Press in Washington, D.C. Canada's green indicators have been mentioned previously, and there is also the *Green Budget* from the British Green Party and Merlin Press of London.

See also ENVIRONMENT; FORESTRY; GREEN REVOLUTION; NATURAL RESOURCES, USE OF; SOCIAL INDICATORS.

BIBLIOGRAPHY

ANDERSON, VICTOR. *Alternative Economic Indicators.* London: Routledge, 1991.
CAIRNCROSS, FRANCES. *Costing the Earth.* Boston: Harvard Business Review Press, 1992.

DALY, HERMAN, and COBB, JOHN. *For the Common Good.* Boston: Beacon Press, 1990.

EKINS, PAUL; HILLMAN, MAYER; and HUTCHISON, ROBERT. *The Gaia Atlas of Green Economics.* New York: Anchor Books, 1992.

HENDERSON, HAZEL. *Paradigms in Progress.* Indianapolis, IN: Knowledge Systems, 1991, chapters 6 and 7.

"Statistical Needs for a Changing Economy." Background Paper, September 1989. Washington, DC: U.S. Office of Technology Assessment.

Hazel Henderson

Environmental Institutions

In June 1972, 113 nations met in Stockholm, Sweden, at the UN Conference on the Human Environment, to assess the conditions of the Earth's land, air, and water systems and to design a program of international cooperation for life and human activities. They mandated the establishment of the United Nations Environment Programme (UNEP) to implement that program.

As an outcome of the 1972 UN conference, UNEP was established in 1973 in Nairobi, Kenya. UNEP serves as a catalyst for environmental policy and management within the United Nations system and among regional, national, and nongovernmental organizations. Areas of concentration include the atmosphere; fresh water; biodiversity; hazardous waste and toxic chemicals; ocean and coastal areas; land degradation; desertification; cleaner production; and technology. Activities include monitoring and sensing; advancing international environmental laws; conventions and protocols; environmental education and training; and mobilizing women, youth, religious leaders, business, and industry on environmental issues and ecosystem management.

The World Commission on Environment and Development (WCED) was introduced by the 1983 Governing Council of UNEP and affirmed by Resolution 38/161 of the UN General Assembly. WCED was charged with proposing long-term environment strategies for achieving sustainable development, recommending ways in which concern for the environment may be translated into greater international cooperation, and helping to define shared perceptions of long-term environmental issues.

The Organization for Economic Cooperation and Development (OECD) promotes economic and social welfare in member countries and the harmonious development of the world economy. Members of OECD are governments of twenty-four industrialized countries in North America and Western Europe, as well as Australia, Japan, and New Zealand.

The *United Nations Development Programme* (UNDP) is the world's largest grant development-assistance organization, drawing on the expertise of specialized and technical UN agencies, to work in over 150 countries in virtually every sector of development. UNDP provides grant assistance to build national capacity and develop resources in areas such as agriculture, industry, health, education, economic planning, transportation, and communications.

The *International Union of Nature and Natural Resources* (IUCN) is an independent international organization including a union of sovereign states, governmental agencies, and nongovernmental organizations concerned with the initiation and promotion of scientifically based action that will ensure the conservation of the natural environment.

The *World Wildlife Fund* (WWF) is the largest private international nature conservation organization promoting public awareness of conservation problems and raising funds for the protection of threatened species and environments.

The *Nature Conservancy* is the leading U.S. private-sector organization working to preserve biological diversity in the United States by protecting natural lands and the life they harbor.

The *International Maritime Organization* (IMO) is an intergovernmental organization concerned with promoting safety at sea and with the threat of marine pollution from ships.

The 1979 Bonn Convention on the Conservation of Migratory Species of Wild Animals established the objective of protecting those species of wild animals that migrate across or outside national boundaries. The Bonn Convention tests approaches to protection of wild migratory species and attempts to restore habitats and reduce factors endangering their existence. There are forty-two assenting members.

Several global and regional agreements regulate the use and conservation of marine animals. For example, the International Whaling Commission (IWC), established in 1946 under the International Convention for the Regulation of Whaling, keeps under review and revises the measures laid out in a schedule of the convention governing the management of whaling. These measures provide for the complete protection of certain species of whales and designate specified ocean areas as whale sanctuaries. The IWC has introduced an international moratorium on whaling. Similarly, the Convention on the Conservation of Antarctic Marine Living Resources provides for the safeguarding of the environment and the protection of the ecosystem of the surrounding seas and for the conservation of Antarctic marine living resources.

Several global and regional agreements regulate the use and conservation of fisheries. For example, the 1949 Washington Convention for the establishment of an Inter-American Tropical Tuna Commission has the objective of maintaining the population of tuna in the eastern Pacific Ocean to permit maximum sustained catches. The 1959 London North-East Atlantic Fisheries Convention was to ensure the conservation and rational exploitation of the fish stocks of the North-East Atlantic ocean and adjacent waters.

The 1982 United Nations Convention on the Law of the Sea covers land-based sources of pollution, ship-based sources, and atmospheric pollution of the oceans. Its objectives are to establish a comprehensive new legal regime for the seas and oceans and to establish environmental standards as well as enforcement provisions dealing with pollution of the marine environment.

The 1979 Geneva Convention on Long-Range Transboundary Air Pollution has the objective of protecting the environment against air pollution while endeavoring to prevent, limit, or, as far as possible, gradually reduce air pollution, including long-range transboundary air pollution.

In 1988, the Intergovernmental Panel on Climate Change (IPCC) was established by UNEP and World Meterological Organization to assess the latest scientific knowledge, socioeconomic impacts, and policy response strategies regarding climate changes. In 1992 the Framework Convention on Climate Change was formed to achieve stabilization of greenhouse gas concentrations in the atmosphere at a level that would prevent dangerous interference with the climate system from human sources. Such a level should be achieved within a time frame sufficient to allow ecosystems to adapt naturally to climate change, to ensure that food production is not threatened, and to enable economic development to proceed in a sustainable manner.

The 1963 Nuclear Test Ban Treaty inaugurated by the U.S. and U.S.S.R. bans nuclear weapon testing in the atmosphere, in outer space, and under water. In 1971, another treaty was signed prohibiting the placement of nuclear weapons on the seabed and the ocean floor. There is also an international convention facilitating the safe transfer of nuclear material and establishing measures for its physical protection. The goal of the 1972 London

Dumping Convention (LDC) is to prevent marine pollution from the intentional dumping of waste materials at sea from ships, aircraft, platforms, and other manmade structures at sea. LDC also prohibits the dumping of low-level radioactive waste. The IMO has issued a code on transporting nuclear wastes and plutonium providing safeguards for shipping.

The 1989 Basel Convention on the Control of Transboundary Movements of Hazardous Wastes and Their Disposal has the objectives of reducing the number of transboundary movements of hazardous wastes to the minimum consistent with the environmentally sound management of such wastes; self-sufficiency in the management of wastes produced locally; their disposal as close as possible to their source of generation; and minimizing the generation of hazardous wastes (quantity and toxicity) at the source. Its immediate target is to impose strict controls on the hazardous wastes that are allowed to cross boundaries and on their ultimate disposal.

Several conventions address the problem of oil spills. The 1972 London Dumping Convention was intended to prevent marine pollution from the intentional dumping of waste materials at sea from ships, aircraft, platforms, and other manmade structures at sea. The 1973/78 International Convention on the Prevention of Marine Pollution from Ships, which established regulations for the prevention of pollution by oil by providing geographical and volume limits, requires reception facilities at oil terminals and repair ports. The 1990 International Convention on Oil Pollution Preparedness, Response and Cooperation (OPRC) requires that all ships, offshore units, and sea ports must have an oil pollution emergency plan. Each party must establish oil pollution reporting procedures in accordance with IMO regulations. National and regional systems for preparedness must be established and parties should facilitate international cooperation and mutual assistance with respect to oil pollution incidents.

The Convention on International Trade in Endangered Species of Wild Flora and Fauna (CITES) plays a major role in controlling the international wildlife trade. One hundred countries are party to the convention whose purpose is not to eliminate the trade, but to encourage rational and sustainable utilization of living resources. CITES lists species threatened with extinction and species that may be threatened in the future. It also establishes a regime on export and import of the species covered and provides for sanction.

See also ENVIRONMENT; ENVIRONMENTAL BE-
HAVIOR; ENVIRONMENTAL ETHICS; ENVIRONMEN-
TAL INDICATORS; ENVIRONMENTAL POLICY
CHANGES; GLOBAL ENVIRONMENTAL PROBLEMS;
GREEN REVOLUTION; NATURAL RESOURCES, USE
OF; RESOURCES.

Joan Martin Brown

Environmental Policy Changes

Environmental policy evolves as we learn more
about how the world works, as new technologies
are developed, as we uncover problems, as efforts
at solution create new problems, as we assign new
responsibilities to government, as we develop
deeper understanding of quality in living, and as
we look further into the future. Contemporary policy making is restrained by old ways of thinking
and by existing structures of government that do
not fit newly discovered realities. In nearly every
country except China the people are ahead of the
government in perceiving environmental problems
and urging corrective action. Wariness about
health threats has been foremost in eliciting concern and demanding action. Victims of dangerous
actions by others have often turned into environmentalists. The visibility of some forms of pollution and their detrimental side effects may be the
reason why many people define environmental
problems as pollution.

The Basic Underlying Learning Curve

A century ago those concerned with the preservation of beautiful natural places called themselves
conservationists. Concern about increasing industrial pollution in the 1950s and '60s led to a sister
movement of persons who called themselves *environmentalists.* Both movements, in those early
days, accepted the premise that while modern society was basically sound, nature would have to be
protected by better technology as well as by better
and more vigorously enforced laws. Current public
discourse about environmental problems is still
based on that premise, which is accepted by most
governments as well.

Future-oriented environmentalists see environmental problems differently. They point out that
the world has a population of 6 billion. This could
double to 12 billion by 2035 (and could double
again to 24 billion by 2075). Economic throughput
(the speed with which we take things from the
earth, process them, use them, and discard them as
waste) grows even faster than population. Meanwhile, mineral stocks are being used up; deforestation is spreading; species extinction is accelerating;
deserts are expanding; soils are depleting swiftly;
fish stocks are diminishing; wildlife habitat is disappearing; toxic poisons are circulating from air to
water to soil to food and bioaccumulating up the
food chain; the protective ozone shield is thinning
rapidly; and greenhouse gases are threatening to
alter climatic systems—perhaps sending them into
chaos. Without intending to, just by doing better
and better that which people had always done, humans are changing the way the planet's life support
systems work. At the very time when increasing
numbers of people need sustenance, we are crippling the ability of life systems to provide it.

It became clear to these environmentalists that
better laws and better technology are unlikely to
reverse the accelerating negative trends; that continued environmental exploitation and ruin is
rooted in the fundamental beliefs and values of
modern society—that society itself must be transformed. But how should we characterize the new
society they seek?

In the later half of the 1970s the phrase "sustainable society" began to be used and soon became
widely accepted. The phrase implies that our present trajectory was not sustainable, that growth in
population and economic throughput has to be
limited. No one argued against the desirability of
sustainability, but there was considerable disagreement about what it would require in everyday
practice. Even so, people of many persuasions felt
comfortable under this umbrella. The perceived
need to address urgently the whole set of interconnected global environmental problems drew the
conservation and environmental movements together so that they are now close partners and
nearly indistinguishable.

The United Nations General Assembly established in 1983 a World Commission on Environment and Development (WCED). In its report, *Our
Common Future* (1987), it called for "sustainable
development." The phrase caught on, becoming
the topic of hundreds of books and thousands of
conferences and discussions. It became the central
focus of the United Nations Conference on Environment and Development held in Rio de Janeiro
in June 1992. This first planet-wide summit of national leaders was soon dubbed the "Earth Summit" and firmly established environmental concerns and the sustainability of society and its
ecosystems at the top of the world's agenda. Today

nearly everyone recognizes that there are severe environmental problems on planet Earth; but are they fixable by better laws and better technology or must our whole society be transformed? Let us call the two camps transformationalists and fixers.

A much quoted definition of sustainable development in *Our Common Future* reads: "Sustainable development is development that meets the needs of the present without compromising the ability of future generations to meet their own needs" (p. 43). The fixers interpret that statement as endorsing economic growth as desirable and sustainable. Transformationalists caution, however, that sustainable growth is an oxymoron; the two terms are contradictory. We must distinguish growth from development. Development implies improvement and has no inherent limit but continuous growth is physically impossible. Tragically, population growth is such a sensitive issue that the WCED did not forthrightly confront it; the topic was even excluded from discussion at the Earth Summit. The United Nations did hold a separate conference on population in Cairo in September 1994. That conference achieved agreement that population growth must be limited and that emancipation of women would be the most effective strategy for doing so. Currently, fixers control nearly every government and economic growth is urgently being encouraged around the planet. Even though humankind continues to desire unlimited growth, that desire will not change the physical reality that growth in population and economic throughput must cease.

Learning a New Way of Thinking

The "let's fix it" mentality dominated early thinking about environmental policy. We sought specific solutions to specific problems: national parks to preserve beautiful places; filtration plants to cleanse dirty water; tall smokestacks to disperse air pollutants; treatments for cancer caused by polluted environments; and so forth. Early efforts to solve discrete problems were assigned to different governmental departments. Even when these disparate efforts were reassigned to newly established environmental ministries to upgrade their effectiveness and improve coordination, the old divisions (air, water, land, etc.) were retained. The U.S. Environmental Protection Agency (EPA) concluded from an internal policy review in the 1980s that this piecemeal approach merely moved problems from one place to another without really eliminating them; but the U.S. Congress still has not seen fit to change the EPA's structure.

Recent studies show that most people, all around the planet, are aware of and highly concerned about environmental problems. They want government and industry to correct these problems, although they have little confidence that they will. Other studies show that most people and their leaders are ignorant of the basic dynamic principles of the planet's life support systems and the interaction of those systems with socio-economic-political systems. For example, every school child should be taught that matter and energy can neither be created nor destroyed, they can only be transformed (the first law of thermodynamics). Environmentalists derive four maxims for everyday living from that basic law of nature: *everything has to go somewhere, we can never do merely one thing, everything is connected to everything else,* and *we should always ask "And then what?"* This new way of thinking can be characterized as holistic, systemic (seeing the world as a system of systems), integrative, and future oriented.

Not only is environmental education absent from the curriculum of most schools, the educational establishment in most places resists adding this new subject. Most young people pick up what little they know from television, which is effective in arousing concern but not very effective in teaching people how to think about the environment.

The effects of ignorance became painfully visible in the 1960s and 1970s as unsophisticated policy makers, who had not yet learned to ask "And then what?", committed new errors with their solutions: tall smokestacks increased acid rain; waste incinerators increased air and water pollution; landfilling toxic wastes polluted groundwater; sludge from sewage treatment plants polluted land; and closing air leaks from buildings to save energy increased indoor air pollution. The "And then what?" question also should have been applied to new technologies but almost never was: widespread use of chlorofluorocarbons dangerously thinned the protective ozone layer; pesticides caused cancer and other diseases in humans and other creatures; widespread use of trucks increased energy consumption; and the invention of new chemicals (4,000 to 5,000 each year) overwhelmed the regulatory capability of the EPA.

More mistakes were made by allowing each level of government to establish its own environmental regulations, thereby introducing competition between cities, states, and nations to lower environmental standards in order to attract industries that pollute. The persistent effort to lower trade barriers between nations has another unintended consequence as footloose transnational corporations will be able to demand greater weakening of environmental standards in nations hoping to attract and retain industry.

Policy makers must learn how policy sectors are interconnected. Policy for transportation, agriculture, energy, commerce, labor, health, foreign affairs, defense, even justice, also impinge on environmental policy. The preservation of life systems on our planet will require transformation in all those sectors.

The Future?

Human civilization is threatening life systems. How much time do we have? Only a few decades. How fast can we learn? That depends. History shows us that social learning is agonizingly slow. Sometimes, however, it is astonishingly swift. As we persist in damaging life systems, nature will be our most powerful teacher. Will we look ahead and learn? Or will we wait for nature to use death to convince?

See also CONSERVATION; ENVIRONMENT; ENVIRONMENTAL ETHICS; EXTINCTION OF SPECIES; GLOBAL ENVIRONMENTAL PROBLEMS; ENVIRONMENTAL REFUGEES; GLOBAL WARMING; MEGACITIES; OZONE LAYER DEPLETION; PUBLIC POLICY CHANGE.

BIBLIOGRAPHY

DALY, HERMAN E. and COBB, JOHN B. JR., *For the Common Good: Redirecting the Economy Toward Community, the Environment, and a Sustainable Future.* Boston: Beacon Press, 1989.

GORE, AL. *Earth in the Balance: Ecology and the Human Spirit.* Boston: Houghton Mifflin, 1992.

MILBRATH, LESTER. *Envisioning a Sustainable Society: Learning Our Way Out.* Albany, NY: SUNY Press, 1989.

———. *Learning to Think Environmentally.* Albany, NY: SUNY Press, 1995.

Lester W. Milbrath

Environmental Refugees

Today, millions of people are fleeing or have been forced from their communities and homelands from the shock of sudden catastrophes or from the accumulated effects of land abuse, overcrowding, industrialization, pollution, severe weather and climate change, and other assaults on ecosystems throughout the world. These effects are often intensified by social prejudices, war, terrorism, chronic poverty, economic failures, unsustainable development, faulty technology, and the ignorance or willful violence that defiles, wastes, and depletes precious natural resources.

Those who flee are becoming known as environmental refugees, although "refugee" has been internationally defined and limited until now to those who have fled their countries because of a well-founded fear of persecution by reason of race, religion, nationality, social group, or political opinion. But people fleeing the environment also fear for their lives. Further, traditional forms of persecution may be part of their predicament; worse, they suffer a singularly bleak future because their homelands may be utterly destroyed, contaminated, or transformed. In the end, they have little or no hope of return.

One of the most frightening environmental disasters was the Chernobyl nuclear reactor accident in April 1986, on the Ukraine-Byelorussia border (Anspaugh, Catlin, and Goldman, 1988). During an experiment, the reactor became uncontrollable; it rapidly heated, and then exploded twice, blowing parts of the molten core through the top of the massive complex and continuing to burn for two weeks (Eisenbud, 1987). While the radioactive plume fell in a wide swath across the Northern Hemisphere, exposing 400 million persons, hundreds of thousands fled the blast area (Lofstedt and White, 1990).

The destinations of those who fled are not completely known, nor is it clear who returned, where they resettled, or who are still unsettled. Approximately 1,000 to 1,100, mostly elderly, returned illegally to Chernobyl's thirty-mile-radius "dead zone" (O'Neill, 1989). In 1988 it was reported that approximately 140,000 people initially evacuated were monitored for radiation effects (Milne, 1988). More than 11,600 Chernobyl children and more than 2,000 mothers were sent for medical treatment in Cuba from 1990 to 1993.

Although Chernobyl caused only a fraction of the environmental refugees in the world, examining the details of such an extraordinary disaster can bring to life the contemporary reality of the term and an appreciation for the human and environmental impacts that occur at the same time within each episode. Because there already may be at least twenty-five million environmental refugees worldwide, and millions more "protorefugees" suffering from near-disaster conditions that could happen at any time, people who are not yet refugees themselves may find it worthwhile to learn how to identify existing crises and anticipate future ones, design and implement preventive measures, and organize the restoration of damaged and abandoned homelands.

Defining and Recognizing Refugees, Evacuees, and Migrants

Refugees flee because they are forced to leave against their will and because their options to remain likely have been exhausted. For those in the shadow of Chernobyl, flight was the only way to avoid death from direct radiation; up to 1 million curies of radioactivity were released, a lethal dose for anyone caught in the open, downwind, within 15 kilometers of the reactor ("The Hard Rain . . .", *New Scientist*, 1986). In villages just beyond, there could be death from inhaling, absorbing, or consuming radioactive substances. Those still farther risked long-term chronic poisoning and cancer, and probably feared that their children and livestock would sicken or die. Women from these areas were advised not to have children; reportedly, forced abortions were given to every woman within a particular distance of the accident.

It is not productive to limit defining refugees to only those who have fled their countries. Environmental disaster episodes are place-specific; therefore, fleeing villages, cities, districts, or bioregions within countries should be sufficient. Some nations and many relief agencies now recognize the existence of these "internal refugees," who may be in hiding or held captive by severe conditions. In total, their numbers likely equal those who have actually crossed frontiers. Relaxing the traditional definition helps nonrefugees grasp the true magnitude of humanity's uprooting; refugees, then, become global indicators of quality of life.

Refugees need to make critical decisions. They have to draw on past experiences, their best guess about the future, and their sense of responsibility for each other's welfare. Their decisions come from (1) what is known for certain about the consequences of not fleeing; (2) what is not known for certain but is suspected to be true; (3) what is not known for certain but is overridden by the fear of staying or being left behind; and (4) what, if anything, can moderate, reverse, eliminate, or adapt to the situation quickly enough to avoid disaster. This is the fundamental predicament of people preparing to flee.

Refugees are "pushed" from danger, whereas migrants are "pulled" or attracted toward more viable destinations (Myers, 1995). Refugees are fleeing someplace they would rather not leave, but migrants are primarily drawn to where they expect better conditions. Without careful study, it may be difficult to make distinctions; at other times, the difference is clear. Emergency workers establishing relief camps, for example, report difficulties predicting where fleeing refugees will appear. Migrants, however, seem to have particular destinations in mind (Lowder, 1974).

There is an important time element involved. If Chernobyl had been simply a large industrial fire, residents may have returned soon after it was extinguished, without fear, and resumed their lives. It would have been an "evacuee" event, no less consequential in the short term, but much less so in the long term. Because, in actuality, Chernobyl was a massive radioactive explosion, the chances for safe return approached zero. Hence, those who fled were refugees.

Consonant with the prevailing definition, refugees not only flee from danger but also cannot expect or depend on their government's support or protection. Instead, they experience abandonment, ambivalence, indifference, incompetence, or outright antagonism. Sometimes governments refuse to address the causes of problems, or they take advantage of disasters to drive unwanted populations away, even out of the country. In the early 1990s, Somalia's answer to its subsistence crisis was the brutal mass-transfer of tens of thousands of people into the Sudan; many of these people were coincidentally government opponents.

The term *evacuees* implies being alerted, informed, and promptly conducted or directed away from harm according to rational and appropriate plans of action, including known destinations and adequate reception. At Chernobyl, a delayed evacuation began thirty-six hours after the explosion, mobilizing 1,100 buses, and was not completed until the tenth day after the accident (Eisenbud, 1987; Lofstedt and White, 1990). Unquestionably, the government's behavior contributed to the residents' peril, so Chernobyl victims suffered the "refugee," not the "evacuee," experience.

There is a perplexing question: "When does a refugee stop being a refugee?" This would normally occur after war or persecution ceases and people are repatriated and resettled, recognizing, however, that refugees have the human right not to be forced back. Alternatively, refugees may have already safely settled elsewhere. But this happens slowly; for environmental refugees, it may be generations or never, especially if homelands have been logged, flooded, depleted, mined, polluted, or irradiated. After Chernobyl, farming was problematic because it was virtually impossible to prevent the spread of radioactive dust as the soil was plowed. Early in 1989, three years after the blast, the Byelorussian government announced that twenty villages were to be evacuated because several hot spots of intensive radiation had been discovered.

Refugees may have trouble resettling anywhere at all. After Chernobyl, some villages resisted welcoming irradiated refugees because of the feared consequences of eventual intermarriage. On April 26, 1993, Byelorussian radio reported that the rate of defects in newborn babies had increased by 18 percent and the number of oncological (tumor-producing) diseases had nearly trebled.

Worldwide, refugee numbers are sharply climbing. Added to each new crisis, there are often longer resettlement times, the children of refugees born in camps or on the run, and the recurrent uprooting of refugees. The reality for most may be, "Once a refugee, always a refugee."

Refugees have identities and life stories to tell, if they survive. As of the mid-1990s, refugees are predominantly women and children, as high as 80 percent of the total. However, they are only the surviving fraction of each crisis; others die or are killed en route, and others may not be able to flee. Thus, relying on refugee counts alone greatly understates the severity of episodes.

Whole communities become refugees: parents and children, teachers, laborers, scientists, artisans, professionals, soldiers, farmers, and politicians. Except for certain tragic circumstances of time and place, refugees share many characteristics with nonrefugees. In other ways, refugees are distinctly vulnerable; as events unfold, they become impoverished, desperate for signs of hope, and driven away by forces beyond their control.

Some people argue "there always will be refugees," and "nothing can be done about it." Some blame refugees for their own misfortune. The fact is, the root causes are often found in the attitudes and practices of people who are not yet refugees themselves.

The Environmental Dimension of Contemporary Refugees

Humans have degraded the environment more than any other species and, in places, the damage appears beyond recovery. Because humans inhabit every continent and virtually every region, it is inescapable that some should become endangered by their own actions or those of others. These actions include denuding the land, generating and discarding toxic and infectious wastes, mining recklessly, shortcutting natural processes, disrupting hydrological cycles, and driving species to extinction. Some of these are disastrous even when minimally undertaken in sensitive areas, but the greatest harm is from the massive scale at which they are promoted and practiced worldwide, and the pace at which the damages outstrip pollution control and prevention, ecological restoration, and natural recovery processes.

Just as inevitable as the effects are the refugees fleeing them. It begins when the environment fails to provide what people demand, and ends after a critical but unsuccessful period of ignoring, denying, acknowledging, and then trying to adapt to the adversities. With the world's population approaching 10 billion by 2050, millions are having trouble staying where they are while their safety and resources disappear.

There are an estimated 25 million environmental refugees, meaning approximately 1 per 200 Earth inhabitants. A doubling is conceivable by 2010, and 100 million or more by midcentury if global warming causes higher sea levels, stronger floods and storms, and generally less favorable weather patterns (Myers, 1995). That would mean approximately 1 per 100 inhabitants.

These numbers firmly support the position that environmental refugees should be included in official estimates kept by governments, refugee organizations, and the U.N. high commissioner on refugees. Official counts are important because they influence the level of effort expended to anticipate, find, and protect refugees, and trigger diplomacy against human rights violators, polluters, and other unscrupulous actors on the international stage. Official tallies neglect not only environmental refugees, but also economic refugees, and all internal refugees regardless of why they flee. If included, the total could be 50 million to 100 million people.

Scientists are reaching a consensus on what conditions produce environmental refugees. They include landlessness, deforestation, desertification, soil erosion, salinization and water logging of irrigated lands, water deficits and droughts, agricultural stress, biodiversity depletion, extreme weather events and climate change, population pressures, diseases and malnutrition, poverty, governmental shortcomings, ethnic and cultural prejudices, warmaking, toxic chemicals, waste disposal, radiation, and a host of pollution problems that plague ecosystems. Many of the "-ation" and "-ition" factors are complexes of problems that cannot be simply attacked and eliminated as one would fight a bacterial infection. They are the end stages of norms and practices that developed over centuries, at great expense to the environment and the well-being of billions of people.

Even with total commitment, it will take decades or generations to correct these deadly flaws. Achieving sustainable development, for example, is still beyond precise definition and experience. Some indigenous cultures may have slowly approached sustainability, but for five centuries they been have conquered, robbed, and eradicated; because much of their wisdom was oral, not written, it largely disappeared with the people. Thus we may be obliged to relearn almost everything, with considerably less time and material available to perfect our own restorations.

Environmental Refugees from Developing Countries

While environmental refugees are worldwide, there are some very large concentrations: 4 million in the Horn of Africa, 2 million in the Sahel, up to 3 million in rural areas of central China, and perhaps 500,000 in Mexico and Central America (Myers, 1995). Their presence is the legacy of years of land abuse, agricultural collapse, drought, starvation, and civil war. There are also pressures to sell scarce resources abroad for currency.

Episodes are predominantly in rural-agricultural areas with high population densities, intense poverty, poor soil, malnutrition, and food and water shortages. Many refugees appear in cities, some of which already hold millions of jobless people; the refugees live on bare subsistence diets and are surrounded by filth and contagion. Refugees are also forced from relatively pristine areas targeted for rapid industrialization by national programs and other interests. These areas are rich in mineral and coal deposits, dense forests, rushing rivers, and valleys suitable for hydropower and fossil fuel plants. The projects are frequently opposed, but proceed anyway with little or no care for the land destroyed or the refugees caused (Shiva, 1991). In India, an estimated 20 million people have been displaced by official projects, including dams, mines, forests preserves, and irrigation, and in Egypt in the 1970s, more than 1 million hectares of soil were stripped from productive farms to make bricks for the Aswan High Dam (International Organization for Migration and Refugee Policy Group, 1992). Since the 1992 Environmental Summit in Rio de Janeiro, however, counterpressures have grown in the Third World, forcing the World Bank and other funders to reconsider such heavy-handed development (World Bank, 1994).

There are many tragic examples in the developing world. For years, Saddam Hussein has waged a vicious war against the Marsh Arabs in southern Iraq. Under the pretense of agricultural development, his army is driving out and killing the inhabitants, some of whom are opposition Shiite Muslims, and draining and burning this 17,000-square-kilometer emerald remnant of the fabled Fertile Crescent (Pearce, 1992). During the Persian Gulf War in 1991, American troops swept right around the marshes, providing no haven for the thousands of people trapped there or fleeing toward Iran.

In the vast Asian desert farther east, the former Soviet Union's thirst for water to irrigate and expand cotton growing has almost totally intercepted the headwaters of the Aral Sea. The sea has precipitously shrunk from 60,000 square kilometers in the 1950s to fewer than 50,000 square kilometers; salinity has trebled since the 1960s, wiping out fisheries that once caught 50,000 tons annually. Generations-old villages have been abandoned; many of them are now as much as 40 to 50 kilometers from the retreating shoreline (Eustis and Micklin, 1993).

During the Vietnam War, U.S. forces conducted environmental warfare against the North Vietnamese, dropping defoliants and other toxic chemicals throughout the war zone. A 1982 U.N. study reported that 15,000 square kilometers of mangrove forest had been destroyed. Other researchers found that countless bomb craters not only halted farming but also harbored the stagnant-water habitat necessary for mosquitoes and other disease vectors. Millions of peasants suddenly became environmental refugees (International Organization for Migration and Refugee Policy Group, 1992).

In Eastern Europe, during Soviet rule, more than 100 villages and the town of Most in northern Bohemia (now in the Czech Republic) were obliterated, and 200,000 people lost their homes to strip miners questing for low-grade coal.

Environmental Refugees from Industrialized Countries

As of the mid-1990s, fewer environmental refugees are found in industrialized countries than in the Third World, but their causes, numbers, and lessons are still important. In many ways, they signal what additional grief is in store as the rest of the world industrializes, only more so, because of the much larger populations involved.

The potential for environmental refugees in the United States and other industrialized countries must be in the millions, but unlike the huge "point" source regions of refugees in the Third World, the impression is one of a multitude of smaller "non-point" sources. Exposure to chemicals, air pollution, and toxic contamination of water supplies are among the most serious threats. In 1991 the U.S. Environmental Protection Agency estimated that 3.3 million people were living within one mile and 41 million people within four miles of 1,134 locations on the national priority list of major toxic sites (National Research Council, 1991). The Congressional Office of Technology Assessment variously estimated that the list of sites could readily exceed 10,000 and might be as many as 439,000 (National Research Council, 1991). Poor rural and urban communities, especially in the southern United States, and near Native American reservations, are especially vulnerable to waste disposers and other handlers of toxic substances. The practice of siting pollution-prone activities in or near relatively defenseless communities has become known as environmental racism.

Outside the United States, a complete accounting of refugees fleeing the vicinity of dumpsites, landfills, refineries, incinerators, military installations, and factories in the rest of the developed world has not yet been found. Nor have estimates of numbers that could possibly be affected by future nuclear accidents. This is becoming a particularly ripe scenario to consider as plants age and spent fuel rods pile up on-site. Worldwide there are more than 500 commercial nuclear power stations (*Nuclear News*, 1990).

In the 1970s, Love Canal, N.Y., and Times Beach, Mo., were the first scenes of major government expulsions from neighborhoods poisoned by toxic chemicals. Conditions at these and other toxic sites have forced the permanent relocation of several thousand families (International Organization for Migration and Refugee Policy Group, 1992). Love Canal refugee Lois Gibbs founded the Citizens' Clearinghouse for Hazardous Wastes, Falls Church, Va., to monitor the battles and fate of toxic victims in the United States and to provide grassroots education. The National Toxics Campaign, Boston, operates a citizens' environmental testing lab to help perform independent investigations.

There have been many reports of adults and children who become extremely sensitive, sometimes deathly ill, when repeatedly exposed to the solvents, synthetic chemicals, fabrics, and plastics found in modern building materials, furnishings, clothing, motor vehicles, electrical equipment, appliances, and cleaning agents. Exposure can cause disabling symptoms and force victims to flee their homes, schools, and workplaces temporarily or even permanently. Widely publicized cases involved reactions to chlordane pesticide that was injected into housing foundations and to the phenolformaldehyde component of woodbinding adhesives formerly used to manufacture cabinets and construction panels. Related to this is the emerging problem of "sick-building syndrome," a complex condition wherein chemicals, microorganisms, or other agents inside poorly ventilated buildings interact to make people so ill they must flee.

Once contaminated, there may be no practical, technical, or affordable method available to detoxify some buildings or neighborhoods. They may have to be closed, abandoned, demolished, or limited to those who can tolerate contaminated surroundings. Widely publicized cases concern high levels of radon, lead-based paint, lead-borne drinking water, or asbestos. In the 1980s, Woodstock, N.Y., suffered a near-catastrophe when asbestos cement municipal water lines disintegrated, sending deadly fibers into household drinking water. In the same era, an eastern Pennsylvania community prepared to flee when formaldehyde appeared in private wells; matters worsened when a major oil pipeline ruptured into a local stream.

In cases such as these, homeowners are agonizingly squeezed. They want to leave immediately, especially for their children's sake. But when toxics are discovered, real-estate values plummet; it becomes impossible to sell homes for enough to permit relocation. The people become refugees-in-captivity, drinking or inhaling chemicals as their fate worsens.

Citizens have been driven from the vicinity of farms, orchards, and forests that broadcast fertilizers and toxic chemicals. During the 1970s and 1980s, campaigns were mounted against aerial spraying of hardwood defoliants such as 2,4-D in U.S. national forests. Spray drift was suspected of contaminating watersheds, endangering homesteaders and their properties. In industrialized countries, toxics victims are often forced to sue to recover the value of homes or to obtain adequate compensation to relocate. Not all cases are decided in the victims' favor.

The United States was once a developing country, and many areas are still being transformed by large public and private projects, with their accompanying share of environmental refugees. Missouri, for example, once had more miles of free-flowing streams than any other state except Alaska; now Missouri is covered with artificial lakes, with remnants of farms and forests lying below. In the mid-1970s, the Army Corps of Engineers threatened to dam the wild and scenic Meramec River flowing through thousands of acres of fertile land and century-old farmsteads. Intimidated by corps tactics, outraged by minimal compensation, and fiercely land-tenacious, a "Free Rivers, Free People" campaign stopped construction of the dam; unfortunately, many had already been forced to sign away their land and homes under threat of eminent domain.

As big cities sprawl out onto coastlines, or atop earthquake zones, or into mountain foothills and dense forests, certain refugee episodes are arising from what could be called "natural backlash." There have been serious near-city forest fires, earthquakes, floods, landslides, and combinations of these in Japan, Australia, Europe, and the United States. Of course, the denser the population, the larger the number of refugees. When Hurricane Andrew struck the built-up southern coast of Florida in 1992, many of the 500,000 evacuees never thought they would spend months in tents and emergency shelters as environmental refugees. They subsisted on charity and government rations; many were jobless, with only the belongings they packed the day of the storm. California's coast has also experienced cycles of storm, drought, fires, and earthquakes, with billions of dollars in damage, causing people to move in a kind of reverse migration toward Colorado.

Worldwide Environmental Refugees from Climate Change

Ominously, effects from future climate changes that could cause sea level rise, severe storms, coastline erosion and surges, and very difficult growing seasons may totally overshadow all other refugee causes experienced in the world to date. There could be large-scale displacements in both rich and poor nations, the difference in severity being that the former will be "susceptible" but likely able to afford timely protection, while the latter, with most of the world's population, will be extremely "vulnerable," not being able to afford the protection or the time to adapt quickly enough or escape disaster. Scientists have forecast 13 million climate-change environmental refugees in Bangladesh, 16 million in Egypt, at least 73 million in China, 20 million in

India, 1 million or more from small island-states, and 50 million additional from agriculturally dislocated regions by the year 2050 (Myers, 1995).

What to Remember

World refugees numbers have probably crossed an important threshold that renders conventional disaster relief assistance (blankets, tents, water bottles, etc.) completely and embarrassingly inadequate for both the magnitude and the complexity of this crisis as it is now developing.

While the very existence of refugees has always indicated major flaws in human coexistence, the "discovery" of immense numbers of environmental refugees also verifies major flaws in relations with natural life support systems.

Beyond the terrible misery and suffering experienced, contemporary refugees, no matter what kind, are basically "people out of place." This suggests that the most productive strategies will put more attention into the "place" (because every episode is place-specific) rather than the "people" (because people are pretty much the same the world over, except for their "sense of place").

"Place" and "environment" are synonymous. Incredibly fast-growing numbers of environmental refugees confirm that the environmental roots, and uprooting, of humanity have been neglected for too long.

Knowing the environment's systems and staying safely within their operating limits is the only way to prevent environmental collapse, the only way to know how to respond when trouble begins, and ultimately the only way to avoid becoming an environmental refugee.

Environmental refugees and ecological restoration are inseparable conceptually. Specializing in the first means treating the symptom, not the cause; it ensures that there will always be more refugees. Specializing in the second is lonely; those who will appreciate it the most are the ones who used to be there.

Clearly, when the first important agreements were drawn up to receive refugees fleeing World War I and World War II, nations never anticipated the need to recognize or protect people fleeing from environmentally caused disasters. All that has now changed. Just as clearly, we are in a transitional period where strict definitions obstruct rather than facilitate addressing the plight of uprooted humanity. In the future we will learn to anticipate and prevent conditions leading to refugee episodes, no matter what may be the direct cause or combination of factors. At minimum, this means challenging the norm that "there will always be refugees" and advocating the right to secure homelands and safe environments for all people.

See also CLIMATE AND METEOROLOGY; DEFORESTATION; DISASTERS, PLANNING FOR; ENVIRONMENT; NATURAL DISASTERS; REFUGEES.

BIBLIOGRAPHY

ANSPAUGH, LYNN R.; CATLIN, ROBERT J.; and GOLDMAN, MARVIN. "The Global Impact of the Chernobyl Reactor Incident." *Science* 242 (December 18, 1988).

EISENBUD, MERRIL. *Environmental Radioactivity from Natural, Industrial, and Military Sources*, 3rd ed. San Diego: Academic Press, 1987.

EUSTIS, MARK, and MICKLIN, PHILIP. "Anatomy of a Disaster: A Bird's Eye of a Man-Sized Problem: A Satellite Records the Draining of a Mighty Sea." *Earthwatch* 12/4 (May–June 1993).

"The Hard Rain Falling Over Europe." *New Scientist* (May 8, 1986).

INTERNATIONAL ORGANIZATION FOR MIGRATION AND REFUGEE POLICY GROUP. *Migration and the Environment*. Geneva, Switzerland: International Organization for Migration; Washington, DC: Refugee Policy Group, 1992.

LOFSTEDT, RAGNAR E., and WHITE, ALLEN L. "Chernobyl Four Years After: Repercussions Continue." *Environment* 32/3 (1990).

LOWDER, STELLA. "Migration and Urbanization in Peru." In B. S. HOYLE, ed. *Spatial Aspects of Development*. London: John Wiley, 1974.

MYERS, NORMAN. *Environmental Refugees: Draft Report*. Washington, DC: Climate Institute, 1995.

NATIONAL RESEARCH COUNCIL, COMMITTEE ON ENVIRONMENTAL EPIDEMIOLOGY. *Environmental Epidemiology: Public Health and Hazardous Wastes*. Washington, DC: National Academy Press, 1991.

O'NEILL, BILL. "Life in the Exclusion Zone." *New Scientist* (July 1, 1989).

SHIVA, VANDANA. *Ecology and the Politics of Survival: Conflicts Over Natural Resources in India*. Tokyo: United Nations University Press; Newbury Park, CA: Sage Publications, 1991.

World Bank. "Involuntary Population Displacement Becoming More Significant." *Environment Bulletin* 6/2 (Spring 1994).

Stuart M. Leiderman

Epidemics

Large-scale, even global epidemics of infectious disease, of which the current pandemic of human immunodeficiency virus (HIV) infection is a powerful example, are likely to become increasingly common in the future. The extraordinary increases in movements of people, goods, and ideas which characterize the modern world provide the critical ingredient for such worldwide epidemics.

The world contains many microbiological threats to health which currently have a limited geographical scope. In addition, new disease-causing agents have been recently discovered, including the agents of Legionnaire's disease, hepatitis C virus, Lassa fever virus, the Hantavirus recently identified in the southwestern United States, and HIV itself. It is generally assumed that these pathogens have existed for a long time.

The recognition of "new diseases" may result from several, often interacting factors. For example, Legionnaire's disease required a cluster of infections at a major urban convention for its discovery. Also while the disease caused by the newly recognized Hantavirus in the United States undoubtedly existed in the past, a specific cluster of infections was required for its identification (as with Lassa fever).

In addition, some "new diseases" may result from changes in human behavior or in related ecologic factors. For example, human exposure to Legionnaire's disease appears related to specific technologies involving water use (i.e., cooling towers which provided the mode for propagation). Human actions, such as inadequate sterilization of medical or other skin-piercing equipment, contribute to the spread of the Ebola virus as well as HIV. Environmental changes, including large-scale problems of global warming, may produce conditions which favor the spread of infectious agents, such as cholera.

Yet the movements of people, goods, and ideas represent the most important underlying stimuli for new global epidemics of infectious disease. Since about 1950, the number of international tourists has increased nearly twenty-fold; travel and tourism is now considered to be the largest industry in the world. In addition to tourists, business travelers, migrants, and refugees contribute to the movements of people within and between countries.

Global economic interdependence is well established, based on the increasingly unconstrained movements of capital, labor, and goods. Goods may carry or help transmit infectious agents directly, as when mosquitoes infected with the dengue virus were carried from Asia to Latin America in used automobile tires. In addition, adverse global economic conditions contribute to or even create the vulnerability of populations to infectious diseases by depressing living standards and diminishing access to health services.

The movement of ideas is also vital. Global communications create and convey powerful images of modernity and sophistication to people around the world. In turn, these images influence individual behaviors in ways that can increase health risks (i.e., sexual behavior, cigarette smoking, and violence).

The combination of social forces described above virtually ensures that new microbial threats to health will emerge on a global scale in the future. The HIV pandemic not only illustrates the speed and intensity of the global spread of an infectious agent, but also demonstrates the high level of global vulnerability to new epidemics.

While the origin of HIV is obscure and may never be known with certainty, the worldwide spread of the virus appears to have started in the mid-1970s. By 1980, an estimated 100,000 people had become infected with HIV; during the 1980s, this number increased about 100-fold, to about 10 million. According to some recent estimates, a cumulative total of between 40 and 110 million people may have been HIV infected by the year 2000. Although first recognized in the United States, HIV infections clearly had occurred in other parts of the world, including Africa and Haiti, prior to its recognition and discovery. By early 1993, not only had virtually every country been affected by HIV, but Asia, a region little affected in the mid-1980s, experienced explosive epidemics of the HIV infection. The future of this dynamic and volatile pandemic will be determined by the scope, intensity, and capacity of the human response to it, which includes both societal and scientific dimensions.

There is a major lesson from the HIV experience beyond the recognition of our modern vulnerability to the spread of infectious agents. The great likelihood that new pandemic threats will emerge, and given the ways in which a new health problem in any country may rapidly become a multinational or even global problem, it is essential to develop a global monitoring, detection, and rapid response capacity. Currently, no such system exists in any meaningful way. For example, the discovery of AIDS in 1981 was highly fortuitous, requiring: (a) the recent scientific advances allowing identification of human retroviruses; (b) the occurrence of AIDS in an industrialized country with excellent diagnostic capacity and a national surveillance system; (c) the appearance of highly unusual infections and cancers which facilitated awareness and recognition of a new health problem; and (d) the involvement of a self-aware and distinct community (homosexual men) which also helped stimulate concern and awareness. Had AIDS involved only developing countries, or caused an increase in "normal" illnesses, or been widely spread throughout society, it would have taken longer to recognize and identify.

A truly global system of disease surveillance and response is the appropriate response to the changes in global society and ecology which will continue to make the modern world highly vulnerable to epidemic disease. Rather than considering infectious diseases as stories of the past (plague, cholera, tuberculosis), the world faces perhaps more danger from epidemic disease than ever before. Still, the conditions of global communication which underlie the threat also offer the potential for scientific and societal collaboration, at a global level, which can make all the difference.

See also BIOETHICS; ENVIRONMENT; ENVIRONMENTAL REFUGEES; GENETIC TECHNOLOGIES; PUBLIC HEALTH.

BIBLIOGRAPHY

Centers for Disease Control. "Addressing Emerging Infectious Disease Threats: A Prevention Strategy for the United States." *Morbidity and Mortality Weekly Report.* No. RR-5 (1994): 43.

GARRETT, LAURIE. *The Coming Plague.* New York: Farrar, Strauss, and Giroux, 1994.

LEVINS, R.; AWERBUCH, T.; BRINKMANN, U., et al. "The Emergence of New Diseases." *American Scientist* 82 (1994): 52–60.

MANN, JONATHAN M.; TARANTOLA, D.; and NETTER, T., eds. *AIDS in the World.* Cambridge, MA: Harvard University Press, 1992.

Jonathan M. Mann

Eschatology.

See APOCALYPTIC FUTURE.

Espionage and Counterintelligence

Intelligence, as it has been understood since the end of World War II, is a dying business. The end of the Cold War brought with it the destruction of a world where each intelligence agency had clear targets, broadly understood the nature of the threat, and had a clear role and the technical means to combat it.

The overwhelming amount of work carried out by the main intelligence agencies in the NATO and Warsaw Pact countries was in support of the Cold War. It was aimed either at gathering intelligence about the enemy or trying to prevent the enemy's spies from gathering information. Despite the end of the Cold War, it is clear that every country needs an intelligence service that can play a part in guaranteeing national security. In those countries of the former communist bloc where new agencies are emerging from the old, they are doing so with the help of their former enemies in the West. Being born with all the safeguards of a modern Western intelligence agency might ensure that they do not become political tools, but are used only for the collection and analysis of information vital to the security of the state (as opposed to individual governments of whatever political complexion).

The end of the Cold War also brought with it calls for cutbacks in both the military and intelligence communities. As a result, every intelligence agency suffered budget cuts—but some less than others. In 1993, for example, Britain's Secret Intelligence Service reduced its staff by only 50 out of around 1,900, while the Security Service maintained its existing staff. The American and Russian intelligence agencies were not so fortunate.

The KGB has been destroyed, its old directorates broken up, and its power cut. Staff abroad has been reduced by 50 percent, and some thirty stations have been closed. As the KGB fell apart after the second Russian revolution, so a new era began that divided the old monolith into a number of different parts, all of which are subject to a form of parliamentary oversight. The old First Chief Directorate, which was responsible for foreign spying, became the SVR but with altered responsibilities. According to Yevgeni Primakov, the head of the SVR, in the future there will be no spying for political rather than national security purposes. Attempts to subvert foreign governments through covert support of terrorist organizations, opposition groups, or even agents in place will not be tolerated. This new pragmatism is driven in part by changing political circumstances, but also because the SVR simply does not have the cash to pay for such extravagance. Greater sharing of intelligence on such matters as drugs, organized crime, and proliferation is being established.

There has been little reduction in the activities of the intelligence arm of the Russian military. They continue to try and steal western scientific and technological secrets to help the struggling Russian industrial base. They are also active in trying to recruit spies in the major industrial countries.

Public protestations aside, many of the old KGB have simply donned new uniforms and overnight become staunch democrats. It is difficult to believe that all these thousands of men and women are genuine converts, and there is ample evidence that at many levels in the current Russian political system the levers are still being pulled by the old KGB operators. At the wish of their political masters, most Western spy agencies, such as those in America, Germany, and France, have been forced publicly to embrace the new KGB, exchanging delegations and declaring their chief spies in each other's capitals.

Aside from Russia, the end of the Cold War has had the most dramatic effect in Britain. In the space of four years, the secrecy that surrounded the three principal intelligence organizations—the SIS (Secret Intelligence Service), the Security Service, and the GCHQ (Government Communications Headquarters)—has ended. Two new acts of Parliament have brought the agencies out into the light, complete with a visible Parliamentary oversight system. For a country like Britain, where the overwhelming majority of the population are tolerant of a secret society in a way that would be both illegal and unacceptable in America, these changes have been little short of revolutionary. In America, Congress cut the budget of the American intelligence community by about 25 percent and a budget of $28 billion was authorized for 1994. The CIA has changed its priorities and has become a more open intelligence service, although the basic structure of American intelligence remains in place.

Military threats to the state, proliferation, counterespionage, drugs, terrorism, industrial espionage, and international financial crime are the new priorities for intelligence agencies around the world. The new world order is so unstable that each of these areas requires additional resources if the challenges are to be met effectively.

The end of the Cold War and the collapse of authoritarian communist states released ethnic tensions that go back hundreds of years and are only now finding expression. In the early part of this century, many of these ethnic tensions were limited in their influence because of a lack of technology or weaponry. Now modern conventional and unconventional weapons are readily available. It is certain that there will be a proliferation of small wars in the future.

Terrorism, arms control, and drugs pose unique challenges to the intelligence community. By the end of this century, a number of Middle Eastern countries are likely to have ballistic missiles that can carry chemical or nuclear warheads and will have the range to reach most of Western Europe. As the intelligence failures in Iraq demonstrated, there must be a determined effort to gather the information and act upon it before it is too late.

Both drugs and terrorism are more insidious, but their impact can be enormous. The cost of fighting the drug war in America is currently over $13 billion a year and rising, without a commensurate reduction either in the amount of drug use or the profits being generated for the drug barons. New patterns of trafficking emerging out of the former communist countries suggest that there will be new sources of supply and an increased number of illegal drugs in the future.

In terrorism, too, the nature of the problem is escalating rapidly, in part through the rise of Islamic fundamentalism, which has produced a new brand of terror. There is no grand conspiracy to replace the illusion of a grand conspiracy of the Marxist-Leninist terrorists of the 1970s. Then it was convenient to think of Moscow as the architect of the bombings and the killings, the single hand controlling the explosion of revolutionary fervor that erupted almost simultaneously all over the world.

There needs to be a greater emphasis on human sources. To a large extent, only personnel on the ground can bring back intelligence on terrorists, underground arms networks, or the release of nuclear materials onto the black market. The illegal operators, be they terrorists or arms dealers, now understand the capabilities of the various technical means of gathering intelligence, and have developed effective methods of combatting them. The terrorists no longer talk on the telephone (unless they are amateurs like those who bombed the World Trade Center in New York), and drug dealers do not communicate by fax or arms merchants through a single front-company via telex. Such communications are easily intercepted. Intelligence increasingly will become a high-tech game.

See also ARMS RACE; INTERNATIONAL TENSIONS; NATIONAL SECURITY; TERRORISM.

BIBLIOGRAPHY

BATHURST, ROBERT B. *Intelligence and the Mirror: On Creating an Enemy*. Newbury Park, CA: Sage Publications, 1993.

JORDAN, AMOS A. *American National Security: Policy and Protest*. 4th ed. Baltimore, MD: Johns Hopkins University Press, 1993.

TOFFLER, ALVIN, and TOFFLER, HEIDI. *War and Anti-War: Survival at the Dawn of the 21st Century*. Boston: Little, Brown, 1993.

James Adams

Estate and Financial Planning

Several trends that have affected estate and financial planning in the latter part of the twentieth century will continue, even accelerate, in the years to come. The role played by financial planners and estate-planning specialists in the wealth transmission process will remain an important one.

The first trend, what might be called the "democratization" of estate planning, has been the most significant one. Until the late 1960s, estate planning—the utilization of trusts and other arrangements to reduce the tax cost of transferring wealth to the next generation—was a concern only to the ultra wealthy. Since World War II, unprecedented wealth has been accumulated by a broad segment of the populace, most notably through the growth of closely held businesses and investments in securities, mutual funds, life insurance, and pension plans, and through increases in the value of homes and real estate. Over the next two decades, all of this wealth—estimates have been as high as $8 trillion—will pass through the owners' estates to the next generation or to charity. Many persons whose parents made do with simple wills (if they had wills at all) will find it essential to employ far more sophisticated arrangements if they do not want the taxing authorities to be major beneficiaries of their estates.

For many years, a $60,000 exemption from the estate tax kept the vast majority of Americans off the transfer tax rolls. By the mid-1970s, the $60,000 figure had become unrealistically low, and in 1976 Congress replaced it with an exemption (actually an "exemption equivalent" tied to a tax credit) of $175,625, to be phased in gradually. In 1981, this figure was increased to $600,000 (again, to be phased in gradually). As wealth continues to accumulate and the value of the dollar declines, Congress is likely to reconsider again the appropriate amount of an exemption from transfer taxes.

A second trend has been the incessant reexamination of our transfer tax laws by Congress. For many years, the tax laws affecting wealth transmission were relatively constant. From the enactment of the Internal Revenue Code of 1954 until 1976, the only major change was a 1969 statute dealing with "charitable remainder" trusts. In this environment, clients could rely on an established and predictable tax system in formulating estate plans for themselves and their families. Persons did not have to review or revise their wills unless their economic circumstances or family situations changed.

Beginning with the Tax Reform Act of 1976, fundamental changes in the transfer tax laws have been made on almost an annual basis. The Revenue Reconciliation Act of 1993 was the tenth major amendment to our tax laws since 1976, not to mention several technical corrections acts in between. Each of these new laws affected existing estate plans, often in major ways. Income-shifting and estate-planning techniques that could be employed in the early 1980s no longer exist and have been replaced with new ones. Authors have despaired of publishing hardcover books, concerned that the printed materials may soon become obsolete or even dangerously wrong. Some of the most intrusive laws, enacted with uncommon haste, proved to be unworkable and were later repealed or replaced. One of the most notable, a "carryover basis" rule enacted in 1976, was repealed in 1979. The notorious "anti-freeze" statute enacted in 1987, overhauled by amendments in 1988 and 1989, was repealed in 1990. A generation-skipping transfer tax enacted in 1976 was repealed retroactively in 1986, only to be replaced with a more draconian measure that taxes offending generation-skipping transfers at a 55 percent rate. In response to these changes, many persons have found it necessary to revise their estate plans in light of a significant new tax law, only to see the law modified, repealed, or replaced a few years later.

Although the estate and gift taxes raise relatively little revenue in the federal scheme, it is likely that the transfer laws will undergo periodic review and revision in the coming decades impelled largely by the federal deficit. Staying abreast of any changes will continue to be important to all persons with accumulated wealth, and to the professionals who advise them.

A third trend has been the increased importance of "nonprobate" assets in the planning decisions of many clients. (Nonprobate assets are interests in property that pass at death other than by will or intestate succession and which are not subject to administration in the probate courts.) Two of the most significant forms of wealth that many individuals have involve such nonprobate assets: life insurance and deferred compensation benefits prominent among them. For an increasing number of individuals, a last will and testament will be the least important document relating to the disposition of wealth—often far less important, in terms of the dollars involved, than life insurance, pension plan, or individual retirement account (IRA) beneficiary designations.

Since World War II, the dollar value of life-insurance coverage has greatly increased, not only for the traditional purpose of providing economic pro-

tection for surviving family members, but also to fund buy-sell agreements and other business arrangements and to address liquidity problems that an estate may face. The Treasury Department can be expected to continue to challenge techniques whereby life insurance proceeds escape transfer taxes on the insured's death. In response, taxpayers' counselors will continue to devise new planning strategies.

A 1980 U.S. Department of Labor report projected that by 1995, the holdings in private pension plans would exceed $900 billion. In fact, figures reported several years later showed that by 1980 there already were assets valued at $642 billion in 480,000 private pension plans. In 1988, 730,000 private pension plans (146,000 defined benefit plans and 584,000 defined contribution plans) held assets worth $1.94 trillion, and by 1992 the value had grown to $3.3 trillion. Adding in the $988 billion in funded state and local government pension plans, $304 billion in the funded federal civil-service and railroad retirement programs, and $647 billion in IRAs, the value of assets in private and public pension plans in 1992 totalled $5.25 trillion (1993 Statistical Abstract of the United States 526 [1994]). All indications are that this form of wealth will continue to grow, not only from continuing contributions by workers and their employers, but because the tax-deferred buildup of investment income make such plans so attractive.

A compex scheme of "minimum distribution rules" reflects a congressional policy that the benefits of qualified pension plans and IRAs are to be used to provide funds for the plan participant's retirement and not for the tax-free buildup of an inheritance for the participant's heirs. Under current law, distributions from a qualified plan or IRA must commence no later than April 1 following the year in which the participant reaches age 70 1/2. Despite this requirement, substantial funds will pass to designated beneficiaries on the participant's death, when the funds are subject to both income tax and estate tax. Without planning, combined taxes on these benefits can reach confiscatory levels. Planning decisions will continue to be challenging, as the rules governing distribution and taxation of plan benefits are dismayingly complex even by Internal Revenue Code standards.

Although all qualified plan benefits ultimately must pass through the income tax mill, the assurance that tax revenues will be received in the future tends not to assuage the appetite of any current administration. In recent years, Congress has limited the amounts that can be contributed to a qualified plan and has enacted a supplemental tax on excess accumulations and excess distributions from a plan or IRA. The phenomenal growth and tempting size of such funds make it likely that additional limits and taxes on plan benefits will be proposed.

Another trend affecting estate planning has been the increase in life expectancies brought about by advances in medical science and technology. The financial and medical problems faced by an aging population will continue to have a profound effect on the estate planning practice. Until very recently, lawyers and other professionals in the estate practice dealt almost exclusively with the property consequences of death. Lawyers drafted wills to govern the disposition of property and then, after the client died, supervised the estate's administration. The lawyer's client was never around to participate in, or obtain directly the benefits of, the estate planning that he or she had paid for. In contrast, estate planning professionals are increasingly involved with events that take place during the client's lifetime and in providing advice and services that benefit the client as well as his or her successors.

With increased longevity have come increased concerns as to the management of property in the event of a temporary or permanent incapacity as well as concerns about who will make health care decisions if the client loses the ability to make them. While guardianship and conservatorship laws have been reformed, in most states these are still seen as the least effective means of handling the property of a disabled person and as the refuge of those who do not plan in advance. Revocable trusts, almost unheard of until the late 1960s, are now staples in estate planning, in many cases supplanting the need for a will. Greater use will be made of revocable trusts, durable powers of attorney, and other property management arrangements in handling the property of incapacitated persons. On another front, heightened awareness of the economic and emotional costs of prolonging life will lead to an increased use and refinement of health care powers of attorney and "living wills."

Finally, the changing structure of American families has made planning decisions more complicated for many couples. The dramatic rise in the divorce rate, with divorce often followed by remarriage, has increased the instances in which one or both spouses have children by an earlier marriage. In this setting, devising an estate plan that will be seen as satisfactory by all surviving family members is no easy task. While the level of will contests may remain relatively constant, fiduciary litigation over the administration of estates and trusts is likely to increase, making one's appointment as executor or trustee a more hazardous undertaking than in the past.

See also AGING OF THE POPULATION; DERIVATIVES; HOME OWNERSHIP; INSURANCE; INVESTMENTS; LONGEVITY; PUBLIC ASSISTANCE PROGRAMS: SOCIAL SECURITY.

BIBLIOGRAPHY

CHRISTENSEN, DONALD. *Surviving the Coming Mutual Fund Crisis*. Boston: Little, Brown, 1994.
CLARK, GORDON L. *Pensions and Corporate Restructuring in American Industry: A Crisis of Regulation.* Baltimore: Johns Hopkins University Press, 1993.
RAPPAPORT, ANNA M., ed. *Demography and Retirement: The Twenty-First Century.* Westport, CT: Praeger, 1993.

Stanley Johanson

Ethics

Contemporary emphasis on autonomy has led us to think of the individual as an isolated being, complete in his or her own self. From this view, the community is frequently seen as an obstacle—if not an outright barrier—preventing the individual from achieving his or her desires or goals.

The most basic reason for this state of affairs is that the society we experience today is the consequence of decades of the determined and single-minded practice of autonomy. Society has reached an impasse. It has arrived at the point of being unable even to suggest a criticism of individual action, regardless of what that act is or what consequences it might have. It means that no one can suggest what might be good or helpful for an individual, whether in the area of individual maturity, design or school curricula, or appropriate health practices.

The consequence of this recent dominance of autonomy, occurring in an arena of rapidly increasing technology, has been the total isolation of the individual from the family and community. The upshot is that autonomy, though an important and critical value in our society, is simply inadequate to help us resolve critical social issues. In particular, what our over-reliance on autonomy has done is seduce us into thinking that all difficulties or dilemmas are individual problems that can be resolved on a purely individual level. That someone makes an autonomous decision does not mean that all impacts on others or on the community should not be taken into account.

Healthcare Ethical Dilemmas

One such impact involves the runaway cost of health care on the community. We are beginning to realize that individual, autonomous choices have social effects that are of profound significance. Medical ethics provides a case study of this phenomenon and its consequences for religion, spirituality, and morality.

Medical ethics has been characterized by two dominant, interrelated realities, one technical and one ethical in nature. We are faced with the continuing pace and implementation of technological and medical developments. Progress in imaging technologies has given us a detailed new look at the human interior. Developments in artificial reproduction have allowed individuals with all manner of reproductive difficulties to conceive and bear children. Increasing success in mapping the human genome has led to success in locating specific genes responsible for various diseases. In turn, this has led to the development of genetic therapies. On the ethical front, it also poses ominous questions involving the ethics of selective genetic engineering.

Increasingly we are recognizing that the cumulative costs of all the autonomous choices in medical care are staggering. We are now recognizing that not everyone receives—or is even able to receive—the same medical therapy, even though everyone's needs may be similar. The shortage of organs for transplantation, for example, continually brings this problem to public awareness.

Another area of concern is the increasingly strident debate over euthanasia, whether done as an individual act or with the assistance of a physician. In addition, given that health insurance in America is largely private and contingent on one's employment, we find autonomy confronting a rather insurmountable corporate barrier.

The second consideration involves the almost exclusive reliance on the autonomy of the individual as the defining and normative ethical concept in decisionmaking, whether on the individual or social level.

Parallel to technological developments has been an increasing focus on the rights of patients. This was the logical consequence of court cases in the early 1940s and '50s that focused on informed consent and the right to know what was going to be done to a patient before a procedure was initiated.

Up to that time medicine was paternalistic, and many physicians were reluctant to tell patients much of anything, especially if the diagnosis was problematic. This tendency has been almost totally reversed, with the obtaining of informed consent for any medical procedure having become an elaborate process accompanied by legal strictures and advice.

The rights of the individual (or the autonomous choices of the individual) are essentially "trumps" that the patient can use either to demand therapy (even when the value of such therapy may be marginal or nonexistent) or to reject any therapy (even when there may be demonstrably positive outcomes from the therapy). The autonomous individual thus stands in final and total judgment of all that affects him or her. The immediate shortcoming of this approach becomes clear and most problematic when the patient is unable to speak on his or her own behalf—that is, if a patient is comatose, unconscious, or in some other way incompetent.

Current attempts to resolve this dilemma are based on the perception that incompetence is not a disqualification for the exercise of autonomy. We are beginning to recognize that some requests or demands made by an autonomous individual can be problematic. The fact that someone chooses a therapy does not automatically qualify that person for that therapy. Furthermore, if one chooses a therapy, it does not mean that the therapy will be successful. Likewise, the fact that one rejects a therapy does not mean that such a decision is an appropriate one.

Community Vision and Standards

All things considered, the most urgent ethical task of the future lies not in resolving particular problems or providing specific social (or medical) programs—though to be sure these are on the substantive agenda to be resolved. The most urgent problem of the present—and therefore of the future—is to develop an understanding of the individual in relation to the community, or to develop a model of the community in which its needs also have standing. A notion of the common good of society or, minimally, of goods we hold in common must be developed.

As things stand, we as a society lack the philosophical basis either to critique individual action or to offer a compelling vision of goods or services incumbent on all which would benefit the community. Already we experience the cost of the lack of such a vision: social isolation, the abandonment of individuals to their own devices or lack thereof, and the indifference to social entities larger than the individual or perhaps that individual's nuclear family. We know that our society cannot bear much more of the same, for these experiences are beginning to overwhelm us.

Just as the seeds of autonomy are present in the traditions of our American culture, so are the seeds of community. Our most serious ethical task is to construct a vision of the community, presenting a compelling social good to which all will aspire and seek to achieve, and creating an ethic that takes seriously the rights of *both* the individual and the community. These seeds now need planting and careful cultivation. For if we do not care for the whole of the harvest, perhaps there may not be a harvest for anyone.

See also COMMUNITARIANISM; DEATH AND DYING; HEALTH CARE: MORAL ISSUES; RELIGION, SPIRITUALITY, MORALITY; VALUES.

BIBLIOGRAPHY

BELLAH, ROBERT; MADSEN, RICHARD; SULLIVAN, WILLIAM M.; SWIDLER, and TIPTON, STEVEN M. *Habits of the Heart: Individualism and Commitment in American Life.* Berkeley, CA: University of California Press, 1985.
_____. *The Good Society.* Berkeley, CA: University of California Press, 1991.
HIMES, MICHAEL J., and HIMES, KENNETH R., O.F.M. *Fullness of Faith: The Public Significance of Theology.* Mahwah, NJ: Paulist Press, 1993.
SULLIVAN, WILLIAM M. *Reconstructing Public Philosophy.* Berkeley, CA: University of California Press, 1986.

Thomas A. Shannon

Ethics, Medical.

See BIOETHICS; HEALTH CARE: MORAL ISSUES.

Ethnic and Cultural Separatism

Since the rise of the nation-state, people have lived within their own ethnic, national, and cultural boundaries. Sometimes those boundaries were between nations, sometimes such boundaries were formed by enclaves within nations. Living within a cultural boundary gave people a distinct sense of identity, of belonging to a clearly defined social unit. Myths and traditions interpreted the meanings of that culture and reinforced the sense of belonging.

Today, through global television, proliferating communications technologies, and jet travel, historic boundaries are falling, and they no longer constitute the outer limits of a people's identity. We have come to the end of several thousand years of different civilizations living side by side without having significant cross-cultural effect on each other. From now on, integration and cross-fertilization will shape cultural, economic, and educational developments. A new uniformity of human experiences is in the making, with more people coming to share similar impressions and experiences more rapidly. Thus the fabric of tradition in countless nations is being shredded, and a new fabric must be woven. In an age of mobility and global impressions, we must foster a sense of rootedness in time and place.

Cultural and national groupings obviously still exist, but they no longer form a relevant psychological boundary. So painful questions face each of us: With whom do I identify? Who is my group? Indeed, do I have a group any longer? As a separate, isolated, psychologically closed unit, all the groups we have known in the past have now been merged with one larger human family. What each person is facing is the painful necessity to adjust to this new reality.

The basic referent is no longer my tribe, my nation, or even my civilization. We have moved from the era of nation-states to the age of a world community as the defining political and economic framework. In this new era, we are incorporating the planetary dimensions of life into the fabric of our economics, politics, international relations, and culture. For the first time in human history, we are forging an awareness of our existence that embraces humanity as a species.

This collapse of boundaries is one of the primary consequences of space exploration. Seeing Earth from the Moon in the 1960s was a seminal event in human history, both scientifically and psychologically. When we saw a picture of Earth from space, our view of who we are and to what cultural group we belong was forever changed. All of a sudden, everyone saw themselves as part of one human community without all the national, cultural, or religious distinctions by which we had defined ourselves for centuries.

We have entered a period when life needs to be seen whole to be understood. For the first time in history, we see that Earth whole, and we need a new understanding that is based on wholeness rather than on reductionism. None of the major issues we face can be resolved within a national context—not the environment, not economic growth, not Third World debt, not even illegal drugs or AIDS.

The collapse of boundaries is bringing with it a redefinition of nationhood. It is happening everywhere—Russia, South Africa, Germany, even the United States. Nationalism—in the nineteenth-century sense of constituting the outer limits of a people's political awareness—is on the wane. What surfaces in places such as Bosnia, Georgia, or Turkmenistan is not historic nationalism but an old ethnicity that cries out for a new expression.

Demography is a major force shaping destiny. Statistical projections precisely laying out population numbers, distribution, patterns, and trends span the next seventy to eighty years with a very high degree of assurance. People already born today fulfill those projections. Because we know human proclivities and can assess the risks, there is a high degree of certainty concerning outcomes. Population trends provide a powerful trajectory into the future.

Barring some unforeseen use of birth control, world population will double from 5.6 billion in 1994 to 12.6 billion by the year 2100. Millions of years were required for population to reach the first billion mark, in 1800. The second billion mark was reached in 130 years. Thirty years later we hit the third billion mark. Fourteen years after that we reached the fourth billion mark. The fifth billion was hit in twelve years, and the sixth billion increment will have been reached in an eleven-year span (by 1997). To put this in perspective, 18 percent of all the people who ever lived since the birth of Christ are alive today.

Hard as it may be to appreciate fully, these population projections mean that globally, the equivalent of an entire second Earth stands in the offing, bringing along with it all the attendant needs of housing, feeding, and jobs. The United States, the third most populous nation in 1994, will drop to eighth by 2050. Nigeria, Pakistan, Indonesia, and Brazil will all pass us by. These are vast nations already struggling to provide the good life for their teeming residents. And India's population is projected finally to overtake and exceed that of currently top-ranked China by the year 2050.

Globally, the political trend is toward separatism. By World War II, 50 independent nations could be counted. That number exceeded 190 by 1993 and could reach 300 by the year 2000. The former Soviet Union—now 15 nations—may fragment into as many as 60 to 70 independent nations. China also could break up into numerous subdivisions.

The breakup of existing nations and the assertion of new rights by separatist groups will punctuate the twenty-first century with a flurry of wars, ethnic and religious violence, coups d'état, border disputes, civil upheavals, and terrorist attacks. These developments have multiplied world dynamics on an enormous scale, and their repercussions reach to the very core of American life.

In the United States, demographic trends indicate that Hispanics will surpass African Americans as America's largest minority by 2020. Ethnic minorities, furthermore, may account for 30 percent of the U.S. population by 2033. And European Americans are projected to become a minority group by 2060.

A key question is whether America's melting pot tradition still will continue and newcomers will be assimilated into a united nation. Or will a mosaic society emerge, marked by separatism and multiculturalism?

The fragmentation of America is representative of a deeper global force at work. The new view is one of a multicultural perspective where ethnic, sexual, and cultural differences are emphasized. Group and ethnic interests are emerging as preeminent, and the very idea of a common culture is under assault.

How does a pluralist society, comprised of diverse cultures and traditions, and daily bombarded by modern communications, divergent themes, and conflicting philosophies cohere and rise above intense parochial interests to forge the larger common interest? Can we successfully come to grips with these changes and evolve some moral consensus and plan that can make a pluralistic world creative rather than destructive? That is a legitimate question, but it is almost impossible to answer. Scenarios could be developed where America becomes so choked by multiculturalism that consensus on how to deal with common problems becomes impossible. In such a case, America could stagnate and lose any sense of common purpose and identity.

In a complete reversal of the historic idea of America, the degree of common ground could be shrinking. "If separatist tendencies go unchecked," writes Arthur Schlesinger, Jr., one of America's most prominent historians, "the result can only be the fragmentation, resegregation, and tribalization of American life."

A nation dwelling primarily on its differences cannot survive. Nationhood grows out of what a people have in common. Multiculturalism must become a means of melding parochial interests with national interests, of enabling diverse views to contribute to a multifaceted political pattern.

See also GLOBAL CULTURE; LIFESTYLE; NATIONALISM; PLURALISM.

BIBLIOGRAPHY

HACKER, ANDREW. *Two Nations: Black and White, Separate, Hostile, Unequal.* New York: Scribner, 1992.

HUGHES, ROBERT. *Culture of Complaint.* New York: Warner Books, 1993.

KENNEDY, PAUL. *Preparing for the Twenty-First Century.* New York: Vintage Books, 1993.

LASCH, CHRISTOPHER. *The True and Only Heaven.* New York: W. W. Norton, 1991.

MCCARTHY, EUGENE. *A Colony of the World: The United States Today.* New York: Hippocrene Books, 1992.

SCHEIN, EDGAR H. *Organizational Culture and Leadership.* 2nd ed. San Francisco, CA: Jossey-Bass Publishers, 1992.

SHAFFER, CAROLYN R., and ANUNDSEN, KRISTIN. *Creating Community Anywhere: Finding Support and Connection in a Fragmented World.* Los Angeles, CA: J. P. Tarcher, 1993.

STEWART, EDWARD C., and BENNETT, MILTON J. *American Cultural Patterns: A Cross-Cultural Perspective.* Rev. ed. Yarmouth, ME: Intercultural Press, 1991.

Graham T. T. Molitor
William Van Dusen Wishard

Ethnic Diversity.

See RACE, CASTE, AND ETHNIC DIVERSITY.

Europe, Central and Eastern

In mid-1995 Central and Eastern Europe (CEE) consisted of Poland, the Czech Republic, the Slovak Republic, Hungary, Bulgaria, Romania, Albania, Bosnia-Herzegovina, Slovenia, Croatia, Macedonia, and the Federal Republic of Yugoslavia (FRY). Strongly religious groups coexist uneasily in the region. The majority of the Poles, Slovaks, Hungarians, Croats, and Slovenes are Roman Catholic. The Czechs are about 40 percent each Roman Catholic and atheists. A majority of the Serbs, Montenegrins, Macedonians, Romanians, and Bulgarians are Orthodox. Seventy percent of Albania and Kosovo and 43.7 percent of Bosnia-Herzegovina are Muslim.

The six-republic multinational Socialist Federal Republic of Yugoslavia (SFRY) had collapsed in 1991. Croatia and Slovenia declared their independence on June 25, 1991, the former Yugoslav Republic of Macedonia on September 17 of that year, and Bosnia-Herzegovina in April 1992. On April 11, 1992, the FRY (Serbia-Montenegro) declared itself as a successor to the SFRY but was not formally recognized by the United States. The Czech and Slovak Republics became independent states on January 1, 1993.

Serbia failed to halt Croatian and Slovenian independence, but the dynamism of ethnic and religious forces, combined with inter-republic tensions, led to the tragedy of Bosnia-Herzegovina. Following the March 1992 referendum in that republic, opting for independence, the ethnic Serbs in Bosnia, supported by Serbia, launched military operations against the Muslim government in opposition to the independence moves. The objective was to partition the republic, with the Serb-held areas to be attached to the Serbian Republic. The Bosnian Croats occupied about 10 percent of Bosnia in 1993. Together with the Bosnian Serbs, they succeeded in controlling over three-fourths of Bosnia's territory. The number of refugees, displaced persons, and those who fled to other countries by September 1992 was over half of the republic's population—4,365,639, according to the 1991 census. The Bosnian government estimated that 200,000 were killed. Acts of "ethnic cleansing" received nearly universal condemnation, as the Bosnian Serbs continued their assault upon the Bosnian Muslims.

The UN, Western institutions, and individual countries, including the United States, became involved defensively. In July 1991 the United States, and in September 1991 the UN Security Council, imposed an arms embargo on Yugoslavia. Many countries considered this as aiding aggression and detrimental to Bosnia. Despite U.S. Congressional and UN (nonbinding) resolutions to lift their embargos against Bosnia-Herzegovina, the ban continued into mid-1995 as the Bosnian Serbs boldly intensified their attacks against the so-called safe-areas. The numbers of killed, homeless, and refugees increased.

Beginning in 1992, humanitarian aid, UN peacekeepers, and international negotiations all sought to help the suffering humanity and to establish peace in Croatia and Bosnia-Herzegovina, but in mid-1995 time was running out. The lack of political will of Western leaders, the seeming reluctance of their publics to commit their troops to combat, as well as jurisdictional and command controversies all conspired to inhibit assertive action against the aggressors.

Even so, some positive steps had materialized. Croatian and Serbian forces in Bosnia agreed to a cease-fire in early 1992. On February 21, 1992, the UN Security Council established a peacekeeping (not peacemaking) force—UNPROFOR—for the former Yugoslavia. Augmented by NATO, in 1995 they numbered approximately 36,000 personnel from twenty-seven countries: over 20,000 providing military escorts for aid in Bosnia, some 14,800 in Croatia, and the rest in Macedonia.

Yugoslav military forces pulled out of Macedonia in April 1992; the country was admitted into the UN, recognized by other states, and welcomed UN, including U.S., peacekeepers. At a U.S.-sponsored event in Washington, D.C., the Bosnian Muslims and Croats on March 1, 1994, established a federation leading to a confederation with Croatia. Instead of being attracted to the idea, the Bosnian Serbs undertook more aggressive military operations, which increased in 1995.

All countries are experiencing various domestic difficulties during the transformation from communist totalitarianism to independence, political pluralism, and a free-market economy. Expectations for a rapid transition into stable, viable, and peaceful entities proved to be unrealistic, particularly in the former Yugoslavia. The war in Bosnia-Herzegovina will inevitably end, but the political and socioeconomic scars may not be healed for decades.

The CEE countries are attempting to establish friendly relations with each other—for example, the historic 1995 Slovak-Hungarian Treaty—but many areas of tension remain, such as Kosovo, a province in Serbia, and the presence of Albanians in Macedonia. Dominant Serbia opposed the emergence of independent states and resorted to military operations. Numerous ethnic groups inhabit Serbia, the largest comprising Albanians (17.2 percent) and Hungarians (3.5), while Muslims are 2.4. In Croatia, 12.2 percent are Serbs. In Bosnia-Herzegovina, 31.4 percent are Serbs and 17.3 Croats. In Macedonia, 21.1 percent are Albanians.

Kosovo, with 90 percent ethnic Albanians, is a time bomb. Serbia claims it on historic grounds, but Albania has recognized Kosovo as an independent state. Another inflammatory region is Vojvodina, also a province in Serbia, with approximately 400,000 ethnic Magyars (Hungarians) and some 300,000 Serb refugees resettled in the region. When the larger conflicts end in the region, the ethnic Magyars, supported by Budapest, will demand political autonomy and the Serbs may retaliate. Ethnic Turks, who suffered from assimilation

attempts in the late 1980s, comprise some 8.5 percent of the population of Bulgaria.

Another potentially volatile territorial dispute involves Transylvania, a historically disputed region in western Romania with a Magyar population of about two million. Bucharest objected to Budapest's "revanchism," but the two countries concluded an "open skies" agreement in April 1992. With the March 1995 Slovak-Hungarian Treaty serving as an example, Hungary and Romania continued their negotiations for a similar pact. Essentially, Bratislava and Bucharest demanded formal recognition of the inviolability of existing boundaries, and Budapest sought guarantees of human rights to Hungarian minorities by those countries.

Restitution of property is still another area of dispute. For example, the Sudeten Germans—over three million before World War II—claim restitution for confiscated property when they were expelled by Prague following World War II, and Slovakia wants a fair redistribution of pre–January 1, 1993, federal property.

Czech and Slovak leaders decided amicably to establish two separate states, pledging cooperation (though former president Vačlav Havel resigned in protest). The approximately 320,000 Slovaks are the largest minority in the Czech Republic, and there are some 60,000 Czechs in Slovakia. The 567,000 Hungarians (1991 census) are the largest minority in Slovakia, while the Slovaks in Hungary number about 117,000. In Hungary, the Gypsies (about 400,000) and Germans (170,000) are the most numerous minorities.

Slovak-Hungarian tensions increased in 1992 with Budapest's abrogation of the 1977 treaty for the construction of the Gabcikovo-Nagymaros dam on the Danube, after Slovakia completed over 90 percent of its construction. A peaceful solution to this dispute, and others like it, may depend on international help.

Population

The population of nearly all CEE countries—estimated at 100.4 million in 1995—is heterogeneous. Poland (97.6 percent) is the most homogeneous and the largest, with 38.8 million people in mid-1995. Slovenia, with 2.05 million, is the smallest. Albania and Macedonia are expected to experience the largest population growth, while Bulgaria, Croatia, Hungary, and Slovenia project a decline in the early twenty-first century. However, Albania's growth rate has been declining since 1980 and is projected to continue on this course well into the

TABLE 1. Population: Central and Eastern Europe (Thousands)

Country	1995	2010	2025	2050
Albania	3,414	4,016	4,591	4,935
Bosnia-Herzegovina	3,202	3,641	3,669	3,375
Bulgaria	8,775	8,757	8,559	7,745
Croatia	4,666	4,805	4,662	4,118
Czech Republic	10,433	10,892	11,010	10,319
Hungary	10,319	10,477	10,418	9,672
Macedonia	2,160	2,394	2,529	2,464
Poland	38,792	41,332	42,733	41,156
Romania	23,198	23,950	24,425	23,473
Slovakia	5,432	5,883	6,141	5,969
Slovenia	2,052	2,094	2,057	1,824
Yugoslavia:				
Montenegro	708	761	786	736
Serbia	10,394	10,965	11,158	10,592

Source: U.S. Department of Commerce, Bureau of the Census. *International Data Base.* Washington, D.C., 1995.

next century. Moreover, some 300,000 Albanians left the country in the early 1990s, mostly males seeking work. (See Table 1.)

Albania has the highest birthrate and the lowest death rate, resulting in the highest rate of natural increase. Croatia has the lowest birthrate and Hungary the lowest life expectancy. By 2030 all countries, except Albania and Macedonia (2035), are expected to have a negative growth. (See Table 2.)

Urbanization and Living Conditions

The CEE countries are not densely populated—for example, Albania with 80 and the Czech Republic with 131 inhabitants per square kilometer. Despite a general movement from agriculture to industry, much of the region remains rural, with Albania having the largest rural population, at 60 percent. Only modest increase in urbanization is foreseen into the next century.

Living conditions vary markedly in the region. Albania's economy had virtually collapsed in 1992, but through reform and Western assistance the country has been revitalized, to the extent that in 1995 economic prospects for the future are hopeful. The damage to Bosnia is so enormous that decades will be required for recovery. Bulgaria's poor conditions lasted longer than most, but promising signs appeared in 1995. Romanian standards have been perennially low for the majority of its people, especially in the urban areas, even by CEE standards. Those with the most encouraging performances are the Czech Republic, Poland, Slovakia, Hungary, and Slovenia. However, all CEE countries lag far behind the EU states.

The cost of living is well below Western standards, with prices rising higher than wages, but the rate of inflation has been reduced substantially. Income disparity has increased under a market economy.

Social Conditions

Under communism there was full employment, at least on paper. After its fall, growing unemployment and a decrease in or loss of social benefits caused additional instability. The size of families has decreased, but housing shortages continue. Many family members work more than one job to make ends meet. Before 1918 the region was largely rural and social mobility was minimal to modest. Under communism, the elitist *nomenklatura* controlled mobility and isolated society from the "capitalist" West. Now, with democracy, pluralism, and a free-market economy the opportunity for social mobility is greater than previously.

Until 1989 all communist countries had a comprehensive social security system, with health care provided without charge, and a universal retirement system. However, this system produced low-quality health care: a legacy of poor and inadequate equipment and facilities, an inadequately educated and low-paying profession, a shortage of medical personnel and medicine, and poor service.

After the fall of communism, the new governments were faced with the enormous task of rehabilitating health care. They continued widespread

TABLE 2.   Demographics of Central and Eastern Europe: 1995

Country	Per Thousand		Infant Mortality	Life Expectancy (Years)		Natural Increase (Percent)
	Births	*Deaths*		*M*	*F*	
Albania	21.70	5.22	28	70.8	77.0	1.65
Bosnia-Herzegovina	11.29	7.51	12	72.8	78.4	.38
Bulgaria	11.75	11.31	11	70.4	77.1	.04
Croatia	11.02	10.55	8	70.6	77.7	.05
Czech Rep.	13.46	10.85	9	69.9	77.4	.30
Hungary	12.65	12.44	12	67.9	76.1	.02
Macedonia	15.82	6.70	24	71.9	76.3	.91
Poland	13.34	9.23	12	69.2	77.3	.41
Romania	13.71	9.93	19	69.3	75.4	.38
Slovakia	14.51	9.12	10	69.2	77.6	.54
Slovenia	11.85	9.27	8	70.9	78.8	.26
Yugoslavia:						
Montenegro	14.39	5.70	10	76.7	82.6	.87
Serbia	14.15	8.72	19	71.4	76.7	.54

Source: U.S. Department of Commerce, Bureau of the Census. *International Data Base.* Washington, D.C., 1995.

coverage but at lower levels. The unemployed receive benefits for limited periods, such as six months in Romania and on a sliding scale in Hungary. Special allowances may be legislated for pensioners and families to offset dramatic rises in inflation. Pay for child care is provided. Income taxes are withheld, and both employers and employed contribute to social welfare. With freedom, democracy, economic restructuring, and human rights have come inflation, unemployment, corruption, and a startling increase in crime.

Economics

The new CEE governments inherited failed communist economies. The transition to a free market is slow and spasmodic, but stabilization and upturn appeared earliest in the Czech Republic, Slovakia, Poland, and Hungary. For much of the area, however, the future appears less promising. The combination of Western investments, international assistance, and improved domestic capabilities nevertheless holds some hope.

Political developments notwithstanding, during the last half century the region has been shifting from agriculture to a diversified industrial stage. All countries are moving from collectivist farms and state enterprises to privatization. Years will be required to unravel property rights and construct a sound industrial foundation.

East European countries are not wealthy, and disparity among them is substantial. Budget deficits are common. After an initial decline in their gross domestic products, these countries have rebounded, with Albania recording the highest growth rate in the region. Following are the estimated 1994 figures (exceptions cited) for GDP in billions of dollars at current prices, and the real growth rate: Albania, 1.4 billion, 7.4 percent; Bosnia-Herzegovina, not available; Bulgaria, 0.97, 1.0; Croatia, 15.0, 0.8; Czech Republic, 31.5, 2.6; Hungary, 40.0, 2.0; Macedonia, 1.54 (1993), –11.0 (1994); Poland, 95.0, 5.0; Romania, 22.5, 1.5; Slovakia, 12.2, 4.7; Slovenia, 11.2, 5.0; FSR, not available (9.5 in 1993, with 6.5 percent social product growth in 1994).

Income and expenditures were controlled under communism. The free market and the removal of or reduction of subsidies brought higher prices and greater disparity in wealth. Average personal income is expected to be low for many years. During the early transition period, annual inflation rates increased alarmingly (e.g., Poland's rose to 900 percent and Bulgaria's to 500), then reduced substantially in some countries (1994 estimates of consumer prices): Albania, 27; Bulgaria, 120, but with a predicted reduction to 80 for 1995; Czech Republic, 10.7; Hungary, 21; Poland, 32; Romania, 150, down from 296 the previous year, and likely to be reduced by half in 1995; Slovakia, 12.1.

Slovenia's percentage was reduced from 201.3 in 1992 to 19.8 in 1994, and is projected to fall to 12 in 1995. Croatia's enormous rate of 1,500 in 1993 was cut sharply to 97 in 1994 and is to be reduced to 10 by 1996. The retail price inflation in FRY skyrocketed to 9,237 percent in 1992 but came down to 116.5 the following year. Macedonia's was lowered from 1,691 in 1992 to 57 in 1994.

During Soviet control, foreign trade was concentrated within the Warsaw Pact and the Council for Mutual Economic Assistance (CMEA) blocs. The new governments have instituted reform—for example, currency, legal, accounting, pricing, and privatization—and have become more closely associated with the West. Western countries, institutionally or individually, injected essential, albeit insufficient, assistance and lifted trade restrictions.

Dependence on Western largesse is temporary, competition for Western markets difficult, and imports from European Union countries debilitating. A more solid foundation for favorable trade began to evolve regionally with bilateral and multilateral agreements providing for increased and more favorable trade relations. The Visegrad governments (Poland, Hungary, the Czech Republic, and Slovakia) created a duty-free zone from March 1, 1993, with complete tariff elimination to occur by 2001.

The region is burdened by convertible foreign debt (amounts listed in billions of U.S. dollars, according to 1994 estimates): Albania, 1.0; Bulgaria, 14.3; Croatia, 3.06; Czech Republic, 9.1; Hungary, 28.06; Macedonia, 1.1; Poland, 41.3; Romania, 4.2; Slovakia, 4.1; Slovenia, 2.65; and Yugoslavia (Serbia-Montenegro), 5.6 (1993). Hard-pressed to repay, the governments require rescheduling over a longer period of repayment.

Labor and Workforce

With a free-market economy, unemployment increased rapidly—in some countries substantially—throughout the region. However, unemployment has been gradually lowered. The disparity between the Czech and Slovak Republics—the latter burdened with a large military industry—has narrowed but is still considerable. At the end of 1994, the unemployment rate in the former was 3.7 percent and in the latter 14.0 percent.

The end-of-1994 unemployment rate for other CEE countries was as follows: Albania, 15.0 percent, but thousands had fled the country; Bulgaria, 18.5; Croatia, 18.0; Hungary, 10.0; Macedonia, 27, (1993 est.); Poland, 15.0; Romania, 15.0; Slovenia, 14.0; and Serbia-Montenegro, over 60 (according to 1993 estimates), but reduced in 1994.

Quality of worklife suffered from low wages, high prices, unhealthy working environments, un-

certainty about the future, and job insecurity. Strikes and demonstrations erupted in Poland during July 1992. However, with greater success of the private sector and of other reforms, as well as international aid, these shortcomings are expected to be repaired in the years to come.

Ecology and Environment

The ecological degradation of the region bordered on the catastrophic. Communist dictatorships generally ignored ecology and environment in their economic plans. The post-communist governments established ministries to cope with the problems. In varying degrees all CEE countries suffer from air and water pollution and deforestation. Pollution has been a serious threat to health. Restoring a healthy environment may take decades, even with the financial aid and expert assistance of the Western states.

Energy

The region, with only limited oil and gas resources and modest production, is exploring and developing environmentally safe and increasingly private energy capacity with international assistance. The Czech Republic's energy resources are inadequate, and the country is burdened by high consumption and costly imports. The major domestic source is coal (about 45 percent), but the goal is reduction to 30 percent by the year 2000. Brown (bituminous) coal is expected to be exhausted before 2010, but hard (anthracite) coal may last another one hundred years.

The Czech Republic has been almost totally dependent on Russian oil, but drastic reductions from that source have contributed to the Czech Republic's economic problems. However, in exchange for the then Czech/Slovak financial support of a natural gas pipeline to East Central Europe, Russia is obligated to supply natural gas to the Czech and Slovak Republics until 2009. Electricity is more than 75 percent thermal, over 21 percent nuclear and less than 3 percent hydroelectric. In addition to the power plant in southern Moravia, a second is being constructed in southern Bohemia.

Primary energy sources are delivered to the Czech Republic through Slovakia. This dependence will be decreased when the pipeline from Ingolstadt, Bavaria, to Bohemia becomes operational. Also, Slovakia furnishes crude oil products to the Czech Republic, receiving in turn hard and soft coal as well as coke from the Czechs.

Bratislava intends to reduce Czech, and increase Polish, coal imports. With meager domestic fuel supplies, Slovakia is dependent on Russia and Ukraine for 90 percent of its needs, a situation expected to continue for some years. However, Slovakia's strategic location affords imports from various sources. It hopes to tap into the transit gas pipeline from Russia to Western Europe. Slovakia's electricity is over 50 percent nuclear; the rest is thermal and imported. An increase in nuclear power, temporarily hampered by costs and foreign pressure, is being aided by the West. Despite Hungary's 1989 suspension and 1992 withdrawal from the 1977 bilateral agreement to construct the Gabcikovo-Nagymaros hydroelectric project on the Danube, Slovakia continued to develop its Gabcikovo segment, employing environmental safety measures.

In Poland, coal is the major energy resource—accounting for about 70 percent of its energy consumption—and a net export. Its anthracite coal reserves in 1994 were estimated at 63.5 billion tons. While the production of brown coal in recent years has remained just below 70 million tons per year, that of hard coal—Poland was a world leader with 193 million tons in 1988—fell drastically to 131 million tons by 1993. Still, coal continues to make up about 70 percent of Poland's energy consumption.

Poland produces only negligible amounts of oil and one-third of its natural gas needs. Since 1980, it has been a net importer of oil and gas, especially from the former U.S.S.R. Because of reduced oil deliveries in 1990, Poland shifted to the higher-priced Western suppliers. Among the initiatives to decrease its dependence on coal, Poland is undertaking offshore drilling in the Baltic Sea. Some 93 percent of the country's electricity is generated by coal. It has no nuclear power. Warsaw announced that power plants would be privatized during the first half of 1995, with Western, including U.S., financial support for the modernization and development of the power sector.

Hungary's domestic energy resources are insufficient; it imports the majority of its requirements. In 1989 it received 7.7 million tons of crude oil, or 90 percent, from the former U.S.S.R. This was reduced to 5 million tons the following year. Hungary's oil production—1.97 million tons in 1990, meeting about 25 percent of its needs—began to fall the following year but reversed the decline by 1994. Oil reserves are 58 million tons, but Hungary's oil has a high sulfur content.

Hungary has 100 million tons of "economically recoverable" hard coal reserves, with 714 million tons total reserves and much more soft coal. Coal output has been decreasing in recent years, from 17.5 million tons in 1990. Budapest has turned to the West for alternate oil supplies and has undertaken privatization. Its gas reserves are about 113 billion cubic meters, but production has declined in recent years as well, now down to approximately 5 billion cubic meters per year. More than half of Hungary's electricity is produced by nuclear power; the rest is mainly thermal and imported. Hungary's uranium ore, although quantitatively sufficient, is dependent on foreign enrichment and processing facilities—Russian at present. Budapest intends to diversify its energy sources, link up with the European grid, and invite foreign exploration.

By the late 1970s Romania became an oil importer, a major factor in the country's stunted development. With the fall of communism, oil imports fell as well but were still 8.5 million tons in 1993, the majority from the OPEC countries. However, Romania is the leading producer of oil and gas in the region—in 1994 6.7 million tons crude oil and 19.6 billion cubic meters of natural gas—and is a world leader in oil-refining industries. It hopes to modernize and increase its oil production to reduce imports of oil and gas by $400 million annually during 1995–2000, a difficult task. Coal output in 1994 was 42 million tons, of which 5 million tons was hard. Bucharest has given top priority to the development of energy, a twenty-year program aided by foreign financing. Electricity is largely thermal.

Bulgaria is a major importer of energy, especially since 1989 due to a substantial decrease in production of oil, gas, and coal. It has large deposits of soft coal but is poor in hard coal. The country imports over 90 percent of its oil and nearly all of its natural gas needs. Imports have shifted from former U.S.S.R. to other suppliers, especially in the Middle East. Its reliance on nuclear power—the sole plant at Kozloduy produced 36.7 percent of total electricity in 1993—has been plagued with safety problems and stoppages. In 1991 the station was found unsafe by the IAEA, and two of its six reactors were closed. However, of the three EBRD-managed energy projects in Bulgaria in 1994, one is to upgrade the safety of the nuclear power plant. Most of the country's electricity is thermal.

Albania is self-sufficient in energy, except for small imports of coking coal. In recent years, however, the output of coal, oil, and natural gas declined, and crude oil was found to contain a high sulfuric content. Some processed oil is exported. About 85 percent of electric power is generated by hydroelectric stations; the aging facilities are being upgraded with financial help from EBRD and Japan. In 1994 six foreign oil companies were exploring offshore, Croatia's state oil enterprise was licensed to explore on land, and Albania itself budgeted substantial funds to rehabilitate the energy sector.

In the former Yugoslavia domestic sources, particularly coal, supplied two-thirds of its needs. Oil topped energy imports, and electricity was generated largely by thermal power plants. Due to the war, information since 1991 has been spotty or lacking for the whole area. Bosnia-Herzegovina has large reserves of coal, and its hydroelectric power was substantial, but it relies on imports for oil and gas. Croatia's production of energy is modest, so it relies heavily on imports. Fuel and lubricants are both imported and exported, but the former predominates. Electricity is nearly equally thermal and hydro-generated. Macedonia has coal (lignite) but must import oil and gas. Its electricity is heavily thermal, with small hydro capacity. Slovenia has meager energy resources, and even these are problematic. Brown coal and lignite—1.2 and 3.9 million tons in 1993—are of a low quality but generate more power than either hydro or nuclear plants. Domestic oil and gas are negligible and must be imported. Serbia has energy resources but relies on imports for its oil needs. Following the end of hostilities, which have affected all the republics, the need for foreign financial assistance to rehabilitate energy facilities will be enormous, especially in Bosnia Herzegovina.

Transportation and Communication

The transportation and communication networks, due to decades of neglect, are obstacles to economic progress. The system is in dire need of modernization, expansion, repair, and maintenance. The relatively inexpensive public transportation—buses, streetcars, trains—continue to be the favorite modes of travel. Links between cities and towns are adequate. Bicycles are popular in rural areas. The development of railroads, roads, and airlines varies widely throughout the region, with the southeastern countries, especially Albania and Macedonia, lagging behind the others. An increasing number of private autos is in evidence, but the extremely high cost of gasoline limits widespread, long-distance travel.

Communications, including telecommunications, telephone service, computers, telex, and facsimile capabilities, are far behind the Western countries. The less impoverished are in the western part of the region; of the rest, Bulgaria has an extensive system but is deficient qualitatively, and Albania is the least developed. In varying degrees, the CEE countries need rehabilitation of the infrastructure, modernization, substantial increase in telephone lines, modern technology including a digital system, and expertise. Rural areas lag far behind the cities in all categories.

The governments are giving this sector priority attention—for example, Romania has a fifteen-year modernization and Bulgaria a twelve-year digital program. Foreign assistance is necessary and is being provided by several international financial institutions of individual countries.

Under communism, the mass media were tightly controlled. With freedom, control ceased or was reduced, the number of televisions and radios increased, while the press and publications expanded rapidly. Former communist organs were renamed or retained their name, as did *Pravda*. In some countries, as in Romania, the government continues to exert control, especially over radio and television. However, privatization is increasing in radio and television, as is access to foreign programs. Tabloids are popular. Some major newspapers represent political parties, while others are independent. Problems of circulation and costs are not uncommon among the latter. English language publications—some owned by Westerners—appear in some capitals. Despite serious problems, the future in communications is hopeful.

Education and Literacy

Education, training, and retraining are essential to successful transformation. During communist control, education suffered from ideology and forced isolation from the West, including limits on language study. Reform began with decentralization and diversity as goals. Educational systems are undoing almost a half century of indoctrination. At least a generation will be required to complete this process. Public education is free and compulsory for ages six to fourteen (or sixteen). Free education continues through secondary school and, in most cases, through the university, some with stipends for living expenses.

Changes can be expected, as with the Czech decision that beginning in 1994—but not yet implemented in mid-1995—university students would pay one-quarter of the cost. With inflation and a markedly increasing number of students in every country, costs will become a greater fiscal burden.

Facilities, equipment, and educational technology are in dire need of modernization. Private schools, mostly at the primary and secondary levels, are also increasing.

Literacy is above 90 percent in all countries except Albania, where it is under 80 percent. Most countries are in the upper nineties, with the Czech Republic, Hungary, Poland, Slovakia, and Slovenia registering 99 percent. The rate is higher for men than for women.

Culture, Arts, and Leisure

Communist ideological control and propagation of "socialist realism" undermined traditional cultural values. Culture and the arts have now to some extent swung to the other extreme. The hunger for things Western includes some of the worst of Western culture, with the free market flooded by Western films, television, and pornography.

Income and prices affect leisure activities. As in much of the West, interest in the fine arts is highest among the better educated. The most popular cultural activities, especially among young people, are movies and rock music, although attendance at the former has been falling, probably as the quality of television reception increases. A majority of the people devote an inordinate amount of time to home improvement.

Many people have sufficient time to travel, but low income limits travel to distant areas. Weekend getaways are popular but not easily affordable.

Alternative Future

While democratic values are favored, the majority consider them in economic terms. Political orientation may well depend on the success of democratization, but the majority believes their future lies in some form of democratic system.

All countries desire to maintain their independence and function actively in a peaceful and stable environment as equals. They want to achieve prosperity and security. Thus there is increasing realization that near-term assistance and longer-term integration into the European system—especially membership in NATO—are contingent on achieving stability and presenting evidence of performance.

Pace-Setting Developments, Laws, Achievements

CEE publics envisioned a dramatic internal transformation and support by the West for a life of prosperity. However, rapid reforms caused political, economic, and social upheavals. The results were political fragmentation, high unemployment, inflation, insecurity, and inertia, causing disillusionment with programs conceived and implemented by inexperienced officials and disappointment with Western assistance.

A hardened realism has replaced exaggerated expectations. The initial governments have been replaced by more pragmatic leaders. In some countries—for example, Bulgaria, Hungary, Macedonia, and Poland—there has been a shift to the Left. This stemmed from a combination of frustrated citizenry, differing agendas of splintered political parties, and the promises of better organized former communists, renamed Socialists or the Democratic Left. In the FRY, the Serbian Socialist Party (the former Communist Party) maintains control. Continuing programs include private enterprise and investment, dismantling or reducing state subsidies, price liberalization and stabilization, and privatization of industry and agriculture.

The countries have become parliamentary democracies where rule of law is replacing "socialist legality." New constitutions have been adopted or, as in Poland and Albania, are being politically negotiated, providing for democratic institutions, separation of power, guarantees for human rights, limited powers for the president, constitutional courts, and checks against the reemergence of dictatorship. Laws and regulations guide the evolution of reform. Some of the communist laws and regulations are still on the statute books.

Progress is visible but problems remain. Evolution toward Western judicial systems will take time. Privatization, restitution, and division of property are making headway despite difficulties. The CEE countries are attempting to construct a democratic political system, a free-market economy, a society in which people will have confidence in the government's adherence to the constitution, and a body of laws that will ensure fairness, equality, and dignity.

See also DEVELOPMENT, ALTERNATIVE; DEVELOPMENT: WESTERN PERSPECTIVE; EUROPE, WESTERN; RUSSIA.

BIBLIOGRAPHY

BUGAJSKI, JANUSZ. *Nations in Turmoil: Conflict and Cooperation in Eastern Europe.* Boulder, CO: Westview Press, 1993.

HAGLUND, DAVID. G.; MACFARLAND, NEIL; and SOKOLSKY, JOEL J., eds. *NATO's Eastern Dilemmas.* Boulder, CO: Westview Press, 1994.

HELD, JOSEPH, ed. *The Columbia History of Eastern Europe in the Twentieth Century.* New York: Columbia University Press, 1992.

KURIAN, GEORGE THOMAS, ed. *Encyclopedia of the Second World.* New York: Facts on File, 1991.

LATAWSKI, PAUL C. *The Security Route to Europe: The Visegrad Four.* London: Royal United Service Institute for Defense Studies, 1994.

MOJZES, PAUL. *Yugoslavian Inferno: Ethnoreligious Warfare in the Balkans.* New York: Continuum, 1994.

MOSS, JOYCE. *Peoples of the World. Eastern Europe and the Post-Soviet Republics: The Culture, Geographysical Setting, and Historical Background of 34 Eastern European Peoples.* Detroit, MI: Gale Research, 1993.

NAGORSKI, ANDREW. *The Birth of Freedom: Shaping Lives and Societies in the New Eastern Europe.* New York: Simon & Schuster, 1993.

SERAFIN, JOAN, ed. *East-Central Europe in the 1990's.* Boulder, CO: Westview Press, 1994.

John J. Karch

Europe, Western

Unity—how much, how soon, what kind? These questions push aside all others as Western Europe approaches the twenty-first century.

The vision of European unity goes back at least as far as the Holy Roman Empire. Correctly dismissed a century ago by Bismarck as no more than a geographic notion, Europe seems, as the next millennium nears, at last to be moving inexorably toward greater unity of the nations that lie westward of the now-defunct Iron Curtain.

Pitfalls to speedy attainment of unity abound. Maastricht (the treaty signed in 1991 which set a path toward rapid integration of the twelve nations that then comprised the European Union) has become a synonym for doubts and confusion rather than a clarion call for relentless movement toward a single currency, a common foreign policy, and a European identity. Still, the single market is a reality, and most European states outside the union of twelve are eager to join up.

The great obstacle to rapid and dramatic movement toward unity is nationalism, that is, loyalty to a homeland nation. Western Europeans differ among themselves regarding territory, law, and religion; they speak twelve languages, not to mention numerous regional dialects. However, they share many traditions, among them political democracy, parliamentary institutions, and Judeo-Christian ethics, as well as such values as humanism and rationalism. The relative strength of forces toward unity and forces against it is an evolving phenomenon. At present (the mid-1990s), nationalism is far stronger than any competing feeling of loyalty to Europe. Indeed, many see in Bosnia, Scotland, the Basque region, the Northern League (in Italy), and elsewhere countercurrents of ethnic separatism that not only challenge European universalism but even well-established nation-states. All told, the day when Europe has a government of its own is not at all imminent: 2020 is an optimistic guess; 2050, or so, is more realistic.

Nevertheless, Austria, Sweden, and Finland have joined the union, and Poland, the Czech Republic, Hungary, and Slovakia will probably follow suit early in the next century. Whether Romania and Bulgaria also will join is far less clear, not to mention Slovenia, Croatia, Serbia, Macedonia, Bosnia-Herzegovina, and Albania. The Baltic states may eventually join, while Russia, Ukraine, and Belarus seem destined to remain outside looking in; they are too distant, too unwieldy, and too exotic to be subsumed into institutional Europe. Switzerland will probably remain in affluent isolation well beyond 2000, but economic pragmatism eventually will overcome Swiss antipathy to opening its borders to other Europeans, and Norway may eventually decide to join.

As for the form that a united—or more united—Europe will take, Switzerland, a decentralized federation, is a more likely model than the United States. The languages and parochialism of Britons, Germans, Spaniards, and Greeks are not going to vanish. Genevois are bound to their French culture and the burghers of Zürich to things Germanic, but the Swiss system accommodates these preferences while generating staunch national feeling. Whatever emerges, the new Europe will be unique.

European security will be far more dependent upon NATO and its American contingents than upon indigenous European forces, much less a single European army. Indeed, European units from members of the union are likely to be formed within ten or fifteen years, but separate national forces will probably survive much longer. NATO may well exist in some form indefinitely, perhaps under another name, including significant numbers of U.S. armed forces on European soil. One reason will be the reluctance of Western Europeans to make the financial outlays and take other measures that would permit Europe to field forces as modern and as powerful as the American. As additional members, notably Poland, the Czech Republic, Slovakia, and Hungary, join the political union, they also are likely to join NATO, with a delay of perhaps a decade. However, Russia, Ukraine, Belarus, and the Baltic states will probably remain outside the alliance.

While progress toward political unity will be gradual if steady, the economic outlook for Western Europe is bright. The integration of the European Economic Area will of itself add significantly to economic growth. The union enjoys high savings rates, impressive investment levels, excellent educational systems (especially for noncollege youth), and a skilled work force. These ingredients of high productivity will be enhanced as new members join the Common Market, especially Eastern European states whose highly skilled workers are much less well-paid than their Western European counterparts. A single currency, which may at first not apply to all union members, will add further stimulus to economic dynamism.

The key economic challenges facing Western Europe are high levels of unemployment and the heavy costs of the welfare state. The best hope for reducing joblessness is to lessen so-called rigidities in labor markets, while the onerous burdens of social welfare (including generous unemployment compensation) must be alleviated if Europe is to remain competitive with Japan and the United States in world markets. To the extent that progress is made to deal effectively with these problems, Western Europe will tend more toward free market than statist solutions to its economic problems. And Western Europe is more likely to be outward-looking than protectionist, though this is by no means certain.

An issue that will become more acute is migration from outside the union. The end of the Cold War and the rise of Islamic fundamentalism in Africa and the Middle East will require the union to deal with mounting pressure from would-be immigrants—mainly political from the south, and mainly economic from the east. Just when many European states are raising barriers to new entrants in response to mounting nationalist and even racist sentiments in their body politics, demography (as well as humanitarian impulses and economic rationality) suggests that the union should welcome newcomers. UN projections suggest that Western Europe's population will decline after 2020.

Will Germany dominate the new Europe? In a sense, Germany cannot avoid being *primus inter pares*, at the least—because of its central location, the size of its population, and its economic prowess. Germany's GNP is 1.5 times larger than Britain's and a third larger than those of France and Italy. Furthermore, it has more armed forces than any other union member. Finally, Germany invests in and trades with Eastern Europe far more than does any other country.

However, Germany still carries the legacy (and guilt feelings) of two world wars and the abomination of the Holocaust. This accounts for its renunciation of weapons of mass destruction and prohibition against sending armed forces abroad. The German national mood borders on pacifism: many Germans feel that their nation should emulate that of the Swiss.

However, Germany will gradually shed its historical baggage and behave more like a normally assertive member of the international community. Still, Germany is unlikely to play as dominant a role, at least politically, as its natural attributes would suggest. Indeed, many Germans and other Europeans feel that the main virtue of the union is to restrain Germany.

The future of Western Europe is brimming with promise. For this promise to be fulfilled, Europe must deal realistically with thorny economic problems and the pressure of migrants. If unity proves elusive, this will be regettable rather than tragic. After all, Europe played a leading role in world affairs for centuries, while consisting of unruly sovereign states that often fought one another. Greater unity will surely enhance Europe's role in the future.

See also DEVELOPMENT: WESTERN PERSPECTIVE; EUROPE, CENTRAL AND EASTERN; FRANCE; GERMANY; RUSSIA; SWEDEN; UNITED KINGDOM.

BIBLIOGRAPHY

ASH, TIMOTHY GARTON. *In Europe's Name: Germany and the Divided Continent.* New York: Random House, 1993.

ATTALI, JACQUES. *Millennium.* New York: Random House, 1991.

KENNEDY, PAUL. *Preparing for the Twenty-First Century.* New York: Random House, 1993.

LUKACS, JOHN. *The End of the Twentieth Century and the End of the Modern Age.* New York: Ticknor and Fields, 1993.

PFAFF, WILLIAM. *The Wrath of Nations.* New York: Simon & Schuster, 1993.

Ernest Schneider

Euthanasia.

See DEATH AND DYING.

Evolution, Biological

With the major developments of the space age, our interest in the question of life's origins has rocketed to new heights. A question which has been asked mainly in the field of metaphysics has emerged in the domain of chemistry and physics. Along with the problem of the origin of the universe and the origin of intelligence, it may be considered to be among the most fundamental questions of all science.

The idea of life arising from nonlife, or the theory of spontaneous generation, had been accepted for centuries. One had only to observe the evidence of the senses, thought the ancients: worms seemed to emerge from mud, maggots from decaying meat, and mice from old linen.

The Darwinian theory of evolution subsequently postulated the unity of the Earth's entire biosphere. According to Darwin, the higher forms of life evolved from the lower over a very extended period in the life of this planet. Alexander Ivanovich Oparin gave us the idea of the continuity of the universe from the inorganic to the organic, from the elements to the small molecules. The concept of cosmic evolution, then, comes to us from his early writings. One could say that what Darwin is to biological evolution, Oparin is to chemical evolution. Oparin spoke of the general origins of life—not as a special event, but as a phenomenon that could commonly take place.

If we go back all the way to the earliest times on Earth, we know that the Earth had been formed from the dust cloud out of which all the planets of the solar system emerged about 4.5 billion years ago. The most recent evidence for the oldest life on Earth from the studies of the Greenland rocks date back 3.8 billion years. Life on Earth must have begun between these two points in time. There was, therefore, a time when no life existed on Earth.

The great impetus, however, to the experimental study of the origin of life began with Oparin pointing out, "that there was no fundamental difference between a living organism and brute matter. The complex combination of manifestations and properties so characteristic of life must have arisen in the process of the evolution of matter." According to Oparin:

> at first there were the simple solutions of organic substances whose behavior was governed by the properties of their component atoms and the arrangement of these atoms in the molecular structure. But gradually, as a result of growth, and increasing complexity of the molecules, new properties have come into being and a new colloidal chemical order was imposed on the more simple organic chemical relations. These newer properties were determined by the spatial arrangement and mutual relationship of the molecules. In this process biological orderliness already comes into prominence.

From a scientific point of view, possibly the greatest contribution Oparin made to the study of the origins of life was his careful analysis of the nature of the primitive atmosphere. He suggested that the carbides in the crust of the Earth may have given rise to hydrocarbons. Indeed, the carbides may have come from meteorites. Here, then, was a source of the reduced carbon necessary for the organic molecule. Oparin also argued that in the amino acids the carbon and nitrogen are in the reduced form and that, therefore, the starting materials for life may have been in that form.

Independently of Oparin, Haldane in 1928, had speculated on the early conditions suitable for the emergence of terrestrial life:

> When ultraviolet light acts on a mixture of water, carbon dioxide and ammonia, a variety of organic substances are made, including sugars and apparently some of the materials from which proteins are built up. Before the origin of life they must have accumulated until the primitive oceans reached the constituency of a *hot dilute soup.*

Experiments in the laboratory have simulated conditions in prebiotic times. The building blocks of life have been synthesized under such conditions. The processes are simple and the pathways are chemically elegant. Amino acids, carbohydrates, and the genetic bases are all sequentially made by such processes such as an electric discharge, simulating lightning, striking a primitive atmosphere of methane, nitrogen, and water. Several attempts also have been made to string these components together to give rise to polymers resembling proteins and nucleic acids. A certain measure of success has also been achieved here and the prerequisite for such processes to take place have been clearly demonstrated.

The energies available for the synthesis of organic compounds under primitive Earth conditions are ultraviolet light from the sun, electric discharges, ionizing radiation, and heat. It is evident that sunlight was the principal source of energy. Photochemical reactions would have taken place in the upper atmosphere and the products transferred by convection. Next in importance as a source of energy are electric discharges such as lightning and corona discharges from pointed objects. These occur close to the Earth's surface, and hence, would more efficiently deposit the reaction products in the primitive oceans. A certain amount of energy was also available from the disintegration of uranium, thorium, and potassium 40. While some of this energy may have been expended on solid material such as rocks, a certain proportion of it was available in the oceans and the atmosphere. Heat from volcanoes may also have been effective in primordial organic synthesis. In comparison to the energy from the sun and electric discharges, this was perhaps not too widely distributed and its effect may have been only local—on the sides of volcanoes, for example. Most of these forms of energy have been used in the laboratory for the synthesis of organic molecules. Simulation experiments have been devised to study the effect of ionizing radiation, electric discharges, heat and ultraviolet light on the assumed early atmosphere of Earth. The analysis of the end products has often yielded, very surprisingly, the very compounds that we consider today as important for living systems.

In the experiments in our own laboratory, we have adopted the simple working hypothesis that the molecules that are fundamental now were fundamental at the time of the origin of life. We are analyzing "the primordial soup" described by Haldane. The various forms of energy that are thought to have been present in the primitive Earth have been used by us in a series of experiments. In the experiments with methane, ammonia, and water, electron irradiation was used as a convenient source of ionizing radiation simulating the potassium on the primitive Earth. The results of this investigation clearly establish adenine (one of the basic chemical components of the genetic code) as a product of the irradiation of methane, ammonia, and water. It is the single largest nonvolatile compound produced. The apparent preference for adenine synthesis may be related to adenine's multiple roles in biological systems. Not only is it a constituent of both the nucleic acids DNA and RNA, but it is also a unit of many important cofactors. In these and other experiments, most of the molecules necessary for life have been synthesized.

Chemical evolution may be considered to have taken place in three stages. From inorganic chemistry to organic chemistry, and from organic chemistry to biological chemistry. The first stage of chemical evolution perhaps began with the very origin of matter. In a series of cataclysmic reactions during the birth of a star, the elements of the periodic table must have been formed. Almost 15 billion years later, when the solar system was being formed, the highly reactive elements that occur in living organisms, probably existed in combination with hydrogen—carbon as methane, nitrogen as ammonia, and oxygen as water. Four-and-a-half billion years ago, when the planet Earth was arising from the primitive dust cloud, the rudimentary molecules, which were the forerunners of the complex biological polymers of today, were perhaps already in existence. Within this framework, life appears to be a special property of matter, a property that arose at a particular period in the existence of our planet and resulted from its orderly development.

The consideration of biological evolution thus leads us logically to another form of evolution, namely, chemical evolution. Recent biochemical discoveries have underlined the remarkable unity of living matter. In all living organisms, from the smallest microbe to the largest mammal, there are two basic molecules. Their interaction appears to result in that unique property of matter that is generally described by the word *life*. These two molecules are the nucleic acids and protein. While each one of these molecules is complex in form, the units comprising them are few in number. The nucleic acid molecule consists of nucleotides strung together like beads along a chain. The nucleotides in turn are made up of a purine or pyrimidine base, a sugar, and a phosphate. In the protein molecule, twenty amino acids link up with one another to give the macromolecule. A study of the composition of living matter thus leads us to the inescapable conclusion that all living organisms must have had some common chemical ancestry. A form of evolution purely chemical in nature must of necessity have preceded biological evolution.

A few years ago *Alvin*, the robotic unmanned submarine that went down to the bottom of the ocean, brought back to us samples from the hydrothermal vents. For almost forty years we had worked in our laboratories on the assumption that the conditions suitable for the origins of life had disappeared. But here we find them anew. Therefore, we must rationally accept the likelihood that life is arising there now. This is perhaps one of the great discoveries of modern biology: that it is possible for life to exist under those conditions. We have worked in the laboratory in the assumption that the conditions that prevailed 4 billion years ago have disappeared from the face of Earth. But we find them now right at the bottom of the ocean. So here we have an opportunity to examine what Oparin described as the general origins of life, that it is not something confined to one place or one time on Earth, but perhaps to the end of the universe. Is it possible that the life is arising right now? Neo-abiogenesis may be a reality.

The sequence from atoms to small molecules to large molecules to life thus appears to be natural. Laboratory experiments have clearly demonstrated that the molecules necessary for life can be synthesized under simulated planetary environments. There is no reason to doubt that we shall rediscover, one by one, the precise processes of physical and chemical evolution. We may even reproduce the intermediate steps in the laboratory. Looking back upon the biochemical understanding gained during the span of one human generation, we have the right to be quite optimistic.

See also BIODIVERSITY; EVOLUTION: LIFE-FORMS IN THE UNIVERSE; EVOLUTION, SOCIAL; EXTINCTION OF SPECIES; GENETIC ENGINEERING; GENETICS; GENETICS, COMMERCIALIZATION OF; GENETIC TECHNOLOGIES; SEXUAL REPRODUCTION: ARTIFICIAL MEANS.

BIBLIOGRAPHY

ANFINSEN, CHRISTIAN B. *The Molecular Basis of Evolution*. New York: John Wiley, 1959.

OPARIN, A. I. *The Origin of Life on Earth*. 3rd ed. New York: Academic Press, 1957.

PONNAMPERUMA, CYRIL, and CHELA-FLORES, JULIAN, eds. *Chemical Evolution: Origin of Life*. Hampton, VA: A. Deepak Publishing, 1993.

YOUNG, J. Z., and MARGERISON, TOM, eds. *From Molecule to Man*. New York: Crown, 1969.

Cyril Ponnamperuma

Evolution, Social

Evolution is rather obvious in a broad sense, because even children understand that life emerged billions of years ago and that beings like ourselves then slowly evolved. Yet this grand process is fraught with controversy, raising such perennial questions as, Does social progress really improve human welfare? For example, the Information Age promises to unify the globe, yet it is also helping to spark wars between ethnic groups, as in the former Yugoslavia, fostering violent youths in the United States and other nations, and swamping people in a morass of data overload.

By analyzing evolution using general systems theory, we can achieve a better understanding of this complex process, and gain insights into the stages lying ahead. From a systems view, the history of change seems to form a great pattern that comprises a life cycle for the planet. This "life cycle of evolution" (LCE) is similar to the life cycle of ordinary organisms, such as humans, but vastly larger in scope and duration. Like any life cycle, life on Earth has evolved from a rudimentary biological level to advanced social, intellectual, and spiritual phases.

The key to understanding evolution is to see that today's changes are cultural equivalents of biological evolution, as shown in Table 1. Biological evolution comprises the first stage in this process, while the remaining six stages involve cultural evolution. A brief outline characterizing how life

TABLE 1.   Stages of Evolution

Main Characteristics	1 Biological Era	2 Tribal Era	3 Agrarian Era	4 Industrial Era	5 Service Era	6 Knowledge Era	7 Existential Era
Technical Base	genetics	primitive tools	agriculture	manufacturing	social structure and interaction	computerized information processing	mental/ spiritual technology
Beginning of Era	4 billion B.C.	3 million B.C.	7000 B.C.	1850 A.D.	1950 A.D.	2000 A.D.*	2100 A.D.†
Initiating Step	appearance of life	development of humans	agricultural revolution	industrial revolution	postindustrial revolution	global information systems	steady-state physical world
Energy Source	biomass	human labor	animals	machines	attitudes and emotions	data and knowledge	symbols, beliefs, and values
Form of Organization	organisms	nomadic tribes	feudal estates	factories and distribution systems	complex organizations	information networks	global community leading to a space age

* This estimate is based on various studies (per #2); margin of error about ± 5 years.

† Based on extrapolating the LCE; probable margin of error about ± 50 years.

evolves through these stages shows the commonality that unites this entire process.

Life on Earth began some four billion years ago and eventually flowered into a rich array of species, including primitive humans. Roughly three million years ago, people formed tribal societies that used stone tools to hunt and gather food. Agrarian civilization emerged about 7000 B.C., when farming permitted settled communities and cities. About 1850 A.D., the Industrial Revolution automated farming, thereby forcing most people to work in factories; today less than 3 percent of the U.S. labor force works on farms.

The next transition in 1950 introduced a service economy consisting predominantly of white-collar jobs in restaurants, hotels, banks, media, government, and the like. Only 20 percent of American workers do blue-collar work now, and that number should fall to 10 percent or less in a decade or two. As the information revolution automates service jobs (ATM machines in banking, and so forth), a Knowledge Society should appear about the year 2000 that focuses on using information to solve difficult problems in education, science, the environment, and so on.

Thinking about the next stage beyond the Information Age is obviously speculative, but many believe it will focus on that vast realm of emotion, awareness, power, choice, wisdom, idealism, and other concerns that transcend knowledge to comprise the human spirit. This poorly understood domain of the spirit does not consist merely of blissful experiences, but a more existential state of being in which people struggle to guide more complex matters. Life at advanced levels of evolution seems to be more *intense;* it requires the careful use of sophisticated capabilities to choose among greater options in order to carry out grave new responsibilities. A good example is the power to control life itself now being conferred by biotechnology.

This systems perspective illustrates the fundamental process that underlies the entire LCE. All forms of evolution experiment with tentative advances, leaving the best adapted inventions to survive. In biological evolution, a struggle takes place among various species, while in cultural evolution it is a competition between machines, information systems, and other cultural artifacts. Passage through these stages is driven by necessity. Each stage presents new problems as well as new gains, disposing civilization to evolve continually toward higher stages of development. For instance, the industrial age produced historic gains in physical comfort, but at the cost of war, pollution, and other drawbacks that re-

quire the powers of a knowledge society to resolve. Thus, evolution is neither "good" nor "bad"; it simply heightens the existential challenge of life.

The LCE can also be plotted, as shown in Figure 1 on page 285, to put this historic process in perspective. The times when each stage occurred are shown on a logarithmic scale in order to compress the enormous differences of early stages and spread out the later stages into a comprehensible figure. Figure 1 illustrates how the planet has evolved through its development along the same S-curve that characterizes all life cycles: a culture of bacteria, a human being, or the overall evolution of life on this planet. A few special points of interest are also highlighted by this S-curve.

The "take-off point" when the LCE begins to rise upward through the industrial, service, and knowledge eras seems to coincide with the end of the Middle Ages. Since then, change has accelerated over time by almost any measure: world population, the speed of travel, and countless other factors all bend sharply upward during the past few centuries. This striking pattern is apparent by noting that the times between stages are shorter by orders of magnitude: four *billion* years of biological evolution were needed to develop humans; three *million* years passed before the onset of an agrarian age; nine *thousand* years later the Industrial Revolution occurred; one *hundred* years after that the service era began, and it required only five *decades* to reach the knowledge age.

This acceleration of evolution reaches its peak at the "pivot point"—the contemporary decades that seem so hectic with chaotic change. The pivot point represents that unique inflection point when physical growth slows down to reach toward an equilibrium. This juncture provokes controversial issues that comprise the "world problematique"— a constellation of interrelated crises involving the environment, population growth, a global economy, and other challenges that require a fundamentally different worldview.

Recently, the arrival of an environmental ethic, the collapse of communism, the onset of the information revolution, and other unprecedented changes suggest that this transformation is likely to be resolved in time, leading to a global maturing into a stable physical system sometime during the twenty-first century. While this may represent the "high point" of our planet, the serious colonization of outer space is expected to become a reality at about that same time, which may then initiate another, even higher life cycle of evolution as the space age launches life into the universe.

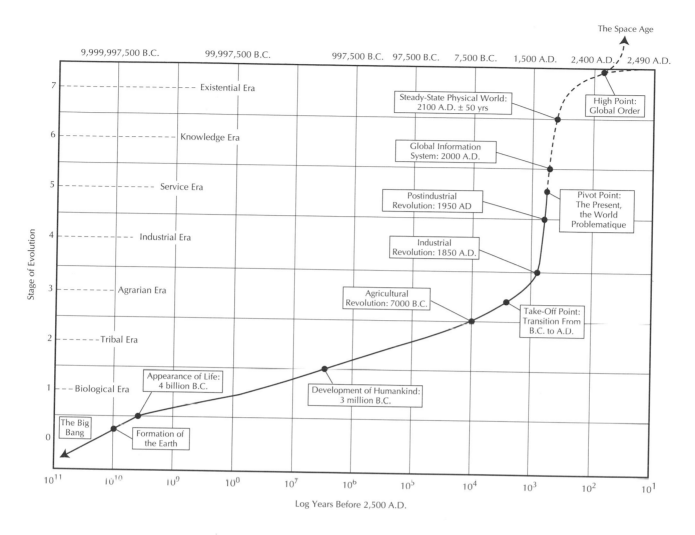

FIGURE 1. The life cycle of evolution.

See also CHANGE; CHANGE, CULTURAL; CHANGE, PACE OF; CHANGE, SCIENTIFIC AND TECHNOLOGICAL; EVOLUTION, BIOLOGICAL; LAWS, EVOLUTION OF; PUBLIC POLICY CHANGE; RECORD SETTING; SOCIAL INVENTIONS; SOCIAL AND POLITICAL EVOLUTION; TECHNOLOGICAL CHANGE.

BIBLIOGRAPHY

HALAL, WILLIAM E. "The Life Cycle of Evolution." *ICIS Forum* (January 1990).

———. "World 2000." *Futures* (January/February 1993).

HARMAN, WILLIS. *Global Mind Change* (Indianapolis, IN: Knowledge Systems, 1991).

MARIEN, MICHAEL. *Societal Directions and Alternatives.* Lafayette, NY: Information for Policy Design, 1976.

SPERRY, ROGER. "Psychology's Mentalist Paradigm." *American Psychologist* (August 1988).

William E. Halal

Evolution: Life-Forms in the Universe

We are awed by the mystery of the universe around us. The question looms larger than ever: "Are we alone in the universe?"

Over 500 years ago, Copernicus showed that the Earth was one of the many planets revolving round the sun. A hundred years ago Darwin pointed out that there was a continuity in the biosphere from the microbe to man. Not since Darwin, and before him Copernicus, has science had an opportunity for so great an understanding of man. The scientific question at stake in exobiology is the most challenging and most profound issue not only of this century but of the entire naturalistic movement that has characterized Western thoughts for over three hundred years and Asian thought for thousands of years.

285

In our search for the existence of extraterrestrial life three possible approaches present themselves. First, the landing of instruments or man somewhere in the universe. With our present knowledge, this attempt would undoubtedly be restricted to our own planetary system. A second method is via radio contact with civilizations in outer space. This presupposes the existence of intelligent beings in space with a technology as advanced as or even greater than our own. Thirdly, we have the experimental attack on the problem. Here life is considered an inevitable consequence of the evolution of matter. Since the laws of chemistry and physics are universal laws, the retracing, in the laboratory, of the path by which life appeared on Earth would give strong support to our belief in its existence elsewhere in the universe.

Alexander Ivanovich Oparin's reflections on the origins of life led him to examine the possibility of life beyond the Earth. He postulated that the conditions suitable for the origins of life had existed on the primitive Earth, but that the primitive Earth was only one of many suitable locations in the universe. Modern astronomy tells us that there are billions and billions of sites in the universe where life is possible. An estimate of the distribution of intelligent life in the universe, made by Carl Sagan of Cornell University, puts the figure at a million in our own galaxy.

On the basis of our sampling of galaxy populations to the limit attainable by present-day telescopes, we can readily compute that there are more than 10^{23} stars in the universe. Each one of these can maintain the photochemical reactions that are the basis of plant and animal life. Let us impose a number of restrictions in considering the stars that can support life. Suppose that because of doubling, clustering, and secondary collisions, only one star in a thousand has a planetary system. Suppose that only one out of a thousand of those stars with planetary systems has a planet at the right distance from a star to provide the water and the warmth that life requires. In our own planetary system we have two such planets. Further, let us suppose that only one out of a thousand of those stars with planets at the right distance has a planet large enough to hold an atmosphere. In our planetary system at least seven of the nine can do that. Suppose a further restriction is made, and we suggest that the right chemical composition for life to arise occurs only once in a thousand times. Assuming all these four restrictions, we come to the conclusion that there are at least 100 million possibilities for the existence of life. This is a conservative estimate made by Harlow Shapley.

More recent studies, taking into account the time scales of stellar, planetary, and biological evolution, reveal to us that at least 1 percent of all stars in the universe must have conditions around them suitable for life. We are still talking about a colossal number: 10^{21} possibilities. Planets are plentiful in the universe.

A starting point for any experimental consideration of the origin of life turns on the question of the cosmic distribution of elements. Astronomical spectroscopy reveals that with surprising uniformity the most abundant elements in our galaxy are, in the order of rank: hydrogen, helium, oxygen, nitrogen, and carbon. Hydrogen, oxygen, nitrogen, and carbon are indeed the basic constituents of living systems. In the presence of hydrogen, carbon will be in the form of methane, oxygen as water, and nitrogen as ammonia. It is this atmosphere of water vapor, containing C, H, N, and O, which is considered in this discussion as the primitive atmosphere of Earth.

Within our own planetary system we have explored the surface of Mars, the atmospheres of the giant planets Jupiter and Saturn, and the surface of many of their satellites. The soil of Earth's moon was brought back, and we have analyzed it in the laboratory. We looked for evidence of organic matter, but there was no evidence of any molecules related to life, and the total amount of carbon was about two thousand parts per million. This was easily understood because the surface of the moon had been exposed to large amounts of ultraviolet radiation and, in the high vacuum, carbon bonds could not survive on the surface. It was inhospitable; life could not have come into being there.

However, like a gift from heaven, we have received on Earth meteorites containing organic molecules. Careful analysis has indicated that several of them contain carbonaceous materials and are therefore described as carbonaceous chondrites. Amino acids of extraterrestrial origin have been found in them. Beginning with the Murchison meteorite, which fell to Earth in 1969 in Australia, the presence of organic molecules have been observed in several carbonaceous chondrites. Expeditions to the Antarctic during the last few years have brought back several thousand samples, many containing organic compounds. They are pristine in not being contaminated by terrestrial organic debris. However, the evidence was clear that they were prebiological. The fact that they were formed so easily suggests that life must be a common process in the universe.

Observations of Halley's Comet reveal the presence of various hydrocarbons, hydrogen cyanide, and so forth. We are moving, then, from the idea of the primitive atmosphere of the Earth to the primitive atmospheres of other planets to the general presence of organic matter under interstellar conditions. If this is indeed the case, surely life would have evolved to the point where intelligent life is present elsewhere.

Moving from the asteroid belt to the giant planets, the Voyager satellite has indicated large-scale processes in the atmosphere of both Jupiter and Saturn and infrared spectroscopy has provided evidence of organic matter. Organic molecules, which are the basis of life, appear to be common in these atmospheres. The satellites of the giant planets have also given us evidence of organic matter. Titan has an atmosphere and there is possible evidence of a very exciting organic chemistry. But, alas, it is too cold for life to begin and evolve. One possibility may be the satellite Iapetus, which has an area covered with dark material, and if there is a heat source inside and the ice is melting there may be possibility for life.

Our effort to land an instrument or eventually a scientist astronaut on a neighboring planet has been primarily directed to the planet Mars. The possibility of life on Mars has often been raised. The canal-like structures on Mars and the seasonal wave of darkening across the planet have led many to believe that there must be some form of life on Mars. Some have suggested the existence of highly intelligent beings that have saved for themselves the depleting water supply on the planet by incredible feats of engineering—that is, the construction of mammoth canals crisscrossing the planet. All these speculations have fired the imagination of planetary scientists and made them determined to find out the answer to the question, "Is there life on Mars?"

A very sketchy survey of the physical parameters of Mars indicate to us that, although the conditions are rigorous as compared to the Earth, they are within the range in which microorganisms can survive. Indeed, laboratory experiments in which these conditions have been simulated have shown that some Earth microorganisms can survive and even multiply under such conditions. Furthermore, if we consider planetary evolution in the context of of the smallness of the planet Mars, the processes of chemical evolution may have proceeded very rapidly. Life may have evolved and disappeared.

Visitors to Mars may be greeted by relics or fossils of a once-thriving biosphere.

Several experiments of interest to the life scientists were performed on the surface of Mars. A handful of soil was analyzed for organic matter. The surprising result was that less than five parts per billion of carbon was detected. This was a figure that was least expected, considering that the moon gave us 200 parts per million. There was less carbon on Mars than on the moon. In the absence of carbon would there be life? It is most unlikely. The Viking missions to Mars provided no evidence of the presence of life on the red planet. Further missions to Mars may explore the ancient history of the planet and give us some information about the early history of life there if it really did exist.

Our studies of the solar system by man and instrumental exploration has not provided any convincing evidence of the presence of life outside the Earth. We have therefore to go beyond our solar system and at the moment this cannot be done except by the use of radio or optical telescopes.

Looking beyond our own solar system, astronomers have discovered a vast array of organic molecules. The latest count gives fifty-three of them. Many of these are intermediates in prebiotic synthesis, such as hydrogen cyanide and formaldehyde. The marriage of chemistry and astronomy gives us the emerging picture of a universe where chemistry related to prebiotic processes is cosmic in nature. God himself must be an organic chemist. The universe appears to be striving to make life. Life itself must be commonplace in the universe. Today our studies of the cosmos are giving us a more profound view of the universe indicating that, indeed, life itself is an integral component of the universe, and that our brothers and sisters may be dwelling in distant planets around far-off stars.

See also EVOLUTION, BIOLOGICAL; EXTRATERRESTRIAL LIFE-FORMS; GENETICS; SPACE TRAVEL.

BIBLIOGRAPHY

CROWE, MICHAEL J. *The Extraterrestrial Life Debate: 1750–1900.* Cambridge: Cambridge University Press, 1992.

SAGAN, CARL, with AGEL, JEROME. *The Cosmic Connection: An Extraterrestrial Perspective.* Garden City, NY: Anchor/Doubleday, 1973.

SHKLOVSKII, I. S., and SAGAN, CARL. *Intelligent Life in the Universe.* New York: Delta/Dell, 1966.

Cyril Ponnamperuma

Executive Branch

The U.S. Constitution assigns to the executive branch the execution of the laws and the administration of the national government other than Congress and the courts. It charges the President with five principal responsibilities:

1. Participating in the creation of laws by assenting to, or vetoing, bills approved by Congress.
2. Commanding the armed forces.
3. Conducting foreign relations.
4. Appointing judges, ambassadors, and subordinate officials.
5. Administering the executive branch.

During the terms of the first thirty-one Presidents, the president largely confined himself to these functions. With the administration of Franklin D. Roosevelt (1933–1945), the role and function of the executive branch increased radically. After five years of rapid, Depression-induced government growth, the Brownlow Committee on Administrative Management recommended, and Roosevelt initiated, a major expansion and reorganization of what is now known as the executive office of the president.

In the postwar years the executive branch mushroomed until (in 1994) it dispensed annual outlays of more than $1.4 trillion, employed 3,000,000 civilians, and maintained more than 1,500,000 in the armed forces. Not since 1969 has the federal government balanced its annual budget; deficits in the 1990s consistently exceeded $200 billion, and by 1995 the gross federal debt is projected to surpass $5 trillion.

The tasks of the presidency have expanded far beyond those envisioned in the Constitution. The President must now be a leader in proposing and managing domestic as well as foreign policy, shaping economic policy, managing crises, building effective political coalitions, and advancing the fortunes of his political party. He must persuade the people to trust him and support his goals, and he must try to implement his policies through the vast and often unwieldy machinery of the branch he heads.

In carrying out these responsibilities, the President is in constant tension with, and often faces outright opposition from, various Nayers in national policy making. He must:

- Constantly resolve disagreements among his own cabinet and executive office appointees and persuade them to stay in line with his policies instead of yielding to the appeals of powerful members of Congress and special-interest groups.

- Struggle to persuade the vast and often lethargic civil service bureaucracy to carry out his policies, but without the ability to fire those who are obstructionist or nonproductive.

- Find some way to work with a Congress that may be dominated by special-interest advocates and controlled by opponents seeking to tie his hands (as with the War Powers Act or the Budget and Impoundment Act) or even bring him down.

- Seek a working arrangement with governors of the states, thwart the aims of political rivals, and withstand or temper the pleadings of organizations representing business, labor, women, veterans, minorities, environmental concerns, and many other special interests.

- Avoid confrontations with the judicial branch and take care to avoid interference with the process of justice.

- Interact constructively with the news media, the principal means for transmitting his message and his performance to the electorate.

- Seek some way to stay in touch with new ideas and the sentiments of the American people, while remaining virtually isolated in the White House.

Numerous proposals have been advanced for reshaping the presidency and the executive. One, debated for more than two hundred years, would require a further limitation of presidential service, most commonly one six-year term instead of a maximum of two four-year terms. Another would give the president new budget management tools, notably: "enhanced rescission power (the line-item veto, including authority to reduce or eliminate appropriations unless overridden by Congress), a federal budget redesigned for sound management, financial controls, reporting, and audits, and a balanced-budget constitutional amendment (not a mere statutory provision that could be ignored at congressional whim). Another proposal would create an executive branch "First Secretary" to free the President from the pressure of managerial duties.

A more sweeping set of proposals aims at diminishing the size of the national government itself, through abandoning functions altogether (such as transportation regulation and farm price supports), redelegating functions to state governments, sometimes with either the funds (Nixon) or the tax sources (Reagan) to pay program costs (welfare, highways, airports, etc.); privatizing government programs (selling off government-owned land and power corporations, competitive contracting for facilities management, shifting grants to public-housing bureaucracies to vouchers for housing consumers); and introducing more market-oriented flexibility in government agencies.

Another type of proposal aims at generating important feedback to the presidency. One proposes the use of interactive video and satellite technology to allow the President and his top officials to converse with ordinary citizens at "town meetings." Another, typical of parliamentary systems, would bring those officials onto the floor of Congress for an open "question period." Another would create a "Council of State" composed of respected senior men and women no longer active in public life to periodically assess for the President the status of the presidency, the condition of the nation, and the concerns of the people.

Finally, there are long-standing proposals for converting to a parliamentary system such as is found in most other Western democracies, notably the United Kingdom and Canada. In such a system the executive branch is managed by the leaders of the legislative branch, selected by the party holding a majority in the popularly elected house of Parliament. The party leader becomes the prime minister and head of government. If the party loses its majority in Parliament, through defections or special elections, it is obliged to call a general election to reestablish a popular mandate to govern.

In authoritarian systems, such as North Korea, Cuba, and many nations in Asia, Africa, and in parts of the former Soviet Union, there is no independent legislative or judicial branch. Instead of a constitutional balance of powers, such nations are ruled by the groups that seize power and maintain control through an army, national police force, and mass party or religious organizations. Fortunately, these models are diminishing in significance.

See also EXECUTIVE BRANCH: THE PRESIDENCY; JUDICIAL REFORM; LEADERSHIP; LEGISLATIVE AND PARLIAMENTARY SYSTEMS.

BIBLIOGRAPHY

CRONIN, THOMAS E. *Inventing the American Presidency.* Boston: Little, Brown & Co., 1989.
_____ *The State of the Presidency.* Boston: Little, Brown & Co., 1980.
HART, JOHN. *The Presidential Branch.* Elmsford, NY: Pergamon Press, 1987.
HESS, STEPHEN. *Organizing the Presidency.* Washington, D.C.: Brookings Institution, 1988.
NEUSTADT, RICHARD E. *Presidential Power and Modern Presidents.* New York: Macmillan, 1990.
ROSSITER, CLINTON. *The American Presidency.* New York: New American Library, 1960.
SCHLESINGER JR., ARTHUR M. *The Imperial Presidency.* Boston: Houghton Mifflin, 1973.

John McClaughry

Executive Branch: The Presidency

After several decades in which governmental power had increasingly been centralized, and in which government had taken prime responsibility for many major societal functions, the United States, like other countries, began in the 1990s a decentralization of governmental power, a devolution to other levels of government and the private sector, and a relaxing of constraints and regulations that were hampering national competitiveness in the world economy.

These changes were taking place in part because of the end of the Cold War and the centralized defense and industrial policies fostered by it. But they also were triggered by the need of the United States and other countries to reduce the burdens of the welfare state, cut government spending as a percent of GDP, and allocate resources more effectively in an increasingly global financial and economic framework.

The American presidency and executive branch, no longer able to mobilize public and congressional opinion behind national security imperatives, had by the mid-1990s lost much of the authority necessary to generate consensus behind anything other than least-common-denominator policies.

Barring an unforeseen international military, financial, or economic crisis—forcing dramatic, unifying actions by the federal government and American people—this diffusion of power is likely to continue into the twenty-first century.

The *international security function* will, of course, remain lodged principally with the president and executive branch. But the use of American military forces, or even the application of major diplomacy, increasingly will require prior congressional and public consensus. The paradigm will be that of World War II rather than that of the Korean or Vietnam wars. Responsibility for *economic growth and job creation* increasingly will be returned to the private sector and financial markets as the federal government loosens regulation and constraints that hamper the United States in international competition.

The *social safety net*, including such programs as Social Security, Medicare, Medicaid, and public welfare, will remain a high national priority. But rather than being funded and administered wholly through federal agencies, they will in some cases be provided through lower levels of government, through contracting with the private sector, or through provision of vouchers to individual recipients so that they can make individual choices.

Federal *regulation* will continue to be enforced over areas where health and safety must be protected. But those areas, in turn, will be more narrowly defined. And economic regulation, not necessarily affecting health and safety, will be diminished as attempts are made to reduce public spending and to remove constraints from institutions whose principal competitors will be offshore. *Competition policy*, relatedly, will be administered by the Justice Department and federal regulatory agencies with international, rather than domestic, criteria in mind.

With the national-crisis mentality fostered over sixty years by challenges of the Depression, world war, and Cold War having been removed, the United States presidency and executive branch will in fact return to the more traditional position they have held within the American system. That is, they will be held accountable for providing for the common defense, in consultation with the Congress, but they will play a more catalytic and less central role in providing for the general welfare.

The imperatives imposed by external economic competition, requiring flexibility and responsiveness, will be fortified by the worldwide trend toward localization (in its more negative forms, "balkanization"), in which states, regions, localities, and particular groups of people seek autonomy within a larger political unit.

In its more positive aspects, this new era will relieve the president and federal government from the performance of functions for which they are not best suited. But there will be a negative side as well. Accustomed to following national leadership only occasionally and in a limited number of areas, the American people will not necessarily respond to their president and the executive branch when difficult and urgent actions are required. The well-told stories of President Abraham Lincoln's attempt to save the Union and avert civil war, of President Woodrow Wilson's inability to gain support for League of Nations membership, of President Franklin Roosevelt's difficulties in mobilizing opposition to Nazi aggression, or even of President Bill Clinton's attempt to mount continuing support for Mexico through its economic and financial crisis will be repeated on many fronts in coming years. In some cases these challenges will be transcended by extraordinary presidential leadership. But the country will not always be able to count on

inspiring presidential leaders with an ability to overcome public resistance and galvanize national opinion. More often, the presidency will as in the past continue to be filled by a series of persons who will alternatively be brilliant, inadequate, or simply ordinary.

The national political process that spawns presidents and presidential candidates also will continue its path since the 1960s toward diffusion and decentralization. Therefore, presidents will continue to come from the cadre of officeholders and ambitious politicians who will be able to mobilize money, media attention, and organizational support without regard for the formal structures of the major political parties. They will emerge not because of respect by their peers, or because their parties judge them qualified for the presidency, but because their skills at campaigning can bring them through a Darwinian selection process in which skills at governance may carry little weight.

The presidency and executive branch of the future, except in times of crisis requiring national unity and uniquely presidential leadership, thus will be less powerful central institutions than those that most living Americans have known. Rather, they are more likely to resemble those of the late nineteenth and early twentieth century in which other institutions were of equal or greater importance. The initial impulse of the country's original settlers—that is, to escape centralized and sometimes oppressive government power—will, as it always has, reassert itself.

At the heart so the unique and unmistakable American character is the notion that free men and women, except in extraordinary circumstances, should be left alone to do as they please and only at their periodic pleasure should invite government to assert itself. Part of that character is illusory. But much of it is authentic. It will be more clearly evident in the years ahead.

See also EXECUTIVE BRANCH.

BIBLIOGRAPHY

CAPLAN, RICHARD, and FEFFER, JOHN. *State of the Union 1994: The Clinton Administration and the Nation in Profile*. Boulder, CO: Westview Press, 1994.

LIGHT, PAUL C. *The President's Agenda: Domestic Policy Choice from Kennedy to Reagan*. Rev. ed. Baltimore: Johns Hopkins University Press, 1991.

WILDAVSKY, AARON. *The Beleagured Presidency*. New Brunswick, NJ: Transaction Publishers, 1991.

Ted Van Dyk

Exercise and Fitness

The writing is on the arterial wall. The American Heart Association recently moved physical inactivity from its list of "contributing factors" for heart and blood-vessel diseases and stroke to the status of "risk factor." This puts the slothful lifestyle on a par with high blood cholesterol, high blood pressure, and cigarette smoking as a deadly killer.

More and more research continues to link regular exercise to lower risk for osteoporosis, heart disease, Parkinson's disease, arthritis, high blood pressure, and diabetes. Without exercise or some kind of leisurely activity, weight-gain develops, which is key in boosting the risk for many of these illnesses.

The popular press has not ignored this information, although much of the American public has. A recent study, for example, found that children weigh an average of 11.4 pounds more now than they did in 1973, while eating the same amount of calories and less dietary fat and without measurable change in height. No longer are kids turning into couch potatoes. They are turning into couches—soft, puffy, and immobile.

No one would argue that exercise and fitness are unhealthy. Being unfit causes a lot of problems that being fit cures. That first step—realizing the necessity of exercise—is easy.

The second step—getting an inactive society active, thus saving thousands of lives and billions of dollars in escalating health care costs—is much tougher. Government cannot force people to exercise and eat bran muffins. Unless we are to become a sweat-suited version of *1984*, with Big P.E. Teacher replacing Big Brother, no one can force people to do things they do not want to do. A democratic society allows each of us the freedom to kill ourselves slowly—with a couch, a remote control, and a bag of fat-laden, calorie-rich, salty, or sugary snacks.

That is why the future of fitness and leisure lies not in new sports, games, or equipment—but in encouragement and incentives. Instead of introducing new gadgets and gizmos to the same group of fitness elites who always buy them, fitness as a general prescription must be introduced to the rest of America. The key is to integrate physical activity into everyday living for everyday people. Call it "fitness populism."

Who Will Take the Lead?

The best way to get people moving toward healthier lifestyles via fitness will be through imaginative, experimental efforts by the private sector—principally our employers and the health club industry. With escalating health care costs burdening all businesses, employers have a huge stake in maintaining the health of their workers. Health clubs and gyms are already realizing that reaching a wider audience through a pro-active approach will help to make them more profitable.

The Workplace Workout

Research already suggests that being in good shape reduces absenteeism on the job. In one study, workers deemed poorly fit had two and one-half times the rate of absenteeism of those who were in excellent shape. Since employers can expect fewer sick days from fit people, they may try to hire more fit people. This trend should encourage more people to keep fit to enhance chances of getting hired. Employers also will encourage employees to get and stay in shape, knowing that over time this will increase productivity and save money.

Companies can experiment with financial incentives to get their employees fit. Bluntly put:

- They can require employees to take part in an exercise regimen to be eligible for health benefits.
- Insurance premiums can be linked to an employee's physical fitness.
- Employees may have to furnish proof of exercise by signing in at their company gym or local YMCA. They can fill out training logs to document the amount of time spent exercising on their own.
- Some companies will experiment with gentler approaches to urge their employees to get healthier, making incentive programs optional instead of mandatory.
- People who fill out activity forms and show improvement through on-site exercise testing may lower their premiums or get rebates—just as a good driver can lower his or her car insurance with a clean record.
- Employees can win awards for reaching new fitness goals. Being able to jog thirty minutes continuously may earn someone a company t-shirt or a free lunch. Bicycling to work once a week might earn a gift certificate at a sporting goods store at the end of the year.
- Employers can make physical fitness infectious, by offering rewards for employees who get *other* employees involved in exercise.

- Incentive programs can reach beyond exercise into other areas of health improvement. Boosting one's use of seat belts or cutting out fried foods are examples that might earn special bonuses or rewards.
- Programs also will offer screening of major disease risk factors. More employers will experiment with weight-loss and quit-smoking clinics, stress management, mammography, blood pressure monitoring and cholesterol-lowering clinics. If you bring your cholesterol out of the danger zone, for example, you may get a reduced insurance premium or a cash prize.

For this culture of fitness to grow, worksite fitness is key. Gyms and clubs will become as ubiquitous at the jobsite as the in-house cafeteria, only healthier in content.

The worksite club will not simply feature a wide range of fitness machines and weights to improve and maintain workforce fitness. The club will become the focal point for all health-promoting behaviors—the place to get blood pressure checked, have a mammogram done, or sign up for the organization's marathon.

Onsite exercise need not be limited to the predictable. Ballroom dancing, walking vigorously, playing tennis, or rollerblading will serve just as fine as calisthenics. The emphasis will be on activity, regardless of what kind.

The Health Club of the Future

The idea of the gym as an arsenal of iron will soon fade.

- To encourage more people to buy memberships, health clubs will offer more options—from beginning weightlifting classes and ballroom dancing lessons to weight-loss clinics and yoga/relaxation workshops.
- Gyms and clubs will go beyond the needs of the baby boomers—and go after their youngsters. Some gyms have already instituted programs designed for children. This approach helps to improve the club image and also brings in cash from a previously untapped source. This trend may also boost the exercise equipment industry—who else would produce the special child-sized equipment needed?
- Competition for the club market will come from an unlikely place—academia. Colleges already have hi-tech gyms—but these state-of-the-art fitness centers will now begin to pull business away from private clubs. Members can be en-

listed from students, faculty, staff, alumni, and their families.
- The sexual revolution will reach the gym as women-only health clubs become more popular and widespread. Co-ed gyms will remain alive and well, preserving healthy terrain for people with more social motives than fitness goals in mind.
- Clubs will soon respond to the needs of the older segment of the fitness market for a place to exercise where they would feel less self-conscious and more comfortable. Fifty-plus gyms will start up, while other clubs may make certain times of the day off-limits to anyone born after 1935. Senior-citizen discounts—prevalent in movie theaters and restaurants—will become commonplace at health clubs.

Profit from Prevention

In the future, the private sector will take the lead in encouraging better health through exercise and fitness. The allure of fitness makes money, and being fit saves money. Preventive health through exercise means profit—and that is all the private industry needs to know to make it work.

See also FOOD CONSUMPTION; FREE TIME; LEISURE TIME; NUTRITION; OUTDOOR RECREATION AND LEISURE PURSUITS; PERFORMING ARTS: DANCE AND THEATER; PERSONAL TRANSPORT; SPORTS AND GAMES, COMPETITIVE.

BIBLIOGRAPHY

"Breaking the Age Barrier." *Prevention* (August 1992).
"Building a Healthy Child." *Prevention* (October 1992).
"Flex Rx." *Prevention* (February 1992).
"The New Club." *Club Industry* (December 1992).
"Worksite Health Promotion: Enhancing Human Resource Capital." *American Journal of Health Promotion* (January-February 1993).

Greg Gutfeld

Extinction of Species

With the development of artificial life, new knowledge in genetics and the postmodern paradigm of complex dynamics, the concept of extinction has lost its crisp definition. As species evolve, the underlying genetic information that defines unique character has changed. At what point in the transition is a species extinct and when does one have a new species? Biologists are not even in total agreement when they try to construct family trees for plants or animals. With experiments in genetic engineering and artificial life systems on computers, questions of what is alive become more than philosophical rhetoric; and the issues of life, death, creation, and extinction are far from trivial.

Some evolutionary models allow for catastrophic changes, calling into question the concept of a continuous evolution which had created the need to locate or identify a lot of missing links in the evolutionary chain. This does not deny the demise of certain living entities; but it does raise the issue of how and when one species may or may not evolve or become extinct. The apparent differences may lead to false organizational perceptions in an evolutionary hierarchy, further confusing extinction and evolution.

Additionally, computer models coupled with work on the human genome project give indications that genetic codes for creation or recreation can be defined, and potentially assembled at will. Even though certain genetic patterns may be "lost," it is understood that such permutations and combinations can be restored given time, even when such efforts are random or semirandom. Thus, if the building blocks are available, but the physical form is no longer extant, is a species extinct?

The importance or interest in extinction rests not with the study of a single species. Rather it lies with the changes in time and space that either lead to such an extinction or the potential impacts that such an extinction may cause or foreshadow. While ostensibly this questions the survival of life on planet Earth, pragmatically the ultimate issue is the survival of human life. Ironically it is possible that humans may become the first species to create its own evolutionary successors. Will this imply the extinction of the human species or the development of parallel life-forms?

Numerous species have become extinct within the historic period. Human intervention has played a significant role in many of these extinctions. The consequences of such actions are not yet fully understood within a larger time/space domain.

The underlying assumption here is that humans are already in their most highly evolved form and that any activity which could significantly alter the larger ecosystem could yield consequences that could only be described as resulting in the extinction of the human race. A potential transformation that significantly altered the genetic materials or the physical appearance would be perceived, in the current environment, as equivalent to extinction.

Extinction is not a value-neutral term. Under certain circumstances it might be considered to be universally beneficial, such as the eradication of smallpox. Yet we realize that such actions have a variety of consequences that might be mixed blessings in the long term. For example, weed elimination may have costs and benefits. Thus, today, concerns have been raised that the loss of even one species may mean the loss of some significant genetic pool with potential benefits as yet to be determined.

This concern operates at two levels. The first is manifest in the potential loss of plant materials, particularly in tropical areas such as the Amazon Basin or Africa. Here the issue is primarily pragmatic. Natural products have potential in the area of medicines that could be beneficial, in the near term, to human life.

The second level comes from a systems perspective and the realization that the biota of the planet are integrated in a poorly understood matrix. There is concern that the extinction of one or more species in, for example, the Amazon may potentially be felt in China (the so called "butterfly effect" of modern "chaos" theory). Additionally, there is uncertainty as to how much of the web can be allowed to become extinct before the system collapses or undergoes significant reorganization.

The question of extinction raises further the relationship between humans and nature, particularly when the dimension of time is taken into consideration. Desertification in the African Sahel has been attributed to mismanagement by humans. Yet, Earth satellite data seem to indicate that the natural ebb and flow of the desert, dancing with the vegetative edge, is significantly larger than any manifestation caused by humans. Similarly, major volcanic eruptions release greater destructive forces and nature recovers more quickly than that expected by any current understanding of modern science. Additionally, models of ocean fisheries show that current management techniques, even in conservative terms, do not stop shifts in relationships between marine populations. Standard equilibrium models do not work in dynamic, open, systems.

Thus, regardless of the problems created by humans and the clearly identifiable destructive forces unleashed by humans, nature in both short and long time cycles creates greater evolutionary changes. Thus, the issue of human intervention in the biosphere may, ultimately, prove to be trivial except where its own survival is concerned.

One of the fears is that humans, with their consciousness and ego, may be driven to try to prove that they can both create life and cause extinctions *pare passu* with nature. Several authors have raised the point that when Mother Nature created humans, she took a chance. Intelligence may not be a survival characteristic.

See also ASTRONOMY; BIODIVERSITY; EVOLUTION, BIOLOGICAL; EVOLUTION, LIFE-FORMS IN THE UNIVERSE; GENETIC ENGINEERING; GENETICS; GENETICS: AGRICULTURAL APPLICATIONS; GENETICS: COMMERCIALIZATION OF; GENETIC TECHNOLOGIES; GREEN REVOLUTION; NATURAL DISASTERS.

BIBLIOGRAPHY

AINSWORTH-LAND, GEORGE. *Grow or Die*, New York: John Wiley, 1986.

CASTI, JOHN, *Complexification*, New York: HarperCollins, 1994.

HAYLES, N. KATHERINE. *The Cosmic Web*. Ithaca, NY: Cornell University Press, 1984.

KELLERT, STEPHEN. *In the Wake of Chaos*. Chicago: University of Chicago Press, 1993.

LASZLO, ERWIN, ed. *The New Evolutionary Paradigm*. New York: Gordon Breach, 1991.

STEIN, WILFRED, and VARELA, FRANCISCO. *Thinking About Biology*. Reading, MA: Addison-Wesley, 1993.

Tom Abeles

Extraterrestrial Life-Forms

Since the dawn of consciousness, human beings have speculated on the possibility that intelligent beings might inhabit other worlds. Since the eighteenth century, science has sought answers to the question "Are we alone?"

Scientists are divided on this issue. In one camp stand those who believe that the laws of the universe are similar everywhere, and what we see in our solar system is likely to have been repeated elsewhere many times. If this assumption holds, then the universe is probably filled with life and intelligence. Our sun is an average star, and there are an estimated 200 to 400 billion stars in our galaxy alone, the Milky Way, with an estimated 100 billion galaxies in the universe. Thus, there are trillions of potential sites where life and intelligence might emerge and evolve.

The numbers dwindle when we ask, "How many stars are like our sun, how many have planets, and how many of those can support life? Once life starts, how often does it evolve into intelligence, and how often does that intelligence attempt to communicate?"

The issues to be considered in determining the likely number of advanced technological communicating civilizations were summarized by Frank Drake in a mathematical statement known as the Drake Equation:

$N = R(s)$ [Rate of Star Formation] $\cdot$ $F(p)$ [Fraction of Stars with Planets] $\cdot$ $N(e)$ [Number of planets ecologically suitable for life] $\cdot$ $F(l)$ [Fraction of planets suitable for life where life has evolved] $\cdot$ $F(i)$ [Fraction of "life-starts" where intelligence has appeared] $\cdot$ $F(c)$ [Fraction of intelligent species who have created technical civilizations] $\cdot$ $F(L)$ [Estimated lifetime of technical civilizations]

The Drake Equation shows that we can derive an estimate of millions of worlds harboring intelligent life, or only one, depending on our assumptions about several variable factors. However, most of these factors can only be estimated, which means that the equation cannot prove anything.

In fact, not all scientists believe that intelligence is common in the universe. They point out that of the nine planets and many more moons in our solar system, only one, Earth, is known to support life and intelligence. How do we know that other solar systems are constructed in the same way, with even one life-supporting planet? Perhaps it would take an entire galaxy to produce the necessary conditions for intelligence to appear on just one planet—or even an entire universe.

The probability that extraterrestrial life-forms—intelligent or otherwise—exist or would want to contact us is unknown. Advanced life-forms, evolving on planets dramatically different from Earth, might never develop our kind of technology and might advance so far beyond human society that they would have no interest in contacting us. It is because of these uncertainties that scientists tend to agree only that experiments should be conducted to determine whether we are living in a universe that is sparsely populated or filled with life.

Types of Contact

Contact between humans and extraterrestrials might occur in a variety of ways. For example, extraterrestrials could send a robot probe from their own solar system to explore nearby systems.

Crews of extraterrestrials in spacecraft might also arrive in our solar system and make direct contact with us. Many people believe that UFOs (unidentified flying objects) are spacecraft and that not only have humans been contacted by the occupants of these vessels but they have even been abducted by them and used for various experiments. So far, we have no confirmation that UFOs are extraterrestrial in origin, or even that they exist, so we cannot yet say that contact with extraterrestrial life-forms has taken place.

Another approach to contact, known as SETI (Search for Extra-Terrestrial Intelligence) refers to the search for artifically created electronic signals emanating from other star systems. SETI commenced in 1959 with a paper by physicists Philip Morrison and Giuseppe Cocconi, who argued that the time might be right for beginning a serious search for extraterrestrial intelligence.

Within a year, Frank Drake, an important SETI pioneer, implemented this suggestion with project Ozma. Using a radiotelescope in Green Bank, West Virginia, he looked for signals from Epsilon Eridani and Tau Ceti, two Sun-like stars situated ten to twelve light-years from Earth.

Until 1992, the most ambitious search ever undertaken was Project Meta, sponsored by the Planetary Society and conducted by Harvard professor Paul Horowitz. Project Meta initiated its searches at a site outside Boston in 1983. On Columbus Day, 1992, NASA began a "targeted search" of some one thousand Sun-like stars and a survey of the entire night sky visible from the northern hemisphere. However, this ambitious project lost its funding when Congress voted to terminate it after about a year of operation.

SETI scientists have yet to find any signals that are undeniably of extraterrestrial origin. Intriguing anomalies were turned up by Project Meta—signals have been detected that seemed to be of unnatural origin. However, the signals do not repeat, and researchers have withheld judgment as to what they are.

The Impact of Contact

What would happen if we made open, unambiguous contact with extraterrestrials? The impact on Earth's society would most likely be significant, but it would depend on several factors:

DISTANCE

Impact will be greater if the signal comes from a star system close to Earth. If the Earth receives a signal from a civilization 100,000 light-years away, it will have been en route for 100,000 years, and any response will take 100,000 years—a round-trip of 200,000 years. If the signal is only a brief "hello," impact will be limited to the knowledge that we are not alone.

On the other hand, if the signal comes from a nearby star system, such as Alpha Centauri, only 4.3 light-years away, an active dialogue would be possible, since round-trip discussions would take only eight years.

PARITY

Impact will vary also according to the differences in development between our society and the contacting civilization. If the contacting civilization is at the same stage of development as ourselves, we may teach as much as we learn. However, if the other civilization is even a few hundred years ahead of us, it may be very challenging for terrestrial society.

Rather than being contacted by a single planet, we may be signaled by an advanced galactic federation consisting of many worlds. After being the most advanced species on Earth for thousands of years, humans may find themselves in a "galactic kindergarten."

VOLUME

Finally, impact will depend upon the volume of information transmitted. If the contacting civilization is far away, but sends us the equivalent of the *Encyclopedia Galactica*, all of its knowledge of the universe, then the impact clearly will be enormous.

These and other variables have been used by this author to develop a "contact impact model," which has several levels of complexity. However, in its simplest form, the model can be expressed in a single expression, known as the White equation:

I (Impact) = Pd (parity difference in years at time of transmission) – D (Distance in light years) · Vi (fraction of extraterrestrial knowledge base transmitted per year)

This equation assumes that the level of impact will depend primarily upon how much new knowledge is transmitted in a given period of time. In terms of getting ready for SETI, the equation shows that we have limited control over the impact of contact, since we cannot predetermine who will contact us, nor how much of their knowledge they will share.

Preparations for contact are already underway. For example, a group of SETI researchers created a set of "detection protocols," including suggested guidelines for what should be done in the event that a signal is found. These activities prepare a worldwide cadre to help our planet respond intelligently to detection of extraterrestrial intelligence.

Summary

The search for extraterrestrial intelligence has long captured the imagination of the human species. By trying to understand the nature of extraterrestrials, we are simultaneously searching for self-knowledge, because we can only define ourselves in relationship to others. For this reason, if for no other, the search will continue.

See also EVOLUTION, BIOLOGICAL; EVOLUTION: LIFE-FORMS IN THE UNIVERSE; GENETICS; SPACE TRAVEL.

BIBLIOGRAPHY

BARROW, JOHN D., and TIPLER, FRANK J. *The Anthropic Cosmological Principle.* Oxford: Oxford University Press, 1988.

COCCONI, GIUSEPPE, and MORRISON, PHILIP. "Searching for Interstellar Communications." *Nature* 184 (1959): 844.

CROWE, MICHAEL J. *The Extraterrestrial Life Debate: 1750–1900.* "The Idea of a Plurality of Worlds, from Kant to Lowell." Cambridge: Cambridge University Press, 1986.

DRAKE, FRANK, and SOBEL, DAVA. *Is Anyone Out There?: The Scientific Search for Extraterrestrial Intelligence.* New York: Delacorte Press, 1992.

EASTERBROOK, GREGG. "Are We Alone?" *Atlantic Monthly* (August 1988).

SHKLOVSKII, I. S., and SAGAN, CARL. *Intelligent Life in the Universe.* New York: Delta Books/Dell Publishing, 1966.

WHITE, FRANK. *The SETI Factor: How the Search for Extraterrestrial Intelligence Is Transforming Our View of the Universe and Ourselves.* New York: Walker, 1990.

Frank White

F

Factories and Manufacturing

Themes likely to dominate manufacturing through the first decade of the twenty-first century include a continued emphasis on quality, concurrent approaches to *everything* (especially design, processing, and distribution), and globalization (especially marketing, distribution, and customer support). Quality will continue to be a major driver, including statistical process control (SPC), quality function deployment (QFD), design of experiments (DoE), "re-engineering" of operating processes, and other quality improvement efforts.

Concurrent engineering will grow and become the standard for development of new products and processes. New products will be configured in a manner that is most "producible" based on existing or planned manufacturing processes, a significant departure from today's standard approach, which involves designing the product and worrying later about how to build it.

Globalization will be a major change agent over the next two or three decades. Led by globalization in markets and distribution activity, mainstream manufacturers from all major industrialized countries will find themselves drawn into multinational status. This will dramatically affect management training and skills, as well as the cultural make-up of multinational manufacturing work forces, particularly in management and technical areas.

Locations for production operations are selected today based on such criteria as the availability of skilled labor, adequate distribution modes, tax breaks, and other political-economic incentives. Over the next ten to twenty years, domestic production facilities will shift from the Midwest to the Sun Belt states and especially to second-tier cities and large-city suburbs. Internationally, fabrication in general (particularly low-tech fabrication operations—metal bending, sewing, etc.) will move from industrialized countries to less developed, industrializing countries. This will allow companies to take advantage of lower labor rates, looser environmental and other regulations, and trade offsets.

Actual factory size is likely to diminish generally as equipment becomes more compact, materials become more adaptable to final fabricated shapes, and efficiency improves, and also as large manufacturers move away from vertical integration. Average factories by the year 2000 will employ half the number of a decade earlier.

Human resources, the most critical aspect of any company's operations, will face new challenges as a result of two primary factors. First, the work force will not have all the education, skills, and training required to operate the increasingly complex manufacturing and information-processing equipment. Educational levels, both in the United States and in most other industrialized nations, are woefully inadequate and may not improve quickly enough to keep pace with future workplace demands. The shortages may be acute in engineering, product and process research, physical sciences, and computer sciences. Secondly, the values of tomorrows' workers will be quite different. People entering the manufacturing work force are less eager for overtime pay and for job stability at any cost, and likely to be more interested in free time and personal fulfillment. As a result, the most talented people will be far less responsive to the deadlines and other regimens imposed regularly in today's manufacturing settings. This will mean rapid expansion of temporary workers contracted for specific assignments, free-lance management specialists and technical people, and telecommuting from distant locations in job categories not requiring face-to-face dealings.

Automation levels through 2010 will grow exponentially. Rather than earlier images of an army of humanoid robots moving up and down aisles and assembling manufactured goods in the place of people, the robotics applications in factories will stem from initial successes in redundant operations, hazardous processes (such as welding and spray painting), in areas requiring precision and high levels of accurate repeatability (such as data entry and mixing of chemical compounds), and in areas where human strength is inadequate (such as the continuous lifting of heavy loads).

2010–2030

Themes that will dominate the manufacturing world between 2010 and 2030 are likely to include knowledge-based systems development and deployment, the development of product and service infrastructures, and the integration of technologies into "seamless" process development activities.

Knowledge-based systems will be used to determine optimum product configurations and availability; to allow materials management professionals to calculate optimum inventory investment levels and procurement timing; to enable finance departments to take maximum advantage of lending rates, tax laws, and other financial opportunities; to allow transportation/distribution professionals to identify the lowest-fare carriers and shortest-time distribution channels; and to let production departments schedule optimum production flow rates so as to maximize direct labor efficiency. These systems will grow out of the converging technologies of expert systems, natural language processors, telecommunications, and computers.

Infrastructure building will likely be recognized as critical for success. Infrastructures, environ-

mental factors, and systems required for support include sales and distribution networks, legislation, and even cultural factors that influence product "demand."

Technology integration will be a distinguishing characteristic as lines blur between materials sciences and manufacturing engineering, between sales and distribution, and between design and production. Cross-training will enhance the breadth of individual expertise levels. Single workstations operated by one or two individuals may be able to take the "design" process from concept through (simulated) testing, (simulated) marketing, production process development and scheduling, packaging development, and distribution channel selection.

Factory locations are expected to follow patterns exhibited in the previous decade. The size of the factories is likely to continue to shrink as personnel are cross-trained, knowledge-based systems provide technical "expertise" as needed, and new materials technologies reduce floor space requirements.

Human resources will continue to be a critical aspect, as more heavily cross-trained and broadly skilled and educated personnel are required. Strategic alliances between manufacturers and trade schools, universities, and community colleges are likely to proliferate.

Automation will continue to grow as a percentage of the value-adding component of manufacturing. Interchangeable "plug-and-play" process component equipment should be available for most standard manufacturing processes during this period, assuming that we have dealt with these interface communications issues.

2030–2050

The period from 2030 through the 2050s in manufacturing will likely be typified by the developments of microfabrication, virtual marketing and testing, and biocomputing. Microfabrication will be the most exciting development for manufacturing since the advent of the computer. It will allow the fabrication of materials and parts at the molecular level, building them with the features we desire (strength, weight, flexibility, and so forth). Left behind will be the era of excavating ore from the ground, refining it, and beating it into the forms we want. Common materials such as sand (silica) will require minor modification to configure them into extremely property-rich materials.

Virtual marketing will move to the forefront of marketing, sales, and distribution activity. Based on enormous volumes of information available through accessible on-line services and data bases, "virtual" markets may be accurately evaluated without major cost.

Biocomputers promise staggering computational power and memory capabilities. Combined with nanotechnology, prodigious information processing capability will easily support "virtual marketing."

Location will begin to wane in importance as microfabrication becomes possible, and the possibility of "portable manufacturing" emerges. Since face-to-face labor requirements will be virtually eliminated, and "pollution" or other environmental side effects will be effectively eliminated, there will be very little restriction as to appropriateness of such "factory" sites.

Factory size will at this point become a function of manufacturing equipment size, which will gradually become smaller just as computers did. Automation will be at the heart of most microfabrication operations, since handling molecules and monitoring molecular construction are not activities for which humans are well suited.

Beyond 2050

Themes likely to dominate include the balance of nanotechnology operations (namely microassembly, disassembly, replication, and altered replication), and the return to space exploration.

Nanotechnology will continue to supplant traditional manufacturing processes, replacing not only fabrication but assembly processes as well. Disassemblers may be constructed that allow virtually any substance to be broken down into its molecular components. We may be able to disassemble just about anything, and reconstruct it molecule by molecule, replicating it over and over again, even with alterations. Manufacturing will most closely resemble today's pharmaceutical industry, with vats and pipes and mixing slurries of chemicals.

As nanotechnology opens new vistas of economy and power for manufacturing, the lure of space exploration will likely become irresistible. New industries supporting space exploration will spring up to expand Earth's domain without ruining our existing habitat. This will also perhaps enable us to do space-based manufacturing of substances that can only be readily generated in gravity-free environments.

In the years ahead, factory size will be gradually reduced as manufacturing processes become encoded in robotic microfabricators and microassemblers. Eventually, as they are catalogued and

made available "over the counter," an entire "factory" may well be comprised of a handful of individuals dedicated primarily to conceiving of, developing, and selling products.

See also APPROPRIATE TECHNOLOGY, BUSINESS STRUCTURE: FORMS, IMPACTS; GLOBAL BUSINESS: DOMINANT ORGANATIONAL FORMS; MANAGEMENT; MATERIALS: RESEARCH AND DEVELOPMENT; NANO-TECHNOLOGY; ROBOTICS; SCIENCE CITIES; WORK, QUALITY OF; WORK ETHIC; WORKFORCE REDISTRIBUTION; WORKING CONDITIONS.

BIBLIOGRAPHY

BOYETT, JOSEPH, and CONN, HENRY. *Workplace 2000.* New York: Dutton, 1991.

CETRON, MARVIN, and DAVIES, OWEN. *American Renaissance.* New York: St. Martin's Press, 1989.

DREXLER, K. ERIC, et al. *Unbounding the Future.* New York: Morrow, 1991.

DUNCAN, WILLIAM L. *Manufacturing 2000.* New York: AMACOM, 1994.

William L. Duncan

Families and Households

Many prognostications about the future devote considerable attention to the potential impact of technological change on various institutions such as the family. This is neither surprising nor inappropriate. Technology is almost always a major force—indeed, at times, the major force driving social and economic change. The Industrial Revolution exerted a profound and far-reaching impact on family life in American society, affecting everything from where families lived to how they organized and carried out their social and economic responsibilities.

Nevertheless, it is a mistaken emphasis, at this juncture in U.S. history, for an examination of the future of family life in American society to focus primarily on the effects of technology. Fascinating though it may be to consider whether twenty-first-century Americans will be flying around in space-mobiles like George and Jane Jetson, the future of the family in American society will be determined far less by technological change than by the outcome of raging conflicts over values. At the heart of this cultural battle is a sizeable and growing gap between traditional standards and actual behavior, between how we want our families to be and how they actually are.

Most Americans want to be happy at home. In survey after survey, Americans consistently identify marital happiness and a strong family unit among their top goals in life. Amidst all of the cultural turbulence in recent years, baby boomers are expressing a growing concern about and interest in family life.

Not only do surveys consistently show a high appreciation for family life, but they consistently produce results that affirm many of the time-honored principles providing a firm foundation for achieving a strong family. According to survey data, Americans believe it is best for marriages to last until the death of one spouse, for married couples to be faithful to one another, for children to be born in wedlock, for children to grow up in a two-parent household, for parents to organize their work-and-family responsibilities in a manner that minimizes time away from their children.

Yet, the reality of family life in American society often falls short of these aspirations:

- America, for better or worse, has the highest divorce rate in the world, with half of all marriages ending in divorce. More than half of all divorces involve children; disrupted family life often results in severe emotional scars, especially for young children.
- Children born out of wedlock constituted 30 percent of all births in 1991 (up from 5 percent in 1960, and projected to reach 40 percent by 2000; among blacks the percent soared from 23 to 68 percent between 1960 and 1991). Illegitimate children incur higher infant mortality, suffer lower birth weights, and are relegated to growing up poor (with increased risks of not completing school or becoming involved in crime).
- Almost 90 percent of all single-parent households in 1991 were fatherless; half of all divorced fathers seldom see their offspring, and most do not provide child support. By the mid-1990s, the number of fatherless households resulting from unwed childbearing is projected to exceed the number created by divorce.
- Among children born in 1980, only 6 percent of blacks and 30 percent of whites will live with their parents through age eighteen. Recent reports indicate that children raised in single-parent households are two to three times more likely to suffer emotional/behavioral problems as children from two-parent families are; also, they are more likely to become high school dropouts, pregnant teenagers, or drug abusers, and to engage in criminal behavior.

No one seriously argues that we are living in an era marked by family strength. Faced with the gap between traditional standards and actual behavior, one side in this cultural conflict calls for lowering or doing away with traditional guidelines governing human behavior and family life. It maintains that eliminating standards will enable people to live any lifestyle they want, to redefine the family in any way they so choose.

Others urge behavioral changes to conform with time-honored guidelines, since such standards have proved throughout history to limit human suffering and promote human happiness. Indeed, they argue that the fall of every great civilization was preceded by a retreat from time-honored principles governing human behavior and family relationships.

Should the proponents of family redefinition prevail, then the families of the future may bear less resemblance to the family pattern to which most Americans today aspire. Instead, the twenty-first century may see more adultery, divorce, and illegitimacy than that found today. Child abuse, neglect, and abandonment also may rise, as children and childrearing become less and less valued. Schools, day care centers, corporations, and governments may be called upon to assume more and more traditional family functions. Ultimately, a system of year-round, all-day, cradle-to-college programs may evolve.

Divorced from the commitments of marriage, sex may become increasingly a mechanical recreational activity, just another pleasurable experience. Traditional taboos against behaviors such as incest and man-boy sex may wane, as practitioners seek "tolerance" from those who do not share their sexual preferences. Advanced contraceptive technologies such as Norplant will be used to lessen the need for responsible decision making about sex among teenagers. RU-486 and other abortion pills will be used to terminate unwanted pregnancies.

Euthanasia may become widely available, particularly when baby boomers reach retirement age and demand old-age entitlement benefits. Genetic engineering could be utilized to provide prospective parents with designer babies, screened to eliminate undesirable genetic hazards (for example, hereditary disposition to cancer). Carried to the extreme, parents may be able to change desired genetically determined traits.

Youth gangs will proliferate by offering youngsters who have been deprived of strong families a group identity and sense of belonging they never had. Violent crime, particularly crimes against women, also may rise. All of the above trends portend disaster. In the wake of their cumulative swathe, social chaos and anarchy will cast dark shadows.

Conversely, if the defenders of time-honored standards prevail, we are apt to see a cultural revamping in which Americans commit or recommit themselves to living up to the ideals of marital fidelity and marital childbearing. In this climate, fewer children would be growing up in homes where parents had divorced or both parents worked. Family incomes would then be reduced to one income rather than two.

Information Era communication technologies also exert important influences on family life. For example, some family-oriented workers will be able to find work that allows them to earn their income by working at home using personal computers, faxes, modems, and interactive television. In addition, parents will make increasing use of these new technologies in educating their children. They also will rely upon these technologies to educate themselves as society relies less upon formal classroom education and moves toward "lifelong learning" that is integrated into economic pursuits. Families will be linked to vast electronic networks of businesses, financial institutions, government agencies, schools, universities, libraries, and museums. All this may be vastly expand a family's access to the wider world. These information and entertainment networks change what is possible for American families and change the family itself.

In many ways, the postindustrial family of the twenty-first century may bear some resemblance to the preindustrial farm or small-town family of the eighteenth and nineteenth centuries. The home, once again, may become more of a place for pursuing economic livelihoods as well as the focus of education and training.

By taking advantage of home-based employment opportunities, fathers and mothers may be able to stay at home and divide their attention between work and family demands. They would be more accessible to nurture their children during the day. In addition, families will find it easier to build and to retain home-based kin networks as more and more jobs in the information-based economy change to brainpower rather than "brawnpower" work. Such change would enhance family responsibilities over a worker's life cycle by lessening the workload when children are young, and would open up opportunities for extending careers well into the worker's sixties and seventies once children have left the home.

Obviously, such transformations will not take place overnight. It is possible that we will continue to see some countervailing trends occurring simultaneously. What happens to families is very responsive to economic and tax policies of the government as well as government regulation of the use of homes as workplaces. Laws were enacted in earlier decades to protect women and children from home-based sweatshop working conditions and to limit child labor for output sold outside the home.

It is unlikely that the turbulent redefinition of "values" will last forever. One side or the other will gain consensus and cultural dominance. A likely key to gaining dominance will be based on framing the issues to one's advantage.

Many of the polarizing issues that lie at the heart of the clash over appropriate values—abortion, illegitimacy, pornography, divorce, TV violence, homosexuality, and day care—involve issues that pit adult liberty against child well-being. Family priorities, choices, and the quality of family life are shaped differently depending upon what is important to a family and to a society. One viewpoint prizes freedom and choice and entrepreneurial liberty. Another perspective reveres an often religiously based tradition, continuity, and conventional standards such as "the sanctity of the family." Such conflicts between "moral relativists" and "religious and cultural traditionalists" are not easily reconciled.

Many issues at the heart of the controversy do not easily lend themselves to compromise. However the current conflict is resolved, the outcome is likely to have a more dramatic effect on the future of the family than will any technological change.

See also ABORTION; CHILD CARE; CHILDREN, LIVING ARRANGEMENTS; DIVORCE; ELDERLY, LIVING ARRANGEMENTS; FAMILY PATTERNS; FAMILY PLANNING; FAMILY PROBLEMS; FAMILY VALUES; HOUSEHOLD COMPOSITION; HOUSING, DEMOGRAPHIC AND LIFESTYLE IMPACTS OF; LIFESTYLES, ALTERNATIVE; MARRIAGE; SEXUAL LAWS; SOCIAL CONTROLS.

BIBLIOGRAPHY

BEUTTLER, WILLIAM. *Family: The Future.* Chicago: Libra, 1990.

FLETCHER, RONALD. *The Abolitionists: The Family and Marriage Under Attack.* New York: Routledge, 1988.

HUTTER, MARK. *The Changing Family: Comparative Perspectives.* New York: Macmillan, 1988.

KIRKENDALL, LESTER A., and GRAVATT, ARTHUR E. *Marriage and the Family in the Year 2020.* Buffalo, NY: Prometheus, 1989.

LEVITAN, SAR A. *What's Happening to the American Family? Tensions, Hopes, Realities.* Baltimore: Johns Hopkins University Press, 1988.

MOYNIHAN, DANIEL PATRICK. *Family and Nation.* New York: Harcourt Brace Jovanovich, 1987.

Gary L. Bauer

Family Patterns

Nostalgic discussion of the "old-fashioned" American family and "family values" idealizes the husband-father as breadwinner, wife-mother as housekeeper, and children who are seen but not heard. These sentiments memorialize patriarchal values, legal restrictions hobbling women's economic independence, and divorce as a seldom-used alternative.

Even in the past there was no one American family, traditional or otherwise. Because families were more economically interdependent, they were more stable. But we do not know how many couples stayed together for lack of acceptable alternatives and how many for love. Wives in black families, in immigrant families, and in working-class families always had to share the breadwinning role with their husbands. The size, the composition, the structure, and the living arrangements of families in the United States and Western Europe have undergone changes so profound as to raise the question, is the family as we have known it becoming outmoded and obsolete?

Cultural experience indicates that children benefit from having two parents who share a stable relationship. Separation and divorce are obvious stressors for children. The long-term outcome depends on the circumstances of the custodial parent after the separation, and on the quality of the children's relationship with each parent. Even after income and ethnicity are taken into account, children from single-parent families simply fare worse.

In 1900, when a woman's life expectancy was about forty-eight years, she spent almost all her adult life bearing and rearing children. Today, with an expectancy of eighty years, women have a long postreproductive life. For most women, that longer life includes years of separation, divorce, or widowhood.

As the result of changes in types and venues of work, in vocational characteristics, in the economics of family life, and in custom and law, the stability of the family has declined sharply in Western Europe and America. Most women today work because they have to and because the economy needs them in the workforce. With paid employment, wives have become less dependent on their husbands. Divorce, once a luxury restricted to the wealthy who could afford to buy it, is now a recourse more common among the working class.

Europe and the United States differ greatly in the percentage of births that take place out of wedlock. In 1992 the percentage for Greece was 2.6, well below that for any other country in the European Union (compare: Italy 5.8, Ireland 11.7, and France 26.3 percent). The figure for the United States is now 27 percent, 2.5 times greater than it was two decades ago. The rate for Sweden is twice again as high; *half the births* take place out of wedlock. Yet there is little public alarm in Sweden but widespread consternation in the United States about an "epidemic of teenage pregnancy." Why the difference?

Out-of-wedlock births occur under entirely different social circumstances in the two countries. Births to unwed teenagers have been increasing in the United States at the same time that they have been decreasing in Sweden. Infants born out of wedlock in Sweden enter a family of two parents most likely living in a consensual union. Such infants in the United States most often have only a mother to care for them—a mother living in poverty, to boot.

Among industrialized nations, the United States has the highest teenage pregnancy rate and the highest teenage childbirth rate. This is *despite* the United States, having the highest teenage abortion rate. All this is *not* because we have the highest rates of nonmarital adolescent cohabitation; the rate for Sweden is actually higher. In Sweden, public school education about human sexuality and access to contraception have been systematically provided to adolescents for many years; in contrast, both education and access have been restricted in the United States for fear of "encouraging promiscuity."

When the data are disaggregated by ethnic group, profound differences become apparent. Overall, 29.5 percent of all 1991 births were to unmarried women; the rate for blacks was 67.9 percent, for whites 21.8 percent, and for Hispanics 38 percent.

Even when they work full time, most single mothers in America remain near or below the poverty line because their wages are so low. They are vulnerable to frequent layoffs; high expenses for child care deplete their meager earnings; they lose Medicaid if they work. In Sweden, the support system is more favorable. Single parents benefit from an extensive social support system—housing subsidies, child support, day care, and medical care—that cushions the mother and her children against adversity.

Why These Social Changes?

What accounts for the increase in consensual unions, the decline in marriage, and the increase in

302

divorce during successive decades in this century? There is no simple or completely satisfactory explanation. The striking differences among countries demonstrate the importance of local variations in custom, in history, in the influence of religion, and in economics. Divorce rates regularly increase with industrialization in the West, yet remain low in Japan.

In earlier centuries, husbands and wives were tightly bound to each other. A traditional family economy enforced mutual dependence. There were simply no viable alternatives for a place to live, for subsistence, and for security. When divorce was difficult or impossible to obtain, abandonment was common. But as women earned wages, they gained independence and it became possible for women to choose to leave.

Decisions about whether to marry, to stay married, and to have children are influenced by job availability, tax structure, housing markets, rules governing social welfare benefits, and other economic considerations. The disappearance of blue-collar jobs has shut low-income and minority youth out of the workforce. For a young woman to marry a man with no prospects for employment is to take responsibility for him as well as the infant.

Does the expansion of welfare benefits account for single motherhood? Both welfare benefits and single parenthood *did* increase in parallel in the 1960s and '70s. During the past twenty years, however, benefits have *declined* in real dollar value by 26 percent, whereas single parenthood has continued to increase.

Looking to the Future

Moral exhortation for premarital chastity and an end to divorce is unlikely to succeed in reconstituting family stability in the future any more than it has in the past. National employment policies in the future may recast work patterns designed to enhance family life. This might include flexible schedules, alternative work locations, and part-time work.

The federal government also may consider implementing a full-employment policy to assure young adults who enter the labor market incomes sufficient to support families. Increasing the minimum wage is merely one step. There is no safety net for poor two-parent families. A comprehensive family assistance policy might embrace a decent basic living standard, cover unemployed two-parent as well as single-parent families, subsidize low-income housing, assure access to health care, and provide work training to enhance adult skills.

Eighteen months (recently scaled back to twelve months) of paid leave after childbirth or adoption, already the case in Sweden, might be made available in the United States for either parent with guaranteed job protection. Paid parental leave permits infant care in the home. Payments to single mothers might include a decent standard of living guarantee, including subsidized housing.

Access to good-quality infant and child day care for all families is also on the agenda. Both parents assume responsibility for children. Nonresident fathers who are employed are expected to share their income with their children; child support awards require vigorous enforcement. Security for mothers and children could be assured by a guaranteed minimum child support benefit paid directly by the government and recouped from the father, so far as possible.

Success in marriage requires shared values, reasonable expectations, willingness to compromise, and moral commitment. These are the family values that make for stability, durability, and fairness in family relationships today and in the future.

Will these policies bring about a golden age of the family? Clearly not. But they will cushion children against neglect and misfortune.

See also CHILD CARE; DIVORCE; FAMILIES AND HOUSEHOLDS; FAMILY PLANNING; FAMILY PROBLEMS; FAMILY VALUES; HOUSEHOLD COMPOSITION; MARRIAGE; SEXUAL BEHAVIOR; SEXUAL CODES; SEXUAL LAWS; SOCIAL CHANGE: UNITED STATES; VALUES; VALUES CHANGE; WOMEN AND WORK; WOMEN'S MOVEMENT; WOMEN'S RIGHTS.

BIBLIOGRAPHY

DAWSON, D. A. "Family Structure and Children's Health and Well-Being: Data from the 1988 National Health Interview Survey on Child Health." *Journal of Marriage and the Family* 53 (1991): 573–584.

GIBBS, J. T. "The Social Context of Teenage Pregnancy and Parenting in the Black Community." In M. K. Rosenheim and F. F. Testa, eds. *Early Parenthood and Coming of Age in the 1990s.* New Brunswick, NJ: Rutgers University Press, 1992, pp. 71–88.

HOEM, B., and HOEM, J. M. "The Swedish Family: Aspects of Contemporary Developments." *Journal of Family Issues* 9 (1988): 397–424.

MASSEY, D. S., and DENTON, N. A. "Hypersegregation in U.S. Metropolitan Areas: Black and Hispanic Segregation Along Five Dimensions." *Demography* 26 (1989): 373–391.

MCLANAHAN, S. S., and SANDEFUR, G. *Growing Up with a Single Parent.* Cambridge, MA: Harvard University Press, 1994.

WILSON, W. J. *The Truly Disadvantaged: The Inner City, the Underclass, and Public Policy.* Chicago, IL: University of Chicago Press, 1987.

Leon Eisenberg

Family Planning

Family planning means, to most people, limiting the number of children born. But it can mean timing births, spacing births, or meeting a large family-size target.

People delay and limit births or voluntarily remain childless for many reasons. Having a child often means doing without something else because childrearing costs time and money. Couples may delay a first birth from a sense of economic insecurity, in order to save, afford more living space or other goods, or retain personal flexibility. Some couples limit family size or avoid childbearing altogether out of concern for the burden that growing populations put on the environment.

Strategies for limiting family size run the gamut from individual to cultural, from benign to brutal. A continuum of strategies and lifestyles worldwide that affect family size can be arrayed approximately from the most to the least acceptable to Western religious and other cultural values. These approaches include abstinence, delayed marriage, premarital virginity, breastfeeding, modern contraception, coitus interruptus, long postpartum-sex taboos, abortion, polygyny (multiple wives, who may be sisters), polyandry (multiple husbands, who are always brothers), arranged marriage combined with discrimination against young widows, subincision (splitting the underside of the penis so that most semen is lost during coitus), infibulation (cutting and joining the labia in order to nearly fuse the vaginal orifice), female infanticide, and the abuse and sexual exploitation or even murder of young women or widows.

Many cultural practices work indirectly and synergistically. For example, a long postpartum-sex taboo is easier to observe when a man has access to more than one sexual partner, as in polygynous marriages. Polyandry limits the total fertility rate because, where one woman weds several men, other women necessarily remain unmarried. Many behaviors are rationalized by values other than limiting family size (e.g., subincised men are supposedly more attractive to women). Others (such as child abandonment or infanticide and bride

murder) are illicit or illegal, although, in some societies, rarely prosecuted.

Intentional family-size limitation and cultural patterns that support it keep population size in balance with resources. Societies lacking self-regulating mechanisms will grow beyond the carrying capacity of their environment and finally disperse or die off.

The great virtue of modern contraception is to offer a humane alternative to such practices. Its shortcoming is that only women or couples who expressly intend to limit childbearing are likely to use it. Total and easy access to modern contraception would probably reduce childbearing by only one-third of the amount needed to bring Third World fertility to a level where parents just replace themselves in the population.

Population policies promulgated by governments, whether pro- or antinatalist, have been somewhat ineffective in gaining public compliance. For example, the later Roman emperors as well as the recent dictator of Romania, Nikolae Ceausescu, pursued aggressively pronatalist policies; but people two thousand years apart in time reacted similarly to their deteriorating economies by avoiding family responsibilities. Likewise, government-sponsored family planning programs fail without incentives which reinforce a desire for small family size.

People want more children when they perceive expanding economic opportunity. Conversely, a sense of limited resources is an incentive for marital and reproductive caution. Government encouragement of small family size is often undermined by the simultaneous subsidy of consumer goods and social services.

AIDS and other endemic diseases can slow population growth. Even in high-fertility countries in Africa, AIDS is expected to stop population growth by the year 2020. Rwanda, Sudan, and other countries experiencing economic downturns since about 1980 have seen fertility rates decline as much as 25 percent in the decade. In Asia, Myanmar has had a similar experience. In Myanmar and Sudan, where less than 10 percent of couples use modern contraception, the decline is attributed to delaying marriage.

See also ABORTION; ARTIFICIAL LIFE; DEMOGRAPHY; DIVORCE; FAMILIES AND HOUSEHOLDS; FAMILY PATTERNS; FAMILY PROBLEMS; FAMILY VALUES; POPULATION GROWTH: UNITED STATES; POPULATION GROWTH: WORLDWIDE; SEXUAL BEHAVIOR; SEXUAL CODES; SEXUAL REPRODUCTION; SEXUAL REPRODUCTION: ARTIFICIAL MEANS.

BIBLIOGRAPHY

ABERNETHY, VIRGINIA DEANE. *Population Politics: The Choices That Shape Our Future.* New York: Plenum Press (Insight Books), 1993.

DEMENY, PAUL. "Social Science and Population Policy." *Population and Development Review* 14 (1988): 451–480.

NAG, MONI. *Factors Affecting Human Fertility in Non-industrial Societies: A Cross Cultural Study.* New Haven: Human Relations Area Files, 1968.

Virginia Deane Abernethy

Family Problems

The future social problems of American families already are on the horizon. Families will become further divided between haves and have-nots. Women with children will be increasingly estranged from the men who fathered those children, and this will deepen the economic and social divisions between the sexes. However, even families that have two parents will struggle to integrate two jobs in a rigid work environment while attempting, simultaneously, to care for children.

Haves and Have-Nots: Homeless Families and Childhood Hunger

There has been an increasing polarization of the rich and the poor, resulting in wide discrepancies between the classes' standards of living. For the poor, this has resulted in the creation of seemingly inescapable conditions of social inequity. Homelessness increased fourfold during the 1980s. Families make up almost 40 percent of the estimated half-million homeless population. These families suffer higher infant mortality rates and their children have a harder time in school.

Struggles to make ends meet are not, however, limited to the homeless. Half of all food stamp recipients are children. In Massachusetts, for example, one in four children under the age of twelve is affected by hunger. Large numbers of the working poor are having difficulty feeding their families. Furthermore, parental unemployment, coupled with cuts in state and local aid, have contributed to childhood hunger. The percentage of children living in poverty will continue to rise unless there is some mechanism for further economic redistribution.

Female Heads of Household: Teen Mothers and Divorced Women

It is increasingly the norm for children to spend a portion of their lives with only one parent—usually their mothers. This development is driven by growth in the size of two groups: teen mothers who may eventually (though not necessarily) marry the fathers of their children; and divorced women who may remarry some other men. Men are increasingly absent or transient members of these households.

Poverty among teen mothers is the major reason why childbearing among this age group has become a social problem. The alternatives have recently been framed as continuing support for welfare versus placing the children of these mothers in orphanages in order to break the cycle of teen pregnancy (and intergenerational poverty). However, pregnancy does not cause poverty. These teens were already poor when they became pregnant. Teenage pregnancy has soared, particularly for African-American teens, but it is also increasingly common among white teens. The social stigma of being an "unwed mother" no longer exists or is waning. In addition, the foster care system commonly used by teen mothers is strained, and in some cities the system is unable to handle the large numbers of children in it. Children pay the price—emotionally and socially—of constantly living in limbo between biological mothers and foster care or between foster care placements.

Policy makers view teen mothers as both victims and creators of their own fate. Some scholars and politicians have argued that the problems of inner-city teens could be solved by providing meaningful jobs for the men. The assumption is that if men had employment that paid a decent wage, they would marry, thus returning the family to a nuclear form of a breadwinner husband and stay-at-home mother. Perhaps this would happen. It remains unclear, however, why men would share their wages with women. What is needed are jobs for women, in order for women to be able to support themselves and their children. Returning women to dependence on men for economic survival is not likely to happen among this welfare group unless the men are given jobs that pay a family wage, something that was long ago eroded. Fatherless homes have higher crime rates, lower educational attainment, and more women and children on welfare—leading to more and more children in the United States living in poverty.

In virtually half of all first marriages and among the divorced, most men abandon the responsibilities of parenthood and fail to pay child support. As a result, women and their children are rapidly becoming segregated economically from their former husbands, particularly among the middle class. Regardless of how they became single mothers, women and children—of all races—are more likely to live in poverty when men are not present. Fathers who do pay child support may spend more time visiting with children, and they often are involved in decisions about their children's lives. However, there is no national policy to enforce child support payments even though social pressure to do so does exist. Efforts are underway to see to it that as a last resort fathers are made to pay up, have their wages attached and garnished, or are arrested for failure to pay.

When men remarry, they remain biological parents to children they do not live with and become social parents to the children of the women whom they remarry. Such families become networks and chains of relations, which are built more upon social ties than upon biological ones. The legal system has yet to formalize these social ties or to give step-family parents legal rights or (economic) responsibilities for these children.

Dual Earner Couples: Asymmetry in Gender Relations

Among married couples today, there is a strain to find adequate jobs, to care for children, and still find time for one another, an increasing but largely unacknowledged social problem. An ideology of equality in marriage is what most newlyweds want, but they find it far from easy to achieve. Women remain the primary childcare providers and continue to do more housework than men. Partly, this is due to the economic reality that women, overall, are paid less than men for doing the same or comparable work. Only a very small percentage of women in the United States—those at opposite ends of the economic continuum—equal or exceed their spouse's earnings. Men are still considered the primary breadwinners, even though women's incomes have become essential to the family's remaining in the middle class. As a result, this pattern of women's employment being of "lesser value," coupled with their continued responsibility for the home and children, makes marriage far from an equal institution.

Among those couples who are economically positioned to choose, women have a broader range of options. They can choose full-time or part-time motherhood. Or they can choose full-time or part-time employment, coupled with some type of day-care. Men's choices are much more constrained: house husbands remain rare. As more men embrace the nurturing of children as an important part of their fathering, they may broaden their view of themselves as caring for their family through their economic contributions and may assume a fuller range of possibilities. In that case women will no longer be the sole socio-emotional conduits of family life. In order for this symmetry in gender relations to occur two related arenas must change: (1) The care of children and household tasks must be equally shared by women and men. (2) Women must be viewed as essential and permanent labor force participants if the sexual division of labor and the devaluation of women's work is to change. The linchpins of dual-earner couples' abilities to integrate their family lives with employment will be employment policies that are family-friendly as well as changes in childcare provisions.

Day Care and Afterschool Programs: The Raising of the Next Generation of Children

Day care remains a leading social problem that families face, regardless of whether the family has two employed parents or is comprised of only one parent—mother or father—living with children. Parents are left to solve this problem by taking personal responsibility for and finding suitable solutions. The responsibility might be passed along to other providers. Since there is no comprehensive national family policy, couples are left to piece together suitable ways to cover child care while trying to meet the requirements set by their employers. In order for parents to give their utmost to their jobs, they need to feel that their children are cared for in safe and loving environments. One of the critical problems in this country is the lack of sufficient child care facilities or arrangements and the failure to regulate such child care. Unlike the day care offered in other industrialized nations, the care that does exist in the United States is not subsidized by the government, nor is parental leave sufficient to cover infant and toddler care. Workplaces are coming around to acknowledging that their employees are parents by becoming more family-friendly. For example, some already provide adequate parental leaves to cover the early years and arrange on-site day care facilities or vouchers for community day care; some also accommodate elder care arrangements and sick leaves. Public policy debates, at bottom, strive to delineate institutional roles—or those of employers, employees, and government itself. Without changes in an inflexible workplace, parents will be caught between their obligations to family and the demands of employers.

The educational system in the United States also may become increasingly involved in caring for children. At the present there is a lack of before-school and afterschool programs. In addition, the school calendar leaves parents without child care for about three months a year. The problem society faces is who will provide all the various child care activities, and how are we going to raise the next generation of children? What kind of care arrangements are best for young children with employed parents? The private and often piecemeal ways that families try to care for their children, and the nature and scope of new arrangements, will be a matter of continuing public debate until those issues are satisfactorily resolved.

See also CHILD CARE; CHILDREN, LIVING ARRANGEMENTS; FAMILY VALUES; WOMEN AND WORK.

BIBLIOGRAPHY

ARENDELL, TERRY. *Mothers and Divorce: Legal, Economic, and Social Dilemmas.* Berkeley, CA, and London: University of California Press, 1986.

HERTZ, ROSANNA. *More Equal Than Others: Women and Men in Dual-Career Marriages.* Berkeley, CA, and London: University of California Press, 1986.

KOZOL, JONATHAN. *Rachel and Her Children: Homeless Families in America.* New York: Fawcett Columbine, 1988.

WILLIAMS, CONSTANCE WILLARD. *Black Teenage Mothers: Pregnancy and Childrearing from Their Perspective.* Lexington, MA: Lexington Books, 1991.

Rosanna Hertz

Family Values

The family values debate in America began with a bang in 1965 when a young assistant secretary of labor in the administration of President Lyndon B. Johnson called attention to the growing number of black children being born into fatherless families. The so-called Moynihan Report, named for author Daniel Patrick Moynihan, who would later be elected to the U.S. Senate, issued a prophetic warning: "A community that allows a large number of young men to grow up in broken families, dominated by women, never acquiring any stable relationship to male authority, never acquiring any set of rational expectations about the future, that community asks for and gets chaos."

That early warning went unheeded. The Moynihan report provoked such a firestorm of protest—with critics unfairly accusing the author of racism—that for more than a quarter of a century the subject of family breakdown became a taboo topic for public discussion. By the early 1990s, when public attention again focused on the problem of fatherless children, the situation had worsened dramatically. Official data showed a soaring number of births to unmarried women of all races and in every social class. By 1991, nearly 30 percent of all births in the United States were to unmarried mothers—about five times what the rate had been only thirty years earlier. Over the same period, the divorce rate almost tripled as well.

The combination of these two trends has produced a social revolution unprecedented in American history. Some experts estimate that fewer than 40 percent of the children born in the decade of the 1990s will have both a mother and a father at home throughout the first eighteen years of their lives.

The widespread breakdown of the traditional family has grim consequences, both for the children who are denied the support and guidance of two parents and for the broader society in which they live. While a small but influential group of elites has attempted to defend the single-parent family as an alternative lifestyle, or as a progressive experiment in nontraditional family forms, a mountain of evidence has accumulated to show that children in single-parent homes have the deck stacked against them.

Fatherless children are disproportionately likely to live in poverty and to lead disordered lives, including as violent criminals. Consider just a few figures: Almost half of all fatherless families receive some form of financial assistance from government. The comparable figure for families with two parents is under 10 percent. Girls who grow up in households without a father are roughly 50 percent more likely to become pregnant out of wedlock than girls who do have a father at home. Nearly two-thirds of the juveniles convicted of rape and three-quarters of those convicted of murder come from fatherless homes. Indeed, more than 70 percent of juvenile criminals who have been imprisoned or institutionalized come from single-parent families.

All of these figures, it should be emphasized, are probabilities or averages. There have always been, and always will be exceptions—children who grow up without both parents certainly can succeed in life. Many always have and many will continue to do so. It should also be emphasized that the millions of women who are struggling, often heroically, to raise their children alone are not necessarily bad parents. They are not the ones who have abandoned their children, shirked their duties, and refused to shoulder the obligations of parenthood.

The urgent question as we look ahead to the twenty-first century is how to reverse these destructive trends. This is a pressing issue not just in the United States but in many industrialized nations, where the illegitimacy rates, while lower than in the U.S., are also rising rapidly.

A combination of private and public efforts will clearly be required. While the rise of the modern welfare state has accompanied the breakdown of the family—and has probably contributed to the problem by cushioning the extreme hardship that once was the common fate of fatherless families—scholars disagree about the precise cause and effect. And even those who attribute a large part of the responsibility for family breakdown to government programs that provide financial support to single-parent households are uncertain whether the ethic of self-sacrifice and obligation that once held families together "for the sake of the children" can be revived even by radical reforms of the welfare system.

The decision to bear children responsibly and to sacrifice for their well-being is fundamentally a matter of personal character and morality. Individuals ultimately must resolve to do the right thing; government, however, can reasonably be expected to encourage those who make the right choices and to discourage those whose irresponsibility profoundly harms the prospects of their children and the health of the larger society. Deliberations over public policy in the years ahead will be increasingly devoted to the question of how precisely government can meet this challenge.

Since the collapse of the Soviet empire at the end of the 1980s, the American people have focused increasingly on this domestic challenge. Their confidence in the future, as expressed in numerous public opinion polls, has been shaken by their recognition that the epidemic rates of illegitimacy and family breakdown have created a society adrift in uncharted waters.

Yet there is reason to believe that Americans will rise to meet this challenge, as they have met other challenges in the past—with sustained personal and community efforts, inspired by their traditional belief in a better future. A heartening number of private, voluntary organizations have already arisen, aiming in different ways to encourage parental responsibility. Some emphasize moral obligations; others aim to provide job training and counseling to unemployed, unmarried young fathers. Still others focus on instilling virtue in young people through traditional religious teachings, encouraging them to marry before having children. These private efforts may hold the best long-term hope for reweaving a social fabric in which two-parent families are the norm.

Twenty years from now—fully a half century since the Moynihan report—America will still be facing the consequences of family breakdown. Daniel Patrick Moynihan's original warning, however, will no longer be controversial. It is customary to think of the future in terms of the novelties it will bring—new technologies, or things that are bigger, better, faster, or simply different than what we are accustomed to. When it comes to the family, however, the America of tomorrow will be a place that has restored the primacy of an institution as old as mankind itself: the tried and true model of the mother and father raising children. The family of the future will look a lot like the family of the past.

See also ABORTION; CHILD ABUSE; DIVORCE; FAMILIES AND HOUSEHOLDS; FAMILY PLANNING; FAMILY PROBLEMS; MARRIAGE; SEXUAL BEHAVIOR; SEXUAL CODES; SEXUAL LAWS; SOCIAL CHANGE: UNITED STATES; WOMEN'S MOVEMENT.

BIBLIOGRAPHY

BLANKENHORN, DAVID. *Fatherless America: Confronting Our Most Urgent Social Problem.* New York: Basic Books, 1995.

HIMMELFARB, GERTRUDE. *The De-Moralization of Society: From Victorian Virtues to Modern Values.* New York: Alfred A. Knopf, 1995.

MOYNIHAN, DANIEL PATRICK. *The Negro Family: The Case for National Action.* Washington, DC: U.S. Department of Labor, 1965.

WHITEHEAD, BARBARA DAFOE. "Dan Quayle Was Right." *Atlantic Monthly* (April 1993).

Dan Quayle

Farm Policy

Farm policy is, generally speaking, the course of action taken by the federal government with respect to farmers and farming, particularly to maintain farm income. Ever since the days when George Washington advocated the establishment of an agency devoted to the welfare of farmers, the government has adopted policies favoring farmers. However, as the twenty-first century approaches there has been a change in attitudes. Perhaps this shift occurred because when Washington was president over 90 percent of Americans made their living from agriculture, while two centuries later less than 2 percent of workers are engaged in farming.

Major policies respecting agriculture have for the most part been adopted during two periods in American history, first in the year 1862 and second in the decade of the 1930s. Although modified in many respects, the legislation passed during these two periods remains the basis of American farm policy. However, in the near future, in part because of the declining numbers of farmers and, indeed, of the success of the past programs, there will be substantial modifications in the farm subsidy programs and pressure for elimination of the Department of Agriculture.

In 1862, President Abraham Lincoln signed three laws primarily devoted to the welfare of family farmers. The first provided for a Department of Agriculture; the second granted 160 acres of unclaimed federal lands to any person who would settle on and farm them; and the third granted federal lands to the states for the purpose of establishing colleges to teach agriculture, mechanical engineering, and the military arts.

The second series of laws was passed during the New Deal of the 1930s. The Agricultural Adjustment Act, signed by President Franklin D. Roosevelt on May 12, 1933, offered farmers specific prices, called parity or fair prices, for compliance with production controls. Invalidated by the Supreme Court, this act was replaced by acts in 1936, 1938, and 1949. The acts of 1938 and 1949, with modifications, are still in effect almost fifty years later.

Most agricultural subsidy programs in the 1990s and beyond will be of an indirect nature, such as the assistance offered farmers by county agents and the increased demand for farm products resulting from the school lunch and food stamp programs, although the county agent program will be sustantially reduced or even eliminated by the turn of the century. Some programs, such as the Reclamation Act of 1903, which provided many farmers with irrigated lands, have a long-term impact and are also indirect in nature.

Price support, also known as commodity stabilization, and soil conservation programs are the most direct in nature. Commodity stabilization is sought through commodity loans, purchases, and payments to eligible producers. Basically, if prices in the marketplace do not reach a particular level, farmers who have allotments from a past history of producing the commodity receive direct payments to make up the difference between what they receive

in the marketplace and what they should receive by law. Only crops specified by law are supported. While the list has varied over the years, few animal products have been supported since World War II.

The Soil Conservation Service is concerned with preserving the soil and water of the nation. Its local agents work directly with farm groups and with individual farmers to develop programs for soil preservation and water conservation. As the century nears its end, the service and farmers are urged by groups concerned with natural resource preservation to cut back on intensive cultivation, the use of fertilizer, and other production stimulants in order to conserve the soil and other resources.

The federal government maintains many programs, including research, regulation, and education, to assist farmers. For example, the Farm Credit Administration, an independent agency, supervises institutions operating under government sponsorship to make credit available to farmers and their credit cooperatives.

Government policy over the years encouraged agricultural exports and protected American farmers from unfair foreign competition. Most of the effort has gone into promoting exports since, except for a few commodities such as seasonal fruits and vegetables and wool, American farm products are competitive in a free market. However, many nations control their imports of farm products. The world prices of those not controlled are sometimes maintained at levels that American farmers cannot compete against.

The Foreign Agricultural Service of the Department of Agriculture and the Agency for International Development are both concerned with exports of agricultural products, the Foreign Agricultural Service mainly from a commercial viewpoint and the Agency for International Development mainly from an humanitarian viewpoint. Both have responsibilities under the Agricultural Trade and Development Act of 1954, known as Public Law 480, passed primarily to help rid the government of surplus commodities. The law authorized the government to make agreements for the sale of farm products for foreign currency, to make shipments for emergency relief and other aid, and to barter farm products for needed materials. P.L. 480 proved so valuable that, in a modified form, it has been extended into the 1990s and doubtless will be further extended, but it has been far from a complete answer to the surplus problem. However, the emergency relief and similar programs have saved and improved the lives of many people around the world.

The Foreign Agricultural Service collects and makes available information on agricultural production in other countries, advises commercial exporters, makes subsidies available to producers or exporters who are suffering from unfair trade practices abroad, and, in general, aids in the export of American farm products. Farm products made up some 20 percent of America's total exports in 1980, but the figure fell to 10 percent in 1992. Farm organizations usually look with favor on international agreements promoting free trade but are wary of the importation of commodities subsidized by other nations.

The GATT Uruguay Round trade agreement proposed the countries mutually dismantle agricultural subsidy programs that artificially skew international commerce. The Blair House accord called for subsidized agricultural exports to be cut by 21 percent in volume (measured against the 1986–1990 base period), and by 36 percent in value; in addition, domestic subsidies were to be cut by 20 percent over six years. Changes are in prospect.

How much farm support programs cost varies from year to year. Direct agricultural support payments averaged about $10 billion a year during the early 1990s. Global cost estimates incurred by the industrial nations of the world mounted to $150 billion.

U. S. farm policies, a patchwork whole made up of literally hundreds of programs and policies, will undergo major changes by the turn of the century, possibly including the elimination of direct subsidy payments. Cost considerations are likely to impose substantial changes, even though the policies and programs result in lower food costs to the consumer. At the same time, future farm policies will keep farmers a small minority of the population and will continue to replace a distinctly rural system with the values of industrial capitalism.

See also ALCOHOL; ANIMAL RIGHTS; FISHERIES; FOOD AND AGRICULTURE; FOOD AND DRUG SAFETY; FOOD LAWS; FOOD TECHNOLOGIES; FOOD AND FIBER PRODUCTION; FORESTRY; GENETICS: AGRICULTURAL APPLICATIONS; NUTRITION; TOBACCO.

BIBLIOGRAPHY

BAKER, GLADYS L.; RASMUSSEN, WAYNE D.; WISER, VIVIAN; and PORTER, JANE M. *Century of Service: The First 100 Years of the United States Department of Agriculture.* Washington, DC: U.S. Department of Agriculture, 1963.

COCHRANE, WILLARD W. *The Development of American Agriculture: A Historical Analysis*, 2nd ed. Minneapolis: University of Minnesota Press, 1993.

HALLAM, ARNE, ed. *Size, Structure, and the Changing Face of American Agriculture.* Boulder, CO: Westview Press, 1993.

RASMUSSEN, WAYNE D. *American Agriculture: A Documentary History.* 4 vols. New York: Random House, 1975.

———. *Taking the University to The People; Seventy-five Years of Cooperative Extension.* Ames, IA: Iowa State University Press, 1989.

Wayne D. Rasmussen

Feminization of Poverty.

See POVERTY, FEMINIZATION OF.

Financial Institutions

Financial services solve business problems, fuel economic growth, and help bring the world closer together. They also can contribute to inflation and instability. As a result, they operate under a highly regulated structure that, in the United States in particular, separates the functions of traditional types of organizations. In the 1980s the separation of powers began to weaken. Dramatic changes occurred in the United Kingdom and Canada, moving them closer in structure to the universal banking systems of continental Europe. The U.S. banking structure has responded slowly to international competition, technology, and a climate in which market forces generally are allowed to have greater reign. Nevertheless, the United States is leading in the extensive financial innovation that this climate engenders.

Financial Innovations

Financial innovations are making it easier to reduce the risks associated with doing business internationally, to make assets more liquid, to economize on capital, and to overcome distance and time. Securitization of assets, which allows financial institutions to sell assets so they can relend the same money, has become commonplace in the United States and has started to become important in Europe and elsewhere. Derivatives and related risk management products (such as options, futures, and interest rate and currency swaps) enable the parties to a transaction to insulate themselves to a degree from fluctuations in interest rates, exchange rates, and securities prices while locking in desired patterns of cash flow. Investment pools have grown to facilitate markets for products from high-grade investment paper to below investment-grade securities and to create vehicles through which institutional investors such as pensions and life insurance companies can easily place funds.

In the future, accepted financial solutions will be more widely used. Impending innovations will allow financing for longer periods of time, provide greater protection against inflation, provide guarantees for funds invested in engineering construction megaprojects, and create much larger risk pools to allow diversification of risky investments—particularly in formerly socialist countries, new industries, and emerging nations.

Technology is at the heart of the revolution in financial services. Powerful and low-cost computers and communications have led to the growth of computer screen-based trading; regional, national and international credit card systems; ATM (automated teller) machines; and electronic data exchange for ordering, shipping, and bill-paying.

The rise of the Internet and the spread of the personal computer, along with developments in software for financial analysis and database management, will enable a new level of electronic banking and merchandising for individuals and businesses. Increasingly sophisticated consumers will do more for themselves, and more of what they do will be done electronically. The United States will remain the leader in creating and promoting new financial instruments and arrangements and increasingly will export its techniques and services to the rest of the world.

U.S. Banks

Financial sectors are subject to their own special pressures and trends. The business of banking has changed dramatically with the advent of money funds, the growth of mutual funds, and the expansion of 401-K plans and other defined contribution pension arrangements. Despite the lifting of interest rate ceilings on deposit interest rates and the creation of certificates of deposit, the banking industry's share of consumer financial assets has declined, particularly for savings and loan associations and savings banks. Higher capital requirements after earlier misadventures with real estate and other loans have raised costs and hampered the competitiveness of banks and S&Ls as holders of assets. No longer as able to profit from intermediating low-cost deposits into loans, and faced with slower mortgage lending as baby boomers passed homebuying age, banks have expanded fee-income. They have increased the charges for many services

to offset the need to pay market interest rates. And they have restructured to make more effective use of assets and provide additional fee-based services.

Banks have created securities pools for fees and sold them to lend again. Larger banks have become more involved in offering risk management services. They have taken on more consumer risk through the expansion of credit cards, which also are an important source of fee-income. Some have provided transaction and other technology-based services, often to other banks.

At times banks have taken on more risk, lending mortgages long term while sources of funds were relatively short term, lending large sums to Third World nations at low margins, lending heavily to real estate developers, lending for mergers and acquisitions, and trading for their own accounts. Banks and S&Ls have gotten into major trouble periodically. As they become more sophisticated and large enough to average some risks internally, it is to be hoped they will not pose new threats for the financial system—but new temptations and unknowns tend to foster history repeating itself.

Banks will continue to consolidate, to move interstate by acquisition under new legislation, and, as permitted, will pursue de novo branching. They will expand further in providing fee-based services to companies, and will provide a growing array of products to consumers through securities subsidiaries. Annuities will be a source of particular growth. Banks will continue to automate and provide enhanced automated analysis and advice, transaction services, and investing. Holding companies will be allowed to operate full-service securities firms and investment banks in subsidiaries, and eventually they they will have a growing role in insurance sales and possibly in underwriting. However, it is unlikely that commercial and industrial firms will be allowed to own banks.

U.S. Securities Firms

Securities firms make their money from a combination of selling securities, underwriting, trading for their own account, and doing deals such as mergers. The industry is composed of firms that specialize in one or more of these functions and large, multiline firms. Since trading commissions were deregulated in 1975, discount brokers have taken market share from other financial houses. The largest discounters have emerged as major offerers of their own mutual funds. There also has been pressure on commissions for underwriting and trading as electronics and global markets have advanced.

Many securities firms have sought additional income in the market for corporate restructuring. Some, especially boutiques such as Kohlberg, Kravis and Roberts, have taken increasingly large equity and "junk bond" positions in commercial and industrial companies, which they hold for some time and later try to sell. This model is more akin to traditional European investment banking and to banking in the United States before the Glass Steagall Act of 1933 separated securities and bank powers. Securities firms also have become quite active in the international arena, including emerging markets. They and mutual fund companies have created numerous investment pools that allow investors to diversify among investments and take advantage of their expertise.

Ownership of unrelated businesses and internationalization will shape the securities industry in the years ahead. So will the acquisition by banks as banking powers are revised. Many of the largest securities firms already are owned by life insurance or other financial firms. The extent of conglomeration will largely depend on whether holding companies that own banks are allowed to own insurance companies.

U.S. Insurance Companies

Insurance companies are adjusting to their heavy real estate losses of the 1980s and a climate of slow growth in life insurance. They are making the transition from selling insurance to cover family needs after death to preparing people for the prospect of long life. An increase of twenty years in the average remaining life expectancy for persons at age sixty-five, together with an average retirement age of sixty-three, have produced a greater need for retirement savings. It has also become more important to have an orderly system of pension withdrawals through annuities, either built into a pension or sold separately, that guarantee payment no matter how long one lives. Life insurance products continue to benefit from important tax advantages: Death benefits are not taxable, and the buildup of investment income in an annuity is only taxed when the funds are withdrawn. The rules may change somewhat, but there are likely to be important continuing tax benefits.

The property/casualty side of the insurance business has had difficulty from increased consumer-oriented regulation and large disasters. However, there are signs that the cycles (as distinct from the supplies) the industry experiences may be moderating, at least for a while. Also new risk coverage needs are evolving. It is likely that in the next generation we will find the amount of insurance business related to computers and communications will become as large as the motor vehicle-related market, which traditionally accounted for 40 to 50 percent of the sector business.

Insurance companies also are taking on a new role in the health field. The traditional claims-based profit center is being supplanted by managed care, with large insurers not only underwriting risks and investing premiums but also operating managed care health delivery systems tied to their insurance plans. Insurers could find some of their role taken over by the government, but it is more likely the government will turn to the industry to handle the system, as it did with Medicare; this time both (1) to enroll and pay and (2) to manage and operate managed care networks that serve the public.

International Financial Services and Capital Flows

European integration has spurred cross-industry and cross-national alliances and mergers in financial services. Universal banking that combines banking, insurance, and brokerage has spread. The United States and Japan have been laggards but are likely to follow. U.S. banks are puny in size compared to those of Europe and Japan—only a half dozen have assets of $100 billion or more compared to banks with $400 billion or more in Europe and Japan. The United States will create many large conglomerates to compete internationally and the efforts of U.S. financial firms will turn more international. Internationalization will mean the expansion of financial firms across regions and between the developed and the developing world. New financial centers will continue to emerge alongside New York, London, and Tokyo in continental Europe, Singapore and other parts of Asia, Latin America, and Africa. Electronic financial services increasingly will be cross-border for households as well as businesses.

Capital flows will rise rapidly with long-term world recovery (*see* ECONOMICS). Net capital flows tended to occur almost entirely among developed countries in 1980s. The coming decades will see a great rise in capital flows to and from the developing world and among its members with the spread of regional arrangements (*see* INTERNATIONAL GOVERNANCE AND REGIONAL AUTHORITIES). There may be global capital shortages from time to time as demands of world growth put pressure on available savings. The financial markets will continue to innovate to solve problems such as managing the risks and needs inherent in international markets and in long-term global economic development.

See also CAPITAL FORMATION; CREDIT, DEBT, AND BORROWING; DERIVATIVES; INFORMAL ECONOMY; INSURANCE; INVESTMENTS; PUBLIC FINANCE.

BIBLIOGRAPHY

Federal Reserve Bank of New York. *International Competitiveness of U.S. Financial Firms.* New York: Federal Reserve Bank of New York, 1992.

International Capital Markets. Washington, DC: International Monetary Fund (annual).

Market 2000: An Examination of Current Equity Market Developments. Washington, DC: U.S. Securities and Exchange Commission, 1994.

World Bank. *Financial Systems and Development, World Development Report, 1989,* Washington, DC: The World Bank, 1989.

Irving Leveson

Fisheries

About 8 percent of the animal proteins consumed in the United States are fish and shellfish. The U.S. industry produced a record 11 billion pounds in 1993, doubling volume during a steady growth period that began in 1977 after establishment of a 200-mile Exclusive Economic Zone encompassing all coastal waters. Globally, fish production grew steadily from the 1950s to the late 1980s, plateauing at about one hundred million metric tons.

Despite the growth, troubling signs have appeared in many fishery resources. The once rich, traditional cod, haddock, and flounder resources off New England have slipped badly. Major stocks in the Chesapeake have dwindled, and salmon runs in California, Oregon, and Washington have declined, some to the point of endangerment.

The declines occurred despite a fisheries management system that sets quotas and other limits on the harvest. The system has been very successful in some fisheries but a failure in others as overly optimistic quotas, unanticipated environmental conditions, and habitat destruction have taken a toll. Faltering catches are generating new approaches to fisheries management, technology, and practice internationally and domestically.

Overfishing, Overcapacity

The world's fishing fleets, including those in the United States, are grossly overcapitalized, with far more capacity than is needed. The U.S. marine fisheries traditionally have been open to all citizens; anyone with a boat can try to make a living by catching fish. Conservation and management controls are in the form of industry-wide quotas, with seasonal and gear-type restrictions. Since difficulties in maintaining fish stocks at maximum yield levels are attributed in part to the overcapacity resulting from open access policies, limited access schemes such as Individual Transferable Quotas (ITQ) are being established. Vessel owners are given rights to a certain percentage of the allowable harvest. These rights, in turn, may be sold or leased. The evolution of open access to individual quotas will inevitably lead to fees from the fishermen to the government to pay for costs associated with managing the fishery, and perhaps lead also to the collection of an economic rent. Even in those fisheries where limited access is not feasible, resource management agencies will implement more restrictive conservation measures.

A precautionary approach is being built into management plans to provide greater assurance against resource depletion. The precautionary approach to resource utilization is finding its way into international fisheries as well. The United Nations is continuously working on multilateral agreements to control fishing in international waters. Some of these will give coastal nations more controls beyond the 200-mile lines.

International concerns over resource depletion and the need for more production to feed growing populations are creating pressure for more selectivity in fishing. As much as 27 percent of fish caught in nets are discarded at sea because they are undesirable species, too small, or restricted by law. Discards become part of the food chain, avoiding biological waste. Yet the pressure for more conservation is intensifying research on more-selective fishing technology. Devices are being developed for insertion in nets to allow non-target fish to escape.

Aquaculture

Even with more effective fisheries management and selectivity, catches from the oceans will not keep pace with fish consumption needs, spurring greatly increased aquaculture production. U.S. aquaculture operations in 1994 produced an estimated one billion pounds of such species as catfish, trout, salmon, shrimp, and striped bass. Throughout the world, aquaculture grew at a compounded rate of 9 percent a year in the 1980s, reaching 16 percent of overall fish production by 1993.

Continued aquaculture growth is dependent on extensive capital investment, primarily in tropical and subtropical areas. Health authority approval of therapeutants necessary to control disease in intensive culture environments will enhance production. Fish-dependent nations will invest more in stock enhancement programs whereby fish are raised in hatcheries to their juvenile life stage and then released to the oceans, protecting the fish during the early life stage when they are most vulnerable to predation.

Whales and Other Marine Mammals

Once a major target species of many fishing nations, whales have been given special protection. Only small harvests are allowed for aboriginal peoples. The conservation has resulted in healthier whale stocks generally, with some species in great abundance.

Eventually commercial harvest on a limited basis will be resumed by nations with a whaling tradition. Unchecked growth of protected seal herds will create renewed pressure to control the populations of animals whose predation has a major impact on fish populations needed for human food.

See also ACID RAIN; ANIMAL RIGHTS; BIODIVERSITY; FOOD AND FIBER PRODUCTION; FRESHWATER; GLOBAL ENVIRONMENTAL PROBLEMS; HAZARDOUS WASTES; OCEANS; OZONE LAYER DEPLETION; RESOURCES; SUSTAINABILITY.

BIBLIOGRAPHY

Aquaculture Situation and Outlook. Washington, DC: U.S. Department of Agriculture, 1994.

Fisheries of the United States. Washington, DC: U.S. Department of Commerce, 1994.

The State of World Fisheries and Aquaculture. Rome: Food and Agriculture Organization of the United Nations, 1994.

Lee J. Weddig

Fitness.

See EXERCISE AND FITNESS.

Food Additives

From almost the beginning, the human species has been involved in a constant struggle to ensure a safe and abundant food supply. Described often as a war, the conflict results from the fact that humans have no natural right to the bounties of nature, but have to compete with rats, mice, locusts, molds, viruses, and bacteria. Among the successful weapons that human society have developed are various chemical additives. Fermentation, salting, and smoking are only a few of the ways in which early societies used chemicals to preserve food. Moreover, these additives not only protect the food, but also improve its nutritive value and palatability. Food is not food until someone eats it. Taste, flavor, texture, and odor are all essential components influencing the acceptability of food. In their concern over the chemicals in food, the public often forgets these aspects of food additives. It is clear that to efficiently supply an increasingly urbanized society with adequate food, many new food formulations will have to be devised: to be nutritionally adequate, to present a variety of organoleptic characteristics, and at the same time to ensure their safety.

Modern biology is spectacularly increasing the possibility of modifying traditional foods and developing new food sources and ingredients to meet newly defined health needs. For the first time the scientific community has the opportunity to design and construct foods having specially desired characteristics based on a more refined definition of human health and nutrition requirements. In other words, new food sources not only meet these newly defined, precise health needs, but are also optimal for the particular environment in which the consumer is living and in which the food is to be grown. The essence of good diet is the consumption of a variety of foods, not food components. The target needs to be to change the nature of foods, rather than to simply add individual nutrients.

It is possible to divide these new foods and additives into several broad categories:

1. Foods that traditionally are not widely used as food, such as foods derived from yeast.
2. Products constructed from food materials that have rarely been used as foods, such as certain fungi.
3. Formulations constructed largely of the products of chemical synthesis or the physical modifications of traditional foods such as artificial sweeteners and fat substitutes.
4. Products constructed from or consisting of organisms resulting from genetic manipulations. These will include such things as food enzymes having greater stability or better control and new plant cultivars having special characteristics such as better shipping qualities. They may

provide better flavor or better profiles or allow many new environments in which the plant could flourish.

5. New packaging materials that offer better protection of the food from the environment. At the same time, these new products will themselves be environmentally friendly. These new packaging materials will permit the movement of gases in and out of the food package in a controlled manner, thus ensuring the quality of the food. Moreover, such packages will contain indicators to demonstrate when the integrity of the package has been broken or when the food has become contaminated with pathogenic organisms. It is also possible that these packages can be designed to combine with new, unique processing methods to produce room-temperature shelf-stable food, thus reducing the number of products requiring refrigeration or freezer storage.

A comment must be made about the safety of these new materials. The public is concerned about modification of their food supply. The same science that will develop these new products will also provide the basis for more accurate and predictable tests for food safety. Not only will it ensure better control over microbial contamination of foods (the greatest threat to human health), but also it will provide the means to better predict the potential toxicity of chemical substances added to food or the safety of new plant and animal varieties.

Over the past two hundred years it has become increasingly evident that diet plays a significant role in human health. Modern food science with its ability to modify existing plant and animal species and to construct new food materials based upon more precise knowledge of human metabolism and needs will bring human society something it has only dreamed of: a supply of high-quality food that will not only nourish but also improve the health of the public.

See also CHEMICALS; FINE; FOOD AND DRUG SAFETY; FOOD LAWS; FOOD TECHNOLOGIES; GENETICS: COMMERCIALIZATION OF; NEW CONSUMER PRODUCTS; NUTRITION; SOIL CONDITIONS; TOBACCO.

BIBLIOGRAPHY

GOODMAN, DAVID, and REDCLIFT, MICHAEL. *Refashioning Nature*. New York: Routledge, 1992.

LEWIS, RICHARD J. *Food Additives Handbook*. New York: Van Nostrand Reinhold, 1989.

SAULSON, DONALD S., and SAULSON, ELIZABETH M. *A Pocket Guide to Food Additives*. Huntington Beach, CA: VPS Publishing, 1991.

Sanford A. Miller

Food and Agriculture

Food and agriculture will continue to be the world's largest productive industry in the twenty-first century, representing over 50 percent of the total activity in individual regions. It will continue to employ more people, develop more technology, and link providers and consumers with more new products and services. It will continue to improve as agriculture moves from the "green revolution" to the "gene revolution" worldwide.

Agriculture operates a highly productive system that provides food, fiber, and timber for basic world sustenance and survival. This system will continue to improve in both industrial and developing countries. But agriculture is shifting its problem-solving talent to the more pressing issues of producing renewable feedstock inputs for basic industries, providing affordable personal health, managing productive ecosystems, and developing thriving communities. In the twenty-first century, agriculture will add four new product services:

1. Fuels, plastics, biochemicals from renewable crop cycles
2. Preventive health, nutrients, vitamins from quality foods
3. Sound productive ecosystems from sustainable conservation
4. Robust rural communities from regional design/development

The 200-Year Agricultural Development Recipe

This can be summarized by the following equation:

$$\text{Agriculture} = \text{Population} + \text{Technology} + \text{Institutions} + \text{Environment}$$

The world's agrifood system is not uniform or monolithic. Each region has its own recipe for development. It depends on the makeup of the population, the availability of technology, the incentive climate of rulemaking institutions, and the natural resource base.

During the past two hundred years agriculture has developed the capacity to supply almost 6 billion customers. This was a remarkable accomplishment that is now taken for granted. Two hundred years ago, feeding a world of one billion people was a controversial topic. T. R. Malthus and William Godwin debated whether man and science together could manage the Earth without catastrophe. In the 1990s, this same debate continues, but with a different focus. The agrifood system has demonstrated that it can feed a sixfold increase in world population, and now it is developing new technologies to tackle other problems.

"Freedom from want" was the clarion call that has empowered and will empower agriculture from 1800 to 2000. "Sustainable human development" will be the theme for the next century. The evolution of the agriculture industry into the ecoculture industry of the next century will be a bridge between the resource-using, person-replacing technologies of the economic growth era and the resource-renewing, person-enhancing technologies of the sustainable human development era.

Quality products and services from the gene revolution will replace the quantity products from the green revolution. The worldwide extension of computers, telecommunications, and biotechnology will provide the operating basis for managing human ecosystems rather than farms.

Agriculture and Renewable Industrial Feedstocks

Genetically engineering new crops and new products is becoming possible with increased computer capacity to process the massive genetic maps of humans, plants, animals, and ecosystems. The combination of computer and recombinant DNA technology will drive the next generation of agriculture technology. This twenty-first-century technology will move agriculture from improved production to improved quality cycles of food, fiber, and timber, as well as new fuels, lubricants, biochemicals, and plastics. This technological shift to bioengineered products will result from the development of a new agro-industrial process relying on renewable crops. The process is already beginning, and laboratory experiments now are exploring a variety of genetic engineering products, such as using tobacco to produce hepatitis B vaccine, the cultivation of milkweed for fuel, and the extraction of renewable chemicals, plastics, inks, and lubricants from oil seeds.

Agriculture and Preventive Health

Access to enough good quality food is basic to providing robust health. Agriculture's green revolution has provided the basis for producing enough food to improve health and longevity. Movement to the gene revolution will continue the ability to produce enough food, but it will also provide the ability to design foods and diets for personal health enhancement. Food processing companies already are designing foods to give athletes peak physical performance, to encourage healthy infant growth, and to provide the vitamins, medicines, and nutrients to

improve the health of the sick and the elderly. Mapping the human genome (chromosome structure) by the year 2000 will provide a more complete understanding of the human biosystem. This, together with maps of animal and plant genomes, will provide food-health scientists with the tools to design foods for individual health. A step in this direction is the development of a detailed food specification database at the U.S. Department of Agriculture, which allows any consumer to identify the precise characteristics of any food.

Agriculture and Sustainable Ecosystem Management

Some 80 percent of the world's arable land and water is directly linked to the food-fiber-fishery-forestry system. Conservation of these natural resources is an investment in long-term productivity. But the conservation technology of the past century is now evolving into a total ecosystem technology to deal with cycles that sustain not only soil and water but the entire biotic and human development cycle. New DNA technology and computer science provide the tools that make ecosystem demographics and design possible for the next century. Some experiments are beginning to demonstrate what this new technology can accomplish. Some cities are using aquatic plants and farmland together with municipal effluent and compost to define a new bioindustrial cycle. The utilization of specific crops to remove toxic materials and radioactive waste from contaminated soil demonstrates the use of agricultural processes to deal with manmade waste cycles. With sufficient investment in research, ecosystem technology will turn wastes from one process into inputs to other processes in a closed-loop sustained human development cycle.

Agriculture and Regional Community Development

More than any other industry, agrifood enterprises link families, communities, commerce, and natural resources in a renewable system. This process of using technology to produce a variety of useful products from the biosphere not only creates jobs and businesses, but also supports basic human needs and links families and their communities into regional socioeconomic systems. The entire cycle creates, sustains, and enhances human interplay. It promotes life, growth, development, and security.

See also FOOD ADDITIVES; FOOD CONSUMPTION; FOOD DISTRIBUTION; FOOD AND DRUG SAFETY;

FOOD AND FIBER PRODUCTION; FOOD LAWS; FOOD SERVICES; FOOD TECHNOLOGIES; GENETICS: AGRICULTURAL APPLICATIONS; NUTRITION.

BIBLIOGRAPHY

AVERY, DENNIS T. *Global Food Progress.* Indianapolis: Hudson Institute, 1991.

BROWN, LESTER R., et al. *Vital Signs: The Trends That Are Shaping Our Future.* New York: Norton, 1992.

Food and Agriculture Organization of the United Nations. *1991: The State of Food and Agriculture.* Rome: FAO, 1991.

Office of Technology Assessment, Congress of the United States. *A New Technological Era for American Agriculture.* Publication No. F-474. Washington, DC: OTA, 1992.

VOSTI, STEPHAN A.; REARDON, THOMAS; and VON URFF, WINFRIED, eds. *Agricultural Sustainability, Growth, and Poverty Alleviation: Issues and Policies.* Washington, DC: International Food Policy Research Institute; Feldafing, Germany: German Foundation for International Development, 1991.

William E. Gahr

Food Consumption

Food preferences are deeply ingrained, but dietary patterns do change over time. It is reasonable to predict that as new food technologies are perfected and as biomedical science uncovers the benefits and risks to human health of various components of food, people will gradually add new foods and drop others from their meals and snacks.

What people choose, and choose not, to eat is also influenced by:

- Broader economic trends such as the widening gap between affluent people and households with very limited food dollars as well as homeless people and those living in poverty
- The relative importance for various population segments of the health benefits versus taste, convenience, and other attributes of food
- Whether people believe food marketing promises and trust health promotion messages
- Changing values regarding the social role of food in family and interpersonal relationships

Dietary surveys are an effective way of documenting current food intake of consumers, and, to a certain degree, of predicting changes in food consumption patterns. Another less quantitative, but very useful, technique for anticipating future consumer preferences is to analyze what people are reading in the popular press about diet/health relationships, food safety, and other topics that influence eating choices. The database for this review includes approximately 250 food and health-related articles per month from 50 U.S. and Canadian monthly consumer magazines from 1989 to 1994.

Nutrition and Dieting

The consumer food press has strongly communicated the dietary recommendations of major health policy documents, especially the advice that people should reduce total dietary fat intake. The advice to reduce saturated fat and cholesterol is given less emphasis. Journalists are writing less frequently now about whether monounsaturated fatty acids are healthier than polyunsaturated fats, but interest in trans-fatty acids is growing.

Magazine editors seem so convinced that dietary fat is dangerous to their readers that they have given much less attention to potential problems caused by fat substitutes than they did with the introduction of sweetener substitutes. However, journalists often point out the lack of controlled studies to document the value of such ingredients for losing weight. A few writers encourage readers to learn how to eat healthily, without relying on "processed" foods that contain fat substitutes; but, in general, the consumer press is promoting consumer acceptance of these products. The availability of fat substitutes could theoretically have a significant effect on total dietary fat consumption, but quantitation of actual change is difficult to predict until taste-related technologies are improved and prices of reduced-fat products become competitive with their traditional counterparts in certain food categories.

Journalists' advice to increase dietary fiber intake declined in the early 1990s. This message was replaced by the more general recommendation in nutrition policy documents to eat more fruits, vegetables, and grain products. The consumer press is giving heavy coverage to this change in advice, especially as biomedical and epidemiological research reveals better understanding of the benefits, and potential risks of antioxidants (such as beta-carotene and vitamin E) supplements versus foods that contain these and other nutrients. Consumption of foods of plant (rather than animal) origin will probably increase, but the evolving consumer interest in moderate, rather than drastic, dietary changes suggests that this transition will probably not be as extreme as is currently recommended by health professionals.

Dieting continues to be a popular topic in the consumer press. Articles on this subject appear frequently in health-oriented magazines for men, as well as mainstream publications for women. The evolving trend that will probably affect future consumer eating patterns most is the advice to lose weight without "dieting," as it has been defined in the past. "Don't diet" articles, which are becoming more common, are based on research relating the dangers of "yo-yo dieting." This change is also being driven by evidence that exercise produces health benefits beyond weight reduction. According to journalists, another reason to avoid strict diets is that the psychological value of liking yourself outweighs the harm that results from being a little overweight.

Combined, these influences suggest that consumers of the future will place more emphasis on exercising rather than on eating significantly more reduced-calorie or low-calorie products. Food choices will probably be based more on fat content than on the caloric value of foods.

A major variable that will affect future food patterns is whether increased Food and Drug Administration control of the truthfulness and consistency of food package information will overcome consumer skepticism regarding health-benefit promises which were used in food marketing prior to 1994. Consumer magazines are emphasizing the reliability of information on food labels, but this focus will probably call attention to the lack of parallel regulation of advertising messages until such changes are made by the Federal Trade Commission.

Looking and Feeling Younger

Another editorial message that will affect future dietary patterns is that the health reward of wise food choices extends beyond simply reducing the risk of heart disease and cancer. The consumer press in the early 1990s had not fully accepted the food technologists' term, "nutraceuticals," but magazines do discuss certain foods that might enable people to live longer, or at least postpone the processes that make their bodies look and feel old.

Part of this trend blends with the emphasis on fruits and vegetables, but magazines are also communicating the potential health benefits of garlic, peppers, and other herbs and spices in the context of articles about the recently funded research program of the Office of Alternative Medicine within the National Institutes of Health. Antiaging articles usually begin with research reports regarding antioxidants and their effects on immune functions, such as infection resistance and protection from environmental pollution. Journalists then exercise their editorial prerogative and weave in themes,

such as herbology, Asian and African medicine, and holistic healing, treatments that are not widely endorsed by the traditional biomedical community (*see* HEALTH CARE: ALTERNATIVE THERAPIES).

The feel-younger, live-longer message will shape future food patterns. More consumers will select diets based on concepts that have not yet been scientifically documented. Self-medication in the grocery store may partially replace reliance on advice from health professionals. Furthermore, as global barriers to food export and import recede, culturally associated ideas about single foods with special healing powers will also cross international borders.

Bioengineered and Irradiated Foods

Although food scientists envision major usage of these technologies in the future of foods, consumers are still evaluating their benefits and risks. The public's concerns are directed not only at the safety of such foods per se, but also at the perceived danger that these processes will unleash unknown, and therefore potentially more frightening, consequences. For example, biotechnology conjures up consumer images of "tinkering with" nature and the possibility that what scientists do intentionally for the benefit of society might lead to other events that are harmful, either through negligence or malicious purpose. Irradiation brings to mind nuclear power plant accidents that not only resulted in immediate, confirmed damage, but also raised the haunting possibility of future harm, perhaps even to children yet unborn.

Biotechnology and irradiation offer many potential benefits: feeding hungry people, reducing postharvest waste, and improving quality attributes of foods. The marketplace acceptance of such foods will probably be determined by the safety records of bioengineering research laboratories and nuclear energy plants. Consumer attitudes will also be influenced by how honestly industry representatives and government officials explain unavoidable risks, regardless of how small, associated with these technologies.

Environmental Influences

Since Earth Day in April 1990, environmental sensitivity has escalated. In the future, protecting the health of the planet may influence food choices more than protecting individual health.

Several comparisons suggest that environmental concerns may shape future eating patterns more than nutrition:

- The benefits of protecting the Earth endure for generations, whereas nutrition benefits last, at most, a lifetime.
- Protecting the Earth helps people everywhere; healthy eating improves only your own life.
- Environmentalists can rally around the "fight the money-hungry industry" flag, whereas opposing food companies has less "David-versus-Goliath" appeal.

The environmental movement, regardless of whether it *competes* with nutrition, will have other effects on food choices of the future. Opposition to excess packaging might drive consumers toward less processed foods. Also, unless the world economy improves, even nonvegetarians will consume fewer meat products. The sustainable agriculture movement will no doubt further affect how and where food is grown.

See also AGRICULTURAL TECHNOLOGY; FOOD ADDITIVES; FOOD AND AGRICULTURE; FOOD DISTRIBUTION; FOOD AND DRUG SAFETY; FOOD AND FIBER PRODUCTION; FOOD SERVICES; FOOD TECHNOLOGIES; NEW CONSUMER PRODUCTS; NUTRITION.

BIBLIOGRAPHY

DUCKHAM, A. N. *Food Production and Consumption.* New York: Elsevier, 1987.

National Research Council Assembly of Life Sciences. *Assessing Changing Food Consumption Patterns.* Washington, DC: National Academy Press, 1981.

Review of Food Consumption Survey. *Household Food Consumption by Economic Groups.* Rome: FAO, 1983.

WORMAN, STERLING, and CUMMINGS, JR., RALPH W. *To Feed the World: The Challenge and the Startegy.* Baltimore: Johns Hopkins University Press, 1978.

Kristen McNutt

Food Distribution

Americans allocated about 11.7 percent of disposable personal income to food in 1992. Approximately 30 percent of this went to purchase the raw agricultural products used in the food supply while the other 70 percent, over $500 billion, paid for the processing, transporting, sorting, distributing, retailing, and servicing of the raw food supply. This intricate and interacting network of institutions that transform the food supply between the farm gate and the consumer is the food marketing system.

The food marketing system includes an estimated 400,000 companies—16,000 food processors, 135,000 retailers, and 200,000 restaurateurs—with a total of well over 1 million places of business.

They distribute the output of nearly 3 million farmers to the nation's 256 million consumers. About 12 million Americans are directly or indirectly employed in distributing this food.

The U.S. food distribution system going into the twenty-first century is considerably changed in size, structure, competitive conduct, and performance from the 1950s. It is considerably more globalized, moving toward larger firms producing more differentiated products, serving a market that is becoming older and more ethnically diverse, yet accounting for a smaller share of the consumer's total budget. The same trends can be expected to continue in the next century.

Declining Growth Rate of Food Marketing

The U.S. food marketing system is the largest aggregate marketing institution in the American economy, but it is growing more slowly than the nonfood sector. This trend will likely continue. In 1972, American food marketers accounted for 15.5 percent of the value added to the nation's Gross Domestic Product; by 1992 this contribution had fallen to 10.5 percent, as fewer and fewer of the nation's resources—land, labor, capital, and management—were devoted to distributing the nation's food supply. It will likely fall to 9 percent in 2010 (see Figure 1). This decline will be caused by two factors: continued efficiency in U.S. food distribution and continued growth in income.

The efficiency of the U.S. food system is reflected by its output growth. About 1,400 pounds of food per person left farms in 1992, a number almost unchanged since 1952. In 1952, food processors

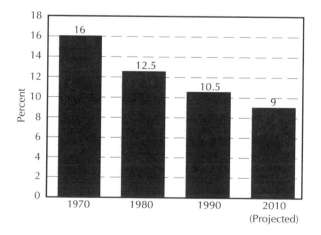

FIGURE 1. Share of Gross National Product generated by the U.S. food marketing system (Source: Gallo, 1992).

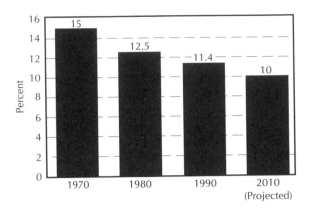

FIGURE 2.   Share of employment generated by the U.S. food marketing system (Source: Gallo, 1992).

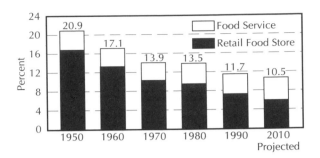

FIGURE 3.   Food marketing system's share of disposable personal income, excluding alcohol and nonfood groceries (Source: Gallo, 1992).

employed 1.8 million workers to feed 150 million Americans. By 1992, fewer workers (1.2 million) were employed to feed more Americans (256 million), and they provided a higher degree of processing in doing so. The farmers' share of domestically provided farm foods fell from 42 percent to 22 percent of the food dollar over the same period while the retailing, wholesaling, and food service share of marketing costs increased because of more service provided by these sectors. Although the food marketing system generated 15 percent of the nation's employment in 1970, this figure had fallen to 11.4 percent in 1990, and will likely drop to 10 percent by 2010 (see Figure 2). As an economy prospers, more of its income is allocated to nonbasic or luxury items. Hence, the share of income directly spent for food declined from nearly 21 percent in 1950 to 11.7 percent in 1992, and will likely decline

to 10.5 percent in 2010 (see Figure 3). The slow-growing demand of the U.S. food market will continue to have implications for U.S. food manufacturers, retailers, and wholesalers throughout the twenty-first century. First, there will be continued competition by fewer and larger firms within the domestic market to acquire or maintain market share. Second, food processors will continue responding to changing U.S. market demographics. Third, the food system will continue expanding into world markets through globalization via foreign investment and exports.

Competition Among Giants

The number of food processors declined from over 32,000 in 1963 to 16,000 in 1987, while the number of foodstores fell by about one-third (Table 1). Within this domestic market, each of the four major food marketing industries has experienced higher market concentration, where a larger share of total

TABLE 1.   Number of Food Marketing Companies

| | | Wholesaling | | Food | Retailing | | |
| | | | | | Food- | Liquor | |
Year	Processing	Grocery	Liquor	Service[1]	Stores[1]	Stores	Total
				Number			
1963	32,617	35,666	7,598	175,117	162,273	28,624	441,895
1967	26,549	33,848	6,246	170,851	131,926	20,200	389,620
1972	22,171	32,053	5,792	179,578	122,592	28,378	390,564
1977	20,616	31,670	5,518	186,625	120,107	29,741	394,277
1982	16,800	31,290	5,158	198,088	109,567	28,977	389,880
1987	15,692	34,155	5,835	191,798	108,439	25,163	381,082
2010	13,000	34,000	5,000	109,000	407,000		

[1] Firms with paid employees.

Source: Gallo (1992).

output is controlled by fewer and fewer firms in either local or national markets. Consequently, fewer firms are controlling a larger share of a slow-growth market, and this concentration will likely continue to rise in the twenty-first century (Table 2). The battle of giant firms for market share will continue well into the twenty-first century. Nonprice competition in the food system throughout the latter part of the twentieth century has been reflected in more product differentiation through new product introductions and advertising. Nearly 17,000 new grocery products were introduced in 1992; about 100,000 have been introduced between 1983 and 1993. Nearly $12 billion was spent on consumer advertising. Food will continue its role as the overwhelming leader among all industries in advertising and new product introductions in the twenty-first century.

Some of the competition will continue to be reflected in the struggle between the at-home and away-from-home food markets. Food service sales accounted for about one-fourth of all retail food sales in 1952; this had increased to 45 percent by 1992. Inroads by restaurants into the at-home food market have stabilized in recent slow-growth years. That stability is likely to persist into the twenty-first century as the saturation point may have already been reached.

Responding to Changing Demographics

Changing demographics dominated changes in the type of food processed and sold in the last half of the twentieth century. Household and family sizes have declined; the proportion of families with more than one wage owner has increased. The nonwhite proportion of the population has increased. More income, less time for food shopping, and interest in convenience and health have resulted in food marketers responding to a changing consumer climate. Changing lifestyles and demographics will mean shifting consumption patterns. As the link between farmer and consumer, the food marketing system will continue to respond to consumer preferences. For example, over the past fifty years, less milk, eggs, pork, and beef and more chicken, fish, fats and oils, and vegetables have been consumed. The degree of processing has changed drastically from less processed to more processed food. And, consumers make the bulk of their purchases in large supermarkets. Fast food restaurants have come to dominate the food service market.

Table 3 contains the projected changes in per capita consumption between 1990 and 2010 due to projected changes in demographic characteristics and to assumed income growth.

Changes in age distribution are likely to have the biggest impact on per person demand. Age distribution changes are projected to increase per capita food expenditures by 1.0 percent over the twenty-year period. Regional population distribution changes are expected to have a slight positive effect on total food expenditures, and changing racial mix will have a slight negative impact.

Competition for Shelf Space

Changing consumption patterns and a slowly growing market will mean continued competition

TABLE 2. Aggregate Concentration in Food Marketing

| Year | *Share of Market Controlled by Top Firms* | | | |
	Top 50 Processing Firms	*Top 50 Wholesaling Firms*	*Top 20 Retailing Firms*	*Top 50 Foodservice Firms*
	Percent			
1967	35.0	NA	34.4	NA
1972	38.0	48.0	34.8	13.3
1977	40.0	57.0	34.5	17.8
1982	43.0	64.0	34.9	20.2
1987	47.0[1]	71.4	36.5	22.3
2010	52.0	78.0	39.0	30.0

NA = not available
[1]Estimated.
Source: Gallo (1992).

TABLE 3. Estimated Percentage Change in Per Capita Food Expenditures, 1990–2010

Food Group	Age Distribution	Regional Distribution	Race	Income	Total[1]
All food	1.0	0.1	−0.2	14.9	16.1
Beef	3.7	0.1	0.1	3.5	7.5
Pork	4.1	−0.3	0.3	1.3	6.2
Poultry	2.7	0.1	0.7	5.3	9.6
Cereals and baked goods	2.6	0.0	−0.2	4.7	7.3
Dairy products	1.5	0.1	−0.4	4.7	6.0
Fruits	3.7	0.1	−0.1	10.5	14.8
Vegetables	4.3	0.5	−0.1	6.1	11.1
Sugars and sweeteners	2.4	0.3	−0.1	6.2	8.8
Fats and oils	4.2	0.2	−0.2	4.6	8.9

[1] Net adjustment after accounting for projected changes in all variables.

Source: Blisard (1993).

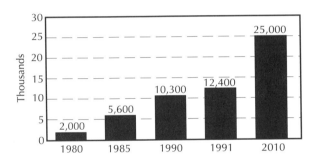

FIGURE 4. New food product introductions (Source: Gallo, 1992).

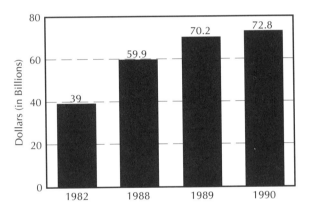

FIGURE 5. U.S. investment abroad in food processing: value of shipments by U.S.-owned affiliates (Source: Gallo, 1992).

TABLE 4. World Trade in Manufactured Foods and Beverages, 1962–1990

Year	Nominal Value	Value in 1987 Dollars[1]
	Dollars (in millions)	
1962	16,219.9	49,749.7
1967	21,973.3	62,496.5
1972	38,033.8	88,801.3
1977	89,084.7	133,083.6
1982	129,838.7	132,318.4
1987	167,916.1	167,916.1
1990	205,955.6	181,298.9

[1] Based on the Producer Price Index for Finished Consumer Foods.

Source: Handy and Henderson (1992).

TABLE 5. U.S. Exports of Manufactured Foods and Beverages, 1962–1991

Year	Nominal Value	Value in 1987 Dollars[1]
	Dollars (in millions)	
1962	1,206.8	3,701.9
1972	2,787.1	6,507.2
1982	11,088.4	12,136.2
1990	17,490.4	15,396.5
1991	20,084.4	17,726.2

[1] Based on the Producer Price Index for Finished Consumer Foods.

Source: Handy and Henderson (1992).

for retail shelfspace. New product introductions have burgeoned from 1,000 in 1964 to over 17,000 in 1992. At the recent rate of increase, about 25,000 could be introduced in the year 2010 (see Figure 4). Although the discontinuance rate on these items is in the 95–99 percent range, they will pose a problem of shelfspace allocation. The average market currently has space for 30,000 items. Superstores carry 40,000 items. The total number of different labeled packaged foods available in the marketplace exceeds 257,000 items. What items will be stocked on shelves? Will small firms be deterred from entering the market?

Global Expansion

The U.S. food distribution system will continue looking to expansion in foreign markets, either through exports or investment. World trade in processed foods rose from $16 billion in 1962 to $206 billion in 1990 (Table 4). In 1990, sales of foreign subsidiaries of U.S. food firms reached $75 billion, up from $39 billion in 1982 (Figure 5). Exports amounted to $20 billion in 1992 (see Table 5). Foreign investment in the United States was reflected in a sales rise from $15 billion in 1982 to $45 billion in 1991. The United States accounted for 8.5 percent of the $206 billion (Table 5) world trade in food and beverages, ranking behind France and the Netherlands (Figure 6).

See also FARM POLICY; FISHERIES; FOOD ADDITIVES; FOOD AND AGRICULTURE; FOOD AND FIBER

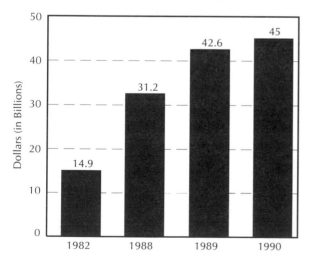

FIGURE 6. Foreign investment in American food processing: value of shipments by U.S. affiliates of foreign firms (Source: Gallo, 1992).

PRODUCTION; FOOD LAWS; FOOD SERVICES; FOOD TECHNOLOGIES; NEW CONSUMER PRODUCTS; NUTRITION.

BIBLIOGRAPHY

BLISARD, NOEL. *Food Expenditure Projections, 1990–2010.* Outlook Conference, November 1993. Washington, DC: U.S. Dept. of Agriculture, n.d.

GALLO, ANTHONY E., et al. *Food Marketing Review* (annual), 1992 edition. Washington, DC: U.S. Dept. of Agriculture, 1993.

MANCHESTER, ALDEN G. *Rearranging the Economic Landscape: The Food Marketing Revolution, 1950–1991.* Washington, DC: U.S. Dept. of Agriculture, Economic Research Service, 1992.

Anthony E. Gallo

Food and Drug Safety

The United States has long been a leader in the establishment of food safety standards. The Delaney Clause, prohibiting the addition of any human or animal carcinogens to food, was adopted as an amendment to the Food, Drug, and Cosmetic Act in 1958. No other country has adopted such a zero-tolerance requirement. Increasingly, however, scientific evidence has provided a basis for modifying this draconian approach to regulation. Indeed, the European Union issued a directive on July 20, 1993, for assessing the risks of chemical hazards embodying the principle that a tolerance can be established for nongenotoxic carcinogens; and any toxic substances, including carcinogens, would be subject to regulation on a case-by-case basis. Differences in national approaches to the regulation of carcinogens can be expected to become issues before the World Trade Organization as it proceeds to carry out its charter in administering the new General Agreement on Tariffs and Trade (GATT).

In a related area, the U.S. Food and Drug Administration (FDA) pioneered the use of quantitative risk assessment methods for evaluating the carcinogenic risks in foods from the residues of veterinary drugs used in the production of food animals and from the residues of agricultural pesticides and other unavoidable food contaminants. These methods have undergone considerable development in the past twenty years, as the United States and other countries have invested considerable regulatory and scientific efforts to rationalize their use.

Notwithstanding these efforts, quantitative risk assessment has not been uniformly adopted by scientific and regulatory organizations around the world. Further, there are marked differences in the ways in which different organizations approach the testing and evaluation of potential carcinogens.

The Codex Alimentarius Commission has established maximum residue levels (MRL) for pesticide residues that may safely exist in foods as a result of agricultural production methods. The MRLs serve as the basis for acceptance and rejection of commodities in international trade. These MRLs are developed without formal risk assessments, but do take into account the "mechanism of action" as a means of evaluating potential cacinogens. Understandably, the Codex MRL standards differ in a number of instances from those established for pesticides by the U.S. Environmental Protection Agency (EPA). The EPA uses the Delaney Clause as well as its own methods of doing risk assessments and conducting tests to evaluate carcinogenic potential.

There is now an organized effort being planned by the Organization for Economic Cooperation and Development (OECD) to achieve international standards for risk assessment. Without a harmonized approach to risk-assessment criteria and methods, the ability of the GATT agreement to reduce trade barriers will be seriously compromised. Reaching agreements on uniform risk assessment approaches will be difficult and will require changes in regulatory standards by all involved.

Biotechnology

The benefits of genetic manipulation in food production have just now begun to be realized. Tomatoes, cheese enzymes, and milk promoters in cows have been the first products to be commercially introduced, not without considerable controversy. Other food products, including squash and oilseeds, are under development and may soon be introduced.

The regulatory approach to such products varies considerably from country to country, and is far from settled. In the United States, regulatory requirements are based on existing laws and regulations, supplemented by policy guidance from the FDA regarding the scientific resolution of safety issues. This approach is intended to assure safety while providing developers of new food products with flexibility, but is opposed by some consumer organizations and anti-biotechnology activists. Under consideration by the FDA is a new regulation that would require premarketing notification for foods produced or manufactured by genetic

manipulation. Labeling of such foods is being approached for the present on a case-by-case basis.

Other countries or political bodies, notably the European Union (EU) and Canada, take a substantially different approach. The concept of "novel foods" has been introduced, which includes foods produced by genetic manipulation and foods produced by nontraditional methods. Both products and processes would be subject to premarketing approval. The inclusion of new production processes would dramatically extend the scope of food regulation. Premarketing approval could significantly impede the introduction of new products and processes, as well as alter the conduct of food research. Researchers and entrepreneurs would seek out those countries that offer the greatest flexibility and opportunity to conduct their activities.

International standards or guidelines for the use of genetically modified foods and conduct of research have not been developed. The OECD has published a description of concepts and principles for evaluating foods produced by modern biotechnology, but these have not been incorporated into the EU and Canadian approaches. Again, the lack of consensus among the largest international trading partners indicates that national regulatory policies will be unsettled and under revision for some time to come, with concomitant disruption in business and agricultural research.

Regulatory Processes

With shrinking resources, governments around the world will find it necessary to reduce certain activities or raise additional revenue sources, including those for regulatory agencies. This is certainly true in the United States, where the president's budget has included user fees to help cover the costs of regulatory agency operations, including the FDA and the U.S. Department of Agriculture (USDA). Such fees also have been imposed in some countries in Europe and elsewhere, where food manufacturers are required to fund the costs of plant inspections. In the United States, user fees have already been adopted to enhance the resources needed for the safety and effectiveness review of new drug applications. The continued pressure to reduce government spending may see an expansion of user fees to other areas of product safety.

The user fee concept, however, can be implemented in ways other than by simply employing additional government scientists for reviewing new product applications, whether they are for food additives, drugs, or medical devices. The EU, for example, contemplates the use of nongovernment experts for safety evaluations of food additives and foods from biotechnology. Preliminary explorations of the use of outside experts for food additive safety evaluations have begun in the United States.

The use of outside experts can be helpful in providing needed expertise and reducing time for safety evaluations by focusing efforts. Such an approach is likely to raise other fundamental questions, for example, whether the recommendations and findings of outside bodies should have regulatory decision status, and whether government agencies should be required to adopt their findings as a default position to reduce the duplication of efforts and to enhance the productivity of both public and private resources. Changes in law would be necessary to accomplish this.

Food Inspection Standards

Resource constraints coupled with interests in tighter regulatory control over microbiological hazards have prompted the FDA and USDA to adopt the use of hazard analysis and critical control point (HACCP) systems as the basis for food plant inspection. Other regulatory agencies are also adopting such regulations, and the Codex Alimentarius Commission is developing HACCP standards for hygiene and for the certification and inspection of imported foods. Although there appears to be consensus on the technical standards for HACCP, there is not yet agreement on how to certify imported foods: The key issues involve how to ensure the competency of certifying organizations and how to judge the acceptability of nongovernment (private sector) groups as certifying bodies. Certification and inspection will become increasingly important with the growth of international trade in food and the inability of resource-limited regulatory agencies to meet the workload created in assuring the safety of both domestic and imported foods.

Conclusion

Food safety regulations will be the subject of change during the next several years resulting from changes in science and the desire of international trading partners to reduce conflicts—or at least to resolve trade issues. National approaches will have to accommodate international standards, and each interested nation can be expected to work to protect its approach.

See also CHEMICALS, FINE; FOOD ADDITIVES; FOOD LAWS; FOOD TECHNOLOGIES; GENETICS, COMMERCIALIZATION OF; HAZARDOUS WASTES; NEW CONSUMER PRODUCTS; NUTRITION; SOIL CONDITIONS.

BIBLIOGRAPHY

GARDNER, SHERWIN. "Food Safety: An Overview of International Regulatory Programs." *Regulatory Affairs Professionals Society Journal* (Spring 1995).

General Agreement on Tariffs and Trade. *Agreement on the Application of Sanitary and Phytosanitary Measures,* 1994.

LISTER, C. *Regulation of Food Products by the European Community.* London: Butterworths, 1992.

Organization for Economic Cooperation and Development. *Safety Evaluation of Foods Derived by Modern Biotechnology.* Paris: OECD, 1993.

Sherwin Gardner

Food and Fiber Production

Food is our most important renewable resource, and agriculture is America's and the world's number one industry. Nearly half of the world's population is engaged in food and fiber production. Nearly 30 percent of the land surface is used for agriculture, 10 percent for raising crops, and nearly 20 percent for grazing livestock. Of the arable land used for crops, the 17 percent that is irrigated contributes one third of the total production.

Plants provide, directly or indirectly, most of the world's food supply. Globally, twenty-one crops stand between people and starvation. In order of importance, they are rice, wheat, corn, potato, barley, sweet potato, cassava, soybean, oat, sorghum, millet, sugar cane, sugar beet, rye, peanut, field bean, chick pea, pigeon pea, cowpea, banana, and coconut. The global importance of these basic crops will continue, with the possible exception of the sugar crops. Sucrose is being replaced by other sweeteners.

Food animals are literally protein factories that convert vegetation and grains into milk, meat, and eggs. Livestock supply one-third of all dietary protein. Milk production provides one-fourth of this, with India and Russia consuming the most in liquid form, and the United States consuming the most as butter and cheese. In addition to 1.3 billion dairy and beef cattle, there are nearly 1 billion pigs, 2 billion sheep and goats, and over 10 billion chickens. China, with its 1.20 billion people, leads the world in both pigs and chickens. Consumption of poultry meat now exceeds that of beef, in both the United States and most of the rest of the world.

Hunger is the world's oldest enemy, but it has been overcome in the developed world of the twentieth century, and portions of the yet developing world during the past two decades. A golden age of agricultural technology is at hand to ensure sustainability and food security. Expansion of the world's food supply will depend, in the future, less on natural resources (climate, land, water, or energy) than on the power of human knowledge and initiative. A larger proportion of the world's human population enjoys adequate nutrition than ever before. This trend will continue.

World food demand will skyrocket. Farm output increases are already winning the race with a population growth of 1.5 percent annually, rice by 3.5 percent, and oilseeds by nearly 5 percent. Globally, there have been path-breaking developments in plant breeding, the hybrid rice of China, Poland's triticale, Brazil's acid-soil corn, Nigeria's soybeans and polyploid cassava, a new grain sorghum from the Sudan, and the Indonesian dry-land sugarcane.

In the future, farm capacities will expand. Land and water resources are sufficient to sustain needed growth into the twenty-first century. In the United States, 25 to 30 million acres of cropland are diverted annually from production, and another 35 million are under the long-term Conservation Reserve. Argentina has 80 million acres of pasture land that could be readily planted with food crops, if there were a market. Even in China, there are an estimated 25 million acres that could yet be converted into food production. For technological inputs, we now have a confluence of major achievements in biotechnology, microbiological transformations, crop and livestock production, controlled environments, and intensive crop and livestock management. These achievements will increase productivity and overall output. Poultry production in the United States has been industrialized and hog production soon will be. With a sustainability of natural resource inputs and no major threats to the environment, a degree of world food security may be realized.

How can all this come about? What are the new developments and changes that will shape food and fiber production for the future? Three general types of food production technologies may be described. All have some common elements that at times overlap and are not always easily distinguishable.

The first entails mechanization involving extensive use of land, water, and energy resources and the moderate use of biotechnologies. This approach is characterized by the United States system. One farmer in the United States now produces enough food for 124 people, enough to feed 94 in the United States and 34 abroad.

The second pattern is labor-intensive, small in size, more biologically based and scientifically oriented, but sparing of land, water, and energy resources. New inventions surmount the land resource constraint; Japan represents this approach with the highest yields of rice of any nation.

A third wave of the future, with elements of the previous two, is the alternative or sustainable approach, defined as the successful management of resources for agriculture to satisfy changing human needs, while maintaining or enhancing the natural resource base and minimizing environmental depredation. The model for this approach is China, where food and fiber are provided for 22 percent of the world's people on only 7 percent of the arable land.

The main adjustable components are fertilizers, pesticides, and cultivations (tillage). Others include rotation, innovative cultural technologies, machinery inputs, organic matter, and crop breeding. There is the challenge to assemble and characterize the plant and animal genetic resources of the world to transform the now conventional biological technology of the twentieth century to a biotechnology-based agriculture for the twenty-first century. Plants, other than the conventional annual grain crops which now contribute over half the world's food and feed, may be developed.

Specifically, we can look forward to the following: The power of technology will expand the resource base, which will change with time and technology. This is true of all the resource inputs (land, water, climate, genetic, and human) into crop and livestock production. Water will become the most critical input. Greater efficiency in crop irrigation will become a high priority. The positive direct effects of a rising level of atmospheric carbon dioxide on increased photosynthetic and water use efficiency in crops will more than offset any adverse affects of climate change or global warming.

The first biotechnological breakthrough during the next decade will be the Bovine Somatotropine (BST) and the Porcine Somatotropine (PST). A 15 to 20 percent increase in milk production for dairy cattle and 10 to 15 percent more lean meat, with 30 percent less body fat, and a 25 percent reduction in feed are projected for hogs and beef cattle. Either the growth hormone will be used directly, or transgenic animals will manufacture their own. An ultra-high-yielding rice, which will produce 20 to 30 percent more (raising yield from 9 to 13 tons per hectare) and be harvestable in 100 to 130 days, may be developed within five to eight years. New processing technologies for cotton, the world's leading fiber crop, will enhance competition with synthetic nonwoven fabrics. Integrated pest management will become an arsenal of tactics favorable to the environment, human health, food safety, economics, food ecology, and sustainability. Crops, including cotton, wheat, soybean, and corn, with genetically built-in protection against pests (bio-pesticides), will reduce chemical pesticide use by 75 percent.

Another breakthrough appears imminent in the controlled ripening of tomatoes and other fruit. Consumer demand for vine-ripened produce is increasing. Tomatoes and many other fruits ripened on the vine are flavorful, aromatic, juicy, and soft, but they quickly rot. Control of the ripening process and ethylene biogenesis now appears possible, through the use of transgenic plants biotechnologically manipulated to control the plant's ethylene output. The first such tomatoes were introduced in 1992 to be followed by other soft and perishable fruits, including raspberries and tropical products.

Dramatic changes are taking place in dietary habits. People are on a health blitz. Fresh fruits and vegetables, along with whole-grain cereal products, fish, and poultry will become increasingly important. Green (environmental, ecological) consumerism will become manifest in America's $280 billion food industry. "Food ecology," the relationship between food products and the environment, will heavily influence consumer choice. The organic movement, food products labeled "natural," the Reform (health food) Stores of Western Europe, and health food stores in the United States will gain in prominence. Nutritional policies will powerfully influence food policies.

Agricultural knowledge is becoming internationalized. Discoveries made in one country will be quickly available in others through literature, computer accessing, FAX transmissions, and personnel exchange. Contributions will be selective, adaptive, and chosen, rather than prescribed. It is easier to adopt than to wholly create the new. Science for the future of agriculturally developing nations will be a mixture of the borrowed and created. Research activities of the thirteen international agricultural research centers will be expanded to include forestry, agroforestry, fisheries, vegetables, bananas, and irrigation management. The cornucopia of the future is an overflowing one.

See also ALCOHOL; FARM POLICY; FISHERIES; FOOD AND AGRICULTURE; FOOD CONSUMPTION; FOOD DISTRIBUTION; FOOD AND DRUG SAFETY; FOOD TECHNOLOGIES; FORESTRY; GENETICS: AGRICULTURAL APPLICATIONS; GREEN REVOLUTION; NEW CONSUMER PRODUCTS; SOIL CONDITIONS; TOBACCO.

BIBLIOGRAPHY

AVERY, DENNIS E. *Global Food Progress 1991*. A Report from Hudson Institute Center for Global Food Issues. Indianapolis: Hudson Institute, 1991.

Board on Agriculture/National Research Council. *Alternative Agriculture*. Washington, DC: National Academy Press, 1989.

GIBBS, MARTIN, and CARLSON, CARLA, eds. *Crop Productivity—Research Imperatives Revisited*. East Lansing, MI: Michigan State University, 1985.

MAYER, ANDRE, and MAYER, JEAN. "Agriculture, the Island Empire." *Daedalus* 103/3 (1974): 83.

PAARLBERG, DON. *Toward a Well-Fed World*. Ames, IA: Iowa State University Press, 1988.

WITTWER, SYLVAN H. "Food Ecology and Choices." *Food and Nutrition News* 64/3 (1992).

WITTWER, SYLVAN H., YU YOUTAI, SUN HAN, and WANG LIANZHENG. *Feeding a Billion: Frontiers of Chinese Agriculture*. East Lansing, MI: Michigan State University Press, 1987.

World Bank. *Agricultural Biotechnology, The Next "Green Revolution."* Washington, DC: World Bank, 1991.

Sylvan H. Wittwer

Food Laws

Since the earliest recorded civilizations, one of the essential functions of government has been to assure the safety, quality, and proper labeling of the food supply. As our scientific base has developed, our regulatory mechanisms have correspondingly increased (see Table 1).

Labeling

When Congress enacted our first national food law, the Food and Drugs Act of 1906, it included no mandatory food labeling. When the 1906 act was replaced by the Federal Food, Drug, and Cosmetic Act (FD&C Act) of 1938, however, Congress included four mandatory elements of food labeling: the name of the food, the statement of ingredients, the name and address of the manufacturer or distributor, and the net quantity of contents.

From 1938 until the early 1970s, food labeling closely followed the requirements of the FD&C Act

Food Laws

TABLE 1. Food Regulation Through the Centuries

Ancient Sumeria	Net weight controls
Biblical era	Dietary restrictions
Roman empire	Food labeling
	Food standards
Medieval England	Prohibition of corrupt or unwholesome food
Nineteenth century	Prohibition of adulterated or misbranded food
1950–2000	Premarket approval of functional food ingredients
	Anticancer provisions
	Labeling of nutrient content
	Control of disease prevention claims
Twenty-first century	Regulation of genetically altered food
	Improved sanitation controls
	Emphasis on diet and health

and thus was relatively simple. In the early 1970s, the Food and Drug Administration (FDA) promulgated a series of regulations that transformed food labeling. Names of foods were required to be more descriptive and informative. Full nutrition labeling was required for any food for which a nutrition claim was made or to which a nutrient was added. The FDA began to define nutrient descriptor terms, such as "reduced" and "low" calorie. Mandatory information was required to appear on a single information panel in a minimum or greater type size. In the mid-1980s, the FDA also began to regulate specific disease prevention claims for food, such as the claim that a food product "helps reduce the risk of cancer."

Congress codified and extended these reforms in the Nutrition Labeling and Education Act of 1990. First, nutrition labeling was made mandatory for all food. Second, the FDA was required to complete the job of defining nutrient descriptors. Third, the FDA was also required to complete the job of regulating disease prevention claims.

As scientific information increases, the food label can be expected to change in the future in two respects. First, the FDA will refine its definitions for nutrient descriptors to be more precise with respect to the levels that represent a low, moderate, or high level of individual nutrients. Second, labeling statements about the relationship of individual nutrients to health and disease will become more focused and precise.

Food Identity and Quality

Since ancient times, attempts have repeatedly been made to describe, and to set standards of identity for, individual food products. Initially these efforts were directed at assuring the basic quality of the food by preventing unintended or purposeful adulteration. Later, these standards of identity were designed to protect the safety and nutritional quality of the food as well.

With increased knowledge about the relationship of dietary components to health and disease, food manufacturers will engineer traditional products to make them more nutritious and less likely to contribute to disease. This will be done in three ways. First, macronutrients and other components that contribute to the potential for disease will be reduced or eliminated through traditional methods of food technology—for example, substituting water for fat. Second, entirely new functional food ingredients will be developed and (after FDA review of safety) used for the same functional purposes as the less desirable macronutrients. Third, raw agricultural commodities will themselves be changed by genetic engineering, to reduce or eliminate undesirable constituents and to increase desirable constituents.

The Nutrient Content of Food

Discrete micronutrients (vitamins and minerals) were first added to the food supply in the 1930s. Modification of the macronutrient content of food began with the invention of saccharin in the late 1800s, but has remained stalled for many years because of the lack of truly adequate substitutes for such important macronutrients as sodium and fat. In the future, based on new technology, the nutrient content of any food will be fine-tuned to meet virtually any nutritional requirement.

Dietary Supplements

Ever since the inception of cod liver oil containing vitamins in the 1920s, the FDA has fought a tireless campaign against dietary supplements of vitamins, minerals, and other dietary substances. For decades, the FDA has preached that, with rare exceptions, people who eat an adequate diet simply do not need nutrient supplementation.

When the FDA has sought to implement this policy, however, it has been brought to a halt both in the courts and by Congress. The FDA retains authority to establish safe limits for any nutrient, but its authority to establish controls for perceived economic or nutritional reasons has been severely limited.

The FDA is unlikely to give up its vendetta against dietary supplement products. Manufacturers and consumers, on the other hand, will continue to argue that these products are safe and provide an important insurance for those who do not consume an adequate or balanced diet. As more detailed scientific information emerges about the biochemistry and nutritional importance of specific nutrients in the daily diet and their relation to health and disease, the arguments in favor of dietary supplements are likely to gain strength and ultimately to overwhelm the FDA objections.

Food Sanitation

From ancient times to the present, contagion and communicable disease have been spread through the food supply. Our modern food supply is unquestionably the safest in history. Nonetheless, such pathogenic organisms as salmonella and listeria continue to elude control.

In the future, new technology will offer the possibility of even more effective antimicrobial agents to reduce the likelihood of food contamination. As public acceptance of irradiation increases, this technique will assume a much larger role in combatting pathogenic organisms. Use of recombinant DNA technology to build antimicrobial capacity directly into raw agricultural commodities themselves is also at hand.

The Safety of Food Constituents

Under the 1906 F&D Act and the FD&C Act of 1938, it has been illegal to add any poisonous or deleterious substance to the food supply. In the Food Additives Amendment of 1958, Congress required that all food additives—food substances not generally recognized as safe—must first be the subject of extensive testing by the food manufacturer and then approval for safety by the FDA before they can be used in the food supply.

Since 1958, the American food industry and FDA have cooperated on a massive review of the safety of functional food ingredients—flavors, colors, emulsifiers, nonnutritive sweeteners, nutrients, and other substances used to achieve a specific intended purpose in the food supply. Raw agricultural commodities, in contrast, have undergone no such review. We continue to eat the same basic food products as our ancestors, without the same assurance of safety that we have imposed on functional food ingredients. As more scientific information becomes available about the relationship of our diet to health and disease, the safety of our natural food products is likely to come into greater question.

The rapid increase in the availability of genetically altered raw agricultural commodities will force even greater scrutiny of the safety of very familiar but significantly changed food items. Completely new approaches to the evaluation of food safety will become essential once the full impact of biotechnology is reflected in the food supply.

Conclusion

Laws and regulations governing the food supply have not changed dramatically in more than one hundred years. What has changed is our knowledge about the safety, quality, sanitation, and nutrient value of the food we eat. Accordingly, it is the progress of science, not the development of laws and regulations, that will determine the course of government regulation of the food supply in the future.

See also CONSUMER PROTECTION/REGULATION; FARM POLICY; FOOD ADDITIVES; FOOD AND AGRICULTURE; FOOD AND DRUG SAFETY; GENETICS: AGRICULTURAL APPLICATIONS; NUTRITION.

BIBLIOGRAPHY

HUTT, PETER BARTON, and MERRILL, RICHARD A. *Food and Drug Law: Cases and Materials,* 2nd ed. Westbury, NY: Foundation Press, 1991.

Peter Barton Hutt

Food Services

Food service is the serving of prepared meals and snacks for immediate consumption away from home. Away-from-home eating has grown faster than at-home eating since the Great Depression. Food service accounted for 45 percent of all food dollars in 1992, compared with 40 percent a decade ago, and 25 percent in 1954 (see Figure 1).

The food-service industry is made up of more than 732,000 establishments comprised of individual market segments commonly divided into two major sectors: commercial and noncommercial. Commercial food service is the largest sector of the food-service industry, accounting for 76 percent of the total $250.5 billion spent in 1992 (Table 1). The commercial segment includes for-profit establishments, such as full-service restaurants and lunchrooms, fast-food/limited-service outlets, cafeterias

Food Services

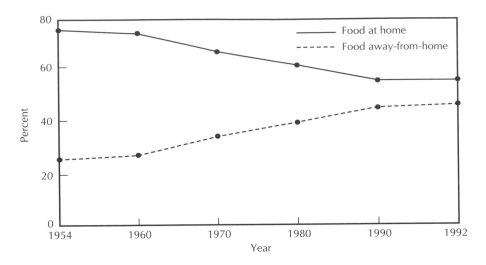

FIGURE 1. Food eaten away from home captures an increasing share of the food dollar. (Source: U.S. Food Expenditures, USDA/ERS)

and social caterers, as well as lodging places, retail hosts, recreation and entertainment facilities, and separate drinking places. The food may be consumed on the premises or eaten elsewhere. Fast-food outlets and restaurants and lunchrooms dominate commercial food-service sales.

The primary purpose of noncommercial food-service operations is to render a service rather than to make a profit. Noncommercial food service provides food in establishments such as nursing homes, child day-care centers, university or school cafeterias, and hospitals.

Fast-Food Outlets

Fast-food outlets are those establishments where food is ordered and picked up from a counter. The menu is limited and seating or stand-up facilities are located elsewhere in the establishment. Other services, such as drive-thru, carryout, and/or delivery may also be offered. Some outlets have only drive-through or carryout service.

Fast-food is the largest segment in the food-service industry with 1992 sales of $83.6 billion—exceeding sales of $72.7 billion at full-service restaurants and lunchrooms. Fast-food began in the 1950s and, because of its speed and convenience, grew rapidly. Fast-food captured an increasing share of separate eating-place sales during the past decade—from 46 percent in 1982 to 52 percent in 1992 (see Table 1).

Domestic market saturation by fast-food outlets led to expansion into other countries in the 1970s. By 1992 there were over 14,000 fast-food outlets of

U.S. companies in other countries, compared to 980 in 1971. Canada, Japan, the United Kingdom, and Australia are popular foreign locations.

Restaurants and Lunchrooms

Restaurants and lunchrooms, the more traditional eating places, now make up the second largest segment of commercial eating places. While fast-foods' share of separate eating place sales increased over the last decade, restaurants and lunchrooms' share decreased from 51 percent in 1982 to 45 percent in 1992. Casual restaurants lead this sector of separate eating places, followed by family dining, and fine-dining restaurants. Cafeterias and caterers accounted for sales of $5.5 billion or 4 percent of eating place sales. In contrast to the commercial sector, noncommercial sales are spread broadly among different kinds of institutional feeders.

Institutions

Over the last decade, institutional food-service sales grew 62 percent from $36.1 billion in 1982 to $58.3 billion in 1992. The transportation segment accounts for the largest percentage increase, followed by colleges and universities, and child day-care centers (see Table 1).

Future Growth

The away-from-home eating market has a bright future. Rising incomes and changing lifestyles have been primary reasons for success in this market.

TABLE 1.   Sales of Meals and Snacks by Foodservice Industry, 1982–1992*

Industry Segment and Type of Establishment	1982	1992	Percent Change
		Billion dollars	
Commercial			
Separate eating places:			
Fast-food outlets	36.5	83.6	129
Restaurants and lunchrooms	40.9	72.7	78
Cafeterias	2.7	3.9	45
Social caterers	——	1.6	——
Total	80.1	161.8	102
Lodging places	6.2	12.4	100
Retail hosts	3.9	8.9	129
Recreation and entertainment	2.8	6.0	115
Separate drinking places	1.1	1.6	46
Commercial feeding total	94.1	190.7	103
Noncommercial			
Institutional:			
Elementary and secondary schools	7.4	10.5	42
Colleges and universities	3.7	9.3	152
Plants and office buildings	5.9	5.3	−11
Hospitals	5.6	3.8	−33
Extended care facilities	4.8	9.3	94
Vending	3.2	6.7	110
Transportation	1.7	4.8	183
Associations	1.4	1.8	29
Correctional facilities	1.0	2.5	150
Child day-care centers	0.6	1.6	167
Elderly feeding programs	0.6	0.2	−67
Other	0.2	2.5	1150
Total	36.1	58.3	62
Military services:			
Troop feeding	1.6	1.0	−38
Clubs and exchanges	0.5	0.5	0
Total	2.2	1.5	−32
Noncommercial feeding total	38.3	59.8	57
GRAND TOTAL	132.4	250.5	90

* Excludes sales taxes and tips.
Source: *Food Marketing Review,* selected issues.

Incomes will continue to rise due to (1) the proportion of women in the labor force continuing to increase (now at an all-time high of 57.8 percent); (2) a high birthrate in the years ahead (Technomic, a research consulting firm, predicts a 10.8 percent increase in the school-age population between 1990 and the year 2000); and (3) an increasing elderly population with more time and money to spend on leisure activities such as travel and dining out. Food-service sales are projected to reach $300 billion by 1995 and $400 billion by the year 2000.

Domestically, fast-food firms will continue to focus more on alternative or nontraditional ways to expand the market and increase sales. Much fast-food is already reaching nontraditional locations such as hospitals, gas stations, department stores, schools, supermarkets, shopping malls, theme parks, stadiums, airports, bus terminals, and practically anywhere else hungry people are found. Though fast-food outlets led the move into nontraditional markets, more casual restaurants going beyond the traditional markets are likely. Foreign countries, particularly in Europe, and also China and Russia, offer opportunities for outlets in the next decade.

As food-service establishments cater to consumers' interest in fitness and nutrition, we will likely see more healthful, low-fat foods on the menu, such as salads and salad dressings, broiled and baked chicken items, steamed rice versus fried rice, and low-fat dairy products. Advancing technology, such as touch screens and other forms of electronic interactive ordering, will likely replace spoken communication at the counter, the drive-through, and perhaps even the table in the next few years. Both concepts are already being tested in some stores.

See also FOOD AND AGRICULTURE; FOOD CONSUMPTION; FOOD TECHNOLOGIES.

BIBLIOGRAPHY

BARTLETT, MICHAEL, and BERTAAGNOLI, LISA. "R&I Forecast 93." *Restaurants and Institutions* (January 1993).
PRICE, CHARLENE C. "Fast Food Chains Penetrate New Markets." *Food Review* 16/1 (January–April 1993).
——. "Foodservice." In *Food Marketing Review, 1992–93.* Washington, DC: U.S. Department of Agriculture, Economic Research Service, Publication No. AER-678.
WALLACE, JANE. "$400 Billion by 2000." *Restaurants and Institutions* (January 1993).

Charlene C. Price

Food Technologies

Prediction of the future of technology is always hazardous. Extrapolating from scientific knowledge results largely in the extension of what already is rather than of what might be. The development of new technology demands new scientific insights. The results of contemporary research will impact on food processing in ways that we do not yet understand.

Nevertheless, ongoing developments in food science and technology permit an attempt at predicting the near future. The three areas of investigation most likely to have their greatest impact on food processing are computer science, genetic modification, and materials science. New computer software and hardware have already had an enormous effect on the practices of the food industry. Not only is modern analytical technology dependent on computers, but process control and automated manufacturing is expanding rapidly with the development of new hardware and software. The availability of software programs to maintain inventory control and the development of automated warehousing technologies will assure consumers that the product they receive will be fresh and of high quality. Totally automated processing, storage, and distribution systems will provide a seamless system from farm to market.

Increasing capability in genetic modification will continue to result in the ability to produce from microbes the specific enzymes used in food processing. Rennin, for example, normally is obtained from higher organisms. This capacity will increase the availability of important processing aids or food components at a much reduced price.

Materials science will provide the foundation for the development of "engineered" foods. Today we see the increasing appearance of reformed meats, diet drinks with alternative sweeteners, and the development of fat substitutes. Not only will these engineered foods deliver a desired characteristic, for example, sweetness, a fat-like mouthfeel or a particular texture, but will also provide enhanced nutritional characteristics. Among the technologies that appear ready to be utilized in the near future is super-critical fluid extraction, which results in the removal of cholesterol from butter and eggs and similar products while maintaining acceptable taste and flavor.

The use of ionizing radiation to ensure the microbial safety of foods will increase. There are few other food processes that permit the same level of assurance of safety from microbial contamination. It is likely that radiation will not be used by itself, but rather in combination with other food-processing methods such as heat treatment, refrigeration, and freezing. This will, in turn, permit the use of lower doses of radiation to accomplish desired preservation tasks. Moreover, it is likely that the use of machine-produced electrons will replace isotope irradiators, reducing significantly the possible risks associated with such facilities.

Membrane processes are common in the food industry today, but new combinations will have the potential to produce novel products such as low-fat, low-sodium cheese. A variety of approaches have been proposed, including reverse osmosis, electrode dialysis, and dialysis.

From the point of view of the consumer, the most obvious changes will occur in the area of engineered foods. The engineering of foods offers major advantages in terms of their flexibility. A processor can vary the source of protein, vary the sweetener, vary the fat source—or any combination of these—and yet end up with basically the same product. The development of other technologies such as microwave processing has also resulted in technologists looking for ways to modify foods to allow preparation with microwave finishing and yet result in the same product that is obtained from preparation by other processes such as heating.

The potential exists for the development of food polymers and lipids that may be engineered to carry functional groups that can signal the presence of pathogenic bacteria or to carry a specific taste or flavor or texture. While we have not yet actually duplicated all the flavors in nature, we are beginning to understand better how the human organism detects and distinguishes among various flavors. If we know how these substances interact with the sensors in the nose or the mouth and how that signal is translated, a revolution in flavor engineering can take place that will permit the design of specific molecules to provide specific tastes. This most important area of food and flavor engineering will be derived from research in the brain and central nervous system. Increasingly we are beginning to understand how to control appetite, where sensory input pathways are located, and how to control these systems. With this information, food technologists will be able to design products that will both provide taste and flavor and, at the same time, control appetite.

It is important to understand that humanity has been modifying and engineering foods from the earliest of times. The development of fermentation technologies such as brewing of beer and the baking of bread are perfect examples of engineered products. Bread, in particular, is an excellent example. It has built into it a range of specific properties such as a certain number of air cells, a crust, a crumb, a caloric content, and a retinue of nutritional values. When combined with advances in the creation of foods and food additives, new technologies will provide an entirely new approach to foods and assure the public that the food they eat not only tastes good, but also fulfills the needs for health and nutrition.

See also CHEMICALS, FINE; FOOD ADDITIVES; FOOD DISTRIBUTION; FOOD AND DRUG SAFETY; FOOD AND FIBER PRODUCTION; FOOD LAWS; FOOD SERVICES; GENETICS, COMMERCIALIZATION OF; GENETIC TECHNOLOGIES; GENETICS: AGRICULTURAL APPLICATIONS; GREEN REVOLUTION; NEW CONSUMER PRODUCTS; NUTRITION.

BIBLIOGRAPHY

BUSCH, LAWRENCE; LACY, WILLIAM B.; and LACY, LAURA R. *Plants, Power, and Profit: Social, Economic, and Ethical Consequences of the New Biotechnologies.* Cambridge, MA: Basil Blackwell, 1991.

GASSER, CHARLES S. "Transgenic Crops." *Scientific American* 266/6 (June 1992).

HOBBELINK, HENK. *Biotechnology and the Future of World Agriculture: The Fourth Resource.* London and Atlantic Highlands, NJ: Zed Books, 1991.

MOLNAR, JOSEPH J., and KINNUCAN, HENRY. *Biotechnology and the New Agricultural Revolution.* Boulder, CO: Westview Press, 1989.

Office of Technology Assessment. *A New Technological Era for American Agriculture.* Washington, DC: U.S. Government Printing Office, 1992.

PALMER, SUSHMA. "Food and Nutrition Policy: Challenges for the 1990s." *Health Affairs* 9/2 (Summer 1990).

ROSENBLUM, JOHN W., *Agriculture in the Twenty-first Century.* New York: John Wiley, 1983.

Sanford A. Miller

Forecasting, Deterministic

In this generation, the world is passing through the greatest evolutionary jump in human history. The immense technological developments since about 1940 have changed human powers, human interactions, and human perceptions, more than any changes before:

- The biotechnology revolution has given us the power to reduce birthrates, control disease, transform farming, manipulate genes, and alter species. This is happening with a speed and on a scale unmatched in evolutionary history.
- Nuclear energy, fission (and, someday, fusion), for power as well as bombs, and cheaper solar-electric power with photovoltaic cells will far surpass our limited supplies of fossil coal, oil, and gas. It is the greatest change in supplies of energy since the development of photosynthesis two billion years ago.
- Our venture into space, with men walking on the moon and unmanned planetary probes, is the greatest jump into a new habitat since the land animals first came ashore.
- Jet planes are the most dramatic advances in travel and global accessibility since the development of seaborne ships five thousand years ago.
- The development of long-range nuclear rockets and of automated factories and automatic feedback-control systems since about 1940 is a new quantum jump.
- The greatest recent development may be in the field of electronics. First, in electromagnetic transmission and communications, public and private, from radar maps to television, FAX, and e-mail, with pictures and data exchanged around the world at the speed of light, by fiber-optic networks or satellite relays 40,000 kilometers up. We spend half our leisure time with television, and today over half the human race can watch a sports event or a catastrophe simultaneously. Even speech and language, writing and printing, pale in comparison to the scale and immediacy

of broadcast vision. And now videocassettes and recorders, with their stored vision, make further worlds available at everyone's fingertips.

- In addition, electronic data processing, transmission, and storage can solve scientific and technical problems at speeds millions of times faster than ever before. Advanced technology has transformed daily life, from the electronic kitchen and living room to electronic schools and offices, from social records to global credit cards, from home camcorders to satellite surveillance.

Possibilities and Uncertainties of Prediction

The coming together of so many factors spreading all over the world in our time is a far more powerful force than the technical changes that produced the Industrial Revolution two hundred years ago. But some of them are already pressing the limits of what is physically possible in several fields, so that their limits can be predicted, if not their speeds of advance or interaction. Thus, there are limits to orbital speeds, atmospheric sinks, food production, and human information capacity. Likewise, there are self-maintaining social patterns or limit-states whose continuity is predictable in sustainable societies, like traffic rules and rules of parliamentary order. Today, the only useful historical comparisons are not with times of constancy but with times of immensely rapid change. Nevertheless, certain aspects of the coming decades may be easier to predict just because of the determinism underneath the changes.

How could we make such predictions? How many of the present developments could have been, or were, predicted? The answer is that it is not as impossible as usually supposed. Throughout his lifetime, for example, H. G. WELLS used his realistic scientific imagination to make many successful forecasts, not just the apparent "fantasies" of space missiles, but wars and their timing and technology, and atomic energy, decades ahead. In *Anticipations* in 1902, he tried to predict for the whole twentieth century, and actually foresaw, for example, many of the social consequences of the horseless carriage in war and peace. But the speed of advances outran even Wells. Just one year before Kitty Hawk, he thought that the airplane was far off and would be unimportant; his century-predictions were fulfilled within twenty-five years and were surpassed by many developments in areas he missed.

Of course, anyone can make fairly reliable predictions of trends and social consequences in certain areas. Barring global catastrophes, we can predict population within a few percentage points one or two decades ahead, because most of that population is already living today. Even a great change in birthrates or death rates would not change the total very fast. The population forecasts, in turn, determine fairly accurately the pressures on food and resources, pollution, and urban growth, for the near term.

Conversely, the prediction of wild and improbable events that change everything—a message from space, or a catastrophic asteroid impact—is obviously impossible. This is also true of really new discoveries or inventions. Heavier-than-air flight had been hoped for and worked on ever since Daedalus, but success was not certain until the Wright brothers solved the problems of power and control. And the dramatic new powers of lasers and recombinant DNA were not anticipated by scientists even three years ahead.

Yet there are constancies even here. Evolutionists like Waddington and others have compared these "evolutionary jumps" to traveling over an unknown landscape and finding a hidden valley. There is a combination of surprise and inevitability, as many paths lead downward to the same pattern at the bottom. While flight was not certain for animals or humans, many ways were finally found to achieve it, from insects to birds to bats to airplanes of many types. And they all look surprisingly alike, because they satisfy the same physical requirements.

Evidently, to make good forecasts, we must look for constancies of these types. Technological constancies are much more predictable than the accidents of fashion or leadership or wars, and technosocial change often rides over this accidental "noise." Nuclear weapons and electronics, for example, seem to have stopped certain kinds of great wars and changed the scale of others. And television and public feedback have changed the responsiveness of presidents and the nature of politics and international interactions.

There is therefore a "technological determinism" that occurs when we are rushing into an evolutionary valley, when technosocial inventions are feasible and desired by all. In an open and diverse society equipped to produce them, such developments become "self-propagating" everywhere, almost invariant to accidents of history or national differences. All want health and longer life; less farm labor and higher yields; cars, television, and cassettes if they can get them. Change feeds on itself. The young rush to it. It crosses borders, sold or smuggled, and undermines old ways and opposition and authority. Television makes addicts, yes, but also inspires instant outrage, stimulates instant imitation, and creates instant demands. Why else the same movements in every country, after it arrived?

Determinisms of this kind can evidently be used, within limits, to make social and global forecasts for the next few decades that will be relatively invariant to the turbulence of events. We find such invariances in three different stages of the technosocial sequence: (1) ongoing consequences of present technology; (2) probable consequences of new self-propagating technologies; and (3) long-range limits of technology and self-maintaining patterns in a sustainable society.

Predictable Invariances from Present Technology

CONVERGENT GLOBAL CHANGES, 1960–1990

First we can look for the ongoing social consequences of present technologies, where parallel effects in different countries already show that there must be common deterministic causal patterns. In the last thirty years, we have seen:

- The end of centuries of colonialism; new nations and their troubles; independence movements. Why? Changes in farm and factory, education, television, national and international awareness.

- The longest period of peace between the European powers in history, with expected economic and political unification, the end of the Cold War, and arms reductions. Why? Nuclear rockets, satellite surveillance, television, tourism, and trade.

- The rise of a multipolar world. Global linkage, trade and business and tourism, with multinational corporations, high-tech banking, and mobility. No country any longer controls its own economy or stock market or exports. One terrorist act may cost billions, showing how intense the positive connection is.

- Global and satellite television, penetrating all borders. Electronics changing all family, society, government patterns.

- The information society. The transformation of agriculture by the Green Revolution, of industry by automation, and of business and government by computers. As labor changes from farming and construction to information handling and services, farms empty and cities explode. Work is light; education is long; retirement can be early;

and television, entertainment, sports, and travel can fill the days. It is the greatest revolution in work and time since the invention of agriculture.

- Mass protest movements everywhere, for rights and other causes. Hundreds of thousands mobilize in the streets as never before. When television makes problems vivid to millions, they become intolerable—a war, injustice, the deaths of seabirds. So television becomes to a surprising degree a conscience machine, a sympathy and tolerance machine, forcing corrections.

- The increase of refugees and migrants and guest-workers, legal and illegal, in all countries and cities. Uprooted by revolution or famine, or seeking jobs, they force cultural diversity and a new underclass on many surprised societies.

- The increase of health and longevity resulting from the conquest of diseases. In the United States, life expectancy has increased by about ten years in the last thirty years. This stretches out the stages of life; childhoods are long and dependent; families age, migrate, and divorce; seniors multiply. And populations explode wherever there is death control without birth control.

- The increase of education, especially higher education, in all countries, with lighter labor and more need for literacy and technical training. The world education budget has exceeded the world military budget in several recent years, surely for the first time in human history. Universities multiply everywhere.

- The decline of mainline Western religions, whose dogmas seem quaint to the liberal world of television and living room immediacy. The rise of dynamic and intolerant fundamentalism simultaneously in Islam, Judaism, and Christianity is a reaction against these modern forces that are threatening tradition.

We could add a hundred other great jumps in this generation: new architecture; electronic social records and global credit networks; the high-tech sciences; universal television and its marketing effects and mental effects, good and bad; and so on and on. All together, this remarkable set of rapid social changes since 1960 or so has no explanation other than the astonishing technical developments of the previous two decades. The surprising thing is that it has been such a great revolution in our minds and in the inner connections of society with so little violence in the streets. With a few awful exceptions—amplified by television—it has not been a blood revolution but an information revolution, a "velvet revolution." Officials often were not fired or hanged, but simply turned their politics around—sometimes within twenty-four hours. This new feedback flexibility is itself a revolution in social organization.

ONGOING CONSEQUENCES 1990–2020

A continuation of these social consequences into the next generation will be almost equally inevitable. For example:

- We may be seeing the end of five thousand years of large-scale armies and wars. Nuclear war seems less likely, with only one dominant power left; and the Persian Gulf War, with its one-sided, high-tech outcome, might be the last war of the great powers. They might now actually unite to stop arms sales and curb the fierce new wars between liberated minorities.

- In the next ten years, millions of species of plants and animals—perhaps 10 percent of those on Earth—will probably be wiped out. Their extinction will be primarily from human destruction of their habitats, from population growth and deforestation and pollution. By great effort a few hundred species may be saved. Zoos may concentrate on rare breeding, and great wild parks of hundreds of square miles, especially in the tropics, will be set up to save a few ecological systems. But it will be only a breath against the juggernaut, perhaps the greatest loss of species since the extinction of the dinosaurs 65 million years ago. Nevertheless the losses will not touch most people, and the biggest effects may be indirect, a permanent heightening of environmental concern and far tighter conservation and controls.

- Other environmental changes and catastrophes are feared by many, such as waste disposal problems, ocean pollution, and atmospheric problems of smog, ozone, and global warming. Television heightens awareness of the damage, but also our sense of the need of uniting to protect nature and our beautiful earth. As a result, within ten years or so, the international environmental movement, growing in all countries, may become the very strongest force for global integration and management for the long-range future.

- Within ten years, the world's dependence on oil may level off or decrease, partly because of these environmental pressures. The watchwords are conservation and improved efficiency; replacement by natural gas or even liquid hydrogen; cleaner nuclear power; and solar power with photovoltaic cells, which may decentralize our living patterns.

- Entertainment and tourism will go on to become our biggest industries. The young and the old, the literate and the illiterate, the well-fed and the hungry, demand television, video entertainment, and computer games. Tourism, whetted by inescapable advertising, with easy travel and credit cards, has become the main income of many cities and countries, with tourists outnumbering the inhabitants. As old cultures are lost or blended together, the strangeness disappears; the world becomes a common ground.

- The man-in-space projects may slow down for several years, along with the attempt to militarize space and other macroengineering projects, because of the costs and difficulties and the low payoffs, in a time of retrenchment and other priorities. But unmanned space projects, for communications, surveillance, navigation, and environmental studies, have value for every country and may continue expanding rapidly.

New Self-Propagating Technologies

Similar consequences may follow from some new technologies just ahead:

- The world's population may begin to level off or drop in the late 1990s, because of several new and more efficient contraceptives or abortifacients such as the French "morning-after pill," RU486. It costs far less and has much smaller side effects than any present contraceptive methods; so it may reduce births much faster and more widely even than the birth control methods of the 1950s, which brought birthrates below replacement levels in one-third of the world in less than twenty years. Because it can replace millions of surgical abortions, it will be pushed for birth control by large countries, such as China, and India. A population peaking below 8 billion by 2005 is now possible.

- New ranges of crime and terrorism will be made easier by mobility and anonymity, automatic weapons, and rich networks of support. The old villages were safe because some Granny Smith was watching, knowing who came and went. In the global village, the answer to modern mobility and anonymity may be modern watching, electronic surveillance and identification. It will surely grow for the poor and the outs, as it has already become universal for the rich and the ins, who need it for their credit cards and computers. Democracies will have to find out how to combine surveillance with safeguards, to reestablish safety and openness for all.

- Direct satellite-to-home television, along with fiber optics and interactive-learning disks, will decentralize and multiply the personal options for entertainment, business, and study. With public or private specialties, and an informational feast, it cannot help but change education, creativity, culture, politics, and global networks of participation.

- Together these massive global changes and dangers in the next ten years or so add up to mounting pressure for global reorganization and integration. The rapid organizing of the European common market and reduction of barriers will be a pattern for many other parts of the world. But the problems of nuclear and other arms control, environmental protection and control, monetary management, rescue for collapsing countries, and other global problems, are too large for any nation or any regional agreements, and they demand new global institutions. These institutions will have to operate by consent and with checks and balances to prevent dictatorial behavior and ensure responsive and competent operation, but they will require some surrender of independent national sovereignties in these areas, just like the European Community.

Such institutions may be set up piecemeal, sector by sector, just as global monetary links and credit and trade and tourism have been set up in the last thirty years. They may be in effective operation long before there are such things as global elections or an individually elected global parliament. As a result, the world may become more and more like an integrated biological organism, with its various feedback loops—the circulatory system, the nervous system, and so on—all stabilizing themselves with responsive connections to each other, without confrontational elections or a parliament. Eventually, a world democracy sensitive to the needs of all its citizens may be more like this pattern than we have supposed; if so, we are surprisingly close to it already.

Long-Range Limits and Self-Maintaining Patterns

Since the globe is finite, we can predict that in the long run, regardless of details, the growth of any technology will reach certain limits on this Earth, such as those we can see already with pollution and extinctions. Three kinds of limits are particularly important:

- *Limits to growth for a sustainable society.* The Club of Rome's hundred-year analysis of *The Limits to Growth*, by Meadows et al. in 1972, is still broadly valid. To keep a high-interaction society from running away to exponential booms and crashes will require hands-on management of population, pollution, resource use, and investment, as well as weapons—with strong agencies for monitoring and anticipatory corrections. We see them coming already, and they will be major parts of global reorganization by 2010 or so. Cleanup and recycling of everything, as in any closed system, will be a major feature.

  The adjustment to sustainable patterns will not happen instantly. It takes time for the effects of new technology to be fully understood, and it always requires "working through," with second-stage and third-stage technology, such as pollution controls, to correct unforeseen dangers or side effects. It is Ashby's Law of Requisite Variety: there must be at least as many controls as there are problems to be solved. The limits to growth will finally be maintained by many social controls.

- *Self-stabilizing patterns in complex systems.* With feedback communication, the subsystems will always develop a working balance, not optimizing but "satisficing," moment by moment. In the future global society, with television and fast communication of complaints and demands, the balancing of interests will require something like John Rawls's idea of "justice as fairness." In his system, any inequalities in shares and privileges can be justified and defended only as long as the lot of the least fortunate improves as much as possible. Probably no other pattern of distribution will be stable in the long run. This means guaranteed entitlements, insurance and transfer payments; ombudsmen in all organizations; and Marshall-type plans for Third World rescue.

  Stabilization will also require real "checks and balances" feedbacks, like those in the U.S. Constitution, so that the governed can control their governments and their economic systems. High-information management elites will always tend to expand and exploit their knowledge and will have to be curbed. Strong autonomous subsystems with their own information networks will be needed, like the organs of a healthy organism.

- *Blocks to technology.* A very different kind of limits would be imposed if science and technology were someday banned, as they were in Islam in the 1100s by a religious hierarchy, and in China in the 1400s by a fearful bureaucracy—which is why both cultures "lost out" to the then-primitive West. Today, some major high-tech catastrophe might likewise unite the antitech fears and the fundamentalists to stop growth around the world, perhaps under a charismatic television revivalist using electronic technology to stop all the rest.

But as Joel Mokyr has convincingly shown in *The Lever of Riches*, the West's explosion of science and technological growth was due to its diversity. New ideas that were blocked by guilds or governments could always find other channels and markets. With world society now moving toward still more diversity—with more individualist and small-group technologies!—there will always be channels of change, and no real blocks to technological determinism seem likely for a long time to come. Even with disasters, risky but useful technologies will be debated and corrected, rather than abandoned.

In the other direction, a great expansion of limits will come if and when *self-supporting space habitats* can be developed outside the Earth, with shielding and artificial gravity for long-run living. With recycling and abundant energy and asteroidal and lunar materials for expansion, different groups could find new evolutionary niches and possibilities. It would complete the evolutionary jump into the new medium of space. Is this possible? Will it happen? As with flying, in the centuries before the Wright brothers, we cannot know ahead of time. But technological determinism—which is another name for intelligence that meets the wants of humanity—says that if it is feasible, it will be done.

Whether this happens or not, with this level of control and communication and mutual interaction, the human race, if it survives, cannot help but become something like an *integrated global organism*. It will not be a dictatorship. People will fight to shape their own tastes and lives, so there will be enormous local autonomy. The world may have more patches than a calico cat; but on the overall problems of survival of ourselves and of our Earth, we will still move together—simply because we have to.

After this great shock wave has passed, we might go on for generations or centuries in the new world with nothing like this rate of change and reorganization again. What we are passing through is a unique metamorphosis in the whole history of the human race—like that of a caterpillar into a butterfly, like the birth of a baby—and this is what it looks like from inside. But the necessary end is so surely visible that many aspects of this remarkable new world of our children and grandchildren can already be broadly predicted.

See also CHANGE, SCIENTIFIC AND TECHNOLOGICAL; FORECASTING METHODS; FORECASTING, MISTAKES IN; SCIENTIFIC BREAKTHROUGHS; TECHNOLOGY FORECASTING AND ASSESSMENT.

BIBLIOGRAPHY

ASIMOV, ISAAC, and WHITE, FRANK. *The March of the Millennia: A Key to Looking at History.* New York: Walker and Company, 1991.

DEUTSCH, K. W.; MARKOVITZ, A. S.; and PLATT, J. *Advances in the Social Sciences, 1900–1980: What, Who, Where, How?* Cambridge, MA: Abt Books, 1986.

FEATHER, FRANK. *G–Forces: Reinventing the World. The Thirty-five Global Forces Restructuring Our Future.* Toronto: Summerhill Press, 1989.

GOODMAN, ALLAN E. *A Brief History of the Future: The United States in a Changing World Order.* Boulder, CO: Westview Press, 1993.

LASZLO, ERVIN, and MASULLI, IGNAZIO, eds. *The Evolution of Cognitive Maps: New Paradigms for the Twenty-first Century.* Langhorne, PA: Gordon and Breach, 1993.

LINSTONE, HAROLD A., and MITROFF, IAN I. *The Challenge of the Twenty-first Century: Managing Technology and Ourselves in a Shrinking World.* Albany, NY: State University of New York Press, 1994.

WAGAR, W. WARREN. *A History of the Future.* Chicago: IL: University of Chicago Press, 1989.

_____ .*The Next Three Futures: Paradigms of Things to Come.* Westport, CT: Greenwood Press, 1991.

John Platt

Forecasting, Mistakes in

Could forecasters have accurately predicted the extent to which the social problems engulfing America would worsen between 1960 and 1993? During that period, total crimes have gone up 300 percent, violent crimes by 550 percent. Illegitimate births have increased by 400 percent overall, with illegitimacies by teenagers up 200 percent. Teen suicides have gone up more than 300 percent. Divorce has risen more than 200 percent. Although elementary and secondary education outlays are up by 200 percent, scholastic aptitude test (SAT) scores have plummeted an average of 73 points.

Political forecasts and prognostications may be even riskier. Half a century after the women's suffrage movement had begun and had gained much public support, Grover Cleveland, America's twenty-second and twenty-fourth president, contended in

1905 that "Sensible and responsible women do not want to vote." Following Barry Goldwater's rout by President Lyndon Johnson in 1964, serious commentators wondered whether the Republican party would survive or would ever again attain the presidency; but Republicans won five of the next seven presidential elections. East German leaders boasted in early 1989 that the Berlin Wall would stand for another hundred years; but several months later it was torn down and the communist tide had turned.

Even moguls of industry go awry in forecasting their might. Thomas Watson, IBM's founder, speculated, "I think there is a world market for about five computers." The president of the Dean Telephone Company made a similar error, prognosticating in 1907, "You could put in this [office] all the radiotelephone apparatus that the country will ever need." Western Union, in another classic miscalculation in 1876, refused to buy Alexander Graham Bell's telephone invention for $100,000; after all, telegraph was "king." At the turn of the century, Britain's Chief Engineer of the Post Office proclaimed, "The Americans have need of the telephone but we do not . . . we have plenty of messenger boys." Harry Warner of Warner Brothers asserted in 1927: "Who the hell wants to hear actors talk?" Introduction of television at the 1939 World's Fair prompted the *New York Times* to report: "The problem with television is that people must sit and keep their eyes glued to the screen; the average American family hasn't time for it." The average daily television viewing per household amounted to 7:04 hours in 1992, by far the greatest leisure time pursuit. The list of errors in calculation could go on endlessly.

At the height of the Information Age, these prescriptions for wrongly estimating communications technologies and social response suggest the need to take matters more seriously. Predicting future developments and trends requires soberly imaginative professional futurists skilled in detecting, interpreting, and anticipating patterns of change.

See also CHANGE, PACE OF; FORECASTING METHODS; PLANNING; SCANNING; SCENARIOS; SURPRISES; WILDCARDS.

BIBLIOGRAPHY

CERF, CHRISTOPHER, and NAVASTY, VICTOR. *The Experts Speak: The Definitive Compendium of Authoritative Misinformation.* New York: Random House/Pantheon Books, 1984.

GOLDBERG, M. HIRSCH. *The Blunder Book.* New York: William Morrow, 1984.

William L. Renfro

Forecasting Methods

There is no one best forecasting technique. The methods used must be tailored to the particular problem and the resources available to complete the forecast. The huge expenditures involved in constructing the dynamic models employed by the Club of Rome would not be appropriate for the entrepreneur wanting to predict short fluctuations in the commodities market. Tremendous efforts to collect detailed energy-sector data for state input/output tables proved "untimely" when, a few years later, the results were available. Senior state officials needed to make broad policy/investment decisions in a period of world energy shortages, not of surpluses. Often a combination of methods produces the best results—perhaps a Delphi approach to frame the problem via expert opinion followed by more quantitative modeling techniques.

There are hundreds of forecasting techniques or approaches from which to choose, as the following list only begins to suggest:

1. Forecasting via surveys
   a. Delphi methods
   b. Panels
   c. Public opinion polls
   d. Surveys of activities, events, units, intentions, attitudes, priorities, hopes, and fears
2. Barometric or indicator forecasting
   a. Economic and social indicators
   b. Precursor events
   c. Signals of change
   d. Technological audits
   e. Analysis of limits and barriers
   f. Prediction of changeover points
3. Forecasting via trends
   a. Trend extrapolation
   b. Exponential smoothing
   c. Time-series data

To begin the selection process, the planner should have the answers to the following questions: What is it you are looking for? What are you going to get when all is said and done? How do you do it? What do you need? A sample write-up for a cross-impact analysis is shown here:

1. What is it?
   - *Name:* Cross-impact analysis.
   - *Definition/description:* Comparison of individual forecasts, on a pairwise basis, to determine whether there are interactions or to provide a systematic method for examining the interactions among several forecasts.

- *History/degree of provenness/promise:* Devised by Theodore Gordon and O. Helmer in the late 1960s. Numerous applications—it works. High degree of promise.

2. What are you going to get?
   - *Uses and limitations:* Comparisons of forecasts and testing policies. Provides greater clarification of issues and better definitions of the risk and uncertainties in the subject being forecast, as well as a more complete and consistent picture of some future time period.
   - *Limitations:* Number of forecasts that can be made and possible methodological inflexibility.
   - *Forms of output:* A matrix of events in rows and columns depicting the interaction between events.
   - *Level of detail:* While extensive detail is possible (more than twenty-five events), the procedure becomes tedious and evaluation complex when too many events are involved.
   - *Level of confidence:* Judgmental, but use of experts and probabilities provides for extensive feedback and review.
   - *Span of forecast:* Flexible (long- or short-term) and determined by the nature of events.

3. How do you do it?
   - *Procedures:* Very systematic. Events are suggested with probabilities and year of occurrence. Events are then arranged in columns and rows. The interaction between events is shown in terms of mode (i.e., whether one event enhances, enables, or prevents another), strength (10–100 percent), and time lag (from immediate to *x* years).

4. What do you need?
   - *Data requirements and availability:* Forecasts—the results of these often is from Delphi methods or panels, but can be from any source.
   - *People, including organizational backup:* Need "experts" to determine events, probability, and time of occurrence. Also, must evaluate the interaction among events.
   - *Time:* One day to one year, depending upon complexity, with a median required duration of one month.
   - *Money:* Cost for such analysis can range from modest to high, depending upon the complexity of events being analyzed, type of "experts" required to take part, and whether a computer is utilized.

To assist the planner in identifying the most appropriate methods, the types of methods discussed in this article are compared with various areas of analysis, resource conditions, and special situations as respectively shown in Tables 1 and 2.

Forecasting Techniques Using Time Series and Projections

These methods may involve pattern identification, trend extrapolation, and probabilistic forecasting. Series of historical data are subjected to various kinds of statistical analysis to generate forecasts of the future. Although the mathematics used is sometimes quite advanced and the concepts may be quite subtle, this type of analysis, on the whole, is the easiest to use and understand of all forecasting approaches. These methods are quite flexible in

TABLE 1. Areas of Analysis

Focus of Forecast	Time Series and Projections			Models and Simulations					Qualitative and Holistic			
	Trend Extrapolation	Pattern Identification	Probabilistic Forecasting	Dynamic Models	Cross-Impact Analysis	KSIM	Input-Output Analysis	Policy Capture	Scenarios and Related Methods	Expert-Opinion Methods	Alternative Futures	Values Forecasting
Economic	X	X	X	X			X		X	X	X	
Technological	X	X	X				X		X	X	X	
Social	X	X	X	X	X	X		X	X	X	X	X
Environmental	X	X	X	X	X	X		X	X	X	X	X
Valucs		X			X	X		X	X	X	X	X
Institutional					X	X		X	X	X	X	X

TABLE 2. Resources Needed to Use the Techniques

Type of Resource	Time Series and Projections			Models and Simulations					Qualitative and Holistic			
	Trend Extrapolation	Pattern Identification	Probabilistic Forecasting	Dynamic Models	Cross-Impact Analysis	KSIM	Input-Output Analysis	Policy Capture	Scenarios and Related Methods	Expert-Opinion Methods	Alternative Futures	Values Forecasting
Data												
Historical	X	X	X	X	X	X	X					X
Public opinion								X				X
Expert opinion				X	X	X		X		X	X	X
Imagination/ speculation				X	X			X	X	X	X	X
Personnel												
Generalists				X	X	X		X	X		X	X
Methodologists				X	X	X	X			X		X
Subject experts		X		X	X	X	X	X	X	X	X	X
Mathematicians/ statisticians	X	X	X	X		X	X					
Writers/communicators									X		X	
Literature searchers									X		X	X
Computer programmers		X	X	X	X	X	X					
Questionnaire and survey experts										X		X
Physical												
Computers	X	X	X	X	X	X	X					
Programmable hand calculators	X							X				
Existing computer programs	X		X	X	X	X	X					
Statistical packages	X	X	X				X	X				
Data banks	X		X				X					

terms of the kinds of problems that can be treated and in terms of the level of detail in the results. Although time series and projection forecasting can be used alone to generate forecasts on specific subjects, they can also be used in conjunction with other methods, such as those based on models or those that are derived from more wholistic, nonquantitative kinds of forecasting.

Trend extrapolation refers to a number of different mathematically based kinds of forecasting. All trend extrapolation seeks to determine the future values for a single variable through some process of identifying a relationship valid for the past values of the variables and determining a solution for future values. This single variable may be highly complex in that it may reflect or be the result of numerous trends. The greatest limitation of trend extrapolation is that it is unable to deal with unanticipated changes in the historical pattern of the data. It does not take into account such wild card phenomena as sudden shifts or breakthroughs. Valid trend extrapolation may include such methods as "eyeballing," moving averages, exponential smoothing, substitution and growth curves, envelope curves, and simple and multiple regression.

Forecasting methods based on *pattern identification* seek to recognize a developmental pattern in historical data and to use it as the basis of forecasting future events. This method is useful both for time-series data, for which more direct extrapolating methods do not work, and for interpreting numerous social trends. The Box-Jenkins method is an example of the former; Normex forecasting and analysis of precursor events are examples of the latter. However, pattern identification methods sometimes suffer from a poor database, varied interpretations, and hence questionable reliability.

Forecasting Methods

Many phenomena for which forecasts are needed appear to change randomly, albeit within recognizable limits. *Probabilistic forecasting* methods use mathematical models of such phenomena. Numerical odds are assigned to every possible outcome or combination of outcomes. On the basis of such assigned odds, predictive statements are made about the future behavior of the phenomenon. Probabilistic forecasts are helpful in discovering where, how, and when a phenomenon may best be anticipated in the future, and where nonpredictable occurrences must be accepted. Such methods should not be used in cases where adequate mathematical models cannot be developed, or when the results must be understood and accepted by decision makers untrained in these specialized techniques.

Forecasting Techniques Using Models and Simulations

These techniques include dynamic models, cross-impact analysis and KSIM, input-output analysis, and policy capture. This group of techniques demonstrates the interactions of the separate elements of a system or problem, as well as their combined overall effect. Such models are helpful in attaining a broad perspective and a better grasp of the totality of a problem and in foreseeing effects that might otherwise be overlooked. These models can range in complexity and difficulty from an easily accomplished graphic display to a comprehensive, formal dynamic model that deals with quantitative relationships over time and requires special skills and computerization.

Dynamic models of complex, nonlinear systems are extremely useful for forecasting futures resulting from interacting events. The simulation model, which is usually numeric, reveals the evolution of systems through time under specified conditions of feedback. By changing equations or adding interacting trends, a large number of possible futures can be explored in computer runs. Dynamic models are also helpful in gaining qualitative insight into the interactions of system elements. Dynamic models require extensive time, resources, and skills on the part of the developers.

Cross-impact analysis strives to identify interactions among events or developments by specifying how one event will influence the likelihood, timing, and mode of impact of another event in a different but associated field. Cross-impact analysis is used not only to probe primary and secondary effects of a specified event, but to improve forecasts and to generate single forecasts from multiple forecasts.

KSIM is a tool that utilizes a small group of people to complete a cross-impact table and evaluate the changes over time in a few significant variables produced by simple dynamic model. Cross-impact analysis is a basic forecasting tool helpful to most forecasters dealing with interacting trends.

Input-output (IO) analysis is a means of interrelating industry inputs and outputs in a single model, showing the consequences to all other sectors of a specified change in one. Different models deal with the nation, with regions, with specific industries, and so on. IO analyses are of great value in quantifying changes in a region's or subregion's commodity flows and likely industrialization patterns resulting from specific projects—such as improved navigational facilities or a new recreational site. Principal problems to its use include lack of detail on coverage in IO matrices, out-of-date data, and the high cost of developing specialty IO tables.

Policy capture involves building a model that, given the same information the individual has, will accurately reproduce his or her judgments and hence policies. The goal is not simply to predict or reproduce judgments accurately; rather, policy capture seeks to generate descriptions of the judgmental behavior that are helpful in identifying characteristic differences between individuals. It is believed that the judgmental process can be described mathematically with a reasonable amount of success.

Qualitative and Holistic Forecasting Techniques

This type of forecasting may involve scenario building and related methods, expert-opinion methods, and values forecasting. These techniques are aimed at portraying the system as a whole. The forecaster typically starts with an intuitive sense of the totality instead of with a specific component of the whole. With the total context in mind, the planner next identifies the elements, how they fit together to make the whole, the driving forces of change, and so forth. Then, such methods as trend extrapolation and modeling come into play, but they are used in the service of explaining the whole. This kind of forecasting thus tends to be more global, more qualitative, and "softer" than more conventional approaches.

Scenarios, alternative futures, modes and mechanisms of change, authority forecasting, and surprise-free futures all depend upon logical, plausible, and imaginative conjectures that are most properly regarded as descriptions of potential futures rather than probabilistic forecasts of actual futures. Such methods are most often used in conjecturing about complex, little-understood social phenomena, for which more rigorous quantitative forecasting methods do not exist.

Expert-opinion methods, including the use of panels, surveys of intentions and attitudes, and Delphi polls, may be used either for actual forecasting or to make conjectural explorations of potential futures. Identifying, qualifying, and making pertinent experts credible is a central issue with these methods. While the findings of expert-opinion studies are usually easy to communicate, it is often difficult to convey the specialized information and the reasoning on which findings are based.

People's values (priorities, opinions, attitudes, and so on) are of crucial importance in judging what public actions and policies they will support. *Values forecasting* usually involves clustering values into topology and forecasting changes in values on the basis of demographic shifts or broad societal scenarios. Values forecasting is essential for the purpose of reflecting soft human factors in long-term planning and policy analysis. Values studies are extremely helpful when used in conjunction with other forecasting methods, but are of limited reliability or detail when used alone.

Conclusion

The methods presented here can be employed for a wide variety of purposes. Forecasting can focus on predicting the future course of events. It can also focus more broadly on identifying a range of *probable* outcomes. At other times it may seek to determine the physical plausibility of achieving some set of results. It can also be an instrument to bring about a specific moral agenda by beginning with a notion of what the future *ought* to be like and then proceeding to map out the actions that are needed to bring about such a future. All of these approaches are characteristic of forecasting, broadly defined.

Forecasting can be short-term, mid-term, long-range, comprehensive, farseeing, logical, deliberate, rational, definite, intricate, elaborate, complicated, detailed, simple, clear-cut, solid, daring, or subtle. It can also be accurate, sophisticated, makeshift, tentative, grandiose, linear, nonlinear, unproductive, frantic, weird, unbelievable. . . . The horizons are limitless.

See also FORECASTING, DETERMINISTIC; FORECASTING, MISTAKES IN; SCENARIOS; SOCIAL INDICATORS; SURPRISES; TECHNOLOGY FORECASTING AND ASSESSMENT; TREND INDICATORS; WILD-CARDS.

BIBLIOGRAPHY

ABRAHAM, BOVAS, and LEDOLTER, JOHANNES. *Statistical Methods for Forecasting.* New York: John Wiley, 1983.

ARMSTRONG, J. SCOTT. *Long-Range Forecasting: From Crystal Ball to Computer.* New York: John Wiley, 1985.

CASTI, JOHN. *Searching for Certainty: How Scientists Predict the Future.* New York: William Morrow, 1991.

LEVENBACH, HANS, and CLEARY, JAMES. *The Beginning Forecaster: The Forecasting Process Through Data Analysis.* New York: Van Nostrand Reinhold, 1981.

Pamela G. Kruzic

Foreign Aid/Assistance

Foreign aid or assistance refers to the flow of resources in the form of money or "in kind" from more wealthy developed countries to poorer developing countries. Two basic kinds of assistance can be distinguished: (1) military assistance provided primarily in pursuit of the defense objectives of the donor, and (2) economic assistance provided primarily in support of the long-term economic development of the recipient. Arms transfers from the developed countries, including the former Soviet Union plus China (a low-income developing country), amounted to $24.7 billion in 1991, the latest year for which data are available. By comparison, the total amount of economic assistance provided in 1993 was $74.8 billion. The end of the Cold War is likely to reduce military shipments. The emphasis now, and even more in the future, will be on economic assistance.

Most of the economic assistance, amounting to $68.5 billion in 1993, consisted of official development finance (ODF) provided by governments (bilateral aid) and by multilateral organizations (multilateral aid) such as the World Bank and regional development banks (e.g., the Inter-American and Asian Development Banks) that have been established to support the economic development efforts of poor countries. A small amount, $6.3 billion, was provided by private voluntary organizations such as CARE and OXFAM. These totals exclude credits provided by the International Monetary Fund (IMF), Official Export Credit agencies, and private banks. The IMF provides credits to all countries, wealthy or poor, to help them cope with temporary balance-of-payments problems, while export credit agencies such the U.S. Export-Import Bank and private commercial banks provide credits in pursuit of private gain.

The terms on which ODF is provided vary. Some development finance is in the form of grants which the recipient does not have to repay. Most are loans at interest rates and maturities (interval to final repayment) more advantageous to the recipient than loans offered by commercial banks. The largest category of aid is entitled Official Development Assistance (ODA). This involves grants or loans provided by governments or multilateral organizations for economic development purposes at interest rates less than 5 percent and maturities longer than ten years. Such aid amounted to $55.2 billion in 1993. The bulk of ODA (which is also called "concessional" assistance) is directed to developing countries with per capita income of less than $765 in 1991. Budgetary constraints in all major donors are likely to limit future ODA levels and reduce its share of development finance.

Some economic assistance is in the form of technical aid to finance the costs of training or the salaries of foreign experts providing technical advice to developing countries. Some of this is in the form of credits to finance the costs of a particular project (e.g., the building of a highway or an irrigation system); some is in kind (e.g., the shipment of food to a country facing famine); and some is in the form of general financing of imports in support of a broad program of development reforms. Doubts about the effectiveness of aid in support of general import financing is likely to reduce its role in future aid programs.

Japan and the United States are the two largest providers of bilateral ODA with net disbursements (i.e., after repayment of the principal on previous loans) of $11.3 and $9.7 billion respectively, in 1993. The World Bank is the largest provider of multilateral assistance, with total gross disbursements of about $18.1 billion in 1993. Of this total, the World Bank provided $4.9 billion in very long-term credits (ODA) to low-income countries and about $13.2 billion in development finance to other countries.

The World Bank finances flows of assistance in two ways. It uses contributions by the developed countries to finance flows of ODA and it borrows in the private capital market and then lends the proceeds to developing countries. Because of its strong credit rating in international capital markets, the World Bank is able to borrow at attractive terms and offer credits to developing countries on terms and maturities more advantageous than

what they themselves could secure by borrowing in the capital markets directly. Most World Bank lending finances discrete projects, especially in infrastructure, energy, the environment, agriculture, health, and education. About 20 to 25 percent of gross disbursements, however, involves credits in support of programs of structural and sectoral policy reform undertaken by aid recipients. This so-called "policy-based" lending, which involves the provision of foreign exchange that can be used for the purchase of imports needed for the overall development effort of the recipient, is conditioned on explicit undertakings by the recipient to put in place specific policies conducive to longer term development. In the future, multilateral programs such as those of the World Bank which are based on capital market borrowing, are likely to continue to be a major source of development finance. But concessional programs are likely to face problems in getting funded.

In 1993 the four largest recipients of ODA worldwide were China ($3.3 billion), Egypt ($2.3 billion), Indonesia ($2.0 billion), and India ($1.5 billion). Most of these large, populous countries received low amounts relative to the size of their economies. The highest aid recipients relative to their gross national product (GNP) are in Africa, where in 1991–1992 Tanzania received ODA amounting to 96 percent of its GNP, Uganda 43 percent, and Ethiopia 15 percent. By contrast, ODA received by China and India was only 0.4 percent and 0.8 percent of their GNP, respectively. Since 1991, a number of countries in Eastern Europe and the former Soviet Union have also received economic assistance. The share of development finance going to these countries is likely to rise in the future, while that going to countries of East Asia which have developed good access to international capital markets, is bound to diminish.

Over the years, many questions have been raised regarding the effectiveness of foreign assistance in promoting development. Critics have argued that assistance has gone to corrupt governments with ineffective policies, which have wasted it, and that assistance tends to substitute rather than augment domestic resource mobilization for development. Experience has shown that while, as with all government programs, some aid resources have been wasted or badly utilized, foreign assistance can make a significant contribution to economic development, if certain conditions are met: First, that the recipient government is committed to a program of effective development policies; second, that the recipient institutions are sound, or can be strengthened, so as to absorb foreign aid efficiently; and finally, that donors provide assistance with the sole objective of promoting the recipient's economic development rather than their own foreign policy or commercial objectives. Because donor governments find it difficult to obtain public support for their assistance, unless they use it in the pursuit of foreign policy or commercial objectives, assistance from multilateral organizations, which are not affected by such considerations to a significant degree, has tended to provide more effective support for development.

See also DEVELOPMENT, ALTERNATIVE; GLOBAL BUSINESS: DOMINANT ORGANIZATIONAL FORMS; INTERNATIONAL GOVERNANCE AND REGIONAL AUTHORITIES; INTERNATIONAL TRADE: SUSTAINING GROWTH.

BIBLIOGRAPHY

CASSEN, ROBERT, et al. *Does Aid Work?* Oxford: Clarendon Press, 1986.
Development Co-operation. Paris: Organization for Economic Co-operation and Development; 1994.
KRUEGER, ANNE O.; MICHALOPOULOS, CONSTANTINE; and RUTTAN, VERNON W. *Aid and Development.* Baltimore: Johns Hopkins University Press, 1989.

Constantine Michalopoulos

Foreign Relations.

See INTERNATIONAL DIPLOMACY; INTERNATIONAL TENSIONS.

Forestry

Urban and community forests mitigate environmental impacts by moderating climate, conserving energy, removing carbon dioxide, storing water, improving air quality, controlling rainfall runoff, minimizing flooding, lowering noise levels, harboring wildlife, and enhancing the attractiveness of cities. Benefits may be partially offset by problems caused by vegetation, including pollen discharges, hydrocarbon emissions, green waste disposal, water consumption, and the displacement of native species by exotic ones (i.e., species that did not evolve there but were imported by humans).

Forestlands

The total forest area of 4.2 billion hectares covers 32 percent of the total land area of 13.1 billion

hectares. Another 675 million hectares are classified as shrub land and 406 million hectares are categorized as forest fallow—lands that have been cleared for shifting cultivation in the past twenty years. The world's coniferous forests cover 1.1 billion hectares, with 83 percent of these situated in North America and the former U.S.S.R. Nonconiferous forests cover 1.7 billion hectares with large areas in Africa, South America, and Asia. Tropical forests cover nearly 3 billion hectares worldwide.

Temperate forest areas in Europe, Asia, and Oceania have grown slightly over the last three decades as reforestation and reversion of cropland to forestland more than offset losses to urbanization, roads, and other uses. Between the 1950s and the 1980s, forest area in Central America declined 38 percent and 23 percent in Africa. Deforestation results from slash-and-burn agriculture, which can lead to land degradation, logging, and demand for fuelwood, fodder, and other forest products.

Forest Management

Most of the world's forests are not consciously managed for sustained production. Most of the managed forest throughout the world is natural forest. If forests are not managed for sustainable harvests, overcutting can result in thinner stands.

Catastrophic wildfires occasionally occur, but prevention, detection, and suppression activities have done much to alleviate fire damage. Nevertheless, millions of hectares are burned each year, with associated damages in the hundreds of millions of dollars.

Forest Pests

Outbreaks of forest insects and diseases commonly occur when forests become stressed because of drought or other environmental factors. Some insects and diseases are endemic to forests. Outbreaks may be widespread, such as the gypsy moth in North America, or more localized. The damage may lead to tree mortality or slow tree growth. Annual mortality from all causes is probably in the hundreds of millions of cubic meters. Wildlife can become a pest by damaging regeneration or by overgrazing.

Watershed Use

The watershed values of forests have long been recognized. For example, the legislation that created the U.S. National Forest System in 1897 stated that the purposes of national forests were to include securing favorable water-flow conditions. Unmanaged harvest of forests in watersheds can aggregate flooding and decrease water quality.

Trees and Forest Products

Trees are converted into fuelwood, lumber, panels, various pulp and paper products, and other miscellaneous products. In 1990, a total of 3.3 billion cubic meters of roundwood was produced worldwide. Some 54 percent of total roundwood production was used for fuelwood, and the remainder is described as industrial roundwood used for the manufacture of products. About 30 percent of the total roundwood production was used as sawlogs and veneer logs, and 13 percent was processed as pulpwood. Chips and byproducts from the manufacture of lumber and panels are also used in the manufacture of pulp.

About 45 percent of the world's roundwood is produced in developed countries and 55 percent in developing countries. Some 87 percent of the fuelwood is produced in developing countries, but only 24 percent of the industrial roundwood. Worldwide, only 0.2 percent of fuelwood and charcoal and 7 percent of industrial wood is exported. About 40 percent of the world's industrial wood exports are shipped to Japan.

The possibility of global warming has heightened interest in the role that forest biomass plays as a carbon sink. Forests act as carbon sinks by absorbing carbon dioxide. Agriculture and burning of tropical forests contribute to global warming, but to a much lesser degree than the combustion of fossil fuels and industrial activities in the developed world.

Logging

Logging practices vary around the world and depend in large measure on forest management practices. Harvest of ancient forests occurs in portions of North America, Russia (the CIS), and the tropical rainforests. Temperate hardwoods tend to regenerate naturally. Logging operations necessitate the development of a transportation infrastructure that, if not well designed, can contribute to soil erosion and water pollution. In the tropics, this infrastructure also provides access for people who develop land for agriculture.

In some countries, development of plantations of quick-growth species has been the choice over management of naturally occurring forests. There has been special interest in the development of these plantations in the tropics, where growth rates can be high. The total area of plantations in tropical areas amounts to some 25 to 35 million hectares. These plantations account for a small portion of the total forest area in the tropics. Worldwide, there are some 130 million hectares of plantations, situated mainly in Brazil, Chile, New Zealand, and the American South.

End Products

The use of end products from timber processing varies with climate, customs, and income. For example, in Japan, the Scandinavian countries, the United States, and Canada, wood is used extensively in framing for home construction. In Mexico, China, and many European countries, wood is used mainly for forming concrete, and in window and door frame applications. Developed countries account for 77 percent of the production of sawnwood and sleepers (railway ties)—486 million cubic meters—and they account for 87 percent of world imports of these products that total 94.6 million cubic meters.

Developed countries account for about two-thirds of the plywood production of 49.7 million cubic meters. Much of the remainder is produced in the Far East; Indonesia is an especially important source of plywood made from tropical species. Developed countries account for about 65 percent of world plywood imports of 14.3 million cubic meters.

About two-thirds of the material used in paper and paperboard production is wood pulp. The other major source of fiber is waste paper. Most wood pulp is made by heating wood chips in a mixture of chemicals that leave the cellulose fibers for further processing into pulp. Recycling of paper and paperboard is increasing rapidly in developed countries and is expected to become a more important source of fiber in the future for the United States and other countries.

Developed countries account for 93 percent of world production of 154.4 million metric tons of wood pulp and 83 percent of world imports of 25.6 million tons. Much of the production in developing countries is in Latin America, especially Brazil.

End products from forests, such as nuts, contribute to the food supply. Forests have long been a source for pharmaceuticals. For example, Andean Indians employed cinchona bark from *Cinchona ledgeriana* trees to fight malaria long before the time of European discovery. Many people claim there are further discoveries to be made. Recently, taxol from the Pacific yew was found to be useful in treating cancer.

Forest preservation looms as an increasingly important issue in the years ahead. Products ranging from food and pharmaceuticals to paper and a profusion of wood products require sound forest management. Touted paperless-office forecasts fade as paper use soars. Vital roles in global climate, preserving biodiversity, contributing to water availability and quality—all these things, and much more, demand nurturing forestlands, one of the world's few sustainable resources.

See also BIODIVERSITY; DEFORESTATION;ENVIRONMENTAL BEHAVIOR; ENVIRONMENTAL ETHICS; GENETICS: AGRICULTURAL APPLICATIONS; GREEN REVOLUTION; PARKS AND WILDERNESS.

BIBLIOGRAPHY

Food and Agriculture Organization of the United Nations. *FAO Yearbook: Forest Products, 1990.* Forestry Series, 25. Rome: FAO, 1992.

OLDFIELD, MARGERY L. *The Value of Conserving Genetic Resources.* Washington, DC: U.S. Department of Interior, National Park Service, 1984.

World Resources Institute. *World Resources 1987.* New York: Basic Books, 1987.

David R. Darr

Forrester, Jay W. (1918–)

Born in Climax, Nebraska, Jay Forrester received engineering degrees from the University of Nebraska and Massachusetts Institute of Technology (MIT). From 1946 to 1951 he was director of the MIT Digital Computer Laboratory, responsible for the design and construction of Whirlwind I, one of the first high-speed computers. He also invented random-access coincident-current magnetic storage, which was for many years the standard memory device for digital computers. He headed the Digital Computer Division of MIT's Lincoln Laboratory from 1952 to 1956, where he guided the development of the Air Force SAGE (Semiautomatic Ground Environment) System. In 1956 Forrester became professor of management at the MIT Sloan School of Management, where he applied his background in computer sciences and engineering to the development of a social science field known as system dynamics, based on simulation and modeling. His first book in this field was *Industrial Dynamics* (1961), followed by *Principles of Systems* (1968), *Urban Dynamics* (1969), and *World Dynamics* (1971). Forrester's work brought him seven honorary doctorates and numerous awards, including the National Medal of Technology (1989), the Computer Pioneer Award from the Institute of Electrical and Electronics Engineers (IEEE) Computer Society (1982), the IEEE Medal of Honor (1972), and the Valdemar Poulsen Gold Medal from the Danish Academy of Technical Sciences (1969). He was inducted into the National Inventors Hall of Fame in 1979. Thomas J. Watson, Jr., endowed the Jay W. Forrester Chair of Computer Studies at MIT in 1986. Forrester's principal contribution to futurism is his development of system dynamics as a tool to study the future of institutions and organizations.

See ECONOMIC CYCLES: MODELS AND SIMULATIONS by Jay W. Forrester in this volume.

BIBLIOGRAPHY

FORRESTER, JAY W. *From the Ranch to System Dynamics: An Autobiography.* New Haven, CT: Jai Press, 1991.

George Thomas Kurian

Fortunetellers.

See PSEUDO-FUTURISTS.

Fragrances

Fragrance in the 1990s is at the center of an olfactory revolution. Its use as a personal adornment continues unabated, but at the same time fragrance has become the focus of scientific study, as olfactory researchers and sensory psychologists search for clues to the human response to odors. Much of this research is being conducted by the nonprofit Olfactory Research Fund, the only charitable organization in the world dedicated to the study of the sense of smell and the psychological benefits of fragrance. The fund studies the effects of scent on human behavior, including such areas as sleep, stress, alertness, and social interaction.

Never have there been so many fragrance choices: over 800 scents are available in America alone. Women's fragrances are available in a broad variety, but the basics are perfume (the strongest, longest-lasting), eau de parfum, or toilet water (the next longest-lasting), and cologne (the lightest form). For men, the most concentrated scent is cologne, followed by body splash and aftershave.

Fragrances

In recent years, an ever-wider variety of soaps, body lotions, creams, shampoos, and gels have become increasingly popular. They offer well-known scents, as well as specially blended fragrances that have been formulated expressly to soothe or stimulate.

Our Unique Sense of Smell

Each person has his or her own individual, unique odor identity, determined by genes, skin type (dry/oily), hair color, diet (high or low fat), mental and physical health, anxiety, fear, happiness, and environmental conditions. The sense of smell is keenest between the ages of twenty and forty. It helps determine our food preferences, warns of danger, helps us make decisions about products, places and people, and enhances our well-being.

Women in general have a keener sense of smell than men, but much of this ability is learned. Women in our society are typically encouraged to use their noses more often than men are through their traditional interest in cooking, flower arrangements, interior environments, and the early use of fragrances. The fluctuations in a woman's sense of smell during a twenty-four hour period is systematically greater than a man's, due in part to female hormones.

Fragrance and Our Environment

Japan led the way in redefining the multifaceted roles of fragrance during the latter part of the twentieth century. The Shimuzu Construction Company of Tokyo developed the first computerized delivery system to circulate fragrance within closed environments (e.g., homes, office buildings, hotels, hospitals), utilizing different fragrances appropriate for each environment.

Shimuzu's studies reveal that subliminally perceived aromas have positive psychophysiological effects. Piped into convention centers, offices, or hotels, lavender, jasmine, and lemon increase the efficiency of meetings and decrease keypunch errors. Scents of seasonal flowers and ocean breezes eliminate anxiety. Lavender and peppermint help lessen mental fatigue and reduce the urge to smoke. Lemon, proven to have a stimulating effect, can energize visitors in morning conferences or inspire a mood of festivity in the banquet rooms in the evening. Jasmine works to soothe weary guests. The scent of Japanese cypress has a relaxing effect. Cinnamon piped into lounges "induces calmness."

Used in an athletic facility, scents activate the circulatory system.

The problem of interior air pollution is known as "sick-building syndrome," a result of the 1973 energy crisis, which led to tighter sealing of the building envelope to conserve fuel. The Shimuzu system is designed to avoid the health hazards of the syndrome. Initially, it filters and purifies recirculated air and conditions new air, which is then fragranced as it circulates. Japan is also leading with sophisticated car deodorants, fragrance alarm clocks, fragrant games for children, and scented containers to attach to telephone mouth-pieces.

Looking to the Future

In the twenty-first century, fragrance will be more than a glamorous fashion accessory or statement of personal style. It may be routinely used to promote relaxation and reduce stress; improve work performance; elevate mood and reduce depression; modify sleep and dreams; enhance self-image; retrieve memories; enhance sexuality; and improve social relationships.

Our new comprehension of the psychological and physiological effects of fragrance will result in scientific and medical applications as well:

- Doctors will use fragrance to reduce anxiety during medical testing.
- Doctors and sensory psychologists may be able to cure functional anosmia (the inability to smell) when it is not due to nerve damage.
- People on weight-loss diets may use flavor enhancers and sprays (of food odors) to satisfy their food craving.
- Our aging population, with diminished sense of taste and smell due to the aging process, may be able to restimulate these functions with fragrance and olfactory exercises.
- Women going through menopause may use fragrances to alleviate related depressions and mood swings.
- An infant's early ability to recognize and respond to smells may be used to diagnose potential learning disabilities later in life.

As virtual reality systems mature, they may be developed to allow a person not only to see, hear, and touch, but also to smell the simulated world and the adventures within it. Fragrances will increasingly play a prominent, positive role in enhancing and expanding our sensory experiences and our daily lives.

See also COSMETICS AND TOILETRIES.

BIBLIOGRAPHY

ACKERMAN, DIANE. *Natural History of the Senses*. New York: Random House, 1990.

JELLINEK, J. STEPHAN. "Aroma-chology: A Status Review." *Perfumer and Flavorist* 19 (September-October 1994): 25–49.

"Living Well with Your Sense of Smell." New York: Olfactory Research Fund, 1992.

Annette Green

France

France, over the next twenty years or more, may be shaped by two contrasting but inextricably related macrotrends: individualism and globalization. The individualist impulse, cited by the statesman Alexis de Tocqueville in the nineteenth century as an essential characteristic of all democratic societies, became dominant during the 1960s and '70s, when such institutions as marriage, the nuclear family, the church, labor unions, political parties, and the military came to be held in less esteem than previously.

Accompanying this inward turning has been a concomitant long-term trend toward globalization, perhaps first identified by philosopher-poet Paul Valéry in 1931, when he described the modern age as the "incipient era of the finite world." More recently, political scientist Benjamin Barber has referred to our age as the "McWorld," alluding to the computers and fast-food so omnipresent today. Advances in communications and other technologies are increasingly making the world seem smaller. Everything in consequence is seen to be interconnected: ecology, pollution, human rights, and trade between nations are increasingly viewed as global issues that transcend narrow, humanmade boundaries and challenge—perhaps even threaten—traditional French insularity. Both of these overarching macrotrends may be simultaneously viewed as sources of fresh opportunity and new sets of obstacles to be overcome.

The nineteenth-century three-tiered native French society of peasantry, working class, and bourgeoisie is rapidly vanishing. These once distinct social classes are metamorphosing into a more complex and fluid social structure that is becoming increasingly homogenized and centrist—at least within its confines. The lifestyles of this centrist core of managers and white collar workers are converging more and more. A recent poll indicates that 40 percent of leisure time is spent watching television. Political dichotomies also are becoming less pronounced for this core group. In 1991, 55 percent of survey respondents in France felt that political parties and politicians no longer could be meaningfully understood as being of the Left or the Right. In 1983, only 33 percent voiced a similar opinion. Thus, as individuals have more and more freedom in determining their own lifestyles, the choices they make are resulting in a society that seemingly allows, overall, for less diversity.

This neat picture of an increasingly uniform society is far from complete, however. For some groups in society, the effects of these dual macrotrends are more difficult to gauge, and prognostications range from uncertain to dire. Listed in increasingly problematic sequence, these groups are: women, the elderly, children, and immigrants.

A sea change in the status of women has recently occurred in France. The rise in status is undoubtedly permanent, but the pace of change is likely to decelerate. In the future, gains for women are likely to be achieved at a much lower psychic cost in France than in the United States, which the French see as more of a "conscience-wracked" nation, to borrow Daniel Boorstin's phrase, than is France regarding matters of gender. One particular source of concern, however, is the possibility that the growing share of women in the French workforce will require drastic readjustments in human resource management.

Tracking the plight of the elderly may be considerably more problematic, largely because there is no historical precedent with which to compare certain developing trends. In France, people over sixty-five will soon make up more than 20 percent of the population, a situation that has never occurred previously. On the one hand, sociologist Henri Mendras argues that new pensioners will be so much better off, in terms of health, educational level, income, and the availability of free time, that they will tend to form a new leisure class, able to customize their lifestyles. On the other hand, the late demographer Alfred Sauvy feared that an ageing population might be less receptive to technological change and cultural diversity. Moreover, elderly people could be affected in contrasting ways by the twin macrotrends. The anti-ageist bias of a culture of individualism tends to favor the elderly. At the same time, the competitive pressures of an increasingly global economy could counteract this bias by reinforcing prior stereotypes about the "unemployability" of ageing employees (i.e., persons over fifty).

The fate of children may be even more problematic. Parental hedonism, the rapidly increasing incidence of divorce and "informal" marriage arrangements, and persistent moral relativism may well jeopardize early childhood socialization. The declining role of the family as the child's first educator, together with the increased importance of peer pressure at an earlier age, may reduce the opportunity for the very young to learn a number of qualities essential for a civilized life. Late socialization may also be at risk because two fundamental rites of passage from adolescence to adult life—marrying and taking one's first stable job—are in a state of decline. Late (or no) marriage greatly lessens the relevance of the first rite to the maturation process. Parallel occupational precariousness ushered in by economic globalization, especially challenges young French jobseekers with inadequate skills who face competition from less costly workers in less developed countries. Young adults confront several highly disruptive trends: looser family structures that are less able to integrate children into society, a labor market less than receptive to first-time job-seekers, and finally the alarming globalization of the availability of illegal drugs, which provides some youths with a high income without any formal skill requirements.

There is an ongoing debate in France about whether immigrants represent a threat to society-at-large. The current percentage of immigrants in the French population is similar to the pre-1914 level, not exceptionally high by historical standards. The problem is that it is high enough to generate a new "demand" for social integration on top of similar demands coming from the growing ranks of people excluded from the labor market. Moreover, the capacity of certain institutions to create a social bond between French residents, native or otherwise, has been diminished by the demystification of institutions and disruption of norms owing to the rise of individualism, and also by the scarcity of jobs resulting from globalization. French society seems to be fragmenting into three strata—the increasingly homogeneous core culture that evolved out of the old tripartite society of the nineteenth century; an occupationally mobile superclass immersed in a cosmopolitan, English-speaking culture; and a poorly integrated underclass, with a disproportionate number of the young, the unskilled, and immigrants who are more likely to espouse extremist viewpoints.

France has experienced great difficulty in adjusting to the globalized economy that has emerged in the aftermath of the Cold War. This difficulty is attributed to a number of long-standing factors: the burden of an oversized welfare state, adversarial labor relations, unfair competitive practices internationally, and an educational system that harbors under the same roof two radically different approaches—one focusing on mass education and the other oriented toward the certification of elites. Further complicating this is the stance that France assumed during the Cold War when it attempted to assert its national identity by pursuing a kind of free-riding, unilateral foreign policy that placed it in relative isolation between the two competing blocs of East and West. The disappearance of that East-West confrontation has made that detached position increasingly unprofitable. Economic globalization runs contrary to a long-standing French preference for international regulation of economic, financial, and other activities according to a rationally designed scheme. France can no longer retreat from the rest of the world via delaying tactics or ineffectual proclamations of its own cultural exemplariness.

There are two great tasks ahead: at present only 25 or so out of the world's 185 nation-states have achieved fully developed market economies. Likewise, many countries have yet to attain truly democratic societies. There is a need to hasten the spread of democracy, and to increase the number of market economies. These two targets are sufficiently grand to appeal to the French liking for the *beau geste*, as well as quite congruent with the practical realities of current politics.

See also EUROPE, WESTERN.

BIBLIOGRAPHY

ARDAGH, JOHN. *France in the 1990s.* New York: Penguin, 1990.

CROZIER, MICHEL. *Strategies for Change: The Future of French Society.* Trans., William Beer. Cambridge, MA: MIT Press, 1982.

HOLLIFELD, JAMES, and ROSS, GEORGE. *Searching for the New France.* New York: Columbia University Press, 1991.

HOWORTH, JOLYON, and ROSS, GEORGE. *Contemporary France.* New York: Columbia University Press, 1989.

PEYREFITTE, ALAIN. *The Trouble with France.* Trans., William R. Byron. New York: New York University Press, 1986.

Bernard Cazes

Free Time

Free time is usually thought of as a prime indicator of the quality of life in society, because free time activities provide individuals with optimum opportunity for choice, involvement, and enjoyment. Shorter workweeks advance the quality of life in Western countries because they increase free time. However, the last half-century has produced remarkably little change in the estimated length of the American workweek. In contrast to a decline of 2.7 hours per decade in the workweek between 1850 and 1940, the per-decade decline has been less than 1 hour per week since 1940, with virtually no decrease since 1950.

These aggregate work data, however, conceal many important changes within the world of work:

- The proportion of men working has declined, particularly in the fifty-five to sixty-four age bracket (from 83 percent in 1970 to 67 percent in 1988). The average workweek for those older men who do work has declined as well.
- At the same time, there has been virtually no increase in the proportion of women aged fifty-five to sixty-four in the labor force.
- With advanced education, most individuals enter the labor force later in their lives.
- More people past age sixty-five have retired from work.
- More vacation days and holidays are available.

All these factors undoubtedly have led to less overall time spent working per lifetime for those who live to sixty-five or beyond, and likewise have reduced significantly the ratio of people presently at work to the total population. These discrepancies between official workweek figures and the "actual" time that people spend working over their lifetime indicate that the role of working time and its impact on contemporary life have been given undue prominence.

Such considerations led to the first calculation of figures for the total years spent in one's work life by the Bureau of Labor Statistics in 1985, estimated at 55 percent (38.8 years) for men and 38 percent (29.4 years) for women. No trend figures have been compiled since then, but there is good reason to expect that they are on the decline.

Data from national time-diary studies suggest that these work estimate figures do not tell the whole story about free time. The time diary is a survey instrument that attempts to account for all the ways that people spend time. Respondents are instructed to begin at midnight on a designated diary day and to report all their activities in the order in which they occurred across that entire twenty-four-hour day. In this way the diary utilizes time as a measuring tool and monitors the trade-offs in time spent on various activities.

Because of its ability to capture all activity with minimal reporting burden, memory loss, and embarrassment to the respondent, time-diary data are now regularly collected by several government agencies in European societies. In time-diary studies free time is defined as what is left over after subtracting the time people spend working and commuting, taking care of families, doing housework, shopping, sleeping, eating, and going about other personal care activities. Stated positively, free time includes the time adults spend going to school; participating in clubs and other organizational activities; taking part in sports, recreational activities, and hobbies; or watching television, reading, and visiting with friends and relatives—as well as all related travel time.

The Americans' Use of Time Project data in Table 1 suggest that Americans of working age have five hours *more* free time now than in the 1960s. In 1985 men had forty-one hours of free time a week, and women had forty hours of free time. Both time and demographic factors underlie this shift.

Two activity-related reasons help to account for this increase in free time: (1) Women are doing much less housework than they did several decades ago, (2) The diary workweek is shorter today than it was in 1965—not the "official" hours of work Americans report, but the work hours they record in their single-day diaries. While official workweek figures have remained fairly constant over the past few decades, the number of work hours people actually record in their diaries has fallen significantly for both men and women between 1965 and 1985 (Robinson and Bostrom, 1994).

The diary evidence is not the only data to suggest that Americans' free time should be expanding. Two demographic trends also indicate this: (1) Fewer households have children. (2) Americans are also spending more of their adult lives unmarried. At the same time, most Americans have more free time today than they did in 1965, regardless of their living arrangements. The ages of such people in the sample need to be taken into account, because people aged from fifty-one to sixty-four have gained the most free time since 1965 due to shorter workweeks.

Today's forty-hour workweek is balanced by a forty-hour play week. Like all averages, the diary data hide much individual variation and the diary data of working parents give evidence of severe time pressure. On balance, however, more people are gaining free time than losing it.

Besides showing the upward trends in the amount of free time since 1965, Table 1 also shows the domination of television in the way free time is

TABLE 1.   How Free Time Is Distributed Across Activities, by Year and
Gender (Hours per Week)

	Total			*Men*			*Women*	
	1985	*1975*	*1965*	*1985*	*1975*	*1965*	*1985*	*1975*
Total	40.1	38.3	34.5	41.1	38.6	35.6	39.6	38.3
TV	15.1	15.2	10.5	15.7	16.2	11.9	14.5	14.1
Visiting	4.9	5.5	6.6	5.0	5.1	5.9	4.8	5.7
Talking	4.3	2.2	2.6	3.5	1.9	1.8	5.1	2.7
Traveling	3.1	2.6	2.7	3.4	2.8	3.2	3.0	2.4
Reading	2.8	3.1	3.7	2.7	3.0	4.3	2.9	3.3
Sports/Outdoors	2.2	1.5	0.9	2.9	2.3	1.5	1.5	0.8
Hobbies	2.2	2.3	2.1	1.9	1.6	1.5	2.6	3.0
Adult Education	1.9	1.6	1.3	2.2	2.1	1.7	1.6	1.3
Thinking/Relaxing	1.0	1.1	0.5	1.2	1.0	0.2	0.9	1.2
Religion	0.8	1.0	0.9	0.6	0.8	0.8	1.0	1.3
Cultural Events	0.8	0.5	1.1	0.8	0.3	1.3	0.8	0.6
Clubs/Organizations	0.7	1.2	1.0	0.8	0.9	0.8	0.6	1.5
Radio/Recordings	0.3	0.5	0.6	0.4	0.6	0.7	0.3	0.4

* 1965 data not available for women.

Source: Americans' Use of Time Project.

spent, and the relatively small difference between men and women in uses of free time. Free time is not likely to decrease unless work hours increase, more adults become married, or more people decide to have children. Data on TV time and free time from other research organizations suggest no decrease in free time since 1985.

Television consumes about 40 percent of free time, and closer to 50 percent of viewing if a secondary activity is included. Reading time has declined, but only because of the decline in newspaper reading; book and magazine reading have increased somewhat. Other ways of spending free time have remained fairly steady across time, although attending social life—the second most popular way of spending free time—has declined somewhat.

Two additional non-diary studies provide a more detailed glimpse into trends on two important free-time activities since the 1980s, namely arts participation and fitness. Arts participation stayed relatively steady between 1982 and 1992, despite difficult conditions for the arts. The increased attendance at arts museums was offset by declines in musical theater and historic parks. Use of radio for classical music and jazz showed a notable increase, although the reading of literature showed some decline.

In the area of fitness participation, the increases found in diary studies between 1965 and 1985 have not held up since then: instead there has been a roughly 10 percent decline in overall fitness partic-

ipation between 1985 and 1991. Most importantly, the declines were greater among the youngest adults (aged eighteen to twenty-five), the group that could be the trendsetters for the future. Much the same decline in arts participation is found in this group, perhaps signaling the arrival of a more passive adult population in the future.

One more hopeful sign in the Table 1 data diary is that the distinctions in free time activities between men and women have decreased since 1965. That does not mean equality has been achieved, only that the trends mainly move in that direction. At the same time, other studies show that young women's fitness activity between 1985 and 1991 declined more than any other group, perhaps signaling a return to less active lifestyles of women.

In summary, Americans in general have more free time than twenty or thirty years ago. This comes both from increased life spans and its consequent increased years in retirement and from more free time for the younger (preretirement) work force. Signs are that this unofficial decrease in work time is also increasing. The lengthening life span will only accentuate that trend.

Unless more adults have children or stay married longer, or need to work longer hours to keep up their standard of living, it is doubtful the American population will experience any significant decrease in free time in the near future. Nor is there any evidence of a decrease in the dominance of TV in free time.

See also ARTS; BROADCASTING; CHANGE, PACE OF; EXERCISE AND FITNESS; GAMBLING; INTERACTIVE ENTERTAINMENT; LEISURE TIME; LONGEVITY; MASS CULTURE AND ARTS; MOTION PICTURES; MUSEUMS; MUSIC; OUTDOOR RECREATION AND LEISURE PURSUITS; SPORTS AND ACTIVITIES, SPECTATOR; SPORTS AND GAMES, COMPETITIVE; TELEVISION; THEME PARKS AND ORGANIZED ATTRACTIONS; TOURISM; VISUAL ARTS.

BIBLIOGRAPHY

DeGrazia, Sebastian. *Of Time, Work, and Leisure.* New York: Free Press, 1962.

Robinson, John P. *How Americans Use Time.* New York: Praeger, 1977.

_____. *The Demographics of Time.* Ithaca, NY: American Demographics, 1994.

Robinson, John P., and Bostrom, Ann. "The Overestimated Workweek: What Time-Diary Studies Suggest." *Monthly Labor Review* (August 1994).

Robinson, John P., and Gershuny, Jonathan. "Measuring Hours of Paid Work: Time-Diary vs. Estimate Questions." *Bulletin of Labor Statistics* (January 1994).

John P. Robinson

Free Trade

Free trade or, more aptly, freer trade, has been a recent hallmark of democratic societies. Unfettered commerce creates wealth by promoting efficient use of resources and provides consumer access to lower prices and greater choice. Even though most agree that free trade has positive results in the long run, its benefits are spread unevenly among nations and groups within nations. This leads threatened groups to seek protection from their governments and leads nations to shape policies that at least attempt to create advantages for themselves in the competition between nations.

Governments intervene in trade and will increasingly do so in the future. By the twenty-first century, national governments will increasingly direct trade in their own self-interest while trying to enlarge the benefits of free trade. This give-and-take will be carried out by trading blocs that will dominate world trade through the first half of the twenty-first century.

The most likely result is a new triad of geopolitical power: one regional trade bloc in North America, another in Europe, and the third in the Pacific Rim. The reason that regionalism in trade is the likely next step in global economic evolution is that jumping from national economies to the world economy is simply too big a leap. Economist Lester Thurow has suggested that it is necessary to take smaller intermediate steps first. Regional trading blocs characterized by free trade combined with managed trade between blocs may be such a necessary step.

Why Free Trade

In 1776 Adam Smith, an early exponent of free trade, wrote in his *Wealth of Nations* that nations benefit when their citizens can buy and sell free of barriers. The low-cost producer of a commodity, Smith argues, has an advantage, because he is able to export to wider markets, while consumers benefit from being able to buy goods at low cost.

In the early 1800s, David Ricardo strengthened the free trade argument with the idea of "comparative advantage." This process leads producers in each nation or area to specialize in industries where their costs are lower. Each nation then imports goods that are relatively costlier for it to produce. Producers follow their comparative advantage, which leads to maximum worldwide production, and consumers have access to the largest possible supply of goods at lower cost.

A Cycle of Winners and Losers— Past and Future

However, there is a pattern of winners and losers in free trade. Nations that are low-cost producers favor free trade (even if they desire to protect their home markets). Their markets are greatly expanded by removing foreign barriers to trade. Nations that run a trade deficit often look to protectionism, as they see their trade position worsen.

That Adam Smith first argued for free trade at the beginning of the British Industrial Revolution is no accident. Britain needed access to large foreign markets to maximize the advantage of its increasing productive capacity. The standard of living of consumers elsewhere was enhanced through access to inexpensive British commodities, but the leaders of those nations often found British trade a disadvantage to their national well-being and attempted to close their borders.

This pattern of a small trading nation needing access to large, relatively wealthy markets recurs. The pattern repeated in the relationship between Japan and the United States. New producers need access to large foreign markets to fuel growth and favor free trade to gain such access. This has limited ill effect on the large nation unless it runs a trade deficit. Trade deficits often lead to limiting imports to create a more favorable trade balance and to shelter the domestic workforce.

Workers in displaced sectors see themselves as losers in a free trade environment and seek government protection. Even if long-term benefits from free trade are admitted, the short-term dislocation in the economy produces problems that can't be ignored.

Contemporary events in the United States show this same pattern of winners and losers. Some economists, such as Paul Krugman, advocate a "strategic trade policy." This approach calls for government protection and incentives for U.S. industries that may not be low-cost producers but are deemed important because of national interests or jobs.

Other economists, such as Robert Kuttner, argue that other countries, primarily Japan, already manage trade in their national interest; therefore, we should too. When Japan or Europe furthers its self-interest with trade policy, it frustrates the reciprocity needed for free trade to work. For example, the effort in Europe to produce a new passenger jet aircraft gave Europe an advantage over the U.S. aircraft industry. This development demonstrates the vulnerability of a strategic export industry to managed trade from other countries.

Strategic trade policy and other protectionist ideas cast a pall on free trade into the next century. Offsetting this trend, a new combination of trading arrangements is coming into being that will maximize many of the benefits of free trade and minimize adverse influences of protectionism. These new arrangements will be established by the end of the 1990s and are likely to persist well into the next century.

A Regional Trading Approach

Three great trading regions are forming. The creation of an expanded European Union (EU) has made greater Europe the leading new trading region. The EU will enlarge its present membership to include Scandinavia, the remaining countries of Central Europe, and most of Eastern Europe. The EU already comprises the world's largest single economy, which will grow as countries are added. It is likely the EU will expand in phases, so that new national economies can be most easily assimilated.

Free trade will come to dominate commerce between member countries. There will be labor mobility and specialization based on the low-cost producers within the trading bloc. They will manage trade with the rest of the world to protect their own strategic industries.

The North American trade bloc had its beginning with the approval of the U.S.-Canada Free Trade Agreement in 1988, capped by the North American Free Trade Agreement in 1993. These agreements bring Canada, Mexico, and the United States into closer trading cooperation. At the turn of the century this union will be strengthened by the addition of the Caribbean nations. Eventually, the rest of the Americas may be included in this trade bloc. Over the short term, however, Latin American economies add little to the North American economies.

The third trading bloc among economies of the Pacific Rim is likely to be centered on Japan and other nations of the Far East. The area could be formed into a regional free trade area, but there are difficulties for the Japanese to open their system enough to admit others. The economies of South Korea, Taiwan, Hong Kong, and Singapore are unlikely to welcome a closer association with Japan and may look toward alliance with China. Any trade bloc formed in this area is likely to be centered on the vast Chinese market. The Japanese may choose to forestall this development by creating what would better be characterized as a Japanese co-prosperity sphere, rather than a European- or North-American-style trading region.

Each of these three mega-regions will attempt to protect their own interests and manage trade accordingly with the rest of the world. International tensions may grow if regional protectionism leads to competition for an extended period. This competition, along with cultural differences could lead to what it has led to in the past, namely, open conflict. A more optimistic scenario features a phased integration of the large trading blocs later in the twenty-first century. What that integrated system would look like depends on which region emerges as the leader of the new economic system.

Future Regional Competitive Advantage

One of the three regions, Europe, North America, or the Pacific Rim, will assume world leadership in the twenty-first century. Momentum is on the side of a Japan-centered Pacific Rim. To continue this momentum, Japan would have to redefine its cultural solidarity, which has been one of its great strengths, to include others. Currently this appears difficult for Japan to do; but it will be a key to any future leadership role the country may have.

The United States, and with it the rest of North America, has great flexibility and an unmatched ability to organize when directly challenged. It starts out with more wealth and power than any other region. The disadvantage for North America in continuing its leadership role is its legacy of military and social commitments that currently exceed its ability to fund. Also working in its disfavor is its current leadership position. If the United States, redefined to include all of North America, assumes leadership of the next century, it will be the first time that the leader of a former system makes the transition to also lead the new.

The strategic advantage is with the Europeans. The EU has no choice but to include Middle and Eastern Europe in what Lester Thurow calls the "House of Europe." If they follow strategic considerations, they will become the leaders of the new economic system. History suggests it will be far easier for the Japanese and the Americans to put off doing what they need to do to win. Future historians may well record that the twenty-first century belonged to the House of Europe.

See also GLOBAL BUSINESS: DOMINANT ORGANIZATIONAL FORMS; INTERNATIONAL TRADE: REGIONAL TRADE AGREEMENTS; INTERNATIONAL TRADE: REGULATION; INTERNATIONAL TRADE: SUSTAINING GROWTH.

BIBLIOGRAPHY

CLEVELAND, HARLAN. *Birth of a New World: An Open Moment for International Leadership.* San Francisco: Jossey-Bass, 1993.

KENNEDY, PAUL. *Preparing for the Twenty-First Century.* New York: Random House, 1993.

KRUGMAN, PAUL. *The Age of Diminished Expectations: U.S. Economic Policy in the 1990s.* Cambridge, MA: MIT Press, 1994.

PORTER, MICHAEL E. *The Competitive Advantage of Nations.* New York: Free Press, 1990.

ROBERTS, RUSSELL D. *The Choice: A Fable of Free Trade and Protectionism.* Englewood Cliffs, NJ: Prentice Hall, 1994.

SMITH, ADAM. *An Inquiry into the Nature and Causes of the Wealth of Nations,* 1776. Reprint. New York: The Modern Library, 1937.

THUROW, LESTER. *Head to Head: The Coming Economic Battle Among Japan, Europe, and America.* New York: Warner Books, 1993.

Scott W. Erickson

Freshwater

Viewed from space, Earth is a strikingly blue planet. The total volume of water, some 1,360,000,000 cu km, would cover the globe to a height of 2.7 km if spread evenly over its surface. But more than 97 percent is seawater, 2 percent is locked in icecaps and glaciers, and a large portion of the remaining 1 percent lies too far underground to exploit.

Fortunately, a tiny fraction of the planet's water is renewed and made fresh by nature's solar-powered water cycle. Each year, evaporation fueled by the sun's energy lifts some 500,000 cubic kilometers of moisture into the atmosphere—86 percent from the oceans and 14 percent from the land. An equal amount falls back to the surface as rain, sleet, or snow, but it is distributed in different proportions; whereas the continents lose about 70,000 cu km through evaporation, they gain 110,000 through precipitation.

As a result, roughly 40,000 cubic kilometers are transferred from the sea to the land each year. This constitutes the world's renewable freshwater supply—what can be counted on year after year. With today's population size, it amounts to an annual average of about 7,400 cubic meters per person, several times what is needed to support a moderate standard of living. But not all this water can be used by humans as it makes its way back to the sea. Two-thirds runs off in floods, leaving about 14,000 cubic kilometers as a relatively stable source of supply. And even this stable supply is distributed very unevenly and is not always available when and where it is needed.

In each major area of water use—agriculture, industry, and cities—demands have increased rapidly. Global water use has tripled since 1950 and now stands at an estimated 4,340 cubic kilometers per year—eight times the annual flow of the Mississippi River. This total, which includes only what is removed from rivers, lakes, and groundwater, amounts to 30 percent of the world's stable renewable supply. But we actually rely on a far larger share since water bodies dilute pollution, generate electricity, and support fisheries and wildlife. And because of improved living standards, world water demand has been growing faster than population: at 800 cubic meters, per capita use today is nearly 50 percent higher than it was in 1950, and in most of the world it continues to climb.

For decades, planners have met this rising demand by turning to ever more and larger "water development" projects, particularly dams and river diversions, to deliver water when and where it is wanted. Engineers have built more than 36,000 large dams around the world to control floods and to provide hydroelectric power, irrigation, industrial supplies, and drinking water to an expanding global population and economy. Rare is the river that now runs freely toward the sea, and many that still do are slated to come under control soon.

But limits to this ever expanding supply are swiftly coming to light. Engineers naturally first selected the easiest and least costly sites for water development. Over time, water projects have become increasingly complex, expensive to build, and damaging to the environment. Fewer dams and diversion projects are making it off the drawing boards, and most of those that do will deliver water at a far higher price than in the past. Worldwide, the rate of dam construction during the last decade has averaged only half that of the preceding 25 years—170 dams annually, compared with some 360 per year from 1951 to 1977. In Australia, North America, and Western Europe, few affordable and acceptable sites remain for damming and diverting more river water.

Desalination of seawater, in a sense the "ultimate" solution to the world's water problems, remains among the most expensive water supply options. At one to two dollars per cubic meter, turning ocean water into drinking water is four to eight times more expensive than the average cost of urban water supplies today, and at least ten to twenty times the prices that farmers pay currently, which are often heavily subsidized. More than 7,500 desalting plants of various kinds and sizes now operate worldwide, collectively producing 0.1 percent of the world's total water use. Desalination will be an expensive lifesaver to a growing number of coastal cities and towns bumping up against supply limits, but it will not solve the bulk of the world's water problems for the foreseeable future.

Meeting human needs while facing up to water's limits—economic, ecological, and political—entails developing a wholly new relationship to water systems. Historically we have managed water with a frontier philosophy, manipulating natural systems to whatever degree engineering know-how would permit. Modern society has come to view water only as a resource that is there for the taking, rather than as a living system that drives the workings of a natural world we depend on. Now, instead of continuously reaching out for more, we must begin to look within our regions, communities, homes, and even ourselves for ways to meet our needs while respecting water's life-sustaining functions.

Conservation, once viewed as just an emergency response to drought, has been transformed in recent years into a sophisticated package of measures that offers a cost-effective and environmentally sound way of balancing water budgets. By using water more efficiently, in effect, we create a new source of supply. Each liter conserved can help meet new water demands without damming another stretch of river or depleting more groundwater. Reducing irrigation needs by one-tenth, for instance, would free up enough water to roughly double domestic water use worldwide.

With technologies and methods available today, many farmers could cut their water needs by 10 to 50 percent, industries by 40 to 90 percent, and cities by one-third, with no sacrifice of economic output or quality of life. Besides being more ecologically sound, most investments in water efficiency, recycling, reuse, and conservation yield more usable water per dollar than do investments in conventional water supply projects. Putting in place the policies, laws, and institutions that encourage the spread of water-saving measures is an urgent challenge in building a society that is sustainable in all respects.

See also ACID RAIN; DEFORESTATION; ENVIRONMENT; FISHERIES; OCEANS; RESOURCES.

BIBLIOGRAPHY

GLEICK, PETER H., ed. *Water in Crisis: A Guide to the World's Fresh Water Resources.* New York: Oxford University Press, 1993.

MOORE, DEBORAH, and WILLEY, ZACH. "Water in the American West: Institutional Evolution and Environmental Restoration in the Twenty-first Century." *Colorado Law Review* 62/4 (1991): 775–825.

POSTEL, SANDRA L. *Last Oasis: Facing Water Scarcity.* New York: W. W. Norton, 1992.

SHIKLOMANOV, I. A. "Global Water Resources." *Nature and Resources* 26/3 (1990): 34–43.

VAN DER LEEDEN, FRITS; TROISE, FRED L.; and TODD, DAVID KEITH, eds. *The Water Encyclopedia.* Chelsea, MI: Lewis Publishers, 1990.

Sandra L. Postel

Fuller, Richard Buckminster (1895–1983)

Born in Milton, Massachusetts, R. Buckminster Fuller was a maverick American inventor, philosopher, and author who steadfastly remained a generalist in an era of specialization. He achieved universal recognition for his contributions to architecture, yet he was not an architect in the strict sense, but an engineer of huge structures. The best-known of these structures are the geodesic domes based on three-dimensional principles that he developed to achieve maximum spans with a minimum of materials. The most spectacular one was built for the Montreal Exposition of 1967. Fuller produced his most important design, the Dymaxion (the name derived from "dynamic plus maximum efficiency") in 1927. He was fascinated with simple, lightweight structures. "How much does the building weigh?" was his favorite question. What set Fuller apart from other architects and engineers was his invincible optimism and his belief in technology as the driver of social change. A rugged individualist, he filled his writings with the spirit of a scientific frontiersman: *Ideas and Integrities: A Spontaneous Autobiographical Disclosure* (1963), *I Seem to Be a Verb* (1970), and *Critical Path* (1983). The word *livingry* (meaning "tools for living," modeled on *weaponry*) was one of his contributions to the English language.

BIBLIOGRAPHY

EDMONDSON, AMY C. *A Fuller Explanation: The Synergistic Geometry of R. Buckminster Fuller.* Boston: Birkhauser, 1986.

SEIDEN, L. S. *Buckminster Fuller's Universe.* New York: Plenum Press, 1989.

George Thomas Kurian

Fundamentalism

Fundamentalism is the name given to a set of reactive movements in various religions and nations. In the post–Cold War era, after the demise of grand ideologies such as communism and during a time when historic nationalisms are being challenged, these movements often bond with aggressive "tribal" impulses by peoples against others or against regimes. They may also serve as new ideologies, to attract people across national boundaries.

The name *fundamentalism* was invented by parties in American Protestantism early in the twentieth century and, for some decades, was confined to them. In older dictionaries it is equated with Protestantisms that teach literal adherence to an inerrant, divinely inspired Bible. However, after about 1970 it came to be used to characterize reactive movements in most of the world religions.

The stress is on "reactive" rather than "reactionary." Fundamentalisms are not usually equated with historic conservatisms or traditionalisms, though they take root on their soil. The word *fundamentalism* is usually reserved for movements of people who fear a threat to their personal and social identity from modernity—though this may be characterized by other terms, such as *Western imperialism, secular humanism,* and the like. Thus threatened, adherents to such movements revert to ancient, usually scriptural, doctrines or laws and fight back. Their militant reassertions of these "fundamentals" allow for no compromise between those who profess them and the threatening modernists or even moderates.

On these terms, fundamentalism is a formal as opposed to a substantive categorization; that is, in substance no two fundamentalisms could be similar, but the forms they take find parallels elsewhere. Fundamentalism is a global phenomenon, present most often in those faiths that have definite scriptures and canons. Thus "the Peoples of the Book"—Protestant Christians, Muslims, and Jews—have readily turned their orthodoxies into fundamentalisms.

While Protestant Christians first spread fundamentalisms, Shi'ite and Sunni Islamic fundamentalisms are likely to have the most impact on world affairs in the immediate future. The Shi'ism led by, among others, the Iranian Ayatollah Khomeini was directed against Shah Reza Pahlavi and his supporters, notably the United States, in 1979. Two years later an assassin identified with Jihad, an extremist group, killed Egyptian President Anwar Sadat, an act that alerted the world to the presence of aggressive and reactive Sunni Islamic forces in the Arab world. Similarly, Hizbullah, a Shi'ite "Party of God," was a major agent in anti–United States and pro-Islamic activities in Lebanon.

These Islamic phenomena derived from the vision of leaders who in the nineteenth century began to react against modern Western intrusions and innovations. They attracted a following among the disaffected, usually but not exclusively the poor. In the Islamic cases, the appeal was not so much to doctrines as fundamentals, but to laws. Some are in the Qur'an, but more are part of Shari'a, the ancient body of Islamic law, now expected to be literally enforced.

In the future, one expects to see Islamic fundamentalisms meet varying fates across a part of the globe that begins at Gibraltar and extends to Indonesia and Malaysia. All northern African nations, especially Algeria and the Sudan, the latter ruled by the fundamentalist National Islamic Front since a coup in 1989, display these reactive forces. The Gulf War in 1991 led to a destabilization across the Middle East, where Iranian fundamentalism was already strong and where fundamentalist-like movements were in power in Saudi Arabia. Fundamentalists led the various Afghan factions against Soviet troops in the 1980s, and made up strong parties in Pakistan. Some fought Hindus and Sikhs on the Asian subcontinent and are trying to increase their power in Malaysia. The nonfundamentalist, sometimes semisecular regimes in some nations have found ways partly to neutralize the threatening effect of these fundamentalisms.

Judaism, a religion with far fewer adherents, has been the breeding ground for only one or two fundamentalist movements. The ultra-Orthodox Haredim in Israel qualify in some respects, but the small Gush Emunim, "Bloc of the Faithful," has been more politically aggressive through its pioneering program of planting settlements on the West Bank. The Gush Emunim insist literally and fundamentalistically that in the Torah, Israel was given a divine charter to settle and rule those territories.

Because the Hindu scriptures are vast and of indeterminate boundaries, it is harder to find the fundamentals of the faith there. But Hinduism has many aggressive quasi-fundamentalist parties, some of them at war with Muslims and Sikhs.

Roman Catholicism, because it professes the "development of doctrine" and does not insist on an inerrant Bible, is less inclined toward producing fundamentalisms than is conservative Protestantism. Catholic fundamentalists, such as those in the Italian *Communione e Liberazione* group or the French followers of the late Archbishop Marcel Lefebvre, make their appeal to Vatican documents from the sixteenth through the nineteenth century but reject the "open" approach of the Second Vatican Council (1962–1965). Sometimes through association by Catholic charismatics with Protestant pentecostals, Catholic charismatics pick up some fundamentalist impulses. But in Latin America they may also adopt the movements' belligerent and reactive styles when called upon to fight back against fundamentalist-like Protestant proselytizations.

While advancing in Latin America through evangelistic and pentecostal movements which are increasingly turning politically fundamentalistic, it is in the United States that fundamentalisms have been most widespread. After losing out in denominational battles in the 1920s, they returned, this time with political interests and in support of conservative "social issues"—for example, efforts to amend the Constitution to prohibit abortions and license prayer in public schools—to new prominence. During the Reagan-Bush administrations after 1980, they won access to governmental ears and had some influence on policy, but their greatest effect has been on the local level.

Tensions rise between the fundamentalist and "open" wings of the various religions. Thus the Protestant version has reacted not only against Protestant modernism-liberalism but also against moderates like evangelist Billy Graham, who agree with fundamentalist doctrine but reject its style. It has led to a split in the largest Protestant denomination, the Southern Baptist Convention, and will continue to trouble the peace of other religious bodies.

Efforts by Egyptian, Malaysian, Algerian, and other nations with strong Islamic fundamentalist presence have met varied successes. In the future, one expects that the number of fundamentalists will increase, since the conditions behind their rise are likely to remain. At the same time, they will display a varied pattern of responses, finding it necessary to innovate in order to advance causes that they believe resist modernity and innovation.

See also ETHNIC AND CULTURAL SEPARATISM; RELIGION: CHANGING BELIEFS; RELIGION: INSTITUTIONS AND PRACTICES; RELIGION, SPIRITUALITY, MORALITY; RELIGIONS, DECLINE OR RISE OF; TERRORISM.

BIBLIOGRAPHY

CAPLAN, LIONEL, ed. *Studies in Religious Fundamentalism.* Albany, NY: State University of New York Press, 1987.
COHEN, NORMAN J., ed. *The Fundamentalist Phenomenon.* Grand Rapids, MI: Eerdmans, 1990.
LAWRENCE, BRUCE. *Defenders of God: The Fundamentalist Revolt Against the Modern Age.* San Francisco: Harper & Row, 1989.
MARSDEN, GEORGE M. *Fundamentalism and American Culture.* New York: Oxford University Press, 1980.
MARTY, MARTIN E., and APPLEBY, R. SCOTT, eds. *Fundamentalisms Observed.* Vol. 1 of *The Fundamentalism Project.* Chicago: University of Chicago Press, 1991.
MARTY, MARTIN E., and APPLEBY, R. SCOTT. *The Glory and the Power.* Boston: Beacon Press, 1992.

Martin E. Marty

Future: Near-, Mid-, and Long-Term

What is the future?

The future is all that is not yet. The future comprises all that could be but is not now. The future is all possible tomorrows taken together. If the present is "now," then the future is all the potential or possible "nows."

What we mean by the present may be as thin a slice of time as the present instant or tick of the clock—or it may be a much looser term, referring to "nowadays," as contrasted with "olden times."

The past also is an imprecise term. Sometimes it means what just happened and everything that preceded it. But at other times we mean by the past everything that happened "before my lifetime" or "before the present era."

What we mean by the future is similarly elastic. On the one hand, the future is what will happen tomorrow, next year, and after we are dead and gone. But the future in considerable measure is also the result of what is being done (or not done) today and was done in the past by people like ourselves.

Not Entirely of Our Doing

The future, like the present and the past, is made possible by all the biological and physical (geological, chemical, meteorological, gravitational, magnetic) processes of planet Earth. The physical energy that drives these processes, and makes life and the future possible, comes to the Earth from Earth's star, our sun. So, like the past and the present, the future is not entirely of our human doing.

The physical energy that makes the future possible is channeled through the succession of present moments like a river. This energy cascades not only through the biological and physical processes of our bodies and the body of planet Earth; it is also directed by our human activities so that it passes through the technologies and institutions and social orders that have been and are being invented by human minds and then fashioned into the human-created worlds of yesterday, today, and tomorrow.

So the making of the future is a very natural thing that happens apart from us. And at the same time it is also a very human process that we all participate in, even if it is not entirely of our doing.

Starting to Map the Future

Maps usually refer to towns and to terrain and geography. But maps also can refer to what is not yet, what we are trying to understand or give shape. For example, before a skyscraper or a new type of airplane is built, there are extensive working drawings or blueprints as well as budgets. All of these are kinds of maps. Such maps of the future help us think through our planning processes. Later, they help guide us in creating the physical embodiments of what we are inventing.

So maps are mental models of a present or future reality (or even of a past reality). Sometimes the maps are detailed and precise; sometimes they are very broad and general. A map of your neighborhood can be very detailed, while a map of a continent necessarily has to be very general and leaves out everything but the most general outlines.

In mapping the future it is helpful to distinguish among several kinds of future maps. One kind of future map lays out what is "in the cards" and nearly certain to happen. For example, if we drop a glass marble out of a window, it is nearly certain to hit the ground. Of course, someone might be passing by and catch it, and then it would not hit the ground. But apart from that sort of major interference, we expect that in the next instant of time a marble we drop will hit the ground.

In a similar way, demographers who study changes in the size of our human numbers can tell us with nearly as great certainty the number of women of childbearing age there will be twenty years from now. The reason for their near-certainty is that these future women are today's young girls.

So in some respects the near and also the more distant future have built-in momentum to them. They are in those respects going to be the consequences of forces and processes that have been (or are just now being) set in motion. So these aspects of the future can already be observed today.

When we can see a future consequence that has this sort of relative clarity, it is part of what it is useful to think of as "the near future." The near future refers to your marble hitting the ground in the next instant as well as to the number of women of childbearing age twenty years from now. Likewise, atmospheric scientists know with reasonable certainty that it will take nearly a century for the upper atmosphere to neutralize the chlorofluorocarbons that are causing the ozone hole there. So the near future that we can see with relative clarity can include events even a century hence.

It is useful also to speak of "the distant future," meaning all the things about future tomorrows that we cannot yet know. This is the portion of the future that is still unforeseeable and is truly a mystery to us.

The person who tonight wins the lottery (or is hit by a car) is experiencing an event that for him or her (and for us) is still in the distant future. These events are in what we are calling the distant future, because they are still over the horizon of the future, beyond our present field of vision and anticipation.

So the term *the distant future* can refer to events as soon as the next instant and also as distant as a very long time hence. The essential thing about the distant future is that it is still unknowable.

Attempting to Explore "The Middle Future"

Then there is another part of the future we can call "the middle future." This is the part of the future we can glimpse in some of its outlines today but that is still very much subject to being reshaped by our human activities and actions and inactions.

By the middle future we mean those parts of the future we can still do something about, to help or to hinder, to accelerate or to slow, to bring about or to prevent totally. The middle future is for many people the most interesting part of the future. Various techniques have been developed to explore the middle future and to study what is becoming more clear to us as within the range of our potential futures.

After one of those possible futures has happened, it becomes the present, and then the past. Then it will appear always to have been inevitable. But as long as it is still in the future, it is uncertain and competing with many other similar (and dissimilar) alternative futures that also might come to be.

Think about it this way: The world we live in today was not inevitable. It very well could have turned out differently.

In a similar way, the rest of the future is not just going to occur. Futures are actively chosen and made *to happen* by individuals, by organizations, by technologies, by entire cultures. We make these choices of our future by what we do—and also by what we ignore or forget or neglect or simply are unwilling to do.

Techniques for exploring the middle future are important tools for helping us imagine, or "see," what we might be doing, or what we might be choosing. These techniques function for us the way headlights do for someone who is driving an automobile at night. They help us see where we will soon be going, so we can choose where to steer, to go faster or slower, or to stop and go by some better way.

Forecasting is a way of extending what has been happening into the future, to see where the present path will take us if nothing intervenes. *Scenarios* of the future usually start with a desired objective or goal and then attempt to find a path from now to that desired future. Scenarios arc like a spotlight into a night sky, in that what is illuminated is a portion (often called "an envelope") of the possible future. Forecasting tells us where we are likely to go, based on the past; scenarios tell us where we might go, if we choose to.

None of these methods prescribes a definite future or completely predicts a future. But like driving a car at night with the headlights turned on, they are better than no light at all.

Computer specialist Douglas Roberts says: "Your future won't announce itself with great fanfare. It is simply the continuous melding of today with tomorrow. It will occur over and over again. Its brightness is a matter of how much of what you do today is usable tomorrow." On a different note, Mostafa K. Tolba says: "The problems that overwhelm us today are precisely those we failed to solve decades ago."

See also APOCALYPTIC FUTURE; CHANGE, CULTURAL; CHANGE, EPOCHAL; CHANGE, PACE OF; CONTINUITY AND DISCONTINUITY; DYSTOPIAS; ECONOMIC CYCLES: MODELS AND SIMULATIONS; FORECASTING METHODS; FUTURES CONCEPTS; FUTURISM; LAWS, EVOLUTION OF; MULTIFOLD TREND; SURVEYS.

BIBLIOGRAPHY

JOUVENEL, BERTRAND DE. *The Art of Conjecture*. New York: Basic Books, 1967.
MARTEL, LEON. *Mastering Change: The Key to Business Success*. New York: Simon & Schuster, 1986.
MERRIAM, JOHN E., and MAKOWER, JOEL. *Trend Watching: How the Media Create Trends and and How to Be the First to Uncover Them*. New York: AMACON/Tilden Press, 1988.
UNITED NATIONS. *Global Outlook 2000: An Economic, Social, and Environmental Perspective*. New York: United Nations, 1990.

David Dodson Gray

Futures Concepts

Futures concepts are among the primary "building blocks" of the futures field. They enhance the capacity to engage in futures work and to create structures of increasing sophistication such as theories, methodologies, and literature. In short, they provide a basis for futures discourse.

Futures concepts can be explored through a core knowledge base. Components of this core knowledge include:

- Language, concepts, and metaphors
- Theories, ideas, and images
- Literature and practitioners
- Organizations, institutions, and networks
- Methodologies, tools, and practices
- Social movements and innovations

Stereotyped accounts of the futures field throw these core elements out of focus and fail to portray the substantive work of practicing futurists. For example, "the future" has been intellectually miscast as an "empty space" rather than as a dynamic field of potentials interacting richly with the present. It also has been overly identified with prediction, forecasting, think tanks, and Western corporate, positivistic "futurology."

Pop futurists, such as John NAISBITT and Alvin and Heidi TOFFLER, achieved widespread attention with concepts such as "megatrends" and "future shock." Futures scholars, however, tend to be critical of the pop futurist perspective, arguing that it takes existing social relations as a given constant, is ideologically naive, provides unconscious support for the status quo, and places undue emphasis on the superficial aspects of technology and science. Much visually compelling but often spurious, pseudo-futuristic imagery from film, television, and science fiction tends to be diversionary or ambiguous. Mass culture material of this sort can stimulate useful questions. On the whole, however, it fails to explore real alternatives or to describe more substantive matters.

Futures studies possesses a developing substantive knowledge base. It can be accessed, in part, through periodicals. Two of the leading journals are *Futures* (U.K.) and *Technological Forecasting and Social Change* (U.S.). These are complemented by *Futures Research Quarterly, Future Survey, The Futurist* (published by the World Future Society), and *21C* (Australia). Others include the *Future Generations Journal* (Malta) and *Social Inventions* (London).

Many publications are put out by futures organizations such as the World Future Society (WFS) based in Washington, and the World Futures Studies Federation (WFSF) with its secretariat located in Brisbane, Australia. The former is the largest such organization in the world. It hosts some fine, well-attended conferences, but it tends to be popular, noncritical, and corporatist in outlook. The much smaller WFSF with about 500 members, is more facilitative, culturally critical, and genuinely international in outlook.

A range of institutions and organizations cluster around the core. They include the Institute for Futures Studies (Stockholm), the Club of Rome (Italy), the Network on Responsibilities to Future Generations (Malta), the Secretariat for Futures Studies (Germany), the Institute for Social Inventions (London), the Robert Jungk Futures Library (Salzburg), and Australia's Commission for the Future (Melbourne). There are a hundred or more of these organizations worldwide. Some are underfunded and understaffed. By pioneering "institutions of foresight" they provide a valuable seedbed for innovation. Overlapping these near-core units is a diverse range of futures-related organizations including private consultancies and other nongovernmental organizations, government bodies, and other international groups. Together these institutions constitute a powerful force for innovation, constructive change, and a means of responding to the challenges of the future.

At the core of applied futures work is methodology. Theodore J. Gordon's summary of forecasting methods follows:

TABLE 1.   An Outline of Forecasting Methods

	Normative	*Exploratory*

Quantitative	Scenarios
	Technology sequence analysis
		Scenarios
		Time series
		Regression analysis
		Multiple-equation models
		Probabilistic models
		  • Trend impact
		  • Cross impact
		  • Interax
		Nonlinear models

Qualitative	Scenarios Delphi In-depth interviews Expert groups Genius Science fiction	Scenarios Delphi In-depth interviews Expert groups Genius

Source: Gordon, 1992.

Martha J. Garret (1993) describes the elements and methods of futures study in terms of a number of categories, or steps: limiting the scope of a particular study; gathering information; determining key variables; examining the past and the present; identifying the actors; choosing the assumptions; constructing scenarios; evaluating choices; and selecting strategies and tactics. Other practitioners have developed a variety of sequenced steps or methodologies that incorporate these and other elements—for example, Michel Godet's *Prospective*, Joseph Coates's *Issues and Management*, and the QUEST technique pioneered by Burt Nanus and Selwyn Enzer. Overall, there are at least three distinct futures traditions: (1) the empirical/analytic tradition, as exemplified by the writings of Herman KAHN and Julian Simon, which is positivist, corporate in nature, and primarily North American in origin and orientation; (2) the critical-interpretative tradition, exemplified by Bertrand de JOUVENEL and Robert Jungk, which can be characterized as comparative, critical, and unaligned, and is primarily European in origin; and (3) the activist-visionary tradition, exemplified by Elise Boulding and Joanna Macy, which is characterized as applied, facilitative, and universal. Although these traditions are quite distinct, they are not completely separate.

In addition, differences of method and approach can be clarified by recognizing distinct levels of futures work: pop futurism, problem-focused futures study, critical futures study, and epistemological futures study.

Pop futurism identifies problems and seeks to explore solutions at an empirical or taken-for-granted level. It overlooks the central role of worldview assumptions and cultural editing. Prime examples include *The Limits to Growth* (Dennis Meadows et al., 1972) and *Engines of Creation* (Eric Drexler, 1986).

Critical futures study involves the comparative analysis of assumptions, presuppositions, and paradigms. It actively considers the influence of different cultural orientations and traditions of enquiry—for example, *Paradigms in Progress* (Hazel Henderson, 1991) and *Global Mind Change* (Willis Harman, 1988).

Epistemological futures study locates and describes sources of "problems" in worldviews and ways of knowing; it sees "solutions" as arising from deep-seated and unpredictable shifts at this level and reveals the deepest sources of cultural innovation and adaptability—for example, *The Reenchantment of the World* (Morris Berman, 1981) and *Eye to Eye: The Quest for the New Paradigm* (Ken Wilber, 1990).

Progression though this tier escalates in sophistication as problems and methods become increasingly challenging. At the same time the ability to grasp and understand deeply embedded cultural and futures concerns is progressively enhanced by increasingly elaborate methods. From this it may be surmised that the "best" futures work and the most productive futures concepts are structurally simple, yet both are capable of substantial elaboration and deepening, according to capacity and need. Most futures studies are likely to draw on more than one level of futures methodology.

See also FUTURE STUDIES; FUTURES EDUCATION; FUTURISM; FUTURISTS; POPULARIZED FUTURES; PSEUDO-FUTURISTS; SCENARIOS; SCIENCE FICTION.

BIBLIOGRAPHY

COATES, JOSEPH F. *Issues Management*. Washington, DC: Lomond, 1986.
GARRETT, MARTHA J. "A Way Through the Maze: What Futurists Do and How They Do It." *Futures* 25/3 (1993): 254–274.
GODET, MICHEL. *From Anticipation to Action*. Paris: UNESCO, 1993.
GORDON, THEODORE J. "The Methods of Futures Research." *Annals* (AAPSS) 522 (1992): 25–35.
HENDERSON, HAZEL. "Social Innovation and Citizen Movements." *Futures* 25/3 (1993): 339–347.
NANUS, BURT. "QUEST—Quick Environmental Scanning Technique." *Long-Range Planning* 15/2 (1982): 39–45.
SLAUGHTER, RICHARD A. *Futures Concepts and Powerful Ideas*. Melbourne: Futures Study Centre, 1991. Revised and expanded, 1995.

Richard A. Slaughter

Futures Education

The fundamental objective of "futures studies" or "future-oriented education" is to gain an awareness of probable and possible future perils, problems, and promises resulting from scientific and technological innovations and their myriad effects upon the global environment, life in general, and humanity. Such studies serve not only to enlighten but also to stimulate timely action to meet the challenges or opportunities that confront humanity.

Futures studies by their nature are interdisciplinary in that they often transcend traditional academic boundaries and avoid narrow specializations. Instead, they concentrate on complex, interrelated phenomena affecting the natural environment, demography, society, economy, politics, and religion.

Futures studies are especially important today as the environmental toll of the worldwide spread of industrial civilization is coming due. The Industrial Revolution improved the living conditions of vast numbers of people, but by the mid-twentieth century it became increasingly clear that a high—but heretofore overlooked—price was being paid for material progress. All too frequently that price was not recognized or regarded with sufficient seriousness. This shortsightedness stemmed more from ignorance or difficulties of calculation than from malice.

High-tech civilization is characterized by ever more ingenious innovations, expanding new fields of scientific exploration, and achievement with expectations of more marvels to come. In the aftermath of these advances there is a growing apprehension about the planet's ecological future.

At present, the power in human hands is awesome and truly unique. The ability to cause widespread or permanent destruction is now being coupled with the capacity to play the role of gods in creating or refashioning life on this planet through biotechnology and genetic engineering. Such unprecedented developments suggest the genuine need for and the wisdom of developing a serious, sustained interest in the future.

The advent of the twenty-first century is being marked by worldwide attempts to conceptualize the likely positive and negative effects of scientific and technological trends and developments. In this context, futures studies can perform a vital role by providing early warning of serious problems ahead and casting new light on today's problems. Other useful functions involve technological forecasting and the creation of imaginative scenarios depicting alternative futures. These studies serve yet another valuable function in providing "self-negating forecasts." These forecasts have considerable social utility in that they elicit positive action to thwart the forecast made and thereby invalidate it.

Growing numbers of educators in the highly developed as well as developing nations recognize the important role such studies play in preparing people for their own future, that of their country, and that of future generations. This situation has given rise to the growth of future-oriented courses and programs worldwide, especially in the Western world, on the Indian subcontinent, and in East Asia.

Following numerous national, regional, and global futurist meetings over several years, the need for improving currently offered courses in futures studies was discussed, and guidance in the development of new courses and programs was sought. In late 1990, following the initial efforts of Michael Marien, editor of *Future Survey*, and Allen Tough, professor of futures studies at the Ontario Institute for Studies in Education, the Prep 21 Project was inaugurated to encourage future-oriented studies in universities and colleges, as well as in secondary schools, worldwide. A core curriculum of courses, it was felt, could help educators to prepare for the challenges and opportunities ahead.

Worldwide examples of futurist courses of study have been gathered together and presented in the *Prep 21 Course/Program Guide*. This selection of future-oriented programs, many of them oriented to higher education, could be modified for use at the secondary level. The Future Problem Solving Program may not constitute futures studies as conceived by many futurists, but it possesses features that most futurists may wish to emulate. An estimated 200,000 students nationally and internationally use the program materials, which cover students from kindergarden through twelfth grade.

A descriptive brochure provides an overview of the educational program:

> The Future Problem Solving Program is a year-long program in which teams of four students use a six-step problem solving process to deal with complex scientific and social problems of the future. At regular intervals throughout the year, the teams mail their work to evaluators, who review it and return it with their suggestions for improvement. As the year progresses, the teams become increasingly more proficient in problem solving. The Future Problem Solving Program takes students beyond memorization. The program challenges students to apply information they have learned to some of the most complex issues facing society. They are asked to *think*, to make decisions, and, in some instances, to carry out their solutions.

Though the challenges before humanity are complex, difficult, and all too frequently may appear daunting, there is cause for tempered optimism. If we are able to enlist the creative imagination, energy, and dedication of the world's students, we have every reason to face the future with confidence. An education which incorporates future-oriented studies may facilitate the achievement of this end.

See also FUTURE STUDIES; FUTURISM.

BIBLIOGRAPHY

CORNISH, EDWARD. *The Study of the Future: An Introduction to the Art and Science of Understanding and*

Shaping Tomorrow's World. Washington, DC: World Future Society, 1977.

DIDSBURY, JR., HOWARD F. *Prep 21 Course/Program Guide. A Selection of Future-Oriented Courses/Programs.* Bethesda, MD: World Future Society, 1994.

JENNINGS, LANE, ed. *The Futures Research Directory: Organizations and Periodicals, 1993–1994.* Bethesda, MD: World Future Society, 1993.

KLARE, MICHAEL T., ed. *Peace and World Security Studies: A Curriculum Guide*, 6th ed. Boulder, CO: n.p., 1994.

World Future Society Project Staff. *The Futures Research Directory: Individuals, 1991–1992.* Bethesda, MD: World Future Society, 1991.

Howard F. Didsbury, Jr.

Future Studies

Future studies lacks a shared understanding of what it is and a shared vision of what it ought to be. The collective study of the future also is known as "futures studies," to emphasize alternative futures. Some term the enterprise futurology. The terms *futurology* or *futurologist*, which suggest some sort of rigorous science, may be overreaching. Future studies has little to do with science fiction, and science fiction authors have made only modest contributions to nonfictional futures thinking. Future studies, at its best, draws from the natural and social sciences.

Some contend that future studies is a field of study or even a discipline. Little evidence is given to support this wishful assertion. In time, the embryonic enterprise of future studies may develop into something resembling an academic field of study or a discipline.

Futures studies may be conceived as a very fuzzy "multifield," or the key integrative core that enables a broad and long-term approach to human understanding. The fuzzy core entity approach derives from looking at the people involved, the topics considered, and the methods used. *Future Survey* (1979–1994) lists 13,000 abstracts of futures-relevant books, reports, and articles; and the two volumes of the *Futures Research Directory* assemble information on 1,172 individuals, 187 organizations, and 124 periodicals. Both the abstracts and the directories identify something less than half of only the English language part of future studies worldwide.

Who Is a Futurist?

There are no set qualifications for someone to be a "futurist." Some call themselves forecasters, trend-watchers, planners, policy analysts, social critics, environmentalists, and so on. Others call themselves futurists, but as a secondary identity thereby retaining their primary identity as a sociologist, consultant, or other professional practitioner. In a 1993 survey only 25 percent identified themselves primarily as futurists, with another 43 percent calling themselves secondarily futurists. The most popular primary identity, indicated by 34 percent of respondents, was as "planners."

Very roughly, about one-quarter of the literature cited in *Future Survey* was written by people who call themselves futurists, primarily or secondarily. Another quarter of the literature—writing that is equally broad and long-term—is published by non-avowed futurists. Roughly half of the literature is written by obvious specialists, albeit "futurized specialists" who are experts in thinking somewhat broadly about the future of their field.

What Does a Futurist Think About?

Statements about what a futurist ought to think about often suggest an informed generalist who can wisely prognosticate about a wide variety of matters. A few futurists approach this ideal, but the vast majority of necessity specialize in one or a few sectors.

Richard Slaughter has recently proposed twenty key concepts (such as sustainability, the metaproblem, choices, and so forth) that *ideally* should be shared by practitioners in the "futures field." A 1989 study by Joseph F. Coates and Jennifer Jarratt covering seventeen aging male futurists (all but one of them American) revealed a surprising diversity of views.

The index in this encyclopedia or the table of contents in *Future Survey Annual* indicates the diversity of "future studies." The fourteen major *FS* categories include: World Futures, the Global Economy, World Regions and Nations, Defense and Disarmament, Sustainability (added in 1993), Environmental Issues, Food and Agriculture, Society and Politics (including Crime, previously a separate category), the Economy and Cities (including Work, previously separate), Health, Education, Communications, Science and Technology, and Methods to Shape the Future.

Futurists think broadly about global issues (or the global aspects of domestic issues), acknowledge the imperatives of sustainability, think about new technologies, consider alternative futures (both possible and preferable), and stress the complexity of a dynamic world.

Four distinct "cultures" of futures studies have emerged in recent years: Science and Technology Futurists (including those who focus on the emerging information society), holding a long-term and optimistic view; Business Futurists (including people in business, consultants, and business school professors), with a short-term and optimistic view; Social Issue Futurists (including those who specialize in education, health, families, cities, or work), with a short-term and pessimistic view; and Green Futurists (including environmentalists and those who advocate a sustainable world, who often hold a long-term and pessimistic view.

How Does a Futurist Think?

Popular myths about futurists associate them with crystal balls, and predictions of what will happen. Futurists think and write in a variety of styles, ranging from lightly popular to impenetrable academic language.

Many futurists believe that the primary activity of future studies is forecasting, or thinking about the most probable future, involving computers and quantifying methods, such as Delphi, cross-impact matrices, and complex models. The Delphi technique, presumably a key method of future studies, is expensive to employ and subject to much abuse. Moreover, there is no batting average for futurists in anticipating various developments.

In an increasingly uncertain world that nevertheless needs some forward-thinking as guidance, there is a movement away from forecasting the most probable future to sketching scenarios of possible futures (e.g., the best possible, best probable, worst probable, and worst possible). In an increasingly complex world, the emphasis shifts from long-term futures to short-term futures and trying to make sense of present trends. With the growing concern for ethics, there is a trend away from passive forecasting of probable and possible futures to advocating preferable futures—what we should do.

Sound thinking about the future involves three obvious "P's": studying the probable, the possible, and the preferable; and, there are three less obvious "P's": studying the present (including recent changes and new ways to think about our condition), studying the past (especially our historical anticipations and how they turned out), and encouraging the panoramic (promoting integration, overviews, systems thinking, and wide-angled views).

Futurists do not predict so much as they portray what is probable, possible, and preferable. Furthermore, when well executed, the present, the past,

and the panoramic are properly addressed. Developing such perspectives is a demanding task. There are many imperfect efforts.

Recent Trends and Possible Futures

People everywhere will always think about the future, in one way or another. As suggested in the introduction to this encyclopedia by Alvin and Heidi TOFFLER, everyone is a futurist.

There is no common background for professional futurists. Only a handful of academic courses and programs in the field of future studies per se are currently available. There are, however, many courses and programs in related subject areas, such as environmental studies, peace studies, science and technology studies, and so on.

Since the early 1980s, there has been a proliferation of futures-relevant magazines, journals, and especially newsletters. The number of new futures-relevant books has remained about the same in recent times.

Currently, the need is greater than ever for some sort of specialty in broad and long-term thinking about human affairs—for "horizontal" thinkers who can integrate the many ideas of the more conventional "vertical" thinkers who are constrained by the boundaries of their traditional disciplines and professions.

There have been several futurist movements throughout American history, and perhaps elsewhere in the world. Edward Bellamy's "nationalist movement" in the 1890s was widely acclaimed. Another future studies movement may well arise, perhaps precipitated by the magic of the millennial year 2000. On the other hand, it may already be under way, building on the widespread interest in sustainability.

See also FUTURES CONCEPTS; FUTURES EDUCATION; FUTURISM; FUTURISTS.

BIBLIOGRAPHY
COATES, JOSEPH F., and JARRATT, JENNIFER. *What Futurists Believe.* Mt. Airy, MD: Lomond Publications; Bethesda, MD: World Future Society, 1989.
KERR, CLARK. *Higher Education Cannot Escape History: Issues for the Twenty-first Century.* Albany, NY: State University of New York Press, 1994.
MARIEN, MICHAEL, ed. *Future Survey Annual, 1995.* Bethesda, MD: World Future Society, 1995.
MASINI, ELEONORA BARBIERI. *Why Futures Studies?* London: Grey Seal Books, 1993.
SLAUGHTER, RICHARD, ed. "The Knowledge Base of Futures Studies." *Futures* 25/3 (1993): 227–274.

Michael Marien

Futurism

In common parlance, the term *futurism* refers either to a belief that human life will be fulfilled in some future epoch or to a movement in the fine arts that repudiates the heritage of the past. In recent decades, it has also become more or less synonymous with the study of possible, preferable, and probable futures. A *futurist*, by the same token, is defined as a practitioner of futures inquiry.

Men and women have tried to foresee the future throughout history. In premodern times, their principal method was divination—the interpretation by priests or oracles of portents in nature, from the movements of the stars (astrology) to the entrails of sacrificial animals (haruspication). In the Jewish tradition, the role of the diviner was played by the divinely inspired prophet, and in the Christian tradition, by the apostles and fathers of the early church. Several books of the Jewish Bible, such as *Jeremiah* and *Daniel*, and the last book of the Christian New Testament, *The Revelation of St. John*, are explicitly futurist texts (*see* JOHN THE DIVINE). Together with a few seminal works by churchmen, notably St. Augustine's *City of God*, these texts shaped serious thought about the future throughout medieval and early modern times.

In the late eighteenth century, a purely secular vision of the future arose, based in good measure on readings of the advancement of mathematics and the natural sciences. Thinkers such as the Marquis de Condorcet argued that the progress of the human mind in the modern era would usher in a golden age of world peace, prosperity, and equality. In the nineteenth century, belief in the general, virtually inevitable progress of humankind became a dogma of social science, as illustrated by the influential treatises of the founders of sociology, Auguste Comte in France and Herbert Spencer in Great Britain. Karl Marx anticipated the future worldwide triumph of socialism on the basis of a reputedly scientific analysis of socioeconomic history. By the second half of the nineteenth century, science had largely replaced magic and divine revelation as the way to fathom the future.

Futurism in the twentieth century continues to be dominated by the conviction that methodologies borrowed from mathematics and the natural and social sciences can yield knowledge of future times. Few practitioners, however, still believe that the future—and in particular the long-term future—can be "predicted" with deadly accuracy. As Edward CORNISH has written, "The study of the future is, strictly speaking, the study of ideas about the future." No one can predict the future, because to some indefinable extent, it is a time that living men and women will shape by their free decisions in the here and now. In effect, futurist inquiry has become the study of possibilities that are plausible in terms of present-day knowledge and theory.

The genesis of contemporary futurism can be traced to the beginning of the twentieth century, when many social scientists and others tried to imagine what life would be like in the new century. The most durable of these efforts was *Anticipations of the Reaction of Mechanical and Scientific Progress upon Human Life and Thought*, written in 1901 and published as a book the following year by the English novelist and social philosopher H. G. WELLS. In 1902 Wells also delivered a lecture, "The Discovery of the Future," in which he called for the founding of a systematic science of the future.

Over the next forty-four years, until his death in 1946, Wells published dozens of prophetic books that made skillful application of his talents as a science writer, historian, and sociologist. The author of *The Time Machine*, *The War of the Worlds*, and *The First Men in the Moon*, he was also one of the founders of modern science fiction, which has made a significant contribution to futurist speculation in this century. As a general rule, what minds can conceive almost always can be created, given the necessary resources and time. In 1914, in his novel *The World Set Free*, Wells foresaw in remarkably prescient detail the coming of the nuclear power industry and the invention and use in warfare of the atomic bomb.

Wells's appeal to establish a science of the future was not answered during his lifetime. But he helped keep futurism alive, as did various thinkers and writers in the generation that followed his. Systematic efforts to probe the future were made during the early and middle decades of the century by several renowned thinkers, including the historians Oswald SPENGLER and Arnold J. Toynbee, who utilized a cyclical theory of comparative world history to forecast the decline and fall of Western civilization, and the Jesuit anthropologist and philosopher Pierre Teilhard de Chardin, who combined insights from science and religion to outline the future societal and spiritual evolution of humankind.

Futures studies as a self-conscious movement of thought and research did not crystallize, however, until the 1960s. A confluence of trends made this possible. These included the urgent need of ever-expanding government departments and multinational corporations for long-range planning, advances in economic and technological forecasting, progress in the policy sciences, and the erosion of disciplinary boundaries in academic life, making it increasingly possible for social and natural scientists and even humanists to work together on common tasks. Associations of futurists such as the World Future Society (founded in 1966 in Washington), the Association Internationale Futuribles (founded in 1967 in Paris), and the Club of Rome (founded in 1968), gave wide publicity to the futures movement.

Soon, hundreds of researchers in various fields who had known little or nothing of one another's work began to interact. Two defining moments in the rise of contemporary futurism were the publication of *Future Shock* by Alvin TOFFLER in 1970 and of *The Limits to Growth* by Donella H. Meadows and associates under the sponsorship of the Club of Rome in 1972. Both books became bestsellers, helping to make the study of the future a matter of broad public as well as scholarly interest. At about the same time, many colleges and universities started to offer courses and interdisciplinary programs in futures studies, especially in the United States. The 1970s were a particularly rich decade for futurism, as major books appeared from such luminaries as Daniel BELL, Herman KAHN, and E. F. Schumacher. Modest growth continued in the 1980s and '90s, in Asia, Africa, and Latin America as well as in North America and Europe.

The methods used by futurists today range from the abstruse, highly technical procedures of econometric forecasters to intuitive speculation by specialists in the psychospiritual future. At least five methodologies are especially popular: trend extrapolation, mathematical modeling, the Delphi technique for pooling expert opinion, scenario building (which may include the more serious sorts of science fiction), and "probabilistic" techniques (e.g., trend-impact and cross-impact analysis). Some futurists outside the mainstream also continue to show interest in the insights of Marxian analysis. Others find stimulus in holistic philosophies grounded in ecological thought and contemporary revivals of traditional religious belief.

The challenge for futurists in the twenty-first century is to develop an integrative methodology that can fuse some or many of these approaches and create what H. G. Wells hoped for in his pathbreaking 1902 lecture—an authentic science of futures inquiry.

See also DYSTOPIAS; FORECASTING METHODS; FUTURE STUDIES; FUTURES CONCEPTS; FUTURES EDUCATION; FUTURISTS; POPULARIZED FUTURES; PSEUDO-FUTURISTS; SCENARIOS; SCIENCE FICTION; UTOPIAS.

BIBLIOGRAPHY

CLARKE, I. F. *The Pattern of Expectation, 1644–2001.* New York: Basic Books, 1979.

GORDON, THEODORE J. "The Methods of Futures Research." *The Annals of the American Academy of Political and Social Science* 522 (1992): 25–35.

HELMER, OLAF. *Looking Forward: A Guide to Futures Research.* Beverly Hills, CA: Sage Publications, 1983.

HUGHES, BARRY B. *World Futures: A Critical Analysis of Alternatives.* Baltimore: Johns Hopkins University Press, 1985.

POLAK, FREDERIK L. *The Image of the Future.* New York: Oceana Publications, 1961.

WAGAR, W. WARREN. *The Next Three Futures: Paradigms of Things to Come.* Westport, CT: Greenwood Press, 1991.

W. Warren Wagar

Futurists

Futurists are people who have a special interest in what may happen in the years ahead and think seriously about what lies beyond the short-term perspective. However, they generally pay little attention to possible developments more than fifty years ahead, which may lie largely beyond the realm of plausible speculation.

Futurists are especially concerned about the impact on the future of what is done in the present. Typically, they focus on the next five to twenty-five years, which are clearly being shaped by current trends in society and technology.

Futurists use rational or scientific methods to understand alternative futures. They do not use the mystical or supernatural means employed by fortune-tellers, seers, palmists, astrologers, and clairvoyants, who claim to foretell future events. A main point in thinking about the future is to change it—to make it better than it would be without deliberate choices and actions. Futurists believe that people shape their own futures by what they choose to do. The futurists' view is that the future is shaped by man, rather than ordained by fate.

The idea that societies change began to be considered seriously in the early seventeenth century, when Francis Bacon argued that advancing knowledge could and should be used to improve the human condition. Bacon's disciples became outspoken prophets for this idea of social progress.

Scholars, such as the Marquis de Condorcet, began to think seriously about what the future would be like as a result of continuing progress. Condorcet's book *A Sketch for a Historical Portrait of the Progress of the Human Mind* offered remarkably accurate forecasts, such as the end of slavery, the political independence of the European colonies in America, and the spread of birth control.

Belief in progress became the conventional wisdom of the nineteenth century. The steady appearance of exciting inventions like railroads and electric lights seemed to prove that the future would bring worldwide abundance and happiness. Social change seemed so positive and continuous that H. G. WELLS proposed, in 1902, the establishment of a "science of the future," so that people could know in advance about the good things to come.

Optimistic confidence in the future fell victim to the horrors of World War I. Progress, it seemed, was not inevitable; on the contrary, the future now seemed nightmarish. Even when progress appeared benign, it held hidden dangers: faster transportation destroyed local communities; the increased production of goods threw people out of their jobs.

After World War II, with its death camps and atomic bombs, pessimism about the future replaced the optimism of the pre–World War I period. The French experience as an occupied nation during World War II produced a powerful philosophical movement, existentialism, which emphasized deliberate human choice as the prime force determining the future. The future is undetermined, argued Jean-Paul Sartre, and therefore must be invented. And if individuals choose their future, so must nations: the new French regime embarked on a series of national plans to shape the nation's destiny. The planners immediately wanted to know what assumptions could be made about the future as a basis for their plans, so they called upon the nation's intellectuals. One who responded to the call was the economist-philosopher Bertrand de JOUVENEL. With Ford Foundation support, his Futuribles group published an influential series of books and papers dealing with the future of France and the world. The most important book, *The Art of Conjecture* (1964), laid down basic principles for intelligently thinking about the future.

U.S. military planners had also been seeking ways to meet the many contingencies posed by the nuclear era. The Air Force created the Rand Corporation, where scholars were paid to think and write about future possibilities, such as new technologies that might be developed and alternative strategies for dealing with foreign nations.

The Rand scholars often found themselves relying on nothing more than people's opinions, an unorthodox methodology that raised eyebrows among many scientists. In justification, Rand mathematician Olaf Helmer and philosopher Nicholas Rescher wrote an influential 1959 paper, "The Epistemology of the Inexact Sciences," which argued that in fields that have not developed to the point of having scientific laws, the testimony of experts provided a useful guide. The paper provided a general rationale for a science of forecasting and specific support for the Delphi method, a technique of getting expert opinions and combining them in ways that avoided follow-the-leader and other tendencies that distort group decision making.

Helmer left Rand in 1968 to head the new Institute for the Future, which has produced numerous papers, reports, and books applying Delphi and other techniques to the study of future possibilities. In 1971, Theodore J. Gordon, a technology-oriented analyst, departed with two colleagues to found the Futures Group, a profit-making research organization emphasizing proprietary research.

Meanwhile, the Hudson Institute, founded by another Rand researcher, physicist Herman KAHN, had become a major center of future-oriented research. Kahn gained notoriety as the author of *On Thermonuclear War* (1961), which described how thermonuclear wars could be fought and even won. In 1967, he and Hudson colleague Anthony J. Wiener published *The Year 2000: A Framework for Speculation on the Next Thirty-three Years* (1967), a book that impressed scholars with its many charts, graphs, and tables.

These new future-oriented institutions and scholarly studies convinced many knowledgeable people that it is possible to think rationally and intelligently about the future. When the World Future Society was founded in 1966, as an association for futurists, it soon enlisted thousands of members, many of whom were well-known and respected scientists, scholars, and public leaders

Since the 1960s, future-oriented governmental agencies have appeared in many nations and at many levels of government. Typically, such agencies prepare a series of reports and disband, having fulfilled their mandate. Permanent bodies also have been established such as the U.S. Office of Technology Assessment, which became operational in 1974. Sweden's Secretariat for Future Studies, established in 1974, was the first high-level governmental office of its kind (it has since closed down).

Business corporations regularly hire futurists to advise them on possible future developments, and numerous colleges and universities offer courses on the future. The University of Houston at Clear Lake City, for example, has developed a future-studies program leading to a master's degree, and many of its graduates have gone on to find employment as consultants in business and government.

Futurists are still popularly thought of as trying to predict the future—and are sometimes scorned for failing to do so. However, futurists have gained increasing respect in recent decades. Top business and government leaders often speak at meetings of the World Future Society. President Ronald Reagan honored futurists with a special luncheon in the White House in 1985. Senator Albert Gore, a committed futurist and regular participant in World Future Society conferences, was elected as vice president of the United States in 1992. Newt Gingrich, another long-time futurist, became speaker of the U.S. House of Representatives in 1995, and many of its graduates have gone on to find employment as consultants in business and government.

See also FUTURE STUDIES; FUTURES CONCEPTS; FUTURES EDUCATION; FUTURISM; PSEUDO-FUTURISTS.

BIBLIOGRAPHY

COATES, JOSEPH, and JARRATT, JENNIFER. *What Futurists Believe.* Bethesda, MD, 1989.

CORNISH, EDWARD J. *The Study of the Future: An Introduction to the Art and Science of Understanding and Shaping Tomorrow's World.* Bethesda, MD: World Future Society, 1977.

DE JOUVENEL, BERTRAND. *The Art of Conjecture.* New York: Basic Books, 1967.

KAHN, HERMAN, and WIENER, ANTHONY J. *The Year 2000: A Framework for Speculation on the Next Thirty-three Years.* New York: Macmillan, 1967.

NANUS, BURT. *Visionary Leadership.* San Francisco: Jossey-Bass, 1992.

Edward S. Cornish

G

Gambling

The United States is experiencing an unprecedented boom in commercial gambling. The casino business is the fastest growing segment of the entertainment industry. There are compelling reasons to expect that casinos, and to a lesser extent lotteries, will continue to proliferate well into the twenty-first century. Psychological, social, and political forces suggest why commercial gambling will thrive in the next two decades.

Games of chance offering prizes have been part of human culture for over 4,000 years, and part of American culture since colonial times. Early settlers in Jamestown sold lottery tickets to pay for their passages from Europe. The Continental Congress in 1776 funded the revolutionary army from the sale of lottery tickets—George Washington purchased the first ticket. Nineteenth-century frontier gambling saloons and riverboat gambling halls are legendary in American history.

In 1993, Americans wagered more than $394 billion on legal gambling enterprises; casinos, lotteries, and pari-mutuel wagering accounted for about 90 percent of the total. Some believe that gambling meets a human need to choose and control one's exposure to risk, while others say gambling is an escape from a humdrum daily existence. Still others assert that people gamble only to win prizes.

The stigma that until recently surrounded gambling behavior has faded. Gambling is now less frequently viewed as a sin or vice, and more frequently as legitimate adult recreation and entertainment activity. A 1994 national survey showed that acceptance of casino gambling—"casino gaming," in today's nomenclature—in the United States now stands at 92 percent, with 59 percent declaring gaming perfectly acceptable for anyone, and 33 percent saying it is acceptable for others, but not themselves.

Casino Gaming

In the United States, the growth of casino gaming will far outpace growth in lotteries and pari-mutuel betting. The number of states permitting casino gaming grew from only two—Nevada and New Jersey—in 1988 to 24 in 1994. There are four kinds of casinos:

- Traditional land-based casinos, like the unlimited stakes casinos in Nevada and New Jersey
- Limited stakes casinos, like those in historic towns in South Dakota and Colorado
- Riverboat and dockside casinos, like those in Illinois and Mississippi
- Tribal casinos owned by American Indian tribes in more than a dozen states, operated under federal law and agreements with state governments

Casino gaming will proliferate during the next decade because

- casinos create jobs and increase tax revenues. Recession and voter resistance to new taxes have stretched thin the budgets of state and

371

local governments, while taxes on casino revenue continue to be more palatable politically than other taxes.

- casinos satisfy the recreational needs of a broad segment of the public. Research shows why people enjoy casinos: First, they provide social environments, where customers share laughter and companionship with other customers and the casino staff. Second, they provide a participatory entertainment experience, whose pace is customer-controlled. And third, they provide competition and a chance to win.
- new casino jurisdictions will demonstrate that the old myths about casino gaming are untrue. Casino gaming neither preys upon the poor nor brings crime, vice, or moral decay. Tomorrow's casino industry will continue to be among the most tightly regulated businesses in America.

Technological advances, some predict, will soon render casinos obsolete. Why visit a casino when you can adopt the persona of, say, Mark Twain and link via the electronic highway to a "virtual" casino filled with similarly colorful characters? Game manufacturers have already taken some first steps: a multiplayer blackjack game with a video-based "dealer" is now available. The technical prowess of future computer wizards, however, cannot displace the personal and social aspects of the casino experience: games of bluff and counter-bluff between stoic "poker-faced" customers; squeals of unbridled delight from the successful slot machine player; and the sympathetic smiles and subtle compassion of dealers whose loyal customers have lost a few hands in a row. The social interactions and the total casino entertainment are among the primary draws to many casino patrons.

The table below summarizes the future of the casino industry in the United States. Rapid growth in riverboat and tribal casino jurisdiction is likely, especially during the mid-1990s. Legalization of full land-based casinos will accelerate after mid-

decade. By 2002, more than two-thirds of the nation's population will live in states with some form of legalized casino gaming. Casinos will be just another choice for adults planning an afternoon or evening's entertainment, and no more expensive than attending a professional football game or a theatrical performance.

Pari-Mutuel Wagering

Legal pari-mutuel wagering—in which bettors wager against each other, as opposed to against "the house"—on races involving horses and dogs took place in thirty-seven states during 1993. Intertrack wagering, off-track wagering, and home-based wagering will expand the distribution of betting locations, but the total amount wagered on pari-mutuel events (horse racing, harness racing, and the like) will continue a slide that began in the 1970s. Pari-mutuel wagering lacks the broad appeal of casino entertainment, spectator sports, and feature films. Adults seeking entertainment are likely to perceive racetracks as places where nothing happens in the long gaps between races.

Off-track and home-based betting could consolidate the pari-mutuel industry, such that ultimately ten to fifteen major tracks would feed a nationwide network of off-track betting parlors and interactive television systems. This scenario is especially likely if smaller tracks find it more economical to stop live racing and become off-track betting facilities.

Another scenario features land-based casinos at pari-mutuel facilities, with some revenues from casino gaming distributed to live race purses. This could increase interest in betting on live races. It is unclear whether this development would be a temporary prop for the pari-mutuel industry or a key to its long-term viability. If they are to reverse their slump, they must attract a new generation of customers.

TABLE 1   Number of States Where Casinos Are/May Be Legal

Casino Type	1994	1998 (estimates)	2003 (estimates)
Riverboat Casinos	6	13	18
Limited Stakes Casinos	2	2	6
Indian Casinos	20	26	27
Traditional Land-Based Casinos	3	8	14

State Lotteries

State lotteries in 1994 operated in thirty-six states and may expand to forty-four states by 2003. Except in new lottery states, lottery revenue of late has been flat or declining. This trend will continue, with temporary jumps in overall lottery play when new states legalize, and stabilization as lotteries mature. About 90 percent of the American public now has access to lottery play. Combined with their inherently low entertainment value, the existing wide access means that overall levels of lottery play will not significantly increase even if lotteries proliferate.

State lotteries have recently begun operation of casino-like games. Video lotteries, which are essentially networks of electronic casino games (poker, blackjack, etc.) linked to a central computer, operate in six states. Video lottery machines are typically found in bars, lounges, and racetracks. Several states also offer keno-like games (keno is a fast-paced variation of lotto). Because video lotteries and keno share the fast action and high entertainment value of casino games, they have the potential for rapid growth.

Gambling and Society

Some people have difficulty controlling how much they gamble. Most of the casino industry and some lotteries now recognize compulsive gambling as a problem for a small percentage of customers and as a detriment to the industry's growth. Socially responsible casino companies are addressing problem gaming: providing funds for treatment and counseling and training employees to identify potential pathological gamblers and steer them to treatment. Socially responsible casino companies are also addressing the problem of underage gambling. How casinos and lotteries respond to the potential social implications of their proliferation will—and should—influence public acceptance of gambling as a form of entertainment and a source of economic growth and tax revenue during the twenty-first century.

In addition to legalized and regulated gambling, there will also likely be a continuation of illegal gambling, mainly involving betting on sports events. In the long term, casino gaming may be only one entertainment option in recreational complexes that will include virtual reality games/rides and other emerging forms of entertainment.

See also CRIME RATES; GAMES AND PASTIMES; INTERACTIVE ENTERTAINMENT; SOCIAL CONTROLS; SPORTS AND ACTIVITIES, SPECTATOR.

BIBLIOGRAPHY

ABT, VICKI; SMITH, JAMES F.; and CHRISTIANSEN, EUGENE M. *The Business of Risk: Commercial Gambling in Mainstream America.* Lawrence: University of Kansas Press, 1985.

CLOTFELTER, CHARLES, and COOK, PHILLIP. *Selling Hope: State Lotteries in America.* Cambridge, MA: Harvard University Press, 1989.

EADINGTON, WILLIAM R., and CORNELIUS, JUDY A., eds. *Gambling and Commercial Gaming: Essays in Business, Economics, Philosophy and Science.* Reno, NV: Institute for the Study of Gambling and Commercial Gaming, 1992.

HELM, MICHAEL. *A Breed Apart: The Horses and the Players.* New York: Henry Holt, 1991.

Philip G. Satre

Games.

See INTERACTIVE ENTERTAINMENT; SPORTS AND GAMES, COMPETITIVE.

Gas.

See INDUSTRIAL GASES; NATURAL GAS.

Genetic Engineering

The term *genetic engineering* refers to a body of techniques used to manipulate DNA (deoxyribonucleic acid) and its products, RNA (ribonucleic acid), and protein. By means of genetic engineering, genes can be isolated, purified, reproduced, and moved from one organism into another. This technique not only contributes to basic scientific research, it also provides procedures for changing the properties of microorganisms, plants, and animals. This ability to transfer genes, and with them specific characteristics, has raised a host of issues—ethical, social, legal, even philosophical. Can the genetic engineering of crops and livestock solve the economic problems of developing countries? Are there hidden dangers that require strict controls? Should experimental procedures be regulated? Should any limits be placed on how far scientists go in investigating the mechanisms of life? Should researchers be allowed to patent cloned genes? What are the ethics of applying these techniques to human beings?

Comprehension of genetic engineering depends on an understanding of DNA, RNA, protein, and the fundamental cell processes of replication and protein synthesis. The basic ideas follow:

- DNA consists of two parallel chains of molecules, called nucleotides or bases, linked together, like beads on a string. There are four nucleotides, A, G, C, and T, which stand respectively for adenine, guanine, cytosine, and thymine. A given sequence on one strand of DNA determines the opposite sequence on the other strand, by the mechanism of base-pairing. That is, A can only pair with T, and G can only pair with C. Thus, the two strands contain the same information. When a cell divides, the two strands separate, and each one then is a template for the formation of a new double helix identical to the original. This is the famous "double helix" model of DNA (see Figure 1).

- DNA is found in the chromosomes of every cell of every organism. Genes—the hereditary units—consist of sequences of nucleotides within these chromosomes. The order of these nucleotides is a "code" which contains the genetic information.

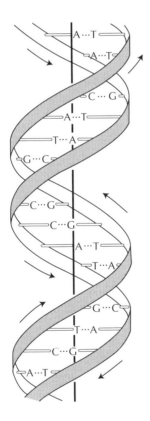

FIGURE 1.   Schematic drawing of the DNA double helix. The sugar-phosphate backbones run at the periphery of the helix in antiparallel orientation. Base-pairs (A—T and G—C) drawn symbolically as bars between chains are stacked along the center of the helix.

- The primary product of each gene is a protein. One gene is said to code for one protein, and when a gene is translated by the cellular machinery into a protein, it is said to be "expressed." This process is carried out or mediated through molecules of *messenger RNA*, short-lived copies of the genes that act as templates for the assembly of the amino acids that make up the protein.

The tools to move genes from one organism to another are referred to as *recombinant DNA technology*. The arts of animal husbandry and plant horticulture have for centuries manipulated the genetic material of organisms indirectly, by means of selection of visible traits. Recombinant DNA technology manipulates the genetic material directly. Theoretically, any gene from any organism may be moved into the genome—i.e., the set of genes—of any other organism. Thus, human genes have been moved into bacteria. Genes from insects have been spliced into the genome of tomatoes and have conferred upon tomatoes the ability to produce natural insecticides. Bacterial genes have been moved into plants. Human genes related to the onset of cancer have been successfully incorporated into yeast, thus providing a simplified biological system in which to study their function.

It is thought that genes control the characteristics of an organism, but this link is clear only in the simplest cases. For example, certain diseases are known to be caused by a defect in a single gene (sickle cell anemia, Tay-Sachs disease, Lesch-Nyhan syndrome). The immediate product of a gene is a protein—and to understand the function of this protein is often very difficult.

The first published example of genetic engineering was reported in a 1973 paper by Boyer, Cohen, Chang, and Helling. Since then, there have been countless other examples. The basic technique of artificial recombination is a patented procedure, licensed by Stanford University.

We now turn to some of the applications which are currently possible, keeping in mind that new ones are being designed literally every day.

Mass Production of Proteins

A common procedure is to turn bacteria into "factories" for a useful protein that is produced in nature only in very small amounts. For example, by isolating the gene for human insulin and inducing its expression in billions of bacteria, this protein, insulin, can be economically mass produced in the lab. The same technique is used to produce proteins of use to medicine, industry, or basic research, including growth hormones, somatostatin (a growth inhibitor), and interferon (a protein produced by the immune system).

Agriculture—Crop Improvement

Tomatoes have been genetically engineered to stay riper longer and to produce their own insecticide. Efforts are focused on producing plants that grow faster, have greater resistance to pests, are cheaper to grow, or are less dependent on water (and thus better able to resist drought). This can be accomplished by incorporating genes from a microorganism or an insect into a plant. Progress in these areas may be crucial to meeting the world's growing demand for food. The first genetically engineered vegetable became commercially available in 1994.

More Productive Livestock

Genetic engineering of the pituitary growth hormone has already produced "giant" mice, and the same technique may be applied to cattle. Researchers are developing methods for transferring genes to commercially capitalize upon important traits, such as milk yield. This is technically difficult because most of these traits are the result of several genes. Another area of exploration involves the creation of new vaccines to protect farm animals from disease.

Waste Management and Mining

Microbes are being designed to break down the waste products of various industries, including the livestock industry and the paper industry; to gobble up oil spills; and to extract minerals from the earth.

Transgenosis

Transgenic animals have been created and patented. These are animals that contain genes from other species. Moreover, these genes have been inserted at a very early stage of development and therefore are also in the sex cells of the animal. Thus, these genes are passed on to their offspring. In the future transgenic animals may be important sources of food and may serve as potent tools for medical and biological research.

Genetic Therapy

Some of the most exciting applications of DNA technology are in the diagnosis and treatment of genetic diseases. Prenatal diagnoses of certain hereditary diseases, using genetic probes extracted from a gene library, are available and becoming more common. Some of these diseases are hemophilia, growth hormone deficiency, and various blood diseases. Genetic therapy is still in a speculative stage, but the idea holds promise. If a disease can be localized to a single gene—and many devastating diseases can—then, if a healthy copy of that gene can be incorporated into the affected cells, the disease could be cured. Now there are viruses—called retroviruses—which stitch themselves into the genome of their host. If such a virus could be stripped of all the "bad" DNA and replaced with the gene of interest, then this gene could be carried into the appropriate target tissues of the patient. Although there are several technical difficulties, such procedures are beginning to be worked out for people who are gravely ill and have no other recourse. It is too soon to know if there are any success stories, but this field is likely to develop very fast.

Even if an individual could be thus cured, his or her children would still be susceptible to the disease. This problem suggests a logical extension of these ideas to the concept of *germ-line therapy*. This would involve the creation of "transgenic" humans—in which the germ line itself had been modified, thus making the change heritable—essentially a change to the species itself. This is very controversial, because any hidden, secondary effects would affect all future generations. At this point, there are no plans to attempt this kind of procedure.

The initial reaction of some scientists to the news that it was possible to move genes among or between organisms was one of alarm. In February 1975, a group of molecular biologists organized a now famous conference in Asilomar, Calif., at which recombination experiments were classified according to risks, containment procedures were recommended, and it was urged that certain experiments be indefinitely deferred. Although some scientists now believe that the Asilomar conference was unnecessary, the episode shows that it is natural even for professionals to react with a certain amount of awe to the development of techniques that allow for the creation of forms of life that could not have been reproduced by nature.

Along with great hopes, these powerful new techniques for experimenting with life-forms have generated fears of three basic types:

1. A dangerous new virus or bacterium might be created and released into the environment. For

instance, when researchers splice a known cancer-causing gene into *Escherichia coli*, a bacterial strain commonly found in the human digestive system, might this not lead to dire consequences? At present the threat of such an accident does not appear likely, since laboratory strains of bacteria do not survive in the wild.

2. Genetic engineering of crops and livestock may reduce the diversity in the biosphere and diminish the robustness of our ecology.

3. The technologies can be applied toward questionable, even evil ends. The example of the Nazi eugenics programs is often cited. Furthermore, the connection with various reproductive technologies is a source of deep ethical debates. To cite one example, a couple at risk of conceiving a child with a genetic disease could produce several embryos by means of in vitro fertilization (fertilization outside the womb). These embryos could then be screened for the disease, and a healthy one selected for reimplantation into the womb of the mother. The others would be disposed of, or perhaps used for fetal research, which itself raises hackles. On the one hand, this seems to guarantee the parents a child free from a particular disease. On the other hand, this sort of procedure is viewed by some as a precursor to people no longer being ends in themselves, but commodities serving the ends of other people.

4. Finally, the development of biotechnologies may well have profound geoeconomic and geopolitical consequences, as do all new technologies. As François Gros puts it in *The Gene Civilization*, "We must not be afraid to acknowledge that the face of the Earth may be changed as a result [of these new technologies." An important issue is how Third World countries will be affected. If, for example, a strain of coffee bean were developed to grow in cold weather, the economy of Brazil could be disrupted. In turn, this would reduce the buying power of an important market and compound the serious debt problem that already exists in that country.

Genetic engineering makes us the first species with the potential power to shape its own evolution. Surely in the next century there will be planned and unplanned actions directed at human enhancement and species improvement.

Conclusion

The industrial use of organisms bred for advantageous and profitable properties is not new. What is new is the ability to directly alter the genotype. Whereas traditional breeding relies on the selection of visible characteristics (phenotype) without fully understanding the underlying changes in the genotype, genetic engineering reverses this pattern by relying on manipulation of the genes without fully understanding all the effects on phenotype. This is a real revolution, and it is reasonable to be amazed as well as concerned. Genetic research is outpacing society's ability to comprehend, integrate, and control its discoveries. The techniques of genetic engineering and their implications are likely to be at the forefront of human concerns for the foreseeable future.

See also BIOETHICS; GENETICS; GENETICS: AGRICULTURAL APPLICATIONS; GENETICS: COMMERCIALIZATION; GENETIC TECHNOLOGIES; LIFE SCIENCES; SCIENTIFIC BREAKTHROUGHS.

BIBLIOGRAPHY

EMERY, ALAN E. H. *An Introduction to Recombinant DNA.* New York: John Wiley, 1984.

GROS, FRANÇOIS, *The Gene Civilization.* New York: McGraw-Hill, 1989.

NOSSAL, GUSTAV, J. V. *Reshaping Life.* New York: Cambridge University Press, 1985.

WATSON, J. D., and TOOZE, J. *The DNA Story.* New York: W. H. Freeman, 1981.

Michael Cook

Genetics

Genetics, as the science of heredity and variation, has undergone the most rapid development of any biological science in the twentieth century. Genetics in the latter half of the twentieth century has increased our understanding of how life on Earth has evolved and how life processes operate, and has provided the potential for the control or alteration of the hereditary material that contributes to the development and expression of traits in all living organisms. The science of modern genetics has spawned a number of new fields of science and technology, including molecular biology, genetic engineering, molecular diagnostics, molecular medicine, gene therapy, and computational molecular biology.

Mendelian Genetics

Mendelian classical genetics up to the 1940s can be summarized as follows:

1. It postulated the existence of a gene as a replicating unit and as the basis for all living activity and the transmission of hereditary information.
2. It proposed that genes are arranged in a pattern or system on a structure, the chromosomes, contained in all cells and transmitted to its progeny.
3. Changes (mutations) in the gene can occur either spontaneously or in response to certain physical (ionizing radiation) or chemical environmental influences.
4. The mutations are the basis for evolutionary changes in species and populations of living organisms.
5. Genes control metabolic processes and the development of organisms.

New Genetics

In the late 1930s and early 1940s a series of experiments were carried out that have transformed genetics.

- Genes have been found to contain deoxyribonucleic acid (DNA).
- Researchers have purified and crystallized DNA so that it can be subjected to the analytical process of X-ray diffraction, the patterns of which give important clues about the relative location of molecular groups.
- In 1953 James D. Watson and Francis H. C. Crick of Cambridge University, U.K., proposed a double-helical structure for DNA. This structure was said to consist of two strands of linearly arrayed nucleotides consisting of two purines, adenine (A) and guanine (G), and two pyrimidines, thymine (T) and cytosine (C), in the form of a double helix. The strands are joined so that a purine is always paired with a pyrimidine and form a strong bond that holds the strands together with the sugar phosphate (ribose) on the outside forming the backbone of the molecule. This structure suggests a mechanism for the storage of information (in the sequence of ATGC) and replication of the information. As the double helix unwinds during cell division, each strand acts as a template for the assembly of identical strands.

Subsequent work confirmed the accuracy of the Watson-Crick proposal. Genes consisting of DNA express their message through another nucleic acid, ribose nucleic acid (mRNA), and the transcription of this message is eventually translated into a protein through certain cellular structures (polysomes) located in the cystoplasm. This has been summarized as the central dogma of molecular genetics:

$$DNA \rightarrow mRNA \rightarrow Protein$$

How DNA replicates and transcribes a message that is subsequently translated into a protein product is the basis of the new molecular biology.

Genes

Genes consist of stretches of DNA that may contain from a few thousand to a million nucleotides and are located in a linear arrangement on the long strands of DNA. Each human consists of more than a trillion cells and each cell contains over six feet of DNA. The strands of the DNA double helix are coiled around cores of protein that together form the structures known as chromosomes. Departures from a normal genetic condition have to be determined by an analysis of the sequence of purines and pyrimidines (the nucleotides) that make up the gene.

The total genetic information contained in the DNA nucleotide sequence is the genome. It is anticipated that by the year 2005 the complete sequence of the three billion pairs of nucleotides that make up the human genome will be known. The Human Genome Project, initiated in 1987 by the U.S. Department of Energy, now involves other U.S. agencies, including the National Institutes of Health. On the basis of techniques currently in use, it will be possible to excise, delete, or insert parts or whole genes in order to correct genetic deficiencies (gene therapy). In 1994, over seventy trials in humans testing the safety and efficacy of gene therapy were under way.

In addition to the development of new methodologies, the various genome projects that are studying humans and a variety of plants and animals of economic and scientific importance are primarily aimed at identifying and physically mapping all the genes on the chromosomes. The tasks of gene identification and determining the gene's physical location on the chromosome will clearly continue well into the twenty-first century and provide the basis for a great deal of exciting and important research.

The number of human genes was originally estimated to be in the range of 50,000 to 100,000. It now appears that there might well be substantially more than 100,000 human genes. In 1994, only a few thousand genes have been identified, and many of these remain to be mapped, sequenced, and their functions determined.

Although many genes consist of an uninterrupted sequence of nucleotides, it is now clear that many other genes are made up of various fragments of DNA that must be assembled (spliced) during the process of transcription and translation to construct a protein coding gene. This phenomenon has been particularly elucidated in the studies on how genes control the production of antibodies (immunoglobulins) that are created in response to the challenges of multiple infectious agents. In the late 1970s it became apparent that many mammalian genes exist in the genome as a discontinuous series of coding (Exons) and noncoding (Introns) regions. The process of excising the noncoding regions and splicing the coding regions into a contiguous gene is under active research. The situation is further complicated by evidence that a mechanism of "proofreading" corrects mistakes in the mRNA and, further, some protein products are "edited" posttranslationally.

The Genetic Code

After the discovery that the hereditary information was somehow encoded in the DNA and in the linear sequences of the four nucleotides ATGC, the unraveling of the genetic code became a major challenge. The code was deciphered in the early 1960s.

As previously indicated, the central dogma of molecular genetics, proven by many experiments, is that DNA replicates itself and also acts as a template for the formation of mRNA. The message encoded in mRNA is translated into protein in the cytoplasm of a cell. Proteins are made from amino acids (AA), of which there are twenty different basic types. The assembly of a specific protein requires the selection and joining together of the correct sequence of amino acids from the pool that exists in the cytoplasm. As a result of the correct sequence of AAs to form a polypeptide, the molecule will fold itself into a three-dimensional structure.

Early on, it was concluded that with an alphabet of four nucleotides (ATGC) it requires a minimum of three bases to code (codon) for a single amino acid. Since the number of coding possibilities is 64, it more than meets the need for protein assembly from a pool of 20 amino acids. Indeed, of the 64 coding possibilities, 61 are used to designate specific amino acids, three codons signal to stop translation of the DNA information, and one codon signals to start. It soon became apparent that some of the different codons designate identical AAs—e.g., ACC, ACA, ACG, ACU all code for the AA threonine (see Table 1).

With the deciphering of the genetic code, it became theoretically feasible to predict from the nucleotide sequence the approximate nature of the protein product. Understanding the mechanisms that are involved in decoding the genetic message and translating the message faithfully into a protein product will provide challenges for researchers for many years.

DNA/RNA

As described above, the information contained in the DNA is transcribed and translated through the agencies of ribose nucleic acids (RNAs). RNA differs from DNA in its sugar component and in the use of the pyrimidine nucleotide uracil (U), instead of thymidine (T), in its base sequence. At least three different RNA molecules are involved in decoding and translating the DNA:

- *mRNA:* Messenger RNA is transcribed on a template of the DNA during gene activation.
- *tRNA:* Transfer RNA recognizes and transfers specific AAs to an anticodon recognition site in the sequence determined by mRNA.

TABLE 1.   The Genetic Code

First Position (5' end)	Second Position				Third Position (3' end)
	U	C	A	G	
U	PHE	SER	TYR	CYS	U
	PHE	SER	TYR	CYS	C
	LEU	SER	Stop	Stop	A
	LEU	SER	Stop	TRP	G
C	LEU	PRO	HIS	ARG	U
	LEU	PRO	HIS	ARG	C
	LEU	PRO	GLN	ARG	A
	LEU	PRO	GLN	ARG	G
A	ILE	THR	ASN	SER	U
	ILE	THR	ASN	SER	C
	ILE	THR	LYS	ARG	A
	MET	THR	LYS	ARG	G
G	VAL	ALA	ASP	GLY	U
	VAL	ALA	ASP	GLY	C
	VAL	ALA	GLU	GLY	A
	VAL	ALA	GLU	GLY	G

Note: Given the position of the bases in a codon, it is possible to find the corresponding amino acid. For example, the codon (5')AUG(3') on mRNA specifies methionine, whereas CAU specifies histidine. UAA, UAG, and UGA are termination signals. AUG is part of the initiation signal, and it codes for internal methionines as well. (After J. D. Watson, J. Tooze, and D. Kurtz, *Recombinant DNA: A Short Course* [1983], p. 38.)

- *rRNA:* Ribosomal RNA constitutes cytoplasmic particles that provide an environment for the assembly of protein.

In the 1980s, it was discovered that certain RNA molecules could act as enzymes (ribozymes) in the absence of protein. The ribozymes have been used to catalyze many chemical reactions, including self-replication. It has been suggested that the first molecules capable of replication in the organic evolution of Earth probably were RNAs.

Cell Biology

The basic unit of life is the cell. In the case of acellular viruses that consist primarily of DNA or RNA, it is necessary to invade a cell to use the host's mechanisms for replication. Bacterial cells (prokaryotes) and more complex animal and plant cells (eukaryotes) have the same basic subcellular components. The majority of early molecular genetics experiments were carried out with viruses that used bacteria as host cells. Eventually it was learned that the basic principles of gene replication, transcription, and translation applied equally to prokaryotic and eukaryotic cells and organisms.

The progress in techniques to cultivate tissues and cells in test tubes (in vitro) facilitated studies that were previously difficult or impossible to do. In vitro tissue culture systems enabled scientists to explore means of excising and inserting genetic material and to learn how genes express their message. Application of these in vitro manipulations has enabled scientists to correct a defect in children born with a genetically transmitted immunodeficiency disease.

Genetic Engineering: Evolutionary Concerns

The techniques that have emerged from the development of the science of molecular genetics have created the power for scientists to do some remarkable things. While much remains to be done to perfect the techniques, the following represent some future prospects:

1. It is increasingly possible to predict future health concerns by genomic analysis. Genetic markers for a number of specific diseases have been identified (cystic fibrosis, Huntington's, Tay Sachs, and others). Markers for heart disease, cancer, and mental health are being sought.
2. Through the methods being perfected for the application of gene therapy, diseases and afflictions such as hemophilia, sickle anemia, dia-

betes, and others may be cured by a single procedure designed to correct the genetic defect.
3. By using genetic engineering techniques for excising, inserting, splicing, and cloning genetic messages, it has become possible to modify many animals and plants. Tomatoes, corn, soybeans, and farm animals are prime targets for such research. Some plants (tobacco) and animals (goats) are being engineered to produce human proteins including antibodies for clinical therapeutic applications.
4. Substances previously not available in adequate amounts are being produced through genetic engineering. Insulin, erythropoietin, granulocytic colony factor, and the interleukins are just a few of the hormones and cell regulator substances becoming commercially available.

Powerful new technologies resulting from molecular genetics have increased the accountability of humans over Earth's evolution. Thousands of years of domesticating plants and animals have sharply reduced genetic diversity and the number of species. Through increasingly efficient hunting and fishing techniques, humans have eliminated or brought to the brink of extinction many thousands of species. Unrestrained population growth, doubling about every twenty-five to thirty years, may overwhelm demands for energy, food and fiber. Already the polluting effects of human activity have stressed and destroyed many ecosystems. Such aspects of human activity can be exacerbated or ameliorated by genetic engineering. Humanity will need all the wisdom it can muster in the way it uses these powerful technologies. Informed laypersons, philosophers, ethicists, ecologists, scientists, and political leaders will need to cooperate in determining appropriate social policies and priorities. This will require a level of commitment and collaboration characteristic of wartime activity. Circumstances justify a similar level of societal response to the opportunities and dangers in the use or misuse of these powerful genetic engineering methodologies.

See also ARTIFICIAL LIFE; BIOETHICS; EVOLUTION, BIOLOGICAL; FOOD TECHNOLOGIES; GENETIC ENGINEERING; GENETICS: AGRICULTURAL APPLICATIONS; GENETICS: COMMERCIALIZATION; GENETIC TECHNOLOGIES; LIFE SCIENCES.

BIBLIOGRAPHY

ANDERSON, WALTER TRUETT. *To Govern Evolution.* Boston: Harcourt Brace Jovanovich, 1987.
SINGER, MAXINE, and BERG, PAUL. *Genes and Genomes.* Mill Valley, CA: University Science Books, 1991.

WATSON, JAMES D.; TOOZE, JOHN; and KURTZ, DAVID T. *Recombinant DNA: A Short Course.* New York: W. H. Freeman, 1983.

Paul H. Silverman

Genetics: Agricultural Applications

Since antiquity mankind has domesticated animals and crop plants to produce food and fiber. In ancient times farmers could only save seed from plants that demonstrated desirable properties. The breeding of animals was often accomplished by trial and error. Gregor Mendel's discovery of the rudiments of genetics in the mid-1800s provided the scientific basis for modern plant and animal breeding. The development of hybrid corn in the 1920s initiated a revolution in plant breeding, increasing the yield of this key crop tenfold.

Developments in molecular genetics or biotechnology over the past forty years give plant and animal breeders new biotechnology tools to feed the ever-expanding world population. It is critical that we use genetic sources wisely to conserve crop diversity and improve the productivity of our farm land. One key aspect of biotechnology that will help in this endeavor is recombinant DNA (r-DNA) technology or genetic engineering.

Twenty years ago, scientists learned how to use special restriction enzymes to cut genetic information out of one organism and splice it into another. At first a laboratory curiosity, r-DNA technology formed the underpinning of the emerging biotechnology industry that formed in the late 1970s and early '80s. While many of the significant advances to date have occurred in health care, the same techniques that allow us to produce human insulin in bacteria can improve agricultural production. Agricultural biotechnology is poised to deliver significant new advances to both farmers and consumers throughout the remainder of this decade. The same techniques that allow us to produce human insulin in bacteria can improve agricultural production.

Plant scientists can add discrete, well-characterized genes to plants to improve their quality, nutrition, and other characteristics. Using new biotechnology approaches, a useful trait found in wheat conferring pest resistance can be transferred to corn. In this manner, plant scientists can harness nature's proteins to improve nutritional factors such as amino acid composition, the degree of un-saturated oils in various seed crops, and increase the use of natural resistance to insects and disease.

Among the major food crops that have been genetically modified are tomato, potato, corn, and soybean. Important traits such as viral resistance, insect resistance, herbicide tolerance, and processing quality have been added. Farmers will benefit from a greater number of pest-management options using environmentally preferable crop protection products and management programs.

The consumer will benefit directly from fruits and vegetables that are tastier and have improved quality and shelf life. Oils that are lower in saturated and higher in unsaturated fat content and grain crops with more balanced protein carry the potential for major health benefits.

The use of microbial pesticides has been increasing in recent years as farmers and foresters have been exploring nonchemical approaches to pest control. *Bacillus thuringiensis* is frequently used to control gypsy moth infestations in forestry settings. New microorganisms are being studied for pesticidal activity. Recently a microorganism has been identified that controls Colorado potato beetles, a key agricultural pest.

Many of these biopesticides produce a toxin with a limited target range. However, the toxin's limited persistence in the environment necessitates frequent spraying. Genetic engineering is being used to improve the field performance of these natural pesticides, making them more appealing for commercial farmers. Over half the pesticides approved by the Environmental Protection Agency during the past three years have been microbial pesticides.

Over 700 million animals (poultry, swine, cattle, and sheep) are raised annually by American farmers. Improving production in this agricultural sector is just as important as it is for the major crops. Protein growth hormones (also called somatotropins) are now being produced in bulk through biotechnology. These natural compounds promote the growth of animals by improving feed efficiency. This shortens the time to market, improving the farmer's profits and assuring a stable meat supply. The use of porcine somatotropin leads to pigs with leaner meat, an important feature for today's nutritionally conscious consumers.

Of all the agricultural biotechnology products, bovine somatotropin (BST) is the most controversial. BST enhances milk production in lactating cows. Questions have been raised about the safety of milk from cows given BST, as well as whether there is a need for the product when we currently produce more dairy products than are consumed.

BST has been the most widely studied animal drug in history. It has been administered to thousands of cows in test herds. The nutritional quality of the milk is unchanged and the Food and Drug Administration (FDA) has approved the sale and use of dairy products from cows given BST. In fact, BST is a natural component of milk and present in every glass we drink.

The issue of dairy surpluses is largely political and is complicated by marketing orders and the price support system. There is no question that BST can improve the efficiency of our nation's dairy farmers. A well-managed dairy farm using BST can reduce the size of the herd without a decrease in milk production. This will reduce the amount of farm labor needed and may be most important for small farmers whose labor costs form the most significant part of the operation.

r-DNA can be used to insert new genetic material into animals to cause them to grow faster, produce valuable pharmaceutical proteins, or improve their resistance to certain diseases. "Transgenic" fish containing genes for growth hormones grow faster and are the subject of research interest because of the shifting dietary preferences of American consumers. Goats and swine have been genetically modified to produce important blood proteins such as human hemoglobin. By the end of this decade, several important pharmaceuticals may be produced more efficiently in animals than through conventional processes.

Enzymes are important to the food processing industry. These proteins catalyze or speed up chemical reactions and are used in the production of a number of key food ingredients. High-fructose corn syrup, commonly used as a sweetener in beverages and baked goods, is one such product. Enzymes are used to degrade the corn starch down to individual sugar units, known as glucose. An enzyme called an isomerase is then used to convert the glucose, which is not sweet, to fructose, which is very sweet.

The production of food enzymes can be enhanced through biotechnology. The enzyme chymosin is used to clot milk, the first step in cheese making. The traditional source of this enzyme has been an extract from the stomachs of unweaned calves. Recently r-DNA has been used to move the calf gene for the enzyme into a microorganism. Chymosin can be produced by microbial fermentation in a cost effective manner. Since this form of the enzyme is identical to that found in the calf's stomach, cheese manufacturers have a reliable supply of the enzyme. Moreover, its cheese-making properties are unchanged.

The current U.S. food safety evaluation system, comprised of plant breeders and food processors, has assured the safest food supply in the world. The developers of these new agricultural biotechnology products regularly consult with federal agencies such as the Food and Drug Administration to assure their safe introduction into the marketplace.

See also BIODIVERSITY; FOOD AND AGRICULTURE; FOOD TECHNOLOGIES; GENETIC ENGINEERING; GENETICS; GENETICS: COMMERCIALIZATION; NUTRITION.

BIBLIOGRAPHY

"Biotechnology and the American Agriculture Industry." *Journal of the American Medical Association* (March 20, 1991).

"Improving Plant Disease Resistance." *Science* (July 24, 1992).

KESSLER, DAVID A.; TAYLOR, MICHAEL R.; MARYANSKI, JAMES H.; FLAMM, ERIC L.; and KAHL, LINDA S. "The Safety of Foods Developed by Biotechnology." *Science* (June 26, 1992).

U.S. Congress, Office of Technology Assessment. "A New Technological Era for American Agriculture." OTA-F-474. Washington, DC: U.S. Government Printing Office, 1992.

Alan Goldhammer

Genetics: Commercialization

Genetic engineering is the altering of plants, animals, and organisms at the molecular level to make or modify products, improve plants or animals, or develop microorganisms. It is a result of the discovery of the double-helix structure of human deoxyribonucleic acid, or DNA, by Francis Crick and James D. Watson in the early 1950s. Since the first cloning of a gene (recombinant DNA) in 1973, scientific research has discovered processes and products of potential social and economic value; these findings have also challenged existing legal and regulatory doctrine.

The genetic revolution has the potential for altering the social, economic, and legal bases of agriculture, medicine, and manufacturing. Potential applications in agriculture are increased crop productivity through the design of transgenic plants and animals with "built-in" disease and herbicide resistance, tolerance to frost or heat, and low-fat and low-cholesterol meat. Potential applications in medicine include better diagnostic procedures through genetic screening, treatment of some diseases with gene therapy, production of medicines based on limited enzymes and hormones, and better preventive medicine due to genetic identification of disease. Potential applications in manufacturing include biosensors to more accurately detect minute traces of various substances and bioremediation, which uses specially designed organisms to break down oil deposits and other hazardous products.

Emerging Commercial Applications

In 1992, there were more than 1,200 companies in some aspect of research, development, or production of genetically engineered products affecting health care, agriculture, energy, or environmental improvement. This fledgling industry employed more than 79,000 persons in 1992, and it is expected to employ more than 200,000 by the turn of the century. Because this is a new and knowledge-intensive industry, firms have high capital needs to sustain large research and development budgets and to long (seven- to ten-year) product approval periods.

Since Genentech, the first U.S. genetic engineering firm, was founded in 1976, the commercialization of genetic engineering has developed on a number of application and regulatory fronts. In 1981, the Food and Drug Administration (FDA) first approved monoconal antibody diagnostic kits, followed the next year by the first approval of a genetically engineered pharmaceutical product (human insulin). Another early medical application of genetic engineering was TPA (tissue plasminogen activator) used to reduce blood clotting and, thus, the probability of heart attacks. In 1990, the FDA approved the first genetically engineered food additive, recombinant renin, an enzyme used to produce cheese. In 1993, the FDA approved the "Flavr Savr" tomato, a genetically engineered vegetable resistant to spoilage that can be ripened on the vine, thus increasing its commercial appeal.

FDA approval of bovine somatotropin (BST), in late 1993, culminated a decade-long controversy about the safety of genetically engineered food products. A naturally occurring hormone, BST increases milk production in dairy cows; it was available only in limited supplies until biotechnological processes to reproduce it were developed.

Current Government Regulation

The Supreme Court decision in *Diamond* v. *Chakrabarty* (1980) that extended patent rights to genetically engineered organisms paved the way for the development of the industry. Prior to this decision, only plants were subject to patent protection under the Townsend Purnell Plant Act and the Plant Variety Protection Act. In 1988, the first U.S. patent on an animal was issued to Harvard University for a mouse genetically engineered to contain a cancer-causing gene.

The Coordinated Framework for Regulation of Biotechnology was established by the U.S. Office of Science and Technology Policy in 1986 to coordinate five federal agencies (Environmental Protection Agency, Food and Drug Administration, Department of Agriculture, Occupational Safety and Health Administration, and the National Institutes of Health) to regulate biotechnology. The Coordinated Framework depends on existing agencies that, under present law, have concurrent jurisdiction. For example, a food product produced using a genetically altered microorganism might be viewed as a "chemical substance" and regulated by the Toxic Substance Control Act administered by the Environmental Protection Agency, or it could be viewed as a food additive normally regulated by the Food and Drug Administration according to the Food, Drug, and Cosmetic Act. And, because of its responsibility to inspect meat and poultry products, the Department of Agriculture has a claim to jurisdiction. While the effectiveness of this regulatory approach has been subject to debate by both proponents and opponents of genetic engineering, its adoption extended the doctrine that chemicals and organisms are usually regulated in the United States according to their intended use and not by their method of production.

The National Institutes of Health, the National Science Foundation, and the Department of Agriculture have funded genetic-engineering-related research programs with animal, plant, and human applications. One highly visible federal policy decision was the $3 billion authorization of the Human Genome Project, which began on October 1, 1990. This project, expected to take fifteen years, is a worldwide research effort to map and define the sequence of all the 50,000 to 100,000 genes in humans.

Public-Policy Concerns

Recent surveys of American public opinion find that while about nine out of ten Americans approve of genetic research and gene therapy, and more than three-quarters would take genetic tests, about seven out of ten support greater governmental regulation of gene therapy and the use of genetic information. Concerns about the more effective genetic testing that will be practical as the Human Genome Project progresses relate to issues of workplace discrimination, legal rights of confidentiality, uncertain effects on life and health insurance, and the effects of more genetic information on reproduction decisions. Two specific problems faced by genetic screening clinics are requests to perform prenatal tests for sex selection, and the generation of "unwanted information." An instance of such information might be learning that one tests positive for a genetic abnormality like cystic fibrosis or Huntington's disease without the ability to correct it, and then facing potential adverse reactions from employers or health-insurance companies. To date, genetic counselors have few public-policy directives to assist them in making such decisions.

There are environmental and consumer concerns about genetic engineering as well. Environmental concerns include the risk of release of genetically engineered organisms into the environment, and the threat of increased pesticide use due to the ability of pesticide-tolerant crops to withstand the previously harmful effects of excessive exposure. Consumer issues involving product labeling and the safety of biotechnology products still surface when new applications of genetic engineering to produce food are announced.

Prospects for Future Developments

Despite an impressive record of scientific advancement, the future of the biotechnology industry is unclear. Like other high-tech industries, the biotechnology industry has large capital requirements, and its ability to attract investments depends on the economic and regulatory climate. Both the direction and pace of applications of genetic engineering in the United States depend on public-policy decisions affecting the legal, economic, and governmental support for further research, development, and, ultimately, applications. There appears to be a public consensus that U.S. international economic competitiveness depends on technological advancement, and biotechnology is widely viewed as one of the nation's most promising advanced technologies. However, harnessing that potential requires that, in addition to continual scientific advancement, intellectual-property rights be modified to protect genetically engineered products and that consumer confidence be maintained through adequate, competent environmental and consumer regulation.

In summary, genetics, particularly the developments in molecular biology and the understanding of the human genome, will for the first time give us direct control over our own evolution. Most visible to us will be the effects on body, brain, and behavior. As the genetic base of those three elements of our lives becomes clearer, there will be many successful positive interventions. Genetics will also bring separate waves of benefits to humankind in agriculture and industrial processes.

See also BIODIVERSITY; FOOD AND AGRICULTURE; FOOD TECHNOLOGIES; GENETIC ENGINEERING; GENETICS; GENETICS: AGRICULTURAL APPLICATIONS; GENETIC TECHNOLOGIES; LIFE SCIENCES.

BIBLIOGRAPHY

BISHOP, JERRY E., and WALDHOLZ, MICHAEL. *Genome: The Story of the Most Astonishing Scientific Adventure of Our Time—the Attempt To Map All the Genes in the Human Body.* New York: Simon & Schuster, 1990.
DAVIS, BERNARD D., ed. *The Genetic Revolution: Scientific Prospects and Public Perceptions.* Baltimore, MD: Johns Hopkins, 1991.
U.S. Congress, Office of Technology Assessment. *Biotechnology in a Global Economy.* Washington, DC: U.S. Government Printing Office, 1991.

David J. Webber

Genetic Technologies

In the second half of the twentieth century, a cascading series of new discoveries in genetics launched a "biological revolution" that soon began to transform medicine, agriculture, and several other fields of human activity. The pace of new discoveries and new applications is certain to increase rapidly in the decades ahead. Biology will become the "master science" of the twenty-first century—as physics was the master science of the twentieth—and biotechnology will replace or perhaps merge with electronics at the cutting edge of technological innovation.

Among the genetic technologies currently in use are the following:

- *Recombinant DNA.* For example, when a gene from one organism is "spliced" into the DNA of another, the host organism can then produce a new protein. In this way, bacteria are used to manufacture products such as human insulin.
- *Protein engineering.* "Conventional" recombinant DNA produces a familiar protein manufactured by a different organism; further genetic

modifications can produce entirely new proteins with different characteristics—such as the ability to metabolize at different temperatures.

- Antisense technology. When an exact but sequence-reversed segment of synthetic DNA is inserted into a cell, it binds with the complementary segment of messenger RNA and prevents the expression of that gene. The first commercial application of this technology controlled the gene that causes softening in tomatoes.
- *Biosensors.* When an organic element is integrated with an electronic system, it makes possible instant detection of the presence or quantity of certain chemicals.
- *Cell and tissue culture.* Although not an entirely new technology, culture has made dramatic advances in the genetic age, enabling cultivation of animal cells—human skin tissue, for example—and plant cells.
- *Monoclonal antibodies.* Antibodies for use in research and therapy were rare and expensive until genetic technology developed a procedure for mass producing them through a new form of cell culture in which a type of cancer cell is fused with the antibody-producing "B" cell.

Applications of the New Genetic Technologies:

The revolutionary impact of the new technologies was felt first in medicine, then in agriculture—two traditionally biologically-based fields of human endeavor. In future the revolution will transform other fields that were not previously biologically based, such as energy production, various kinds of manufacturing, and possibly even computer electronics.

MEDICAL APPLICATIONS

Diagnosis. Monoclonal antibodies are a useful tool for medical diagnosis, since they quickly and accurately identify various diseases such as malaria, schistosomiasis, and some types of cancer. They also are used in kits for detecting pregnancy. Another tool, the DNA probe—a specific piece of selected or synthesized DNA that recognizes the DNA of an infectious organism—is an effective diagnostic method that replaces tedious and expensive laboratory analysis. Likely future development: instant and precise diagnosis of most diseases.

Gene Therapy. Many serious diseases are caused by the malfunctioning of a single gene. When healthy genes are inserted into defective cells, they enable the cell to function properly. This approach is called "somatic" gene therapy because it treats

only the cells of the patient; its effects are not inherited. A more controversial but highly probable future development, germline therapy, would correct genes in the germline (reproductive) cells, and the effects would be inherited. Antisense technology opens up yet another approach to genetic therapy: It can block the activity of an infectious organism such as a malaria parasite or an AIDS virus, or stop the proliferation of artery-hardening cells on the inner walls of blood vessels. Ultimately, such genetic therapies could make drugs obsolete.

Immunology. When people learned that deliberate infection with the relatively mild cowpox could produce resistance to smallpox, immunology began. Later, vaccines against viral diseases such as polio generally employed a weakened form of the virus. In either case, the general idea was to trick the body into producing enough antigen to confer immunity. New genetic technologies perform this same operation with greater precision and less danger. The future of immunology includes protection against an increasing number of diseases, including malaria caused by parasites, and new ways of getting the vaccine into the body (e.g., by pills or nasal spray).

AGRICULTURAL APPLICATIONS

As new knowledge about human genetics leads to fundamentally new kinds of medicine, so does new understanding of plant and animal genetics lead to new kinds of agriculture—it begins to redefine completely what agriculture is. We will soon see traditional food and fiber products coming out of factories rather than farms. At the same time, many more farms will be used to grow products other than food and fiber.

Modified Crop Plants. Through recombinant DNA and other methods (generally in combination with traditional methods of plant breeding), crop plants with a host of new characteristics—such as self-fertilization, pest resistance, and new flavor and nutrition qualities—are being developed.

Pharming. "Pharming" is the name given to a new kind of agriculture, in which pharmaceutical proteins can be produced in the milk of genetically modified domestic animals. Scientists also see a good possibility of modifying tobacco plants to produce medically useful chemicals, so that tobacco farming can become a socially beneficial form of agriculture.

Food Without Farms. In 1991 a California biotechnology company took out a patent on a process to manufacture "real" vanilla extract through tissue culture. The resultant product has much richer flavor than the synthetic vanilla extract used in most commercial products and is also far lower in cost than the extract produced from beans hand-picked from the vanilla orchid, which grows in a few tropical regions such as Madagascar. This approach will be used to produce many kinds of food products such as "real" fruit juices, fibers such as cotton, and plant-derived medicines such as the cancer treatment taxol, which comes from the bark of yew trees.

INDUSTRIAL APPLICATIONS

Chemicals for various industrial purposes can be produced from organic materials through biotechnology, making it possible to replace petrochemicals for manufacturing or fuel with similar chemicals produced from farm crops. This is already being done in a limited way, but more effective ways of biologically processing common substances such as lignocellulose (present in wood chips, straw, corncobs) will greatly increase the economic independence of developing countries. Biotechnology can also yield entirely new industrial products. Some scientists propose, for example, that a spider's genetic code might be used to make a polymer that would be five to ten times stronger than steel and could be pulled out by 20 percent of its length without breaking.

Environmental Cleanup. Bacteria already are being used to clean up oil spills and other forms of environmental pollution. With genetic modification, they promise to become capable of biodegrading a wide range of toxic substances.

Biotechnologies of the Future

Bioelectronics began in the 1980s with the first use of biosensors. A possible future development will be protein-engineered "biochips" that usher in a new generation of computer technology.

Nanotechnology is the term for a predicted next generation of engineering as people learn how to manufacture machines of microscopic dimensions—small enough to travel through capillaries and operate within living cells. Such devices might then be able to cure diseases, reverse aging, and give the body new strengths and abilities.

See also BIOETHICS; GENETIC ENGINEERING; GENETIC REGULATION; GENETICS; GENETICS: AGRI-CULTURAL AND FORESTRY APPLICATIONS; GENETICS: COMMERCIALIZATION; LIFE SCIENCES; NANOTECHNOLOGY; SCIENTIFIC BREAKTHROUGHS.

BIBLIOGRAPHY

ANDERSON, WALTER TRUETT. "Food Without Farms: The Biotech Revolution in Agriculture." *Futurist* 24 (1990): 16–21.

———. *To Govern Evolution: Further Adventures of the Political Animal.* Boston: Harcourt Brace Jovanovich, 1987.

DREXLER, K. ERIC. *Engines of Creation: The Coming Era of Nanotechnology.* Garden City, NY: Doubleday, 1986.

FISHER, JEFFREY A. *Rx 2000: Breakthroughs in Health, Medicine, and Longevity by the Year 2000 and Beyond.* New York: Simon and Schuster, 1992.

Office of Technology Assessment, U.S. Congress. *Commercial Biotechnology: An International Analysis.* Washington, DC: U.S. Government Printing Office, 1984.

ZIMMERMAN, BURKE. *Biofuture: Confronting the Genetic Era.* New York: Plenum, 1984.

Walter Truett Anderson

Geriatrics.

See AGING OF THE POPULATION; ELDERLY, LIVING ARRANGEMENTS.

Germany

Tomorrow's Federal Republic of Germany will be very different from the country that existed in the four decades following World War II for reasons that go considerably beyond the impact of unification. Among the large, industrialized countries, Germany is unique in the pressures it faces to redefine its social contract and its external relationships simultaneously.

Pressures Within and Without

On the economic side, Germany must respond to three challenges at the same time. First, it must complete the economic unification of the country, a process of rebuilding that will extend well into the twenty-first century. Massive infrastructure projects will be continued for at least the next two decades in the fields of energy, environmental cleanup, housing, transportation, and telecommunications. Private investment and entrepreneurial initiatives are needed to create jobs for the almost three million unemployed eastern German workers.

Second, Germany must halt and, it is to be hoped, reverse a startling decline in its global economic competitiveness. The development of technology in Germany is held back by intense regulation, the difficulty of financing risky ventures, a bureaucratized research-and-development (R&D) culture, and a widespread pessimism about the effects of new technology on social life and the environment. Germany's widely heralded status as a major exporter masks the fact that its global share of the high-technology export market is significantly smaller than its overall market share in manufactured goods (15 percent as opposed to 20 percent in 1992). That condition does not bode well for the future, since it is primarily in the most advanced sectors that German firms will be able to hold off low-wage competitors. Labor costs in Germany are the highest in the world, and German labor-market regulations are highly rigid, discouraging part-time and short-term employment, shift work, and the employment of pensioners and students. German workers—who enjoy six- to eight-week vacations and more than a dozen annual holidays—put in 15 to 20 percent fewer hours on the job each year than their Asian and North American counterparts. Not surprisingly, the Federal Republic's attractiveness to investment is in decline.

The third element in this mix of economic challenges is a major actuarial problem. Germany stands at what might be called the limits of the welfare state and must discover a means to balance its entitlements accounts and/or reduce the expectations of its citizens drastically. It is common for university students to reach the age of thirty before entering the workforce, even as the average retirement age in Germany creeps down to fifty-nine and life expectancies increase. Meanwhile, the range of benefits promised to the German population surpasses what might be called a safety net and now constitutes a cradle-to-grave cushion against every conceivable setback. For many large firms operating in Germany, contributions to mandated entitlement and insurance programs account for more than eighty-five pfennig on top of every deutsche mark that is paid in wages.

The future of Germany will be shaped as well by the demands of its new place on the world stage. For the foreseeable future, Russia's behavior toward Central and Eastern Europe probably will be an uncomfortable mixture of disinterest and intimidation. While Russia offers little that might ease the economic difficulties and political tensions of the region, its powerful militarists will remain jealously opposed to the incorporation of the Soviet Union's former satellite countries into the North Atlantic Treaty Organization (NATO) and other Western security organizations. At the same time, the European Union (EU) maintains trade barriers to eastern goods and offers no time tables for eventual Central and Eastern European membership in a united Europe. The net effect is the virtual isolation of the entire region astride Germany's eastern border.

If countries such as the Czech Republic, Hungary, Poland, and Slovakia fail to achieve sustained economic growth, political stability, and external security in the 1990s, they may instead be a source of large refugee flows into Germany. Military violence within and between the Central European countries cannot be ruled out. Such developments would destroy German hopes for expanded trade and investment opportunities in the region and further diminish Germany's competitive position worldwide.

A New Social Contract

In the twenty-first century, Germany will move in the direction of the market and away from social security. That is not to say that Germany will dismantle its social welfare system. The Federal Republic will be a more competitive society, one in which more is expected of individuals and private firms while less is expected of governments.

Job creation in the Federal Republic seems likely to override the traditional resistance of policymakers and unions to a more flexible labor market. Some firms may preserve jobs during difficult periods by combining shorter work weeks and reduced wages, and others may experiment with part-time and shift work. Forty-hour work weeks may once again become the norm. Labor mobility almost certainly will increase. German firms will seek strategic alliances worldwide in an effort to improve their technological capacities, while both public and private R&D places more emphasis on industrial applications and less on basic research.

The creation of new jobs in Germany will do much to balance the country's social-welfare accounts, but not enough. To sustain its social safety net and vast retired population in the twenty-first century, the country will need to address its demographic problems. Subreplacement birthrates persist in the Federal Republic, which means that Germany's closed-door policy on immigration is not sustainable. In the effort to accommodate foreign workers, enlightened Germans will accept more liberal immigration and citizenship laws. Many other Germans will resist such changes, heightening social tensions in Germany for the foreseeable future and leading to occasional violent outbursts against foreigners.

Income disparities seem likely to increase. Violent strikes and other forms of economic protest (such as traffic blockades) may become relatively common features of German life. Extremist political groups almost certainly will seek to incite or take advantage of such developments. While Germany's 5 percent threshold for parliamentary representation will keep most of those groups away from the halls of power, some will be successful—and mainstream political parties will be tempted to pander to their constituencies. Germany's firm moorings in liberal democracy are not in doubt, but the long periods of stable coalition government to which the Federal Republic is accustomed could give way to more frequent transitions and unlikely political bedfellows.

If it can create jobs by reducing the excesses of the welfare state, foster technological development, and accept foreigners as an asset rather than a liability, twenty-first century Germany will be more humane, more competitive, and ultimately more powerful than ever before.

An Assertive Foreign Policy

West German governments spent forty years telling the rest of the world, in effect, that Germany had no national interests—that it was tied inextricably to the Atlantic Alliance and that what was good for Western Europe as a whole was good for Germany. There was no deliberate deception in that message. National interests were sublimated in the effort to rehabilitate Germany from its aggressive, criminal reputation in World War II.

German unification and the collapse of the Soviet Union marked the beginning of the end of that Federal Republic. Gone are the ultimate carrot (the prospect of unity), and the ultimate stick (the prospect of Soviet invasion) that kept Germany from deviating too far from plans laid out in the meeting rooms of the EU and NATO. The new Germany will not revert to aggression. But Germany also will not remain forever enthralled by what are now quite vague understandings of Europe's greater good. Germany's current leaders still are afraid to speak and act forcefully in the name of their country's own interests. Their successors, however, will not hesitate to do so.

Germany almost certainly will try to turn the EU eastward at the expense (at least for the foresee-able future) of grandiose plans for a common currency and political federation in Europe. Germany will find many reasons—including access to much-needed markets, political stability on its borders, and the creation of a buffer against an unpredictable Russia—for expanding the EU's membership and its trade to Central and Eastern Europe. If the EU does not follow Germany eastward, then Germany will go alone—spreading aid and investment and thereby gaining political influence.

Similarly, Germany will convince NATO to take responsibility for the security of Central and Eastern Europe or it will try to do the job itself. *Der Osten* (the East) has been an obsession of German leaders throughout their nation's history and it will remain so. Germany's future policy in the region, if NATO holds back, will be some combination of several elements: diplomatic understandings with Russia, a defensive military buildup, more visible military exercises with its neighbors, preferential trade deals, and/or the creation of a separate Central European trading sphere under German tutelage.

Gradually putting aside its reputation for pacifism during the Cold War and resolving its constitutional conundrum on the use of military force, Germany in the 1990s and beyond will play an occasional military role in safeguarding its economic interests and contributing to crisis management outside of Europe. So long as the U.S. continues to respond to the most egregious threats against global resource and trade flows, however, Germany will find few reasons to make independent investments in power-projection capabilities.

Summary

Germany will change quite dramatically by the early twenty-first century—emphasizing market mechanisms over government intervention, striving to accommodate ethnic diversity, enduring greater political and social volatility, articulating new or rediscovered national interests, and shedding its geopolitical reticence. At the same time, however, the Federal Republic seems likely to retain many familiar reference points: the guarantee of basic social welfare, the belief in universal economic opportunity, a preference for multinational over independent actions, and a primary focus on Europe rather than the global political arena. Observers will recognize the Federal Republic of Germany, even as it moves well beyond its one-time economic miracle, its division, and the constraints of the Cold War.

See also DEVELOPMENT: WESTERN PERSPEC-
TIVE; EUROPE, WESTERN.

BIBLIOGRAPHY

BERGNER, JEFFREY T. *The New Superpowers.* New York:
St. Martin's Press, 1991.

GEIPEL, GARY L., ed. *Germany in a New Era.* Indianapolis: Hudson Institute, 1993.

HUELSHOFF, MICHAEL G., MARKOVITS, ANDREI S., and
REICH, SIMON, eds. *From Bundesrepublik to Deutsch-
land: German Politics After Unification.* Ann Arbor, MI:
University of Michigan Press, 1993.

MATTOX, GALE A., and SHINGLETON, A. BRADLEY, eds. *Germany at the Crossroads.* Boulder, CO: Westview Press,
1992.

SMYSER, W. R. *The Economy of United Germany.* New
York: St. Martin's Press, 1992.

STARES, PAUL B., ed. *The New Germany and the New Europe.* Washington, DC: Brookings, 1992.

Gary L. Geipel

Global Business: Dominant Organizational Forms

The global corporation has not yet arrived; it has long been predicted but will arrive only when all countries are open economically. Its size and shape will differ from that envisioned by many, for it will not be monolithic either in size or construct. Rather, it will develop in response to the emerging patterns of international economic integration, as determined by governments and influenced by markets around the world.

The evolution of global business began with the joint ventures across national boundaries prior to the advent of the Industrial Revolution and capital-ism. These early units were essentially trading or financial ventures. A distinguishing feature of the nineteenth- and early twentieth-century organiza-tional forms in Europe and the United States was the rise of investment in manufacturing operations abroad. These international corporations largely served local national markets ("market-seekers") or brought resources back to the parent company ("resource-seekers"). Organizationally, this corpo-rate form was often separate from operations in the home country, being legally incorporated as a separate entity.

Following World War II, international business became characterized by foreign affiliates estab-lished to develop the most effective organization for production among several locations to serve multiple national markets at least cost ("efficiency seekers"). Known as the "multinational enterprise" (MNE), or the "transnational corporation," this form became the basis for closer international inte-gration of economies through mobility of capital, technology transfers, exchange of management, greater access to resources, and dispersion of cor-porate cultures.

It now became evident that international eco-nomic integration, formerly presumed to occur through trade, was more effectively accomplished through foreign direct investment (FDI). Trade, after all, could be terminated much more readily than direct investment, and the presence of an or-ganization in a country built ties that became per-manent. By the 1930s, international businesses conducted over half of international trade in man-ufactures within their corporate structures—i.e., as intra-company trade. Furthermore, if trade with nonaffiliates was included, such global trade ac-counted for an overwhelming majority of total in-ternational industrial trade. Government efforts to alter the trade balance of a country, therefore, had to take fully into account the nature of trade among these major worldwide corporations.

Reception by Governments

There was considerable opposition initially to each of the three forms of international business be-cause they were regarded as an extension of colo-nialism. By the 1990s, no significant country con-tinued to oppose internal FDI. To the contrary, virtually all countries were seeking to attract MNEs as a key means of stimulating economic growth and increasing higher-skilled employment. Even former communist countries have now be-come eager to join the world economy through ties with MNEs. Many developing countries still pre-ferred or required joint ventures (JVs), especially in key sectors, with local investors to reduce the "presence" of or control by foreigners.

Experience with JVs has not always been favorable in the view of Western international corporations, who preferred 100 percent ownership for its neat lines of authority and the absence of extraneous in-terests. However, JVs were formed when necessary because of a partner's strength in the local market, access to needed capital, unique management skills within a foreign culture, technology position and strength, or insistence by host governments.

Diverse Forms

Different corporate organizationsl forms arose in Europe and Asia. European enterprises, formed similarly to those in the United States, combine forces by integrating operations more closely through a variety of cartel arrangements. Similar arrangements, illegal in the United States, are permitted under European laws as long as their power is not abusive. In some instances, as with the OPEC arrangements among Arab countries, cartel activity was mandated by the governments.

The Japanese *keiretsu* and the Korean *coebol* (types of holding companies) are the major forms for large corporations in these respective countries. Structural ties link dozens and even hundreds of companies together in mutual shareholding, cross-directorates, and close supplier-vendor relationships. This organizational form permitted ready international expansion of several companies simultaneously and promoted collaboration and inter-company trade as suppliers or vendors. Such ties and collaboration, regarded as "anticompetitive" in the eyes of many observers, are not opposed openly in Europe, but they are considered a significant threat to competition.

Future Integration

The structure of international business began to change in the late twentieth century as economies became more open and more closely integrated. As a consequence, the markets that could be served became larger and also more diverse in the styles and qualities of products demanded. Size and diversity opened up "niche" markets that fostered multiple ties or "strategic alliances" among major corporations to build competitive strength in particular functions or product lines. Within and among countries, alliances were formed in marketing, in production, and in research and development. The new arrangements led to reliance on "comparative advantage" among enterprises rather than among countries. These developments reflected the opening of economies worldwide and the reduction of governmental intervention in the flow of FDI.

The opening of global markets will give further impetus to the grouping of nations into regional economic associations. Within these regional trade alliances or blocs, markets will be virtually wholly open. Sectoral agreements within these blocs will set the rules for FDI in specific industries, such as autos, pharmaceuticals, chemicals, and electronics. These agreements are likely to provide a perceived *equity* in the distribution of the benefits of economic growth among participating nations through the allocation of investment, thereby creating employment, promoting new skills, and offering additional choices for consumers.

Regulation

Government regulation of trade, technology, transfer, investment, and ownership has controlled and curtailed the development of international business, but this is likely to change. Efforts at intergovernmental regulation through the United Nations will continue to be largely ineffective, since it will not be perceived as needed. With the eagerness of all governments to attract these engines of growth, intervening rules will become fewer.

National governments are likely to have less to say about where investment takes place. Municipalities and state governments eager to attract FDI, to establish ties with local industry, to promote local R&D activities, and to enhance employment opportunities within their jurisdiction will have more of a say. The regulations will be few and the incentives large. However, the competitive use of incentives will be costly to the hosts of global corporations.

Given the competition to attract FDI, the creation of social responsibility within the global corporation may not be demanded by the local government. However, these companies will be influenced by consumer and community attitudes and will move toward self-regulation because of public awareness of the impacts of what they are doing.

The future structure of the global corporation will permit a high degree of mobility. Thus, governments, local as well as national, will be induced to learn more about the activities of the companies and to work with them to increase both the volume and quality of the benefits to each.

Benefits

The development of the global corporation awaits a fully global economy, which is not yet in sight. Its rise will be favorable in that it will spread the benefits of employment, trade, and technology (providing higher skills and opportunities for creativity) among more countries. And it will achieve long-term objectives of *efficiency*, *equity*, and *participation* by more peoples and countries, as corporations are drawn to address the social as well as economic objectives of their hosts. Further, the opening of more opportunities will permit small companies to become global also, reducing the dominance of large corporations.

The remaining challenge to these corporations is to adopt policies attuned to the cultures and sociopolitical interests of host countries so that they are seen less as "foreign" and more as locally oriented.

See also BUSINESS STRUCTURE: FORMS, IMPACTS; GLOBAL CULTURE; INTERNATIONAL TRADE REGULATION; INTERNATIONAL TRADE: SUSTAINING GROWTH; MANAGEMENT; PARTICIPATIVE MANAGEMENT.

BIBLIOGRAPHY

BEHRMAN, JACK N. *Industrial Policies: International Restructuring and Transnationals.* Lexington, MA: Lexington Books, 1984.

BEHRMAN, JACK N., and GROSSE, ROBERT E. *International Business and Governments: Issues and Institutions,* Columbia, SC: University of South Carolina Press, 1990.

DUNNING, JOHN H., and USIU, MIKOTO, eds. *Structural Change, Economic Interdependence and World Development.* London: Macmillan, 1987.

MORAN, THEODORE H., ed. *Multinational Corporations: The Political Economy of Foreign Direct Investment.* Lexington, MA: Lexington Books, 1985.

ROBINSON, RICHARD D. *Direct Foreign Investments: Costs and Benefits.* New York: Praeger, 1987.

Jack N. Behrman

Global Consciousness

The central evolutionary trap in human history can be described as follows: When one species attains a position of dominance over all the other species in the ecology of its planet, if it is both egocentrically greedy and has a powerful set of technologies through which to amplify the expression of that greed, unless that dominant species can find a way to limit or to transform its egocentric greediness into something more wholesome, it will foul its planetary nest as surely as the night follows the day . . . perhaps even to its own extinction. This is an accurate synopsis of the writings of Olaf Stapledon and Gregory Bateson.

Olaf Stapledon (1886–1950) is an author whose visionary contributions to the futures community are perhaps underrecognized. Of Stapledon's many multifaceted themes, perhaps the most provocative is what nowadays is useful to call *global consciousness*—a phrase meaning at least two kinds of things:

- Improved awareness of our planetary ecology as a whole system of physical and nonphysical interactions across time.

- The expansion of consciousness beyond the confines of an egocentric sense of self to include transpersonal experiences and/or transcendent self-identity as well.

At issue is whether or not the widespread attainment of global consciousness could provide a necessary (and sufficient) set of conditions for preventing the ecological carrying capacity of the planet from being overshot by runaway growth in "ecological load"—precisely what is currently destabilizing the essential life-support systems of Spaceship Earth. (See Figure 1.)

Stapledon's two main books for futurists are: *Last and First Men* (1931) and *Starmaker* (1937). Together, they stand out as key classics in the field, each being something of a visionary "Encyclopedia of Alternative Futures"—both for humankind as a species unto itself and as depictions of the various ways in which humankind might co-evolve with other intelligent life-systems within and beyond this universe.

Last and First Men

Last and First Men (1931) is an extended scenario in which "Last Men" contact "First Men" (us) in order to communicate a better understanding of the future, which they believe critically important for us to grasp. The book traces a plausible, alternative future history spanning some eighteen separate species of humankind across some 22 billion years between "First and Last Men" and the facing of ultimate physical limits such as the universe entropically "winding-down" as implied by the Second Law of Thermodynamics. Each chapter spans an order of magnitude of ten times more time than the preceding one—a task that, when realized, has much in common with the fugue form perfected by J. S. Bach (but along many more dimensions and exploring many more types of cyclic alternatives). It has even more in common with the system dynamics modeling approach pioneered by Jay FORRESTER and his colleagues at M.I.T.

Evidence of Stapledon's capacity as a true visionary is the fact that the book, although written in 1930, contains highly accurate descriptions of such technological innovations as nuclear fission and global mainframe computers (at that time undreamt of) as well as a genetically engineered species of humankind ("Fifth Men"). It is also shown by the fact that he wrote his manuscript in much the same way as Mozart composed music: He wrote the first draft cleanly and straightforwardly,

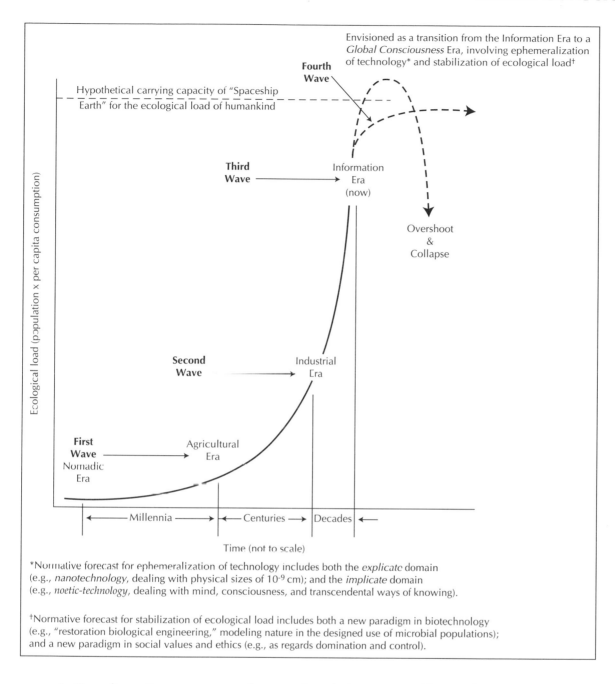

FIGURE 1. Two alternative outcomes to the central evolutionary trap of human history.

and made only relatively minor, cosmetic changes in the second and published version. *Last and First Men* is a veritable handbook of alternative-future scenario possibilities and has been used as such by science fiction writers—e.g., Arthur C. CLARKE—for decades. It could similarly be used to great advantage by scenario writers and futurists who wish to expand their personal repertoires of alternative future possibilities.

Starmaker

Stapledon's masterwork *Starmaker* (1937) is a high-water mark in the science fiction literature dealing with global consciousness. Using the concept of *mindedness*, Stapledon explores various ways in which capacity for global consciousness in a species can give it the resources it needs to resolve, transform, and transcend the "Evolutionary

Trap" summarized in the opening statement of this article. By *mindedness* is meant "a state/process of global consciousness involving the integration of individual minds in such a way that each is a sentiently knowing part of each other and of the whole." And Stapledon explores the possible ramifications of the phenomenon of mindedness in a way parallel to that used in the earlier book. (Where each chapter of *Last and First Men* covers an order-of-magnitude greater span of *time*, each chapter of *Starmaker* covers ten times greater *space*, while at the same time expanding the time dimension even further.)

Species Death and the Nature of Source Causality

Stapledon treated two additional themes having great relevance for the human species as it confronts the "Central Evolutionary Trap" noted above. How future generations of humankind might respond to the threat of species death is a theme explored in both *Last and First Men* and *Starmaker*. In both, Stapledon provides a range of plausible and highly relevant alternative conjectures, all described with the highly sensory concreteness that is desired in a good scenario.

The nature of ultimate source causality—a theme left virtually untreated in the modern futures literature—was an important theme for Stapledon, and the way he treated it could be important for the integration of currently competing paradigms. Stapledon's conception of God (the Starmaker) integrates essential elements of *both* the "Creationist" and "Evolutionary" paradigms of thought about source causality. As such, Stapledon's vision of the divine has an as yet unrealized potential for helping to generate a new paradigm of understanding in Judeo-Christian-Islamic cultures—one that could integrate the religious and the secular in a way that is inclusive, rather than exclusive.

Related Writings of Importance for Futurists

The global consciousness thread that flows through Stapledon's writings can also be found in other works of considerable relevance for futurists. The Stapledonian vision of global consciousness is undoubtedly carried forth in its purest form in Peter Russell's *The Global Brain* (1983) and *The Global Brain Awakens* (1995). By way of exploring Stapledon's concept of mindedness at a planetary level, Russell accurately anticipated the synthesis of computer-based systems and human consciousness that is emerging in the mid-1990s with the development of artificial intelligence, virtual reality, and Information Era arts, sciences, and technologies.

From within this viewpoint it is straightforward to envision how a transition from the "runaway ecological load" to "sustainable, humane culture" might be possible and even feasible. Just as the Third Wave is thought to be bringing a transition from the Industrial Era to the Information Era, at some reasonably close distance in the future there could be a further transition: a Fourth Wave transition from the Information Era to a new era, called the Era of Global Consciousness, organized around the "ephemeralization of technology" and "stabilization of ecological load," rather than "overshoot and collapse"—the other alternative future possibility. (See Figure 1.)

Russell's exploration *The White Hole in Time* (1992) further expands on this theme by exploring the evolutionary significance of light and time—especially the significance of *now*.

Other complementary, Western writings of relevance for futurists include:

- *The Image of the Future* (1954; trans. 1961), the epic treatise of the Dutch social philosopher Fred Polak, who feared the demise of Western culture due to a dearth of adequate "guiding images" for the future.
- *The Phenomenon of Man* (1959), the classic work of the late French Jesuit paleontologist Pierre Teilhard de Chardin, who foresaw the rise of global consciousness in his concepts of *Noosphere*, and *Omega Point*.
- The writings of Willis Harman and his colleagues, which deal with noetic arts, sciences, and technology (defined as dealing with mind, consciousness, and transcendental ways of knowing), including *Old Wine in New Wineskins* (Harman, 1967), *The Emergence of Paraphysics* (O'Regan, 1974), *Changing Images of Man* (Markley and Harman, 1974/1982), *Voluntary Simplicity* (Elgin, 1981/1993), *Global Mind Change* (Harman, 1988), *Hero with a Thousand Faces* (Campbell, 1949/1990), *With the Tongues of Men and Angels* (Hastings, 1991), *Awakening Earth* (Elgin, 1993); and *Using Depth Intuition Methods for Creative Problem Solving and Strategic Innovation* (Markley, 1988/1992).

A Potential Breakthrough in Theory

One of the major barriers to a satisfactory theory of consciousness (ego-centered *or* global) lies in the difficulty of explaining the causal relationship between what the late physicist David Bohm termed the *implicate* and the *explicate* domains of reality (e.g., how is it that free will and determinism interact, as when one decides to bend one's elbow?). A recent article in *The Sciences* offers a concise, nonmathematical, and easy-to-read introduction of a new mathematical-physics theory of "Zero-Point Energy"—a type of energy that may in the near future be shown to be the *source* of the explicate domain—and may also be a direct expression of the source of the implicate domain. (The energy density of the Zero-Point Field is theoretically derived to be proportional to the cube of the frequency: if you double the frequency, you get eight times more energy density!) This theory potentially may form a key part of the technical underpinnings supporting the emergence of a transphysical theory of global consciousness. The article is: "Beyond $E = mc^2$" (Haisch, Rueda, and Puthoff, 1994).

See also APOCALYPTIC FUTURE; CONSCIOUS EVOLUTION; EVOLUTION, LIFE-FORMS IN THE UNIVERSE; GLOBAL CULTURE; HOLISTIC BELIEFS; MIND: NEW MODES OF THINKING; NONRELIGIOUS BELIEFS; SCIENCE FICTION.

BIBLIOGRAPHY

BATESON, GREGORY. *Mind and Nature: A Necessary Unity.* New York: Bantam Books, 1988.

CAMPBELL, JOSEPH. *Hero with a Thousand Faces*, rev. ed. Princeton, NJ: Princeton University Press, 1990.

ELGIN, DUANE. *Awakening Earth: Exploring the Evolution of Human Culture and Consciousness.* New York: William Morrow, 1993.

_____. *Voluntary Simplicity: Toward a Way of Life That Is Outwardly Simple, Inwardly Rich*, rev. ed. New York: William Morrow, 1993.

HAISCH, BERNHARD; RUEDA, ALFONSO; and PUTHOFF, H. E. "Beyond $E = mc^2$." *The Sciences* (November–December 1994): 26–31.

HARMAN, WILLIS. *Global Mind Change: The New Age Revolution in the Way We Think.* New York: Warner, 1988.

_____. "Old Wine in New Wineskins," Chapter 33 in J. F. T. Bugental, ed. *Challenges of Humanistic Psychology.* New York: McGraw-Hill, 1967.

MARKLEY, O. W. "Using Depth Intuition Methods for Creative Problem Solving and Strategic Innovation." *Journal of Creative Behavior* 22/2 (1988): 85–100.

MARKLEY, O. W., and HARMAN, WILLIS W. *Changing Images of Man.* New York: Pergamon Press, 1982.

MOSKOWITZ, SAM. *Far Future Calling: Uncollected Science Fiction and Fantasies of Olaf Stapledon, with an Authorized Biography.* Philadelphia: Oswald Train, 1979.

O'REGAN, BRENDAN. "The Emergence of Paraphysics: Theoretical Foundations." In E. Mitchell, ed. *Psychic Explorations: A Challenge for Science.* New York: G. P. Putnam, 1974.

RUSSELL, PETER. *The Global Brain Awakens.* Palo Alto, CA: Atrium, 1995.

_____. *The White Hole in Time: Our Future Evolution and the Meaning of Now.* San Francisco: Harper San Francisco, 1992.

STAPLEDON, OLAF. *Last and First Men* (1931), bound together with *Starmaker* (1937). New York: Dover, 1968.

TEILHARD DE CHARDIN, PIERRE. *The Phenomenon of Man.* New York, Harper & Row, 1959.

Oliver W. Markley

Global Culture

Global civilization is here, yet its era has scarcely begun. Although this civilization has been slowly developing for centuries, its emergence in these times has been hastened by the end of the Cold War and also by rapid increases in human mobility and communications. In coming decades, globalization will proceed at a rapid, even dizzying, pace.

The present global culture includes a global economy, a rudimentary system of global governance, and a rapidly growing common storehouse of ideas, symbols, values, and beliefs.

The most visible part of this—so conspicuous that one might easily take it to be the whole thing—is a global *popular* culture linked to the mass entertainment media. Global pop culture was dominated at first by products from the West, particularly the United States: rock music, television shows, Hollywood movies. Now it is becoming truly international as other entertainments—such as Asian martial-arts films and Latin American soap operas—find widespread mass followings. In the future, popular culture will become even more international—with constant fads and many combinations of the cultures of different times and places. There are already Japanese salsa bands and Polish rap singers. As globalization proceeds, all cultural styles and symbols become part of a common storehouse. Clearly there is much more to global culture than popular entertainments. All the things we associate with tribal and national cultures— including stories, myths, rituals, structures of thought, and social institutions—now have their global counterparts.

Coming Together, Spinning Apart

Like all great historical processes, cultural globalization produces its own reactions. As the world becomes more unified it also becomes, in many ways, more divided.

To many people, the pervasive encroachment of global culture is a highly undesirable development. Their greatest fear is that it will bring universal standardization and homogenization, the loss of all differences. This fear has produced a variety of counter-globalization movements. Patriots struggle to protect the classical cultures of the nation-states. Other activists lament the loss of tribal cultures with their rich heritages of language, art, and ritual. Religious fundamentalists of various persuasions see global culture as a vehicle of permissiveness and materialism; they struggle—sometimes violently—against its corrupting influences.

Yet at the same time that globalization brings trivialities and troubles, it also brings new freedom, political maturity, and a sense of responsibility for the biosphere. The last years of the twentieth century achieved a rapid, sometimes turbulent, spread of democracy as countries with no history of it leaped into free elections and constitution writing. Theorists who studied "political culture" as a phenomenon of specific bounded societies are now discovering that a global political culture—with common ideas about human rights—is rapidly taking form. Just as artists and performers borrow from around the world, national leaders borrow freely from the world's common pool of political ideas and methods of governance.

Among the forces that have contributed to this globalization of political culture are the consciousness aroused by the women's movement and concern about the global environment. The women's movement is an international one, with common goals that transcend boundaries. Global environmental awareness comes with an image of the world as a whole and of trans-boundary threats such as ozone depletion. These globalizing forces are empowering for certain people and groups, but also strongly threatening to many established cultural and political orders.

So globalization itself becomes a global political issue as people take sides for and against it. The world becomes accustomed to a new kind of polarization: conflict between those who seek to hasten the development of a global civilization and those who yearn to return to simpler and more familiar forms of life. And, as the game is played out, the shape of the playing field keeps changing.

Postmodernism: New Creations, New Diversities

Global civilization is a postmodern civilization in which people everywhere recognize that the forms of culture are socially constructed. They cannot avoid developing such a postmodern consciousness: Life in pluralistic societies, with constant exposure to the news and entertainments of the mass media, generates many daily encounters with deeply different ways of being. The stressful experience called "culture shock" becomes commonplace in everyday life, and people regard turning from one cultural form to another as similar to the transience of buildings and works of art: They are regarded as things that people create and can modify as they choose. Postmodernity nurtures eclecticism, choice, and improvisation—and continual cultural change. All of this change can be unsettling.

Where will it go from here? Three scenarios can illuminate possible change in the twenty-first century:

1. Back to Basics

The world separates into a number of distinct social entities. Different regions become bastions of fundamentalist Christianity, fundamentalist Islam, Marxism, or clearly defined ethnic groups such as Basques, American Indian tribes, Palestinians—each group maintaining its traditions and lifestyles with minimal change or outside interference. (This scenario is popular with cultural preservationists and enthusiasts for the currently fashionable agenda of "devolving" global society into smaller social and political units.)

2. Tomorrow the World

Global civilization comes together under one belief system. Peace and stability are achieved as all learn to understand reality according to the same teachings. (Although most of us would regard this scenario as highly unlikely, many people still hope to unite the world as one great Christian, Islamic, Marxist, or otherwise monolithic society. New Age fundamentalists have their own agendas for cultural unification, different in kind but similar in intent.)

3. A Plurality of Pluralisms

All regions of the world become pluralistic, with people of different races, religions, worldviews, and traditions living in close contact with one another and exposed to global events. There are not only many beliefs, but many beliefs about belief. People inhabit cultures in different ways, improvise, create new forms. "Culture war" (conflict between traditionalists and innovators) becomes a familiar part of social and political life every-where.

See also CHANGE, CULTURAL; CHANGE, EPOCHAL; CULTURE AND SOCIETY; GLOBAL TURNING POINTS; HUMAN RIGHTS; LIFESTYLES, ETHNIC; LIFESTYLES, VALUE-ORIENTED; MASS CULTURE; MULTIFOLD TREND; VALUES CHANGE; VALUES FORMATION.

BIBLIOGRAPHY

ANDERSON, WALTER TRUETT. *Reality Isn't What It Used to Be.* San Francisco: HarperCollins, 1990, 1991.

CLEVELAND, HARLAN. *Birth of a New World.* San Francisco: Jossey-Bass, 1993.

DAYAN, DANIEL, and KATZ, ELIHU. *Media Events: The Live Broadcasting of History.* Cambridge, MA: Harvard University Press, 1992.

GERGEN, KENNETH J. *The Saturated Self.* New York: Basic Books, 1991.

HUNTER, JAMES DAVISON. *Culture Wars.* New York: Basic Books, 1991.

ROSENAU, JAMES N. *Turbulence in World Politics.* Princeton, NJ: Princeton University Press, 1990.

Walter Truett Anderson

Global Environmental Problems

What are the long-term options for growth that are still available to humanity? What are the physical dimensions of growth that are still possible in population, food production, pollution, industrial production, and our use of energy and resources?

The Limits to Growth, a 1972 study for the Club of Rome, examined the long-term causes and consequences of physical growth on the planet. Twenty years later, *Beyond the Limits* updated the data and conducted new computer-simulation studies.

The genius of Aurelio Peccei, who founded the Club of Rome, was that he was several decades ahead of his audience. Many of the world's leaders today have finally achieved an understanding of global problems akin to what Peccei set forth almost a quarter-century ago in his 1969 book *The Chasm Ahead.* National leaders today are joining the struggle to find an appropriate response. Peccei wrote in his last book, *Before It Is Too Late,* published after his death in 1984, about the preconditions for a sustainable society. Despite world leaders' perception of the threat of emerging environmental problems, they still do not understand the profound changes required to deal fundamentally with problems of growth. So what we have experienced is a quarter century of delay, without significant corrective actions being taken. This delay has allowed the problems to intensify, and it has di-

minished the physical resources available for their solution.

Beyond the Limits reaffirmed the urgent importance of bringing coordination among the family of nations in an effort to reduce drastically humanity's assault on the environment and to pursue deliberately the preconditions for a sustainable world.

Transition to a Stable World Future

The Limits to Growth (1972) warned that if the present growth trends "continue unchanged, the limits to growth on this planet will be reached sometime within the next one hundred years. The most probable result will be a rather sudden and uncontrollable decline in both population and industrial capacity." In 1995 global systems are already above sustainable levels.

Because the systems responsible for population growth and economic output have a momentum that keeps their growth going, delays in making appropriate adaptations to the new conditions are almost certain. These delays will make the final changes harder and more abrupt. But within the next fifty years humanity, in order to survive, will finally be forced to reduce its numbers and to economize drastically its use of energy, raw materials, and environmental resources.

There are three different ways in which this transition can occur. The first, and most probable, is that we will overshoot some important global thresholds such as global climate change, the hole in the ozone layer, or massive radiation releases.

Such an overshooting is inevitable because it takes considerable time for political, technological, and ecological systems to respond *after* something drastic happens. The full knowledge of the consequences of such an overshoot usually comes considerably later. It is later still that those consequences become obvious to everyone. It takes even longer before appropriate alternative responses are discovered or invented. These ecological, technological, and political alternatives must then be tested—and only then are appropriate political and economic decisions made and acted upon. If climate patterns shift drastically or ultraviolet radiation increases rapidly not just at the North and South poles but in the lower latitudes, then the reductions in populations and material economies would occur everywhere around the globe.

The second possibility is that, probably through sheer luck, we manage not to trespass beyond important global thresholds. For example, we might stave off ozone depletion, avert climate change, avoid further nuclear disasters like Chernobyl and Three Mile Island. Then the rich countries might continue to grow for at most another fifty years. But the poorer nations would pay the environmental costs of providing ever more raw materials and energy to the richer countries, and stockpile for the richer countries ever more toxic wastes and pollutants.

The third possibility is that humanity understands what it is up against and takes universal corrective measures. Population would decline, not because of famine and epidemics but because people decide that they want to have smaller families. Energy use and resource use would diminish, not because of scarcities but through universal gains in the desire as well as the capability to do more with less. In this scenario, societies worldwide would work deliberately to achieve dramatic economies in their use of energy and resources. Major initiatives in environmental protection would be undertaken everywhere. And people everywhere would work for a more equitable distribution of the goods and services and technologies required for a humane existence.

Living Held Within the Web of Life

Whatever the path we take, the final result will be the same: Human numbers and human consumption will decline until they reach an equilibrium, or balance, within the resource limits and the ecological limits of the globe.

Humanity cannot avoid making some choice among these three options. To ignore the issue is merely to opt for the first or second possibility, with chance determining the final outcome. Human life always exists in the interrelated web of pressures that the environment exerts on any physically expanding system which has grown large enough to encroach on planetary limits.

But it is clear that the three paths would entail radically different implications for what life would be like after the transition. There would be major differences in each path for our morality, environment, political and military institutions, and the quality of political and economic life after the transition.

The fundamental question with which we are left is this: How do we harmonize human systems and the life-supporting systems of our planet?

The Sustainable Society

Beyond the Limits outlined not only our present predicament but also what it will take for society to be sustainable over the long haul, for generations. A sustainable society is one that is farseeing enough, flexible enough, and wise enough not to undermine either its physical or its social systems of support. In the words of the World Commission on Environment and Development, it is a society that "meets the needs of the present without compromising the ability of future generations to meet their own needs."

The current global economy is so wasteful, inefficient, and inequitable that, in a perverse way, it also has tremendous potential for reducing both what it requires from the planet and also what it then spews back into natural systems as pollution and wastes. So in these circumstances it is still possible greatly to reduce total throughput while at the same time raising the quality of life for everyone.

A sustainable society is not necessarily a "zero growth" society, a society in continual economic recession or depression. Rather, in a sustainable society the population and the leaders would ask what growth is for; who would benefit; what it would cost; how long it would last; and whether it can be accommodated by the Earth's storehouse of raw materials and its capacities to recycle, store, or dispose of resultant pollutants and wastes. The difference between the transition to a sustainable society and a present-day economic recession can be likened to the difference between stopping an automobile using its own brakes or by crashing it into a brick wall. A deliberate transition to sustainability would take place slowly enough and carefully enough so that people and businesses could find their proper place in the new society.

There is no reason why a sustainable society has to be either technically or culturally primitive. Nor would a sustainable world have to be a rigid one, or a centrally controlled one. Like every human culture, a sustainable society needs its own rules, laws, standards, boundaries, and social agreements. Rules for sustainability, like every workable social rule, would be put into place not to remove freedoms but to create them and to protect them against their enemies. Such rules could permit many more freedoms than would ever be possible in a world that continues to crowd against its limits.

Diversity is both a cause and a result of sustainability in nature, and therefore a sustainable human society would be diverse in both nature and culture.

A sustainable society could and should be democratic, evolutionary, technically advanced, and challenging. It would have plenty of problems to solve and plenty of ways for people to prove themselves, to serve each other, to realize their abilities, and to live good lives—perhaps more satisfying lives than any available today.

See also ACID RAIN; APOCALYPTIC FUTURE; CHANGE, OPTIMISTIC AND PESSIMISTIC PERSPECTIVES; CLIMATE AND METEOROLOGY; CONSERVATION; CONTINUITY AND DISCONTINUITY; DEFORESTATION; DEMOGRAPHY; DEVELOPMENT, ALTERNATIVE; ENVIRONMENT; ENVIRONMENTAL POLICY CHANGES; ENVIRONMENTAL REFUGEES; EXTINCTION OF SPECIES; GLOBAL WARMING; HAZARDOUS WASTES; OZONE LAYER DEPLETION; RESOURCES; SUSTAINABILITY; TREND INDICATORS.

BIBLIOGRAPHY

MEADOWS, DONELLA H., et al. *The Limits to Growth.* New York: Universe Books, 1972.

MEADOWS, DONELLA H.; MEADOWS, DENNIS L.; and RANDERS, JORGEN. *Beyond the Limits.* Post Mills, VT: Chelsea Green Publishing, 1992.

PECCEI, AURELIO. *The Chasm Ahead.* New York: Macmillan, 1969.

PECCEI, AURELIO, and IKEDA, DAISAKU. *Before It Is Too Late.* Tokyo: Kodansha International, 1984.

Dennis L. Meadows

Global Paradox

A bigger and more open world economy will be dominated by smaller and middle-sized companies, compounding entrenched expectations. Fortune 500 companies now account for only 10 percent of the U.S. economy, down from 20 percent in 1970. This is news to most Americans because the U.S. business media are passionately devoted to covering the Fortune 500 companies almost exclusively, even though small- and medium-sized companies account for 90 percent of the economy. Individual entrepreneurs are creating the new U.S. economy, and entrepreneurs everywhere are recasting the global economy.

Big companies today are trying to act like small companies in order to survive. Jack Welch, the CEO of General Electric, says: "What we are trying relentlessly to do is get that small-company soul—and small company speed—inside our big company body." In today's competitive world, quality can be replicated anywhere. The competitive edge is marketing innovation and swiftness. Small, agile companies will beat big bureaucracies every time. It is not that small is beautiful. Small is powerful.

The most decentralized of the large companies is Asea Brown Boveri, the world's largest power engineering company with annual revenues exceeding $30 billion from 1,200 companies. Each company averages 200 people. CEO Percy Barnevik says, "We are not a global business. We are a collection of local businesses with intense global coordination."

In the center of Europe sits European Telecom, a Belgian phone company that helps Europeans save money by routing their international calls through American carriers in California. This arrangement saves customers one-third against the costly European rates. European Telecom has only three employees and only $50,000 worth of equipment.

The almost perfect metaphor for the movement from bureaucracies of every kind to small, autonomous units is the shift from the mainframe to network PCs. What is unfolding is a global paradox. The bigger the world economy, the more powerful its smallest players: countries, companies, right down to the individual.

As the world integrates economically, the component parts are becoming smaller and more numerous and more important. At once, the global economy is growing while its parts are shrinking. The bigger the system, the more efficient its parts must be. The great negative example is the former Soviet Union, whose inefficient parts brought about its collapse. Business units must become smaller in order to more efficiently globalize the world economy.

The paradox continues: The huge economy is generating smaller and smaller market niches. A Mexican company saw a market niche for small refrigerators for hotel rooms, dormitory rooms, and offices. Today that company sells more refrigerators to the United States than any other company in the world. Thus, the more the world's economies integrate, the more they will differentiate. Differentiation is now a powerful driver of change.

The more democratic the world, the greater the number of countries. In Barcelona in the 1992 Summer Olympics, there were teams representing 172 countries. Well over 200 countries will paricipate in the 1996 Olympics in Atlanta and as many as 300 countries in the 2000 Olympics in Sydney.

This spread of self-rule will characterize the decade ahead of us. As 200 countries become 300 countries, heading toward a world of 1,000 countries, along the way it will become overwhelmingly apparent that the idea of countries and borders is less and less relevant. Boundaries may be important symbolically and culturally, but not too relevant in a single world economy dominated by person-to-person communications.

The global paradox is being powered by the revolution in telecommunications. Enhanced communication is the driving force that simultaneously is creating the huge global economy and making its parts smaller and more powerful.

We are moving toward a world where everyone will be hooked up with everyone else in the world, able to communicate with anyone in the world by voice, data, and image, all by wireless transmission. It will take a long time to get there, but that is where we are going.

Today a person's business card might list a phone number for office and home, a fax number, an E-mail number, an Internet number, and car phone number. But in the not too distant future, each of us will be assigned a lifelong number. Personal computer assistants (carried by persons) will sort out what messages go where. Individuals will phone others wherever they are in the world—without knowing their actual location. Until now we have always called a place and asked for a person. In the new world, we will call a person's unique number and the computer in the sky will ring him or her.

The new telecommunications revolution, zeroing in on the individual, will give new and powerful meaning to the global paradox. The bigger the world economy, the more powerful its smallest players.

Another major paradox that helps us sort out what is going on in the world is, the more universal we become, the more tribal we act.

The tension between the tribal and the universal has always been with us. Now democracy and the revolution in telecommunications (which spreads the word about democracy and gives it urgency) have brought a need for balance between tribal and universal to a new level.

As we globalize the world's economies, many more things will become universal. Yet at the same time, what remains tribal will become more important and powerful. Take language. Even as English becomes the language of the world, non-English languages are gaining in importance within their national boundaries.

The tribal/universal paradox accounts for the ambiguity being experienced throughout Europe. All over the world, people are agreeing to trade more freely with each other, but at the same time are asserting their independence, sovereignty, and distinctiveness. The economic interdependence of the European Union has led people in its member nations to otherwise want to hold on to their identity, their language, their culture, their history.

The riddle of the 1990s is: What will become universal? What will remain tribal?

With the new emphasis on what is tribal in a world increasingly global, the New Age mantra, "Think globally, act locally," is turned on its head. It is now, "Think locally, act globally."

We have witnessed the end of communism, the decline of the nation-state, the emergence of a single-market world economy, the spread of democracy throughout the world, and the new revolution in telecommunications. What we do not yet understand is that these changes set the stage for extraordinary new opportunities for entrepreneurs and small companies. The global paradox tells us that the opportunities for each of us as individuals are far greater than at any time in human history.

See also CHANGE, CULTURAL; ECONOMICS; GLOBAL BUSINESS: DOMINANT ORGANIZATIONAL FORMS; GLOBAL CULTURE; GLOBAL ECONOMY; MULTIFOLD TREND.

BIBLIOGRAPHY

ABURDENE, PATRICIA, and NAISBITT, JOHN. *Megatrends for Women.* New York: Villard Books/Random House, 1992.

NAISBITT, JOHN. *Global Paradox: The Bigger the World Economy, the More Powerful Its Smallest Players.* New York: William Morrow, 1994.

_____. *Megatrends: Ten New Directions Transforming Our Lives.* New York: Warner Books, 1982.

NAISBITT, JOHN, and ABURDENE, PATRICIA. *Megatrends 2000: Ten New Directions for the 1990's.* New York: William Morrow, 1990.

_____. *Reinventing the Corporation: Transforming Your Job and Your Company for the New Information Society.* New York: Warner Books, 1985.

John Naisbitt

Global Statistics

Detailed statistical projections estimating the size of major categories for future years are an essential component of any long-term global program. From the founding of the United Nations in 1945, that organization has spearheaded this task by compiling and regularly publishing every two years global statistics including future projections.

The following table, "Global Statistics of the Future," describes the global situation in past, present, and future covering twenty-three major subject spheres.

The base demographic statistics come from two United Nations publications. The first is *World Population Prospects: The 1992 Revision* (New York: United Nations, 1993). Its future projections to 2025

TABLE 1. Global Statistics of the Future, 1900–2200

	Year			
	1900	*1995*	*2025*	*2200*
GLOBAL POPULATION				
World	1,620 million	5,759 million	8,472 million	11,600 million
Males	818 million	2,900 million	4,256 million	5,810 million
Females	802 million	2,859 million	4,217 million	5,790 million
Ratio males to females	1.020	1.014	1.009	1.003
Population density, per sq. km.	12	42	62	85
Age distribution, as % of world:				
Infants, ages 0–4	12.0	11.5	8.4	5.0
Children, ages 5–14	18.0	20.4	16.5	12.7
Children under 15	30.0	31.9	24.9	17.7
Youths, ages 15–24	25.0	17.9	15.9	13.0
Seniors, ages 60 or over	2.5	9.5	14.1	30.0
Elderly, ages 65 or over	1.3	6.5	9.7	24.6
Aged, ages 80 or over	0.2	1.0	1.6	10.6
School-age children (6–11)	10.0	12.4	9.9	6.0
School-age children (12–14)	4.0	5.8	4.9	3.0
School-age children (15–17)	5.0	5.4	4.9	3.0
Student-age youths (18–23)	13.0	10.8	9.5	7.0
Median age, years	15.0	25.1	31.0	42.7
VITAL STATISTICS				
Population increase p.a.	14.6 million	93.3 million	84.5 million	2.3 million
Births p.a.	58.3 million	144.8 million	147.9 million	141.5 million
Deaths p.a.	43.7 million	51.5 million	63.4 million	139.2 million
Natural increase, % p.a.	0.90	1.63	1.02	0.02
Birth rate % p.a.	3.60	2.51	1.79	1.22
Death rate % p.a.	2.70	0.89	0.77	1.20
Life expectancy, years	36.2	65.4	72.5	84.9
Males	34.0	63.4	70.2	82.5
Females	39.0	67.5	75.0	87.5
CITIES WORLDWIDE				
Metropolises (over 100,000 population)	300	3,780	6,800	65,000
Megacities (over 1 million population)	20	380	650	3,050
Urbanites (urban dwellers)	233 million	2,603 million	5,185 million	10,440 million
Ruralites (rural dwellers)	1,387 million	3,156 million	3,287 million	1,160 million
Urbanites, % of world	14.4	45.2	61.2	90.0
Ruralites, % of world	85.6	54.8	38.8	10.0
Urban poor	100 million	1,640 million	3,050 million	100 million
Urban slum dwellers	20 million	810 million	2,100 million	50 million[1]
GEOPOLITICAL WORLDS				
Group I (UN terminology)	*501 million*	*1,126 million*	*1,288 million*	*1,182 million*
Europe	287 million	516 million	542 million	420 million
Northern America	82 million	292 million	361 million	306 million
Oceania	6 million	29 million	41 million	41 million
Eurasia (former U.S.S.R.)	126 million	289 million	344 million	415 million
Group II	*1,119 million*	*4,633 million*	*7,185 million*	*10,418 million*
Africa	108 million	744 million	1,582 million	3,130 million
Latin America	65 million	482 million	702 million	1,125 million
China	472 million	1,238 million	1,540 million	1,383 million
India	230 million	931 million	1,394 million	1,955 million
Other Asia	244 million	1,238 million	1,967 million	2,825 million[2]
GLOBE	*1,620 million*	*5,759 million*	*8,472 million*	*11,600 million*

Global Statistics

TABLE 1.   Global Statistics of the Future, 1900–2200 *(continued)*

	Year			
	1900	*1995*	*2025*	*2200*
STATUS OF WOMEN				
Global female population	802 million	2,859 million	4,217 million	5,790 million
% literates among women	15	56	70	85
Female life expectancy, years	39.0	67.5	75.0	87.5
Women denied full rights or equality	750 million	2,500 million	1,800 million	100 million[3]
% world income received by women	1	10	20	40
% world property owned by women	0	1	3	20
Women as % of all poor	80	70	60	55
Women as % of all illiterates	80	66	55	52
Women as % of all refugees	65	80	70	60
Women as % of all ill/sick	60	75	57	52
Female urban poor	20 million	700 million	1,400 million	80 million
Female urban slum dwellers	2 million	320 million	980 million	40 million
MOTHERHOOD				
Women of childbearing age (15–49)	389 million	1,341 million	2,041 million	2,320 million
Ditto, % of world population	24.0	25.3	24.7	20.0
Fertility rate (births per woman)	4.0	3.17	2.36	2.06
Gross reproduction rate, per woman	2.0	1.55	1.15	0.7
Net reproduction rate, per woman	1.8	1.36	1.08	0.6
Contraceptive prevalence rate, %	5	56	75	95
Birth rate, % p.a. (males, females)	3.60	2.51	1.79	1.22
Births p.a. (males, females)	58.3 million	144.8 million	147.9 million	141.5 million
Induced abortions, p.a.	5 million	60 million	130 million	500 million
Maternal mortality, p.a., total	550,000	500,000	400,000	80,000[4]
Ditto due to abortion	210,000	200,000	150,000	30,000
FAMILIES				
Families/homes/households	324 million	1,339 million	2,118 million	3,135 million
Household size, persons	5.0	4.3	4.0	3.7
Households headed by women, %	3	33	55	70
New families each year	12 million	34 million	38 million	39 million
% women 15–19 already married	15	23	25	35
Dependency ratio, %	70.0	62.6	52.1	45.0
Marriage rate per 1000 population p.a.	3	4	5	6
Divorce rate per 1000 population p.a.	0.05	0.4	1	3
Battered women	95 million	200 million	500 million	100 million[5]
Women raped p.a.	10 million	15 million	25 million	5 million[6]
Child-abuse incidents p.a.	15 million	90 million	70 million	30 million[7]
CHILDREN				
Infants (0–4 years)	194 million	662 million	712 million	580 million
Children (5–14)	292 million	1,175 million	1,398 million	1,473 million
School-age children (6–14)	227 million	1,048 million	1,254 million	1,044 million
Babies born malnourished, p.a.	8 million	10 million	25 million	1 million[8]
Sick/ill children	300 million	600 million	1,000 million	200 million[9]
Exploited child labor	30 million	50 million	200 million	20 million[10]
Orphans	150 million	450 million	1,000 million	1,500 million
Abandoned children and infants	140 million	60 million	260 million	500 million
Homeless/familyless children	250 million	300 million	700 million	1,000 million
Magacity street children	1 million	100 million	300 million	800 million
Infant mortality (under 1), % p.a.	9.0	5.9	3.1	0.5
Toddler mortality (1–4 years), % p.a.	3.0	1.0	0.7	0.1
EDUCATION				
Primary schools	300,000	3.2 million	4 million	5 million

Pupils in school	35 million	980 million	1.5 billion	1.3 billion
Adults, primary-educated	100 million	1.2 billion	3.3 billion	7.5 billion
Adults without primary education	926 million	2.7 billion	3.1 billion	2.0 billion
School teachers	2 million	39 million	50 million	100 million
University campuses	500	20,000	30,000	100,000
College students	2 million	65 million	120 million	500 million
Foreign students	20,000	3 million	15 million	100 million

ILLNESS AND DISEASE

Sufferers from disease or illness	420 million	1,152 million	1,395 million	15 million[11]
Sufferers experiencing chronic pain	350 million	900 million	1,400 million	14 million[12]
Nonsighted (totally blind)	9 million	28 million	35 million	50 million
Hearing-impaired (deaf)	90 million	320 million	500 million	700 million
Leprosy sufferers (lepers)	5 million	13 million	1 million	0[13]
New malaria cases p.a.	100 million	400 million	30 million	0
Psychotics	10 million	51 million	10 million	0
Schizophrenics	2 million	10 million	0	0
Psychoneurotics	150 million	950 million	1.1 billion	1.5 billion
Suicides per year	300,000	410,000	500,000	1 million
Disabled (handicapped)	400 million	1.6 billion	1.8 billion	2 billion
Handicapped children	100 million	340 million	500 million	700 million
Severely mentally-retarded	40 million	130 million	50 million	0
Arthritics	80 million	300 million	50 million	0
Persons not immunized	1.4 billion	4 billion	100 million	0
Diarrheal deaths of under-5-year olds, p.a.	2 million	5 million	700,000	0
AIDS carriers	0	70 million	400 million	0
AIDS-related deaths p.a.	0	500,000	10 million	0
Tobacco smokers	42 million	650 million	20 million	0
Tobacco-related deaths p.a.	150,000	2.6 million	5 million	0
Drug addicts (illicit drug users)	1 million	65 million	100 million	0

HEALTH CARE

Persons in good health	300 million	1.1 billion	2.4 billion	7 billion
Physicians	1 million	5.2 million	7.9 million	13 million
Nurses and midwives	2 million	7.7 million	10.5 million	16 million
Dentists	100,000	500,000	800,000	1,400,000
Pharmacists	50,000	520,000	1 billion	1.6 billion
World pharmaceutical market, $ p.a.	200 million	130 billion	400 billion	2 trillion
Hospitals	60,000	240,000	300,000	500,000
Hospital beds	4 million	18.2 million	23 million	35 million
Mental institutions	20,000	150,000	200,000	1,000[14]
Health care costs, $ p.a.	10 billion	2,500 billion	4 trillion	10 trillion
Population per doctor	9,500	3,780	2,500	500

HUMAN RIGHTS AND ABUSES

The poor (living in poverty)	1.2 billion	2.4 billion	3.3 billion	100 million
Absolutely poor (in absolute poverty)	900 million	960 million	700 million	0[15]
Undernourished	1.2 billion	1.8 billion	500 million	0
Hungry	700 million	950 million	400 million	0
Severely malnourished	500 million	550 million	300 million	0
On verge of starvation	200 million	400 million	200 million	0
Starvation-related deaths p.a.	20 million	20 million	10 million	0
Without safe drinking water	1.4 billion	1.3 billion	1 billion	0
With unsafe water and bad sanitation	1.5 billion	3.0 billion	1 billion	30 million
Killed by dirty water, per day	20,000	25,000	10,000	0
With no access to electricity, %	86	41	30	0
With no access to radio or TV, %	100	67	20	0
Without adequate shelter	200 million	1.1 billion	700 million	10 million
With no shelter whatsoever	50 million	100 million	30 million	0
No access to schools	1.2 billion	1 billion	500 million	0
Without money to buy food	500 million	1.1 billion	700 million	0

Global Statistics

TABLE 1. Global Statistics of the Future, 1900–2200 *(continued)*

	Year			
	1900	*1995*	*2025*	*2200*
HUMAN RIGHTS AND ABUSES *(continued)*				
With no access to medical care	1.1 billion	1.5 billion	700 million	0
Cave-dwellers	200 million	50 million	10 million	0
Stateless (with no nationality)	1 million	10 million	5 million	0
Prisoners	5 million	100 million	50 million	10 million
Prisoners being tortured	500,000	100,000	0	0
Disenfranchised (no control by vote)	1.2 billion	2.1 billion	100 million	0
Non-readers (orate, illiterate adults)	739 million	1,392 million	1,171 million	382 million
Permanently unsettled refugees	50 million	14 million	10 million	0
Persons abused in childhood	400 million	300 million	350 million	0
Persons with human rights violated	1.4 billion	2,590 million	1.7 billion	30 million
COMMUNICATION				
Languages	11,600	9,500	8,000	2,000
Trade languages	200	700	800	2,000
Official state languages	25	95	150	500
Countries with own radio services	0	270	300	100
Countries with own TV services	0	150	250	100
Radio sets in use	0	1.8 billion	5 billion	9 billion
Radio hours broadcast p.a.	0	24 million	60 million	1 billion
Television sets	0	850 million	5 billion	10 billion
TV hours broadcast	0	21 million	70 million	1 billion
Ham radio operators	0	1.2 million	2 million	30 million
Daily newspapers	750	8,300	7,000	20,000
Newspaper circulation	70 million	590 million	1 billion	3 billion
Newsprint per global inhabitant, pounds p.a.	0.1	12	10	10
Mail, pieces p.a.	1 billion	280 billion	450 billion	2 trillion
Electronic mail messages p.a.	0	6 billion	50 billion	1 trillion
Telephones	3 million	750 million	1.1 billion	4 billion
Direct-dial telephones	0	710 million	1.1 billion	4 billion
Telephone calls made, p.a.	150 million	120 billion	300 billion	1 trillion
Fax machines	0	35 million	350 million	10 billion
Videocassette recorders (VCRs)	0	500 million	2 billion	10 billion
Cinemas	100	250,000	400,000	2 billion
Cinema seats	5,000	75 million	200 million	1 billion
Cinema attenders p.a.	200,000	15 billion	30 billion	1 trillion
General-purpose computers	0	150 million	850 million	700 billion
Computer sales p.a.	0	35 million	80 million	1 billion
Computer power, MIPS (world total)	0	29 million	500 million	25 trillion
Electronic bulletin boards	0	100,000	1 million	100 million
Internet computer users	0	18 million	80 million	2 billion
TRANSPORTATION				
Roads, length in miles	1 million	17 million	25 million	40 million
Bicycles	10,000	850 million	1.7 billion	2 billion
Commercial vehicles	0	120 million	250 million	300 million
Passenger cars	30,000	410 million	500 million	700 million
Cars produced p.a.	3,000	45 million	40 million	50 million
Railway track, length in miles	454,730	880,000	1.5 million	5 million
Rail passenger-miles p.a.	10 billion	1,100 billion	2 trillion	3 trillion
Air traffic, passenger-miles p.a.	0	950 billion	3 trillion	10 trillion
Airport and airfields	0	67,000	100,000	500,000
Sea traffic: merchant ships	2,000	75,300	100,000	300,000
Sea freight, tons p.a.	10 million	3.6 billion	10 billion	100 billion
Seamen (merchant seafarers)	300,000	10 million	15 million	10 million

AGRICULTURE AND LIVESTOCK

Agricultural land, sq. km.	15 million	46.5 million	55 million	70 million
Agricultural land as % all land	11	34	40	51
Forest land, sq. km.	100 million	40.1 million	20 million	5 million
Harvested land as % all arable land	15	77	90	98
Global agricultural research, $ p.a.	3 million	9 billion	20 billion	50 billion
Tractors in use	0	22 million	40 million	200 million
Fish catches, metric tons p.a.	1 million	91 million	100 million	150 million
Cattle	80 million	1.3 billion	1.0 billion	300 million[16]
Sheep	200 million	1.1 billion	800 million	100 million
Chickens	600 million	9.0 billion	5 billion	1 billion
Horses, mules, asses	20 million	120 million	150 million	300 million
Rats	500 million	20 billion	10 billion	1 billion[17]
Food/property destroyed by rats, $ p.a.	5 billion	350 billion	100 billion	500 million
Domestic pets	5 million	1 billion	1.5 billion	100 million
Nomads and pastoralists	40 million	220 million	100 million	10 million

INDUSTRIALIZATION

Economically active persons	300 million	2.4 billion	3 billion	5 billion
Labor force, persons	100 million	1.9 billion	2.5 billion	4 billion
Unemployed	10 million	100 million	200 million	500 million
Underemployed	30 million	600 million	1 billion	2 billion
Beggars	10 million	80 million	150 million	300 million
Scientists and engineers	1 million	38 million	60 million	100 million
Pure scientists	10,000	1 million	1.3 million	2 million
Scientific research, $ p.a.	100 million	125 billion	200 billion	400 billion
Industrial robots	0	14 million	25 million	100 million
Known chemicals	5,000	7 million	10 million	20 million
New chemicals created p.a.	200	10,000	50,000	60,000
Police officers	400,000	5.1 million	6 million	7 million
Professional firefighters	100,000	2 million	2.5 million	3 million
Lawyers	300,000	6 million	8 million	9 million
Labor migrants	2 million	150 million	300 million	500 million

ENERGY PRODUCTION

Primary energy, quads BTU p.a.	10 billion	3.2 quadrillion	9 quadrillion	10 quintillion
Coal, known reserves, metric tons	50 billion	7,600 billion	8 trillion	4 trillion
Coal, kg mined per capita p.a.	1,000	1,870	2,000	2,500
Electricity, kilowatt hours p.a.	100 million	9.7 trillion	100 trillion	1 quadrillion
Petroleum, known reserves, metric tons	0	91 billion	100 billion	1 billion[18]
Oil, total recoverable reserves, barrels	1 billion	1,635 billion	2 trillion	0
Oil, output in barrels p.a.	1 million	19.8 billion	30 billion	1 billion
Nuclear power produced, kilowatt hours p.a.	0	630 billion	1 trillion	100 trillion
Natural gas, known reserves, cubic meters	100 billion	86 trillion	100 trillion	200 trillion

TOURISM

Foreign tourists p.a.	1 million	350 million	600 million	2 billion
Domestic tourists p.a.	5 million	3.7 billion	4.5 billion	5 billion
Registered hotel beds	500,000	15.0 million	30 million	100 million
Religious pilgrims p.a.	2 million	350 million	800 million	1.5 billion

FINANCE AND TRADE

Gross world product, $ p.a.	200 billion	18 trillion	30 trillion	300 trillion
World imports, $ p.a.	30 billion	2,200 billion	4 trillion	25 trillion
World exports, $ p.a.	25 billion	2,100 billion	3 trillion	20 trillion
Balance of trade, $	5 billion	100 billion	1 trillion	5 trillion
Gold reserves, kg	2 million	32 million	50 million	1 billion
Foreign economic aid, $ p.a.	50 million	60 billion	200 billion	2 trillion
Average income per person, $ p.a.	125	3,120	3,540	25,860
Average family income, $ p.a.	625	13,440	14,160	95,700
Transnationals (TNCs, multinationals)	400	10,800	20,000	300,000

TABLE 1. Global Statistics of the Future, 1900–2200 *(continued)*

	Year			
	1900	*1995*	*2025*	*2200*
FINANCE AND TRADE *(continued)*				
Nongovernmental organizations (NGOs)	50	3,500	10,000	100,000
Millionaires (each worth over $1 million)	20,000	2.5 million	6 million	300 million
Billionaires (each worth over $1 billion)	10	400	600	10,000
Cost of advertising, $ p.a.	300 million	120 billion	300 billion	2 trillion
Betting and gambling, $ p.a.	1 billion	700 billion	1,500 billion	3 trillion
Business failures (bankruptcies) p.a.	5,000	250,000	300,000	100,000
MILITARIZATION				
Military expenditures, $ p.a.	500 million	950 billion	100 billion	20 billion[19]
Troops in regular armed forces	5 million	25 million	15 million	2 million
Paramilitary troops	2 million	280 million	5 million	1 million
Military supply personnel	200,000	52 million	20 million	30 million
Combat aircraft	0	60,000	20,000	2,000
Nuclear warheads	0	65,000	1,000	0[20]
Submarine-borne SLBMs	0	9,200	500	0
Chemical weapons, tons	1,000	300,000	10,000	0
International arms trade, $ p.a.	5 million	42 billion	20 billion	0
Handguns (personal firearms)	1 million	600 million	100 million	0
CRIME				
Crimes (registered) p.a.	5 million	500 million	400 million	10 million[21]
Property crimes p.a.	2 million	100 million	50 million	1 million
Violent crimes p.a.	2 million	27 million	30 million	1 million
Criminals	4 million	550 million	350 million	15 million
Murders p.a.	500,000	950,000	800,000	10,000
Terrorist incidents p.a.	100	4,000	2,000	200
Cost of all varieties of crime, $ p.a.	750 million	3,300 billion	2 trillion	10 billion
White-collar crime, $ p.a.	200 million	1,000 billion	500 billion	1 billion
Financial fraud, $ p.a.	150 million	900 billion	400 billion	1 billion
Organized crime, $ p.a.	100 million	600 billion	1 trillion	2 billion
Credit card fraud, $ p.a.	0	550 million	200 billion	1 billion
Alcohol/liquor expenditures, $ p.a.	50 million	380 billion	50 billion	0[22]
World purchases of cigarettes, $ p.a.	30 million	290 billion	10 billion	0
Illegal drug traffic, $ p.a.	20 million	150 billion	10 billion	0
Shoplifting, $ p.a.	20 million	95 billion	5 billion	0[23]
Computer crime, $ p.a.	0	60 billion	10 billion	1 billion
Major art thefts, $ p.a.	100 million	25 billion	1 billion	0
Pornography, $ p.a.	20 million	20 billion	1 billion	0
Automobile thefts, $ p.a.	0	20 billion	1 billion	0
RELIGION				
Christians	558,056000	1,923,812,000	3,022,623,000	4,397,929,000
Muslims	200,102000	1,047,616,000	1,716,091,000	2,624, 567,000
Nonreligious	2,923,000	931,409,000	1,279,525,000	1,62 6,497,000
Hindus	203,033,000	772,896,000	1,113,103,000	1,398,32 9,000
Buddhists	127,159,000	336,742,000	484,432,000	607,601,000
Atheists	226,000	231,150,000	237,257,000	249,000,000
Chinese folk-religionists	380,404,000	195,156,000	233,813,000	253,162,000
New-religionists	5,910,000	151,209,000	217,314,000	272,280,000
Tribal religionists	106,340,000	99,460,000	77,026,000	15,416,000
Sikhs	2,961,000	19,811,000	28,370,000	35,434,000
Jews	12,270,000	16,986,000	21,468,000	24,697,000
Shamanists	11,341,000	11,057,000	15,849,000	19,859,000
Confucians	640,000	6,357,000	9,142,000	11,459,000

Baha'is	9,000	5,892,000	9,544,000	14,559,000
Jains	1,323,000	4,003,000	5,795,000	7,351,000
Shintoists	6,720,000	3,399,000	4,892,000	6,138,000
Other religionists	470,000	19,541,000	27,978,000	36,273,000
LITERATURE				
Adult population (over 15)	1,026 million	3,937 million	6,421 million	9,547 million
Literates	287 million	2,545 million	5,250 million	9,165 million
Nonliterates	739 million	1,392 million	1,171 million	382 million
Literates, % of adults	27.9	54.7	81.8	96.0
Nonliterates, % of adults	72.1	45.3	18.2	4.0
New book titles yearly	40,000	880,000	950,000	3 million
Books printed yearly	900 million	30 billion	50 billion	100 million
Scientific journals	15,000	350,000	450,000	2 million
Scientific articles published yearly	60,000	2 million	3 million	10 million
Periodicals	9,000	130,000	180,000	500,000
Magazines	40,000	500,000	700,000	3 million
Encyclopedias	100	500	1,000	3,000
General encyclopedias	20	70	200	500
Subject encyclopedias	80	430	800	2,500
Bookshops	65,000	600,000	1 million	10 million
Public libraries	30,000	270,000	500,000	2 million
Library volumes (books)	70 million	3.7 billion	10 billion	100 billion

Notes: p.a. – per annum (per year); all sums of money are given in U.S. dollars ($).
Notes for 2200 (end column):

[1] Likely to decrease drastically as urban planning tackles the problem.

[2] Countries are specified, and Groups I and II defined, in the UN's *Long-Range World Population Projections* (1992).

[3] Falling dramatically over 200 years as women's full rights are established.

[4] Falling with enforced universal medical coverage.

[5] Falling as the practice becomes fully exposed and unacceptable.

[6] Dropping due to public awareness and universal protection.

[7] Falling with massive public determination and safeguards.

[8] Dramatic reduction due to strict medical requirements.

[9] Falling with fuller medical programs.

[10] No longer acceptable, legal, or in most countries even possible by 2200.

[11] Drastic decline as universal health care spreads.

[12] Controlled then virtually eliminated by medical advances.

[13] Leprosy and the other diseases or disabilities enumerated in the 13 lines with zeros in this section are likely to have been eradicated medically by 2200.

[14] Disappearing as medical science conquers all mental illnesses as anticipated.

[15] All lines in this section reaching zero by 2200 reflect successful worldwide campaigns to completely eradicate unacceptable aspects of poverty and other human rights abuses as politically and ethically intolerable.

[16] Declining in numbers as the global beef industry yields to varieties of vegetarianism for a number of reasons (likewise with the next two lines).

[17] Expected to be finally eradicated within two centuries, with scientific solutions.

[18] Petroleum and oil reserves (next two lines) are likely to be fully used up within 200 years.

[19] Expected to fall drastically from their untenable high point in 1995.

[20] Nuclear weapons may well be totally eliminated within 20–200 years, likewise (next four lines) other mass-destruction weapons. The arms trade could be liquidated through political action, and handgun epidemics through bans on manufacture and through rigid electronic monitoring.

[21] Virtually eliminated in many categories through strict electronic monitoring.

[22] Likely to follow tobacco and other drugs as harmful, hence undesirable.

[23] Fully eliminated through rigid electronic monitoring and policies.

are given under four alternate scenarios. These are labeled Medium-Variant, High-Variant, Low-Variant, and Constant Fertility Variant projections.

The United Nations has also published *Long-Range World Population Projections: Two Centuries of Population Growth, 1950–2150* (New York, 1992). Statistics are provided for seven alternate scenarios: a Medium-Fertility, High-Fertility, Medium/High-Fertility, Low-Fertility, Medium/Low-Fertility, Constant-Fertility, and Instant-Replacement-Fertility extensions. This table utilizes the most likely of the seven, namely the Medium-Variant and Medium-Fertility extensions.

Comprehensive demographics for the year 1900 were collected in national population censuses by all countries of the world at that time. These have been compiled in the *World Christian Encyclopedia* (Oxford University Press, 1982 and subsequently).

Past and present figures for a vast number of nondemographic categories are given in B. R. Mitchell, *International Historical Statistics, 1750–1988* (Macmillan/UK, 1990, three volumes). Future figures shown here for the years 2025 and 2200 have been published, in the *AD 2000 Global Monitor*, issues numbers 23–27 (September 1992–January 1993). Other topics come from a handbook of global statistics entitled *Our Globe and How to Reach It* (1990). Some data sets are repeated under a second heading to improve comprehensiveness.

The two columns for the years 2025 and 2200 should not be considered as concrete predictions. They give only the figures considered most likely in the present investigation or by authorities in their fields.

There are numerous appearances of *0* (zero) in the first column, for over thirty categories. These simply mean that in the year 1900 they did not exist or had not yet started. Radio and television, for instance, had not yet been invented. The AIDS epidemic had not begun.

Another surprising aspect is the string of forty-six zeroes in the last column representing the most likely situation in 2200. Zeroes are not due to naive utopianism. Many represent a realistic assessment of what would appear very probable after 250 years of determined, informed, aggressive, democratic activism. Many futurists see various diseases or social disorders as certain to be eliminated once and for all by advances in medical expertise. Also, total electronic monitoring may well eliminate crime, fraud, and an extensive array of other antisocial behavior patterns.

A number of other categories that have declined dramatically in numbers do so for similar reasons.

It means that the world's activists are dealing successfully with the intolerable situation of earlier years.

David B. Barrett

Global Turning Points

How are we to understand the turbulence of our times? Is there a frame of reference within which we can make sense of the American experience as the twentieth century draws to a close? A look at the past may offer us a clue.

Many historians divide Western history into clearly defined periods, shaped by unique characteristics. This demarcation is never neat or tidy. The characteristics that shape a particular period also influence the succeeding phase of history. The shift from one age to the next has always produced a time of dissolution of old patterns or paradigms of life, of turbulence as old forms lose their force, and of creativity as new patterns of life and organization evolve. Such major changes in perspective have sometimes been described as *paradigm shifts*.

The American story encompasses what is generally referred to as the modern age, which began around 1500. Characteristics defining the modern age include geographical exploration, the expansion of Europe, and the creation of colonial empires; the rise of the nation-state; the Newtonian view of the universe and of physical reality; the printing press with the subsequent diffusion of knowledge that followed its invention in 1453; the introduction of gunpowder; the predominance of sea power; progress defined as the expansion of the scientific and material realms; the triumph of reason over faith as the perceived foundation of reality; and an enlarged understanding of liberty.

The twentieth century marks the end of the modern age and the beginning of a new epoch of history. The forces that shaped the last five hundred years are giving way to a new set of defining impulses. Thus, we live in a century characterized by the massive dissolution of authority, the decline of established institutions, and fundamental shifts in the patterns of life. It is, as well, a time of unprecedented creation of new understandings and possibilities. This shift has shaped the twentieth century. It has been the seedbed of two world wars, of the rise and fall of communism, and of great economic/material growth and political independence.

What are some of the characteristics shaping the future?

- We are moving from the era of nation-states to the age of a world community as the defining political and economic framework. All of the major issues confronting America—economic growth, energy resources, finance capital, AIDS, protection of the environment, immigration, drugs, institutional stability—are global issues.

- Electronics is challenging print as the main medium of visual communication. Any change in the primary mode of communication in a society has significant consequences for other aspects of life such as culture, education, and the family.

- Interdependence is becoming the dominant requirement for future progress. In biology and the natural world, the progression of life goes from dependence to independence, to interdependence. The same is true of the social/political realm. We are moving into a phase where we are adapting to the imperatives of interdependence just as we adapted to the evolution of independence two hundred years ago.

- We are the first generation to seek an empirical/scientific comprehension of the origin of the universe. We have come to see ourselves as part of an unfolding story, and we are trying to understand the human relationship to the beginnings of time and matter. This alters our view of who we are and where we come from.

- We have the potential to become partners with nature in defining what constitutes a human being. With genetic engineering, we can determine some characteristics of unborn children—in effect, create *designer children*. It may be possible to transfer genetic traits between species, thus blurring the distinction between species—hopefully with more positive results than imagined by H. G. WELLS in *The Island of Doctor Moreau*.

- Whereas the masculine impulse was predominant in the modern age, the feminine instinct, as expressed in both men and women, is becoming more pronounced in shaping the future. We see this in the collapse of hierarchical structures and the emergence of more cooperative modes of organization, in a new emphasis on intuition, in an effort to reintegrate ourselves with Earth and the natural order from whence we tore ourselves during the industrial revolution and subsequent urbanization, and in an increased emphasis on *being* rather than *having*.

- The assumptions underlying almost five hundred years of Western science are yielding to new assumptions. The scientific enterprise was built on the belief that there is an objective universe that can be explored by methods of scientific inquiry (the objectivist assumption); that what is scientifically real must take as its basic datum only that which is physically observable (the positivist assumption); and that scientific description consists in explaining complex phenomena in terms of more elemental events (the reductionist assumption). The new assumptions for the science of the future are likely to be an emphatic departure from many of these past assumptions. For example, quantum mechanics is beginning to suggest that consciousness may not be the end-product of material evolution; rather, that consciousness was here first. Consciousness may be causal.

Such trends bring us to one of the major watersheds of history. André Malraux, a noted French cultural authority, suggested that the historical shift the world is experiencing "has but one precedent; the discovery of fire." Czech writer and political leader Václav Havel warned that some of the tasks we face "might be as extended and complex a process as the creation of a Christian Europe" in the centuries following the bifurcation and collapse of Roman Empire.

What is the core challenge as we move deeper into a new historical era? It is to evolve a legitimizing vision of life that expresses the spiritual essence of the human journey with such force and resonance as to define world purposes and standards of conduct for a new epoch of history. For each one of us, it means thinking through who we are, what we believe, and what we are living for.

No generation was ever offered a challenge of greater magnitude, possibility, and hope.

See also CHANGE, EPOCHAL; EVOLUTION, BIOLOGICAL; EVOLUTION, SOCIAL; GENETIC ENGINEERING; GLOBAL CONSCIOUSNESS; GLOBAL CULTURE; LITERATURE; MIND: NEW MODES OF THINKING; PRINTED WORD.

BIBLIOGRAPHY

ATTALI, JACQUES. *Millennium*. New York: Random House, Inc., 1991.

DRUCKER, PETER F. *The New Realities*. New York: Harper & Row, 1989.

HALBERSTAM, DAVID. *The Next Century*. New York: William Morrow, 1991.

HARMAN, WILLIS. *Global Mind Change*. Indianapolis, IN: Knowledge Systems, 1988.

HAVEL, VÁCLAV. *Disturbing the Peace*. New York: Knopf, 1990.

LUKACS, JOHN. *The End of the Twentieth Century and of the Modern Age*. New York: Ticknor & Fields, 1993.

MAY, ROLLO. *The Cry for Myth.* New York: Norton, 1991.
POSTMAN, NEIL. *Technopoly.* New York: Knopf, 1992.
SWIMME, BRIAN, AND BERRY, THOMAS. *The Universe Story.* New York: HarperCollins, 1992.

William Van Dusen Wishard

Global Warming

During the 2-million-year-long great, or Pleistocene, Ice Age which ended about 10,000 years ago, several intensely cold periods known as *glacials* alternated with much warmer periods called *interglacials*. These warming and cooling trends were caused by natural climatic factors—complex interactions of the sun, Earth, atmosphere, and ocean. In more recent times, warming and cooling trends have continued, but on a much smaller time scale. For example, the "Medieval Warm" extended from about 700 AD to about 1150 AD, while the "Little Ice Age" began about 1180 AD and ended only a century ago.

The Little Ice Age was characterized by glacial advances in both North America and Europe. Moveover, alpine glaciers in New Zealand and the Andes moved further downslope than at any time in the previous 8,000 years. By the late 1400s, the sea ice had completely blocked the shipping lanes between Iceland and Greenland and elsewhere. It was so cold that farmers could no longer raise grain in Iceland. Eventually, however, the glacial shrinking of the late nineteenth century signaled that the Little Ice Age had come to an end.

For hundreds of years, astronomers have tried to link the twenty-two-year sunspot cycle with temperature changes on Earth. Sunspots are caused by turbulence in the sun's magnetic field. During one phase of the cycle, the spots are most numerous in the northern hemisphere, while in the southern hemisphere there is a simultaneous minimum. A few years later, the pattern is reversed. With the aid of satellite imagery, astronomers have succeeded in measuring solar energy production throughout a given cycle. They noticed that solar energy generation declines somewhat when the sunspots disappear. Most climatologists have concluded, however, that the change in energy production has very little influence on the actual temperature of the Earth.

The oceans, which cover over 70 percent of the Earth's surface, are active components of the global climatic system. They can influence long-term variations in the temperature of our planet. The oceans' most important feature, in this regard, is their ability to absorb, recirculate, and release heat. The surface temperature of the ocean varies from 28° F (–2° C) near the North and South poles to a maximum of 86° F (30° C) near the equator. The ocean currents, in particular, are dynamic forces in the transfer of warmth from one region of the Earth to another. Two of the most important currents in this regard are the Gulf Stream and El Niño.

The Gulf Stream has its origin in the western Caribbean, where it is warmed up by the equatorial sun. It then flows through the Gulf of Mexico, around the tip of Florida, and then northward along the Atlantic coast of the United States to North Carolina. From there it passes northeastward across the Atlantic. While off coastal North Carolina, the Gulf Stream is about 15° F (6° C) warmer than the water around it, and during winter, it is actually warmer than the overlying atmosphere. As a result, the winds that blow toward Europe are warmed considerably as they move eastward over the Gulf Stream. This results in unusually mild winters for Great Britain and Norway.

El Niño is another major ocean current that may have a warming influence on certain regions of the Earth. With the aid of satellites and computers, scientists have recently learned a great deal about it. El Niño has its origin in the eastward shift of a pool of warm water that usually is confined to the equatorial Pacific, just northeast of Australia. This shift occurs at intervals of three to seven years, the last two occurring in 1986 to 1987 and 1991 to 1992. The tropical heat that is released into the atmosphere from El Niño displaces eastwardly, blowing jet streams high in the atmosphere to new positions over North and South America, generally resulting in highly unusual weather conditions. For example, El Niño in 1991 to 1992 brought torrential rainfall along the Gulf Coast and shirtsleeve weather to the region around Fargo, North Dakota. After reaching the Pacific Coast of North America, El Niño flows southward and warms up the weather in Ecuador and Peru.

The Earth's atmospheric temperature would be considerably higher were it not for the heat "sink" function performed by the global oceans. These vast bodies of water, up to six miles deep, absorb a considerable amount of atmospheric heat. Then, over a period of years, this heat is slowly released back into the atmosphere. Scientists are still not exactly sure of the role played by the oceans in shaping the world's climate. There is no doubt, however, that major ocean currents like the Gulf Stream and El Niño and the ocean's function as a thermal sink must have a major influence on the warming phenomenon, highly publicized in recent years, known as the *greenhouse effect.*

Have you ever parked your car on a sunny summer day with the windows closed? When you reentered your car some time later, it felt like an oven. Why? Because of the greenhouse effect. The solar (short-wave) radiation freely passed through your car's glass windows. These short waves were then converted into long-wave heat (infrared) radiation, much of which could not pass back through the glass to the outside. As a result, the car warmed up because of the greenhouse effect.

Carbon dioxide operates very much like the windows of your car, or like greenhouse glass, in trapping heat and preventing it from passing out of the atmosphere. However, since the dawn of the Industrial Revolution in the mid-nineteenth century, large quantities of carbon dioxide generated by human activities have been released into the atmosphere from factories, coal-fired power plants, gasoline-powered motor vehicles, and the consumption of fossil fuels for the purpose of warming homes, stores, and industries. In addition to carbon dioxide, however, modern society has also been releasing ever-increasing amounts of other greenhouse gases, such as methane, nitrous oxide, and ozone.

Atmospheric levels of carbon dioxide, the most important greenhouse gas, remained at about 270 parts per million for thousands of years. Then, with the beginning of the industrial age and the accelerated consumption of fossil fuels (coal, oil, and natural gas), the carbon dioxide levels rose substantially, from 270 ppm to 350 ppm by 1990—an increase of almost 30 percent.

As of 1990, the burning of fossil fuels worldwide has been causing the release of five billion metric tons of carbon dioxide into the air every year— almost one ton for each person on Earth, and about 53 times the rate back in 1860. The burning of tropical forests to clear areas for cattle ranching and farming causes the annual release of still another 1.6 billion tons. Many climatologists predict that if CO_2 levels continue to increase at the current rate, the average global temperature could rise 5° F (3° C) by 2035. However, the increase at the poles would be considerably greater—about 13° to 18° F (7° to 10° C).

This artificially induced global warming is reinforced by a natural phenomenon known as the *albedo effect*—the reflection of light (and hence heat) back into the atmosphere from rocks, soil, water, homes, factories, highways, plants, animals,

and all other entities on the surface of this planet. Darker materials, like rocks, soil, and trees, have relatively little albedo effect. On the other hand, materials like snow and ice reflect light more intensely. One major effect of the man-induced greenhouse effect will be the melting of glaciers, snow fields, and icecaps in the polar regions. The eventual result will be the exposure of increasingly large areas of rocks, soil, and water—all materials with much lower albedo values. The net effect would be a warming of the planet due to the increased absorption of sunlight.

Many experts agree that the global warming that has already resulted because of the artificially induced greenhouse effect caused ocean levels to rise 1 foot (0.3 meters) in the past century due to the melting of glaciers, ice fields, and polar icecaps. The U.S. Environmental Protection Agency predicts that the oceans could rise another 3.3 feet (1 meter) by 2035. This would be catastrophic for millions of people occupying lowland areas bordering the sea. Among the most vulnerable (and highly populated) regions would be Indonesia, Pakistan, Thailand, the Ganges Delta of Bangladesh, and the Nile Delta in Egypt. Of course, the inundation not only would displace large numbers of people but, especially in the case of the fertile lowlands along the Nile and Ganges, would permanently submerge extremely fertile farmlands, upon which considerable segments of humanity depend for food.

What about the situation in the United States? There is no doubt that a 3.3-foot (1-meter) rise in ocean levels by 2035 would cause a dramatic reshaping of our Atlantic and Gulf shorelines. The seas would move an average of about one hundred feet (30 meters) inland. Extensive low-lying areas in coastal Louisiana and Florida would become part of the ocean floor. "Environmental evacuees" from the flooded seaboards would number in the millions. Multibillion-dollar devastation would be caused by the massive flooding of highways, railroads, homes, schools, stores, and factories. It is estimated that the rising seas would wreak $650 million in damage in Charleston, S.C., alone. Even greater destruction would be experienced by Boston, New York City, Philadelphia, Norfolk, Miami, New Orleans, and Houston. Human anxiety, emotional stress, severe discomfort, as well as serious financial setbacks would be commonplace.

Although the human-caused greenhouse phenomenon will certainly be highly destructive, it will have some redeeming features. One beneficial effect would be lengthened growing seasons in northern latitudes. A predicted warmup of 5° F

(3.5° C) or more by 2035 would be a boon to residents of Canada and northern Europe. For one thing, the cost of heating homes, shops, and factories during winter would be sharply reduced. Moreover, the longer growing seasons in these regions would boost agricultural production. For example, the relatively brief 110-day growing season in Canada's wheat belt would be extended to 160 days—an increase of more than 45 percent, thus permitting more diverse crop production. As Robert Stewart, an agricultural climatologist with the Canadian government, remarked, "The greenhouse effect will not be gloom and doom for Canada in any sense."

See also ACID RAIN; CLIMATE AND METEOROLOGY; DEFORESTATION; DISASTERS, PLANNING FOR; OZONE LAYER DEPLETION; RESOURCES.

BIBLIOGRAPHY

BEARDSLEY, TIM. "Add Ozone to the Global Warming Equation." *Scientific American* (March 1992).
BENEDICK, RICHARD ELLIOTT. "Essay: A Case of Déjà Vu." *Scientific American* (April 1992).
KERR, RICHARD. "A Successful Forecast of an El Niño Winter." *Science* 255 (1992): 402.
MONISTERSKY, RICHARD. "Do Clouds Provide a Greenhouse Thermostat?" *Science News* 141 (1992): 69.
OWEN, OLIVER S. "The Heat Is On: The Greenhouse Effect and the Earth's Future." *Futurist* (September—October 1989).
———. *Natural Resource Conservation: An Ecological Approach.* New York: Macmillan, 1990.

Oliver S. Owen

Governance

Governance, in all its forms, must undergo radical transformation to meet the needs of the future: Increasingly powerful instruments at the disposal of humanity make failure rates too costly; globalization of problems and processes (such as climate changes and financial markets) can no longer be handled by national governments or by existing supranational authorities; changing values require novel political expressions; the growing power of non-Western cultures makes present Western-based political ideologies increasingly obsolete; and so on. In short, a high-technology, multicultural, increasingly integrated world of 10 to 15 billion people cannot be managed by present governance slightly reformed. Needed instead are radically novel forms of governance.

Future governance will be pluralistic and based on different values, conditions, and traditions. But to meet emerging challenges, all undertakings will have to meet requisites not satisfied by present governance. Seven requisites illustrate future requirements that are becoming increasingly pressing. The contradictions between some of them exposes the tensions that will characterize governance debates.

Requisites of Future Governance

BASED ON CONSENT

Governance that does not enjoy broad consent will not work and will not be acceptable valuewise. Democratic elections will provide a main consent procedure, as will electronic direct democracy based on emerging technologies. Other forms of consent, such as those based on religious beliefs, also will characterize future governance.

INTELLIGENT PUBLIC OPINION

For governance to handle complex issues on the basis of consent, public opinion in turn must be based on better understanding. Generating intelligent public opinion will become an increasingly necessary government task. But being "intelligent" does not necessarily mean being "enlightened." Fundamentalist worldviews, for example, may well go together with intelligent public opinion, producing high-quality governance on very different lines than Western democratic ones.

SOME DETACHMENT FROM SHIFTING PUBLIC OPINION

Based on intelligent consent, governance will also require detachment from shifting public opinion, in order to accommodate the needs of future generations, to cope with issues too complex for general understanding, and to generate more intelligent public opinion. This means that there may be limits on direct or popular democracy; intervals between elections may have to be increased; nondemocratic institutions, such as central banks, special project agencies, and "councils of state" may be left in charge of important functions; and that professional elites will be allowed to fulfill major roles in governance. In democracies, all governing institutions will be subject to override by majority rule.

BETTER INTEGRATION OF KNOWLEDGE INTO POWER

Governance will be based on full utilization of all available knowledge requiring novel forms of integrating knowledge with power. This might include new types of professional senior civil services, extensive training, and the conferring of autonomous knowledge-bodies such as "think tanks," with statutory powers.

UPGRADING POLITICIANS

Hand in hand with consent and better-informed publics, governance will become elitist. Approaches will differ between countries and cultural areas, but in all of them political elites will be of crucial importance. Deliberate efforts to upgrade the quality of politicians will become essential, however taboo such measures may seem according to present political myths.

Interdependent steps in this direction include

- elimination of corruption, by reducing the dependence of politicians on money, providing politicians with adequate remuneration, and punishing corruption harshly
- changing the rules of democratic elections by requiring full disclosure of personal histories and subjecting candidates to intensive public interrogations—to break through "television masks" so the public will be better informed
- integrating systematic learning opportunities and incentives into the career of politicians, such as by paid study leaves and establishing policy colleges for politicians
- imposing strictly enforced codes of ethics for politicians, including accountability for all aspects of their private behavior that might adversely affect their public functions

NEW BALANCE BETWEEN LEVELS OF GOVERNANCE

To handle human problems well, local governance will become more important. To handle economic and social issues, multistate governance will also become more important, along the lines of the European Union. But to handle the problems of humanity as a whole, global government will become much stronger and be equipped with effective enforcement powers and instruments. As a consequence, the importance of states in their present formats will diminish.

TOWARD A NEW POLITICAL PHILOSOPHY

Governance is grounded in political philosophies. However, available political philosophies are grossly inadequate, especially concerning increasingly crucial issues such as "global equity," public control of biotechnology and of mass media, and space travel. New political philosophies will emerge, driven by the inadequacies of present ones.

There is no strong reason to presume that these new political philosophies will be based on what we at present regard as "obvious." If and when radically new political philosophies emerge, governance will undergo transformations. To perform effectively, it will have to satisfy many of the requirements postulated above.

Future-shaping issues of globalization, population growth, economic and social disparities, climate change, space travel, uses and misuses of new technologies, ideological conflicts, and many more will prove increasingly unmanageable by market processes and civil societies. Therefore, politics and governance will rise again as master architects of social life on a global scale, for better or worse.

The basic choice between good and evil governance will continue to vex humanity, becoming more important than ever. Optimistic assumptions on a benign "end of history" have no basis, either in human experience or in what we know of human nature. Conscious efforts to move toward good governance, subject to changes in what constitutes "good" governance, are imperative. The outcome is not preordained, but depends on our ideas and deeds.

The more we engage in deliberative governance redesign to better fit the future in moral ways, the higher are the chances that governance will operate for the better. But if we leave unavoidable shifts in governance to chance and shock effects, the future of governance may be dismal indeed.

Adequate action depends on ideas. Present thinking on the future of governance is quite inadequate, suffering inter alia from fixation on western experiences and reliance on overoptimistic assumptions. Creative thinking on the future of governance is, therefore, urgently needed.

See also EXECUTIVE BRANCH; EXECUTIVE BRANCH: THE PRESIDENCY; GLOBAL BUSINESS: DOMINANT ORGANIZATIONAL FORMS; INTERNATIONAL GOVERNANCE AND REGIONAL AUTHORITIES; LEADERSHIP.

BIBLIOGRAPHY

DROR, YEHEZKEL. *The Capacity to Govern: A Report to the Club of Rome.* English version in publication.

———. *Public Policymaking Reexamined.* Scranton, PA: Chandler Publishing, 1968.

PAGE, WILLIAM, ed. *The Future of Politics.* London: Frances Pinter, 1983.

The Report of the Commission on Global Governance. *Our Global Neighborhood.* Oxford, UK: Oxford University Press, 1995.

Yehezkel Dror

Government Organization

The most remarkable political development in the closing decade of the twentieth century was the rise of liberal democracy as the chosen form of government for most of the world's nations. This dramatic shift raises a profound question for governance: will this represent the "end of history"—or a new beginning? Francis Fukuyama, in a provocative book entitled *The End of History and the Last Man*, argues that history has progressed to liberal democracy and capitalism, and that while changes and refinements will be made and are needed, no other forms of human political and economic organization will replace liberal democracy and capitalism. Forces in place give credence to the accuracy of Fukuyama's prediction, but there are some trouble spots.

The biggest source of trouble is nationalism. Given license, old hatreds and rivalries have been reignited and magnified in ways that challenge the new world order and threaten the stability and promise of liberal democracy. Various regions of the former Soviet Union, the countries of Eastern Europe, India, Pakistan, Bangladesh, Lebanon, Sri Lanka, and Nigeria are among those countries dangerously divided along ethnic lines in a manner that calls into question their capability to secure and maintain liberal democracy. Can Russians who live in Georgia or Serbs who live in Croatia ever be reconciled to the political boundaries that existed at the time of the breakup of the Soviet bloc?

The essential challenge is whether nations can modify the liberal democratic form in ways that reconcile unity and diversity to deal with ethnic rivalries and nationality tensions. Some form of federalism is seemingly vital for the survival of liberal democracy.

Federalism

Federalism requires recognition of and respect for individual rights, a democratic form, and a substantial political, financial, and programmatic role for regional governments that are the arbiters of the local units of which they are composed. Prior to the U.S. Constitution, the idea of federalism referred to a league that formed a club of states. Each state was a member of a central body. The U.S. founding fathers, in James Madison's words, invented a "new composition" that is "neither wholly *federal* nor wholly *national.*" In this new federal form, citizens acquired dual citizenship of both the national and the state government, and secured rights to participate in the affairs of both.

Conceptual boundaries of this federal-state relationship were deliberately blurred to accommodate shifts in the way responsibilities, functions, and finances were divided between the national government and the states.

American federalism when diagrammed shows a steady accretion of central powers, but with a wavy upward line reflecting cyclical variations in the relative strength in different periods of the role of state governments vis-à-vis the central government (see Figure 1). The 1980s and early 1990s brought about increasing reliance on the states under Reagan and the Republicans, as contrasted to the accretion of national governmental power in domestic affairs over the period from Franklin Roosevelt's New Deal through the late 1970s. Other periods in U.S. history—the 1880s and 1920s—also were characterized by the rising role of the states. Despite advancing and retreating state power, the trend, overall, has been toward centralization. Similar centralization trends are found in other federal nations, including Germany, Australia, and Canada.

The best way to understand modern federal systems is to compare the relative role of the states, which are called by different names in different federal countries—provinces in Canada, *Länder* in Germany, and cantons in Switzerland. A continuum of "federalness" showing relative roles would place Switzerland at one end as the most decentralized federal country. It would place Brazil, India, and Australia at the opposite end as the least decentralized federal countries in terms of the power of regional governments in relation to the central government.

Federalism as defined so far is described in terms of structure. Left out is something very important—a spirit of community. The regions in federal nations are rooted in tradition and history with which citizens identify, often in very strong ways. In the early history of the United States, citizens might have described themselves as Vermonters, New Yorkers, or Virginians, but not as Americans. Among modern federal countries, Switzerland is the most clearly divided between different nationality groups, with Germans, French, and Italians concentrated in different cantons. In this respect, the Swiss brand of federalism offers the best model of a country that has successfully dealt with geographically differentiated nationality groups.

Governance Issues

Beyond the idea of federalism as a way to reconcile unity and diversity, and the way it relates to the current challenge of ethnic and national divisiveness, are important questions of form and function in the United States.

INTERGOVERNMENTAL FINANCE

In the United States, federal grants-in-aid are made to state governments, and also to localities, in some cases. They can be: broad, like revenue sharing; focused on functional areas, like education, health, the environment, and so forth; open-ended, like welfare grants; closed-ended; conceived for narrow or for broad purposes; based on a formula or a project basis; or targeted at capital, operating, or income-transfer purposes. Needed for the future are new intergovernmental fiscal mechanisms much more selective than past grants. States differ greatly in their governmental and managerial capacity. A new form of what might be termed "functional-flexibility" grants is needed to take these state differences into account. Conditional grants conferring upon states wide discretion in the absence of failure to conform with acceptable standards might also specify a national government takeover or close federal supervision when activities funded under that grant failed to conform.

MANAGERIAL EFFICIENCY

Liberal democracy needs constant refinement. In an increasingly interconnected global economy, the managerial efficiency of democracy requires a delicate balancing of time-consuming open decision processes, and the ability to make and execute policies on a timely basis. Vibrant political pluralism enables the nation to deal with stalemates between political leaders and the public who want to make changes, against other powerful stakeholders whose interest is to prevent change. Institutional arrangements are needed in these confrontational situations (health policy is a good example) to permit specially created bodies to develop and advance plans for systemic change. The legislative and executive branches might be given the power to reject these plans, but not to modify them. This would provide a way to break stalemates while preserving political legitimacy. Military base closing commission recommendations that could be voted up or down, but not modified by carving out politically inspired base-saving exceptions, set a poignant precedent.

METROPOLITAN GOVERNMENT

The fragmentation of local government in the United States also presents a governance challenge that in many regions requires new instruments. Regional government is usually not the answer, but the establishment of regional service compacts in major functional areas often is. This solution reflects the "public choice" theory that says, in effect, that the geographic service area for different functions should vary, but that common matters may be dealt with collectively, often with considerable savings.

ROLE OF COMMUNITY-BASED ORGANIZATIONS

In the United States, the biggest recent structural change in urban policy has not been "privatization," but the *nonprofitization* of social services. Many government-funded social services that are operated by nonprofit community-based groups now perform in a competitive marketplace where urban services are rewarded for efficiency, managerial talent, and entrepreneurial skills. This trend towards "nonprofitization" will continue; however, refinement of the basic organizational model is needed.

All over the world, liberal democracy as a governmental form is on the march. Its future seems bright. But problems of ethnic and nationality rivalries and institutional rigidities challenge liberal democratic governments to be inventive in the twenty-first century. Federalism has great potential as a formula for stabilizing and buttressing the liberal democracies of the future.

See also CAPITALISM; COMMUNISM; CONSERVATISM, POLITICAL; DEMOCRACY; DEMOCRATIC PROCESS; GOVERNMENT: FORMS OF; INTERNATIONAL GOVERNANCE AND REGIONAL AUTHORITIES; LIBERALISM, POLITICAL; POLITICAL CYCLES; POLITICAL PARTY REALIGNMENT; SOCIAL DEMOCRACY; SOCIALISM.

BIBLIOGRAPHY

HAMILTON, ALEXANDER; MADISON, JAMES; and JAY, JOHN. *The Federalist Papers.* New York: New American Library, 1961.

FUKUYAMA, FRANCIS. *The End of History and the Last Man.* New York: Free Press, 1992.

NATHAN, RICHARD P. "Federalism—the Great Composition," In Anthony King, ed. *The New American Political System.* Washington, DC: American Enterprise Institute Press, 1990.

Richard P. Nathan

Gray Market Goods

Gray goods are defined as products purchased in the low-price market, repackaged, and diverted to other markets by means of a distribution system not authorized by the manufacturer. Manufacturers are not obligated to honor warranty claims for such goods. The terms *gray market* and *parallel import* have been used interchangeably to describe the unauthorized sale of products both *across* and *within* country markets. The question of the legitimacy of gray marketing does not involve the legality of the products themselves, but the legality of the means by which the products are distributed. (Pirated items, stolen goods, and so forth are not part of the gray market.) The major motivation for the gray marketer is to take advantage of the price discrepancies of the goods.

Gray markets arise and diminish in various product areas in response to ever-changing patterns of trade, supply, and demand, and have involved diverse products such as computers, consumer electronics, toys, or pharmaceuticals.

Gray markets can occur both *within* domestic markets (i.e., channel flow diversion) and *across* international markets (i.e., parallel importing). Some have distinguished between a parallel import (where the good is purchased in a low-price country and sold to a high-price country at a price below the domestic price) and a parallel reimport (where the manufacturer sells the product to a low-price country or jurisdiction, and the wholesaler in the low-price market resells the good to a high-price country or jurisdiction at a price below the domestic price).

Necessary Market Conditions for Gray Markets

For a gray market to exist, now or in the future, the gray marketers must have a source of supply, trade barriers between countries must be low enough or configured to provide the gray marketer with easy access from one market to another, and price differentials must be large enough to be profitable. In addition to the price differential, factors that make certain products more attractive to gray marketers include the volume of demand in the market to be supplied; the availability of supply in the exporting country; the extent of repackaging that may be required; and the degree to which the product resembles the product sold in the domestic market. For example, a low price differential but a high volume, or vice versa, makes a product more susceptible to parallel trade. In addition, homogeneous product presentation throughout the various markets, such as identical brand name, packaging, color, and the like would create the ideal product to be parallel-imported. Finally, the growth of parallel trade may be hindered if a steady supply of the product in the exporting country cannot be procured.

In the United States, the gray market can arise in several ways. For example, a U.S. firm may purchase rights from an *independent* foreign firm to register and use the trademark of the foreign firm within the United States. The U.S. firm can sell the products, which are manufactured abroad, in the United States. This has been called the "prototypical" gray market case.

A gray market also can arise when a U.S. firm registers the U.S. trademark for goods that are manufactured abroad by an *affiliated* company. In most cases, the foreign company wishes to control the distribution of its products in the United States by incorporating a subsidiary in the United States. Then the subsidiary registers a U.S. trademark under its own name. This trademark is identical to the parent company's foreign trademark. A gray market is then created when a third party buys the goods abroad and imports them into the United States.

In another situation, a U.S. company may establish a manufacturing division or subsidiary overseas to produce its goods that bear a U.S. trademark. The U.S. firm then imports these foreign-manufactured goods into the distribution channel of the United States. The holder of the trademark or its foreign subsidiary may then elect to sell the trademarked goods in another country, such as Italy. If these Italian goods are reimported into the United States, they will compete on the gray market with the domestic sales of the company holding the U.S. trademark.

In another case, a U.S. firm that holds a U.S. trademark may authorize an *independent* foreign manufacturer to use the trademark. The U.S. firm holding the trademark usually sells an exclusive right to the foreign manufacturer to use the trademark in a particular foreign location. In exchange for this right, the foreign manufacturer must promise that it will not import the trademark goods into the United States. If the foreign manufacturer violates this agreement, the goods manufactured abroad will compete on the gray market against the domestic goods of the U.S. firm.

The emergence of significant trade blocs, such as the European Union (EU), may provide fertile ground for gray markets in the future. The European Court of Justice generally has ruled in favor of parallel imports. Articles 30 and 36 of the Treaty of Rome have been interpreted to prevent significant trade barriers for gray markets in the EU. Article 30 ensures the free movement of goods in the EU. Article 36 permits exceptions to this policy based on public morality, public policy, or public security.

United States Regulation of Gray Market Goods

In the United States, the Tariff Act of 1930 prohibits the importation into the United States of any merchandise manufactured abroad that bears a trademark registered in the United States and owned by a U.S. citizen or corporation unless the owner of the trademark has consented in writing. Thus, importing gray market goods usually infringes the trademark of those goods.

For this reason, the United States Customs Service regulations prohibit the importation of most gray market goods. The Customs Service does permit, however, the importation of gray market goods that are manufactured abroad by the owner of the U.S. trademark or by someone *affiliated* with the owner of the trademark. This is known as the "common-control" exception.

Anti Gray Market Strategies

Both *reactive* and *proactive* strategies are being employed and will continue to be used to retaliate against gray marketers. The reactive strategies include price cutting, strategic confrontation, participation, supply interference, promotional bursts, collaboration, and acquisition. For example, the tactic of strategic confrontation requires the manufacturer to support the authorized dealers of its product by means of education (e.g., providing them with an understanding of the gray market, why it happens, and how they can combat it) and creative merchandising (e.g., plans to develop product differentiation).

Proactive strategies designed to avert gray markets include strategic pricing, product or service differentiation, dealer development, marketing information systems, long-term image reinforcement, establishing a legal precedent, and lobbying. For example, estimating the size of the gray market for a firm can be arduous. A common method used to trace a gray good is to secretly encode a warranty card with an identification of the original dealer who procured the product. Thus, the development of a marketing information system assists the manufacturer in identifying the point of access for gray marketers in the distribution channel. Technological advances in the future will no doubt aid in combating the gray market, though in the future, as in the present, larger companies will continue to be better able to effectively combat the efforts of gray marketers than will smaller firms. Doubtless, the gray marketers will likely themselves make use of new high-tech ploys to thwart their more legitimate adversaries.

See also CONSUMER PROTECTION/REGULATION; COUNTERFEITING; INTERNATIONAL TRADE: REGULATION; MARKETING: INTERNATIONAL TRADE: SUSTAINING GROWTH.

BIBLIOGRAPHY

CAVUSGIL, S. TAMER, and SIKORA, ED. "How Multinationals Can Counter Gray Market Imports." *Columbia Journal of World Business* (Winter 1988): 75–85.

CESPEDES, FRANK V., COREY, E. RAYMOND; and RANGAN, V. KASTURI. "Gray Markets: Causes and Cures." *Harvard Business Review* (July–August 1988): 75–82.

CHARD, J. S., and MELLOR, C. J. "Intellectual Property Rights and Parallel Imports." *World Economy* (March 1989): 69–83.

DUHAN, DALE F., and SHEFFET, MARY JANE. "Gray Markets and the Legal Status of Parallel Importation." *Journal of Marketing* (July 1988): 75–83.

HOWELL, ROY D.; BRITNEY, ROBERT R.; KUZDRALL, PAUL J.; and WILCOX, JAMES B. "Unauthorized Channels of Distribution: Gray Markets." *Industrial Marketing Management* (November 1986): 257–263.

LOWE, LARRY S., and MCCROHAN, KEVIN F. "Minimize the Impact of the Gray Market." *The Journal of Business Strategy* (November–December 1989): 47–50.

WEIGAND, ROBERT E. "Parallel Import Channels— Options for Preserving Territorial Integrity." *Columbia Journal of World Business* (Spring 1991): 53–60.

WILSON, W. WELDON. "Parallel Importation—Legitimate Goods or Trademark Infringement?" *Vanderbilt Journal of Transnational Law.* (1985): 543 576.

Peggy Chaudhry
Michael G. Walsh

Green Revolution

As long as there is hunger in developing nations, the "green revolution" will pit scientists, farmers, agricultural researchers, and health activists against the forces of nature and industry. By 2050 or so, when the world's population peaks at ten to twelve billion, the winner—either sustainable, self-sufficient agricultural systems or a perpetual cycle of poverty and famine in some lands—will be apparent.

The green revolution (GR) began in the mid-1960s, launched by agricultural researchers concerned about sustaining life on an increasingly crowded planet. Their goal was to maximize harvest yields and to end hunger. GR technologies departed from conventional farming methods in three ways: planting high-yield grain varieties, expanding irrigation, and increasing the use of chemical pesticides and fertilizers.

In its first thirty years, the revolution boosted land productivity and crop yields in many developing countries, where agriculture not only is a primary food source but also generates up to sixty percent of the Gross Domestic Product (GDP). By the early 1990s, the International Food Policy Research Institute reported that GR investments exceeded expectations: crop yields in many developing countries showed significant gains with no sign of slowing down.

Challenges

Despite impressive achievements, the green revolution is far from complete. More than half a billion people worldwide live in a constant state of hunger, according to the 1992 annual report of the Bread for the World Institute on Hunger and Development. In addition, another one billion people cannot afford an adequate diet to sustain an active worklife.

Several obstacles keep GR proponents from reaching their ultimate goal. One is that GR methodologies have not reached many regions. Until they do, and until these areas' infrastructures can accommodate greater use, population growth will continue to exceed food production growth. Another is the environmental impact. Deforestation and overgrazing accelerate soil erosion and degrade land. The loss of natural ecosystems threatens genetic raw materials critical to agriculture. Similarly, the expansion of cultivated land—a key GR strategy—is nearing its physical limits. Future growth must come not from increased acreage, but from yet higher yields.

Other factors are beyond science's control. Most hungry people starve not because of a global food shortage, but because of political instability or lack of money. More ominous is global climate change. The greenhouse effect on temperature and rainfall patterns could reduce agricultural output by fifteen to twenty-five percent over the next fifty to one hundred years.

Theories

Because there is no single cause for hunger, no one strategy can end it forever. Immediate, short-term "cures" such as emergency food shipments are no panacea: food aid has never freed a country from famine. Instead, to become famine-free long term, a developing country must have a sustainable agricultural system.

GR proponents agree that strong infrastructures and agricultural research systems are essential for achieving sustainability. Equally important are elements such as stable and open international markets, broad participation achieved by expanding education to rural areas, and decentralized, competitive domestic markets to encourage small farmers to adopt new technologies. China, for instance, became the world's biggest food producer in the 1980s by adopting reforms linking farmers' rewards to output.

Pierre Crosson, a senior fellow at Resources for the Future, argues that a system's success hinges upon its ability to mobilize "social capital," or energy, land, irrigation water, plant genetic material, climate, and knowledge.

The Bread for the World Institute offers concrete suggestions. They include establishing policies that merge new agricultural techniques with support for small rural enterprises, and integrating ecological and development concerns such as environmentally sound tourism. It also recommends nonagrarian tactics, including food stockpiling.

David Norse, a research associate for the Overseas Development Institute, advocates grass-roots empowerment. He calls for local level husbandry and development through organizations such as grazing associations and water user groups.

The single most important element of a sustainable agricultural system is knowledge—individual, technological, and institutional. Knowledge imbues developing countries with self-reliance. It is also subject to few physical constraints.

Efforts to build managerial and analytical skills in developing countries have been successful and relatively inexpensive. Given the necessary training, poor farmers are quick to adopt new technologies when it's in their interest to do so.

The best hope in the years ahead may come from foreign donors. Developed nations will boost their funding of, and provide more expertise for, schools and research centers, and will enable more students from developing countries to study agriculture abroad.

Strategies for the Future

Little new land is available for cultivation, but the global food supply must increase threefold by 2030 to sustain population growth. The best hope for meeting this need lies in science, especially in bioengineered crops—genetically altered to produce higher, hardier yields that defy drought, resist disease and spoilage, withstand pests, and require no fertilization. By the early 1990s, biotechnology brought tremendous gains to Asian countries such as China and Thailand, but found few takers in other developing nations. Biotechnology not only is environmentally benign, but also is a cheaper and more effective way to manage weeds and pests than conventional herbicides and pesticides.

A movement to revive ancient food sources is another approach to help resolve the challenges ahead. Just 150 of 4,000 or so edible plant species are widely cultivated. In 1993, the Food and Agriculture Organization launched an effort to identify and protect the other 3,850 or so, as well as animals with livestock potential. Among early successes were the maram bean, which resists drought, tastes good, and has more protein than peanuts, and the min pig, which is low in fat, tolerates extreme temperatures, is highly fertile, and survives well on poor feed.

Similarly innovative is the "perennial polyculture" or "domestic prairie" theory, which turns modern science—and the green revolution—on its head. The Land Institute, in Sierra, Kansas, answers the sustainability question by crossing a wheat field with a prairie—planting three or four perennial crops, adding no chemicals, and leaving the field untilled for years at a stretch. As a result, roots survive, while creating more soil and finding their own moisture and sustenance. The domestic prairie yields prolifically, requires little labor, and does not pollute. Its main detractor, however, is time: in an era of rapid change and instant results, a program that could take one hundred years to reach fruition wins little attention.

Numerous other initiatives will add fuel to the fire of the green revolution in the twenty-first century. Some, such as tree-planting schemes to regenerate woodlands or to protect pastures and fields from wind and sun, are not new. More laborious efforts—controlling runoff, erosion, and damage to rivers from siltation, for instance—may be improved with technology. Other strategies include using fast-growing trees and grasses as "biofuels" to reduce reliance on fossil fuels, curb carbon emissions, and revitalize rural economies.

See also FOOD AND AGRICULTURE; FOOD AND FIBER PRODUCTION; FOOD TECHNOLOGIES; GENETICS: AGRICULTURAL APPLICATIONS; GENETICS: COMMERCIALIZATION; GLOBAL WARMING; NEW PRODUCTS; SOIL CONDITIONS.

BIBLIOGRAPHY

BORLAUG, NORMAN E., and DOWSWELL, CHRISTOPHER R. "World Revolution in Agriculture." In *Encyclopaedia Britannica 1988 Book of the Year.* Chicago: Encyclopaedia Britannica, 1988.

NORSE, DAVID. "Feeding a Crowded Planet." *Environment* 34/5 (1992): 6–11, 32–39.

CROSSON, PIERRE. "Sustainable Agriculture: A Global Perspective." *Choices* (Second Quarter 1993): 38–42.

MELLOR, JOHN W., and RIELY, FRANK Z. "Expanding the Green Revolution." *Issues in Science and Technology* (Fall 1989): 66–74.

Leah Thayer
Jerry Kline

Guns.

See LETHAL WEAPONS.

H

Handicapped, Rights of.

See DISABLED PERSONS' RIGHTS.

Harassment, Sexual.

See SEXUAL HARASSMENT.

Hardware, Computer.

See COMPUTER HARDWARE.

Hazardous Wastes

Human activities create "wastes"—the by-products of daily life that were not there the day before. Wastes appear and then accumulate, and have no apparent use or desirability to whomever leaves them behind. Households generate literally mountains of trash annually. Riding to work leaves rubber on the road, exhaust fumes in the air, and brake lining dust on the ground. On the farm, spoiled hay, rusty tools, and runoff (including fertilizer and pesticides) abound. In strip-mine country, acidic tailings; in foundries, broken castings. In outer space, old satellites and rocket parts. In the ocean below, radioactive wastes and sewage sludge.

The United States alone creates more than 6 billion tons of waste of all kinds annually, nearly 50,000 pounds per person (NRC, 1991, p. 1). Some of these wastes are innocuous and others are mostly harmless, except that the principles of ecology recognize that all wastes must eventually go somewhere.

Some wastes are harmful, even deadly, or can become so under certain circumstances. About 10 percent to 15 percent of all wastes generated in the United States are hazardous (Wentz, 1989, p. 13).

The documented history of human and environmental health toxicology is fascinating. One classic account is W. Eugene and Aileen M. Smith's *Minamata* (1975). Their description and pictures portrayed the crippling spread of mercury poisoning among Japanese coastal families during the 1950s and '60s. The culprit was methyl mercury waste from the manufacture of acetaldehyde and vinyl chloride discharged into Japan's Minimata Bay. By 1959, mercury concentration in the bay's bottom mud exceeded 2,000 parts per million. The mercury entered the bay's food chain, passing from smaller life-forms to fish and eventually to human consumers of fish. By sharing a common bay, the people and the poisons were on a collision course. The adverse health effects, known as "Minamata disease," ranged from debilitating to deadly. Subsequently the disease was eventually found in communities throughout the Shiranui Sea in southern Japan. Over one hundred Japanese died from mercury poisoning between

1953 and 1965, and the problem persisted for more than twenty years (Smith and Smith, 1975).

Social and Economic Contexts of Hazardous Wastes

It appears to be getting more difficult to stay one jump ahead of disaster. In time, Minamata disease was found outside of Japan. Then, poisonings from other hazardous wastes were discovered—pesticides, lead, and asbestos, among them. Minamata signaled the beginning of the Toxics Era, not a surprising development for several reasons: the crushing increase in world population, the burgeoning demand for material goods, the growth of organic chemistry based on cheap petroleum, the related increase in synthetics production, the attendant wastes, and the release of toxins into the environment.

Society's ability to detect danger or act on warnings tends to lag behind the inclination to pursue profits, power, or special interests, no matter what the cost to the environment or human communities. The damage created "by the few on the many" spawns suspicion, polarization, and conflict within and among societies.

Finding, controlling, and removing hazardous waste creates major economic crises. It is estimated that there are 300,000–400,000 or more toxic sites in the United States alone (NRC, 1991, p. 9). The bill for hazardous-waste management and cleanup easily exceeds $6 billion annually (Mucci, 1987, p. 8). These outlays compete with society's other basic funding priorities: education, old-age security, health, conservation, agriculture, transportation, community improvement, and international peacemaking. Further, the labor requirement is immense and will continue to be; it will divert the talents of millions of workers who might otherwise be involved in more productive livelihoods.

Dimensions of Hazardous Wastes Exposure

Many believe that there is far more hazard in our lives than need be. How has this occurred? First, we have altered or countermanded nature by dividing and then valuing higher the parts most immediately used or demanded ("the products"), while valuing lower what we leave behind ("the wastes"). These priorities virtually ensure that resources will be used inefficiently and wastes will accumulate. Second, we pursue lifestyles that have seemingly insatiable, material demands, coupled with a consumer ethic based on the "freedom to waste." Economies consequently take great risks in acquiring, producing, and delivering goods. Third, we have poorly defined and underestimated the significance and volume of the wastes generated—their monetary, social, and environmental costs, now and for future generations.

Hazardous waste troubles have been experienced in all the basic sectors of our society, including energy, petrochemicals, fertilizers, metals, communication, transportation, and military defense. In the chemicals industry, 80,000 chemicals are in commercial use today and about 1,000 more are introduced each year (Gerrard, 1994, p. 7). Annual chemical production exceeds 300 billion pounds (Epstein, 1982, p. ix). Only a few hundred chemicals are regulated under hazardous-waste laws, and only a small fraction of the rest have been thoroughly tested for toxicity (Gerrard, 1994, p. 7). There are serious questions about which of these untested chemicals are, indeed, innocuous. For example, of approximately 1,200 "inert" ingredients in pesticides, the U.S. Environmental Protection Agency claims that about 50 are of significant toxicological concern and an additional 60 are considered potentially toxic (NRC, 1991, p. 110). Even silicone, originally promoted as inert and user-friendly, is now suspected to be chemically reactive within the human body.

Wastes have the tendency to degrade or transform over time. However, they do not always become less toxic. The anaerobic microbial transformation of inorganic mercury into methyl mercury is an example of the secondary compound being much more troublesome than the first.

When toxic wastes are loose in the environment, both the routes and the intensity of exposure may drastically change. For example, workers' exposure to certain volatile dry-cleaning solvents, some of which are known cancer-causing agents, is typically by inhalation or absorption. Waste solvents also may find a way down a drain, onto the ground, or into a landfill, exposing unsuspecting people to groundwater and drinking water pollution. Each year, thousands of wells are closed because of hazardous-waste contamination (NRC, 1991, p. 5).

The human body's capacity to detoxify chemicals is definitely limited. At first, there may be no symptoms, but with prolonged exposure, a variety of symptoms can appear. Adverse health consequences may include modified or irregular behavior, central-nervous-system disorientation, impairment of body functions, allergic reactions, skin and eye irritation or damage, respiratory distress and cardiac collapse, pulmonary edema, or less obvious delayed reactions that may take years before producing carcinogenic, mutagenic, or teratogenic effects in essential organs (Fawcett, 1988, p. 84). Pregnant women and nursing mothers, babies, children, the elderly, and others in poor health or recovering from surgery or other medical treatment are especially vulnerable.

The "Catalog" of Hazardous Wastes

One taxonomy of waste problems consists of five categories: (1) parent materials or derivatives; (2) reactions and transformations over time and under various conditions; (3) interactions with other substances, including other wastes; (4) range and severity of effects on life-forms; and (5) relative difficulty in locating, identifying, isolating, and assimilating or disposing of wastes. To address the hazardous waste problem, it is essential to understand how each waste fits these categories, how it got there, and how to remove it without causing yet another waste problem.

Hazardous wastes come from both natural materials and synthetic compounds. Some 90 percent are generated by manufacturing. More than 99 percent are produced by large-quantity generators—that is, sources accounting for more than 1,000 kg per month. Just 1 percent of all generators create 97 percent of all hazardous wastes in the United States, and three plants—operated by DuPont, Dow Chemical, and Eastman Kodak—generate 57 percent of all hazardous wastes nationwide (Gerrard, 1994, p. 8). It has been estimated that the chemical and petroleum industries account for approximately 70 percent to above 88 percent of hazardous wastes, and the metal-related industries for 22 percent (Mucci, 1987, p. 10; Wentz, 1989, p. 2).

The U.S. military is a significant hazardous-waste generator, accounting for approximately 700,000 tons of hazardous wastes annually, including paint thinner, spilled solvents, hydraulic fuel, aviation fuel, fuel tank and sewage sludges, and herbicides. A total of 1,877 installations have been targeted for cleanup, with an estimated total cost of $24.5 billion (Gerrard, 1994, p. 15). Extensive soil contamination has occurred at hundreds of air bases and elsewhere, and upwards of 100 million tons of military ordnance require disposal. There is also an estimated 10 million tons per year of waste munitions and more than 1 million tons per year of naval paint and plating wastes (Dawson, 1986, p. 120). No matter where one looks, it is obvious that the dimensions of the problem are immense.

Radioactive wastes, mostly from atomic weapons manufacture and nuclear power plants, are classified as high-level or low-level. Included are wastes that will be dangerous for thousands of years. Many people believe that this generation of high-level wastes has been totally immoral, amounting to an undeclared war on future generations. Highly radioactive wastes from plutonium warhead production are stored at government installations in Washington state and South Carolina. Most of the approximately 10,000 cubic meters of radioactive spent-fuel rods from more than 100 nuclear power plants are being stored on site. About 1,900 tons of spent fuel are generated each year (Gerrard, 1994, pp. 29–30). There are almost 3 million cubic meters of low-level wastes from nuclear weapons manufacture in Washington State, South Carolina, and Tennessee, mostly buried in shallow trenches; prior to 1970 the U.S. military practiced ocean dumping (Gerrard, 1994, p. 33). Most civilian wastes have been stored at six sites, all of which will be closed before the end of the century, leaving it up to individual states to establish their own disposal sites. Siting has become a very controversial issue. Finally, there are more than a dozen extremely contaminated sites (collectively known as the Nuclear Weapons Complex), where atomic weapons were made. Cleaning up these sites will cost more than $200 billion and will take at least twenty to thirty years (Gerrard, 1994, p. 36).

The Citizen Factor

Since the beginning of the Toxics Era, from the mid-1960s through the '70s, concerned citizens have been in an intelligent debate with scientists, engineers, politicians, and others to (1) find, study, and rank the hazards of wastes as a guide to assessing the threats to health, aesthetics, and the environment; (2) try to arrive at "acceptable limits" of environmental concentrations and personal exposure for various compounds; (3) direct the investment of public and private funds and technology development to minimize or eliminate the damage caused; (4) prevent the worldwide proliferation of wastes and waste-causing activities; and (5) explore pathways to a world where no wastes would be hazardous.

Little initiative and follow-up has come from government and industry; the U.S. National Research Council concluded, ". . . The intent of Congress in creating Superfund (the Comprehensive Environmental Response, Compensation, and Liability Act of 1980) has not been realized, in that the public health consequences of exposures to substances from hazardous-waste sites have not been adequately assessed. Moreover, there is little reason to believe that current procedures identify the most important abandoned hazardous-waste sites, from the point of view of public health" (NRC, 1991, p. 6).

Too often, citizens have had to hire lawyers to sue their own governments—first, to hold hearings on hazardous wastes; then to propose and enact legislation; and then to force slow, indifferent, or even belligerent agencies to release information on waste generators and disposal sites and to implement the authorized programs. Although much has been attempted in the way of mediation and conflict resolution, the adversarial relationship, backed by the threat of litigation, is still the prime mover. This situation has persisted regardless of changes in political administrations.

The continuing suspicion and animosity are fueled by the media's vivid reporting of new toxic-waste catastrophes. Among these are: oil spills, truck and rail accidents, community evacuations, toxic building fires, medical wastes washing up on beaches, garbage barges wandering the oceans, leukemia and cancer clusters near toxic sites. Public opinion surveys consistently rank hazardous-waste sites among the most serious environmental risks, and the environment as an issue of great public concern (NRC, 1991, p. 5).

Tens of thousands of recognized toxic sites and more than 16,000 active landfills in the United States (NRC, 1991, p. 112)—a large portion of them designated as federal "Superfund" sites—has prompted ad hoc voluntary organizations of impacted or frightened residents. Other organizations and union research committees have formed at industrial plants, mining sites, and military installations. A recent U.S. Environmental Protection Agency survey found that more than 40 million people live within four miles and about 4 million within one mile of a Superfund site (NRC, 1991, p. 2). Group leaders are often those who believe they are the most immediately or severely affected: people with unexplained cancers, metabolic diseases, sick children.

Worldwide, hazardous-waste sites probably number in the millions. They may be small, concealed, and dispersed "nonpoint" sources of gasoline-soaked subsoil or leaking underground storage tanks. In the United States alone, the latter are estimated to be a third of the 2.4 million to 4.8 million tanks holding kerosene, heating oil, cleaning solvents, and other dangerous fluids (Mucci, 1987, p. 22; NRC, 1991, p. 112). Or they may be "point sources," large enough to be visible from space, such as Chernobyl's 30-kilometer-radius intensely radioactive "dead zone."

The Hazardous-Wastes Industry

The public's concern about hazardous wastes has stimulated tremendous growth in technology to deal mostly with the wastes already generated. The major focus has been on learning how to handle wastes at contaminated sites. Remote sensing and sophisticated subsurface investigation try to track and predict the movement of toxic plumes. Highly selective, large-capacity filtration systems have been designed to intercept advancing wastes. A variety of on-site air strippers and combusters, and experimental in situ waste treatment—solidifiers, vitrifiers, and broths of microorganisms, for example—are beginning to fill the catalog of available equipment and methods.

In the United States and other industrialized countries, hazardous-waste cleanup and disposal have become a profitable industry of major proportions, supporting engineers, on-site investigators, waste detection technologists, instrumentation specialists, laboratory personnel, and research and education centers. The entire national cleanup program, known as Superfund, is under fire for spending billions of dollars on what might be termed glorified landscaping and pork barrel projects for engineers and contractors without actually cleaning up the sites.

Looking Forward

Remember that the hazardous-waste crisis is made by people. Thus, even before speculating on its outcome, we must ask, "Who wants what to happen when?" The "who" is basically three categories of actors, although they sometimes overlap: concerned citizens, government, and business.

The agenda for the future of hazardous wastes is being hammered out publicly and privately, from small towns to international conferences. It is being punctuated and pushed along in the media whenever, for example, a tank truck jackknifes on a highway, or a new microbe is discovered with an appetite for leachate.

In 1992, thousands of representatives from around the world addressed hazardous wastes at the United Nations' Earth Summit in Rio de Janeiro.

Chapter 20 in the summit's culminating *Agenda 21* acknowledges that "human health and environmental quality are undergoing continuous degradation by the increasing amount of hazardous wastes being produced. There are increasing direct and indirect costs to society and to individual citizens in connection with the generation, handling, and disposal of such wastes. It is therefore crucial to enhance knowledge and information on the economics of prevention and management of hazardous wastes. . . . One of the first priorities in hazardous waste management is minimization, as part of a broader approach to changing industrial processes and consumer patterns through pollution prevention and cleaner production strategies. Among the most important factors in these strategies is the recovery of hazardous wastes and their transformation into useful material. . . ." (United Nations, 1992).

Major citizen efforts are already under way to reject certain products, processes, and classes of compounds whose waste products are hazardous. The antichlorine movement, for example, changed circuit-board and computer manufacturing in fewer than five years: Once the pressure was applied, closed-loop and water-based methods for cleaning high-tech components replaced chlorinated solvents.

The most significant trend has been the emergence of "pollution prevention" as part of the environmental ethic. The U.S. Environmental Protection Agency and many states now subscribe to pollution prevention as the preferred way to meet current and future environmental goals. Front-end prevention is generally less expensive and hazardous than rear-end control.

"NIMBY"

"Not in my backyard!" the people shout. Since the 1970s, this cry has been a shield for millions of citizens all over the world in defense against the twin plagues of pollution and life-threatening wastes that have been spread over the land; injected into the soil, water, and air; and passed through virtually every corner of the planet, often while no one was looking.

It is not by coincidence that the tone of defiance in "Not in my backyard!" echoes Benjamin Franklin's famous "Don't tread on me!," which landed hard on the chin of the British monarchy and unified the American colonies into a groundswell for complete independence two hundred years ago. "Not in my backyard!" and its global extension, "Not in anyone's backyard!," bring this revolution-

ary challenge up to date. They invoke the moral obligation to reject any conditions where pollution and disaster endanger the well-being of communities. Two hundred years ago, the battle was political; today, for many, it is clearly environmental.

See also ACID RAIN; DEFORESTATION; DISASTERS, PLANNING FOR; FACTORIES AND MANUFACTURING; FRESHWATER; NUCLEAR POWER: CON; OCEANS; SOIL CONDITIONS; SOLID WASTE.

BIBLIOGRAPHY

DAWSON, GAYNOR W., and MERCER, BASIL W. *Hazardous Waste Management.* New York: John Wiley & Sons, 1986.
EPSTEIN, SAMUEL S.; BROWN, LESTER O.; and POPE, CARL. *Hazardous Waste in America.* San Francisco: Sierra Club Books, 1982.
FAWCETT, HOWARD H. *Hazardous and Toxic Materials: Safe Handling and Disposal.* New York: John Wiley & Sons, 1988.
GERRARD, MICHAEL B. *Whose Backyard, Whose Risk: Fear and Fairness in Toxics and Nuclear Waste Siting.* Cambridge, MA: MIT Press, 1994.
MUCCI, NICK. *Hazardous Waste Industry: Overview.* Braintree, MA: Clean Harbors, 1987.
National Research Council [NRC], Committee on Environmental Epidemiology. *Environmental Epidemiology: Public Health and Hazardous Wastes.* Washington, DC: National Academy Press, 1991.
SMITH, W. EUGENE, and SMITH, AILEEN M. *Minamata.* New York: Holt, Rinehart, & Winston, 1975.
United Nations. *Agenda 21.* New York: U.N. Department of Public Information, 1992.
WENTZ, CHARLES A. *Hazardous Waste Management.* New York: McGraw-Hill, 1989.

Stuart M. Leiderman

Health Care

Health care—the management of the resources of healing—is one of the most complex and difficult enterprises on the planet, and in the mid-1990s it is changing with great speed and turbulence. This turbulence is likely to continue for some time into the future, for a combination of reasons both within health care and outside it.

Where We Are Now

In the mid-1990s, relatively few nations are satisfied with their health-care systems. In the United States, health care costs have ballooned to $1 trillion, accounting for nearly 15 percent of the U.S. economy. Yet the United States consistently falls behind many other industrialized nations in infant mortality, longevity, and other benchmarks, and some 40 million Americans lack health insurance. Despite these facts, the chance for significant health care reform seems to have come and gone after the defeat of President Bill Clinton's plan and all of its rivals in late 1994.

Other developed nations, though their per capita costs are far lower, also face tough political struggles over rising costs and constricted resources. At the other end of the scale, the World Health Organization (WHO) estimates that more than half of the world's 5.6 billion people lack access to the most essential drugs—vaccines, antibiotics, and painkillers—and more than one-third of the world's children are malnourished. Many Third World governments spend less than 1 percent of gross domestic product on health care.

Factors in the Future of Health Care

A number of outside factors will affect health care in the future. A less predictable climate worldwide means an increase in natural disasters such as floods, droughts, famines, and typhoons. The absence of the constraints of the Cold War, the continued devolution of the former Soviet countries, the increase in effectiveness and the lower cost of many weapons (especially conventional small arms), growing atomization along ethnic and nationalist lines, and the growing scarcity and depletion of natural resources, point to the likelihood of increased chaos and war. For health care this means an increase in trauma, in malnutrition (as the chaos disrupts food supplies), of infectious disease, and stress-induced illness, as well as a diversion of resources away from health-care toward arms and reconstruction.

Other trends point toward continued and locally increased industrial pollution, which affects people's health over wide areas. Continued population growth will stretch all resources thinner. Increasing industrialization and urbanization around the world tend to break up the family, clan, and village support systems that have traditionally supported health. The increasing power and size of global corporations, less stable global finances, the increasing influence of donor nations, of central finance agencies such as the World Bank and the International Monetary Fund, and of the central government banks and finance ministries of wealthy countries, may mean even more constraint on resources for health care in many Third World countries.

Finally, certain medical changes endanger health care around the world. In the ongoing war between pathogens and antibiotics, overused antibiotics seem to be losing their effectiveness against the rapidly evolving pathogens. And the rapid increase in cheap international travel allows new epidemics to rapidly become global. The spread of human immunodeficiency virus (HIV) has gone essentially unchecked in much of the world. As of 1994, HIV was infecting 13 million adults a year. The WHO expects that 5 million children worldwide will become infected with HIV between 1995 and 2000. Southern Asia and sub-Saharan Africa are expected to bear the brunt of this epidemic.

All these changes will tend to push national health systems increasingly into crisis and chaos. The effect will be most marked at the ends of the economic spectrum, in the bloated U.S. health care industry, and in the highly strained economies of the Third World. It will be least marked in the other industrialized nations and in the robust "tiger" economies of East and Southeast Asia.

China, with the world's largest population (1.17 billion), presents an enigmatic future. Since the 1949 revolution, China has built a health care infrastructure that has been widely admired for its comprehensiveness, wide social base, preventive focus, and efficient use of the country's scant economic resources. China's economy is growing rapidly, and it is expected within a decade or so to become an economic powerhouse, a middle-income country, which always bodes well for health care. But early signs warn of an increasing gap between classes, urban and rural areas, and coastal and inland areas. There are also signs of increasing social strain, such as the open reemergence of infanticide, baby-selling, and prostitution, and a rise in the death rates of children under five. Some observers, as well, express concern over China's long-term political stability. The most hopeful signs for the future of health in China are: (1) the government's strong, widespread family planning programs, (2) its focus on strengthening the corps of low-cost primary health professionals in the neighborhoods and villages, and (3) its focus on educating girls and the relatively high literacy rate of its women (68 percent). Studies by the World Bank and the WHO have shown the education of females to be the most effective method of improving the health of populations.

Technical Advances

We cannot expect technical developments with anything like the life-changing power that the inventions of antibiotics, antisepsis, painkillers, and X-rays brought to the early decades of this century. And some technical advances, such as distance surgery, may be spectacular but are unlikely to have a large effect on the health of most people. The areas that show the most promise for actually improving people's health include:

- the Human Genome Project, which may isolate the genetic roots of many human diseases—including many that are not generally considered genetic.
- the use of genetic markers to screen mass populations and prevent (through diet, gene substitution, or other special therapies) the specific diseases that individuals are likely to develop.
- nanotechnology, the newly developed craft of building molecular-scale machines, which holds the promise of completely new types of drugs: tiny machines with the tools and intelligence to perform specific tasks, kill certain viruses, repair certain cells, and manufacture certain necessary proteins or enzymes.
- new modes of pharmaceutical research that go far beyond the old, blind trial-and-error techniques to actually building the molecules (or evolving the bacteria) that can carry out specific tasks, lock onto specific receptor sites in the body, or defeat specific pathogens.

In fact, the most important effect of technical advances will not come through the invention of new medical techniques, but in the more effective use of the techniques that already exist.

Shifts in Direction

We can expect to see four major types of change in health care around the world in the coming decades, and two others that will be most pronounced in the United States.

- *Computers, Telecommunications, Databasing.* Advances in health-oriented telecommunications, medical imaging, massive databasing, memory miniaturization, satellite technology, and other information systems lay the groundwork for fundamental changes in the organization of health care. These new technologies will allow doctors to communicate far more easily and quickly and will allow health-care managers to drive their systems in real time. At the same time that they push consumer awareness about health to an entirely new level through the use of interactive cable systems, on-line forums, and personal health-information systems in a wide variety of formats.

- *Outcomes Management and Expert Systems.* Outcomes measurement uses massive databases scanning millions of cases to determine what therapies actually work best in particular circumstances. Its use as a management tool tends to make the practice of medicine more of a science and less of a craft, decreasing costs and increasing quality at the same time. Broadly applied, it will also open the gates to a number of highly effective and inexpensive nonmedical methods that are considered "alternative" or "complementary" in the Western countries. The ability to measure all interventions by outcome and cost will push all therapies toward greater unity, bring a wider range of therapies into official payment systems, and allow true comparison of intervention and prevention strategies. Outcomes management is spreading rapidly in the United States, but has only begun to penetrate other countries. Medical knowledge is expanding faster than any human can learn it. Computer programs called "expert systems" help physicians and other health practitioners move much more rapidly and effectively through the decisions of diagnosis and therapy, isolating rare diseases, differentiating among similar syndromes, and discovering the latest research on the most effective therapies. Their widespread use is likely to significantly change the role of a doctor away from knowing facts and toward the more human elements of the craft, such as making difficult decisions and helping patients change their behavior.

- *Going "upstream."* The focus of health care will move increasingly out of the acute-care hospital to clinics, doctors' offices, and even into schools, workplaces, and the home. The focus will change as well, away from intervening in the acute phase of the disease toward early screening, detection, treatment, and even toward preventing the disease in the first place. This will happen because it is not only more effective to diagnose diseases early, it is far cheaper.

- *Population health.* According to the National Institutes of Health, about half of all health problems are caused by behavior such as smoking, excess drinking, and poor diet. Many of the rest are caused by problems in the environment, such as pollution and unsafe working conditions. All of these are preventable. A growing number of health care professionals around the world view changing the behavior of populations (as Americans changed their smoking habits) and cleaning up the environment as a highly effective use of health care funds. One expression of this is the rapid growth of the WHO's "Healthy Cities" movement.

U.S. Trends

Within the United States, two trends stand out:

- *Restructuring.* As health care moves "upstream," acute health care will continue to shrink drastically. In 1982, for every 1,000 U.S. citizens, American hospitals logged 1,132 nights in a hospital bed—more than one night per citizen. By 1992, that had dropped to 607. By 1995, some states were as low as 225, with some specific markets (such as San Diego County in California) as low as 160. Health futurist Jeff Goldsmith estimates that within a decade, most markets will log only seventy or eighty nights in a hospital per year for every 1,000 citizens. One-third to one-half or more of all hospitals will close. The rest will shrink and become much more intensive. Almost all will join one of the many different large-scale organizations that are bringing together hospitals, doctors, payment structures, and many other services under single ownership.
- *Reform.* Congress is not likely to enact significant health care reform anytime soon. But we will see a wide array of experiments at the local and state level. Business will become more heavily involved in health care negotiations, but in an increasingly sophisticated way, moving from simply bargaining for cheaper rates, to working with the doctors and hospitals to keep quality up and costs down, and finally to working with people from government, health care, education, and other sectors to make the whole community healthier.

See also HEALTH CARE: ALTERNATIVE THERAPIES; HEALTH CARE COSTS; HEALTH CARE FINANCING; HEALTH CARE: MORAL ISSUES; HEALTH CARE: TECHNOLOGICAL DEVELOPMENTS; MEDICAL CARE PROVIDERS; MENTAL HEALTH; NURSING; PSYCHIATRY; PUBLIC HEALTH.

BIBLIOGRAPHY

ANNIS, EDWARD R. *The Future of Health Policy*. Cambridge, MA: Harvard University Press, 1993.
GRAIG, LAURENE A. *Health of Nations: An International Perspective on U.S. Health Care Reform*. 2nd ed. Washington, DC: Congressional Quarterly, 1993.
FUCHS, VICTOR F. *The Future of Health Policy*. Cambridge, MA: Harvard University Press, 1993.
HAMMERLE, NANCY. *Private Choices, Social Costs, and Public Policy: An Economic Analysis of Public Health Issues*. Westport, CT: Praeger/Greenwood, 1992.
LATHROP, J. PHILIP. *Restructuring Health Care: The Patient-Focused Paradigm*. San Francisco: Jossey-Bass, 1993.
SCHECHTER, MALVIN. *Beyond Medicare: Achieving Long-Term Care Security*. San Francisco: Jossey-Bass, 1993.

Joseph Flower

Health Care: Alternative Therapies

Alternative therapies have grown into a multibillion-dollar-a-year industry. As the new century approaches, people are determined to find what to them constitutes acceptable total health care. Among the more acceptable remedies are the following:

Folk Remedies

These treatments have long been regarded as little more than superstition or witchcraft. In all parts of the inhabited world, recipes, ingredients, and remedies have been handed down from one generation to another. Many treatments and alleged cures have passed the test of centuries and now merit serious scrutiny for their valuable contribution to medicine. In Native American societies a medicine man could read the mysteries of nature. He knew the curative properties of roots, leaves, seeds, blossoms, tubers, berries, and fruit of almost every plant, shrub, or tree. Every old woman in a community gathered her own medicine, and medical doctors were called only in extreme circumstances.

Now medical science wants to know the secrets of the medicine man and the old woman. Was it more than belief in the magical power of the healer that brought about the wonderful cures?

Folk remedies from the past that continue to be used include: white willow for pain, catnip for colic, ginger for digestion, and purgatives such as castor oil, rhubarb, or calomel.

Herbal Healing

"A weed is a plant whose virtues we do not yet know," said Emerson. Pliny the Elder (c. 79 A.D.), a

Roman naturalist who wrote the book *Natural History*, held a similar view. He stated that every plant had a special medicinal value if only we could discover it, and that for every disease there was a plant that would cure it.

Herbs grow everywhere: in fields or forest, along roadsides, mountains, backyards, nurseries, or on a windowsill.

For common ailments the home medicine shelf may stock arnica for bruises and pain, echincea for immune building, golden seal as an antiseptic/bacteriostatic agent, valerian for calming and insomnia.

Even in the high-technology world of drug design the search continues for the fountain of youth in a jar or the secret of longevity and rejuvenation harvested from botanical sources.

Acupuncture

The use of acupuncture as a healing technique is over four thousand years old. It is practiced not only in the Orient but generally worldwide. The oriental explanation of its mode of function is that in addition to the flow of blood, lymph, and nervous impulse there is also a flow of energy in the body that is called Chi. Chi flows along pathways called meridians. Whenever the flow of energy is obstructed, the potential for disease is present. The acupuncturist is able to diagnose the obstruction and to release normal energy flow by inserting needles to stimulate the appropriate meridian at specific points. In the days of the *Yellow Emperor's Classic of Internal Medicine,* stone needles were used; then iron needles progressed to silver or gold. Today stainless-steel needles of very fine caliber are used.

The general requirements in basic training that are essential for the safe and competent practice of acupuncture are a knowledge of anatomy, physiology, pathology, medicine, pharmacology as well as diagnostic skills. Acupuncture is a unique system for pain relief. Supporters claim it can cure many ailments and maintain health.

Chiropractic

Ever since chiropractic was founded in 1895, it has focused on the nervous system and its lifeline, the spinal column, as the integrator of all body functions.

In chiropractic, disease is attributed to a misalignment of individual vertebrae that creates pressure on nerve tissue and interferes with nerve impulses. Although the traditional treatment focuses mainly on spinal manipulation, many chiropractors also work with nutrition and physiotherapy.

Rigorous studies have shown manipulations of the spine to be effective in relieving lower-back pain. Claims are that chiropractic outdistances drugs for long-term management of headaches. As a holistic healing art it is considered whole-person therapy.

Faith Healing

Although one can be helped without expressing faith, it is the healer who must have real faith in the power to heal. Human beings, like all other living systems, possess great powers of spontaneous recovery, and often a healer can effectively trigger such an occurrence.

Studies have been made of the effectiveness of so-called places of miracles such as Lourdes, sacred shrines, holy water, holy objects, the touch of a priest, and blessed amulets or talismans.

Spiritual Fate

The motive of the practitioner is of prime concern. Those who believe in karma or cause and effect do not take lightly their capacity to influence profoundly on all levels of health.

Criminal Liability

As an adjunct to medicine, faith healing is subject to the same creed, "Do good if you can, but do no harm," observing the Hippocratic oath. Sometimes failure to resort to conventional medical intervention based on beliefs denying outside intercession can be surmounted and help in grave situations mandated by public authorities.

Natural Healing

Self-care and the people's responsibility for their own health can no longer be ignored. Every doctor and patient can work out guidelines for maintaining optimal health.

The body will often heal itself without any intervention. The revolution in health practices reveals the requirements for optimal health and the way to avoid debilitating diseases. Longevity and good health are synonymous with the way we think about the future in medicine.

Natural healing is assisted by balanced nutrition including herbs to prevent illness, exercise, vitamins, and a collection of easy, safe home remedies for common ailments, The media offer free advice on avoiding major illnesses such as heart attacks, cancer, and strokes. Mind power is a recognized factor in health: It can influence illness or wellness. Breath is the basic life energy, and together with mind power it can be a transformative tool for healing. Natural healing is the new medicine for the year 2000 and beyond.

Holistic Health Care

Holistic is the term used to describe alternative healing therapies from acupuncture to Zen macrobiotics. The treatment views the patient as a whole: body, mind, attitude, and emotions. It is considered drugless because it concentrates on diet, exercise, meditation, and natural medications. The healers include not only medical physicians but lay practitioners skilled in the art and science of healing to expand the spectrum of holistic treatment.

The cornerstone of holistic philosophy is the sharing of responsibility equally by physician and patient. The physician assumes the greater role as health educator. As adviser the holistic doctor may ask questions instead of giving answers to help redefine the problem. Holistic prescriptions are more likely to be books, workshops, health spas, support groups, and nutrition counseling. Symptoms are analyzed to determine what changes in lifestyle might prevent recurrences and would inspire them to take responsibility for their own health.

Yoga

Yoga systems include raja, kundalini, hatha and tantra, inherited from the five-thousand-year-old tradition of the Himalayan sages. These teachings promise to develop a physical, mental, and spiritual life leading to total well-being. Karma yoga also teaches how to apply the principle of cause and effect to enhance daily living.

The practice of yoga is organized around meditation to bring harmony to body, mind, and spirit. The stillness of body and mind is achieved by rest, breath, sound, rhythm, simplicity, and wholeness. Various postures for balancing the body are designed to improve health in general or to correct specific spinal problems such as lumbar lordosis or misalignments.

Homeopathic Medicine

Homeopathy is a complete system of healing discovered two hundred years ago by a German physician, Dr. Samuel Hahnemann. The basic belief is: "Like cures like." In conventional medicine, the suppression of disease is considered the cure. Homeopathy sees the symptoms as evidence that the body is working in a healthy way to overcome the condition by stimulating the body's own self-healing power.

There is increased interest in homeopathy because of growing concern about toxic side effects used in mainstream medicine. Homeopathy has been the focus of scientific research. The medicines are prepared from fresh plant, animal, or mineral sources. One part of the original substance is mixed with nine parts of an inert substance or liquid. Potencies are then formulated for a wide variety of ailments. Homeopathy can be used without harm by following recommended dosages exactly.

Allopathic Medicine

Medical practice that seeks to cure disease by producing a condition incompatible or antagonistic to the condition to be cured is termed *allopathic medicine.*

Almost all conventionally trained physicians are specialists. Whether they are general internists, pediatricians, or family physicians (the major primary-care specialties), they are board-certified and go through a residency after medical school.

Hippocrates, the father of medicine, was the first to examine the sick carefully and record the signs and symptoms of disease. His accumulation of facts is among the first organized and systematic knowledge on which modern medicine rests.

The sophisticated scope of future medicine will enable the physician to control and stimulate healing at will. Science fiction healing increasingly becomes reality.

Rehabilitative Therapies

Illness that requires rehabilitation involves psychological as well as physiological trauma. Therapy centers report that treatment must take into account mind, body, and emotions. Stressful emotions resulting from traumatic injuries, fear, anger, frustration, and depression all stimulate the body to produce excess adreline and cortisone that upset the balance of body functions.

Rehabilitation requires specialized training with more communication, more interaction between therapist and patient.

Among therapies used are the following examples: guided imagery and hypnosis for pain control, massage for muscular disease, exercise, and mutrition to build immunity.

Empowerment is a potent medicine that gives freedom in decision making and responsibility for each individual's recovery and health.

See also HEALTH CARE; HEALTH CARE FINANCING; HEALTH CARE: MORAL ISSUES; HEALTH CARE: TECHNOLOGICAL DEVELOPMENTS; NUTRITION; SEXUAL REPRODUCTION, ARTIFICIAL MEANS.

BIBLIOGRAPHY

Huard, Pierre, and Wong, Ming. *Chinese Medicine.* New York: McGraw-Hill, 1968.

Meyer, Joseph E. *The Herbalist.* Chicago: Rand-McNally, 1960.

Vithoulkas, George. *Homeopathy: Medicine for the New Man.* New York: Arco, 1979.

Weil, Andrew. *Natural Health, Natural Medicine.* Boston: Houghton Mifflin, 1990.

Etel E. De Loach

Health Care Costs

In the mid-1990s, the United States was spending more than a trillion dollars a year on health care, 15 percent of the nation's gross domestic product. Americans were paying $4,000 a year for the health care of each man, woman, and child. Hospitals, doctors, pharmaceutical companies, medical equipment manufacturers, insurers, and nursing homes were billing the country $3 billion a day, an amount equal to more than the daily production of goods and services of half the states in the country.

Every president since Harry S. Truman has tried to restructure America's health care system in an effort to assure every citizen access to quality care at reasonable cost. While progress was made, the cost of the system continued to grow and the number of citizens who lacked health insurance increased to 40 million. Driven by the sober realization that the nation could no longer afford the rising costs of care or tolerate the social injustice of gaps in health coverage, the president, the Congress, and the country's leading employers reconsidered the foundations and operation of a system providing the most technologically advanced care in the world.

Health care reform involves the training of doctors and paramedicals, the regulation of research, the role and funding of hospitals, the financing mechanisms of insurers and health maintenance organizations (HMOs), the pricing of pharmaceuti-

cals and medical devices, the provision of nursing home care for the expanding elderly population, and the lifestyle of individual patients with regard to diet, exercise, stress, sex, and substance abuse (including legal and illegal drugs, nicotine, and alcohol).

Further complicating the task, the health industry contributes millions of dollars to presidential candidates and members of Congress to protect the industry's financial interests in the details of health legislation. The same individuals who on the one hand believe the nation must control its health care spending and that doctors charge too much, insist on the other hand that no care is too expensive for their sick parents, spouse, and children, and that their own doctors' fees are reasonable.

In 1965, when President Lyndon B. Johnson persuaded Congress to enact Medicare, which provides insurance for the elderly, and Medicaid, which provides insurance for poor Americans, the health system accounted for less than 6 percent of the domestic economy. In the mid-1990s, advocates of reform believed that without radical reform the health industry would absorb $2 trillion annually and account for close to 20 percent of the economy by the year 2000.

By the mid 1990s, health was America's biggest business. It employed almost 11 million people, more than the number working in transportation and construction combined. The nation spent on health twice what it spent on defense or education. Gaining control of health spending, the fastest-growing component of the federal budget, was essential in efforts to close the budget deficit, which threatened to reach $500 billion by the year 2000. At the state level, only the rate of increase in prison costs comes close to the rise in health care spending.

The United States spends more on health care per person than its international peers. In 1993, the U.S. paid $3,300 per capita, compared to $1,900 in Germany and $1,500 in Japan. But Americans have a shorter life expectancy than Germans or Japanese.

The American health care system has produced miraculous achievements in the quest to solve the riddles of the human body and mind. The nation's medical centers are the envy of the world for their advanced technology and innovative treatment, attracting patients from around the globe. In 1993, the federal government spent $12 billion on health research and development, with the bulk supporting basic research. The private sector spent another $16.8 billion, with most supporting applied research.

Yet the rising price of advanced technology pushed the highest-quality care above what many insurance policies cover and beyond the reach of many Americans. At the same time, waste, fraud, and abuse consumed at least $250 billion—a quarter of all health spending in 1994, and despite its spectacular technological abilities, the country ranks below most developed countries in its ability to prevent infant deaths. A quarter of all pregnant women do not get early prenatal care, an important factor in preventing infant mortality.

The United States also has one of the lowest rates in the Western Hemisphere for preschool immunizations against diseases such as measles, mumps, and polio. From 1989 to 1991, a decade after the country was on the verge of eradicating measles within its borders, 55,000 Americans contracted measles and 130 of them died. Only about half of all urban preschoolers are fully immunized.

Measuring the quality of health care has always been a difficult task. The American system intensively uses high technology and innovative drugs. These expenses may be sensible if they prevent ill health, pain, and suffering, as many do. But striking variations in the level of care across the country have raised the question of whether the nation's health care dollars are buying unnecessary or inappropriate care.

Research has found, for example, that if you are a man who retires in Florida rather than in Maine, you are four times as likely to have your prostate surgically removed. If you are a woman with localized breast cancer, your chances of a radical mastectomy are a third higher if you live in Iowa rather than Seattle, Washington. Much of the variation reflects uncertainty among doctors about what works in treating illness, but in some cases it reflects inappropriate care. Some experts believe the country could eliminate one-quarter of all surgical and medical procedures without any impact on health.

Beginning in the 1980s, variations in practice combined with rapidly increasing costs prompted many employers and insurers to question the autonomy of the nation's 600,000 active doctors. The special expertise of physicians had generally shielded them from scrutiny outside their professional domain. But they suddenly found themselves answering questions from a host of nonphysician reviewers, who created a mound of paperwork for America's health care providers. Today the proportion of health spending devoted to administrative expenses in the American system is extraordinarily high—roughly twice the share of administrative costs in the Canadian system.

Furthermore, the growing distrust of doctors, combined with the litigious American legal system, sparked an explosion in malpractice suits, costing $10 billion a year in the early 1990s. In turn this prompted roughly $10 billion in unnecessary tests and procedures that doctors ordered to protect themselves from potential litigants. Such "defensive medicine" contributes precious little to health outcome. All of these forces have demoralized many doctors; some are retiring early or going into other fields.

The increasing number of elderly citizens also adds to the challenge of providing quality care for every American. Not only is the elderly population growing in size, but more of its members are living longer and using the health care system frequently. The number of people age sixty-five in the U.S. increases by nearly 6,000 every day. Many of them can now expect to live past age eighty. By 2010, the elderly will total 40 million. By 2030, the group will number 70 million as baby boomers enter their golden years.

The elderly already account for a heavy share of the nation's health care budget and its high-technology miracles. They use almost four times as much health care per capita as people under age sixty-five. Medicare, the primary source of insurance for the elderly's hospital and doctor bills, covered 37 million Americans, most sixty-five or older, at a cost of $160 billion in 1994.

The growing elderly population has caused expansion of the nursing home industry as well. Back in 1985, the country spent $34 billion on long-term care. The bill doubled in eight years, and will double again by the year 2000. Nearly a third of the Medicaid budget, which reached $150 billion in 1994, pays nursing home bills for the elderly. In 1993, Medicaid spent $9,595 for the average elderly patient, compared to only $1,444 for each poor child and $2,419 for each poor adult.

The nation's 6,500 hospitals, which house 1.2 million beds, account for 40 percent of every health care dollar. Since the middle of the twentieth century, hospitals have largely enjoyed full reimbursement from government and private insurers for the services and new technologies they offered. Hospitals competed for the best doctors and the most patients by offering the latest technological advances and procedures, regardless of cost.

Beginning in the 1980s, government and private insurers pushed hospitals to reduce expensive hospital stays. In 1983, the federal government introduced Diagnosis Related Groups (DRGs), a prospective payment system affecting hospitals receiving Medicare. By notifying hospitals how much payment they would receive for a certain patient or therapy, DRGs prevented hospitals from providing unlimited care with the expectation that Medicare would pay the bill. In response, hospitals ratcheted up their patients to the highest intensity care possible, cut their costs, or shifted them to privately insured patients whose health plans lacked such limits.

Pressured by public and private insurers to eliminate unnecessary admissions, hospitals also cut the number of patients hospitalized from 36 million in 1982 to 31 million in 1992. Hospitals eliminated 182,000 beds. Hundreds of hospitals closed their doors. At the same time, patient stays in hospitals grew shorter, especially among the elderly. The average length of stay among seniors fell 18 percent from 10.1 days in 1982 to 8.3 in 1992. After leaving the hospital, many received care at home or in hospices.

Even with these changes, higher costs related in part to the use of expensive technology more than doubled the price of hospital stays from 1982 to 1992. Meanwhile, the number of outpatient visits grew by 40 percent, providing a surge of income for hospitals. Both developments helped ease the pressure to eliminate empty beds. On a typical day, only two-thirds of all beds are occupied. Hospitals have at least 250,000 more beds than the nation needs, costing more than 8 billion dollars a year to maintain.

How doctors receive payment for their services has become another focus of reform. The nation's doctors consume 20 percent of every health care dollar, but their decisions affect about 75 percent of all spending. Traditionally, doctors collected fees for the services they provided, giving them a financial incentive to provide more care than absolutely necessary. Well-insured patients, who usually paid little or none of their medical bills, had no incentive to minimize their use of the health system and little ability to second-guess their doctor's decisions.

Beginning in the 1980s, many doctors responded to concerns about costs by moving to a payment system in which they collected an annual salary, rather than individual fees for each procedure they performed. This migration was part of the shift to "managed care" in which HMOs encouraged doctors to consider costs when treating their patients, and insurance companies hired reviewers to look over the shoulders of doctors to weed out unnecessary care.

Employers, who pay more than a quarter of the nation's personal health expenditures, have nur-

tured many of the financing and delivery innovations that continue to redraw the face of health care in the U.S. Many employers encourage workers to use "preferred providers" who offer care at reduced prices. They push employees to negotiate doctor bills just as they would question the sticker price on a new car. They give workers incentives to use HMOs, forcing them to pay higher prices for care outside the HMO of the company's choice.

Employers also have restrained their health spending by shifting costs to employees in the form of lower wages. Many companies shed the burden of health benefits by moving cafeteria workers, janitors, and entry-level staff from full-time status to contract status without benefits, or by discontinuing coverage for full-time employees. Others increased deductibles, copayments, and employee contributions to premiums.

While these tactics have produced savings, fundamental problems—such as substance abuse and addiction, poverty, violence, and individual behaviors that adversely affect health—continue to fuel the demand for health care. In the early 1990s, legal and illegal drugs, alcohol, and tobacco were responsible for some $200 billion in health care costs annually. Half of the nation's hospital beds held victims of violence, auto and home accidents, cancer, heart disease, AIDS, tuberculosis, liver, kidney, and respiratory illnesses, all caused or exacerbated by the abuse of tobacco, alcohol, and drugs.

Much of the effort to restructure the health system has focused on the challenge of assuring universal access to care. As the twenty-first century begins, public and private leaders alike will also face the tasks of reducing waste, fraud, and abuse, emphasizing health promotion and disease prevention, providing care for the elderly that enables them to live their final years independently and in dignity, and freeing every American from the dehumanizing grip of substance abuse and addiction. An agenda of this urgency and complexity will keep health care at the center of the nation's radar screen well into the twenty-first century.

See also DEATH AND DYING; ENTITLEMENT PROGRAMS; HEALTH CARE; HEALTH CARE FINANCING; HEALTH CARE: MORAL ISSUES; HEALTH CARE: TECHNOLOGICAL DEVELOPMENTS; MEDICAL CARE PROVIDERS; PUBLIC HEALTH; SOCIAL WELFARE PHILOSOPHIES.

BIBLIOGRAPHY

AARON, HENRY J., and SCHWARTZ, WILLIAM B. *The Painful Prescription.* Washington, D.C.: The Brookings Institution, 1984.

BOVBJERG, RANDALL R.; GRIFFIN, CHARLES C.; and CAR-
ROLL, CAITLIN E. "U.S. Health Care Coverage and
Costs: Historical Development and Choices for the
1990s." *The Journal of Law, Medicine and Ethics* 21
(Summer 1993): 141–162.

BURNER, SALLY T.; WALDO, DANIEL R.; and MCKUSICK,
DAVID R. "National Health Expenditures Projections
Through 2030." *Health Care Financing Review* 14 (Fall
1992): 1–29.

CALIFANO, JOSEPH A. *Radical Surgery: What's Next for
America's Health Care.* New York: Times Books, 1994.

Congressional Budget Office. *Economic Implications of
Rising Health Care Costs.* Washington, DC: C.B.O.,
October 1992.

National Center for Health Statistics. *Health, United
States, 1991.* Hyattsville, MD: Public Health Service,
1992.

SCHROEDER, STEVEN A. "A Comparison of Western European and U.S. University Hospitals; A Case Report
from Leuven, West Berlin, Leiden, London, and San
Francisco." *Journal of the American Medical Association* 252 (July 13, 1984): 240–246.

STARR, PAUL. *The Social Transformation of American
Medicine.* New York: Basic Books, 1982.

WOOLHANDLER, STEFFIE, and HIMMELSTEIN, DAVID. "The
Deteriorating Efficiency of the U.S. Health Care System." *The New England Journal of Medicine* 324 (May
2, 1991): 1253–1258.

Joseph A. Califano

Health Care Financing

Public policy in health care financing has to answer three basic questions:

- Who is covered?
- What is covered?
- How is it paid for?

The U.S. federal government, and virtually every
state, is working to reform health care delivery and
financing systems and to establish some form of
universal care covering all citizens, with a standard
package of at least basic benefits. Assuming the
continued goal of universal coverage, policy makers face three financing options:

1. Separating health care coverage from employment and financing it by general taxation. This
   option can be made much more progressive and
   avoids forcing employers to trade off health care
   benefits against job creation.
2. A totally private system that will shift financing
   to the individual by mandating that every citizen have health insurance. Upon examination,
   simply ordering people to have health insurance

is an impractical alternative. The government
must do more than mandate individual action
because, among other reasons, many people
cannot afford or will not buy health insurance
privately.

3. A public/private partnership system, which is
   essentially the model that the United States now
   follows, however inadequately. Public policy
   makers have to decide what is covered by the
   public system and what is covered by the private
   system. While the delivery systems vary considerably, the financing under this alternative generally provides public funding for the medically
   indigent, the blind, and the elderly, while the
   employers continue to finance employees (who
   usually also are required to contribute). These
   latter systems subsidize small employers, or
   allow a phase-in period.

Those who argue for health care market reform
usually also limit the amount that employers can
deduct for providing health insurance to the cost of
a basic benefit package (thereby creating an incentive for employers to select an efficient plan), and
requiring the cost of any plan more expensive than
a basic benefit package to be included in the employee's income (creating an incentive for the employee to select an efficient plan). Many proposals
also include a small copayment for most medical
services to make patients think twice before accessing the system.

What Does the Future Hold?

Reforming one-seventh of the national economy is
a gargantuan task filled with a myriad of special
interest pitfalls. Many congresspersons and legislators never had to deal with the health issue and are
loathe to interject themselves into a subject that
has so many conflicting interests. Members of
Congress who have studied the issue are split between those who want a single payor (Canadian-
type) system and those who want to reform the
health care market. It is hard to see these two
deeply held, but inconsistent, philosophies reconciled—but it will and must happen because health
care costs are growing at two and one-half times
the rate of inflation and unduly interfering with
other important public and private needs.

The most likely scenario will be for a national
bill that will encourage a number of states to reform their systems in the interim until a more
comprehensive national legislation can be instituted in 1996. The most probable form that legisla-

tion will take will be for employer mandate with a phase-in for small employers. A Canadian-type system would require shifting over $300 billion (1992 dollars) in premiums now paid by employers to new taxes. This seems unlikely, however powerful the arguments supporting it are. The least political resistance will be to build on the existing system, and the fact that over three-quarters of U.S. employers now voluntarily cover their employees (and dependents) will furnish a model that requires the least amount of new taxes and generates the least amount of political opposition. Evolution is always more likely than revolution in a democracy.

Government will cover those who are not connected to the workplace, most likely out of "sin" taxes and general revenues. Medicaid will be folded into the new system, but Medicare will initially be maintained separately because of the power of the elderly lobby. Eventually, Medicare will be eliminated and its beneficiaries will be added to the new plan.

Health care reform will not be a one-time event, but an incremental and evolutionary process which will likely last at least a decade. If employer mandate proves inefficient or does not generate the expected stability of health care costs, new reforms will be initiated. No nation can tolerate health care doubling its share of the GDP every twenty years. If market reform does not produce a high level of health care at affordable prices, government will redeploy much more blunt instruments to achieve this goal.

See also DEATH AND DYING; ENTITLEMENT PROGRAMS; HEALTH CARE: MORAL ISSUES; HEALTH CARE: TECHNOLOGICAL DEVELOPMENTS.

BIBLIOGRAPHY

AARON, HENRY J. *Serious and Unstable Condition: Financing America's Health Care.* Washington, DC: Brookings Institute, 1991.
CALIFANO, JOSEPH A., JR. *America's Health Care Revolution.* New York: Touchstone Books, 1986.
FUCHS, VICTOR R. *The Health Economy.* Cambridge, MA: Harvard University Press, 1986.

Richard D. Lamm

Health Care: Moral Issues

Who lives, who dies, and how much public money should be spent determining the answers to these questions are moral issues that will continue to challenge our society in the twenty-first century.

New knowledge will reframe these issues and confront old beliefs. Knowledge of genetics and complex systems will lead people to rethink moral choices. This new knowledge can help society distinguish practices that are based upon carelessness from those resting on deeply held beliefs.

Careless allocation of health care resources creates one of the future moral issues likely to be reshaped by new knowledge. Early in the twenty-first century, the map of the human genome will be largely filled in and many genes will be fully sequenced. Geneticists will provide far better predictions about the potential for long life, early sickness, or susceptibility to specific environmental exposures. These predictions will both illuminate and trouble the decisions of individuals and organized health care providers who determine the allocation of health care dollars. It is hard to stop trying to save a life, even when realistically the effort holds little help. Although genetic information will be incomplete and probabilistic, it is still likely to be used to ration such care. Rationing of care in the mid-1990s is less informed and will likely be seen to be morally repugnant. Enormous expenditures are made on futile, heroic measures to stave off death for short periods during which people are incapacitated. The ability to more accurately predict probable deaths through molecular genetics will help society confront the moral question about who receives expensive treatments and who does not.

Social values are visible in both cases where health care dollars are spent and where they are not. As we create better models, using concepts from the growing field of evolutionary systems (sometimes called complexity, dynamic systems, or chaos theory) and supercomputers to perform massive computations, the economics of the health care system will be better understood. More people will see what society buys with its health care dollars and what it fails to buy. Fewer allocation decisions in the future will profit from the ignorance of true costs and social benefits than is the case in today's world.

The money spent on children, for example, exemplifies the high value placed on technological intervention and the low value placed on community health. Neonatal intensive care units (NICUs) have grown capable of saving premature babies who would die without the use of expensive technology. Months after these low-birthweight babies leave the NICUs, however, studies show a high proportion are plagued with problems that lead to early death or severe impairments. Many may go to homes or institutions to suffer horrible childhoods with little community support. Knowledge of long-term (more than a year) outcomes of saving premature infants at the edge of viability is incomplete. Our fragmented information system fails to keep track of most health care results over time.

Answers dealing with these vexing problems will likely not resolve fully the questions raised. Compelling studies do show, however, that dollars spent to foster healthy communities can create higher-quality life, particularly for children in poverty. Looked at from a systems perspective, health care allocations show a kind of carelessness about children, a fact that is mirrored by society's poverty rates for children, educational failures, and divorces. The allocation of health care resources tends to go to the extremes—the end of life and the beginning of life—which has been described as "the zone of medical futility." If those resources were spent to create healthy environments that support the maximum capacity of individuals within a community, health care would be very different. Expenditures would go to prevent problems that are currently treated, and children, in particular, would receive more care.

Hopeful forecasts anticipate that values will shift in our society as idealistic baby boomers mature into a generation that makes the care of children more important. Already the first baby-boom president and his wife represent a hope for rekindled commitment to America's children. They began the health-care reform debate with childhood vaccination. While this debate appears to be stalled, or even failed, it is likely to be simply the beginning of another reform era that will reflect the ascending leadership of the baby-boom generation. As the debate moves to the Medicare program, which represents the many dollars spent on the burden of illness borne by the elderly, the hope remains that a new selflessness might arise in our society.

When health care reform is marked by selflessness instead of selfishness, the debate can move from illness to health. When institutions and individuals throughout the nation answer the callto idealism, the commitment shifts to creating healthy people in healthy communities. Then the use of resources changes. Children who have a hope for a better life will receive more care. Those likely to die may receive more humane care that does not sap dollars that can be better used to support health. These resource issues are ultimately moral issues. The twenty-first century will see a healthy society and a caring society only if the moral issues are embraced during the era of reform that lies ahead.

See also ABORTION; BIOETHICS; DEATH AND DYING; DISABLED PERSONS' RIGHTS; EPIDEMICS; FAMILY PLANNING; GENETIC TECHNOLOGIES; HEALTH CARE; HEALTH CARE: TECHNOLOGICAL DEVELOPMENTS; SEXUAL REPRODUCTION: ARTIFICIAL MEANS.

BIBLIOGRAPHY

BIEMESDERFER, SUSAN C. *Healthy Babies: State Initiatives for Pregnant Women at Risk.* Denver, CO: National Conference of State Legislators, 1993.

HUROWITZ, JAMES C. "Toward a Social Policy for Health." *New England Journal of Medicine* 329/2 (July 8, 1993): 130–133.

KIMBRELL, ANDREW. *The Human Body Shop: The Engineering and Marketing of Life.* San Francisco, CA: Harper Collins, 1993.

"Your Final 30 Days—Free: Let's Ban Doctor and Hospital Bills for Futile Care of the Dying." *Washington Post,* May 2, 1993.

Jonathan Peck

Health Care Providers.

See DENTISTRY; MEDICAL CARE PROVIDERS; MENTAL HEALTH; NURSING; PSYCHIATRY.

Health Care: Technological Developments

Human health services stand at the threshold of a new revolution. The process of creating health care breakthroughs is accelerating and producing revolutionary consequences for medicine in the next century.

Early in the century the primary cause of death and disability was disease organisms. Due to advances in medicine and public health (including waste disposal and sanitation systems), many infectious diseases have been eliminated or reduced. But new ones have been added, such as AIDS and environmental risks posed by toxic substances. One by one, disfiguring and disabling childhood diseases have succumbed to breakthroughs in medical science. Rubella, mumps, and measles have been almost relegated to history books in the aftermath of vaccinations. Next, medical advances could eliminate cancer and heart disease as the main killers and bring vaccines for other diseases—genital herpes, flu, AIDS, and so forth.

Now the health issues have been redefined to include those matters once considered social problems: drunkenness, smoking, chemical dependency, environmental concerns, workplace management matters, and so on. In developed countries today worries about the drunken driver have replaced worries about Typhoid Mary. Concerns about the outpouring of noxious vapors from automobiles and factories have replaced concerns about microbes in drinking water (which, before sanitation systems, killed millions yearly). Tobacco smoke now is the major destroyer of our lungs, not tuberculosis. Up to age forty in the U.S., auto accidents are the major killer. After age forty, the biggest health problem and killer of humans is attributable to smoking. Auto accidents kill about 40,000 Americans per year, whereas smoking has been traced to cause over 300,000 deaths per year. Our own actions or inactions relative to our lifestyle decisions have become the chief causes of disability and death. High-tech medical R&D is beginning to attack such "health" problems.

Lengthening Life

Developing trends create forces-of-change that weave the fabric of the future—this is especially true in the medical field as it relates to the elderly. Because we are learning more about how to initiate and implement change, we are beginning to realize that the future is coming more under our control. Certainly, death is predictable from the viewpoint of the knowledge that all of us will die sometime, as we have in the past. So far we can only predict the event but not the date—will it always be thus?

Throughout human history, life expectancy has been increasing. Back in the Stone Age, the average life expectancy was about eighteen years. By the year 1900 Americans had an average life expectancy of slightly over forty years of age. Today, in the U.S., the average life expectancy is approaching age eighty. Will this trend continue? Recent research indicates that our life span can be significantly increased.

The next question for each of us is, can we expect to live to be more than one hundred years old? Or, when can we expect to live two hundred years or more? Obviously, living longer is desirable only if we can live more years of calendar time to reach a physical age of considerably fewer years—for example, to take 150 years of calendar time to reach a physical age of sixty. With recent advances in our knowledge of why and how we age, resulting from genetic and computer studies, many scientists are now optimistic that such agendas for the future are now opening to the human race.

Now, with the new high technology of computers and recombinant-DNA genetics, scientists see pathways into the future for moving the end-point of death farther out. This process is known as life-span-extending. Thus, scientists and futurists, finding life expectancy too difficult to predict, invent ways to prolong life and thus bypass the need to predict death!

Living longer shifts major diseases and health concerns from youth to the elderly. Average life expectancy at the turn of the century in the U.S. was somewhat over four decades; now it is nearly eight decades. Research points toward another doubling in the next century with humans living to 150 years of age. Beyond this, farther advances are not possible without genetic intervention. Knowledge gained from genetic mapping suggests that there is no genetically programmed upper limit to life! Of course, longer life spans equate to a growth of trips to hospitals—ever more, the older we get.

Gene Technology

The genetic revolution portends a bigger breakthrough than any previous one in human history. New knowledge of the human gene, advances in genetic engineering will drive health care advances and preempt trial-and-error evolution by nature.

Modifying defective genes by replacing or augmenting them with nucleotide sequences of predeterminable specificity and design stand in the offing. The power to intervene genetically, to edit and redesign humans, is awesome.

Prenatal life is already open to genetic scrutiny. Prognostic genetic screening of adults, children, and embryos is becoming ever more routine and prevalent. Gene therapies for correcting congenital disorders, proven in animal models, is poised for application soon in humans—even to grow new limbs and other organs. We are already modifying germ lines of livestock and plants—soon such procedures could become commonplace even for humans. Soon we will be re-engineering immune systems. It is inevitable that somatic cell gene therapy will be eventually adapted to the treatment of diseases and enhancements of the central nervous system—the last frontier or the beginning of a new frontier, depending on one's point of view of molecular genetics.

DNA/RNA intervention technology has augmented the power of medical diagnostics several orders of magnitude, especially through monoclonal antibody re-engineering. This same technology has made somatic gene therapy a reality. In the

435

future it may be possible to piggyback specific genetic materials aboard "tame" viruses that could be sprayed over large areas to eliminate an oncoming flu outbreak or to "cure" plant disease.

Molecular medicine raises ethical issues and challenges for coping with inherited disorders, programs for genetic screening, genetic counseling, radical modification of humans, and power to enhance (accelerate) human evolution. These awesome new powers require societal and political guidance.

Computers, previously used for paperwork, administration, patient record keeping and accounting, and intensive care monitoring, are moving into the diagnostic arena and toward doctor/nurse/patient cognitive skill amplifiers. Artificial intelligence (AI) or applied intelligence amasses expert knowledge for syndication by others. Imagine a future in which all health care knowledge is available to everyone, in an understandable and usable form, in the real-time of need and continually updated as new knowledge is developed! This will first be used by health professionals to amplify their practice, and may be mandated by law to assure use of the best available skills.

Hospitals of the Future

Computers will further automate the hospital and health care. Some trends and issues involved are:

- Intelligent (AI [Artificial Intelligence] expert knowledge-based) health machines—X-rays, CAT and NMR scanners, intensive care units, beds, patient/doctor/nurse/lab technician amplifiers.
- Computer-automated operations and the OR (operating room).
- Self-cleaning/deodorizing rooms, ORs, labs, floors, clothes, and so on.
- Super-cleaning and perpetually sterile instruments—e.g., using a new form of Teflon so slick that even bacteria cannot adhere to it.
- Soft systems (machines, walls, floors) with computerized sensors/detectors and actuators/controllers to prevent hard falls, slips, and damage to limitedly ambulatory patients.
- Totally automated record keeping—without clerks.
- A move away from "pill hill hospitals," toward preventive-medicine practice—e.g., computerized collision-avoidance equipment in automobiles to prevent auto accidents and thus largely eliminate the need for hospitals to patch up people after accidents. A paradigm change is forecast for the medical field and hospital research toward the microminiaturization of hospitals via computer technology, which may prevent or lessen the need to go to the hospital.
- Hospitals becoming more like networks, regional specialists, consortia, health centers with distributed and remote health-delivery nodes, and the like—i.e., a new form of high-tech hospital.

Computers in Medicine

New health/medical opportunities are resulting from the continued speedup of computer technology advances:

- Speech recognition and reply—talk, listen, and dialogue-producing medical hardware and systems—resulting in next-generation, "user-friendly" systems.
- Intelligent expert-knowledge-based systems—medical tools and instruments that permit health professionals to have access to the total knowledge of their special area to apply for personal, professional, embedded amplification in the real-time of their need.
- Computers and AI (Artificial Intelligence) embedded in all manner of medical equipment—"smart" and "intelligent" medical high-tech devices.
- Health computers—eventually worn as part of one's attire.
- Sense environment and take-initiative health systems—health-wellness sensors and controllers.
- Health high-tech microsensors—future "source-date collection automation" devices for automating the sensing and recording of health data.
- Convivial and congenial computers—smart and intelligent health machines that are nice, friendly, easy to use, aware, and so on.

HEALTH PROFESSIONALS/PRACTITIONERS IMPACTS

- High-tech capabilities that "de-skill" the medical professions—impacting on doctors, nurses, and other health professionals, resulting from future, deeper penetration of PCs (personal computers) and AI (Artificial Intelligence).
- Doctors and other health professionals turning more toward research rather than being a prime factor in the delivery of health services
- Reduction of hospital, nurses, and health-services paperwork.
- Upturn of emergency medicine/doctors—as other areas are "de-skilled" and/or automated.
- Expertise of doctors contained in knowledge-based expert systems, allowing growth of the

vocation of health technicians—and eventually allowing the average person/patient to perform health care functions at the same level of expertise, or above, of today's doctor or medical practitioner.

Patient Impacts

The real winner in the accelerating advances of computers and medical technology is the future patient, who would benefit from developments such as these:

- Patient becomes more of a health consumer and/or client.
- New patient rights achieved.
- Patient as a habitual seeker of second and third opinions—often using computers or knowledge-based expert systems.
- Patient shopping around to get "best" (cost and expertise) health deal—often via computer—without a reduction in the level of care.
- Patient being better informed to the "expert" level, allowing for self-help scenarios and getting away from being administered to by a health professional/practitioner.
- On-line health utility services remotely available and deliverable to patient—via high-tech medical/health information utility services or computer networks.
- Longer life with a higher quality of health.

The roles of doctors and nurses also are in transition. The nature of the doctor-patient interaction is changing from the family general practitioner toward clinical settings. Doctors are better trained and more specialized. Hospitals and doctors have more high-tech instruments for diagnosis, the operating room, intensive care, and health care/medical administration. Currently, the medical field is under siege, beset with paperwork, requirements for tests to avoid malpractice claims, and a public and politicians screaming for lower costs. Physicians are delivering more cognitive services and fewer procedural services, which increasingly are being performed by nurses and technicians. Machines are becoming more automated, making the health technician's job easier, but also more cognitive. One possible future is a "post-physician" or computer-delivered health care era wherein health technicians, paraprofessionals, and "health care robots" deliver health services while doctors work more to advance the medical state-of-the-art.

Information technology has recently entered a new era of end-user computing, user-friendly systems, networked personal computing, information centers/utilities, office automation, expert systems, health management systems, and much more. Trends allow medical practitioners to more easily apply advanced technology to amplify what they can do. As a result, a new medical computer technology revolution definitely seems to be in the making that will greatly reduce the paperwork of health professionals (especially supervising nurses), allowing them more time to deal with each patient's health/medical problem.

Nanotechnology

Breakthroughs portending even greater impact on health care and society than molecular cell biology or AI involve nanotechnology. Nanotechnology can use the same DNA/RNA mechanisms in living systems to grow all manner of biological, chemical, and physical things. In this future, which has already begun, the production of things is replaced by the means to grow them—including everything from body parts to new species. Nanotechnology, in the eyes of many researchers and futurists, may become the biggest breakthrough in history.

Feats of genetic engineering spawn new forms of medical diagnostics, new therapies, new roles for health care professionals and hospitals, new "cures," and now, new life forms and new futures. It is hardly deniable that the fruits of scientific discovery color our perception of the world and increase our odds for a healthier life.

Health Care Costs

To reiterate, as we learn more about how to keep people healthier, younger, and living longer, it obviously should cost more to do so. That is, as we continue to evolve a better medical and health science, the percentage of GNP spent on health care must go up. This truism is perhaps the hardest trend challenge for the future that politicians will increasingly need to deal with and resolve. The current push to lower the costs of health care will speed high technology into the health care field to raise the productivity of hospitals, professionals/people, energy, and so on, and to:

- Expand the role of health centers and HMOs.
- Advance computer technology for microminiaturizing expensive health care machinery and to reduce the cost of such machinery in the future.
- Develop medical technology to raise the productivity of the health care industry—e.g., using

NMR and CAT scanners to eliminate the need for exploratory operations.

- Encourage more cooperative sharing between hospitals linked via computer networks, especially initial costly medical high technology.

Medical/health care technology, rather than a villain, is a lifesaver as well as a long-term cost reducer. Non-invasive imaging technology, for example, often eliminates the need for more expensive exploratory operations. Computers reduce paperwork and administrative costs. Technology used for early diagnoses and prevention radically reduces mortality and medical costs. Computers will be used to lower the cost of health care services, thereby increasing availability, especially for persons of limited means.

Demanding health as an entitlement means that more medical technology will be required. Society in the future will not opt for lesser health care than made possible by the health knowledge available to it, at least not for long.

With an accelerating growth of knowledge about human health and the means for improving it, high medical advances, especially with future molecular genetics, nanotechnology, computers, and AI (Artificial Intelligence), there should be little doubt of the future direction of health care and health delivery. For each of us, it means a higher health-quality-of-life.

See also AGING OF THE POPULATION; ARTIFICIAL LIFE; BIOETHICS; DEATH AND DYING; GENETIC ENGINEERING; GENETIC TECHNOLOGIES; HEALTH CARE; HEALTH CARE: ALTERNATIVE THERAPIES; HEALTH CARE COSTS; HEALTH CARE FINANCING; HEALTH CARE: MORAL ISSUES; HIGH TECHNOLOGY; LONGEVITY; MEDICAL CARE PROVIDERS; NANOTECHNOLOGY; NUTRITION; PHARMACEUTICALS; SEXUAL REPRODUCTION: ARTIFICIAL MEANS.

BIBLIOGRAPHY

BUNTON, ROBIN, and MACDONALD, GORDON, eds. *Health Promotion: Disciplines and Diversity.* London and New York: Routledge, 1992.

EMMECHE, CLAUS. *The Garden in the Machine: The Emerging Science of Artificial Life.* Princeton, NJ: Princeton University Press, 1994.

FOOTE, SUSAN B. *Managing the Medical Arms Race: Public Policy and Medical Devices.* Berkeley, CA: University of California Press, 1992.

FUCHS, VICTOR R. *The Future of Health Policy.* Cambridge, MA: Harvard University Press, 1993.

HUBBARD, RUTH and WALD, ELIJAH. *Exploding the Gene Myth: How Genetic Information Is Produced and Manip-*

ulated by Scientists, Insurance Companies, Educators and Law Enforcers. Boston, MA: Beacon Press, 1993.

KIMBRELL, ANDREW. *The Human Body Shop: The Engineering and Marketing of Life.* San Francisco, CA: Harper San Francisco, 1993.

LAFAILLE, ROBERT, and FULDER, STEPHEN, eds. *Towards a New Science of Health.* London and New York: Routledge, 1993.

LARUE, Gerald A. and BAYLY, RICH. *Long-Term Care in an Aging Society: Choices and Challenges for the '90s.* Buffalo, NY: Prometheus Books, 1992.

Earl C. Joseph

Higher Education

The evolution of higher education has seen several major periods of development. As American higher education is poised for a similar major readjustment, elements of past periods are still evidenced in its basic values structure and will play a part in how higher education evolves to about the year 2015. Originally, higher education was a personal relationship between teachers and students. The students studied with only a few scholars and paid for their education after the class was over, according to their feeling of the worth of the class. If the scholars felt mistreated by the town, they would move to another town, taking their students with them. Colleges were gradually formed as an administrative conveyance primarily to provide better facilities. In the Middle Ages, the primary source of an advanced education was provided through the most educated profession: the clergy. Because of the near monopoly that the church had on education, there developed the concept of separation and isolation of higher education from the secular and political world. The college as an intellectual sanctuary comes directly from the role that churches played as a spiritual sanctuary.

The Evolution of Higher Education in America

The first college in America was Harvard, founded in 1636. For the first two hundred years the American college was modeled after the English college, where faculty and students lived and learned together. The primary goal was to form the "whole" student based on a classical and spiritual education. In the mid-1800s the German university concept, with its emphasis on graduate research and intellectual and spiritual separation between faculty and students, appeared at the same time that there was a general discontent with the English/classical model.

This discontent resulted in the passage of the Morrill Act of 1862, which established the land-grant, state-supported universities that were charged to focus on agriculture, mechanical subjects, and the applied arts. In the 1950s there was an increased demand for postsecondary education training that was less than the traditional four-year college. This lead to the development of the comprehensive two-year community college. The creation of the land-grant public college system and the community college led to the establishment of a fundamental value that all citizens who are intellectually qualified for college should be able to attend regardless of income.

Thus the characteristics and values of the independent faculty entrepreneur, intellectually separate from the community; religious and sectarian control; private and public support; and classical and applied education could be found throughout American higher education. Each institution was distinctively different from the other. However, prior to the 1960s, what was common to all was that they were small in size because the majority of Americans did not feel that higher education was very important to their success. In the 1930s fewer than 5 percent of Americans had any post–high school education. In the 1990s more than 50 percent of the population have had some post–high school education, and nearly 25 percent of the population have a baccalaureate degree. Although higher education has grown from fewer than one million students in the 1930s to more than twelve million students in the 1990s, the basic academic values and governance structure have remained essentially the same.

Why higher education is poised for a major change to the year 2015 is due to three converging forces of increased accountability. The first force is the realization that higher education is too important to the economy and social structure of our society to allow it to remain basically unaccountable for the quality of its outputs (i.e., the educational quality of its students, the relevance of the research being performed by its faculty, and the amount of public service provided to society). The second force for greater accountability is due to a decrease in the amount of available funds from all sectors—personal, corporate, and public—to support higher education. Having citizens graduate from college is no longer enough; how well they are educated is also important. The third force comes from an evolution in the management of businesses. Starting in Japan after World War II and spreading in the 1970s and '80s to the United States and Europe, the concept of managing through carefully defining results, relating accomplishment of these results to

refining the systems or interrelations within the organization, and giving decision-making authority to the people at the lowest possible level became the dominate management paradigm. Thus the future of American higher education will be shaped by these three external changes: a public's unwillingness to allow higher education institutions total autonomy because they have become too important to the individual and society; restricting resources that demand greater efficiencies; and new management concepts that will allow for responsible academic independence while providing for accountability to the various publics.

Demographics

Until the year 2005 there will be an increase of 20 percent in the traditional group—eighteen to twenty-four years old—that attends college. This increase in potential college students will be reflected in the enrollments shown in the accompanying table.

The expenditure for higher education over this same period of time will increase from $171.1 billion (1993–1994) to $229.4 billion (2004–2005). This projection represents an average annual increase of 3.4 percent. At the same time, support from state and federal sources are projected to remain stable at best, and some projections indicate dramatic decreases. As of the mid 1990s the cost of going to a public institution is approximately 15 percent of the disposable income for middle-income families; for a private education this figure is closer to 35 percent. If current trends continue, the differences in cost between public and private institutions will become even greater, resulting in more students applying to public institutions.

Pressures for Change

Keeping the expenditures and cost of college in mind, the changing enrollment figures indicate several sources of conflict for higher education. During the 1980s, when the number of traditional college-age students was decreasing, institutions developed new but more costly programs that attracted older students, minorities, and students with learning or physical disabilities. With an increase in enrollment of the more traditional students, colleges will feel pressure to lower costs by eliminating these more costly programs that are serving people with disadvantages.

The pressure for demonstrating greater education outcomes will come from the increasing

TABLE 1. Higher Education* (numbers in thousands)

Enrollments	1982–1983	1993–1994 (estimate)	2004–2005 (projected)	Percent Change 1982–1983 to 1993–1994	Percent Change 1993–1994 to 2004–2005
Total	12,426	14,762	15,976	19	8
Control of institution					
Public	9,696	11,569	12,529	19	8
Private	2,730	3,193	3,447	17	8
Type of institution					
4-year	7,654	9,073	9,818	19	8
2-year	4,772	5,689	6,158	19	8
Sex of student					
Women	6,394	8,119	8,745	27	9
Men	6,031	6,643	7,231	10	8
Age					
19 yrs. and under	2,959	2,861	3,501	–3	22
20–21 yrs. old	2,539	2,762	3,108	9	13
22–24 yrs. old	2,081	2,596	2,798	25	8
25–29 yrs. old	1,995	2,091	1,915	5	–8
30–34 yrs. old	1,263	1,538	1,406	22	–9
35 yrs. or over	1,589	2,915	3,248	83	11
Attendance Status					
Full-time	7,221	8,220	9,053	14	10
Part-time	5,205	6,542	6,923	26	6
Level					
Undergraduate	10,825	12,686	13,969	17	10
Graduate	1,322	1,774	1,810	34	2
First professional	278	302	295	34	–2
Full-time equivalent	9,092	10,579	11,548	16	9

Source: National Center for Educational Statistics, *Projections of Education Statistics to 2005.* Washington, DC: U.S. Department of Education, 1995.

number of students who are thirty-five years or over. A majority of these students will not be entering college for the first time but will be returning to college through employer-assisted tuition programs to develop additional job skills. Both the students and the employers will be insisting that colleges demonstrate that the education offered is relevant to their needs.

Changing Accountability—Changing Learning—Changing Management

The changing demographic and continued financial pressures will foster a demand for greater accountability for higher education institutions to demonstrate that what they are doing is worth the investment of time and resources. The adversarial tension that these demands for accountability gen-

erated in the 1980s and early '90s will change to a greater sense of partnership. This change will first be promoted by a need for institutions to gain financial support from the business and foundation sectors to supplement loss of support from the public sector.

A second reason will be the rapid expansion of knowledge that will occur in many fields, especially in areas such as computers, genetics, and health. This expansion of knowledge will be faster than most colleges can keep up with under traditional ways of educating faculty and having them keep abreast of their field by taking sabbaticals every seven years. Instead, there will be a need for greater sharing of technology, equipment, and experiences. The process to do this will be developed through cooperative agreements with business and industry.

A third pressure for better assessment of the teaching-learning process will come from within the institutions, with faculty and administrative leaders developing a link between the values of education and the usefulness of using purpose or outcome-driven teaching and management problem-solving techniques. Learning these techniques will be encouraged through grant programs sponsored by corporations using the same techniques, state and federal quality award programs, and college reputational ranking surveys that will begin to assess institutions by how well they can document their educational practices.

The end result will be an integration of all parties that play a role and receive a benefit from higher education. This integration will take the form of establishing outcome expectations for the education process, greater awareness of the teaching-learning process, and a more continuous flow of faculty in and out of noncollegiate settings.

Curriculum

For the curriculum the changes will be significant. Historically the primary teaching method has been lecturing. At first this style was used to transfer basic knowledge because of the scarcity of books; later this style was used to integrate knowledge from a variety of sources. However, with the development of the electronic transfer of information, such as computer networks, CD-ROM discs, and videotapes, much of which has been combined into one source, the lecture style no longer will be acceptable. A second pressure to move away from the passive lecture style to a more active faculty-to-student and student-to-student style of learning involve the findings of education research that have developed considerable evidence on the effectiveness of other teaching styles as well as the necessity to accommodate different individual learning styles.

The pressure for changing teaching styles will be heightened by both the development of new knowledge bases and areas of study and rapid changes in the delivery of education through electronic transfer of data. Specialty academic programs never conceived of in the 1960s will emerge at the turn of the century. Courses dealing with new health fields involving genetics, new technology systems, or new areas of study such as dealing with social discontent, will emerge. Advances in computer, video, and audio technology will allow for greater distant interaction between the professor and the student. CD-ROM and holographic projections will allow an interconnectivity that will make education available regardless of geography and time.

Since the publication of *Scholarship Reconsidered: Priorities of the Professoriate* (Boyer, 1991) there has been a debate concerning what activities should be considered appropriate scholarship for faculty. For most of the twentieth century, original research, published in refereed journals and presented at national conferences, was considered the only legitimate form of scholarship. This was a process approach to scholarship. As an outcome approach—creating, discovering, or combining knowledge that expands the knowledge base—becomes more acceptable, then different forms of scholarship will become more recognized. This new scholarship would include the creation of new computer programs, excelling in the performing arts, or teaching. One of the discoveries concerning the judging of scholarship is the recognition that what is considered scholarship is partly a product of a process: The product is often the result of collaborative efforts, the end product is documented well enough so it can be replicated by others, it appears in a form than can be observed and judged, two or more colleagues make a judgment on its contribution to the knowledge base, and others build on it to create new knowledge. These elements of collaboration, visibility, and documentation will be taken into other areas of higher education, especially teaching, to create a more open, valued, and respected part of higher education.

Class Society Based on Levels of Education

Increasingly there is concern over the possibility of the United States developing a class society based on levels of education. One of the consequences of evolving into a postindustrial society with an information and service industry base is the elimination of many middle management positions. This will create a bimodal job force of lower-paid service workers and a much smaller number in a highly educated professional, technical, and managerial class. With a decrease in the availability of student aid, which will provide both access to a higher education and the ability to select the best possible institution, regardless of cost, there will be an increasing gap of haves and have-nots based on education.

During times of prosperity this gap will not be noticeable, but by the year 2005, as the number of workers decreases in relation to nonworkers (primarily retired individuals), the economy will begin to feel the strain. In the 1990s the unemployment rate for a person with a college degree was 2.9 percent, while for a person without a high school diploma the unemployment rate was 13.5 percent. Combining this aspect with the decline or lower levels of participation of male African Americans and Hispanics in higher education, the likelihood of increased social discontent based on the availability of a higher education is very high. As this becomes more apparent, both government and industry will take steps to build a more equitable system that minimizes financial barriers to attend college and accepts the reality that in a nation of great diversity, the educational system must also be diverse at all levels to provide opportunities for all.

As outcome-driven decisions become the common method of problem-solving, only the quality of the final education outcome will be important; all other parts of higher education will be subject to being questioned and changed. This will be the true revolution of higher education.

See also ADULT LEARNING; EDUCATIONAL TECHNOLOGIES; ELEMENTARY AND SECONDARY EDUCATION; LIBERAL ARTS.

BIBLIOGRAPHY

BOYER, E. L. *Scholarship Reconsidered: Priorities of the Professoriate.* Princeton, NJ: Princeton University Press, 1991.

CAFFEE, ELLEN EARLE, and SHERR, LAWRENCE A. *Quality: Transforming Postsecondary Education.* Washington, DC: George Washington University Graduate School of Education and Human Development, 1992.

National Center for Educational Statistics. *Projections of Education Statistics to 2005.* Washington, DC: U.S. Department of Education, 1995.

SIMS, RONALD R.; and SIMS, SERBRENIA J., eds. *Managing Institutions of Higher Education into the 21st Century: Issues and Implications.* Westport, CT: Greenwood Press, 1991.

Jonathan D. Fife

High Technology

Technology is moving so fast today that it carries its own warning: keep up, retrain, or drop out. Technology is changing not only the rules but the game itself. As change accelerates, it is not impossible that the bulk of all the goods and services that humans will be interacting with by the start of the third millennium have not yet been developed. This acceleration will make many things obsolete within the next decade. Traditional approaches will be left in the dust.

The turn of the millennium could be termed the end of the age of credentialism. The prime requisites for the employment of tomorrow are going to be attitude and aptitude. People with the right attitude and aptitude can be trained for anything—and rapidly. Many conventional paths to learning will no longer exist or will become unrecognizable in the future. Those who expect to survive on past talents and beliefs will fare badly.

New opportunities will continue to open in fields now unknown or only vaguely seen. Technology is no longer limited to the manipulation of the inorganic. Organic fields beckon. Biotechnology will allow the creation of new life-forms that in time may more than replace the species disappearing due to a changing planetary environment.

Biohackers—young, probably undisciplined minds who, for various reasons, do not find a suitable mode to enter exciting fields of science and technology—will create their own laboratories. They will use equipment and techniques not unlike those used by young, 1970s computer geeks who created in a garage what highly trained and conformist computer scientists were unable to accomplish in multimillion-dollar institutions. The origin of the Apple Computer Company is one such example.

Many such new life-forms will be chimeras—living organisms containing tissues of varied genetic structure. Previously forbidden boundaries already have been crossed with transmission into a tobacco plant of the gene that causes the glow in a firefly. Such experiments suggest that many unthinkable things are possible. The spectrum of life-forms that can be created with biogenetics may be totally open-ended and have no end.

Totally new forms of entertainment, created especially for the home, will appear quickly and dramatically. Virtual reality (VR), the result of a computer designing a real world or other worlds that could not exist under natural laws yet which viewers can enter, will change humans more than the automobile has. VR will become the preferred mode of training for most fields. It will, for example, enable an eighty-five-year-old bedridden grandmother to get together with her grandson and go skydiving or scuba diving. VR will provide emotional as well as visual and aural experiences. People will become participants, not passive spectators. VR will revolutionize show business as we know it.

Coupled with ground-linked, global fiber-optic networks, satellite transmissions—a concept introduced to the world by visionary author and scientist Arthur C. CLARKE in 1945 before anyone but astronomers thought a satellite was anything but our moon—will radically transform our lives. They will bring unlimited knowledge to anyone with the right attitude and aptitude. The continuing technological advance of relatively inexpensive equipment for use in the home will pave the way for previously unimaginable New Age breakthroughs.

Medical technology, which has doubled lifespans in technologically advanced societies since the agricultural age, will make astounding forward strides. Such advances will ultimately allow some humans to "grow" themselves back to health.

Technology that can convert once harmful pollution into viable and valuable new compounds or easily detoxify hazardous ones will shortly spring forth from Japan and other locations. Developments could make former sterile lands productive and reduce toxic substances in the atmosphere. Conversion of seawater into potable water is already possible, though at prices somewhat above present usual water costs, in some arid areas. At the same time, and possibly built into desalination plants, converters will produce hydrogen for powering the nonpolluting vehicles of tomorrow.

The development of efficient modes of transportation on land, sea, and in the air may be accomplished in months compared with what required years previously. The development and application of super and paralleled computers will vastly accelerate and bring forth vehicles previously unimaginable. Newly developed transport systems should perform flawlessly during their first demonstrations. They will have been repeatedly tested and improved and tested again on computers before being introduced to the public.

Technology will invade home and workplace as ceramics, new materials, and innovative techniques penetrate and replace traditional building construction. "Smart" materials that can transform the shape of airplane wings or ship hulls as they respond to changing conditions will spread to buildings and bridges, making them more malleable and responsive to forces acting on them.

Such developments will come from the five billion minds now on the planet. Working more and more with emerging computer technologies, enhanced by optical and crystal storage units such as SERODS (Surface Enhanced Optical Data Storage) capable of storing on one twelve-inch disc all the information contained in an entire large university library. Information will be accessible from anywhere in the world at costs lower than what you now put in a parking meter in front of present libraries. The possibilities are limitless.

See also CHANGE, PACE OF; GENETIC TECHNOLOGIES; INTERACTIVE ENTERTAINMENT; MEDICA LAB; SATELLITE COMMUNICATIONS; SPACE SATELLITES; TECHNOLOGICAL CHANGE.

BIBLIOGRAPHY

BRAND, STEWART. *The Media Lab: Inventing the Future at M.I.T.* New York: Penguin, 1988.

COGHLAN, ANDY. "Smart Ways to Treat Materials." *New Scientist* (July 4, 1992).

OGDEN, FRANK. *Dr. Tomorrow's Lessons from the Future.* Bellingham, WA: 21st Century Media Communications, 1992.

RHEINGOLD, HOWARD. *Virtual Reality.* New York: Summit Books/Simon and Schuster, 1992.

Frank Ogden

Hinduism

There are more than 750 million Hindus around the world who trace the sources of their religion to the coming together of the Harappa Civilization (ca. 3000 B.C.E.) and the culture of the Indo-European people who may have settled in India around 1500 B.C.E.

The Future According to Hindu Sacred Texts

The epic *Mahabharata* (ca. 400 B.C.E.) and Sanskrit texts known as *puranas* (composed between 300 and 1200 C.E.) speak of the Earth being created and destroyed in cycles. The ideal age (*krta yuga*) lasts 1,728,000 human years, and righteousness flourishes. During the next three ages, righteousness is on the decline; the final age of *kali*, in which we live, is the most corrupt. At the end of the *kali* period, Vishnu, an important Hindu God, is to incarnate himself as a person called Kalki, and destroy evil.

Leaving aside now the future anticipated in Hindu sacred texts, one may cautiously project some prominent trends currently shaping the future of the Hindu people. But first it must be noted that in Hinduism there is no single, centralized authority or text that legitimates any of these activities. Trends and practices described here may be supported (or opposed) by particular religious leaders of the various disparate Hindu communities.

Technology in the Service of Hinduism

One of the most striking features of the Hindu tradition in the twentieth century has been the ease with which technology has been used to facilitate and selectively fulfill religious and cultural norms.

The Vedas (collections of prayers and liturgy) were considered to be revealed by listening (aurally). They were then transmitted orally, without transformation, through generations of male brahmins. The Vedas and later the devotional songs were to be recited and sung in an atmosphere of piety, either in a domestic ritual or in the temples. Today these devotional songs are sung on the secular stage and disseminated through the mass media. This movement from the shrine onto the secular stage is an important transition in the history of the holy word in the Hindu tradition.

Cassettes of popular devotional songs are bestsellers. A new orality has surfaced through the electronic media, one that combines the personal articulation through voice with the impersonal distance of the mass media.

"Do-it-yourself" rituals on audiocassettes are also popular in the Indian marketplace. Both in rural areas within India and in the worldwide diaspora there are no Hindu priests available to conduct rituals, so audiocassettes are increasingly popular as a way of leading men and women through particular rituals.

In a similar way, visual technology is bringing new meaning to the notion of *darsan*, a central practice within the Hindu tradition; it is to behold with faith, to see and be seen by a teacher or the deity. With the advent of the videocassette recorder and television set, a new visualization has emerged. The largest audiences on national television broadcasts are for visual reenactments of the epics *Ramayana* and the *Mahabharata*, portraying the life of Krishna, who is perceived to be an incarnation of the deity Vishnu.

Television increasingly beams images of rituals from sacred places all over India into homes. Videocassettes replay them so that one can vicariously experience the joys of a pilgrimage that someone else has taken. Once a priestly guide, later a flimsy little pamphlet, informed the eager pilgrim of the hierophany that took place in a holy site. Today a videotape made by the temple authorities will tell all in exquisite detail. While it may not seem that viewing the videotape gives the spiritual merit that accompanies the actual experience of being in a holy place, it is certain that exploring the sacred geography of Hinduism has never been more popular.

Abortion and Reproductive Technologies

The books on dharma written around the beginning of the Common Era emphasized the importance of procreation. Male children were considered to be more important than female. By having sons a man fulfilled his religious debt to his ancestors. In later centuries, gifts to a daughter at the time of her marriage became a significant family burden. For all these reasons, male children were more welcome in many Hindu families.

These values, embedded in the Hindu tradition through many centuries, may explain the enthusiasm with which many Hindus today accept advances in reproductive technology. Abortion seems to have been accepted in India without any editorial debate, strong statements from religious leaders, or lingering questions raised by the legislative or judicial systems. The practice of abortion will probably continue to increase both for sex selection of male babies after amniocentesis and as a form of birth control.

Religious texts in the Hindu tradition condemn abortion and say that killing the embryo is ethically reprehensible. But abortions are conducted legally in India, and apparently are accepted and utilized by large numbers of Hindu couples. One reason is that many religious texts simply do not have (and have not ever had) the compelling authority that scripture may have in some other religious traditions. Statistics from some states show that in recent years there has been a dramatic decline in the number of live births of girls. This trend will probably continue into the future.

Hinduism in the Diaspora

Until the early twentieth century, Hindus believed that living in any place other than India was ritually polluting. Hindus who traveled abroad had to undergo purification rites when they reentered India. Almost five million Hindus now live in other countries and the situation has drastically changed.

New temples are being erected in all the major cities of North America. But despite the desire to remain faithful to the code and sequence of rituals, there are some compromises and innovations. The sacred-time orientation of the temple is made to coincide, as far as the ritual almanac will allow it, with the secular calendar of the country in which it is located. Hindu traditions retain and reinforce selective features of the scriptures and adapt to changing times and different local customs.

See also ASIA; BUDDHISM; CHRISTIANITY; INDIA; ISLAM; JUDAISM; RELIGION, SPIRITUALITY, MORALITY.

BIBLIOGRAPHY

BAKHLE. S. W. *Hinduism: Nature and Development.* New Delhi: Sterling Publishers, 1991.

COWARD, HAROLD G. *Modern Indian Responses to Religious Pluralism.* Albany, NY.: State University of New York Press, 1987.

EMBREE, AINSLIE T. *Hindu Tradition.* New York: Random House, 1971.

KLOSTERMAIER, KLAUS K. *A Survey of Hinduism.* Benares, India: Manoharlal, 1989.

MISHRA, R. P. *Hinduism: The Faith of the Future.* New Delhi: S.S. Publishers, 1981.

SONTHEIMER, GUNTER, and KULKE, HERMANN. *Hinduism Reconsidered.* New Delhi: Manoharlal, 1990.

WALKER, BENJAMIN. *Hindu World: An Encyclopedic Survey of Hinduism.* Philadelphia: Coronet Books, 1983.

Vasudha Narayanan

Holistic Beliefs

From 1970 on there have been many indications of a shift toward a more holistic view in health, ecology, education, management, the feminist movement, and so on. Among the factors promoting such a shift were dissatisfactions with conventional medicine, consequences of the fragmentation of knowledge, perceived failures of education based on such a fragmentary view, reaction of feminists to the nonholistic features of patriarchal society, environmental mishaps resulting from the failure to take a holistic view of ecological systems, and a rising appreciation of the holistic worldview of the world's indigenous peoples.

Such a shift in worldview has the most profound implications for prevailing values in a society. Values can be thought of as particular kinds of beliefs—namely, beliefs about the desirability of something. Viewed in that way, a person's values are part of the total belief structure, some parts of which are relatively superficial and easily changed, while other parts are partly or largely unconsciously held and relatively resistant to change. For example, some value changes are matters of fluctuating fashion or taste; others may be variations in the way a deeper-level value or belief is expressed (as, for instance, in the shift from emphasis on outer to inner indicators for validating one's feeling of self-esteem). The most powerful values are derived from the deepest, core beliefs—about individual identity, the nature of the universe, the role of the self in the total environment, and a sense of what is most important. For example, values in modern society with regard to nature, other living creatures, and the land are very different from those in Native American culture with a more holistic worldview.

Thus, although changes in value emphases are taking place in society all the time, and superficial value changes may be influenced by fashion, education, or advertising, major and persistent shifts tend to be associated with changes in the collectively held worldview.

As the findings of modern science made increasing impact on society, the power of the religious foundations of values decreased, with the result that by midcentury little value consensus remained. This general confusion about values was a consequence of the fact that modern society was attempting to operate from two different and contradictory worldviews—one scientific-economic, the other humanistic-spiritual. The tension brought about by this situation resulted in continued attempts to reconcile science and spirituality. These only began to appear successful in the 1990s, due to two important developments.

One of these developments was in comparative religion. Essentially, it was the discovery that diverse as the exoteric or public forms of the world's religious traditions may be, their esoteric, inner-circle forms—which typically are more experiential, involving some kind of meditative discipline—are quite compatible with one another. This common core of the world's spiritual traditions has been termed the "perennial wisdom."

The other development, reassessment of the suitability of positivistic, reductionistic science to provide a complete and adequate societal worldview, has been gaining strength since the 1960s. One form of the reassessment, which we shall examine below, challenges the fitness of the metaphysical foundations of modern science.

The Western industrial, "modern" paradigm amounted to a shift from the more holistic medieval paradigm to one more characterized by separateness. This is exemplified in politics by the emphasis on individual rights; in economics by emphasis on competition; in science by the ontological assumption that ultimate reality is "fundamental particles." By the early 1990s there were multifold indications of a shift away from the reductionistic, positivistic paradigm of mid-twentieth-century science, toward a more holistic paradigm, with more attention to subjective experience as allowable data, and with a more participatory methodology.

In reassessing the consequences of the ontological assumption of separateness, it appears in retrospect that practically all of present science remains in place if a different assumption is made—namely the assumption that *everything in human experience, mental as well as physical, is part of a unity, an intercommunicating oneness.* This implies that the positivistic epistemological assumption, that the only way we contact reality is through the physical senses, is replaced by an assumption that we contact reality in not one, but *two* ways. One is through the physical senses; the other is (since we are each ineluctably part of the oneness) through deep intuition. Reductionistic science is then seen as a special case, valid in its realm but not suited to be elevated to the position of a worldview by which we live our lives and guide society. For science to merit that position, it would have to be restructured on the basis of an ontological assumption of wholeness, and an epistemological assumption that subjective experience is potentially a valid source of knowledge of the whole.

Such an "extended" science is potentially compatible with the "perennial wisdom" of the world's contemplative traditions, and hence a complete reconciliation of C. P. Snow's "two cultures." It is also in accord with cultural shifts that are perhaps most obviously manifested in transpersonal psychology and the so-called "New Thought" churches.

Basic to the contemplative traditions is the proposition (or, rather, the experiential *knowing*) that human beings have a higher spiritual nature; that in that nature each is part of, and in touch with, the Whole; and that basic to that state of being is a natural compassion and love for other humans, and indeed for all of nature and all aspects of the Whole. Contemplative traditions generally concur that in our usual state we are estranged from our higher nature by our attachments, in particular to our own belief structures—we are estranged by our beliefs in separateness.

If we are correct in our premise that the future prevailing worldview will be something like this reconciliation of an "extended" science with the understandings of the contemplative traditions, then the prevailing value emphases can be anticipated to be those which follow from that worldview. It is not accidental that those values are essentially those of the contemporary eco-feminist movement.

These arguments would forecast very strong emphasis on the value of human growth and development, to the point that this represents the lodestar of society's "central project." The economy and technological advance will be seen, properly, as *means*, rather than mistakenly perceived as ends in themselves (the present position). Cultural diversity will be valued, not only because it makes for a more resilient global society, but because it adds to the richness of the experience of all.

The essence of their worldview was once described by one Native American as (a) *everything* in the universe is *alive;* and (b) we are *all relatives!* The future worldview we are describing will have something of this flavor, and will cherish all creatures and everything in nature. Thus preserving biodiversity will be a strong value, and not because plants with as yet undiscovered properties will be valuable to the pharmaceutical industry.

Creative altruism—altruism guided by an intuitive sense of what will be in the real interest of the other—will be a widespread human trait. Because it is recognized as a natural trait, society will be dedicated to removal of the obstacles that inhibit its expression. This will be characteristic of education and indeed of all social institutions.

Society will value freedom—the freedom to discover and be oneself. This involves valuing the inner life, being in touch with the deep Center. But it also values finding one's purposeful work in the work—work which not only contributes to the whole, but also, through accomplishments and failures, provides feedback from the universe to help bring one back to being "on purpose." Society will value balance—between contemplation and action, masculine and feminine.

Most of these value emphases are not new. They will be in a new context, however—not authoritarian or inflexible religious tradition, but vibrant, living, transcendent spirituality.

Because people will be in varying states of clarity and self-understanding, even if the above value emphases predominate there will be need for political institutions such as the rule of law, disciplinary strictures, and a balance of powers. People will not be morally perfect, but the society-wide commitment to, and realization of, the highest values may well in the long run be greater than at any previous time in human history.

See also GLOBAL TURNING POINTS; GREEN REVOLUTION; LIFESTYLES, ALTERNATIVE; MIND: NEW MODES OF THINKING; NATIVE AMERICANS; SUSTAINABILITY.

BIBLIOGRAPHY

BERMAN, MORRIS. *The Reenchantment of the World.* Ithaca, NY: Cornell University Press, 1981.
BERRY, THOMAS. *The Dream of the Earth.* San Francisco: Sierra Club Books, 1988.
BOHM, DAVID, and PEAT, F. DAVID. *Science, Order, and Creativity.* New York: Bantam Books, 1987.
GRIFFIN, DAVID, ed. *The Reenchantment of Science.* Albany, NY: State University of New York Press, 1988.

HARMAN, WILLIS W. *Creative Work.* Indianapolis: Knowledge Systems, 1991.

HAYWARD, JEREMY W. *Shifting Worlds, Changing Minds: Where the Sciences and Buddhism Meet.* Boston: New Science Library, 1987.

HENDERSON, HAZEL. *Paradigms in Progress: Life Beyond Economics.* Indianapolis: Knowledge Systems, 1992.

SMITH, HUSTON. *Forgotten Truth: The Primordial Tradition.* New York: Harper and Row, 1977.

Willis W. Harman

Home Ownership

Home ownership seems likely to continue to be the preferred form of housing for most Americans. The proportion of Americans owning their homes will rise slowly throughout the next half century as incomes increase and families and individuals seek privacy, security, and an investment for the future.

Determinants of Home Ownership

As in the past, demand for home ownership will depend on demographics, economics and tax policy. The demographic trends important to home ownership are population growth and household formations and to a lesser extent the social acceptance of different living arrangements. The economic trends affecting home ownership are incomes, housing costs, including taxes. Deviations from the trend will occur as interest rates rise and fall, as the general economy grows or diminishes, and as different regions fare better or worse than others.

The primary determinant of how many households there will be is the rate at which the adult population forms and maintains separate households. The level of household formations is driven by the age distribution of the population and by social trends in living arrangements and family formations. Most new household formations occur when people are between twenty and thirty-four years old. Home ownership occurs later, when the household head is in his or her late twenties or thirties. Social and individual acceptance of living arrangements further influence the amount of home ownership by permissive (or nonpermissive) attitudes toward singles living alone, unmarried couples living together, and single parents staying single.

The single largest determinant of whether households will be owners or renters is household income. For instance, the rate of ownership is 25 percent greater for households with incomes around $50,000 than it is for households with incomes around $25,000.

Similarly, housing prices determine the amount of home ownership, although there is a dual effect that sometimes obscures the relationship. Higher house prices mean that households must devote a greater share of their income to a home purchase and that fewer households are willing to purchase. In addition, because most households borrow to purchase a home, the credit criteria of mortgage lenders limit the proportion of income that can be devoted to mortgage obligations.

Home ownership offers three benefits not available to renters. First, an owned home allows the household to provide the members with exactly the type, condition, and appearance of shelter that they want. Their home can be adapted (within the local zoning and use restrictions) to suit their needs without permission from an outside owner. Their length of stay and most of their costs are determined by their use rather than by a landlord or property owner. Second, an owned home is also a source of wealth, allowing families and individuals to put money into an asset that presumably will grow in value and yield a return that has historically risen at a rate greater than the general rate of inflation. The third benefit is subsidization in the form of tax relief.

Because an owned home serves as an asset as well as providing shelter, higher home prices have a dual effect on the number of households that choose home ownership. Higher prices deter some from owning because they require of buyers a greater down payment and more of their income than they are willing or financially qualified to spend. But rising prices are often seen as precursors of future rising prices. In addition, capital gains can offset the increased monthly costs.

Production Levels

Housing production for home ownership will increase as the population and numbers of households increases. However, slow growth and a decline during the early twenty-first century in the population group of ages twenty-five to thirty-nine will slow production, which could mean some declines in the annual output of new homes.

The production level of homes intended for ownership exceeded 1.5 million homes per year in the late 1970s, averaged 1.1 million homes in the 1980s, and dropped to 1.0 million homes per year in the early 1990s. The late 1990s will see an average annual production of 1.2 million homes intended for ownership. The early 2000s will see declines, as the people born in the low-birthrate years of the late 1960s and '70s reach home-buying age.

Although the number of new homes produced each year could dip in the first two decades of the twenty-first century, the value of the construction should continue to increase as homes become larger and more amenities are installed. New homes are more likely to be purchased by households that already have a home or are selling it and therefore have sufficient equity to purchase a larger, more elaborate home. The median sales price of new homes has increased 2 percentage points above inflation rates since 1970. The increase in prices is expected to continue as present home owners use their earned equity in their present home to trade up to a larger home with more amenities.

Type of Home

Eighty-six percent of the owned homes in 1991 were single-family homes, either freestanding, detached, or attached in a row as townhouses. Another 8 percent were manufactured housing, produced in a factory and shipped to the location. Most of these were in rural areas, and half were in the South. The remaining 6 percent were in buildings with more than one housing unit (multifamily housing). Ninety-two percent of the multifamily, owner-occupied homes were in urban areas.

The median size of all owner-occupied homes was 1,775 square feet, the median number of rooms was 6.1, the median number of bedrooms was 2.9, and the median number of bathrooms was one. Half of the owner-occupied homes were built in the previous twenty-five years.

Over 90 percent of the single-family homes built in the early 1990s were single-family detached. Owned multifamily homes account for about one in every five new multifamily units and about 5 percent of the homes built for an owner-occupant.

New single-family detached homes are larger than the existing stock of single-family homes. The median size (in square feet) of a new home increased slightly more than 1 percent per year in the 1970s and about 2 percent per year in the 1980s. By the early 1990s, the median square footage of new single family homes was just over 1,900 square feet. The space increases occurred in the family areas of the home: the family room, den, kitchen, entry foyer, and halls. Bedroom and bathroom sizes have not increased significantly.

The size of new single family homes will continue to increase in the range of 1 to 2 percent per year. Average size will increase because fewer new homes will be sold to first-time buyers, thereby leaving more of the market to trade-up buyers who prefer larger homes. Amplifying the trend, the trade-up buyers will want even larger, more elaborate homes than previous trade-up buyers because they will have more housing equity to roll over into a new home.

Space allocations in the new homes built in the late 1990s and early twenty-first century will increase in the informal areas of the home such as family rooms and will decline in the formal areas such as dining rooms and formal living rooms. Bedroom space will expand, especially for the master bedroom. Special-use rooms will also be more prevalent, like exercise rooms, home office space, and hobby or workshop areas.

Single-family detached homes will remain the preferred style of home for most home owners. However, the size of the lot upon which the home is built will not increase as much as the home. Lot sizes for single-family homes increased 1 percent per year in the 1980s, but that trend will be more difficult to maintain as concerns about growth, environmental impact, traffic congestion, and the need for more local services increases. Lower residential density requires more roads, greater amounts of infrastructure, and public utility investment. Even if new home buyers are willing to bear their private costs for the lower densities, local governmental bodies will apply restrictions that address the social costs of development.

See also ELDERLY, LIVING ARRANGEMENTS; HOUSEHOLD COMPOSITION; HOUSING, AFFORDABLE; HOUSING, COST AND AVAILABILITY OF; HOUSING, DEMOGRAPHIC AND LIFESTYLE IMPACTS ON.

BIBLIOGRAPHY

APGAR, WILLIAM. C., JR., et al. *The Housing Outlook 1980–1990.* Westport, CT: Greenwood/Praeger, 1985.

DRAKAKIS-SMITH, DAVID. *Urbanization, Housing, and the Development Process.* New York: St. Martin's Press, 1980.

GALSTER, GEORGE C. *Homeowners and Neighborhood Reinvestment.* Durham, NC: Duke University Press, 1986.

RANSOM, P. *Healthy Housing: A Practical Guide.* New York: Van Nostrand Reinhold, 1991.

TURNER, JOHN F. Housing by People: *Towards Autonomy in Building Environments.* 2nd ed. New York: Marion Boyars, 1990.

David Crowe

Homosexuality.

See SEXUAL BEHAVIOR; SEXUAL LAWS.

Hospitality Industry: Lodgings and Accommodations

The astonishing events at the close of the twentieth century, including the fall of the Berlin Wall and the lifting of the Iron Curtain, signalled the end of the Cold War and the beginnings of freedom of movement for hundreds of millions of people. In fact, one of the first rights demanded by Eastern Europeans as they regained control of their governments was the right to travel.

Paralleling these events has been a rapid globalization of economic enterprise, lowering of trade barriers, transition to free-market economies, and in general a global trend toward democratization leading to higher standards of living. The continual expansion of world trade is generating growth in international business travel.

The confluence of these trends, coupled with the emergence of global communication technology, has made Marshall McLuhan's notion of the "Global Village" a reality. There is now a general awareness of people of other nations, their cultures, landscapes, and cityscapes, creating a strong desire among more and more people to want to experience these destinations firsthand.

Economic Significance of Tourism

Travel and tourism became the world's largest industry in the 1990s and the largest generator of jobs. The World Travel and Tourism Council (WTTC) estimates that the travel and tourism industry worldwide will generate a gross output of U.S. $3.4 trillion in 1995 when expenditures for both business and consumer travel, plus capital investment and government expenditures for tourism are included. By 2005, the figure is projected to double to U.S. $7.2 trillion (hereafter all dollar amounts are in U.S. dollars).

If all the people whose jobs are generated by the world travel and tourism industry lived in one country, that country would rank fourth in population (after the United States) with 212 million people. The gross domestic product (GDP) of that country would be $3.4 trillion, second only to the United States. And that country, according to WTTC statistics, would account for 10.9 percent of the world's GDP and 11.4 percent of the world's capital investment (see Table 1).

TABLE 1.   Travel and Tourism, World Estimates*

	1995	2005
Jobs	212 million	338 million
Output	$3.4 trillion	$7.2 trillion
GDP	10.9%	11.4%
Investment	11.4%	11.8%
Taxes	$655 billion	$1.4 trillion
Real Growth	5.5% p.a.	na.a

*Source: World Travel & Tourism Council.

While Western Europe and North America are currently the dominant markets for the industry, major gains will be made over the next ten years in Latin America, Central and Eastern Europe, and the Asia Pacific Region. China is expected to be both a major generator of tourists, as well as a major destination market early in the twenty-first century.

Tourism's Contribution to Emerging Economies

Tourism offers excellent potential for sustained economic development of emerging economies. In 1991, tourism earned developing countries $312 billion in foreign currency, second only to oil revenues. Table 2 demonstrates the impressive growth of tourism over a ten-year period to selected countries.

Tourism in the Caribbean for example, is the major industry of each of the thirty states in the region, contributing an estimated 25 percent of the regional economy. Tourism has been the only industry in the Caribbean has demonstrated steady growth over the past twenty years. The travel and tourism industry has provided the thirty diverse

TABLE 2.   Growth of Tourism to Selected Destinations*

	Tourist arrivals (thousands)		Tourism receipts (US $ millions)	
	1981	1990	1981	1990
Belize	93	222	8	91
Costa Rica	333	435	94	275
Ecuador	245	332	131	193
Dominica	16	45	2	25
Kenya	373	801	175	443
Botswana	227	844	22	65
Madagascar	12	53	5	43
Maldives	60	195	15	85

*Source: World Tourism Organization.

states of the region—states with different languages (French, English, Dutch, Spanish) and cultures a reason to come together to collaborate in the common purpose of marketing tourism on a regional basis. More recently they have been collaborating in meeting other challenges faced by this industry, such as environmental protection.

Protecting Environment and Heritage

Beyond its potential as an engine for economic development, the travel and tourism industry can make a major contribution to protecting both environment and heritage. Approximately 650 million people visit the national parks and protected areas in Kenya each year, spending some $350 million. A World Bank study has estimated that an average elephant herd generates $610,050 per year in income, or an individual elephant approximately $900,000 over the course of its sixty-year life span.

Tourism provides both the audience and economic engine for museums, the performing and visual arts, and the preservation of heritage. Singapore, for example, has recently set aside $1 billion to preserve the city's architectural heritage and culture.

Indigenous people, as well, are increasingly responding to the opportunities provided by tourism to preserve unique aspects of their heritage in the form of dance, music, and artifacts.

Global Leadership—The Green Globe Program

"Nature tourism," or ecotourism, is the most rapidly growing segment of the travel and tourism industry. Much of the potential for ecotourism is in the rich, biodiverse areas of developing countries. Revenues generated from ecotourism have provided an economic rationale for setting aside vast tracts of land as parks and wilderness areas in countries around the world. Visitors to these areas experience the beauty and majesty of the world's finest natural features and come away with a heightened appreciation of environmental values.

Leaders within the travel and tourism industry have recognized that the environment is its basic product. It is one of the first industries to respond to the challenge of the UN Conference on Environment and Development (UNCED), held in Rio de Janeiro in 1992 by introducing a "Green Globe" program. Green Globe has been developed by the World Travel and Tourism Council as a worldwide environmental management and awareness program. The program is designed to encourage all companies in the Travel and Tourism Industry to commit to environmentally compatible development and sound environmental-management techniques based on environmental guidelines and international best practices.

Tourism—The World's Peace Industry

With the end of the Cold War came an end to a world divided by two opposing ideological camps. A wave of democratization and economic liberalism soon followed. Ironically, the end of the Cold War also heightened the incidence of ethnic violence in certain regions of the world. The United Nations declared 1995 as the International Year of Tolerance in recognition of the need for promoting greater tolerance within the global family.

The challenge facing the travel and tourism industry is to take a leadership role in promoting greater tolerance, to help bring about greater understanding and respect among members of the global family in a spirit of joy and appreciation of the diversity which illuminates and strengthens us as a global family. Through travel, people are finding friends in every corner of the Earth, establishing common bonds with other members of the global family, and spreading messages of hope for a peaceful world. Through travel, people are discovering one another and the beauty of nature. In the process they are discovering themselves.

By creatively nurturing and facilitating this act of discovery, the tourism industry has the potential to become the world's peace industry, an industry that recognizes, promotes, and supports the belief that every traveler is potentially an ambassador for peace within the global family and with nature.

See also AIR TRANSPORT; FREE TIME; GLOBAL CULTURE; INTERACTIVE ENTERTAINMENT; LEISURE TIME; MASS CULTURE; OUTDOOR RECREATION AND LEISURE PURSUITS; SPACE TRAVEL; TOURISM; WORKFORCE DISTRIBUTION.

BIBLIOGRAPHY

POON, AULIANA. *Tourism, Technology and Competitive Strategies.* Wallingford, Oxon, U.K.: C.A.B. International, 1993.

RITCHIE, J. R. BRENT, and HAWKINS, DONALD E., eds. *World Travel and Tourism Review: Indicators, Trends, and Issues.* Vol. 3. Wallingford, Oxon, U.K.: C.A.B. International, 1993.

ROBINSON, JAMES D., III. *Travel and Tourism: The World's Largest Industry.* Brussels: The World Travel and Tourism Council, 1992.

WATERS, SOMERSET R. *Travel Industry World Yearbook: The Big Picture, 1993–94.* Rye, NY: Child and Wages, 1993.

Louis J. D'Amore

Household Appliances

Technology and the miniaturization and falling prices of microprocessors will transform everyday objects and appliances into high-tech appliances. For example, "smart" electrochromic windows that automatically vary their transparency at specified optical wavelengths will save energy by reflecting sunlight in hot weather and letting the sun shine in during cold weather.

Japan's NTT Company has already introduced a tankless, microprocessor-controlled toilet that flushes by pushbutton and has a heated seat. A warm water spray function followed by an air dry cycle is supposed to make toilet tissue unnecessary. The toilet has a built-in urine analyzer that measures levels of sugar, protein, red and white blood cells, and ketones. The user can stick a finger into a specially defined armrest to measure blood pressure, pulse, and body temperature. This diagnostic information can be displayed to the toilet user on a small screen informational display or relayed by modem to a doctor.

In addition to technology, home appliance design in the future will be shaped largely by three other factors: shrinking living space, easier-to-use controls, and growing environmental regulation.

Shrinking Living Space

Much of the impetus for smaller-scale living space comes from Japan, where living quarters already are very small by North American standards. While it may be a while before America living space shrinks to Japanese dimensions, this trend will have major effects on both the functionality and styling of tomorrow's appliances.

FUNCTIONAL INTEGRATION

The design of future appliances will be altered to save space (particularly floor space) and there will be a trend toward combining related appliances into multifunction units:

- Consumer electronics: Audio and video equipment will be increasingly combined into all-in-one entertainment modules, reversing the component trend of the middle-to-late twentieth century.
- Television: The exception to this trend will be television sets. These will remain separate as they grow to become ubiquitous. High-resolution, flat screens will transform the television from a box to a wall hanging with integral high-fidelity speakers. Every room in the house will

have a screen, which will function as a video intercom system, house controller, and access point for on-line services. When not being used for communications or control, televisions will function as an art gallery or "virtual interior design." Homeowners will be able to select paintings or even complete audio/video environments with a touch of a button, from a library of images stored on interactive CD-ROM.

- Telecommunications: The telephone, computer/house controller, and fax machine will merge into an electronic voice and data transfer system. For example, when a fax is sent to the home, it will automatically print out on the laser printer. The home controller will respond to voice commands phoned in from a remote location.
- Laundry: Clothes washers and dryers will be combined into a single unit that washes and dries clothes all in one operation. A combination of much higher washer spin speeds and microwave clothes drying (which operates at lower temperatures than hot-air drying) will conserve energy, extend clothing life, and reduce dryer exhaust problems.
- Cooking: Combination microwave/conventional ovens will both optimize use of kitchen space and provide larger oven cavities for microwaving food.
- Water heating: Small point of use instantaneous water heaters mounted beneath sinks will replace large forty- to fifty-gallon storage tank water heaters. These small local water heaters will be combined with electronically controlled faucets that provide one-touch temperature control and adjust automatically to maintain a steady water temperature. Clothes washers will have integral "booster" water heaters as dishwashers do today.

APPLIANCE STYLING

Shrinking living space will mean that reducing visual "clutter" due to appliances and other consumer products will be more than just an aesthetic concept. It will become more psychologically important as dozens of differently styled products, in the same small space, compete for visual attention and jar the senses.

The need to reduce visual clutter and save floor space will lead appliance styling in two contradictory directions:

1. Blending: The inconspicuous blend-in look is the wave of the future. Those home appliances with which consumers have a merely functional relationship (laundry, area heating, ventilating,

air conditioning, water heating) will be chameleonlike products that blend with any decor (their surroundings).

2. Furniture: Those appliances with which consumers have a more personal relationship (cooking, audio/video, telecom) will be designed more as art objects that express an individual vision and substitute as furniture.

COOKING TECHNOLOGY

Microwaving will become the dominant food preparation mode due to its speed, convenience, and improvements in cooking ability. Increasingly, foods will go from freezer to ready-to-eat in a single operation, nearly untouched by human hands.

Various "niche" cooking technologies will gain in popularity. Induction cooking using magnetic energy to heat food in ferrous pans, without creating a touch or fire hazard, for example. Induction units built into dining tables will gently heat ferrous inserts in dinnerware to keep food warm.

Easier-to-Use Controls

Controls on every type of appliance will become simpler, more "intelligent and adaptive," and easier for homeowners to use. Just as high-end audio appliances are using fewer controls today, so in the future will all appliances.

Ideally, appliance controls will become so intuitive that user manuals would be unnecessary. But the drive toward higher levels of features inevitably adds complexity.

Greater use of graphic displays on appliances will help solve this problem. Touch screens will simplify the user interface by storing control and on-screen "help" features in software. The ubiquitous wall-screen television will become the control interface for major house systems. A screen showing the layout of your house will let homeowners control the HVAC system with an easy-to-use universal remote control.

Intelligent adaptive controls will "learn" homeowner patterns [routines] of behavior so that the home and its appliances function in various "default" modes that the user can interrupt and change as desired.

Improvements in speech recognition will replace remote controls with speech commands, at least for controlling basic functions.

Growing Environmental Regulation

While there is little evidence that North American consumers will pay extra for "green" appliances,

government regulation is driving appliances in the direction of increasing environmental friendliness. Three major trends for the future:

1. Ozone-safe cooling appliances: Increasing government regulation will eliminate the use of refrigerant chemicals with ozone-depleting potential or global-warming potential. Future household cooling appliances will use hydrocarbon chemicals such as cyclopentane and isobutane. Because these replacement chemicals are less energy-efficient than the CFCs and HFCs they replace, refrigerators will be built with improved insulation such as vacuum panels to replace the polyurethane insulation used today. Many of these changes will be invisible to consumers.

2. Design for recycling: Future appliances will be constructed of fewer materials and constructed so that they can be disassembled more easily, to facilitate recycling. Home appliances will be manufactured to a greater extent from recycled materials.

3. Water conservation: Laundry appliances and plumbing fixtures will use less water and energy. Government regulation will eliminate garbage disposers and trash compactors as methods of disposing of kitchen waste. Some observers see waterless toilets that use microwave energy to reduce human wastes to powder, and microwave home incinerators for kitchen waste.

See also CLOTHING; ENVIRONMENT; HOUSEHOLD COMPOSITION; INTERACTIVE ENTERTAINMENT; TELECOMMUNICATIONS.

BIBLIOGRAPHY

BABYAK, RICHARD J. "Designing the Future." *Appliance Manufacturer* 41/7 (July 1993): 31–39.

"Domotechnica: The World's Fair of Appliances." *Appliance Manufacturer* 41/4 (April 1993): 28–40.

KESSELRING, JOHN. "Microwave Clothes Dryers." *EPRI Journal* 24/6 (June 1992): 15–17.

NORMAN, DONALD A. *The Psychology of Everyday Things.* New York, NY: Basic Books, 1988.

STAUFFER, H. BROOKE. *Smart House Wiring.* Albany, NY: Delmar Publishers, 1993.

H. Brooke Stauffer

Household Composition

The gigantic demographic tsunami called the Baby Boom can be easily tracked from its origin between 1946 and 1964. We can watch it rush past us into the future all the way to 2047 when the first of these "baby boomers" become centenarians. The effect of the Baby Boom upon household composition is already visible to us.

The U.S. Bureau of the Census defines a household as "all the persons who occupy a housing unit. These persons may be related, unrelated, or living alone." The Census Bureau then goes on to define "a family household" as one consisting of "the householder, and at least one additional person related to the householder through marriage, birth, or adoption" (U.S. Bureau of the Census Report. *Households, Families, and Children: A 30-Year Perspective*, P23–181, pp. 14, 15. Washington, DC, November 1992).

A "housing unit" may consist of a single-family home, duplex, multifamily dwelling, or mobile home (home to 6.75 percent of all Americans). Not to be discussed here are what the Census Bureau calls "group quarters," where all those individuals not living in households, live in schools, hospitals, mental hospitals, treatment centers, nursing homes, orphanages, as well as in correctional facilities (prisons, jails, military stockades), college dormitories, military barracks, and various kinds of shelters.

Diversity—it becomes glaringly evident—is the word which best describes the dramatic changes that have taken place in where we live, and especially within households during the first fifty years of the Baby Boom. Let us look first at changes in one type of household, the family household.

Changes in the Family Household

During the 1930s, 1940s, and 1950s the predominant model of the idealized family consisted of two parents and two or more children. The father was the breadwinner and the mother the homemaker. This is still held by many as an ideal. But as early as 1980 one survey showed that this type of family household represented only 7 percent of the U.S. population.

By 1991 one in eight households was headed by a single parent, with 25 percent of all children living with only one parent. Children who were living with grandparents had increased from 3 percent in 1970 to 5 percent in 1991. Among African-Americans, 12 percent of children live with grandparents; 6 percent of Hispanic children live with their grandparents.

More than half of those ages eighteen–twenty-five in 1991 lived with their parents in 1991. The median age for getting married and starting a new household was twenty-four for women and twenty-six for men. With the increase in the divorce rate, the expectation of remaining married was about 50 percent.

Waning disapproval of divorce and increasing ease of remarriage have been partially responsible for a cycle of marry-divorce-remarry-divorce-remarry, which has been reflected in household composition. Children often have multiple parents and siblings, stepmothers, stepfathers, stepsisters, and stepbrothers. One divorced couple, to provide the continuity and emotional stability and security of a family household for their twelve-year-old son, set up a separate apartment for him, with the mother spending one week with him, the father the next. Clearly, diversity and often ingenuity characterize family household composition in the 1990s.

There are also often important surrogate members of households. Sometimes these are live-in companions or nursing aides for the elderly. Sometimes these are close friends who are perceived as "belonging" to the family group.

The television set has introduced important new relationships to households, marked by new electronic surrogate-family members (98.2 percent of all households have an average of 2.1 TV sets according to Arbitron). The most immediate and important emotional attachments, especially among the elderly living alone (the center of their sense of companionship and the focus of their day-to-day concern), is sometimes with the lives and roles portrayed by actors in the dramas of daytime "soaps" and everyday primetime "reruns." The emotional depths of immediacy and caring evoked by these relationships with figures in television dramas often surpasses those with members of one's own often distant family.

In 1990 54.8 million households also shared their living space with a companion animal ("pet"), according to the American Veterinary Medical Association. For many years dogs, cats, and numerous other animals have served as emotionally important participating members of families and households. The value of animals has been proven in assisting the blind, and there is growing appreciation of the benefit of pets for the elderly. An aging population coupled with increased longevity means that housing needs to accommodate age-related limitations will have to be met. Special household arrangements will include nursing homes, retirement settlements, and hospices. Similarly, needs will be posed by disabled and handicapped individuals who want to live independently.

Changes in Nonfamily Households

Nonfamily households are made up of (1) single men or women living alone (widowed, divorced, never-married), or (2) unrelated persons living together in groups. With the growing acceptance of divorce, childlessness, and singleness, single occupancy households have risen from one in eight of all households in 1960 to one out of every four in 1992. In 1991, one quarter of these occupants of nonfamily households are under the age of thirty-five, one quarter between thirty-five and fifty-five, and half older than fifty-five. These singles constitute nine-tenths of all nonfamily households. Women living alone (13.9 million) are the largest group after married couples with or without children (52.3 million). Nine million men live alone.

In 1992 there were 4.3 million households made up of "unrelated persons living together." These include boarders and apartment sharers in high-rent areas, older unmarried couples sharing social security benefits, people of the opposite sex sharing living quarters, gay and lesbian couples, college students not living in dormitories or with their parents, and unrelated refugees and ethnic groups sharing housing. Unmarried couple households will continue to raise many legal issues related to inheritance and other rights of such "partners."

New Utilization Patterns of Households

How many hours or days are "homes" used during a given period—day, week, month, year? With parent(s) working during the day and children in nursery school, day care, school, or with baby sitters, many living units are completely unoccupied more and more during certain time periods.

But there is also a movement to reclaim this "empty" time for homes and use it in new ways. The networks of telecommunications embedded in cellular phones, pagers, faxes, notebook and laptop computers, are transforming many cars and homes into minioffices. Many of workers are being encouraged by their companies to substitute their own living space for some or all of their working time, and in response they are creating "work centers" within their homes. These trends, combined with the increase of home businesses, are changing the function of households at a time when their composition has already been changing rapidly.

See also DEMOGRAPHY; DIVORCE; FAMILIES AND HOUSEHOLDS; FAMILY PATTERNS; FAMILY VALUES; HOUSING, DEMOGRAPHIC AND LIFESTYLE IMPACTS ON; MARRIAGE; PETS; SOCIAL CHANGE: UNITED STATES.

BIBLIOGRAPHY

AHLBURG, DENNIS A., and CAROL J. DEVITA. *New Realities of the American Family. Population Bulletin* 47/2 (1992).
DYCHTWALD, KEN, and PLOWER, JOE. *Age Wave.* Los Angeles: Jeremy P. Tarcher, 1989.
HUGHES, JAMES W., and ZIMMERMAN, TODD. "The Dream Is Alive." *American Demographics* (August 1993): 32–37.
RUSSELL, CHERYL. *The Master Trend.* New York: Plenum Press, 1993.
TOFFLER, ALVIN. *The Third Wave.* New York: William Morrow, 1980.
_____. *War and Antiwar.* New York: Little, Brown, 1993, chapters 10–11.
U.S. BUREAU OF THE CENSUS, and LUGALLA, TERRY. *Households, Families, and Children: A 30-Year Perspective.* Washington, DC: Current Population Reports P23–181, 1992.
_____, and SALUTER, ARLENE P. *Marital Status and Living Arrangements.* Washington, DC: Current Population Reports P20-468, 1992.

Robert E. Maston

Housing, Affordable

One of the fundamental needs of modern life among people of all classes is for a place to live that is affordable. Though what may be affordable to a bricklayer in Glasgow is something quite different than what is affordable to an investment banker in New York City or a civil service official in Lagos, Nigeria, the common denominator of affordable housing functions as a cornerstone for how well or poorly people live together.

Regardless of contemporary densities, all nations will be challenged in the twenty-first century to construct sustainable living conditions that enable the majority of their citizens to live decently and affordably by their own country's standards. This will be achieved not through technological advances in materials or methods. And it will not be materially achieved through alterations in the structure of housing finance.

Rather, achievements in constructing sustainable living conditions in the United States, Russia, or elsewhere, will be made for three principal reasons: (1) Alterations in land-use development patterns must effectively curb low-density development. (2) Land-use patterns must begin to reflect a reliance on mass transit-oriented development rather than freeway-oriented (auto) development. (3) Each country facing housing affordability crises in the first decades of the twenty-first century will need to accept and cope with the interrelationship between air quality, housing affordability, and surface transportation.

As the twentieth century draws to a close, the concept of housing is defined quite differently around the world. In Port-au-Prince, basic shelter remains a distant goal for large numbers of Haitians living in a country atrophied by despotism and civil unrest. In Tokyo, an 800-square-foot apartment can rent for 10,000 times as much as the annual per capita income for a Palestinian in Gaza. And in San Francisco, a well-educated teacher with advanced degrees earning only 30 percent of the area median income will find the goal of home ownership utterly unattainable without significant public subsidy.

For better or worse, public subsidy, in one form or another, has thus become the essential ingredient in making housing widely affordable, whether in the United States, Australia, or Mexico. Since sustainable urban living is related to air quality, housing affordability, and surface transportation, the major issue facing governments will be what form their housing subsidies take, and to whom those subsidies flow.

If housing affordability for the vast majority of people is thus a reality that is going to be made possible only with public participation, it raises the issue of the relationship between the individual and society.

Countries that achieve a sustainable balance between the rights and privileges of individual citizens and the country as a whole will reap the rewards of a preserved civic realm. Continued public participation whose effect is to increase affordability without sacrificing the quality of the civic realm is the seed corn for sustainable high-density living.

But because high-density living inevitably suggests mixed-class living, there will be considerable resistance to public efforts either to mandate outright or passively to permit such arrangements. It will always be more politically remunerative in the short run for jurisdictions to gobble up land and to separate citizens according to wealth. But the intersection of global economic interdependency and land scarcity at precisely this moment in history suggests that such actions will prove costly in the long run.

The cauldron of low-wage workers from all countries being necessarily mixed together in the modern era means that for the foreseeable future, industrial countries will see an ever widening gap between what housing costs and what low-skilled workers can afford. When juxtaposed alongside of low-density development patterns fostered by public land-use and tax policies, the distance between the haves and the have-nots will be nowhere more evident than in housing disparity.

It will be inevitable that this disparity, in Canada, Australia, or Israel, will be momentarily closed by concomitant subsidies for highways that enable low-wage workers to live in one place and work in another. But the resulting reductions in air quality are not long supportable, especially since such arrangements only serve to perpetuate harmful land-development tendencies.

In the end, failure to reckon with the absolute necessity for people of differing classes to live in closer proximity to one another will only prove calamitous. In such instances there will be increased tendencies to look to technology and housing finance for remedies. But only in altered outlooks on the relationship of individual and society, the pluses and minuses of dense urban living, the preservation of agricultural space and ecosystems made possible by the elimination of low-density sprawl, and an enhanced belief in the importance of the civic realm, will housing affordability be achieved in any meaningful way.

See also ENTITLEMENT PROGRAMS; HOME OWNERSHIP; HOUSING, COST AND AVAILABILITY OF; HOUSING, DEMOGRAPHIC AND LIFESTYLE IMPACTS ON; LAND USE PLANNING.

BIBLIOGRAPHY

JENCKS, CHRISTOPHER. *The Homeless*. Cambridge, MA: Harvard University Press, 1994.
NATHAN, RICHARD P. *The New Agenda for Cities*. Washington, DC: National League of Cities, 1992.

Charles Buki

Housing, Cost and Availability of

The market is positive for owner-occupied housing over the next ten years or so. The pace of housing construction activity and housing price appreciation will probably fall short of that experienced during the 1970s, but ought to exceed the rate that occurred through most of the 1980s. The reasons underlying these opinions and a brief review of the performance of the housing market during the past three decades follow.

Housing, Cost and Availability of

Review of Recent Housing Market Activity

Volatility in the U.S. housing market has been particularly apparent during the past thirty years or so. The numerous causes include: severe ebbs and flows of funds into financial institutions that specialize in housing finance (as in the mid-1960s to late 1970s); the demand surge caused by the "baby boom" generation coming of age during the late 1970s to late '80s; a high and unstable interest rate environment (in the 1970s and '80s); and substantial income growth and decline among many local housing markets—e.g., the Texas oil boom and bust. Few local housing markets have been immune from the unexpected surges and declines in the price of housing associated with these volatile factors.

Time series of owner-occupied housing costs are compared with an index of the purchase price of a constant-quality new house in Figure 1. The cost of owner-occupied housing represents the sum of the mortgage payment, the interest that could be earned on the household's housing equity, property taxes, and miscellaneous expenses, less income tax benefits and capital gains. Both series are smoothed using a four-quarter moving average and are expressed in real terms (1964 dollars). The two series demonstrate the volatility in housing prices during the past twenty-five years. Note especially the surge in housing prices in the late 1970s, which was largely fueled by the entry of the baby boom population into the market for owner-occupied housing. Prices in real terms were lower at the end of the 1980s than at the beginning. A

high and volatile interest rate environment combined with a reduction in capital gains expectations triggered this decline.

Volatility in the housing market is especially noticeable in the construction statistics presented in Figure 2. The two series are smoothed using a four-quarter moving average of the housing start data. The construction of housing experienced wide swings in the 1960s as a result of fluctuations in the supply of funds available to financial institutions. A record number of houses were built in two major housing booms during the beginning and end of the 1970s. The 1980s began with a sudden reversal of this trend. Interest rates rose dramatically, the national economy experienced a recession, and some regions of the country such as Texas suffered a severe depression. Although the late 1980s witnessed improvements in the economy and housing, the final scorecard showed a decline in home ownership, a rise in the cost of owner-occupied housing, and a slowdown in household expectations and realizations of capital gains.

The rental housing market also experienced its ups and downs. Multifamily housing construction (housing structures with five or more housing units) boomed in the early 1970s, due in part to large government rental-housing programs. Tax legislation enacted in the early 1980s and excessive investment in all forms of commercial real estate associated with the savings and loan (S&L) debacle were major causes behind the increase in the construction of multifamily housing in the early and mid-1980s. The Tax Reform Act of 1986

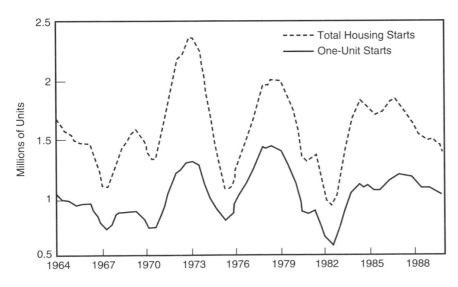

FIGURE 1.   Housing starts, 1964–1989.

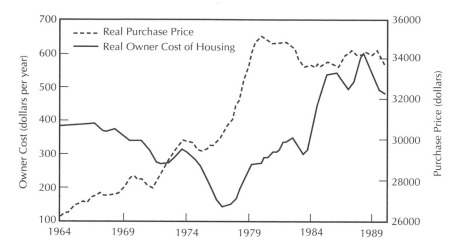

FIGURE 2.   Home owner cost versus purchase price (in 1964 dollars).

and resolution of the savings-and-loan crisis brought this rental housing boom to a sharp and sudden conclusion.

Forecasts of Future Housing Market Directions

The primary basis for optimism regarding owner-occupied housing is posited on the population of potential home buyers that will continue to grow during the 1990s. Total population growth will probably be around 7 to 8 percent during the 1990s, representing about 15 to 20 million people. If income growth is modest (1.5 percent real growth per year) and interest rates remain in the 7 to 8 percent range, the number of owner-occupied households can be expected to increase from about 60 million to well over 65 million.

The percentage growth in the number of renter households will probably exceed that of homeowners. Population growth also will stimulate the demand for rental housing. Growth among the elderly, especially those above seventy years of age, and among persons in the age group from twenty-five to thirty-four years will be especially important in prompting this increased demand. Rental housing also will benefit from the slow growth and even decline in real wages among segments of the population; those without a college education and those adversely affected by declining job prospects in manufacturing will be most susceptible to real wage declines.

The housing construction industry has a strong history of responding adequately to demand. As a consequence, housing prices for the most part follow trends in the overall price level. Price "bubbles," like the one experienced during the late-1970s tend to be short-lived and concentrated in rapidly growing urban areas. There is good reason to remain confident in the ability of the housing construction industry. As a consequence, housing prices will probably not appreciate much beyond the average rate of inflation for the entire economy in most parts of the country during the 1990s.

This forecast comes with one important caveat: Growth management strategies may lead to sizeable increases in housing prices in some fast-growing areas. Society has yet to settle upon appropriate strategies with which to manage the impact of population growth on local housing markets. Many current growth management policies—e.g., zoning and large development-fees—tend to drive up the cost of housing in ways that help those already in the select neighborhoods and hurt those who wish to enter them. Until more equitable and efficient strategies can be developed, the cost of housing will exceed the cost of construction in the areas in which growth controls are most prevalent.

Many other government policies also will affect the housing market, such as "affordable" housing programs designed to assist low- and middle-income households to switch to home ownership. The federal government will likely continue to pressure Fannie Mae, Freddie Mac, and other financial institutions to offer low down-payment programs with flexible underwriting criteria in order to improve access to mortgage credit and home ownership for low- and middle-income households. Some of these efforts are worthy; however, these programs will be unable to offset the deeper economic problems faced by many young people who enter the labor market with inadequate job training and

457

education. For many of these would-be homeowners, the primary obstacle to home ownership is an inadequate and unstable income, not a poorly performing housing or mortgage housing market.

Will the 1990s be a good time to buy a house? Homebuyers ought to be more selective in the 1990s than in the past ten to fifteen years. They cannot count on substantial capital gains to offset the high cost of entering home ownership, although some lucky households will reap such rewards. The tax advantage of owning versus renting remains, but its absolute size has declined for many in the middle class. Regardless, home ownership remains a good economic decision for most middle-income households who expect stable employment and to remain in their houses for several years. Home ownership will also be attractive to those fortunate ones able to participate in affordable housing initiatives. For those with less secure employment prospects and lower incomes, rental housing is likely to be the preferred form of housing tenure.

See also ELDERLY, LIVING ARRANGEMENTS; FAMILIES AND HOUSEHOLDS; HOME OWNERSHIP; HOUSEHOLD COMPOSITION; HOUSING, AFFORDABLE; HOUSING, DEMOGRAPHIC AND LIFESTYLE IMPACTS ON.

BIBLIOGRAPHY

FOLLAIN, JAMES R. "The Outlook for Owner-Occupied Housing in the Year 2000." In Frank Bonnello and Tom Swartz, eds. *Upheaval in Urban Housing Markets.* Sage Press, 1993.

FOLLAIN, JAMES R., PATRIC H. HENDERSHOTT, and DAVID C. LING. "Real Estate Markets Since 1980: What Role Have the Tax Changes Played?" *National Tax Journal* (September 1992): 253–266.

James R. Follain

Housing, Demographic and Lifestyle Impacts on

Demographic change and social adaptation have produced dramatic shifts in housing patterns in the past, and can be expected to do so in the future. In Europe, the character of most old cities and towns, with their dense honeycombs of houses and courtyards, is the direct result of seventeenth- and eighteenth-century property owners' practice of building homes for their relatives or employees on back-garden plots. The overcrowded tenements of early industrial Europe and

America were largely the consequences of extended families' occupying living quarters that factory owners originally had designed to house working couples and their children.

In modern times, the bleak economic conditions of the 1930s caused a one-third drop in marriage rates. As a result, the proportion of single Americans nearly doubled, from 15 percent in 1930 to 29 percent in 1940. Depression-era singles often rented modest but genteel quarters from the managerial-professional class, many of whom were unemployed and impoverished following the 1929 financial collapse and converted their large, formal homes into boarding and rooming houses. When prosperity returned after World War II, marriage rates soared and the U.S. middle class expanded. The rebound was so great that builders and developers had to mass-produce millions of "tract houses," standardized on the statistically dominant nuclear family: one married couple and their offspring. By 1950, only 3.2 percent of Americans lived alone.

While industrial era economists from Adam Smith (1723–1790) to 1992 Nobel Laureate Gary Becker have detailed the benefits of monogamous marriage, both to its participants and to society as a whole, it is not clear that the nuclear family will remain the dominant household form. By the 1980s, many social scientists had become comfortable with the idea that the nuclear family's predominance in Western industrial nations was a temporary, circumstantial phenomenon. Currently, nearly 12 percent of American adults live alone. Steadily increasing longevity, and high divorce rates suggest that marriage may become a temporary stage of adulthood—for parenthood—before and after which most people will live alone or in small, intentional groups. Meanwhile sequential marriages are creating extended and blended "co-families" or network households. Above all, economic restructuring in the United States has curtailed the growth of prosperity during the past twenty-five years, fostering greater intergenerational interdependence, including more extended, multigenerational households.

From 1990 to 2010, new household formation rates will be at a seventy-five-year low, due largely to the low birthrates of the 1970s and '80s. The housing industry during this period will largely be involved with: (1) responding to government and community mandates for more "affordable" housing, and (2) adapting existing housing stock to the changing needs of an aging population. Current U.S. housing, built almost entirely for nuclear families, will have to accommodate a growing diversity of living arrangements, including singles; unrelated roommates ("mingles"); childless couples, including gay and lesbian partners; and groups of three or more unrelated adults, especially young adults and self-sufficient seniors living together as a family (in congregate or group housing). Simultaneously, there will be an ongoing construction boom in additions to existing housing, to accommodate mother-in-law wings and granny-flats, as greater longevity and the high cost of housing and health care promote the increase of three- and four-generation households.

The rise of home-based self-employment and salaried work-at-home ("flex-place") also will reshape U.S. housing arrangements in the future. Because the great productivity achieved by labor-intensive mass-market economies requires large-scale physical facilities such as factories, offices, schools, or service facilities, most high-value jobs in such economies are necessarily located away from employees' homes. Because electronics make it much cheaper and faster to move information than to move people, enormous efficiencies will be achieved in the information-intensive economies of the future by bringing office work to the employees rather than vice versa. The movement of gainful employment back into the home, the locus for most employment in agrarian and mercantile economies, will strengthen the family both economically and culturally. Substantial rearrangement of metropolitan traffic and energy flows will fundamentally alter the nature of residential neighborhoods and suburban communities.

Demographic and lifestyle changes shape housing patterns on a national scale, as well as at the neighborhood and community levels. Cities grew from the Civil War until 1950, as the industrial share of U.S. jobs grew. Millions of rural Americans, their jobs eliminated by agricultural mechanization, migrated to cities in search of employment. From the 1950s on, however, most older central cities in *all* mature industrial countries began to lose population. First the exodus was to the suburbs, and after 1970, to exurban and rural areas. As technology reduces the amount of direct labor needed for manufacturing, some producers relocated to rural communities where business operating costs are characteristically 15 to 20 percent lower than in cities and suburbs. Simultaneously, a substantial portion of current rural population growth is due to in-migration of people, including many information workers and retirees, whose income is not geographically dependent. In the United States, fully one-third of seniors who relocate when they retire now move to rural communities near where they lived for most of their lives, rather than moving to areas such as the Sun Belt.

So long as the costs of urban life and work continue to rise and the quality of urban life and work continue to decline, the dispersion of population and production to rural areas and the exurban fringes of metropolitan regions will grow. This shift will accelerate if less developed areas retain fewer statutory restrictions upon innovative land use, residential living arrangements, and working arrangements. Urban and suburban jurisdictions that accommodate innovative lifestyles—such as congregate living, greater residential-commercial integration, and flexible cohousing—will compete more effectively for productive populations than those communities that adhere to restrictive twentieth-century zoning, building, and land-use codes intended to protect existing property values.

See also DEMOGRAPHY; FAMILIES AND HOUSEHOLDS; HOME OWNERSHIP; HOUSEHOLD COMPOSITION; HOUSING, COST AND AVAILABILITY OF; LIFESTYLES.

BIBLIOGRAPHY

BECKER, GARY E. *A Treatise on the Family.* Cambridge, MA: Harvard University Press, 1981.

GIROUARD, MARK. *Cities and People.* New Haven, CT: Yale University Press, 1985.

MORRISON, PETER A., *Demographic Factors Shaping The U.S. Market For New Housing.* Santa Monica, CA: The Rand Corp. Population Research Center, 1988. Monograph.

SNYDER, DAVID PEARCE. "The Corporate Family: A Look at a Proposed Social Invention." *The Futurist* (December 1976): 323–335.

_____. The Family in Post-Industrial America. Boulder, CO: Westview Press, 1979.

David Pearce Snyder

Humanism.

See NONRELIGIOUS BELIEFS.

Human Resources Development

Human resources development will change dramatically as the twentieth century draws to a close. The work force will be older, more stable, and more diverse. Compensation costs will increase as workers try to regain ground lost in the 1980s.

The American Work Force Is on the Move

The U.S. Bureau of Labor Statistics (BLS) estimates that nearly one in five workers changes jobs in a given year. Half or more of these changes involve occupational changes as well.

Job mobility may decline over the next few decades. The post–World War II baby boom generation, which now accounts for more than half of the work force, will reach its mid-thirties to mid-fifties at the turn of the century. Older workers change jobs less frequently than younger workers do.

The impending bulge in experienced workers could benefit firms trying to boost efficiency and competitiveness. The changing work force is also changing human resource management practices. A larger number of seasoned workers competing for fewer senior positions, portends that a promotion increasingly means a change, rather than an increase, in responsibilities. Likewise, frequent job changes by a worker now indicate broadened experience, not instability.

Some companies are responding to changing work force dynamics by investing more in their workers to keep them challenged, productive, and committed. New investments include additional benefits such as child care centers, sabbaticals to pursue professional or personal interests, and worker retraining.

The Challenge of Diversity

The workforce is becoming more diverse. In 1970, nearly 62 percent of the workforce was male and nearly 90 percent was white. In 1991, men accounted for 55 percent of the workforce and whites for 86 percent.

Government, the courts, and employees themselves expect employers to accommodate diversity. Numerous court decisions have found that employers are responsible for ensuring that the workplace is not just physically safe, but also psychologically safe. As a result, increasing attention will be directed at harassment, prejudice, and discrimination.

The Americans with Disabilities Act of 1990 (ADA), one of the most important pieces of civil rights legislation in a generation, imposes special responsibilities on employers. The law prohibits employers from discriminating against a current or prospective employee with certain handicaps, so long as the employee can perform the essential functions of the position with reasonable accommodation on the part of the employer. Among the protected groups of employees and applicants are those with HIV/AIDS, alcoholics. AIDS has already become the most litigated disease in history. Pursuant to statutory protection of the ADA, other conditions may be not far behind.

The farsighted employer will inventory its employees' skills and responsibilities and implement performance evaluations that accurately reflect the responsibilities of each position. Finally, the employer will state its personnel policies clearly and apply them equitably. For example, prohibitions against drinking on the job may not be enforced against alcoholics if violations by occasional drinkers who are not alcoholics are routinely ignored.

Americans Are Working Harder

The decline or death of the American work ethic has been exaggerated. More Americans are working than ever before, and they are working longer hours.

In 1970, 60 percent of the population aged sixteen and older was either working or looking for work. By 1991, this share had risen to over 66 percent, higher than that in all developed, industrialized countries other than Sweden and Canada.

In 1970, 70 percent of those at work worked full-time (at least thirty-five hours weekly). By 1991, this share was up to 81 percent. Over the last two decades, the proportion of workers holding more than one job rose from just over 5 percent to just over 6 percent.

Money Matters

While American workers are working harder, they are losing purchasing power. Between 1981 and 1990, inflation averaged just under 5 percent annually and labor productivity grew nearly 1 percent annually. Average hourly earnings, over the same period, grew just over 3 percent per year. Wages thus fell behind over 2 percent each year. Workers will expect to catch up over the next decade.

The relative position of women workers has improved. In 1991, women working full-time earned seventy-four cents for every dollar earned by men, up from sixty-two cents a decade ago. Much of this increase reflects women's expanded opportunities. Women working full-time are now as likely to be employed in high-paying professional, technical, and managerial jobs as men are.

Women, however, still earn less than men in similar industries or occupations or with similar characteristics. The male-female earnings gap has narrowed, in part because women's earnings have improved and in part because men's earnings have declined after adjusting for inflation.

White workers earn more than African-American workers, but the earnings differential by race is not as large as that by gender. Full-time African-American workers earn seventy-eight cents for every dollar earned by white workers. However, this figure is down from eighty-one cents a decade ago.

Employee Benefits

In 1990, employers spent $375 billion on employee benefits other than Social Security. Contributions to retirement plans accounted for 34 percent of the total, while health benefits accounted for 47 percent. As recently as 1980, these proportions were reversed; retirement benefits accounted for 48 percent of employer spending, while health benefits took up only 31 percent.

The increased importance of health care benefits reflects their growing cost. General inflation reached historic lows during the 1980s and early '90s, but employers' health care costs continue to rise at 10 to 20 percent yearly.

This growth reflects several factors. Sixteen percent of the U.S. population under age sixty-five lacks health care coverage from any source. Physicians and hospitals often raise charges to those with coverage to reflect uncompensated or undercompensated care. Providers who fear malpractice litigation may add to overall costs by overtreating or overtesting patients. Medical advances add treatment options, but often raise costs as well.

Most ominously, more than ten cents of every dollar paid out in health care claims pays for mental health care, substance abuse treatment, or both, and these costs are among the fastest-growing health care costs. Employers can no longer consider drug abuse a law enforcement problem; it is now an employee compensation issue.

Employers are responding to growing health care costs in many ways. Flexible benefit plans have allowed employers and employees to get more for their money, particularly in health care spending. In these plans, also called cafeteria plans, employees choosing less-generous health care plans "earn" credits that can be applied to other benefits. According to the BLS, about one in four employees in firms with one hundred or more employees is now eligible to participate in some type of flexible benefit plan. Forty percent of employees in these firms also participate in retirement plans offering a choice between current cash and deferred compensation.

Runaway health care costs have also prompted interest in comprehensive health care reform. Just as retirement benefit security was the major compensation question of the 1960s and early '70s, health care reform will be the major compensation question of the late twentieth and, perhaps, early twenty-first centuries. In the 1990s, policy makers will have to find a way to expand health care coverage while containing the growth of health care costs, maintaining U.S. competitiveness, and reversing the erosion of real wages and living standards.

See also DISABLED PERSONS' RIGHTS; HEALTH CARE: FINANCING; INSURANCE; UNEMPLOYMENT; UNEMPLOYMENT INSURANCE, WORKMEN'S COMPENSATION, JOB SECURITY; WORK; WORK ETHIC; WORK, QUALITY OF; WORKING CONDITIONS.

BIBLIOGRAPHY

Executive Office of the President. *Economic Report of the President.* Washington, DC: U.S. Government Printing Office, 1992.

PIACENTINI, JOSEPH S., and FOLEY, JILL D. *EBRI Databook on Employee Benefits.* Washington, DC: Employee Benefit Research Institute, 1992.

U.S. Department of Commerce, Bureau of the Census. *Statistical Abstract of the United States 1991.* Washington, DC: U.S. Government Printing Office, 1991.

U.S. Department of Labor, Bureau of Labor Statistics. *Employee Benefits in Medium and Large Firms, 1989.* Washington, DC: U.S. Government Printing Office, 1990.

Kenneth E. Feltman

Human Rights

After World War II, "human rights" began to refer to claims (or demands) to be legitimated in the future for all human beings. It also was used to prohibit certain forms of barbarism and to protect specified groups of people who might otherwise suffer from oppression, deprivation, or discrimination. Commitment to future fulfillment was intended to help the weak enjoy rights already available for the strong.

Actually, the basic substance of many ethical ideals now called human rights began with the first human beings. Anthropologists report that early kinship groups were knit together by tacit standards specifying what people had no right to do—such as committing incest. Other social norms established hunting, fishing, or grazing rights in territories regarded as their collective, often "God given," property. They also imposed responsibilities not only for the division of labor but also for nurturing infants, sharing food, honoring elders, and favoring kinsfolk. These responsibilities conferred implicit rights on the beneficiaries. To this day, the notion of interweaving rights and responsibilities (or duties), together with some action to attain these ideals and contend with transgressions, drives most serious human rights efforts.

Long before recorded history the strongest people proved that they could suppress many rights of weaker people. With the help of superior weaponry, numbers, and force, they secured widespread acceptance for slavery: "might makes right." They established patriarchal subordination of women: "male makes right." For themselves, they won various privileges, immunities, and entitlements. These included the power to make war, seize the property and women of others, build empires, settle disputes, and levy taxes. They also were able to control coinage and accumulate wealth: "money makes right."

With the development of writing came codification of evolving standards. The code of Hammurabi (ca. 1750 B.C.) set forth the rights of rulers, fathers, mothers, and children, together with penalties for wrongdoing. The Hindu Code of the Manus listed hundreds of written rights, duties, and penalties; these were amplified in the *Bhagavad-gita* and *Ramayana*. The many authors of the Hebrew scriptures went far beyond the basic ten commandments and compiled 613 rules, over 400 of which were about what people have no right to do. Generations of commentators went still further. The Christian scriptures and the sacred texts of Islam, Buddhism, Shintoism, and Taoism developed similar traditions. All of these codes included some standards that transcended particular religions by expressing shared human values that protect weaker or poorer people. These codes stood alongside other religious doctrines that justified the right of one group to dominate another, or even to wage "just" wars.

Supported by priests, many rulers were deified. As "gods," these humans enjoyed the right to make law and to stand above it. Aristocrats did not always accept this situation. They often banded together to overthrow rulers. English barons and bishops staged a rebellion in 1215 against King John, forcing him to promulgate a "Magna Carta." This Great Charter denied the monarchy's right to ignore law, gave aristocrats rights to be consulted, and conferred a few rights on lesser folk. Gradually, elected assemblies became forums for consultation with nobles, ecclesiastics, city people, merchants, and other mercantile capitalists. The members of these parliaments gradually established stronger rights of consultation and rights to override a monarch's decree and actually to enact law. The 1689 English Bill of Rights limited the monarchy and established many civil and religious rights.

Expanding wealth and sea power allowed the English the unwritten right to build a huge empire. Later, English power was temporarily checked by the rebellion of its North American colonies. The 1776 Declaration of Independence, the 1789 U.S. Constitution (ratified the same year as the French Declaration of the Rights of Man and the Citizen), and the 1791 U.S. Bill of Rights helped shape the new country's character in the capitalist-industrial era. In the United States and England, as in Western Europe generally, profit-seeking corporations became "fictitious persons" enjoying many of the rights accorded individual males. Backed by armed might and bolstered by dedication to a "civilizing mission" ideology, industrialized nation-states competed with each other in exercising their "sovereign rights and responsibilities" to control lives, governments, and cultures in Africa, Asia, Latin America, and Oceania. After the mid-nineteenth century abolition of slavery, the United States entered this fray with a "Manifest Destiny" to dominate the whole North American continent. This ideology put armed power behind the concept that "white (or lighter-skinned) makes right."

After taking over the former Tsarist empire in 1917, the Russian communists built a regime immensely destructive of human rights. Yet they attained international prestige by guaranteeing some minimal economic rights (particularly paid employment), supporting anticolonial movements, opposing South African apartheid, and helping defeat the fascist Axis powers in World War II. In many countries during the early twentieth century women won the right to vote and labor unions won rights to organize and bargain collectively.

After World War II, the victors established the United Nations. This institution created a Security Council with the right to use military force, as a last resort, for keeping or making peace. Its charter gave each permanent member of the Security Council (originally the Republic of China, France, the United Kingdom, the United States, and the Soviet Union) a veto right over Security Council actions. After abstractly encouraging member states to respect "human rights and fundamental freedoms," the United Nations created a human rights commission to prepare an international bill of rights treaty. Since support could not be obtained for any treaty that might conflict with prevailing elite interests, the "nonbinding" 1948 Universal Declaration of Human Rights (UDHR) was adopted by the General Assembly as "a common standard of achievement for all peoples and all nations." This 1948 resolution combined economic, social, and cultural rights (including property rights) with civil and political rights.

The UDHR has since been endorsed in many national constitutions and international agreements and is widely regarded as part of humankind's "common law." But efforts to expand its generalities into the specifics of a single treaty were blocked by those who opposed giving equal weight to economic rights, then widely regarded as socialist inventions. The outcome was two treaties: a weak UN Covenant on Economic, Social, and Cultural Rights (with property rights omitted), and a stronger UN Covenant on Civil and Political Rights. The right to self-determination was added to both. An optional protocol gave persons the right to appeal to the UN over the head of their own government concerning alleged violations of civil and political rights. These four documents were temporarily labeled the "International Bill of Human Rights." They were soon followed by other UN treaties dealing with genocide, torture, racism, discrimination against women, employee and employer rights of association, war crimes refugees, and children. New treaty ideas deal with the disabled, sustainable development, and peace. Regional human rights charters or conventions have been established in Western Europe, Africa, and the Western hemisphere.

Of the treaties already formally proposed, many remain unratified by many countries. In the name of "sovereignty rights," most governments have refused to endorse the Optional Protocol. The United States has been pondering ratification of the Covenant on Economic, Social and Cultural Rights and the Convention on the Rights of the Child. Ratification, once it occurs, is often a stealth process, with neither governments nor media informing people about treaty-protected rights or governments' responsibilities toward them. Officials may then more readily ignore violations, evade responsibilities, and deny remedies.

In the world of events rather than ideals, the greatest human rights triumph has been the end of the Cold War. Human rights activists played notable (although not exclusive) roles in the collapse of the Berlin wall, the Solidarity victories in Poland, the Charter 77 success in Czechoslovakia, and the breakup of the Soviet Union. They also were crucial in displacing authoritarian regimes in Greece, Spain, Portugal, the Philippines, Argentina, Chile, and Brazil. They demonstrated their power in the conversion from apartheid to constitutional democracy in South Africa. In many other countries, partial triumphs have been won concerning the rights of women, ethnic or religious minorities, homosexuals and bisexuals, children, older people, criminals, crime victims, prisoners, students, teachers, tenants, consumers, and the disabled.

Some people shirk the language of rights on the ground that hypocritical rhetoric may render overly abstract rights meaningless. Commitment to a well-defined right provides explicit responsibilities, remedies, and resources nurturing expectations that fine words really may be followed by specific actions. Those whose perceived interests could be even slightly compromised may find rights (such as the right to earn a living at decent wages) too meaningful a threat. In response, they may try to delegitimate that right, remove it from the agenda of accepted policy discussion, or weaken it by restrictive reservations, understandings, and declarations.

In balancing conflicts among human rights and responsibilities, power is usually decisive. Much more than physical force is entailed. Power (or influence) may be understood as the ability to have some effect on some part of the world. Religion, love, beauty, philosophy, and law, as well as organization, leadership, and nonviolent activism, all may be sources of power. The legitimacy of such power (actual or potential) depends on the depth and breadth of acceptance through silent, grudging, or active consent. To the extent that it is dispersed widely and deeply, the relative power of males, money or the light-skinned might decline. Through the spirit and machinery of democracy, might (widely dispersed) might make right.

Whether it does so depends on millions of people resisting the barbarous enemies of human rights: poverty, hunger, disease, environmental depredation, ignorance, sexism, homophobia, ageism, repression, corruption, nationalist extremism, dehumanizing technologies, violence of all sorts, and war. For human rights ideals to be realized, action is needed to strengthen private and public structures—local, national, regional, and global—of rights, responsibilities, action, and resources. Human rights advocates would have to recognize the importance of labor and management rights. Civil liberties specialists would have to recognize the importance of international law. International human rights law might thus become a stronger global force as an evolving bill of human rights and responsibilities. In a world suffering from hopelessness and chaos, leadership along those lines could help build foundations for "human rights democracies." More and more people—particularly women and children—might thus enjoy economic, social, cultural, civil, and political rights, signaling the emergence, however slow, of a more civilized world society.

See also BEHAVIOR: SOCIAL CONSTRAINTS; BIOETHICS; CHILD ABUSE; CHINA: ETHNIC REAWAKENING; CIVIL PROTEST; COMMUNICATIONS: PRIVACY ISSUES; COMMUNITARIANISM; CRIMINAL JUSTICE; CRIMINAL PUNISHMENT; DEATH AND DYING; DISABLED PERSONS' RIGHTS; ENTITLEMENT PROGRAMS; ETHNIC AND CULTURAL SEPARATISM; LAWS, EVOLUTION OF; MEDIA CONSOLIDATION; MIGRATION; REFUGEES; RELIGION: CHANGING BELIEFS; SOCIAL CONTROLS; SOCIAL WELFARE PHILOSOPHIES; WOMEN'S RIGHTS.

BIBLIOGRAPHY

ADLER, MORTIMER J., "From Political to Economic Rights." In Mortimer J. Adler, *We Hold These Truths: Understanding the Ideas and Ideals of the Constitution.* New York: Collier Books, 1987.

ALDERMAN, ELLEN, and KENNEDY, CAROLINE. *In Our Defense: The Bill of Rights in Action.* New York: Morrow, 1991.

BURNS, MCGREGOR JAMES, and BURNS, STUART. *A People's Charter: The History of Human Rights in America.* New York: Knopf, 1991.

DORSEN, NORMAN, ed. *Our Endangered Rights.* New York: Pantheon, 1984

DRINAN, ROBERT F. *Cry of the Oppressed: The History and Hope of the Human Rights Revolution.* New York: Harper & Row, 1987.

GLENDON, MARY ANN. *Rights Talk: The Impoverishment of Political Discourse.* Free Press, 1991.

HENKIN, LOUIS. *The Age of Rights.* New York: Columbia University Press, 1990.

LAQUEUR, WALTER, and RUBIN, BARRY, eds. *The Human Rights Reader.* Rev. ed. New American Library, Penguin, 1990.

NICKEL, JAMES. *Making Sense of Human Rights.* Berkeley, CA: University of California Press, 1987.

SIEGEL, RICHARD LEWIS. *Employment and Human Rights: The International Dimension.* Philadelphia: University of Pennsylvania Press, 1994.

WILLIAMS, PATRICIA J. *The Alchemy of Race and Rights.* Cambridge, MA: Harvard University Press, 1991.

Bertram Gross

Hydroelectric Power.

See ELECTRIC POWER.

Illiteracy

Global literacy is a goal of the United Nations and a specific undertaking of the United States for its people by the year 2000. In the United States, state governors have set a goal of 100 percent literacy by the year 2000. The United States has the largest number of functional illiterates of any industrialized nation—an estimated 60 million adults in 1990, and the number may reach 90 million by 2000. UN surveys rank the United States forty-ninth among 158 member states—not an impressive record. Remedial efforts will have to continue until well into the next century.

As the twentieth century closes, no universal definition of literacy has been settled upon, and strategies to overcome illiteracy are varied. Controversy about the nature of the problem and disagreement concerning which skills and functional levels of performance will be adequate to meet living and working needs beyond the year 2000 are mostly unsettled.

In the past, literacy meant the ability to read and write one's name, together with some degree of reading skill. Later, literacy was defined as the attainment of a fourth-grade level of ability, essentially restricted to "the three R's"—reading, writing, and arithmetic. World War II, however, fundamentally changed the nature of literacy. Soldiers were given paper-and-pencil tests, and the results were used to sort out intelligence and literacy levels. Intelligence required the ability to read questions and select or write answers. Levels of schooling defined literacy.

By standards applied a few decades ago, today's young adult population (ages twenty-one to twenty-five) would be 95 percent literate. This standard, based on a fourth-grade level of reading and writing, was established fifty years ago. By the 1960s, the War on Poverty standards were based on young adults meeting or exceeding eighth-grade levels of literacy performance.

These earlier definitions of literacy have become inadequate. These times require information manipulation and application as a part of our work or social world. As we attempt to define new standards and prepare ourselves for literacy demands of the twenty-first century, we must realize that 80 percent of the workforce in the year 2000 is already at work today. Therefore, to reduce illiteracy, programs will have to be applied in the workplace and include lifelong learning. Literacy training can never again be viewed solely as a school-based problem.

Other challenges in eliminating illiteracy involve skill level change and new criteria to meet the new requirements of the Information Era. Already, demands of information age technology and the skills required of new job opportunities not dreamed of a decade ago have drastically changed the old definitions.

Literate high school graduates in the year 2007 must be ready for livelihoods that did not exist when a majority of the new workers started school in 1994. Furthermore, students preparing to be "literate" in science, mathematics, computer use, or in any discipline, can expect that preparation to be outmoded in a short time. Constant upgrading of skills is becoming imperative. Accelerating change illustrates the obvious: old concepts of literacy, of life and job preparation, and of schooling, must continue to change and keep pace with the times.

The dictionary defines *literate* as "educated: especially able to read and write" and "having or showing extensive knowledge, experience, or culture." This description does not suggest the flexibility required for lifelong learning or for undergoing rapid changes essential for survival in the future.

Literacy surveys by the U.S. Department of Labor of the twenty million people engaged in DOL programs concluded that 40–50 percent need literacy training to qualify for new jobs. An estimated 22 percent of U.S. adults are considered illiterate, and an additional 23 percent are functionally illiterate.

An Office of Technology Assessment study concluded: ". . . we as a nation must respond to the literacy challenge, not only to preserve our economic vitality, but also to ensure that every individual has a full range of opportunities for personal fulfillment and participation in society." (U.S. Congress, 1993).

Literacy rates vary worldwide from 99 percent in Sweden and Korea to 14 percent in Mozambique. However, comparisons can be misleading due to widely differing definitions. The Educational Testing Service has defined literacy as ". . . using printed and written information to function in society, to achieve one's goals, and to develop one's knowledge and potential" (Campbell et al., 1992). Definitions of this type may be helpful in developing measuring instruments, but in societies in which citizens get most of their information by viewing television screens (video or computer), we must move beyond reading and writing. Literacy in the future will have to be defined in terms of the media in which it is practiced. Future trends indicate that functional, practiced literacy includes the ability to:

1. Read about, observe, and listen to information and be able to communicate and demonstrate understanding.
2. Possess lifelong learning skills that enable self-directed, necessary changes in work and lifestyle.
3. Have the necessary skills to function in society and to pursue self-directed achievements.

Future prospects for reaching toward universal, global literacy are positive. New technologies are about to unleash better tools with which to teach and learn. The new literacy for the twenty-first century must not ignore the 98 percent of the world's illiterates who live in developing countries. Dignity and respect for a diversity of cultures and pluralistic ideologies must not be glossed over; nor should singular and unified efforts be allowed to homogenize differences. There is strength in diversity, and proper recognition of that elemental truth must not be allowed to wither and wane.

See also ADULT LEARNING; DEVELOPMENT, ALTERNATIVE; EDUCATIONAL TECHNOLOGIES; ELEMENTARY AND SECONDARY EDUCATION; HIGHER EDUCATION; LIBERAL ARTS; LITERATURE.

BIBLIOGRAPHY

APPLEBEE, ARTHUR N.; LANGER, JUDITH A. M.; JENKINS, LYNN B.; MULLIN, INA V. S.; and FOERTSCH, MARY A. *Learning to Work in Our Nation's Schools.* Princeton, NJ: Educational Testing Service, 1990.

BHOLA, H. S. *Evaluating "Literacy for Development" Projects, Programs and Campaigns.* Quebec: UNESCO Institute for Education and German Foundation for International Development, 1990.

HAUTECOUER, JEAN-PAUL. *ALPHA 92 Current Research in Literacy: Literacy Strategies in the Community Movement.* Quebec: UNESCO Institute of Education, 1992.

KIRSCH, IRWIN S., and JUNGEBLUT, ANN. *Literacy: Profiles of America's Young Adults.* Princeton, NJ: Educational Testing Service, 1986.

KIRSCH, IRWIN S.; JUNGEBLUT, ANN; and CAMPBELL, ANN. *Beyond the School Doors: The Literacy Needs of Job Seekers Served by the U.S. Department of Labor.* Princeton, NJ: Educational Testing Service, 1992.

KIRSCH, IRWIN S.; JUNGEBLUT, ANN; JENKINS, LYNN; and KOLSTAD, ANDREW. *Adult Literacy in America.* Princeton, NJ: Educational Testing Service, 1993.

LANGER, JUDITH A.; APLEBEE, ARTHUR N.; MULLIS, INA V. S.; FOERTSCH, MARY A. *Learning to Read in Our Nation's Schools.* Princeton, NJ: Educational Testing Service, 1990.

LIB, BARBARA, and STACEY, NEVZER, COCHAIRS, et al. Office of Educational Research and Improvement (ORE), *Reaching the Goals: Adult Literacy and Lifelong Learning.* Washington, DC: U.S. Government Printing Office, 1993.

U.S. Congress, Office of Technology Assessment. *Adult Literacy and New Technologies: Tools for a Lifetime,* O.T.A.–SET-550. Washington, DC: U.S. Government Printing Office, 1993.

Le Roy Owens

Immigration.

See MIGRATION, INTERNATIONAL.

India

Like the rest of the world, India is undergoing such rapid change that predictions of future scenarios are tentative at best. Above all, the industrial structure and socioeconomic framework of recent decades are falling apart. Money and power seem to be losing their importance. The growing feeling among Indians is a sense of helplessness and uncertainty coupled with a tenacious resolution to look for and implement alternatives.

Politics and Governance

Since India gained freedom from British rule in 1947, the major party in power has been the Congress party, with brief interruptions since 1976. However, a significant continuing trend is the declining trust and support of the Indian people for their government, which is widely viewed as becoming too large, too complex, and too distant from the common citizenry (Drucker, 1992). A crucial factor is the loss of the faith that problems can be solved by government.

Internationally, India's policy has been one of nonalignment. However, with the collapse of communism the dynamics of international diplomacy are changing dramatically worldwide. Moreover, the Indian government's fascination with large-scale industrial and economic projects will increasingly require outside financial support. Meanwhile, the industrialized countries will continue to get deeper into economic messes themselves, consequently losing their former glamor and role-model appeal for other countries. India, like other Asian and African nations, will therefore pay increasing attention to its internal affairs.

Sources of Potential Conflict

In India poverty and unemployment loom large as the major source of internal conflicts. Even when these conflicts appear to be social (such as those arising from job discrimination against socially "backward" classes) or linguistic (such as those arising from the formation of states on the basis of language or dialect), the underlying element is economic—i.e., the effect of such policies on the growth of income and jobs.

Population and Demographics

India's population is huge. Every seventh person in the world is Indian. With 880 million people, India ranks second only to China, and is in fact the world's largest democracy. The size and growth rate of the Indian population are shown in Figure 1 below.

Population control policies have, therefore, assumed a top priority. Some crucial reasons for the explosive increase in population, particularly among low income groups, can be traced to their economic predicament.

Physical labor is the major source of livelihood for the poor. In old age, therefore, the poor must rely on their children. Just as a large bank balance

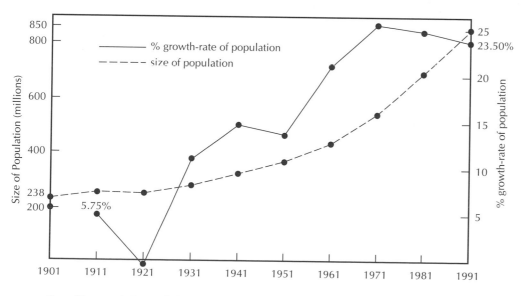

FIGURE 1. Size and Growth-Rate of the Indian population, 1901–1991.
(Source: *India 1992,* p. 54.)

or insurance policy is a hedge against old age for the rich, so is an abundance of children for the poor. Children are their only asset in cases of emergency, disability, and old age. Another reason for the high birthrate among the poor is the high mortality rate in families due to malnutrition and other scarcities. In the future it will become imperative to create alternative sources of livelihood and better standards of living to solve the population explosion problem.

Urbanization

In recent decades, all village-based occupations, beginning with cloth production, have been destroyed by the massively aggressive industrialization of cities. There are literally no jobs and no industries in the smaller villages. This has forced large rural populations to migrate to cities in search of livelihood (*India 1992*, p. 66). Contrary to western economic theories, in India urbanization has led not to economic growth but to massive, crowded, filthy slums, which have become breeding grounds for crime and disease.

In coming years, however, the failure of industrialization will revive rural industries, rendering them economically more viable and profitable, and populations will shift back from cities to villages.

Social Conditions

For thousands of years, Indian society and its central units, the family, were peaceful, rural, and flourishing. But the industrial revolution, which spread worldwide through international trade during the last two centuries, tore apart this smooth and colorful social fabric.

Economic production in India had been cottage-based, involving all family members. But with in-

TABLE 1. Trends of Urbanization

Year	Population (Millions)		% of Total Population	
	Rural	Urban	Rural	Urban
1901	213	25	89	11
1971	439	109	80	20
1981	525	160	77	23
1991	627	217	74	26

dustrialization, husbands left home to work in urban factories and wives became unemployed and dependent on them. In the future, when industries return to villages, Indian society will regain its social and economic well-being.

Quality of Life

Measured in terms of a wide variety of indicators, the quality of life of Indians has rapidly deteriorated in recent years. For example, in India divorce was unheard of, or at least stigmatized, only a few decades ago. Now marital separations are commonplace. Drinking and drug addiction are spreading among all age groups. Reverence, consideration, and care, not only for fellow citizens but for family members and friends, have become concepts of the past. Violent crimes, arson, and terrorism are rampant.

Economic Scenario

Modern industries must survive in international markets. In the future, a lack of international competitiveness will become a major hurdle to the progress of Indian industry.

Nevertheless, some Indian industries have shown remarkable growth recently, as indicated in Table 2.

TABLE 2. Growth of Production of Selected Industries

Industry	Unit (Millions)	1987–88	1990–91
Petroleum	Metric tons	30	33
Steel castings	Metric tons	0.170	0.256
Machine tools	Rupees	3,900	7,650
Automobiles	Rupees		366
Paper and boards	Metric tons	1.6	2
Cement	Metric tons	40	49
Sugar	Metric tons	9	12
Cotton cloth	Square meters	12,626	13,400
Power transformers	KVA	25	37
Electricity generated	Billion kwh	202	265

In 1992, reports of major Indian companies show a decline in production, sales, and profits, causing deep concern, if not alarm. In the future, a crucial advantage India holds is its own local markets, which it can acquire by revitalizing village industries and, in turn, Indian agriculture. Agricultural workers in India are mostly landless and work only during the farming seasons. The shift of industries to villages will provide work and livelihood to these people year-round and will substantially strengthen agriculture.

International Trade

International trade has been the harbinger of economic growth only in the Western industrialized countries. For India—as for a few other countries of Asia, Africa, and Latin America—international trade has brought colonialism, the destruction of villages, unemployment, and poverty. Instead of reducing scarcities, it has led to the concentration of incomes in a few pockets in other, often distant countries.

India's share of world exports amounted to only 0.5 percent in 1988, and even that consisted of primary materials like tea, spices, iron ore, leather, precious stones, and cloth. India's trade balance (exports f.o.b.–imports c.i.f.) declined from Rs.-93 billion in 1987 and 1988 to Rs.-124 billion in 1989 and 1990 (*India: 1992*, p. 162).

It would be nearly impossible for India to raise the standard of living of its huge population through international trade, as it would entail earning unrealistically large profits abroad. Moreover, India should not even wish to raise the living standards of its people through international trade, because the latter often creates prosperity in one country at the expense of other countries. Instead, by relying on rural industrialization, India can bring itself prosperity in both a sustainable and humane way.

Transportation and Communication

Scientists in industrialized countries have labeled the present as "the Information Age." Such a description is meaningless for most of the world community living in Asia, Africa, and Latin America, as a few statistics about transportation and communication facilities in India attest.

Although India has intensively planned for modern technology since 1951, according to Indian government data, approximately 400,000 villages out of a total of 600,000—comprising 75 percent of the country's population—do not have an access road in the monsoon season. Out of these, about 200,000 villages do not have an access road for the rest of the year either. About 450,000 villages do not have a post office, and 540,000 do not have telephone service. Still, the initial hope is being nurtured that an industrial-information revolution will be advanced with the use of even more advanced technology.

Education and Health Care

On the educational and health fronts, facilities have improved in recent years but still remain scanty, considering the size of the total population, as shown in Table 3.

Alternative Futures and Sustainable Development (2000 and Beyond)

India's economic future lies in changing to the new system of local-production-for-local-markets by revitalizing village industries, beginning with cloth-production using the spinning wheel and then exchanging cloth with other commodities by gradually reestablishing local, cottage-based production.

Times are changing so rapidly that projections for the year 2000 and beyond cannot be made simply by extending the statistical trends mentioned

TABLE 3.   Education and Health Care in India

	1980–81	1987–88
Primary school enrollment (millions)	69	93
Middle school enrollment (millions)	18	30
Secondary school enrollment (millions)	9	18
Hospitals and dispensaries (thousands)	23	38
Beds per million population	8.3	9.1
Medical practitioners per million population	3.9	4.2

Source: *India 1992*, pp. 252–253.

above. Widespread unemployment, escalating inflation, rising crime rates, and increasing scarcity of food supplies are among the many factors which will bring fundamental changes. Forces are already on the move to launch a new rural industrial revolution in India. The new local-production-for-local-market will eliminate the present huge overhead and thus curb inflation.

By virtue of the spinning wheel's widespread availability, the weaker sections of society will produce cloth, the pivotal commodity. This will enable all the rest to be productive, using simple tools, local materials, and other commodities and services to barter local cloth with one another, leading to full employment and self-sustaining growth.

The new system of rural industrialization will eliminate most poverty and unemployment, inflation and sluggishness in effective demand, energy prices and costs of high-tech machinery, bureaucratic red tape and the burden of middlemen chains, environmental damages and ecological imbalances, pressures due to urbanization and loss of contact with nature, subordination of women and mistreatment of minorities, destructive use of scientific knowledge and the lack of relevance of the educational system, increasing crime rates, and escalating arms production.

See also ASIA; DEVELOPMENT, ALTERNATIVE; HINDUISM.

BIBLIOGRAPHY

DRUCKER, PETER F. *Managing for the Future: The 1990s and Beyond.* New York: New American Library/Dutton, 1992.

GALBRAITH, JOHN KENNETH. *The Nature of Mass Poverty.* Cambridge, MA: Harvard University Press, 1979.

GANDHI, MOHANDAS K. *Constructive Programme.* Ahmedabad, India: Navjivan, 1945.

India 1992. New Delhi: Observer Research Foundation, 1992.

JOSHI, NANDINI. *Development Without Destruction: Economics of the Spinning Wheel.* Ahmedabad, India: Navjivan, 1992.

Nandini Joshi

Industrial Design

Industrial design and the industrial designer are at the center of the transformation of mass production manufacturing and the globalization of culture. Industrial design is emerging as a major strategic tool in international economic competition. Industrial designers are an inseparable part of product development groups, working with engineers, marketing staff, accountants, and strategic planners from concept to market, bringing better products to market faster. The role of the industrial designer and the designer's relationship to the consumer are being transformed as consumers increasingly demand that products meet their specific needs, possess utility, and delight their individual sensibilities.

The industrial designer is moving out of the studio and away from the drafting table to the computer console. Computer technology has allowed more people, from engineers and planners to marketers and consumers, to input more data into the design process. Up-to-the-minute consumer data and wider access to critical decision points has increased the possibility that consumers are offered products they need, want, and will buy.

Computer chips and circuit boards having led to the miniaturization of many products for the office and home, human scale is often the only reason for mass and size. Components inside the product are very tiny. The size of the product need not be determined by the size of its internal components, but by the size, dexterity, and comfort level of the user.

Aesthetics in design are changing. A transcultural, global aesthetic is emerging as technology links people and cultures worldwide. Technology has made it possible for the same product designed and manufactured by different manufacturers to have the same basic functions. The design's competitive edge goes beyond utility to delight the user aesthetically or to perform additional, desired functions beyond the basic ones. User delight is value added.

Technology has brought the consumer right to the heart of the design process. Manufacturers are increasingly attentive to the needs and concerns of consumers. As global competition has forced more manufacturers to compete for the same consumer, manufacturers have begun to ask consumers what they want and need, and then use this data in product planning and design. Nowhere is this more evident than in the international automotive industry. The success of Japanese manufacturers was largely based on creating products that were excellent in quality, economical, and aesthetically pleasing. The Japanese were also the first to shorten drastically the time in getting products to market; they were able to provide products when they were needed. North American and European manufacturers, as they adopt similar consumer-centered practices, are closing the competitive gap and surpassing their rivals.

The development of "expert" software systems makes it possible for the consumer to custom-design products. Soon, the consumer will meet with a designer-facilitator and work at a design kiosk using computer technology to assemble a product to meet that consumer's individual needs, wants, and aesthetic sensibilities. Virtual reality technology also should allow the consumer-designer to "try on" the product and make changes, before the product is manufactured. There will be no warehouse or inventory as the product is built and delivered direct to the consumer. The industrial designer has two key roles in this process: first by developing the "expert" software systems that provide the design components for the consumer to manipulate, next by helping the consumer make design decisions during the consumer-centered design process.

Second only to computer technology in significance, environmental concerns are transforming design and manufacturing. The need to eliminate materials that are toxic or cannot be recycled, as well as concerns involving the depletion of global resources, have drawn new, "green" design solutions from industrial designers. Increasingly, as manufacturers are being held accountable by consumers and by government, they are taking responsibility for recycling or disposing of toxic and waste components in their products. It will become commonplace for manufacturers to retain ownership of selected products, lease them to consumers, then take them back for recycling or environmentally safe disposal.

As technology and green design push back the limits of design possibilities, industrial designers are being challenged to solve design problems wherever they occur. A laptop computer with a modem can take the design process to the problem site. Designers in the remotest areas can draw on "expert" systems software and databases around the globe to create customized, indigenous solutions. As designers work on-site rather than remotely, local traditional design and aesthetics will influence specific design solutions. Perhaps more significantly, the global exposure of the industrial designer together with the transglobal popularization of aesthetics are shaping global design. Industrial designers are responding to the increasing value placed on handmade, ethnic, one-of-a-kind products by the globally conscious consumer. Most industrial designers will work in multidisciplinary product development teams much of the time. Individual designers will also take "time out" to work in fluid, changing coalitions with other designers, enabling them to practice as "artisan designers," creating custom, one-of-a-kind products.

Historically, the industrial designer became involved near the end of the product development process to make the product look attractive. The engineer was typically at the center of the process, the product being "engineered" rather than "designed." By training, engineers push a process or product to its capacity, to see how far it can go; industrial designers are trained to begin with the consumer. Manufacturers have discovered that complexity, incorporating all the functions possible in the product, creates serious problems for the consumer. Consumer complaints and returns often are based on complexity, which often perplexes them, rather than on quality problems. Many manufacturers have redesigned their products, substituting utility for complexity. Utility means: Does it work? Is it useful? Can I operate it? As the consumer becomes central to product development, industrial design will become a coordinating, synthesizing discipline. Industrial designers should become the multiskilled project synthesizers who integrate input from all of the disciplines in the product development group, keeping the consumer central to the process.

The transformation of industrial design poses serious implications for the training of industrial designers. All industrial design curricula will place increasing emphasis on developing designers' skills in three key areas: (1) Industrial designers will learn how to make maximum use of state-of-the-art computer-aided design hardware and software. (2) They will be trained to push designs beyond utility to delight, stressing the value-added qualities of aesthetics. (3) A new emphasis will be placed on team building and team work skills, as well as human factors and psychology.

Industrial design is emerging as both a tactical and a strategic tool in world competition. Design is no longer an afterthought, but is emerging as the core of the product development process. Intrinsic factors, aesthetics, and human factors provide the competitive edge. As the project design group takes hold and becomes the normative approach to product development, industrial designers will become project integrators and multiskilled synthesizers.

Industrial design is emerging as both a tactical and a strategic tool in world competition. Design is no longer an afterthought, but is emerging as the core of product development. At the extrinsic level, involving such factors as technology and engineering, competitors are on essentially equal footing.

Intrinsic factors, such as aesthetics and human factors, provide the source of any competitive edge. As the product-design-group approach takes hold and becomes the typical approach to product development, industrial designers will become project integrators and multiskilled synthesizers.

See also ARCHITECTURAL DESIGN; COMPUTERS: SOFTWARE; CREATIVITY; MARKETING BREAKTHROUGHS; NANOTECHNOLOGY; VISUAL ARTS.

BIBLIOGRAPHY

CAPLAN, RALPH. "Designers and Engineers: Strange but Essential Bedfellows." *Technology Review* (February–March 1983).

HAWKEN, PAUL. "The Ecology of Commerce." *INC.* (April 1992).

HAWKEN, PAUL, and MCDONOUGH, WILLIAM. "Seven Steps to Doing Good Business." *INC.* (November 1993).

SEDGEWICK, JOHN. "The Complexity Problem." *Atlantic Monthly* (March 1993).

SMITH, P. G., and REINERTSEN, D. G. *Developing Products in Half the Time.* New York: Van Nostrand Reinhold, 1991.

Josephine Kelsey

Industrial Gases

Industrial gases are an important, growing component of our economy. Industrial gases are commonly categorized in terms of the containers in which they are stored or shipped. The most common container is the relatively compact cylinder, followed by the larger tank or tanker and then the pipeline. Such gases are respectively referred to as "cylinder," "bulk," or "pipeline" gases. The atmospheric gases oxygen, nitrogen, and argon are the most commonly used and bring in the most revenue. Other commonly used gases are hydrogen, helium, carbon dioxide, and acetylene. Industrial gases are used in a wide variety of industrial applications, ranging from basic metals to chemicals, food processing, and medicine.

New applications are bringing gases closer to the customer in uses never before contemplated. Some applications require a greater degree of purity and extremes of temperature in the cryogenic (supercooled) range. Probably the most opportune use for industrial gases in the future is in cleaning up our environment. Applications of gases, primarily oxygen, for environmental cleanup extend from actual remediation of contaminated land and water to reducing pollution in various manufacturing processes. Hydrogen can be mixed with other fuels to increase reactivity, which also reduces the level of pollution.

At the same time that we are discovering new applications for gases, we also are discovering new, more efficient methods of separating the atmospheric gases. These new methods of air separation are noncryogenic (i.e., they do not require very low temperatures to take place). Two commonly used noncryogenic air-separation methods are pressure-swing absorption and membrane filters. While noncryogenic gases are cheaper to produce, they have a more limited degree of applicability. Noncryogenic gases are generally not as pure as those produced by the cryogenic process, and since they are not liquid, they cannot be used for applications requiring extremes of cold. However, the noncryogenic gases can be produced by a relatively small "black box" installed at a manufacturing site, eliminating the need for cylinders or bulk gas transport and pipelines. As gases are used more broadly, the noncryogenic processes are likely to become more refined and competitive so that by the turn of the century, a significant amount of the new growth in atmospheric gases could be satisfied by noncryogenic gas processes.

Even though noncryogenic gases will enjoy significant growth, cryogenic gases will always fill an important need. Cryogenic liquid gases are much more efficient to transport (700 times more compact as a liquid than as a gas), and liquefied gases represent the only way to achieve the cold temperature essential for superconductivity. Present commercial applications of superconductivity require liquid helium (–452° F). The principal use of liquid helium for superconductivity is in magnetic resonance imaging (MRI) technology for noninvasive medical diagnostic applications.

Recent discoveries of higher-temperature superconducting materials have increased the enthusiasm for superconducting. This has meant more use of liquid helium, both for commercial and research applications. As higher temperature superconductivity materials are discovered, other higher temperature cryogenic liquids are likely to be used, such as liquid nitrogen (–346° F). Since nitrogen is far more plentiful than helium, and requires less energy to liquefy, the cost of superconducting systems will be more affordable and therefore more commercially viable.

High-temperature superconductivity (HTS) will have major applications for the generation, transmission, and use of electric power. HTS will revolutionize our use of power and help solve our need for cleaner, less-polluting transportation.

Hydrogen also holds great potential for our transportation needs in the future. Hydrogen is very clean-burning, producing only heat and water. Currently, hydrogen is supplied for many essential uses including aerospace, chemicals, food, electronics, glass, metals, nuclear power, petroleum, and pharmaceuticals.

Demand for cleaner air has created a need for transitional low-emission motor vehicles (TLEV), low-emission vehicles (LEV), ultra-low-emission vehicles (ULEV) and zero-emission vehicles (ZEV). California already has an emission-reduction plan in place; other states will follow. Hydrogen is likely to be a key component in satisfying emission-reduction plans. In addition to battery-driven electric vehicles, only hydrogen with a fuel-cell/electric-motor drive can meet the zero-emission vehicle requirements. With the advent of the 1990 Clean Air Act amendments, refineries are required to produce cleaner-burning fuels. This is most effectively accomplished through hydrogen processing to significantly reduce the sulfur, olefins, and aromatics content in the transportation fuels a refinery produces. Clean-burning hydrogen, or blends of hydrogen and natural gas in internal combustion engines are candidates to meet less-stringent, but still challenging, ultra-low-emission vehicle standards.

Gases can themselves be pollutants. Carbon dioxide has many beneficial uses, but is a product of combustion. The level of carbon dioxide in our environment is increasing, due largely to the burning of fossil fuels and deforestation. At the beginning of the Industrial Revolution, there were about 280 parts per million (ppm) of CO_2 in the atmosphere. Today, there are about 360 ppm, a 30 percent rise. The annual increase is 2 ppm and rising. If present trends continue, the concentration of CO_2 in the atmosphere will double to about 700 ppm in the latter half of the twenty-first century. This increase would not be a direct threat to human life, but it does pose an indirect threat due to the greenhouse effect. Man-made change of such magnitude requires careful consideration to understand the consequences. Scientists have developed models to show the effect of the global warming caused by the rise of CO_2 and other so-called greenhouse gases. The debate rages on with other scientists refuting the global warming hypothesis. Nevertheless, we are now changing the composition of our atmosphere. We are in effect conducting a global environmental experiment without knowing the result. While some of the change that higher levels of CO_2 in our atmosphere will bring about may raise concerns, it is also important to stress the beneficial aspects of higher CO_2 concentrations for some food crops, trees, and plants.

While there is significant disagreement about the global warming phenomenon, there is agreement that rising concentrations of CO_2 in the atmosphere will increase the growth of plant life. A doubling of CO_2 concentrations will cause plants to grow larger and faster, with increases in leaf size and thickness, stem height, branching, and seed production. Fruits and flowers will also increase in size and number.

Industrial gases will also be a factor in sewage conditioning and garbage disposal. In areas of high geothermal activity, deep shafts can be drilled into areas of high temperature. Sewage can be injected with oxygen and pumped down the shaft where the oxygen and high temperature work on the sewage making it into an easily manageable and safe compost suitable for gardening.

Everywhere we look, industrial gases play an important part in the way we live: in processing and serving food, steel production, making semiconductors, treating the sick, carbonating beverages, and providing fuels, to cite but a few examples. Industrial gases will continue to be used in commerce as well as on the leading edge of technology. Gases will also be important in finding ways to satisfy our growing need for energy and to help clean up our environment. Industrial gases will continue to be an essential part of our economy while enhancing our quality of life.

See also ACID RAIN; BATTERIES; CHEMICALS, FINE; CHEMISTRY; GLOBAL WARMING; MAGLEV; MOTOR VEHICLES, ALTERNATIVELY POWERED; NATURAL GAS; OZONE LAYER DEPLETION; SPACE TRAVEL; SUPERCONDUCTORS.

BIBLIOGRAPHY

Carbon Dioxide. Publication No. CGA C-6. Arlington, VA: Compressed Gas Association, 1993.

Handbook of Compressed Gases. Arlington, VA: Compressed Gas Association, 1990.

Proposed Regulations for Low Emission Vehicles and Clean Fuels. Sacramento, CA: California Air Resources Board, 1990.

Safe Handling of Cryogenic Liquids. Publication No. CGA P-12. Arlington, VA: Compressed Gas Association, 1993.

WITTWER, SYLVAN H. "In Praise of Carbon Dioxide." *Policy Review* (Heritage Foundation) (Fall 1992).

Carl T. Johnson

Industrial Policy.

See BUSINESS STRUCTURE: INDUSTRIAL POLICY.

Informal Economy

The informal economy consists of all productive but unpaid work, including household maintenance, do-it-yourself repairs, and home building; food growing for personal use; child care; looking after the sick, elderly, and disabled; and volunteer work. These vast informal sectors are generally ignored by economists and do not show up in their money-dominated, macroeconomic statistics such as gross national product (GNP), gross domestic product (GDP), savings investment rates, and so forth.

The enormous contribution to national wealth made by these informal sectors led to reappraisal during the 1980s. Figure 1, "Total Productive System of an Industrial Society," shows both the paid and unpaid sectors. This four-layer cake shows the GNP, money-denominated sectors as the two top layers that correspond to the more familiar econo-mists' pie charts: the private and public sectors, as well as the underground economy of cash-based drugs, off-the-books work, money laundering, and other illegal activities. Below the middle line are the unpaid or unaccounted productive activities of the informal, unpaid "love economy." The bottom layer of the cake diagram consists of nature's productivity.

A very important subdefinition for all activities of the informal economy differentiates between (1) the love economy: altruistic, largely local activities such as volunteering, family and community care, mutual aid, subsistence work, and local skills (sharing, bartering), and (2) the underground economy: activities that are criminal, quasi-criminal, tax-avoiding in nature, involving gray and black markets and unreported trade, and often national and international in scope.

Bartering

Bartering is ubiquitous in all human societies, from ancient times to the present, and is found across all societies in both legal and criminal activity. Countries experiencing shortages of foreign exchange—

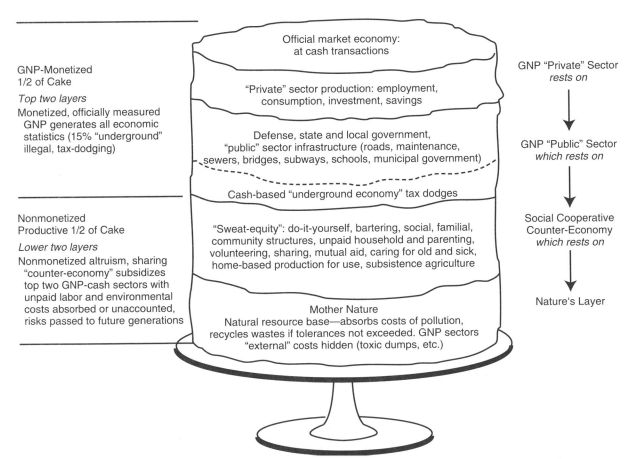

GNP-Monetized
1/2 of Cake

Top two layers
Monetized, officially measured GNP generates all economic statistics (15% "underground" illegal, tax-dodging)

Nonmonetized
Productive 1/2 of Cake

Lower two layers
Nonmonetized altruism, sharing "counter-economy" subsidizes top two GNP-cash sectors with unpaid labor and environmental costs absorbed or unaccounted, risks passed to future generations

Official market economy: at cash transactions

"Private" sector production: employment, consumption, investment, savings

Defense, state and local government, "public" sector infrastructure (roads, maintenance, sewers, bridges, subways, schools, municipal government)

Cash-based "underground economy" tax dodges

"Sweat-equity": do-it-yourself, bartering, social, familial, community structures, unpaid household and parenting, volunteering, sharing, mutual aid, caring for old and sick, home-based production for use, subsistence agriculture

Mother Nature
Natural resource base—absorbs costs of pollution, recycles wastes if tolerances not exceeded. GNP sectors "external" costs hidden (toxic dumps, etc.)

GNP "Private" Sector
rests on
↓
GNP "Public" Sector
which rests on
↓
Social Cooperative Counter-Economy
which rests on
↓
Nature's Layer

FIGURE 1.   Total productive system of an industrial society (three-layer cake with icing metaphor).

for example, Russia and China—often resort to barter. Such bartering is usually facilitated by intermediaries and referred to as countertrade. Some of this countertrade is undertaken to avoid taxes, or to take advantage of loopholes that allow global intra-company trading to escape or minimize host-country taxes. Global bartering is thought to encompass almost one-quarter of all world trade.

Within a love economy, bartering is very different, embracing cooperative and altruistic undertakings and activities of simpler village life so as to optimize community resources in societies where little money is used. Barter such as this escapes statistical report or review.

Barter often resurges in economies hit by hard times and also in more isolated communities. Forms of such barter include exchange clubs for used clothing and appliances, baby-sitter co-ops, community workshops where tools can be shared, mutual aid networks, and even local "currencies" (such as the "local exchange trading systems" invented by Michael Linton in Vancouver, Canada).

Black Markets

Black markets occur in situations where there are shortages of needed goods and services. Transactions usually involve hoarders, speculators, and middlemen who try to corner the market on scarce goods. Objects of such trade include legal commodities such as food and housing, or illegal ones such as narcotics, and may be widely practiced where political controls are weak.

Causes

Informal economies are, and have been throughout history, at the base of all human societies. In a very real sense, informal economies are statistical artifacts born of excessively narrow economic theories, models, and statistics that defined such activities as "uneconomic" and outside the scope of GNP/GDP national accounts. Economic theory holds that most caring, cooperative, unpaid, and volunteer work, such as is characteristic of the love economy, is "irrational." Persons operating in the underground economy, on the other hand, work surreptitiously and hide their activities to avoid persecution for tax avoidance or other crimes.

During the 1970s and '80s, GNP/GDP and national statistical accounts began to be readdressed by documenting some sectors of the informal economy such as unpaid work, unreported international trade, and barter transactions. Governments, however, have often avoided documenting large areas of informal activities, notably global and domestic drug trade.

Another problem highlighted by studies of informal economies involved methods used to compile labor statistics, such as unemployment. Until the late 1970s, textbooks defined an economy as fully employed when only approximately one-half of the adult population was working in a paid job. That half of the population consisted primarily of heads of households. This household model assumed there was a breadwinner (usually male) with a dependent wife and children.

Surprisingly, even among the world's twenty-four major industrial countries that are members of the Organization for Economic Cooperation and Development (OECD), such unpaid activities account for approximately half of all productive hours worked. In the United States, unpaid work accounted for an estimated 60 percent of GNP (according to Burns, 1977). In the U.S. "love economy" some 94.2 million Americans performed 20.5 billion hours of volunteer work in 1991, valued at $176 billion. In developing countries, where approximately three-quarters of the world's population live, unpaid work accounts for three-quarters of all productive hours worked. This reflects the persistence in these countries of large subsistence sectors and traditional communities that still function outside of the money-based economy, or that only use cash for items that cannot be produced or bartered locally.

Information quantifying these informal economies is collected by the United Nations. For example, household work is usually reported in terms of the unpaid hours. No OECD country includes this data in GNP/GDP figures, but some (Canada, Denmark, and Finland) have officially worked up the statistics. Denmark values household work the highest (at 50 percent of GNP), with Norway at 41 percent and Finland at 31 percent. A 1929 report estimated that household work was valued at 25 percent of GNP in the United States, but since then only a few privately commissioned studies have been made.

Data is very sparse in developing countries. Venezuela's Central Bank estimated household work at 22 percent of GNP in 1982. In the same year, the National Committee on the Role of Filipino Women estimated the value of household work at only 11 percent of GNP. The collection of such data is affected not only by the economic biases mentioned but also by cultural values such as male dominance.

During the 1980s, household incomes in the United States eroded. Not only were women obliged to enter the paid work force, but male household heads often held down two jobs to make ends meet. Full-time jobs shrank while enormous numbers of 20-hour-a-week jobs were created.

Today, some 30 percent of U.S. workers shed from company payrolls have become "contingency" workers, while part-time jobs have also burgeoned. During the 1990s, with fewer at-home unpaid spouses doing household, parenting, and community duties, new businesses providing such services have boomed. They include: fast foods, day care, home helpers, visiting nursing and rehabilitation services, child minders, self-help seminars, and preschools.

Informal economies will likely remain unmeasured as long as nations have crime and other illicit activities, and as long as some types of work, particularly that performed within homes and communities, go unrecognized and financially unrewarded. However, there are signs that some of this activity is being acknowledged as societies modernize and women enter the work force. Illicit aspects of the underground economy are likely to remain unless laws prohibiting "immoral" behavior, such as drug use, are dropped and these activities become accepted as economic undertakings.

See also DRUGS, ILLEGAL; GRAY MARKET GOODS; WOMEN AND WORK; WORK; WORKFORCE DIVERSITY; WORK, QUALITY OF.

BIBLIOGRAPHY:

HENDERSON, HAZEL. *Paradigms in Progress,* Chapters 4 and 6. Indianapolis: Knowledge Systems, 1991.

NICHOLLS, WILLIAM M., and DYSON, WILLIAM A. *The Informal Economy.* Montreal: VIS Publication Renouf, 1983.

SCHUMACHER, E. F. *Small Is Beautiful.* New York: Harper & Row, 1973.

SHANKLAND, GRAEME. *Wonted Work, A Guide to the Informal Economy.* New York: Bootstrap Press, 1988.

UL HAQ, MABUB, ed. *Human Development Report.* New York: United Nations Development Program, 1990, 1991, 1992.

WARING, MARILYN. *If Women Counted.* San Francisco: Harper & Row, 1989.

Hazel Henderson

Information Overload

It is well known that the primary force driving the world economy and most other aspects of society is the flood of new information and knowledge. General information doubling time occurs about every 2.5 years (each 900 days).

As of the mid-1990s, 90 percent of all the scientists who ever lived are still alive. Scientific information doubles about every 12 years (1994). The number of scientific articles, as such, doubled every 5.5 years during the early 1980s. The number of scholarly scientific journals rose from 70,000 in 1970 to 108,590 in 1990. One million papers published in mathematics found their way into the literature between 1984 and 1994. Scientific knowledge itself doubles every decade or so. More scientific knowledge has been produced since 1960 than was produced in all history prior to 1960. This is generating a torrent of information and fostering a trend toward specialization.

Since the mid-1950s, science has learned more about how the world and universe work than had been learned in the previous 5,000 years. By the year 2000, the base of scientific knowledge is likely to grow by 200 percent. In 1945 we could identify two galaxies. Today we can identify 2 billion galaxies. We even seem to have made contact with radiation left over from what some scientists consider to be the Big Bang, which took place perhaps fifteen billion years ago. Thus it appears that we may have established a direct link with the beginnings of time and space.

Earth's galaxy, the Milky Way as we call it, is comprised of 250 billion to 400 billion stars. It is only a single galaxy of 100 billion galaxies within our universe. There may be 10,000 to 100,000 advanced civilizations in this galaxy alone! Carl Sagan estimates that up to one million technical civilizations may exist in Earth's galaxy alone. If we are alone—and we may know the answer within the next twenty-five to fifty years—that poses an enormous responsibility. If we are only one of millions, that, too, is equally mind-boggling. One thing for certain is that a little humility as well as awe are in order. Whatever the outcome, the immensity of, the sheer magnitude of knowledge throughout an expanding universe is awesome to contemplate.

The number of printed articles soars. More than 12,000 magazines were published in America in 1990. Over the same period, 350,000 new books were published worldwide. The number of books in our leading libraries doubles every fourteen years. Literature overall doubles every ten to fifteen years.

This torrent of new knowledge means that most technology is obsolete within five to seven years. In certain areas, particularly computers and electronics, technology becomes obsolete usually within two to three years.

The pace of technological catch-up is so fast that a company has to recover its production costs in three to six months on a new electronic product, for example. After that, rivals will have produced a competitive look-alike for the market. As product life cycles are getting shorter (half of what they were a decade ago), corporations are seeking greater flexibility. Technology is changing so quickly that companies do not necessarily want to tie themselves down to making a particular product. Joint ventures and other alliances offer far more flexibility in a fast-changing environment.

Accelerating growth of knowledge looked at in another manner means that by the time a child born today finishes college, knowledge may have increased fourfold. By the time that person reaches fifty years of age, accumulated knowledge may have grown thirty-two fold. It means that 97 percent of all knowledge will have been acquired since that person was born.

Increased Speed of Communication

Long-distance transmission of data has accelerated from two bits per second by smoke signals to unbelievable new speeds. Beams of light, for example, may transmit a mind-boggling one million times more information in a given unit of time than present radio wave technology. Electromagnetic fields conceptualized as beams of light change polarity approximately one trillion times per second. The ability to transmit bits of data on light waves at rates of one trillion bits per second means that someone could transmit 200,000 average-size books in one second! The Library of Congress's entire 1991 collection of books, amounting to 25 terabits, could be transmitted in just over five minutes (312.5 seconds). A gigabyte (one billionth of a second) is to one second what one second is to 31.7 years. Just as we are becoming familiar with "megabytes" in mere thousandths, technology is ushering in terabytes—rates of data handling equivalent to 1 trillion bits per second.

The first edition of the *Encyclopaedia Britannica*, published in 1771, ran only three volumes in length, with 2,659 pages. The thirty-two volume *Encyclopaedia Britannica*, published in 1993, included 44 million words (300 megabytes) and 23,000 illustrations (600–700 megabytes)—in electrical data processing terms, 1 gigabyte total.

New fiber-optic cables developed during the mid-1990s by AT&T advance transmission capability over today's standard by at least sixteen-fold. By substantially reducing interference between wave-

lengths (colors), the new cables can transmit 80 gigabytes per second. Thus the entire contents of the *Encyclopaedia Britannica* (1 terabit) could be transmitted in about one-eightieth of a second!

Information Overload

The profusion of scientific information has generated a Niagara of information. This cascade of information inundates the American mind daily. A person reading the entire Sunday edition of the *New York Times* would be exposed to more information in that one reading than was absorbed in a lifetime by the average American living in Thomas Jefferson's day. (On November 13, 1987, the *New York Times* published an edition that was 1,612 pages long and contained more than 12 million words.)

By one estimate the amount of information an individual uses in a lifetime is equivalent to 20 billion bits of data. That amount of data can be transmitted in the parsing of a second. In other words, everything one will ever think or say in an entire lifetime can be flicked around the globe in a millisecond.

This onrush of information has brought us to a point where we have more information than we can possibly use. We may have reached the point of what's called "negative information" so much information that the quality of decision is actually decreased. No longer does the assumption that says more information produces better solutions hold. Too much information creates a sense of numbness and discouragement. What is needed is an understanding of the contexts and cultures in which all this information is embedded. In a negative information environment, the very concept of civil society loses focus and form. The civil society is, in part, an outgrowth of human relationships, and the avalanche of information swamping us every day means that we tend to develop "contacts" rather than human relationships, the latter of which are of a deeper quality and character and can only grow over time.

The positive results of all this information are obvious. People's lives have been enriched in countless ways. But we have yet to find a way of compensating for other, less obvious consequences. For example, psychologists tell us that information overload is now a significant cause of mental illness.

In the past, the transmission of information, ideas, and images took place slowly, sometimes taking centuries to move around the world. This gave people time to adjust psychologically to a new information environment. But today, children who use computers in classrooms represent a generation that grows impatient with teachers and parents whose explanations are drawn out or too wordy. Impatience and expectation of perfection from spouse or child is increasing as an attitude of those whose work involves extensive use of computers. Computer operators internalize the computer's standards for speed, accuracy, perfection, and yes or no answers. They show little patience for nuance or ambiguity, and none for error. In an age where students have access to all knowledge by the mere press of a button, how does education develop the judgment and wisdom an individual needs to use that knowledge to best advantage?

The sheer volume of the data confronting us daily—information overload—virtually forces a reduction in our span of focus on events. No human brain can begin to comprehend the sum total of the mass-produced data we generate. Thus we lose context and perspective, and with them, a clear sense of the meaning of the information we amass; the tie between information and human purpose is severed.

Compare this endless stream of data with the elegant simplicity of our basic communication symbols:

- A mere twenty-six letters comprise the English alphabet. Despite the tiny number of symbols, the language derived from them is limitless.
- A scant ten Arabic symbols comprise our number system, yet calculations and manipulation of these numbers into combinations is circumscribed only by time.
- Just twelve notes make up our basic chromatic scale for music, yet infinite combinations are possible.
- From the basic ten commandments, basic tenets of those principles have been recast into well over three million laws, with more coming every day.

The whole of our civilized life has rested on these few communication symbols. This should remind us that human affairs are infinite, not finite; limitless, not limited.

Exponential Rate of Change

Trillions of calculations per second usher in a rate of speed that divorces time from any human comprehension. We solve problems now in seconds that, in bygone ages, would have taken armies of people, working their entire lifetimes, to solve. In a world of super speeds, the human reaction time of 1.5 seconds to push a button is far too slow. Combat jets rely, to a large extent, on machines performing with split-second timing.

The marriage of information and communication technologies has created a new force—telepower—which is the driving force of global change. Computers, telephones, television, faxes, and robots—connected by wire or satellites—constitute the largest technical machine in the world. In terms of technology, the telecommunications industry is going to see more change in the next six years than it has seen in the past ninety-four years.

Building the next phase of the American Experiment requires a new form of leadership. And that's because instant information has virtually eliminated the knowledge gap between the leaders and the led.

One thing has become clear: The more information we amass, the more important context and meaning become. We live in two worlds—the world of data and the world of meaning. Knowledge does not exist in a vacuum. It always moves forward and demands the application of meaning.

Meaning requires reflection and time-consuming thought. In this respect, Harvard Business School, AT&T, Pepsi, Aetna, and numerous other companies are training managers in the exercise of reflection, in various forms of inner awareness. This is based on the belief that the key trait of a good leader is having an inward center of reflection from which to make considered decisions. While information agents such as "wildfire" may help filter out overload, such an inward center can only emanate from an internal search in life that has noting to do with technology.

As life becomes more information-driven, it becomes more essential for each manager to know how to provide his or her personnel with the requisite meaning and context.

See also COMMUNICATIONS TECHNOLOGY; INFORMATION SOCIETY; INFORMATION TECHNOLOGY; LIBRARIES; LIBRARIES: ELECTRONIC FORMATS; TELECOMMUNICATIONS.

BIBLIOGRAPHY

BATHURST, DIANA, and BATHURST, ROBIN. *The Telling Image: The Changing Balance Between Pictures and Words in a Technological Age.* Oxford, UK: Oxford University Press, 1990.

GLASTONBURY, BRYAN, and LEMENDELA, WALTER. *The Integrity of Intelligence: A Bill of Rights for the Information Age.* New York: St. Martin's Press, 1992.

McLuhan, Marshall, with introduction by Lewis H. Lapham. *Understanding Media: The Extensions of Man.* Reprint. Cambridge, MA: MIT Press, 1994.

Postman, Neil. *Technopoly.* New York: Alfred A. Knopf, 1992.

Sakaiya, Neil. *The Knowledge-Value Revolution.* New York: Kodansha America, 1991.

Wurman, Richard Saul. *Information Anxiety.* New York: Bantam Books, 1989.

Graham T. T. Molitor
William Van Dusen Wishard

Information Society

Information society, service society, postindustrial society, technological society, computer society, knowledge society—all of these terms are labels that attempt to make sense of the profound transformation wracking industrial societies since the mid-1950s. Regardless of which label is used, the central assertion is that industrial societies are evolving into a new form of society.

While the term *postindustrial* first appeared in print in 1917, the term *information society* was not used until 1968. *Service society*, describing a slightly different economic base, was the preferred term in the 1970s. Peter Drucker referred to our *knowledge society* in 1969. The earliest substantial book on a knowledge-based society is Daniel Bell's 1973 *The Coming of Postindustrial Society*, although nowhere therein does he actually refer to the phrase *information society*. The Organization for Economic Cooperation and Development published a report entitled *The Information Society* in 1975, and by the early 1980s the term *information society* started to come into common use, prompting John NAISBITT to declare in 1982 that "it is now clear that the postindustrial society is the information society" (Naisbitt, 1982, p. 4).

Even today there is no widely accepted formal definition of either the industrial or the information stages of socioeconomic development. However, the following features are commonly used to distinguish between them:

- *Industrial societies* are dominated by blue-collar workers who labor in large organizations under close supervision, using industrial technologies to process physical materials in order to mass-produce physical goods. Few of these goods require high levels of information or information technologies to design, manufacture, sell, or maintain.

- *Information societies* are dominated by team-based knowledge workers who add value by strategically utilizing high-quality information in the creation of goods, services, and relationships. All of these undertakings require high levels of information and information technologies to create, market, and maintain.

Two major developments—one technological, the other human—dominate information society discussions: The first is the emergence of powerful, computer-based information technologies that for the first time in history make the sharing of information, regardless of its form or content, cheap, easy, and distance-independent. The second is the corollary requirement that, in order to sustain success, individuals, organizations, and societies must develop an ability to routinely utilize high-quality information and to do so strategically.

These are startling developments when seen against the taken-for-granted world of the mid-twentieth century. Then, communications and travel over long distances were occasions for excitement; personal long-distance phone calls, always operator-dialed, often meant very special circumstances such as births, deaths, or a year-end holiday. Boundaryless networks of self-managed work teams did not exist and were in fact virtually unimaginable.

Diverse developments heralded the demise of the industrial order:

- In 1954 only twenty computers were shipped to customers in the United States. In Europe, in 1958, only 160 computers were in use. In contrast, by the early 1990s, 140 million personal computers were in use worldwide, and over 400 million microprocessors were embedded in autos, telephones, televisions, and a variety of appliances. By 1994, the Internet had over 30 million users worldwide.

- In the mid-1950s, 80 percent of the cost of a new car represented materials and wages. The cost of services and information—design, marketing, engineering, management, and health care—accounted for the rest. By the mid-1980s, these ratios had reversed.

- In 1956, for the first time, white-collar workers outnumbered blue-collar workers in the United States. This date, well before the advent of the microprocessor, is customarily used to mark the arrival of the information society in the United States.

- By the early 1990s, national politics, professional sports, entertainment, and evangelism had all developed a significant dependence on their electronic audiences. Live performances still brought in substantial sums, but proportionally much less than previously.

- By the early 1990s, every form of information—data, text, pictures, sound, art—could be fully digitized and therefore integrated. The familiar distinctions among media delivery systems—computers, telephones, cable, radio, CDs, wireless, publishing, movies, and databases—were becoming increasingly blurred.

- By 1991 computer hardware and software exports from the United States were almost $48 billion—more than double the value of exported autos and auto parts ($22 billion).

- In 1993, Americans spent $341 billion on entertainment and recreation, almost ten cents of every nonmedical consumer dollar. This was more than the worldwide value of computer hardware and software sales ($300 billion). The amount of information available continues to double roughly every five years.

Such far-reaching developments herald the end of the industrialized world as we have known it. The significance of such events began to be apparent by the 1970s. Reports were commissioned by governments: e.g., the 1972 Computer-Communications Task Force report of the government of Canada. National policy conferences were organized—e.g., the annual Telecommunications Policy Review Conference, first held in 1973. Journals were established such as *The Information Society*, which appeared in 1981. Consultants developed management information systems (MIS). Database libraries were created—e.g., Dialog and Lockheed in the late 1960s. Computer-conferencing systems were developed: Internet in the 1970s.

In the 1970s and '80s, many people welcomed the information age, whether or not they really understood its significance. Others, however, worried about the negative effects of the emerging informational order. The sheer volume of information that could be created, stored, and accessed, many people felt, would prove to be unmanageable. There was much talk about the "mass production" of information, the "information explosion," and the possibility of informational overload or "infoglut." People were also concerned about the number of blue-collar and clerical jobs that would be lost because of the widespread use of information technologies. (Interestingly, though, the decimation of middle management, now a reality, was seldom foreseen.) There was fear, too, that privacy might be severely threatened, that individuals would be

depersonalized, and that a centralized surveillance society might develop. As if confirming this, there was bold talk about the need for public bodies to exert control over these new technologies and determine who would benefit from their use. The "new world-information order" discussed by developing nations at the United Nations was but one example. Few persons then understood that in an information society such control by governments or others would become increasingly difficult.

In the twenty-first century, similar discussions may be dominated by considerations such as the following:

- Because knowledge is inherently a personal, social, and cultural creation, an information society is ultimately more, not less, personal than an industrial society. This means that an information society requires new epistemological foundations—a new understanding of what knowledge is, how it is created, and how it is validated. Knowledge can no longer be seen merely as complex information. Rather, knowledge is information that has been internalized and made useful by users.

- Knowledge-in-use, not merely the possession of information, is the key to sustained success in every area of life. The new challenge—for individuals, families, organizations, or societies—is not merely to possess quality information but to digest it and put it to use.

- Attention is increasingly focused on the creation, testing, and use of knowledge and not merely on the technologies by which we possess and transmit information. This human dimension is revealed in the growing preoccupation with the formation of subcultures—within families, organizations, or societies—that are able to sustain self-critical learning and self-monitored performance.

- The most profound question facing the information society is this: When many citizens are well educated, widely traveled, and linked to quality sources of information, how can sound and binding judgments and consensus be developed? Increasingly, it is apparent that this can no longer be achieved by the assertion of one's authority—technical or structural—or by the use of majority votes. Unconvinced minorities now undercut virtually every majority decision. Yet a community will disintegrate and become ungovernable without the capacity to create and act upon knowledge which is commonly accepted. Survival as free persons and societies requires a much greater capacity than is now possessed by any industrial society to democratically deliberate, to cocreate, and to achieve consensus.

The ultimate challenge facing us in our transition to an information society, therefore, is to mature into a truly responsible, deeply thoughtful democracy.

See also COMMUNICATIONS; COMMUNICATIONS TECHNOLOGY; COMPUTERS: OVERVIEW; EVOLUTION, SOCIAL; GLOBAL PARADOX; ILLITERACY, INFORMATION OVERLOAD; INFORMATION TECHNOLOGY; INTELLECTUAL PROPERTY; LANGUAGES; LITERATURE; MULTIFOLD TREND; TELECOMMUNICATIONS; WORKFORCE DIVERSITY.

BIBLIOGRAPHY

BELL, DANIEL. *The Coming of Post-Industrial Society: A Venture in Social Forecasting.* New York: Basic Books, 1973.

CLEVELAND, HARLAN. *The Knowledge Executive.* New York: E. P. Dutton, 1985.

DRUCKER, PETER F. *The New Realities.* New York: Harper & Row, 1989.

NAISBITT, JOHN. *Megatrends: Ten New Directions Transforming Our Lives.* New York: Warner Books, 1984.

ROSELL, STEVEN A., ed. *Governing in an Information Society.* Montreal: Institute for Research on Public Policy, 1992.

ZUBOFF, SHOSHANA. *In the Age of the Smart Machine: The Future of Work and Power.* New York: Basic Books, 1988.

Ruben F. W. Nelson

Information Technology

Information technology will shape the future, because information is central to the organization and coordination of social activities. Technology that supports and extends the ability to generate, use, transmit, and store information will grow in importance as social institutions continue to become more complex, powerful, and global. The term *information technology* spans the inventions of writing, the printing press, nineteenth-century telegraphy and telephony, and now includes computers, telecommunications, and dependent technologies such as software, computerized databases, numerically controlled machines, and robots.

Driving Forces

Rapid development of information technology since 1950 has been driven by the burgeoning services sector of the economies in postindustrial nations. Most services, beyond those of simple personal or domestic labor, involve the generation, processing, dissemination, or transmission of information.

"Technology push"—the imperative to develop new areas of technology long before useful applications are identified—drove the early years of information technology. "Market pull," or response to corporate and consumer demand, drives present and future developments. The development of global markets and transnational enterprise further reinforces the demand for information technology. Most large corporations have national or even global telecommunications and computer networks.

Long-Range Technological Trends

Four phases of computer development have occurred: large central mainframes for scientific research and then for institutional data management; personal computers and decentralized data processing; networking of personal computers within organizations; and the convergence of computing and communicating technology and the creation of farflung networks. Consistently information technology is becoming more powerful, faster, and cheaper. Other dominant trends include development of packaged easy-to-use software so that users need less training, increasing compatibility of systems enabling interconnecting components from many sources; and increasing mobility enhanced by the development of portable computers, cellular telephones, and similar devices.

Distinctions between computing and communicating technologies have become progressively blurred: telephone switches are really computers; data flow from computer to computer over cables also may carry voice, graphics, and video signals; information is switched from satellite to microwave to cable channels by computer controllers and routers; the household telephone touch-tone pad serves as a computer input device. Information technology has become both more versatile (a single workstation may function as computer, telephone, fax, printer, and copier) and more specialized (computer chips embedded in household appliances or a plastic "smart card"). Enormous interconnected computerized databases have become a striking characteristic of modern society.

Other technological trends that will shape the future of the technology are the digitization of data and their "capture at the source," the evolution of artificial intelligence, and the search for new interfaces between people and information machines.

Increasingly, useful information—whether in the form of text, numerics, sound, images, or pictures—is "digitized" or converted to binary signals that can be manipulated, stored, transmitted, and reconverted using information technologies. This common machine language enables data to pass from computer to computer through telecommunications networks without human handling. Data are increasingly captured at the source by electronic scanners, bar code readers, or consumer input (e.g., at automated teller machines, voting machines, and the like). Among the third-order effects are reduced demand for clerical labor (so-called technological unemployment) and the creation of interconnected data banks that contribute greatly to scientific research, corporate productivity, and government efficiency. One disturbing threat posed involves the invasion of individual privacy.

Artificial intelligence, or the emulation of human mental functions by computers, has progressed to the point that knowledge and decision-rules gleaned from experts are available to nonspecialists through interactive software packages. Work continues to equip computers and robots, physically active forms of information technology, with sensors and effectors allowing them to perform many routine human tasks.

Outlook for Information Technology

New advances are likely in person-machine interfaces, artificial intelligence, advanced processing, and miniaturization. So that information technology can be thoroughly integrated into nearly all kinds of human activity, the present cumbersome and restricting channels of interaction between people and technology—keyboards, mouses, number pads, artificial languages, and stationary display screens—will be eliminated. Computer voice recognition and generation, long promised advances, are on the verse of major breakthroughs. Optical character recognition (computer scanning of printed material) also should improve. "Virtual reality" is being developed to combine computer capabilities and human sensibilities in a three-dimensional interface that uses goggles, gloves, and other appliances to allow people to interact with computer-manipulated perceived environments.

We can expect greater ability to store, manipulate, and transmit both two-dimensional and three-dimensional (holographic) images; high definition imaging systems for medical and other important applications as well as for television are already close at hand. Near-term advances can be expected in parallel and neural net processing. In order to escape what now look like ultimate limits on speed and size-reduction, scientists are developing ways to build molecule-scale computers (nanotechnology) and photonic computers, which will use light rays rather than electrons.

Information technology will become more pervasive in two ways. As passive technology, computer chips will increasingly make familiar objects and surroundings (from kitchen tools to automobiles) more responsive to users' needs. Actively manipulated computers, no longer tied to a desk and requiring no more specialized knowledge than is necessary for telephoning or driving an automobile, will increasingly be used in a wide range of household, sports, consumer, and educational activities. Computer systems will become, like traffic lights and public telephone booths, part of the social infrastructure serving the community as a whole.

Impacts on Employment, Industry, and Government

Growing demand for information in developing nations and slow-to-modernize industries (such as mining, education, and aids for the disabled) should create many future jobs. Some experts argue that increasing productivity and encouragement of innovation through information technology will benefit most production and services sectors, reducing the costs of consumer goods and stimulating economic growth. Others, pointing out that demand for information may not be indefinitely insatiable, expect eventual reductions in white-collar employment. This would result from elimination of much clerical work associated with keyboarding, a reduced need for middle-level managers, and computer support or substitution for professional tasks such as diagnosis, research, auditing, and drafting.

Many industries face restructuring as technological change introduces new competitive rivalries. For example, banks now operate electronic networks, telecommunications operators offer financial services in competition with banks, cable television providers may be allowed to transmit telephone messages, and television companies may offer a wide range of videotext and other information services.

Consequences for People and Institutions

Both electronic databases and remote sensors (another type of information technology) pose intrusions on individual privacy and otherwise increase the potential for the misuse of personal information. Safeguarding "intellectual property" (the unique representation of artistic, scientific, or intellectual work, traditionally protected by copyrights or patents) has been compromised by the new capability to copy or change such work, even with inexpensive home equipment. Decision-support technology, such as models, decision systems, and expert systems, can be misused to the harm of individuals or groups—for example, models for predicting criminal recidivism that use race or ethnic origin as indicators. Such Information Era issues may become increasingly troublesome in the future.

Information technology is inherently democratizing because it makes state monopoly of information difficult to maintain. At the same time, it could foster economic elitism if important information, once widely shared in simpler societies, is increasingly digitized, commercialized, and accessible only through technology that may not be universally available. Zbigniew Brzezinski and George ORWELL have anticipated that future society may be the privileged domain of "technocrats" whose power is based on information rather than birth, property, or armed force. Daniel BELL pictured these experts somewhat less threateningly as a "meritocratic elite." Nevertheless, these and many more recent thinkers agree that we have entered an age of information, and the way that we organize and manage information technology will determine how good or bad that future will be.

See also ARTIFICIAL INTELLIGENCE; COMMUNICATIONS; COMPUTERS: OVERVIEW; DIGITAL COMMUNICATIONS; INFORMATION OVERLOAD; INFORMATION SOCIETY; MULTIFOLD TREND; NANOTECHNOLOGY; TECHNOLOGICAL CHANGE; TECHNOLOGICAL INNOVATION; TECHNOLOGY DIFFUSION; TELECOMMUNICATIONS.

BIBLIOGRAPHY

BELL, DANIEL. *The Coming of Post-Industrial Society: A Venture in Social Forecasting.* New York: Basic Books, 1973.

BRZEZINSKI, ZBIGNIEW. *Between Two Ages: America's Role in the Technetronic Age.* New York: Viking Press, 1968.

LEEBAERT, DEREK, ed. *Technology 2001: The Future of Computing and Communications.* Cambridge, MA: The MIT Press, 1991.

SOLA POOL, ITHIEL DE. *Technologies of Freedom.* Boston: Harvard University Press, 1983.

(The views expressed in this article are solely the responsibility of the author and not those of the Office of Technology Assessment or its governing board.)

Vary T. Coates

Institutions, Confidence in

Business, government, education, and other social institutions can be thought of as the major organs of the body politic, and public support of them is essential. Surveys are conducted periodically to assess the confidence people place in those institutions. Despite differences among various institutions and nations, decline has swept across most institutions over the past two decades. Confidence fell by more than half during this period, declining a combined average of 48 percent in 1966 to 22 percent in 1992. While nearly a majority of Americans once felt confident toward key institutions, currently only a small minority express confidence in government, major companies, educational, and other major institutions.

The meaning of this decline is open to controversy because it involves many diverse causes. Historically it reflects the passing of a simpler "Industrial Age" which prevailed at least through the 1950s when approval of institutions was high because they served the needs of the time. Social disorders of the 1960s marked the onset of a postindustrial society or an information age, which introduced a new economic order based, among other things, on television, global communications, computer networks, and other powerful new information technologies.

As a result of this historic shift, people have become better educated and ever more critical just when these old industrial-based structures are unable to cope with the emerging, knowledge-based global economy. Changes wrought by this shift are so pervasive that they also were responsible for the collapse of authoritarian governments in the Communist bloc. Lech Walesa contended that the underlying force that powered the revolutionary reforms in Poland were the result of computers, communication satellites, and television.

Trust in the U.S. government has eroded steadily since the Reagan Revolution, reaching a new low in 1992, when Congress and the President proved unable to control federal spending to reduce the budget deficit, revitalize the economy, or resolve other key issues. Business confidence decline may be ascribed to eroding global dominance of companies like GM and IBM, heightened competition, and overconcern with short-term profits that often places them at odds with environmental protection, employee welfare, and other long-term public interests. Education also has been widely criticized for failing to train young people for a modern world. A recent study ranked American student achievement at the bottom of the list of industrialized nations.

Other institutions suffer from similar problems. Military services may be an exception, owing to public approval of the military's performance in the Gulf War.

Public discontent manifested by these declines also exerts pressure for innovative reforms. A mere 33 percent of voters bothered to vote in the midterm 1990 congressional elections. Roughly forty states are resorting to a more entrepreneurial form of government in order to rejuvenate economic progress and, hopefully, more effectively serve public needs. Corporate structural changes introduced since the 1980s include decentralization of large bureaucratic companies like IBM into flexible systems composed of small internal enterprises. "Quasi-democratic" business forms in which managers collaborate with their employees, customers, suppliers, and government have been introduced in firms like the Saturn division of GM. Education also is on the verge of historic change. Some communities are permitting students a choice of schools in order to replace the former bureaucracy with market accountability, and a new concept of local control is emerging in which teachers, parents, and educators work together on policies to mange schools.

Three scenarios seem most likely as these conflicting forces of declining confidence grapple with change. Perpetuating the status quo of low confidence in a slowly declining society, it is possible that many institutions will remain unaffected by these innovations. There is also the possibility that the situation will deteriorate to such an extent that all public confidence will collapse and a state of crisis may come into being. A third possibility is that there will be a progressive swing in national opinion that will stimulate a major restructuring of institutions, thereby producing a broader social renaissance of sorts.

Environmental scanning suggests the likelihood of some type of major transition in American institutions during the 1990s, as is summarized in the following list:

- *Liberal phase in the political cycle.* Historian Arthur Schlesinger, Jr., has described a twelve- to thirty-year cycle in American politics alternating between liberalism and conservatism, between public purpose and private interest, with a new phase of progressive change likely to occur in the mid- to late 1990s.
- *Move to social values.* Author Tom Wolfe, who predicted the "me-decade" of the 1970s and the "money madness" of the 1980s, now sees a swing toward social values. "There will be a lot of dis-

cussion in the '90s about morality," he said recently, "and it has already begun."
- *Revival of political activism.* Robert Teeter, chief opinion analyst for President George Bush, thinks the nation is heading toward a revival of political activism akin to the disorders of the 1960s.
- *Rise of economic populism.* Kevin Phillips, a political analyst who invented the successful Republican "southern strategy," counsels that a "political counterreaction" is coming, "a resurgence of economic populism based on a concern over the decline of the U.S. economy, and maldistribution of income among the super-rich.
- *Shift in power structures.* Futurist Alvin TOFFLER anticipates a coming "powershift" to a decentralized, participatory social order driven by today's revolution in information technology. This agrees with the views of Frank Doyle, a senior GE executive who claims that "the power of the nineties will be people power."
- *Transition to a new paradigm.* Futurists Herman KAHN and Willis Harman began stressing that a paradigm shift was underway during the 1970s. *Time* magazine noted, "The 1990s has become a transforming boundary between one age and another, between a scheme of things that has disintegrated and another taking shape." The industrial paradigm—a rational, technocratic, linear, quantitative, materialistic, utilitarian, male-centered model—is being replaced by another model based on collaboration, common good, global concern, pluralism, and critical dialogue.
- *Institutional changes.* Studies show that widespread institutional changes are underway. Surveys of scholars and executives in the United States, Europe, and Japan concur that a more entrepreneurial, participative "New Capitalism" is emerging and should enter the mainstream during the next five to ten years.

According to this viewpoint, the United States appears to be heading toward a major turning point as increasing dissatisfaction strengthens the resolve of liberals to confront the conservative policies that have dominated over the past two decades.

Environmental scanning also indicates a growing consensus in favor of a "powershift" involving decentralized, democratic institutional forms suitable for a new era and roughly similar to the "Renaissance" scenario. The transformation of the former Soviet Union into a modern society, despite all the uncertainty ahead, illustrates the enormous power of historic change when the time has arrived.

Today's movement of communist states to free markets and democracy, the imminent unfication of Europe, and the emergence of a global economy are an essential part of this historic transition, which is causing wrenching institutional changes all around the world. The Industrial Revolution introduced similar transitions, so this process in not unprecedented. Current trends indicate that the early phase of this societal restructuring is underway. Barring unforeseen events, the forecasts summarized here suggest that institutions are reforming in ways that may restore public confidence over the next decade or so.

See also CHANGE; CHANGE, CULTURAL; CHANGE, OPTIMISTIC AND PESSIMISTIC PERSPECTIVES; CIVIL PROTEST; CONTINUITY AND DISCONTINUITY; GLOBAL CULTURE; GLOBAL TURNING POINTS; INFORMATION OVERLOAD; INSTITUTIONS AND ORGANIZATIONS; MEDIA CONSOLIDATION; PUBLIC OPINION POLLS; SOCIAL CHANGE: UNITED STATES.

BIBLIOGRAPHY

BELL, DANIEL. *The Coming of Post-Industrial Society*. New York: Basic Books, 1973.

CETRON, MARVIN, and DAVIES, OWEN. *American Renaissance: Life at the Turn of the 21st Century*. New York; St. Martin's Press, 1989.

DOYLE, DENIS. "America 2000." *Phi Delta Kappan* 73/33 (November 1991): 185–191.

HALAL, WILLIAM E. *The New Capitalism*. New York: John Wiley, 1986.

————. "The New Management: Business and Social Institutions for an Information Age." *Business in the Contemporary World* (Winter 1990).

LIPSET, SEYMOUR MARTIN, and SCHNEIDER, WILLIAM. *The Confidence Gap: Business, Labor, and Government in the Public Mind*. New York: Free Press, 1983.

OSBORNE, DAVID, and GAEBLER, TED. *Reinventing Government*. Reading, MA: Addison-Wesley, 1992.

SCHLESINGER, ARTHUR M., JR. *The Cycles of American History*. Boston: Houghton-Mifflin, 1986.

TOFFLER, ALVIN. *Powershift*. New York: Bantam, 1990.

VICKERS, GEOFFREY. *Making Institutions Work*. New York: John Wiley, 1973.

YANKELOVICH, DANIEL. *The New Morality: A Profile of American Youth in the '70s*. New York; McGraw-Hill, 1974.

William E. Halal

Institutions and Organizations

People create organizations and negotiate rules, rights, and responsibilities to govern their activities. Organizations allow people to combine their knowledge, skills, and resources and to allocate tasks among the participants, who benefit from greater accomplishment than they could achieve individually. They also share in the profits and losses, acclaims, and defeats resulting from their collective actions. Thus organizations are built on collaborative relationships established by agreement to carry out recurring specified transactions. Groups of organizations that perform similar social and economic functions are called institutions, such as churches and religion, or banks and banking.

Spanning Traditional Boundaries to Create Networked Institutions for the Future

In earlier eras, most relationships and transactions occurred within a local marketplace, with only a few national institutions. In the twentieth century, relationships and markets expanded to a national scale, with hierarchical industrial organizations such as automobile companies dominating. People migrated from communities to cities where the factories and jobs were located.

In the past few decades, the technological capacity to quickly move ideas, information, financial resources, and products and services across global boundaries has encouraged the formation of new types of relationships and transactions. Thinking and acting internationally, as well as nationally and locally, is now possible and often necessary.

The transformation of long-distance travel and communications illustrates forces prompting these changes. Industrial era society was dependent upon railroads, highways, airlines, and telephones organized with rigid structures and dominated by a few huge companies. Our modern society is shifting to a wide array of services for moving people, information, and materials while providing individuals and business the means to design their own routes and timing relative to needs and budgets. Meeting basic mobility needs is now the end purpose of numerous organizations working in networked relationships to provide continuous worldwide service, including transportation reservation systems; airport and airline operating systems; and hotels, rental cars, food service, telecommunications, police and protection services, and local transportation services.

Central to the change in organizations from hierarchies to networks is the shift of the "middle manager" from controller to boundary spanner. In rigidly hierarchical relationships, the middle levels control the processes, which are highly structured and routinized. Relationships are defined by the design and rules of the process—a manufacturing task or the processing of an item of information. Beyond the designers of such systems most people's knowledge is limited to the domain of the specific tasks they perform. There is no need to know about the entire process or the overarching social purpose of the organization. Contact with people in other parts of the organization and other organizations is minimal. This approach makes optimal use of physical plants and equipment, which is the bedrock infrastructure of industrial organizations. Rigorous control to reduce the risk of deviation from norms requires close supervision performed by layers of middle managers. Large inventories and available, unemployed people provide backup to reduce the risk of running out of resources or production capability to meet changing demand. People are a resource in the industrial processes. This industrial model for institutions continues to dominate today, in part because many people prefer the perceived security of such long-standing, bureaucratic organizations.

The new era of networked relationships will require the spanning of boundaries across organizations, disciplines, cultures, and time. In a commercial setting, the connections among diverse groups must be managed—each with the capability of providing only part of the products and services required to seamlessly meet customers' needs. Networks and boundary spanning require that all participants have a general understanding of essential needs and of the integrated capacity of the network, so they can contribute most effectively and efficiently. Networked organizations are driving the creation of "hyphenated disciplines" such as bio-engineering, the growth of multidisciplinary fields such as ecology, and the search for new leadership capabilities for integrating and guiding—but not controlling—the networks across new frontiers with clear and shared visions of just what is possible.

Networks are built upon mutual respect, and the sharing of information, ideas, and trust. Creating or joining a global networked organization means respecting both emerging international norms and diverse cultures with their varying foundation of rights and responsibilities. This does *not* mean imposing U.S. norms on other cultures. The U.S. government, businesses, and American interest groups are working with representatives of other countries to adopt common international rules for trade and investment that will allow unrestricted flows of goods, services, and investments among nations. Similar international work is addressing ways to

strengthen mutual security, to achieve basic human rights for everyone, and to protect the environment while developing at sustainable levels. At the same time, the United States is changing its rules and practices to conform to the new international standards and is working with individual countries to seek compliance and resolve disputes. Multinational institutions such as the World Trade Organization provide a means to achieve a consensus on rules for international relationships and transactions and to resolve disputes that cannot be settled directly.

"Real time" is a central concept for this new era. Long lead and lag times are inherent in industrial processes, which are by nature slow to change and lack mobility. Today, information about changing conditions is broadcast worldwide continuously, reaching everyone at the same time. The challenge is to be able to respond quickly to new opportunities, while avoiding or minimizing new threats. Networks have substantial capabilities for meeting these types of challenges. Because participants share information and ideas, their collective knowledge base can be used for anticipating changes and considering alternative actions, as well as acting quickly when changes do occur. Similarly, commercial networks are better able to meet changes in customers' needs quickly by altering priorities and reconfiguring flows rather than waiting for the activation of excess capacity (unemployed people and unused plants). Operating in real time requires flexible, dynamic, and trusting relationships.

Peter Drucker's idea of the "network society" (summarized in *The Wall Street Journal*, March 29, 1995) emphasizes these changes. He argues that increasingly, people will not be employees of organizations, but contractors, part-timers, and temporary workers. Among businesses, alliances and consortia are among the techniques that will be used increasingly to build partnership rather than ownership connections. Drucker says that "in a partnership one cannot command. One can only gain trust."

Institutional Change in the Future

Organizations engaged in change throughout the world use terms such as *restructuring, reinventing, reengineering, outsourcing, rightsizing, privatizing, deregulation,* and *liberalization.* What is involved is disintegrating obsolete institutions and integrating new ones, although most change has been in the direction of disintegration. Businesses are cutting layers of middle managers, outsourcing functions that others can perform better, selling units that are incompatible with core businesses, reengineering processes to make them more efficient, and changing policies to set the stage for integration of the remaining functions into networks. Similarly, governments are deregulating; privatizing functions that can be performed by businesses; and restructuring policies and programs to shift greater responsibility to individuals and business. For example, after the collapse of the Soviet Union, the former communist countries are restructuring their policies, institutions, and organizations to comply with international norms and become more fully integrated into global institutions and markets.

Creating networked organizations that have global capabilities requires expanding the foundation of rights, responsibilities, and rule of law upon which they are built. This is being done through changes in national laws, development of new legal systems in the nations in transition from communism, and through international treaty institutions. Changing the rules of the game is the work of political institutions. Throughout the world, they are under pressure to overhaul policies and programs as well as to provide relief and assistance to the people and organizations affected by changing conditions. Political institutions are always the battleground of special interests. They are the places where consensus is developed or where gridlock and barriers to change are played out. In transformational processes, political institutions normally are better able to adapt policy to fit a redefined world based on a clear demonstration of what that world might look like. Thus, pioneering organizations are those that are able to overcome barriers and invent new institutions of value that meet people's basic needs and provide a benchmark for changing the rules of the game. Businesses and governmental institutions are now in the midst of such transformational processes, and this process is likely to dominate legislative bodies and international treaty institutions for another decade or more.

Education and training for working effectively in these new networked institutions are at the core of transition-support services. This in turn will require the restructuring of education and training institutions to become institutional change leaders and focal points for transition-support services. The critical resources of organizations—their infrastructure—are their human knowledge, boundary-spanning skills, and trust-building capabilities. Ac-

quiring the ability to learn and work collaboratively is critical to the success of individuals and organizations.

Other Futures Are Possible

The changes described here are based on fuller use of existing technologies, primarily the integrated use of computer, communications, and management technologies. Breakthroughs in biotechnology, energy capabilities, and materials could reinforce or shift the direction of development. Similarly, failure to control the proliferation of weapons of mass destruction, to contain ethnic conflicts and terrorist actions, and to continue the process of liberalizing international trading and investment practices while integrating the countries in transition into the global economy could undermine progress in human development and alter the opportunities available to individuals and organizations. Without doubt, we are living in interesting, uncertain, and challenging times.

See also BUSINESS GOVERNANCE; BUSINESS STRUCTURE: FORMS, IMPACTS; GLOBAL BUSINESS: DOMINANT ORGANIZATIONAL FORMS; INSTITUTIONS, CONFIDENCE IN.

BIBLIOGRAPHY

COWHEY, PETER F., and ARONSON, JONATHAN D. *Managing the World Economy: The Consequences of Corporate Alliances.* New York: Council on Foreign Relations Press, 1993.

DICKEN, PETER. *Global Shift: The Internationalization of Economic Activity.* New York: The Guildford Press, 1992.

DRUCKER, PETER. "The Network Society." *Wall Street Journal,* March 29, 1995.

DUNNING, JOHN H. *The Globalization of Business: The Challenge of the 1990s.* New York: Routledge, 1993.

Kenneth W. Hunter

Insurance

Insurance is a social device for managing the financial consequences of risk. The future of insurance depends on the risks faced by individuals and organizations in the future and on the decisions made about the use of alternative devices for managing risks and allocating the costs of uncertain events.

Risks are created by the environment. Although death may be certain, its time and financial consequences are uncertain. In addition, financial losses due to illness, accidents, fires, storms, earthquakes, and economic fluctuations are inevitable, but their size and timing are uncertain.

Society creates incentives for individuals and organizations to adopt safety and loss-prevention measures. Beyond that, systems are adopted for allocating the costs of risk events that persist despite efforts to reduce their frequency and severity. These costs can fall on individuals, families, businesses, governments, or on special-purpose financial security (insurance) organizations created to pool the costs. The allocation system selected usually depends on the degree of economic development of the society and its political organization. For example, the replacement of earned income because of premature death might be borne by the family in an agricultural society, by a life insurance company in an industrial market economy, or by government in a socialist state. Similarly, health care costs can be allocated through the tax structure, individual payments to health care providers, insurance premiums, or reduced wages.

Trends

Insurance is shaped by the same forces that form other aspects of a society:

MORTALITY

Mortality has declined in Europe and North America for more than five hundred years. In the past century, the rate of decline has been especially significant. In the first seventy years of the century, the decline was largely among the young because of improved sanitation, nutrition, and medical advances against infectious diseases. In the last twenty-five years, the improvement has been in the middle and older ages and is attributable primarily to success against cardiovascular diseases.

HEALTH COSTS

The allocation of income to purchase health care increased in developed nations over the past fifty years. In the United States, approximately 14 percent of gross domestic product went for health care in 1993. Productivity gains in manufacturing and agriculture facilitated this reallocation.

AGING

The combination of reduced mortality and fertility increased the portion of older persons in most developed countries. The rate at which the proportion of the population over age eighty-five is increasing in a given country depends primarily on

when the post–World War II boom in the fertility rate peaked. In the United States the peak occurred in approximately 1960.

TECHNOLOGY

The development of medical technology influenced the cost of health care, and the associated reduction in mortality rates contributed to the aging of the population. New technology also created hazardous wastes and associated disposal costs that must be allocated. Other technical developments now permit the identification and measurement of particular risks, such as radiation, that previously were not readily discernible or were assumed to be a part of general background hazard.

ECONOMIC DEVELOPMENT

The transition from an agricultural to an industrial economy also drove the development of insurance. The costs of risk no longer are borne by families but are absorbed by insurance organizations. Economic development also concentrated risks and increased the severity of losses. Industrial and residential development in coastal areas subject to tropical storms provide examples.

INTERNATIONALIZATION

The growth of global trade is intertwined with economic development and the growth of technology. The internationalization of commerce has increased the demand for insurance to facilitate trade. This was historically the first application of insurance. Internationalization permitted the pooling of losses over the world through reinsurance contracts. It also created a host of regulatory issues when insurance transactions bridge traditional national regulation.

CONSERVATISM

The dominant political trend of the past decade has been toward conservatism and a more individualistic ethic. The collapse of the U.S.S.R., shifts in the political organization of Eastern Europe and election results in the United States and Western Europe affirm this trend. The consequences for the allocation of the costs of risks is a trend away from distribution through the tax structure.

NEW IDEAS

During the past fifty years new ideas in the theory of finance rapidly developed. These developments involved creating models for pricing and managing uncertain future cash flows. This set of new ideas was applied almost immediately in existing financial markets and helped to create new markets such as those for futures and options. It is not known how these ideas will influence insurance management or how insurance markets will be absorbed into general markets for future uncertain cash flows.

Insurance Implications

The study of insurance has traditionally been organized by the nature of the risk insured.

LIFE INSURANCE

The life insurance industry grew in importance both for its role in pooling the costs of premature death and in marshalling savings. These savings have been intended primarily for use in financing old-age income. The relative emphasis in the function of bearing mortality risk and managing savings shifted toward the savings function in recent years. The shift had important implications on managing a life insurance company. The decline in mortality and the prevalence of multiple family members in the work force providing income security retard the growth of the risk-pooling aspect of life insurance. The aging of the population and the decline in the reliance on government and corporate old-age income systems will also give impetus to the role of life insurance companies in marshalling, investing, and dispersing old-age income funds.

OLD-AGE INCOME

In response to the aging of the population, old-age income systems that are funded on a current-cost basis must dramatically increase required contributions. This includes the U.S. Social Security system. To moderate higher contribution rates, increases in the age of normal retirement are expected. Funded old-age income systems can escape increases in required contributions to maintain level real-benefits only if, in the aggregate, their investments succeed in significantly increasing the per capita productivity of the working population.

PROPERTY

Competitive forces work toward an efficient insurance market. In a technically efficient insurance market, premiums are based on expected losses. These market forces tend to provide cost incentives to inhibit building in high-risk areas such as flood plains, earthquake zones, high-crime districts, and coastal areas subject to storms. Regional political pressure that attempts to force insurance prices that are not based on expected losses will continue.

ENVIRONMENTAL RISKS

The costs of environmental degradation have been borne directly or allocated through the tort liability system (see below). In the future there will be a search for a cost allocation system that builds expected environmental cleanup costs into the prices of the goods creating the hazards. Long-term financial security systems will have to be developed because frequently there is a delay between the manufacture of a good and its ultimate cleanup.

LIABILITY

Tort liability is a judicial process for allocating the costs of some unforeseen events by using the concept of fault. Liability insurance was designed to spread damage-award costs, imposed by the judicial system, to a broad group of insureds. The control issue in the tort system involves prudently balancing its incentives with the relative high cost of the judicial process and the pooling of these costs through insurance. Early in the twentieth century, a political decision was made to create a separate system—workers' compensation—for allocating the cost of industrial accidents. The same sort of decision may have to be made regarding the cost/benefits of the tort liability system for other ubiquitous risks.

HEALTH CARE

Health care costs have been a perplexing problem. For individuals, part of health care costs are not unexpected, others are candidates for insurance pooling. The scope of health care and its cost has been influenced by technology, which has vastly expanded the scope and induced an upgraded demand for health care. Competitive forces tend to push premiums in an open insurance market as a function of expected costs; those individuals with high expected health costs pay high premiums in such a market. These high premiums may be viewed as socially unacceptable. As of 1994, the United States was using the political process to make basic decisions about providing incentives for efficiency in health care and for allocating the costs.

See also CONSERVATISM, POLITICAL; ENTITLEMENT PROGRAMS; FINANCIAL INSTITUTIONS; GLOBAL CULTURE; HAZARDOUS WASTES; HEALTH CARE COSTS; SOCIAL WELFARE PHILOSOPHIES.

BIBLIOGRAPHY

FROOT, KENNETH A.; SCHARFSTEIN, DAVID S.; and STEIN, JEREMY C. "A Framework for Risk Management." *Harvard Business Review* 72/6 (November-December 1994).

HUBER, PETER. "Environmental Hazards and Liability Law." *Liability: Perspectives and Policy*. In Robert E. Litan and Clifford Winston, eds., Washington, DC: Brookings Institute, 1988.

World Bank Research Report. *Averting the Old Age Crisis: Policies to Protect the Old and Promote Growth*. New York: Oxford University Press, 1994.

James C. Hickman

Integrated Performance Systems

Whether you are running a small business or a global corporation, the customary job is to gather the components which you then have to assemble to serve some need. In the construction business, for instance, the installation of energy-using systems in buildings includes buying steam boilers and air-conditioners, oil/gas/electricity and pipes/wiring to run them and conduits to distribute their output; hiring skilled workers to assemble them all into a workable system; and buying light fittings and more electricity for illumination.

Such aggregations and combinations of components lead to systems that are wasteful of energy, people, resources, and capital. Energy use in buildings, for instance, could now be cut by one-third, if all cost-effective, energy-efficient technologies were used. But incentives to make such innovative investments are stymied by the jerry-built characteristics of the system itself.

The integrated performance system concept (IPS) denotes that, in the future, organizations will contract to provide performance of a total—integrated—system to serve the functional needs of society. Thus, the business of the future will supply functions, not hardware or people. The hardware and people will be the organization's means to an end.

IPS can go a long way toward achieving desired goals (e.g., energy conservation in our example) while opening up exciting new commercial opportunities. IPS holds the greatest appeal for the principal stakeholders of the enterprise. In the case of energy efficiency in buildings, these are the public utilities now supplying electric power and gas, as well as the companies now supplying heating oil.

- What if these organizations—for example, under the leadership of the electric power company—were to take the initiative in forming a consortium of business entities that comprise all the complementary resources—technical, human, and financial—to put in place complete systems to perform all the energy-performing functions in buildings?
- What if this consortium were thereby able to offer arrangements for supplying building occupants with all the energy-consuming amenities (heating, cooling, lighting, and so on) using the consortium's *own*, state-of-the-art equipment and systems?
- What if this selling of performance were cost-effective—i.e., competitive—with the customary cost of products and their operation (e.g., heating and air-conditioning equipment) that building occupants must now own, operate, maintain, upgrade, and finally dispose of themselves?

This significant institutional innovation—IPS—will quite possibly be seen as the means of satisfying market demands for efficiency, quality, service, and socioeconomic well-being: in short, as a means for propelling American business and industry into the forefront of twenty-first-century competition.

Energy efficiency in buildings is but one example to introduce the concept of IPS. This concept has limitless applications. IPS calls for no basic change from our profit-motivated, market-driven system. This system can be strengthened and the corporation's competitive edge can be sharpened when business focuses its strategy on performance rather than on particular products or services.

In every key function—health, shelter, food, education, energy, transportation, communication—society needs systems offering competing performance of these functions. IPS is a package of complementary technologies—hardware, software—operated by an umbrella organization so that its customers can buy as much of the system's performance as they need, with a minimum of transaction costs and wasted resources. The umbrella organization would most often be a consortium of companies whose complementary resources and capabilities are needed for the research-and-development, production, operation, maintenance, and continued upgrading of the integrated performance system.

Inherent advantages of the IPS approach include the following:

For business:

- Business practices are formulated that are more capable of higher risk taking by virtue of managing all the elements that make for systems efficiency and innovation.
- There is an increased perception of, and demand for, continuous technical and institutional innovation—i.e., "market-pull for the better."

490

- Acting is more often in anticipation of needs rather than in reaction to crisis. Fear of product obsolescence is abated.
- Functional performance-oriented enterprises can better gain international competitiveness through greater pull for and better management of advanced technology. Their enhanced power to absorb and employ technologies will accelerate the commercialization of new ideas, increase productivity, reduce costs of industrial production, and increase consumer satisfaction.
- It is easier to implement a closer approach to quality, service, and reliability in all aspects of the business, particularly in meeting customer needs.
- There is greater facilitation of access to foreign markets by providing a unique competitive edge.
- There is an increased demand for higher skills in management, engineering, and labor: employment opportunities are upgraded.

For the nation:

- There is increased productivity, leading to better allocation of resources as the key to achieving multiple national goals simultaneously.
- There is improvement in the quality of human life through *humane* technology, inasmuch as the advent of new technologies can be significantly influenced by consideration of societal good through an IPS enterprise's pursuit of total system cost-effectiveness.

For the consumer:

- Advantageous new market choices are possible: there is a new-found ability to buy performance of functional needs, realizing that the technical and institutional means reflect the best available at a competitive price, without any concomitant burden of product ownership. For those who prefer to continue owning products, better ones will be available as a result of the advances made by IPS enterprises and their equipment suppliers.

IPS goes far beyond vertical or horizontal integration and alliances, or the usual approaches to efficiency, quality, service, and reliability. Integrated performance systems are the business of the the future.

See also BUSINESS STRUCTURE: FORMS, IMPACTS; BUSINESS STRUCTURE: INDUSTRIAL POLICY; ENERGY CONSERVATION; FACTORIES AND MANUFACTURING; MANAGEMENT; PRODUCTIVITY; ROBOTICS; VISIONARY THINKING.

BIBLIOGRAPHY

BAND, WILLIAM A. *Touchstones: Ten New Ideas for Revolutionizing Business.* New York: John Wiley, 1994.

CAMPBELL, ANDREW, and NASH, LAURA L. *A Sense of Mission: Defining Direction for the Large Corporation.* Reading, MA: Addison-Wesley, 1993.

HAMMER, MICHAEL, and CHAMPY, JAMES. *Reengineering the Corporation: A Manifesto for Business Revolution.* New York: HarperBusiness/Harper Collins, 1993.

HAYES, ROBERT H., WHEELWRIGHT, STEVEN C., and CLARK, KIM B. *Dynamic Manufacturing; Creating the Learning Organization.* New York: Free Press, 1988.

QUINN, ROBERT E., and CAMERON, KIM S. *Paradox and Transformation: Toward a Theory of Change in Organization and Management.* Cambridge, MA: Ballinger, 1988.

SHETTY, Y. K., and BUEHLER, VERNON B., eds. *Competing Through Productivity and Quality.* Cambridge, MA and Norwalk, CT: Productivity Press, 1988.

TOMASKO, ROBERT M. *Rethinking the Corporation: The Architecture of Change.* New York: AMACOM, 1993.

Michael Michaelis

Intellectual Property

The notion of private property—distinguishing private ownership of land and goods from other forms of rights to use—has been central to economic thought for centuries. Marxists opposed private ownership of "the means of production," but this argument would have been meaningless before private ownership had become established as a concept. Until recent centuries, the idea of property was largely limited to land or tangible goods. The first major extension was to include debt instruments (e.g., mortgages) or shares in joint stock companies, as a form of property. Much more recently, the notion of products of the human mind as a form of wealth—and therefore, of property—has begun to take legal form. The generic term is *intellectual property.* Such works have commercial value to the extent that they can be protected.

There are many types of intellectual property but only four methods of protection, the choice depending on circumstances. The first approach, applicable to inventions (and possibly to computer programs and synthetic bio-molecules) is to rely on patents. These are published descriptions of operating principles, specific designs, formulas, processes, or end uses. The second alternative is the secret process or formula: a plan or process, tool, mechanism, or compound known only to its owners or other confidants. The famous "secret formula" of Coca-Cola is an example. The third possibility is the trademark, a unique name, symbol, mark, motto, device, emblem, or distinctive logo that identifies the commercial products of a particular manufacturer or other organization. Trademark protection can be indefinite. The fourth and last protection is the copyright. This applies to written material, including artwork, music, and computer programs.

Patents

Patents are the most important form of intellectual property from an economic perspective. A patent is a form of publication that contains a detailed description of the invention, as well as a list of related prior inventions. In theory, the award of a limited monopoly (protection against competition) for a limited time is provided simply as an inducement to publish new ideas, thus benefitting society as a whole. Considerable debate rages among economists as to the optimum degree of protection from the societal perspective.

Worldwide approximately one million patent applications are filed yearly; 166,000 applications were filed in the United States in 1989 and 102,712 were granted. There is a growing trend toward internationalization of U.S. patent applications. In 1967 only 20 percent of the patent grants in the United States went to foreigners as compared to 47 percent in 1989. The United States in that year, granted 21,090 patents to Japanese, 8,560 to West Germans, 3,299 to the French, and 3,281 to citizens of the United Kingdom.

Any invention can be patented provided (1) that it is novel and resulted from an act of invention (i.e., it cannot be derived by a practitioner in a clear-cut way from the state-of-the-art in that field) and (2) that it has a practical application. In principle a patent grants an exploitation monopoly on the invention to the patent holder for a period of years (seventeen in the United States) and within a specific country. A patent (backed up ultimately by know-how) is an incorporeal or intangible good that can be sold or licensed either exclusively or not in exchange for money or reciprocal licenses. A very few important patents in the past have brought fortunes to their inventors. In most such cases the inventor secured "blanket" patents that covered all of the likely alternatives, associated process technologies, and end-use applications. In addition, such innovators were commercially oriented enough to build a successful manufacturing business based on the technology. George Eastman

of Kodak and Edwin Land of Polaroid are familiar examples. However, some of the more valuable inventions, such as the telephone, the vacuum tube, FM radio, and the computer, resulted in expensive litigation that took many years to resolve and often left the inventors with very little at the end.

In practice, the protection provided by a patent registered in the United States or elsewhere is minimal. Foreign patents are not effectively enforced against domestic infringers by many governments. Many Asian and Latin American governments make it difficult for foreign firms to obtain patent protection; some, including Brazil, Taiwan, and South Korea, go further and actively encourage national firms to evade or infringe on patents held by foreign firms. Deficiencies in international patent protection were a major topic of the 1993 "Uruguay Round" negotiations of the General Agreement for Tariffs and Trade (GATT).

Trade Secrets

Chemical processes, as well as processes for the manufacture of specialized food products (e.g., food additives and sauces), perfumes, liqueurs, and cosmetics, are sometimes kept as trade secrets because of the relatively short life and often ineffective protection offered by patents. Trade secrets have been held for considerable periods, an example being the secret "Chatham process" discovered in the 1940s for manufacturing synthetic gem-quality emeralds, rubies, and sapphires sold in jewelry shops. Some trade secrets have been held for a century or more.

The economic value of trade secrets is problematic because they are difficult to buy and sell. A usual prerequisite to the sale of secret technology is the release of a certain minimum amount of technical and commercial data. Theoretically, this is protected by a "nondisclosure agreement." Civil codes of most industrialized countries provide penalties for violating such agreements. However, legal proof of a violation is very difficult to establish.

Trademarks

Trademarks, brand names, logos, and other symbolic devices are means of identifying a product or service (and its producer/supplier) as it is presented in the marketplace. A distinctive label constitutes an almost indispensable support in developing a market and an advertising campaign. For example, "Bibendum" has contributed to global product-recognition for Michelin tires. In the United States in 1989,

63,100 certificates were issued in 1989, of which 7,800 were renewals. The total number in force is around 500,000. An international classification system of thirty-four product and eight service categories has been established under which trademarks can be officially registered. Protection is renewable and lasts for ten years. This protection, such as it is, can be acquired in many countries.

Copyrights

Copyrights are applicable to written documents, computer software (which also may be patentable), sound recordings, and works of the visual arts (including movies). When these materials can be shown to be original and the personal work of their creator, they can be protected by a copyright under international agreements. This prohibits the reproduction (including photocopying) without authorization from the originator. In 1989, 618,300 copyrights were issued in the United States, of which 38,600 were renewals. Written materials (categorized as monographs and serials) accounted for 187,000 of the total, while musical works accounted for 197,200. It is of interest that 1,200 copyrights were issued for semiconductor chip products. (Software is included under "monographs.")

Infringements, Clones, and Counterfeits

Imitation may be the sincerest form of flattery, but it can also be very damaging to inventors and innovators. New products, even when protected by patents, trademarks, copyrights, and model registration, have always been a target for fraudulent and illicit reproduction. The Museum of Patent Infringement in Paris displays some particularly spectacular examples. When a company is a market leader, its products are relentlessly imitated. This process is sometimes beneficial to the consumer, at least in the short run, since it minimizes monopoly profits and (possibly) encourages even more rapid technological improvement by the market leader in its effort to stay ahead of the pack.

On the other hand, unrestrained imitation deprives innovators of the needed return on research and development (R&D) costs, not to mention entrepreneurial risk-taking. If expensive R&D is not rewarded, there is little if any economic incentive to undertake it. This would have a harmful effect on the main source of economic growth. The biotechnology and pharmaceutical industries provide clear examples. Research needed to develop new drugs can be exceedingly costly. Most biotechnology companies have yet to reap any significant return on capital invested; most of the costs went for investments in R&D and clinical testing. Even so, drugs can be fairly easy to manufacture. There are a number of firms (many in Italy) that specialize in generic versions of proprietary drugs, which can sell at prices far below those set by the original manufacturers. Italy is unique in that it does not allow patents for pharmaceuticals. Carried to a logical extreme, such practices could destroy the economic incentive for pursuing drug-related research.

Another form of industrial piracy is the unauthorized use of trademarks to sell cheap copies of expensive, premium-quality consumer goods such as Rolex watches, Parker pens, Gucci luggage, videocassette recordings, and so on. Both the customer and the manufacturer whose trademark has been violated are victimized by this practice. Gullible customers do not get the "bargain" they think they are getting, and the reputation of the name-brand is smirched. Nevertheless, this sort of theft is tolerated, or even actively encouraged, by a number of unsympathetic or unscrupulous governments, especially in Asia.

Unfortunately, piracy seems to be a growth industry, as modern communications and "reverse engineering" technology (the ability to disassemble and dissect a product with intent to replicate it) have made it possible for design-based products (especially computer software and hardware) to be copied and reproduced in weeks if not hours. This reduces the inherent advantage of the innovator and helps the imitator.

If protection for intellectual property is not significantly strengthened by international agreement in the next few years, it is likely that R&D investment in design-based products will decline, with more investment going to process technologies (which are more difficult to copy). The economic value of patents is also likely to decline, as businesses seek other means of protecting themselves.

See also ARTIFICIAL LIFE; COUNTERFEITING; CREATIVITY; GRAY MARKET GOODS; MARKETING BREAKTHROUGHS; RESEARCH AND DEVELOPMENT; TECHNOLOGICAL CHANGE; TECHNOLOGICAL INNOVATION; TECHNOLOGY DIFFUSION.

BIBLIOGRAPHY

DIMANESCU, DAN, and BOTKIN, JAMES. *The New Alliance: America's R&D Consortia.* Cambridge: MA: Ballinger, 1986.
HIPPEL, ERIC VON. *The Sources of Innovation.* New York: Oxford University Press, 1988.

"In the Realm of Technology, Japan Looms Ever Larger." *New York Times*, May 28, 1991, p. c–1.

National Science Board. *Science and Engineering Indicators*. 10th ed. Washington, DC: U.S. Government Printing Office, 1991.

SAMUELS, JEFFREY M., ed. *Patent, Trademark, and Copyright Law*. Washington, DC: Bureau of National Affairs, 1985.

SERVI, ITALO S. *New Product Development and Marketing: A Practical Guide*. New York, Praeger, 1990.

Robert U. Ayres

Interactive Entertainment

Interactivity has attracted considerable press attention lately, and most major entertainment/media companies are becoming involved in or are seriously exploring the interactive entertainment market. Interactive entertainment is part of the natural evolution of media/entertainment, a rapidly changing market in which new products/services are introduced only to become obsolete within a matter of a few years. The term "interactive" has been applied to so many disparate products, services, and programs that its exact meaning has become elusive. It is broadly defined here as any entertainment in which the user can participate. There are many different levels of interactivity, ranging from simply selecting programming of interest and watching it at one's convenience to substantially shaping, manipulating, or exercising control over a particular program/experience.

An array of key factors has created a hospitable environment for interactive entertainment: (1) the growing desire of consumers to control their entertainment habits, as shown by the success of video games and the strong market penetration of VCRs; (2) the growing familiarity of consumers, especially young people, with computers and other interactive devices; (3) the increasing fusion of education and entertainment; (4) the growing convergence of computers and video and of computers and telecommunications; (5) the trend toward experiential entertainment (realistic simulations and fantasies); (6) the increasing drive of entertainment/media companies to generate new sources of revenue and open up new markets; (7) the rise of narrowcasting; (8) the increasing popularity of new forms of programming that could lend themselves well to interactivity, such as hybrid programming (i.e., docudramas) and segmented programming, especially magazine-style programming; (9) the rise of special interest programming and special interest publications; (10) the increasing desire and need for enhanced social communication, especially among people with special interests; (11) the arrival of more advanced, economical, and convenient technologies; (12) the integration of interactive technologies with other new technologies, such as high-definition television, in new home entertainment systems; (13) the strong impact of direct marketing and the growing effort of advertisers/ad agencies to devise more effective and targeted ways of reaching consumers; and (14) increased competitiveness in the highly crowded media/entertainment industry.

Forms of Interactive Entertainment

VIDEO GAMES

These consist of electronic game cartridges with audio and animation played on special consoles. There are a variety of video game systems, including hand-held systems and systems that display images on full-size consoles and television sets. Coin-operated video games are typically found in video arcades, family amusement centers, bars, and other public places. Joysticks or more elaborate game pads are typically used to control game action on regular-size video games.

COMPUTER SOFTWARE

This category includes entertainment, educational, and other types of software. Typically computer games offer a higher level of interactivity and greater audiovisual capability than video games. Keyboards, joysticks, and mice are used to access material on computers. Computer software can offer graphics, text, animation, audio, still video, and limited full-motion video with the help of video compression techniques.

VIDEOTEXT/ONLINE SERVICES

Interactive services can be accessed by modem-equipped personal computers or by "dedicated" videotext terminals hooked up by phone or cable, or by other link with a central computer. These services, which include informational (news), entertainment (games), and transactional (home shopping) services, provide text and graphics. A few computer games allow play-by-modem provided that all participants have computers, input devices, monitors, and copies of the game software.

AUDIOTEXT

Audio programs and services of an informational or entertainment nature can be accessed over the telephone for free or for a (sometimes substantial) charge, as in the case of 900 phone numbers. Audiotext programs vary in their degree of interactivity.

INTERACTIVE TELEVISION

A range of interactive television services permit viewers to interact with their televisions. These services include: (1) video-on-demand, which allows users to view programs of their choice at a time of their choosing (at present most such services require a short waiting period before users can watch the program of their choice); (2) play-along systems, which allow viewers to play along with programs on the air (i.e., responding to a trivia question on a game show), typically using some kind of console device, without actually affecting the program content; (3) audiotext-based interactive television services, which allow viewers to either play along with programming on the air or to exercise some influence or control over program content using the phone; and (4) branching/video manipulation systems, which allow viewers to manipulate/influence/control the program content in some way, typically using a console or other device (these systems vary considerably in the degree of video manipulation they afford, with fiber optic systems offering a much higher degree of control). Play-along and branching systems can be one-way or two-way interactive. Interactive television services are delivered over a variety of media, including cable television, satellite television, broadcast television, and fiber optics.

Interactive Multimedia

This term refers to interactive optical disk technologies that offer a combination of visuals, sound, and text on optical disks, primarily compact discs. These technologies include:

INTERACTIVE VIDEODISCS

Offering full-motion video, graphics, animation, still video, audio, and text, these 8″ and 12″ interactive (analog) optical disks have different levels of interactivity—generally they become more truly interactive when hooked up with computers.

CD-ROM

An interactive compact disc technology offering audio, text, graphics, animation, and still video on a 5″ compact disc, CD-ROM players are attached to personal computers. CD-ROM players (and other interactive CD players) have a large storage capacity. Limited full-motion video can be offered on CD-ROM using video compression techniques, such as Quick Time and MPEG, though the quality of that video was initially mediocre. Full-motion video chips and modules are being added to several CD-based platforms and feature-length movies with laser-disc quality video are expected to become widely available in the very near future. All interactive CD systems play regular compact (audio) discs, and there is a smaller degree of cross-platform software compatibility between certain types of CD-ROM devices and software.

CD STAND-ALONES

Interactive compact disc stand-alone systems that hook up with the television and/or monitor and the stereo also offer audio, graphics, animation, still video, and text on a 5″ compact disc. There are also some dedicated CD-based game systems that hook up to existing video game systems from those systems' manufacturers, and a few CD stand-alone devices can even be upgraded into computers with add-on keyboards, disk drives, and the like. At present some of these CD stand-alones are hampered by extremely limited save-game capacities, overall program storage capacity notwithstanding.

KARAOKE

First developed by the Japanese, these audio/video systems permit the user to "sing along" with recorded music using a microphone. (The original vocal tracks are deleted, while the backing music is retained.) These systems use a number of different technologies, including regular CDs, videotape, laser-discs, and interactive CDs.

INTERACTIVE LIVE THEATER

The level of participation varies widely in these live plays. Audience participation ranges from simply voting on the identity of the culprit in murder-mystery plays to actually playing a role in the drama itself (as in *Tony 'N' Tina's Wedding*).

INTERACTIVE FILMS

In these movies, which are shown in movie theaters, museums, amusement parks, and other public places, the audience can make plot choices at particular points, and influence the action on the screen by pressing buttons near their seats or through some other means. Such interactive technologies as laser-discs are used for interactive films in theaters and other public places. These interactive films are not to be confused with "interactive movies" on computer software, interactive compact discs, and other media in the home.

VIRTUAL REALITY

The term *virtual reality* has many different connotations. Sometimes it is merely empty media hype, but generally speaking, it refers to computerized systems that place the users in a simulated 3D graphic environment: (1) immersive systems that seemingly plunge the user directly into a particular environment, typically using head-mounted displays and data gloves; or (2) nonimmersive systems, which project the user into an environment and allow him or her to interact directly with that environment without the use of such external devices as head-mounted displays.

Current Market Analysis and Future Prospects

The largest segment of the interactive entertainment industry by far is video games, with home video games generating currently about $5 billion in revenues. Despite all the hype about multimedia and other new advanced interactive products, the most successful forms of interactive entertainment to date have been fairly simple, easy to use, lower-level interactive, more convenient, and less expensive. These forms include video games, audiotext, interactive live theater, and karaoke. The most promising interactive products in the short-term future are likely to be similar in nature. As consumers become more acclimated to interactivity, a higher level of interactive sophistication is likely to emerge. Interactive CD products are not likely to have a significant impact until the late 1990s, when player prices will be more affordable. At that time there will be a greater supply of higher quality software and full-motion video products, dominant standards will emerge, consumers will be better acclimated to interactivity, and young people raised on video games will reach a purchasing age and be prime consumers of multimedia products. When reasonably priced recordable-and-erasable CDs and CD players appear on the home market, the new home entertainment center will begin to take shape and become more firmly established.

There has been much talk about electronic databases and special interest interactive programming, but up to now entertainment (especially games) has been the driving force behind interactive media. Broad-appeal entertainment programming, such as movies, science fiction, games, and music, is likely to dominate the interactive market

initially. Children's programming may also fare well initially, but special-interest interactive programming is not likely to sell well early on. The electronic database design model may work in education and other institutional/industrial markets, but it has little appeal with most consumers, as indicated by the poor early performance of videotext. Consumers need to have a clear idea of precisely what these devices are to be used for before they will be willing to buy them. In order to succeed in the broader consumer market, interactive entertainment programs will need to offer strong dynamics, storylines, and characterizations—not merely dazzling graphics but meaningful opportunity for user involvement—elements that consumers have come to expect from mainstream linear entertainment. Social interaction will also be a key element in interactive entertainment of the future, especially given the rising popularity of chat/bulletin board services.

Interactive entertainment in video arcades, amusement parks, museums, movie theaters, and other public places will play a central role in educating consumers about interactivity by allowing them to try out new interactive products/experiences at little or no risk. These places provide an ideal testing ground for new interactive products/experiences. Such interactive products/experiences as interactive lasers, interactive CDs, videotext, virtual reality, interactive rides/interactive simulators, and teleconferencing are likely to figure more prominently in amusement parks and other public places of the future.

Interactive entertainment is likely to develop into a broader, more substantial market over the next ten years and will have a strong impact on media/entertainment in general. Although the technical aspects of the media are rapidly changing, the actual growth of the market will be a slower, more evolutionary process.

See also COMMUNICATIONS; COMPUTERS: SOFTWARE; GAMES AND PASTIMES; TELECOMMUNICATIONS; THEME PARKS AND ORGANIZED ATTRACTIONS.

BIBLIOGRAPHY

MORRISON, MIKE and SANDIE, C. *The Magic of Interactive Entertainment.* Indianapolis: SAMS Publishing, 1994.

MORROW, CINDY, ed. *Cyberlife.* Indianapolis: SAMS Publishing, 1994.

RHEINGOLD, HOWARD. *Virtual Reality.* New York: Touchstone Books, 1991.

Michael Mascioni

Internal Migration, United States

In common parlance, *internal migration* refers to the geographic relocation of persons within a given country. *International migration* relates to geographic relocation across national boundaries. In official U.S. statistics, *internal migration* is defined more narrowly as the movement of persons from one usual residence to another that involves crossing a county line and is intended to be for an indefinite period. As a rule, the volume of residential movement within counties exceeds that of such movement between counties. In the following discussion, we adopt the first-cited, broader concept of internal migration but make distinctions among types of mobility and migration where relevant.

Migration combines with fertility and mortality of an area to determine its relative population change. The smaller the geographic area, the greater likelihood that migration will be the critical component of population change. Because migration rates typically vary from area to area more than do fertility and mortality rates, migration contributes substantially to population redistribution within the country.

Not all people are equally likely to move. In the recent history of the United States between 15 and 20 percent of the population moved each year. At least one-third of persons in their twenties, but less than 10 percent of those forty-five and over, move in any one year. These age differences hold despite the distance of the move. Hispanics and blacks are more likely than whites to move locally but less apt to move across county or state lines. Education makes little difference with regard to local mobility, but the better-educated are likely to move longer distances. The unemployed are more likely to migrate than those who work or are out of the labor market. Among the regions of the United States, the West exhibits the greatest degree of within-county mobility, and the South has the highest rate of between-county migration.

Migratory patterns are fairly stable over short periods, but are apt to vary over longer intervals. This makes estimation of future migration difficult. Three factors that most influence the level and variation in mobility and migration patterns are the vibrancy of the economy, especially job availability; the changing size and composition of households; and the condition of residential areas. Business closures lead to net out-migration. Economic development causes in-migration. Lower fertility, longer life expectancy, and population aging increase the number of smaller households, alter housing de-

mand, and stimulate mobility. Decaying urban neighborhoods can result in structural renewal projects that displace people en masse.

The most widely consulted source of information about future migration and redistribution of population within the United States is probably the Census Bureau's recurrent series of population projections for states. The most recent of these, by Campbell (1994), is the first to have been prepared after completion of the 1990 census. It contains more detailed race/ethnicity information than was in predecessor studies. Scenarios based on the latest census data do not suggest any dramatic break from trends of the recent past with respect either to favored destinations of migrants or to differences in migration behaviors among demographic groups. The Census Bureau figures suggest a continued pattern of movement away from the Northeast and Midwest toward the South. In the 1990s, the census forecast a net out-migration of 3.3 million persons from the Northeast and the same magnitude of net in-migration to the South. The census study suggests that while the volume of internal migration is likely to diminish, the Northeast and increasingly the Midwest should lose population from internal migration directed almost exclusively to the South. In every five-year period between 1990–1995 and 2020–2025, the state of Florida is projected to gain about 600,000 persons from net internal migration, more than twice the levels anticipated for the second through fourth states on this list (North Carolina, Washington, and Georgia).

A principal reason for the expected decline in internal migration is the aging of our population. While migration will vary according to other demographic variables, the relationship between chronological age and the limited tendency for migration is well known and consistent over both time and place (Rogers and Castro, 1984). Applying the most recent figures (for 1991–1992) showing the proportion of each group that moves during a year to the current population reveals that 16.8 percent of all Americans aged one and over would live in a different *house* from the one they had lived in at the beginning of the year, and that 6.0 percent would live in a different *county*. Taking the same set of movement rates, but using the population as projected to the year 2020, we find that 15.4 percent of all Americans aged one and over will live in a different *house* from the one they lived in at the beginning of the year, and that 5.6 percent will live in a different *county*. Even though the number of persons moving and migrating will grow with the population, the changes in age distribution should reduce the fraction of the population moving and migrating.

Zelinsky (1971) proposed that societies go through mobility transition stages much as they go through mortality and fertility transition stages. Based on what he saw as logical extension of earlier mobility stages, he projected these probable trends:

- A decline in the level of residential migration
- Most migration occurring between cities
- Acceleration in circulatory mobility, as people identify with multiple residences
- Stricter political controls on internal migration

Whether or not Zelinsky's conjectures are correct, mobility and migration patterns of the recent past in the United States will continue in the near future, barring cataclysmic events. Modifications of those patterns may take place in later years as the country's social institutions are reshaped by economic, social, and environmental changes.

See also DEMOGRAPHY; ENVIRONMENTAL REFUGEES; LAND USE PLANNING; LIFESTYLES, REGIONAL; MEGACITIES; MIGRATION, INTERNATIONAL; MULTIFOLD TREND; POPULATION GROWTH: UNITED STATES; POPULATION GROWTH: WORLDWIDE; REFUGEES.

BIBLIOGRAPHY

CAMPBELL, PAUL R. "Population Projections for States, by Age, Sex, Race, and Hispanic Origin: 1994 to 2020." *Current Population Reports.* Series P-25, No. 1111. Washington, DC: U.S. Bureau of the Census, 1994.

HANSEN, KRISTIN A. "Geographical Mobility: March 1991 to March 1992." *Current Population Reports.* Series P-20, No. 473. Washington, DC: U.S. Bureau of the Census, 1993.

ROGERS, ANDREI, and CASTRO, LUIS B. "Model Migration Schedules." In A. Rogers, ed. *Migration, Urbanization and Spatial Population Dynamics.* Boulder, CO: Westview Press, 1984.

ZELINSKY, WILBUR. "The Hypothesis of the Mobility Transition." *Geographical Review* 61 (1971): 219–249.

Charles B. Nam
William J. Serow

International Diplomacy

The end of the Cold War between communism led by the Soviet Union and the West led by the United States revealed a world, part of which was different than anything that had gone before. The security of almost all of the greatest powers came less from their military forces and alliances than from the fact that their neighbors were all democracies—and no one thought that any of the modern democracies would attack another.

At the turn of the new millennium, the great powers of the world are the United States, Japan, Germany, France, Great Britain, Italy, and China. Russia, despite its nuclear weapons, is too internally divided and unstable to be a great power except defensively. India, as the second most populous country in the world, expected to become nearly China's equal, also has special importance and may soon become a great power.

Because all of the great powers except China are modern democracies, they do not fear attack from one another, and because all of them except China are among the most productive in the world, their actual and potential power frees them from fear of attack by other countries. Therefore the areas where only these and other democracies are located are "zones of peace and democracy."

Some traditional questions about the relation between power and law in international affairs have become obsolete for the great powers, because for the first time in history these countries are not divided into competing military-political power blocs whose balance determines the security of all nations. During the twenty-first century a new diplomacy of "geoeconomics" will develop for the relationships among powers in the zones of peace, to replace traditional diplomacy based on concerns about alliance needed to provide fundamental safety.

During the next century or two the rest of the world will go through the process that the countries of the zones of peace went through during the last two centuries. Most countries will move from poor to wealthy, from authoritarian to democratic, and from a diplomacy dominated by the need to protect against military conquest or domination, to a diplomacy concerned with less vital national interests and concern for the quality of the international order.

The worldwide passage from a poor and natural world to a world of wealth, democracy, and peace, will be the central feature of the history of the next two centuries; it will be the environment that shapes international diplomacy. This passage began as recently as the end of the eighteenth century. By the end of the twentieth century one-seventh of the world had completed it—and most of the rest of the world was already greatly changed by beginning to move through it. Before the passage there were no wealthy countries in the world—measuring by absolute standards.

The twenty-first century will see the countries with more than half of the world's expanding population cross the threshold of absolute wealth that was crossed for the first time by the United States early in the twentieth century. As a result, by the end of the twenty-first century about three-quarters of the world's eight to twelve billion people will live in countries where life expectancy is well over seventy, where almost all children get a high school education, where most people work indoors with their minds and their fingers—rather than working with their backs and muscles while exposed to the elements—and where most people have at least potential access to the whole world and to many choices.

The twenty-first century will also see a change in the role of and threat from nuclear weapons. In 1989 the United States and the Soviet Union had nearly 50,000 nuclear weapons, all or most essentially aimed at each other. Nuclear deterrence was the centerpiece of national security policy. Nuclear weapons posed a danger of killing hundreds of millions of people in a week. With the end of the Cold War these dangers have largely disappeared, and the number of nuclear weapons has begun to come down.

In the twenty-first century the threat from nuclear weapons will change to be primarily a threat from weak countries (or subnational groups) and probably mostly a threat to cities rather than nations—except for Israel, the most likely target, which is so small that it could be destroyed by a relatively small number of nuclear weapons, and which is confronted by enemies whose goal is its destruction.

The twenty-first century will also see the world choose between two possible nuclear paths: the first involves the further spread of nuclear weapons to twenty or forty or more countries and groups, or, alternatively, a path which reverses direction and leads to a smaller number of nuclear powers, and possibly to the practical removal of nuclear weapons from the field of diplomacy. If this second path is chosen, it will not be based on a new global idealism, but on a sophisticated understanding of the realities of power and of national interest.

The fundamental features of the nation-state system will continue through the twenty-first century—although there will be a substantial evolution in its character. The basic security and identity of countries will continue to be organized by sovereign na-

tions; no world government will supersede national governments or gain the power to protect against strong nations. But the end of military dangers to the integrity of states will gradually lead to the division of many states into smaller units for most political activities and ordinary economic management. Some of these smaller units will be separate states, but most of them will continue as units of larger national governments which continue to provide the primary identity of their citizens.

Simultaneously with the devolution of governmental power to smaller units, other governmental functions will be delegated by nations to international organizations—either regional, like the European Union, or functional, like the World Postal Union and other specialized agencies.

The United Nations will continue through the twenty-first century as the institutional forum for considering worldwide issues—the only organization in which virtually all peoples are represented. However, it will continue to be based on the equal dignity—and voting power—of all sovereign states, from tiny island nations with less than 100,000 population to continental-wide nations with 1,000,000,000 or more people, from democracies whose governments legitimately speak for their citizens to absolute tyrannies where the government speaks for no one except a dictator who rules by fear and force. The threat of war will be reduced, not neatly by the establishment of a super authority, but gradually by fallible human measures by which nation after nation becomes part of zones of peace and democracy where live those countries who have painfully learned the lessons of peaceful self-government.

The most important result of international diplomatic development will be that by the end of the twenty-first or twenty-second century the great majority of the world's population will live in zones of peace and democracy, and the fear of war between great powers will seem to be a thing of the past.

See also COMMUNISM; DEMOCRACY; ESPIONAGE AND COUNTERINTELLIGENCE; GLOBAL CULTURE; NATIONALISM; PEACEKEEPING; WEAPONS OF MASS DESTRUCTION.

BIBLIOGRAPHY

SINGER, MAX. *Passage to A Human World*. New Brunswick, NJ: Transaction Publishers, 1989.

SINGER, MAX, and WILDASKY, AARON. *The REAL World Order: Zones of Peace/Zones of Turmoil*. Chatham, NJ: Chatham House Publishers, 1993.

Max Singer

International Governance and Regional Authorities

For the last fifty years, global politics and economics have been largely divided along ideological and development lines: communism versus market economies, totalitarianism versus democracy, developed versus developing nation. Institutions and alliances developed to support the divisions, among them the North Atlantic Treaty Organization (NATO), the Organization for Economic Cooperation and Development (OECD), the Council for Mutual Economic Assistance (COMECON), and the UN Conference on Trade and Development (UNCTAD).

The relative stability of these divisions has been ruptured in recent years by the collapse of Soviet-style communism, the rise of Islamic fundamentalism, the eruption of ethnic hostilities, and the spread of nuclear weapons that created new potential threats and alliances. At the same time, economic development differences shifted the center of economic activity away from the United States–Western Europe and COMECON axes toward Asia. Differences in economic development among developing countries and intractable differences between developed countries on certain fundamental economic issues have rendered the "north/south" or "developed/developing" divisions less important in international economics and politics.

In such a setting it is hardly surprising that international and regional organizations face an uncertain future. Current security structures, especially the United Nations and NATO, are struggling to better define their purpose in an era in which threats to international security are not marked by a superpower struggle. China, a second military superpower, albeit weakened, continues to exist and could potentially become a third superpower through complex issues such as ethnic conflict and nuclear proliferation. At the same time, regional economic organizations are proliferating, both to facilitate international competitiveness and to secure access to important or fast-growing markets.

In terms of economic integration, the most comprehensive effort to date has been accomplished by the European Union (EU) through the establishment of the Common Market and political institutions including the European Parliament and Commission. The EU has political and economic goals, seeking both to institutionalize the balance of power needed to minimize the recurrence of military conflicts on the Continent and to promote greater economic growth through regional integration. However, efforts toward deeper integration, such as the introduction of a common European currency, will continue to present challenges to the EU, as will efforts toward broader integration through eastward expansion.

To initiate the expansion effort, the EU has signed agreements with Poland, Hungary, the Czech and Slovak republics, Bulgaria, and Romania to expand trade relations and provide trade preferences. The expense of extending EU benefits to Eastern European countries will, however, cause enormous debate within the EU member states as public opinion may not support the large expenditures needed. Further, this issue has caused tension between the EU leading members, as Germany's interest in promoting expansion is not matched by other members who believe eastward expansion will allow for German domination of the group. Competing interests of European nation-states will likely limit the speed and degree of integration in coming years.

Other regional political and economic organizations, such as Mercosur in Latin America, ASEAN in Asia, or ECOWAS, UDEAC, PTA, and SADCC in Africa allow for regional dialogue on political and economic issues, but there is presently no real effort toward integration in terms of establishing common institutions or policies on the scale accomplished in Europe.

The leading trend toward increased economic integration has been accomplished through trade arrangements. The highlight of multilateralism in trade was realized through the successful conclusion of the Uruguay Round and the establishment of the World Trade Organization. Simultaneous to those developments was a proliferation of regional trade arrangements. In the Western Hemisphere, this included the United States–Canada Free Trade Agreement, followed by the North American Free Trade Agreement (NAFTA). The Summit of the Americas in December 1994 formally initiated the effort to expand NAFTA to include Chile. In addition to NAFTA expansion, the summit also produced an initiative to create free trade in the hemisphere early in the next century.

The existence of other regional trade blocs such as Mercosur and that of the Andean countries is creating an interrelated web of trade preferences for much of the hemisphere. Among the reasons for this move toward regional trade blocs in the hemisphere has been the desire to offset the European-centered trade focus of the European Union. One result of the NAFTA and Summit of the Americas efforts has been to prompt negotiations between the European Union and the Mercosur countries for a possible free trade agreement.

In Asia, APEC has evolved institutionally in recent years and now includes numerous committees and working groups that promote regional cooperation on issues as divergent as customs, investment, transportation, and education. APEC has received most attention for its initiative to achieve regional free trade for member countries on both sides of the Pacific—by 2010 for developed countries and 2020 for developing nations. Activities of the working groups and committees indicate further integration beyond trade relations. Evolving political alliances and dramatic existing differences in level of development and economic philosophy caution that the road to economic integration in the Pacific area will be difficult to achieve.

While not indicative of increased economic integration, international financial institutions such as the World Bank and the International Monetary Fund (IMF) play an important role in economic development. The IMF is also relied upon in economic crises, as was demonstrated recently by the joint IMF-US effort to bolster the Mexican peso. Competing interests and priorities currently plaguing member states of international security institutions could reduce support for multilateral economic cooperation. These institutions will be hard pressed to meet the substantially expanded needs of both countries in transition and other developing countries.

On another front, there is growing uncertainty and confusion regarding the purpose of multilateral and regional security organizations. NATO and the United Nations have lost prestige due to their inability to resolve regional conflicts, particularly in Bosnia. These organizations are currently in a stage of disengagement regarding the ethnic conflicts that have escalated and proliferated in recent years.

Declining international support for the United Nations will likely lead to funding reductions, especially for international peacekeeping activities. It is likely that the UN will seek to limit operations to more clearly defined and supported objectives, such as humanitarian aid and disaster relief.

The leading regional security organization, NATO, is also struggling to redefine its purpose in the aftermath of the Cold War. The potential for further balkanization of Europe could require NATO to rapidly redefine how it will approach conflicts on the Continent. NATO's principal response to redefining regional security has been to focus on expanding the organization by including states in Central and Eastern Europe. NATO is likely to focus more on is-

sues outside of Europe as they emerge as potential threats to international security.

In the future, security threats will also increasingly emerge from Asia and the Persian Gulf region, especially as states in these regions seek nuclear capability, as already demonstrated by North Korea, Iran, and Iraq. There are also increasing concerns in Asia regarding the prospects of an aggressive China that might launch a military campaign toward Taiwan or attempt to resolve regional territorial claims by force. Regional security organizations, such as the Gulf Cooperation Council (GCC), originally established in response to the Iranian revolution, or the ASEAN Regional Forum (ARF), which held the first ever regional security forum for the Asia-Pacific region in 1994, will play an increasingly important role in security matters.

Thus, as the world approaches the next millennium, one is likely to see increasing economic integration for much of the Americas and Europe and possibly Eastern Asia. Such regional economic integration will also benefit multilateralism in trade and investment. More uncertain will be the evolution of alliances to deal with the political crises flowing from some of the remaining isolated (or partially isolated) countries—China, North Korea, Iran, Iraq—and from the traditional sources of international conflict. The perceived recent ineffectiveness of international organizations—principally the UN and NATO—in resolving conflicts successfully or cost-effectively is likely to result in reduced multilateral funding of these institutions. In turn this may increase local conflicts, which are unchecked by international groups and which foster the reemergence of armed conflicts with local or regional defenders.

See also FREE TRADE; GLOBAL CULTURE; GLOBAL ENVIRONMENTAL PROBLEMS; GOVERNANCE; HAZARDOUS WASTES; HOLISTIC BELIEFS; HUMAN RIGHTS; INTERNATIONAL DIPLOMACY; INTERNATIONAL TRADE: REGIONAL TRADE AGREEMENTS; INTERNATIONAL TENSIONS; LAWS, EVOLUTION OF; MULTIFOLD TREND; PACESETTER GOVERNMENTS; PEACEKEEPING.

BIBLIOGRAPHY

CAMERON, DAVID M. *Regionalism and Supranationalism.* Brookfield, VT: Gower, 1981.

FELD, WERNER J., and JORDAN, ROBERT S. *International Organizations: A Comparative Approach.* Westport, CT: Greenwood Press, 1988.

MITRANY, DAVID. *The Progress of International Government.* Northford, CT: Elliot Books, 1983.

Terence Stewart

International Tensions

International tensions in political, military, economic, technological, and sociocultural relationships are the main sources of international conflict. International conflicts created by international tensions range from nonviolent but vigorous competition, through heavily armed, potentially violent "cold war," to escalating degrees of local conventional warfare, all the way to the threat of global war employing atomic, biological, and chemical weapons of mass destruction.

International tensions can be both creative and destructive, but most are seen as destructive and leading to costly diversions of national resources to military forces for containing or fighting wars if deterrence fails. Creative international tensions include peaceful positive-sum competitions in the arts and sciences, business, commerce, education, sports, and trade that benefit all participants but some more than others. Examples abound in the sciences and arts, where international competition and cooperation stimulate and support mutual achievement.

Recent major international *political* tensions include those between politically different forms of national government, such as those between democratic and authoritarian governments. At their most intense, these political tensions are strongest between countries actually at full-scale war with each other, or that regard each other as enemies or potential aggressors. Current examples of warring nations include countries in each of the four major continents and the Middle East: in North America, Mexico and its southernmost state as well as Guatemala and the Mayan Indians; in South America, Ecuador and Peru; in Europe, Bosnia and Serbia, Russia and Chechnya, and Russia and Moldova; in Asia, South and North Korea, Afghanistan, Kashmir, Sri Lanka, and Timor; in Africa, Burundi; in the Middle East, Israel and Lebanon, Syria, Gaza, and the West Bank, and in Turkey and Iraq with the Kurds.

Countries not engaged in major shooting wars with each other, but engaging in limited violence through terrorism and counterterrorism, include Iran, Iraq, and Libya vis-à-vis the United States; in Europe, the United Kingdom and Ireland, Croatia and Serbia, and others. In all of these cases, political tensions—some associated with cultural and religious tensions, as in Bosnia between Eastern Orthodox and Muslims—have resulted in violent conflict and warfare.

In the next century these international political tensions are likely to persist as a major cause of militarization—war preparations and arms races—and actual shooting wars and their subsequent recovery and rehabilitation efforts (which, in wars involving weapons of mass destruction, may exceed war preparation and war fighting costs and duration). New international political tensions that threaten to increase military costs and increase war risks are likely to intensify between new global military-economic powers such as China, and large neighboring and competing countries such as Russia, Japan, South Korea, Taiwan, Vietnam, Malaysia, India, the United States, the Philippines, and Indonesia. The first eight of these ten countries have experienced war with China in this century. To the extent that China increases international tensions in the ongoing dispute over the ownership of the Spratly Islands oil fields, the risk of arms buildups and war between China and several of these countries will increase.

The internal tensions of the great power coalitions of the Cold War have fragmented some and stressed others. In the decade after World War II the world went through a fragmentation of old colonial empires as former colonies became independent nations. At the same time the Soviet empire extinguished the independence of most of the Eastern European nations. That same Soviet empire of the Soviet Union and its satellite states ended in 1991, and the union of Yugoslavia ended shortly thereafter, both breaking up into smaller, independent states—some parting peacefully, others with violence and civil war. In the former Yugoslavia and the Caucasus, the overriding powers relaxed their superordinate, political-military suppression of ethnic, religious, and economic/ideological conflicts among these smaller, independent nation-states.

Currently the major international tension of the nuclear and conventional stalemate between the old Communist Bloc/Warsaw Pact and the U.S.-led Western alliances of NATO, CENTO, and SEATO has abated into international cooperative threat reduction and conversion of surplus militarized resources to cooperative and technically assisted economic development. What lies ahead in international tensions is the proliferation of democratized communications and the technologies of freedom, apace with the proliferation of the technologies of war and oppression. The most socially advanced, wealthiest, and industrialized nations such as the United States, Japan, the United Kingdom, France, Germany, and Italy, as well as economies in transition, such as Russia and China, are suffering from varying but generally increasing degrees of domestic violence and disorder, from drug abuse and family breakdown to increases in violent crime resulting from the growth of organized crime, local vigilantism, and mass terrorism. It is not clear yet if democratic institutions of the rule of law, civil liberties, and freedom of expression will be able to provide sufficient physical security to law-abiding citizens to withstand these assaults.

The inexorable diffusion of the weapons technologies of mass destruction—nuclear, biological, and chemical—together with cheap and pervasive communications, computing, and sensor systems for targeting and intelligence, threaten the domestic peace of all countries. Where the international arms trade—in which the major nuclear powers are the market leaders—together with domestic internal conflicts supported by nationally sponsored international-terrorist and other violent, criminal organizations interact, we have a rapidly growing source of international tensions. The major powers cannot totally defend themselves from smaller-state–sponsored terrorism, whether conventional or nuclear, without ultimately threatening massive retaliation and destruction of the terrorist-sponsoring government. Whether internal pacification of such national sponsors of international terrorism is feasible without recourse to war by the larger countries remains to be seen. In any case this development will be one of the most ominous sources of international tensions in the next century.

Major current sources of international tensions are likely to continue to grow or evolve in the next century, involving a variety of forces or factors, as outlined here:

- Cultural: Judeo-Christian versus Islamic or Confucian/Buddhist.
- Economic: Rich versus poor; capitalist versus socialist systems.
- Military: Nuclear versus conventional warfare; strong, global nuclear powers versus weaker, local, or regional ones.
- Political: Democracy versus authoritarianism.
- Technological: Advanced technologies, versus those trying to catch up, versus backward ones, who may have piecemeal access to some elements of advanced technology.

In particular, the miniaturization and diffusion of cheap, easy-to-manufacture biological, chemical, or nuclear weapons of mass destruction may serve to exacerbate these growing social, political, and economic conflicts into violent military engagements.

See also APOCALYPTIC FUTURE; ARMS RACE; CHINA: ETHNIC REAWAKENING; ENVIRONMENTAL REFUGEES; ESPIONAGE AND COUNTERINTELLIGENCE; ETHNIC AND CULTURAL SEPARATISM; FUNDAMENTALISM; GLOBAL STATISTICS; HUMAN RIGHTS; INTERNATIONAL TRADE: SUSTAINING GROWTH; MIGRATION, INTERNATIONAL; NATIONALISM; PEACEKEEPING; POPULATION GROWTH: WORLDWIDE; TERRORISM; WEAPONS OF MASS DESTRUCTION; WORLD: PROLOGUE AND EPILOGUE.

BIBLIOGRAPHY

BANKS, MICHAEL. *Conflict in World Society: A New Perspective on International Relations.* New York: St. Martin's Press, 1984.

BARTLETT, C. J. *Global Conflict: International Rivalry of the Great Powers.* White Plains, NY: Longman, 1984.

BLOOMFIELD, LINCOLN P. *Management of Global Disorder.* Lanham, MD: University Press of America, 1988.

BRECHER, MICHAEL, and WILKENFELD, JONATHAN. *Crisis, Conflict and Instability.* Elmsford, NY: Pergamon, 1989.

HOLSTI, KALEVI J. *Peace and War: Armed Conflict in International Order.* New York: Cambridge University Press, 1991.

KLARE, MICHAEL T., and THOMAS, DANIEL C. *World Security: Trends and Changes at Century's End.* New York: St. Martin's Press, 1991.

MANDEL, ROBERT. *Irrationality in International Confrontation.* Westport, CT: Greenwood Press, 1989.

MATTHEWS, ROBERT O. *International Conflict and Conflict Mangement.* New York: Prentice-Hall, 1994.

ORDESHOOK, PETER C. *The Balance of Power Stability and Instability in International Systems.* New York: Cambridge University Press, 1989.

STILLMAN, EDMUND O., and PFAFF, WILLIAM. *The Politics of Hysteria: The Sources of Twentieth Century Conflict.* Westport, CT: Greenwood Press, 1981.

Clark C. Abt

International Trade: Regional Trade Agreements

Regional trade agreements (RTAs) have proliferated since World War II, and more than eighty have now been notified to the General Agreement on Tariffs and Trade (GATT). This survey only considers the most active groups (see Table 1). The two most common variants of RTAs are Customs Unions (CUs), which impose a common external tariff (CET) on nonmembers, and Free Trade Areas (FTAs), in which individual members maintain their separate tariff schedules for nonmembers. The motivations for RTAs are both political (to alleviate political tensions between neighboring countries) and economic (to gain the benefits of mutual trade liberalization). In principle, multilateral liberalization on a global scale could confer greater economic benefits, but RTAs are often justified as a quicker means for achieving deeper liberalization within a smaller group of countries. Countries outside the trade "blocs" fear that they will lose export markets to countries within the group; GATT rules minimize these adverse impacts.

Europe

The European Economic Community (EEC), also known as the European Common Market, was launched in 1957 with the passage of the Treaty of Rome specifying "four freedoms"—free movement of goods, services, capital, and people. A classic customs union, the group adopted the name European Community and then changed it to European Union (EU) in 1993. The initial membership of six grew to twelve countries by 1986 (see Table 1). Austria, Finland, Norway, and Sweden are scheduled

TABLE 1.   Summary of Regional Trade Agreements

Name and Year Signed	*Membership (Year signed, if not original member)*
Europe European Union (EU, 1957)	Belgium, Denmark (1973), France, Germany, Greece (1981), Ireland (1973), Italy, Luxembourg, the Netherlands, Portugal (1986), Spain (1986), and the United Kingdom (1973).
European Free Trade Association (EFTA, 1960)	Austria, Finland (1961), Iceland (1970), Liechtenstein (1991), Norway, Sweden, and Switzerland.
North America North American Free Trade Agreement (NAFTA, 1993)	Canada, Mexico, and the United States.
Pacific Rim Association of Southeast Asian Nations (ASEAN, 1967)	Brunei (1988), Indonesia, Malaysia, the Philippines, Singapore, and Thailand.
Asia Pacific Economic Cooperation (APEC, 1989)	Australia, Brunei, Canada, Chile (1994), China (1991), Chinese Taipei (Taiwan, 1991), Hong Kong (1991), Indonesia, Japan, Korea, Malaysia, Mexico (1993), New Zealand, Papua New Guinea (1993), the Philippines, Singapore, Thailand, and the United States.
Australia–New Zealand Closer Economic Relations Trade Agreement (ANZCERTA, 1983)	Australia and New Zealand.
Latin America Latin American Free Trade Association (LAFTA, 1960), renamed Latin American Integration Association (LAIA, 1980)	Mexico and all the South American countries except Guyana, French Guiana, and Suriname.
Central American Common Market (CACM, 1960)	Costa Rica (1962), El Salvador, Guatemala, Honduras, and Nicaragua.
Caribbean Community (CARICOM, 1973)	Antigua and Barbuda, the Bahamas (1983), Barbados, Belize (1974), Dominica (1974), Grenada (1974), Guyana, Jamaica, Montserrat (1974), St. Kitts and Nevis, St. Lucia (1974), St. Vincent and the Grenadines (1974), and Trinidad and Tobago.
Andean Pact (1969)	Bolivia, Colombia, Ecuador, Peru, and Venezuela (Chile withdrew in 1976).
Mercado Común del Sur (MERCOSUR, 1991)	Argentina, Brazil, Paraguay, and Uruguay.

TABLE 1. (CONTINUED)

Name and Year Signed	Membership (Year Signed, If Not Original Member)
Africa	
South African Customs Union (SACU, 1910)	Botswana, Lesotho, Namibia, South Africa, and Swaziland.
South African Development Coordination Conference (SADCC, 1980)	Angola, Botswana, Mozambique, Tanzania, Zambia, and Zimbabwe.
Economic Community of West African States (ECOWAS, 1975)	Benin, Burkina Faso, Cape Verde, Côte d'Ivoire, The Gambia, Ghana, Guinea, Guinea-Bissau, Liberia, Mali, Mauritania, Niger, Nigeria, Sénégal, Sierra Leone, and Togo.
Communauté Economique de l'Afrique de l'Ouest (CEAO, 1973)	Benin (1984), Burkina Faso, Côte d'Ivoire, Mali, Mauritania, Niger, and Sénégal.
Mano River Union (MRU, 1973)	Guinea (1980), Liberia, and Sierra Leone.
Customs and Economic Union of Central Africa (UDEAC, 1964)	Cameroon, Central African Republic, Congo, Gabon, Chad, and Equatorial Guinea.
Preferential Trade Area for Eastern and Southern African States (PTA, 1981)	Angola, Burundi, Comoros, Djibouti, Ethiopia, Kenya, Lesotho, Malawi, Mauritius, Mozambique, Namibia (1991), Rwanda, Somalia, Sudan, Swaziland, Tanzania, Uganda, Zambia, and Zimbabwe.

Sources: International Monetary Fund, *World Economic Outlook*. (May 1993): 107–108; De Melo and Panagariya. *New Dimensions in Regional Integration*. Cambridge, U.K.: Cambridge University Press.

to join in 1995, and the group may be enlarged to include Eastern European countries within another ten years. The "Europe 1992" program, launched in 1985, sought to eliminate all residual barriers to achievement of the four freedoms before January 1993. The Maastricht Treaty of 1991 set out to create a single currency and the same degree of economic cohesion as in the United States. Though unification is far from complete, the EU already has achieved more integration than any other regional group.

The European Free Trade Association (EFTA) was created in 1960 as a free trade area. Membership dwindled with the departure of the United Kingdom, Ireland, and Denmark in 1973, and three of the six remaining EFTA members are seeking to join the EU.

North America

The North American Free Trade Agreement (NAFTA) augments the U.S.–Canada Free Trade Agreement of 1988 by the addition of Mexico. Basically, the NAFTA provides for free trade in goods and services, and the free movement of capital after a phase-in period of about ten years.

Pacific Rim

In the Asia-Pacific region, formal economic cooperation originated in 1967 with the creation of the Association of Southeast Asian Nations (ASEAN). The inspiration for ASEAN was political (as a regional security body), not economic. Only with the 1991 agreement to create an ASEAN Free Trade Area (AFTA) did the nations seriously turn to economic integration. AFTA's progress is still hampered by nonbinding liberalization schedules, lengthy transition periods, and an unwillingness to commit to free trade in sensitive products.

The Australia-New Zealand Closer Economic Relations Trade Agreement (ANZCERTA or CER) entails strong economic cooperation between two countries that have long been political allies. Since its creation in 1983, ANZCERTA has removed all merchandise trade barriers between Australia and New Zealand, and has instituted precedent-setting rules on trade in services, harmonization of commercial codes, and competition policies.

The newest regional umbrella organization, the Asia Pacific Economic Cooperation (APEC), contains eighteen members (Table 1). APEC was created in late 1989 to provide a consultative forum in which the members can discuss economic policy issues, somewhat similar to the OECD (Organization for Economic Cooperation and Development). Since 1992, APEC has begun strengthening its institutional structure, by creating a permanent secretariat in Singapore, an Eminent Persons Group to lay out a vision for the organization, and a Committee on Trade and Investment. At the 1994 summit in Bogor, APEC leaders resolved to achieve free trade and investment in the region by 2020 (2010 for industrialized countries).

Lastly, a number of subregional economic zones (SREZs) have been created in Southeast Asia in recent years. SREZs usually include parts of neighboring countries, rather than the entire countries themselves. Examples include the SIJORI growth triangle, covering Singapore, Malaysia's Johor province, and Indonesia's Riau province; the Greater South China Economic Zone, covering coastal South China, Taiwan, and Hong Kong; and the Yellow Sea Economic Zone, covering Northern China, Japan, and South Korea.

Latin America

Economic integration in Latin America originated in the early 1960s, inspired by the political doctrines of import substitution and self-sufficiency. The hope was to expand exports and overcome foreign exchange shortages through greater trade within the region, but little integration was achieved until the mid-1980s, when regional pacts were rejuvenated on the basis of market-oriented principles. At the Miami Summit of the Americas in December 1994, Western Hemisphere leaders agreed to integrate existing subregional agreements into one encompassing "Free Trade Area of the Americas."

The Latin American Free-Trade Association (LAFTA)—replaced by Latin American Integration Association (LAIA) in 1980—and the Central American Common Market (CACM) were created in 1960. LAIA has remained a talk-shop organization, which ambitiously encompasses all of South America and Mexico. Because of political turmoil in Central America, CACM accomplished little until the late 1980s. Since then, the CACM members have agreed to drop internal duties on agricultural trade, impose a CET by 1995, and establish a free trade area with Mexico by 1997.

The Andean Pact was created in 1969. Encouraged by market-oriented reforms of the mid-1980s, its members agreed in 1990 to achieve regional free trade by 1992; Bolivia, Colombia, and Venezuela eliminated tariffs on schedule, while Ecuador has fallen behind and Peru has withdrawn from the group.

The Caribbean Community (CARICOM) evolved from the Caribbean Free Trade Area (CARIFTA) in 1973. The group, with a membership of thirteen Caribbean nations, became active in the late 1980s, but has repeatedly postponed deadlines for establishing a CET, while trade liberalization among members has progressed at different rates.

The Mercado Común del Sur (MERCOSUR) is the youngest of Latin America's regional trading blocs. Created in 1991, MERCOSUR's schedule calls for free internal trade and a CET by 1995. This schedule is proceeding as planned, although macroeconomic instability in Brazil has created severe strains.

Africa

African regional integration attempts have been mostly unsuccessful, with the exception of South African Customs Union (SACU) and South African Development Coordination Conference (SADCC). SACU, created in 1910 by South Africa, Botswana, Lesotho, and Swaziland (Namibia joined in 1990), has a CET and a centralized monetary policy. SADCC was created by the other southern African states to reduce their dependence on South Africa during the apartheid era.

Other "paper" groups include the Economic Community of West African States (ECOWAS); Communauté Economique de l'Afrique de l'Ouest (CEAO); Mano River Union (MRU); the Customs and Economic Union of Central Africa (UDEAC); and the Preferential Trade Area for Eastern and Southern African States (PTA). None of these groups has achieved meaningful trade liberalization or established a CET.

Do Regional Trade Agreements Presage Global Integration?

The proliferation of regional trade agreements raises the question whether RTAs create commercial tensions between regions, or whether they presage global economic integration. The GATT requires that participants in RTAs eliminate barriers on "substantially all" trade; that average external duties in a customs union should not "on the whole be higher or more restrictive" than the duties previously imposed by the member countries; and that interim agreements should lead to CUs or FTAs "within a reasonable amount of time." All of these conditions are criticized as too vague, permitting

TABLE 2.   Intraregional Exports as a Share of Total Regional Exports

Regional Trade Agreement	1970	1975	1980	1985	1990
EU	51.0	50.0	54.0	54.4	60.4
EFTA	28.0	35.2	32.6	31.2	28.2
NAFTA	36.3	35.0	33.6	31.2	28.2
ASEAN	20.7	15.9	16.9	18.4	18.4
ANZCERTA	6.1	6.2	6.4	7.0	7.6
LAFTA/LAIA	9.9	13.6	13.7	8.3	10.6
CACM	25.7	23.3	24.1	14.7	14.8
ANDEAN PACT	2.0	3.7	3.8	3.4	4.6
SADCC	2.6	3.7	2.1	3.9	4.8
ECOWAS	2.9	4.0	3.5	5.3	5.7
CEAO	6.3	12.7	8.9	8.7	10.5
MRU	0.2	0.4	0.5	0.4	0.1
UDEAC	4.8	2.7	1.6	1.9	3.0
PTA	8.0	9.3	7.6	5.5	5.9

Sources: De Melo and Panagariya. *New Dimensions in Regional Integration.* Cambridge, UK: Cambridge University Press, 1993: 247–248; International Monetary Fund. *World Economic Outlook* (May 1993): 112.

too much discrimination against nonmembers. Meanwhile, it is an open question whether, over the next decade, RTAs will inspire or impede the newly created World Trade Organization.

Trade Patterns

Intraregional exports as a percentage of total regional exports are depicted in Table 2, which shows that intraregional trade has increased over the last two decades for the larger groups (especially EU and NAFTA). This relative growth in intraregional trade can be interpreted in two ways. It could come at the expense of trade with nonmembers ("trade diversion"); or it could result from an overall increase in trade due to liberalization ("trade creation"). Research suggests that trade creation is generally more important; but countries that are not members of a particular group are especially sensitive to trade diversion.

See also FREE TRADE; GLOBAL BUSINESS; INTERNATIONAL TRADE: REGULATION; INTERNATIONAL TRADE: SUSTAINING GROWTH.

BIBLIOGRAPHY

ANDERSON, KYM, and BLACKHURST, RICHARD. *Regional Integration and the Global Trading System.* New York: St. Martin's Press, 1993.

DE MELO, JAIME, and PANAGARIYA, ARVIND. *New Dimensions in Regional Integration.* Cambridge, U.K.: Cambridge University Press, 1993.

GARNAUT, ROSS, and DRYSDALE, PETER. *Asia Pacific Regionalism: Readings in International Economic Relations.* Pymble, Australia: HarperEducational, 1994.

HENNING, C. RANDALL; HOCHREITER, EDUARD; and HUFBAUER, GARY C. *Reviving the European Union.* Washington, DC: Institute for International Economics, 1994.

HUFBAUER, GARY C., and SCHOTT, JEFFREY J. *NAFTA: An Assessment.* Washington, DC: Institute for International Economics, 1993.

HUFBAUER, GARY C., and SCHOTT, JEFFREY J. *Western Hemisphere Economic Integration.* Washington, DC: Institute for International Economics, 1994.

(The author would like to acknowledge the invaluable assistance of Gautam Jaggi in the preparation of this article.)

Gary Hufbauer

International Trade: Regulation

From a strictly economic perspective, there are only two valid reasons for international trade: to expand markets (and demand) for domestic capacity and to acquire something of value not comparably available from domestic sources. However, actual trade involves a more complex rationale flowing from a diverse network of geopolitical and social purposes. This forecast delves into trends and changes affecting international trade between 1955 and 2020, chiefly from a U.S. perspective.

Historic Perspectives

Two methods of calculating U.S. trade trends in quantitative terms—the five-year moving average and the exponential fit—make it dramatically apparent that the United States cannot remain either a major world power or a leading world economy if ongoing trends are projected ahead twenty-five years. Therefore, U.S. trade policies will have to change if a major, more favorable shift in these trends is to occur. More careful forecasts require an understanding of the policy dynamics that underlie these numbers.

An analysis of socioeconomic history and a cursory review of the trade agreements, policies, and programs of the United States summarizes the sweep of history. This pattern of U.S. trade history is consistent with the global patterns.

From this historical perspective, significant changes in philosophy or policy features determine each "new" historic era. This "historic era" concept is an important construct or tool in any forecast. If the forecasting horizon does not involve a transition into a "new era," one can more confidently assume a "strategic stability" in the underlying driving forces. Impending transition into a new era supports (selectively) more reliance upon projections. At the same time, when an "era transition" is in progress, projections are more likely to yield inaccurate results.

On the basis of these few foundations, a new era is probably emerging today. The following forecasts are based upon this premise. This estimate is based upon the unacceptability of projected trends, the dynamics associated with emerging technologies, and institutional changes within the emerging global economy.

Forecasts

The emergence of global telecommunications, manufacturing technologies, the weaponry of sabotage, global finance, the emergence of the global market, and the emerging dominance of the transnational corporation (replacing the international and multinational-type companies) are the principal forces driving the future of international trade.

Given the geographic redistribution of manufacturing and value-added roles associated with the evolving transnational corporations, the volume of world exports is expected to grow rapidly. The U.S. effort to capture 20 percent of world exports will require a major expansion of exports. As the value-added functions of trade shift from national concentrations of commercial enterprise toward global optimization based on global markets and global manufacturing/services, wherever they might be located, imports will steadily rise. Imports will continue to be carefully controlled, but the onus of regulation will gradually shift from treaties, compacts, and trade agreements toward voluntary controls involving new accountability standards related to processing quality and production costs.

The U.S. economy will remain a major import market, but the comparative attractions will erode considerably. This shift will lower U.S. trade negotiation leverage. However, efforts will be undertaken to offset this eroding influence in other ways.

International trade will become much more a function of marginal economic advantage. Subsidies intended to spur economic development or bestow political reward (i.e., the awarding of most-favored-nation status and the like) will wane.

Forecasts

U.S. policy goals can be summarized as follows:

- To remain a "dominant" world power, with the military capability to back up that role.
- To sustain democracy as the predominant political system of choice.
- To maintain market-driven capitalism as the economic system of choice.
- To retain effective sovereignty of the nation-state by selectively delegating sovereignty to world trade regulatory bodies, though limiting this sovereignty to specified circumstances.
- To redefine national security so that it includes many aspects of economic and sociopolitical value protection. This will lead to a world power–based economy capable of supporting with minimal dependency the military capability required to support the world role and the protection of U.S. freedoms and living standards.
- To implement import controls that will prevent imports from eroding the strategic power of the U.S. economy.
- To sustain national competitiveness within the global economy
- To attain for the United States at least 20 percent of the world's exports, with two or more U.S.-based transnational companies among the top-ten global firms within each major industry or economic sector. (A result of this strategy will be the development of new kinds of partnerships between the U.S. government and various transnational firms.)
- To achieve a strategic equilibrium of trade and monetary exchange balances.
- To establish global production and trade standards that assure certain quality and "compar-

ability" in labor rates and environmental standards.

- To achieve regulatory control of the transnational "corporate state."
- To foster developmental economics that will shift the focus from the nation-state to identifiable population subsets within nation-states.

Ultimate Sovereignty

The most significant judgment to be made is the estimate of where the ultimate sovereignty will reside—i.e., in the political configuration (whether nation-states, regional federations, or a global government) or the corporate state (i.e., the network of emerging global corporations). The assessment must go beyond rhetorical structures to an estimate of where the effective operational power to define and control policy lies.

Continued erosion of the relative power and effective sovereignty of the nation-states will occur over the next five to ten years. Some sovereignty will be relegated to regional coordinating bodies (e.g., the European Economic Community) and ultimately to their political counterparts (e.g., the United States of Europe).

Regional entities (economic and geopolitical) will reflect matrices of geographically contiguous areas (Europe, the Americas, Asia/Pacific) and political alliances (the Muslim states). Culturally based concepts such as "Western civilization" will gradually be eroded as the amalgamation of cultures progresses within nations. (Only states clearly defining cultural values as a heritage to be protected and propagated will involve themselves in transregional/transnational alliances.)

Regional entities will contend for increased power via delegated sovereignty from constituent nation-states. Accelerating concentration of global economic wealth and power in the top transnational corporations will occur in the near term. Before the end of the first decade of the next century, the concept of the corporate state as a geopolitical power will be well defined. Many current U.S. philosophies and goals will be at serious risk unless "national interests" are reinstated as the primary criteria governing international policies and relations. (At this point there will be a major drive to rebuild the nation-state(s) as the primary sovereign entity.) The ultimate outcome will depend upon the network of nations, and their related philosophies, goals, and economic resources. The United States will adjust its policy structure and evolve a coherent industrial policy of the type required to remain a major factor in this block of world power nations.

Controlling Transnational Corporations

If current trends continue through the forecasting period, the corporate state, composed of fewer than 400 transnational corporations, will represent a power base that will erode and eventually dominate the policy structures within which trade is conducted. National interests will increasingly be defined by economic determinism based upon "optimization" of the corporate economy.

New controls over transnational corporate communities will evolve. One major mechanism for this regulatory control will be new process quality standards and audit systems. (Whatever the ultimate form, the corporate state will remain subject to the collective authority of nation-states.)

There should be no underestimation of the influence that the corporate state can bring to bear on the network of national and regional policies. It is not likely that a renewal of isolationism will materialize. There may be some degree of nationalistic "protectionism" on a selective basis, but this phenomenon is not likely to become widespread. Similarly, total subservience of the corporate state to any particular nation states will not occur.

These tensions will exert a dominant influence over the dynamics of international trade for the next twenty-five years.

Cross-National Equity in Process Quality and Costs

The current drive in the EEC for "uniformity" in product reliability as a function of specific process and quality standards will become a global model. Process standard concepts will be extended to services such as stock market operations, banking, and other major economic undertakings. Process standards and audits will become major mechanisms for equalizing such factors as environmental quality and labor costs. Ultimately, all goods and services entering global markets will compete, with the competitive edge determined by productivity, innovation, and other legitimate differentiating factors.

These developments will shift much of the trade regulatory function onto individual company behavior, with less emphasis upon nations or entire industries. Compliance with process and quality standards will require certification by independent audits, much like today's independent auditor certifications of financial statements.

Legally Regulated Transactions

Regulated transactions will be expanded to encompass financial services and, ultimately, capital investment. A coherent U.S. industrial policy will evolve that sustains industrial capabilities associated with national security on a minimum dependence basis. Provision also may be made to protect selected key employment centers required to sustain continued growth of the U.S. national markets so that they remain attractive to imports and investments, protect overall U.S. standards of living, and sustain ecological standards, intellectual property rights, and so forth.

Illegal Transactions

Banned imports or exports will expand to include the following:

- Items or goods that pose public health risks (e.g., certain drugs and adulterated or contaminated foods or beverages).
- Items or goods found to be in noncompliance with process and quality standards or that have not been audited or tested to see if they are in compliance.
- Items or transactions that pose a threat to national security or sovereignty.

Barter Exchanges

Trade regulatory systems will require companies engaging in global trade to report transactions on a value-added basis. Data acquired will be used to monitor the financial dealings of each nation and company. Black market bartering among transnational companies intended to circumvent regulations standing in the way of the company goals will increase, driven by economic motives. Tensions between accountable barter and black market barter will become a major problem in international trade during the next century.

See also FREE TRADE; GRAY MARKET GOODS; INTERNATIONAL GOVERNANCE AND REGIONAL AUTHORITIES; INTERNATIONAL TRADE: REGIONAL TRADE AGREEMENTS; INTERNATIONAL TRADE: SUSTAINING GROWTH.

BIBLIOGRAPHY

ADELMAN, CAROL C., ed. *International Regulation: New Rules in a Changing World Order.* San Francisco, CA: Lehrman Institute/Institute for Contemporary Studies Press, 1988.

BROWN, MICHAEL B. *Fair Trade: Reform and Realities in the International Trading System.* Atlantic Highlands, NJ: Zed Books, 1993.

HOWELL, T. R.; WOLFF, A. W.; BARTLETT, B. L.; and GADBAW, R. M., eds. *Conflict Among Nations: Trade Policies in the 1990s.* Boulder, CO: Westview Press, 1992.

OHMAE, KENICHI. *The Borderless World: Power and Strategy in the Interlinked Economy.* New York: HarperCollins, 1990.

RUNNALLS, DAVID, and COSBY, AARON. *Trade and Sustainable Development: A Survey of the Issues and a New Research Agenda.* Winnipeg, Manitoba: International Institute for Sustainable Development, 1992.

STARR, MARTIN K. *Global Competitiveness: Getting the U.S. Back on Track.* New York: W. W. Norton, 1988.

VERNON, RAYMOND, and SPAR, DEBORA. *Beyond Globalism: Remaking American Foreign Economic Policy.* New York: Free Press, 1989.

Charles W. Williams
Wesley H. Williams

International Trade: Sustaining Growth

The United States has been promoting a multilateral open trade policy since the end of World War II. This policy is expected to continue for the remainder of this century. U.S. economic policy analysts expect that international exports will become a major factor in sustaining U.S. economic growth and living standards during this time. This entry looks at historic data regarding the growth of world trade and the U.S. economy, particularly as it pertains to these expectations.

World merchandise trade (in current dollars) has more than doubled over the past decade. In the process, however, persistent bilateral trade imbalances emerged. Advocates of multilateral open trade minimize the significance of these bilateral imbalances, claiming that multilateral balance will be achieved over time. Even so, the persistence of the imbalances of the United States and Japan, not just with each other but with the world, suggests that multilateral balance may be a long time in coming.

Another problem associated with imbalances is how they transmit recessions among trading partners. For example, in the 1990–1991 period, while the U.S. economy was in recession, U.S. imports declined slightly but recovered vigorously shortly thereafter. In contrast, the Japanese recession, which also began in 1990, has persisted through 1994 and is not expected to end before the end of 1995. Not only do American exporters suffer from the shrinking export market, but attempts to bring the national trade accounts into balance will invariably fail, along with the political friendships that inevitably develop between trading partners.

Over the past few decades, the United States has gone from being the world's largest creditor to the world's largest debtor, with Japan becoming the world's largest creditor. This does not augur well for claims about multilateral accounts balancing over the long term.

U.S. budget deficits are commanding an enormous amount of political attention today. As devastating as the overall budget deficit is to the U.S. economy, it pales in importance with persistent current account deficits. The cumulative current account imbalances indicate that the United States ran up deficits totaling about $1.2 trillion over the past decade. This debt is somewhat offset by U.S. holdings of international assets, but a growing portion of U.S. debt is held by foreigners—in 1992, about 15 percent of the national debt was held by foreigners.

The reasons foreigners hold U.S. dollars, or invest in dollar-denominated assets, are quite different than they are for Americans. Foreigners hold U.S. dollars to facilitate trade (since most international trade is denominated in dollars) and as an investment. As foreign dollar holdings increase, the investment value becomes more important. If the return on dollar investments erodes or if the creditors need domestic currency (e.g., if the Japanese need more yen), they will become sellers of their dollar holdings. This would in turn cause a decline in the value of the dollar and reduce the return on dollar-denominated assets—a vicious cycle. Recent experiences with Mexico provide a good example of how this phenomenon works. While there are vast differences between the United States and Mexico, the United States may not be far behind with regard to currency crises. Clearly, the U.S. ability to regulate the dollar or intervene in international economic crises has been strongly eroded by foreign dollar holdings.

With regard to the U.S. living standards, current account deficits have both positive and negative aspects. On the positive side, they allow the United States to consume more than it produces. On the negative side, they create a dependence on foreign goods. And since these goods are bought on credit, they produce a debt that will have to be serviced until it is repaid. However, the debt will never be re-

paid until the United States runs a current account surplus. In addition, transferring wealth to international creditors makes it more difficult for the Federal Reserve to control the domestic economy and erodes the strength of the U.S. economy in general.

U.S. trade deficits over the past decade are the result of a three-pronged U.S. policy: (1) to reduce inflation; (2) to increase military spending (during the Cold War); and (3) to promote multilateral open trade by unilaterally offering itself as an example of the benefits that accrue to an open-trader (especially one with a sound currency and high interest rates). In many ways, the policy has been successful. U.S. inflation rates have been held in check despite a horrendous rise in budget deficits. The Soviet Union actually collapsed—exceeding the most optimistic expectations of its supporters, and, because of America's willingness to accept imports, the United States was able to get others to support U.S. living standards by exporting goods to the country on credit. Unfortunately, this policy had many side effects, which are now extremely difficult to correct.

In addition to the transfer of economic power discussed previously, the world has come to rely on U.S. markets and trade deficits. But, perhaps more important, the United States has become dependent on exporters for a wide variety of industrial and consumer products. These conditions make it very difficult for the United States to deal firmly with trading partners who deny American companies access to the markets that their own companies enjoy in the United States. Therefore, notwithstanding the fact that the United States is currently among the most highly productive nations in the world, it is virtually unable to increase its exports or even gain access to many of its trading partners' markets or to protect its intellectual property rights, the old (but real and important) unleveled playing field argument.

Some economists expect that services trade will be the means by which the United States reverses it trade deficits. The country currently runs a surplus of about $50 billion in its service trade, but this will be difficult to increase. The U.S. services trade is less than 25 percent of its merchandise trade, and most services trade is for tourism, shipping, and royalties. Potentially expandable services trade (e.g., financial services) is tied to capital, and because of America's international indebtedness, it has little capital to support these opportunities should they materialize. Japan is far better positioned to take advantage of such opportunities. The only real hope for an increase in U.S. services trade surpluses is from open and protected markets for intellectual property. It will take more than reluctantly signed trade agreements to secure meaningful protection of intellectual property.

Japan's merchandise trade picture stands in dramatic contrast. Japan runs a trade surplus with all of its trading partners except for raw materials exporters (e.g., oil, copper, steel ore) While the Japanese consumer may be paying more than Americans for many consumer products, even for those produced in Japan, this may be offset by greater economic stability.

The difficulty America has had in negotiating a greater access to the Japanese marketplace is not going to change without increased American pressure. Furthermore, America's ability to apply such pressure weakens steadily as America's international debt continues to rise, as the dollar weakens, and as the world military threat declines.

Statistically the European Community (EC) is the world largest trade group. However, most EC trade is conducted with the other member states under economic agreements that make their behavior resemble a single nation. The EC's external trade provides a somewhat more accurate picture of their international trade. However, the pending expansion of the EC is not reflected in these data.

The EC merchandise trade picture is changing dramatically as a result of new European countries joining the EC and an internal restructuring of the rules moving them toward greater economic unification. Nonetheless, EC trade is more balanced than that of either the United States or Japan.

The EC is still in a recession. However, with the end of the recession expected by 1996 and with the opening of the East European economies imminent, the EC economic outlook is bright.

In spite of an orchestrated effort to create an open multilateral trade system, and without any formal constituency to promote it, the international economy is organizing itself into three major trading blocs. Collectively these three blocs account for more than 80 percent of world trade, more than half of which is intrabloc trade.

A glaring distinction between these blocs is that the Asia/Pacific-10 has been in surplus for more than a decade, and (barring any major shifts in the international economy) this is expected to continue for many years to come. The question is whether or not the other blocs or the international financial markets will permit these trade surpluses to continue.

Also, the internal trade of the West European bloc is more than double its external trade. The trend toward greater concentration of bloc trade is likely to increase as internal economic consolidation continues.

Many global companies recognize this tripolar trend and are positioning their divisions to locate in each of these three blocs in ways that make them appear as if they were "naturalized citizens" of the regions in which they operate.

U.S. macroeconomic trends are as follows: (1) U.S. total trade (merchandise and services exports plus imports) and (2) individual income taxes and social insurance payments have been increasing far more rapidly than (3) U.S. GDP, and all three have been expanding more rapidly than (4) median U.S. family incomes.

These measures clearly show that U.S. family incomes have been lagging behind both trade and GDP trends. Furthermore, the net income has been declining even further since taxes have also been increasing more rapidly than incomes and because more family members had to work to maintain the low levels of growth in family incomes shown here.

Many argue that these conditions are not a result of international trade or global competition, but a consequence of technological progress that has eliminated many highly paid jobs while creating primarily low-paying jobs. Others consider the primary cause to be a result of U.S. companies outsourcing high-paid, labor-intensive jobs that have been made more easily transferable by technological progress. Clearly both technology and the globalization of business have contributed to the trends.

Regardless of the degree to which trade or technology has contributed to the present trends, if they continue, American attitudes toward multilateral open trade will turn increasingly protectionist. But it is not likely that American support for technology will decrease. Americans will continue to have faith in technology and in their ability to develop technology. They will be firm in their belief that if they use the technology they develop wisely (i.e., do not give it away), American living standards will improve. However, if the United States continues to pursue policies directed toward promoting a global multilateral open trade system, and if American living standards do not improve, the political backlash against these trade policies will be severe, at least at the ballot box.

While no one would seriously argue that this is strictly a result of America's pursuit of multilateral open trade policies, it can certainly be argued that globalization of business has put highly paid American workers in direct competition with low-paid foreign workers, and that the American worker is the loser in the process. In an attempt to offset the erosion of income, more women in general, and wives in particular, entered the labor force despite the tax consequences, the fact that they were underpaid (relative to men), and the job-related expenses incurred.

In order to change these trends, the United States must break the deficit mentality that is built into U.S. economic policies. Instead, there must be a focus on measures that will bring production and consumption into balance. Even before the recent decline in the dollar, the United States was among the most productive nations in the world. Nevertheless, the United States cannot sell sufficient product on the domestic and export markets combined to equal its consumption. Hence the country runs trade and current account deficits—deficits that are major factors in the U.S. inability to bring the overall budget into balance. When the United States runs a current account deficit in excess of $150 billion, as it did in 1994, it further debases the dollar as the world's reserve currency.

To change this, Americans will have to muster all of the country's technological and innovative skills to increase the competitiveness of American companies and to support this effort with appropriate economic policies—especially leveling the playing field and keeping it level.

The importance of the level playing field is not because of the export opportunities it will present to U.S. businesses, but because leveling the playing field abroad will also level it at home. Anyone who has traveled to Japan knows that one can usually buy Japanese products at lower prices in the United States than one can in Japan. This procedure, whereby an exporter earns excess profits from domestic sales and uses the surplus to offset lower profits (or even losses) from exports, is often referred to as cross-subsidization.

An American business in a domestic market where a foreign competitor employs cross-subsidization can be at an impossible disadvantage. Furthermore, it is almost impossible to design regulations to prevent cross-subsidization. For example, it is impossible to distinguish between selling at a loss during a "clearance sale" and cross-subsidization. The only effective way to prevent cross-subsidization is to level the playing field so that an exporter's domestic market is not protected, and therefore cannot be used for cross-subsidization. In short, leveling the playing field not only opens foreign markets to U.S. products, it levels the competition at home as well.

One way to accomplish this that would be supported by most Americans is to demand bilateral reciprocity. If the United States were to seek reciprocity via the kind of trade negotiations recently witnessed, it would be negotiating forever, or so it seems. Bilateral reciprocity will have to be unilaterally imposed prior to the usual hearings from the opposition as to issues of unfairness. And since the only trade regulations that the United States controls are U.S. regulations, unilateral change means that the United States will only limit its trading partners to the same privileges American businesses enjoy in other countries.

The details of how to implement this policy will be very contentious, but the specifics are less important than the commitment to changing the rules and U.S. economic policies to make it possible for U.S. businesses to once again produce an amount at least equal to America's consumption. There will surely be many complaints from U.S. companies who depend on foreign production sources and technology, and from those trading partners whose competitiveness would be threatened by such a policy. This should not prevent the United States from following this course. It may be the only way to (1) balance domestic accounts; (2) save the dollar; and (3) prevent the international economy from complete collapse.

See also FREE TRADE; GLOBAL BUSINESS: DOMINANT ORGANIZATIONAL FORMS; GLOBAL CULTURE; INTELLECTUAL PROPERTY; INTERNATIONAL TRADE: REGIONAL TRADE AGREEMENTS; INTERNATIONAL TRADE: REGULATION; TOURISM.

BIBLIOGRAPHY

BATRA, RAVI. *The Myth of Free Trade: A Plan for America's Revival.* New York: Charles Scribner, 1993.
BROWN, MICHAEL B. *Fair Trade: Reform and Realities in the International Trading System.* London and Atlantic Highlands, NJ: Zed Books, 1993.
HOWELL, THOMAS R., and WOLFF, BRENT L. *Conflict Among Nations: Trade Policy in the 1990s.* Boulder, CO: Westview Press, 1992.

Selwyn Enzer

Investments

The importance of investments in any assessment of the future cannot be overestimated. Following the dramatic collapse of communism in 1989–1991, and the subsequent rise of democratic free enterprise worldwide, investments of all types are taking on vital significance as the *sine qua non* of world economic development and prosperity. The United States has been the global leader for democracy and free enterprise for the community of nations. One of the reasons for the political/economic ascendance of the United States was the rapid development of its capital markets, especially in the period following the Civil War.

A brief survey of different investment terms follows.

Debt Instruments

A "debt security" is evidence of borrowing that must be repaid, stating the amount, maturity date (or dates), and a specific rate of interest (or discount). Debt securities can be traded among investors before they mature. A corporate bond is a certificate of indebtedness extended over a period of from several years to a century. It is issued by a company which also has common stock. Bonds are considered a senior security in the capital structure of the corporation and have first call on revenues of the corporation to pay their interest and also preference over the assets of the company to insure the return of money lent when the bonds were issued. Bonds are rated based on the outlook for the corporation's business and other factors, with "Triple A" being the highest bond rating. The federal government also issues debt securities ranging from short-term Treasury bills, maturing in a year or less, to the well-known thirty-year Treasury bond. Since Washington is assumed to be able always to raise taxes to pay interest, the quality of the $4 trillion federal debt is considered to be the highest. There is varied tax treatment of different types of debt securities. Municipal bonds, issued by local governments, for example, pay interest that is not taxed by the federal government. The dollar value of trading in the bond market surpasses that of the stock market.

Stocks

Stocks or equities represent ownership in companies. Common stock is issued to shareholders when a company first "goes public" in a "primary offering." The company then uses the money from the offering to develop a business providing a product or service. After the initial stock sale to investors, shares of stock are traded in "secondary markets"—i.e., on the major exchanges (such as the New York Stock Exchange or the American Stock Exchange) or through the over-the-counter dealer network. Stockholders, as owners of a company, benefit when the company earns profits and

suffer when it is unprofitable because stock prices and dividends rise and fall, in each respective situation.

The "dividend yield" on a stock is a function of its dividend and price per share. A "cash dividend" is a cash payment to a company's stockholders made from current earnings or accumulated profits. Investors can also benefit from "dividend reinvestment" plans—i.e., purchasing more shares of a company with its cash dividend payments. Some companies have automatic reinvestment programs for their dividends. In contrast to dividend income, "capital gains" on stocks result when share prices appreciate and are defined as the selling price minus the cost basis. The tax rate on long-term capital gains is currently a 28 percent maximum, contrasted to a much higher maximum marginal rate of 39.6 percent for ordinary income.

"Options" are contracts giving the right to buy (a *call* option) or to sell (a *put* option) a stock, commodity, or financial instrument at a predetermined price and within a preset time period. In the context of a specific company, employee options usually refer to the right to purchase shares of the company, usually below their value in the secondary market, as an incentive for superior performance by employees.

Investors can purchase stocks directly from some major companies without transaction costs, or through discount brokers that charge low commissions or at full-service brokerage firms. It is also possible to purchase shares of companies that are listed on foreign stock exchanges by buying American Depository Receipts for those stocks on our exchanges.

Stock investment strategies range widely from simple value investing, which focuses on share prices selling at low multiples of earnings, to exotic "arbitrage," the practice of buying and selling two different but related securities to profit from a temporary divergence in their values.

Stock Market

The stock market is composed of a large number of individual stocks. There are approximately 2,200 common stocks listed on the New York Stock Exchange and several times that number are traded on the American Stock Exchange and in the NASDAQ market. The number of publicly traded companies in America totals approximately 8,000.

The long-term return for the stock market, which may be thought of as an "investment yield," is approximately 9 percent per year. This return includes both price appreciation and dividends. During the 1980s, when the Dow Jones Industrial Average of thirty well-known stocks rose from 1,000 to nearly 3,000, the return was twice the long-term norm.

While an individual stock can rise and fall substantially based on company developments, the entire stock market is usually less volatile and reflects not only the diverse movements of many common stocks, but also broad factors like economic recoveries and recessions that influence the overall level of corporate profits and interest rates. Also, political developments, such as changes in taxes, and monetary policies implemented by the independent Federal Reserve Board can affect the stock market. There are brief periods when influences on the entire stock market can overshadow all company-level factors. The 1987 stock market crash is an example where the widely watched Dow Jones Industrial Average plunged approximately 1,000 points in only a few weeks, with one giant drop of over 500 points occurring on October 19, 1987. Economic events that may have been responsible for the initial part of the decline included an increase in interest rates by the Federal Reserve. Importantly, another relatively new instrument in U.S. financial markets, termed a "derivative," was responsible for the extreme nature of decline.

A "derivative" product is a contract that has its price determined by an underlying asset such as a stock index, a currency, or a commodity. In the 1987 case, the derivative in question was stock index futures. While the intended use of derivatives by large institutional investors was to reduce risk, the result was just the opposite. A tactic called "portfolio insurance" resulted in the selling of stock index futures as the market began to decline. When the value of these futures dropped below the value of the underlying stock market index, interaction with another derivative tactic termed program trading resulted in a "meltdown." The aforesaid sounds confusing because it is, and the message is that today's financial markets are increasingly complex and subject to forces well beyond fundamental developments in individual companies and normal economic trends. Precautions have, of course, been taken by the exchanges and regulatory authorities to prevent a repeat of the fall of 1987.

Another risk factor in the stock market is related to the purchase of stocks on "margin"—i.e., with borrowed money. While this enhances gains during rising markets, when sudden declines in a common stock, or worse in the entire market, occur, the declining value of stocks held on margin requires that they be sold if new money is not deposited. In most cases, including the fall of 1987, the stocks held on margin are sold, adding to the downward pressure on prices. A long-term investor holding stocks that were fully paid, however, could ride through the 1987 crash without being forced to sell.

Commodities

The original definition of "commodities," bulk goods such as metals or foodstuffs, has been expanded to include financial instruments. Commodity prices are determined by competitive bids and offers, similar to the pricing of stocks. Trading in commodities is usually confined to the futures markets. "Futures" are exchange-standardized contracts for the purchase or sale of a commodity at a future date. Gold is one well-known futures contract, as is the thirty-year Treasury bond. Options can be purchased on commodity futures contracts, just as with stocks. Commodity contracts usually involve high risk.

Mutual Funds

An increasingly popular investment medium in recent years is the "mutual fund," an investment company offering its fund shares for purchase by the public and investing on behalf of its shareholders who may also sell their shares at will, usually at net asset value in the case of open-end funds. Mutual funds can invest in stocks, debt instruments, and even commodities. Specialized funds invest in sectors of the equity market, such as environmental stocks. Over two thousand funds now offer professional management and diversification to investors, but superior performance is not assured.

Future Investment Trends

What might be termed "future shock" certainly characterizes the investment world today—i.e., an increasingly rapid pace of change involving new capital markets, new financial instruments, and new investment strategies. With the collapse of the Berlin Wall, new stock exchanges are opening all around the globe. If one thinks Hong Kong is a frontier stock exchange, what about Mongolia? In Poland, market for the exchange of stock shares began its trading in a building formerly used to store Marxist papers? By the twenty-first century there may well be over one hundred active stock exchanges around the world, many increasingly linked by instant telecommunications and around-the-clock trading. Such growing capital markets will foster the spread of democratic free enterprise.

New financial instruments will continue to offer opportunities, but not without risks. Possibly financial futures will emerge on the gross domestic products of leading industrial countries so that investors can actually buy and sell proxies for the major global economies for both speculative and hedging purposes. On the regulatory front, government policymakers are expected to index capital gains for inflation so taxes will not be paid on phantom gains.

Innovative investment strategies will also characterize the twenty-first century. Asset allocation among various stock markets around the globe will certainly become increasingly popular and rewarding. Possibly one of the most exciting investment philosophies of the future—one that is now crystallizing—is democratic capitalism. This philosophy for managing portfolios seeks to invest in companies where workers at all levels own shares in the enterprise that employs them. If the worker is also an owner and decision maker, there is a growing body of evidence that the company is more productive and profitable. The shares of productive and profitable companies rise faster and higher than the average stock, and both investors and employee/owners benefit accordingly. Significantly, democratic capitalism is not just a investment phenomenon, but a tangible reality that will make all economies where it is practiced more prosperous.

Despite periodic crashes and other shocks that will always occur, stock markets around the globe offer the most exciting investment opportunities for the twenty-first century as an increasing number of the world's more than six billion inhabitants become sufficiently affluent to invest in their own future. In America, a Dow level of 10,000 will probably be one of the first investment milestones of the new century.

See also CAPITALISM; CAPITAL FORMATION; CREDIT, DEBT, AND BORROWING; DERIVATIVES; FINANCIAL INSTITUTIONS; MONETARY SYSTEM; SAVINGS; TAXES; WEALTH.

BIBLIOGRAPHY

ALEXANDER, GORDON J., and SHARPE, WILLIAM F. *Fundamentals of Investment.* New York: Prentice-Hall, 1989.

DELACO, ENRICO, and HORNELL, ERIK. *Technology and Investment: Crucial Issues for the 1990s.* New York: St. Martin's Press, 1991.

WOOD, JOHN H., and WOOD, NORMA L. *Financial Markets.* Fort Worth: Dryden Press, 1990.

David B. Bostian

Islam

Islam, the faith of more than a billion people—a quarter of humanity—is not just a religion. The diversity of cultures and peoples that embrace Islam and the areas of the world they inhabit also make Islam a global culture. The Muslim world embraces some fifty-four sovereign countries. In discussing the future of Islam we thus have to examine both the faith as well as the culture.

Islam is best understood and appreciated as a worldview, as a system of knowing, being, and doing. The literal meaning of Islam is submission and peace. To be a Muslim is to submit voluntarily to the will of "One God" and to seek peace on the basis of this submission through exploration and practice of the teachings of the Qur'an and the Prophet Muhammad. Schools of thought within Islam range from groups who insist on literal interpretation, to those who lean toward mystical elucidation, to those who emphasize the legalistic rulings of classical scholars.

Because Islamic fundamentalism is the most talked-about and politicized aspect of contemporary Islam, it is easy to assume that the future of Islam will be dominated by fundamentalism. But Islamic fundamentalism has no long-term future, largely because as a modern, concocted political dogma, it goes against the history and tradition of Islam. What distinguishes fundamentalism from traditional Islam is the fact that the state, and state power, are fundamental to its vision and represent a paramount fact of its consciousness. Thus, from a total, integrative, theocentric worldview and a God-centered way of life and thought, Islam is transformed into a totalitarian, theocratic world order that submits every human situation to arbitrary edicts of the state. Given the fact that Muslim societies are intrinsically heterogeneous and diverse, a single, dominating interpretation of Islam that excludes all other historical and traditional interpretations cannot survive for long.

The global decline of the sovereignty of the nation-state will also make the fundamentalist quest for a utopian "Islamic state" superfluous. There is a resurgence of a medieval world order in which monarchs and feudal lords are forced to share power and authority with a variety of subordinate and higher powers. The "state" is no longer located in a single place and thus has almost become immune to "capture" by a single party or group. This trend makes the fundamentalist strategy of seizing state power by force unworkable because "the state" is no longer in one place to be "seized."

Fundamentalism will remain a major factor in the Muslim world for at least another decade. It is largely a product of the secular nationalism and imported modernism of the Muslim world. Dictatorial nation-states have stripped Muslim societies of their diversity, concentrated power in the hands of westernized elites, and marginalized and ruthlessly suppressed all other segments of society. Ill-fitting modernization and development schemes are destroying the very foundation of traditional lifestyles. Displaced from their land and unable to sustain themselves, millions of farmers and rural folk are migrating to overcrowded cities, without infrastructure, adequate housing, sanitation, or employment. Deprivation and bitterness breed extremism, and, when combined with a strong sense of religious identity, generate fundamentalism. Islamic fundamentalism will thus be with us as long as these basic problems of Muslim societies remain.

However, both due to the failure of modernity and the threat of fundamentalism, Muslims everywhere have become acutely aware of the need for new ideas. This realization has led to a number of efforts to spawn new disciplines within the Islamic purview. "Islamic futures" is the new area of inquiry perhaps most relevant to futures studies. It focuses on articulating visions of future Muslim civilizations, critiques of contemporary Muslim thought from a futures perspective, and a consideration of the impact on Muslim societies of developments in modern biology and information technologies. These varied studies have played a major part in raising the level of consciousness about future possibilities in the Muslim world. The worldwide "Islamization of knowledge" movement is based on the realization that both modernity and traditionalism have failed Muslim societies. It aims to develop new, pluralistic interpretations of Islam that could be used both to manage as well as usher positive change in Muslim societies and thus create a distinct and different future for Muslim civilization. The emerging ideas on "Islamic science" have generated considerable debate regarding appropriate science and technology policies for Muslim countries. Whatever the outcome of such debate, there can be no doubt that the future of Islam will be considerably different from that envisaged by simply concentrating on Islamic fundamentalism.

The end of the Cold War has already had a profound effect on the Muslim world. The war was cold because it froze history in Europe and abandoned the fate of some 150 million Muslims to communism. The emergence of the six new Muslim republics in central Asia—Azerbaijan, Kazakhstan, Kyrgyzstan, Tadjikistan, Turkmenistan, and Uzbekistan—as well as Albania and Bosnia-Herzegovina has enhanced the power of Islamic civilization. Once these countries acquire a modicum of infrastructure, they will become thriving economies.

Chechnia, Dagestan, Abkhazia, Adzhar, Kabardino-Balkar, Tataristan—all of these are likely to become independent states within the next two decades. The emergence of a new Chinese Muslim republic, Xinjiang, is also likely.

In addition to the emergence of new Muslim republics, some old ones will undergo major transformations. Both Iran and Saudi Arabia will collapse as authoritarian and fundamentalist states; both will move toward some form of participatory governance. The new, enlarged Muslim world will not only provide a battleground for economic interests, it will also be seen in the West as the most hostile emerging contender for international influence, not the least because it will be the only nonsecular participant in the global power game. Broadening of the cultural base of Islam also will serve to increase its negotiating and political power.

The second transformation concerns the leadership of the Muslim world. Up to now, Saudi Arabia has been the *de facto* leader of the Muslim world. However, there is serious disillusionment with Saudi Arabia, both at the popular level and at the level of international relations. As Saudi Arabia itself comes under pressure for reform, the leadership of the Muslim world will move eastward toward central and southeast Asia. A fully developed Azerbaijan, with all its oil reserves, will become the new Kuwait and will command considerable attention and respect from Muslim countries, but it will be Malaysia that will emerge as the new, undisputed leader of the Muslim world.

Malaysia, a new tiger in Asia, is one of the fastest-growing economies of the world. Its success as a multicultural, power-sharing democracy will serve as a galvanizing model for other Muslim countries. Disillusioned by extremes of arid, alienating modernity and rigid, authoritarian fundamentalism, most Muslim countries will readily adopt the Malaysian route to development. This political stability will be accomplished with power-sharing and participation from all segments of society, and industrialization with due emphasis on rural development, education, and distribution of wealth. Malaysian Islam has a particularly moderate and humane characteristic, encompassing a "middle path" of balance and toleration.

The third transformation concerns the *ulama*, the religious scholars of Islam, who have commanded unprecedented respect and power in the Muslim world. In some countries, like Iran, they have led revolutions and hold power; in others, like Saudi Arabia, they shape the politics of the state by collaborating with the rulers. The power base of the *ulama* is about to change drastically. In the classical Muslim civilization, the *ulama* were not so much a priestly class as independent custodians of Muslim thought and behavior. After they banned independent and reasoned struggle in matters of religion, they became the sole guardians of Islamic knowledge. The source of the power of the *ulama* is their role as repositories of Islamic knowledge, a function they performed by becoming walking data banks who could retrieve citations from the Qur'an and traditions of the Prophet Muhammad, opinions of classical jurists, historical incidents, and anecdotes almost instantly. This function of the *ulamas* is now being overtaken by the computer revolution. Already, all the classical texts of Muslim thought—including the Qur'an, numerous commentaries, the books of traditions of the Prophet Muhammad, major texts of jurisprudence, major works of classical authors, including translations in major Muslim languages —are all available on a single CD-ROM. Thus, ordinary Muslims, instead of turning to the *ulama* for help and guidance, can go directly to the sources, cutting out the middlemen. The *ulama* thus face two choices: extinction or a transformation back to their original role as the independent—i.e., politically nonaligned and autonomous from structures of power—conscience of the Muslim community.

The coming decade will be crucial in determining whether Islam goes forward toward democratic ways of governance and indigenous forms of multiculturalism or backward toward an idealized medieval past. Much of contemporary Muslim scholarly and intellectual effort is aimed at checking the latter possibility. Preliminary indicators point toward a dynamic, pluralistic future.

See also BUDDHISM; CHRISTIANITY; DEVELOPMENT, ALTERNATIVE; FUNDAMENTALISM; HINDUISM; JUDAISM; MIDDLE EAST; VALUES, NONWESTERN.

BIBLIOGRAPHY

AL-FARUQI, ISMAEL RAJI, ed. *Towards Islamization of Disciplines*. Herndon, VA: International Institute of Islamic Thought, 1989.
ANEES, MUNAWAR AHMAD. *Islam and Biological Futures: Ethics, Gender, and Technology*. London: Mansell, 1989.
BUTT, NASIM. *Science and Muslim Societies*. London: Grey Seal, 1991.
CHAPRA, M. UMAR. *Islam and the Economic Challenge*. Leicester, U.K.: Islamic Foundation, 1993.
DAVIES, MERRYL WYN. "Rethinking Knowledge: Islamization and the Future." *Futures* 23/3 (1991): 231–247.
MANSOOR, S. PARVEZ. "The Future of Muslim Politics: Critique of the Fundamentalist Theory of the Islamic State." *Futures* 23/3 (1991): 289–301.
SARDAR, ZIAUDDIN. *Explorations in Islamic Science*. London: Mansell, 1989.
_____. *The Future of Muslim Civilization*. 2nd ed. London: Mansell, 1987.
_____, ed. *An Early Crescent: The Future of Knowledge and Environment in Islam*. London: Mansell, 1989.

Ziauddin Sardar

Israel.

See JUDAISM; MIDDLE EAST.

Italy

Italy was governed by a totalitarian regime for twenty years between the 1920s and 1940s, but it has functioned as a democracy since World War II. During this same period the basically agricultural Italian society was rapidly transformed into first an industrial and later (in the 1980s) a postindustrial society with the development of advanced electronic industries and sophisticated services in the public and especially the private sector. Although there has been considerable progress in public areas such as education and health, there were signs of deterioration by the late 1980s and early '90s.

The 1970s were marked by a dangerous resurgence of terrorism aimed at destabilizing the system. This unsettled period was followed by prolonged internal stability enabling Italy to prepare for participation in the European Union, which has long been part of its political and economic agenda. More recently, there has been a renewed proliferation of "secret" groups accompanied by a worrisome degeneration of political institutions. The global economic crisis of 1992 has possibly contributed to a healthy reaction against corrupt institutions and chronic governmental crises.

In the future, Italian society will be characterized by continued uncertainty and the danger that the more reactionary political forces will try to take advantage of the situation. Hopefully democracy will prevail.

International diplomacy has always been vital to Italy as a small country occupying an interesting but difficult position in geopolitical terms. In recent years Italy has been pursuing a policy of balanced relations with other Mediterranean countries. The main threat at present derives from the conflict under way in the former Yugoslavia and Italy's ethnic and religious ties with parts of Croatia and Slovenia.

In Italy there are no internal ethnic, linguistic, or religious sources of conflict. The minorities of the bordering regions of Aldo Adige and Valle d'Aosta and of Istria have been peaceful for more than forty years. However, conflicts may arise from the increase in immigrants from Africa, most of whom are Muslims. Although Italy has been traditionally a nonracist country, xenophobia is on the rise, especially in the more conservative north.

Population and Demographics

Italy's current population is about 58 million but declining. Together with Germany and Japan, Italy has the lowest rate of fertility in the world: 1.3 children per fertile woman. Because of a corresponding increase in life expectancy, 14 percent of Italy's population is over sixty-five years of age. By the year 2005, this figure will have increased to 17 percent. As in all industrialized countries, women live longer than men: female life expectancy is eighty years, and male life expectancy is seventy-three. The over-eighty age group is also increasing rapidly. An even higher rate of immigration can be expected in the future because of the aging population and decreasing working population.

Urbanization

The population of medium-sized towns has been increasing but not that of cities with a population of more than one million.

Social Conditions

Contrary to some forecasts, the family remains strong in Italy, but today the family is no longer necessarily based on marriage, especially among the younger generation. There has been no significant increase in the number of couples separating and divorcing, although the number of consensual unions with children born outside marriage is increasing. There is, however, no evidence of a marked increase in the number of households headed by women.

Social mobility was very high in the 1960s and '70s, with an increase in the middle class and a decline of the working class and former aristocracy (tied mainly to the loss of land). In the 1980s, and particularly in the '90s, there have been signs of increasing poverty in the middle class, aggravated by the economic recession.

Welfare has played an important role in Italian society since World War II. Italian maternity laws offer the best protection in the world, and great progress has been made in all sectors. Various factors—not the least of which are the economic crisis, the aging of the population, and the increase in the number of people living on welfare—point to a decrease in welfare expenses. The current countertrend toward privatization of services parallels similar moves in many other countries in the European Community (EC).

Regarding security and law enforcement, a prolonged period of strong support for individual rights, followed by a certain *laissez-faire* due mainly to political alliances, is now being offset by stronger law enforcement campaigns against groups trying to destabilize the state.

On the whole, quality of life is high in terms of living conditions except at either ends of the economic spectrum, though more recently there is evidence that the poor are increasing in numbers while the ranks of the very rich are getting thinner.

Labor and Worklife

Quality of Italian worklife is highly protected in the formal economy, but hardly at all in the informal economy, where the majority of the workforce is composed of women and older and young people. The trend toward an increase of the informal economy is obviously linked to the high cost of social benefits to be paid for the formal workforce.

Science and Technology

Although the Italian state still invests insufficient resources in science and technology, private industry has been very enterprising in this area. Italy's electronic, clothing, food, and fashion sectors are among the best in Europe.

Ecology and Environment

Economic and social issues are very important in Italy. The level of public awareness is high and very much part of politics. All nuclear power plants have been forced to close down in Italy. However, the issue is still being debated, following the EC orientation. Italy is lacking in natural resources, unless one considers beautiful countryside and historic sights a resource. Of course, tourism is one of Italy's greatest assets.

Education, Schooling, Training, and Literacy

There has been great progress in the field of schooling and literacy, and virtually 99 percent of Italy's population is literate. As in all other postindustrial societies, functional illiteracy is a problem, especially for the older population. Education is still not sufficiently flexible and has not adapted to the changing requirements of the labor market or kept pace with technological advances—hence the high rate of unemployment (second in the EC only to Ireland), which is approximately 12 percent of the working population.

Decline of the Communist Party

Concurrent with the collapse of the Soviet Union, the previously strong Italian Communist party has transformed its policy, moving toward a more Social Democratic orientation. It is being further weakened by the unexpected emergence of center-right parties—a reaction by Italians to perceived corruption in the previously governing parties.

Alternative Futures

In the throes of an economic crisis that is expected to last for at least two to three years, Italy can choose to weather the crisis with other European countries or move toward a more authoritarian system. A period of relative indifference on the part of the Italian people for social and political issues seems to be coming to an end, possibly under the impetus of the economic crisis. This change could lead to a renewal of democratic institutions, the division of the country into federations or regions (a trend evident in recent elections), or an authoritarian regime.

In social terms, with its aging population and increased immigration, Italian society will undoubtedly develop into a multicultural society in the long term. This will also involve changes in religious beliefs, due to Islamic migration and mixed marriages. In a sense, Italy may act as a kind of laboratory for other European countries, given the rapidity of the aging of the population and the inflow of migrants with too little time for mutual adaptation and hence possible cultural and economic tension or conflicts.

See also EUROPE, WESTERN.

BIBLIOGRAPHY

PROCACCI, GIULIANO. *History of the Italian People.* London: Penguin, 1968.

SUISBORG, PAUL. *History of Contemporary Italy.* London: Penguin, 1991.

Eleonora Barbieri Masini

Japan

The maturing of the Japanese economy is producing long-run changes, not only in economic life, but also in politics and society. Accumulated social changes are beginning to affect politics, with consequences for the economy. Political choices will determine whether Japan's maturity will be vigorous or stagnant. Many policies and behavior linked to Japan's post–World War II economic success could endanger transformation into a successful twenty-first-century society if left unchanged.

The Japanese economic miracle peaked in the early 1970s. From a 10 percent real annual per capita growth rate of gross national product between 1955 and 1970, Japan's economy slowed to 3 percent growth in the following fifteen years. The 1990s and beyond are likely to witness further declines because the sources of earlier growth—investment, increases in labor supply, and productivity growth—are slowing. Higher productivity is key because it allows greater outputs from the same inputs, higher personal income, superior products, more convenience, and additional leisure. Higher productivity also makes business more competitive by reducing costs and improving products.

Economists have long recognized the possibility of economic stagnation as the returns to investment decline with the increasing capital intensity of production. Japan's economic growth, in particular, is susceptible to that prospect since it was driven by high rates of business investment. In the 1960s, for example, more than one out of every five yen of output was plowed back into equipment investment. As the capital intensity of Japanese production overtook levels in the United States and other advanced industrial economies, the nation's industries earned ever-lower returns on their investments. Economists estimated that the 1990 marginal returns to capital in Japan were about one-third less than in the United States.

Prior to the 1980s, high domestic savings channeled to favored industries through regulated financial institutions provided a below-market cost of funds to many Japanese manufacturing firms. Now, however, Japanese companies pay competitive global rates because of financial market globalization and liberalization. In contrast to the time when companies could rely on large profits or low interest rates, they will now have to make investment decisions balancing real financial costs against declining investment returns. This changing financial reality will require shifting focus from growth to profits. Investment, therefore, is likely to decline.

Demographic shifts in Japan will cause the labor force to decline during the late 1990s. As wages rise due to the falling supply, more older people and women will be drawn into the labor force, which will somewhat mitigate the shortage. Nevertheless, higher wages could raise the cost of output in Japan and erode the share of income going to profits, which in turn would further reduce the internal company funds available for investment.

Investment in education, which complements investments in physical capital, plateaued in the 1970s with almost 100 percent literacy and a large proportion of the population completing secondary education. The average level of formal education barely has changed since then. The gains from further extensions of educational attainment will have to come primarily from increasing the share of people with university degrees, which in 1995 is almost 30 percent below the American level for twenty-two-year-olds. Impending labor shortages and a shift to electronics technologies in manufacturing and services could increase the demand for more educated employees to help offset higher real wages and to operate the more complex technology. A similar shift in the demand for educated workers has occurred in the United States since the 1970s.

Productivity growth and investment are related because new equipment and technology typically include the most advanced capabilities. As investment falls, productivity growth from this source is likely to follow. Another retarding factor is that countries gain an extra boost from their investment when they are technological laggards. Japan's manufacturing productivity seemed to have stopped benefiting from the laggard effect in the 1970s when its capital stock was the youngest of the industrial countries.

Productivity gains among mature economies, however, need not go to zero. Over the twenty-year period from 1969 to 1989, the so-called total factor productivity (which accounts for the contributions of all inputs) of the ten industrial countries with the highest per capita incomes increased at an annual rate of 1 to 2 percent. Although explanations for this growth and its variations are not fully satisfactory, international openness and competition, research and development (R&D), especially basic research, and the adaptability of the economy seem to be the key factors for success of the mature economy. Japan's prospects in these areas are mixed.

Several indicators place Japan's R&D efforts ahead of the United States; for example, Japan's ratio of research scientists and engineers to the labor force was 17 percent higher than in the United States in 1989. In absolute terms, however, American R&D was approximately twice as great. Moreover, Japan is relatively weak in basic research, which seems to have several times more impact on productivity than either physical investment or applied research. On another front, American authors turned out more than 35 percent of the

world's scientific and research literature in 1991 versus 8.5 percent for Japanese scientists; this difference is twice as large as would be expected on the basis of expenditures.

Cross-country studies of productivity conclude that variations in the intensity of competition faced by managers and their exposure to producers on the leading edge are the factors most closely linked to productivity leadership. Illustrating these findings is the Japanese productivity in motor vehicles, automotive parts, steel, consumer electronics, and machine and precision tools, which were all above American levels in 1990. These industries faced high levels of domestic or international competition and were challenged to come up with better ways of making things while adopting the best practices of others. One of the outstanding innovations of the twentieth century, the Toyota production system, came out of this experience.

Japanese manufacturing productivity averages only 80 percent of the American level. The partially regulated food processing business, for example, was two-thirds below American levels in 1990. Japanese economywide productivity was even lower. Gross domestic product per employee in the market sector, which accounted for 81 percent of GDP and 87 percent of employment in 1990, was only 61 percent of the American value and also fell below the levels of France, Germany, and the United Kingdom.

Slower economic and productivity growth and significant lags in productivity levels combine with other forces to increase the pressure for change. The principal reason for lagging productivity is overt regulation or other forms of noncompetitive behavior condoned and sanctioned by the government. According to Japanese government estimates, approximately 40 percent of the economy is subject to explicit regulation. Regulatory constraints are retarding Japanese innovation in several of the most dynamic new industries such as multimedia, which combines telecommunications, computing, and the broadcast media. Without significant deregulation, Japanese participation in these emerging industries will be thwarted.

The Japanese are more likely in the future than in the past to question policies that have favored the narrow interests of producers and the special interests of politically favored groups over those of individuals. The pressure for change arises in part from demographic and economic changes. Relatively fewer people work in the formerly favored sectors. Manufacturing employment fell from a 1970s high of almost 30 percent of all workers to

24 percent in 1991. Heavy industries such as steel and petroleum products lost more than one-third of their employees. Services (including transport, communications, wholesale and retail trade, finance, insurance, real estate, government, and others) rose from 40 percent to 60 percent of the labor force between 1960 and 1991. Over these same years, agricultural employment fell by more than 10 million—from 30 percent of the labor force to 6 percent. From 1966 to 1991, the number of small retail shops fell by 22 percent and employed 430,000 fewer people while the economy as a whole grew by 400 percent. The inhabitants of smaller towns and villages fell from 36 percent to 23 percent of total population. All of these trends are continuing.

Despite these substantial shifts, politics remained straitjacketed. Incomplete adjustment of legislative districts left rural areas overrepresented in the national parliament by more than three to one over urban districts. The political alignments that brought the Liberal-Democratic party to power in 1955 managed to hold the reins of government until 1993. In the meantime, producers (especially heavy industry), agriculture, small shopkeepers, and small-town and rural interests continued to be favored by government policy.

Negative side effects of regulations intended to protect the public or support industrial growth became more apparent as economic growth slowed and as millions of Japanese who traveled abroad each year could see directly that other policies were both feasible and desirable. Additional pressures for change come from the internationally competitive business sector whose efficiency is dragged down by their inefficient domestic suppliers. The international community is also urging Japan to continue the deregulation and market-opening process initiated in the late 1970s. Foreign companies that believe they could be profitable in more open and less regulated Japanese markets are pressuring their governments to negotiate market-opening arrangements.

Change will be profoundly political. Many benefit from the status quo and will fight deregulation and procompetition policies. Inefficient firms, workers facing job loss, cities and regions confronting decline, and government ministries giving up their authority all face real losses. Other political forces, though, push in the opposite direction. Political reforms passed in 1994 under the first non–Liberal-Democratic administration in thirty-eight years should go a long way to begin shifting the balance of legislative influence in favor of urban and consumer interests and away from the old power structure.

In the meantime, slower economic growth is transforming customary relations. Lifetime employment patterns, which made sense when growth was rapid, have declined since the 1970s slowdown; its erosion will accelerate in the coming decade. High levels of corporate cross-shareholding, an effective tool against takeovers when profits seemed to be perpetually rocketing upward, is a costly practice when capital is less available and profits grow more slowly. Similarly, the deep pockets of *keiretsu*—the large vertical or horizontal groupings of companies either in the same business or affiliated with a corporate family bank—that could sustain unprofitable diversifications and ward off acquisitions and mergers will not be as deep or effective as they once were. Therefore, we are likely to see more unfriendly business acquisitions—both domestic and foreign.

Labor market shortages could have significant consequences for the role of women in society. Women are the great underused resource in Japan's economic life. Slow progress has been made by women in penetrating the upper levels of management and technical jobs. Higher labor costs and the gradual decay of the rigid lifetime employment system will aid in prying open opportunities for women. Already more women are attending four-year universities than previously, although their proportion is lower than that of men, which is the reverse of American experience. Also, women's age of marriage is on the rise as they take more time to try their hands at careers. However, sociologists suggest that changes in the attitudes of men and women toward work and family roles will probably be the slowest to occur. Substantial change is only likely as new groups of both men and women move through gradually shifting work and home patterns. Economic forces could take a long time to alter traditional Japanese gender roles, although the direction of change is toward fuller participation by women in the work of the nation.

See also ASIA; FREE TRADE; INTERNATIONAL TRADE: SUSTAINING GROWTH.

BIBLIOGRAPHY

ALEXANDER, ARTHUR J. "Japan as Number Three: Long-Term Productivity and Growth Problems in the Economy." *JEI Report* 17A (1994): 1–15.

BRINTON, MARY C. *Women and the Economic Miracle: Gender and Work in Postwar Japan.* Berkeley, CA: University of California Press, 1993.

ITO, TAKATOSHI. *The Japanese Economy.* Cambridge, MA: MIT Press, 1992.

Japan, Statistics Bureau, Management and Coordination Agency. *Japan Statistical Yearbook: 1993*. Tokyo, 1993.

World Bank. *The East Asian Miracle: Economic Growth and Public Policy*. New York: Oxford University Press, 1993.

Arthur J. Alexander

Job Security.

See UNEMPLOYMENT INSURANCE, WORKMEN'S COMPENSATION, JOB SECURITY.

John the Divine (c. 50–100 A.D.)

According to Christian tradition, John—also known as John the Evangelist, John the Apostle, or Saint John—was a disciple of Jesus and the author of the fourth gospel of the New Testament, three epistles, and Revelation. He is thought to have died c. A.D. 100. Modern biblical scholars doubt that all five books are the work of the same man. Purportedly written by John while in exile on the Aegean island of Patmos, Revelation may have been assembled from the writings of several visionaries who date from near the end of the first century. Whatever its authorship, Revelation is generally regarded as the most influential text in the history of Western futurism. It foretells a time of calamities inflicted on sinful humankind by God, a terrible war between the forces of Satan and the forces of God, and the return of Christ to earth at the head of a victorious army of martyrs. Christ will rule for a thousand years—the Millennium—after which Satan will be loosed, defeated once more, and cast into a lake of fire. The damned will join him in the lake, and a bejewelled city will descend from Heaven where the faithful will spend eternity in glory and honor.

See also APOCALYPTIC FUTURE.

BIBLIOGRAPHY

BULLINGER, E. W. *Commentary on Revelation*. Grand Rapids, MI: Kregel Publishers, 1984.

ELLUL, JACQUES. *L'Apocalypse: architecture en mouvement*, 1975. Translated by George W. Schreiner as *Apocalypse: The Book of Revelation*. New York: Seabury Press, 1977.

FORD, J. MASSYNGBERDE. *Revelation*. Anchor Bible annotated text and commentary. Garden City, NY: Doubleday, 1975.

THOMAS, W. H. *The Apostle John: Studies in His Life and Writings*. Grand Rapids, MI: Eerdmans, 1946.

W. Warren Wagar

Jouvenel, Bertrand de (1903–1987)

The son of a prominent diplomat, the French economist, political philosopher, and futurist Bertrand de Jouvenel wrote extensively on politics and foreign affairs for the French press between the two World Wars. His first book, *L'Economie dirigée* (1928), was a discussion of state economic planning. In mid-life he published an important series of theoretical works, including *Du Pouvoir* (1945; in English, *On Power*, 1949); *De la Souveraineté (1955;* in English, *Sovereignty*, 1957); and *De la Politique pure* (1963; in English, *The Pure Theory of Politics*, 1963). At the same time he became a leading world figure in the burgeoning futurist movement. The activities of the international study group that he organized in 1960, known as Futuribles (a word of his own coinage), led eventually to the founding of the leading French futures journal *Futuribles: Analyse, Prévision, Prospective*. He made his greatest theoretical contribution to futures research in *L'Art de la conjecture* (1964; in English, *The Art of Conjecture*, 1967), a sophisticated analysis of the limits and possibilities of forecasting in human affairs. In this work he defined futuribles as states of affairs in the future whose "mode of production from the present state of affairs is plausible and imaginable."

See also FUTURISTS.

BIBLIOGRAPHY

CORNISH, EDWARD, et al. *The Study of the Future*. Washington: World Future Society, 1977, Chapter 9.

SLEVIN, CARL. "Social Change and Human Values: A Study of the Thought of Bertrand de Jouvenel." *Political Studies* 19 (March 1971): 49–62.

JOUVENEL, BERTRAND DE. "Introduction." In Dennis Hale and Marc Landy, eds., *The Nature of Politics: Selected Essays of Bertrand de Jouvenel*. New York: Schocken Books, 1987.

W. Warren Wagar

Judaism

It is impossible to separate religious from social and political developments when speaking about the future of the Jewish people. Judaism is not a religion like Islam and Christianity where one avows belief, it is rather a religious tradition that reflects the historical development of a particular people. Jewish religiosity and Jewish peoplehood are inseparable. Thus any discussion of the Jewish future must be conducted within a historical context.

In the twentieth century three historical events have dominated the spiritual development of the Jews: the Holocaust, the transformation of American Jews into the largest, most dynamic Jewish community in the world (as a consequence of the physical and spiritual destruction of Eastern European Jewry by the Nazis and the Communists), and the creation of the state of Israel. The Holocaust and Israel have given birth to new prayers and new religious holidays. The preeminence of American Jews has made Conservative and Reform Judaism the numerically dominant form of religious identification in the Jewish world.

As we approach the twenty-first century, demographic developments will radically change the social, cultural, political, and psychological context in which Jewish spiritual development takes place. Israel will become the largest Jewish community in the world by the year 2010. Israel's Jewish population will be greater than the entire Diaspora by the year 2020. Every Jewish community in the world is experiencing negative population growth, with the exception of Israel.

English Jews have declined in number from 400,000 in the 1960s to about 250,000 today. The 700,000 strong French Jewish community is wracked by mass intermarriage (estimated by some to be around 70 percent). Since the fall of communism, over half a million Jews have left the former Soviet Union. The Jewish communities of Latin America and South Africa are being drained by mass emigration. Within the next several decades, given current demographic trends, less than two million Jews will live in all of Europe, less than a half million in all of Latin America, and less than 100,000 in all of the Islamic countries.

The American Jewish Committee's yearbook (the authoritative source of information about American-Jewish communal life) has reported that the number of American Jews is shrinking by about one-half of one percent a year (other sources claim that the rate of shrinkage may be as high as 3 percent). There are indications that the rate of shrinkage is likely to grow. By the year 2000, it is estimated that 70 percent of all marriages in which Jews are involved will be intermarriages. In age, Jews are already the eldest ethnic group in the United States; some reports claim their median age to be over forty-five—that is, predominantly beyond the age of reproduction. By comparison, thirty-five is the median age of the general population with twenty-

five being the median age of the black and Hispanic communities.

Additionally, Jews within the age of reproduction tend to marry later than other ethnic groups because of a variety of social factors, such as a proportionately higher feminist consciousness. Despite the very large influx of Israeli, Latin American, and Soviet Jews, the American Jewish community is still shrinking and, together with Canadian Jewry, will probably number less than 5 million by 2010. At the same time, the Israeli Jewish community will be close to 6 million in number. By the year 2020, the Israeli Jewish community will probably be close to 7 million, while the Jews in the entire rest of the world will be less than 7 million.

These are quantitative extrapolations. Qualitative developments, such as the advent of Mideast peace and a sustained economic boom in the region, could even speed up these trends.

Israeli Jews surpassing American Jews in population will have tremendous symbolic, psychological, and spiritual impact on both communities. Israel will no longer be the "little brother" depending on American Jewry. The impact of Conservative and Reform Jewry could decline. Neither has succeeded in planting authentic roots in the Israeli reality. Israelis define themselves as being secular or being religious in the Orthodox sense. A very large third group (mostly of Oriental and Sephardic origin) would describe themselves as traditional—neither religious nor secular. However, Conservative and Reform initiatives in Israel have failed to attract significant numbers of this group, and for all intents and purposes they have remained a marginal offshoot of American Jewry. One may perceive two possible scenarios: (1) As the demographic balance changes, these small Conservative and Reform communities will gradually lose their overseas support and become even more marginal to the Israeli reality. (2) Without significant overseas support, both Conservative and Reform communities might finally find their authentic Israeli voice and play an ever-growing role in the spiritual development of the Israeli community.

What about the future of Jewish religious thought per se? This is problematic. Judaism has always concerned itself primarily with practical commandments. There has never been an official Jewish theology, doctrine, or dogma. As in the past, the future will be rife with a myriad of philosophical approaches. The real question concerning Jewish identity is which practical commandments can serve as the unifying force around which the Jews can organize their communal identity and find a sense of unity. Which communal "projects" can unify the disparate factors of Jewish life? We may imagine innumerable alternative Jewish futures as they are refracted through the prism of the interaction between an evolving Diaspora and an evolving Israel, between the secular, Reform, Conservative, Orthodox and ultra-Orthodox communities, as well as the interaction between all of these and the social, economic, cultural, spiritual, and political developments of the world at large.

The central question is one of Jewish identity, an identity which cannot be founded on a commonality of religious faith. The question is whether Judaism and the Jewish people will continue to develop spiritually as, over the course of the twenty-first century, Judaism becomes increasingly coextensive with a national state. The question is why a young modern Jewish individual (in the Diaspora or in Israel) should even care about remaining Jewish. If Judaism cannot renew itself in line with the demands of the postmodern world and with the spiritual requirements of the modern Jewish individual and be a unifying force in a pluralistic world and a pluralistic Jewish community, then it may become an increasingly irrelevant concern for all but the ultra-Orthodox, who will become a cultural curiosity like the Amish.

Israel is the key. Let us assume that the state of Israel will continue to guarantee the physical survival of an ethnic identity called the Jews. Who is to say that that entity will continue to make meaningful contributions to world civilization or will provide meaningful frameworks for the self-realization of the individual Jew? Only if Israel can develop new expressions of Judaism, will it have significance for Jewish history. With the advent of peace in the Middle East, these questions will preoccupy the Jewish people in the twenty-first century, to the same extent that the question of physical survival preoccupied them in the second half of the twentieth century.

See also BUDDHISM; CHRISTIANITY; HINDUISM; ISLAM; MIDDLE EAST; RELIGION, CHANGING BELIEFS; RELIGION, SPIRITUALITY, MORALITY.

BIBLIOGRAPHY

ELLENSON, DAVID. *Tradition in Transition: Orthodoxy, Halakah and the Boundaries of Modern Jewish Identity.* Lanham, MD: University Press of America, 1989.
FACKENHEIM, EMIL W. *To Mend the World: Foundations of Future Jewish Thought.* New York: Schocken, 1982.
KAPLAN, M. MORDECAI. *Future of the American Jews.* Wyncote, PA: Reconstructionist Press, 1981.
VITAL, DAVID. *The Future of the Jews.* Cambridge, MA: Harvard University Press, 1990.
WIGODER, GEOFFREY, ed. *Encyclopedia of Judaism.* New York: Macmillan, 1989.

Tsvi Bisk

Judicial Reform

Seven judicial problem areas can be identified where reform is needed in the near future, involving criminal and/or civil cases: (1) problems involving pretrial release and bail procedures; (2) difficulties in finding and providing adequate legal counsel for the poor in criminal and civil proceedings; (3) delays in criminal and civil cases resulting from overcrowded dockets or other factors; (4) problems with media coverage of pending cases and cases in progress; (5) judicial selection; (6) jury shortcomings; and (7) judicial nullification of legislative and administrative laws.

Pretrial Release and Bail Reform

Releasing or not releasing suspects prior to trial depends on (1) whether they can deposit sufficient money to assure that a suspect on trial will return for the trial (the traditional bail bond system) or (2) whether personal circumstances are such that return for trial is a near certainty (release on one's own recognizance, often referred to as the ROR system). Bail has been the dominant method, because individuals were economically motivated and partly because it favored the middle-class interests that dominate legal rulemaking. Reform is likely to occur in the direction of a more objective and scientific variant on the ROR system.

Studies by the Vera Institute in New York City show that screening to separate suspects into good- and bad-risk groups (largely based on community roots and affected by the seriousness of the crime) can be equally as effective in assuring court appearance as the traditional money-deposit system. Trial-day mail or phone reminders also help assure appearances. Studies show that the screening and notification system enables more arrested suspects to be released from jail pending trial than is allowed under the money-deposit system. Released suspects can (1) continue their jobs, (2) better prepare their cases and prove their innocence, (3) save taxpayers money by not being jailed and (4) be less embittered than if time were spent in jail and they were then acquitted. The money-deposit system so inherently discriminates against the poor that the Supreme Court may declare that it violates the equal-protection constitutional guarantee.

One objection to the ROR system is that it may sometimes release arrested suspects who will commit additional crimes while awaiting trial. One response to this objection is to require that dangerous persons be detained regardless of their ability to post a large bail or bail bond. It may be, however, that pretrial crimes are more often due to long delays prior to trial than to poor screening or the lack of a bail bond.

Legal Counsel for the Poor

Since 1962, criminal defendants who cannot afford an attorney have been entitled to be provided one by the government, at least for crimes with penalties involving more than six months imprisonment. The big problem now is how, not whether, to provide counsel. Alternatives include: (1) using unpaid or paid volunteer attorneys, (2) using court-assigned attorneys, or (3) hiring full-time public defenders salaried by the government.

The unpaid volunteer system too often attracts young attorneys seeking experience to the detriment of clients whose liberty might be jeopardized. The paid volunteer system works well if only well-qualified attorneys are allowed and if they are fairly compensated for their services. Where assigned counsel is used, clients are frequently represented by reluctant attorneys or by attorneys with little or no criminal case experience. The full-time public defender system is being increasingly used, although many such offices are underfinanced and understaffed.

Although the Supreme Court has not yet required free counsel for the poor in housing eviction, motor vehicle repossession, or other civil cases, the federal Office of Economic Opportunity (OEO) and most local communities have sought to provide it. These efforts promote respect for the law, protect the innocent, promote orderly law reform, and educate the poor concerning their legal rights and obligations. Civil legal aid alternatives are similar to those for criminal legal aid. The traditional system has involved volunteer attorneys whose availability is generally limited. The OEO has provided many cities with full-time civil legal services programs similar to public defender offices in recent years. A "judicare" system would provide civil legal aid enabling poor clients to hire attorneys of their choice, for which the government would pay, as in Medicare.

Legal insurance and plans designating attorneys for unions or other organizations to represent individual members also have been developed. Bar associations object that organization attorneys will lack a close attorney-client relationship, and they oppose the economic competition posed to traditional lawyers. Certain of these organizational schemes, already declared by the Supreme Court to be protected by the freedom of assembly clause of the Constitution, may flourish.

Court Delays

Increased industrialization and urbanization have contributed to undesirable delays in civil as well as criminal cases. Automobile accidents are mainly at fault in causing the long delays in civil cases. Urbanization and concomitant increased crime add to criminal court docket congestion.

When personal injury cases are delayed, the injured party may be unable to collect because of the forgetfulness or unavailability of witnesses and may be unduly pressured to settle for quicker (though reduced) damage payments. Although criminal case delays tend to be shorter, they become objectionable if the arrested suspect must wait in jail pending trial, and all the more objectionable when an acquittal or a sentence shorter than the time already spent in jail results.

Civil case reforms designed to encourage out-of-court settlements provide for impartial medical experts, pretrial settlement conferences, and pretrial proceedings to enable the parties to know where they stand with regard to each other's evidence and to impose interest charges beginning with the day of the accident. Other reforms remove personal injury cases from the courts by shifting them to less formal administrative agencies for speedier disposition or by requiring injured parties to automatically collect from their own insurance company, regardless of their negligence (as with fire insurance).

Protracted jury trials can be reduced by imposing high jury fees, providing quicker trials for non-jury cases, randomly picking twelve jurors (thereby avoiding lengthy selection), and by separating the liability and damage issues (so there is no need to discuss damages if the defendant is found nonliable, and settlement can be facilitated if liability is established). Reformers also have recommended that delay be reduced by having more judges, and more work days and/or work hours per day, shifting judges from low-volume to high-volume courts, and conserving judges' time to resolve situations such as those involving the simultaneous scheduling of the same attorney in two different courts, for example.

Reforms to reduce criminal case delays include: better screening of complaints; more encouragement of guilty pleas, if merited; more criminal court personnel; less use of grand jury indictments; more pretrial proceedings to narrow the issues; random jury selection; and release of the defendant within a specified period of time if not tried.

Media Reporting

Mass media reporting on pending criminal cases involves conflict between two civil liberties: freedom of speech and freedom of the press, which includes the right to report on pending cases; and the constitutional right to a fair trial unprejudiced by distorted reporting, by reporting evidence inadmissible in court, or by sensational coverage.

The Supreme Court favors holding sensational trials away from the community where the crime was committed; reprimanding attorneys for gossiping to reporters; keeping jurors and sometimes witnesses from seeing newspapers; holding in contempt reporters who print gossip while a trial is still in process; and limiting the number of reporters allowed in the courtroom.

Many newspaper and newspaper association rules establish voluntary press restraints. American Bar Association rules restrain attorneys in criminal cases from communicating prejudicial information to the press. Reformers favor the British system holding newspapers in contempt of court for publishing almost anything other than the barest facts about criminal trials until the trial is completed.

Judicial Selection

Judges are chosen by two basic methods: (1) they may be appointed by the president, governor, or mayor—with or without the approval of a bipartisan nominating commission or the legislature; or (2) they may be elected by the general public under partisan or nonpartisan election procedures. Originally, nearly all United States judges were appointed. Federal judges have always been appointed as specified in the Constitution. During the period of Jacksonian democracy, however, a shift toward electing state and local judges began. In the last few decades, there has been a shift back to gubernatorial appointment of state and local judges.

Those favoring elected judges point out that judicial decision making frequently involves subjective value judgments that should reflect public opinion. Electoral advocates also point out that elected judges will come closer in their backgrounds to the general public than appointed judges, especially if the nominating commission tends to be dominated by the state bar association.

Those favoring appointed judges contend that appointed judges are less partisan in their judicial voting behavior. This outcome may be due more to the bipartisan approval needed for appointment, to appointment across party lines by some governors, or to the differences in how appointed judges view their roles, rather than being directly related to the selection process. Appointment advocates also argue that appointed judges are technically more competent because they tend to come from better law schools and colleges than elected judges do, a conclusion not supported by empirical evidence.

Judicial reformers usually advocate both appointive selection and longer judicial terms. Longer terms give a judge more independence from political pressures. Such terms, however, are likely to make judges less responsive to public opinion, although possibly more sensitive to minority rights.

Some jurisdictions provide for regular elections to fill vacant judgeships (with provision for opposition candidates), to be followed periodically by retention elections (whereby each sitting judge runs against his record with the voters being able to vote only yes or no on his retention). Such compromises will probably become increasingly prevalent.

Jury Shortcomings

Jurors in medieval England were originally persons from the community who had actually witnessed the facts in dispute. Eventually, the jury evolved into a group of community representatives who resolved factual disputes in cases, while the judge determined the applicable law. Traditionally the jury has consisted of twelve people chosen by both sides from a list of voters charged to determine guilt in criminal cases and liability in civil cases by unanimous decision. The idea of having juries to supplement the work of judges has come under attack in recent years.

Critics contend that jury trials consume too much time, suggesting that jurors often lack competence and sometimes ignore the legal instructions given them.

Defenders point out that a jury trial is more likely to free the innocent than a bench trial, because all jury members must agree to convict and because jurors tend to be more like defendants than judges are. Judges and juries agree approximately 83 percent of the time in criminal cases, but when they disagree, the jury is nearly always pro-defendant and the judge pro-prosecutor. They also argue that juries, by providing public participation, encourage respect for the law. Before-and-after tests show that serving as a juror does improve one's attitude toward the legal system. Public participation of jurors also resolves ambiguities in the facts or law in accord with public opinion.

The trends point toward juries smaller than twelve persons who decide by less than a unanimous vote. This trend has been especially evident in civil cases, and recently was extended by the Supreme Court to criminal cases.

Judicial Nullification of Legislative and Administrative Laws

The most controversial aspect of appellate and trial court decision making is the court's power to nullify legislative laws and administrative regulations. Congress, it is argued, cannot be trusted to police itself since it has a vested interest in its own legislative edicts. Another strong point is that unpopular minority viewpoints need the courts to protect them. It is also said that constitutional interpretation requires technical legal training, which the courts have, and that the courts have less political bias than legislatures do.

Arguments against judicial review emphasize that Congress is more responsive to public opinion. Past attacks stressed the conservatism of the courts, particularly with regard to economic regulation. It is further noted that the lack of preciseness in the Constitution makes it more a political than a legal document.

Between the positions of complete judicial review over all types of statutes and no judicial review at all, there are many intermediate ways to restrict judicial review: (1) by requiring more than a simple majority of judicial votes; (2) by providing for congressional override or veto; (3) by limiting judicial review to legislation relating to matters involving special protective interests, state legislation (to preserve American federalism), or civil liberties (to protect ideological, ethnic, or other minority interests). The trend is toward a civil-liberties-oriented judicial review. Other ways to make the Supreme Court more responsive include: (1) requiring that the Court be composed of representatives of all three branches of government, as in some Western European systems; (2) giving justices an elected or fixed-term tenure; or (3) providing for representation on an expanded court from all fifty states (proposed in a constitutional amendment already passed by some states).

A Changing Environment

The fact that reform is needed does not necessarily indicate that the American system of justice has been inefficient or discriminatory. It is indicative of organizational changes affecting efficiency and reflecting a keener sensitivity to discriminatory injustices. Encouraging as it is that courts and other policy-making bodies have recently instituted innovations in an attempt to cope with the problems raised by pretrial release, legal aid, court delay, pretrial reporting, judicial selection, the jury system, and judicial review, much more remains to be done.

See also CRIME, NONVIOLENT; CRIME, VIOLENT; CRIME RATES; CRIMINAL PUNISHMENT; LAWMAKING, JUDICIAL; LAWS, EVOLUTION OF; LAWYERS AND THE LEGAL PROFESSION.

BIBLIOGRAPHY

ARON, NAN. *Liberty and Justice for All: Public Interest Law in the 1980s and Beyond.* Boulder, CO: Westview, 1989.

DEAN, H. *Judicial Review and Democracy.* New York: Random House, 1966.

DUBOIS, PHILIP. *The Analysis of Judicial Reform.* Lexington, MA: Lexington-Heath, 1982.

FREED, D., and WALD, P. *Bail in the United States.* Washington, DC: U.S. Government Printing Office, 1964.

GOLDFARB, R. *Ransom: A Critique of the American Bail System.* New York: Harper & Row, 1965.

HANDLER, JOEL. *Social Movements and the Legal System: A Theory of Law Reform and Social Change.* New York: Academic Press, 1978.

JOINER, C. *Civic Justice and the Jury.* Englewood Cliffs, NJ: Prentice-Hall, 1962.

JONES, H. *The Courts, the Public, and the Laws Explosion.* Englewood Cliffs, NJ: Prentice-Hall, 1965.

KALVEN, H., and ZEISEL, H. *The American Jury.* Boston: Little, Brown, 1966.

SIGLER, JAY, and BEEDE, BENJAMIN. *The Legal Sources of Public Policy.* Lexington, MA: Lexington-Heath, 1977.

SILVERSTEIN, L. *Defense of the Poor.* Boston: Little, Brown, 1966.

SKOONICK, J. *Justice Without Trial: Law Enforcement in a Democratic Society.* New York: John Wiley, 1967.

WATSON, R., and DOWNING, R. *The Politics of the Bench and the Bar: Judicial Selection Under the Missouri Nonpartisan Court Plan.* New York: John Wiley, 1969.

WILSON, JAMES Q., ed. *Crime and Public Policy.* New Brunswick, NJ: Transaction, 1983.

ZEISEL, H.; KALVEN, HANS; and BUCHHOLZ, B. *Delay in the Court.* Boston: Little, Brown, 1959.

Stuart S. Nagel

Kahn, Herman (1922–1983).

A native of Bayonne, N.J., American defense analyst and futurist Herman Kahn became a staff physicist for the Rand Corporation in 1948 and went on to build a formidable reputation as one of the world's preeminent students of nuclear war strategy. His books, *On Thermonuclear War* (1960) and *Thinking About the Unthinkable* (1962), made the case that nuclear war is not only probable at some time in the future but can also, at certain levels of intensity and with adequate civil defense precautions, be survived. In 1961 in collaboration with Max Singer, Kahn founded the Hudson Institute. Under Kahn's leadership, the institute won many civilian as well as defense-related research contracts. He spent most of his later years in nonmilitary areas of futures inquiry. *The Year 2000* (1967), written with Anthony Wiener and others, is one of the most influential futures books of the century. Other books include *The Next 200 Years* (1976, with William Brown and Leon Martel), and *The Coming Boom: Economic, Political and Social* (1982). *Thinking About the Unthinkable in the 1980s* (1984), a revisiting of his earlier studies of nuclear war strategy, was published posthumously. Despite his reputation as a prophet of nuclear war, Kahn was always an optimist, displaying a reasoned faith in the power of science, technology, and capitalism to solve the pressing problems of modern civilization.

See also FUTURISTS.

BIBLIOGRAPHY

CORNISH, EDWARD, et al. *The Study of the Future.* Washington, DC: World Future Society, 1977, Chapter 9.
CLARKE, I. F. "Obituary." *Futures* 15 (December 1983): 540–544.

W. Warren Wagar